Service Industries in the Global Economy
Volume II

The International Library of Critical Writings in Economics

Series Editor: Mark Blaug

Professor Emeritus, University of London
Professor Emeritus, University of Buckingham
Visiting Professor, University of Exeter

This series is an essential reference source for students, researchers and lecturers in economics. It presents by theme a selection of the most important articles across the entire spectrum of economics. Each volume has been prepared by a leading specialist who has written an authoritative introduction to the literature included.

A full list of published and future titles in this series is printed at the end of this volume.

Wherever possible, the articles in these volumes have been reproduced as originally published using facsimile reproduction, inclusive of footnotes and pagination to facilitate ease of reference.

For a list of all Edward Elgar published titles visit our site on the World Wide Web at
http://www.e-elgar.co.uk

Service Industries in the Global Economy
Volume II
Services, Globalization and Economic Development

Edited by

J.R. Bryson

Lecturer in Economic Geography, Service Sector Research Unit,
School of Geography, University of Birmingham, UK

and

P.W. Daniels

Professor of Geography and Director of the Service Sector Research Unit,
School of Geography, University of Birmingham, UK

THE INTERNATIONAL LIBRARY OF CRITICAL WRITINGS IN ECONOMICS

An Elgar Reference Collection
Cheltenham, UK • Northampton, MA, USA

Published by
Edward Elgar Publishing Limited
Glensanda House
Montpellier Parade
Cheltenham
Glos GL50 1UA
UK

Edward Elgar Publishing, Inc.
6 Market Street
Northampton
Massachusetts 01060
USA

A catalogue record for this book is available from the British Library.

Library of Congress Cataloguing in Publication Data
Service industries in the global economy / edited by J.R. Bryson and
  P.W. Daniels.
      (The international library of critical writings in economics)
      Includes bibliographical references and indexes.
      Contents: v. 1. Service theories and service employment—v.
  2. Services, globalization, and economic development.
      1. Service industries. I. Bryson, J.R., 1963–   . II. Daniels,
  P.W. III. Series.
  HD9980.5.S42515   1998
  338.4—dc21   98-27692
                                                      CIP

ISBN 1 85898 718 0 (2 volume set)

Contents

PART II PRODUCER SERVICES

PART III   MULTINATIONAL SERVICE FIRMS

PART IV   SERVICES, TECHNOLOGICAL CHANGE AND GLOBALIZATION

Acknowledgements

The editors and publishers wish to thank the authors and the following publishers who have kindly given permission for the use of copyright material.

Edward Arnold Publishers Ltd for articles: P.W. Daniels (1989), 'Some Perspectives on the Geography of Services', *Progress in Human Geography*, **13** (3), September, 427–37; Stephen Britton (1990), 'The Role of Services in Production', *Progress in Human Geography*, **14** (4), December, 529–46.

Blackwell Publishers, Inc. for articles: Barney Warf (1989), 'Telecommunications and the Globalization of Financial Services', *Professional Geographer*, **41** (3), August, 257–71; Niles Hansen (1990), 'Do Producer Services Induce Regional Economic Development?', *Journal of Regional Science*, **30** (4), November, 465–76; Alan MacPherson (1997), 'The Role of Producer Service Outsourcing in the Innovation Performance of New York State Manufacturing Firms', *Annals of the Association of American Geographers*, **87** (1), March, 52–71.

Blackwell Publishers Ltd for article: Brian Hindley and Alasdair Smith (1984), 'Comparative Advantage and Trade in Services', *World Economy*, **7** (1), March, 369–89.

Carfax Publishing Ltd for articles: Mark Hepworth (1986), 'The Geography of Technological Change in the Information Economy', *Regional Studies*, **20** (5), October, 407–24; Peter Enderwick (1987), 'The Strategy and Structure of Service-Sector Multinationals: Implications for Potential Host Regions', *Regional Studies*, **21** (3), June, 215–23; Mitchell L. Moss (1987), 'Telecommunications, World Cities, and Urban Policy', *Urban Studies*, **24** (6), December, 534–46; J.N. Marshall (1989), 'Corporate Reorganization and the Geography of Services: Evidence from the Motor Vehicle Aftermarket in the West Midlands Region of the UK', *Regional Studies*, **23** (2), 139–50; Martin Perry (1990), 'Business Service Specialization and Regional Economic Change', *Regional Studies*, **24** (3), June, 195–209; W.R. Goe (1990), 'Producer Services, Trade and the Social Division of Labour', *Regional Studies*, **24** (4), August, 327–42; J. Howells (1990), 'The Internationalization of R & D and the Development of Global Research Networks', *Regional Studies*, **24** (6), December, 495–512; William J. Coffey and Antoine S. Bailly (1992), 'Producer Services and Systems of Flexible Production', *Urban Studies*, **29** (6), August, 857–68; Barney Warf (1995), 'Telecommunications and the Changing Geographies of Knowledge Transmission in the Late 20th Century', *Urban Studies*, **32** (2), March, 361–78.

Frank Cass & Co. Ltd for articles: John H. Dunning (1989), 'Multinational Enterprises and the Growth of Services: Some Conceptual and Theoretical Issues', *Service Industries Journal*, **9** (1), January, 5–39; Martin Perry (1992), 'Flexible Production, Externalisation and the

Interpretation of Business Service Growth', *Service Industries Journal*, **12** (1), January, 1–16; Kim Wai Ho, Yan Chin Lim and Thian Ser Toh (1997), 'The Perceived Advantages, Disadvantages and Strategic Responses of International Stockbroking Firms in ASEAN Countries', *Service Industries Journal*, **17** (2), April, 264–77.

Elsevier Science Ltd for articles: Martin Perry (1990), 'The Internationalisation of Advertising', *Geoforum*, **21** (1), 35–50; Roger Mark Selya (1994), 'Taiwan as a Service Economy', *Geoforum*, **25** (3), 305–22.

European Communities for article: Michael Green (1985), 'The Development of Market Services in the European Community, the United States and Japan', *European Economy*, **25**, Chapter 3, September, 69–96.

Growth and Change for article: James W. Harrington, Alan D. MacPherson and John R. Lombard (1991), 'Interregional Trade in Producer Services: Review and Synthesis', *Growth and Change*, **22** (4), Fall, 75–94.

International Regional Science Review for article: Amy Glasmeier and Marie Howland (1994), 'Service-Led Rural Development: Definitions, Theories, and Empirical Evidence', *International Regional Science Review*, **16** (1&2), 197–229.

NTC Publications Ltd for article: Dong-Sung Cho, Jinah Choi and Youjae Yi (1994), 'International Advertising Strategies by NIC Multinationals: The Case of a Korean Firm', *International Journal of Advertising*, **13** (1), 77–92.

Pion Ltd for article: P.W. Daniels, J.H.J. Van Dinteren and M.C. Monnoyer (1992), 'Consultancy Services and the Urban Hierarchy in Western Europe', *Environment and Planning A*, **24** (12), December, 1731–48.

Regional Science Association International for articles: William B. Beyers and Michael J. Alvine (1985), 'Export Services in Postindustrial Society', *Papers of the Regional Science Association*, **57**, 33–45; William J. Coffey and Mario Polèse (1989), 'Producer Services and Regional Development: A Policy-Oriented Perspective', *Papers of the Regional Science Association*, **67**, 13–27; William B. Beyers and David P. Lindahl (1996), 'Explaining the Demand for Producer Services: Is Cost-Driven Externalization the Major Factor?', *Papers in Regional Science*, **75** (3), July, 351–74.

Revue d'Economie Régionale et Urbaine for article: Riccardo Cappellin (1989), 'The Diffusion of Producer Services in the Urban System', *Revue d'Economie Régionale et Urbaine*, **4**, 641–61.

Royal Dutch Geographical Society KNAG for article: P.W. Daniels (1986), 'Foreign Banks and Metropolitan Development: A Comparison of London and New York', *Tijdschrift voor Economische en Sociale Geografie*, **LXXVII** (4), 269–87.

Sage Publications, Inc. for article: Wendy Patton and Ann Markusen (1991), 'The Perils of Overstating Service Sector Growth Potential: A Study of Linkages in Distributive Services', *Economic Development Quarterly*, **5** (3), August, 197–212.

Taylor & Francis Ltd for articles: Sven Illeris (1989), 'Producer Services: The Key Sector for Future Economic Development?', *Entrepreneurship and Regional Development*, **1** (3), July–September, 267–74; John Bryson, Peter Wood and David Keeble (1993), 'Business Networks, Small Firm Flexibility and Regional Development in UK Business Services', *Entrepreneurship and Regional Development*, **5** (3), July–September, 265–77; John R. Bryson (1997), 'Business Service Firms, Service Space and the Management of Change', *Entrepreneurship and Regional Development*, **9** (2), April–June, 93–111.

United Nations Conference on Trade and Development for article: Frederick F. Clairmonte and John H. Cavanagh (1984), 'Transnational Corporations and Services: The Final Frontier', *Trade and Development: An UNCTAD Review*, **5**, 215–73.

John Wiley & Sons Ltd for article: Praveen R. Nayyar (1990), 'Information Asymmetries: A Source of Competitive Advantage for Diversified Service Firms', *Strategic Management Journal*, **11** (7), November–December, 513–19.

Every effort has been made to trace all the copyright holders but if any have been inadvertently overlooked the publishers will be pleased to make the necessary arrangement at the first opportunity.

In addition the publishers wish to thank the Library of the London School of Economics and Political Science, the Marshall Library of Economics, Cambridge University and B & N Microfilm, London for their assistance in obtaining these articles.

Part I
Services and Economic Development

[1]

Some perspectives on the geography of services

by P.W. Daniels

A good deal of the geographical literature on services has been concerned with questions and problems with their roots in the developed countries (see for example Noyelle and Stanback, 1988; Commission of the European Communities, 1987; Bailly and Maillat, 1988). But the developing countries must also be cognizant of the contribution of services to their economic and social health. After all, the existing evidence from developed countries suggests that harnessing services effectively will promote other economic activity, exports and, ultimately, the overall welfare of national economies (Aronson, 1988). A recent publication by UNCTAD (1988) stresses the strategic role of producer services in the regional and international development of developing countries and explores strategies and opportunities for improving their role. As the service economy becomes more globalized (Nusbaumer, 1987) there is a danger that unless the developing countries adopt a more constructive view of trade in services they will miss the opportunities afforded by its official recognition in the Uruguay Round of GATT negotiations (Veale, Spiegelman and Ronkainen, 1988).

Such considerations are particularly important in relation to advanced business and professional services. These are of course already growing rapidly in developed countries and without them most developing countries will not only continue to have service economies dominated by low wage activities but will also continue to penalize domestic firms trying to produce more exportable products and services (Veale *et al.*, 1988). By protecting the limited advanced services that they already have the developing countries may well be protecting outdated infrastructure and practices which could be upgraded to make a more positive contribution to overall national development. Therefore almost '. . . every developing country needs to reform and revitalize its knowledge-based service sectors' (Aronson, 1988: 54). To do so, however, the developing countries may have to endorse greater factor mobility, of both labour and capital, than they currently believe prudent. Inward movements of foreign labour and services is an integral part of the right-to-establish concepts valued by knowledge-intensive legal services and management or engineering consultancies (Bhagwati, 1988).

The locational impacts of these requirements are likely to be very narrowly confined; Meyer (1986) shows that almost half of the offices of international banks (mainly developed-country banks) in South America are in just three national metropolises: Sao Paulo, Caracas and Buenos Aires. This is perceived, perhaps rightly, as immediately stengthening the already considerable comparative advantage of developed countries exporting these services, but for many services temporary factor relocation is feasible. This would ensure that the developing countries gain from knowledge transfer, and in the medium or longer term improve the overall export competitiveness of indigenous service producers. Bhagwati (1988) cites the increased share of the world market of medium-level developing countries such as Korea, Brazil or Taiwan in international design services, of Korea (Republic) in construction, or India in computer software, as indicative of the opportunities to develop their own comparative advantage. Hence, it is likely that there is a higher proportion of third-world multinationals (TWMs) in the service sector than developed-country multinationals. The TWMs have skilled workers and managers that can be transferred abroad at low cost and some can also offer state-of-the-art technology in shipping, construction or banking services (Lecraw, 1988). Trade in services will inevitably remain one-sided, however, if the developing countries choose not to participate in multilateral negotiations in which they seek to protect as well as to enhance any existing strengths in the crucial knowledge-intensive and circulation services.

In some respects the spatial inequalities, encapsulated by the relationship between development and services at the international level, are even more significant at the national scale. The actual and potential role of services in restructuring economy, space and society continues to be the focus of attention and debate (Massey and Allen, 1988; Marshall, 1988; Buck, 1988). Coffey and Polese (1988a) conclude that it is still optimistic to expect footloose services to move away from metropolitan areas since the attraction of agglomeration economies seems to be as strong as ever. This may, however, be overly pessimistic. Van Dinteren (1989), for example, distinguishes two urban networks in the Netherlands; the first operates at the international level and is dominated by headquarters activities of service or manufacturing corporations, while the second involves financial and business services functioning at a national level. Each functions within different urban networks with the latter extending well into the intermediate region outside Randstad and sustained by exporting output in the way now fully recognized in the research literature (see also Lambooy, 1986; Illeris, 1988; Stabler and Howe, 1988; Harrington and Lombard, 1988). In the particular case of financial services employment, northern provincial cities in the UK have recently experienced widespread growth (Leyshon, Thrift and Tommey, 1988; Lewis, 1988; Morris, 1988). Demand-led indigenous expansion and inmigration of multilocational firms has, however, played a larger part than decentralization of operating divisions from London; this has largely been confined to locations in the southern UK (see for example Hampshire Development Association, 1987). The process has advanced far enough for it to be suggested that there '. . . is increasing evidence that the influx of international financial and producer service firms into provincial financial centres will soon breach London's virtual monopoly on the organization of cross-border business in financial and producer services' (Leyshon, Thrift and Tommey, 1988). It is interesting to note, however, that the concentration which has accompanied the continued internationalization of producer services is also happening within the UK regions, as Manchester asserts its dominance over Liverpool in the northwest, and Birmingham asserts its over Nottingham and Leicester in the Midlands. Other evidence for some relative decentralization of producer services has been assembled by Moulaert, Chikhaoui and Djellal (1988) in a study of the locational behaviour of French high-technology consultancy firms. France is now the second largest producer in the world of these services which are found to be torn between regional decentralization and the conventional need for agglomeration economies in a bid to achieve market penetration through good client orientation (see also Tordoir, 1988). Thus Rhône-Alpes and Provence as well as the Paris Region are prominent locations, but regions with well established low growth profiles continue to be marginalized despite the evidence for relative decentralization. Similar conclusions can be drawn from a study of the multiplant strategies of a range of producer services in Italy (Bitetti and Senn, 1988).

Although regional concentration is a significant feature in the relative decentralization of producer services, regional performance is also determined by the growth of services in rural areas and small towns (Bender, 1987; Miller and Bluestone, 1987). Lensink (1987) has painstakingly accumulated establishment and employment data for small towns (5000–50 000) in three rural regions of the Netherlands, and concludes that the development prospects for intermediate services appears to be best in centres with a population of 30–50 000 where they operate most effectively as basic activities. Although approached from the wider issue of the office development potential of rural Washington State, Conway and Associates (1988) have demonstrated that rural communities with populations of 10 000 or more are the only locations with a realistic potential for attracting footloose offices (see also Miller and Bluestone, 1987). It is stressed that this potential can only make a partial contribution to the economic health of rural communities; they will still need to rely on traditional basic industries in resources and manufacturing. An emphasis on indigenous rather than externally controlled firms is also desirable since Black's (1989) ongoing study of business-service supply and demand in the Highlands of Scotland again demonstrates that the latter still tend to maintain service linkages well outside the region. Deficiencies in the supply of rural business services are therefore much more likely to hit indigenous enterprises and can hold back their development.

A possible way of compensating for these difficulties is for firms in rural areas to obtain specialized services through electronic information networks. Thus in the Fjordane region of northern Noway, Sjoholt (1988) found that only one-third of the enterprises in his sample used electronic data processing in 1982 but by 1988 all had installed capacity. It would be a mistake to conclude that the ability that this confers upon users to import services from Bergen or elsewhere is satisfactory; supply of services as near as possible was still considered essential

430   *Some perspectives on the geography of services*

by the majority of the enterprises in the Fjordane region (see also Tweeten, 1987). This accords with one of a number of conclusions derived by Illeris (1989) from a synthesis of the findings of several studies of the supply/demand and local/distant consumption of producer services. Big and/or innovative firms require a more diversified set of service inputs; independent firms buy more services externally than branch establishments and are more likely to purchase from their immediate environment; local or regional trade (purchases and sales) predominates but the considerable (and increasing) purchases between regions involve transactions across the central place hierarchy rather than from smaller to larger centres, with multilocational firms exporting more than independent service producers. In some respects such conclusions provide encouragement to noncentral regions such as Noord Brabant (1988) at one end of the spectrum, or major metropolitan areas such as Vancouver (Vancouver Economic Advisory Commission, 1988) at the other, that are actively exploring possible proactive approaches to policies for services and economic development. Equally, it may well be that the long-term prospects and appropriate policies for incorporating technology, innovation and concentration which accompany metaindustrialization (Commission of the European Communities, 1988) are best devised and applied at the international scale, i.e. within the area of the Internal Market which is due to come into existence from 1992.

The difficulties confronting rural areas and small cities trying to participate more fully in the service economy continue to be exacerbated by location preferences of firms which export beyond their national market. An empirical study of almost 600 business-service firms in the Netherlands (Bureau Goudappel Coffeng, 1987) shows that those firms employing more than 50 persons, with a turnover greater than 5 million guilders, anticipating growth in personnel, engaged in exporting their output to international clients and showing the highest relative shares in exports as part of total turnover are most likely to be located in the four largest cities (Amsterdam, Den Haag, Rotterdam and Utrecht) and the rest of the western region. The national average for the latter is 10% but rises to 20% for business services in Den Haag, 13% for Rotterdam and 11% for Amsterdam compared with 4–5% for business services in Brabant, Zeeland and Limburg provinces. When asked why they did not engage in exports outside the Netherlands only one in three firms indicated that they did not believe they had a service to export although almost two out of three firms positively discriminated in favour of the national market. Of the business services without exports 19% expected to engage in this activity within a few years and only 11% of those already doing so expected exports to decrease rather than remain stable or to increase. About 10% of the firms had branches overseas and most were headquartered in the four major cities and in the intermediate zone. Rimmer (1988) draws attention to similar problems, but at the global level, in relation to the internationalization of engineering consultancies.

The degree to which business and professional services can perform a basic role depends on access to good telecommunications facilities. Many of the issues here are highlighted by Gillespie and Williams (1988) in terms of the implications of telecommunications innovations for intercorporate and intracorporate spatial relationships. Telecommunications provide opportunities for innovation in the distribution, manufacture, transactional and managerial activities of services. Information-intensive environments in cities already well established as diversified service centres are becoming even stronger as telecommunications hubs (Moss, 1987). Not only must policy makers anxious to incorporate services in their economic development objectives for metropolitan areas recognize the pervasive impact of telecommunications they must also appreciate that deregulation has passed responsibility for investment and location decisions to private firms. The indications are that they prefer to invest and reinvest in established business concentrations, thus reaffirming the recentralization of many producer services in recent years. In some cases, such as Brazil (Cordeiro, 1988) this may be paralleled by the investment policies of public telecommunications and other services. O'hUallacháin (1988) suggests that in addition to the ability to control geographically extensive markets from centres well served by telecommunications, search costs for skilled labour, knowledge and markets which have resulted from rapid technological change in services and market uncertainty generated by government deregulation, have encouraged concentration of growing service industries. The effects of bank deregulation in the USA seem to encapsulate many of those processes (Wheeler, 1988; Holly, 1988; Lord, 1987). At another level locational proximity between specialist (technical) consultancy services and small manufacturing firms (SMFs) in major cities has been responsible for innovative behaviour and employment growth. Indeed, '. . . technical consultants in the service sector may in some instances act as important "facilitators" of SMF export activity' (McPherson, 1988a; 1988b). Small firms with backward linkages to specialized producer services are more likely to be able successfully to penetrate foreign export markets.

Systematic studies of specific producer-service activities or explorations of their economic development potential for regions and cities continue in parallel with a number of large scale national studies (Coffey and Polese, 1988b). A good example is Beyer's detailed work on trends in the growth of producer-services employment in the USA during the decade since 1975 (Beyers and Hull, 1988). His results point to wide variations among sectors in growth rates, locational trends, the balance between metropolitan and nonmetropolitan areas, in levels of concentration and export activity potential. Perhaps the most interesting finding is that different regions have developed strengths in different producer services, depending on the contribution of particular types of service to the performance of individual economies. Other national-level work includes the first major study of the service economy of New Zealand (and the role of Auckland within it) (Perry, 1988) and a comprehensive analysis of the service sector in Italy (ISCOM, 1988). The most recently available comparative data on service-sector employment, productivity and related indices for a number of OECD countries has been asembled by Elfring (1987) and by Noyelle and Stanback (1988).

432   *Some perspectives on the geography of services*

All these analyses indicate that service employment continues to increase its share of all employment with producer services making a notable contribution (Giarini, 1987; Van der Aa and Elfring, 1988). A number of anxieties connected to this have begun to surface. These include: the quality of the jobs accompanying this growth (Bednarzik, 1988; Loveman and Tilly, 1988), the significance of the shift out of manufacturing (Hirschorn, 1988), the characteristics of the emerging new service class and sociopolitical change (Savage, Dickens and Fielding, 1988), and the impacts on local labour markets (Buck, 1988). In the USA jobs in the service sector have lower average real wages and slower rates of productivity growth than the manufacturing sector and the real wage gap has widened between 1973 and 1986 (Loveman and Tilly, 1988). Such trends are linked to a deterioration in job quality although there is no agreement about the causal factors, which may be structural or cyclical depending on whether they are viewed from the labour supply or labour demand sides. As might be anticipated, the debate is not helped by the problem of defining and measuring job quality; attributes considered appropriate to high quality service-sector jobs need not be the same as for the manufacturing sector, while perceptions of quality may well vary between different geographical areas or between metropolitan and nonmetropolitan aareas. Although earnings do not provide a full description of job quality, Bednarzik (1988) finds that females have increased their share of jobs in the top one-third of the earnings range and decreased their share of the bottom third. Females have therefore not been adversely affected by the shift to services but men have, since their share of the bottom third of earnings has increased and their share of middle earnings has also declined. However, it remains unclear whether this reflects, for example, the changing gender composition of employment or changes in the occupational mix of the labour force.

Nevertheless, it should be recognized that services, and producer services in particular, exhibit self-propelled growth and trade in which they are market makers and innovators and are responsible for substantial value added to services as well as to goods. Hirschorn (1988: 36) suggests that the manufacturing and service sectors are converging, with the latter playing a '. . . critical role in helping manufacturing attain high levels of productivity and customization. Services do not displace manufacturing, and manufacturing does not compete with services, rather they each reinforce the other' (see also Miles, 1986; Unvala and Donaldson, 1988). But, it should be recognized that perhaps it is necessary to look more closely at the reasons for the continuation of service activity through the creation of new jobs. This will, for example, require further refinement of the characteristics of services (see for example, Gadrey, 1988; Flipo, 1988; Millward, 1988; Harrington, 1988) which will improve our understanding of the causes of differential growth rates. But this will only be possible if research is undertaken on the differences and the similarities between services at corporate, industrial and unit level (Unvala and Donaldson, 1988).

The conceptual distinction between producer and consumer services provides an example of the characterization problem. Although now used extensively by geographers (see for example Marshall *et al.*, 1988; Price and Blair, 1989) there remains uncertainty about the validity of the distinction. Allen (1988a: 16) suggests that such a simple dichotomy '. . . undermines empirical work on the service industries. . . .' since it mistakenly includes services in the sphere of circulation as well as those in the sphere of production. The expansion of banking and finance, which are more appropriately considered as circulation services, is the result of very different causal processes to those affecting business (producer services). The net result is the emergence of a different geography of these activities (Allen, 1988a).

The clearest expression of this is the concentration of finance and banking services in the premier global metropolitan areas (Drennan, 1988; Noyelle, 1989; Price and Blair, 1989; Edward Erdman, 1989; Allen, 1988b). While most observers chart the principal attributes, the explanatory factors and the consequences of the concentration of these services, Noyelle's (1989) collection of papers is one of the first to consider the practical and policy issues that a key city such as New York needs to evaluate as we move towards the 1990s. Rajan and Fryatt (1988) have also attempted an assessment of the human resource needs created by the City of London's unique labour market both at present and in the future. The central concern for New York, and similar financial centres such as London, Tokyo or Singapore, is how to maintain their leading positions as information technology, diffusion of expertise and knowledge or improved competition from rivals threatens to undermine their apparently invincible comparative advantage. In New York's case it is concluded that '. . . preparing for the future will require a much more pro-active role on the part of state and local officials than was needed in the past' (Noyelle, 1989: 6). Perhaps this is also true for London (Cundell, 1988). New regulations relating to foreign company registration and capital requirements are seen as a potential threat to the City's international competitiveness (Edward Erdman, 1989) particularly as the transition towards a unified European Market in 1992 continues. Such strategic approaches will not, however, overcome the exposure of London, New York and similar centres to sharper fluctuations in financial markets. The stock market crash in October 1987 has sharpened the existing disparities in the social and economic topography of New York and its region (Cox, Warf and Preston, 1988). Because technology has created such an integrated system of service transactions focussing on selected cities, it has become more difficult to confine such impacts to one country or metropolitan area (Dobilas, 1988).

Portsmouth Polytechnic, UK

References

Allen, J. 1988a: Service industries: uneven development and uneven knowledge. *Area* 20, 15–22.

434   *Some perspectives on the geography of services*

1988b: The geographies of service. In Massey, D. and Allen, J., editors, *Uneven re-development: cities and regions in transition*. London: Hodder and Stoughton, 124–41.

Aronson, J.D. 1988: Services and development: an analysis of options. *Economic Impact*, September/October, 54–58.

Bailly, A.S. and **Maillat, D.** 1988: *Le secteur tertiaire en question*. Paris: Economica.

Barcet, A. 1988: The development of tertiary services in the economy, labour market and employment. *The Service Industries Journal* 8, 39–48.

Bednarzik, R.W. 1988: The 'quality' of US jobs. *The Service Industrial Journal* 8, 127–35.

Bender, L.D. 1987: The role of services in rural development policies. *Land Economics* 63, 62–71.

Beyers, W.B. and **Hull, T.J.** 1988: Understanding the growth of producer services employment in the United States: 1974–85. Paper presented at 35th North American Meetings of the Regional Science Association, Toronto, November, Mimeo.

Bhagwati, J.N. 1988: Trade in services: developing country concerns. *Economic Impact* 62, 1, 58–64.

Black, J.S. 1989: Explaining the demand for business services: some preliminary results from a survey in the North of Scotland. Paper presented at IBG Annual Conference, Coventry Polytechnic, Coventry, January, Mimeo.

Bitetti, F. and **Senn, L.** 1988: Multiplant strategies of service activities. Paper presented at 4th Seminar on the Service Economy, Geneva, 30 May–1 June, Mimeo.

Buck, N. 1988: Service industries and local labour markets: towards 'an anatomy of service job loss'. *Urban Studies* 25, 282–96.

Bureau Goudappel Coffeng 1987: *Regionale Verschillen in Internationalisatie in de Zakelijke Diensten*. Deventer: Bureau Goudappel Coffeng.

Coffey, W.J. and **Polese, M.** 1988a: Service activities and regional development: a policy-oriented perspective. Paper presented at 35th North American Meetings of the Regional Science Association, Toronto, November, Mimeo.

1988: Locational shifts in Canadian employment 1971–81: decentralization versus decongestion. *The Canadian Geographer* 32, 248–56.

Commission of the European Communities 1987: *Services Europe: the essential change (synthesis of FAST research on changes in services and new technologies)*. Brussels: Directorate-General Science Research and Development.

Conway, D. and **Associates** 1988: *Rural office development in Washington State: its feasibility and the role of telecommunications*. Seattle: Report prepared for Washington State Department of Community Development.

Cordiero, H.K. 1988: The major control points of the urban transactional economy in Brazilian space. Melbourne: Paper presented at IGU Urban Groups Pre-Congress Meeting, August, Mimeo.

Cox, J.C., Warf, B. and **Preston, V.** 1988: Black Monday and the Big Apple: the impacts of the October 19, 1987 stock market crash on the New York economy. Toronto: Paper presented at 35th North American Meetings of the Regional Science Association, November, Mimeo.

Cundell, I. 1988: *Planning for city offices in the 1990's: a challenge unmet?* London: Geography Discussion Papers, New Series No. 22, Graduate School of Geography,

London School of Economics.

Dobilas, G. 1988: *Information technology and simultaneous financial markets: the crash of October 1987.* London: Geography Discussion Papers No. 23, Graduate School of Geography, London School of Economics.

Drennan, M. 1988: New York in the world economy. *Survey of Regional Literature* 4, 7–12.

Erdman, E. 1989: *London's office market: the overseas influence.* London: Edward Erdman Research.

Elfring, T. 1987: Service employment in advanced economies. Unpublished Ph.D. Thesis, Rotterdam: Erasmus University School of Management.

—— 1988: *Service employment in advanced economies.* London: Gower.

Enderwick, P., editor, 1988: *Multinational service firms.* London: Routledge.

Gadrey, J. 1988: Rethinking output in services. *The Service Industries Journal* 8, 67–76.

Giarini, O., editor, 1987: *The emerging service economy.* Oxford: Pergamon.

Gillespie, A. and **Williams, H.** 19888: Telecoms and the reconstruction of regional comparative advantage. *Environment and Planning A* 20, 1311–21.

Hampshire Development Association 1987: *Relocation trends in the financial services sector.* Winchester: Report prepared by Coopers and Lybrand.

Harrington, J.W. 1988: Towards an understanding of trade in services: Canada and the US. Buffalo: Canada-United States Trade Centre, Department of Geography, University of Buffalo, Mimeo.

Harrington, J.W. and **Lombard, J.R.** 1988: Producer service firms in a declining manufacturing region. *Environment and Planning A* 20, 65–80.

Hirschorn, L. 1988: The post-industrial economy: labour skills and the new mode of production. *The Service Industries Journal* 8, 19–38.

Holly, B.P. 1988: Spatial aspects of banking industry deregulation. Paper presented at Association of American Geographers Annual Meetings, Phoenix, April, Mimeo.

Illeris, S. 1989: *Local and distant producer service provision: a survey of quantitative studies.* Copenhagen: Nordic Institute of Regional Policy Research (forthcoming).

ISCOM, 1988: *Il sistema terziario en Italia.* Roma: ISCOM.

Lambooy, J.G. 1986: Information and internationalization: dynamics of the relations of small and medium-sized enterprises in a network environment. *Revue d'Economie Régionale et Urbaine* 5, 719–31.

Lazerson, M.H. 1988: Organizational growth of small firms: and outcome of markets and hierarchies? *American Sociological Review* 53, 330–42.

Lecraw, D.J. 1988: Third world multinationals in the service industries, in Enderwick, P., editor, *Multinational service firms.* London: Routledge, 200–12.

Lensink, F. 1987: Small towns and the service sector: some indications of spatial contrasts in development prospects. Paper presented at Second Dutch-Hungarian Seminar, Kecksemet, April, Mimeo.

Lewis, J.R. 1987: *Employment in financial services.* Durham: Middlesbrugh Locality Working Papers No. 6.

Leyshon, A., **Thrift, N.** and **Tommey, C.** 1988: *South goes north: the rise of the British financial centre.* Bristol and Portsmouth: Working papers on Producer Services No. 9, University of Bristol and Portsmouth Polytechnic.

Lord, J.D. 1987: Interstate banking and the relocation of economic control points.

436   *Some perspectives on the geography of services*

Urban Geography 8, 501–19.

Loveman, G.W. and Tilly, C. 1988: Good jobs or bad jobs: what does the evidence say. *New England Economic Review*, January/February, 46–65.

Marshall, J.N., editor, 1988: *Services and uneven development.* Oxford: Oxford University Press.

Massey, D. and Allen, J., editors, 1988: *Uneven re-development: cities and regions in transition.* London: Hodder and Stoughton.

McPherson, A. 1988a: Small firm export behaviour and technical service linkages: survey evidence from metropolitan Toronto. Toronto: Paper presented at 35th North American Meetings of the Regional Science Association, November, Mimeo.

1988b: Industrial innovation and technical service linkages: evidence from Toronto. *Urban Geography* 9, 464–84.

Meyer, D.R. 1986: The world system of cities: relations between international financial metropolises and South American cities. *Social Forces* 64, 553–81.

Miles, I. 1986: *The convergent economy: rethinking the service economy.* Brighton: Science Policy Research Unit, University of Sussex.

Miller, J.B. and Bluestone, H. 1987: *Prospects for service sector employment growth in non-metropolitan America.* Washington, DC: Government Printing Office.

Millward, R. 1988: The UK services sector, productivity change and the recession in long-term perspective. *The Service Industries Journal* 8, 263–76.

Morris, J. 1988: Producer services and the regions: the case of large accountancy firms. *Environment and Planning A* 20, 741–59.

Moss, M. 1987: Telecommunications, world cities and urban policy. *Urban Studies* 24, 534–46.

Moulaert, F., Chickaoui, Y. and Djellal, F. 1988: Locational behaviour of French high tech consultancy firms. Toronto: Paper presented at 35th North American Meetings of the Regional Science Association, November, Mimeo.

Noyelle, T.J., editor, 1988: *New York's financial markets: the challenges of globalization.* Boulder: Westview Press.

Noyelle, T.J. and Stanback, T.M. 1988: *The post-war growth of services in developed economies.* Geneva: Report for UN Commission on Trade and Development.

Nusbaumer, J., editor, 1987: *Services in the global economy.* Boston: Kluwer.

O'hUallacháin, B. 1988: Agglomeration of services in American cities. Paper presented at Association of American Geographers Annual Meetings, Phoenix, April, Mimeo.

Perry, M. 1988: *New Zealand's service economy 1956–86: a preliminary examination of employment and output trends.* Auckland: Working Papers on Auckland's Producer Service Industry No. 1, Department of Geography, University of Auckland.

Price, D.G. and Blair, A.M. 1989: *The changing geography of the service sector.* London: Belhaven Press.

Provincie Noord-Brabant, 1988: *Kansen voor professionele Diensten in Noord-Brabant.* Hertogenbosch: Einrapport van de Adviescommissie Diensten, Provincie Noord-Brabant.

Rajan, A. and Fryatt, J. 1988: *Create or abdicate: the city's human resource choice for the 1990s.* London: Institute for manpower Studies.

Rimmer, P.N. 1988: The internationalization of engineering consultancies: problems of breaking in to the club. *Environment and Planning A* 20, 741–59.

Savage, M., Dickens, P. and Fielding, A. 1988: Some social and political implications of the contemporary fragmentation of the service class. *International Journal of Urban and Regional Research* 12, 455–76.

Sjoholt, P. 1988: *Use of producer services by manufacturing industry: a comparative pilot study in metropolitan and non-metropolitan Norway.* Bergen: NORAS Program Forskning for Regional Utvikling Report No. 6, Institutt for Geografie, Norges Handelshoyskole.

Stabler, J. and Howe, E.C. 1988: Service exports and regional growth in the post-industrial era. *Journal of Regional Science* 28, 303–15.

Tordoir, P. 1988: Management consultancy services: an analysis of demand. In UFR de Sciences Economiques et sociales, *La Demande de services complexes des firmes multinationales et l'offre correspondant*, Lille: Research Report for le Commisiarat Général du Plan.

Tweeten, L. 1987: No great impact expected on rural areas from computers and telecommunications. *Rural Development Perspectives* 3, 7–15.

UNCTAD 1988: *Trade and development report: part II, services in the world economy.* Geneva: UNCTAD.

Unvala, C. and Donaldson, J. 1988: The service sector: some unresolved issues. *The Service Industries Journal* 8, 459–69.

Van Der Aa, W. and Elfring, T. 1988: *Dynamiek in de Dienstensector: Strategie, Innovatie et Groei.* Amsterdam: Kluwer.

Van Dinteren, J.H.J. 1989: The enlargement of the Dutch metropolitan complex. *Tijdschrift voor Economisch en Sociale Geografie* (in press).

Vancouver Economic Advisory Commission 1988: *Vancouver: a strategy framework for economic development.* Vancouver: Vancouver Economic Advisory Commission.

Veale, S.E., Spiegelman, J.M. and Ronkainen, I. 1988: Trade in services: the US position. *Economic Impact* 62(1), 53–57.

Wheeler, J.O. 1988: The corporate role of large metropolitan areas in the United States. *Growth and Change* 19, 75–86.

[2]

EXPORT SERVICES IN POSTINDUSTRIAL SOCIETY

William B. Beyers
Department of Geography
University of Washington
Seattle, Washington 91985

Michael J. Alvine
Central Puget Sound Economic Development District
Seattle, Washington

ABSTRACT While it is evident that employment in services now dominates the U.S. economy, we still have relatively little understanding of the spatial structure of trade in services. This situation is in part a legacy of our historic tendency to focus on the markets of manufacturing and primary production sectors on the theory that they are "basic." However, the great expansion of services employment in our economy in recent decades means this assumption needs reexamination. This paper reports the results of interviews with 2,200 service sector firms in the Central Puget Sound region, exploring their degree of export orientation. These interviews show a striking degree of export orientation within these sectors. This study suggests that interregional trade in services is probably extremely important in the economic base of all major metropolitan regions.

1. INTRODUCTION

While it is evident that employment in services now dominates the U.S. economy, we still have relatively little understanding of the spatial structure of trade in services. There is disagreement among scholars as to the degree of interregional trade in services. Some feel that trade of services is largely defined by central place hierarchical positions of places, while others have argued for the essential substitution of service sectors for the primary and secondary sectors as the driving forces in regional economies.

This paper presents selected results from a study of service sector firms in the Central Puget Sound region. These results indicate that interregional trade in services is significant and growing, and they imply the need for a reorientation of our view of the growth-inducing role of the services in "postindustrial society."

Given the relative stagnation of manufacturing sector employment in this country in recent years, it has become popular to think of our society as "postindustrial," meaning that traditional manufacturing industry is no longer the only key agent in regional economic change. Writers such as Daniel Bell (1973) emphasize the expanding power of new elements in the industrial order — the tertiary, quaternary, quinary sectors — including activities that did not exist a decade or two ago and that have come to be regarded as bellweathers of economic change in advanced economies. Information processing, design, communications management, organizational management, software, etc. are examples of these sectors, which contrast with the "industrial" society driven by manufacturing and primary processing activities.

A variety of forces are responsible for the growth of industrial society. These forces include the development of more narrowly defined product lines and consequent regional specialization, technological change in products and processes, and the development of more complex organizations for management and product distribution. But to what extent have elements of the "postindustrial" economy also demonstrated these same growth properties? To what extent is the postindustrial society, composed of highly specialized organizations delivering their output to clients, located with the same spatial diversity as is the case for goods producers in the "industrial" society? We really do not have a body of empirical evidence on trading structures, or a location theory developed for this class of activities, which can help us answer this question very elegantly. We recognize that the Central Administrative Office (CAO) functions of large (usually manufacturing) corporations are located typically in the laborsheds of our largest cities, and that the suppliers of inputs to these organizations are agglomerated near these headquarter cities. But beyond this top of the hierarchy layer, and beyond the specialized services cities such as Washington, D.C. or Las Vegas, what is the degree of interregional trade in the more "normal" complement of these activities which are found in almost every metropolitan region?

2. SELECTED TREATMENT OF SERVICES EXPORTS IN THE LITERATURE

A considerable literature has developed in regional science, geography, economics, and planning regarding the economic base of communities, a literature which makes various assumptions about trade in different industries. Let us review some of this literature vis-à-vis trade in services.

At one end of the spectrum, there are those who regard interregional trade in services to be an insignificant activity. This group acknowledges that services are exported, but argues that their trade is governed by central place principles. Reifler (1976) has taken this position, arguing that exports from larger metropolitan centers filter to places farther down the hierarchy. Using data for Bureau of Economic Analysis (BEA) urban-focused regions, he finds an association between services earning per capita and size of place, and he interprets this as evidence of increased export activity in services from large size places. But what of exports to other large size places, internationally, or into smaller places in another subregion in the lattice of places of a given size: " . . . these activities are likely to respond to, but not initiate, regional growth" (Reifler 1976, p. 100). Hence, in this view we should expect that service exports, if any, from a region such as the Seattle area would be localized in nature, flowing to nearby (BEA) regions.

Riefler's analysis was national in scale. However, the same posture is evident in many studies at the regional scale. This has been a convenient means of accomplishing economic base analyses for agencies without the resources to conduct survey research on the structure of their regional economies. Recently produced studies in the Pacific Northwest by the Northwest Power Planning Council (1983) and the State of Washington Emergency Commission on Economic Development and Job Creation (1983) are exemplary of this posture.

In some ways it is curious that this tradition has developed, since some of the earliest empirical work on the nature of the regional economic base emphasized the prospective contribution of any sector to this component of any regional economy (Tiebout 1962; Blumenfeld 1955; Alexander 1954).

In striking contrast to the work of scholars taking a pessimistic view of the role of services in the regional economic base is the work of scholars such as Noyelle (1983, 1984), Stanback and Noyelle (1982), Stanback, Bearse, Noyelle and Karasaek (1981), Pred (1977), Polese (1982), and Ullman and Dacey (1960).

Pred undertook an analysis of "job-control" in large corporations, headquartered in a sample of western United States metropolitan centers in the 1970s. He reasoned from their organizational structure to probable interregional trading relationships, and was struck by the nonhierarchical nature of the locations of jobs "controlled" from his sample of cities. Smaller places such as Boise, Idaho were endowed with headquarters of some very large corporations. On a per capita basis, Pred argued that an equal amount of this type of employment was found in Boise as in the biggest of places. Pred reasoned that much services trade was associated with these headquarters functions, but he did not exploit the possibility that linked services sectors are also highly externalized (although he did not foreclose the prospect of such interaction).

Stanback and Noyelle have recently published a number of papers focusing on the services in the context of urban change (Stanback, Bearse, Noyelle, and Karasek 1981; Noyelle 1983, 1984; Stanback and Noyelle 1982). They have repeatedly argued that services have become more important elements in the economic base of large cities, particularly those that they refer to as the "complex of corporate activities." Included in this set are Central Administrative Offices (CAO's) of manufacturing firms and primary producers, finance, insurance and real estate, business services, legal services, membership organizations, miscellaneous services, and social services. While not presenting data on trade, they make interesting arguments regarding the growth of these sectors in an export context.

Noyelle and Stanback argue that as the economy has grown, services inputs to producers and CAO's have grown rapidly. R&D, planning, engineering, customizing, stylizing, corporate management, etc. are described as examples of these enlarged input streams from the services. In a sense, they argue that these services have grown as indirect exports, arguing that their rise has been stimulated primarily by the expansion in demand for them by increased purchases as inputs to other sectors which are in turn exporting. Noyelle and Stanback also present a classification of cities, based on an analysis of the structure of their economies, to bolster arguments regarding their vision of the possibility of an impending polarization of the nation's urban places. They conclude that the potential exists for the very largest of places to capture much of the expansion of the traded services, with some disenfranchisement of the set of places below the level of the diversified service centers from this new era of trade in services in advanced societies (Stanback and Noyelle 1982).

In considering structural change, they see advanced services as becoming more important in community economic bases:

> Until recently, manufacturing had been a principal component of the export base of many of the current diversified and specialized service centers. Increasingly, however, it is advanced services that constitute the vital sector of their economies (Noyelle 1983, p. 286).

It should be noted that these authors provide no data on trade to confirm their arguments.

Writers on the economic base concept have also sometimes included services in their "basic sector." Ullman and Dacey's work on the minimum requirements concept is probably the best example of this, in that every sector is to some degree basic or exporting (except in the place that is the observed minimum for a sector) (Ullman and Dacey 1960). Similarly, input-output accounts make no assumptions about such bifurcations; any sector may be selling locally or nonlocally in empirically observed proportions. Mulligan and Gibson (1984) provide similar evidence for a set of small places in Arizona.

It is instructive to review evidence from the survey-based input-output models to focus on assumed trade in services. Table 1 shows percentages of exports in some services sectors in a sample of such studies. It is striking that the widely cited Washington model shows large trade exports, and modest exports in business and personal services.

Several years ago Beyers explored spatial patterns in the interregional economic system. Noting the openness of regional economies documented in input-output studies, and the significant degrees of external linkage suggested by Pred's work, an effort was made to document the spatial structure of trade between regions. Survey work revealed that the pattern of interregional interaction was complex at the level of the establishment, but followed a gravity model for all firms in a sample of manufacturers. It was found in this study that the degree of interregional trade was growing more complex over time. These results led to the development of a speculative interregional model which has been recently reported (Beyers 1983). A follow-up study was conducted with a small sample of Puget Sound region service sector firms, and similar spatial and temporal results were obtained.

This earlier study also analyzed changes in the interindustry linkage system in the Central Puget Sound region. Two aspects of this work are germane here: changes in the apparent structure of the region's economic base, shown in Tables 2 and 3, and changes in requirements for services as inputs by various sectors, as shown in Table 4. Table 2 shows changes in overall markets for the Puget Sound region service sector in these input-output data. Services exports grew from 17.6% to 27.9% of total sales and the local intraservices sales market share expanded slightly, while market shares tied to regional final demand declined strongly.

Table 3 shows the percentage contribution of various services sectors to the regional economic base (as measured by value of sales) in 1958 and 1977. Services sectors can be seen to almost double their share of the regional economic base over this time period, with a corresponding decline in the proportional contribution of the manufacturing and primary products sectors.

Table 4 shows data on changes in input requirements proportions from services sectors in the Puget Sound regions over the 1958-1977 time period. Developed from analyses of changes in the structure of input-output models

TABLE 1.   External Sales of Services for Selected Input-Output Models
Percentage of Sectoral Output Sold as Export

	Georgia	W. Virginia	Kansas	Washington	Hawaii
Trans. Services	63.5	50.3	48.5	47.3	47.9
Comm/Util	10.4	15.2	3.4	4.6	5.5
Trade	20.1	16.4	1.0	25.9	31.7
F.I.R.E.	18.5	5.7	14.6	25.3	14.2
Business and Personal Services	23.2	7.1	4.7	1.9	28.7

Sources: Emerson and Hackmann 1971; Schaffer, Laurent and Sutter 1972; Hawaii Department of Planning and Economic Development 1972; Bourque and Conway 1976; Miernyk et al. 1970.

TABLE 2.   Service Sector Sales in the Puget Sound Region, 1958-1977
(Percentage of Total Output)

	Regional Interindustry Sales:		Regional Final Demand	Exports
	To manufacturing	To services		
1958 sales	7.2	13.7	61.6	17.6
1977 sales	7.4	14.1	50.6	27.9

TABLE 3.   Contributions of Services Sectors to the Economic Base
Puget Sound Region, 1958-1977

	Percentage of the Regional Export Base	
	1958	1977
Transport Services	4.5	7.6
Communications	0.4	1.1
Electricity	0.0	0.3
Natural Gas	0.1	0.2
Other Utilities	0.5	2.7
Trade	1.0	12.2
FIRE	4.1	6.2
Business & Personal Services	4.2	1.7
Subtotal	14.8	32.0
Other Industries	85.2	68.0
Total	100.0	100.0

TABLE 4.   Puget Sound Region Direct Requirements
(Services Purchases Per Dollar of Output)

	1958 (cents)	1977 (cents)	Change 1958-1977 (cents)
All Sectors	8.78	11.40	2.69
Manufacturing Sectors	5.48	6.82	1.34
Services Sectors	12.40	14.31	1.91

paralleling the work of Carter (1970), these data show that in 1958 services inputs accounted for $.0871 per dollar of inputs to all sectors, but only $.058 to nonservice sectors and $.124 to service sectors. By 1977, services inputs had grown to $.1147 per dollar of inputs to all sectors, to $.0682 in non-services sectors, and to $.1431 in service sectors. These data clearly indicate that intraservices trade represents a much stronger linkage than services input requirements in nonservices sectors. Moreover, the growth in this interdependence has also been stronger within the services than it has been for services inputs by nonservice sectors. This finding is somewhat at odds with arguments made by Noyelle (1983) and Stanback and Noyelle (1982), who argue that a major basis of services sector expansion has been increases in requirements for their output by goods producing sectors. While there have been these increases in the Central Puget Sound region, their magnitude seems to be overshadowed by increased intraservices interdependence, and by the growth in the exports of service activity.

A recent study by Polese (1982) has also documented the importance of interregional trade in services. This study by Polese focused on the source of services consumed by enterprises in a rural area of Quebec, and he found:

> ... over half of regional service demand is satisfied by imports. This indicates a high level of interregional trade in services, perhaps higher than is usually suspected (p. 158).

The study documented the fact that a large proportion of these traded services are intrafirm, and covered a variety of manufacturing and services sectors firms.

3.   EXPORT SERVICES IN THE CENTRAL PUGET SOUND REGION

The preceding review suggests that it is likely that services sectors are engaged in export or interregional trading activity to a greater extent than commonly realized. In order to evaluate this issue, a research project was undertaken involving a broad cross-section of service sector establishments in the Central Puget Sound region.

This section of the paper provides selected findings from this project. More detailed findings are available in Beyers, Alvine, and Johnsen (1985).

The desire in this project was to undertake "exploratory analysis," focusing on sectors which have been previously more or less overlooked. Thus, retail and wholesale trade activity was not focused upon because it has been the subject of so many central place market studies, and tourism-related sectors were bypassed because of the relative wealth of information about this activity. A set of (business) service sectors was identified at a four-digit SIC level of detail which we felt was likely to have export markets.

We obtained a list of firm names in these sectors from Contacts Influential, a private firm that collects information on individual business establishments primarily for market research purposes. Almost 19,000 establishments were identified in the study region in the four-digit SIC codes selected for study. This was a much larger sample than we could interview, so we chose to contact all firms with six or more employees, and 5% of firms with five or fewer employees. This led to a sample size of about 5,000 establishments. Almost 2,200 of these firms were contacted by telephone, and probed about their degree of export market orientation. We chose to conduct detailed interviews with those reporting more than 10% of their business in export markets, and sought limited information from the balance of the sample. About 1,105 firms met the 10% export threshold; these firms employed approximately 85,000 persons, while the other approximately 1,100 firms employed about 35,000 persons. (About 5% of the firms contacted refused cooperation in the survey.) The in-depth interviews probed the level of export business, its dynamics, factors associated with the firms choice of location in the region, changes in location, and factors affecting business success. Interviews were conducted by students with key executives in these firms. It appears as though our overall sample size is about 40% of employment in the sectors which we chose to study, a very large level of coverage by survey research standards.

Location of Markets

Respondents to the in-depth interviews had nonlocal sales of more than 55% of their revenues. Table 5 shows the size of this sample by broad SIC groups, and the location of revenues for these establishments. In almost every grouping, the nonlocal revenue proportion is significant; in about a third of these categories the non-Washington sales component was over half of their business.

Sectors with particularly striking export proportions include transportation services, research and development labs, insurance, and real estate services. In contrast, a more local orientation is evident in advertising, commerical photography and art services, and bookkeeping services. Beyond these extremes, it is fascinating to note the almost generic strong ties to external markets in a variety of sectors heretofore considered largely local in their focus: communications, banking, and computer services.

The tally of regions identified is shown in Figure 1 for domestic regions. While the pattern shows a dominance of ties to Alaska, Oregon, and California, this regional focus should not be interpreted as a central place like market structure. One would be hard pressed to consider California to be in Washington's hinterland. Portland, Oregon is a metropolitan place in the national settlement system only slightly smaller than Seattle. And as with California, it is probably

TABLE 5.   Distribution of Revenues[a] by SIC Groups

SIC Group	No. of Firms	Sum of Emp.	Local	Other WN	Other US	Foreign
				Percent of Revenues		
Transport Carriers	75	6,327	35.8	3.5	52.0	8.7
Transport Services	68	1,388	29.2	10.1	47.1	13.6
Comm/Util	31	8,155	48.1	26.6	24.8	0.5
Finance	57	13,587	47.8	26.9	16.3	9.0
Insurance	129	7,701	39.1	17.6	43.0	0.3
Real Estate	43	1,702	41.9	8.6	45.2	4.2
Adv/Comm Art	47	2,781	64.2	24.2	11.5	0.1
Computer Prog/Serv	93	9,944	47.1	5.2	41.4	6.3
R&D Labs	36	3,125	15.1	2.9	67.0	15.1
Mgmnt/Pub Rel	91	1,812	45.4	11.3	40.1	3.2
Other Bus. Serv.	75	2,308	57.5	11.7	27.0	3.8
Legal Services	81	3,620	57.5	13.0	24.4	5.1
Equip Rental	20	320	56.6	20.3	20.3	2.8
Arch/Engr	162	4,707	46.2	15.5	34.3	4.1
Acctg/Bkkeep	40	1,286	76.3	10.5	12.4	0.8
Other Services	51	15,511	39.8	19.5	37.9	2.8
All Responses	1,099	84,274	44.5	16.5	34.1	5.0

[a] Firm responses weighted by employment.

erroneous to consider most Oregon sales as within a central-place hinterland of Puget Sound services firms. The foreign regions identified most commonly were Canada and the Far East, followed by Europe and Latin America.

Slightly less than half of the firms in the sample responded in more general terms about their market locations, e.g. they did not identify a particular state or foreign country. Most of these were responses indicating spatially extensive marketing patterns.

Firm Size and Export Markets

It has been common for scholars to consider the small firm as having a regional market focus, with arguments made about the impediments associated with communicating about the firm's products and services in distant markets. In contrast, the large firm is seen as having a spatially extensive marketing network or corporate organizational structure, which would enable it to penetrate distant markets (Molander 1966). We found absolutely no correlation between firm size and the degree of export market orientation. For our very large size sample, the simple correlation coefficient between firm size and percent export sales was an insignificant .02.

This is a very significant finding, for it totally defuses the notion that the small firm cannot be quite successful in obtaining spatially extensive business. The tendency of regional planning organizations to seek large businesses to locate branches of their organizations in their territory has long been an issue needing evaluation. To the extent that small businesses — which tend to slip through the net of concerns of public and private sector development organizations — have the degree of interregional business suggested in this project and in work of scholars such as Birch (1984), there can be no doubt but that many current development efforts need reprogramming.

Changes in Sales

Interviewees were asked about changes in their sales over the past five years, and if there was a change to describe the change in terms of previous shares of nonlocal business and geographical patterns of markets. They were also asked

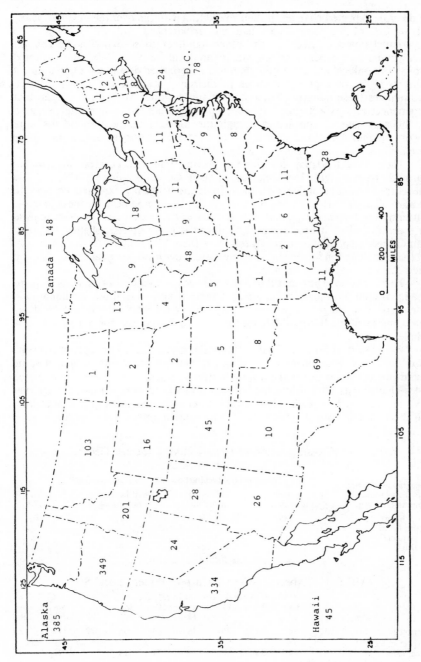

FIGURE 1.   Regions Cited by Respondents (Number of Citations)

to describe expected changes in their marketing patterns over the next five years. About half of the respondents had not experienced and did not expect to experience much change. On the other hand, of those experiencing change, many more had experienced growth in nonlocal markets (34%) and expected growth in nonlocal markets (30%) than had experienced declines in their nonlocal markets (13%) or expected declines in their nonlocal markets (15%). Table 6 summarizes these patterns. Responses off the diagonals in Table 6 suggest that experiences and expectations are more complex than the simple totals suggest. In the aggregate, it appears as though the markets of the respondents were becoming more nonlocal and they expected their business to become more nonlocal.

There is a tendency for those expecting nonlocal business to grow to currently have a highly localized market, as is shown in Table 7. Table 7 shows the current percent of local business juxtaposed against expected changes in market locations. Half of the firms expecting their nonlocal business to grow currently sell between 10% and 30% of their output externally. The distribution of those expecting it become more localized is more diverse; slightly less than half of these respondents currently sell more than 70% of their services externally, so there is some tendency expressed by those now most externalized to develop their local market in the near future.

There was no significant difference between the pattern of markets of firms headquartered in the Central Puget Sound region and those headquartered elsewhere. One might have thought that branches would have had localized operating territory, but that did not turn out to be the case for our sample as a whole.

We also asked firms to forecast their sales and employment change over the next five years. Most firms had strong expectations of growth, although some could not or would not make a quantitative estimate. The median anticipated sales change was 60%, while the median anticipated employment change was 33% in the next five years. That median level of employment growth translates to about a 6% annual growth rate. The annual growth rate in all services

TABLE 6.   Crosstabulation of Historical vs. Expected Geographical
Orientation of Sales

Geographically, how has distribution of your sales changed?	Geographically, how will your sales change?			
	Expect no change	Will be more local	Will be more non-local	TOTAL
No Change	388	66	97	551
More Local	57	39	36	132
Less Local	132	42	174	348
Total	577	147	307	1031

TABLE 7.   Expected Sales vs. Current Percent Local Sales

	Current Percent Local Sales									
	0-9	10-19	20-29	30-39	40-49	50-59	60-69	70-79	80-90	Total
Expect no change	102	54	51	36	36	63	56	72	119	589
Expect more local sales	30	14	24	14	9	21	14	15	10	151
Expect more export sales	10	13	27	15	27	32	32	44	109	309
Total	142	82	102	65	73	116	102	131	238	1051

employment in the Central Puget Sound region was 4.5% per annum over the 1958-1977 time period.

The firms we interviewed were probed for information on their mobility. Given that many had grown rapidly, it should be expected that they have had a dynamic locational history. This was borne out by the interviews. Fully half had moved in the last five years, mostly to gain space or to be nearer to sites important to principal officers in the firm. Most of the firms we interviewed were young — half had been started since 1971, and one quarter since 1978. They were small — median size was only fifteen employees — hence it is likely that they were short of space as they were and are growing. Most moved only short distances, and interestingly many fewer anticipated not having to move in the next five years than had recently moved (additional detail can be found in Beyers, Alvine, and Johnsen 1985).

Other Establishments.

The preceding discussion has referred to those firms meeting our interview screen of 10% export business; this sample must be placed in context of all firms in the services sectors in this survey to get a more accurate image of overall interregional trade in services. Firms with less than 10% export business were asked their export sales percentage, and their level of employment.

In striking contrast to the 1,100 firms that met our 10% screen, the approximately 1,000 firms which we interviewed by telephone had only about 2% of their business in export markets. These firms tended to be slightly smaller than the median size of firms in the in-depth interview sample, and collectively had about 35,000 employees. Extrapolation of the results for the sample of firms meeting our export-sales screen and the sample with less than 10% export sales as a whole in the Contacts Influential listing leads to a level of export orientation in the 33%-37% range. This level is well above those reported in Table 1 for the various input-output studies in the sector focused upon in this survey. While this is the case, these studies are somewhat dated, and given the growth in export-market sales reported by firms in our interviews, there is good reason to expect higher export-service estimates than found in these earlier research efforts.

The contrasting levels of export orientation of firms in the same four-digit SIC codes in our sampling plan is a major finding of this study. Why is it that firms in narrowly defined categories of services studied here have highly varying degrees of export market ties? Expressed alternatively, what determines what degree of the business activity is export-tied in given sectors?

4. CONCLUSIONS

The data presented in this paper indicate that service sectors probably have significant export markets in larger metropolitan regions. The linkages found in the Central Puget Sound region service sectors to larger urban regions (e.g. New York, San Francisco and Los Angeles) are contrary to central place theory notions that Puget Sound region service firms' exports are exclusively to their surrounding periphery. Many service sectors have a base of income which is as external and spatially diverse as many sectors traditionally considered key to the local economy. This finding means that many state and local economic development initiatives need rethinking, even in the absence of changes in federal programs. Clearly, one of the most important results of the project reported here is documentation of the fact that a broad cross section of service sectors are strongly dependent upon interregional trade — trade in distant parts of the United States and in foreign countries. Moreover, these are growing sectors in the national economic context, and the degree of their external trade is also growing. This is clear not only from the recent history of sales of respondents but from their expectations of changes in sales relationships.

The data presented in this paper tend to support analyses of structural change using input-output data, but do not necessarily support some more qualitatively oriented interpretations of studies of structural change. In this regard, the work of Noyelle and Stanback deserves reexamination. Noyelle and Stanback argue that much of the growth of the local services (wherever) is due to their greater input requirements by the "key" (i.e., export) sectors found in each region. Yet the data presented in this paper suggest that while the significance of these inputs has risen, proportionally they did not increase as much as intraservices input purchases. The survey research reported here also suggested a strong market tie within the services: more than half of the contacts reported by our respondents were with services or public sector markets. Evidence gathered in this paper suggests that growth of services exports was not primarily associated with the movement of goods, or because of export market linkages to goods producing or moving sectors. Rather, the growth of the services seems to be more tied to complex intraservices sector demands, and final demands for services by consumers and government. The research results presented here lead to a number of research needs.

To what extent are these findings unique to Seattle or generalizable to larger metropolitan regions? Without comparable survey research in other places we are not in a position to answer this question definitively. However, the Central Puget Sound region's industrial structure is not vastly different than the nation as a whole, as shown in Table 8, and fits Noyelle and Stanback's concept of a diversified service center. This similarity in structure makes it likely that the results reported here would be broadly applicable to other places, but clearly it would be highly desirable to have validation of these results through comparative research efforts.

We noted a great bifurcation in service sector firms' export orientation — even within fairly narrowly defined SIC codes. What factors lead some service sector firms to be highly involved in export markets, while others in the same sector have local market orientation? The interview process used in this study did not probe this matter in nearly the depth which it could have, since this would have required some effort at contrasting business development strategies of those exporting with those not exporting. For the latter group, we developed only minimal data, and did not explore why they had only localized markets.

In developing a location theory for the services — beyond central place theory and industrial location theory of the Weberian and "behavioral" type —

TABLE 8.   Non-Agricultural Wage and Salary Employment
Central Puget Sound Region and the United States 1981
(Percent of Total)

Sector	Central Puget Sound	United States
Manufacturing	20.0	22.1
Wholesale & Retail Trade	23.9	22.6
Government	18.0	17.6
Services	20.3	20.4
Transportation, Utilities	5.2	5.7
Finance, Insurance, Real Estate	6.8	5.8
Construction	4.7	4.6

we really need to have a micro level understanding of the location factors of significance to these sectors. This means a comparative evaluation of the importance of various input factors. Given the significance of labor costs to these sectors it is likely that qualities of labor would figure centrally in the development of a location theory for service export firms. Given the small size of many of these establishments, and the apparent key role of their founder in their siting decision (or nondecision?), any such theorizing about their location must have a focus on these entrepreneurs.

Many current regional development program efforts seem typically focused on attracting manufacturing industry; industrial policy discussion has largely focused on manufacturing to the exclusion of much consideration of the role of the services as basic industry in a national or regional context. The data presented in this paper indicate that this view must be augmented. Given the continuing growth of employment in services through the recent recession, and given the data provided to us by the respondents about their recent history of growth, it is clear that structural change in the export base of the Central Puget Sound region has continued as suggested in Tables 2 and 3. This suggests the need for careful consideration of service sectors in any national or regional industrial policy.

The results presented in this paper are exploratory. While they need verification in other settings to confirm their generality, there is good reason to believe that the spatially extensive characteristics of the markets of services firms in the study region are common to most large metropolitan regions, and may also characterize many smaller regions' economic base in "postindustrial" society. Hopefully, regional scientists, geographers, planners, economists and others interested in understanding forces leading the growth and development of our economy will help in obtaining the understanding we need of the role of export service activity in contemporary economic development processes. At the same time, new perspectives are probably necessary on location theory for the services, and in "industrial policy" for America in the 1980s.

ACKNOWLEDGMENTS

Funding for the research reported in this paper was provided by the Economic Development Administration, Grant No. 07-15-11071, and by the College of Arts and Sciences at the University of Washington. The views expressed are those of the authors; they do not necessarily represent the views of the supporting institutions. The assistance of J. Scott MacCready, Dean Hansen, John W. Tofflemire, Barney Warf, David Baltz, Jonathan Van Wyk and Nancy White, in conducting interviews is gratefully acknowledged. Mr. Erik Johnsen, Executive Director of the Central Puget Sound Economic Development District, was instrumental in the development of this project. Support from the National Science Foundation under Grant No. SES 8109290 to William Beyers also played a critical role in this project.

REFERENCES

Alexander, J. W. 1954. The basic-nonbasic concept of urban economic functions. *Economic Geography* 30: 246-61.
Bell, D. 1973. *The coming of postindustrial society: a venture in social forecasting.* New York: Basic Books.
Beyers, W. B. 1983. The interregional structure of the U.S. economy. *International Regional Science Review* 8: 213-31.
Beyers, W. B., Alvine, M. J., and Johnsen, E. 1985. *The service economy: export of services in the Central Puget Sound Region.* Seattle: Central Puget Sound Economic Development District.

Birch, D. 1984. The changing rules of the game, finding a niche in the thoughtware economy. *Economic Development Commentary* 8, 1: 12-16.

Blumenfeld, H. 1955. The economic base of the metropolis. *Journal of the American Institute of Planners* 21: 114-32.

Bourque, P. J. and Conway, R. S., Jr. 1976. *The input-output structure of Washington state.* Seattle: Graduate School of Business Administration, mimeographed.

Carter, A. 1970. *Structural change in the American economy.* Cambridge, MA: Harvard University Press.

Emerson, M. J. and Hackmann, D. G. 1971. *The 1969 Kansas input-output study.* Topeka: Kansas Department of Economic Development, Planning Division.

Hawaii Department of Planning and Economic Development. 1972. *Interindustry study of the Hawaiian economy.*

Miernyk, W. H., Shellhamer, K. L., Brown, D. M., Coccari, R. L., Gallagher, C. J., and Wineman, W. H. 1970. *Simulating regional economic development.* Lexington, MA: D.C. Heath and Company.

Molander, J. D. 1966. Geographic isolation and market area expansion; a study of small Washington state firms attempting to sell in the national market. D.B.A. dissertation, Graduate School of Business Administration, University of Washington.

Mulligan, G. and Gibson, L. 1984. Regression estimates of economic base multipliers for small communities. *Economic Geography* 60: 225-37.

Northwest Power Planning Council. 1983. *Economic and Demographic Assumptions,* mimeographed.

Noyelle, T. J. 1983. The rise of advanced services. *American Planning Association Journal* 49, 3: 280-90.

Noyelle, T. J. 1984. The service era, focussing public policy on people and places. *Economic Development Commentary* 8, 2: 12-17.

Polese, M. 1982. Regional demand for business services and interregional service flows in a small Canadian region. *Papers, Regional Science Association* 50: 151-63.

Pred, A. 1977. *City-systems in advanced economies.* New York: Wiley & Sons.

Riefler, R. 1976. Implications of service industry growth for regional development strategies. *Annals of Regional Science* 10: 88-103.

Schaffer, W. A., Laurent, E. A., and Sutter, E. M., Jr. 1972. *Introducing the Georgia economic model.* Atlanta: The Georgia Department of Industry and Trade.

Stanback, T. M., Jr. and Noyelle, T. J. 1982. *Cities in transition.* Totowa, NJ: Allenheld, Osmun.

Tiebout, C. M. 1962. *The community economic base study.* New York: Committee on Economic Development.

Ullman, E. L. and Dacey, M. J. 1960. The minimum requirements approach to the regional economic base. *Papers, Regional Science Association.* 6: 175-94.

Washington State. 1983. *Report of the emergency commission on economic development and job creation.* Volume III.

[3]

Urban Studies, Vol. 29, No. 6, 1992 857–868

Producer Services and Systems of Flexible Production

William J. Coffey and Antoine S. Bailly

[Paper first received, February 1991; in final form, October 1991]

Summary. During the decade of the 1980s, regional science began to devote more and more attention to the influence of two phenomena upon the structure and functioning of the space-economy: (1) service activities, in general, and producer services, in particular; and (2) flexible production systems. This paper explores the extent to which these two major preoccupations of contemporary regional science can be integrated, and attempts to contribute to the understanding of the growth and location of producer services by examining the manner in which an analytical framework based upon flexible production may be applied to the latter. The exploration begins with a summary and criticism of the flexible production approach. This is followed by a discussion of the growth of producer services and of the trends towards the increasing externalisation of these activities. Next, the appropriateness of employing a flexible production framework in the case of producer services is examined. The significance of the concept of flexible production for understanding the location of producer services is then explored. Finally, the paper examines the effects upon the labour force of flexibility in the production and use of producer services.

1. Introduction

In the view of an increasingly wide range of authors, flexible production (or flexible accumulation) has become the driving force underlying the restructuring of the space-economies of many industrialised nations. Indeed, since the mid-1980s researchers have increasingly employed a flexible production framework in their analysis of the structure and evolution of both national and regional economic systems. In this context, it is therefore surprising to note that, with very few exceptions (e.g. Moulaert *et al.*, 1988; Scott, 1988a; Christopherson, 1989; Beyers, 1990; Coffey and Bailly, 1991; Wood, 1991), analyses of flexible production systems have completely ignored the role played by service activities. On the one hand, certain services represent basic elements of the manufacturing process, and are often essential for achieving flexibility; on the other hand, many services may be viewed as production systems in their own right, and thus are characterised by specific strategies designed to achieve flexibility.

The omission of services from the flexible production literature is especially difficult to understand given the strong performance of service activities relative to manufacturing in all developed economies over the past 15 years. Producer services, especially, have been the subject of particular attention on the basis of their growth rates, their acknowledged status as an important component of a region's export base, and their strategic role in promoting

William J. Coffey is at the Département d'études urbaines, University of Quebec at Montreal, and Antoine S. Bailly is at the Département de géographie, University of Geneva, Uni-Mail, 1211 Genève 4, Switzerland. The authors are indebted to the European Science Foundation for its support of this research through its programme, Regional and Urban Restructuring in Europe (RURE).

innovation and technological change in other economic sectors (Marshall, 1988; Coffey and Polèse, 1989; Illeris, 1989).

This paper explicitly seeks to explore the role of producer services in systems of flexible production, as well as the manner in which the flexible production framework can be extended so as to include these high-order service functions. The approach adopted here is conceptual rather than empirical; indeed, at present, there are few empirical investigations of these issues in the literature. Our exploration begins with a brief summary of the characteristics of flexible production. This is followed by a discussion of the growth of producer services and of the trend towards the increasing externalisation of these activities. The appropriateness of employing a flexible production framework in the case of producer services is then examined, followed by an analysis of the ways in which a knowledge of flexible production aids us to understand the location of producer services.

2. Flexible Production

A flexible production system, it is often argued, is the antithesis of the rigidities inherent in the Fordist system of mass production. As its name implies, the basis of a flexible production system is *flexibility* of production processes and labour markets; its principle dimensions include:

(1) programmable, and hence flexible, forms of production automation;

(2) socially fragmented, but inter-connected and organisationally pliable, units of economic activity; and

(3) more fluid labour market structures.

The hallmark of flexible production is *vertical disintegration*. Here, the entire production process is not internalised by one enterprise, as in the case of vertical integration. Rather, the main enterprise controls only the final product and the key technology; activities that are not strategic to the production process itself, together with the production of parts, components

and ancillary services, are *contracted-out* to other firms. An inter-firm, inter-establishment structure thus emerges, one in which a network of small and medium-sized specialist enterprises supports the activities in the main establishment. The functioning of this type of production system relies upon the *social division of labour*, that is the division of labour between firms. Here production becomes more externalised among a set of individual firms with input–output linkages and, in organisational terms, more flexible; the notion of 'the firm as an organisation' is replaced by that of 'the organisation of firms' (Scott, 1988b). In addition, the internal economies of scale and scope that have characterised traditional Fordist modes of production are replaced by *external* economies of scale, creating intense agglomeration economies.

3. Producer Services: Growth and Externalisation

Producer services are intermediate-demand functions that serve as inputs into the production of goods or of other services; they enhance the efficiency of operation and the value of output at various stages of the production process, broadly defined so as to include activities that are both upstream and downstream of actual production (e.g. research and development, marketing). A wide range of empirical evidence (e.g. Gershuny and Miles, 1983; Daniels, 1985; Bailly and Maillat, 1988; Marshall, 1988; Beyers, 1989; Coffey and McRae, 1989; Illeris, 1989) has demonstrated that producer services occupy a major and expanding role in the space-economies of developed countries.

Where the production of either goods or services is concerned, producer service inputs may be provided either *internally* by the firm or the establishment itself, or *externally* by a free-standing specialist firm. While the extent and the growth of employment in free-standing producer service firms have been more readily documented, the magnitude and increase of non-production employment in the goods-producing sectors are also quite significant. For example, in 1981 approximately 30 per cent of employment in Canada's goods-producing sectors was non-production related (Coffey and McRae, 1989); this figure rises to over 50 per cent in certain sub-sectors such as chemical products and petroleum refining.

Producer Service Growth

The rapid growth of producer services involves several factors related to the increasing complexity of both the external environment of the firm and its internal organisation. In general, the amount of information that a firm must process (gather, store, analyse, distribute) is continuously increasing. The opportunities and constraints presented by its social and economic environment, as well as those imposed by its internal structure and functioning, need to be constantly evaluated. In addition, certain interventions or adjustments must often be initiated as a result of this process of evaluation.

More specifically, the following factors are widely recognised to play significant roles in producer service growth (Coffey and Bailly, 1991). *First*, there have been transformations in which goods and services are produced. Here the trend has been towards increased *product innovation and differentiation*. The research and development, design, advertising, marketing and distribution aspects of the production of goods and services have thus become increasingly important.

Second, transformations have also occurred in how goods and services are produced. In parallel with product innovations, process innovations are also occurring. New tasks, functions and techniques have appeared in the organisation of production systems, permitting greater efficiency and rapid adjustment to changing economic circumstances. The pace of technological change, in particular, has forced a growing number of firms to seek specialised help or to develop specialised capacities, notably in fields such as information processing, industrial engineering, process design and research.

Third, the national and international environments within which firms must operate are becoming increasingly complex, in terms of finance, production and distribution. Functions relating to raising capital, foreign exchange and mounting or resisting take-overs and/or mergers are occurring over wider geographical areas. Firms must also be increasingly concerned with the development and exploitation of foreign markets, the maintenance and administration of relations with foreign affiliates and trading partners, and the direction of offshore production and sales units.

Fourth, the increased government intervention and regulation that characterise certain (mostly European) developed nations have necessitated reactive and proactive responses by firms seeking to conform to the norms imposed by society. In addition, however, this expanding regulatory framework has increased the consumption of producer services by the various levels of government themselves. *Finally*, the range of tasks related to the internal management and administration of the firm, and to the co-ordination of inter-firm transactions, has expanded rapidly. The more complex the firm becomes, and the more intricate each of its individual elements, the greater the need for a general management function whose task is to choose strategies, plan, organise, co-ordinate and control at all levels.

All of the functions referred to above require the intervention of specialists—engineers, lawyers, accountants, management consultants, advertising professionals, and so forth—who can analyse situations, process information, produce required documentation, and assist in decision-making.

The Externalisation of Producer Services

A given firm or establishment has the choice between providing some or all of its producer services internally through its own personnel, or purchasing these inputs from separate specialist organisations. The latter, free-standing producer service activities, have achieved the highest rates -of employment growth among all sectors of advanced economies (141.2 per cent in Canada over the period 1971–81, according to Coffey and McRae, 1989). These activities now account for between 25 and 30 per cent of the US's GNP (Noyelle and Stanback, 1984; Beyers, 1989), the equivalent of that resulting from the physical production of goods; in most European countries producer services create over 20 per cent of the GNP (Bailly and Maillat, 1988).

In view of the growing economic significance of free-standing producer services, it becomes important to understand the factors that induce a firm to purchase these inputs externally, rather than to provide them internally. The principal factors identified in the literature may be summarised as follows. *First*, firms are subject to in-house technical limitations. While consuming greater quantities of producer services, the capacity of a given firm to develop the level of expertise required to provide effectively a particular service input may be restricted by knowledge, personnel or cost limitations. *Second*, advantages of external economies are associated with the contracting-out of services. Firms are often able to purchase specialised producer services from outside sources less expensively than they can provide them internally due to scale economies in the specialised free-standing service firm.

Third, where the required service inputs involve highly diverse and constantly shifting mixes of information and expertise, and where the demand for these inputs is both sporadic and unpredictable, it may not be economically feasible for a firm to engage sufficient personnel to deal effectively with the entire range of demand. *Fourth*, there are certain economic and organisational advantages in maintaining a small and highly focused pool of human resources. Many firms seek to restrict their activities to core functions, those that they accomplish better than other organisations; the remaining service inputs are purchased externally. *Finally*, firms may reduce their costs of participation in social insurance programmes and of other overheads through the externalisation of service inputs. Similarly, the risks associated with unstable demand for particular services are transferred to the external service supplier.

The latter four factors, in particular, are explicitly related to the concept of flexible production; indeed, they help to define the notion of flexibility in a production system. It is interesting to note, however, that the majority of these factors were first identified in the management economics literature (Chandler, 1977; Williamson, 1981; Leibenstein, 1987). A multi-divisional (or M-form) governance structure has long been recognised as having a greater degree of autonomy and flexibility than alternative forms; it is the result of the organisational strain of trying to cope with increasing complexity. Thus the M-form corporation takes on many of the properties of, and is usefully regarded as, a miniature market system, and provides a high degree of operational flexibility, both in terms of the sources and mix of available inputs, and in terms of its ability to minimise the transaction costs of acquiring these inputs.

4. Producer Services: Growth, Vertical Disintegration and the Social Division of Labour

Is the growth of producer services (both internal and external) real or illusory? Certain authors (e.g. Gershuny and Miles, 1983) have argued that the increase of producer services is largely a statistical artifact due to an elasticity of demand greater than unity, and a lower level of productivity compared to the goods-producing sector. In addition, it has been argued that the 'growth' of free-standing producer services may simply be due to a displacement effect—i.e. the shift away from in-house service production by firms and towards their external purchase from specialised establishments.

The empirical evidence concerning these issues is categorical, however not only has producer service growth been found to be real, but output and employment growth have been achieved in internal and external producer services simultaneously; a displacement of internal services is not occurring. Illeris (1989) comes to this conclusion after reviewing a wide range of European research, as do McCrackin (1985), Tschetter (1987), Kutscher (1988) and Beyers (1989) in the context of the US economy. "Thus our research indicates little support for the argument that the growth of producer services is illusory, attributable to the transfer of certain occupational categories out of the goods sector" (McCrackin, 1985, p. 20). Beyers (1989) argues that much more producer service growth has resulted from fundamental changes in the types of services consumed than in the simple externalisation of certain functions. Technical change within the services in both 'product' and process appears to have been a more significant factor than the exploitation of economies of scale in given pre-existing producer service activities (i.e. than an internal–external shift).

As defined in the literature, the principal characteristics underlying a flexible production system are vertical disintegration and the social division of labour. Given that vertical disintegration (the net displacement of internal producer services to free-standing firms) is not occurring, is it inappropriate to apply the notion of flexible production to producer services? Logically, if the presence of vertical disintegration is a necessary element of flexible production, the response is affirmative. The situation must, however, be viewed in a more nuanced manner. The key characteristic of a flexible production system is not vertical disintegration, narrowly defined to indicate the divestment of functions (here, internal producer services) on the part of firms, but rather a deepening social division of labour—that is, an incremental growth of the proportion of external activities utilised due to the complex set of reasons identified in the previous section. This phenomenon is indeed occurring in the area of producer services, where available evidence clearly indicates a proliferation in the number and the utilisation of specialised establishments. Thus, using a less rigid interpretation of the characteristics of flexible production, there is no logical difficulty in interpreting the dynamics of producer service activities within this context.

5. Producer Services and Flexible Production

With very few exceptions, the flexible production framework has completely ignored producer services; rather, it has been restricted to the analysis of manufacturing activities, specifically dealing with the vertical disintegration of material inputs (parts and components) among a network of independent sub-contractors. In the present section, we explore the manner in which the scope of the flexible production framework may logically be extended so as to include producer service activities. This extension involves two specific elements: (1) the explicit acknowledgement of producer services as inputs in the goods production process; and (2) the increasing vertical disintegration or unbundling of activities within producer service establishments themselves.

In the *first* case, producer services may simply be grafted onto the existing goods-production focus of the flexible production approach. As exemplified by the work of Piore and Sabel (1984), Holmes (1986),

Scott (1988b) and others, the flexible production framework represents a highly incomplete perspective on the modern production system, in which the fabrication of goods and the production of services are highly integrated. Manufacturing inputs include more than raw materials, parts and components, and labour; as we have seen, services play an important and expanding role in the production of goods. The forward and backward linkages of a manufacturing enterprise involve not just the transport of physical objects, but also the communication of information, expertise and technical ability. Thus, a manufacturing establishment's substitution of externally-purchased service inputs for internally-provided services may be seen to represent a form of organisation by which the establishment in question is able to increase the level of flexibility of its production process. In addition, as Hatch (1987) notes, many service activities play a strategic role in facilitating the operationalisation of the flexible manufacturing concept, which places heavy demands on the firm's ability to co-ordinate and to manage the flow of production.

The *second* case, involves the increasing externalisation and specialisation of inputs purchased by producer service establishments themselves. As in the case of the goods-producing sector, producer service activities are increasingly marked by a social division of labour; firms are becoming more and more specialised as the range of services available becomes increasingly diversified, and as evolving technological changes require narrower and deeper types of expertise. Similar to the well-known situation in high technology manufacturing, much of this social division of labour occurs through spin-offs of key employees from existing service firms and results in a dense network of intra- and inter-sectoral firm linkages (Marshall, 1988). Thus, as in the case of high technology manufacturing and of other 'new production ensembles', the producer service sector is characterised by high levels of new firm formation and of

small firm growth (Wood, 1991). Further, increases in complexity and inter-penetration within the producer service sector have created new and rather intricate corporate structures.

As in the case of manufacturing activities, the externalisation of functions within producer service establishments causes internal economies of scope to be replaced by external economies of scale as a set of highly specialised producers interact with one another. The advantages of this externalisation of producer service inputs are analogous to those resulting from the external purchase of services by a manufacturing establishment: firms may obtain increased flexibility, substitute variable costs for fixed costs, and spread their risk in several ways. Logically, a firm will seek to externalise services with high fixed costs; if the volume of work is changing, unused capacity may be avoided through the purchase of services from sub-contractors at peak periods or when a rare need occurs. Externalisation also puts the risk of coping with periods of unstable demand on the sub-contractor. In these respects, the process of service production is directly comparable to the goods-production process.

Under what conditions is the externalisation of functions within producer service establishments likely to occur? In addition to the factors identified in Section 3, the following conditions (which are similar to the circumstances identified by Scott (1988b) under which an extensive social division of labour is apt to occur among manufacturing firms) are likely to lead to externalisation. *First*, where complementary producer services have widely varying scales of production. Small firms may contract out certain tasks (e.g. legal counsel or tax accounting) because they do not have the volume of demand required to employ economically the specialised personnel required to perform the function internally. Conversely, specialised sub-contractors (e.g. in the legal or tax fields) can achieve internal economies of scale by pooling a wide range of external demand. *Second*, where segmented labour markets prevail. Here the possibility exists for some work tasks to be sub-contracted out from firms in high-wage primary labour market sectors (e.g. technical and professional occupations) to firms in lower-wage secondary labour market sectors (e.g. maintenance, security or data-input personnel). *Third*, where the spatial agglomeration of producer service activities exists. In this situation, external transaction costs will fall due to close physical proximity, encouraging the social division of labour.

6. The Spatial Dimension

What are the implications of flexible production for producer service location? Before addressing this question, it would be useful to review briefly the conventional wisdom concerning the effects of flexible production methods upon *manufacturing* location. As in the case of the narrower application of flexible production to manufacturing activity, its extension to producer services has implications at both inter-regional and intra-regional scales.

Geographically, the Fordist system is said to have generated large industrial conurbations (e.g. Detroit, Birmingham and the Ruhr valley), possessing essential agglomeration economies; only plants not needing to avail themselves of such benefits were able to decentralise. With the rise of flexible forms of production, and due to the imperatives of increased international competition, the geography of economic activity began to change (Scott, 1988b). At the *inter-regional* level, it has been argued that the range and diversity of feasible locations have been greatly extended, all the more so when the shift to flexible production is accompanied by a high degree of technological innovation and by the rise of new production ensembles (e.g. high technology industries). The result is both the internal restructuring of older industrial regions and the expansion of production activity into 'new industrial spaces'. The latter phenomenon is related to a number of factors (e.g. higher rates of unionisation, rising land prices and local taxes, and increasing congestion and pollution) which render traditional manufacturing regions increasingly unattractive to new industrial investments, in general, and above all to the formation of flexible production complexes. These new growth centres based on flexible production systems often tend to be found in places such as Silicon Valley, Phoenix or Boulder—areas that are either socially insulated or geographically isolated from the main foci of earlier industrialisation (Scott, 1988b).

At the *intra-regional* (metropolitan) level, it is argued, the system of flexible production creates the spatial clustering, in various locations, of functionally differentiated and organisationally distinct enterprises which exhibit close forward and backward linkages. By concentrating in geographical space, the linkage costs of vertically disintegrated producers can be reduced. Thus, the social division of labour provokes spatial agglomeration as a way of lowering external transaction costs. On the other hand, however, because it lowers costs, agglomeration also encourages the further social division of labour and the in-migration of new producers (Scott, 1988b).

Inter-regional Scale

At the inter-regional level, the spatial behaviour of producer service firms motivated by considerations of flexible production is somewhat different from that of manufacturing establishments. In the latter case, as we have seen, flexible production has sometimes encouraged the creation of 'new industrial spaces' isolated from traditional industrial centres. In the case of producer services, however, activity has generally remained concentrated in large metropolitan areas, many of them in the traditional industrial heartlands (Noyelle and Stanback, 1984). Table 1 indicates

Table 1. The spatial concentration of producer service employment in Canada, 1986

	Population		All services		Producer services	
	Percentage of all Canada	Cumulative percentage	Percentage of all Canada	Cumulative percentage	Percentage of all Canada	Cumulative percentage
Toronto	12.3	12.3	15.8	15.8	27.4	27.4
Montréal	11.6	23.9	12.8	28.6	16.1	43.5
Vancouver	5.2	29.1	6.8	35.4	10.0	53.5
Ottawa-Hull	3.0	32.1	4.4	39.8	5.2	58.7
Edmonton	2.7	34.8	3.8	43.6	5.0	63.7
Calgary	2.4	37.2	3.3	46.9	7.3	71.0
Winnipeg	2.4	39.6	3.2	50.1	2.8	73.8
Québec	2.4	42.0	2.9	53.0	2.2	76.0
Hamilton	2.2	44.2	2.2	55.2	2.3	78.3
St Catharines	1.3	45.5	1.1	56.3	1.2	79.5

the high degree of spatial concentration in the Canadian space-economy, where the three largest metropolitan areas account for 53 per cent of national producer service employment. The imperatives of flexible production do not negate the factors that have created the metropolitan concentration of producer services; on the contrary, flexibility in the production of producer services is actually facilitated by these factors, which combine to create massive external economies of scale. The factors promoting spatial concentration and facilitating flexible production may be summarised as follows.

First, a pool of appropriately skilled human resources. There is general agreement in the literature that human resources represent the principal factor underlying the location of producer services; the latter are generally much more labour intensive than manufacturing. Since labour is a factor of production with limited mobility, especially in the current era of two-breadwinner households, the job must often come to the person. On the one hand, many producer services require a labour force with high qualifications, as manifest in a professional, university-type education. Generally, a significant concentration of highly educated people is found in metropolitan areas: not only is this where a large proportion of them have been edu-

cated, but they are also attracted by high quality cultural and public services and by the large labour market. On the other hand, increasing externalisation within high-order producer services also requires a pool of labour with lower qualifications. Such personnel are similarly available in metropolitan areas.

Second, opportunities for backward linkages. Like manufacturing, the production of intermediate-demand services requires a particular mix of inputs. The spatial proximity between producer services and the sources or creators of knowledge, information and technical ability is crucial. A given producer service establishment must therefore have linkages to specialised consultants, complementary producer services, research institutions, universities, government organisations, hardware producers and so forth. In general, such facilities are available in greater scope and quantity in large urban areas.

Finally, opportunities for forward linkages. Here the market for producer services is the issue. Approximately one-half of the output of the producer service sector is typically purchased by other service establishments; a wide range of empirical evidence has shown that the latter tend to be concentrated in metropolitan areas. Further, in those cases in which producer services are purchased by the manufacturing sector, it is generally not by the production units themselves but, rather, by head offices or regional headquarters (Marshall, 1982, 1985). As corporate control and its associated spatial division of administrative functions tend to be highly concentrated in a small number of large metropolitan areas (Noyelle and Stanback, 1984; Daniels, 1985). It follows that the demand for producer services will be similarly concentrated. Thus the spatial pattern of corporate headquarters imposes a marked centralising influence upon the location of producer services (Wheeler, 1988). Further, the linkages between producer service establishments and head offices are becoming even stronger and more self-reinforcing than in the past. As firms increase their product range and their use of technology, so their need for specialised producer services increases.

Where both forward and backward linkages are concerned, the concentration of producer services in a small number of large cities enables the transaction costs associated with the production and delivery of such services to be minimised. In particular, it is the cost of maintaining face-to-face contact between the producers, on the one hand, and their inputs and markets, on the other hand, that is potentially the most expensive element of intermediate-demand service production; this expense can be significantly reduced by spatial agglomeration. Evidence indicates that, unless the information transmitted is relatively standardised, new telecommunications technologies cannot be successfully substituted for face-to-face contact (Törnqvist, 1970; Pred, 1975; Gottmann, 1977). The conventionally held view that telecommunication technology will supplant face-to-face contact and thus produce a decentralisation of producer services may be over-optimistic. On the contrary, it is possible that evolving telecommunications technologies will have the effect of increasing the concentration of these activities.

In sum, in large cities these forces of agglomeration tend to produce what may be termed a 'complex of corporate activities'; the spatial clustering and mutual symbiosis of (1) the head or divisional offices of primary, secondary and tertiary sector firms; (2) high-order financial establishments; and (3) the producer service firms that provide inputs to the first two types, as well as to each other. This complex of corporate activities is analogous to the complex of manufacturing activities that characterises a 'new industrial space', in terms of its tightly woven network of input–output linkages. Thus the agglomerative tendencies that are commonly identified as one of the hallmarks of 'new' methods of flexible production are a well-established phenomenon among producer service firms. Further, with increasing vertical disintegration in the producer service sector, the external economies of such corporate complexes are becoming more pronounced.

Intra-regional Scale

At the intra-regional level, the spatial behaviour of producer service activities is generally analogous to that of manufacturing establishments in new industrial spaces: a geographical clustering of functionally different enterprises which exhibit close forward and backward linkages. More so than in the case of manufacturing, however, this clustering tends to occur in major metropolitan areas. Such spatial concentration is most evident in the case of the above-mentioned 'complex of corporate activities', which establishes itself in the central business district of a large urban area in order to facilitate face-to-face contact. The spatial concentration of producer services in the CBD is, however, only one element of a more intricate locational pattern. Associated with the increasing social division of labour in this set of activities is a spatial separation of: (1) high-order 'front office' functions that require face-to-face contact, and thus remain centralised; and (2) routinised 'back office' functions that do not necessitate high-level personal contact, and may thus 'decentralise' in order to take advantage of cost savings associated with 'peripheral' locations. Unlike the case of manufacturing, however, when the 'decentralisation' of producer service functions occurs, it tends to be towards the suburbs of the same metropolitan area in which front office functions are located (Marshall, 1985; Moss and Dunau, 1986; Nelson, 1986).

While the lower land prices of non-CBD locations certainly play a role in the decoupling of back office functions, the structure of the metropolitan labour market may also be an important factor (Nelson, 1986). Metropolitan areas are generally characterised by extremely segmented labour markets: highly skilled, expensive professional personnel are juxtaposed with lower skilled, relatively inexpensive (and possibly part-time) labour. While the former type of labour input is necessary for many kinds of producer service functions, particularly those found in the CBD, many routinised or standardised functions can be carried out by the latter type. Further, the latter type of labour is generally characterised by higher levels of instability; these kinds of workers tend to be non-unionised and non-organised and thus are likely to offer minimal levels of resistance to erratic and insecure conditions of employment. The possibility of utilising such labour inputs adds considerably to the flexibility of a firm. In the manufacturing sector, it is principally immigrants and women who play this role; organised male labour forces that were formed under the Fordist system are highly rigid and are actively avoided by firms operating under the flexible production system (Scott, 1988b). In the case of producer services, certain authors (e.g. Nelson, 1986) have argued that producer service back offices tend to locate in suburbs to ensure the supply of a large and flexible labour force, primarily composed of suburban housewives. This point of view is not universally accepted, however;

in certain cities, producer service back offices employ large proportions of males and full-time workers (Huang, 1989).

In sum, the result of the locational response of producer services to the structural and locational characteristics of the metropolitan labour force is a functional segmentation of metropolitan space. To the extent that certain producer service functions are actively attempting to avoid the rigidity associated with the downtown primary labour market, the suburbs of metropolitan areas have begun to play the role of the 'new industrial spaces' of the service era.

7. Conclusion

The rise of flexible production methods in both goods-producing and service-producing sectors has stimulated the growth of producer service activities; on the other hand, however, increases in the number and variety of available producer services have clearly contributed to the development of flexible production systems. It must be emphasised that the types of processes that have been considered in this paper did not just suddenly appear when the term 'flexible production' entered current usage. Rather, such processes have existed to varying degrees for centuries, within both manufacturing and service production activities; however, these processes have become increasingly present during the past decade.

A modern economy must be regarded as an integrated system in which the fabrication of goods and the production of services are not viewed as dichotomous functions but, rather, as intersecting zones along a continuum. In this respect, the vast majority of research on flexible specialisation in manufacturing, which entirely ignores the role of producer services in the production process, represents a highly fragmentary view of both production systems and the available methods for achieving flexibility.

Although supported by the relevant literature, the approach taken here has remained at a conceptual level. The arguments that have been presented concerning the relationship between producer services and flexible production require further and systematic empirical investigation. For example, what types of producer services are most subject to the social division of labour? Is this process increasing over time? Are there spatial variations in the level of externalisation of particular producer service functions? Do the motivations, factors and processes underlying the decision to externalise specific types of producer services vary according to establishment or firm size, geographical area, or sector? What is the role of labour-force structure in inducing externalisation? What is the impact of technical change on the decision to externalise producer services?

Many of the issues that have been raised in this paper will specifically involve a micro-level of investigation. Indeed, it is clear that, in order better to understand the observed macro-scale patterns and processes of producer service activity, it is necessary to devote more attention to the underlying micro economic factors and mechanisms.

References

BAILLY, A. and MAILLAT, D. (1988) *Le secteur tertiaire en question*, 2nd edn. Geneva and Paris: Editions Régionales Européennes and Economica.

BEYERS, W.B. (1989) *The Producer Service and Economic Development in the United States: The Last Decade.* Washington, DC: Economic Development Administration.

BEYERS, W.B. (1990) *Changing business practices and the growth of the producer services: geographical implications.* Paper presented at the *Annual Meeting of the American Association of Geographers*, Toronto.

CHANDLER, A.D. (1977) *The Visible Hand: The Managerial Revolution in American Business.* Cambridge, MA: Belknap Press.

CHRISTOPHERSON, S. (1989) Flexibility in the US service economy and the emerging spatial division of labour, *Transactions, Institute of British Geographers*, 14, pp. 131–143.

COFFEY, W.J. and BAILLY, A.S. (1991) Producer services and flexible production: an exploratory analysis, *Growth and Change*, 22(4), pp. 95–117.

COFFEY, W.J. and McRAE, J.J. (1989) *Service Industries in Regional Development.* Montreal: Institute for Research on Public Policy.

COFFEY, W.J. and POLÈSE, M. (1989) Producer-services and regional development: a policy-oriented perspective, *Papers of the Regional Science Association*, 67, pp. 13–27.

DANIELS, P.W. (1985) *Service Industries: A Geographical Appraisal.* London: Methuen.

GERSHUNY, J.I. and MILES, I.D. (1983) *The New Service Economy.* London: Frances Pinter.

GOTTMANN, J. (1977) Megalopolis and antipolis: the telephone and the structure of the city, in: I. DE SOLA POOL (Ed.) *The Social Impact of the Telephone*, pp. 303–317. Cambridge, MA: MIT Press.

HATCH, C. (1987) Learning from Italy's industrial renaissance, *The Entrepreneurial Economy*, 1, pp. 4–11.

HOLMES, J. (1986) The organisation and locational structure of production subcontracting, in: A. SCOTT and M. STORPER (Eds) *Production, Work and Territory: The Geographical Anatomy of Industrial Capitalism*, pp. 80–106. Winchester, MA: Allen and Unwin.

HUANG, S. (1989) *Office suburbanisation in Toronto: fragmentation, workforce composition and laboursheds.* Unpublished PhD thesis, Department of Geography, University of Toronto.

ILLERIS, S. (1989) *Services and Regions in Europe.* Aldershot: Gower.

KUTSCHER, R.E. (1988) Growth of service employment in the United States, in: B. R. GUILE and J. B. QUINN (Eds) *Technology in Services: Policies for Growth, Trade and Employment.* Washington, DC: National Academy Press.

LEIBENSTEIN, H. (1987) *Inside the Firm: The Inefficiencies of Hierarchy.* Cambridge, MA: Harvard University Press.

MARSHALL, J.N. (1982) Linkages between manufacturing industry and business services, *Environment and Planning A*, 14, pp. 1523–1540.

MARSHALL, J.N. (1985) Services in a postindustrial economy, *Environment and Planning A*, 17, pp. 1155–1167.

MARSHALL, J.N. (1988) *Services and Uneven Development.* New York: Oxford University Press.

McCRACKIN, B. (1985) Why are business and professional services growing so rapidly?, *Federal Reserve Bank of Atlanta Economic Review*, August, pp. 14–28.

Moss, M.L. and Dunau, A. (1986) *The Location of Back Offices: Emerging Trends and Development Patterns.* New York: Real Estate Institute, New York University.

Moulaert, F., Swyngedouw, E. and Wilson, P. (1988) Spatial responses to Fordist and post-Fordist accumulation and regulation, *Papers of the Regional Science Association,* 64, pp. 11–23.

Nelson, K. (1986) Labour demand, labour supply and the suburbanisation of low-wage office work, in: A. Scott and M. Storper (Eds) *Production, Work, and Territory: The Geographical Anatomy of Industrial Capitalism,* pp. 149–171. Winchester, MA: Allen and Unwin.

Noyelle, T.J. and Stanback, T.M. (1984) *The Economic Transformation of American Cities.* Totawa, NJ: Rowman and Allanheld.

Piore, M.J. and Sabel, C.F. (1984) *The Second Industrial Divide.* New York: Basic Books.

Pred, A.R. (1975) Diffusion, organisational spatial structure, and city system development, *Economic Geography,* 51, pp. 252–268.

Scott, A.J. (1988a) *Metropolis: From the Division of Labour to Urban Form.* Berkeley, CA: University of California Press.

Scott, A.J. (1988b) *New Industrial Spaces.* London: Pion.

Törnqvist, G.E. (1970) *Contact systems and regional development.* Lund Studies in Geography, Series B, No. 38, University of Lund.

Tschetter, J. (1987) Producer service industries: why are they growing so rapidly?, *Monthly Labor Review,* 12, pp. 31–40.

Wheeler, J.O. (1988) The corporate role of large metropolitan areas in the United States, *Growth and Change,* 19, pp. 75–86.

Williamson, O.E. (1981) The modern corporation: origins, evolution, attributes, *Journal of Economic Literature,* 19, pp. 1537–1568.

Wood, P.A. (1991) Flexible accumulation and the rise of business services, *Transactions, Institute of British Georgraphers,* 16, pp. 160–172.

[4]

Strategic Management Journal, Vol. 11, 513–519 (1990)

INFORMATION ASYMMETRIES: A SOURCE OF COMPETITIVE ADVANTAGE FOR DIVERSIFIED SERVICE FIRMS

PRAVEEN R. NAYYAR
Stern School of Business, New York University, New York, New York, U.S.A.

Information asymmetries are generally considered as leading to costs for both parties in an exchange transaction. They can, however, also be a source of competitive advantage. Potential buyers face information asymmetries in evaluating services prior to purchase. Since such asymmetries impose costs on buyers, there exists an incentive to lower such costs. This incentive may be exploited by service firms that diversify into other services that meet the needs of existing customers.

Previous research on diversification has focused on the potential benefits from shared resources, both tangible and intangible, among the businesses of a diversified firm as a rationale for related diversification (Montgomery, 1979; Rumelt, 1974, 1982; Teece, 1980; Palepu, 1985; Porter, 1985, 1987; Chatterjee, 1986; Day, 1986). While economies of scope, especially in marketing costs, based on shared customers in multi-product firms are widely recognized, benefits of related diversification need not arise from such production cost savings alone.

Buyers face a difficult and costly task in ascertaining the attributes of services before purchase due to information asymmetries in buyer–seller relationships. Though information asymmetries present a problem to both buyers and sellers of services, such asymmetries could, in fact, be exploited by diversified service firms. Service firms can develop a competitive advantage by exploiting the potential buyer's incentives to lower information acquisition costs when buying new services. This constitutes a powerful potential revenue side benefit from related diversification in contrast to the potential cost side benefits from shared resources within firms. Such buyer incentives that indicate benefits from corporate

diversification have previously neither been discussed in the literature on diversification nor explored in the vast literature on services.

Buyer incentives to lower information asymmetries suggest that 'exploiting' existing relationships with buyers in the provision of multiple services by diversified service firms could lead to significant competitive advantages. The search for such advantages may explain why American Express, a travel-related services company, diversified into financial services; why Sears, Roebuck & Co. is attempting to grow its financial services business; and why accounting firms have so successfully developed their management consulting practices.

An in-depth understanding of mechanisms, other than economies of scope, that underlie potential benefits from related diversification is crucial to determining corporate and business strategies for service firms and finding effective ways to actually realize those benefits. In this paper we depart from the 'internal focus' on resources owned by firms and, instead, adopt an 'external focus' on existing customers of service firms to suggest another potential benefit of related diversification by service businesses. This benefit does not rely on the traditional production

0143–2095/90/070513–07$05.00
© 1990 by John Wiley & Sons, Ltd.

Received 27 January 1989
Final revision received 2 April 1990

514   P. R. Nayyar

cost reduction logic of related diversification, but on a new information asymmetry reduction logic that results in direct benefits to buyers. The potential for such benefits can lead to competitive advantages and economic benefits for diversified service firms.

INFORMATION ECONOMICS AND RELATED DIVERSIFICATION

Buyer behavior is crucially dependent upon the information that is available before and after purchase. In order to make choices, buyers need to at least know the price and quality of the various alternatives that they are considering. But service quality is difficult to evaluate due to the intangibility and simultaneous production and consumption of services (Holmstrom, 1985). Further, since service delivery is a social interaction in which service providers and customers are involved, significant quality variations could occur.

This potential for variation in service quality, and the general difficulty in assessing service quality, makes the evaluation of services difficult. This complicates the choice decision for potential buyers. Hence, buyers seek information to help make better choices. Information search, however, is costly (Stigler, 1961). Parties to an exchange transaction usually have different information sets about the object, tangible or intangible, that is the reason for the transaction. These information sets may contain relevant data on what is being exchanged such as its quality, price, performance, specifications, and circumstances of delivery. Differences in the information sets of buyers and sellers cause problems in the exchange transaction that leads to costs for both parties to the exchange.

COSTS OF INFORMATION ASYMMETRIES

When there exist information asymmetries between buyers and sellers, high- and low-quality goods and services can coexist in the marketplace (Akerlof, 1970). This coexistence requires buyers, *ex ante*, to determine the quality of goods and services they buy. Given information asymmetry, this is an inherently problematic, and costly,

task.

Problems resulting from incomplete or asymmetric information may be classified into either moral hazard or adverse selection problems, depending on the type of information asymmetry present (Holmstrom, 1984). Moral hazard refers to problems associated with the buyer's inability to observe actions taken by the seller. With service quality being difficult to judge, service being generally impossible to reverse, and service outcome being uncertain because of exogenous factors, it is impossible for the buyer of services to evaluate whether the sellers' actions were proper and adequate (e.g. did my attorney or physician exercise due care?). Adverse selection problems arise when the buyer is unable to observe either the seller's characteristics or the contingencies under which the seller operates. For instance, the seller often has greater information about the contingencies under which he or she operates than the buyer (e.g. did my car really need those expensive repair services?). Also, if buyers cannot ascertain the competence of the service provider, quality and value of the service and the risks of malpractice cannot be predicted. Further, in such a case, 'bad-quality' providers can enter the market and drive out the 'good quality' providers by so lowering price that the latter cannot obtain economic returns on their investments for competence enhancement (Akerlof, 1970).

REMEDIES FOR INFORMATION ASYMMETRIES

While there exist several potential remedies for information asymmetries, such as contingent contracts including liability contracts and warranties, signaling, and certification and monitoring (Holmstrom, 1985), most are generally not satisfactory. For instance, the inability to fully anticipate all contingencies that may arise in the execution of a contract prevents the writing of complete contingent claims contracts, and therefore limits their usefulness in information asymmetry reduction. Similarly, warranties covering services are impossible to administer since failure to perform a social interaction is generally indeterminable. Certification, too, is so widely prevalent as to make it of no consequence in consumer choice behavior. Further, it is no guarantee of performance. Instead, it merely serves as an attestation to having met some minimally acceptable standards that are often unknown to buyers.

Monitoring is inadequate because it suffers from information asymmetries between the monitor and the person or facility being monitored. All the facts and contingencies prevailing at the time of service production and delivery cannot be fully known to the monitor, and sometimes are even partially unknown to the service provider as, for example, in the case of medical diagnostic and treatment services and automobile repair.

Firms may, nevertheless, attempt to signal the quality of their products by writing contracts (though they might be imperfect) and making firm-specific investments in specialized education and equipment and advertising (Nelson, 1970, 1974). Both approaches seek to assure potential buyers that the firm is committed to providing high quality. High prices, too, may act as signals of high quality (Klein and Leffler, 1981; Shapiro, 1983; Allen, 1984). In a competitive market for services, when quality is unobservable, each firm has no incentive to lower price to equal marginal cost since that would make it more profitable for the firm to produce low, rather than high, quality (Allen, 1984); but consumers know this. When faced with low prices they judge quality as being low and do not buy from the low-priced firm. Therefore, firms do not cut price because that would change their incentives and consumers would refuse to buy their services. Hence, in a competitive market, high prices signal high-quality services. The distribution of prices alone, however, is insufficient to reliably signal quality because of the existence of adverse selection problems. Fly-by-night, low-quality producers could also charge high prices, and thereby distort the expected monotonic relationship between prices and service quality.

THE ROLE OF REPUTATION

In addition to signaling quality, firms may attempt to provide potential buyers with greater information in order to reduce information asymmetries between buyers and sellers. Recall that buyers attempt to ascertain various attributes of goods and services prior to making their purchase decisions. Services (and goods) may be described by the mix of three qualities that consumers use to evaluate them: search qualities, which are attributes that a consumer can determine prior to purchase; experience qualities, which are attributes determined only after purchase or during consumption; and credence qualities, which are intangible qualities that a consumer may be unable to evaluate even after purchase and consumption (Darby and Karni, 1973).

The mix of search, experience, and credence qualities of goods and services in question moderates the role of information in buyer behavior. The availability of information before purchase is considerably more important in the case of services which are high on experience or credence qualities, such as medical services and consulting services, since they are more difficult for potential buyers to evaluate. Note that the value of prior information to buyers in assessing the quality of services is directly proportional to the severity of the consequences suffered by consuming services of less than anticipated quality.

Buyers seek information about quality and other characteristics of goods and services either by search prior to purchase or by experience through purchase and use. Search is limited by the cost incurred in obtaining information by experience. Experience is used to judge quality when search becomes too expensive. Prior to sampling different brands of a product, consumers may obtain information about various brands from several sources, such as advertisements and word-of-mouth.

Advertisements provide direct information about the search qualities of a brand. However, in the case of experience qualities the most important information conveyed by advertising is simply that the brand advertises (Nelson, 1974). For experience qualities, word-of-mouth information may, reasonably, be considered as constituting better information than advertising since, in a sense, it provides an avenue for evaluation of the good or service through a vicarious experience. As buyers rely more on word-of-mouth, they will respond less to advertising (Nelson, 1974).

Each sampling, by search or experience, contributes toward the information bank which buyers maintain about the various brands sampled. When the producer of a brand

516   *P. R. Nayyar*

introduces another brand, buyers may draw upon their information banks to form associative evaluations of the likely properties of the new brand. This 'carry-over' of evaluative information tends to reduce information acquisition costs for buyers. Hence it can be expected that customers who have favorable impressions of current service providers will tend to favor such providers when making purchase decisions about other services that these providers may offer. As a corollary, service providers who have formed favorable impressions on existing customers may find it easier to influence them, as opposed to entirely new customers, to try the producer's new brands or, by extension, new goods or services. Hence, from the perspective of potential buyers, reputation is potentially a stronger remedy than signaling to reduce information asymmetries in buyer–seller relationships.

Reputation performs as an implicit contract. It is enforced by the seller's concern about future demand for the service provided. The size of demand, and the way in which information is disseminated among buyers, determines the efficacy of reputation as a remedy for information asymmetries. Subject to the constraints of legitimate transferability across services, reputation is likely to exhibit characteristics of a public good. Once acquired it can be used over and over again in the context of other services or markets. It should be cautioned, however, that it is equally possible that lapses in quality or value in these other services or markets could quite easily be transferred back to the original services provided by the firm and, quite literally, destroy the reputation built up in those services, too.

In the presence of difficulties in determining quality, when consumers are sure that firms will provide good quality, it pays firms to cheat and provide bad quality, since learning about quality will be very slow, or zero, due to the lack of information (Allen and Faulhaber, 1986). Consumers know this, however, and so they will expect some firms to supply bad quality. Consumers, therefore, will be skeptical and upon the receipt of new information they will rapidly adjust their beliefs about the quality of a firm's products. This rapid adjustment will make it very expensive for firms to cheat. Conversely, this same rapid adjustment will reward consistent good quality.

In sum, it can be expected that buyers of services will attempt to economize on information acquisition costs by exhibiting a tendency to transfer reputation effects to other goods or services offered by a firm. In fact a firm that diversifies into services that its existing customers may buy from it could create a competitive advantage, since it could potentially exploit the favorable alteration in the information asymmetry distribution faced by potential buyers when they consider buying the new service offered by the firm. Quasi-rents (Klein, Crawford and Alchian, 1978) may therefore be obtained, since the buyer–seller relationship represents a firm-specific investment on the part of the buyer which gives rise to switching costs (Porter, 1980).

Conversely, firms that offer a narrower line of services could potentially be at a competitive disadvantage in selling their services if their competitors are diversified. Potential buyers actively seeking to reduce their information acquisition costs when choosing service providers would favor the firm with a wider line of services. The similarity in the portfolios of many diversified service firms is likely a result of such imperatives.

Hence, possible differentiation through the lowering of information acquisition costs for potential buyers constitutes a legitimate potential benefit for service firms that leverage customer relationships across service businesses. Related diversification may, therefore, be beneficial even without any resource-sharing economies. Unrelated diversification, however, does not derive benefits from information asymmetry reduction. Of course, firms also face costs in alleviating information asymmetries. Assuming that firms wish to maximize profits (or shareholder wealth), they will seek to economize on information dissemination costs by leveraging whatever reputation they have built on other goods or services offered.

There exist, however, limits to the transferability of reputation effects that, in turn, limit the diversification opportunity set for any service firm. Reputation must transfer legitimately in order for information asymmetry to be reduced. In other words, potential buyers must believe that the diversifying service firm can and will deliver the expected quality in the new service. For example, it is reasonable to expect an accounting firm also to provide some management consulting services, since it has a proven expertise in evaluating accounting and management control systems. In addition, the typical accounting firm also has a rich knowledge base on the design of such systems derived from its experience in auditing several clients. Similarly, advertising agencies could legitimately claim to provide good-quality market research and media planning services. In contrast, it is highly unlikely that potential clients will believe that an accounting firm can also operate an airline. Also, a reputable retailer does not necessarily appear to possess the requisite skills and competence to provide a wide array of specialized financial services, just as even a reputable management consulting firm does not appear to have the skills required to provide accounting services.

These limits to the transferability of reputation effects arise from the difficulty in evaluating services high on experience and credence qualities. Prerequisites, whether real or perceived, for providing good quality differ across some services while being similar across others. In the former case reputation does not play an important role in informing potential buyers about the likely quality of the new service, while in the latter case it does. A retail services firm diversifying into financial services is an example of the former case.

Further, even if reputation effects do transfer, there exist several organizational and other barriers to successful related diversification. Note that related diversification implies interrelationships among business units in diversified firms. The need for a clear conceptualization of the services offered, and the intimacy of the buyer and service provider in the service delivery process, limit the flexibility of service firms to grow without limits by offering new services and entering new markets (Carman and Langeard, 1980) since the presence of interrelationships contaminates each service delivery process. Porter (1985) lists several impediments to achieving interrelationships among businesses in diversified firms. Among these are asymmetric benefits to the business units involved, perceived or actual loss of autonomy and control, biased incentive systems, and differing business unit circumstances. In a similar vein, Riordan and Williamson (1985) discuss internal transaction costs that arise in managerial hierarchies due to governance structures, bureaucratic distortions, and incentive degradation. These internal transaction costs

need to be balanced against the potential benefits of relatedness. When the former exceed the latter, firms limit their growth. Similarly, Reed and Luffman (1986) and Kanter (1989) have noted that the benefits of synergy among businesses in diversified firms are not automatically attained. They suggested that firms often forego the potential benefits of related diversification when they incur substantial costs in seeking synergies.

CONCLUSIONS

Information asymmetries cannot be viewed as merely another obstacle in the competitive battle, because they can be a potent source of competitive advantage for those service firms that consciously develop new services for their existing customers. This source of competitive advantage for diversified service firms does not rely on any resource-sharing mechanisms within the firm. It relies, instead, on information asymmetry reduction by potential buyers through the transfer of reputation for quality services across multiple services offered by diversified service firms. The mix of search, experience and credence qualities of the services involved moderates the role of reputation in reducing information asymmetries between buyers and sellers. Reputation plays a more important role when services high on experience and/or credence qualities are involved. In the case of services high on search qualities, however, potential buyers do not rely on the reputation of the service provider since they can adequately assess service quality prior to purchase. Hence, we have:

Proposition 1: If reputation can legitimately be transferred, diversification into services high on experience or credence or both qualities will reduce information acquisition costs for potential buyers.

Proposition 2: Diversification into services high on search qualities will not reduce information acquisition costs for potential buyers.

These variations in the importance of information asymmetries in buyer behavior with variations in the characteristics of services with respect to the mix of search, experience and credence qualities suggest that the strategy of sharing customers across businesses in a diversified service firm

518   *P. R. Nayyar*

offers greater potential benefits when services high in experience or credence or both qualities are involved. In fact, the value of such a strategy when services high on search qualities are involved is questionable. Hence, we have:

Proposition 3:   If reputation can legitimately be transferred, service firms will gain a competitive advantage by serving multiple needs of their clients for services high on experience or credence or both qualities.

Proposition 4:   Service firms will not gain a competitive advantage by serving multiple needs of their clients for services high on search qualities.

Finally, since the benefits of relatedness do not flow automatically, effective customer sharing needs to be consciously managed by diversified service firms in order to ensure that information asymmetry is attenuated, not accentuated, by the multiple sources and pieces of information about the multiple services offered by the firm that are available to potential buyers. This management of information about the firm and its services translates to the dual requirements for the need for an appropriate organization design and an effective communications strategy to reinforce the information asymmetry reduction mechanisms discussed in this paper.

ACKNOWLEDGEMENTS

This paper is based on the author's Ph.D. dissertation. I thank Robert K. Kazanjian for supervising that work. I also thank two anonymous reviewers for their detailed and thoughtful comments that contributed significantly toward improving this paper.

REFERENCES

Akerlof, G. 'The market for "Lemons": Quality uncertainty and the market mechanism', *Quarterly Journal of Economics*, 1970, pp. 488–500.

Allen, F. 'Reputation and services'. Fishman-Davidson Center Discussion Paper, Wharton School, University of Pennsylvania, Philadelphia, PA, 1984.

Allen, F. and G. R. Faulhaber. 'Optimism invites deception'. Fishman-Davidson Center Discussion Paper, Wharton School, University of Pennsylvania, Philadelphia, PA, 1986.

Carman, J. M. and E. Langeard. 'Growth strategies for service firms'. *Strategic Management Journal*, 1980, pp. 7–22.

Chatterjee, S. 'Types of synergy and economic value: The impact of acquisitions on merging and rival firms', *Strategic Management Journal*, 1986, pp. 119–139.

Darby, M. R. and E. Karni. 'Free competition and the optimal amount of fraud', *Journal of Law and Economics*, 1973, pp. 67–86.

Day, D. L. 'A contingency theory of relatedness in corporate venturing and venture performance'. Unpublished doctoral dissertation, Columbia University, New York, 1986.

Holmstrom, B. 'The provision of services in a market economy'. Fishman-Davidson Center Discussion Paper, Wharton School, University of Pennsylvania, Philadelphia, PA, 1984.

Holmstrom, B. 'The provision of services in a market economy'. In R. P. Inman (ed.), *Managing the Service Economy: Prospects and Problems*. Cambridge University Press, Cambridge, UK, 1985.

Kanter, R. M. K. *When Giants Learn to Dance: Mastering the Challenges of Strategy, Management, and Careers in the 1990s*, Simon & Schuster, New York, 1989.

Klein, B. and K. B. Leffler. 'The role of market forces in assuring contractual performance', *Journal of Political Economy*, 1981, pp. 615–641.

Klein, B., R. G. Crawford and A. A. Alchian. 'Vertical integration, appropriable rents, and the competitive contracting process'. *Journal of Law and Economics*, 1978, pp. 297–326.

Montgomery, C. A. 'Diversification, market structure, and firm performance: An extension of Rumelt's model'. Unpublished doctoral dissertation, Purdue University, West Lafayette, IN, 1979.

Nelson, P. 'Information and consumer behavior', *Journal of Political Economy*, 1970, pp. 311–329.

Nelson, P. 'Advertising as information', *Journal of Political Economy*, 1974, pp. 729–754.

Palepu, K. 'Diversification strategy, profit performance and the entropy measure', *Strategic Management Journal*, 1985, pp. 239–255.

Porter, M. E. *Competitive Strategy: Techniques for Analyzing Industries and Competitors*, Free Press, New York, 1980.

Porter, M. E. *Competitive Advantage: Creating and Sustaining Superior Performance*, Free Press, New York, 1985.

Porter, M. E. 'From competitive advantage to corporate strategy', *Harvard Business Review*, 1987, pp. 43–59.

Reed, R. and G. A. Luffman. 'Diversification: The growing confusion', *Strategic Management Journal*, 1986, pp. 29–35.

Riordan, M. H. and O. E. Williamson. 'Asset specificity and economic organization', *International Journal of Industrial Organization*, 1985, pp. 365–378.

Rumelt, R. P. *Strategy, Structure and Economic Performance*, Harvard University Press, Boston, MA, 1974.

Rumelt, R. P. 1982. 'Diversification strategy and profitability', *Strategic Management Journal*, 1982, pp. 359–369.

Shapiro, C. 'Premiums for high quality as returns to reputations', *Quarterly Journal of Economics*, 1983, pp. 659–680.

Stigler, G. J. 'The economics of information', *Journal of Political Economy*, 1961, pp. 213–225.

Teece, D. J. 'Economies of scope and the scope of the enterprise', *Journal of Economic Behavior and Organization*, 1980, pp. 223–247.

[5]

The Perils of Overstating Service Sector Growth Potential: A Study of Linkages in Distributive Services

Wendy Patton
Ann Markusen
Rutgers University

The export potential of services has been assessed without regard to forward and backward linkages. Yet regional service sector growth is often associated with three factors: the displacement of manufacturing functions into service establishments, the marketing role of manufacturing-displacing imports, and locational shifts toward customer sites. Many services remain locationally linked to suppliers and buyers, with no net gain to the regional economy. In addition service gains may be temporary, associated with cyclical or abnormal business conditions. In the case of steel service centers, which grew rapidly in the early 1980s to account for 25% of all steel sales, employment gains were largely attributable to the spin-off of steel manufacturing functions and to opportunities for marketing imported steel. Eventually, the growth trend tailed off as macroeconomic factors (recovery from recession and the fall of the dollar) restored the relative profitability of the steel industry and enabled it to "learn" flexibility from service center pioneers. Economic development planners should assess service sector potential in light of such linkages and dynamics.

Wendy Patton is a Fellow on the Project on Regional and Industrial Economics, Rutgers University. Ann Markusen is Director of the Project on Regional and Industrial Economics, Rutgers University and Professor of Urban Planning and Policy Development. Both consulted for the City of Chicago on its Steel Industry Task Force, and were coauthors of Steel and Southeast Chicago: Reasons and Remedies for Industrial Renewal, *a report to the Mayor's Task Force on Steel and Southeast Chicago (1985). Both have published on industrial development in declining as well as fast-growing regions.*

Long overdue attention has recently been focused on the role of service activities in urban economic development. Much of it has been preoccupied with export potential. The fact that service exports have grown faster than manufacturing exports has been interpreted to mean that services may be an autonomous and even preferable form of job creation. However, far from bringing "new" dollars into the region, and creating net new jobs, some service sector employment is simply the result of "spin-off" from manufacturing, where work is displaced from factories into linked service sectors. Furthermore, some service growth is linked to heightened levels of imports into the local economy, because the new market penetrators buy advertising, accounting and

AUTHORS' NOTE: This research was conducted under a contract with the Department of Economic Development, City of Chicago. We would like to thank Jean Ross, Judy Schneider, Rob Mier, Steve Alexander, Julie Putterman, Tom Dubois, Josh Lerner, Wim Wievel, Frank Cassel, Andrew Sharkey, Amy Glasmeier, Candace Howes, Scott Campbell, and several anonymous reviewers for their help and comments on the research, and Vickie Gwiasda, Jim Day, Wei Ping Wu, and Kim Smith for research assistance. We are especially grateful to Gertrude Scott of the Steel Service Center Institute in Cleveland for helping us with data and carefully reading our article.

ECONOMIC DEVELOPMENT QUARTERLY, Vol. 5 No. 3, August 1991 197-212
© 1991 Sage Publications, Inc.

distributive services from local firms even as they displace local producers. In both cases, service sector exports' contribution to net job creation may be overestimated.

We argue that a proper assessment of service sectors' development potential must evaluate spatial linkages between services and their suppliers and customers. Service sector contributions cannot be judged simply on the basis of their apparent net growth rates or survey responses stating that they export substantial shares of their output. The interregional locational tendencies of service sectors — whether they are drawn to suppliers, toward customers, or are truly footloose — must be incorporated into the analysis. We also argue that because services sectors vary dramatically in composition and market structure, they can best be evaluated at a relatively highly disaggregated level. In other words, the locational calculus will be quite different for some types of services than for others. Finally, we suggest that interpretations of industry trends are often made on the basis of short time series, hence the roles of economic cycles and policy-induced abnormalities are often not taken into account. This can result in mistaken prediction and prescription.

We demonstrate the power of linkage and locational analyses with a case study of one distributive sector — steel service centers. This is an industry formally catalogued in the wholesaling sector but actively engaged in marketing, warehousing, and some processing of steel and others materials. The industry grew robustly in the late 1970s and early 1980s, even as steel mill employment dropped. Several cities welcomed steel service center growth, advocating public sector nurturance of the industry. To determine its independent ability to generate jobs, we develop a number of hypotheses on the geographical proclivities of the industry, based on a prior study of its linkages with consuming and producing sectors, and test them against data for the 1980s.

We find, overall, that steel service centers are highly sensitive to the location of producers and/or the ports at which imports enter, the location of consuming sectors, the changing technology and relative costs of transportation, and an evolving internal division of labor among service centers. The more sophisticated, headquarter functions of these firms remain concentrated in the largest centers of supply and importation — namely Chicago, Los Angeles, and New York. Some warehousing and processing functions have been dispersing from centers like Chicago and New York following the decentralization of major steel-using manufacturers.

We conclude that the economic development potential of this service industry is almost entirely dependent on the existence of a concentration of either steel producers, steel importers, and/or steel users. The spatial links with producers of steel remain quite strong, while the links to customers are relatively more varied and volatile over time. We find that the 1980s employment boom in steel centers was largely a result of the transfer of major marketing and processing functions from steel mills to service centers, whose viability thus remains almost entirely dependent on the continued production of steel in major steel-producing metropolises.

Macroeconomic forces also left their mark on the local expansion of this industry in the 1980s. The growth of steel service centers, exceeding that of steel production in the first half of the decade, was artificially induced by a recession during which steel mills abandoned many marketing functions, and by an overvalued dollar, which resulted in dramatic penetration of imports, which were marketed through service centers. After 1985, as the dollar fell and the steel industry recovered, the steel service industry stagnated as imports levelled off and mills began to sell more of their own steel. Thus, forecasts of the autonomous employment growth of service centers turned out to be overly optimistic. However, the growing importance of "just-in-time" practices and the externalization of services are both forces encouraging continued growth of the industry.

... 1980s employment boom in steel service centers was largely a result of the transfer of major marketing and processing functions from steel mills to service centers, whose viability thus remains almost entirely dependent on the continued production of steel in major steel-producing metropolises.

SERVICES AND ECONOMIC DEVELOPMENT

A number of analysts have argued in favor of the economic development potential of service sectors. They rightfully challenge the assumption that only manufacturing and primary activities like mining and agriculture constitute an area's export base. The major evidence offered for the export potential of service industries is interview and survey data which indicate that service sector firms sell substantial amounts of their product to customers outside of the region.[1]

We see two conceptual problems with this type of evidence. First, a service sold (exported) to a company outside of the region may be associated with the downstream sale (import) of the final product back into the local region. Suppose a local advertising firm or wholesaler sells its services to an outsider, say Sony, who uses such services to win sales in the local market. The local consumer is actually paying the bill for both the importer's product and the local firm's sale of services. In other words, the ability of that firm to exist is still dependent on the size of the local market.[2] Furthermore, if the imports themselves have displaced local factory production, then the net job gain may actually be negative. What the service-exporting local firm represents, in this case, is the vestigial survival of local production-associated activities through the successful sale of its services to the production-displacing importer — a consolation, because it moderates the negative multiplier effect, but hardly cause for celebration.

Second, export base studies, by not addressing the linkages among sectors locally, cannot elucidate the dependence of a particular sector on a local supplier whose presence explains the location of the former. A wholesaling firm or an engineering service may apparently export outside the local economy, but be positioned there because a major input to their activity is rooted locally. In the case of the industrial engineering firm, it might be the presence of a large chemical or machinery complex that is a major source of talent and information. In the case of wholesalers or truckers, it might be a set of food processors, steel mills, or garment plants which provide the bulk of the product shipped. The fact that the firm in question bills its services to an outside customer is not as significant as the fact that its viability in this location is dependent on a set of local suppliers. If the latter should fold, the locational incentive anchoring the firm locally is gone, and the service is free to move elsewhere, closer to new sources, import entrepots, or customers.[3]

Both these criticisms suggest that a fuller understanding of both forward and backward linkages, and the associated locational calculus of the firm, are essential to a comprehensive evaluation of any service sector's economic development potential. Indeed, their omission may explain an apparent paradox in the literature — that most aggregate studies still suggest the overwhelming significance of manufacturing to an area's economic base and the tight geographical connection between services and manufacturing, despite service firm survey responses showing high levels of export activity.[4]

Using interview and survey data to assess the export potential of services is problematic precisely because it divorces an immediate buyer/seller relationship from the more extensive spatial and interindustry relationships in which it is embedded. This is a major technical problem. Suppose a local steel mill, in addition to direct exports of 30%, sells 40% of its output to a local wholesaler, who in turn markets half of that outside the region. The steel mill would then respond on a survey that it exports only 30% of its output when, in fact, 50% is bound for external markets. In this case, the wholesaler gets the credit for being a substantial exporter, although its sales take place only because the sheet metal is made in the region. If the wholesaler were to bill its services to the steel mill, rather than buying and reselling, they would be all be counted as local income and this, too, would be inaccurate. The wholesaler is part of an export base, surely, because its jobs are funded from export income; but it is not a stand-alone independent facility. Similarly, a distortion is introduced in the case of the exporter whose service is immediately incorporated into an import. The source of the income paying for the "export" is not external at all, but local.[5]

The service firm will be a part of an export base when its jobs are funded in whole or part from export income. Some are predominantly exporters, and some can be treated as stand-alone entities — major money center banks, stock and other financial exchanges, for instance. But the export promise of many service sectors may be illusory, because of the presence of one or both of these linkages: service exports directly tied to downstream imports or service exports as part of a larger complex of production activities. The true income-generating potential of a service firm can be determined only empirically, not hypothetically, and only with techniques more extensive than surveys that partition sales destinations from domestic ones. For that reason, we chose to examine in greater depth one particular service sector — distributive services — and within that, the steel service center industry.

200   ECONOMIC DEVELOPMENT QUARTERLY / August 1991

DISTRIBUTIVE SERVICES

Service subsectors have been distinguished by generic types: distributive services, producer services, personal services, business services, among others.[6] Of these, business services have perhaps been the best analyzed for their economic development potential, both in aggregate studies and case studies. Few studies have been done on distributive services, despite the fact that they have grown substantially in the past decade (though not as fast as business services) and have shown rather high differential growth rates by city and region.[7]

Distributive services have been broadly defined to include transportation, communication, wholesale, and retail services.[8] We prefer a narrower definition which is more precisely associated with commodity trade — transportation and wholesaling. Together, these two sectors accounted for over 8% of national employment by the 1970s.[9] Studying distributive services permits us to investigate directly the manufacturing spin-off argument — that at least some of the apparent service sector growth in the economy are functions simply displaced from manufacturing toward service categories.[10]

Few have written on the geographical distribution of wholesaling. Much of the literature in business and economics treats it as one function of a larger production complex. Vance's seminal study of wholesaling is an important exception, as is Glasmeier's recent work on distributors.[11] Both demonstrate that wholesalers participate in the economic development process, by transforming themselves from trade outposts to exporters, and by signalling effective demand to potential plant entrants eager to become import substitutors.

Which cities will be favored with distributive-related economic activity depends heavily on individual firms' locational calculus vis-à-vis the location of demand, the location of supply, technology, economies of scale, and industry structure. Hypothetically, given what we know generally about change in the American economy over the past 2 decades, we might expect the following:

1. The growth in the absolute volume of trade internationally will be reflected in the growth of total trade in and out of urban areas, including possibly heightened interregional trade, as a result of increasing specialization of local economies. As total trade rises, the amount of distributive activity should rise as well, although economies of scale may result in less-than-proportional increases.
2. As the share of international trade in all goods traded and consumed rises, coastal locations should be favored as centers of export- and import-related activity.
3. Countervailing the previous tendency, containerization favors interior locations, where imports are unbundled for distribution regionally or exports are packed into containers near their production site.
4. To the extent that distributive sector growth reflects the transfer of functions from within manufacturing, it will favor existing and new manufacturing concentrations.[12]
5. The decentralization of manufacturing from the northeastern industrial core toward sunbelt and exurban locations should draw the simpler distribution functions in its wake.

In addition, a number of other hypotheses about distributive service industry location and growth potential will evolve out of the specific features of the industry, as we show in our case study below.

The economic development questions which must be asked of such a sector are the following. How locationally sensitive is this sector to linkages on both the forward and backward sides of its market? How stable are its existing technology and the industry structure? Is apparent job growth a real net addition to the local economy, or does it simply represent economic activity that has been transferred from other existing local industries, and if so, is its net contribution larger or smaller?

We chose to investigate these questions with evidence on the steel service center industry, assessing its performance as a "basic," export income-producing activity. Steel service centers, being a fast-growing industry, have been welcomed as the silver lining on a dark cloud, especially in aging steel cities like Chicago, Cleveland, and Pittsburgh, where the steel-based manufacturing complex has declined dramatically. At least one big-city task force has recommended the fostering of steel service centers as a target economic development activity.[13]

THE STEEL SERVICE CENTER INDUSTRY

Steel service centers sell both domestically produced and imported steel. They not only wholesale it but store it, market it, and perform a number of final processing functions including slitting, pickling, levelling, cutting, sawing, and quality control. Steel service centers illustrate how thorny the question of service classifications can be: their functions span steel processing, fabricating, warehousing, wholesaling, marketing, and even transportation. The more diversified steel service centers buy from a large number of suppliers and sell to a large number of buyers, often ranging widely across the construction, machinery, auto, oil, shipbuilding, and metalworking industries. As critical middlemen, their locational tendencies provide insights into spatial links between manufacturing production and distributive services more generally.

Industry Structure

The metal service center originated in the 1800s from warehouses that served the needs of blacksmiths and builders in frontier towns. The steel mills themselves were instrumental in establishing an enlarged role and market niche for steel service centers in the late 1940s and 1950s: that of buying and marketing the mills' secondary materials and production overruns. Today steel service centers distribute a quarter of all steel produced in the United States and about 20% of the steel imported into the American market.

Service centers market both products and services. In terms of product, they supply ferrous metals ranging from basic steel forms (such as wire, bar, and sheet) to processed steel pieces or components. Many service centers also stock nonferrous metal, plastic and ceramic supplies. Traditionally, most sales consisted of small lots of specialized metals, often for machinery repair or replacement parts, but, over time, centers have enjoyed larger and more reliable orders from the large original-equipment manufacturers like auto companies.

Services provided include processing, cutting, finishing, and inventory control. The importance of "service" to the steel service center industry cannot be overstated. In this era of "lean" manufacturing, firms live and die by the quality of their product and the reliability of their deliveries. To the extent that these services are important, they may favor locations nearer to steel users than steel producers.[14]

Steel service centers are classified as metals distributors.[15] Within the industry, there are three categories of distributors: (a) merchant wholesalers, who are independent service centers or branch plants serving customers from inventory-on-hand; (b) agents, brokers, and traders, who are members of large and diversified wholesaling firms serving as commodity brokers between foreign and domestic suppliers and foreign and domestic customers; and (c) manufacturers' sales branches and offices, the sales arms of steel producers. The bulk of the industry is concentrated in the merchant wholesale segment, and this is the fastest growing segment of the industry as well. Employment in steel merchant wholesalers establishments rose by 36% in 1987 over 1977. By contrast, total employment of manufacturers' sales branches and offices shrank by 7% over the same period of time.[16]

Barriers to entry and exit in the steel service industry have traditionally been very low. All an entrepreneur needed was a building and an inventory. Technology was rudimentary: shelves, forklifts, cranes, maybe some cutting machinery. The work force was not skilled. Even management requirements were not sophisticated. Competition was based on price and customer proxim-

> Steel service centers sell both domestically produced and imported steel. They not only wholesale it but store it, market it, and perform a number of final processing functions including slitting, pickling, levelling, cutting, sawing, and quality control.

ity alone. Profit margins were thin. Service centers appeared overnight and vanished as quickly. This feature argues for considerable locational flexibility in the industry, so that present locations can be read as more or less optimal ones.

Macroeconomic Factors and Structural Change

A number of macroeconomic peculiarities helped to shape the steel service center industry and its geography in recent years. Expensive credit and cheap imports favored service centers over steel producers, as well as favoring the larger among the service centers. Escalating interest rates in the late 1970s made steel customers seek "lean" inventory systems. Because capital-intensive steel mills produce in tremendous bulk and quantity, steel service centers, which specialize in inventory control, were well positioned to respond. Stiff foreign competition forced domestic manufacturers to adopt new practices, especially quality control. Steel service centers, leaner and more entrepreneurial than the mills and with different technology and capital structures, were better able to provide the timely delivery of guaranteed quality goods.[17]

However, new customer demands required significant capital investments on the part of service centers. The high cost of money of the late 1970s and throughout the 1980s meant that in this industry of razor-thin profit margins, only the biggest and strongest service centers were able to serve the new and sophisticated customer demand. The result was consolidation, mergers and plant closures within the steel service center industry. In addition, growing emphasis on capital investment, computer capability, and skilled management raised barriers to entry. As independent medium-sized wholesalers disappear, the industry is shifting toward a three-tiered structure of large headquarters plants, branch plants, and small companies that feature an exotic product line. This new division of labor within the steel service center industry is associated with a growing hierarchy of sites, with the more sophisticated processing and accounting functions performed at larger-than-ever headquarters plants of the largest firms and dispersed branch operations serving regional markets. Specialized steel distributors tend to agglomerate in major steel production centers.

Successful foreign penetration of the domestic market, in large part a response to the persistently overvalued dollar in the early 1980s, also favored steel service centers in other ways. As domestic production declined and some product lines were abandoned, the steel service center industry captured whole market segments by distributing imported steel products.[18] Our interviews with industry sources revealed that the service center industry supplies a number of steel products no longer produced in this country from an international network of suppliers. Moreover, service centers picked up steel business from smaller steel customers dropped by the mills when the latter slashed marketing staffs in the early 1980s in an effort to cut costs.

In short, the steel producers abandoned whole market segments in the early 1980s which were captured by the steel service center industry. Thus, the dramatic increase in steel service centers' business was not due to overall market growth, but to its possession of an expanding piece of a shrinking pie. Steel service centers have not been adding net output or employment at the national level.

This is not to say that the industry is not a significant element in a newly competitive American economy; it is. The share of domestic steel distributed for industrial purposes by steel service centers has increased by 20% since 1980, and 40% since 1960. But these gains do not imply a permanent trend. Since 1985, when service centers controlled 30% of the market, their share has been whittled back to 25%, as a falling dollar and economic recovery shifted the advantage back toward the steel producers (see Table 1).

All of the factors cited affect the locational array of service centers. Assumption of mill functions and consolidation in larger operations favor agglomerations located closer to the sites of domestic supply. Increased marketing of imported steel favors sites of importation as well as major steel-using areas. Thus cyclical and structural features peculiar to the industry add dimensions to its spatial restructuring beyond those expected for distributive services in general.

TABLE 1
**Shipments of Domestically Produced Steel Products
to Steel Service Centers, 1960-1989 (Millions of Tons)**

Year	Total Industrial Steel Product Shipments	Percentage of Total
1960	7.4	16.2
1961	6.9	16.8
1962	6.8	15.2
1963	7.6	15.6
1964	9.3	17.2
1965	9.9	16.8
1966	9.8	17.2
1967	9.0	17.3
1968	9.7	17.2
1969	11.3	19.4
1970	11.6	21.3
1971	10.2	18.9
1972	12.5	21.2
1973	15.3	21.1
1974	15.2	22.0
1975	9.3	19.0
1976	11.0	18.9
1977	11.5	19.6
1978	12.8	20.7
1979	13.6	21.9
1980	11.8	24.2
1981	13.1	25.2
1982	10.2	28.0
1983	12.9	29.4
1984	14.2	30.2
1985	14.6	30.8
1986	13.8	29.9
1987	14.9	29.5
1988	15.8	26.9
1989	15.3	25.8

SOURCE: William Hogan, *Economic History of the Iron and Steel Industry in the United States* (Lexington, MA: D. C. Heath, 1971), 2023; American Iron and Steel Institute, *Annual Statistical Report* (Washington, DC: AISI, various years); Steel Service Center Institute, Cleveland, OH, unpublished data, 1990.

THE LOCATION OF STEEL SERVICE CENTERS

Steel service centers can thus be hypothesized to be subject to conflicting locational pulls. Will the links to centers of steel supply dominate over the links to decentralizing steel user sites? On the supply, or upstream, side, will links with domestic steel producers dominate over the entrepots where imported steel first enters the country? Will the tendency for increased centralization in headquarters operations, and among centers with highly specialized product lines, dominate over the user-chasing dispersal of branch and independent operations? Throughout the following empirical analysis, we probe the question of linkages: how locationally sensitive is the steel service center industry to forward and backward linkages? Can it be regarded as a stand-alone export-income generating industry, or is it part of a larger production complex? Is it footloose or rooted, and what are the implications for job creation and retention?

To gauge the relative strength of these forces, we analyzed published data on steel service center plants and employment patterns at the metropolitan level for the top 35 steel service center cities. We also conducted a series of interviews with steel service centers in California and Chicago. Our interviews covered firms which, in 1985, accounted for 5 out of the top 10 companies. In 1990,

TABLE 2
Employment in Top Metal Service Center Cities, 1982-1987

		Service Center		Manufacturing
Rank	SMSA	Employment 1987	% Change 1982-1987	% Change 1982-1987
1	Chicago	15,030	2.2	−14.1
2	Los Angeles	7,838	−6.1	−1.3
3	Detroit	7,250	31.6	7.6
4	New York City	6,972	−11.3	−14.2
5	Philadelphia	4,312	−0.1	−9.3
6	Cleveland	3,926	−3.7	−12.3
7	Houston	3,893	−48.8	−39.0
8	San Francisco-Oakland	2,846	16.0	−5.3
9	Atlanta	2,636	8.7	26.1
10	Dallas	2,500	−31.5	3.3
11	Pittsburgh	2,391	−6.6	−37.7
12	Minneapolis	2,071	24.2	−0.9
13	Birmingham	1,963	−17.4	−10.7

SOURCE: U.S. Department of Commerce, *County Business Patterns* (Washington, DC: GPO, 1982, 1987).

we updated must of this information by working directly with the Steel Service Center Institute in Cleveland. Our informants ranged from large center operations, with many branch plants around the country, to smaller ones with a single plant.

Leading Steel Distribution Cities

Wholesale trade in manufacturing supplies is generally concentrated; steel wholesaling is one of the most concentrated. As of 1987, Chicago led the hierarchy, with almost double the jobs of the next largest city (Table 2). Most of the rest of the top cities were either the largest industrial era cities (New York, Philadelphia), major steel-using cities (Detroit, Los Angeles), and/or major steel-producing cities (Cleveland, Pittsburgh, Detroit, and Birmingham). Job change in steel services was not closely correlated with overall manufacturing job change. Some cities, like Chicago and San Francisco, managed to post job gains despite general manufacturing losses, whereas in others, like Atlanta or Dallas, steel service center expansion lagged behind manufacturing gains.

To determine where the steel service center industry is disproportionately concentrated, and therefore of greatest importance to the local economy, we calculated location quotients for the top standard metropolitan statistical areas (SMSAs) in 1982 and 1987 and looked at the change in the concentration of each SMSA between these two dates (Table 3). The top cities by this measure demonstrate that supply is an important factor in spatial concentration: the top 6 SMSAs are major steel-producing areas. Many are also major steel-using areas, because of the historical gravitation of steel producers and users toward each other.[19] No clear pattern of increasing or decreasing intensity occurred over the period.

Upstream Linkages

The importance of proximity to steel supply in service center location is evident in the top service center cities: only Dallas, Atlanta, and Minneapolis are not either the site of major domestic integrated steel mills or the location of a major international port (Table 2). According to our informants, the headquarters plants of the largest steel service center companies are inextricably linked to major points of supply because of the variety of steels available, the potential for special steel products, and discounts for purchasing in bulk. Recently achieved economies in long-distance hauling through deregulation of transportation reinforce concentration of the industry in these centers of supply.

TABLE 3
Change in Metal Service Center Industry Location Quotients 1982-1987

Rank	SMSA	Location Quotient 1987	% Change in Location Quotient 1982-1987
1	Birmingham	3.84	-11.0
2	Cleveland	3.27	13.1
3	Chicago	3.07	17.0
4	Detroit	2.92	32.1
5	Houston	2.01	-27.6
6	Pittsburgh	1.99	16.7
7	Tulsa	1.83	-28.1
8	Minneapolis	1.67	26.6
9	Cincinnati	1.60	8.8
10	Grand Rapids	1.60	5.0

SOURCE: U.S. Department of Commerce, *County Business Patterns* (Washington, DC: GPO, 1982, 1987).

TABLE 4
Change in Employment in Basic Steelmaking (SIC 331) and
Metal Service Center Industry (SIC 5051) in Steel Cities, 1982-1987

City	Service Center Employment 1987	% Change 1982-1987	Basic Steel Employment 1987	% Change 1982-1987
Birmingham	1,963	-17.4	3,080	-58.0
Chicago	15,030	2.2	41,372	-43.4
Cleveland	3,926	-3.7	7,560	-32.4
Pittsburgh	2,126	-17.0	16,568	-69.5
Youngstown	772	5.8	5,407	-41.4

SOURCE: U.S. Department of Commerce, *County Business Patterns* (Washington, DC: GPO, 1982, 1987).

Over time, as steel employment and output have declined in traditional steelmaking cities, local service centers have experienced difficulties also. However, their losses have been mitigated by the shift in functions from mills to service centers and because local steel customers still require steel. Between 1982 and 1987, the five largest traditional steel areas lost more than 30% of their steelmaking jobs (see Table 4). In all five, steel service center losses were considerably smaller, and in some, service centers actually added jobs in the same period. In Birmingham, the city which suffered the steepest decline in service center employment, steel distribution declined by much less than the 58% drop in employment in basic steel production. In Chicago, basic steel production employment fell by 43%, yet employment in steel distribution grew by 2.2%. In part, this growth represents the marketing of imported steel to area steel users. But the more important explanation, according to our interviewees, was the relative success of service centers in winning distribution business from the mills as the latter retrenched. Neither source of new job growth represents a net gain to the cities involved.

The draw of domestic steel production centers as locations for service centers has been challenged by the growing importance of foreign steel, another upstream location force. We expected this to lead to growth in service center concentration in port cities, or alternatively, in nonport cities where containerization has allowed break-of-bulk for intermodal shipping to take place in cheaper settings than major port locations.[20] On average, concentration in port cities grew by 3.3% between 1982 and 1987, as compared with a zero growth rate for nonport cities (see Table 5). Removing steel-producing cities from both groups heightened the difference: concentration in port cities grew by 5.2% versus -0.4% percent for nonport cities by that measure. This suggests that imported steel depots are a major attraction for steel service center firms. It also demonstrates that containerization has not seriously affected the pattern of steel wholesaling. Steel comes in bulk

Between 1982 and 1987, the five largest traditional steel areas lost more than 30% of their steelmaking jobs. In all five, steel service center losses were considerably smaller, and in some, service centers actually added jobs in the same period.

TABLE 5
Metal Service Center Concentration in Port and Nonport Cities, 1982-1987

Port Cities (SMSAs)	Growth Rate 1982-1987	Nonport Cities (SMSAs)	Growth Rate 1982-1987
Baltimore	−20.1	Anaheim	−2.8
Boston	7.7	Atlanta	−3.4
Buffalo	−20.4	Birmingham	−11.0
Chicago	17.0	Charlotte	−6.1
Cleveland	13.1	Cincinnati	8.8
Detroit	32.1	Dallas	−30.4
Houston	−27.6	Denver	−3.8
Los Angeles	2.4	Grand Rapids	5.0
Miami	10.2	Hartford	26.9
Milwaukee	7.5	Indianapolis	9.4
Nassau-Suffolk	−1.4	Kansas City	16.8
New Orleans	−34.2	Minneapolis	26.6
New York City	−0.4	Phoenix	−1.8
Newark	20.7	Pittsburgh	16.7
Philadelphia	6.1	St. Louis	−22.7
Portland	12.4	Tulsa	−28.1
San Francisco-Oakland	26.9		
Seattle	22.5		
Tampa/St. Peterburgh	−11.5		
Average	3.3	Average	0.0
Average without steelmaking cities	5.2	Average without steelmaking cities	−0.4

SOURCE: U.S. Department of Commerce, *County Business Patterns* (Washington, DC: GPO, 1982, 1987).

and is transshipped onto trucks at port sites, encouraging the sale of steel at dockside. Industry sources confirm that not much steel is subject to containerization.

Port cities do stand to gain from the encouragement of distributional activities associated with international trade. They can add net new employment which would otherwise have not occurred within the region. However, from a national point of view, such employment represents a shift from other, interior locations, not a net gain. When it is associated with the shift toward imports and away from domestic steel production, it is in fact a consolation prize for the loss of many more steelmaking jobs.

Downstream Linkages

The strength of steel production and importation centers as wholesaling centers appears to contradict Vance's argument that wholesalers who provide a service will gain market advantage by being near customers. Vance argued that demand factors outweigh supply factors in most wholesale location decisions, because the wholesaler's ties with suppliers tend to be formalized, while ties with customers change and shift. The real advantages accrue to the wholesaler who locates near an enlarged and clustered customer group.[21]

To the extent that steel user pulls are effective, we would expect to see some degree of decentralization in the industry. In the last 20 years, steel consumption has grown at above-average rates in regions of the United States where little efficient steelmaking capacity exists. The rise of the "gunbelt" — the siting of aerospace, communications, and electronics activities far from the industrial heartland — has resulted in remarkable regional growth rate differentials in manufacturing generally.[22] Our informants confirmed that the large, national service centers have responded by establishing branch plants, some of them buyouts, in regionally dispersed locations. The

TABLE 6
Change in Metal Service Center Employment and Manufacturing Employment by Region

Region	Average Change in Metal Service Center Employment 1982-1987	Average Change in Manufacturing Employment 1982-1987
Northeast	−1.1	−11.5
Midwest	5.5	−4.1
South	−21.6	−7.5
West	3.2	0.7

SOURCE: U.S. Department of Commerce, *County Business Patterns* (Washington, DC: GPO, 1982, 1987).

headquarters plants of these large firms are free to concentrate on supply, and the branch plants focus on serving customer demand.

Overall, however, the shift away from the industrial heartland has not uniformly drawn steel service center activity with it. The relationship between metropolitan manufacturing employment growth and steel service growth is not particularly strong (Table 2). When pooled regionally, service center growth rates of 45 SMSAs, all with wholesale trade location quotients close to or greater than one, show no consistent pattern of replicating manufacturing growth rates. Despite heavy losses in both manufacturing and steel intensive industries, Midwest cities fared best of all in terms of service center employment change (Table 6). In contrast, Southern cities lost relatively more service center jobs than they did manufacturing employment. Of course, the particular industrial composition of these regions may explain these differentials. For example, the decline in service center employment in Southern cities may be associated with the depression in the steel-intensive oil industry.

The steel service center industry in the Midwest is stabilized by an enduring agglomeration of steel suppliers and steel-using manufacturers. Steel trade is heavily internalized within the regional economy. Steel trade in other locations may be dependent on undiversified and more cyclically sensitive sectors, such as oil, aerospace, defense or construction, producing greater volatility in the industry over time.[23]

To the extent that service centers have decentralized, they are increasingly apt to be the arms of a large corporate parent rather than independent operations. These branch centers service the steel users, also chiefly branch plants, in exurban and rural settings far from centralized headquarters in the heartland. In these outposts, they become import-substituting activities, where they unequivocally add to local net job creation if they displace the importation of such services from other regions. However, their ability to operate in these metropolitan areas is dependent on the steel users and their locational calculus. Their employment is export financed only to the extent that the steel consuming sectors reexport their product. Furthermore, if the new users are, for instance, foreign auto plants in the upper South whose output is displacing domestic auto employment, then the related steel service center employment represents merely a shift from other locations.[24]

CONCLUSION

The steel service center industry is tightly enmeshed in larger geographical production complexes. Rarely can it be found as a stand-alone activity in a local or regional economy. It is either linked to sources of steel supply, both domestic mills and ports of entry for imported steel, and/or linked to centers of steel-using activity. Local economic development analysts, viewing its divergence from area growth rates in the early 1980s, believed that it was a bright spot on a dark horizon and sought ways of encouraging its growth. But its relative superior growth performance through most of the 1980s, compared with steel and manufacturing in general, was a function of three major factors: the shedding of functions from steelmakers in a period of profit squeeze, the rising share of imported steel in the domestic market, and changes in technology and inventory practices by steel users and distributors. The first two of these were in turn products of a severe recession coupled with high interest rates and an overvalued dollar — conditions that were reversible. Even "just-in-time" innovations do not unequivocally favor service centers over steel makers, as we argue below.

Our research on the steel service center industry offers some interesting insights into the role of distributive services in regional development generally. First, it demonstrates that the links with supplier industries can be strong, and can anchor a distributive sector in an older industrial district, even if supply is decentralizing over time.[25] Indeed, we detected within this industry a hierarchical structure similar to that of many manufacturing industries, where headquarters, operations with heavy fixed capital commitments and/or speciality products, remain centralized in historic core cities, while regional depots and subdepots spread out to reach customer demand. These latter segments remain less capital intensive, less specialized, more volatile, and vulnerable to changes in the fortunes of consuming sectors. We do not find much evidence that steel service centers have acted as a vanguard for manufacturing relocation or new industrial complex building, although some steel minimills in decentralized locations have grown out of distributor activities.

Second, a relatively sophisticated analysis is required to determine the degree of export orientation of service sectors. The tight links among steel service centers and their customers and suppliers make an evaluation of them as "exporters" or "local-serving" difficult without direct evidence on the entire metals-related complex. Wholesalers operating in Chicago, distributing Chicago area steel, may be selling it to an American automaker in the region who is embodying it in cars sold locally, or nationally, or to the Canadian market. They may also be selling imported steel to local manufacturers. Determining whether the income to steel service centers is ultimately "export earnings" or domestic in origin cannot be read from statements about the first-round destination of their metals. In many ways, using the crude location quotient device is as good a method as any for determining export orientation.[26] Up-to-date input-output data, with regional trade coefficients, would be even more desirable.

Third, understanding macroeconomic, structural, and technological changes affecting an industry's performance is essential before economic development prescriptions can be written. Technological change has been a force in facilitating the growth of steel service centers at the expense of both customers and suppliers. Shifts among transportation modes, inventory control techniques and new, relatively inexpensive machinery for slitting, pickling, and other finishing operations have encouraged vertical disintegration. In the process, these changes have statistically shifted the employment in metal-based industries from what were previously entirely manufacturing categories toward the "service" categories, without substantially changing the nature of the work involved. Steel service center employment can not be seen as a detached activity without significant links to local manufacturing. Survival remains contingent on mills making steel and/or auto, machinery, and parts makers providing the market demand.

External structural changes, both cyclical and secular in nature, also appear to have affected locational tendencies in the industry. A profit squeeze on steel makers over the period studied quickened the pace of externalization, where large steel mills yielded marketing and distribution operations to the service centers as a way of cutting costs and coping with uncertainty.[27] In addition, when the recession hit in 1982, financial managers for steel-using companies decided to cut inventories dramatically, buying "hand to mouth." Inventory functions were thus abandoned to the steel service centers, who were willing to take on the higher risk, at a premium of course. In this recession, as in other downturns, the centers increased their market shares. In general, service centers' growth has been countercyclical — a downturn in the auto industry almost always means a shift in market share toward their operations and away from steel makers. Secular factors, too, like the just-in-time emphasis and the spreading of low-cost labor and shared equipment over a number of individual customers, help to explain the longer term trend toward externalization in the industry.

Such shifts in favor of distributional services may be temporary or periodic. By the late 1980s, big steel mills were recapturing steel markets. The mills had learned to tailor supply to demand more closely, eliminating surpluses once dumped on service centers. They refashioned long-term deals, especially with large buyers, as a part of "vertical alignment." Particularly in flat-rolled products, sold predominantly to the auto industry, greater direct ties between auto companies and steel mills eroded service center sales. Automakers are experimenting with new "resale" programs, where they buy the steel directly from big steel mills and then sell it to their suppliers for making parts, bypassing service centers. The big mills also began to sell smaller quantities again to the small buyers they had once shunned and sent to service centers. As a result, the incidence of steel service center bankruptcy rose in the late 1980s, and some smaller centers sold out to larger operations.[28]

The short-term effects of an overvalued dollar, peaking in 1985, may account in part, through its favoring of imports, for the increase in steel service center activities over the period studied. As the dollar declined and as steel imports levelled off in the later part of the decade, the centers' advantages in offering "supermarket" shopping for both domestic and imported steel have diminished in importance. Centers had increased their market share from 25.7% to 28.8% from 1982 to 1986, but saw it erode back to about 25% by 1990. If these cyclical causes account for the flurry in activity in the first half of the decade, then future growth for steel service centers is in doubt.[29] In general, economic development planners should use caution in interpreting short-term trends when assessing industry segments for targeted economic development aid.

Finally, using growth rates as a proxy for growth potential is no substitute for careful analysis of long-term shifts that may indeed favor an area as a center of service sector exports. In steel, longer-term secular trends in trade and technology may ensure a growing role for such centers. Over the long term, steel imports have risen as a share of the domestic market, although in absolute terms they have not grown much over the past 2 decades. The new Korean mills coming on line in the 1990s, aimed at the American market, may set off a new round of successful imports based on low wages and state-of-the-art technology. Furthermore, as manufactured goods like machine tools and tractors are increasingly imported, they embody steels which displace domestic producers and domestic demand for steel. As imports become more important, and the market disperses with sunbelt and gunbelt tendencies, the favored position of cities like Chicago as central steel distributors may indeed be eroded, as port cities and the new manufacturing cities of the nation become attractive locations.

Locations near customers, rather than steel sources, may benefit from another trend. The service centers are fighting their recent losses to the big mills by emphasizing their "just-in-time" services. A recent survey of steel customers found that only 37% were using "just in time techniques."[30] Surprised at these low levels, the Steel Service Center Institute, the industry's trade association, is actively promoting "just-in-time" and computerized electronic data interchange to their clients. If "management gets on the stick," reports Gertrude Scott of the Institute, "there is a huge opportunity for us. In twenty-four hours, we've got it on your dock!" However, the big mills are also learning the advantages of such flexibility and are responding by creating their own "outside processing systems," where they run steel through a separate facility before delivering it to the automotive user. Such processors would be considered manufacturers, not service establishments, and they can be located either at the mill end or the user end. If these mill-related outlets dominate, user-oriented shifts will occur, but will be tabulated as manufacturing rather than service sector gains.

The steel service center case demonstrates the perils of overstating service sector growth potential and treating it as an autonomous activity. Not taking linkages, macroeconomic forces, and structural changes into account can lead to a mistaken economic development strategy. In the mid-1980s, the Chicago's Mayor's Steel Task Force debated whether to target steel service centers independently of the larger steel complex. We did the research which underscored the recent gains of the service centers, but during meetings we cautioned against seeing them as isolated phenomena. If the city had indeed pursued extensive targeting of service centers, it would have been

Our study of the steel service center industry underscores the importance of industry-by-industry analysis in determining locational tendencies in services. We suspect that the characteristics of this industry may be quite different from those of other distribution sectors, not to mention financial or business services.

disappointed in the outcome, as service center employment levelled off in the late 1980s. The city was better advised to concentrate its efforts on shoring up the competitiveness of both steel-producing and steel-using activities — service center gains would keep pace.

Our study of the steel service center industry underscores the importance of industry-by-industry analysis in determining locational tendencies in services.[31] We suspect that the characteristics of this industry may be quite different from those of other distribution sectors, not to mention financial or business services. The fact that steel, for instance, is not sold to household customers but to steel-using factories, energy, and construction firms means that its location will be much more concentrated than the population in general. Steel is also a heavy, bulky commodity, restricting its distributional possibilities, especially by brokers whose transshipment costs add considerably to the sales price. The distribution of household goods, coming in from Asia in enormous containers, may follow a completely different pattern, favoring low-cost interior locations where it is not tied to supplier nor consumer sites.

Our research leads us to question the extent to which a policy approach should focus on manufacturing industries to the exclusion of services, or vice versa. Any interpretation of the job generation potential or economic development needs of an industry like steel or steel service centers cannot be made without serious analysis of the upstream and downstream industries from which it buys and to whom it sells, and the locational tendencies within the complex.[32] In the 1980s, the steel service centers were a bright spot for state and local analysts interested in stabilizing the steel industry, because they were adding jobs while the mills were eliminating them. But most of the job growth was accounted for either by taking over sales functions from the mills, or by selling their importing competitors' steel. In the first case, the centers' future depended wholly on the viability of the mills. In the second case, small job gains in selling imports could not possibly compensate communities or cities for the associated losses in steel mill jobs displaced by those imports. In either case, service centers should not be targeted for economic development assistance in the absence of an appreciation for their interrelationship with steel suppliers and steel buyers. It *is* time that economic development planners paid close attention to the service sectors, but not by isolating them from their links to manufacturing.

NOTES

1. See, for instance, William Beyers and M. J. Alvine, "Export Services in Postindustrial Society," *Papers of the Regional Science Association* 57 (1985): 33-45; Stanley Keil and Richard Mack, "Identifying Export Potential in the Service Sectors," *Growth and Change* 55 (1986): 1-10; Jack Stabler and Eric Howe, "Service Exports and Regional Growth in the Postindustrial Era," *Journal of Regional Science* 28 (1988): 303-15; and Martin Perry, "Business Service Specialization and Regional Economic Change," *Regional Studies*, (1990): 195-209. The conceptual case for services as export base components is made by William Gillis, "Can Service-Producing Industries Provide a Catalyst for Regional Economic Growth?" *Economic Development Quarterly* 1 (1987): 249-56.

2. This criticism is a complement to one sometimes made about the absence of the import element in economic base theory generally; that is, that the implicit favoring of import substitution as a development strategy ignores the possibility that the income earned by a foreign firm or resident in the sale of an import can be recycled back into the local economy through heightened demands for exports.

3. The issues of linkage and locational ties are also raised by W. Richard Goe and James Shanahan, "A Conceptual Approach for Examining Service Sector Growth in Urban Economies: Issues and Problems in Analyzing the Service Economy," *Economic Development Quarterly* 4 (1990): 144-53.

4. Robert Reifler, "Implications of Service Industry Growth for Regional Development Strategies," *Annals of Regional Science* 10 (1976): 88-103; Laurence Falk and Adam Broner, "Specialization in Service Industry Employment as a State Policy," *Growth and Change* 49 (1980): 18-23. See Gillis, "Service-Producing Industries," p. 250, for a discussion of the paradox.

5. These problems could be remedied with a more extensive survey questionnaire or interview, but we are dealing here with an important conceptual problem, not just a methodological weakness. For an excellent challenge of the whole notion of services as distinct from goods producing sectors, see Richard Walker, "Is There a Service Economy? The Changing Capitalist Division of Labor," *Science and Society* 49 (1985): 42-83.

6. Distributive services are an explicit category in H. C. Browning and J. Singelmann, *The Emergence of a Service Society* (Springfield, VA: National Technical Information Service 1975). M. A. Katouzian, "The Development of the Service Sector: A New Approach," *Oxford Economic Papers* 22, No. 3 (1970): 362-82, uses complementary services for a somewhat

broader group which includes finance. Dorothy Riddle, *Service-Led Growth* (New York: Praeger 1986), separates transportation and communications from wholesaling and retailing. See also the discussion in Thomas Stanback and Thierry Noyelle, *Cities in Transition* (Totowa, NJ: Allanheld, Osmun, 1982), and T. R. Lakshmanan, "Technological and Institutional Innovations in the Service Sector," in *Knowledge and Industrial Organization*, ed. Ake Andersson, David Batten, and Charlie Karlsson (New York: Springer-Verlag, 1989).

7. One excellent case study of how the changing patterns of both international trade and technology have affected the geographical location in a distributive sector can be found in Scott Campbell, "The Transformation of the San Francisco Bay Area Shipping Industry and its Regional Impacts" (Working Paper No. 454, Institute of Urban and Regional Development, University of California, Berkeley, 1986).

8. Retail services are eliminated from the definition by some researchers in order to focus on the intermediate goods level; by this measure, distributive services grew in national output share from 13.4% to 16.5% between 1947 and 1977 (Browning and Singelmann, *The Emergence of a Service Society*, p. 18.) Several innovative schemes for dealing with sectoral boundaries have been offered recently. See Goe and Shanahan, "A Conceptual Approach," and Antoine Bailly, Louise Boulianne, Denis Maillat, Michel Rey, and Laurent Thevoz, "Services and Production: For a Reassessment of Economic Sectors," *Annals of Regional Science*, July 1987, pp. 45-59.

9. Transportation has been gradually losing aground over the years while wholesaling has been gaining. Wholesaling accounted for 4.97% of national employment in 1948 and 5.68% in 1977, a share gain of 14%. Stanback and Noyelle, *Cities in Transition*, pp. 8-13.

10. For the argument that a substantial share of service growth is activity displaced from manufacturing, see Ann Markusen, "Chicago Still a Factory Town," *Chicago Tribune*, December 29, 1985; Ann Markusen, *Steel and Southeast Chicago: Reasons and Remedies for Industrial Renewal*, (Evanston, IL: Center for Urban Affairs and Policy Research, Northwestern University, 1985 [Report to the Mayor's Task Force on Steel and Southeast Chicago]), Steven Cohen and John Zysman, *Manufacturing Matters* (New York: Basic Books, 1987); Lynne Browne, "High Technology and Business Services, *New England Economic Review*, July/August 1983, pp. 15-17; and Nicholas Perna, "The Shift From Manufacturing to Services: A Concerned View," *New England Economic Review*, January/February 1987, pp. 30-38.

11. James Vance, *The Merchant's World: The Geography of Wholesaling*. (Englewood Cliffs, NJ: Prentice-Hall, 1970); Amy Glasmeier, "The Missing Link: The Role of Wholesaling in Regional Development" (Working Paper No. 1, University of Texas, Austin, Graduate Planning Program, 1988); and Amy Glasmeier, "The Role of Merchant Wholesalers in Industrial Agglomeration Formation, *Annals of Association of American Geographers*, 80 (1990): 394-417. Among Glasmeier's insights is the tendency over time for distributors to act as the vanguard for manufacturing, drawing in new plants as they signal steady demand.

12. The disintegration of manufacturing, with increasingly more functions subcontracted out, outsourced, and/or abandoned to new competitors in surrounding sectors, creates the statistical appearance of the decline of manufacturing and a growth in service sector functions, with no actual change in function. Much of this "spun off" service sector activity will remain in the same area as the production plant itself.

13. Chicago Steel Task Force, *Betting on the Basics* (Chicago: Mayor's Department of Economic Development, 1986).

14. Vance, *The Merchants World*, argues that customer-oriented locational choices, which he sees as increasing regional self-sufficiency in trade or "internalization," are most common in the branches of wholesale trade wherein the service component is the greatest.

15. Steel service centers are assigned the specific SIC (Standard Industrial Classification) of 5051311, a subcategory of metals and minerals wholesalers. Steel is the primary product stocked and distributed by steel service centers, but by no means is it the only product handled by the industry. Many service centers stock products made of other metals, industrial plastics, and ceramics. As manufacturers begin to substitute alternative materials for steel, steel service centers also begin to stock and supply the substitute materials. Steel remains the primary material used in most manufacturing, however, and continues to dominate the inventory of the steel service centers.

16. Census of Wholesale Trade, 1977 and 1987, *Geographic Series, U.S. Summary*, Tables 1, 3 (Washington, DC: GPO).

17. By the early 1980s, service centers offered a standard delivery time of 24 to 48 hours after the order had been placed. This contrasted with a minimum of 4 to 6 weeks from a domestic mill, and 8 weeks or longer for foreign producers.

18. Hans Mueller, *Protection and Competition in the United States Steel Market: A Study of Managerial Decision Making in Transition* (Middle Tennessee State University: Business and Economic Research Center, Monograph Series No. 30, May 1985).

19. Ann Markusen, "Neither Ore, Nor Coal, Nor Markets: A Policy-Oriented Analysis of Steel Siting in the U.S.," *Regional Studies* 20 (1986): 499-62.

20. In his work on the impact of trends in port facilities on San Francisco's economic development, Campbell argues that containerized shipping conventions allow cargo to pass expeditiously through the port of entry to inland sites where land costs and inventory taxes are lower. See Campbell, "The Transformation of the San Francisco Bay Area Shipping Industry."

21. Vance, *The Merchant's World*. This view is shared by Robert Hayes and Steven Wheelwright, *Restoring our Competitive Edge: Competing through Manufacturing* (New York: Wiley, 1984), who argue that proximity to markets is a key source of competitive advantage in service oriented industries.

22. See Ann Markusen, Peter Hall, Scott Campbell, and Sabina Deitrick, *The Rise of the Gunbelt* (New York: Oxford University Press, 1990), and Ann Markusen and Virginia Carlson, "Deindustrialization in the American Midwest: Causes and Responses," in *Deindustrialization in the U.S.: Lessons for Japan*, ed. Lloyd Rodwin and Hidehiko Sazanami (Boston: Unwin Hyman, 1989).

23. Elsewhere, we compare the period from 1982 to 1985 with that from 1982 to 1987. Although growth rates are lower over the former period, a time of recession and initial recovery, the overall patterns we describe here are not significantly different. See Wendy Patton and Ann Markusen, "The Development Potential of Distributive Services: A Case Study of Steel Service Centers" (Working Paper No. 18, Center for Urban Policy Research, Rutgers University, 1990).

24. For an interpretation of the relationship between the entry of foreign auto branch plants and changing regional auto supply patterns, see Candace Howes, "The Future is Now and It's all Going Wrong: Foreign Direct Investment in the Auto Parts Industry" (Working Paper No. 4, Center for Urban Policy Research, Rutgers University, 1990).

25. Research on producer services comes to much the same conclusion. Several researchers find them heavily anchored to major urban areas and unsuitable, for the most part, for rural and smaller city growth. Beyers' ambitious study concludes that "growth rates of producer services in individual regions were found to be functionally tied to the success or failure of key traded sectors." William Beyers, *The Producer Services and Economic Development in the United States: The Last Decade* (Final Report to the U.S. Department of Commerce, Economic Development Administration, April 1989: i). See also Robert Gilmer, Stanley Keil, and Richard Mack, "The Service Sector in a Hierarchy of Rural Places: Potential for Export Activity," *Land Economics* 65 (1989): 217-27; and William Coffey and Mario Polese, "Producer Services and Regional Development: A Policy-Oriented Perspective," *Papers of the Regional Science Association* 67 (1989): 13-27.

26. For the use of location quotients in gauging export potential of services, see Erica Groshen, "Can Services Be a Source of Export-Led Growth? Evidence From the Fourth District," *Economic Review*, Federal Reserve Bank of Cleveland, Quarter 3 (1987): 2-35; Ziona Austrian and Thomas Zlatoper, "The Role of Export Services," *REI Review*, Fall 1988, pp. 24-29, (Center for Regional Economic Issues); and Robert Gilmer, Stanley Keil, and Richard Mack, "The Export Potential of Business and Financial Services: Methodology and Application to the Tennessee Valley (Working Paper, Central Washington University, Department of Economics, 1990).

27. For an analysis of the steel industry in the 1980s, and the nature of its difficulties from an economic development point of view, see Ann Markusen, "Planning for Communities in Decline: Lessons from Steel Communities," *Journal of Planning Education and Research* 7 (1988): 173-184.

28. Mike Beirne, "Steel Distribution Undergoing Major Changes?" *American Metal Markets*, April 13, 1990, pp. 4, 8; Tom Balcerek, "ASD Members See Dwindling Profits," *American Metal Markets*, March 27, 1990, p. 1; William Gimbel, "Service Centers Link Producers, Consumers," *American Metal Markets*, February 13, 1990, p. 1; Judy Paprock, "Small Service Centers Fret New Auto 'Resale' Programs," *American Metal Markets*, August 13, 1989.

29. Peter Scolieri, "Centers Eye Erosion of Flat-Roll Sales," *American Metal Markets*, May 8, 1989, p. 1.

30. Brian Moskal, "Just in (the wrong) Time," *Industry Week*, August 15, 1988, p. 28.

31. In a study of the "externalization" of services, Esparza and Krmenec found that industry differences were as important as geographical differences in the degree of externalization. See Adrian Esparza and Andrew Krmenec, "Regional Differences in the Externalization of Producer Services" (Paper presented at the American Association of Geographers Meetings, Toronto, May, 1990).

32. Indeed, linkage issues go beyond just the first exchange in the sequence of sales. In research on producer services, Beyers (*Producer Services and Economic Development*) and W. Richard Goe, "Producer Services, Trade and the Social Division of Labor" (Working Paper, Center for Urban Studies, University of Akron, 1989), both find high intraservice sector linkages. This does not tell us, however, whether these services are or are not ultimately sold to manufacturers.

[6]

© *International Regional Science Review*, Vol. 16, Nos. 1 & 2, pp. 197–229, 1994

Service-Led Rural Development: Definitions, Theories, and Empirical Evidence

Amy Glasmeier

Department of Geography
Pennsylvania State University
University Park, Pennsylvania 16802-5011 USA

Marie Howland

Urban Studies and Planning Program
University of Maryland
College Park, Maryland 20742-8225 USA

ABSTRACT Two opposing views of service-led development contend, on the one hand, that services can be a propulsive force in rural economic development and, on the other, that services are neither independent of, nor a replacement for, older forms of rural industrialization such as agriculture, mining, and manufacturing. Both views fail to account for the dualistic nature of rural services growth, which does not mirror the developmental experience commonly associated with services in the nation's cities. This article reviews the literature on services and economic development, summarizes definitions, discusses national growth of rural services and recent trends, examines models of spatial distribution of services, and identifies gaps in existing knowledge.

1. Introduction

For more than two decades the service sector has employed the majority of rural workers. Yet the lion's share of rural research has centered on the agriculture, mining, and manufacturing sectors. Amidst the growing recognition that some service employers are more than passive players in the national economy, a number of researchers have begun to explore what the growth in service jobs means for rural areas.

This research was generously funded by the Rural Economic Policy Program, a jointly sponsored program of the Ford Foundation and the Aspen Institute, and by the National Rural Studies Committee, funded by the Kellogg Foundation. A previous article, coauthored with Gayle Borchard (Glasmeier and Borchard 1989), formed the basis of this review of the literature on services and economic development. Amy Kays and Mei Zhou provided excellent editorial and research assistance. Shirley Porterfield, Calvin Beale and four anonymous reviewers gave helpful comments. Nonetheless, any remaining errors are the responsibility of the authors.

Received 13 August 1991; in revised form 23 June 1992.

198   INTERNATIONAL REGIONAL SCIENCE REVIEW   VOL. 16, NOS. 1 & 2

There are two opposing views about service-led development. One contends that services can be a propulsive force in rural economic development, and the other, that services are neither independent of, nor a replacement for, older forms of rural industrialization such as agriculture, mining, and manufacturing. A middle ground probably exists between these two opposing perspectives. Neither accounts for the dualistic nature of rural services growth. The service sector in rural America does not mirror the developmental experience commonly associated with services in the nation's cities. Few rural services have export potential, and the level of employment in export-oriented services is low relative to that in urban areas. Too narrow a focus on the export potential overlooks other changes that influence service sector growth. Specifically, these changes are the growth of indirectly exported services, the loss or addition of residentiary services, the capacity of local services to attract manufacturing jobs, and issues surrounding enterprise ownership.

Intertwined with limited development models are, with few exceptions, spatial models applied to services that borrow erroneously from the experience of manufacturing. There is an expectation that services start as innovative products produced by small firms in urban areas and then decentralize to rural areas as labor-intensive standardized service operations, i.e., service branch plants (Glasmeier and Borchard 1989; Glasmeier and Howland 1989; Dickstein 1991; Reich 1988a, 1988b). Those sectors most likely to create branch plants are not proliferating in rural areas. Moreover, rural establishments, even the unsophisticated, export-oriented back office service activities such as data entry, are generally sole proprietorships. These rural firms not only compete with low-wage workers in other communities around the world, but now face the prospect of displacement as computer technology entirely obviates the need for human keystroke entry.

Beginning with a summary of the various definitions that frame the service sector, this article reviews the accumulating literature on services and economic development. The national growth of services is discussed generally, and then recent trends in rural service growth over the past two decades are reviewed. Models of the spatial distribution of services are examined along with the implications of these models for future rural service growth. A summary of the major gaps in existing knowledge concludes the article.

2. Defining Services

Current debate regarding the growth and distribution of services is hampered by the lack of a common definition of services and the absence of appropriately disaggregated data (O'Farrell and Hitchens 1990; Marshall et al. 1988). The obvious limitations are due in part to the traditional view of services as residual. In spite of their majority share of all jobs in most developed countries, services received little attention until the late 1970s, when manufacturing began to falter. In general, service industries have been seen as nonproductive and derivative of other sources of growth. Until recently, more precise definitions and disaggregated service industry data were not in great demand by scholars.

Although questions of definition and classification remain problematic, the need to differentiate between services and other sectors necessitates the identification of meaningful boundaries. Traditionally, sectors were defined by the physical characteristics of an activity or output of that activity: primary (extractive), secondary (manufacturing), and tertiary (service) functions (Quinn, Baruch, and Paquette 1987; Quinn 1988; Quinn and Doorley 1988; Quinn and Gagnon 1986; Quinn, Baruch, and Paquette 1988). In the earliest studies, the service sector was a convenient grouping for all activities that defied definition as either extractive or manufacturing. The problem with this scheme is that it does not reveal what services are, only what they are not.

As a way of defining services more precisely, some scholars have emphasized their qualitative nature. In the past, services were considered intangible or impermanent — consumed at the moment or near moment of production (Enderwick 1987). With this distinction in mind, it was relatively easy to identify service activities. With the advent of new technologies, however, the basis of this scheme has eroded because some outputs of the service sector are tangible, permanent, storable products. New service products, such as the magnetic storage of information, belie the impermanent or unstockable concept (Marshall et al. 1988). More importantly, services increasingly take on a quality of permanence when linked in package deals with tangible products such as hardware and software.

As a practical matter, service definitions are largely captive to industry classification schemes that may no longer precisely delineate distinctions among industries (Duncan 1988). As attempts are made to be more precise about which activities constitute services, the debate revolves around the inclusion or exclusion of activities that take on the characteristics of a tangible product (e.g., software). At least one author argues that services are really misclassified forms of manufacturing rather than distinct, and therefore separable, activities (Walker 1985). From a slightly different perspective, using occupational data, Beyers (1991) notes that occupations important to producer services are found throughout the economy. This only adds to the debate about what should be included in a definition of services. Finance, insurance, real estate, and business and personal services are most commonly considered core services. But what of construction, utilities, transportation, communications, and government (Daniels 1982)? Construction and utilities are the most frequently excluded industries. The argument for their not being considered services is

200   INTERNATIONAL REGIONAL SCIENCE REVIEW   VOL. 16, NOS. 1 & 2

that their product, production technology, and physical plant are more akin to the goods-producing, manufacturing sector.

Because the physical quality of a service provides no conclusive basis for definition, scholars have looked toward the embedded composition of labor to distinguish among sectors. Services have been defined as activities that create or transform information and require cognitive skill, knowledge, and experience. This is in contrast to manufacturing, which involves the chemical or physical transformation of materials and relies much more directly on physical labor. According to this definition, white-collar workers within manufacturing, such as clerical workers or engineers, are identified as service workers. Again, putting such a definition into operation is difficult. For example, a high proportion of the value-added of some tangible or manufactured products is created by knowledge-intensive service inputs. The pharmaceutical industry is classified under manufacturing although production costs represent a tiny fraction of value. Most of the costs of pharmaceutical products are derived from research and development, clinical trials, patent applications, regulatory clearances, drug marketing, and distribution (Reich 1991).

An advantage of the occupational approach is that it resolves some of the confusion surrounding the growth of the service sector. The decade of the 1980s witnessed an unprecedented movement of tasks out of the firm and into the market. Activities previously performed within agriculture, mining, and manufacturing firms are increasingly executed outside these sectors. Because of this job shifting, a standard industrial classification (SIC) code-based definition of services overstates the growth of jobs since many activities previously belonging to the traditional basic sectors are now counted as services, in spite of the fact that no new employment is created for the national economy and the same jobs are performed.

The potential for overestimating job growth in services using an industry-based definition argues for measuring services in terms of occupation. While occupational data circumvent the problem of embedded service activities, there is unfortunately no adequate source of occupational data that allows analysis on a highly spatially disaggregated basis. The *Census of Population* and *Current Population Survey* are sources of occupational data, with managerial, professional, technical, sales, and administrative occupations generally defined as service jobs. Both data sets are based on self-selection, however, rather than job task content, thus leaving substantial room for error. One advantage of the industry-based approach is that it best corresponds to a wide range of geographically disaggregated employment data classified by SIC categories.

Service Classification Schemes

Definitional problems arise not only in making the distinction between services and nonservices, but in identifying internally coherent groupings of services. Current classification schemes are based on markets, tradability across international boundaries, occupation, and various combinations.

Market-based schemes categorize services according to whether their clients are business and government or households (Marshall et al. 1988). Attempts to define services by the nature of the purchaser are problematic in practice, if not concept, since individual establishments can serve all three sectors. Once establishments are aggregated to the industry level, the potential for error is even greater. For example, Greenfield (1966) found that the industries most considered to be producer services sold large portions of their output to households. Using detailed data on the revenues of individual firms, he found that approximately 50 percent of the revenues in legal services, finance, insurance, and real estate are derived from households. Even research attempting to link services and manufacturing has shown that an end user definition lacks precision. Services firms are found to sell more to each other than to manufacturing industries. Therefore, accurate identification of markets cannot be extracted from published data. The only method of classifying markets is through the painstaking process of individual firm interviews (see, for example, Beyers and Alvine 1985; Coffey and Polèse 1987; Kirn, Conway, and Beyers 1990).

Tradability across geographic and political borders is a second classification scheme relevant to the study of rural services. Tradable services, according to this breakdown, are those with the capacity to be consumed at a site distinct from where they are produced.[1] This framework is valuable for analyzing the location decisions of multinational service firms (Enderwick 1987) and international trade in services (Sauvant 1986), but it overlooks instances in which the production site moves to the consumption site, as is the case for consulting. Moreover, existing data sources make such a scheme difficult to implement in practice. The conceptualization of tradable services is particularly germane for the study of rural economies in which tourism is an important export service, and the degree to which rural services are exported is critical to the potential of services for development.

Within services, an occupation-based classification scheme inventories occupations by their degree of information processing. Hepworth (1990) uses this approach in his study of the information economy, for which labor's role in the manipulation of symbols and information is critical. Based on earlier work by Porat (1977),

---

[1] Boddewyn, Halbrich, and Perry (1986) and Enderwick (1987) distinguish between services in which the commodity can be separated from the production process and can therefore be traded across country boundaries (e.g., computer software); services that are location-bound and therefore necessitate a foreign presence to sell (e.g., hotel accommodations); and combination services where locational substitution is possible.

202   INTERNATIONAL REGIONAL SCIENCE REVIEW   VOL. 16, NOS. 1 & 2

Hepworth groups service occupations as either information producers (e.g., chemists, economists, accountants, lawyers); processors (e.g., production workers, office supervisors); distributors (e.g., teachers, librarians); or infrastructure workers (e.g., computer operators, printers). While this scheme includes most service workers across industries, it completely excludes some occupations traditionally considered service-oriented, such as bus drivers and shop assistants.[2]

One of the most widely used service classification schemes relies on a combination of more than one principle (Singlemann 1979; Noyelle and Stanback 1983; Fuguitt, Brown, and Beale 1989). The Singlemann (1979) categories differentiate services by markets, final versus intermediate consumers, and by the nature of the provider: private, nonprofit, or public. Services are arranged into distributive, corporate, nonprofit, retail, mainly consumer, and government services. Employees performing tasks in the central administrative offices and in auxiliary establishments of agriculture, mining, and manufacturing are included as a subset of the producer services category. Aside from the capture of a sizable portion of service occupations in other sectors through the reallocation of central administrative office employment to the service sector, the Singlemann breakdown is subject to all of the shortcomings of any scheme based on the SIC code classification.

Problems of Classification in Rural America

None of the above classification schemes was developed with rural areas in mind. Extremely disaggregated and detailed data would be needed to make any of these definitions relevant to rural communities. Small counts, mainly a problem in low population areas, are not reported in census industry publications. Consequently, studies of rural areas cannot be performed with the same precision as studies of urban areas.

Three available sources of rural employment and earnings data are the *County Business Patterns*, the Bureau of Economic Analysis (BEA) data, and the Dun and Bradstreet data. All three sets are industry-based rather than occupation-based. The *County Business Patterns* and Dun and Bradstreet data provide information on rural services disaggregated to the 4-digit SIC code level. The BEA data are disaggregated to the 2-digit level. Only the Dun and Bradstreet data will permit an analysis of services by town size. Both *County Business Patterns* and BEA data are available geographically disaggregated to the county level.

---

[2] While the *Current Population Survey* would permit an occupational approach, the analyst could extract only limited geographical detail. For example, these data will not illuminate differences in occupational structure between larger and smaller rural jurisdictions, or between rural counties adjacent and nonadjacent to metropolitan counties.

A serious shortcoming of either the *County Business Patterns* or the BEA data for rural analysis is that information for low population counties is suppressed when the confidentiality of an individual establishment's identity is in jeopardy. Researchers have developed algorithms which allocate missing industry/county data based on column and row totals for the states. Such enhancement of the *County Business Patterns* circumvents some of the biases that may result from concealed employment totals in rural economies. Confidentiality is not an issue with the Dun and Bradstreet data because it is not a government data source.

A second problem with both the *County Business Patterns* and BEA data is that establishments designated as sole proprietorships are not included in either establishment or employment totals. This omission is particularly worrisome for analyses of the service sector, which contains a high proportion of sole proprietorships. This bias affects employment and establishment counts for the service sectors of both urban and rural areas. The Dun and Bradstreet data do include sole proprietorships.

Another concern with classification schemes is that even when industry data is available for a rural region and disaggregated to the 4-digit level, urban and rural comparisons can be misleading. The nature of urban versus rural activities within SIC codes are varied. Service firms located in Boston are likely to be centers for research and development, while a plant in rural Texas in the same SIC code is more likely to be engaged in routine, low value-added activities. And, the New York financial sector in no way resembles banking in rural America.

Some service definitions are not really relevant to the study of rural economies. For example, the Porat-Hepworth groupings break out the information-intensive, high-skilled, or producer services, which are notably under-represented in rural areas, and aggregate the more commonplace residentiary services, which are over-represented in rural economies.

While the appropriateness of a scheme varies by the intent of study, variants of the Singlemann (1979) classification scheme have several advantages for studying rural areas. A market-based taxonomy is valuable. Regardless of the current enthusiasm about the potential of service exports, the major share of services in general, and rural services in particular, is market driven. Additional advantages are the Singlemann classification's SIC code foundation, since the best rural data are based on SIC codes. The classification gives equal weight to the less knowledge-intensive industries, apropos for the study of rural economies where workers are generally less educated. And it gives equal weight to residentiary services, traditionally considered the dominant rural service activities. The Singlemann classification is at the core of current research on services in the rural economy (Glasmeier and Howland 1989).

204   INTERNATIONAL REGIONAL SCIENCE REVIEW   VOL. 16, NOS. 1 & 2

3. Growth of the National Service Sector

The service sector is claiming center stage in rural development discussions for at least three reasons. First, services have grown rapidly over the post–World War II period, and until very recently seemed immune to economic recession. Second, with the decline of traditional industries, rural and peripheral areas are grappling with uncertain futures. Services are seen as both a potential source of export activity and a component of modern infrastructure critical to future development. Finally, a reexamination of the development path of rural areas in the 1970s and 1980s suggests that places outside the influence of metropolitan areas have made little progress toward improving economic opportunity and human well-being. Like the nation's urban areas, rural America is beginning to show the effects of a decade of neglect. What role services can play in this period of uncertainty rests in large part with the underlying bases for services growth.

The post–World War II years witnessed a major transformation in the industrial structure of the U.S. economy. These changes are widely heralded as the advent of the service or information economy. Twenty years ago service employment represented only two-thirds of all workers. At present, service workers account for three out of every four workers in the United States. Since 1982, nine out of every ten jobs added to the U.S. economy have been in the service sector (Buck 1988; Kahan 1990).

While there is wide agreement that services are the major source of employment growth, there is less consensus about why they are currently growing so rapidly (Eckstein and Heien 1985). The literature includes a number of potential explanations (Tschetter 1987; Moore 1987; Kirk 1987). Part of services growth reflects general economic expansion. Gross national product growth accounts for 40 percent of the expansion of producer services between 1972 and 1985.

Growth of the world economy, increasing complexity of corporations, and expansion of foreign trade also explain some of services' growth (Dunning and Norman 1987). Financial services are particularly sensitive to worldwide economic trends — deregulation, world markets, and volatility of currency. Their growth is both a reflection of the increasingly complex system of trade and a response to, for example, nation-based policies that regulate international trade (van Dinteren 1987).

Another contributing factor to services growth is the low potential for realizing productivity increases in service employment. Services are considered by some to be less susceptible to productivity increases than manufacturing (Gershuny and Miles 1983; Kahan 1990). If service sectors have lower per capita productivity levels, all else being equal, they will employ more (less productive) workers to meet market demand. The view on this issue is not unanimous. Some researchers speculate that in the future, services are likely to create fewer jobs as pressures to raise productivity result in capital intensification of service production processes. Marshall, Damesick, and Wood (1987) note that relatively low-productivity services are becoming more capital intensive, which results in lower employment multipliers. An article in the *New York Times* (1988) about the American Express Corporation indicates the possibilities for productivity increases. Generating the Corporation's monthly credit card billing once required hundreds of data entry processors, but new electronic scanning technologies have cut the size of American Express' data entry staff by as much as 90 percent in some cases.

Additional factors related to changing modes of production also account for some service employment growth. Manufacturing firms now subcontract many services previously supplied in-house (Buck 1988). Certain kinds of activities such as janitorial, food service, and landscaping are increasingly being acquired from firms classified in the service sector. Many of these functions were formerly done in-house by manufacturing firms, and thus were classified in the manufacturing sector. They are not additions to the economy but have merely been redefined.

Another example of increased demand for services arises from growing specialization among manufacturers. As incomes rise, consumers are demanding higher quality and more specialized products. Manufacturers are responding by making products for narrower market niches. This results in more extensive demand for business services such as market analysis, advertising, and distribution services (Stanback and Noyelle 1982). Rapid rates of technological innovation in information and goods processing are also exerting a positive impact on the growth of producer services (Gillespie and Green 1987; Hepworth 1990). As the cost of obtaining information declines, demand increases, stimulating this industry. The introduction of information-based technologies in industry generally creates additional demand for workers in such industries as software and computer equipment consulting. This technological innovation contributes to the growth of service sector jobs. There are also important developments in the nature of consumer demand that are influencing the growth of services (Moore 1987).

In spite of the attention paid to producer services, expansion in consumer services contributed most of the new jobs in services in the 1980s. There are several explanations for this development. The income elasticity of demand for services exceeds that for manufactured goods. As consumers gain personal wealth, they spend proportionally more of their income on consumer services. Dual wage-earning families have resulted in increased disposable consumer income and account for some growth in trade (the trend toward convenience over price), recreation, and restaurants (Mawson 1987; Miller and

Bluestone 1988). Other authors argue that the dual-income household has become a necessity due to wage stagnation. Thus, expansion of consumer services is due to the gradual incorporation of household functions into the formal economy (Illeris 1989). Still others suggest that a major source of services growth in the 1980s was expansion in retail operations. This type of employment is notorious for its part-time status and lack of benefits. As incomes fell and retail profits were squeezed, firms eliminated full-time employees and hired part-time workers (Christopherson 1989).

Medical services were also a major component of services growth. The administration of medical services, encompassing highly sophisticated testing and caregiving procedures, has become increasingly complex. Simultaneously, trends toward extreme specialization of service delivery through outpatient clinics and the fixing of remuneration rates for procedures covered under federally sponsored health care assistance have contributed to increased numbers of both medical service establishments and auxiliary administrative personnel.

Other major sources of consumer services growth are tourism and retirement-related development (Reid and Frederick 1990). Selected locations with high amenity resources experienced dramatic growth in the 1980s, with tourism bringing in export dollars as visitors occupied hotel rooms, bought gasoline at convenience stores, and ate in restaurants. Although detailed consumer surveys of the elderly are lacking, secondary evidence suggests that retirees have relatively high and stable incomes, a portion of which is spent on local services. In addition to the expansion of the medical services sector, the mobile elderly also contribute to the expansion of other sectors, including eating and drinking establishments, convenience stores, and membership organizations. Tempering the benefits of this type of development is the fact that services consumed by the elderly are largely tied to consumer spending and pay relatively low wages to workers.

The explanations for services growth have all been made on an aggregate basis. There has been a tendency to gloss over issues of spatially uneven development of services (see Marshal et al. 1988, and Marshall and Jaeger 1990 for an exception). Moreover, there has been a tendency to treat services expansion outside the context of very real changes occurring in the economic base of peripheral areas.

4. The Growth Experience of Services in Peripheral Areas

While services have been a major source of employment for decades, most geographic research has been biased toward manufacturing (Redwood 1988; Bender et al. 1985). Hence, conceptual models of both service location and development are primarily derived from the experience of the goods-producing sectors. Much of the language

and discourse about services in rural areas reflects the expectation
that rural service industrialization is a response to urban development
forces and not an organically derived process. For example, the
assumption that services will decentralize out of urban areas and into
rural communities draws upon a model of manufacturing decentralization. The efficacy of this formalization is questionable. Instead,
rural services' location and development must be seen in light of
trends that are both distinctly rural (that is, associated with the
underlying rural economic base and demographic trends) and global
in nature. Thus, research that sheds some light on the growth
experience of the service sector in rural areas is reviewed first.

There is broad evidence of services growth and possible decentralization over the last four decades (Garnick 1983). National data
for the 1958–79 period show service sector employment growing
almost as rapidly in rural as in urban counties. Between 1969 and
1979, the service sector (measured as employment outside of agriculture, construction, and manufacturing) grew at an annual average
rate of 2.9 percent per year in metropolitan counties and 2.7 percent
per year in nonmetropolitan counties (Majchrowicz 1989). Further
verifying the tendency toward decentralization, Kirn (1987) studied
the periods from 1958 to 1967 and from 1967 to 1977, and found
that producer services such as banking, finance, real estate, advertising, management consulting, membership organizations, miscellaneous services, and accounting had all become less urbanized in 1977
than they were in 1958.

European and Asian examples further confirm the tendency
toward decentralization of services over the last two decades (Gillespie
and Green 1987; Green 1987). Howells and Green (1986), writing
about Great Britain, demonstrated that location quotients for producer services decreased in London from 2.04 in 1971 to 1.85 in
1981, while the location quotient for southern rural areas increased
from .72 to .89 over the same period. Some suggest that growth of
the Third Italy provides evidence that both consumer and producer
services can assist in job expansions in provincial areas (Aydalot 1984;
Coffey and Bailly 1990; Bailly 1986; Bailly and Maillat 1986; Planque
1982). Martinelli (1989, 1986), on the other hand, argues that there
has been only limited filtering of service employment toward the
Mezzogorno, Italy's traditionally underdeveloped region. And, Corey's (1991) study of the electronics industry in Singapore illustrates
that services accompanied the development of manufacturing within
this small island country.

While reconsidering the motivations for services expansion, researchers have called for greater precision in defining the basis for
service sector growth and its geographic expression. Marshall and
Jaeger (1990) cite tendencies toward vertical disintegration and
corporate organizational decentralization as major factors that have
loosened former ties between services location and hierarchical cor-

porate organizations. The fragmentation of corporations has led managers to recognize the benefits of subcontracting specialized services rather than maintaining an in-house staff. While this process has been and is still occurring, there is little theoretical argumentation or empirical evidence suggesting that the effect of disintegration will be manifested in rural areas (Miller 1987; Barkley 1978; see Pulver 1987, and Porterfield and Pulver 1991 for an important exception). The suggestion that these new developments might lead to services' spatial decentralization would be more precise if the authors specified that the emerging service opportunities are in suburban and adjacent hinterland locations rather than remote rural locations (Drucker 1989; Drennan 1989; Kellerman 1985; Wheeler 1986). Use of the term "peripheral" to describe hinterlands becomes problematic. In most literature the term appears to be interchangeable with suburban, nonurban, exurban, deindustrialized regions, and in isolated cases, rural areas. Lack of precision in specifying what peripheral means reduces this discussion's applicability to sparsely populated and isolated locations.

The recession of the early 1980s slowed the process of services expansion (Richter 1985). Rural economies were especially hard hit by the weakening manufacturing, mining, and agricultural sectors. An overvalued dollar and a worldwide economic slowdown hurt rural manufacturing. Agriculture suffered from low prices and high debt-to-land-value ratios, and mining was depressed by falling energy prices. While employment growth in the services sector also slowed, it continued to outpace that of the goods-producing sectors.

The slowdown in services expansion highlights the distinction between urban and rural experiences. During the 1980s, traditional rural sectors such as mining and agriculture declined. Industry-based demand for services consequently diminished. Services declines further reflected lost incomes paid to workers in traditional rural sectors. Deregulation of key sectors such as transportation and telecommunications has made rural locations more isolated and therefore less profitable for business, further contributing to a decline of services in rural areas. Prior to deregulation, rural areas' access to trucking and air services was cross-subsidized by urban areas (Abler and Falk 1981). The same held true for telecommunications services for which low-traffic rural connections were cross-subsidized by high-volume interurban connections. With the end of regulation, rural communities lost important access to affordable transportation and telephone services.

During the recovery that began in 1983, nonmetropolitan job growth improved but did not keep pace with metropolitan job growth. Nor did rural areas recapture the dynamic expansion of the 1970s. Rural manufacturing and construction employment exhibited strong growth, but the other goods-producing sectors languished. The rural service sector grew more rapidly than the goods-producing sector, but continued to lag behind services growth in metropolitan counties (Majchrowicz 1989). For the most recent year of data, 1986–87, manufacturing grew faster in rural than urban counties, and the metropolitan-nonmetropolitan gap in services growth narrowed to 0.8 percentage points (Majchrowicz 1990).

5. The Service Sector and Rural Development

Although the rural services sector grew rapidly during at least part of the last 20 years, the rural share of overall employment in service industries remains lower than that of metropolitan areas (Bluestone and Hession 1986; Beale and Fuguitt 1986). Furthermore, the proportion of producer, personal, and social service workers as a share of all occupational classes is lower in rural than in urban areas (Fuguitt, Brown, and Beale 1989).

From a developmental standpoint, the composition of services growth is more problematic. Producer services and management and technical occupations are conspicuously underrepresented in nonmetropolitan areas (McGranahan et al. 1988; Kirn, Conway, and Beyers 1990). Fuguitt, Brown, and Beale (1989) found that 13.3 percent of metropolitan counties' employment was in producer services, compared to only 7.7 percent of rural counties' employment. The difference was made up by rural economies' greater dependence on extractive industries. Other researchers have demonstrated persuasively that advanced producer services such as advertising, banking, insurance, and computer services are concentrated in the largest cities, a pattern consistent in the United States and across the developed world (Daniels 1985; Marshall, Damesick, and Wood 1987; Coffey and Polèse 1987). It can then be concluded that advanced producer services are underrepresented in the rural regions of the same countries. While these findings underscore the importance of services to rural economic growth, they also highlight the fact that urban centers are more likely than rural areas to accommodate advanced services.

Over the last three decades, the locational experience of services in rural areas has differed from that in urban areas. By and large, rural areas have not received producer service shares comparable to population. The majority of service sector growth has occurred in income-dependent sectors. Consequently, the development implications of services in rural areas should differ from those of the nation's cities. Or should they? Examining the extent that services are tradable commodities, transferable among different places based on population size, may help answer this question. This means also examining the development theory literature to ascertain the role of service economic development.

210   INTERNATIONAL REGIONAL SCIENCE REVIEW   VOL. 16, NOS. 1 & 2

Export Services

If direct export service employment is to be a source of economic vitality for rural communities, two conditions must be met. There must be a sizable export base component to national service employment, and at least some of the export-oriented service industries must decentralize to rural areas.

The literature on producer services emphasizes that services can initiate export-led development (Harrington 1992). To what extent service industries are capable of initiating economic growth, however, is hotly debated in the current literature on U.S. international competitiveness and regional development (Cohen and Zysman 1987; Guile and Quinn 1988; Guile 1988; Reich 1991). Most scholars would now agree that selected service industries are capable of generating export revenues for a country or a region. The most widely traded services include consulting, banking, insurance, and data processing facilities (Riddle 1986), and accounting, design and engineering, and legal services (Sauvant 1986; van Dinteren 1987). Just what proportions of these service activities are exported is unclear, however.

According to conventional theory, service sector growth depends on growth in the basic or export sectors of the local economy, assumed to include agriculture, manufacturing, and natural resource extraction (North 1955; Tiebout 1956). Based on empirical evidence, some scholars maintain that the major share of service activities remains market-oriented. Thus, services are likely to respond to, but not initiate, regional and national growth (Falk and Broner 1980; Riefler 1976). Riefler (1976) found that all services, with the exception of government, are closely tied to market size. Moreover, he found that services became more, rather than less, market-oriented over time. While Riefler shows that a large and perhaps growing proportion of the service sector is market-oriented, he does not prove that all services are. His model explains only about 50 percent of service sector growth in terms of markets.

Another group of scholars argues that services can be an engine for regional and national growth and that the notion of a merely passive service sector is out of date. Some postulate that advanced services are increasingly exported either directly as final services or, more often, indirectly as intermediate services to national and international markets (Noyelle and Stanback 1983; Beyers and Alvine 1985). Other studies (Daniels 1985; Marshall et al. 1988; and Harrington and Lombard 1989) consistently report that corporate services, especially advertising, management, and computer services, are the most commonly traded services, and they are exported more often than previously assumed. In an exhaustive review of location quotient-based studies designed to identify export services, Harrington, Macpherson and Lombard (1991, 88) concluded that "the broad category of finance, insurance, and real estate exhibited high variation, along with its specific constituent sectors of insurance underwriters and trust companies. Outside of this sector, advertising, R&D, and miscellaneous professional services had large variations in location quotients across regions." Nonetheless, due to empirical limitations, it is impossible to determine whether these findings support the possibility of service exports from rural areas. In all these cases, findings highlight the potential of service exports from major U.S. cities, but suggest little about the potential for rural economies.

There is some indirect evidence that identifies the potential for service exports from smaller cities and towns. Using quantitative measures of export behavior, scholars show that sectors such as retail demonstrate little variation in share of jobs to total population. Other sectors, such as colleges and universities, show large variations in employment relative to total local population (Keil and Mack 1986). Commercial research, management services, and data processing also exhibited large variations in location quotients, suggesting these services are often traded between different cities and non-SMSA counties. Keil and Mack (1986) calculated location quotients for service industries for non-SMSA counties and for each SMSA with a population of 250,000 and above. Because data were missing for most SIC codes for non-SMSA counties of 50,000 population and below, their results do not hold for the smallest population rural towns.

More geographically focused research in the United States also notes the tradability of services across regions. Porterfield and Pulver (1991) surveyed service firms in the upper Midwest region of the United States and found that rural service producers exported 16.7 percent of sales out of state. They also point out that service firms generally export less than manufacturing firms, but partial compensation may occur because rural services buy more of their inputs from within the state. Smith and Pulver (1981) found that rural Wisconsin service firms export a portion of their output. In this instance, export orientation was dependent on size and ownership of firms. Larger, nonlocally owned firms were more likely to export. Beyers (1991) also finds that larger establishments and core regions dominate the interregional trade in services. Smith (1984) noted that distance from metropolitan areas is an important explanation of rural export service growth. At a certain threshold distance, nonadjacent rural areas appear capable of supporting exportable services.

International evidence also supports the view that services are traded across regions. Using a survey of firms' sales patterns, Polèse (1982) identified substantial interregional trade in services in a rural area of Quebec. Stabler (1987) and Stabler and Howe (1988) examined exports from the four western provinces of Canada and found that in 1974, service exports accounted for between 22 and 44 percent of total direct plus indirect exports, and by 1979, services accounted for between 38 and 53 percent of total exports from the

212 INTERNATIONAL REGIONAL SCIENCE REVIEW VOL. 16, NOS. 1 & 2

western Canadian provinces. They concluded that service exports made a substantial contribution to the economic growth of the four western Canadian provinces during the 1970s. In a study comparing nine firm surveys, including eight in Europe, Illeris (1989) found that, in general, firms purchased marketing services long distance and accounting and personnel services locally. The results of these studies indicate that service exports can be significant in regions that contain only small or intermediate-sized metropolitan centers. These studies also suggest that remote rural areas have some chance of developing an export base that includes services. The results, however, should not be overstated. Other researchers have found only a limited capacity for rural service firms to export across spatial boundaries (Kirn, Conway, and Beyers 1990).

While recent literature generally finds evidence of a growth-inducing role for services, the extent to which exportable services will decentralize and diversify rural economies is less clear. Such a prospect assumes that export-oriented services will follow the path of manufacturing and decentralize to rural areas in search of low wages and cheap land. Anecdotes aside, there is no conclusive evidence that this is indeed happening. Decentralization is often associated with nonlocal ownership, but it is not known whether producer service firms presently found in rural areas are locally or nonlocally owned. Also, existing empirical research does not accurately measure the extent that services are indirectly exported. That is, existing survey studies do not capture local sales to exporters, the value added of service inputs to exported products, or the extent that exported services are immediately reimported.

Two different lines of reasoning try to explain export service decentralization. One is that many entrepreneurs would rather live in less congested, more pastoral environments (Bradshaw and Blakely 1979). A second draws upon the spatial division of labor and product cycle models to argue that routine service functions of large corporations may decentralize to rural areas to take advantage of low-wage, nonunionized labor (Hepworth 1990). Both possibilities hinge on innovations in telecommunications technologies, an issue discussed in more detail below.

An export base can also take the form of pensions, investment returns, and social security checks to rurally based retirees. In this case, it is not the geographical base of the resident but of the income source that is fundamental. Transfer payments to rural residents contribute to a local economy in the same way as tourism, or the export of computer or advertising services (Gillis 1987). Such dependence on passive income is another way that rural and urban economies differ. In many rural communities and labor market areas, passive income is more than half of total regional personal income (Hirschl and Summers 1982).

Interindustry Dependence

While it is difficult to ascertain the extent that services are exported and hence capable of increasing local incomes in rural communities, there is substantial evidence of the productivity-enhancing role played by services as inputs to other industries. Thus, even if services are not exported, their presence in a local economy presumably adds to the quality and competitiveness of other local business activities. The service content of manufactured goods, for example, is significant. Service occupations provide the research, development, engineering, and design essential for creating products and processes. Consulting services identify markets and production problems. Service firms are also responsible for the storage, delivery, marketing, and sales of commodities, and financial and management services broker the above transactions. It is estimated that only 10 to 15 percent of the purchase price of an IBM personal computer reflects the actual cost of manufacturing. The remaining value is from research, design, engineering, sales, and maintenance services (Reich 1991). The productivity of the goods-producing sectors has been substantially enhanced over recent decades by improvements and increasing specialization in transportation, wholesaling, financial markets, and business services (Kuznets 1977; Gillis 1987; Marshall et al. 1988).

There is also evidence that producer services play a strategic role in altering the organization of firms by expanding the division of labor (Hansen 1990). As labor becomes more specialized, economies of scale are achieved, and the workforce becomes more productive. Manufacturing success requires feedback from the marketplace, more specialized products in tune with consumer demands, and more reliable delivery and service. When these activities are provided by specialized producer services firms instead of in-house employees responsible for numerous tasks, output per worker increases. Hansen provides empirical support for this argument, and for the critical role of education services in enhancing the productivity of the work force. Comparing measurements across MSAs, he finds that the more dense the producer services and the higher the education levels, the higher a city's per capita income.

While services do contribute to the productivity of the goods-producing sectors, a more significant issue is whether proximity between service inputs and the rural goods-producing sectors is required, and if so, under what circumstances it occurs. While few authors address this question directly, several presuppose spatial propinquity between services and other industries. The relationship between producer services and regional productivity differences assumes tight geographical linkages between producer services and the goods-producing sectors (Hansen 1990). The spatial relationship between services and other income-producing activities still remains at the level of assertion, however. Few scholars have tested whether the patterns thought to accompany urbanization and service development spill over into rural areas.

There is considerable evidence suggesting that services remain tightly linked to urban population concentrations. Italian studies suggest that services are strongly market-oriented but will not decentralize to rural areas (Cappellin 1988). Based on survey studies, Cappellin showed that intra-industry transactions among service sector firms are more complex than among manufacturing firms. In fact, the largest market for service firms is other service firms. Marshall et al. (1988) estimated that only 11 percent of service sector output went to manufacturing, compared with nearly 35 percent that was sold to other service firms. These results suggest that services are tied in many instances to other service firms, not manufacturing firms. Since services are still concentrated in metropolitan areas, dispersal is unlikely. Consequently, the urban-to-rural shift of manufacturing may not accurately predict the behavior of service firms.

The high concentration of manufacturing branch plants and subsidiaries in rural economies further weakens the locational bond between producer services and manufacturing. Branch plants purchase few of their legal, insurance, or banking services on location (Howland and Miller 1990). The major share of services are purchased by urban-centered head offices. Majchrowicz (1991) conducted one of the few recent studies to examine the service/agriculture linkage. Using the *County Business Patterns,* he found that between 1975 and 1987, farming and agriculture services employment declined 16.3 percent in rural counties but grew slightly in urban counties. While the rural decline may not be surprising in light of the hardships faced by agriculture during this period, the decline is noteworthy in light of employment gains in agricultural service employment in metropolitan counties. One possible interpretation to these findings is that the agricultural sector is turning to metropolitan areas for service inputs.

Other researchers reverse the causal relationship and hypothesize that a complex service sector enhances the prospects for attracting and promoting manufacturing (Goode 1990; Hansen 1990). Services may also perform a role in local economic development through the enhancement of productivity in existing export-oriented firms. A local and well developed service sector may reduce a client's production costs and widen and deepen markets for more traditional rural exports.

Finally, new modes of production and organization may strengthen the relationship between distributive services and manufacturing (Scott 1988). For example, just-in-time operations minimize on-site inventories. A smaller stockpile requires proximity to wholesalers and suppliers to insure quick deliveries and minimize down-time. Again, such changes cannot be separated from the revolution in telecommunications options. But as Kirn, Conway, and Beyers (1990) note, telecommunications and transportation advances provide urban firms with relatively easy access to rural markets. Urban-based producer service firms are therefore able to reach into rural areas and provide efficient and cost-competitive services.

Services Largely Dependent on Local Incomes and Population

Although research on services and economic development focuses on the relationship between income growth and service exports, the vast majority of service employment in urban and rural areas remains tied to exogenously derived income. There is a well-established history relating the level of community development to size of place. Central place theory, formulated by Christaller (1966), is the preeminent model of service location in an agrarian economy. In the context of an industrialized urban economy, central place theory is most relevant for residentiary services, particularly retailing and consumer services. Density of demand (determined by income, population, and frequency of purchase), transportation costs, and economies of scale are determinants of the settlement pattern.

The dynamics outlined in this model are still at work in the spatial pattern of retail and consumer services within selected U.S. regions. Anding et al. (1990) found that the geographic structure of trade center systems showed remarkable stability over the 1963 to 1989 period. Morrill (1982) and Stone (1987) showed that during the years that population decentralized, retailing revenues followed suit. This dependence has sustained the argument that service industries cannot stimulate labor demand in rural labor markets, but rather that they merely follow population (Miller and Bluestone 1988; Summers, Horton, and Gringeri 1990).

This argument overlooks the fact that residentiary services can play a role in economic growth when locally produced services substitute for imported services. For example, where a new medical center provides medical services not previously available in the region, local dollars flow to local factors of production — reducing the dollar outflow (Gillis 1987). In the case of rural areas, however, the trend may be in the wrong direction as a larger and larger share of rural dollars is spent in metropolitan economies. Anding et al. (1990) found a disproportionate share of service growth occurring as one moves up the trade center hierarchy. This finding is supported by the work of Stone (1987), Stabler (1987), and Deller and Holden (1991). Other evidence suggests that the growth of corporate retailing and reduced transportation costs have contributed to slow retail and consumer service growth in the smallest rural towns (Stone 1989). Deller and Holden (1991) found that between 1978 and 1988, 38 states witnessed shifts in retail employment out of rural areas. This problem is especially significant in rural areas adjacent to larger cities. Thus, while the residentiary sector has some ability to expand the local income multiplier, this growth stimulus is lacking in the smallest rural towns and those towns adjacent to metropolitan centers.

6. Models of Service Industry Development and Location

So far, this article has viewed services outside the context of sectoral and global change. At least some of the literature suggests that services decentralization is part of an evolutionary process of industrialization, and while the bulk of service employment in rural areas is primarily residentiary in nature, areas will eventually receive employment as it abandons urban areas. More general issues surrounding service industry growth and location attempt to understand global trends and context, particularly the role of nonmetropolitan regions in an integrated international economy.

Researchers examining the service sector in the context of regional development implicitly use one of three models to conceptualize the spatial realignment of services. The product cycle, spatial division of labor, and neoclassical models frame the relationship between the rural service sector and the national and international economies.

Product Cycle Models

Perhaps the most widely cited model of industrial evolution and spatial decentralization is the product cycle. As applied to manufacturing in the post–World War II period, the product cycle theory provides a context for understanding the hypothesized decentralization of tradable services. Nilles et al. (1976) proposed a four-stage locational model for the service sector that is derived from the product cycle model for manufacturing (Thompson 1965; Vernon 1966). In the first stage, employment centralizes in urban areas. Most services, especially information-using industries, are currently in this phase. In the second stage, decentralization will begin to occur, primarily through the outward movement of subunits such as back office functions. For example, fragmentation of this sort may affect branch banks or accounting departments that use mail and telecommunication technology to maintain contact with head offices. Further dispersion may occur in a third stage when previously central functions are shifted to peripheral sites. A fourth phase occurs when employees work at home, connected to their offices by computers and modems (Nilles 1985). During this last phase only a small core of senior personnel will concentrate at a single central location. Nilles' model (Nilles et al. 1976) closely follows the innovation diffusion model for manufacturing in which firms spin off branch plants to rural communities while headquarters stay close to the capital markets and high-skilled labor forces of urban areas. Other researchers have also speculated on a filtering down process for services similar to the pattern experienced by manufacturing (Smith 1984; Dunning and Norman 1987; Price and Blair 1989; Summers, Horton, and Gringeri 1990).

Whereas Nilles' model hypothesizes employment dispersion, there is an equally compelling argument that services will not behave as manufacturing has. One reason is that services are much more dependent than manufacturing on sophisticated telecommunications technologies, and rural areas lag behind cities in obtaining the investments required to link them into the information economy — a necessity for attracting service firms. Many rural counties lack digital switching equipment and fiber optic connections. Data transmission in analog form, the current technology in many rural communities, is unreliable and slow, resulting in higher transmission costs. Installation of digital switching and fiber optic cables is only justified if volume of use is high, making these investments uneconomic in many rural areas (Price and Blair 1989; Parker et al. 1989).

This uneven distribution of telecommunications services is largely the result of deregulation and the switch to marginal cost pricing in the communications industry. Prior to deregulation, the Bell system set average nationwide rates. The cost of communications systems to rural areas and small towns was cross-subsidized by the more profitable high-demand metropolitan routes. Since deregulation, service providers have competed to carve out market shares in the heavy traffic intercity routes by undercutting previous monopoly rates and attracting urban customers with enhanced services. This competitive strategy of skimming off the most profitable routes has forced AT&T to abandon geographical cross-subsidization and to respond to competition with marginal cost pricing on its interurban routes and a greater range of services between major cities.

The result is that rural and small towns face higher costs because of higher average costs incurred in serving low population areas. Rural clients also have access to a narrower range of telecommunications options in places where limited demand does not justify the high fixed costs of state-of-the-art telecommunications investments (Abler and Falk 1981; Langdale 1983).

As a consequence, service employment, which is increasingly dependent on telecommunications technology, is unlikely to decentralize to nonmetropolitan areas. In fact, it should centralize. Headquarters officials making location choices for their branches and subsidiaries are deterred from locations where data transmission technologies are inferior. According to this scenario, service sector jobs will not compensate for the loss of jobs in the goods-producing sectors of peripheral regions.

Gottman (1983) makes another argument for the continued concentration of service employment. Telecommunications are not a substitute for face-to-face contacts, but rather are a complement or contributor to them. For example, say a telephone call leads to a face-to-face meeting. According to the argument, the new telecommunications revolution generates in-person interactions, which promotes concentration, not dispersal.

Telecommuting — once thought an ideal basis for rural economic development — has failed so far to have the expected dramatic impact (Miles 1988; Forester 1988; Metzger and Glinow 1988; Kraut 1989; Lohr 1989). Serious personnel, productivity, and technological problems are warnings to those who would propose telecommuting as the future model of rural development (Kirkland 1985). For example, studies verify that telecommuting workers need access to head office personnel to secure job advancement and job security. Thus, while some facets of the global factory no doubt exist and others are developing (Hamilton 1990), the consensus at this point is that telecommuting will not displace people's need to congregate in one location to work, pass on information, and maintain social creativity.

Cycle theories tend to overgeneralize industry and firm behavior. Moreover, they ignore the role of new technology which can alter the cost structure of the firm and truncate the process of spatial decentralization. Such models also overlook noneconomic factors that influence the spatial distribution of industry.

Spatial Division of Labor Models

The spatial division of labor model provides a more qualitative basis for service industry location by allocating the functions of the modern corporation according to the characteristics of the labor force. Knowledge-intensive industries tend to concentrate in metropolitan centers with more highly educated labor forces, while routine tasks are implemented in regions of the nation and the world where low-skilled, low-wage labor predominates. Again, the model for the service sector is derived from experience in manufacturing. In its application to service industries, it is most relevant for large service companies, which are likely to be firms selling to markets beyond their local jurisdiction.

Recent attempts to theorize the spatial location of producer services identify the critical role played by markets and key personnel in the spatial distribution of producer services. Harrington (1992) argues that

> [markets exert] a distance-measured pull common in classic location analysis: the opportunity cost of serving the market and the danger of losing clients to competitors increase with distance. The importance of personnel increases with the entrepreneurial nature of the firm, the rarity of key personnel for the particular activity, and the relative immobility of professional workers. The personnel factor exerts a more

absolute pull than the distance-dependent cost of market
distance, in that it is critical to be within commuting range
of founding or key associates. (p. 11)

Given these two dominating factors, service firms tend to agglomerate in places where producer service firms complement the
underlying industrial specialization of a region. Thus, in rural areas
producer services would be associated with the dominant industrial
base, such as agriculture or mining. Given transaction costs, producer
services in remote locations are at a disadvantage. Harrington (1992)
notes four solutions for firms to overcome the absence or under-
served demand for producer services: (1) provide services within the
firm at great inefficiency, given economies of scale and scope; (2)
provide services within a branch plant; (3) seek the service from a
multilocational service firm; or (4) acquire the services from a local
firm. Harrington's model suggests that rural areas' producer service
needs would be served in an inferior fashion unless services were
either provided by the parent of a large corporation or purchased
from firms located outside the region.

Much of what rural communities can hope to attract in the
nature of producer services are the routinized, labor-intensive back
office operations. Rural areas compete best with urban economies on
the basis of low-wage labor (Hepworth, Green, and Gillespie 1987).
In contrast to low-skilled manufacturing, however, services require
that low-wage labor be coupled with a degree of literacy and numeracy
that exists in some but not all rural counties (Fuguitt, Brown, and
Beale 1989). Therefore, service industries may not decentralize in
the same way as manufacturing.

Moreover, advanced telecommunications make possible more far-
reaching locational alternatives than was the case with manufacturing.
Back office services may decentralize to sites directly offshore, bypassing nonmetropolitan regions entirely. The nature of many service
sector products lends itself to relatively low cost movement across
space because activities can be transmitted into appropriate markets
via satellite and fiber optic technology. Thus, service companies
looking to locate their back office functions may face greater opportunities for combining appropriate skill levels with low wage labor in
regions outside the United States (Howland 1993).

Recent articles in both the *Washington Post* (1989) and the *New
York Times* (Lohr 1989) verify that low-skilled service production jobs
are not alone in taking advantage of the spatial division of labor. A
major U.S. insurance firm shifted its software division from the
United States to Ireland where they hired highly skilled software
engineers at two-thirds the cost of comparably trained U.S. workers.
The company is taking advantage of satellite communications linking
the two countries. By using advanced information technology, this
company reduced its labor costs while maintaining — or even improving — quality. If this indicates a trend, then the simple spatial

220   INTERNATIONAL REGIONAL SCIENCE REVIEW   VOL. 16, NOS. 1 & 2

division of labor model used for manufacturing may operate even more rapidly for services, and service employment may bypass rural America completely.

Neoclassical Models

In the absence of a definitive theory of services industry development and location, scholars have focused on place-based factors associated with the cost of doing business. Most studies indicate that factors associated with services' location do not deviate substantially from those that motivate manufacturing location decisions (Nilles et al. 1976; Daniels and Lapping 1988; Gillespie and Robbins 1989; Price and Blair 1989; Howells and Green 1986). Although some authors highlight the differences, which largely relate to the knowledge-intensive nature of many services (Noyelle 1987), the literature generally repeats what is known about manufacturing, although with greater specificity. Six factors are usually cited as relevant: market size, agglomeration economies, labor costs and quality, infrastructure, and nonconventional factors such as quality of life. A review of service sector location studies indicates variations in the importance of these elements.

Markets. In traditional models of service location, proximity to market is the driving force. Consumer, business, and nonprofit services — particularly those with an ephemeral product, complex output, and small economies of scale — are especially driven by markets in their location decision. And given the highly linked character of producer services, both intrasectorally and with other activities such as manufacturing, it is generally agreed that proximity to markets is a major determinant of their location as well (Noyelle 1986).

Most research identifying the importance of markets in service location is based on the workings of metropolitan economies or residentiary services in agricultural economies. Less studied is the extent to which government installations and retirement communities draw market-oriented services (Coffey and Polèse 1987; Mawson 1987; Bailly, Maillat, and Coffey 1987).

Since service firms are the most important market for other services, and services are concentrated in metropolitan areas, cities will continue to draw most market-oriented services (Goe 1990; Marshall et al. 1988; Cappellin 1988; Harrington 1992).

Agglomeration Effects. Industrial agglomeration — the synergy arising from the clustering of industries at one location — contributes to the spatial concentration of services (Coffey and Polèse 1987; Dunning and Norman 1987; Hepworth, Green, and Gillespie 1987; Harrington and Lombard 1989). In contrast to views that services are likely candidates for decentralization, most researchers argue that urban and localization economies are critical to the majority of services — particularly producer services — and that decentralization is unlikely. Specific subsectors of services, such as trade, banking, finance, and other knowledge-intensive services, are increasingly seen as urban industries (Noyelle and Stanback 1983; Stanback 1979; O'Connor 1987). For the major share of services, there appears to be a point where increased operating costs inside metropolitan areas (e.g., rent, wages, commuting time) are offset by reductions in communications costs when activities are spatially concentrated (Mawson 1987).

Labor. Since labor costs are the most important expense for the average service firm, labor availability and cost become critical factors in the location decision. Skill requirements for workers in the service sector differ markedly from those in manufacturing. For the service sector as a whole, there is greater demand for two extremes, very low-skilled workers and labor at the highest end of the education continuum. A service firm frequently requires both types, and unless the firm is large enough to separate functions and relocate back office tasks elsewhere, location is constrained to large, diverse labor markets. Whether tested with large data sets or small samples of firms, researchers find labor availability and cost to be critical to the location decision (Enderwick 1987; Coffey and Polèse 1987).

Infrastructure. Along with labor, infrastructure levels are also considered influential in service firm location. Discussion of this factor in the literature tends to be vague, however. For example, O'Connor (1987) refers to an unspecified "well-developed local services infrastructure" as an important locational asset — particularly for trade-related service activities. Enderwick (1987) and Daniels (1987) find that services are pulled toward educational facilities and academic/industrial collaboration. The causal relation may be just the opposite, however, with service sector growth resulting from income-derived demand and institution-based need for clerical and other support services.

Telecommunications infrastructure is particularly important. Dillman and Beck (1986) note that rural areas have antiquated and inadequate telecommunications systems (party lines and mechanical versus digital switches), which hamper their ability to support new service industries. While the potential for on-site satellite links may diminish the importance of inadequacies in rural telecommunications capacity, these options are not feasible for any but the largest firms. For example, it currently costs a quarter of a million dollars for corporations to buy a channel on an existing satellite that would circumvent the need for publicly provided telecommunications infrastructure.

On-site telecommunications technology may dramatically alter the importance of infrastructure levels as a location factor. For example, in Bengalore, India, Texas Instruments Corporation has established a software design center linked by satellite to headquarters in Dallas. If Texas Instruments were dependent upon local infrastructure (such as telephone and roads), the operation could not exist in this location. A former resident of Bengalore noted that the city's telephone system is severely deficient, making even cross-town communication next to impossible. With advanced technology, however, local telecommunications infrastructure is less of an impediment to business.

Transportation infrastructure is also deemed important to service firm location decisions by some researchers. High quality air transport is referenced by Dunning and Norman (1987) and Howells (1984). Others discount air transport quality in light of technological advances in information technology (Thurow and Billard 1989). The importance to all services of a "movement" network — either physical or electronic — is obvious.

Amenities. Speculation exists that nontraditional location factors, especially quality of life, may influence future rural service growth (Bradshaw and Blakely 1979). The importance of amenities is well supported, especially for services requiring a highly skilled labor force. For example, Howells (1984) interviewed pharmaceutical firms in Great Britain to assess factors important in locating their research and development facilities. Aside from proximity to other organizational units, residential attractiveness, good schools, adequate services, and good cultural amenities ranked highest on the list.

For the most part, literature on the location of service firms focuses on the location decisions of private firms. Public services, however, also play an important, if less studied, role in service growth. A recent Government Accounting Office study (U.S. Congress 1990) found that although federal agencies are required to give first priority to rural areas, this has not been an important factor in location decision. The preference for urban locations was explained by short-run budget pressures, political inertia, and the need for agencies to be close to the population they service.

7. Conclusions

Despite a decade of research, it is still difficult to precisely describe the distinguishing characteristics of a service industry. This problem is compounded by the fact that the composition of a service, even as it is identified by the SIC code system, varies across different locations. The development implications of services growth are therefore difficult to discern without close examination of actual organizations engaged in service businesses.

Although there is considerable empirical evidence concerning the function of certain types of services, such as producer or business services, in a local economy, much still needs to be learned about how the operations of such industries vary across space. It is also necessary to view this type of industrialization dynamically. Past justification for the existence of services in rural communities may be obviated by developments in new technologies.

While much of the attention in the 1980s focused on producer services, the service sector employment base is still largely tied to other sources of income generation. Thus, the magnitude of service employment in local communities is very much affected by national and increasingly global economic events. The State of Massachusetts' economic downturn of the late 1980s is a striking illustration of the extent of services' dependence on other sources of economic growth (Browne 1992). Even producer services are tied to more fundamental elements of a local economy. When the computer manufacturers close shop, the demand for software designers declines.

Models applied to service industry location behavior largely draw from manufacturing's experience. For a variety of reasons, the services sector in rural areas has not "matured" and resulted in branch plant proliferation. The majority of service jobs are tightly tied to labor markets — hence the nation's suburbs. Rural services are largely locally owned and, in some sectors, operate with mature technologies. There is little evidence that services will be the next propulsive industry in rural areas.

Theorizing service industry location requires recognizing the dualistic nature of the sector. Face-to-face contact remains important for the more advanced services. Labor intensiveness also necessitates access to large, inexpensive, educated labor markets — hence suburbs. Given advances in technology, many service activities that might have decentralized domestically enjoy even more far flung locational options. Assisted by new technology, transportation, and communications, labor-intensive services can find low cost labor half way around the world. Thus, decentralization can entirely skip a domestic stop and go international.

Perhaps the single largest limitation of existing literature on services and economic development is the lack of specificity in the use of terms such as hinterland, peripheral, provincial, rural, and so on. Empirical evidence documents the tendency for services decentralization to occur within close confines of large population concentrations. Remote and sparsely settled areas have limited options to attract services, much less producer services. A point may have been reached where the notion of dependency no longer accurately describes the relationship between the core and the periphery. More detailed theorizing about the problem of core-periphery in an era of globalization can lead to improved policy that is focused on the problems of peripheral areas in advanced economies.

References

Abler, R., and T. Falk. 1981. Public information services and the changing role of distance in human affairs. *Economic Geography* 57: 10–22.

Anding, T., J. Adams, W. Casey, S. de Montille, and M. Goldfein. 1990. *Trade centers of the Upper Midwest: Changes from 1960 to 1989.* Minneapolis: University of Minnesota, Center for Urban and Regional Affairs.

Aydalot, P. (ed.) 1984. *Crise economique et espace.* Paris: Economica.

Bailly, A. 1986. Le sectuer des services: Une change pour le development local. In *The present and future role of services in regional development,* ed. S. Illeris. Brussels: Commission of the European Communities, OP-74.

Bailly, A., and D. Maillat. 1986. *Le secteur tertiaire en question.* Paris: Anthropos.

Bailly, A., D. Maillat, and W. Coffey. 1987. Service activities and regional development: Some European examples, *Environment and Planning A* 19: 653–68.

Barkley, D. 1978. Plant ownership characteristics and the locational stability of rural Iowa manufacturers. *Land Economics* 54: 92–99.

Beale, C., and G. Fuguitt. 1986. Metropolitan and nonmetropolitan population growth in the United States since 1980. In *New dimensions in rural policy: Building upon our heritage,* ed. Joint Economic Committee. Washington, D.C.: Government Printing Office.

Bender, L., B. Green, T. Hady, J. Kuehn, M. Nelson, L. Perkinson, and P. Ross. 1985. *Diverse social and economic strategies of nonmetropolitan America.* Washington, D.C.: U.S. Department of Agriculture Economic Research Service, Rural Development Research Report 49.

Beyers, W. 1991. Service industries, service occupations, and the division of labor. Paper presented at the North American Regional Science Association Meetings, New Orleans.

Beyers, W., and M. Alvine. 1985. Export services in postindustrial society. Papers of the Thirty-First North American Meetings of the Regional Science Association 57: 33–45.

Bluestone, H., and J. Hession. 1986. *Patterns of change in the nonmetro and metro labor force since 1979.* Washington, D.C.: U.S. Department of Agriculture, Economic Research Service.

Boddewyn, J., M. Halbrich, and A. Perry. 1986. Service multinationals: Conceptualization, measurement, and theory. *Journal of International Business Studies* 17(3): 41–57.

Bradshaw, T., and E. Blakely. 1979. *Rural communities in advanced industrial society.* New York: Praeger.

Browne, L. 1992. Why New England went the way of Texas rather than California. *New England Economic Review.* Jan/Feb: 23–42.

Buck, N. 1988. Service industries and local labor markets: Towards an anatomy of service job loss. *Urban Studies* 25: 319–32.

Cappellin, R. 1988. The diffusion of producer services in the urban system. Regional Science Association European Summer Institute on Theories and Policies of Technological Development at the Local Level. Department of Economics, July 1–23. Milan, Italy: Universita Luigi Boccone.

Christaller, W. 1966. *Places in Southern Germany.* Translated by C. W. Baskin. Englewood Cliffs, N.J.: Prentice-Hall

Christopherson, S. 1989. Flexibility in the U.S. service economy and the emerging spatial division of labor. *Transactions of the Institute of British Geographers* 14: 131–43.

Coffey, W., and A. Bailly. 1990. Producer services and the rise of flexible production systems. Paper presented at the Western Regional Science Association Meetings, Bilingual Special Session on Services and Regional Development, Molokai, Hawaii.

Coffey, W., and M. Polèse. 1987. Trade and location of producer services: A Canadian perspective. *Environment and Planning A* 19: 597–611.

Cohen, S., and J. Zysman. 1987. *Manufacturing matters: The myth of the post-industrial economy*. New York: Basic Books.

Corey, K. 1991. The role of information technology in Singapore's planning and development. In *Collapsing time and space: Geographical aspects of communications and information*, eds. S. D. Brunn and T. R. Leinbach. London: Unwin Hyman.

Daniels, P. 1982. *Service industries: Growth and location*. Cambridge: Cambridge University.

Daniels, P. 1985. *Service industries: A geographical appraisal*. London: Methuen & Co. Ltd.

Daniels, P. 1987. The geography of services. *Progress in Human Geography* 11: 433–47.

Daniels, T., and M. Lapping. 1988. The rural crisis and what to do about it: An alternative perspective. *Economic Development Quarterly* 2: 339–41.

Deller, S., and J. Holden. 1991. Rural retail market development: A policy for economic development. In *Proceedings from the Conference on Rural Planning and Development: Visions of the 21st Century*, February 13–15. Orlando, Fla.: University of Florida.

Dickstein, C. 1991. Offshore competition for back offices: Policy implications for promotion of back offices in West Virginia. Morgantown: West Virginia University, Report to the Institute for Public Affairs.

Dillman, D., and D. Beck. 1986. The past is not the future: Urban quality of life as we approach the 21st century. *Urban Resources* 3(3): 43–47.

Drennan, M. 1989. Information intensive industries in metropolitan areas of the United States of America. *Environment and Planning A* 21: 1603–18.

Drucker, P. 1989. Information and the future of the city. *The Wall Street Journal*, April 4, A22.

Duncan, J. 1988. Service sector diversity — A measurement challenge. In *The Service Economy* 2(2): 1–5. Washington, D.C.: Coalition of Service Industries.

Dunning, J., and G. Norman. 1987. The location choice of offices of international companies. *Environment and Planning A* 19: 613–31.

Eckstein, A., and D. Heien. 1985. The U.S. experience: Causes and consequences of service sector growth. *Growth and Change* 16(2): 12–17.

Enderwick, P. 1987. The strategy and structure of service-sector multinationals: Implications for potential host regions. *Regional Studies* 21: 215–23.

Falk, L., and A. Broner. 1980. Specialization in service industry employment as a state policy. *Growth and Change* 11(4): 18–23.

Forester, T. 1988. The myth of the electronic cottage. *Futures* 20: 227–40.

Fuguitt, G., D. Brown, and C. Beale. 1989. *Rural and small town America*. New York: Russell Sage Foundation.

Garnick, D. 1983. Shifting patterns in the growth of migration in metro and nonmetro areas. *Survey of Current Business* 63(5): 39–44.

Gershuny, J., and I. Miles. 1983. *The new service economy*. New York: Praeger Publishers.

Gillespie, A., and A. Green. 1987. The changing geography of producer services employment in Britain. *Regional Studies* 21: 397–411.

Gillespie, A., and K. Robins. 1989. Geographic inequalities: The spatial bias of the new communications technologies. *Journal of Communication* 39(3): 7–18.

Gillis, W. 1987. Can service-producing industries provide a catalyst for regional economic growth? *Economic Development Quarterly* 1: 249–56.

Glasmeier, A., and G. Borchard. 1989. From branch plants to back offices: Prospects for rural services growth. *Environment and Planning A* 21: 1565–83.

Glasmeier, A., and M. Howland. 1989. Services in the rural economy. A collaborative research proposal to the Ford Foundation Rural Economic Policy Program, Washington, D.C.

Goe, R. 1990. Producer services, trade, and the social division of labor. *Regional Studies* 24: 327–42.

Goode, F. 1990. Community service sector structure as an industrial location determinant. University Park: Pennsylvania State University, unpublished paper.

Gottman, J. 1983. *The coming of the transactional city.* College Park: University of Maryland Institute for Urban Studies.

Green, A. E. 1987. Spatial prospects for service growth in Britain. *Area* 19: 111–22.

Greenfield, H. 1966. *Manpower and the growth of producer services.* New York: Columbia University.

Guile, B. 1988. Introduction to services industries policy issues. *Technological Forecasting and Social Change* 34: 315–25.

Guile, B., and J. Quinn. 1988. *Technological forecasting and social change.* 34: 313–14.

Hamilton, J. 1990. *Entangling alliances: How the Third World shapes our lives.* Cabin John, Md.: Seven Locks.

Hansen, N. 1990. Do producer services induce regional economic development. *Journal of Regional Science* 30: 465–76.

Harrington, J. 1992. *Information-intensive services and local economic development.* Paper presented at the Southern Regional Science Association Meetings, Charleston, S.C.

Harrington, J., and J. Lombard. 1989. Producer-service firms in a declining manufacturing region. *Environment and Planning A* 21: 65–79.

Harrington, J., A. Macpherson, and J. Lombard. 1991. Interregional trade in producer services: Review and synthesis. *Growth and Change* 22(4): 75–94.

Hepworth, M. 1990. *Geography of the information economy.* New York: Guilford.

Hepworth, M., A. Green, and A. Gillespie. 1987. The spatial division of information labor in Great Britain. *Environment and Planning A* 19: 793–806.

Hirschl, T., and G. Summers. 1982. Cash transfers and the export base of small communities. *Rural Sociology* 47: 295–316.

Howells, J. R. L. 1984. The location of research and development: Some observations and evidence from Britain. *Regional Studies* 18: 13–29.

Howells, J., and A. Green. 1986. Location, technology, and industrial organization in U.K. services. *Progress in Planning* 26(2): 85–183.

Howland, M. 1993. Technological change and the spatial restructuring of data entry and processing services. *Technological Forecasting and Social Change* 43: 185–96.

Howland, M., and T. Miller. 1990. UDAG grants to rural communities: A program that works. *Economic Development Quarterly* 4: 128–36.

Illeris, S. 1989. *Services and regions in Europe.* Avebury, England: Aldershot.

Kahan, S. 1990. The service economy — At present, employment tells the whole story. In *The Service Economy* 4(2): 1–8. Washington, D.C.: Coalition of Service Industries.

Keil, S., and R. Mack. 1986. Identifying export potential in the service sector. *Growth and Change* 17(2): 1–10.

Kellerman, A. 1985. The evolution of service economies: A geographical analysis. *The Professional Geographer* 37: 133–43.

Kirk, R. 1987. Are business services immune to the business cycle? *Growth and Change* 18(2): 15–23.

Kirkland, R., Jr. 1985. Are service jobs good jobs? *Fortune* (June 10): 38–43.

Kirn, T. 1987. Growth and change in the service sector of the U.S.: A spatial perspective. *Annals of the Association of American Geographers* 77: 353–72.

Kirn, T., R. Conway, and W. Beyers. 1990. Producer services development and the role of telecommunications: A case study in rural Washington. *Growth and Change* 21(4): 33–50.

Kraut, R. 1989. Telecommuting: The trade-offs of home work. *Journal of Communication* 39(3): 19–47.

Kuznets, S. 1977. Notes on the study of economic growth of nations. *Economic Development and Cultural Change* 25: 300–14.

Langdale, J. 1983. Competition in the United States' long-distance telecommunications industry. *Regional Studies* 17: 393–409.

Lohr, S. 1989. The growth of the 'global office.' *New York Times* February 2, p. 27.

McGranahan, D., J. Hession, F. Hines, and M. Jordan. 1988. *Social and economic characteristics of the population in metro and nonmetro counties, 1970–80.* Washington,

D.C.: U.S. Department of Agriculture Economic Research Service, Rural Development Research Report 58.

Majchrowicz, T. 1989. *Patterns of change in the rural economy, 1969–86.* Washington, D.C.: U.S. Department of Agriculture Economic Research Service, Rural Development Research Report No. 73.

Majchrowicz, T. 1990. Regional economic performance of nonmetro counties, 1969–87. Paper prepared for the Southern Regional Science Association Meetings, Washington, D.C.

Majchrowicz, T. 1991 Employment changes in rural America's farm and farm-related industries during 1975–87. In *Proceedings from the Conference on Rural Planning and Development: Visions of the 21st Century,* February 13–15. Orlando: University of Florida.

Marshall, J., and C. Jaeger. 1990. Service activities and uneven development in Britain and its European partners: Determinist fallacies and new options. *Environment and Planning A* 22: 1337–54.

Marshall, J., P. Damesick, and P. Wood. 1987. Understanding the location and role of producer services in the United Kingdom. *Environment and Planning A* 19: 575–95.

Marshall, J., P. Wood, P. W. Daniels, A. McKinnon, J. Bachtler, P. Damesick, N. Thrift, A. Gillespie, A. Green, and A. Leyshon. 1988. *Services and uneven development.* New York: Oxford University.

Martinelli, F. 1986. Producer services in a dependent economy: Their role and potential for regional economic development. Ph.D. dissertation, University of California, Berkeley.

Martinelli, F. 1989. Business services, innovation, and regional policy: Consideration of the case of Southern Italy. In *Regional policy at the crossroads,* eds. L. Albrechts, F. Moulaert, P. Roberts, and E. Swyngedouw. London: Jessica Kingsley Publishers.

Mawson, J. 1987. Services and regional policy. *Regional Studies* 21: 471–75.

Metzger, R., and M. Glinow. 1988. Off-site workers: At home and abroad. *California Management Review* 30(3): 101–11.

Miles, I. 1988. The electronic cottage: Myth or near-myth? *Futures* 20: 355–66.

Miller, J. 1987. *Recent contributions of small businesses and corporations to rural job creation.* Washington, D.C.: U.S. Department of Agriculture Economic Research Service, Staff Report AGS H61212.

Miller, J., and H. Bluestone. 1988. Prospects for service sector employment growth in nonmetro America. In *Rural Economic Development in the 1980s: Prospects for the future.* Washington, D.C.: U.S. Department of Agriculture Economic Research Service, Rural Development Research Report 69.

Moore, G. 1987. The service industries and the business cycle. *Business Economics* 22(2): 12–24.

Morrill, R. 1982. Continuing deconcentration trends in trade. *Growth and Change* 13(1): 46–48.

New York Times. 1988. American Express goes high tech. July 31.

Nilles, J. 1985. Teleworking from home. In *The information technology revolution,* ed. T. Forester. Oxford: Basil Blackwell.

Nilles, J., R. Carlson, P. Grey, and G. Heineman. 1976. *Telecommunications-transportation trade-offs: Options for tomorrow.* New York: Wiley.

North, D. 1955. Location theory and regional economic growth. *Journal of Political Economy* 63: 243–58.

Noyelle, T. 1986. Economic transformation. *Annals of the American Academy of Political and Social Science* 488(November): 9–17.

Noyelle, T. 1987. *Beyond industrial dualism: Market and job segmentation in the new economy.* Boulder: Westview.

Noyelle, T., and T. Stanback, Jr. 1983. *The economic transformation of American cities.* Totowa, N.J.: Rowman and Allanheld.

O'Connor, K. 1987. The location of services involved with international trade. *Environment and Planning A* 19: 687–700.

228   INTERNATIONAL REGIONAL SCIENCE REVIEW   VOL. 16, NOS. 1 & 2

O'Farrell, P., and D. Hitchens. 1990. Producer services and regional development: Key conceptual issues of taxonomy and quality measurement. *Regional Studies* 24: 163–71.

Parker, E., H. Hudson, D. Dillman, and A. Roscoe. 1989. *Rural America in the information age: Telecommunications policy for rural development.* Boston: University Press of America.

Planque, B. 1982. *Le développment décentralisé.* Paris: Litrec.

Polèse, M. 1982. Regional demand for business services and interregional service flows in a small Canadian region. *Papers of the Regional Science Association* 50: 151–63.

Porat, M. 1977. The information economy: Definition and measurement. Washington, D.C.: U.S. Department of Commerce Office of Telecommunications, Special Publication 77–12(1).

Porterfield, S., and G. Pulver. 1991. Services producers, exports, and the generation of economic growth. *International Regional Science Review* 14: 41–59.

Price, D., and A. Blair. 1989. *The changing geography of the service sector.* London: Belhaven.

Pulver, G. 1987. The changing economic scene in rural America. Paper prepared for the Center for Agriculture and Rural Development, Council of State Governments, Lexington, Ky.

Quinn, J. 1988. Technology in services: Past myths and future challenges. *Technological Forecasting and Social Change* 34: 327–50.

Quinn, J., and T. Doorley. 1988. Key policy issues posed by services. *Technological Forecasting and Social Change* 34: 405–23.

Quinn, J., and C. Gagnon. 1986. Will services follow manufacturing into decline? *Harvard Business Review* 86(6): 95–103.

Quinn J., J. Baruch, and A. Paquette. 1987. Technology in services. *Scientific American* 257(6): 50–58.

Quinn J., J. Baruch, and A. Paquette. 1988. Exploiting the manufacturing services interface. *Sloan Management Review* 29(4): 45–56.

Redwood, A. 1988. Job creation in nonmetropolitan communities. *The Journal of State Governments* 61: 9–15.

Reich, R. 1988a. The rural crisis, and what to do about it. *Economic Development Quarterly* 2: 3–8.

Reich, R. 1988b. Response to letter from Daniels and Lapping. *Economic Development Quarterly* 2: 342.

Reich, R. 1991. The real economy. *The Atlantic Monthly.* 267(2): 35–52.

Reid, N., and M. Frederick. 1990. *Rural America: Economic performance, 1989.* Washington, D.C.: U.S. Department of Agriculture Economic Research Service, Agriculture and Rural Economy Division, Agriculture Information Bulletin No. 609.

Richter, K. 1985. Nonmetropolitan growth in the late 1970s: The end of the turnaround? *Demography* 22: 245–63.

Riddle, D. 1986. *Services-led growth.* New York: Praeger.

Riefler, R. 1976. Implications of service industry growth for regional development strategies. *Annals of Regional Science* 10: 88–103.

Sauvant, K. 1986. *International transactions in services: The politics of transborder data flows.* Boulder: Westview.

Scott, A. 1988. *New industrial spaces.* London: Pion.

Singlemann, J. 1979. *From agriculture to services.* Beverly Hills: Sage.

Smith, S. 1984. Export orientation of nonmanufacturing businesses in nonmetropolitan communities. *American Journal of Agricultural Economics* 66: 145–55.

Smith, S., and G. Pulver. 1981. Nonmanufacturing business as a growth alternative in nonmetropolitan areas. *Journal of the Community Development Society* 12: 32–47.

Stabler, J. 1987. Nonmetropolitan population growth and the evolution of rural service centers in the Canadian prairie region. *Regional Studies* 21: 43–53.

Stabler, J., and E. Howe. 1988. Service exports and regional growth in the postindustrial era. *Journal of Regional Science* 28: 303–15.

Stanback, T. 1979. *Understanding the service economy: Employment, productivity, location.* Baltimore: Johns Hopkins University.

Stanback, T., and T. Noyelle. 1982. *Cities in transition.* Totowa, N.J.: Allenheld, Osmun.

Stone, K. 1987. Impact of the farm financial crisis on the retail and service sectors of rural communities. Paper presented at the American Agricultural Economics Association (AAEA) Symposium on Farm Debt Stress, Kansas City, Mo.

Stone, K. 1989. The impact of Wal-Mart stores on other businesses in Iowa. Ames: Iowa State University, unpublished paper.

Summers, G., F. Horton, and C. Gringeri. 1990. Rural labor market change in the U.S. In *National Rural Studies Committee: A Proceedings* (Cedar Falls, Iowa). Corvallis: Oregon State University Department of Agricultural Economics.

Thompson, W. 1965. *A preface to urban economies.* Baltimore: Johns Hopkins University.

Thurow, L., and G. Billard. 1989. Service activities and deindustrialization.In *Deindustrialization experiences of the U.S. and Japan*, ed. L. Rodwin. London: Allen and Rowenfeld.

Tiebout, C. 1956. Exports and regional growth. *Journal of Political Economy* 64: 160–64, 169.

Tschetter, J. 1987. Producer services industries: Why are they growing so rapidly? *Monthly Labor Review* 110(December): 31–39.

U.S. Congress. Government Accounting Office. 1990. *Facilities location policy: GSA should propose a more consistent and businesslike approach.* (September 28), pp. 1–31.

van Dinteren, J. 1987. The role of business service offices in the economy of medium-sized cities. *Environment and Planning A* 19: 669–86.

Vernon, R. 1966. International investment and international trade in the product cycle. *Quarterly Journal of Economics* 80: 190–207.

Walker, R. 1985. Is there a service economy? The changing capitalist division of labor. *Science and Society* 49: 42–83.

Washington Post. 1989. Global offices on rise as firms shift service jobs abroad. April 20.

Wheeler, J. 1986. Corporate spatial links with financial institutions: The role of the metropolitan hierarchy. *Annals of the Association of American Geographers* 76: 262–74.

[7]

The development of market services in the European Community, the United States and Japan

By Michael Green
Directorate-General for Economic and Financial Affairs

Chapter 3

List of tables

List of graphs

Corrections

Chapter 3: The development of market services in the European Community, the United States and Japan

Page 73:   *Table 2: The second line of the heading should read:* 'Based on data at constant prices'.

Page 76:   *Second column of text. The last two lines should read:*
'In the United States, over the 10 years to 1980–82, there was no clear shift in the structure of total investment away from...'.

Page 77:   *First column of text. The first two lines should read:*
'... manufacturing and towards market services except possibly when allowance is made for the decline in investment in dwellings'.

Page 78:   *Graph 1: The graph should be labelled:*
'Based on data at constant 1975 prices'.
For the USA, data for 1980–82 are not available (n/a).

Corrections continued

Page 79:   *First column of text, last paragraph. Fourth sentence should read:*
           'Thus in 1970–72 the gross profit share in market services in the Community as
           a whole, was a substantial 43.2% above that for manufacturing activities'.

Page 81:   *Second column of text. Equation 2: The second term on the right-hand side*
           should read:
           $$\frac{`b`}{Y_1}.$$

Page 93:   *Second column of text in box, last paragraph. Second sentence should read:*
           'However, the data on hours worked per week available from Eurostat (see
           Table 3) suggest that the result would be broadly the same if account were
           taken of changes in the weekly hours worked per full-time employee'.

Chapter III: The development of market services in the European Community, the United States and Japan

The purpose of this chapter is to examine the development of market service activities in the European Community, the United States and Japan over the decade to the early 1980s, and to throw some light on why these developments have taken place. The term 'Market services' is used to cover all services which can be the object of purchases and sales on the market, and which are produced by a unit whose resources are mainly derived from the sale of its output. In the present study the term 'Total market services' covers a wide range of activities for example; wholesale and retail trade; lodging and catering services; all transport and communication services; the services of insurance credit and financial institutions and personal and business services of various kinds (including the renting of dwellings). Market services excludes collective services produced by general government.

The chapter is divided into two parts:

(i) the first describes the changes in economic structure that have occurred in the 10 years to 1982 and points to the increased importance of market service activities in the Community and the United States;

(ii) the second examines the pattern of demand for market services and shows that, in recent years, in the Community, the growing demand for services by industry has been the major influence on the growth of market services output.

The analysis in the first part of the text together with the supporting tables and graphs are based upon the data given in the Eurostat sectoral data bank.[1] This bank provides data on value-added employment, investment and related variables for the Member States of the European Community, according to the concepts and definitions of the European System of Accounts (ESA) and the associated nomenclature of economic activities, the NACE.[2]

Comparable data have also been prepared by the Directorate-General for Economic and Financial Affairs, for the United States and Japan.

It should be stressed that there are gaps in the data. For certain countries and certain activity branches observations are missing for a number of years. These gaps make it difficult to construct figures for the Community of 10

countries. Consequently the figures given in the text, tables and graph, for the Community, are for the grouping of six countries - Belgium, FR of Germany, France, Italy, the Netherlands and the United Kingdom. This group of countries accounted for more than 95 % of Community GDP in 1982.

1. A comparison of changes in the structure of the European, American and Japanese economies

This first section summarizes the more general changes in structure that have occurred, in the above three economies, over the past decade. In particular attention is focused upon changes in:

(i) the structure and the growth of value-added;

(ii) employment and labour productivity;

(iii) the structure of gross fixed investment;

(iv) earnings and gross profits.

In the tables data are given for market services and, for comparative purposes, for manufacturing industry and the whole economy.[3]

1.1 Increased contribution of market services to total gross value-added

There are a number of ways in which the contribution of market services to total economic activity can be measured. One is to consider the the proportion of total gross value-added (TGVA), measured at current prices, generated by market services and to estimate how this proportion has changed. The available data point to a significant increase in the value-added contribution by market services, in the Community, the United States and Japan over the period 1970-72 to 1980-82[4] with the movement for the Community more marked than elsewhere. Over the same period the contribution of manufacturing activities fell. The details are set down in Table 1. In interpreting this table it should be kept in mind that data are only given for the activities market services, manufacturing and for the totals of each of the economies in question. Thus in 1980-82 market services

---

[1] For a detailed description of this bank see 'Studies of national accounts — No 4 Structural Data Base. Tables by branch 1960-1981', Eurostat, 1984.
[2] For a more detailed description of the concepts and definitions used see annex.

[3] The other four activity branches included in the totals in the tables, but for which data are not given separately are 'Agriculture, forestry and fishing', 'Fuel and power', 'Building and construction' and 'Non-market services'.
[4] To improve the estimation of changes in longer-term trends the figures are based on three-year moving averages.

A comparison of changes in the structure of the European, American and Japanese economies

Table 1

Contributions of market services and manufacturing to total gross value-added, 1970-72 and 1980-82[1]
Based on data at current prices

(%)

	Market services			Manufacturing industry			Total		
	1970-72	Change	1980-82	1970-72	Change	1980-82	1970-72	Change	1980-82
D	35,8	5,6	41,4	35,6	− 5,6	30,0	100	—	100
F	40,4	4,5	44,9	28,5	− 2,6	25,9	100	—	100
I	38,8	0,7	39,5	28,3	0,5	28,8	100	—	100
UK	40,1	0,9	41,0	31,2	− 6,4	24,8	100	—	100
EUR 6[2]	38,8	3,5	42,3	31,0	− 4,3	26,7	100	—	100
USA	47,1	2,5	49,6	24,7	− 3,5	21,2	100	—	100
Japan	43,5	2,7	46,2	32,8	− 4,6	28,2	100	—	100

[1] To improve the estimation of changes in longer-term trends, the figures in Tables 1 to 9 are based on three year moving averages.
[2] Unless otherwise stated throughout this note the term EUR 6 covers the grouping Germany (D) + France (F) + Italy (I) + United Kingdom (UK) + Belgium (B) + the Netherlands (NL).
Source: Eurostat and Commission services.

Table 2

Contributions of market services and manufacturing to total gross value-added, 1970-72 and 1980-82
Based on data at current prices

(%)

	Market services			Manufacturing industry			Total		
	1970-72	Change	1980-82	1970-72	Change	1980-82	1970-72	Change	1980-82
D	36,7	4,6	41,3	33,9	− 2,9	31,0	100	—	100
F	40,1	4,7	44,8	27,5	− 0,3	27,2	100	—	100
I	37,8	2,0	39,8	29,3	2,3	31,6	100	—	100
UK	40,0	2,8	42,8	29,8	− 5,9	23,9	100	—	100
EUR 6	38,8	3,7	42,5	29,7	− 1,6	28,1	100	—	100
USA	45,5	4,2	49,7	23,7	− 0,9	22,8	100	—	100
Japan	44,0	− 0,3	43,7	28,7	5,7	34,4	100	—	100

Source: Eurostat and Commission services.

and manufacturing contributed 42,3 % and 26,7 % respectively to the total gross value-added of the Community. The remainder was accounted for by the other four main activity groups; Agriculture (3,3 %); Fuel and power (6,4 %); Building and construction (6,8 %) and Non-market services (14,5 %).

The figures for the Community are the result of somewhat different changes in each of the four large Community countries. Thus in Germany, the increase in the contribution of services, and the decrease for manufacturing, were very marked indeed. On the other hand, in Italy, the current price data point to a modest increase in the contribution to the total by both market services and manufacturing. In the United Kingdom the increase in the contribution of market services was modest and the fall for manufacturing substantial, although the latter movement was offset by the increased contribution of energy producing activities.

The data in Table 1 combine the effect of both volume and price movements. Changes in the contribution of each activity to total gross value-added based on constant price data (see Table 2) provide a measure of volume movements alone.

The data show that, both for the Community and the United States, the increases in the contribution of market services to TGVA were greater, and the declines in the contribution of manufacturing were less marked when measured at constant prices, than when measured at current prices; this contrast is also to be seen in the data for each of the large Community countries except Italy (see Table 2). Indeed, in Italy, the manufacturing contribution, when measured at constant prices, rose significantly. It is possible to explain these differing structural changes by noting that in Europe and the United States, over the period 1970-72 to 1980-82, the prices of manufactured goods increased more slowly than prices in market services and indeed in the economy as a whole, so that any analysis based on current price data exaggerates the decline of manufacturing activities.

However, it is for Japan that the contrast between the current and the constant price data is particularly marked. Thus although, when measured at current prices, the changes in the structure of value-added in Japan were similar to those observed elsewhere, a completely different picture emerges from the constant price data, with the contribution of market services falling (albeit modestly) and that of manufacturing increasing substantially.

These movements reflect the small increase in the price index of gross value-added for Japanese manufacturing industry of 3,0 %. at an average annual rate, over the 10 years to 1980-82, compared to an average annual increase of 7,2 %

Table 3

Average annual growth rates of gross value-added at market prices over two five-year periods: (i) 1969-71 to 1974-76; (ii) 1975-77 to 1980-82

Based on data at constant 1975 prices

(%)

	Market services		Manufacturing industry		Total	
	(i)	(ii)	(i)	(ii)	(i)	(ii)
D	3,7	4,0	2,1	1,4	2,9	2,7
F	5,4	3,7	4,9	2,0	4,3	2,6
I	4,0	3,4	4,2	3,8	3,3	2,9
UK	2,7	2,0	1,0	−2,2	2,4	0,8
EUR 6	4,0	3,4	3,0	1,4	3,3	2,3
USA	3,8	3,8	2,7	2,1	2,8	2,9
Japan	5,0[1]	5,1	5,3[1]	8,8	4,7[1]	5,6

[1] 1970-72 to 1975-77.
Source: Eurostat and Commission services.

for market services. The difference between these two growth rates, 4,2 percentage points, was much greater in Japan than in the Community or the United States.[1]

Thus, when measured at constant prices, the shift in the structures of value-added in the Community and the United States towards market services was not repeated in Japan; instead manufacturing industry increased its strength and importance.

The difference in volume movements are also illustrated by the growth rates of gross value-added as measured at constant prices. These are summarized in Table 3. In the period to the early 1970s, in the four major European countries, the average annual growth rate of value-added in manufacturing was greater than that for the economy as a whole, whereas that for market services was broadly the same or somewhat less. However there is now evidence to suggest that the roles of market services and manufacturing have been reversed. Thus for the Community, over the period to 1980-82, the value-added growth rate for market services moved further and further ahead of both that for manufacturing, and for the economy as a whole. This experience was shared by each

---

[1] The average annual growth rates of the price indexes of gross value-added for market services and manufacturing, between 1970-72 and 1980-82. were 9,5 % and 8,5 % for the Community, and 6,8 % and 6,0 % for the United States.

A comparison of changes in the structure of the European, American and Japanese economies

of the major Community countries with the exception of Italy where gross value-added in manufacturing continued to grow significantly faster than the total economy.

The change in the structure of growth in the United States was marked by a significant weakening in the growth of value-added in manufacturing whereas growth in market services remained close to 4 % per annum at an annual average rate.

In contrast in Japan the gross value-added of market services, in the five-year period to 1980-82, grew more slowly than the economy as a whole and growth in manufacturing accelerated sharply.

1.2 A marked change in the pattern of employment, and in Europe, an improved labour productivity performance in market services

In the European Community, the change in the pattern of value-added growth noted in Table 3 was associated with a change in the structure of employment with the numbers employed in market services increasing by 15 % (see Table 4). This increase more than offset the decline in manufacturing, and overall employment increased slightly.

In the United States the steady growth of market services was associated with a massive increase in market service employment (33 %). There was also a very small increase in manufacturing activity employment. When account is taken of the increase in employment in other activity branches

(largely non-market services), then total employment increased by more than 21 % over the 10 years to 1980-82.

In Japan, the vigorous growth of manufacturing gave rise to little change in manufacturing employment, whereas market service employment advanced strongly.

In the Community, the United States and Japan the growth of gross value-added per head (labour productivity) in manufacturing industry has, in the past, been greater than that for the economy as a whole, whereas that for market services has been less. The explanation normally advanced for this difference is that the labour intensive and personal nature of many service activities makes it difficult for them to enjoy the kind of productivity gains that are normal in manufacturing industry. Indeed many economic commentators have argued that this difference of labour productivity growth rates, reflecting the nature of the production processes for goods and services, accounts for the shift in the structure of employment towards market services that has occurred in Europe and the United States

This pattern of labour productivity growth rates appears to have persisted until the mid-1970s. However, there is some evidence that, in the major European countries (with the exception of Italy), the Community as a whole, and the United States, the gap between labour productivity growth rates in services and manufacturing has narrowed and that labour productivity growth in services has moved close to that for the total economy (see Table 5). This convergence of labour productivity growth rates occurred at the same time as an underlying slowdown in labour productivity growth.

Table 4

Employment: 1970-72 and 1980-82

(' 000)

	Market services			Manufacturing industry			Total		
	1970-72	Change	1980-82	1970-72	Change	1980-82	1970-72	Change	1980-82
D	8 262	702	8 964	9 561	− 1 347	8 214	26 647	− 692	25 955
F	6 974	1 538	8 512	5 577	− 429	5 148	20 942	575	21 517
I	5 728	1 336	7 064	5 464	95	5 559	19 728	1 190	20 918
UK	9 171	1 053	10 224	8 098	− 1 691	6 407	24 426	117	24 543
EUR 6	33 529	5 123	38 652	31 019	− 3 889	27 130	100 180	1 199	101 379
USA	37 642	12 282	49 924	19 178	948	20 126	87 117	18 855	105 972
Japan	21 249	5 512	26 761	14 512	− 26	14 486	54 630	5 490	60 120

Source: Eurostat and Commission services.

Table 5

Average annual growth rates of labour productivity over two five-year periods: (i) 1969-71 to 1974-76; (ii) 1975-77 to 1980-82

	Market services		Manufacturing industry		Total	
	(i)	(ii)	(i)	(ii)	(i)	(ii)
D	2,9	2,8	3,9	2,2	3,3	2,4
F	3,1	1,8	4,1	3,8	3,8	2,5
I	2,3	0,9	3,5	4,0	3,0	2,2
UK	1,7	0,9	2,8	0,6	2,2	0,9
EUR 6	2,6	1,8	3,9	2,9	3,2	2,1
USA	1,2[1]	0,6	2,8[1]	1,2	1,2[1]	0,6
Japan	2,6[1]	2,7	5,8[1]	8,4	3,8[1]	4,4

[1] 1970-72 to 1975-77.
Source: Eurostat and Commission services.

As the massive increase in employment would suggest labour productivity growth rates also declined in the United States; indeed they were virtually negligible both in the service activity branch and for the economy as a whole in the five years to 1980-82.

In Japan, labour productivity growth for the whole economy remained substantially greater than in the United States or Europe. At the individual branch level however, productivity performances differed markedly. Gross value-added per head in market services grew at a steady 2,6 % per annum whereas in manufacturing activities a much more impressive average annual rate of 8,4 % was recorded towards the end of the period considered.

The results for the four large Community countries given in Table 5 may be grouped into two categories. In Germany and the United Kingdom labour productivity growth in market services moved ahead of that for manufacturing activities and, in the former case, ahead of that for the economy as a whole. On the other hand, in France and Italy labour productivity growth in manufacturing maintained an impressive strength, whereas that for market services weakened considerably.

By comparing Tables 3 and 5 it will be seen that, in the European Community and for the economy as a whole, output and labour productivity growth were broadly the same. However, in the United States although output growth remained relatively vigorous, productivity growth was virtually zero, particularly in the five years to 1982, so pointing to a substantial increase in employment.

In Japan the growth of output remained perhaps 1 % ahead of output per head so ensuring that the impressive productivity gains were not reflected in a loss in employment. For a more detailed examination of these points see box 'Changes in employment and hours worked in certain market service activities'.

1.3 Market service activities increase their contribution to total investment

For the European Community the changes in the patterns of growth of gross value-added, productivity and employment, already noted, have been associated with changes in the structure of gross fixed investment and, as a consequence, of the capital stock. Thus over the decade to 1980-82, there was an increase in the proportion of the volume of total gross fixed investment undertaken in market services, offset by a decrease in the proportion undertaken by manufacturing (see Table 6). When allowance is made for investment in dwellings, the increase in the total accounted for by other market service activities is even more marked. Thus following national accounts conventions investment in dwellings is included in the activity market services and Table 6 presents these data separately so as to reveal the changes in the contribution of market services in the narrower sense. (However, it should be noted that a significant part, although by no means all, of the structural shift which this disaggregation reveals, will be the result of investment undertaken by various financial institutions, for the purpose of leasing to companies engaged in manufacturing activities.) This change in structure, and its implications for the capital stock, when combined with the movements in labour productivity already noted, suggests there may have been a process of both capital widening and of capital deepening in the service activities. Such a process could well lead to a change in the nature of service producing activities with perhaps less emphasis on labour intensive personal services and more on capital intensive services provided to enterprises (see box on 'Changes in employment and hours worked').

These developments are broadly reflected in each of the four large Community countries (see Table 6) with their magnitude being particularly substantial in Germany and the United Kingdom, countries where, however, in recent years investment by enterprises classified to market services, for the purposes of leasing to manufacturing undertakings, has been important (see box 'The leasing of investment goods' for more details).

In the United States over the 10 years to 1980-82, there was no clear shift in the structures of investment away from

A comparison of changes in the structure of the European, American and Japanese economies

Table 6

Contributions of market services and manufacturing to total gross fixed investment
Based on data at constant 1975 prices

(%)

	Market services			Manufacturing industry			Total		
	1970-72	Change	1980-82	1970-72	Change	1980-82	1970-72	Change	1980-82
D	50,8	5,1	55,9	20,8	−3,4	17,4	100	—	100
F	53,6	2,0	55,6	19,0	−2,2	16,8	100	—	100
I	52,5	2,8	55,3	22,1	−3,3	18,8	100	—	100
UK	50,6	4,8	55,4	18,1	−4,6	13,5	100	—	100
EUR 6	51,5	3,9	55,4	20,0	−2,9	17,1[2]	100	—	100
USA	50,4	5,0	55,4[3]	11,5	2,3	13,8[3]	100	—	100
Japan	44,0	−2,6	41,4	22,7	−3,5	19,2	100	—	100

[1] The contributions in % for Market services excluding investment in dwellings are:

	1970-72	Change	1980-82
D	23,0	7,5	30,5
F	23,8	4,7	28,5[2]
I	23,8	7,0	30,8
UK	16,0	10,7	26,7
EUR 6	24,3	6,1	30,4[2]
USA	24,8	13,3	38,1[3]
Japan	22,1	0,9	23,2

[2] 1979-81.
[3] 1978-80.
Source: Eurostat and Commission services.

manufacturing and towards market services even when allowance is made for the decline in investment in dwellings.

In contrast to the developments observed for Europe and the United States there appears to have been, in Japan, a decline in the contributions of both market services and manufacturing activities to total gross fixed investment as between 1970-72 and 1980-82. However, an analysis of the year-to-year changes in structure shows that it was in the mid-1970s that the contribution of manufacturing to total investment fell markedly, by some five percentage points. By 1980-82 the contribution was increasing again towards the levels recorded in the early 1970s. In contrast, the contribution of market services increased over the first part of the decade but then fell somewhat. Over this period the declines in the contributions of manufacturing and market services were offset by increases from the activities energy and non-market services. These developments are also illustrated by the growth rates of investment set down in Graph 1. The

substantial increase in manufacturing investment occurred in the early 1980s at the same time as the acceleration in labour productivity in manufacturing activities given in Table 5. Over the same period investment in market services activities grew at a modest but relatively steady pace.

In the United States, on the other hand, it was market services investment which declined after the first oil price shock and then recovered strongly whereas manufacturing investment continued to grow at a strong pace.

In Europe the growth performance of market service investment was somewhat stronger than that of manufacturing throughout the 10-year period, a development which confirms the change in structure already noted. However, both rates of growth remained modest compared to those reached in the United States and Japan.

GRAPH 1

Growth rates of gross fixed investment

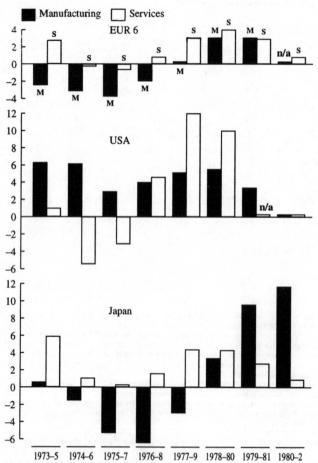

Average annual growth rates over three year period (%) vertical scale.
Growth rates calculated using three-year moving averages of annual data. The end period for calculation of
the growth rates is given on the horizontal scale.

A comparison of changes in the structure of the European, American and Japanese economies

1.4 The growth of earnings per head in market services below that observed for manufacturing

It can be argued that the increase in market service employment and, in Europe, the change in the structure of fixed investment, should be reflected in the development of earnings per head, and indeed this does appear to be the case. Thus in the Community, the United States and Japan, through the 10 years to 1980-82, earnings per head advanced more slowly in market services activities than in manufacturing, although there is evidence that the growth rates were converging towards the end of the period (see Table 7). From these data, it is not possible to judge whether the slower growth in earnings in market services reflects actual differences in hourly earnings paid (for example) or the greater number of part time workers employed by undertakings such as shops and hotels.

The figures for the Community broadly follow developments in each of the large Member States with the exception of Italy where the growth of earnings per head in services had, by 1982, moved ahead of that for manufacturing.

Similar results are obtained if growth rates for real earnings per head are calculated. Thus in Europe and the United States the growth of earnings per head in real terms, in market services, remained significantly below that recorded for manufacturing activities (see Table 8) and this lends support to the view that the growth of employment in market services has been partly in response to favourable developments in labour costs.

1.5 In the European Community and the United States, the share of profits in value develops more favourably in market services

The movements in gross value-added, employment and earnings per head already noted, imply a change in the structure of gross profits. Indeed there have been marked changes in the share of gross profits in gross value-added in market services and manufacturing as between 1970-72 and 1980-82. Figures of relative gross profit shares for these two sectors are set down in Table 9. Thus, in 1970-72 the gross profit share in market services in the Community as a whole, was a substantial 49,4 % above that for manufacturing activities. However, a marked increase took place between 1970-72 and 1980-82 with the relative market services gross profit share becoming 66,4 % greater than that for manufacturing.

This increase in relative gross profit shares also occurred in the four large member countries with the exception of Italy.

A similar increase also occurred in the United States with the relative gross profit share in market services rising to almost 100 % above the level for manufacturing.

Table 7

Average annual growth rates of the compensation of employees per head over two five-year periods: (i) 1969-71 to 1974-76; (ii) 1975-77 to 1980-82

(%)

	Market services		Manufacturing industry		Total	
	(i)	(ii)	(i)	(ii)	(i)	(ii)
D	9,7[1]	5,8	10,2[1]	7,1	9,7[1]	6,0
F	12,5[1]	12,9	14,4[1]	14,1	14,8[1]	13,6
I	17,4	18,4	18,7	18,0	17,6	19,5
UK	16,3[1]	14,4	18,7[1]	14,3	17,7[1]	14,0
EUR 6	13,4[1]	11,0	14,7[1]	11,5	14,1[1]	11,1
USA	7,4	8,6	8,0	9,1	7,5	8,5
Japan	16,7[1]	7,2	17,0[1]	7,4	17,2[1]	7,2

[1] 1970-72 to 1975-77.

Source: Eurostat and Commission services.

Table 8

Average annual growth rates of earnings per head deflated by the price index for gross value-added, over two five-year periods: (i) 1970-72 to 1975-77; (ii) 1975-77 to 1980-82

(%)

	Market services		Manufacturing industry		Total	
	(i)	(ii)	(i)	(ii)	(i)	(ii)
D	3,8	1,6	4,2	2,9	3,8	1,9
F	2,6	2,0	4,4	3,0	4,7	2,6
I	4,0	0,8	5,1	0,5	4,0	1,8
UK	1,6	0,4	3,7	0,4	2,9	0,1
EUR 6	3,2	1,6	4,4	2,1	3,8	1,8
USA	0,7	0,6	1,6	1,1	0,9	0,5
Japan	6,0	3,5	6,2	3,7	6,4	3,5

Source: Eurostat and Commission services.

The development of market services

The picture for Japan is very different. Indeed, the relative gross profit share for market services fell by five percentage points over the decade to 1980-82.

It can be argued that these changes in the structure of gross profits provide some explanation for the changes in the structure of fixed investment already noted.

1.6 *Summary of the points made*

For the European Community:

(i) The contribution of market services to total gross value-added has increased markedly, broadly offsetting the fall in the contribution of manufacturing activities. At the same time, the pattern of growth of value-added has changed, with market services growing faster than the economy as a whole, and manufacturing activities more slowly.

(ii) There has been a marked increase in employment in services, and a decline in employment in manufacturing. Moreover, labour productivity growth in market services has been catching up with labour productivity in the economy as a whole. The growth of earnings per head in market services both in nominal and real terms has, however, remained below that observed for manufacturing.

(iii) There is evidence of a shift in the structure of both investment and gross profits towards services although, to a limited extent, these changes will reflect leasing activities.

The developments in each of the four large Member States have been somewhat different with both France and perhaps more notably Italy recording more vigorous performances by manufacturing activities, whereas in Germany and the UK the growth of manufacturing was much weaker than market services and the decline in employment more marked.

For the United States:

(i) There has been a marked increase in the contribution of market services to total output, largely offsetting the fall in the contribution of manufacturing. At the time market services output growth has remained vigorous, with the growth of manufacturing much weaker.

(ii) The change in the pattern of output growth has been associated with a massive increase in market service employment and a small increase in manufacturing employment. Labour productivity growth has been negligible in market services, and in the economy as a whole.

For Japan:

(i) The growth rate of manufacturing output has remained, in recent years, well above that for the economy as a whole, and for all the other branches, including market services.

(ii) Nonetheless, because output per head in market services has advanced slowly, employment has expanded markedly.

2. The changing pattern of demand for market services

Part 1 sets down the broad changes in economic structure that have occurred in the European Community, the United States and Japan during the decade to 1980-82. In both Europe and the United States the contribution of market services to economic activity has increased; this is the case whether gross value-added, employment, investment or gross profits are considered. The purpose of this second part is to examine the factors on the demand side that have been associated with this change in structure. To begin with, the well-documented link between rising living standards and increases in employment in market services is confirmed.

Table 9

Share of gross profits in gross value-added in market services relative to manufacturing activities[1]

Indices: Manufacturing = 100

	Market services		Manufacturing industry	
	1970-72	1980-82	1970-72	1980-82
D	149,4	210,9	100	100
F	163,1	187,9	100	100
I	132,4	92,9	100	100
UK	131,4	137,7	100	100
EUR 6	143,2	166,4	100	100
USA	164,6	191,7	100	100
Japan	90,7	85,7	100	100

[1] For the purposes of this table, gross profits equal gross value-added at market prices less compensation of employees corrected for the self-employed. The share of gross profits in gross value-added equals gross profits divided by gross value-added. The relative gross profits share for market services equals the gross profits share for market services divided by the gross profit share for manufacturing.
Source: Eurostat and Commission services.

This link is usually attributed to a change in the pattern of private consumption following a rise in living standards.[1] This explanation is then examined and, in the case of the European countries, is shown to be inadequate. Rather the growth of market services owes much to the growth of the consumption of services by industry, as intermediate inputs into production. This finding throws light on the structural changes that have taken place within industry and services, and has implications for the debate on so-called de-industrialization.

To confirm the link between living standards and market service employment a start is made by plotting the proportion of the employed labour force engaged in market services (see Table 4), against the level of real income per head, measured as gross domestic product, at constant 1975 prices and exchange rates, per head. This is done for the Community, the United States and Japan in Graph 2.

The graph shows that, for each of these economies, the link between the proportion of the employed labour force engaged in market services, and real income per head, is close. Moreover, in each case, the proportion of the labour force engaged in market services appears to be related to the level of constant price GDP per head, by a function that has the property of approaching an asymptotic value or limit as GDP/head increases. A possible asymptote is indicated on the graph. A number of functions exhibit this property. One particular relationship is based upon the exponential function:

$$L_s/L = a . \exp (b/Y) \qquad [1]$$

or $\log (L_s/L) = \log a + b/Y$

where L_s denotes the number employed in market services, L total employment, and Y, GDP/head.

This equation has the property that as Y increases so b/Y approaches zero and L_s/L the value a.

Equation [1] also has the property that the elasticity of changes in the employment proportion (L_s/L) with respect to changes in income (Y) is a declining function of the variable Y, implying that the rate of change of the structure of employment generally slows down as GDP per head increases. This property would appear, *prima facie*, to be plausible and so Equation [1] has been tested against the data.

[1] See the earlier chapters in *The New Service Economy*, Gershuny and Miles; Pinter 1983 and the discussion in 'The Growth of Service Employment: A reappraisal', Momigliano and Siniscalco, Banca Nazionale del Lavoro: *Quarterly Review*, No 142 and references cited therein.

To permit ordinary-least least squares techniques to be used the hypothesis has been tested in its logarithmic form

$$\log (L_s/L)_t = \log a + \frac{b}{y_t} + e_t \qquad [2]$$

where t denotes the time period of the observations and the error term e_t is normally distributed $N(0,S^2)$.

The least squares estimates of Equation [2] using data for the Community of Six, the United States and Japan are set out in Table 10.

The results show that:

(i) The proportion of variance explained, R^2, is more than 90 % for the Community and Japan. The proportion is somewhat less for the United States but remains significant. All the regression coefficients are significant. Moreover, they have plausible magnitudes and the expected signs.

(ii) The estimated employment elasticities for 1982, linking income per head and the proportion of the employed labour force in market services, are very close for the Community, the United States and Japan. Thus for each of these economies it is estimated that a 1 % increase in GDP per head will lead to 0,3 % increase in the proportion of the total labour force employed in market services.

However as the discussion in the first part of this study has shown, the results for the Community may not be a good guide to the developments in the individual community countries and so the hypothesis set out in Equation [2] has also been tested using data for Germany, France, Italy and the United Kingdom (see Graph 3). The results are set out in Table 11 where it will be noted that the results again provide high levels of variance explained (R^2) and the expected signs for the coefficients. The results cluster closely around those for the Community. The market service employment proportion elasticity is highest for the United Kingdom and lowest for Germany.

The estimates set out in Tables 10 and 11 show that for the European Community, the four large Community countries (considered separately), the United States and Japan, there is marked correlation between GDP/head and the proportion of the labour force employed in the activity branch market services and in particular, that as GDP/head increases so does the proportion of the labour force employed in market services. These conclusions are consistent with a hypothesis frequently repeated and discussed in the economic literature and often called the theory of stages of econo-

GRAPH 2

GDP per head and the proportion of the employed labour force in market services:
European Community, the United States and Japan

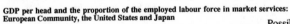

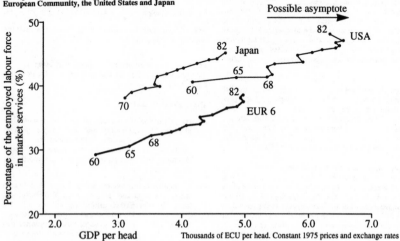

GDP per head   Thousands of ECU per head. Constant 1975 prices and exchange rates

GRAPH 3

GDP per head and the proportion of the employed labour force in market services:
the four large European countries

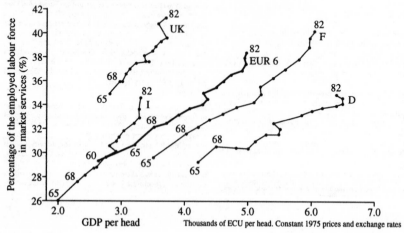

GDP per head   Thousands of ECU per head. Constant 1975 prices and exchange rates

mic growth.[1] This theory attempts to explain the relative growth of market services by suggesting that, as an economy grows and income per head increases, so the demand for services increases faster than the demand for consumption goods in general. As a consequence, the structure of consumption changes and this change, combined with the assumed tendency for the production of services to exhibit a slower rate of labour productivity growth than the production of goods, leads to the shift in the pattern of employment already noted.

To complete the picture it is also usually asserted that the consumption of services is price inelastic, so that the more rapid rise in the price of services, due to slow labour productivity growth, has only a negligible effect on the volume of services consumed.

Clearly it is important to establish whether these speculations are consistent with the developments observed in the

European Community, the United States and Japan. Indeed the link between increases in GDP/head and the rise in the numbers employed in market services may be explained by the following developments on the demand side.

As already noted, there are changes in the pattern of private consumption, with market services accounting for an increasing proportion of total household expenditure; however, it may also be necessary to take into account:

(i) increased purchases of services as intermediate inputs into production activities; and

(ii) an increasing contribution from international trade in services.

2.1 For the European Community and the United States no clear shift in the pattern of private consumption towards market services

In this subsection, the point of departure will be 1975 — a year for which consistent input-output tables are available

---

[1] See the earlier chapters in *The New Service Economy*, Gershuny and Miles; Pinter 1983 and the discussion in 'The Growth of Service Employment: A reappraisal', Momigliano and Siniscalco, Banca Nazionale del Lavoro: *Quarterly Review*, No 142 and references cited therein.

Table 10

Employment in market services and GDP per head
Least squares estimates of Equation [2] for the Community, the United States and Japan

EUR 6	$\log(L_s/L) =$	3.9143	—	1 510.6	•	$\dfrac{1}{\text{GDP/head}}$	:	$R^2 = 0.9028$
		(0.0319)		(128.0)				
USA	$\log(L_s/L) =$	4.1262	—	1 948.5	•	$\dfrac{1}{\text{GDP/head}}$	:	$R^2 = 0.7634$
		(0.0494)		(280.1)				
Japan	$\log(L_s/L) =$	4.1268	—	1 512.1	•	$\dfrac{1}{\text{GDP/head}}$	:	$R^2 = 0.9545$
		(0.0281)		(104.4)				

Estimated elasticities of market services employment proportion (L_s/L) with respect to GDP/head in 1982 are:
EUR 6 0.305;
USA 0.307;
Japan 0.323.
The least squares regressions for EUR 6 and the USA are based on data for 1960, 1965, 1968 to 1982; for Japan on data from 1970 to 1981.
Source: Eurostat and Commission services.

The development of market services

Table 11

Employment in market services and GDP per head
Least squares estimates of Equation [2] for the four large Community countries

D	$\log(L_s/L)$ =	3,7631	—	1 560,0	•	$\dfrac{1}{\text{GDP/head}}$	:	R^2 = 0,8732
		(0,0295)		(153,5)				
F	$\log(L_s/L)$ =	3,9665	—	1 991,8	•	$\dfrac{1}{\text{GDP/head}}$	:	R^2 = 0,9024
		(0,0363)		(169,1)				
I	$\log(L_s/L)$ =	3,7819	—	1 003,8	•	$\dfrac{1}{\text{GDP/head}}$	:	R^2 = 0,8802
		(0,0371)		(95,6)				
UK	$\log(L_s/L)$ =	4,0816	—	1 405,7	•	$\dfrac{1}{\text{GDP/head}}$	:	R^2 = 0,8477
		(0,0477)		153,8				

Estimated elasticities of market services employment proportion (L_s/L) with respect to GDP/head in 1982 are:
D   0,243;
F   0,331;
I   0,305;
UK 0,385.
The least square regressions are based upon data for the years 1960, 1965 and 1968-82.
Source: Eurostat.

Table 12

The allocation of the output of market service activities in the European Community. Data for 1975

(%)

NACE activity number	Proportion of output allocated to:				
	Intermediate consumption by industry[1]	Intermediate consumption by services[1]	Final demand by households[2]	Exports of households[2]	Total
57 Wholesale and retail trade	17,5	7,7	64,7	10,1	100,0
59 Lodging and catering services	6,7	11,0	82,3	—	100,0
61 Inland transport[3]	34,2	24,9	31,4	9,5	100,0
63 Maritime and air transport[3]	19,9	27,9	9,0	43,2	100,0
67 Communication	19,1	45,8	31,8	3,1	100,0
69 Services of credit and insurance institutions	7,5	73,7	16,2	2,6	100,0
73 Renting	2,1	9,7	87,3	0,9	100,0
79 Other services[4]	22,8	29,1	44,0	4,1	100,0
Total excluding 57 and 73[5]	19,2	34,5	38,7	7,6	100,0
Total excluding 73	18,7	26,6	46,4	8,3	100,0
Grand total	16,8	24,6	51,1	7,5	100,0

[1] In this table the term industry covers all activities except market and non-market services; the term services covers the sum of market and non-market services.
[2] Final demand by households includes expenditures by foreign tourists in the Community.
[3] Including the relevant parts of activity 65: Auxiliary transport services.
[4] The sum of NACE activity branches 71 + 75 + 77 + 79.
[5] For the reasons justifying this grouping of activities see annex.

Source: Eurostat; input-output table for 1975 for EUR 8 (EUR 6 as defined plus Ireland plus Denmark).

for each of the Member States of the Community and the Community itself. These data make it possible to calculate for the Community, the allocation of market service output, in 1975, to various categories of intermediate and final demand. The output allocation proportions are given in Table 12. According to the grouping of activities considered, final demand by households, in 1975, accounted for between one third and one half of market service output. Tables 13 and 14 show how the proportion of private consumption devoted to market services has changed over the period 1975 to 1982 for the European Community, the four large Community countries, the United States and Japan. Amongst the market services included in this analysis are those that might be considered, *a priori*, to have a high income elasticity such as expenditure on entertainment and cultural services, and expenditure in restaurants, cafes and hotels, etc.

The figures in Table 13 show that the proportion of final consumption expenditure devoted to the purchase of such market services, in the European countries, increased somewhat over this seven-year period. For the Community aggregate, the average annual rate of growth of market services expenditure at current prices was almost 1 % ahead of that for total expenditures.

Such a result is consistent with the hypothesis that the income elasticity of market services is greater than unity. However, it is important to disentangle the effect of prices from the calculation. Thus the change in the proportion of expenditure on market services at current prices, noted above, could well reflect price movements and low price elasticities, in addition to movements associated with income. Figures based on data at the constant prices are set out in Table 14.

These show that for the countries of the Community, but with the exception of the United Kingdom, the income elasticity of market services is only just greater than unity. Thus, over the seven years to 1982, expenditure on market services in the Community increased at an annual average rate of about 2,4 % whereas the volume of total consumption increased at an average annual rate of 2,3 %.

For the United States, the volume growth of private consumption of market services at 3,0 % has been slightly less than that for consumption as a whole (3,1 %).

For Japan, the data used to calculate the growth of the consumption of market services have a much broader coverage than those for the European countries, or the United

Table 13

Final consumption of households: market services (% based on data at current prices)

	Average annual growth rates 1975-82		Proportion of total consumption devoted to market services	
	Consumption of market services[1]	Total final consumption[2]	1975	1982
D[3]	7,1	6,4	10,7	11,2
F[3]	15,3	14,5	13,7	14,5
I[3]	20,2	20,4	15,2	15,0
UK[3]	14,6	14,3	22,7	23,2
EUR 6[3]	12,7	11,6	14,6	15,6
USA[4]	11,0	10,8	27,7	28,1
Japan[5]	11,4	9,0	43,9	51,0

[1] Final consumption codes 46 + 63 + 64 + 72 + 83 + 84 + 85 + 86 (see ESA 1979).
[2] Exact ESA terminology: Final consumption of households on the economic territory.
[3] *Source:* Eurostat.
[4] *Source:* OECD; for the United States the definition of market services retained is close to that used for the European countries.
[5] *Source:* OECD; for Japan the definition of market services retained covers all expenditure on services.

Table 14

Final consumption of households: market services (% based on data at 1975 prices)

	Average annual growth rates 1975-82		Proportion of total consumption devoted to market services	
	Consumption of market services[1]	Total final consumption[2]	1975	1982
D[3]	3,4	1,9	10,7	11,8
F[3]	3,1	3,4	13,7	13,8
I[3]	2,5	2,7	15,2	14,5
UK[3]	0,6	1,4	22,7	21,6
EUR 6[3]	2,4	2,3	14,6	14,7
USA[4]	3,0	3,1	27,7	27,6
Japan[5]	4,5	3,4	43,9	47,2

[1] Final consumption codes 46 + 63 + 64 + 72 + 83 + 84 + 85 + 86 (see ESA 1979).
[2] Exact ESA terminology: Final consumption of households on the economic territory.
[3] *Source:* Eurostat and Commission services.
[4] *Source:* OECD; for the United States the definition of market services retained is close to that used for the European countries.
[5] *Sources:* OECD; for Japan the definition of market services retained covers all expenditure on services.

The development of market services

States, and so considerable caution is needed in interpreting the figures. Nonetheless these do point to a growth of market services expenditure, at constant prices, significantly greater than that for total consumption (4,5 % compared to 3,4 %).

Thus, for the European Community and the United States, the more vigorous growth in the output of market services (relative to manufacturing and the economy as a whole) in more recent years (see Table 3) and the associated rise in employment does not appear to have been entirely due to a marked shift in the pattern of private consumption in favour of private market services. Other components of demand for market services must have been growing vigorously.

2.2 In the European Community, vigorous growth in the volume of consumption of services by industry

As Table 12 shows, for the Community, a significant proportion of the output of most service activities is purchased as intermediate consumption by industrial and service activities; indeed for many service activities 50 % of the output is accounted for by intermediate demand.

The Europe-wide annual enquiry[1] into the structure and activity of industry, provides a measure of the changes in the purchases of services by manufacturing industry. Table 15 sets down the relevant rates and growth rates for the period 1975-81 (the latter being the most recent year for which suitable data have been published). It will be observed that the growth of the value of purchases of both industrial and non-industrial services is in excess of the growth of the value of production, often substantially so. Consequently, for the Community, the ratio of the total purchases of services to production increased from 13,1 % to 14,9 % over the six years to 1981.

Estimates of the associated rates of price increase over the same period are given in Table 16. On combining the value data in Table 15 with the price data in Table 16, it is possible to conclude that, for the Community as a whole, over the period 1975 to 1981 the average annual growth rate for the volume of services purchased by industry was in the range 3,5-4 % per annum. This compares to an average annual growth of manufacturing gross value-added in real terms for the same six-year period of 2,4 % per annum.

---

[1] *Structure and Activity of Industry: Annual Enquiry — Main results 1980/81*, Eurostat, 1984.

Table 15

The purchases of services by industry
Data at current prices

(%)

	Average annual growth rates 1975-81			Ratio of expenditure on services to the value of production			
	Purchases of industrial services[2]	Purchases of non-industrial services[2]	Value of production	Industrial services		Non-industrial services	
				1975	1981	1975	1981
EUR[1]	13,7	12,7	10,6	3,2	3,8	9,9	11,1
D	10,4	7,8	6,9	3,1	3,8	9,7	10,3
F	—	14,1	13,1	—	6,3	15,1	15,9
I	25,3	22,3	20,1	3,9	5,1	9,8	11,0
UK	10,4	18,3	10,3	2,9	2,9	4,8	7,2

[1] The figures given for the European Community cover those countries for which data are available. For industrial services the figures cover Germany + Italy + the United Kingdom + Denmark. For non-industrial services: Germany + France + Italy + United Kingdom.
[2] Purchases of industrial services cover repair and maintenance work, installation work and technical studies, etc. Purchases of non-industrial services cover the cost of legal and financial services, communication transport, travel and other business services and the cost of leasing investment goods.
Sources: Eurostat and Commission services.

The difference between these two figures suggests that the growth of market service output and employment, in the Community, owes much to the rapid volume growth of the consumption of services by industry.

Unfortunately it has not been possible to construct comparable figures for the United States. For Japan certain estimates have been made. However these lead to different conclusions from those made for the Community namely that in Japan:

(i) significantly more than 60 % of the output of market services, in 1975, was accounted for by final demand;

(ii) the growth of the volume of services purchased by industry was broadly the same as the growth of market services output.

2.3 Exports and imports of market services have grown rapidly

The balance-of-payments data published by Eurostat[1] provide figures for total trade in services analysed both by type of service imported/exported and by geographical area of origin/destination. Using Eurostat's nomenclature and terminology, an aggregate 'International trade in market services' may be derived as the sum of the items set down in Table 17.

These items when added together equal the total 'Services' given in Eurostat balance-of-payments tables, less 'Investment income' and 'Government transactions not indicated elsewhere', neither of which have been considered market services in the strict sense.

Table 17 summarizes the developments in international trade in services for the period 1975 to 1982, based upon data using this framework. Figures for total merchandise trade are provided for comparison.

An examination of these data suggests that developments in international trade in services may have been somewhat unfavourable for growth and employment in the Community. Thus for Community trade with non-Community countries, market service debits (or imports) measured at current prices grew slightly faster than credits (or exports) over the seven year period to 1982, reducing the surplus on market service trade from 1 500 million ECU to virtually zero.

---

[1] See for example *Balances of Payments: Geographical Breakdown*, Eurostat, Luxembourg.

However, it is possible to estimate the growth of exports and imports of services in volume terms; these estimates are set out in Table 18. The figures suggest that the difference between the growth in the volume of service exports, and the growth in the volume of service imports, is even more marked than the differences for values. This further reinforces the idea that the overall export performance of services has been somewhat weaker than that for imports. Nonetheless, exports of market services still exhibited an impressive average annual volume growth of almost 7 %.

Table 16

The purchases of services by industry: value, price and implied volume movements.

Average annual growth rates 1975-81

(%)

	Value	Output prices[2]	Implied volume
Purchase of services by industry[1]			
EUR	13,0	9,1	3,6
D	8,5	3,9	4,4
F	15,0[3]	10,8	3,8
I	23,2	17,3	5,0
UK	16,0	13,3	2,4
Memorandum item: Industrial production			
EUR 6	10,6	8,0	2,4

[1] Calculated by weighting together the figures for the purchases of industrial and non-industrial services given in Table 15. For definition of the Community aggregate see footnote 1 to Table 15.
[2] Implied value-added deflators.
[3] Estimate.
Source: Eurostat and Commission services.

2.4 In the European Community, the growth of the consumption of services by industry and by services accounts for the major part of market services output growth

It is possible to put all these estimates together and to show which components of demand (intermediate or final) have made the major contribution to the growth of market service output, in the Community, between 1975 and 1982.

As already noted, Table 12 shows how the output of the various services activities distinguished in the 1975 input-output tables for the Community is distributed in 1975 between intermediate consumption (by industries and by

The development of market services

services), and final consumption (by households and by non-resident consuming units).

Between 1975 and 1982 the annual rate of volume growth of the output of market services in the Community (as

measured by gross value-added) is estimated to have been 3.2 %.

The following estimates of volume growth rates (at annual averages for the seven-year period to 1982) can be drawn

Table 17

Community trade with non-Community countries/areas: merchandise and services[1]
Average annual growth rates 1975-82 and net balances

(% and millions of ECU)

All non-Community countries	Export (credit) weights 1982 (total goods and services credits equal to 100)	Growth rates		Net balance 1975	Net balance 1982
		Credits (Exports)	Debits (Imports)		
Merchandise (fob)	61.7	13.8	14.8	7 275	− 442
Total market services[2]	22.3	16.9	17.6	1 476	38
2.1 Transport	6.9	13.3	13.5	751	1 292
2.2 Insurance on transport	0.2	18.6	19.1	− 40	− 165
2.3 Travel	3.5	14.3	14.3	− 2 317	− 5 815
2.5 Labour income	0.9	20.6	18.6	84	744
2.7 Other services	10.8	20.5	23.3	2 998	3 982
Property income	0.6	:	:	:	− 1 379
Banking	0.4	:	:	:	− 46
Non-merchandise insurance	0.6	:	:	:	981
Construction/engineering	2.5	:	:	:	7 638
Films/broadcasting	0.1	:	:	:	− 89
Other	6.6	:	:	:	− 3 123

[1] In this table the term Community refers to the Community of nine, i.e. the present Community excluding Greece.
[2] The numbers attached to the headings are those given in the Eurostat balance-of-payments tables.
Source: Eurostat and Commission services.

from the above discussion on the growth of demand for services:

(i) intermediate consumption:
- •3,6 % for the consumption of services by industry([1])

(ii) final consumption:
- •2,4 % for the consumption of services by households;
- •6,9 % for the export of market services.

Given the requirement to balance demand and output for market services, the growth of market services output between 1975 and 1982 must equal the weighted sum of the growth rates of the components of demand for market services. The contribution of each component of demand to the growth of market services is given in Table 19. It can be shown that the growth of market services output balances the growth of demand provided that the intermediate consumption of services, by the market service sector itself,

grows in line with market service output; that is at an average annual rate of about 3 % per annum.

Thus, from the third line of Table 19 it will be seen that for the period 1975-82:

(i) more than half of the growth of market services output is accounted for by the growth of intermediate consumption by industry and by services;

(ii) less than one-third of the growth of output is accounted for by the growth of household consumption of services.

Similar calculations for the four large Community countries are given in Table 20. For three of the four large Community countries, the Federal Republic, France and Italy, the results obtained are close to those for the Community as a whole and the conclusions that can be drawn from these tables are broadly the same. For the United Kingdom, however, the results are somewhat different. In particular the combined contribution of the two components of final demand to market service output is virtually negligible and the estima-

[1] The estimate for the period 1975-81 is assumed to apply to the period 1975-82.

tions needed to balance the table, point to the intermediate consumption of services by services growing very vigorously indeed.

The average annual growth rate of manufacturing industry output in the Community of Six, for the period 1975-82 is estimated to have been 1,6 % (compared to 2,4 % for the period 1975-81). Consumption of the services by industry are estimated to have grown at an average annual growth rate of about 3,5 % in volume terms. The faster rate of growth of services consumption, compared to manufacturing output, is an indication of both:

(i) the rapid development of specialist service activities serving industry;

(ii) the separation of certain technical service activities from manufacturing industry itself, and their deplacement to the service sector.

The latter structural change will reflect the externalization of service activities by manufacturing industry in response to the demands of efficiency, technical change and the presence of economies of scale.

2.5. Summary of points made

The regressions set out in this section confirm the close link between the number employed in market services and the level of GDP/head. It has been argued that this link could be due to consumers spending an increased proportion of

their income on services as their real incomes rise (that is to say that services have a high income elasticity). The subsequent analysis suggests this is only part of the explanation. A more important development has been that, as the Euro-

Table 18

Community trade in market services with non-Community countries[1]
Average annual changes 1975-1982

(%)

Credits (exports)	Value	Estimated prices[2]	Implied volume
Total market services	16,9		6,9
Transport	13,3		6,0
Insurance on transport	18,6	9,4	8,4
Travel	14,3		4,5
Labour income	20,6		10,2
Other services	20,5		10,1
Debits (imports).			
Total market services	17,6		8,1
Transport	13,5		4,3
Insurance on transport	19,1	8,8	9,5
Travel	14,3		5,1
Labour income	18,6		9,0
Other services	23,3		13,3

[1] In this table the term Community refers to the Community of nine, i.e. the present Community excluding Greece.
[2] Implied deflators for the item exports of services given in the national accounts statistics.
Source: Eurostat and Commission services.

Table 19

The growth of services output in the European community (EUR 6) the balance between demand and output

	Components of demand for services				
	Intermediate consumption by industry	Intermediate consumption by services	Final consumption of households	Exports of services	Total
Weights from input-output tables for 1975[1]	0,192	0,345	0,387	0,076	1,000
Estimated volume growth rates[2](%)	3,6	3,1	2,4	6,9	3,2
Contribution to growth of services activity output[3](%)	0,69	1,07	0,93	0,52	3,2

[1] For definition of activity grouping see Table 11 and annex.
[2] Estimated average annual growth rates 1975-82.
[3] There is a slight discrepancy between the sum of the components, and the total given, due to rounding.
Source: Eurostat and Commission services.

The development of market services

pean economies have expanded, so the purchase of services by industry (and by services) has grown rapidly. Thus in Europe, the growth of services is closely linked to the growth of industry in the broad sense.

Consequently the link between GDP/head and market service employment in the Community, reflects more the growth of indirect demand for services, as a result of the increased consumption of services by industry and services, rather than the growth of direct demand itself. The attached box 'Changes in employment and hours worked in certain market service activities' – provides further evidence, on the employment side, for this conclusion.

3. Overall conclusions

The above discussion leads to the following conclusions;

(i) Part 1 has shown how in terms of the growth of value-added and employment, market services have increased in importance over the past decade, particularly in the European Community and the United States. The movement has been less marked in the case of Japan. Moreover, in the European countries, labour productivity growth has been catching up with that observed for manufacturing, traditionally the activity where labour productivity growth is most vigorous. There is also evidence of a shift in the balance of investment and profits away from manufacturing. The data are consistent with the view that the growth of employment in market services has benefited from the lower growth of earnings per head in service activities, both in nominal and in real terms.

(ii) The discussion in Part 2 leads to the conclusion that, for the large European countries, the major part of the recent growth of market services has been due to the increased purchase of services by industry (and by services themselves) rather than the growth of the consumption of services by households. This development is likely to reflect an important structural change, namely the separation of certain technical service activities from industry and their reallocation to services. This amounts to a change in the boundary of manufacturing or industrial activities, and throws doubt on the notion that Europe has been experiencing, in recent years, a process of de-industrialization. This conclusion is consistent with the change in structure commented upon in Part 1, insofar as it affects value-added, employment, productivity, investment and gross profits, to the extent that this change in structure reflects the shift in the boundary of industrial activities.

Table 20
Part A

The growth of services output in Germany: the balance between demand and output

	Components of demand for services				
	Intermediate consumption by industry	Intermediate consumption by services	Final consumption of households	Exports of services[4]	Total
Weights from input-output tables for 1975[1]	0,219	0,345	0,388	0,048	1,000
Estimated volume growth rates[2](%)	4,4	3,7	3,4	5,3	3,8
Contribution to growth of service activity output[3](%)	0,96	1,28	1,32	0,25	3,8

[1] For definition of activity grouping see Table 12 and annex.
[2] Estimated average annual growth rates 1975-82.
[3] There is a slight discrepancy between the sum of the components, and the total given, due to rounding.
[4] These growth rates refer to the total of exports of services as defined for the purpose of the Eurostat balance of payments and the national accounts. They therefore refer to a broader aggregate than that included in Table 18.

Source: Eurostat and Commission services.

**Table 20
Part B**

The growth of services output in France: the balance between demand and output

	Components of demand for services				
	Intermediate consumption by industry	Intermediate consumption by services	Final consumption of households	Exports of services[4]	Total
Weights from input-output tables for 1975[1]	0.289	0.219	0.404	0.088	1.000
Estimated volume growth rates[2](%)	3.8	4.1	3.1	5.2	3.7
Contribution to growth of service activity output[3](%)	1.10	0.90	1.25	0.46	3.7

[1] For definition of activity grouping see Table 12 and annex.
[2] Estimated average annual growth rates 1975-82.
[3] There is a slight discrepancy between the sum of the components, and the total given, due to rounding.
[4] These growth rates refer to the total of exports of services as defined for the purpose of the Eurostat balance of payments and the national accounts. They therefore refer to a broader aggregate than that included in Table 18.
Source: Eurostat and Commission services.

**Table 20
Part C**

The growth of services output in Italy: the balance between demand and output

	Components of demand for services				
	Intermediate consumption by industry	Intermediate consumption by services	Final consumption of households	Exports of services[4]	Total
Weights from input-output tables for 1975[1]	0.176	0.328	0.421	0.075	1.000
Estimated volume growth rates[2](%)	5.1	2.8	2.5	3.4	3.1
Contribution to growth of service activity output[3](%)	0.88	0.92	1.05	0.26	3.1

[1] For definition of activity grouping see Table 12 and annex.
[2] Estimated average annual growth rates 1975-82.
[3] There is a slight discrepancy between the sum of the components, and the total given, due to rounding.
[4] These growth rates refer to the total of exports of services as defined for the purpose of the Eurostat balance of payments and the national accounts. They therefore refer to a broader aggregate than that included in Table 18.
Source: Eurostat and Commission services.

The development of market services

Table 20
Part D

The growth of services output in the United Kingdom: the balance between demand and output

	Components of demand for services				
	Intermediate consumption by industry	Intermediate consumption by services	Final consumption of households	Exports of services[4]	Total
Weights from input-output tables for 1975[1]	0,164	0,362	0,328	0,146	1,000
Estimated volume growth rates[2] (%)	2,4	4,2	0,6	−0,9	2,0
Contribution to growth of service activity output[3](%)	0,34	1,59	0,20	−0,13	2,0

[1] For definition of activity grouping see Table 12 and annex.
[2] Estimated average annual growth rates 1975-82.
[3] There is a slight discrepancy between the sum of the components, and the total given, due to rounding.
[4] These growth rates refer to the total of exports of services as defined for the purpose of the Eurostat balance of payments and the national accounts. They therefore refer to a broader aggregate than that included in Table 18.
Source: Eurostat and Commission services.

ANNEX

Explanation of the terms and symbols used in the tables

The tables set down data for the total market service activity, distinguished by the NACE-CLIO nomenclature (as used to compile the Community's input-output tables) established according to the concepts and definitions of the European System of Accounts (ESA). In addition, in Tables 1 to 9, comparable data are given for the branch 'Manufactured products', and for the economy as a whole. Further details of the ESA concepts and definitions are given in the volume European System of Integrated Economic Accounts (ESA) Eurostat 1979.

For reference purposes the total for 'Market services' (NACE-CLIO code No 68) equals the sum of:

56 Recovery and repair services, wholesale and retail trade services equal to the sum of:
    55 Recovery and repair services
    57 Wholesale and retail trade
59 Lodging and catering services
61 Inland transport services
63 Maritime and air transport services
65 Auxiliary transport services
67 Communication services
69 Services of credit and insurance institutions
74 Other market services equal to the sum of:
    71 Business services provided to enterprises
    73 Renting of real estate
    75 Market services, education and research

77 Market services: Health
79 Other market services.

The figures given in the tables for the European Community are for the aggregate EC 6 which is the sum of Belgium (B) the Federal Republic of Germany (D), France (F), Italy (I), the Netherlands (NL) and the United Kingdom (UK). The proportion of total Community GDP accounted for by this aggregate, in 1982, was 95,1 %.

The data for the United States (USA) and Japan (J), which have been brought into line with the concepts and definitions of the ESA, are derived from national sources.

In certain tables there are minor discrepancies between the totals given and the sum of the individual components.

In constructing input-output tables activity 56 often plays a special role in balancing the tables and so it has been excluded from the analysis of Part 2. Activity 73, which includes substantial imputed transactions for the housing services consumed by owner-occupier households, has also been excluded.

Many of the points made in the text depend upon a comparison of measures of gross value-added for market services and manufacturing. As a rule it is more difficult to measure the value-added of market services than it is for manufacturing activities, and the measures for the former may be subject to a wider variance than those for the latter. This point should be borne in mind when interpreting the data.

Changes in employment and hours worked in certain market service activities

The analysis set out in Part 1 was concerned with changes in the structure of employment at a relatively macroeconomic level, and showed the increased importance, particularly for the European Community and the United States, of total market services both from the point of view of employment and of gross value-added. Part 2 showed that, in Europe, increases in intermediate demand for services by industry and services themselves accounted for the major part of the growth of the output of market services. It can be shown that this development is also reflected in changes in the structure of market service employment itself. Unfortunately, owing to a lack of data for earlier years. it is not possible to estimate changes in the structure of market service employment for the Community as a whole, nor for the Community of Six (D + F + I + UK + B + NL) for which details are given in the main part of the chapter. However, it is possible to observe changes in the structure of market service employment for the following grouping of six countries D + F + I + NL + B + DK which accounted for some 82 % of Community GDP in 1982. Data for this grouping of countries are given in Table 1. In the table the total activity branch market services has been subdivided into five smaller service branches of which 'Other market services' covers a wide range of activities including the activity group 71 'Business services provided to enterprises'. From Table 1 it will be seen that, in all three economies, the proportion of total market service employment accounted for by 'Credit and insurance' and 'Other market services' taken together increased markedly between 1970-72 and 1980-82, and the increase appears to be greatest for the Community. A whole range of services provided to enterprises are included in these two activities and this change in structure is consistent with the results given in Part 2 of Chapter 3. This interpretation of the data is also confirmed by a recent analysis of employment trends in the Federal Republic

of Germany and the United States.[1] It must also be noted that, in all three economies, there was a drop in the proportion of total market service employment accounted for by 'Retail and wholesale trade', and by 'Transport and communication'.

These developments in employment trends in certain service activities are confirmed by the data given in the annual publication of Eurostat *Employment and Unemployment*.

Trends in employment in NACE class 8 'Banking and finance, insurance, business services and renting' between 1980 and 1983 are given in Table 2 together with trends for the total of service employment (including 'Non-market services'), NACE classes 6-9, for the aggregate D + F + NL + B + UK + DK (which accounted for 83 % of Community GDP in 1983).

Table 2 shows that business service employment continued to grow more vigorously than total service employment between 1980 and 1983 despite the sharp decline in industrial production between 1980 and 1982 and only a modest recovery in 1983. Moreover the growth of employment for females was much greater than that for males.

The improved labour productivity performance of market services in Europe, noted in Table 5 is based on calculations of growth rates of value-added per head. However, the data on hours worked per week available from Eurostat suggest that the result would be broadly the same if account was taken of changes in the weekly hours worked per full-time employee.

---

[1] See M. Wegner, 'Die Schaffung von Arbeitsplätzen im Dienstleistungbereich': *IFO Schnelldienst* 6/85.

Table 1

Changes in the structure of market service employment

	EUR 6[1]		USA		Japan	*(%)*
	1970-72	*1980-82*	*1970-72*	*1980-82*	*1970-72*	*1980-82*
Retail and wholesale trade	44,7	41,2	39,5	38,7	42,9	40,7
Lodging and catering	8,3	8,2	11,2	11,3	13,5	14,8
Transport and communication	17,2	16,0	11,1	9,7	14,9	13,1
Credit and insurance	6,1	6,9	5,9	6,3	4,7	4,6
Other market services	23,8	27,6	32,4	34,0	23,9	26,8
Total market services	100,0	100,0	100,0	100,0	100,0	100,0

[1] EUR 6 = D + F + I + NL + B + DK.
Source: Eurostat.

The development of market services

Table 2

Trends in employment in certain service activities
Indexes 1980 = 100

	1980	1982	1983
NACE Class 8: Total	100	102,1	103,0
of which: Female employees	100	103,6	105,0
NACE Classes 6-9: Total services	100	100,6	100,9
Memorandum item; Industrial production	100	96,2	97,1

Source: Eurostat.

Thus on the basis of the data set out in Table 3 there is no evidence that hours worked per week in services, taken as a whole, have evolved significantly differently from those in industry.

Table 3

Weekly hours worked
Indexes 1973 = 100

		1973	1981	1983
NACE Class				
Industry	2	100	94,4	94,1
	3	100	94,7	95,2
	4	100	94,6	95,0
Services[1]	6	100	94,3	94,6
	7	100	93,9	93,6
	8	100	95,7	96,4
	9	100	94,1	95,6

[1] These codes stand for the following NACE classes:
6: Distributive trades, hotels, catering, repairs;
7: Transport and communication;
8: Banking and finance insurance, business services, renting;
9: Other services.
Source: Eurostat.

The leasing of investment goods

In Part 1 a change in the structure of investment in the European Community was noted (see Table 6) with (apparently) market services making an increased contribution to total investment and the contribution of manufacturing industry declining. It was noted, however, that these figures could be influenced by changes in the extent to which capital goods are leased by one enterprise (the user) from another (the owner). The data upon which the investment analysis given in Table 6 is based, provide a measure of the ownership, rather than the use, of investment goods. However, some information is available on the patterns of ownership and use of investment goods, for two of the large Community countries, the Federal Republic of Germany and the United Kingdom.

For some years the IFO Institute has published data for the Federal Republic of Germany giving the distribution of fixed investment and the capital stock by both user and owner industry/activity group. The investment data are summarized in Table 1 where it will be seen that:

(i) the differences between the structures of fixed investment by owner and by user, increased markedly between 1970 and 1982;

(ii) consequently although between 1970 and 1982 there has been a shift in the structure of fixed investment when ana-

lysed by user activity, this change in the structure is much less marked than when analysed by owner activity. Indeed, on the former basis the increase in the contribution of market services to total fixed investment between 1970 and 1982 is perhaps half the increase measured on the latter basis.

For the United Kingdom a similar though somewhat less detailed analysis is possible. This is set out in Table 2. Here again it will be noted that the impact of leasing is to modify substantially the shift in the structure of investment between 1975 and 1982 (the former year being the earliest one for which data on leasing are published). Thus on the ownership concept the contribution of market services (in the narrower sense, that is excluding dwellings) to total investment increased from 23,7 % to 31,3 % over this seven-year period. However, when allowance is made for leasing and the figures are converted to a user basis, the increase in the market services contribution was a more modest six percentage points, from 23,0 % to 29,0 %.

In conclusion therefore, it would appear that on the basis of the limited information available, perhaps as much as one quarter to one half of the shift in the structure of investment, noted in Table 5, in favour of market services, reflects the increased importance of leasing activities.

Table 1

The Federal Republic of Germany: the impact of leasing on the structure of fixed investment[1, 2]
Based on data at constant 1976 prices

(%)

	1970			1982		
	(i)	(ii)	(iii)	(i)	(ii)	(iii)
Manufacturing[3]	24,0	24,7	0,7	17,9	20,8	2,9
Market services[3]	46,9	46,0	−0,9	56,1	51,9	−4,2
— Retail and wholesale trade	5,0	5,9	0,9	4,6	6,7	2,1
— Transport and communications	8,3	8,5	0,2	8,9	9,4	0,5
— Credit and insurance	1,5	1,6	0,1	1,8	2,5	0,7
— Ownership of dwellings	25,8	25,8	—	25,1	25,1	—
— Other services	6,3	4,2	−2,1	15,7	8,2	−7,5
Market services, excluding dwellings	21,1	20,2	−0,9	31,0	26,8	−4,2
Total	100	100	—	100	100	—

[1] *Source: IFO Studien zur Strukturforschung Num. 6. Investitionen und Anlagevermögen der Wirtschaftszweige nach Eigentümer- und Benutzerkonzept, Gerstenberger, Heinze and Vogler-Ludwig.*
[2] Key to columns: (i) Structure by ownership; (ii) Structure by user; (iii) Difference.
[3] The figures are drawn from an analysis based upon the official German classification of activities.

Table 2

The United Kingdom: The impact of leasing on the structure of fixed investment[1, 2]
Based on data at constant 1980 prices

(%)

	1975			1982		
	(i)	(ii)	(iii)	(i)	(ii)	(iii)
Manufacturing[3]	16,2	0,7	16,9	11,5	2,3	13,8
Market services[3]	23,7	−0,7	23,0	31,3	−2,3	29,0
— Retail and wholesale trade, hotels, etc.	6,0	—	6,0	7,7	—	7,7
— Transport and communications	10,4	—	10,4	7,0	—	7,0
— Financial and business services	7,3	−0,7	6,6	16,6	−2,3	14,3
Total	100,0	—	100,0	100,0	—	100,0

[1] *Source:* Department of Trade and Industry and Central Statistical Office.
[2] Key to columns: (i) Structure by ownership; (ii) Adjustment for leasing; (iii) Structure by user.
[3] Data according to national industrial classification. The total for market services excludes dwellings and certain other services. These figures are therefore not directly comparable with those in Table 1.

[8]

Regional Studies, Vol. 24.3, pp. 195–209.

Business Service Specialization and Regional Economic Change

MARTIN PERRY

Department of Geography, National University of Singapore, 10 Kent Ridge Crescent, Singapore 0511

(Received May 1989; in revised form October 1989)

PERRY M. (1990) Business service specialization and regional economic change, *Reg. Studies* **24**, 195–209. Business services are experiencing rapid employment growth, but there is uncertainty over the interpretation of this trend. Three surveys assess changes in the demand and supply of business services in the Auckland Region, New Zealand 1983–8. The data indicate that employment growth is 'real' in that it is not caused by a transfer of activities that were formerly retained within other industries. Most manufacturing firms have adopted a pragmatic purchasing policy, externalizing and internalizing services on an individual basis with increased internalization dominant for data processing and accountancy services. A survey of business service suppliers indicates the greater importance of service exports, demand from other services and product innovation as the basis for growth.

Business services   Service subcontracting   Auckland   New firms   Innovation

PERRY M. (1990) La spécialisation des services aux entreprises et l'évolution régionale économique, *Reg. Studies* **24**, 195–209. Les services aux entreprises entraînent actuellement une croissance d'emploi rapide, mais l'interprétation de cette tendance reste floue. Trois enquêtes évaluent l'évolution de l'offre et de la demande des services aux entreprises pour la zone de Auckland, en Nouvelle-Zélande, sur la période de 1983 à 1988. Les données laissent voir que la croissance d'emploi est réelle dans la mesure où elle ne s'expliquent pas par le transfert des activités antérieurement effectuées au sein d'autres secteurs. La plupart des entreprises industrielles ont adopté une politique d'achat pragmatique, à savoir le développement de services externes ou internes, comme il leur convient, avec un développement plus important des services internes dans les domaines du traitement des données et de la comptabilité. Une enquête des fournisseurs des services aux entreprises démontre que les services-export, la demande des autres services, et l'innovation de produits sont plutôt à la base de leur croissance.

Services aux entreprises   Sous-traitement des services
Auckland   Nouvelles entreprises   Innovation

PERRY M. (1990) Spezialisierung bei Geschäftsdienstleistungen und regionalwirtschaftlicher Wandel, *Reg. Studies* **24**, 195–209. Geschäftsdienstleistungen verzeichnen ein rapides wirtschaftliches Wachstum, doch es besteht Ungewissheit über die Interpretation dieser Tendenz. Drei Erhebungen schätzen Wandlungen in Angebot und Nachfrage nach Geschäftsdienstleistungen im Zeitraum 1983–88 im Gebiet von Auckland, Neuseeland. Die Angaben deuten darauf hin, dass eine "echte" Zunahme von Arbeitsplätzen stattgefunden hat insofern, als sie nicht durch Übernahme von Leistungen zustande gekommen ist, die zuvor in anderen Industrien enthalten waren. Die Mehrzahl der Firmen der herstellenden Industrie haben sich eine praktisch orientierte Einkaufspolitik zu eigen gemacht, wobei Dienstleistungsbedürfnisse von Fall zu Fall als Aufträge nach aussen abgegeben oder innerhalb der Firma erledigt werden; bei Datenverarbeitung und Buchhaltung überwiegt zunehmend die innerbetriebliche Ausführung. Ein Überblick über Firmen, die Geschäftsdienstleistungen anbieten, bezeugt die zunehmende Bedeutung von Dienstleistungsexperten, Nachfrage von anderen Dienstleistungsfirmen und Produktinnovation als Grundlage des Wachstums.

Geschäftsdienstleistungen   Dienstleistungszulieferung
Auckland   Neue Firmen   Innovation

INTRODUCTION

Despite the widespread increase in employment in service industries, doubts remain about the ability of the service sector to generate jobs. There is uncertainty as to how far service industry expansion reflects the sector's own strength and capacity for innovation, or whether it is the residual consequence of developments elsewhere in the economy. Questions have also been raised about the quality of service employment and the extent to which new jobs in service industries adequately substitute for the jobs lost in manufacturing. To assess the significance of statistics on changes in business service employment, the interaction between the demand and supply of these services requires examination. It is important to know how much of the growth (or decline) of business services represents a displacement, that is, a shift of these activities from within existing firms to a specialist service supplier and/or an absolute increase in the demand for services. Other influences can then be assessed including spatial expansion in the area served and innovation in the provision of new types of services.

The causes of the fast growth in business service employment in the Auckland Region during 1983–8 were examined in three surveys. The findings of these surveys provide the main contents of the present paper. The primary objective of the research was to determine the importance of the 'contracting out' or externalization of service functions that were once retained within manufacturing firms. Externalization was, therefore, the subject of the first survey. Other possible causes of service employment growth were examined in surveys of: (1) the origins of new firms in the business service sector; and (2) the market base of new and established service firms, changes in these market characteristics and the significance of subcontracting between other services as well as manufacturers. While the study provides a picture of the demand and supply of services in a region, over a particular period, it is not a comprehensive modelling exercise or an examination of all the possible causes of service employment change. The findings of the paper confirm earlier work in identifying intra-service sector reorganization as the main form of externalization, rather than shifts between enterprises in different sectors, but overall neither process is found to be a significant influence on service sector employment growth.

The paper focuses on service activities that could be provided internally or purchased from independent suppliers. Within this group of 'transferable services' the main interest is in those which have been growing most strongly in employment, reflecting the aim of the paper to examine externalization as a cause of service industry employment expansion. Prior to presenting the survey evidence and background to the study region, some further discussion of the recent debate on the dynamics of the service sector is appropriate.

SERVICE SECTOR GROWTH

A number of explanations have been proposed to account for the growth in business services. GERSHUNY and MILES, 1983, argue that in aggregate the increased share of service jobs is a consequence of their slower productivity growth compared with manufacturing. Related to this, the faster growth of service employment has been interpreted as a residual consequence of the competitive weakness of manufacturing (CAMBRIDGE ECONOMIC POLICY REVIEW, 1982). The growth of large, complex and multinational organizations has enhanced the demand for services as they require more inputs than small, single-line

producers (MARSHALL, 1982). At the same time, successful technology-based enterprise of whatever scale would seem to require more producer service inputs (MACPHERSON, 1988). Product differentiation strategies are increasingly based on the conjuction of material and non-material goods, for example, computer hardware and software (ENDERWICK, 1987). Changes in technology have provided new market opportunities connected with data processing (BARRAS, 1985) and financial services (LANGDALE, 1985), while an increase in international trade in financial and business services has facilitated service expansion, particularly in countries with established financial centres (THRIFT, 1987). Finally, it has been argued that the externalization of service demands, from within goods-producing firms to specialist service suppliers, has made an important contribution to service employment expansion (HOWELLS and GREEN, 1986).

Externalization occurs when companies shed service functions formerly classified as part of that industry and which are then transferred to the service sector through subcontracting. Where the firm shedding the service is a manufacturer, the outward effect of externalization will be a reduction in 'manufacturing' jobs and an increase in 'service' jobs, although the overall net effect for the economy is often no change or indeed a slight employment reduction to the extent that service firms provide the function more efficiently (HOWELLS and GREEN, 1986). If externalization is significant, it casts doubt on the capacity of producer services to generate jobs as employment 'growth' may be confused with employment change.

Three main motives for externalizing services were suggested by HOWELLS and GREEN, 1986: potential cost savings; the ability to obtain a better quality of service; and the increasing technical complexity and specialization of service functions. The potential to externalize services has been linked to the 'maturity' of the service sector in that improved marketing by business service firms is encouraging externalization (DANIELS and THRIFT, 1987). It is also suggested that, in a recession, firms tend to streamline their administration in favour of subcontracting.

The decentralization of service purchases has been associated with the development of new locational and organizational structures, partly facilitated by advances in information technology (HEPWORTH, 1986). In turn, decentralization has been pursued, according to some researchers, to allocate activities between areas with different social and labour force characteristics so as to minimize employee resistance to company objectives (SCOTT, 1988; NELSON, 1986). In the manufacturing sector, the decentralization of production seems to have been more prevalent than office functions (SHUTT and WHITTINGTON, 1987), although the need to co-ordinate more complex organizations can lead to new service purchasers which are externalized from the outset.

The recent debate on externalization has focused on the employment implications of reducing the size of the 'core' workforce as part of a flexible labour strategy. The flexible firm model argues that companies are shifting toward an employment strategy based on functional and numerical flexibility. Functional flexibility embraces the crossing of occupational boundaries while numerical flexibility is achieved through such means as part-time and temporary work and subcontracting. Firms' pursuit of flexibility is motivated by the alleged advantages of reducing the secure workforce to a core group of activities, while more 'peripheral' workers are employed via arrangements that allow for their disposal or employment according to the level of demand.

Employment flexibility is one of several goals pursued by firms so that the ability to exploit the alleged labour advantages of externalizing peripheral activities may conflict with other business goals (MACINNES, 1987). Most work situations require a stable, experienced and co-operative workforce so that high rates of labour turnover, which poor terms of employment encourage, need to be minimized. At the same time, the difficulty of achieving both numerical and functional flexibility is easily overlooked. MACINNES, 1987, reports how part-time staff in a bank were unable to cover peaks in demand because of their limited range of skills compared with full-time staff. Neither is the combination of job security for core workers and more contracting out necessarily compatible. One response of firms to recession has been to use their own 'core' staff whom they wish to retain to undertake tasks done previously by contractors (*ibid.*) This implies that subcontracting might fall in a recession, at the time when the financial advantages of using outside suppliers are greatest. Conversely, in a boom subcontractors can exploit a sellers' market, encouraging internalization.

The capacity to internalize and to centralize service provision has been viewed as one reason for the success of multi divisional corporations (WILLIAMSON, 1981). Internalization overcomes the risk of 'adverse selection' associated with the uncertainties of small-firm contract relationships. The problem of quality control is particularly severe in relation to service purchases (HOLMSTROM, 1985). Three 'moral hazards' jeopardize service purchases: ascertaining the quality of the service; the inability to observe the actions of the provider; and difficulty in establishing an incentive to obtain the desired level of effort (HOLMSTROM, 1985). In the case of physical goods, delivery standards can be more readily established, overcoming these three hazards. Moreover, where quality can be judged, services are still less easily returned for improvement than physical commodities. As POLLERT, 1987, notes, the protagonists of the flexible firm model fail to address the problems of control, efficiency and the costs of fragmented market relations. This failure would seem to be particularly relevant to the use of service subcontractors.

While some activities may have become more specialized, it is not clear that this is a universal trend. Advances in micro computing and packaged software have, for example, considerably cheapened and simplified data processing activities, causing a decline in bureau services (WEIL, 1982). The relative cost of internal and external services is influenced by economies of scale and, as CRUM and GUDGIN, 1977, indicated, the proportion of non-production specialists (particularly computer and other technicians, service workers and managers) in manufacturing declines with establishment size. Consequently, the pressure to externalize may be limited to medium-sized enterprises (small firms having few internal services to subcontract). If recession encouraged externalization, service industry growth would differ from the business cycle, but the general pattern seems to be that producer services experience the same cyclical employment variations as manufacturing (DRIVER and NESBITT, 1987).

Externalization is, of course, the theoretical end point of an evolutionary process which may fall short of the disposal of the service (HOWELLS and GREEN, 1986; SHUTT and WHITTINGTON, 1987). The process commences with the conversion of an existing service function into an unit which remains within the company but offers its services internally and on the open market. As the external market for the service expands, the department may be given more autonomy and become a profit centre in its own right. If this expansion continues, the activity may be *decentralized* to a subsidiary or associate company to market the service more extensively. Later the parent may dispose of the company, possibly for financial gain, but more likely, according to Howells and Green, because the new company does not fit with the main interests of the group. At this point it may *devolve* the activity by licence or franchise agreements, or it may *disintegrate* its ownership links entirely. To the extent that this type of evolution is typical, externalization should be a continuous process connected with the dynamics of individual enterprises, rather than being a new economy-wide phenomenon as in the flexible firm model.

MARSHALL, 1989, shows that both internalization and externalization processes are occurring depending on the character of the firm and the nature of the service being purchased. MASON *et al.*, 1989, found that there had been no major increase in subcontracting by manufacturing firms located in one part of the southern England 'sunbelt' during the 1980s. RAJAN, 1987, has suggested that up to 50% of the jobs created in the UK in services and lost in manufacturing are due to externalization, but this evidence is questionable. The survey reported in RAJAN and PEARSON, 1986, recorded subcontracting activity as a percentage of turnover and this includes the firm working as a subcontractor, as well as the subcontracting of its own production. It is, therefore, more surprising that around two thirds of surveyed manufacturers reported no change or a decline in subcontracting.

The main evidence supporting the importance of externalization is limited to a small number of case studies including those in HOWELLS and GREEN, 1986; RAJAN, 1987; SHUTT and WHITTINGTON, 1987). These examples illustrate major shifts in service expenditure, although mostly between service organizations, rather than from manufacturing to service firms. The reorganization of the public sector has involved an increase in the contracting out of services, but this has been motivated by reasons other than those in the flexible firm model (POLLERT, 1987). Generally, it remains uncertain as to whether the level of subcontracting out of service demands is greater than the general rise in internal service overheads, less than, or equal to them (DANIELS and THRIFT, 1987). The present study concentrates on the redistribution of service expenditure by manufacturing firms as this process has most implication for the interpretation of secondary employment data which was the starting point for the present study (PERRY, 1989a). As previous evidence has suggested that subcontracting within the service sector has increased to a greater extent, some consideration of the latter phenomenon was also given.

SURVEY CONTEXT AND ORGANIZATION

The long term trend in the New Zealand economy has been towards diversification but this has not pre vented a deterioration in the country's economic performance which commenced in the 1960s (EASTON, 1982). Up to 1984, the state sought to arrest this decline by encouraging economic diversification through financial and tax incentives to the primary sector, border protection for manufactured goods and through the promotion of large-scale investment in land development and energy, culminating in the 'think big' energy and transport projects. The links between New Zealand and the international economy were controlled through foreign exchange restrictions, a closely controlled banking and finance sector and regulation of the transport industry (LE HERON, 1988). Since 1984, a new Labour government has reduced industry subsidies, regulation controlling entry to industries and border protection. The impact of these reforms has been uneven. Rural New Zealand suffered from the devaluation of its assets as agricultural subsidies were withdrawn and expenditure on rural services declined. In the main metropolitan centres, the liberalization of the financial market encouraged new activities and an associated property development boom (HARPER, 1986). More recently, there are signs of this prosperity being reversed as agricultural exports grow and the finance sector remains weakened by the decline in sharemarket values.

Against this backdrop, the service sector has grown consistently but the relative importance of different components has changed. From the mid 1950s to the mid 1970s the government and welfare sector made the biggest contribution, while more recently private producer services[1] have been the fastest growing component (PERRY, 1989a). During 1976–86, the service sector grew by 18% compared with a 2% decline in manufacturing employment (Table 1). The Auckland region accounted for 43% of the national increase in service employment and an even higher proportion of the expansion in producer services (57·3%). The region is also the main manufacturing centre accounting for 35·5% of national employment in 1986 and this share has also been increasing. During 1981–6, the expansion of business service employment in the region accelerated: over this period the growth rate was 48% compared with 20·6% in 1976–81. In the more recent period, less than 8% of new jobs in business services were part time, although the proportion is 21% for female jobs.

The dominance of Auckland derives from its long standing role as New Zealand's main link to the international economy from which it attracted a large manufacturing base and the service activities to support trade. More recently, it has also become the location for an increasing number of head offices, a role traditionally taken, and still dominated by the

Table 1. *New Zealand and Auckland employment change, 1976–86*[1]

	Manufacturing		All services		Producer services[2]		Business services[3]	
	No.	%	No.	%	No.	%	No.	%
Auckland	2,610	2·5	52,429	29·1	20,123	52·1	10,867	78·0
New Zealand	−6,291	−2·0	121,227	18·1	35,094	25·9	23,009	54·8

Notes: 1. All employment data refers to those working twenty hours or more per week.
2. Wholesale, road haulage, storage and warehousing, shipping, accountancy, data processing, architecture, engineering and technical services, advertising, business services n.e.c., labour and professional organizations, office cleaning.
3. Legal, accountancy, data processing, architecture, engineering and technical services, advertising, business services n.e.c.
Source: New Zealand Census of Population and Dwellings.

capital, Wellington (AUCKLAND CITY COUNCIL, 1986).

It has been suggested that New Zealand's isolation, the limited size of the market and the extensive regulation of accumulation may have stifled organizational transformation in different parts of the economy (LE HERON, 1988). Evidence that the primary and manufacturing sectors have been slow to adapt in the past exists (LE HERON, 1977, 1988) and that regulation encouraged a preponderance of small manufacturing firms (BOLLARD, 1987) and the internationalization of capital was restricted by foreign ownership controls. A programme to modernize manufacturing commenced in the mid-1970s through the establishment of sector working parties to review the trade protection afforded individual industries. The reform emanating from this programme, coupled with the wider deregulation of the economy post-1984 have encouraged a considerable reorganization of productive capital. These changes have seen large companies become more internationalized (LE HERON, 1988), an increase in mergers (FOGELBERG, 1984) and an increase in the integration of the New Zealand and Australian economies (BOLLARD and THOMPSON, 1988). During 1983–7, manufacturing output grew in real terms by 11·1%, although there has been an absolute decline since a peak in 1985. Manufacturing has been under pressure to reappraise its activities. Case studies of individual industries reveal many firms responding to the changed operating environment by introducing new technology, work force reductions and changes in product lines (BROWN, 1986; MACCOMBE, 1989).

None of the research on New Zealand industry has referred to the externalization of service functions. A preliminary assessment of its potential significance can be gauged from industry occupation data. If part of the explanation for the recent 'growth' in business services is the decentralization of these functions to independent service firms, a diminution in business service occupations within manufacturing might be expected. In fact, the proportion of administrative, technical and clerical occupations (ATCs) in manufacturing enterprises increased from 15·3% in 1956 to 23% in 1986 which is still around 5% below the equivalent UK figure. The growth of ATCs in manufacturing has slowed since the mid 1970s, but this coincides with an absolute decline in manufacturing employment. During 1976–81, manufacturing ATCs fell by almost 4% whereas during 1981–6 there was a 8% growth (PERRY, 1989a). In the UK, the long-term trend has been for ATC jobs in manufacturing to increase, although since 1980 there has been an absolute and percentage decline during a recession in manufacturing activity (MARSHALL *et al*, 1987).

Aggregate trends in the distribution of service occupations may obscure changes amongst those occupations most susceptible to externalization. This possibility has been examined but the pattern remains largely unchanged. Table 2 identifies business service occupations which producers may retain in-house or buy-in from independent sources. Four occupations have declined or changed little within manufacturing alongside an expansion within the business service sector. In the case of industrial engineers and draughtsmen, the decline within manufacturing reflects major reductions in capacity in the car assembly and electrical goods industries over the period examined. Industry occupation data therefore suggest that vehicle mechanics, cleaning, and security are the main

Table 2. Business service occupations by sector affiliation Auckland Region, 1976–86[1]

Occupation	% change 1976–86			% total in manufacturing	
	Business[2] services	Manufacturing	All industries	1976	1986
Architect	25·6	50·0	12·8	1·2	1·6
Legal	71·7	—	74·9	0·0	0·8
Industrial engineers	209·0	−59·7	66·9	48·4	11·6
Draughtsmen	53·6	−33·7	9·4	25·0	15·2
Vehicle mechanics	31·2[2]	−28·0	26·2	12·2	8·9
Data scientists	194·1	114·7	26·2	10·4	17·7
Data processor operatives	165·3	172·0	258·7	29·0	22·0
Personnel management	265·4	34·5	194·4	35·2	16·1
Market research	188·0	30·7	82·9	37·4	26·7
Accountant	60·6	8·4	37·6	26·3	20·7
Goods vehicle driver	−5·1[3]	−12·0	−9·3	20·3	19·7
Cleaners caretakers security	86·5[4]	1·3	40·4	23·4	17·3
All ATCs[5]	72·1	12·5	37·5	21·1	23·0

Notes: 1. Employment data covers all those working twenty hours or more per week: 1986 figures estimated on this basis.
2. Legal, accountancy, data processing, architecture, engineering and technical services, advertising, business services n.e.c.
3. Employment in transport measured rather than business services as drivers mainly classified in this group.
4. Employment in personal services measured rather than business services, mechanics and cleaners classified mainly in this group.
5. Administrative, technical and clerical occupations.
Source: New Zealand Census of Population and Dwellings.

occupations to have been externalized. This is interesting as the latter three industries are commonly as amongst the services most affected by externalization. Personnel and marketing occupations grew in the manufacturing sector and significantly more so in the service sector. In contrast, data processing operatives have grown at a similar rate within business services and manufacturing while architecture and legal services have no significant internal presence.

Industry occupation data suggest that trends in the mode of service procurement vary between activities. Had all the service occupations in manufacturing industry potentially supplied by independent business services been externalized, the 'growth' generated would have been equivalent to around a third of that actually experienced in the business service sector during 1981–6. The actual contribution looks to have been less significant than this, although it is possible that the industry occupation data disguise changes within particular types of firm. For example, employment data may not reflect changes in the status of service functions within manufacturing. Thus the service occupations remaining in manufacturing may simply administer and implement outside expertise.

To assess the importance of externalization in the recent growth of service activity, empirical data were collected via three surveys covering the demand and supply of services in the Auckland Region. The data for the study were derived from postal and personal interview questionnaires as this facilitated the widest possible coverage. POLÈSE, 1982, notes that there is a tendency for firms to underestimate business service expenditure as internal overheads are sometimes overlooked or not known and services supplied with capital purchases may also be excluded. Fortunately such under recording is not all in one direction so that shifts in the balance of expenditure should still be identified. The present study acknowledges the difficulties of obtaining absolute data by restricting the analysis to proportional change and grouping responses into broad magnitudes of change. In addition, the study sought to verify its findings by examining both the demand and supply of services. The three surveys covered: (1) changes in the mode of service procurement by manufacturing and wholesale firms (the *demand* survey); (2) the origins of new business service firms started 1983 onwards (the *new firm* survey); and (3) the market base of new and established business service firms (the *supply* survey)—see Appendix. The surveys were commenced sequentially so that the sample of business service firms could be informed by preliminary findings on changes in demand.

SUMMARY OF SURVEY RESULTS

Demand

Table 3 shows the structure of service demand existing in 1988. Five services were mainly supplied internally; these were (in order of concentration) financial planning, strategic planning, accounting, data processing and payroll services. Eight services were mainly externally supplied; these were (in order) legal services, waste disposal, vehicle maintenance, security, cleaning, road haulage, advertising and public relations. The balance between intra- and inter-firm procurement is broadly consistent with previous research (MARSHALL, 1982; POLÈSE, 1982).

In the next part of the exercise respondents were asked to contrast the present distribution of expenditure with that five years earlier and to indicate, where appropriate, the percentage shift in the allocation of expenditure as between internal and external sources. The focus of the survey was, therefore, on the redistribution of expenditure affecting established service demands. The results are examined, firstly, in terms of the propensity of firms to redistribute expenditure and, secondly, in terms of the services affected. Note that where the firm has commenced use of a service within the study period this is not included. To the extent that services used for the first time are disproportionately supplied externally, the study underestimates externalization.

Slightly under half (47·5%) the sample firms had externalized expenditure on at least one service. On the other hand just under a third (30·3%) had internalized more expenditure on at least one service. A trend towards externalizing more service purchases was evident, but firms undertaking no change or a combination of more externalization and internaliza-

Table 3. *Distribution of business service expenditure (% of respondents)*

Service	User rate	Source of supply[1]		
		Intra-firm	Inter-firm	Mixed
Data processing	99·3	56·2	21·5	22·3
Legal services	96·5	0·0	95·6	4·4
Accounting	98·6	60·1	11·1	28·8
Payroll services	98·6	47·5	31·4	21·1
Financial planning	96·5	65·7	11·4	22·9
Market research	87·5	31·5	43·2	25·3
Advertising	91·7	14·3	58·5	27·2
Public relations	66·9	26·8	47·4	25·8
Personal recruitment	97·2	23·4	31·4	45·2
Strategic planning	87·5	61·4	16·2	22·4
Security	94·5	12·4	75·1	12·5
Road haulage	95·2	7·9	65·2	26·9
Vehicle maintenance	99·3	5·5	86·8	7·7
Building maintenance	97·9	7·0	3·5	89·5
Cleaning	100·0	17·2	66·9	15·9
Waste disposal	97·2	2·1	94·3	3·6
Industrial engineering	77·9	32·7	28·3	38·9

Note: 1. Excludes non users.

Table 4. Changes in the mode of service procurement by activity (no. firms)

Industry	Total	No change	External[1]	Internal[1]	Mixed/minor change
			Major trend		
Food, beverages, tobacco	24	13	6	1	4
Textiles, clothing	18	7	5	1	5
Chemicals, plastics, non-metallic minerals	32	11	9	2	10
Metals, machinery	36	13	2	1	20
Wood, paper, printing	13	9	1	0	3
Wholesale	32	12	4	3	13
Total	145	63	28	8	54

Note: 1. Shift of over 50% of expenditure on at least one service and/or lesser shifts on two or more services generating a net trend in the direction shown.

Table 5. Changes in the distribution of service expenditure (% firms reporting)[1]

Service	No change	More externalization		More internalization	
		Minor[2]	Major	Minor	Major
Data processing	72·2	6·2	1·4	14·6	5·6
Legal services	91·4	7·9	0·0	0·7	0·0
Accounting	88·8	2·1	1·4	6·3	1·4
Payroll	88·1	3·5	2·8	4·9	0·7
Financial planning	92·8	2·1	0·0	2·9	2·2
Market research	90·6	7·1	0·0	2·3	0·0
Advertising	78·2	13·5	4·5	3·8	0·0
Public relations	94·8	3·2	1·0	1·0	0·0
Personal recruitment	92·2	6·4	0·0	0·7	0·7
Strategic planning	96·8	1·6	0·0	1·6	0·0
Security	94·2	5·8	0·0	0·0	0·0
Road haulage	80·5	13·0	2·9	2·9	0·7
Vehicle maintenance	92·4	4·8	1·4	1·4	0·0
Building maintenance	98·6	0·7	0·0	0·7	0·0
Cleaning	93·1	4·1	1·4	1·4	0·0
Waste disposal	94·3	4·9	0·0	0·8	0·0
Industrial engineering	90·2	4·4	2·6	0·9	1·8

Notes: 1. Firms with no current use of the service are excluded.
       2. Minor shift equals 10% or less, major is above this.

tion across different services accounted for 72% of the sample. The main trends are summarized in Table 4 and this highlights the small proportion of firms with an overall strategy of externalizing services. Moreover, most cases of externalization had involved minor shifts in expenditure: just six firms had externalized expenditure on an individual service by more than 50% (the most 'active' firm had externalized three services by this amount).

The stability in the mode of service procurement is further emphasized when individual services are considered (Table 5). In respect of all but five services, over 90% of firms had made no change in the balance of their expenditure. These five services where changes in the mode of procurement were more frequent comprised data processing, advertising, road haulage, payroll and accounting. In two of these five cases (data processing and accounting) the major trend had been to internalize more expenditure and in a third case (payroll) a difference of one firm created a net trend to externalization. Low-skill activities, such as cleaning and security, were absent from the group of

most frequently externalized services in contrast to the expectation expressed by other researchers and suggested by the industry occupation data. These activities were predominantly obtained externally (Table 3) as part of an established pattern.

As the number of firms externalizing a high proportion of expenditure is small, any noticeable impact on the location of service jobs would depend on: (1) expenditure changes being most common amongst major expenditure items; and (2) large firms having the greatest propensity to switch their service demands to independent supplies. These two possibilities are now considered.

The services most frequently identified as the three largest expenditure items were, in order, advertising, road haulage, data processing, accounting, vehicle maintenance and industrial engineering.[2] Two of the six most frequently purchased services, advertising and road haulage were externalized by more than 10% of firms, but the scale of the shift was usually minor.

A slightly greater propensity to externalize amongst larger firms was discovered (Table 6). In

Table 6. *Changes in mode of service procurement by size of firm*

| | % of firms reporting change in mode of service procurement | | | |
| | Increased internalization: employment level | | Increased externalization: employment level | |
	50–99	100+	50–99	100+
Data processing	21·3	17·8	8·0	6·6
Legal services	1·1	0·0	7·3	8·8
Accounting	9·1	4·4	4·1	2·2
Payroll	7·0	2·2	4·1	11·1
Financial planning	4·2	6·8	3·1	0·0
Market research	3·4	0·0	6·6	8·1
Advertising	1·6	4·6	16·3	22·2
Public relations	0·0	2·3	4·3	8·8
Personal recruitment	1·0	2·4	7·2	4·4
Strategic planning	1·1	2·7	2·2	0·0
Security	0·0	0·0	1·0	14·3
Road haulage	3·2	0·0	13·6	22·2
Vehicle maintenance	0·0	2·3	5·0	8·8
Building maintenance	1·0	0·0	0·0	2·3
Cleaning	2·0	0·0	5·0	6·6
Waste disposal	0·0	0·0	2·0	13·6
Industrial engineering	1·2	5·7	7·5	15·5

firms with over 100 employees, there was a more consistent pattern to externalize services, where a change had been made, although the tendency to internalize data processing was maintained. Once again, however, most shifts involved less than 10% of total expenditure on the individual service. There were only five services—payroll, advertising, public relations, road haulage and industrial engineering—which more than 5% of large firms (and never more than 7·5%) had externalized expenditure by over 10%.

Finally, respondents were questioned on their overall strategy towards the procurement of services. The majority of firms indicated that they had no strategy (36·5%) or that they had a policy of reviewing each service individually (55%). Consequently, those with a consistent policy to externalize or internalize their service demands were a small minority (6% and 2·5% respectively).

New firms

New firms comprise an important source of employment in Auckland's business service sector. One estimate indicates that around 16·5% of business service employment in 1987 was in 'new' enterprises started from 1983 onwards (*Business Directory*, Department of Statistics). This is an uppermost estimate which includes some branch office openings, partnership changes and failed new firms (the directory removes inactive enterprises more slowly than new firms are added). All of these were excluded from the survey reported here. Nonetheless, new advertis-

ing and data processing firms retained their employment significance with their revised share being 7% and 18% respectively, although in the latter case one firm accounted for over half the employment. In the other sectors, new firms accounted for around 4% of total employment.

There are three main links that are possible between new firms and service externalization: (1) the service division of an existing enterprise may become an independent enterprise, through *decentralization, devolvement* or *disintegration* (SHUTT and WHITTINGTON, 1987); (2) individual proprietors and/or employees may leave an enterprise to establish an independent undertaking; and (3) an externalizing enterprise may create a market for an unrelated new firm. All these potential avenues were examined.

Over half of the sample of new firms were independent of changes in an established enterprise. Six new enterprises resulted from a parent-company decision to externalize an existing service division. These six cases were, with one exception, in data processing (Table 7). Three of these five new data processing firms were established by an existing data processing organization to provide a new service. Consequently, out of the total sample there were three new firms with a parent company in an unrelated activity, of which one was in the manufacturing sector. The latter involved a management buy-out affecting the data collection section of a multinational food and pharmaceutical's market research division. The buy-out was encouraged by the parent because of the high cost of maintaining a small unit in a local branch and unwillingness to invest in a peripheral activity. The other two cases resulted from an insurance company decentralizing its data processing division and through an accountancy firm establishing an information technology consultancy.

Amongst other non-independent new starts, there were twelve firms resulting from a split between the proprietors of a small firm (Table 7). In most of these cases as well, the new and original enterprises were similar activities.

Table 7. *Profile of new firm sample*

| | Firms origins (% of sample) | | | |
Industry	Independent new start	Partnership split	Established by parent	Other
Accountancy	62(10)[1]	19(3)	0	19(3)
Data processing	69(11)	0·0	31(5)	0·0
Engineering and technical services	40(2)	20(1)	0	40(1)
Advertising	56(17)	27(8)	3(1)	14(4)
Other business services	83(23)	0	0	17(5)
Total	68(63)	12(12)	6(6)	14(14)

Note: 1. Number of firms in parenthesis; % figures rounded.

On a more minor scale, individual employees may also contribute to externalization when they leave a company and continue their occupation in a new enterprise. In fact 60% of the new firm founders had owned or worked previously in a similar firm. In addition, 13% had worked in unrelated occupations, leaving just over a quarter of founders (twenty-five) who had previously been engaged in the same activity but for a different type of firm. Out of this last group, five had previously worked for a non-service organization. Consequently, even at the level of individuals there is little evidence of mobility across sectors.

The third possible link between new firms and externalization is through the creation of new markets. New-firm proprietors identified three main markets which had motivated their enterprise, none of which was to capture the redistribution of expenditure. The principal opportunity encouraging new firm formation was the market for a new, or at least differently delivered, service. A second group of new firms were influenced by a perception that there was a general increase in service demand, providing opportunities for new business. A separate small group of firms had formed following the award of a single key contract but these cases were also not the result of externalization.

Having found little direct relationship between existing firms in the goods-producing sector and new enterprise, it is worth noting the sometimes extensive market area served by new enterprise. Over half the new firms served markets outside the Auckland region and these non-local markets generated almost 40% of total revenue. Almost a quarter of firms served overseas markets and these customers generated 50% of the non-local revenue, mostly earned by data processing and engineering consultancies. The wide market area served by some firms is particularly significant in view of the short time most had been in operation.

Supply

In the *supply* survey, the managers of business service firms were questioned on the importance of externalization and other markets in their recent growth. The data for this part of the study were collected through personal interviews. Resource limitations made it necessary to concentrate on a more limited range of services than covered in the *demand* survey. Four activities were selected based on their combination of high job growth and evidence from the *demand* survey that changes in the mode of procurement had been relatively significant. These activities were advertising, marketing, computer services and engineering and technical services.

The externalization of previously internally-supplied services was assessed as an 'important' source of growth by only 20% of respondents (Table 8).

Table 8. *The importance of contracting out as a source of new markets*

	% of firms		
Industry	No influence	Minor significance	Important
Data processing	37(10)[1]	22(6)	41(11)
Engineering and technical services	43(10)	35(8)	22(5)
Advertising	90(26)	7(2)	3(1)
Other marketing	62(17)	19(5)	19(5)
Total	59(63)	20(21)	21(22)

Notes: 1. Number of cases shown in parenthesis; % figures rounded.

Almost 60% of respondents stated that externalization had been of no importance to the firm's development, while in a further 20% of cases it had been of minor significance. The share of current business acquired through externalization was not always identifiable, but generally was estimated not to exceed 10% of the revenue from all new contracts (1983–8), even when 'important'.

The proportion of service firms indicating that externalization had been important was low, but still suggests that the process may be more widespread than indicated in the *demand* survey. The earlier evidence showing that data processing was increasingly internalized also requires reconciliation with the supply evidence which shows that some data processing activities had been externalized. The discrepancy occurred because contracting-out arose from changes in the public sector and retailing. As part of a wider reform of the public sector, government agencies have been instructed to subcontract services such as computing and engineering services. The propensity of retailers to change their mode of procurement was, according to interviewees, a reflection of their reorganization into larger nationwide operations. Increased scale has produced greater demands for data processing services to assist stock management, marketing and internal communications. Against the more usual trend for organizations to internalize more of their data processing requirements, some large retailers have switched to using bureau services. The national communication networks already established by bureaux was cited as a reason for the preference to externalize.

The contracting out of former public sector services is occurring on a significant scale. One data processing firm had recently taken over the Department of Health computer service employing over 100 people, while another had replaced the computing division of the Forestry Corporation and acquired the telegram service formerly provided by the New Zealand Post Office. Several small data processing consultancies were assisting the establishment of decentralized facilities within public agencies that were no longer tied to the centralized resources provided by the government's computing service. Amongst the engineering consultancies, several noted how they had recently obtained contracts that would formerly have been awarded to the Ministry of Works and Development.

A broad estimate of the significance of externalization within the current employment of business service firms can be made based on the following assumptions: (1) that in firms where externalization was important, 10% of employment growth results from this process and 5% in firms where it was of minor significance; and (2) that externalization occurs at the same rate for the total population of firms as in the sample. On this basis, then around 15% of the employment increase in data processing, 4·5% in engineering and technical consultancies and 13·5% in advertising and other marketing services may result from externalization. These are uppermost estimates for several reasons: the sample of business service firms was skewed to include the firms most likely to have gained from externalization; it is a gross estimate omitting increased internalization, which was particularly important in the case of data processing. The figures include all sources of subcontracting and, as noted, manufacturing enterprises were a minor contributor to this employment displacement.

As externalization does not account for a significant proportion of service activity growth, it is interesting to consider what markets had been increasing. Non-local income (i.e. outside the Auckland Region) accounted for over one third of current revenue. While markets beyond the Auckland Region were important to all industries, engineering and data processing had particularly high export markets. Out of the total sample, there were forty-four firms (45%) which derived 25% or more of their revenue from outside the region, including seventeen firms with 50% or more. In the case of data processing, 51% of sample firms derived at least a quarter of their income non-locally, while 73% of the engineering sample achieved this status. These data have two implications. First, they indicate the strength of the service sector in terms of its ability to supply a wide market area. Second, they may indicate that the present study underestimates the significance of externalization to the extent that only regionally-based enterprises were covered in the demand survey.

Interviewees were asked about changes in the distribution of their income over the past five years: three quarters of the respondents indicated that no significant geographical shift had occurred. Of the thirty firms indicating a change in their market base, thirteen had experienced an increased concentration of income derived from outside the region, including five where this was from an overseas market. On the other hand, the dominant market shift was for the proportion of local income to increase. Two causes were given for this trend: the loss of rural-sector customers, or at least a reduction in their expenditure, and the transfer of economic activity to Auckland (which might involve physical relocation, and/or ownership changes affecting the location of corporate control). Auckland as a market was, therefore, growing at the expense of the rest of New Zealand, rather than overseas markets.

In addition to examining the spatial distribution of income, the survey considered its sectoral pattern. Six broad income sources were differentiated, of which the manufacturing and construction sector was the most important for all the survey industries except data processing (Table 9). In the latter case, other services (finance, insurance and business services) were the most important market. The public sector (local and overseas) is a particularly important market for engineering services. The relative insignificance of the primary sector is surprising in view of its importance in the national economy, but this may reflect the recession in rural industries over the survey period. It should also be noted that producer boards were incorporated with state-owned enterprises so that some demand from the primary sector is recorded elsewhere.

Slightly over half the survey firms indicated that the relative importance of the six sectors had changed in the previous five years. Such income changes were characteristic of all the business services, although the markets generating the change were different. In the case of data processing and engineering, the public sector had been the fastest growing market, while retail and distribution was the most rapidly expanding market for other marketing services. In the case of advertising, a similar proportion of firms identified the manufacturing and retail sectors as their main growth.

It is clear, therefore, that most services had not

Table 9. Sectoral distribution of revenue by industry

| Industry | % of annual revenue from | | | | | |
	Government	State-owned enterprises	Primary	Manufacturing and construction	Retail, distribution, travel	Other services
Data processing	14·7	4·0	2·9	27·8	18·4	32·2
Engineering and technical services	20·6	9·6	6·1	45·9	12·4	5·4
Advertising	0·3	7·1	4·1	57·8	22·8	7·9
Other marketing	2·0	2·4	3·1	42·5	31·6	18·4
Total	12·6	5·4	3·7	36·9	18·9	22·5

grown because of demand from the manufacturing sector. Indeed the primary and manufacturing sectors were the most frequently mentioned markets which had become less important.

DISCUSSION

Changes were being made in the mode of service procurement by many manufacturing firms, but most firms had adopted a pragmatic approach, internalizing some services and externalizing others. On balance there has been a modest trend to reduce internal expenditure in favour of external suppliers. Data processing was the service most frequently affected by changes in the mode of procurement, but the major trend has been towards greater internalization. The economics of computer technology initially encouraged the establishment of bureau services for all but the largest organisations (WEIL, 1982). In New Zealand, few enterprises below 1,000 employees invested in their own computing system (BEARDON, 1985). More recently, the use of microprocessors has simplified the technology and reduced costs, facilitating internalization. At the same time, large organizations have reviewed the efficiency of centralizing their data processing capacity. The comments of data service suppliers indicated that there is now a variety of different attitudes amongst large organizations. Some large firms have opted to externalize, others have decentralized data processing to internal divisions, while some have adopted a mixture of these options.

The externalization of road haulage from wholesaling was identified as another relatively important trend. In this case legislative change has been an influence. The removal of government regulations placing restrictions on independent operators has been a significant influence reducing the attractions of internal transport operations (BOLLARD, 1985). Advertising expenditure had been externalized by a similar number of firms, although most changes were minor and not reflected in the responses of advertising agencies.

In line with the demand evidence, changes in the mode of procurement were not a significant cause of new firm formation. New firms generated through the fragmentation of existing organizations were rare, but their subsequent growth rate is exceptional. The data processing firm which started as the division of an insurance company, had grown from around fifty employees to 1,443 in 1988. Of its present employment, 20% is in New Zealand, 65% in Australia and the balance in the UK, Asia, Canada and the USA. Such a rapid expansion has been achieved through the acquisition of seventeen companies, funded partly from the resources of the parent company which has retained a majority ownership of the company.

The market research firm created through a management buy-out is now among the top five companies in its segment of the industry: employment rose from six to thirty in five years, and income by around 50% a year. Part of the explanation for this growth was the secure income provided by the original owner in the early years of operation. This subcontracted income provided investment in computerized techniques which has subsequently been the basis of the firm's continued expansion.

The *supply* survey identified two further cases of *decentralization* that had occurred prior to the time period covered in the *new firm* survey. Both these additional cases were data processing firms and both had their origins in other service organizations—one a freight distribution company and the other an insurance company. These organizations have also experienced rapid growth. The five data processing firms resulting from *decentralization* collectively account for 20% of regional employment in the sector, although less than a third of these jobs were actually transferred. Fragmentation is more important for generating fast-growth firms than for the direct displacement of employment between sectors. The *disintegration* of public sector computing has displaced more jobs, but was too recent to have influenced the employment trends prior to 1986.

The survey indicates that the rising demand for services is the overwhelming cause of the expansion of service industry employment rather than a transfer between sectors. The overall increase of expenditure on business services by individual enterprises was noted by some respondents to the *demand* questionnaire. In additional comments, twenty-two respondents indicated their change in total expenditure on business services as a proportion of all purchases; seventeen reported that the proportion had increased, including ten cases where the increase was over 50%.

A further influence on business service expansion was the high level of innovation in introducing new products and services. This innovation is worth illustrating as it shows how business service activity is not a direct substitute for existing in-house services. Two themes tend to link many of the forms of innovation and diversification followed: the increased standardization of services; and the packaging of complementary services.

A third of data processing firms indicated that their range of activities had changed over the previous five years. Some changes have resulted from the decline in bureau services which has caused firms in this activity to seek additional functions. As bureau services operate an extensive communication network, they have capitalized on the growing demand for computer communications by providing value-added network services. Diversification has also been into software development and business consultancy to provide guidance on information technology needs and systems design. One firm commented that their functions had gone through four 'iterations' in response to market changes: from hardware vendor, through customized programme writing, to implementation services and, finally, packaged software development.

Amongst marketing firms a significant innovation was database management consultancy. This service aims to exploit more effectively, for product research and direct marketing purposes, the existing information collected by companies on their customers. At the quantitative data collection end of the market research industry, the installation of scanner-based information retrieval has been a major new service. On a smaller scale, public relations firms have added new marketing and strategic planning skills, particularly connected with retail promotion, broadening their previous focus on brochure and news release writing. Advertising agencies have computerized their media placement services and are introducing new organizational structures to increase their buying power and to exploit the economies of scale in this new technology. Almost half the engineering consultancies surveyed had broadened their activities over the study period. One of the most common developments was the addition of project management services, a new specialization (at least in the local context) arising from the growing scale and complexity of commercial building investment.

CONCLUSION

The purpose of this paper has been primarily to examine one possible contribution to the fast growth of business service employment, namely, changes in the mode of procurement. The study found that the majority of business service users had made little or no change in the allocation of their service expenditure over a five-year period. Where changes have occurred, they were not exclusively towards greater externalization and, overall, service firms have a greater propensity to externalize service functions than manufacturing. Few new firms were identified that had originated through the externalization of service demands, but the importance of this process for generating fast growth was noted.

The present research findings conform with recent studies completed by MASON *et al.*, 1989, and MARSHALL, 1989, and may largely be explained by three reasons. First, service innovation and new firms tend to originate from within existing service firms because this provides the most appropriate training ground and awareness of new opportunities. Second, the option of subcontracting services is not new and decisions affecting the internal/external balance of expenditure are now sometimes historic. For example, the first advertising agencies in New Zealand date from the last century and it was in the 1930s that major companies *decentralized* internal divisions (PERRY, 1989b). There has been a public relations industry

since the mid 1950s. The first computer was installed in New Zealand in 1960 and within five years bureau and consultancy services were widely established (BEARDON, 1985). Thirdly, the assumptions in the model of the flexible firm overlook the multiple goals pursued by firms and the difficulties that can be associated with subcontracting relationships.

The New Zealand experience indicates that the growth of business services is not a reflection of restructuring strategies predicted in the flexible-firm model. Externalization is occurring but on a modest scale and rarely to gain labour control advantages. The privatization of state trading activities and the break-up of centralized service provision has reshaped activities that were classified formerly as non-market services. The motivations for this type of subcontracting are expenditure savings and the preparation of services for further privatization, rather than to exploit a more peripheral labour market. The shift from the public to private sector is the single most important externalization process affecting service provision in New Zealand and probably in other economies pursuing similar reforms. In New Zealand, the immediate impact has been to remove the main source of job growth from provincial regions because of the reduction in government activities, while metropolitan-based private services have acquired new markets and prospered. The long term implications for the quality of service provision and access to services by different client groups are important areas for future research.

Within the private service sector, the process of externalization and specialization is primarily a consequence of growing demand and the generation of new activities. A significant proportion of the fragmentation of service firms results from individuals, either small-firm proprietors or large-firm managers, exploiting new markets. As noted, there is a high level of innovation within the service sector and this tends to provide many opportunities for small firms able to respond rapidly to new ideas. The *decentralization* of data processing from large service organizations has been a significant trend mainly to maximize the growth potential of this activity. Within manufacturing, a pragmatic attitude to the acquisition of services seems to prevail. More research into the variations in purchasing practices is required to determine whether systematic influences exist or whether it is simply related to individual preferences and experience. In this latter respect, the recent work by MARSHALL, 1989, has provided a valuable lead.

Meanwhile, the main conclusion from the present study is that the rapid growth in business service employment is the outcome of the sector's real expansion rather than a consequence of employment relocation.

Acknowledgement—This work was completed during

the author's tenure as a post-doctoral research fellow in the Department of Geography, University of Auckland. The financial assistance of the New Zealand Social Science Research Fund Committee and the research assistance of Danny Vadnjal is acknowledged.

NOTES

1. Wholesale, road haulage, storage and warehousing, shipping, accountancy, data processing, architecture, engineering and technical services, advertising, business services n.e.c., labour and professional organizations, office cleaning.

2. The frequency of relative importance may give a misleading impression of overall service expenditure, if large enterprises have different expenditure priorities. A chi-square test of differences in the importance of services between firms with more and less than 100 employees found no significant difference at the 99·9% confidence level.

APPENDIX

The organization of the surveys was as follows. The *demand* survey was conducted by a postal questionnaire addressed to the accountant or financial director (as identified prior to dispatch of the survey) in the head office or main establishment of all enterprises located in the Auckland Region with regional employment of fifty or more in the following industries: food and drink; textiles and clothing; chemicals and non metallic minerals; paper and wood products, metals and machinery; and wholesaling. Firms with less than fifty employees were excluded as previous research indicated that small firms have few non-production workers (CRUM and GUDGIN, 1977) so that the opportunities to externalize expenditure are less. This survey population comprised 374 firms, or 35% of the region's total workforce in manufacturing and wholesale activities. Engineering and manufacturing n.e.c. were both omitted because of their preponderance of small firms with few internal services. Wholesale was included to obtain comparative data on changes within the service sector. The usable response to the survey was 145 (38·8%) completed questionnaires. Chi-square tests were conducted to compare the distribution of the sample and survey population by industrial sector, employment size and proportion with overseas ownership: in no case was the sample significantly different at the 99·9% confidence level. The sample employment was 14,013 or 11% of total regional employment in the manufacturing and wholesale sectors and 32% of the survey population. The current distribution of expenditure on seventeen business services was identified and respondents then indicated whether, and in what way, this balance had changed over the previous five years.

The *new firm* survey was based on the population of

new firms identified in the *Business Directory* (Department of Statistics). The *Business Directory* listing available to the author excluded enterprises with less than three employees and for the purposes of the survey a number of adjustments to the directory definition of a new firm were required. Branch openings and new firms arising from name and partnership changes were excluded as well as those that were not traceable. Legal services, architectural practices (part of the engineering and technical services category), publishing and corporate headquarters (both included in other business services) were omitted because earlier evidence indicated there was little internal provision or because they were outside the interest of the study. Table A1 indicates the size of the remaining population, of which a 100% coverage was achieved in a telephone interview survey.

Table A1. *New business service firms in the Auckland Region, 1987*

Industry	Total firms, 1987[1]	Total 1987 firms started post-1982	Excluded from survey[2]	Survey sample
Accountancy	159	33	17	16
Data processing	86	30	14	16
Engineering and technical services	213	36	31	5
Advertising	161	52	22	30
Other business services	359	106	78	28
Total	978	257	162	95

Notes: 1. Table covers enterprises with three or more employees.
2. Firms excluded are new enterprises created through name and partnership changes, branch establishment openings, untraceable firms, architecture, publishing and headquarters of corporate enterprises.

Source: *Business Directory*, Department of Statistics.

The *supply* survey covered 106 managers of firms drawn in roughly equal numbers from the following industries: advertising, other marketing services, data processing and engineering and technical consultancies. These activities were selected as they have experienced high employment growth and early responses to the demand survey indicated that they had been the most affected by changes in the mode of procurement. Within each industry, the sample was structured to include some new and established firms, large and small enterprises (although firms with fewer than five employees were excluded), locally and overseas-owned firms. While the sample covers around half of the firms in each industry, and is broadly representative in terms of size and ownership (Table A2), it was not a random sample. In the data processing industry, small firms which were primarily retailers were omitted. In advertising, small non-accredited agencies were given less emphasis than accredited agencies.

208   *Business Service Specialization and Regional Economic Change*

Table A2. *Profile of the supply survey sample*

Industry	Total number of firms[1]		Employment >39		Overseas ownership		Sum of employment	
	BD[2]	sample	BD	sample	BD	sample	BD	sample
Data processing	55	27	16	11	8	4	1,704	1,368
Advertising	51	29	6	6	17	11	958	685
Other marketing	43	27	3	2	7	6	608	414
Engineering and technical services	59	23	11	5	6	3	1,946	999
Total	208	106	36	24	38	24	5,216	3,466

Notes: 1. Firms with fewer than five employees excluded.
        2. BD = *Business Directory 1987*, Department of Statistics.

REFERENCES

AUCKLAND CITY COUNCIL (1986) Distribution of economic activity in Auckland, Department of Planning and Community Development, Auckland.

BARRAS R. (1985) Information technology and the service revolution, *Policy Studies* **5**, 14–24.

BEARDON C. (1985) *Computer Culture*. Reed Methuen, Wellington.

BOLLARD A. (1985) Regulatory changes and prices in the freight haulage industry, in BOLLARD A. and EASTON B. (Eds) Markets, regulation and pricing, Research Paper 34, New Zealand Institute of Economic Research, Wellington.

BOLLARD A. (1987) *Small Business in New Zealand*. Allen & Unwin, Wellington.

BOLLARD A. and THOMPSON M. A. (1988) Trans-Tasman trade and investment, Research Monograph 38, New Zealand Institute of Economic Research, Wellington.

BROWN A. (1986) Industrial restructuring and employment: the Auckland apparel industry, unpublished M.A. thesis, Department of Geography, University of Auckland.

CAMBRIDGE ECONOMIC POLICY REVIEW (1982) *Prospects for the UK in the 1980s*. Gower, Aldershot, Hants.

CRUM R. E. and GUDGIN G. (1977) Non production activities in UK manufacturing industry, Regional Policy Series 3, Commission of European Communities, Brussels.

DANIELS P. and THRIFT N. (1987) The geographies of the UK service sector, Working Paper 6, University of Liverpool and University of Bristol.

DRIVER C. and NESBITT B. (1987) Cyclical variations in service industries employment in the UK, *Appl. Econ.* **19**, 613–31.

EASTON B. (1982) External impact and internal response: the New Zealand economy in the 1970s and 1980s, Discussion Paper 26, New Zealand Institute of Economic Research, Wellington.

ENDERWICK P. (1987) The stragegy and structure of service sector multinationals: implications for potential host regions, *Reg. Studies* **21**, 215–24.

FOGELBERG G. (1984) Acquisitions and their impact upon strategy and performance: a preliminary investigation of the New Zealand experience, paper presented at the Strategic Management Conference, Philadelphia, October.

GERSHUNY J. and MILES I. (1983) *The New Service Economy*. Francis Pinter, London.

HARPER D. (1986) The financial services industry: effects of regulatory reform, Research Paper 35, New Zealand Institute of Economic Research, Wellington.

HEPWORTH M. (1986) The geography of technological change in the information economy, *Reg. Studies* **20**, 407–24.

HOLMSTROM B. (1985) The provision of services in the market economy, in INMAN R. (Ed) *Managing the Service Economy: Prospects and Problems*, pp. 183–213. Cambridge University Press, Cambridge.

HOWELLS J. and GREEN A. (1986) Location, technology, and industrial organisation in UK services, *Progr. Plann.* **26**, 88–183.

LANGDALE J. (1985) Electronic funds transfer and the internationalisation of the banking and finance industry, *Geoforum* **16**, 1–13.

LE HERON R. (1977) Patterns of company control and regional development in New Zealand, *Pacific Viewpoint* **18**, 58–78.

LE HERON R. (1988). State, economy and crisis in New Zealand in the 1980s: implications for land-based production of a new mode of regulation, *Appl. Geogr.* **8**, 273–90.

MACCOMBE G. (1989) Restructuring in the New Zealand footwear industry, M.A. thesis, Department of Geography, University of Auckland.

MACINNES J. (1987) *Thatcherism at Work*. Open University Press, Milton Keynes.

MACPHERSON A. (1988) Industrial innovation in the small business sector: empirical evidence from metropolitan Toronto, *Environ. Plann. A* **20**, 953–71.

MARKS P. (1983) The slowdown in labour productivity growth rates 1961–1981, *New Zeal. Econ. Pap.* **17**, 1–16.

MARSHALL J. N. (1982) Linkages between manufacturing industry and business services, *Environ Plann. A* **14**, 1,523–40.

MARSHALL J. N. (1989) Corporate reorganization and the geography of services: evidence from the motor vehicle aftermarket in the West Midlands Region of the UK, *Reg. Studies* **23**, 139–50.

MARSHALL J. N., DAMESICK P. and WOOD P. (1987) Understanding the location and role of producer services in the UK, *Environ. Plann. A* **11**, 575–93.

MASON C., PINCH C. and WITT S. (1989) Inside the 'sunbelt': industrial change in Southampton, in BREHENY M. and

CONGDON P. (Eds) *Growth and Change in the South East of England*, pp. 55–86, London Papers in Regional Science 20. Pion, London.

NELSON K. (1986) Labour demand, labour supply and the suburbanisation of low wage office work, in SCOTT A. J. and STORPER M. (Eds) *Production, Work and Territory: the Geographical Anatomy of Industrial Capital*, pp. 149–71. Allen and Unwin, Boston.

PERRY M. (1989a) The contribution of services in New Zealand's economic development, *Austr. J. Reg. Studies* (forthcoming).

PERRY M. (1989b) The international and regional context of the advertising industry in New Zealand, Occasional Paper 24, Department of Geography, University of Auckland.

POLÈSE M. C. (1982) Regional demand for business services and interregional service flows in a small Canadian region, *Pap. Reg. Sci. Ass.* **50,** 151–63.

POLLERT A. (1987) The 'flexible firm': a model in search of reality (or a policy in search of a practice)?, Warwick Papers in Industrial Relations 19, School of Industrial and Business Studies, University of Warwick.

RAJAN A. (1987) *Services: The Second Industrial Revolution*. Butterworths, London.

RAJAN A. and PEARSON R. (Ed.) (1986) *UK Occupational and Employment Trends to 1990*. Butterworths, London.

SCOTT A. J. (1988) Flexible production systems and regional development: the rise of new industrial spaces in North America and Western Europe, *Int. J. Urban Reg. Studies* **22,** 171–85.

SHUTT J. and WHITTINGTON R. (1987) Fragmentation strategies and the rise of small units: cases from the North West, *Reg. Studies* **21,** 13–23.

THRIFT N. (1987) The fixers: the urban geography of international commerical capital, in HENDERSON J. and CASTELLS M. (Eds) *Global Restructuring and Territorial Development*. pp. 203–33. Sage, London.

WEIL U. (1982) *Information Systems in the 80s*. Prentice Hall, Englewood Cliffs, NJ.

WILLIAMSON O. (1981) The modern corporation: origins, evolution, attributes,. *J. Econ. Lit.* **19,** 1,537–68.

[9]

ENTREPRENEURSHIP & REGIONAL DEVELOPMENT, 1 (1989), 267–274

Producer services: the key sector for future economic development?

SVEN ILLERIS
Local Governments' Research Institute, Copenhagen

This paper has two messages. First: producer services should no longer be considered costs or necessary evils in the economy, but he understood as the dynamic components of the extremely integrated system of activities which a modern economy forms. Second: in a local context, producer services no longer simply passively follow the development of the goods-producing sectors, but increasingly play a leading role, partly through exporting their services to other regions and partly through the synergies which their services create in the local goods-producing sector. Hence, local economic policies should also be directed towards the producer services.

1. The traditional understanding of services

The purpose of this paper is to discuss – in an extremely simplified way – the role of service activities in economic development in general and in local economic development in particular. The focus will be on the profound transition which currently takes place in the European economies.

The way we have understood the economy of our countries until recently was founded in the late eighteenth century. At that time fundamental changes in the old, predominantly agricultural and feudal, society started in some parts of Europe. The first man to grasp this and to form concepts and ideas which could describe the emerging industrial society, was Adam Smith.

In the old society some service workers, for instance clergymen, had been held in high esteem. Adam Smith argued that this was wrong, since service workers did not contribute to the 'wealth of nations'. Only goods-producing activities did that.

This view has thoroughly influenced our thinking since then. In this respect, Karl Marx agreed completely with Adam Smith and labelled service activities as 'non-productive'. To this day, the East European countries do not include services when they calculate the value of the total production in their countries.

In our part of the world, services are included in the GNP and similar measures. But at the back of our heads, our understanding of the economy has still very much the shape of figure 1: a chain of agricultural or mining production of raw materials which subsequently are manufactured, distributed and consumed. In this model, there is no room for services, except transport, trade and a little government regulation. Most services belong to the sphere of consumption – as the barber who is often used as an example – or is a necessary cost for the producers, as the lawyer or the auditing which they are compelled to use.

A more sophisticated version of this view has been expressed for instance by the British economist Kaldor in recent decades, when the share of goods-production in the total production value and even more in the total employment has gone down, and the share of service activities has increased. These people fear that the so-called 'deindustrialization' is a disaster for our economies. They claim that services can rarely be exported, and that the rising share of services will spoil our current account balances. They argue that growth in

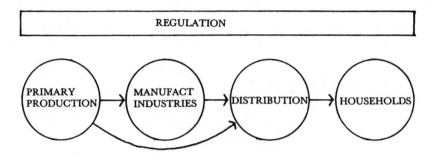

Figure 1.   The Industrial Economy

production depends on growth in productivity ('Verdoorn's law'), and that productivity cannot easily increase in service activities. This means that when we all become barbers or school teachers, when the share of service activities approaches 100%, the economy will simply suffocate in low and stagnating productivity.

2.   Producer services as the dynamic components of the economy

My first message is that this understanding of the economy is gradually becoming outdated. We are once again in the middle of fundamental changes in our economies. And – just as at the time of Adam Smith – we need new concepts and ideas in order to grasp what is happening.

When we are in the midst of radical and turbulent changes it is of course difficult to sort out the main trends from the surrounding 'noise'. However, many theories have been suggested – but hardly proven – in recent years. According to them, some of the most important characteristics of the emerging economy are:

(*a*) Repetitive and standardized work is largely being automated.

(*b*) Markets are becoming increasingly differentiated. This is a result partly of internationalization, partly of the growing segmentation of domestic markets. Firms and households demand goods and services according to their individual needs and preferences.

(*c*) Quality means more, quantity and prices less in the competition. Innovation and creativity, in other words the quality of the personnel, becomes a crucial factor of production.

(*d*) The development of microprocessors makes it possible to produce in short and differentiated series, in contrast to the economies of scale based on long, standardized series which characterized the industrial mass-production society. The assembly line production which Chaplin described in 'Modern times' is vanishing, though it still looms large in political rhetorics.

(*e*) These trends taken together mean that fewer and fewer people work directly with goods manufacturing of the traditional blue collar type. On the other hand, more and more people are involved in the invention, design, planning, managing and

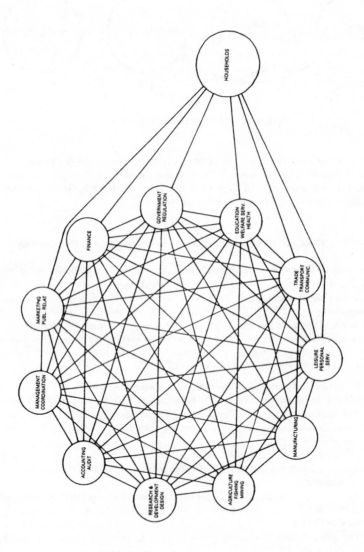

Figure 2:   The Service Economy

marketing of the differentiated commodities, in other words, in producer service activities. They may be performed inside or outside the user firms.

(f) It is nonsense to measure the productivity of these service activities in an isolated way. Service activities are not only an indispensable part of the operation of the total productive system and the productivity gains which can be obtained in the system as a whole. Service activities are also responsible for creativity and dynamism in the system, for instance R & D, design, new management and human relation methods. The question of goods production *or* services is false, there is complementarity rather than competition between goods production and service production. The system may be depicted as in figure 2.

(g) Even many services to households form an important part of the system, since the quality of the labour force – which depends on the health, educational and other services – is the most important condition for the operation of the emerging productive system. Thus in figure 2, one could add lines leading back from the households to all economic sectors. (Of course, some services, e.g. barber shops, form sheer consumption, but they are rather few).

Societies which have tried to restrict the development of services, have run into sclerosis – as is the case in Eastern Europe. It is the irony of history that they have forgotten Marx's elementary statement, according to which societies must find a way of organizing themselves which is adapted to the contemporary mode of production.

Whether productivity can increase faster in this complex society than in the mass-producing society or not, it seems to be a necessary condition for its functioning that services mediate the relationships between all its actors and components.

Many labels have been suggested to describe the society which now emerges. The 'post-industrial' society is not a good label, since goods production remains an important economic activity. On the other hand, flexible production, the information society, the communication society, the knowledge society, or the service society are labels which characterize important aspects of the new – in Toffler's terminology the third – wave of societal transformations.

3. The traditional role of services in local economic development

Just as services have been perceived as playing no role in the development of national economies, they have been thought to be a totally passive element in local economies. The traditional model of a local economy had the form of the cipher 9 (see figure 3).

We thought that the basis of a local economy was activities such as agriculture, mining or manufacturing. They produced goods which could be sold elsewhere and thus bring money into the local economy. Some of this money was used to pay the people who worked in the basic activities. These people spent some of their money on services – private services like retailing and public services like schools – which had to be provided locally, since retailing and school teaching cannot normally be sold over long distances. Such service activities employ other people, who in their turn buy still other services locally.

Thus at the end of the day, all service activities and incomes depended on the money which the 'basic' activities brought into the local area. Therefore, local and regional development policies could ignore the services. They would automatically follow, if only the policies aimed at manufacturing growth were successful.

What was 'the local area'? That would depend on the type of services. Widely used service activities, for instance all-round lawyers, could get sufficient business from a quite

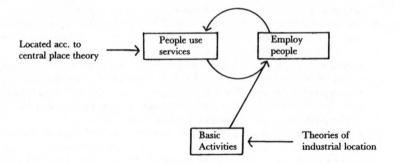

Figure 3.   The '9' Model (Economic Base Model)

small town and its immediate surroundings. More specialized services, like consulting engineers or management consultants, could be based only on larger areas and were located only in medium-sized or larger towns. The most sophisticated producer services would only be found in national capitals or other major cities, from where they served entire regions or whole countries. Thus a hierarchy of service centres or 'central places' on different levels served smaller and larger 'local areas' in such a way that distances between customers and service suppliers always were as short as possible.

4.   Producer services as basic activities in local economic development

My second message is that producer services do not any longer play such a passive role in local economic development. There are two reasons for this: First that new transport and communication technologies have made it possible to sell services over much longer distances. And second, the already described vital role which service activities increasingly play in the economic system.

It is well known that dramatic improvements are taking place within telecommunications, especially when they are combined with computers into what is sometimes called 'telematics'.

We are only beginning to explore the potentials of transmitting data over the new communication networks. This means that all information services which can be transcribed into the standardized, digital form can be sold anywhere at relatively low costs, on condition that the necessary infrastructure is provided. Bank branches can get all data necessary to make a decision from the bank's computer system, and complicated calculations can be transmitted from a computer on the other side of the globe!

Not all services can be carried out through telecommunications, however. Whenever you try to get orientation about new problems and opportunities, deal with complicated questions with many qualitative aspects, or develop services through an interaction between producer and client, personal meetings remain necessary. But meetings between distant partners have also become much easier and faster, thanks to airlines, cars and rapid trains. People come together in meetings and conferences more than ever.

So altogether, we can talk of 'distance shrinking' as a major tendency in our societies. Services which consist of information can increasingly be sold over long distances. This means of course that they can locate independently of the local number of customers or buying power. They may become part of the economic base of a local area and bring money into it.

This is not only a theoretical possibility. In countries where statistical data showing the sales of services between regions exist, such as Canada, we can observe that inter-regional trade with services increases rapidly, and that a growing share of the total service production is sold in other provinces (Stabler & Howe 1988). Also, a number of studies in different countries show that the traditional pattern of service provision from a hierarchy of centres is no longer the only way services are distributed. In figure 4, the thick arrows represent the traditional service provision from high-order centres. The thin arrows, however, show that there are substantial and growing service sales from smaller towns to larger ones, and often to quite distant parts of the country or abroad. (Ireland, however, seems to form an exception, where the provincial towns are unusually weak) (Illeris, forthcoming, and Lensink, 1985).

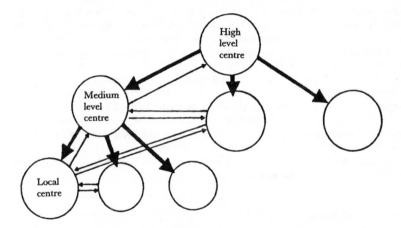

Figure 4.   Modifications of central place theory

The thick arrows represent traditional central place theory, according to which services are always provided from the nearest centre where the threshold in question is available. Thin arrows show the service flows crossing the traditional hierarchy, which are observed today: from low-level to higher-level centres, between centres on the same level, and 'diagonally' to centres which are not the nearest ones.

Thus many – though not all – service activities, and in particular producer services, are no longer tied to locate close to their clients. But this does not mean that they can operate equally well everywhere. It only means that other factors of location become decisive; for instance, the possibilities of finding qualified staff members is a very important factor for many service activities.

There are always factors pulling in different directions. Some non-metropolitan areas may have environmental advantages and show good performance based on trade with distant places. Big cities may be attractive because of big local markets, high accessibility, a large supply of qualified people, and high-quality services. (The latter factor shows that services may become 'basic' activities and thus turn the traditional model upside down, a tendency already foreseen by Blumenfeld in 1955). The resulting pattern of location may be different from one country to another.

The fact that many services are no longer restricted by the local market also means that local and regional development policies can influence the location of services. Among the steps that could be taken, I should mention the provision of infrastructure, and improvement of such 'consumer services' as education, in order to offer qualified personnel.

5.   Interaction of service and goods production in a dynamic local economy

However, while distances shrink, they do not vanish. Not only do consumer services by and large remain tied to locate close to their customer basis. But some producer services too have so frequent personal contact with their clients that geographical proximity remains imperative, or at least raises the quality of the service producer-user relationships. (Often they are organized internally in the user firm). We apparently have to realize that there is no simple truth in this matter: Firms *both* need specialized information services which often only can be bought far away, *and* need frequent interaction with service providers which must be local.

In other words: the closely integrated system of goods production and service production, which is the condition for dynamism of the emerging economy, is from a geographical point of view a complex phenomenon. Some of the linkages which figure 2 displays operate over long distances. Others require that the partners are located in the same local area. Qualified producer services, on which local firms can draw, are increasingly important for the dynamism of a local area.

This is a second reason for local and regional development policies to consider producer services as a target sector for stimulation.

References

Andersen, Ole Winckler (1987) Elementer til en 'ny-institutionalistisk' kritik af de-industrialiseringsdebatten. Roskilde Universitetscenter.

Barcet, André (1987) Tertiarisation de l'économie, marché du travail et emplois. *Economie et Humanisme*, no. 295, pp. 44–53.

Beyers, W. B., Alvine, M. J. and Johnsen, E. G. (1985) The Service Economy: Export of Services in the Central Puget Sound Region. Central Puget Sound Economic Development District, Seattle.

Blumenfeld, Hans (1955) The Economic Base of the Metropolis: Critical Remarks on the 'Basic – non-basic' Concept. *Journal of the American Institute of Planners*, vol. 21 no. 4, pp. 114–132.

Bonamy, J. & Mayère, A. (1987) Logiques des activités de service et inscription spatiale. Pp. 59–183 in D. Barbier de Reulle *et al.*, Mutations des services et dynamiques urbaines. *Economie et Humanisme*, Lyon.

Bonamy, Joël (1988) Business Services and the Transformation of the Productive System. Pp. 10–37 in O. W. Andersen, J. S. Pedersen and J. Sundbo (red) Service- og erhvervsudvikling. SamfundsAkonomi og Planlægning, Roskilde.

Browne, Lynn, E. (1986) Taking in Each Other's Laundry – The Service Economy. *New England Economic Review*, July/August, pp. 20–31.

Gadrey, Jean (1987) The Double Dynamics of Services. *The Service Industries Journal*, vol. 7 no. 4, pp. 125–138.

Gadrey, Jean (1988) Des facteurs de croissance des services aux rapports sociaux de service. *Revue d'Economie Industrielle*, no. 43, pp. 34–48.

Giarini, Orio (1986) Coming of Age of the Service Economy. *Science and Public Policy* vol. 13 no. 6, pp. 209–215.

Illeris, Sven (1987) The Metropolis, the Periphery and the Third Wave. *Town Planning Review*, vol. 58 no. 1, pp. 19-28.

Illeris, Sven (1989) *Services and Regions in Europe* (Avebury/Gower, Aldershot).

Illeris, Sven (forthcoming) Local and Distant Service Provision. In S. Illeris & L. Jakobsen (eds) *Networks and Regional Development* (NordREFO, Helsinki).

Kaldor, N. (1966) *The Causes of the Slow Rate of Growth of the United Kingdom* (Cambridge).

Lambooy, Jan Gerard (1988) Intermediaire dienstverlening en economische complexiteit. *Economisch en Sociaal Tijdschrift*, 42ste jaarg. nr. 5, pp. 617-629.

Lensink, E. (1986) De zakelijke dienstverlening in landelijke gebieden. pp. 65-82 in J. H. J. van Dinteren & H. W. ter Hart (red) Geografie en kantoren 1985. Koninklijk Nederlands Aardrijkskundig Genootschap, Amsterdam.

Monnoyer, M.-C. & Philippe, J. (1989) Facteurs de localisation et stratégies de développement des activités de servies aux entreprises. Pp. 199-214 in F. Moulaert (éd) La production des services et sa géographie. Université de Lille I.

Pedersen, Mogens Kühn (1988) Service i det postmoderne samfund. Pp. 66-95 in O. W. Andersen, J. S. Pedersen and J. Sundbo (red) Service- og erhvervsudvikling. SamfundsAkonomi og Planlægning, Roskilde.

Stabler, J. and Howe, E. C. (1988) Service Exports and Regional Growth in the Postindustrial Era. *Journal of Regional Science*, vol. 28 no. 3, pp. 303-316.

Stanback, T. M. and Noyelle, T. (1988) Productivity in Services: A Valid Measure of Economic Performance? Rapport présenté au colloque international sur le thème 'Productivité et valorisation dans les services aux entreprises'. Paris.

Walker, Richard A. (1985) Is There a Service Economy? *Science & Society*, vol. XLIX, pp. 42-83.

[10]

Pergamon

Geoforum. Vol. 25, No. 3, pp. 305–322, 1994
Copyright © 1995 Elsevier Science Ltd
Printed in Great Britain. All rights reserved
0016–7185/94 $7.00+0.00

0016–7185(94)00013–1

Taiwan as a Service Economy

ROGER MARK SELYA,* Cincinnati, U.S.A.

Abstract: Although Taiwan has been extensively analyzed as an industrial economy, data on the origins of GDP and employment suggest that Taiwan by 1970 had evolved into a service dominated economy. Data supporting this view indicate that services in general have grown faster than manufacturing, been less prone to adverse effects of recession and quicker to recover from economic downturns. Spatially the *distribution* of services follows the dictates of a population/market oriented explanation as suggested by central place theory. The *concentration* of services is better explained by the different locational orientations of consumer and producer services, and by diffusion theory. Four assumptions about anti-service attitudes possibly harbored by planners are tested and found not to apply to Taiwan. The logic and possible limitations of future investment in services are reviewed.

Introduction

The economic development of Taiwan (Republic of China) has been extensively studied. Literally hundreds of articles and books have explored the change in the Taiwan economy from a basically agrarian structure in 1949 to a robust, industrial one in 1992. For the most part, the literature on the economic development of Taiwan has focused on several narrow questions including description and explanation of change, and the role of the government in fostering change (e.g. Kuo *et al.*, 1981; Wu, 1985). Discussions on specific sectors of the economy have been concerned mainly with the successful expansion of manufacturing and trade, although both the positive and negative impacts of modernization on regional development and agricultural change have appeared (Bello and Rosenfeld, 1990a, 1990b; Ho, 1979). The published research of geographers parallels these general topical trends (Selya, 1975, 1982, 1993; Shaw and Williams, 1991; Todd and Hseuh, 1988; Williams, 1988a, 1988b; Williams and Chang, 1989). Overall the impression one gets from the

*Department of Geography, University of Cincinnati, 714 Swift Hall, Cincinnati, OH 45221-0131, U.S.A.

voluminous literature is that Taiwan is basically an industrial economy with increasing per capita income and a weakening agricultural base.

The data on employment and origins of GDP, however, suggest that Taiwan should be considered a service dominated economy. In this article this argument is presented and analyzed. First the problems of definitions, data sources, and measurement of services are reviewed. Second, the data on employment and origins of gross domestic product are presented to quantitatively indicate the central role of services. Third, the spatial distribution of services over time is compared to that of manufacturing. Fourth, policy considerations are presented in the form of four hypothetical reasons why Taiwanese economic planners have ignored services and five arguments for giving services the same investment attention previously given to manufacturing. Finally, in the concluding section the potential positive impact of growing services sector is contrasted with their limitations in solving all of Taiwan's problems regarding unbalanced regional development. Unless otherwise indicated, all calculations are by the author using data from sources described in the next section.

Geoforum/Volume 25 Number 3/1994

Definitions, Sources and Measures

Before presenting and analyzing the data, the questions of definition of services, data sources, and measures to be used must be discussed. The term services is often seen as a vague term, especially when contrasted with manufacturing (Britton, 1990; Riddle, 1986) since frequently there is no tangible 'product'. According to the Standard Industrial Classification, services include groups 40 through 99. These groups include transportation, communications, electric, gas, and sanitary services, wholesale and retail trade, finance, insurance, and real estate, fifteen separate groups of personal services (such as hotels, business services, repairs, entertainment, education, and professional societies), and public administration.

The Industrial and Commercial Censuses of Taiwan, one of the two major sources used in this paper, employs this SIC format. The tables in the 1971 and 1986 editions of the census include groups 40 through 99 even when presenting data at the smallest level of enumeration, *hsiang* (urban township), *chen* (rural township), and city level. In contrast, when presenting data on manufacturing data at this geographic level of enumeration, the censuses only present total manufacturing with no industry by industry breakdown. In fact then, despite the impression that services is an overly-vague term, the data for services on Taiwan, in contrast to other countries (Marshall *et al.*, 1988), are much more refined and detailed than that of manufacturing and permit a more detailed analysis of services than can be done for manufacturing.

Despite its greater detail, the census data do display one major shortcoming: they only report on registered enterprises and establishments. It is well recognized however that extensive informal, or underground, service and manufacturing sectors exist in Taiwan (Huang, 1993). To compensate for incomplete coverage of the census data, when discussing the distribution and concentration of services, employment data from the *Taiwan-Fukien Demographic Yearbook* have been used in this study. The use of employment data from the *Demographic Yearbook* to measure services does not limit the analysis since the three measures of services reported in the Census, number of establishments, employment, and reve-

nues, correlate very highly, with the exception of construction (Table 1). [The construction exception is eliminated if the impact of urban based central offices and support staffs are discounted.] In turn, the Census data correlate highly with data from the *Demographic Yearbook*.

Use of these employment data from the *Demographic Yearbook* does involve the loss of some spatial precision. For example, according to the industrial census, there were some 12 townships in 1971 and 21 townships in 1986 with no factories, and therefore no industrial employment. Employment data from the *Demographic Yearbook* for 1971 and 1986 record all cities and townships as having some workers engaged in manufacturing. The disparity between the two sets of data can be traced to delays in changing residential registrations, or to commuting from a township with no factories to one with. Both sources show no township or city lacking in some type of service employment. Both data sources show that one township lacks employment in transportation, three lack employment in finances, five employment in the general category 'other', and thirty-one lack employment in construction. Regardless of the reasons for the differences in the two sets of data for manufacturing, the *Demographic Yearbook* data provide more complete and accurate better measures of employment in the various sectors of the economy.

Evidence that Taiwan is a Service Economy

Figures 1 and 2 display the data which support the contention that Taiwan is best understood as a service economy. In terms of employment and origins of GDP it is clear that not only are services the largest single contributor to the economy and but also by far the major employer as well. In the 38 years of economic development of Taiwan, growth in services has outperformed growth in manufacturing around half the time. In general both the absolute and relative (percentage) growth of services have been less volatile, less affected by recession, and quicker to recover from recession than the manufacturing sector. These growth patterns are found in other service dominated economies (McKee, 1988; Price and Blair, 1989). In terms of absolute changes in employment, some 56.82% of all the new jobs added to the economy since 1952 have been in the service sector; jobs in

Table 1. Correlation coefficients for various measures and types of services

	No. of establishments	No. of employees	Revenues
1971: All services			
No. of establishments	1.00	0.9879	0.9732
No. of employees	0.9879	1.00	0.9964
Revenues	0.9732	0.9964	1.00
1986: All services			
No. of establishments	1.00	0.9814	0.9812
No. of employees	0.9814	1.00	0.9909
Revenues	0.9812	0.9909	1.00

1986: Employment by sub-sector

	Commerce	Transport	Finance	Other	Construction	All
Commerce	1.00	0.9575	0.9252	0.9651	0.2923	0.9905
Transport	0.9575	1.00	0.9464	0.9801	0.3987	0.9790
Finance	0.9252	0.9464	1.00	0.9898	0.5480	0.9633
Other	0.9651	0.9801	0.9808	1.00	0.4353	0.9633
Construction	0.2923	0.3987	0.5480	0.4353	1.00	0.4005
All	0.9905	0.9790	0.9633	0.9884	0.4005	1.0 0

1971 and 1986: Employment by broad sub-sector

	1986 Commerce	1986 Other	1986 All
1971 Commerce	0.9414	0.9227	0.9291
1971 Other	0.9145	0.9012	0.9067
1971 All	0.9289	0.9129	0.9188

services have been added on average at a rate 2.62 times that of manufacturing positions. Since 1987 services have added more jobs and more GDP than manufacturing in both absolute and percentage terms. Growth in services has not been uniform however. Although total service employment in the period 1971 to 1986 increased some 120.69%, some services, such as commerce and finance grew more rapidly. Within the lagging social and personal ser-

vices sector some types, such as real estate and recreation, actually contracted (Table 2).

As the economy of Taiwan has grown in size and sophistication, so too the number and type of services has expanded. For example, totally new business services enumerated in the 1986 census include market place management, consulting services, data processing and information services, advertising ser-

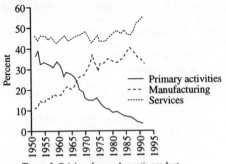

Figure 1. Origins of gross domestic product.

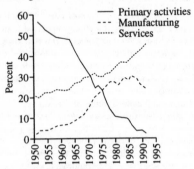

Figure 2. Employment by economic sector.

308   Geoforum/Volume 25 Number 3/1994

Table 2. Growth in service employment

Sector	Percentage growth 1971–1986
Construction	87.29
Commerce	169.54
Transportation	86.93
Finance	150.12
Social	54.62
of which:	
Hotels, restaurants	203.97
Real estate	−54.55
Recreation	−10.71
Personal	27.88

vices, product and packaging services, and machinery and equipment renting and leasing. One new social service category, mass media, was also added. In contrast, some 29 categories of manufacturing were either eliminated or consolidated. As with the growth in service employment, so too in the growth in the number and sophistication of Taiwan's experience mimics that found elsewhere (Price and Blair, 1989). However, Taiwan's experience can also be seen as a mix of the recent experience with services and manufacturing in both developed and underdeveloped countries. In terms of changes in the origins of GDP and employment, Taiwan resembles the developed world; in terms of retaining a sizeable manufacturing sector it resembles many developing countries (Britton, 1990; Daniels, 1985, 1993; Dicken, 1992).

The service sector shares one important trait with Taiwanese manufacturing: it is dominated by small establishments (Table 3). The mean number of employees for all services except insurance are well below that of manufacturing. Small size is an additional trait which Taiwanese service industries also share with services elsewhere (Daniels, 1983). It has been suggested that most Taiwanese service firms are in fact too small to operate efficiently (Wieman, 1987).

Spatial Distribution of Services

There is an interesting spatial parallel to the time series data which show services dominating the economy: as is found elsewhere (Marshall *et al.*, 1988) services are more evenly distributed spatially than is manufacturing. Gini coefficients from Lorenz curves comparing the distribution of services to that of

population, and manufacturing to that of population (Table 4), clearly show that services are more equally distributed. Such an observation suggests that the distribution of services in Taiwan can be explained by central place theory (Daniels, 1982, 1983, 1993; Dicken, 1992; Kirn, 1987). Larger population centers presumably have larger levels of demand and income levels (Allen, 1988; Kirn, 1987), and therefore more types of services and higher employment in services. Accessibility and consumer sophistication is also thought to be higher in larger centers (Daniels, 1982). But demand exists everywhere and therefore all townships and cities have some services. The merit of using central place theory and the above interpretation is perhaps attested to by the very high correlations (0.956087 and 0.93694) between the distribution of population and the number of service employees for 1971 and 1986, respectively.

The observation that services are somewhat equally distributed is contradicted by Figure 3 which shows the distribution of employment in services. [Given the high correlations for services by sector for both years in this study (Table 1), Figure 3 serves as surrogate for all services for 1971 and 1986.] Clearly the major cities and *hsien* (county) capitals dominate the pattern, a distribution found elsewhere (Coffey and McRae, 1989; Dunning, 1989; Marshall *et al.*, 1988; McKee, 1988; Price and Blair, 1989). This urban orientation is confirmed by location quotients of services comparing the distribution of services to that of population (Figure 4). Only 28 townships and cities out of 318 in Taiwan had location quotients of one or higher. All of these areas are either cities or *hsien* capitals. There are several reasons to expect that services should be highly concentrated. On the one hand services may have located in urban centers since these areas traditionally have contained larger pools of highly skilled labor, and because urban areas are the location of both competing and complimentary economic activities. Similarly, an urban location may be preferred as it may reduce the cost of delivering the service to the market (Coffey and McRae, 1989). It may also be the case that service industries prefer rich information environments (Daniels, 1982), and obviously cities have an advantage in this regard over more remote areas. Part of that rich information environment is improved telecommunications (Daniels, 1983; Marshall *et al.*, 1988); in Taiwan improved telecommunications are found in

Table 3. Scale of services and manufacturing, 1986

Sector	Mean number of employees	% Sector with more than 10 employees	Mean net dollar value of assets
Commerce	3.15	5	82,437
Wholesale	5.96	15	149,182
Retail	2.14	2	44,165
Hotels/restaurants	5.16	8	123,704
Finance	21.16	45	13,700,000
Insurance	118.41	56	30,200,000
Business	8.78	22	1,100,000
Real estate	9.16	27	2,100,000
Social	3.91	4	97,257
Social	8.00	6	276,473
Recreation	7.15	15	282,187
Personal	2.42	2	34,106
Manufacturing	24.23	63	742,821

major cities. Furthermore, the business environments of major cities tend to be more complex, and therefore attract more services (Kirn, 1987). The concentration in and about Taipei City is traceable to the fact that Taipei is at the lower end of the World City hierarchy (Friedman, 1986; Friedman and Wolff, 1982), and displays many of the functions and characteristics of a world oriented service economy (Selya, 1994). On the other hand, the better showing of services as compared to manufacturing in the Gini coefficients no doubt reflects the fact that many service industries are more footloose (than manufacturing) and thus have greater locational choices (Allen, 1988; Daniels, 1982; McKee, 1988).

One approach to interpretation of the differences between the Gini coefficients and location quotients would focus on the differences between consumer oriented and producer oriented services (Marshall *et al.*, 1988; Price and Blair, 1989). Consumer oriented services could account for the more equal coefficients for services, while the map of distribution location quotients could show the influence of producer oriented services. Figure 5 supports this conjecture. The ratio of service to manufacturing employment

shows only a small cluster of townships in the northwest coastal area, a small cluster around the southern city of Tainan, and two isolated townships in the south where manufacturing dominates. What is especially noteworthy is that in the isolated, and poorer, central mountain areas where topography and inaccessibility limit industry, services dominate the local economy. Without these service industries these remote areas might very well be even poorer and less developed than they are.

Another classification of services which might explain the differences between the Gini coefficients and the map of location is that of Bhagwati (1987), who distinguishes between those services where physical proximity to the consumer is essential, and those where it is inessential. Financial services tend to be strongly concentrated (Dicken, 1992) since proximity to the consumer, and government institutions, is essential. In contrast, other services, even within the financial sector such as banking (Dicken, 1992), or retailing by catalogue (Bhagwati, 1987) are not dependent upon physical proximity, and therefore these services will concentrate in large urban areas, where communications systems are more developed. If

Table 4. Gini coefficients derived from Lorenz curves

Population compared to:	Services		Manufacturing	
	1971	1986	1971	1986
Number of establishments	16.54	18.22	30.97	24.50
Number of employees	32.78	22.05	34.48	29.13
Revenues	38.75	34.69	38.38	41.86

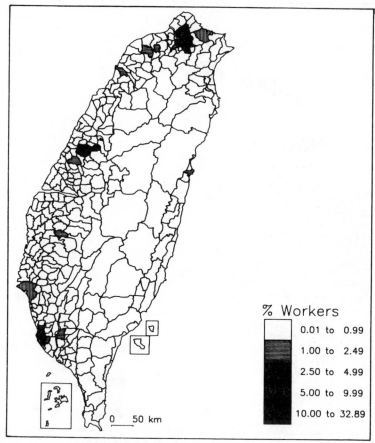

% Workers

	0.01 to 0.99
	1.00 to 2.49
	2.50 to 4.99
	5.00 to 9.99
	10.00 to 32.89

0   50 km

Figure 3. Distribution of employment in services, 1986.

communications services are highly developed enough then such services may place their front office functions in urban areas, and their back office functions in more decentralized locations (Dicken, 1992). It does not necessarily follow that those services which require close physical proximity between providers and users of services will be evenly distributed. In some cases providers can be mobile, while in others, the user may be mobile, or it may be that both have a high degree of mobility. The spatial orientation of these services then can be quite varied, suggesting both equal distribution and a high degree of concentration.

A third classification of services, public *vs* private, can also elucidate the differences found between the distribution and concentration of services. It is generally the case that public services are evenly distributed, whereas private services, and among those producer and business services in particular, are concentrated in major urban areas (Marshall *et al.*, 1988).

Diffusion theory of services (Daniels, 1982) can also be used to explain the seeming disagreement of the measures of service location. According to diffusion theory, service industries occupy specialized buildings whose construction is dependent upon a constel-

Geoforum/Volume 25 Number 3/1994   311

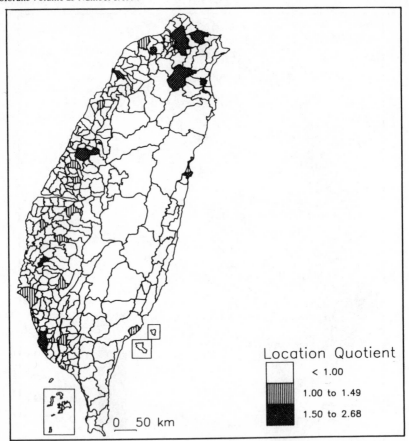
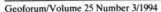

Figure 4. Location quotient of employment in services, 1986.

lation of entrepreneurs, landlords, financiers, and construction companies which is normally found in larger urban areas. In addition services are influenced by the institutional environment. As such the location of government bodies and officials is a strong pulling force for services. In Taiwan specialized buildings are found in the major urban centers, and the institutional environment is well-known as a locational factor (Selya, 1993). As such we would expect to see all services favoring urban settings. A good example of these principles can be seen in the introduction and diffusion of multi-national chain stores such as 7-Eleven and their Taiwan clones. Although the num-

ber of such stores has increased rapidly since their introduction in 1980, they are located in the major cities and *hsien* capitals (Yeung, 1990).

Another perspective on the true nature of the distribution of services and their local impact can be derived from Figures 6, 7, and 8. Figure 6 shows the per cent change in service employment from 1971 to 1986. Significantly some remote rural areas experienced contractions in service employment as did the southern port city, and center of heavy industry, Kaohsiung City. In contrast the remaining cities and *hsien* capitals and the industrial suburbs of all the five

312 Geoforum/Volume 25 Number 3/1994

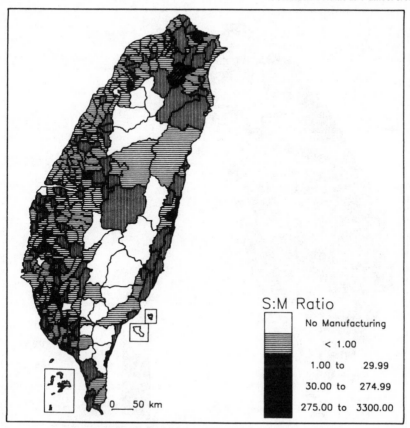

Figure 5. Ratio of employment in services to employment in manufacturing.

major cities experienced significant growth in service employment. These patterns no doubt show the extreme sensitivity of services to changes in population distribution (Daniels, 1982; Green and Howells, 1987). The patterns of service changes closely resemble changes in population distribution which occurred in Taiwan between 1971 and 1986 (Selya, 1988).

Figure 7 shows the results of a modified shift share analysis. The analysis is termed modified as only net shift was computed using the formulae in Stead (1967). A complete shift-share analysis was not done since only the regional share of change was of interest. Here only Taichung and Tainan Cities and the industrial suburbs of Kaohsiung and Taipei, as well as *hsien* capitals, experienced growth in service employment greater than the expected national rate. In fact the isolated areas of the central mountains fared especially badly by this standard. Figure 8 compares the rates of growth in service and manufacturing employment. Service employment expanded in those very areas which are the fastest growing industrial areas (Selya, 1993). A similar comparison of location quotients for manufacturing and services shows just the opposite pattern: here the remote rural townships

Geoforum/Volume 25 Number 3/1994   313

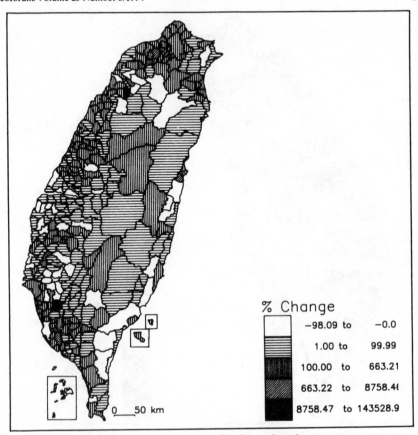

Figure 6. Percentage growth of employment in services.

show much stronger location quotients for services. Interestingly this relationship applies to the five major cities and to all *hsien* capitals.

We are left then with a very mixed view of the spatial distribution of service employment. It is possible to argue that service industries are more equally distributed than manufacturing, although the growth of services in absolute terms favored urban and suburban areas and not remote rural areas. It might be argued that the apparent disparities in the measuring of service location are inherent in the ambiguity of services in regard to what constitutes demand and market (Allen, 1988). As such the growth, and distri-

bution, of different types of services are the function of different causal processes which will be reflected in different measures of location. Finally the possible impact of government policies regarding access to public services and restructuring of the economy on understanding the distribution of services must be raised (Daniels, 1982). It is not possible to clearly indicate what role government policies favoring equal access to public, as opposed to private services, may have on our ability to accurately measure the distribution of services, although one would expect the emphasis on improvements in the social and cultural life included in government development projects would lead to a more equal distribution of public

314 Geoforum/Volume 25 Number 3/1994

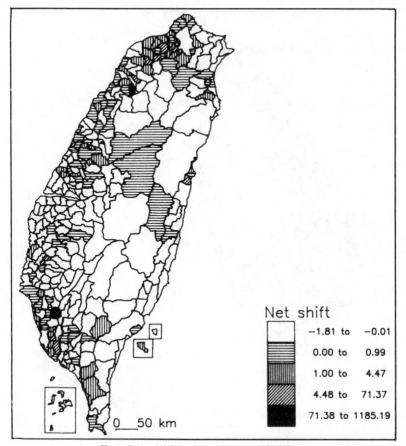

Figure 7. Net shift in service employment, 1971–1986.

services. It is too early to know whether or not government policies regarding restructuring of the Taiwan economy have had a major impact on the distribution of services.

Policy Considerations

If services do truly dominate the Taiwan economy and if they do have locational attributes which suggest they provide greater spatial equality in employment than manufacturing, why, then, is it that in the various development plans, and their implemen-

tation, for the Republic of China services have not received the same degree of attention that manufacturing has? Similarly, when assessing the origins of successful economic development in Taiwan, why have Taiwanese politicians, planners and government officials not mentioned or analyzed the role of the service sector (Wieman, 1987)? In answering these questions several issues must be kept in mind. First, the successive development plans did include macro-economic goals and objectives for services, although they tend to be subsumed in sectoral programs such as transportation and communications, social welfare, tourism, and research and develop-

Geoforum/Volume 25 Number 3/1994   315

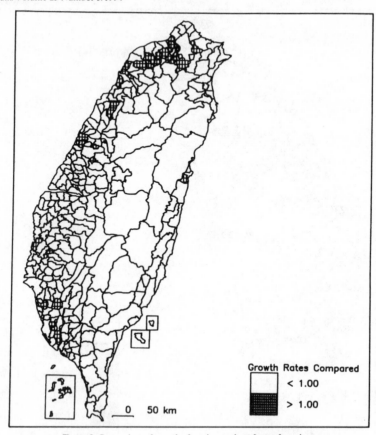

Figure 8. Comparison of growth of services to that of manufacturing.

ment. That is, services are never the focus of development for their own sake. They are mainly seen as means to improving the manufacturing and trade components of the economy, and as such investment in services usually involves investment in physical or material projects rather than quality of life or skills programs. Second, services have not been targeted for development with special legislation aimed at attracting foreign investment or upgrading existing technologies as has been the case for manufacturing (Council for Economic Planning and Development, 1993; Industrial Development and Investment Center, 1991; Wu, 1985). In these regards Taiwan appears to have been typical of most countries in its

lack of conscious comprehensive development planning for services (Riddle, 1986).

Given this treatment of services in the planning process, the questions of neglect must be approached indirectly using material from the literature on the role of services in economic development. This literature suggests that, apart from conceptual and definitional difficulties associated with the study of services (Marshall *et al.*, 1988), there are at least four hypotheses which when tested will at least give indirect answers to the issue of possible neglect. These hypotheses will be introduced in the form of possible assumptions held by Taiwanese planners and government officials and then tested as hypothesis. However in evaluating the results of each test it must be remembered that all data which are used underestimate the importance of services (Dicken, 1992).

Possible Reasons for Neglect

One assumption, which derives from the widespread belief that manufacturing is the engine which drives an economy, is that salaries are lower in services than in manufacturing (Gershuny and Miles, 1983; Ofer, 1967; Riddle and Sours, 1984). If this is the case, since increasing per capita income to a level as high as possible is a goal of the development plans, then increased employment in services would be less desirable and thus encouragement of services would not be advantageous. The data from the Censuses are somewhat ambiguous on this point (Table 5). On average salaries in service industries are higher than those in manufacturing. However, the advantage has declined on average and especially in the two service sectors (transportation and real estate/business) where the ratio was particularly favorable in 1971. The ratio remained unfavorable in commerce, construction, hotels/restaurants, and personal services. In two, commerce and hotels/restaurants, the disfavor has increased, in one, construction, there has been no change vis-à-vis manufacturing, while in personal services there has been some improvement to the point where there is almost equity with manufacturing. A comparison of shifts in salary and employment

shows that the two sets of shifts correlate very highly (0.833 when the shifts for services alone are compared, and 0.989 when shifts in services and manufacturing are compared). The weak advantage for services erodes further when salaries in specific manufacturing sectors are compared to specific service sectors. This weakened advantage for services is true when spatial comparisons are made as well. So although the hypothesis is not confirmed, the slight advantage of services would most likely not convince planners and government officials that investments in services *qua* services would be advantageous.

A second assumption perhaps held by planners would be that services are not as productive as manufacturing (Daniels, 1983; Riddle, 1987). Four measures can be used to test this assumption: value of output per worker, value added per worker, and percentage changes in the two per worker measures (Riddle, 1986). Before analyzing the data one important caveat must be issued. Financial and income data from Taiwan are thought to be notoriously inaccurate (Moll, 1992). In many cases companies are said to have four sets of accounting books: one for the family, one for the government, one for the banks, and one for foreign investors. Since it is not clear how errors are distributed between or within sectors of the economy, the data in the *Industrial and Commercial Censuses* may not reflect true differences between manufacturing and services. With this in mind, as with the first assumption, the data (Table 6) are inconclusive but certainly do not support the overall assumption. In 1971 financial services and commerce

Table 5. Average annual salaries in New Taiwan dollars in manufacturing and services, 1971 and 1986

Sector	1971		1986	
	Salary	S/M* Ratio	Salary	S/M Ratio
Manufacturing	21,329.03		144,354.95	
Commerce	18,804.49	0.88	116,181.16	0.80
Construction	17,021.46	0.80	126,129.16	0.80
Hotels†	16,156.96	0.76	99,122.45	0.69
Transport	31,898.15	1.50	170,181.00	1.18
Finance	42,018.14	1.97	236,286.82	1.64
Real Estate‡	26,860.59	1.26	150,971.61	1.05
Personal	15,130.40	0.71	141,788.19	0.98
Average§	23,984.31	1.12	146,860.00	1.02

*S/M = Services/manufacturing
†Includes restaurants
‡Includes business services
§All services

Table 6. Output and value added per worker

	1971		1986	
Sector	Output	Value added	Output	Value added
Manufacturing	202,235	34,453	1,218,389	341,829
Construction	74,202	21,258	552,071	170,225
Commerce	241,839	29,622	344,368	227,434
Transportation	120,313	44,771	856,509	462,266
Finance	229,623	143,198	1,272,803	680,741
Social services	43,329	21,118	432,955	244,627

had higher output per worker than manufacturing and financial services and transportation had higher value added than manufacturing. In 1986 only financial services had higher output per worker, but both financial services and transportation had higher value added. Preliminary data from the *1991 Industrial and Commercial Census* show the same pattern as 1986, although construction is now achieving 95% of the manufacturing per worker value of output. In terms of shifts in the two measures for 1971 to 1986 and 1971 to 1991 identical patterns show: for value of output per worker manufacturing exceeds only commerce and financial services. For 1971 to 1986 in changes in value added per worker, the same pattern is found. One possible conclusion from these data is that services have the potential to be every bit as productive as manufacturing.

A third anti-services assumption could be that services are less desirable since there is no 'product' to sell or to export (Daniels, 1983, 1993; Dunning, 1989; Price and Blair, 1989; Riddle, 1986; Shlep *et al.*, 1984), or, the concept of comparative advantages does not seem to apply to services (Katouzian, 1970). Parenthetically it should be noted that Taiwan does have a long history of selling 'productless' educational services to Overseas Chinese wishing to enroll in Chinese universities, and foreigners wishing to learn Chinese and to do research. Whether or not there is no product to actually export and, therefore, no sales for other services can be tested in two ways. First, for many developed countries such as France, Switzerland, the United Kingdom and the United States, services are traded with a net positive balance, and the size of the credit provided by services is often large enough to cover a large portion, if not all, of the deficit in merchandise trade. Second, although it appears that since 1986 Taiwan has been running a negative balance of services, the balance is narrow-

Table 7. Sex ratios (males/females) of employment by sector (and selected sub-sectors), 1986

Sector	Sex ratio
All economic activities	1.37
Manufacturing	1.15
Construction	5.79
Commerce	1.19
Wholesale	1.58
Retail	1.29
Department stores	0.47
Restaurants and hotels	0.77
Transportation	4.50
Fire	1.15
Social and personal services	0.96
Mass media	1.78
Social	0.76
Health	0.63
Cultural	0.90
Personal	1.15

ing. Furthermore, the growth in the sale of services in the period 1986 to 1992 has averaged 18.43% per annum, while the growth in merchandise trade has increased on average by 13.21% per annum. In some cases Taiwan's export of services involves materials 'produced' in Taiwan, such as the growth of flight kitchens supplying meals for the 20,000 to 30,000 passengers who leave Taiwan daily. The two major flight kitchens in 1993 employed some 1092 workers (Shen, 1993). Other services are directly supplied in a second country as was the case of construction of major roads and the staffing of a major hospital in Saudi Arabia. In short then, there is a great potential for the export of services.

The last anti-service assumption that planners may hold is that services are somehow inferior as economic activities since they are female dominated (Daniels, 1983). The data from all sources in this paper do not support the idea that services are dominated by female employees (Table 7). The one major

318   Geoforum/Volume 25 Number 3/1994

sector where the sex ratio falls below one, social and personal services, is close to one. It is true that certain sub-sectors are dominated by females, such as restaurants, hotels, department stores, and health services. However, this generalization only holds true for private and public non-incorporated establishments; incorporated establishments in these sectors have sex ratios above one.

Spatially the average sex ratio of employment by broad economic sector is well above one except for commerce in some 56 rural aboriginal areas in the eastern parts of the central mountains of Taiwan. Interestingly, there are also 35 rural and urban townships where the sex ratio for manufacturing is well-below one; this group includes a major urban industrial center—Changhwa City—as well. These female dominated manufacturing centers are located in the more remote parts of the western coastal, central mountain, and southeastern coastal areas. It is hard to image planners arguing that since female employment dominates industry in these areas that incentives for attracting more industry should be cut. As such the data on the sex ratios of employment by sector should dispel any notions that services are uniquely female occupations and therefore somehow inferior.

If the four anti-service assumptions do not seem to hold, then perhaps planners should begin to focus more specific programs on enhancing the growth of services. It is possible to frame a more positive argument in favor of services too. As in the case of trying to infer possible attitudes towards services held by Taiwan planners, the literature on services can provide the framework for advocating investment in services. There are at least five arguments which can be put forth.

Reasons for Investing in Services

First, the growth of services can raise the degree of sophistication, and the overall efficiency and productivity of an economy (Marshall *et al.*, 1988; Price and Blair, 1989) by providing current information regarding raw materials and their prices, exchange rates, returns on investments, and risks (Dicken, 1992). Second, growth of services can act as an impetus to the growth and improved competitiveness of manu-

facturing (Coffey and MacRae, 1989; Gershuny and Miles, 1983; Dunning, 1989; Price and Blair, 1989; Riddle, 1986). There are several routes by which this occurs. Services can insure more efficient delivery of raw materials to factories, and quicker delivery of finished products to retailers. This can be achieved, for example, through the use of distribution centers which avoid the traditional multi-layered distribution system now in place (Shen, 1993a). Similarly, services can adopt new technologies, such as office computers or photocopy machines. The continued use of these new technologies unto themselves also provide a future source of growth in both manufacturing and services since such commodities as paper or toner or ribbons will be needed and technicians will be needed to maintain and repair the new technologies (Dicken, 1992; Marshall *et al.*, 1988). In addition, services can design new products for specific markets. This could help liberate Taiwan from its reputation of merely copying or cloning existing products. Services can provide improved packaging and advertisements to enhance sales. Taiwan already has a positive experience with this process, as seen in the successful export of processed agricultural products such as mushrooms, baby corn, asparagus. One reason these crops were successfully exported is that the manufacturers' associations set standards for the products, including attractively designed labels with correct spellings. Services in some cases may be able to extend the product cycle for some goods by providing information regarding new markets (Daniels, 1993; Dunning, 1989).

A third way in which investment in services can be justified is their ability to assist in the diffusion of manufacturing out of crowded urban centers (McKee, 1988). Given the range of spatial distributions which services can display, they can play a role in changing the distribution of manufacturing. Since Taiwan planners seek to remove industry from major urban centers and spatially restructure manufacturing (Selya, 1993), investment in services can assist in achieving their goals. Although the goal of spatial restructuring of manufacturing seems to ignore the interests and needs of urban-based workers dependent upon industry for their livelihoods, manufacturing workers have displayed a high degree of spatial mobility in the past and continue to do so now (Liu and Tsai, 1990) and planners may have too easily just assumed that they would be willing to move or

Geoforum/Volume 25 Number 3/1994   319

alternatively to find positions in services. Furthermore, industrial workers also suffer from the dirt, noise, and congestion associated with manufacturing in Taiwan cities and it is surely to their benefit to work and live in surroundings where pollution levels are reduced. Fourth, services can help to improve the quality of Taiwan's physical environment. As was the case with new technologies, a growing environmental consulting sector has the potential to help clean up the deteriorated Taiwan environment (Williams and Chang, 1989), and foster both new manufacturing and new service employment. Fifth, and finally, services can assist in improving the quality of life for Taiwan residents. Taiwanese now have more leisure time available (*Asian Affluents 2*, 1992), yet seem unaware or unsure of how to enjoy this time apart from watching television (Anon., 1991). New services can provide new outlets which could both provide meaningful activities and contribute to the growth of manufacturing and other services.

In fact since 1987 government officials and planners seem to be taking service industries more seriously. Their attention to the central economic role and potential of services actually lags behind that of the popular Taiwan print medium (Leu, 1990). Be that as it may, since 1987 the government has started to lift restrictions on foreign and overseas Chinese investments in services. According to officials at the Ministry of Economic Affairs, investment in public utilities, insurance, and news publishing are to be permitted first with other sectors such as banking and securities investments to follow (Pun, 1992). The government thus has come to recognize that a poorly performing service sector can be a detriment to the overall economic health of Taiwan (Leu, 1990), and in particular that expansion of manufacturing will be difficult without an expansion, improvement, and restructuring of services such as research and development, retraining, health and education, sales and marketing techniques, and banking and finance (Daniels, 1983).

A second area where the government has started to emphasize its concern for services is in the area of manpower training. Such an emphasis shows that manpower projections for the year 2000 which estimate that some 90% of new entrants to the labor force will be employed in service industries (Leu, 1990) are now taken seriously. Since 1986 then,

administrators of existing employment and vocation programs within the Ministries of Economics and Education have been directed to expand their training programs (Leu, 1990; Wieman, 1987). Unfortunately these programs are thought to have been grossly understaffed so that older manpower projects were not even adequately, let alone fully, implemented (Leu, 1990; Wieman, 1987).

This new attitude towards services derives from three sources: a realization that current levels of services may no longer be adequate to meet the needs of growth in manufacturing and the subsequent distribution of goods (Wieman, 1987), that special programs to attract foreign investment in services are necessary if Taiwan is to develop a planned regional operations center for high-tech industries, and that foreign investment in services is necessary to off-set a marked decrease in foreign investment in manufacturing (Pun, 1992; Wieman, 1987). The new attitude also reflects a realization that current methods of insuring an adequately trained service sector—using either legal or illegal foreign nationals or pirating staffs from other companies (Liu, 1991)—are counterproductive and will not raise professional standards.

Conclusions

In arguing that Taiwan is best analyzed as a service economy and that more attention should be given to services in the planning process, it is important not to overstate the case and to avoid unrealistic expectations. On the one hand, given the complex relationships between manufacturing, services, and international trade (Dicken, 1992) more research must be done so that the linkages between economic growth, expansion of manufacturing, improvements in the quality of life in Taiwan, the internationalization of Taiwan's services, and the growth of the service sector can be better described and analyzed. More research is also needed regarding the relative impact of manufacturing and services on the local income and income multipliers, and overall value added (Daniels, 1983; Dicken, 1992), and on whether or not expansion of services occurs at the expense of manufacturing (Kirn, 1987), as has been claimed by government officials (Leu, 1990). More research too is needed whereby the different types of services are

320   Geoforum/Volume 25 Number 3/1994

analyzed using alternative classifications to consumer/producer or public/private schema. It is also of interest to establish the conditions under which firms either internalize or externalize their use of services (Dicken, 1992). To do this more detailed information on the input–output functions of service industries are needed (Marshall *et al.*, 1988).

In terms of expectations it must be realized that there will be limits as to what an expanded service sector can do. For example, it is most likely that services will not be able to restore completely the comparative advantage that Taiwan used to enjoy in textiles and clothing. It may assist textile and clothing manufacturers in discovering and capturing new niche markets. Similarly, while in general, services seem to be the only economic sector with the possibility of offering large-scale employment opportunities (Green and Howells, 1987), growth of the service industry should not be seen as an overall panacea for joblessness in other sectors of the economy (Gershuny and Miles, 1983), and especially in manufacturing (Daniels, 1983). This may be less important in the short run, given Taiwan's low unemployment rate, and because there is no significant rural surplus of workers to be absorbed into the urban economy. In the long run, the growth of services may come to compete for workers in manufacturing for two reasons. First, as the Taiwan population continues to age, new services such as adult or senior day-care, nursing homes, and physical and occupational therapy will emerge as growth areas. Second, residents of Taiwan, like those elsewhere, seem to prefer working in services (Anon., 1991a, 1992; Gold, 1991; Riddle, 1987). Women in particular do not see careers in manufacturing as more than temporary situations before marriage (Kung, 1983), and/or opening a small shop (Gold, 1991). Such preferences may be interpreted in many ways. It may well be that women say that they would rather work in their own shops because of the long term impact of wider systems of patriarchy and gender inequality (Diamond, 1979; Gates, 1979; Gallin, 1984; Gannicott, 1986; Thornton *et al.*, 1984). Or the preferences may reflect genuine shifts in the economic, political, and social status of women wherein they are increasingly able to make their own career choices and control their own economic resources (Chou *et al.*, 1990; Lu, 1992; Parish, 1993). Regardless of which interpretation is preferred there are two practical consequences of such preference statements. First they represent a warning to planners that women may no longer be relied upon to automatically become a part of the manufacturing sector. Second they represent major shift in the perception of services as a socially acceptable career area. There is a long time Chinese aversion to serving other people since such activities appear to be undignified (Wieman, 1987). Training programs and the lure of higher salaries than available in manufacturing should help to overcome any lingering inhibitions to employment in the service economy. Finally, while expansion of services may foster regional economic development by creating new businesses, by increasing demands on existing ones, or expanding the export base of an area (Kirn, 1987), in fact any such expansion may also lead to a reaffirmation of existing regional economic disparities, or may even exacerbate them. This may be true for both services and industry (Daniels, 1983; Green and Howells, 1987). Service industries then may be limited in their ability to radically change or regenerate regional and local economies (Green and Howells, 1987), while at the same time the lack of services may be a crucial factor in the stagnation of manufacturing (Kellerman, 1985). Growth of services may then require the same type of policies already in place to redress regional imbalances in Taiwan industry (Selya, 1993). Regardless of these limitations, the development of services via the processes of deregulation and internationalization appears to be a necessary condition if Taiwan is to restructure and thereby insure the long term health of its economy (Dicken, 1986, 1992).

References

Allen, J. (1988) Service industries: uneven development and uneven knowledge, *Area*, **20**, 15–22
Anon. (1991) Leisure life spent idly, survey finds, *Free China J.*, **Jan 28**, 3.
Anon. (1991a) Youths motivated for service jobs, *Free China J.*, **May 6**, 3.
Anon. (1992) 'Be-A-Boss' mentality saps industrial labor force while service sector soars, *Free China J.*, **Mar 6**, 3.
Asian Affluents 2. (1992) Far Eastern Economic Review, Hong Kong.
Bello, W. and Rosenfeld, S. (1990a) *Dragons in Distress. Asia's Miracle Economies in Crisis.* Institute for Food and Development Policy, San Francisco.
Bello, W. and Rosenfeld, S. (1990b) High speed industrialization and environmental devastation in Taiwan, *Ecologist* **20**, 125–132.
Bhagwati, J. (1987) International trade in services and its

Geoforum/Volume 25 Number 3/1994   321

relevance for economic development, In: *The Emerging Service Economy*, pp. 3–34. O. Giarini, (Ed.). Pergamon Press, New York.

Britton, S. (1990) Role of services in production, *Progr. Human Geog.* **14**, 529–546.

Chou, B.-E., Clark, C. and Clark J. (1990) *Women in Taiwan Politics. Overcoming Barriers to Women's Participation in a Modernizing Society*. Lynne Rienner Publishers, Boulder.

Coffey, W. J. and McRae, J. J. (1989) *Service Industries in Regional Development*. Institute for Research on Public Policy, Halifax.

Council for Economic Planning and Development. (1993) *Economic Revitalization Program, An Action Plan for the Promotion of Private Investment*. Executive Yuan, Taipei.

Daniels, P. (1982) *Service Industries: Growth and Location*. Cambridge University Press, Cambridge.

Daniels, P. W. (1983) Service industries: supporting role or centre stage, *Area* **15**, 301–309.

Daniels, P. W. (1985) *Service Industries. A Geographical Appraisal*. Methuen, London.

Daniels, P. W. (1993) *Service Industries in the World Economy*. Blackwell, Cambridge.

Diamond, N. (1979) Women and industry in Taiwan, *Modern China* **5**, 317–340.

Dicken, P. (1986) *Global Shift. Industrial Change in a Turbulent World*. Harper and Row, New York.

Dicken, P. (1992) *Global Shift. Internationalization of Economic Activity*, 2nd edn. Guildford Press, New York.

Dunning, J. H. (1989) Transnational corporations and the growth of services: some conceptual and theoretical issues, *UNCTC Current Studies, Series A*, **no. 9**.

Friedman, J. (1986) The world city hypothesis, *Dev. and Change* **17**, 69–83.

Friedman, J. and Wolff, G. (1982) World city formation: an agenda for research and action, *Int. J. Urban Region. Research* **6**, 309–344.

Gallin, R. (1984) Entry of Chinese women into the rural labor force: a case study from Taiwan, *Signs* **9**, 383–398.

Gannicott, K. (1986) Women, wages and discrimination: some evidence from Taiwan, *Econ. Del. Cul. Change* **34**, 721–730.

Gates, H. (1979) Dependency and the part-time proletariat in Taiwan, *Modern China* **5**, 381–407.

Gershuny, J. I. and Miles, I. D. (1983) *The New Service Economy*. Praeger, New York.

Gold, T. B. (1991) Taiwan: in search of identity, In: *MiniDragons. Fragile Economic Miracles in the Pacific*, pp. 22–47. S. M. Goldstein (Ed.). Westview, Boulder.

Green, A. E. and Howells, J. (1987) Spatial prospects for service growth in Britain, *Area* **19**, 111–122.

Ho, S. P. S. (1979) Decentralized industrialization and rural development: evidence from Taiwan, *Econ. Dev. Cul. Change* **28**, 77–96.

Huang, H. (1993) Success of roadside stalls makes crackdown difficult, *Free China Journal*, **March 9**, 6.

Industrial Development and Investment Center (1991) *Statute for Upgrading Industries*. IDIC, Taipei.

Katouzian, M. A. (1970) The Development of the Service Sector: A New Approach, *Oxford Ec. Pap.* N. 5, **22**, 362–382.

Kellerman, A. (1985) Evolution of the service economy: a geographical perspective, *Prof. Geog.* **37**, 133–142.

Kirn, T. J. (1987) Growth and change in the service sector of the United States: a spatial perspective, *An., Am. Ass. Geo.* **77**, 353–372.

Kuo, S. W. Y., Ranis, G. and Fei, J. C. H. (1981) *The Taiwan Success Story: Rapid Growth With Improved Distribution in the Republic of China*, 1952–1979. Westview, Boulder.

Kung, L. (1983) *Factory Women in Taiwan*. UMI Research Press, Ann Arbor.

Leu, C.-A. (1990) It's a new ball game, *Free China Rev.* **40**, 4–11.

Liu, P. (1991) 5-Star service, *Free China Rev.* **41**, 38–45.

Liu, P. K. K. and Tsai, H. H. (1990) Urban growth and employment restructuring in Taiwan, *Indust. Free China* **74**, 17–33.

Lu, Y.-H. (1992) Married women's informal employment in Taiwan, *Proc. Nat. Sci. Counc., Part C: Hum. and Soc. Sci.* **2**, 202–217.

Marshall, J. N., Wood, P. and Beyers, W. (1988) *Services and Uneven Development*. Oxford University Press, Oxford.

McKee, D. L. (1988) *Growth, Development, and the Service Economy in the Third World*. Praeger, New York.

Moll, T. (1992) Mickey Mouse numbers and inequality research in developing countries, *J. Develop. Stud.* **28**, 689–704.

Ofer, G. (1967) *The Service Industries in a Developing Economy. Israel as a Case Study*. Praeger, New York.

Parish, W. L. (1993) Daughters, education, and family budgets, *J. Human Resources* **28**, 863–898.

Price, D. G. and Blair, A. M. (1989) *The Changing Geography of the Service Sector*. Belhaven Press, New York.

Pun, A. (1994) Foreigners Allowed to Form Bank, *Free China J.*, Jan. 10, 3.

Riddle, D. I. (1987) The role of the service sector in economic development: similarities and differences by development categories, In: *The Emerging Service Economy*, pp. 83–104. O. Giarini, (Ed.). Pergamon Press, New York.

Riddle, D. I. (1986) *Service-Led Growth. The Role of the Service Sector in World Development*. Praeger, New York.

Riddle, D. I. and Sours, M. H. (1984) Service industries as growth leaders in the Pacific Rim, *Asia Pacific J. Manag.* **1**, 190–199.

Selya, R. M. (1975) Trading under duress: the case of Taiwan, *Asian Profile* **3**, 441–446.

Selya, R. M. (1982) Contrasting measures of changing industrial distribution in Taiwan, *Asian Geographer* **1**, 35–50.

Selya, R. M. (1988) Changing patterns of population distribution and density in Taiwan, *Program and Abstracts, AAG Annual Meeting*, 170.

Selya, R. M. (1993) Economic restructuring and spatial changes in manufacturing in Taiwan, 1971–1986, *Geoforum* **24**, 115–126.

Selya, R. M. (1994) *Taipei*. John Wiley and Sons, Ltd., London.

Shaw, S.-L. and Williams, J. F. (1991) Role of transportation in Taiwan's regional development, *Transp. Quart.* **45**, 271–296.

Shen, D. (1993) Travel boom boosts competition among inflight meals businesses, *Free China J.*, **Nov 12**, 8.

Shen, D. (1993a) Distribution centers hasten goods delivery, *Free China J.*, **Nov 26**, 8.

322   Geoforum/Volume 25 Number 3/1994

Shlep, R. K., Stephenson, J. C., Truitt, N. S. and Wascow, B. (1984) *Service Industries and Economic Development: Case Studies in Technology Transfer*. Praeger, New York.

Stead, G. (1967) Locational change: a 'shift and share' analysis of Northern Ireland's manufacturing mix, 1950–1964, *Tijdschr. econ. soc. geogr.*, **58**, 265–270.

Thornton, A., Chang, M.-C. and Sun, T.-H. (1984) Social and economic change: intergenerational relationships and family formation in Taiwan, *Demography* **21**, 475–499.

Todd, D. and Hsueh, Y.-C. (1988) Taiwan: some spatial implications of rapid economic growth, *Geoforum* **19**, 133–145.

Wieman, E. (1987) Growth in services, *Free China Rev.* **37**, 40–45.

Williams, J. F. (1988a) Urban and regional planning in Taiwan: the quest for balanced regional development, *Tidj. econ. soc. geogr.* **79**, 175–187.

Williams, J. F. (1988b) Vulnerability and change in Taiwan's agriculture, *Pacific Viewpoint* **29**, 25–44.

Williams, J. F. and Chang, C.-Y. (1989) Paying the price of economic development in Taiwan, environmental degradation, *J. of Oriental Stud.* **27**, 59–78

Wu, Y.-L. (1985) *Becoming an Industrialized Nation, Republic of China's Development on Taiwan*. Praeger, New York.

Yeung, I. (1990) Chain, chain, chain, *Free China Rev.*, **40**, 28–34.

Part II
Producer Services

[11]

Regional Studies, Vol. 23.2, pp. 139–150.

Corporate Reorganization and the Geography of Services: Evidence from the Motor Vehicle Aftermarket in the West Midlands Region of the UK

J. N. MARSHALL

Department of Geography, University of Birmingham, P.O. Box 363, Birmingham B15 2TT, UK.

(Received July 1988; in revised form October 1988)

MARSHALL J. N. (1989) Corporate reorganization and the geography of services: evidence from the motor vehicle aftermarket in the West Midlands region of the UK, Reg. Studies 23, 139–150. Research suggests that a corporate complex of administrative managerial and technical staff in the hinterland of capital cities underpins the spatial centralization of service activities in the economy. There have been important changes in corporate structures during the last decade. Firms have reduced their in-house provision of some services, resorting to external contractors instead. Divisional and middle management activities have been rationalized, and more autonomy delegated to lower levels in the corporate hierarchy. Using new technology firms have also expanded the range and quality of services provided in-house. This paper explores the geographical implications of these and other changes in business organization. A case study of the motor vehicle aftermarket in the West Midlands region of the UK suggests that simple generalizations concerning the geography of services based on the location of head offices and branch plants are inappropriate. An analysis of the dynamics of vertical integration and disintegration of service activities by firms is proposed as an alternative to the conventional approach to the analysis of corporate structure.

Corporate reorganization   Vertical integration and disintegration   Service location

MARSHALL J. N. (1989) La restructuration de l'entreprise et la distribution des services: des preuves provenant du marché pour les services après-vente dans l'industrie automobile dans la zone West Midlands du Royaume-Uni, Reg. Studies 23, 139–150. Des recherches laissent supposer qu'un complexe qui comprend l'administration, les cadres et les techniciens, et situé dans l'arrière-pays des capitales sous-tend la centralisation géographique des services dans l'économie. Au cours de la dernière décennie il y a eu une restructuration importante des entreprises. Les entreprises ont réduit leur taux d'auto-approvisionnement en services, ayant recours à des prestataires externes. Les fonctions des cadres moyens et de la gestion départementale ont été rationalisées, et les niveaux inférieurs de la hiérarchie de l'entreprise se voient accorder plus d'autonomie. En utilisant la nouvelle technologie les entreprises ont élargi la gamme et la qualité des services auto-approvisionnés. Cet article cherche à examiner les retombées géographiques de ces développements entre autres dans le contexte de l'organisation de l'entreprise. Un cas d'étude du marché des services après-vente dans l'industrie automobile dans la zone West Midlands du Royaume-Uni laisse supposer que de simples généralisations concernant la géographie des services et fondées sur la localisation des sièges sociaux et des établissements ne conviennent pas. Une analyse de la dynamique de l'intégration et de la désintégration verticale des services fournis par les entreprises se voit proposer

MARSHALL J. N. (1989) Korporative Neugliederung und die Geographie der Dienstleistungen: Beweise von Kraftfahrzeugskundenbetreuung im West Midlandsgebiet des Vereinigten Königreichs, Reg. Studies 23, 139–150. Untersuchungen legen es nahe, dass die räumliche Zentralisierung von Tätigkeiten auf dem Gebiet von Dienstleistungen im Wirtschaftssytem sich auf einen korporativen Komplex leitenden, administrativen und technischen Personals im Hinterland von Hauptstädten stützt. Im letzten Jahrzehnt haben im korporativen Gefüge bedeutsame Umwälzungen stattgefunden: Firmen haben die Bereitstellung von Dienstleistungen im Hause reduziert, und stattdessen Lieferanten von ausserhalb zugezogen. Die Aufgaben von Abteilungsund mittleren Betriebsleitern sind wirtschaftlicher gestaltet, und den niedrigeren Stufen der korporaten Hierarchie grössere Selbstständigkeit eingeräumt worden. Mit Hilfe der neuen Technologie haben Firmen auch Umfang und Qualität der im Hause verfügbaren Dienstleistungen ausgeweitet. Dieser Aufsatz untersucht die geographischen Implikationen dieser und anderer Änderungen in der betrieblichen Organisation. Eine Untersuchung des Falles der Kraftfahrzeugskundenbetreuung im West Midlandsgebiet des Vereinigten Königreichs lässt vermuten, dass einfache Verallgemeinerungen in bezug auf die Geographie der Dienstleistungen auf der Basis des Standorts der Hauptgeschäftsstelle und der Zweigstellen ungeeignet sind. Eine Analyse der Dynamik der vertikalen Integrations-und comme une autre façon d'analyser la structure de l'entreprise.

Restructuration de l'entreprise
Intégration et désintégration verticale
Localisation des services

Disintegrationstätigkeit auf dem Gebiet der Firmendienstleistungen wird als Alternative zu der üblichen Stellungnahme zur Analyse korporativer Organisation vorgeschlagen.

Korporative Neugliederung
Vertikale Integration und Disintegration
Dienstleistungsstandort

INTRODUCTION

Corporate structures have a major influence on the location of service employment. Studies suggest that the concentration of corporate administrative and managerial staff in the hinterland of capital cities underpins the spatial centralization of service activity in national economies.

Such work highlights an important reason for the uneven location of services, but it has failed to acknowledge the complexity of business organization, simply concentrating on the influence of external ownership and control on the location of services. More fundamentally, many studies are based on an outdated picture of business organization. The hierarchical model of firm organization described in the literature has been modified during the last decade as firms have reorganized their in-house provision of services, and resorted to external contractors

This paper explores the geographical implications of such changes in business organization in the UK. A case study is presented of the changing demand for services in the motor vehicle aftermarket in the West Midlands region. This suggests that simple generalizations concerning the geography of services based on the location of head offices or branch plants are inappropriate. A dynamic market-based perspective, which appreciates of the fluidity of corporate structures and the interdependence of services and other activities is proposed as an alternative.

CORPORATE STRUCTURE AND SPATIAL STRUCTURE

The growth of large organizations, and the associated dominance of a small group of companies in the economy, has produced an extensive debate on the impact of organizational structures on regional economies (see for example WATTS, 1979, 1980). The argument that the uneven distribution of administrative, technical and managerial staff in dominant enterprises is in large part responsible for the spatial centralization of service work in the economy has been a significant theme in this debate.

Early work demonstrated that the head offices of the largest companies were located close to London (PARSONS, 1972; EVANS, 1973). CRUM and GUDGIN'S, 1977, detailed analysis of non-production workers in manufacturing also showed that managerial and technical functions were largely carried out at head or divisional office, while branch plants primarily performed a production role. In MASSEY'S, 1979, analysis, which draws on these studies as well as work by HYMER, 1975, and WESTAWAY, 1974, the hierarchy of ownership and control in large organizations is a fundamental part of new patterns of uneven development, transforming established forms based on the specialization of localities in differing industrial sectors. The technical separation of production activities, and managerial structures of administration and control within organizations, underpin a spatial division of labour which, 'is increasingly based on the geographical separation of control and research and development functions from the process of direct material production still requiring skilled labour, and of those in turn from the increasingly important element of mass-production and assembly work for which only semi-skilled workers are needed'. (MASSEY, 1979, p. 237).

Massey's 'part-process' structure in which differing stages of production are located in different places was based on an analysis of the electronics sector, and the author argues that it is only typical of 'advanced' industrial sectors (MASSEY, 1984; ALLEN, forthcoming). Nevertheless, a popularization of this and earlier work has attained the status of a general model (SAYER, 1985). It is argued that white collar management and control functions at head offices are attracted by centres of government, international airports, existing pools of managerial labour and major businesses in large metropolitan regions. In turn the important role of the head office in both in-house service provision and the purchase of external services encourages a dense network of local specialist suppliers in central locations. Thus, head offices close to the capital place major contracts with locally-based national and international service companies with the capacity to service their operating units.

In contrast, blue-collar manual production has been shifted out to peripheral locations. Much of the time, this industrialization produces little in the way of service development. While service functions directly supplying production tend to be decentralized to branch plants, many of the services they use are imported from head and divisional offices, and this in turn truncates the development of the service supply sector in peripheral regions.

The insights of the original work on corporate

structure have been very valuable in assisting our understanding of both service dynamics and broader processes of uneven development. However, a considerable simplification of the relationship between corporate and spatial structure has taken place. As SAYER, 1986, p. 109, argues, it is all too common for 'research to try to "read off" the form of uneven development from the corporate hierarchy and locational strategies of the leading firms on the grounds that the economic characteristics of places come to reflect the place of their industry in the international corporate division of labour'. There is also a tendency to neglect the complexity and variety of corporate structures (MARSHALL, 1983; MARSHALL *et al.*, 1988). Corporate hierarchies have been simplified to include a limited variety of sites, for example, head and divisional offices as well as the ubiquitous branch plant. The latter, of course, is frequently erroneously viewed as simply a mass-production unit with little autonomy, low-technology production and links with only head and divisional office.

Research also over-emphasizes the impact of external ownership and control. This is particularly clear in work on the impact of corporate structure on changes in service location. Studies of the development of large firms show that after acquisition head office functions in acquired companies are frequently switched to the headquarters of the acquiree, and links with specialist suppliers of services are broken. Given the tendency of acquiring companies to be larger national and international companies based close to the capital, this in turn implies a growing spatial centralization of service activity (GODDARD and SMITH, 1978; LEIGH and NORTH, 1978. This, so it is argued, is reinforced by the decline of indigenous firms in established industries in provincial regions, and their gradual replacement by branch plants from the corporate sector with fewer service requirements. However, areas adjacent to the capital may benefit from the localized decentralization of head offices from urban centres as cost pressures encourage the relocation of administrative and clerical staff.

Such arguments accurately reflect the dynamics of acquisition activity but, as a framework for understanding the changing location of services, they emphasize only the processes of centralization, and pay insufficient attention to the diverse changes taking place in service location outside southern Britain. In addition, they tell us little about how a reorganization of corporate structures brought about by changes in business demand, or the introduction of new products or processes might affect service location. All too often we have a largely timeless model of corporate structure which is divorced from the technical and historical context of individual industries or economies.

NEW FORMS OF ORGANIZATION

This is problematic because the relationship between organizational structure and spatial structure appears to be changing. A number of authors argue that the links between corporate and spatial structure described above are typical of a specific 'Fordist' phase of capitalist development in which a rigid specialization of tasks and the separation of conception from execution within organizations underlies the spatial separation of corporate activities (PERRONS, 1981; 1986; SCOTT and STORPER, 1986; STORPER and CHRISTOPHERSON, 1987).

This phase of development has been modified during the last two decades. Slower growth in the key markets which have fuelled post-war expansion has been accompanied by an intensification of international competition. Keynesian demand management which helped to sustain a growing demand for output has fallen into disfavour as supply-side and monetarist policies have gained in popularity (LIPIETZ, 1986). Strict Taylorist forms of organization have also proved unsatisfactory in rapidly changing businesses.

A growing flexible response on the part of firms to these developments has been documented (BLACKBURN, COOMBS and GREEN, 1985; HARVEY and SCOTT, forthcoming). These include a more flexible use of labour (ATKINSON, 1984), the installation of more flexible capital equipment (COOMBS and JONES, 1988), the development of flexible forms of inventory control and distribution (ESTALL, 1985; KAPLINSKI, 1984) and the concentration of companies on their core expertise (GILLESPIE AND WILLIAMS, 1988). These changes are increasing the speed with which companies can respond to market demands and rigidities in organizational structures have been reduced. The historical links between automation and scale of production have also been modified and firms are being encouraged to integrate previously separate parts of the production process.

As a consequence, complex changes in the source of service production have taken place. In the harsh climate of recession, companies have become more conscious of the cost of their administrative overheads and have sought to cut back, using computer technology to improve the efficiency of their service workers. This has been associated with attempts to make management structures simpler and more responsive to change. To this end greater accountability has also been introduced at lower levels in the corporate hierarchy (CLUTTERBUCK, 1985).

There has been a growth in the contracting out of services (RAJAN, 1987). This trend goes back to the early 1970s in the case of physical distribution, where its reorganization to form a separate managerial function promoted tighter cost control and encouraged contracting out. There is evidence, however, that contracting has intensified and spread to white collar functions. RAJAN and PEARSON, 1986, for example, on the basis of an extensive employer survey in the UK suggest that out of 700,000 jobs created in distribution (including on their definition retailing), finance and business services between 1979 and 1985, as many as 300,000 were due to contracting out by non-specialist producers. They expect the externalizations process to increase and between 1985 and 1990 possibly 60% of the job creation in distribution, finance and business services could come from a transfer of service work across the sectors.

However, it is too simplistic to view contracting out as the only change taking place in organizational boundaries; both internalization and externalization processes are at work. For example, dramatic market changes and the need for firms to be sensitive to the changing demands of their customers has encouraged them to internalize critical market-related services. For other firms the quality of service they provide to customers is becoming increasingly important to their success, and here again internalization of these services is encouraged (MARSHALL, 1988). Technology has played a critical part in enhancing such fluidity in organizational boundaries. The introduction of computer technology has expanded both the range of services in-house service workers can perform and created new demands for external services.

The geographical implications of these organizational changes remain largely uncharted territory. However, the relationship between corporate and spatial structure appears to be changing. CHRISTOPHERSON and STORPER, 1986, and STORPER and CHRISTOPHERSON, 1987, for example, link corporate reorganization with the further agglomeration of services in major urban centres. In their work on the motion picture industry, they document the emergence of small firms working for independent producers, following the vertical disintegration of the major studios, and show that this coincided with the reconcentration of the industry in Los Angeles. They conclude that the developing vertical disintegration requires a close symbiotic relationship between customer and supplier and a local pool of skilled and flexible labour, both of which favour spatial concentration.

Caution is necessary, however, in generalizing the results of such work because the significance of recent organizational changes is not entirely clear (contrast, for example, PIORE and SABEL, 1984, and ASHIEM, 1988). The extent of the dominance of 'Fordist' structures during previous decades, and the nature, permanence and extent of recent changes is open to question. New relationships between corporate and spatial restructuring are also difficult to unearth in a period of experimentation when industry is making an increasingly subtle use of space (HARVEY and SCOTT, forthcoming).

Clearly, however, a new analysis is needed of the impact of corporate structures on the location of services. The reorganization of business described above suggests that an analysis of the processes of vertical integration and contracting out of services by firms offers a more appropriate framework than changes in ownership and control for understanding the recent changes in the location of services in the UK. Locational changes will then be related more directly to changes in the organization of service production. The impact of the rationalization of corporate administration on the spatial balance of in-house service activities within large companies can be explored, and the impact of changes in internalization or contracting out of services on location will also become clearer.

To understand the way in which locational changes in service activities result from the dynamics of vertical integration and disintegration this study adopts a market-based perspective. It focuses on a *filière* or 'linkage chain' of firms serving the motor vehicle aftermarket; including component manufacturers and assemblers, intermediate services such as wholesalers, and also retailers. This approach enables the research to monitor shifts in service provision between the in-house operations within firms and specialist operators in service industries, to relate these to broader economic changes through the operation of the market, and to trace locational outcomes as the balance of service functions within the *filière* changes.

THE MOTOR VEHICLE AFTERMARKET IN THE WEST MIDLANDS

The size of the motor vehicle aftermarket for replacement parts, equipment and accessories is difficult to estimate. The Monopoly and Mergers Commission estimated the total wholesale supply of replacement parts in Britain to be of the order of £2·48 billion per annum in 1980, and GRAY, 1986, considered £2·0 billion and 100,000 jobs to be a fairly accurate estimate in 1985. Respondents to the author's survey believed replacement parts for motor vehicles to be worth £2·5–3·0 billion in 1987. These estimates include parts which are replaced routinely during servicing such as spark plugs, points and brake pads. Batteries, tyres and exhausts which need to be replaced during the life-time of a vehicle, and clutches, body panels and windscreens which only need to be to replaced following breakdown.

Though it is difficult to be precise, the West Midlands is regarded as the main region for aftermarket supply (BESSANT *et al.*, 1984; GRAY, 1986; MILLER, 1983), and it is argued that as much as 30% of regional employment is dependent on the motor vehicle sector as a whole. The manufacture and distribution of replacement parts for motor vehicles in the West Midlands is complex, fragmented and fluid, and it has in recent years been characterized by considerable changes in vertical integration and disintegration (FRIEDMAN, 1977; WEST MIDLANDS ENTERPRISE BOARD, 1986). This makes it a good example of the changing relationships between non-specialist producers of services and service organizations.

Ten companies were interviewed in a survey of the motor vehicle aftermarket. These were selected to illustrate the key features of the industry in the West Midlands. The companies were chosen using industry sources (WAGSTAFF, 1986; KEYNOTE PUBLICA-TIONS, 1985; ICC BUSINESS RATIOS, 1986; EURO-MONITOR PUBLICATIONS, 1984) and research carried out by the West Midlands Enterprise Board (GRAY, 1986). Firms were asked to describe their main source of supply for physical distribution, transport, insurance, finance, legal, advertising and marketing, design, consultancy, computer, maintenance and training services. Changes in the supply of these services were documented, and these were related to trends in the industry as a whole. The results of the survey were sent to the interviewed firms. In some instances survey material was regarded as confidential, and in the presentation of these results the identity of the firm has been disguised. In other cases only selected examples of general trends have been presented to preserve confidentiality. The general validity of all the results has been tested by discussions with industry experts and a trade association.

Replacement 'original equipment' suppliers

The supply of replacement 'original equipment' (OE) or longer-life parts accounts for close to half of the aftermarket. These parts are largely fitted under warranty on newer vehicles through the franchise dealer network of the motor vehicle manufacturers. This sector of the West Midlands aftermarket industry was represented in the study by Motaquip, the aftermarket retailing arm of Peugeot Talbot.

The motor vehicle manufacturers obtain many parts from other manufacturers of OE components. Some of these manufacturers in turn have their own wholesale or retail outlets. GKN Autoparts, surveyed in this research, is one of four national aftermarket parts wholesalers, as well as a major components supplier of OE equipment. Quinton Hazell, also surveyed in this part of the aftermarket, have developed the quality and design expertise to become a significant OE manufacturer, while remaining the market leader in the supply of parts to the budget sector of the aftermarket.

The motor vehicle manufacturers rely on the demand for parts generated by the workshop business of their dealer network. This is threatened by the expansion of specialist quick-fit operators and retailers

supplying the DIY market. Until recently Peugeot Talbot have had the additional problem of a declining share of the new car market which has had a negative effect on sales of replacement parts.

Motor vehicle manufacturers have counteracted these trends by extending their activities in the aftermarket, supplying their own range of 'all makes' parts and accessories, most of which are bought-in. By developing and distributing an 'all makes' range of products through a brand name such as Motaquip, vehicle manufacturers can supply the smaller independent factors and garages and offer the trade the advantages of the purchasing power and contacts of a major manufacturer.

The non-OE 'budget sector'

The second part of the motor vehicle aftermarket, the 'budget sector', supplies lower cost parts primarily for fitting to older vehicles. Component manufacturers of 'original equipment' also supply this market but in addition there are a number of 'budget sector' manufacturers. Terry Fasteners, a smaller specialist company, was surveyed as an example of this part of the aftermarket.

Retail distribution in this sector is primarily through the independent garage trade, specialist fitting centres, high street shops and edge-of-town superstores. In the retail sector the expansion of new entrants such as B & Q into edge of town self-service retailing, the attempt of Halfords and Kwik-Fit to combine such developments with vehicle service centres and garage facilities and the efforts of others such as Asda to sell cars is breaking down boundaries in the trade. Halfords and Kwik-Fit were included to indicate trends in the retailing and fitting end of the industry.

The outlets of such companies can be supplied directly by component manufacturers, or by an intermediary such as a national factor or wholesaler. Brown Brothers, a major national factor, was included in the survey. Motaproducts Automotive, a smaller distributor acting as an intermediary for national factors and obtaining 20% of its business from overseas, was also included. Smaller wholesalers to the garage trade were represented by the Motor Factors Association.

As well as the retail sector, some factors supply parts and accessories to the major vehicle operators. SERCK Marston, a specialist factor of radiator systems, was chosen to represent this type of activity.

Clearly it is difficult to draw hard and fast distinctions between the different parts of the retail, wholesale and manufacturing sectors of the motor vehicle aftermarket and an appreciation of the interdependence of the industry is essential to an understanding of the dynamics of the changing demand for services. Wincanton Distribution Services Ltd, a

specialist transport company working for both component and vehicle manufacturers, was chosen to
indicate some of the interdependencies of the aftermarket.

THE ROLE OF SERVICES IN THE AFTERMARKET

Changes in demand

The recessions during the 1970s reduced demand for
both new cars and replacement parts. A growth of
import penetration in vehicles and components,
increases in the working life of some parts and reduced
service intervals for motor vehicles intensified the
downturn.

The increasing variety of model types and the
flexibility afforded to vehicle manufacturers by computer aided design and manufacture have also increased the diversity of products in the aftermarket. In
addition, the decline in inflation in the early 1980s has
altered the economics of stock holding. Stock appreciation has been replaced by depreciation, which
requires a more rapid and efficient system of distribution.

The aftermarket operators have responded to these
changes by reducing stock levels for individual
components. They, therefore, require a more rapid
response from suppliers to their orders. This has
resulted in shorter production set up and change over
times for manufacturers, and shorter lead-times for
wholesalers to deliver products to their customers.
Related to this, greater discipline is also required of
suppliers so that customer production schedules are
not disrupted by delays in the delivery of parts.

In addition, suppliers have been encouraged to
produce and deliver parts in smaller batches, and to
take on the responsibility for storage of stock in the
slower moving lines. They must also brief and train
the sales staff of the distributor or retailer concerning
the characteristics of their products and put more
informative instructions to the customer on the
packaging.

The increasing importance of service activities

These changes have required firms in the aftermarket
to be more sensitive to the changing needs of their
customers. Services have played a critical role in this:
1. The changing demands of customers require a
   greater emphasis on market research, marketing,
   advertising, selling, design and packaging services.
2. Training and personnel services have been used to
   improve the quality of staff and enhance the service
   provided to customers.
3. Computer technology has been used to increase the
   flexibility of production, improve information and
   control in the office and provide greater discipline
   in the distribution and supply of components.

MANUFACTURING FIRMS IN THE AFTERMARKET

The recent recession brought about a major change in
corporate behaviour and attitudes in companies
manufacturing for the aftermarket. Non-production
staff are now more closely scrutinized. The number of
layers in corporate structures have been reduced and
the remaining managers have become more accountable for the costs in their part of the business. The
number of non-production workers has been reduced
to match the reduced operations of the manufacturers,
and the remaining workers have become more capital
intensive.

The reduction in the operations of manufacturing
companies increased contracting out. As firms cut
back their production activities they could no longer
justify all their in-house support services and contracting out was used instead. A recent increase in demand
has resulted in the manufacturers' service needs
exceeding the reduced capacity of their in-house staff,
and contractors have been used as a means of dealing
with the fluctuating workflow. Managers did not
want to expand in-house services in case they lost
control over their staff.

The contracting out process has increased most in
blue-collar services which are more routine and easily
programmed. In addition, there is a temporary
element in the contracting out of many production-
related office services. Component manufacturers
have invested heavily in computer aided design and
manufacture to meet the increasingly variable production requirements of their customers. This has
increased their demand for specialist advisory and
training services related to the technology. But as the
manufacturers develop expertise in these areas, close
to the heart of their business, this externalization is
likely to be reduced.

WHOLESALE DISTRIBUTION IN THE AFTERMARKET

Prior to the recessions of the 1970s, manufacturing
companies were heavily involved in wholesale distribution as a means of protecting the outlets for their
products. The current character of the distribution
sector of the industry reflects the decisions of a number
of manufacturing companies to withdraw. Following
these re-organizations, a small number of specialist
national factors have emerged which are responsible
for approximately 30% of the 'free' wholesale business in the aftermarket.

The history of GKN Autoparts is an interesting
example of these developments. Now a specialist
operator in the industrial services division of GKN,
the organization evolved in a haphazard manner
during the 1970s. The manufacturing companies
Vandervell and Sheepridge Engineering were ac-

quired by GKN and both incidentally possessed distribution outlets, namely Replacement Services and Advanced Motor Supplies. Later, GKN acquired Armstrong Engineering and with this came Armstrong Automative, a distribution outlet. When the recession in manufacturing had been weathered, GKN turned its attention towards its loosely integrated distribution outlets and questioned their future in a difficult market. Ultimately it was decided that for their distribution operation to be viable a full national system of branches was required and the opportunity was taken to acquire Godfrey Holmes and Affiliated Factors, the distribution arm of Smiths Industries. These have now been welded into a unitary organization.

A significant feature of the evolution of such firms in the distribution sector of the aftermarket has been their progressive specialization. One company identifies specific market areas, namely paint and body equipment, vehicle workshop supplies and garage forecourt services, and concentrates on factoring products in these areas. Another identifies market niches for each of its branch outlets based on extensive customer and market research and focuses within its broader product range on those products which sell well.

Leading on from this, wholesale distributors have placed a greater emphasis on the quality of service supplied. This includes satisfying customer demands in terms of the quality, availability and speed of delivery of parts. As a result, distribution companies have internalized related services within their company to improve their control of this part of their business.

For example, the distribution end of the aftermarket has had a reputation for low pay, non-unionized and poorly skilled labour. Improving the quality of service provided in the business requires a more highly skilled workforce. New training programmes are usually carried out in-house because it is a high corporate priority.

One organization which had contracted out the design of the packaging for its products regarded this as unsatisfactory because the trend towards increased DIY on the part of motorists meant that the colour, style and instructions for the fitting of the product were critical selling points. External suppliers were unable to satisfactorally reflect the image and culture of the company which must be incorporated in the packaging for it to sell well, so the business was brought in-house.

Another distributor supplied a more complete service to its customers, using the provision of professional services as a means of 'locking-in' customers to the company. In return for purchasing their products, garages received free consultancy on how to design their workshop, how to charge for their business and how to manage the company. To cater

for this new development a special team of consultants had been set up at head office by the distribution company.

All distributors are becoming increasingly sensitive to market changes. Marketing and selling tasks have been re-emphasized. Distributors feel they know their market better than any supplier of services and, therefore, are inclined to carry out these tasks themselves.

Similarly, the computer service function, which is central to the storage and distribution of stock is carried out largely in-house. A strong software department and distribution systems team are necessary to maintain the smooth day-to-day delivery of the products of the company and to develop the software necessary to monitor the flow of stock both of which are critical to the profitability of the business.

RETAILERS IN THE AFTERMARKET

Changes in management practice have been less dramatic in large retailers than elsewhere in the market and have often occurred as a consequence of expansion. Local managers have been made more responsible for the operation of their sales outlet and intermediate levels of management have been pruned. In Halfords, the regional level of management has been reduced and, in Kwik-Fit, the regional and area structure has been combined into a division. The impact on the organization of in-house services has been muted, however, and there have been few transfers of staff because the regional level was not strong prior to reorganization.

Considerable resources have been devoted to the in-house development of computer monitoring of storage, delivery and sales of parts. A sophisticated computer system of stock control and sales, providing up-to-date and detailed information, permits flexibility in pricing policy. It also allows the company to minimize the number of parts in the firm and to reduce the cost of stockholding.

The retailers have also expanded into the distribution of parts, not only because of the stock requirements of a large company, but also because seen from their point of view the supply and distribution system in the aftermarket is too fragmented. By controlling distribution from a central distribution centre and sourcing from major manufacturers and factors, they can obtain greater control of the supply of stock to the company.

In recent years, productivity exercises designed to improve the efficiency of distribution have been introduced and this is encouraging contracting out. The warehouse in each Kwik-Fit division has been reduced to catering for stocks of imported parts. Suppliers are now usually made responsible for delivery. Such an arrangement is not practical in Halfords, however, due to the greater variety of parts required and the larger number of suppliers. However, there is a possibility that the distribution activities of the firm will be set up as a separate company. Greater independence and specialization would, it is believed, produce further productivity improvements.

Other blue-collar services (e.g. cleaning and transport) and routine services such as payroll are largely contracted out. But for office services the retailers occupy a position somewhere between the manufacturers and the distributors. In contrast to manufacturing, market-related services such as advertising, selling and store design are largely internalized but there is a greater tendency for wholesale distributors to externalize management consultancy and market research.

CORPORATE REORGANIZATION AND SERVICE LOCATION
In-house services

Changes in the location of services evolved from the reorganization of service production described above. The relocation of in-house services reflected the rationalization of non-production workers in the manufacturing sector, and the continued growth of retailers less affected by the recession and the growth of import penetration in motor vehicle components. The contraction of non-production staff in manufacturing companies as their operations were reduced was substantial. One company, for example, had experienced a 30% decline in staff in the last five years. The bulk of Quinton Hazell and Peugeot Talbot's operations were located in the West Midlands conurbation so contraction was concentrated there. But contraction was also associated with locational change. Peugeot Talbot, for example, relocated their parts operation from Birmingham to Tile Hill near Coventry because the site in Birmingham was too large and not well suited to distribution operations. Tile Hill in contrast offered a more suitable site close to the centre of the company's operations.

In retailing, the West Midlands benefited from the expansion of Kwik-Fit and Halfords. Kwik-Fit expanded its turnover by 58% and Halfords by 42% in current prices over the last four years. In Halfords this was reflected nationally in an increase of more than 1,000 jobs over the same period. Increased computerization and rationalization of head-office procedures, however, reduced employment in Halford's Redditch base in the south Midlands. Head-office employment declined from 279 to 252 jobs in the last five years. The distribution operations of the company were increasingly concentrated at the Redditch site because the economics of distribution (e.g. larger vehicles and reduced transport costs) favoured a centralized operation. Even so productivity exercises reduced employment in distribution at Redditch from 253 to 238 jobs

over the last five years. Employment growth in in-house support services in the West Midlands was associated with new edge-of-town superstores, eight of which have been established. These sites are increasingly being used not only as sales outlets but also as staging posts in the distribution system.

The impact of contracting out on service location

The (possibly temporary) externalization by manufacturers of technical, advisory and computer services related to the production process produced a leakage of service demand up the urban hierarchy because manufacturers used companies with a national reputation, and these were usually based close to the capital. In contrast, the growth in contracting out of distribution services resulted in *in-situ* reductions of employment within manufacturing companies and a smaller intra-regional shift in jobs to locations often on the edge of the urban area and offering better motorway access.

Lucas Electrical's decision to contract out its transport operations to Wincanton Distribution Services resulted in job loss at the former's Birmingham factory because the supplier was able to introduce newer vehicles which required less maintenance and repair. The supplier already served Austin Rover, a customer of Lucas, and was able to a large degree to integrate both operations. Although the maintenance operations at Lucas were reduced, many drivers remained with their existing employer, and simply used Wincanton vehicles. Job losses were also muted by the establishment of a Wincanton depot at the Lucas site. There was, though, a transfer of employment from Lucas, and the Wincanton operation at Darlaston employs thirteen people, some of whom had formerly been employed at Birmingham.

Reorganization in the distribution sector as manufacturers have reduced their involvement has tended to favour smaller towns. For example prior to the GKN Autoparts re-organization in the early 1980s the distributor had: (1) a branch network of approximately 250 sites grouped very loosely into four regions; (2) three distribution centres in Weedon (Northamptonshire), Doncaster and Peterborough employing approximately 40 people in each; and (3) head offices in Lincoln (65 jobs), Doncaster (60 jobs) and Nottingham (80 jobs).

The branch network was reduced to 200 sites by closing those with overlapping market areas and little prospect for growth. Distribution was concentrated in Weedon which employed an extra ten to twenty people. It had more modern facilities, greater scope for expansion and the best location relative to the motorway network. In contrast, a greenfield site was chosen for the head-office facility. The existing head offices were all closed and a new Banbury (Oxfordshire) office established employing 100–110 people.

This made it easier for the rationalized company to develop a new corporate ethos, rather than simply adopting the head-office approach to the business of one of the original firms. Banbury was chosen as the location for the head office because it was a short distance from the distribution centre at Weedon. It was also relatively close to the Midlands, the main centre for aftermarket suppliers, and it would have good motorway access with the extension of the M40.

The merger of SERCK and Marston Radiators in 1984 produced another major reorganization the results of which reflected the differing expertise of the two companies. Together the two organizations employed 1,850 people. But not all of the business was profitable, and the workforce was reduced to 1,200 partly through a reduction of the branch network of distribution outlets. Marston Radiators manufactured radiator core for the aftermarket from a base in Narborough (Leicestershire) and this was distributed from there to a national branch network. Although SERCK had a small manufacturing facility at Redditch its main strength was in distribution through its Redditch distribution centre. Following the merger the head-office and distribution functions of Marston were transferred to the headquarters of SERCK at Redditch, and approximately 70–80 people were made redundant in Narborough. In contrast, the manufacturing facilities at Redditch were transferred to Narborough and the sister company's facilities were adapted to produce OE radiators.

The subsequent internalization of office services within the distribution sector has re-inforced the effect of the locational transfers described above. Contracts placed with suppliers usually located in major cities have been replaced by in-house service provision in the head office of the distribution firm often in a less major centre. Those services affected by internalization (sophisticated office services) are also those in which there is some leakage of service demand out of the Midlands largely to the South East where major national suppliers are based. It can be argued therefore that internalization has produced a gain in employment in the Midlands at the expense of suppliers located elsewhere.

VERTICAL INTEGRATION AND CONTRACTING OUT PROCESSES

The survey of the motor vehicle aftermarket highlights the way in which changes in the internalization and externalization of services play an important role in locational change. The following section highlights the factors which influenced internalization and externalization decisions in the aftermarket.

This is not straightforward. The insights derived from existing work are limited by the fact that much of it concentrates on physical production activities. Developing detailed distinctions between contractor and subcontractor, which are an important feature of this literature, are of limited value as far as services in the motor vehicle aftermarket are concerned. In this study, contractors have been taken to include outside firms who supply, to a specification, inputs (either directly or through an intermediary) to the production process.

RUBERY and WILKINSON, 1981; HOLMES, 1986; and IMRIE, 1986, identify three broad sets of factors which influence the internalization–externalization decision. It is argued that different parts of the production process will require different scales of production to be economic, and depending on the demand of a company for a particular product or service, differences in internalization and contracting out will emerge. Fluctuations in product markets, by altering a firm's demand for an activity, can also lead to changes in internalization or contracting out. For example, firms may contract out activities where demand is uncertain to smooth-out irregularities in their own production process. Labour demand and supply characteristics are also significant. Differences, for example, in the cost, availability, skills or unionization of labour forces in in-house operations and supplier firms can influence the dynamics of internalization and externalization.

Many of these considerations were significant in the aftermarket, but most important was the perceived expertise of the firm in its core business and the resulting skills of its staff. The following factors influenced the internalization–externalization decision:

1. The significance of the service to the company, with services which were either vital to business or commercially confidential tending to be carried out in-house.
2. The specialist knowledge or expertise required to carry out the service. If knowledge or skills held by the user were important in the service, or if the user had considerable expertise in a particular area then internalization was preferred.
3. The frequency with which a service was required; with infrequently used services being contracted out because they did not justify an in-house capacity.
4. The predictability of a service contract, with unpredictable service needs tending to be internalized and routine or programmed services externalized.
5. The cost of a service, with an external contract having the advantage of a clear measure of expenditure.

In the aftermarket, the nature of in-house and external service provision and the balance between them changed in response to: (1) changes in the demand for motor components which affected the requirements of the companies for service products; (2) the introduction of computer technology which affected the expertise, skills and costs of production of in-house operations and the specialist supply sector; and (3) changes in management.

The importance of these factors differed between different parts of the aftermarket. A fall in the demand for UK manufactured products and resulting cost pressures encouraged specialization and retrenchment in non-production activities in the manufacturing sector. This increased the contracting out of services, both because it was no longer economic to provide some services in-house given the reduction in the manufacturers' operations, and because using external suppliers was believed to reduce costs. Such contracting out was further encouraged by the introduction of more flexible computerized methods of production which required support services in which manufacturers had little expertise.

Wholesale distribution was transformed by the growth in contracting out by manufacturers, and a small number of national suppliers increased their hold on the business. In this sector, quality of service was seen as vital to competitiveness, and where external suppliers were believed to have insufficient expertise or knowledge of the industry, internalization of office services increased.

In retailing, which was less affected by recession, less dramatic increases in contracting out resulted largely from changes in management practice, which encouraged the view that outside suppliers of services were likely to be more efficient than in-house operations. In contrast, retailers also expanded into physical distribution because of the fragmentation of the component supply industry, though this development was curtailed by the rationalization of their in-house distribution during the 1980s.

Throughout the aftermarket the introduction of computer equipment changed the balance between internalization and externalization of services by enhancing the capacity of service workers to carry out new tasks and allowing companies to develop new services, but at the same time creating new demands for external support services.

The result was complex and dynamic shifts in the source of service production. Peugeot Talbot, for example, initially carried out manually the production of its catalogue for the Motaquip range of parts and simply contracted out the final printing of the booklet. Developments in the processing and printing of text using computers encouraged it to contract out the production of the catalogue to a data processing firm which could store the catalogue on file, update it annually and then print the document. This proved unsatisfactory because revisions to the document were not always communicated successfully to the computer services company. Peugeot Talbot in the meantime had updated its in-house computer and was therefore able to take back responsibility for the storage and updating of the catalogue and simply

deposited the final version with the computer firm for printing. In the immediate future, however, further updating by the company of its computer printing facilities would provide the capacity to carry out the whole catalogue in-house and then full internalization would again be a possibility.

In a similar vein, one company contracted out the data processing of its vehicle tachograph returns so that it could analyse driver performance, highlight ways of improving driver productivity and identify incidents of illegality. The company was unhappy with the incomplete data supplied by the computer firm and so they decided to specify their data processing requirements more clearly. Having done this it was realized that this framework offered the company an opportunity to sell a new service to vehicle operators. New computer equipment was purchased to process the tachograph returns and a new tie up with a computer service firm which could provide more specialized computing was arranged (the computer service firm was restricted from offering the service independently themselves) and the company sold a new tachograph monitoring service to transport operators.

Unlike the other processes described here, the locational outcome of these changes was not so clear. However, the examples above reinforce the view that, in the aftermarket, firms were not simply contracting out their service needs. Many services remain internalized and for some internalization was increasing. Both examples also open up the possibility that computer technology will allow non-specialist service producers outside major service centres to develop their in-house service capacity.

But we should be careful not to generalize too readily from these results, because a wide variety of factors influence internalization and externalization processes in services (PEAT MARWICK McLINTOCK, 1988) and the importance of these will differ between industries, places and time periods (HOLMES, 1986).

CONCLUSIONS

Since, despite reorganization, many services continue to be internalized by firms at head office, it follows that the established view of the relationship between corporate structure and the location of services, which highlights the role of head-office control functions in the uneven geography of services, retains some value.

However, the conventional description of the role of corporate structure in the space economy with its emphasis on changes in ownership and control does not explain the dynamics of service location very well. It does not do justice to the diversity of change in service location in provincial parts of the UK, nor does it take account of the way in which corporate structures have changed. Generalizations about the dynamics of service development on the basis of the location of head offices or branch plants can easily be inappropriate. The West Midlands did not, for example, benefit in terms of employment growth from the location there of the Halford's head office even though the company as a whole was growing. The contracting out services and in-house productivity exercises produced a decline of head-office employment. It was the expansion of branch operating units in the West Midlands which expanded services there.

A different approach is clearly needed to understand the changes in corporate structures described in this paper. In the motor vehicle aftermarket, at least, an analysis of the processes of integration and externalization of service activity by organizations presents an appropriate framework within which to understand changes in service location during the 1980s. It highlights the interdependence of service and other activities, identifies shifts in provision between service and non-service organizations, acknowledges the diversity of corporate structures and provides a sophisticated account of the way in which they change in response to external events.

The conclusion of this study—that manufacturing industry is contracting out technical services to firms close to the capital—supports the work of CHRISTOPHERSON and STORPER, 1986, and STORPER and CHRISTOPHERSON, 1987. However, several other results are at odds with their view that organizational changes are encouraging the centralization of services. In contrast to the results reported above on white-collar services, in physical distribution services, where the location of goods production is more important, the decentralization of services to smaller town locations with good motorway access to manufacturing and retail outlets seemed to be occurring. This has encouraged local agencies to invest in this sector in the West Midlands (MARSHALL, 1988). In addition, vertical disintegration, though important, was ba-

lanced in the aftermarket to some degree by the internalization of services by non-specialist producers. This appeared to offer scope for the development of in-house services by dynamic companies in provincial Britain. An important conclusion of this study is, therefore, that a judicious understanding of the processes of vertical integration and disintegration could offer new opportunities for regional agencies to develop services in provincial parts of the UK. Such options are all too readily ignored in established research on corporate structures which emphasizes the need to decentralize head-office functions to provincial regions or change the function of branch plants, both of which are very difficult to achieve.

Many questions, however, remain unanswered by this paper. For example, to what extent will the limited recovery of manufacturing in provincial regions more deeply affected by recession than the West Midlands circumscribe the new options for service development described above. Or assuming that the rationalization of head-office, divisional and regional management described in this paper is more widespread, what impact will it have on the space economy? Is the contracting out process described here influenced by variations in the local supply of services, and if so might it be constrained by the truncated service supply sector in some provincial regions? Where in aggregate are those dynamic companies which are internalising new services likely to be located? Such questions clearly demonstrate that the time has come for a thorough reassessment of the role of corporate structures in uneven development.

Acknowledgement—This paper is based on research carried out for the West Midlands Enterprise Board. The author wishes to acknowledge the kind co-operation of the Board and the companies involved in the research in the publication of the results. The views expressed are those of the author.

REFERENCES

ALLEN J. (1988). The geographies of service, in MASSEY D. and ALLEN J. (Ed.) *Uneven Redevelopment: Cities and Regions in Transition.* Open University Press, Milton Keynes.

ASHIEM B. T. (1988) Innovation diffusion and small firms: between the agency of lifeworld and the structure of systems, paper presented at the Regional Science Summer Institute, Arco, Italy, 17–23 July.

ATKINSON J. (1984) Flexibility, uncertainty and manpower management, Report 89, Institute for Manpower Studies, University of Sussex, Brighton.

BESSANT J., JONES D. and LAMMING R. (1984) *The West Midlands Automobile Components Industry.* West Midlands Enterprise Board, Birmingham.

BLACKBURN P., COOMBS R. and GREEN K. (1985) *Technology, Economic Growth and the Labour Process.* St Martin's Press, New York.

CHRISTOPHERSON S. and STORPER M. (1986) The city as studio: the world as backlot: the impact of vertical disintegration on the location of the motion picture industry, *Environ. Plann. D* **4**, 305–20.

CLUTTERBUCK D. (1985) *New Patterns of Work.* Gower, Aldershot, Hants.

COOMBS R. and JONES D. (1988) Alternative successors to Fordism, paper presented at the Information, Society and Space conference at the Swiss Federal Institute of Technology, Zurich, January.

CRUM R. E. and GUDGIN G. (1977) Non-production activities in UK manufacturing industry, Regional Policy Series 3, Commission of the European Economic Communities, Brussels.

150 *J. N. Marshall*

ESTALL R. C. (1985) Stock control in manufacturing: the just-in-time system and its locational implications, *Area* **17**, 129–33.
EUROMONITOR PUBLICATIONS LTD (1984) *The UK Motor Components Industry, 1984.* EPL, London.
EVANS A. W. (1973) The location of the headquarters of industrial companies, *Urban Studies* **10**, 387–95.
FRIEDMAN A. (1977) *Industry and Labour: Class Struggle at Work and Monopoly Capitalism.* Macmillan, London.
GILLESPIE A. and WILLIAMS H. (1988) Telematics and the reorganisation of corporate space, paper presented at the International Symposium on Telematics Transportation and Spatial Development, The Hague, April 14–15.
GODDARD J. B. (1979) Office location in urban and regional development, in DANIELS P. W. (Ed.) *Spatial Patterns of Office Growth and Location,* pp. 37–62. Wiley, London.
GODDARD J. B. and SMITH I. J. (1978) Changes in corporate control in the British urban system, *Environ. Plann. A* **10**, 1,073–84.
GRAY P. (1986) *Unipart and the Aftermarket.* West Midlands Enterprise Board, Birmingham.
HARVEY D.and SCOTT A. J. (forthcoming) The practice of human geography: theory and empirical specificity in the transition from Fordism to flexible accumulation, in MACMILLAN W. (Ed.) *Remodelling Geography.* Basil Blackwell, Oxford.
HOLMES J. (1986) The organisation and locational structure of production subcontracting, in SCOTT A. J. and STORPER M. (Eds.) *Production, Work. Territory,* pp. 80–106. George Allen and Unwin, Boston.
HYMER S. H. (1975) The multinational corporation and the law of uneven development, in RADICE H. (Ed.) *International Firms and Modern Imperialism,* pp. 29–60. Penguin Books, Harmondsworth, Middlesex.
ICC BUSINESS RATIOS (1986) *Motor Component and Accessories Manufacturers.* ICC Business Ratios, London.
IMRIE R. F. (1986) Work decentralisation from large to small firms: a preliminary analysis of subcontracting, *Environ. Plann. A* **18**, 949–65.
KAPLINSKI R. (1984) *Automation the Technology and Society.* Longman, London.
LEIGH R. and NORTH D. J. (1978) Regional aspects of acquisition activity in British manufacturing industry, *Reg. Studies* **12**, 227–45.
KEYNOTE PUBLICATIONS LTD (1985) *Autoparts: An Industrial Sector Overview.* Keynote, London.
LIPIETZ A. (1986) New tendencies in the international division of labour: regimes of accumulation and modes of regulation, in SCOTT A. J. and STORPER M. (Eds.) *Production, Work, Territory.* George Allen and Unwin, Boston.
MARSHALL J. N. (1983) Business service activities in British provincial conurbations, *Environ. Plann. A* **25**, 1,343–60.
MARSHALL J. N. (1988) *Producer Services and the Manufacturing Sector in the West Midlands.* West Midlands Enterprise Board, Birmingham.
MARSHALL J. N. *et al.* (1988) *Services and Uneven Development.* Oxford University Press, Oxford.
MASSEY D. (1979) In what sense a regional problem, *Reg. Studies* **13**, 233–43.
MASSEY D. (1984) *Spatial Divisions of Labour.* Macmillan, London.
MILLER D. (1983) The role of the motor car industry in the West Midlands regional economy, *Reg. Studies* **17**, 53–6.
PARSONS G. (1972) The giant manufacturing corporations and balanced regional growth in Britain, *Area* **4**, 99–103.
PEAT MARWICK MCLINTOCK (1988) The 'cost of non-Europe' for business services, Research on the 'Cost of Non-Europe', Basic Findings, Volume 8, Commission of the European Communities, Brussels.
PERRONS D. C. (1981) The role of Ireland in the new international division of labour: a proposed framework for regional analysis, *Reg. Studies* **15**, 81–100.
PERRONS D. C. (1986) Unequal integration in global Fordism: the case of Ireland, in SCOTT A. J. and STORPER M. (Ed.) *Production, Work, Territory,* pp. 246–64. George Allen and Unwin, Boston.
PIORE M. and SABEL C. (1984) *The Second Industrial Divide.* Basic Books, New York.
RAJAN A. (1987) *Services: A New Industrial Revolution?.* Butterworth, London.
RAJAN A. and PEARSON R. (1986) *UK Occupation and Employment: Trends to 1990.* Butterworth, London.
RUBERY J. and WILKINSON F. (1981). Outwork and segmented labour markets, in WILKINSON F. (Ed.) *The Dynamics of Labour Market Segmentation,* pp. 115–32. Academic Press, London.
SAYER A. (1985) Industry and space: a sympathetic critique of radical research, *Environ. Plann. D* **3**, 3–29.
SAYER A. (1986) Industrial location on a world scale: the case of the semiconductor industry, in SCOTT A. J. and STORPER M. (Eds.) *Production, Work, Territory,* pp. 107–23. George Allen and Unwin, Boston.
SCOTT A. J. and STORPER M. (Eds.) (1986) *Production, Work, Territory.* George Allen and Unwin, Boston.
STORPER M. and CHRISTOPHERSON S. (1987) Flexible specialisation and regional industrial agglomerations: the case of the US motion picture industry, *Ann. Ass. Am. Geogr.* **77**, 104–17.
WAGSTAFF I. (1986) The UK market for replacement car parts, Automotive Report No 5, Economist Intelligence Unit, London.
WATTS H. D. (1979) *The Branch Plant Economy.* Longman, London.
WATTS H. D. (1980) *The Large Industrial Enterprise.* Croom Helm, London.
WESTAWAY E. J. (1974) The spatial hierarchy of business organisations and its implications for the British urban system, *Reg. Studies* **8**, 145–55.
WEST MIDLANDS ENTERPRISE BOARD (1986) *The Motor Vehicle and Component Industries.* West Midlands Enterprise Board, Birmingham.

[12]

PAPERS OF THE REGIONAL SCIENCE ASSOCIATION, VOL. 67, 1989, pp. 13–27

PRODUCER SERVICES AND REGIONAL DEVELOPMENT: A POLICY-ORIENTED PERSPECTIVE

William J. Coffey
Département d'études urbaines
Université du Québec à Montréal
C.P. 8888, Succ. A
Montréal, Québec H3C 3P8

Mario Polèse
INRS-Urbanisation
Université du Québec
3465, rue Durocher
Montréal, Québec H2X 2C6

ABSTRACT There is a certain optimism among policy makers concerning the ability of producer services, viewed as locationally flexible, to stimulate economic growth in lagging regions. Four issues related to the location of producer services are used to critically examine this notion: (1) observed centralization and decentralization trends, (2) the influence of corporate ownership and control, (3) intrafirm functional separation, and (4) the impact of telecommunications technology. Producer service growth has not benefited central and peripheral regions equally. The empirical and conceptual evidence presented suggests that these activities have little positive impact upon lagging regions. Some essential elements of a regional strategy involving producer services are proposed.

1. INTRODUCTION

Since the latter part of the 1970s, in both academic and government milieux, considerable optimism has been generated concerning the potential of service industries to stimulate economic development in lagging or peripheral regions. A now widely held view suggests that service industries (along with high-technology activities, in whatever manner that the latter may be defined) will ultimately aid in the solution of the longstanding economic development problems of disadvantaged regions. At the root of this optimism is the perception of these types of activities as relatively footloose; that is, they are free of the locational constraints that have made such regions relatively unattractive to investment in traditional forms of manufacturing. Slowly, during the early and middle 1980s, government administrative structures and policy initiatives in various countries and at various levels have begun to acknowledge explicitly the perceived capacity of service industries to influence regional economic problems (Marshall and Bachtler 1987).

In light of the growing interest on the part of decision makers in this sector of the economy, this paper critically examines the potential role of a specific set of service activities — producer services — in regional development. In carrying out this examination, we rely upon two principal sources: a broad range of empirical and conceptual research that we have undertaken in this area in recent years (for example, Coffey and Polèse 1986, 1987a, 1987b, 1987c, 1988; Coffey and McRae 1989), and the fairly substantial international literature on this topic that has arisen over the past decade (and which we review in the course of our

14   PAPERS OF THE REGIONAL SCIENCE ASSOCIATION, VOL. 67, 1989

discussion). This analysis is undertaken from a policy perspective: it seeks, generally, to evaluate whether policies targeted at producer service activities are likely to be effective instruments of regional development and, more specifically, to explore some of the characteristics that could potentially enhance the impact of such policies. Although most of our observations are directly related to the Canadian context, they have, in our view, a broader degree of applicability.

Our analysis begins with an examination of the role of producer services in a regional development context. This is followed by an investigation of a set of issues related to the key issue of locational flexibility, and then by an exploration of existing and potential policy interventions involving producer services and regional development.

2. THE ROLE OF PRODUCER SERVICES IN REGIONAL DEVELOPMENT

It is the set of activities referred to as *producer services,* those intermediate demand functions that serve as inputs into the production of goods or of other services (and that, as such, are perhaps more correctly characterized as indirect elements of the production process), that has the greatest potential for stimulating the economic development of lagging regions. There are four reasons why this is so.

The first reason is that producer services comprise the most rapidly growing sector in the majority of developed economies. In Canada, over the period 1971 to 1981, employment in producer services experienced a growth rate of 141.2 percent, nearly twice that of its closest competitor, the finance, insurance, and real estate (FIRE) sector (Coffey and McRae 1989). In the United States, 25 percent of GNP now originates from producer services alone, the equivalent of the portion of GNP that results from the physical production of goods (Noyelle and Stanback 1984). This increased demand for producer services is, in turn, a function of the changing organizational structure of goods-producing activities, and of the enhanced role of product innovation and of market differentiation. Modern economies are witnessing important transformations in *what* types of goods are being produced and in *how* these goods are produced. It must also be recognized that, due to the strategies of individual firms in internalizing or externalizing certain management-related functions (the overall trends in the organizational structure of firms being to promote increasing externalization), the extent of the growth of free-standing producer service activities may represent an overestimation. For example, when a manufacturing firm decides to replace internalized accounting or legal functions with those purchased from external producer service firms, the extent of the producer service *function* in the economy has not grown, although the statistics show a net shift from manufacturing towards producer service employment. This has led some authors (e.g., McRae 1985) to argue that the observed growth of producer services (and, more generally, of the entire range of service activities) is largely a statistical artifact. On the other hand, it can be argued that the producer service *function* (as opposed to *sector*) is underrepresented due to the internalization of these activities in many goods-producing firms.

The second reason why producer services are so important from a development perspective is that they can constitute an important element of the economic base of a region. For many years, services had been viewed in the framework of the traditional Fisher-Clark typology of economic activity which relegated them to a "residual" category composed of "nonproductive" activities. It is now widely recognized, however, that a significant proportion of producer services, in particular, must be regarded as basic activity in that they are not only exportable (tradeable) but also highly responsive to external demand. Producer services have emerged as one of the fastest growing components of both interregional and international trade. Canadian-based consulting and professional services, alone, accounted for $987 million worth of international exports in 1985, representing a 24-fold increase over the 1969 value (Statistics Canada 1988). Further, at the beginning of this decade, legal services established themselves as the principal export of the New York City economy (Ginzberg and Vojta 1981). Export-oriented business and corporate services grew at an annual rate of 10.1 percent between 1977 and 1986, attaining a total of over $50 billion in 1986, and accounting for approximately two-thirds of New York City's export earnings (Drennan 1987).

The third reason follows from the previous point: producer services *may* be characterized by a spatial distribution that is significantly different from the population-based ones of the range of residentiary (principally consumer) services (Marquand 1983; Coffey and McRae 1989). Due to their potential tradeability, producer services do not face the same constraint of physical proximity to their market. In theory, the less populated, peripheral regions should be able to develop export-oriented producer services.

The fourth, and perhaps most important reason, is that through their role in investment, innovation, and technological change, producer services may contribute to spatial variation in the economic development process (Marshall 1988). They may be regarded as playing a strategic role ("the locus of competitive advantage," according to Walker 1985) within production systems of which they constitute one part of the overall division of labor. The key position that producer services occupies is essentially based upon the contribution that they can make to promoting or facilitating overall economic change and adaption. In an age of rapid technological change, certain producer services provide the source and mediators of that change (Marquand 1983). Marshall, Damesick, and Wood (1985) argue that producer services are an important part of the supply capacity of an economy: they influence its adjustment in response to changing economic circumstances; and they may help to adapt skills, attitudes, products, and processes to changes, or to reduce the structural, organizational, managerial, and informational barriers to adjustment.

In concluding this examination of the role of producer services in regional development, we make the obvious but important observation that the ability of these activities, or of any other element of the economy, to influence the level of economic development in a region is a function of the definition of development employed. If development is defined modestly in terms of incremental job creation, it may well be that public sector functions or consumer services (demand for which, in lagging regions, is perhaps largely financed by transfer payments) will be as effective an instrument as producer services. On the other hand, if development is measured in a more rigorous manner involving considerations of structural change, productivity increase, market-earned income, and so forth, producer services stand alone among service activities as a possible focus for policy intervention.

3. TRENDS IN THE LOCATION OF PRODUCER SERVICES

Where the subject of producer services and regional development is concerned, the notion of *location* is of prime importance. *Where* are these high-order services located? where are they likely to be located in the future? and what factors govern their spatial distribution? It is only those activities that are characterized by some degree of locational flexibility ("footlooseness") that are likely to enhance the economic development prospects of peripheral regions. The principal issue that needs to be examined is, therefore, that of whether high-order producer services, those capable of contributing to the development of a region, are sufficiently footloose to locate in peripheral regions or, at least, outside of large metropolitan areas. This section addresses this issue by examining four of its individual elements: (1) centralization, intrametropolitan deconcentration, and interregional decentralization tendencies; (2) the role of corporate ownership and control; (3) the spatial separation of functions within firms; and (4) the impact of telecommunications technology.

Centralization, Deconcentration, and Decentralization

In their research on the location of service industries in the Canadian space-economy, Coffey and Polèse (1987a, 1987c, 1988) and Coffey and McRae (1989) have found a high level of spatial centralization of producer service activities in the largest urban centers. Over the period 1971 to 1981, approximately 80 percent of employment growth in producer services occurred in metropolitan areas. (While the highest *rates* of growth were found in rural regions and smaller urban places, these high growth rates translated into relatively small absolute change. Metropolitan areas, on the other hand, experienced more modest growth rates that manifested themselves in large absolute increases.) Further, more than one-half of the remaining employment growth (approximately 12 of the residual 20 percent) was located within the urban fields (a 100-km radius) of these metropolitan centers. Using shift-share and location quotient analysis, Coffey and Polèse (1988) and Coffey and McRae (1989) conclude that where producer service employment growth did occur beyond the boundaries of metropolitan areas, it was principally in the form of deconcentration (i.e., extended suburbanization), rather than a true decentralization into peripheral areas. The veritable decentralization of producer services that did take place during this period was closely related to the decentralization of traditional forms of manufacturing activity and to increased natural resource exploitation in rural areas. Further, this decentralization appears primarily to have involved standardized and routinized functions.

Gillespie and Green (1987) report similar results in the British context: a centralization at the national scale of producer service employment within metropolitan areas and, at the intrametropolitan scale, a relative deconcentration within large urban regions. They, too, cite the varying locational trends of more and less standardized functions. Centralization trends in the location of producer services are also reported in Britain by Marshall (1982, 1985a, 1985b, 1988), Howells (1987), and Howells and Green (1986); in France by Philippe (1984) and Philippe and Monnoyer (1985); in the U.S. by Stanback et al. (1981), Noyelle and Stanback (1984), and Beyers (1988); and across a range of countries by Daniels (1985), Moss (1987), Cohen (1981), and Hall (1985).

Although an examination of the locational factors underlying these observed centralization trends in producer services is beyond the scope of the present paper, the principal determinants may be readily identified. Coffey and Polèse (1986, 1987c) have produced a model (derived both inductively and deductively) of producer service location that recognizes the contribution of three factors: a pool of highly skilled labor, complementary economic activities (largely office functions, financial institutions, and complementary services), and the costs involved in "delivering" the "product" to market. The relative importance of the first two elements to an individual establishment is related to its preference for the internalization or the externalization of knowledge-related inputs. This choice, in turn, is a function of considerations related to levels of confidentiality, standardization, and the uncertainty of the economic environment under which the establishment operates. Taken together, these may be considered as externalities or, more precisely, economies of urbanization, which reduce the transaction costs of producer service firms. An additional factor also may be significant. Although more difficult to measure, a strong argument may be advanced concerning the role of the environment (broadly defined to include social, cultural, political, and physical elements) in attracting the skilled labor and complementary activities referred to above. In this sense, a locality's level of public investment may be a significant factor.

Corporate Ownership and Control

The spatial pattern of corporate headquarters imposes a marked centralizing influence upon the location of producer services. More precisely, there is a high level of locational correspondence between producer service firms and the head (or divisional) offices of major corporations (Wheeler 1988). There is strong evidence to suggest that headquarters and divisional offices purchase from sources in their direct proximity an important proportion of those services consumed by their various establishments, irrespective of the geographical location of the latter (Marshall 1982, 1985b).

As corporate control and its associated spatial division of administrative functions tend to be highly concentrated in a small number of large metropolitan areas (Noyelle and Stanback 1984; Stanback et al. 1981; Daniels 1985; Cohen 1981; Moss 1987), it follows that the demand for producer services will be concentrated similarly. Therefore, an urban center well endowed with head office establishments is in a particularly favorable position in terms of the level of demand generated for local, high-order services.

The spatially proximate linkages between head office functions and the external producer service sector, and the resulting concentration of these activities within the largest metropolitan areas, are usually explained by some variant of contact theory (Tornqvist 1970). Face-to-face contacts reflect qualitative characteristics that cannot be reproduced by long-distance communication (Goddard 1975).

Coffey and Polèse (1986) argue that the linkages between head offices and business services are becoming even stronger and more self-reinforcing than in the past. The growth of industrial concentration and corporate enterprise in itself results in a gravitation of head office activities towards the largest metropolitan areas, with their diversity of producer service firms. As firms increase in size and product range, so their need for nonstandardized and non-industry-specific services increases; these needs are increasingly being met by external, specialized producer service firms.

The other side of the corporate control equation involves the impact upon the demand for producer services in nonmetropolitan regions. To the extent that the establishments of multiregional or multinational firms that are located in a peripheral region channel their purchases of producer services through a headquarters located in a metropolitan area — the general pattern in developed economies — the demand for producer services in such peripheral regions will be severely constrained, particularly if the region has essentially a "branch plant" economy. In the extreme case, a branch plant of an externally controlled multinational or multiregional firm may have no producer service linkages with the local economy.

It is locally controlled or managed firms that furnish most of the demand for locally produced business services (Marshall 1982). Where the level of local control over a regional economy is low, it follows that the potential for the development of local producer services will be modest. Regional producer service firms find it difficult to break into the multiestablishment firm market because of their small size and limited branch network. (In addition, it must be noted that local branch offices of national producer service firms add to regional employment, but, having limited autonomy, they carry out predominantly marketing and brokerage tasks, and their local multiplier effect is thus limited.) The acquisition of locally owned manufacturing or resource firms by external interests can thus have a debilitating effect upon the demand for local producer services. After indigenous companies are acquired, certain of their key producer service inputs are usually transferred to the new headquarters where, as noted above, they are purchased from firms in the vicinity of the head office (Leigh and North 1978).

In sum, considerations of firm creation (entrepreneurship), of head office location, and of corporate control are vitally important for understanding the spatial distribution of producer service activities.

Intrafirm Functional Separation

The concept of the spatial division of labor within an economic system is now well accepted; all activities are not found in all locations. In addition, at a microeconomic scale, the division of labor *within* individual firms is increasingly taking on a spatial dimension (Massey 1984). This is evident in the case of producer services (and, indeed, of all office activities) where a clear distinction is beginning to appear between "front office" functions — higher order, management tasks generally requiring face-to-face contact — and those of a "back office" nature — lower order, routinized and standardized functions. The emerging consolidation and decoupling of back office activities enables noncentral locations to be utilized for these latter functions. There is general agreement in the literature, however, that the spatial separation of back office activities involves deconcentration rather than decentralization; that is to say, the "back office" of a firm is usually found on the periphery of the same metropolitan region as its "front office" (Moss 1987; Moss and Dunau 1986; Gillespie and Green 1987; Nelson 1986; Marshall 1985b). Front office functions, on the other hand, are being increasingly centralized in a decreasing number of large metropolitan areas that are becoming functionally more specialized; at the intrametropolitan scale, these activities are becoming concentrated within the central business districts.

It is worth noting, further, that employment in the more routinized producer service functions is contracting, while employment in high-order tasks is expanding (Daniels 1987; Van Haselen, Molle, and De Wit 1985; Moss and Dunau 1986). Combined with the spatial separation tendencies described above, the result is that it is the largest metropolitan centers that can be expected to experience employment growth in producer services; at an intrametropolitan scale, growth can be expected to occur in the metropolitan core rather than on the periphery. These trends have the potential to create a dramatic spatial segregation of jobs according to rank, pay, and gender.

There are two principal factors underlying this spatial division of labor at the intrafirm level. First, there has been an evolution in the organizational structure of firms: a shift towards more complex and advanced managerial structures which involves the relocation of high-order service functions from the establishment level to the firm level. In part, this shift is a result of attempts to achieve scale economies and to enhance administrative control (Stanback et al. 1981). At the same time, however, this macroscale centralization is marked by a microscale separation of functions so that those activities not requiring face-to-face contact can take advantage of cost savings associated with locations not in the dense urban core of a metropolitan area. While our discussion has focused primarily on producer service firms themselves, it is clear that analogous developments in management functions across the whole range of economic activities have contributed to trends in the producer service sector. The external purchase of all but industry-specific services is now recognized as a preferred strategy to reduce overall production costs.

In the following section, the second factor underlying the spatial division of labor within firms is examined: the proliferation and differentiation of back office functions may be seen as a result of developments in information and communications technology (Nelson 1986; Netherlands Economic Institute 1986; Goddard and Gillespie 1986).

The Impact of Telecommunications Technology

There are two major schools of thought concerning the effects of advances in telecommunications technology upon the location of high-order office functions, including producer services. The first (see, for example, Webber 1973; Downs 1985; Kellerman 1984; Kutay 1986) reflects what might be termed the conventional wisdom: that new information and communications technology will permit the *decentralization* of office-based activities by making it possible to transact business without face-to-face contact. These technological changes will, it is argued, reduce the effects of distance and thus eliminate the differences between home and office, between city and country, and between center and periphery.

The second school of thought adopts a viewpoint that is diametrically opposed to the first: that new information and communications technologies free office functions from the necessity of locating in proximity to the operations that they direct. This contributes to the growing *centralization* of office-based activities in a small number of metropolitan areas (subject, of course, to the separation of front and back offices at the intrametropolitan scale), while at the same time permitting the decentralization of goods-producing activities into areas characterized by lower factor costs. The greater the extent of the geographic decentralization of production activities, it is argued, the greater the need for the centralization of key control activities.

Although there is a paucity of empirical research on the spatial impacts of the evolution of telecommunications technology, that which does exist lends strong support, on balance, to the latter viewpoint. Hepworth (1986) demonstrates that firms in Canada are using telecommunications technology to maintain and to increase the level of spatial centralization in their organizational structures. Howells (1988), Daniels and Thrift (1986), Goddard and Gillespie (1986), Goddard et al. (1985), Moss (1987), and the Netherlands Economic Institute (1986) similarly show that, across a range of countries, advanced information and telecommunications technology has facilitated the greater centralization, diversification, and internationalization of producer services. Further, much of the empirical work cited above (e.g., Beyers 1988; Coffey and Polèse 1988; Coffey and McRae 1989; Noyelle and Stanback 1984; Gillespie and Green 1987) provides indirect evidence to support this view. While not focusing explicitly on the impacts of technology, this research indicates that, during the recent period marked by significant evolution in telecommunications technology, very little decentralization has occurred. Rather, the centralization trends that have been observed in a broad set of countries have developed in parallel with, and very possibly as a direct result of, advances in telecommunications technology.

The principal factor underlying this failure of producer services and other high-order office functions to behave in the manner suggested by conventional wisdom relates to the pattern of technological diffusion: there is generally a time lag in the adoption of telecommunications technologies, with the process of diffusion following the urban hierarchy. Thus, firms in metropolitan areas are able to enjoy an initial advantage in acquiring new technologies and, due to the availability of skilled human resources, are generally better able to benefit from the options presented by these technologies (Lesser and Hall 1987; Goddard et al. 1985). The flexibility of modern technology can compensate the generally smaller firms in peripheral regions by allowing them to obtain economies of scope to replace the disadvantages of small scale, but small firms in the more highly industrialized regions also obtain this advantage. In the final analysis, the difficulty facing peripheral regions in benefiting from telecommunications advances once again reflects the traditional problems of the latter: their less diversified economic base, smaller local markets, and limited labor skills, all of which impede the rate of adoption of new technologies. Thus, the very cities that have been the customary centers for face-to-face communication appear to be the ones that will benefit most from the spread of advanced telecommunication technologies (Moss 1987).

The evolution of telecommunications technology appears to be a two-edged sword. In theory, it has the potential to free various types of economic activities from the locational constraints that have ruled them in the past, as well as to permit firms in peripheral regions to manage multi-site organizations without establishing any part of their operations in a metropolitan area. This evolution also, however, enables head offices and producer service firms in large urban centers to centralize their high-level management, scientific, and technical functions. The problem of regional disparities will very likely intensify in this age of new telecommunications technologies (Lesser 1987; Marshall 1988).

To end this section on trends in the location of producer services, we make the following observation: neither an analysis of spatial patterns across a broad set of countries, nor an exploration of the question from a more conceptual perspective, indicates that there is much cause for optimism concerning the capacity for producer services to have an impact upon the level of economic development in peripheral regions. This is the underlying reality that public policy must confront. The following sections examine existing and potential policy directions involving producer services.

4. AN OVERVIEW OF SOME EXISTING POLICY INITIATIVES

To date, the level of experience with regional policy involving services has been relatively slim. The case of the European Economic Community countries is somewhat instructive, however, given that such policy has existed for more than 20 years. Marshall (1988) and Marshall and Bachtler (1987) observe that, within the EEC, regional policy targeted on services has taken three forms. First, during the 1960s and early 1970s, Britain and France sought to encourage the decentralization of high-order services (and other office-based functions) by establishing disincentives that restricted the creation of new activities of this type in large metropolitan areas. The "decentralization" that did occur involved, however, very short distances: between 1963 and 1970, only one percent of the 70,000 jobs decentralized from London went to peripheral regions (Daniels

1976). These policies were relaxed during the 1970s and have now mostly been abolished, as they can disadvantage both firms which need a central location and metropolitan centers which are competing with other international cities.

A second regional policy has been the attempts in Britain, France, and the Netherlands to relocate public service office functions. Although this has proven to be more successful than the disincentive approach, it has primarily produced the spatial redistribution of clerical functions (Marshall and Bachtler 1987). Further, since the general level of government expenditures has contracted recently in most countries, the possibilities for the use of this strategy have consequently diminished.

During the 1970s, a third, incentive-policy approach was introduced. This involved, on the one hand, the creation of service-specific incentives (e.g., in Britain, France, and Ireland, employee transfer grants, rent relief, capital grants, training and job-creation grants) and, on the other hand, the extension of existing regional incentives to include services. Both categories of incentives tended to be restricted to service firms with a choice of location ("mobile offices") or with a certain proportion of exports outside the destination region. Alternatively, in a variation upon the "picking winners" theme, attempts were made to identify and support specific sectors of major national significance (in terms of export orientation or job creation). Among the difficulties encountered with the incentive approach were low funding priorities, low levels of assistance, and a lack of publicity (Marshall and Bachtler 1987).

An issue related to the creation of a service-specific regional policy involves the implementation of a supply-side service approach to regional development. Here, the reasoning is that government policies to expand the supply of producer services in specific peripheral regions will attract other types of industries and, hence, increase the level of economic development. In the early 1980s both academics (e.g., Marshall 1982; Goddard 1980) and governmental organizations (Northern Region Strategy Team 1977) advocated such an approach, arguing that it could be more easily pursued by government than the traditional, more costly forms of regional policy. During the course of the decade this strategy was implemented to some degree in several countries, but at this time it is not clear to what extent the policy has been successful. It is perhaps significant, however, that the more recent literature has not dealt with this approach.

An important impetus towards the development of service-specific policies has been provided by the changing economic context created by the recession of the early 1980s; most developed countries are now witnessing a greater emphasis on national innovation and science policies, and the restriction of public expenditure. Although regional development policy, per se, has come under strong pressure, the level of interest in service activities has increased. This is due to the perceived ability of the latter to provide low-cost job creation, particularly at a time when manufacturing's contribution to employment growth is limited (Marshall 1988). The perception has recently resulted in a more favorable treatment for services in the context of existing regional policy (e.g., in Germany, Ireland, Britain, and Italy) and in the introduction of new service incentive schemes (e.g., in France).

After the more than twenty years of experience with some form of regional policy targeted on service activities, European initiatives in this area cannot be qualified as conspicuously effective in generating development or, even more narrowly, in creating employment in lagging regions (Marshall and Bachtler 1987). The emphasis upon services in regional policy remains tentative and, in some instances, may be regarded as cosmetic. Marshall (1985a) posits that there are several likely explanations for this lack of success: the continued focusing of assistance upon manufacturing industry; an incomplete understanding of the economics of the service sector; the fact that much service employment is tied to levels of local consumer expenditure and that, thus far, regional policies intent on creating additional employment have not been able to satisfactorily distinguish these from tradeable services; and the spatial concentration of corporate control and the associated division of administrative functions between office sites and subordinate organizational units. A further problem is that the overwhelming majority of service policies are conceived in isolation, in the sense of not considering the interdependence between high-order services and other forms of economic activity.

The prospects for service-oriented regional initiatives must also be viewed in light of the existing policy context in most developed countries, where regional and national policies are often in direct opposition, with the latter generally providing assistance to firms in more prosperous areas. Marshall (1985a) notes that where national policies towards services exist, they tend to contradict the goals of regional policy; assistance is channeled to the more developed regions. On the other hand, although services are now eligible for mainstream regional development assistance in most countries, expenditure on regional policy is declining.

In sum, based upon the European experience, the prognosis is not highly positive; the impact of a service-oriented regional policy on peripheral areas could be quite modest. It is unlikely that government policies of any type will be able to combat the observed centralizing tendencies of high-order producer services (Marshall 1985b). Although there is a case for including producer services in a regional development policy on the grounds of their contribution to employment creation, such policy must confront the fact that employment growth in these activities has not benefited central and peripheral areas equally. This does not suggest that an emphasis upon services in regional policy is entirely impractical; for it to be effective, however, it will need to have access to more resources and to be more sophisticated than past attempts. In the following section, we present some ideas concerning the specific directions that such policies might take.

5. POLICY PRESCRIPTIONS

It follows from the empirical and conceptual evidence reviewed thus far that, in most instances, producer services cannot be regarded as the answer to the economic development problems of lagging regions, many of which are small and geographically peripheral. Although there are specific exceptions, and although there are *relative* trends towards decentralization observable, high-order services — those with a high propensity for export and, therefore, for the stimulation of economic growth — generally continue to be highly concentrated in major urban centers. Nevertheless, it is useful to explore some of the essential elements that a service-oriented regional strategy might include. In presenting these ideas, we draw heavily upon our own research on the Canadian space-economy and, as well, upon the international literature.

Perhaps the first point that needs to be made concerns the complementarity between goods production and producer services. A number of authors (Gershuny 1978; Gershuny and Miles 1983; Noyelle and Stanback 1984; Stanback et al. 1981; Bailly and Maillat 1988) have conclusively demonstrated the close interdependence of physical production and high-order services; the latter may correctly be regarded as integral elements of any modern production process. It therefore follows that a regional policy aimed either at "productive" activities (i.e., primary and secondary activities) or at producer services, in isolation, will be destined to a suboptimal degree of effectiveness. Regional policy towards both will need to be integrated.

Stated in slightly different terms, regional policy must concern itself with both supply-side and demand-side aspects of producer services in lagging regions. Supply-side incentives will only be effective if there is a demand for the service that is produced; in most instances, this will involve local demand, because producer service firms in peripheral regions cannot realistically be expected to export a large proportion of their output in the short term. Thus an important constraint upon the development of producer services in such areas is the poor performance of indigenous, nonservice industries and the internalization of demand within large firms. This problem will not be resolved easily by a supply-side policy; a more proactive approach is necessary on the demand side.

More tangibly, a supply-side approach needs to include such measures as human resource policies designed to create skilled labor pools and, at a different scale of organization, incentives aimed at the creation of producer service firms themselves. In theory, a substantial supply of skilled labor will assist a region in attracting or in generating high-order producer service (and other knowledge-intensive) firms. In addition to training and education initiatives, human resource policies may also include measures designed to improve a city's social-cultural-political environment, thus making it more attractive to a highly skilled labor force. Similarly, the presence of a range of producer service firms may enable a region to attract or to create complementary (i.e., nonservice) forms of economic activity.

The demand-side approach consists of generating sufficient demand to stimulate the initial creation and subsequent growth of high-order service firms. The growth of engineering services in Québec is a particularly good example of this strategy which we shall describe in some detail later in this section. Another element involves regional import substitution in producer services — the encouragement of externally owned firms operating in a region to increase their purchase of locally produced services. In this manner one can attempt to avoid the classic "branch-plant-economy syndrome" in which multinational or multiregional firms operating in a region have virtually no backward linkages with the local economy. Similarly, a regional strategy towards the creation of local business might require that the latter make significant use of local services.

Either a supply-side or a demand-side approach, in isolation, is a fragile one; if policy intervention is to be attempted, both avenues need to be pursued simultaneously. It is, for example, well and good to pursue human resource policies, but if parallel efforts are not made to stimulate the demand for this resource the result will likely be the out-migration of the newly created skills.

In our view, the possibilities for the development of services in nonmetropolitan regions appear to be limited to the following:

1. producer services that respond to the demands of local economic activities (e.g., local manufacturing or primary sector firms)
2. producer services that respond to local public sector demand
3. certain standardized and routinized "back office" service functions (e.g., data-processing or mail-order activities)
4. tradeable specialized services derived from longterm local expertise in the primary or manufacturing sectors.

In the case of options (1) and (2), services are fulfilling a principally residentiary function. They may, however, assist the economic growth of the local economy to the extent that they create jobs and that they may be substituted for service imports from the exterior. Option (3) may be important in the provision of employment opportunities in a local area, but is unlikely to stimulate economic growth. Further, as we already noted, the available evidence suggests that these types of activities tend to deconcentrate on an intrametropolitan scale rather than to decentralize on an interregional scale. Option (4) represents the principal possibility for export development; the current expertise (and predominant position) of Québec-based engineering consulting firms is a useful, concrete example of this phenomenon and, as such, warrants a brief summary.

In the 1960s and 1970s, partially to resolve, and partially to avoid, union problems, Hydro-Québec, a provincial crown corporation, began to use the services of independent firms to provide the engineering and management for their vast hydro-electric projects. This contracting-out strategy is clearly one of the major factors (along with an enhanced educational system that was able to assure a supply of highly skilled human resources) in the success story of the Québec engineering consulting sector. Due to this decision, local firms, at first in cooperation with external partners such as the American giant, Bechtel, were able simultaneously to establish a viable level of activity, to develop a base of expertise, and to acquire foreign technology. Over time, this combination has propelled several Québec firms, which now work without foreign assistance (e.g., Lavalin, SNC), to the status of major actors in the global context. The evolution of the Québec engineering sector may be contrasted with that of Ontario, whose crown corporation, Ontario Hydro, chose to maintain a large internal engineering department (Verreault and Polèse 1988).

Finally, the need for locationally-specific policies must be stressed. Our research on the Canadian space-economy suggests that small and medium-sized cities (in the 25,000 to 100,000 population range) that are not in the zone of influence of a large metropolitan center have some potential for the development of producer service activities to serve local demand. Centers within the "shadows" of major urban areas, and places below this size threshold, do not appear to have such potential. Thus, if a regional policy based upon high-order service activities is to be attempted, it needs to be tailored according to the characteristics of individual areas; a blanket approach will likely prove to be highly counter-productive.

CONCLUSIONS

The evidence that we have presented suggests that the conventional wisdom concerning the capability of "footloose" producer service activities to enhance the economic development prospects of peripheral regions is unjustifiably optimistic. The potential for high-order producer services to locate outside of major metropolitan centers is highly limited. The main locational shifts of producer services that most developed economies are witnessing are occurring primarily at the intrametropolitan level. In terms of specific policy interventions to stimulate service activities in lagging regions, considerable caution must be exercised. It is not at all clear that such interventions will have a high probability of success; even more than in the case of manufacturing, the forces of spatial concentration are very strong.

Attempts to create an effective service policy for peripheral regions need to be grounded in a better understanding of the economics of high-order services and, particularly, of the factors governing the location of these activities. Further, such considerations cannot be divorced from the broader issues concerning the future of regional policy, nor from those concerning the greater integration of national science and technology policies with regional policy. Perhaps even more fundamentally, we are led once again to the classic existential question of the regional development practitioner: is it really worthwhile to expend so much effort in attempting to resist the "natural" market trends?

ACKNOWLEDGMENTS

This research was conducted in the context of a larger project on service industries in regional development financed by the Department of Regional Industrial Expansion and Statistics Canada, and coordinated by the Institute for Research on Public Policy.

REFERENCES

Bailly, A. S. and Maillat, D. 1988. *Le secteur tertiaire en question,* 2nd ed. Geneva: Editions Régionales Européennes.

Beyers, W. B. 1988. Trends in the producer services in the U.S.: the last decade. Paper presented at the Annual Meetings of the Association of American Geographers, Phoenix.

Coffey, W. J. and McRae, J. J. 1989. *Service industries in regional development.* Montreal: Institute for Research on Public Policy.

Coffey, W. J. and Polèse, M. 1986. The interurban location of office activities: a framework for analysis. In *The Canadian economy: a regional perspective,* ed. D. J. Savoie, Toronto: Methuen, pp. 85–103.

Coffey, W. J. and Polèse, M. 1987a. The distribution of high technology manufacturing and services in the Canadian urban system, 1971–1981. *Revue d'économie régionale et urbaine,* no. 5: 279–99.

Coffey, W. J. and Polèse, M. 1987b. Intra-firm trade in business services: implications for the location of office-based activities. *Papers of the Regional Science Association* 62: 71–80.

Coffey, W. J. and Polèse, M. 1987c. Trade and location of producer services: a Canadian perspective. *Environment and Planning A* 19: 597–611.

Coffey, W. J. and Polèse, M. 1988. Locational shifts in Canadian employment, 1971–1981: decentralization versus decongestion. *The Canadian Geographer* 32: 248–56.

Cohen, R. 1981. The new international division of labor, multinational corporations and urban hierarchy. In *Urbanization and urban planning in capitalist society,* eds. M. Dear and A. Scott, New York: Methuen, pp. 287–315.

Daniels, P. W. 1976. Office employment in new towns. *Town Planning Review* 47: 210–24.

Daniels, P. W. 1985. *Service industries: a geographical appraisal.* London: Methuen.

Daniels, P. W. 1987. The geography of services. *Progress in Human Geography* 11: 433–47.

Daniels, P. W. and Thrift, N. J. 1986. *Producer services in an international context.* Liverpool: University of Liverpool, Working Paper on Producer Services, no. 1.

Downs, A. 1985. Living with advanced telecommunications. *Society* 23: 26–34.

Drennan, M. 1987. New York in the world economy. *Survey of Regional Literature,* no. 4: 7–12.

Gershuny, J. I. 1978. *After industrial society: the emerging self service economy.* London: Macmillan.

Gershuny, J. I. and Miles, I. D. 1983. *The new service economy.* London: Frances Pinter.

Gillespie, A. E. and Green, A. E. 1987. The changing geography of producer services employment in Britain. *Regional Studies* 21: 397–411.

Ginzberg, E. and Vojta, G. J. 1981. The service sector of the U.S. economy. *Scientific American* 244, 3 (March): 48–55.

Goddard, J. B. 1975. *Office location in urban and regional development.* Oxford: Oxford University Press.

Goddard, J. B. 1980. *Industrial innovation and regional economic development in Britain.* Newcastle-upon-Tyne: Centre for Urban and Regional Development Studies, University of Newcastle-upon-Tyne, Discussion Paper 32.

Goddard, J. B. and Gillespie, A. E. 1986. *Advanced telecommunications and regional development.* Newcastle-upon-Tyne: Centre for Urban and Regional Development Studies.

Goddard, J. B., Gillespie, A., Robinson, F., and Thwaites, A. 1985. The impact of new information technology on urban and regional structure in Europe. In *Technological change and regional development,* eds. R. Oakey and A. Thwaites, London: Frances Pinter, pp. 215–41.

Hall, P. 1985. The world and Europe. In *The future of urban form,* eds. J. Brotchie, P. Newton, P. Hall, and P. Nijkamp, Sydney: Croom Helm, pp. 84–109.

Hepworth, M. 1986. The geography of technological change in the information economy. *Regional Studies* 20: 407–24.

Howells, J. 1987. Developments in the location, technology and industrial organization of computer services: some trends and research issues. *Regional Studies* 21: 493–503.

Howells, J. 1988. *Economic, technological and locational trends in European services*. Brookfield, VT: Gower.

Howells, J. and Green, A. E. 1986. Location, technology and industrial organization in U.K. services. *Progress in Planning* 26: 85–183.

Kellerman, A. 1984. Telecommunications and the geography of metropolitan areas. *Progress in Human Geography* 8: 222–46.

Kutay, A. 1986. Effects of telecommunications technology on office location. *Urban Geography* 7: 243–57.

Leigh, R. and North, D. 1978. The spatial consequences of takeovers in some British industries and their implications for regional development. In *Contemporary industrialization: spatial analysis and regional development*, ed. F. E. I. Hamilton, London: Longman, pp. 158–81.

Lesser, B. 1987. Technological change and regional development. In *Still living together: recent trends and future directions in Canadian regional development*, eds. W. J. Coffey and M. Polèse, Montreal: Institute for Research on Public Policy.

Lesser, B. and Hall, P. 1987. *Telecommunications services and regional development*. Halifax: The Institute for Research on Public Policy.

Marquand, J. 1983. The changing distribution of service employment. In *Urban and regional transformation of Britain*, eds. J. B. Goddard and A. G. Champion, London: Methuen, pp. 99–134.

Marshall, J. N. 1982. Linkages between manufacturing industry and business services. *Environment and Planning A* 14: 1523–40.

Marshall, J. N. 1985a. Business services, the regions and regional policy. *Regional Studies* 19: 353–63.

Marshall, J. N. 1985b. Services in a postindustrial economy. *Environment and Planning A* 17: 1155–67.

Marshall, J. N. 1988. *Services and uneven development*. New York: Oxford University Press.

Marshall, J. N. and Bachtler, J. 1987. Services and regional policy. *Regional Studies* 21: 471–75.

Marshall, J. N., Damesick, P., and Wood, P. 1985. Understanding the location and role of producer services. Paper presented at the European Congress of the Regional Science Association, Manchester.

Massey, D. 1984. *Spatial divisions of labour*. London: Macmillan.

McRae, J. J. 1985. Can growth in the service sector rescue western Canada? *Canadian Public Policy* 11: 351–53.

Moss, M. L. 1987. Telecommunications, world cities, and urban policy. *Urban Studies* 24: 534–46.

Moss, M. L. and Dunau, A. 1986. *The location of back offices: emerging trends and development patterns*. New York: Real Estate Institute, New York University.

Nelson, K. 1986. Labor demand, labor supply and the suburbanization of low-wage office work. In *Production, work, and territory*, eds. A. Scott and M. Storper, Boston: Allen and Unwin, pp. 149–71.

Netherlands Economic Institute. 1986. *Telecommunications and the location of producer services in The Netherlands*. Brussels: Commission of the European Communities, FAST Occasional Paper 98.

Northern Region Strategy Team. 1977. *Strategic plan for the Northern Region. Volume 2: economic development policy*. London: HMSO.

Noyelle, T. J. and Stanback, T. M. 1984. *The economic transformation of American cities*. Totawa, NJ: Rowman & Allanheld.

Philippe, J. 1984. Les services aux entreprises et la politique de développement régional. Paper presented at the annual meeting of l'Association de science régionale de langue française, Lugano, Switzerland.

Philippe, J. and Monnoyer, M. C. 1985. *L'interaction entre les prestations de service et le développement régional*. Aix-en-Provence: Centre d'économie régionale, Discussion Paper.

Stanback, T. M., Bearse, P. J., Noyelle, T. J., and Karasek, R. A. 1981. *Services: the new economy*. Totawa, NJ: Rowman & Allanheld.

Statistics Canada. 1988. *Quarterly estimates of the Canadian balance of international payments*. Catalogue no. 67-001.

Tornqvist, G. 1970. *Contact systems and regional development*. Lund: Lund Studies in Geography (B), no. 35.

Van Haselen, H., Molle, W., and De Wit, R. 1985. Technological change and service employment in the regions of Europe: the case of banking and insurance. Paper presented at the conference on Technological Change and Employment, Zandvoort, The Netherlands.

Verreault, R. and Polèse, M. 1988. L'exportation de services par les firmes canadiennes de génie-conseil: évolution récente et avantages concurrentiels. Montréal: INRS-Urbanisation, unpublished paper.

Walker, R. A. 1985. Is there a service economy? the changing capitalist division of labor. *Science and Society* 49: 42–83.

Webber, M. M. 1973. Urbanization and communications. In *Communications technology and social policy,* eds. G. Gerbner, L. P. Gross, and W. H. Melody, New York: John Wiley & Sons.

Wheeler, J. O. 1988. The corporate role of large metropolitan areas in the United States. *Growth and Change* 19: 75–86.

[13]

The Role of Producer Service Outsourcing in the Innovation Performance of New York State Manufacturing Firms

Alan MacPherson

Canada-United States Trade Center, Department of Geography, University at Buffalo

This paper assesses the contribution of external technical services to the innovation initiatives of New York State manufacturing firms. The results of a spatially and sectorally stratified postal survey of more than 400 manufacturing firms are presented. A major finding of the paper is that specialized technical services can support the product development efforts of innovative firms. The empirical results also point to significant spatial variations in technical service utilization. Some of these variations reflect different supply and accessibility conditions among the state's major regions and urban centers. The survey results are discussed in the context of recent empirical and theoretical findings on the role of producer services in urban and regional development. Particular attention is given to the empirical connection between producer service accessibility and industrial innovation. Key Words: external technical services, new product development, New York State manufacturing firms, regional patterns of service consumption.

A substantial body of literature now highlights the importance of advanced producer services to urban and regional development (see Harrington 1995). Specialist firms in this sector of the economy typically supply other business units with high-order informational inputs (e.g., management advice or market intelligence). Significantly, recent reviews by Daniels (1989), Goe (1993), Hansen (1994), and Illeris (1994) suggest an international convergence of opinion regarding the contribution of these types of services to the operational efficiency and/or commercial performance of client firms—including manufacturers.

In this regard, policy interest in the industrial role of producer services has expanded quickly over the last few years (Britton 1993; Kelley and Brooks 1991; National Research Council 1993). In the U.S., a general lack of product and/or process innovation has seriously constrained the international competitiveness of domestically owned firms (Shapira et al. 1995), many of which lack the in-house skills to keep pace with current rates of technological change

(U.S. General Accounting Office 1995). Recourse to external assistance is a partial corrective to this problem (Feldman 1994), notably for small and medium-sized firms (SMFs). From a policy standpoint, growing attention has focused upon the extent to which independent consultants can assist the commercial and/or technological efforts of SMFs (Shapira 1990). Evidence is mounting that we can trace part of the vitality of the SMF sector to specialists that sell technical expertise in such spheres as production engineering (O'Farrell 1995), contract R&D (Haour 1992), industrial design (O'Connor 1996), and management support (Sinkula 1990). Across most of the advanced market economies, innovative industrial firms have become important buyers of these types of inputs, suggesting a technological interface between goods production and producer service activity (Freeman 1991).

Although nonindustrial clients are the main buyers of high-order producer services (see Beyers and Lindahl 1994), recent work on industrial demand suggests that service-to-manufacturing linkages are especially important in terms

Annals of the Association of American Geographers, 87(1), 1997, pp. 52–71
©1997 by Association of American Geographers
Published by Blackwell Publishers, 350 Main Street, Malden, MA 02148, and 108 Cowley Road, Oxford, OX4 1JF, UK.

of scientific and technical (S&T) interactions (Illeris 1994). According to Tyson (1993), these types of interactions can play a key role in the innovation performance of users, notably with regard to new-product development. Simply stated, the evidence suggests that professionally qualified consultants can deliver strategic benefits to industrial clients, often at remarkably low cost (Berman 1995; Smallbone et al. 1993).

Keeping these points in mind, this paper examines the role of technical outsourcing in the innovation performance of New York State (NYS) manufacturing firms. The results of a recent postal survey show that the propensity to successfully bring new products to the marketplace is often contingent upon the use of different blends of external expertise. The results also suggest that a firm's regional context can influence the depth and nature of its outsourcing activity. On balance, firms that reside in service-poor regions tend to be relatively weak performers in terms of successful product development. And, as we shall see later, part of the explanation for this pattern can be traced to supply-side problems in terms of the local availability of external technical and/or management inputs.

Set against this backdrop, the following analysis tackles three main questions. First, to what extent does technical service demand by industrial firms vary across regions of different types? Second, to what degree is technical service consumption a positive factor in the innovation performance of buyers? And, third, does the geography of supply and demand affect the structure of service-to-industry linkages at the regional scale? Partial answers to these questions come from an empirical investigation of NYS industrial firms across a range of locational settings. Additional insights come from a series of telephone interviews with a subsample of firms. Before reviewing the results, however, it is appropriate to sketch a brief theoretical context for the inquiry.

Theoretical Context

Three interlinked strands of theory inform the empirical thrust of the paper. First, internal diseconomies of scope typically prohibit firms from achieving in-house competence across a full range of S&T functions (Rothwell 1992). This idea flows from the ongoing division of

labor that has been taking place between and within business units since the advent of industrialization (Scott 1986; Walker 1985; Young 1928). As such, there is nothing new about the rising segmentation of tasks between different parts of the economy. Rajan and Pearson (1986) trace at least some of the post-1945 growth of specialized producer services to an efficiency-driven fragmentation of jobs between firms, following the classical logic of structural change outlined by Adam Smith. A formal economic model proposed by Lentnek et al. (1992) presents this logic from a spatial standpoint. According to this model, firms will choose external vendors whenever the relative costs of in-house supply are higher. This model also implies that time lags in the delivery of key inputs will force vendors to optimize their location with respect to client demand, leaving peripheral buyers in a potentially disadvantaged position.

A second line of theory comes from policy-oriented work on the technical links between innovative industrial firms and external consultants (Bessant and Rush 1995; Lefebvre et al. 1991). Evidence dating back to the 1950s shows that many firms can sharpen their technological edge by subcontracting specialized work to outside experts (Carter and Williams 1957; Myers and Marquis 1969). This literature indicates that in-house resources are best allocated toward core activities that match the firm's existing skills, whereas esoteric or infrequently required jobs are better handled by independent vendors (Britton 1989). This body of theory differs from the question of scope economies in that outside talent is often solicited in response to in-house technical limitations (Haour 1992). Unlike the fragmentation thrust noted above, then, this second strand of theory stems from the idea that technological factors may force certain types of firms to seek outside help in fields that go beyond their in-house competence (Feldman 1994).

A third body of theory comes from a number of spatially focused ideas that have cropped up in the recent work on producer services and regional economic change. Several authors have proposed that regions with weak producer service endowment are unlikely to support major levels of new industrial expansion, innovation, and/or job growth (Coffey and Bailly 1993; Hitchens et al. 1994). An implication here is that certain types of firms may need quick access to a locally rooted supply of advanced services

(Harrington and Lombard 1989). While certain types of inputs can be moved up or down the urban system via electronic means (or by mail), others require face-to-face meetings for proper delivery (Daniels 1989). For companies that depend upon a wide mix of services, then, the spatial implications that flow from alternate delivery options are partially analogous to a Weberian problem. In this case, however, the raw materials consist of knowledge, information, or skills, rather than physical resources.

From a policy viewpoint, current interest in the locational relations between industrial and producer service establishments flows from a suspicion that close proximity between these sectors is a necessary condition for efficient interplay (Porter 1990). We can trace empirical support for this idea to Ellwein and Bruder (1982), Feldman and Florida (1994), and Meyer-Krahmer (1985), while theoretical support has come from Britton (1989), Daniels (1989), and Goddard (1978). Other things being equal, manufacturers in service-poor regions are likely to exhibit weaker performance than comparable firms in large urban centers (O'Farrell et al. 1995). Moreover, if we accept the balance of technological evidence noted by Feldman (1994), Malecki (1994), and Rothwell (1991), then a further possibility is that certain types of firms may be locationally disposed toward inferior performance. Although there is little doubt that successful SMFs can be found in a variety of regional settings, including unfavorable ones (Vaessen and Keeble 1995), few analysts would deny that spatial proximity to the human capital resources of major metropolitan centers can offer strategic benefits to potential innovators (Britton 1991; Feldman 1994; Malecki and Tootle 1996).

On this note, four sets of empirical results from earlier studies offer a comparative context for the paper. First, Rothwell's (1977, 1992) work shows that innovative firms usually obtain at least some of their S&T inputs from external sources. Significantly, Rothwell's data suggest an important role for such linkages, especially in spheres that pertain to technology development, product design, and/or management. Second, successful recourse to outside help is often contingent upon a firms's ability to identity, specify, and evaluate its internal weaknesses across key areas of production and marketing (Sinkula 1990). The evidence also shows that in-house technical competence is a first requirement for

successful retrieval of outside help (Rothwell and Dodgson 1991). Third, the need for specialized support varies by type of client. At one extreme, for example, plants that belong to multinational firms can often bypass the external service environment by tapping the internal resources of the corporation as a whole (Malecki 1991). Fourth, the types of outside inputs that manufacturers seek vary considerably in terms of function, cost, and impact (Chandra 1992). Here the evidence implies that a firm's position along the product life-cycle (PLC) can influence the structure of external input demand. In terms of innovation support, for instance, firms in mature markets typically want services that relate to process improvement (new production methods), whereas firms in younger markets more often demand inputs that assist product development (Britton 1989). This is not to deny the existence of intermediate positions among firms of different types, nor is it to suggest that a focus upon one mode of outside help is better than another. Rather, the suggestion is that a firm's PLC position may influence the balance of inputs demanded (Utterback and Abernathy 1975).

Taken together, these findings imply that single-plant firms in peripheral regions are less likely to enjoy good access to high-order services than comparable firms in more central places. While firms can trade almost all types of advanced producer services between regions, the option to import is far from universally applied (Malecki 1994). A limiting factor is that strategic services often require face-to-face interactions for efficient delivery. According to O'hUallacháin (1991), for instance, the need for face-to-face discussions varies directly with the potential ambiguity of the information sought. For peripheral firms that need external help in complex areas, then, human skills must often be imported—either by sending in-house people to the supply-source or by bringing the vendor's boffins to the production site. Significantly, there is evidence that these types of contact requirements can limit the external options of peripheral firms, especially those operating with restricted financial resources (Gertler 1995).

Today, of course, the distance separating vendors from buyers might seem rather trivial as far as interaction potential is concerned. After all, modern telecommunications technologies have surely rendered some aspects of relative location less crucial than before (Hepworth 1989). Lest we get too cozy with the notion of a wired world, however, recent work on producer service delivery suggests a continuing role for face-to-face meetings at the consumption point (Goe 1991). Contemporary research on technology diffusion also points to a major role for physical and/or cultural proximity between buyers and sellers (Cornish 1997). For detailed examples of the transactional problems that can hinder peripheral firms, see Gertler (1995) in the context of after-sales-servicing contracts for Canadian users of advanced machinery; for more general examples, see Lundvall (1988), Sabel et al. (1987), and Porter (1990). Additional evidence from Canada shows that more than 40 percent of the technical services consumed by goods-producing firms in Montreal come from independent producer service establishments (Coffey et al. 1994). These authors also show that face-to-face interaction is the main mode of input delivery, with about half of all such contacts taking place at the client's production site.

On balance, then, the recent literature implies that service accessibility has a potentially important bearing upon innovation success. In addi-

tion, service accessibility would also appear to play a role in the inclination of industrial firms to seek external help in the first place (Chandra 1992). If these types of connections have validity beyond the regional contexts covered by he studies cited thus far, then a logical conjecture is that peripheral firms must expend more effort on competitive positioning than their metropolitan counterparts. Is this the case?

In attempting to answer this question, however, I should note that the taxonomy of producer services employed in this paper is a narrow one (Table 1). For instance, the financial, insurance, real estate, and legal subsectors of the producer services have been ignored, because the original goal of the project was to examine only those services known to contribute directly toward the scientific, technical, and/or management dimensions of the production/innovation efforts of individual plants. While lawyers and bankers are important from an enabling point of view (try launching a new product without a good line of credit or a patent search), they rarely contribute to the hands-on work of problem solving on the shopfloor. In employment

Table 1. Classes of External Producer Services for the New York State Survey[a]

Service Category	Selected Studies	Examples of User Impact
Private services		
Industrial design	Chandra (1992), O'Connor (1994)	New or better products
Contract R&D	Haour (1992), Lawton-Smith (1993)	New products or procedures
Management consulting	Berman (1995), O'Farrell et al (1995)	Better ways of doing business
Marketing	Sinkula (1990), Coffey et al (1994)	Improved sales performance
Advertising	Beyers and Lindahl (1994)	Finding new customers
Export counseling	Berman (1995), Britton (1989)	Finding new export markets
Equipment repair	Lentnek et al. (1992)	Reduced downtime/lower costs
Data processing	Hepworth (1989), Phillips (1995)	Lower costs/professional quality
Business software	Phillips (1995), Yap et al. (1992)	Improved management efficiency
Laboratory testing	Feldman and Florida (1994)	Essential product information
Production engineering	Rothwell (1992), Britton (1993)	New or better production methods
Public services		
Government agencies	Chrisman and Katrishen (1995)	Market data and business planning
Hospital research units	Chandra (1992), MacPherson (1995)	Clinical trials and research
Technical colleges	Lawton-Smith (1993)	Applied R&D, engineering help
Universities	Haour (1992), Rothwell (1991)	Basic and applied research
Informal/nonmarket services		
Other manufacturing firms	Lipparini and Sobrero (1994)	New ideas and engineering advice
Informal business networks	Malecki and Veldhoen (1993), Malecki (1994)	Market leads, business information
Suppliers	Gertler (1995), Soni et al. (1993)	Innovative inputs, new ideas
Customers	Von Hippell (1978, 1988)	Feedback on design flaws
Distributors	Glasmeier (1990)	Hints on customer/market needs

[a]This table is not designed to supply a comprehensive or representative summary of the recent empirical or theoretical contributions by scholars in this field. Instead, the intent is simply to provide a snapshot of the types of inquiries conducted, along with some of the general impacts identified either explicitly or implicitly.

terms, then, the taxonomy shown in this paper captures only a small part of the producer services—not the whole sector.

Methodology

In order to assess the service-to-industry relationship at the firm level, I mailed self-administered questionnaires to more than 1,700 New York State manufacturers across four sectors (furniture, scientific instruments, fabricated metals, and electrical industrial products). These sectors were chosen for several reasons: first, to obtain a technological cross section of firms, notably in terms of R&D effort, market focus, and export activity; second, to find a sector-mix that would closely mirror the structure of industrial employment across the state as a whole; and third, to focus on sectors in which SMFs[1] enjoy a prominent economic role. Earlier studies have shown that SMFs are potentially prime targets for external support, if only because this size-class often lacks a full range of in-house skills (Shapira 1990). In sum, the sample was designed to reflect the typical scale and sector-mix of manufacturing activity within the state's main regions.

The survey consisted of two rounds, spread over a period of fourteen months. In the first phase of the project (September/October 1994), questionnaires were mailed to a systematic sample of 1,700 firms (covering roughly half of the total population across the four sectors). This phase was designed to obtain detailed information on service spending, geographical sourcing, delivery methods, and user impact (among other things). Of the 1,700 firms in the sampling frame, 326 were subsequently eliminated as a result of either incorrect SIC listings (n = 75), recent business failure (n = 62), or job-shop status (n = 189), bringing the N-size down to 1,374. A total of 472 valid returns were received, giving a 34 percent response rate. A second survey was mailed in the autumn of 1995, covering the other half of the population. This phase comprised an abbreviated and categorically structured version of the original questionnaire (focusing upon key areas of variation gleaned from the earlier survey). Because this phase of the project remains as a work-in-progress (to be reported upon at a later date), the discussion which follows confines itself to the results of the first survey. Additional data come from the re-

sults of 255 telephone interviews with business executives from a range of sectors and locations.

In a preliminary effort to assess regional patterns of service demand, I divided New York State into a variety of areal groupings to test for scale and zoning effects. Here the goal was to find a set of regional boundaries that would best reflect the underlying spatial features of the data. While the resulting regionalization (Figure 1) does not provide a perfect delineation as far as aggregation problems are concerned, the three divisions provide acceptable delineations for the purposes of this paper (for a discussion of the regionalization process and its attendant methodological problems, see Curtis and MacPherson 1996).

On this note, Table 2 shows that the spatial and sectoral pattern of responses broadly matches the population distribution for each region. While this implies an element of representativeness in terms of regional and sectoral coverage, the data mask a number of distortions. For one, the sample exhibits a size-mix that is biased toward SMFs (Table 3). Although this is not too surprising, especially in light of the rising prominence of SMFs in the state's industrial base, the relatively low response rate for larger firms is troublesome.

A second caveat is that this SMF bias is strongest for the electrical products sector, notably within the Buffalo and New York City metropolitan areas (for further details, see MacPherson 1997). This is problematic because these two areas contain the lion's share of the state's largest electrical products firms. Although several efforts were made to mitigate these

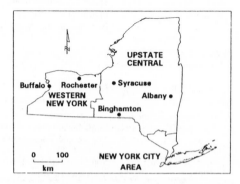

Figure 1. New York: the study regions and main urban centers.

Table 2. Response Rates by Sector and Location

Sector	New York City			Upstate/Central			Western New York			All Regions		
	N	n	%	N	n	%	N	n	%	N	n	%
Metal	159	56	35.2	128	41	34.1	188	52	27.6	475	149	31.3
Electrical	206	71	34.4	144	41	28.4	122	49	40.1	472	161	34.1
Instruments	106	38	35.8	39	15	38.4	89	28	31.4	234	81	34.6
Furniture	78	24	30.7	64	29	45.3	51	28	54.9	193	81	41.9
Total	549	189	34.4	375	126	33.6	450	157	34.8	1374	472	34.3

N = sampling frame population; n = number of valid responses; % = response rate.

biases, the discussion that follows should be treated with caution. In particular, I should note that the results pertain mainly to business units with 500 or fewer workers (Table 3), most of which (84 percent) are single-plant firms as opposed to branches of multilocational companies (16 percent). While several distinctions emerged between these two groups (i.e., single vs. multiplant units), plant status did not turn out to be a significant variable in regard to the key factors discussed later.[2] Keeping these caveats in mind, then, I will summarize some of the main results of the survey below.

Survey Results

Table 4 shows the regional pattern of external service spending by sector (annual averages for the period 1989–1993), aggregated for the full range of private input classes listed in Table 1.[3] At least three notable patterns can be discerned here. First, aggregate levels of spending vary appreciably across the state. A locational rank-size effect can be seen, in that the largest region in terms of economic activity (the New York City metropolitan area) exhibits the highest spending estimates overall, whereas the smallest region (Upstate/Central) exhibits the lowest estimates. These differences are statistically significant at $p = {<}0.05$ for all regional combinations (one-tailed t-tests). At the county level, moreover, a positive correlation ($r = 0.5952$; $p = 0.05$) was found between the external service expenditures of the survey firms (scaled as a proportion of their 1993 sales) and the regional distribution of business service employment (scaled as a percentage of total county employment). Although several important outliers emerged from this exercise, it is fair to say that the geography of external spending closely matches the distribution of business service supply at the county level. In short, external spending is generally higher in supply-rich locations.

A second aspect of the data is that the rank-orders for sectoral spending also vary by region. For example, the scientific instruments sector emerged as the biggest spender in the NYC region (US$68,000 per annum/per firm). In contrast, the biggest spenders from the Upstate/Central region (UC) were metal fabricators (US$33,000), whereas the dominant

Table 3. Size-Classes, Response Rates, and Plant Status of the Survey Respondents

Employment Range[a]	Sampling Frame Population		Valid Responses[b]		Single-Plant Firms		Response Rates[c]
	N	%	n	%	n	%	%
1–49	689	50.1	254	53.8	232	91.3	36.8
50–99	274	19.9	103	21.8	87	84.4	37.5
100–199	217	15.8	67	14.2	54	80.5	30.8
200–499	116	8.5	31	6.6	19	61.2	26.7
500+	78	5.7	17	3.6	3	17.6	21.7
Total	1374	100.0	472	100.0	395	83.6	34.3

[a]Full-time job counts (ranges taken from the Commerce Register [1994] database).
[b]Purged of incorrect listings.
[c]Response by size-class.

Table 4. Average Annual Spending on Producer Service Inputs (US$000s)[a]

	New York City			Upstate/Central			Western New York			All Regions		
Sector	[b]All	Users	Main Input[c]	All	Users	Main Input	All	Users	Main Input	All	Users	Main Input
Metal	20.4	32.6	PE	21.8	32.9	ER	33.3	48.2	ER	25.3	38.3	ER
Electrical	47.6	66.2	PE	17.1	25.0	TS	41.7	56.3	MG	38.1	53.1	PE
Instruments	59.7	68.7	DS	4.0	14.1	DS	23.5	34.6	DS	36.2	52.3	DS
Furniture	7.2	14.4	MG	7.9	17.7	ER	14.5	33.9	ER	10.0	21.9	ER
Total	36.6	52.7	MG	15.0	26.1	ER	30.8	46.9	ER	28.9	44.5	DS

[a]Average annual spending on producer services over the period 1989–1993.
[b]Where All = average spending across all firms in each group; Users = spending by firms that have at least one significant link (> US$5000) to private producer service vendors.
[c]The single largest external spending category by sector.
Where: PE = production engineering
         MG = management consulting
         DS = industrial design
         ER = equipment repair
         TS = testing services

spenders from Western New York (WNY) were electoral equipment producers (US$56,000). Interestingly, the data also point to regional variations in the types of services that firms buy across the four sectors. To keep the description as simple as possible, the service-specific examples listed in Table 4 refer to the single most important external spending categories by sector. On this basis, NYC furniture producers allocate more of their external budgets toward management services than their counterparts to the north (where equipment repair is the single most expensive external link). In the case of the electrical products sector, moreover, the data show that NYC firms are more oriented toward engineering consulting services than comparably sized firms elsewhere in the state (the top-ranking inputs for electrical products manufacturers in UC and WNY are testing and repair services, respectively). With the exception of the scientific instruments industry, where design services consistently rank first across all three regions, it would appear that NYC firms exhibit more sophisticated external purchasing practices than their UC and WNY counterparts.[4]

A third feature of the data is that average spending on external help does not appear to amount to very much in absolute dollar terms.[5] For this sample, in fact, average total spending per annum roughly translates into no more than the annual salary equivalent of a single skilled worker. At first glance, then, this finding might appear to support the contention that industrial demand for external technical inputs has not been a potent factor in the recent growth of

producer service activity. In spite of this, the data conceal other facets of industrial demand that ought to be considered.

To begin with, Table 4 provides a snapshot of average spending for the sample as a whole. Note that there is major variability between the survey firms. Among service users themselves (defined as firms that annually spent at least US$5,000 on external help from private sources), 4 percent spent more than US$250,000 per year, and 5 percent spent between US$100,000 and US$249,000, while a further 5 percent spent between US$75,000 and US$99,000. In short, the sample has captured a small but significant nucleus of "important spenders." Second, the data pertain to a sample of only 472 respondents. If these estimates are even remotely reflective of typical spending levels for the manufacturing sector as a whole, then it is safe to infer that industrial clients generate multibillion dollar earnings for the state's technical advisory units. Third, and perhaps more important, modest spending on external help does not necessarily translate into modest impact. Indeed, as shall be shown presently, some of these seemingly minor expenditures are of considerable significance to the production and/or innovation initiatives of buyers.

A crude but suggestive illustration of this point is shown in Table 5, which collates the incidence of successful new product development against the presence of external linkages.[6] Here the term "innovation" refers to the introduction and subsequent commercialization of a new or substantially improved product. Given

Table 5. Producer Service Linkages and Innovation: Regional Cross Tabulations

		No. of Firms with/without Producer Service Linkages[a]							
		New York City		Upstate/Central		Western New York		All Regions	
		Yes	No	Yes	No	Yes	No	Yes	No
No. of firms with/without innovation[b]	Yes	81	22	31	11	52	12	164	45
	No	50	36	41	43	51	42	142	121
Total		131	58	72	54	103	54	306	166
Chi-square		8.32 $p = 0.0039$		6.16 $p = 0.0131$		10.57 $p = 0.0011$		29.51 $p = 0.0000$	

[a]Defined as the presence of at least one significant external link to the producer service environment.
[b]The introduction and successful commercialization of at least one entirely new product over the study period.

that the survey firms were asked to list only those new products that had successfully moved through the research, design, and development stages to the marketplace itself, the data exclude product failures and/or aborted initiatives. On this basis, Table 5 shows that external linkages are positively associated with new product development across all three regions ($p = 0.05$ or better).[7] In the case of NYC, for example, 62 percent (n = 81) of the 131 service-linked firms introduced successful product innovations over the study period, compared to 38 percent among their nonlinked counterparts. Broadly similar proportions can be seen for the other two regions, suggesting a spatially consistent relationship between external linkages and innovation.[8]

At first blush, these findings are perhaps a little surprising. Despite relatively low levels of external spending in the UC region, for instance, more than 70 percent of the UC innovators exhibit technical links to the producer services (the comparable proportions for NYC and WNY are not significantly higher). It should also be mentioned that linkage propensity does not vary appreciably across the state. Fully 69 percent of the NYC firms reported having significant external linkages over the study period, compared to 66 percent for WNY and 57 percent for UC. While a locational rank-size effect might again appear to be in place as far as linkage propensity is concerned, the results are not statistically significant in this instance.

On closer inspection of Table 5, however, it seems that the incidence of product innovation is much higher among NYC firms than among their more northerly counterparts. For example, 54 percent of the NYC firms launched new products over the last five years, compared to 41

percent and 33 percent for WNY and UC firms respectively. These regional differences are statistically significant at $p = 0.0006$ (chi-square = 14.90). Interestingly, data presented elsewhere (MacPherson 1997) reveal that NYC consistently emerges as the innovation leader across other measures of product development, including innovation share (the percentage of current output represented by products that were developed over the last five years), innovation frequency (the number of new products introduced over the study period), and design innovation (the incidence and/or frequency of quality-oriented product redesign). In terms of innovation share, for example, service users from the NYC region derived (on average) roughly 20 percent of their 1994 sales from new products, compared to 11 percent for UC firms and 14 percent for WNY firms (the comparable proportions for nonusers were 12 percent [NYC], 3 percent [UC], and 4 percent [WNY]). Although there appears to be a spatially consistent association between innovation propensity and the incidence of producer service contact, there is no such uniformity in terms of the distribution of innovative activity itself.

In an effort to probe the data in more detail, Table 6 shows the regional distribution of the sample's top five external spending categories. Although this table contains more data than can be discussed here, several key patterns warrant special mention. First, the innovation/linkage connection implied in Table 5 can be traced to certain types of services. For instance, the industrial design category is positively associated with new product development across all three regions ($p = 0.05$), whereas the advertizing category is not. Repeating these types of comparisons across all of the services listed in Table 1

Table 6. Top Five Service Spending Categories (US$000s) by Region

Region	Average Outlays[a]	No. of Users	% of Firms in User Group	Impact Rating[b] %	Rank
New York City					
Management consulting	6.61	[37]	19.6	59.4	2
Industrial design	6.43	[51]	26.9	49.0	4
Advertising services	5.42	63	33.3	49.2	3
Contract R&D	4.57	[31]	16.4	61.2	1
Production engineering	4.26	[46]	24.3	43.4	5
Upstate/Central					
Equipment repair	3.61	33	26.2	87.8	1
Industrial design	3.23	[31]	24.6	67.7	3
Contract R&D	2.99	[28]	22.2	75.0	2
Advertising services	2.41	20	15.8	55.0	5
Testing services	1.96	[33]	26.2	57.5	4
Western New York					
Equipment repair	6.14	58	36.9	84.4	1
Production engineering	6.01	[48]	30.5	72.9	2
Industrial design	4.02	[47]	29.9	70.2	3
Testing services	3.71	[56]	35.6	64.2	5
Advertising services	3.69	56	35.6	66.1	4
All Regions					
Industrial design	4.91	[129]	27.3	61.2	3
Management services	3.99	[99]	20.9	64.6	2
Advertising services	3.82	139	29.4	56.8	5
Equipment repair	3.76	156	33.0	72.4	1
Contract R&D	3.49	[83]	17.6	57.8	4

Where: [a]average annual expenditures (1989–1993) among users of that input.
[b]% = percentage of users that identified the input as being very important; Rank = rank-order of %.
[ ] = indicates a significant (p = 0.05 or better) chi-square for service use by the incidence of successful product innovation.

revealed a further set of innovation-connected inputs that are consistent among all regions, including business software (p = 0.01), government support (p = 0.05), and university research facilities (p = 0.001). For now, however, one can state with reasonable confidence that the significance of Table 5 flows mainly from the items flagged in the second column of Table 6. In short, the innovation/linkage effect is service-specific rather than service-wide.

Table 6 also shows that NYC firms typically spend more on their top-ranking services than the average for the sample as a whole. Despite relatively high spending estimates for NYC's top-ranking services, however, the data also imply that firms in this region (as a group) attach less importance to their service inputs than buyers from other parts of the state. This finding flows from the fourth column of Table 6, which lists an "impact rating percentage." This rating refers to the proportion of service users that identified the service in question as being "very important" in terms of technical and/or business

impact (ranked along a 5-point Likert scale). While at least 40 percent of the NYC firms rated the impact of their top-ranking inputs as being very important, the figures for UC and WNY are in the order of 55 and 64 percent respectively.

To illustrate this point more vividly, let us consider the top-ranking spending category for the sample as a whole (industrial design). For this service category, NYC firms spent an average of US$6.4 thousand per annum over the study period, and 49 percent of these users rated their design contracts as being very important. In contrast, UC firms spent half as much on these services as their NYC counterparts, yet more than 65 percent of the UC users rated such inputs as being very important (the comparable figure for WNY is 70 percent). Adding to the puzzle, the service with the highest impact-rating for NYC (contract R&D) occupies the fourth rank in terms of average spending. For all regions, in fact, there is no consistent relationship between external spending and perceived impact. The only cogent exceptions can be found in WNY and UC, where many firms rank equipment repair services highly (notably metal fabricators).

To an extent, of course, part of the spatial variability shown in Table 6 might reflect differences in the size distribution and sector-mix of the regional samples themselves. At the state level, for instance, there is a general tendency for service spending to increase with establishment size. From a sectoral perspective, moreover, there is a tendency for R&D-oriented firms in the scientific instruments and electrical products sectors to spend more on high-order technical inputs (e.g., industrial design, contract R&D) than comparably sized firms in the other two sectors.[9] Having said this, I must point out that the regional samples do not differ significantly in terms of the size and sector-mix of respondents, and the same holds true for establishment age. In short, Table 6 is not simply the result of industrial-mix or establishment-size effects.

This being so, I should mention that several of the patterns shown in Table 6 were not fully anticipated during the early days of the study. In view of the significantly higher levels of external spending among NYC firms, the relatively low impact ratings reported by these respondents gave cause for unease. So also did the emergence of seemingly low amounts of external spending at the service-specific level. While previous surveys have reported low spending estimates for firms in Upstate New York (Chandra 1992; MacPherson 1992), the fact that no regional spending average for any service category exceeds US$7,000 remains puzzling. After all, recent evidence from Europe points to the emergence of major service-to-manufacturing consulting projects across a variety of technology-related fields, including several of the categories listed in Table 1. In the case of external R&D, for instance, Haour (1992) documents the emergence of multimillion dollar subcontracting projects between European manufacturers and big producer service units like Batelle (France), TNO (Netherlands), and Germany's Fraunhofer Institutes. Are these types of large-scale/service-to-industry interactions simply absent in the case of New York State? Or do the low estimates shown in Table 6 simply reflect the SMF-dominated nature of the sample?

Although full answers to these questions cannot be given at this stage, at least three possible

factors are worth considering. First, of the 306 service-linked firms in the sample, many have multiple links to a variety of outside vendors (Table 7). While these data show that NYC firms are more likely to exhibit multiple external links than their counterparts from the other two regions, follow-up telephone interviews uncovered extra dimensions to this pattern. Specifically, the linkage arrangements of multi-input users were typically found to reflect combinatorial or synergistic approaches toward service mixing. Thus, for example, a US$5,000 contract-R&D project generally does not stop (or start) with the initial US$5,000 outlay. In many cases, related types of service contracts either precede, follow from, or contemporaneously interact with each other. In short, the low average spending estimates for individual service categories can mask the full extent to which outside expertise is acquired to solve specific types of technical problems.

A second factor is that many of the survey firms have been informally acquiring useful technological inputs at either very low cost or, more commonly, at no cost at all. More than 60 percent of the respondents stated that they frequently obtain knowledge-based inputs from the technical units of other manufacturing companies (usually nearby), almost always on an informal or nonmarket basis (for a review of this topic from a "networking" perspective, see Malecki 1994). Significantly, informal interactions of this ilk were generally ranked high in terms of perceived impact, yet monetary transactions and/or contractual obligations were rarely in place. Clearly, then, the seemingly low spending estimates listed in Tables 4 and 6 need to be reviewed in light of several other factors.

Finally, for the sample as a whole, part of the divergence between spending and perceived impact stems from the fact that most of the input-classes listed in Table 1 are nonsubstitutable. More specifically, an expenditure switch from a relatively high-cost/low-impact service to a lower-cost/higher-impact category would not necessarily deliver a superior package of benefits overall. Instead, it would appear that the data are picking up the service-mixing effect noted earlier. To paraphrase one business executive interviewed, "we spent a lot on contract-R&D to get a product idea off the ground, but it was low-cost market research that gave the crucial feedback to our production people. . . ." In

Table 7. Multiple-External Linkage Patterns among the Survey Firms

	External Contact Diversity (# of different input sources)											
	New York City			Upstate/Central			Western New York			All Regions			
	1	2–3	>3	1	2–3	>3	1	2–3	>3	1	2–3	>3	Total
n	48	43	40	46	21	5	57	26	20	151	90	65	306
Regional %	36.6	32.8	30.5	63.8	29.1	6.9	55.3	25.2	19.4	49.3	29.4	21.2	100.0

Chi-square for contact diversity by region = 21.67, p = 0.05.

these types of cases, "impact" and "cost" can easily diverge, if only for psychological reasons.

To rejoin the introductory tone of the paper, however, several patterns in the data merit reiteration at this point. First, there are significant regional variations in external spending. At the same time, there are no major regional variations in linkage propensity (an exception to this pattern is that NYC firms are more likely to exhibit multiple links to a wide range of sources). Second, there is a regionally consistent relationship between innovation success and the incidence of external linkages. Although NYC firms are more likely to innovate than firms from other parts of the State, most of the innovators across all regions exhibit external linkages. Third, there are regional differences in the relationship between external spending and perceived impact. At this juncture, then, it is appropriate to explore the data at a finer level. Why are external linkages initiated? And what does the geography of external spending actually look like?

Results of Follow-Up Telephone Interviews

Of the 306 service-linked firms in the sample, 255 participated in follow-up telephone interviews. In the case of smaller firms (less than fifty workers), the interviewee was typically the CEO and/or owner. For most other firms, the interviewee was either the vice president, a senior engineer, or a specialist with R&D responsibilities. These interviews were designed to explore three main aspects of the outsourcing relationship, including: (1) motives, objectives, and expectations; (2) modes of service delivery; and (3) the geography of supply linkages. In all cases, the interviewees were asked to describe their experiences regarding only their most important

services (not the full range). Once data relating to these areas had been obtained, unstructured discussions were initiated within the scope of several interlinked themes, including: (a) the usefulness of external inputs, (b) levels of exposure to these inputs over time (an experience-based dimension), (c) the extent to which services were bought in multiple combinations, and (d) problems with vendor identification and/or service acquisition.

In terms of outsourcing motives, Tables 8 and 9 show the main factors that emerged from the telephone interviews. For the sample as a whole, outsourcing was found to be driven mainly by necessity (defined as a condition where the firm had an urgent need but no in-house resources to satisfy that need). Examples included a NYC metal fabricator that wanted access to new adhesives technology for steel-to-plastic bonding applications, a UC furniture company that needed external help to solve materials wastage problems, and a WNY medical devices producer that required ongoing access to advanced testing equipment. In these types of cases, in-house technical resources were simply unavailable. In most of these cases, moreover, service quality was cited as a more critical factor in supplier selection than cost. In terms of Rothwell's (1989) research on the motives that encourage outsourcing, then, there is good evidence that firms explore external options mainly in response to internal limitations (for comparable evidence from a supply-side perspective, see Beyers and Lindahl 1994).

Nevertheless the necessity factor was found to be unevenly spread across the three regions. For instance, NYC firms were less likely to cite this factor than their more northerly counterparts. Roughly 14 percent of the NYC firms cited "necessity" as the chief reason for outsourcing, compared to 47 percent and 40 percent among WNY and UC firms respectively. An implication here is that NYC firms internalize a larger

Table 8. General Reasons for Recourse to External Producer Services

	New York City			Upstate/Central			Western NY			All Regions*		
	n	%	Rank	n	%	Rank	n	%	Rank	n	%	Rank
Quality[a]	33	41.2	(1)	13	15.5	(3)	19	20.8	(2)	65	25.5	(2)
Cost[b]	13	16.2	(3)	10	11.9	(5)	14	15.3	(3)	37	14.5	(3)
Necessity[c]	15	18.7	(2)	34	40.5	(1)	43	47.2	(1)	92	36.0	(1)
Infrequent need[d]	10	12.5	(4)	14	16.6	(2)	10	10.9	(4)	34	13.3	(4)
Other[e]	9	11.2	(5)	13	15.4	(4)	5	5.4	(5)	27	10.5	(5)
Total	80	100.0		84	100.0		91	100.0		255	100.0	

Where: [a] = outside suppliers deliver superior inputs, but "adequate" inputs could be produced in-house if absolutely necessary.
[b] = outside suppliers deliver lower-cost/comparable quality inputs relative to those that could be produced in-house.
[c] = urgent technical need, but no in-house capability whatsoever.
[d] = sporadic/unpredictable demand for service (in-house ability not desired).
[e] = a wide mix of motives that defy easy classification (see text).
*Regional differences for items 1 and 3 are statistically significant (p = 0.05 or better) on the basis of a chi-square test (where location is crosstabulated against each item [yes/no]).

proportion of their technological activities than firms from other parts of the state. Curiously, however, there is no discernible connection between this pattern and the size/age mix of firms across the regions. Furthermore, for the state as a whole, no clear relationship emerged between the size of the respondent and the probability of citing the "necessity" factor. We shall return to these points later.

Regional variations also emerged for the second most important motive (quality)—defined as the existence of superior external supply, even though in-house resources could be used if necessary. Roughly 25 percent of the survey firms cited this factor as the main reason for outsourcing. At the regional level, however, NYC firms were more strongly featured in this category than firms from elsewhere in the state. This again suggests that NYC firms exhibit stronger in-house technological competence, in that the "quality" factor describes activities that could be internally handled.

The third ranked category (cost) describes the motives of some 15 percent of the survey firms. While there are no major regional contrasts in the distribution of this factor, the fact that this motive was not highly ranked implies that the oft-cited externalization of service tasks for cost reasons may not be as extensive as once thought. Of the thirty-four firms that cited this factor, moreover, twenty-nine indicated that their external links were to relatively routine or low-order services such as data processing, payroll management, and/or equipment repair.

The fourth ranked category (infrequent/unpredictable demand) also turned out to be

weaker than initially expected. Although recent literature has identified this factor as a potentially important motive for outsourcing (Coffey and Bailly 1993), the results from this sample suggest that other reasons are more popular. Only 13 percent of the survey firms cited this factor as the main reason for outsourcing.

The final category ("other") refers to a mixture of context-specific factors that defy easy classification. For example, several firms indicated that they buy external services only to compensate for periodic upswings in workload. Although few of the firms in this category viewed their outsourcing activities as being of any technological significance, most respondents noted that outside help is generally useful from a logistical standpoint.

Overall, however, the data point to regional variations in the mix of outsourcing motives. Moreover, even when the firms were asked to specify the nature of their outsourcing activities in terms of technical objectives, regional variations again emerged (Table 9). These data suggest that in-house problem-solving capacities vary across the State. For example, of the fifty-four service-linked NYC firms that buy external inputs to support product innovation, the average contribution of outside advice to the product development process was 10 percent. In the case of UC and WNY, however, the comparable proportions were 28 and 43 percent respectively.

Interestingly, telephone interviews revealed only minor regional differences in service delivery modes. Table 10 shows that face-to-face interaction is the most common delivery style for all regions (weighted average = 78 percent), fol-

Table 9. Service Spending Motives and the In-House/External Input Balance

	New York City			Upstate/Central			Western New York			All Regions		
	n	%	EC%	n	%	EC%	n	%	EC%	n	%	EC%
Product innovation[a]	54	67.5	(10)	29	34.5	(28)	48	52.8	(43)	131	51.4	(22)
Process innovation[b]	17	21.2	(26)	23	27.4	(40)	31	34.1	(35)	71	27.8	(41)
Management[c]	7	8.7	(15)	15	17.8	(17)	8	8.8	(16)	30	11.7	(15)
Other[d]	2	2.5	(12)	17	20.2	(22)	4	4.4	(10)	23	9.0	(13)
Total	80	100.0	n.a	84	100.0	n.a.	91	100.0	n.a.	255	100.0	n.a.

Where: [a] = external inputs that are sourced ultimately with a view to improving an existing product, creating an entirely new product, evaluating a new product, or suggesting strategies for product development.
   [b] = external inputs that are sourced ultimately with a view to improving the firm's manufacturing methods or procedures.
   [c] = external inputs that are sourced mainly to assist organizational and/or management aspects of the production, distribution, marketing, or after-sales-servicing components of the manufacturing effort.
   [d] = a mixture of categories (see text).
EC% = estimated percentage of the external (producer service) contribution to the technical goal in question.

lowed by fax/phone (14 percent), mail (6 percent), and "other" (2 percent). Although UC stands out as having a stronger orientation toward electronic modes of input delivery (28 percent), especially for nonlocal services, the weighted average for the State as a whole is only 14 percent. At first glance, then, it appears that the "information highways" of the Internet and related communications systems are not well traveled—at least not in terms of service delivery. This is not to deny the importance of electronic interactions in terms of other functions. Many firms exploit these types of communications methods with a view toward contact-initiation, supplier search, and/or day-to-day progress monitoring. Nevertheless, it seems fair to say that electronic systems are not the preferred choice as far as strategic aspects of service delivery are concerned.

This said, the data point to regional differences in terms of local versus nonlocal sourcing. This latter mode of service acquisition is more

prevalent outside NYC. The tenth column of Table 10 suggests that WNY and UC are import-intensive regions when it comes to advanced services, whereas NYC is as close to self-sufficiency as any region might conceivably be. The regional pattern of import sourcing is also revealing, in that nonlocal provision for the two import-oriented regions can be traced to a narrow range of sources (Table 11). For instance, 78 percent of WNY's recent imports came from Canada, and almost 80 percent of these expenditures leaked northward to Toronto. Among importers from UC, however, only 11 percent of recent nonlocal expenditures went to Canada—but, in this case, almost 70 percent of the remainder went to New York City. For the NYC region, Canada supplied only 5 percent of total imports, yet more than 20 percent of this region's services came from Western Europe. In this regard, it is not possible to infer a clear proximity effect as far as external sourcing is concerned. While the data suggest relatively

Table 10. Modes of Producer Service Retrieval by Region (% of All Inputs)[a]

		Face-to-Face		Fax/Phone		Mail		Other		Total		
Region	(%)	L	NL	L	NL	L	NL	L	NL	L	NL	L + NL
New York City		53	17	9	8	5	4	2	1	69	31	100
Upstate/Central		28	38	2	26	1	4	1	0	32	68	100
Western New York		44	46	2	4	3	1	0	0	49	51	100
NYS average[b]		42	34	4	13	3	3	1	0	50	50	100
Weighted[c]		57	21	5	9	4	2	1	1	67	33	100

[a]These data come from 255 telephone interviews with service users.
[b]This is a simple average calculated from the columns.
[c]This average is weighted by the total spending patterns of users by region, giving a more representative picture in aggregate terms.
Where: L = sourced from within the local area (home region).
   NL = sourced nonlocally (outside the home region).

Table 11. Service Imports: Regional Patterns of Nonlocal Sourcing

	International			Domestic		
(%)	Canada	Europe	Other	NYS[a]	Beyond[b]	Total
New York City	5	22	1	5	57	100
Upstate/Central	11	2	0	75	12	100
Western New York	78	4	1	14	3	100

[a]Within New York State but outside the home region.
[b]Outside New York State but within the U.S.

short-distance/international sourcing among northerly firms (perhaps reflecting a Canada/U.S. border effect), one would be hard pressed to argue that European supply sources are significantly more accessible to NYC firms from a logistical perspective.

At this point, however, it should be noted that Tables 8–11 present data that were collected via structured questions. Not tabulated here are several sets of impressionistic results that were gleaned from unstructured discussions. In this regard, telephone interviews revealed that regional differences in the relationship between external spending and perceived impact may partly be explained by three sets of factors, including: (1) the relative balance between internal versus external service provision, (2) the degree of service exposure/experience gained over time, and (3) the existence of informal service inputs that are delivered either at minimal cost or at no cost at all.

With regard to the first factor, it would appear that NYC firms spend a good deal more on both internal and external S&T activity than their more northerly counterparts.[10] Scaled as a percentage of total S&T spending, however, external expenditures among NYC firms are noticeably smaller than the average for both UC and WNY. For instance, the external component of total S&T spending among NYC firms lies between 5 and 10 percent, whereas the typical range among WNY firms was between 30 and 35 percent (the range for UC was between 10 and 15 percent). In relative terms, then, average levels of external service dependence are stronger outside NYC.

A further point is that NYC firms appear to have been buying external inputs for longer than firms in the other regions. Although the evidence for this is partial (due mainly to the fact that few interviewees were able to accurately assess the nature of their firms' external contacts over time), the evidence that did emerge merits

attention. In the case of NYC, for instance, most interviewees stated that recourse to external support is "nothing new." Aside from several young firms, most of these people (>70 percent) stated that they had been buying outside technical inputs for "as long as I can remember," "since I joined the firm," or "for a long time" (paraphrased by the author). Outside NYC, however, more than half of the interviewees stated that significant external links had only "recently" been initiated. Although hard data were difficult to obtain, phrases such as "we have only been doing this for the last few years" or "we are new to this game" turned out to be much more common among firms outside NYC. As noted earlier in the paper, moreover, these types of contrasts are not clearly attributable to regional differences in the age, size-mix, or market characteristics of the survey firms.

These types of experience-based contrasts may also explain why service-mixing is more common in the NYC area than elsewhere. Broadly speaking, firms that have been buying external services for a "long time" exhibit a deeper familiarity with the external input environment than firms that are "new to the game." In the case of one NYC producer of electronic testing equipment, for example, recent dealings with a local management consultant led to the suggestion that the firm's product market be broadened within its existing sphere of expertise. In an effort to follow this advice, contract R&D specialists were hired to assess alternative applications for the firm's products. This external contract, in turn, was followed by a subsequent demand for design and engineering services, with a view to developing "makeable" products. While several examples of service-mixing emerged from the telephone interviews, the key point is that multiple-sourcing was particularly noticeable among innovative NYC firms, a majority of whom have been exploiting external talent for a long time.

It is also noteworthy that many firms obtain technical help from sources other than those mentioned thus far. Examples include distributors, suppliers, customers, informal business networks, and industry associations. It is important that expenditures on these types of informal or nonmarket inputs are generally either very low or zero, yet their respective impact rankings are consistently high. While recourse to these modes of external help varies little by region (at least in terms of contact incidence), there is a paucity of interaction between small and large firms within the manufacturing sector itself, especially outside NYC. Although most interviewees stated that they often obtain useful inputs from other industrial companies (notably suppliers and/or clients), very few of the UC or WNY firms indicated having significant links with corporations or large-scale producers. Even within the NYC region, moreover, only 16 percent of the interviewees indicated that large companies act as important sources of technical assistance. Given that several scholars have identified small/large firm technical interactions as being of potentially major relevance to the industrial development interests of peripheral regions (see Rothwell 1992), the sparsity of such interaction in New York State ought to be of concern to policy analysts.

Finally, I should note that the relatively strong level of service import activity among firms outside NYC is not without its problems. For instance, very small firms are generally reluctant and/or unable to access nonlocal inputs. Common reasons cited in this regard include (in rank order): (1) difficulties associated with identifying nonlocal specialists, (2) the perception that nonlocal consultants would not consider these firms important enough to deliver a quality service, (3) a lack of faith in the ability of nonlocal consultants to offer problem-specific inputs, and (4) the perception that nonlocal suppliers are too expensive. For these reasons, among others, small firms outside NYC are less likely to be familiar with a full range of external options. Moreover, of the import-oriented firms from these regions that do explore nonlocal vendors on a systematic basis, several expressed diluted versions of the problems cited above. In most of these cases, import activity continues today mainly because the central factor that drives the outsourcing relationship is "necessity." Despite the advent of advanced communications systems that can link peripheral firms with service-rich regions, relative location may still be an important factor in the performance potential of manufacturing firms, especially small ones.

Conclusions

Evidence shown earlier reveals that external technical services can assist the innovation efforts of New York State manufacturing firms. At the regional level, however, ease of access to these external services varies appreciably. While firms that reside in service-poor areas can import strategic services, this option is not widely practiced by very small SMFs. Peripheral firms in this category operate with fewer external options than their counterparts in the New York City area. Given that innovation is known to play a critical role in the commercial success of manufacturing firms, an important implication is that locational factors may predispose certain types of firms toward weak business performance.

Nevertheless there is no single causality chain that can fully explain the links between innovation and external sourcing. At one extreme, many of the more innovative NYC firms explore multiple external options with a view to complementing specialized aspects of internally conceived projects. Here external spending is mainly a function of in-house creativity. In contrast, several of the more innovative WNY firms exploit outside expertise in order to innovate. Here external talent plays a stronger, more direct role in the innovation process. The existence of intermediate positions between these extremes suggests that a single explanatory model is unlikely to emerge—nor should it.

Although high-order technical services appear to help firms across the state as a whole, the geography of external spending does not match the geography of perceived impact. One possible reason for this pattern is that NYC firms have been using outside services for a long time, perhaps reflecting the existence of strong local supply. In addition, NYC firms have been spending more overall on both internal and external S&T activity than the other firms in the sample. Many of these NYC firms appear to expect, obtain, and/or utilize outside services in ways that are viewed as "routine" by those executives who authorize outsourcing activity. In contrast, this type of perception was rarely found outside the NYC area, where recourse to external help appears to be a somewhat "newer" practice.

Significantly, the survey results lend extra weight to Feldman and Florida's (1994) work on the geography of innovation in the U.S. These authors point to a connection between the regional incidence of industrial creativity and the spatial distribution of external technological resources. From a policy perspective, the present study adds a set of potentially practical angles to the results noted by these authors. For instance, more than 60 percent of the firms in this sample reported an important business impact as a result of external management inputs which cost, on average, less than US$4,000 per year. A comparable proportion of firms reported important product development impacts from industrial design contracts that cost, on average, less than US$5,000 per year. It would appear that worthwhile results can be obtained from relatively small outlays. In policy terms, then, it might make sense to broadcast this type of message to as wide a population of firms as possible. In this regard, public efforts to connect potential buyers with vendors (an information brokerage function) might be incorporated within existing technological outreach initiatives (see Shapira et al. 1995).

A second and related topic for policy research concerns the potential impact of public subsidies to support first-time contacts between firms with specific technical needs and vendors that can deliver suitable skills. Britton (1993) has argued in favor of this type of initiative in a Canadian context for many years, reflecting, in part, the success of the UK's Enterprise Initiative (which is organized as a first-time/once-only contact subsidy for British firms). Both of these policy dimensions (information brokerage and contact subsidies) can be justified by the presence of flawed information markets in which needy buyers fail to connect with appropriate sellers, often as a direct result of the spatial separation of potential demand from supply (Smallbone et al. 1993).

Policy matters aside, however, it should be emphasized that access to outside expertise constitutes only one facet of the innovation relationship among industrial firms. Although there is a growing body of international evidence that confirms the importance of external talent (see Freeman 1991), the task remains to assess this aspect of innovation support in concert with other elements of the performance equation, in-

cluding the role of demand (customer sophistication), the educational and entrepreneurial characteristics of the firm's managers and/or workers (a human capital component), and the various milieu or business network factors suggested by Camagni (1995), Maillat (1990), and Malecki (1994) among others. In short, this paper has merely etched the surface of what must surely be a more structurally and geographically complicated nest of connections between the internal and external technical environments of firms.

Acknowledgments

The views expressed in this paper are those of the author, and in no way represent policy statements of the State University of New York at Buffalo or the Canada-U.S. Trade Center. This research was wholly funded by the National Science Foundation under grant No. SBR-9312630. The author wishes to thank Andrew Curtis for help with data analysis, Pat Randall for assistance with the design of the survey instrument, David Howes for graphics assistance, and the hundreds of New York State business executives who took the time to participate in this research project. Thanks are also extended to three anonymous referees and the former editor of the *Annals*, Carville Earle, for helpful and significant suggestions regarding the shape of this manuscript. All errors and omissions are the sole responsibility of the author.

Notes

1. The term "small and medium-sized firm" (SMF) is defined by the U.S. Small Business Administration as a business entity with fewer than 500 employees. The results shown in this paper do not distinguish between small/medium-sized establishments and small-medium-sized firms. While individual establishments may employ less than 500 workers, such units may also belong to larger multilocational organizations that collectively employ more than 500 workers. The text employs the terms "establishment" and "firm" interchangeably. Although there are significant organizational differences between these two groups of respondents, there are sufficient similarities in terms of the key variables considered in this paper to warrant an aggregated treatment of the sample as far as plant status is concerned.

2. While 69 percent (n = 53) of the establishments that belong to multilocational organizations enjoy access to technical inputs on an intrafirm

basis, no statistically significant differences emerged between this group of establishments and the remainder of the sample in terms of external service spending (scaled as a proportion of establishment sales), geographical sourcing, or the nature of the technical outsourcing pattern (types of services used). There was, however, a general tendency for multiplant respondents to indicate lower levels of external service spending than the sample average, in part because of intrafirm transactions.

3. These data are for private producer services only. Average external spending (total) for the four sectors exceeds the estimates presented in Table 4 because some firms (a small minority) spent significant amounts of money on public sources of assistance. The spending estimates are restricted to private services in Tables 4 and 6 because these services account for more than 90 percent of total external spending for a substantial majority of the survey firms.

4. This interpretation is a subjective one, supported in part by the fact that average costs per contract for management, design, and engineering services far exceed the comparable averages for testing and repair services. I should also note that testing and repair services are typically bought on a relatively frequent basis (3–5 contracts per year, on average), whereas average contract frequencies for the three other service classes listed above rarely exceed one per year. A more detailed discussion of these types of issues is planned for a separate paper.

5. In the absence of comparative sectoral data on external service spending for different regions or nations (disaggregated by establishment size), it is difficult to assess whether the estimates shown in Table 4 are high, low, or average. The term "low" is employed in a purely descriptive/intuitive sense, in that the absolute dollar outlays are rather minor in comparison with the other operating expenses of a typical manufacturing firm.

6. In Table 5, externally linked firms are defined as firms that spent an annual average of at least $5000 on private services over the study period. This threshold was set by a natural break in the spending distribution. Below this threshold, most firms indicated having only insignificant/exploratory links with outside vendors, typically at spending levels of no more than a few hundred dollars spread over the entire study period.

7. The innovation/linkage relationship holds true across all four sectors (and for all regions) at $p = 0.05$ or better on the basis of 2×2 chi-square tests.

8. No significant size differences were found between innovators versus noninnovators, or between externally linked versus nonexternally linked respondents.

9. Another noteworthy sectoral effect concerns the propensity of older firms in the furniture and metal fabricating industries to use external services to support the adoption of process innovations (e.g., new production methods) rather than to promote new product development (which is a more conspicuous phenomenon among scientific instruments and electrical industrial equipment producers). Although an assessment of possible PLC effects would go beyond the scope of this paper, the survey data are well suited to testing the dynamic-stages model of innovation suggested by Utterback and Abernathy (1975).

10. Telephone interviews also revealed that certain types of external linkages are forged with a view to internalizing specific strands of expertise upon completion of the outsourcing contract. This practice was particularly noticeable among NYC respondents. Although the evidence for this was too anecdotal to merit tabulation, several of the NYC interviewees indicated that in-house personnel were expected to learn the ropes for many of the specific contract R&D tasks that were recently outsourced. Whether or not this phenomenon implies shrinking market opportunities for contract R&D companies over time is an issue that cannot be tackled with the data on hand. Suffice it to say, for the moment, that certain types of firms outsource specific technical jobs with a view toward never outsourcing the same types of jobs in the future.

References

Berman, D. 1995. The Internationalization and External Knowledge Acquisition Processes of Small Manufacturing Firms: Empirical Evidence from Metropolitan Toronto. Ph.D. dissertation, Department of Geography, University at Buffalo.

Bessant, J., and Rush, H. 1995. Building Bridges for Innovation: The Role of Consultants in Technology Transfer. *Research Policy* 24:97–114.

Beyers, W. B., and Lindahl, D. P. 1994. Competitive Advantage and Information Technologies in Producer Services. Paper presented at the Annual Meetings of the Association of American Geographers, San Francisco.

Britton, J. N. H. 1989. A Policy Perspective on Incremental Innovation in Small and Medium-Sized Enterprises. *Entrepreneurship and Regional Development* 2:179–90.

———. 1991. Reconsidering Innovation Policy: The Canadian Case. *Environment and Planning C* 9:189–206.

———. 1993. A Regional Industrial Perspective on Canada under Free Trade. *International Journal of Urban and Regional Research* 17:559–77.

Camagni, R. P. 1995. The Concept of Innovative Milieu and Its Relevance for Public Policies in European Lagging Regions. *Papers in Regional Science* 74:317–40.

Carter, C. F., and Williams, B. B. 1957. *Industry and Technical Progress.* New York: Oxford University Press.

Chandra, B. 1992. High-Technology Manufacturing in Western New York: An Assessment of the Internationalization Processes of Innovative Firms. Ph.D. dissertation, Department of Geography, University at Buffalo.

Chrisman, J. J. and Katrishen, F. 1995. The Small Business Development Center Programme in the USA: A Statistical Analysis of Its Impact on Economic Development. *Entrepreneurship and Regional Development* 7:143–56.

Coffey, W. J., and Bailly, A. S. 1993. Producer Services and Systems of Flexible Production. *Urban Studies* 29:857–68.

Coffey, W. J.; Drolet, R.; and Polese, M. 1994. Make or Buy: Internalization and Externalization of Producer Service Inputs in the Montreal Metropolitan Area. Paper presented at the North American Meetings of the Regional Science Association, Niagara Falls, Canada.

Cornish, S. 1997. Product Innovation and the Spatial Dynamics of Market Intelligence: Does Proximity to Markets Matter? *Economic Geography* (forthcoming).

Curtis, A., and MacPherson, A. 1996. The Zone Definition Problem in Survey Research: An Empirical Example from New York State. *The Professional Geographer* 48:310–20.

Daniels, P. W. 1989. Some Perspectives on the Geography of Services. *Progress in Human Geography* 13:427–37.

Ellwein, T., and Brudre, W. 1982. *Innovationsorientierte Regionalpolitik.* Opladen: Westdeutscher Verlag.

Feldman, M. P. 1994. Small Firms, External Resources and New Product Introductions. Paper presented at the North American Meetings of the Regional Science Association, Niagara Falls, Canada.

Feldman, M. P., and Florida, R. 1994. The Geographic Sources of Innovation: Technological Infrastructure and Product Innovation in the United States. *Annals of the Association of American Geographers* 84:210–29.

Freeman, C. 1991. Networks of Innovators: A Synthesis of Research Issues. *Research Policy* 20:499–514.

Gertler, M. S. 1995. 'Being there': Proximity, Organization and Culture in the Development and Adoption of Advanced Manufacturing Technologies. *Economic Geography* 71:1–28.

Glasmeier, A. 1990. A Missing Link: The Relationship between Distribution and Industrial Complex Formation. *Entrepreneurship and Regional Development* 2:315–34.

Goddard, J. B. 1978. Office Location and Urban and Regional Development. In *Spatial Patterns of Office Growth and Location,* ed. P. W. Daniels, pp. 28–60. Chichester: John Wiley.

Goe, R. W. 1991. The Growth of Producer Service Industries: Sorting through the Externalization Debate. *Growth and Change* 22:118–41.

Hansen, N. 1994. The Strategic Role of Producer Services in Regional Development. *International Regional Science Review* 16:187–96.

Haour, G. 1992. Stretching the Knowledge-Base of the Enterprise through Contract Research. *R&D Management* 22:177–82.

Harrington, J. W. 1995. Producer Services Research in U.S. Regional Studies. *The Professional Geographer* 47:66–69.

Harrington, J. W. and Lombard, J. R. 1989. Producer-Service Firms in a Declining Manufacturing Region. *Environment and Planning* A 21:65–79.

Hepworth, M. 1989. *The Geography of the Information Economy.* London: Belhaven Press.

Hitchens, D. M. W. N.; O'Farrell, P. N.; and Conway, C. 1994. Business Service Use by Manufacturing Firms in Mid-Wales. *Environment and Planning* A 26:95–106.

Illeris, S. 1994. Proximity between Service Producers and Service Users. *Tijdschrift voor Economische en Sociale Geografie* 85:185–96.

Kelley, M. R., and Brooks, H. 1991. External Learning Opportunities and the Diffusion of Process Innovation to Small Firms: The Case of Programmable Automation. *Technological Forecasting and Social Change* 39:103–25.

Lawton Smith, H. 1993. Externalization of Research and Development in Europe. *European Planning Studies* 1:465–82.

Lefebvre, L. A.; Harvey, J.; and Lefebvre, E. 1991. Technological Experience and the Technology Adoption Decisions in Small Manufacturing Firms. *R&D Management* 21:241–49.

Lentnek, B.; MacPherson, A.; and Phillips, D. 1992. Optimum Producer Service Location. *Environment and Planning* A 24:467–79.

Lipparini, A., and Sobrero, M. 1994. The Glue and the Pieces: Entrepreneurship and Innovation in Small Firm Networks. *Journal of Business Venturing* 9:125–40.

Lundvall, B.-A. 1988. Innovation as an Interactive Process: From User-Producer Interaction to the National System of Innovation. In *Technical Change and Economic Theory,* ed. G. Dosi,

C. Freeman, R. Nelson, G. Silverberg, and L. Soete, pp. 349–69. London: Pinter.

MacPherson, A. 1992. Innovation, External Technical Linkages and Small Firm Commercial Performance: An Empirical Analysis from Western New York. *Entrepreneurship and Regional Development* 4:165–84.

———. 1997. *Technical Outsourcing among New York State Manufacturing Firms*. Canada-United States Trade Center, Occasional Paper #18, Department of Geography, University at Buffalo, forthcoming.

Maillat, D. 1990. SMEs, Innovation, and Territorial Development. In *Technological Development at the Local Level*, ed. R. Cappelin and P. Nijkamp, pp. 331–51. Aldershot: Avebury.

Malecki, E. J. 1991. *Technology and Economic Development: The Dynamics of Local, Regional and National Change*. London: Longman Scientific and Technical.

———. 1994. Entrepreneurship in Regional and Local Development. *International Regional Science Review* 16:119–54.

Malecki, E. J., and Veldhoen, M. E. 1993. Network Activities, Information and Competitiveness in Small Firms. *Geografiska Annaler* (B) 75:131–47.

Malecki, E. J., and Tootle, D. M. 1996. The Role of Networks in Small Firm Competitiveness. *International Journal of Technology Management* 11:43–57.

Meyer-Krahmer, F. 1985. Innovation Behaviour and Regional Indigenous Potential. *Regional Studies* 19:523–34.

Myers, S., and Marquis, D. G. 1969. Successful Industrial Innovation. National Science Foundation 69-17, internal document.

National Research Council. 1993. *Learning to Change: Opportunities to Improve the Performance of Smaller Manufacturers*. Washington: National Academy Press.

O'Connor, K. 1994. Industrial Design as a Producer Service: Shifts in Function and Location. Paper presented at the Annual Meetings of the Association of American Geographers, San Francisco.

———. 1996. The Use of Industrial Design Services by Firms: A Case Study of Producer Service-Industrial Linkages. Paper presented at the Annual Meetings of the Association of American Geographers, Charlotte, NC.

O'Farrell, P. N. 1995. Manufacturing Demand for Business Services. *Cambridge Journal of Economics* 19:523–43.

O'Farrell, P. N.; Hitchens, D. M.; and Moffat, L. A. R. 1995. Business Service Firms in Two Peripheral Economies: Scotland and Ireland.

Tijdschrift voor Economische en Sociale Geografie 86:115–28.

O'Farrell, P. N., and Moffat, L. A. R. 1995. Business Services and Their Impact upon Client Performance: An Exploratory Interregional Analysis. *Regional Studies* 29:111–24.

O'hUallacháin, B. 1991. Industrial Geography. *Progress in Human Geography* 15:73–80.

Phillips, D. 1995. The Outsourcing of Computer Services: Toward an Explanation of the Externalization Process. Manuscript, Department of Geography, University at Buffalo.

Porter, M. E. 1990. *The Competitive Advantage of Nations*. New York: Free Press.

Rajan, A., and Pearson, R. 1986. *UK Occupation and Employment Trends to 1990*. Guildford: Butterworth.

Rothwell, R. 1977. The External Consultant and Innovation in the Mechanical Engineering Industry. *Engineering* October:838–39.

———. 1989. SMFs, Inter-Firm Relationships and Technological Change. *Entrepreneurship and Regional Development* 1:275–91.

———. 1991. External Networking and Innovation in Small and Medium-sized Manufacturing Firms in Europe. *Technovation* 11:93–112.

———. 1992. Successful Industrial Innovation: Critical Factors for the 1990s. *R&D Management* 22:221–39.

Rothwell, R., and Dodgson, M. 1991. External Linkages and Innovation in Small and Medium-Sized Enterprises. *R&D Management* 21:125–37.

Sabel, C.; Herrigel, G.; Kazis, R.; and Deeg, R. 1987. How to Keep Mature Industries Innovative. *Technology Review* 90:27–35.

Scott, A. J. 1986. Industrial Organization and Urbanization: A Geographical Agenda. *Annals of the Association of American Geographers* 76:25–37.

Shapira, P. 1990. Modern Times: Learning from State Initiatives in Industrial Extension and Technology Transfer. *Economic Development Quarterly* 4:186–202.

Shapira, P., Roessner, J. D., and Barke, R. 1995. New Public Infrastructure for Small Firm Industrial Modernization in the USA. *Entrepreneurship and Regional Development* 7:63–84.

Sinkula, J. M. 1990. Perceived Characteristics, Organizational Factors, and the Utilization of External Market Research Suppliers. *Journal of Business Research* 21:1–17.

Smallbone, D.; North, D.; and Leigh, R. 1993. The Use of External Assistance by Mature SMEs in the UK: Some Policy Implications. *Entrepreneurship and Regional Development* 5:279–95.

Soni, P. K.; Lilien, G. L.; and Wilson, D. T. 1993. Industrial Innovation and Firm Performance: A Reconceptualization and Exploratory Structural Equation Analysis. *International Journal of Research in Marketing* 10:365–80.

Tyson, D. 1993. Consultants Ease the Way to Industrial Innovation. *Physics World* January:57–58.

U.S. General Accounting Office. 1995. Manufacturing Extension Programs: Manufacturers' Views of Services. Briefing Report to the Chairwoman, Subcommittee on Technology, Committee on Science, House of Representatives. Washington.

Utterback, J. M., and Abernathy, W. J. 1975. A Dynamic Model of Product and Process Innovation. *Omega, The International Journal of Management Science* 3:639–56.

Vaessen, P., and Keeble. D. 1995. Growth-Oriented SMEs in Unfavourable Regional Environments. *Regional Studies* 29:489–502.

Von Hippel, T. 1978. Users as Innovators. *Technology Review* 11:31–39.

———. 1988. *The Sources of Innovation.* New York: Oxford University Press.

Walker, R. A. 1985. Is There a Service Economy? The Changing Capitalist Division of Labour. *Science and Society* 1:42–83.

Yap, C. S.; Soh, C. P. P.; and Raman, K. S. 1992. Information Systems Success Factors in Small Business. *Omega, The International Journal of Management Science* 20:597–609.

Young, A. 1928. Increasing Returns and Economic Progress. *Economic Journal* 38:527–42.

Correspondence: Canada-U.S. Trade Center, Department of Geography, University at Buffalo, Buffalo, NY 14261-0023, email geoadm@ubvms.cc.buffalo.edu.

JOURNAL OF REGIONAL SCIENCE, VOL. 30, NO. 4, 1990, pp. 465–476

DO PRODUCER SERVICES INDUCE REGIONAL ECONOMIC DEVELOPMENT?*

Niles Hansen†

ABSTRACT. Goods production and services have become increasingly integrated within a flexible, information-oriented system of production organization. In this context, it is argued here that producer services—carried out both within manufacturing firms and by "independent" enterprises—play a pivotal role in expanding the division of labor, productivity, and per capita income. This proposition is supported by results of an empirical analysis of metropolitan areas in major U.S. regions and in the nation as a whole.

1. INTRODUCTION

In the first part of this paper, I discuss the rapid growth of the services sector, particularly producer services. I then argue that a growing economy shows an increasingly complex division of labor, not only within, but also among, firms and industries. In an increasingly information-oriented economy, producer services play a pivotal role in the complex, expanding division of labor, which in turn creates productivity increases throughout the economy. Regions that have a high density of producer services are, thus, likely to have higher per capita incomes than other regions. The expanding division of labor also has a qualitative dimension that requires increasing skill and education levels, especially with respect to sophisticated producer services. While producer-services density and education can be expected to be directly associated with productivity and income, they alone cannot account for all of the productivity gains arising from growing markets and divisions of labor. However, metropolitan population size may reflect many of these other complex, productivity-increasing interrelations. Thus, while producer services, education, and metropolitan size may be interrelated, it is hypothesized that each of these variables makes a significant contribution to productivity and income gains at the metropolitan level in its own right. These propositions are examined in terms of an empirical analysis of metropolitan areas in major U.S. regions and in the nation as a whole.

2. THE EXPANDING ROLE OF PRODUCER SERVICES

Because of the emphasis on producer services, I should point out that in some contexts they have been defined to include a broad range of activities, such as finance, insurance, and real estate; legal services; transportation and communica-

---

*The author wishes to thank E. Anthon Eff for valuable research assistance.
†Professor, Department of Economics, University of Texas.

Received August 1989; in revised form December 1989; accepted February 1990.

tions; accounting; advertising and marketing; research and development; data processing; and worker and management training. However, conventional government data on employment and output lack the level of detail required to clearly identify and measure producer services. Hence, it is difficult to distinguish between those activities included in the complexes that mostly or exclusively serve firms and those that cater to a much larger public. Moreover, in addition to services provided to business enterprises on a fee or contract basis, many industrial corporations have been moving into territories that were once the sole domain of independent producer-service firms. Thus, corporate offices and producer-service firms need to be examined in conjunction with one another because of the strong complementarities and substitutabilities between their outputs (Noyelle and Stanback, 1984). In light of these considerations, the empirical analysis of producer services includes only (1) those services classified by the U.S. Bureau of the Census as business services (SIC 73)—although the degree of their use may also reflect the degree of producer service use more broadly defined—and (2) the nonproduction payroll outlays of manufacturing firms.

The data in Table 1 indicate that between 1970 and 1986, the U.S. gross national product increased by 53.7 percent and total national employment grew by 39.3 percent. During the same period the value of services output increased by 91.0 percent and services employment rose by 85.3 percent. However, the growth of producer services was even more striking; the value of output in this sector increased by 173.3 percent while employment tripled. Meanwhile, in the manufacturing sector the payroll share accounted for by nonproduction workers increased from 39.9 percent in 1970 to 46.7 percent in 1985; and nonproduction employment rose from 29.7 percent of total manufacturing-sector employment in 1970 to 35.2 percent in 1985 (U.S. Bureau of the Census, 1978, 1987).

In keeping with the traditional economic-base model of regional development, it is still sometimes argued that manufacturing activities are a prerequisite for strong growth in the services sectors (Rones, 1986). Nevertheless, there is a growing literature that emphasizes the importance of services, and especially producer services, in enhancing the prospects for attracting and retaining manufacturing and other firms (Monnoyer and Philippe, 1985; Pedersen, 1986; Gillis, 1987; Bailly and Maillat, 1988; Quinn 1988; Stabler and Howe, 1988; Illeris, 1989a,

TABLE 1: Value of Output (billions in constant 1982 dollars) and Employment for the U.S. Economy, Services, and Producer Services, 1970 and 1986

	U.S. Economy		Services		Producer Services (SIC 73)	
	Value of Output	Employment	Value of Output	Employment	Value of Output	Employment
1970	$2,416	78,678,000	$295.7	13,380,000	$47.5	1,666,000
1986	3,713	109,597,000	564.9	24,794,000	129.8	5,012,000
Change	1,297	30,919,000	269.2	11,414,000	82.3	3,346,000
Percent Change	53.7	39.3	91.0	85.3	173.3	200.8

Source: U.S. Bureau of the Census (1987, pp. 365, 407, 732–734).

1989b; Hansen, 1990). Producer services have even had attributed to them the development-inducing role that Perroux (1964) once attributed to key industrial growth poles in an input-output context. However, the analogy is inexact because the inducing effects of producer services cannot be fully evaluated in terms of purely technical relations and input-output multipliers. Rather, producer services tend to have a strategic role in changing the organization of firms and industries by enlarging the division of labor.

An accurate appreciation of the contribution of producer services to the regional development process has been impeded by measurement difficulties with respect to productivity, arising from problems of numerically defining output units and quality differences in services. In practice, the measurement of productivity in services is usually based on input volumes or ad hoc assumptions. In any case, attempts to measure sector-specific productivity do not reveal much about more significant phenomena, namely the nature of interdependencies among industries or the ways in which technological change affects the organization of production.

The organization of productive activity has increasingly been characterized by a merging of all relevant activities—managerial and production, white and blue collar, design and marketing, economic and technical—into a single, integrated information-intensive system for turning out flexible outputs of goods and services (Perez, 1985). In this process, the goods-producing and services sectors are so interrelated that policy considerations for one cannot be meaningful without carefully examining impacts on the other. Manufacturing success requires rapid feedback from the marketplace, more customized products, and more reliable delivery in shorter time cycles—all of which depend on downstream services integration (Quinn and Doorley, 1988). Moreover, the rapid growth of producer services in recent years cannot be explained by the *unbundling* hypothesis, which suggests that *external* producer services have grown as a result of manufacturers shifting in-house operations to outside service providers, with no increase in the volume of producer-service activities in the economy as a whole. Rather, Kutscher (1988) has shown that most of the growth in U.S. output of producer services between 1972 and 1985 can be attributed to changing business practices, that is, to changes in the structure of production as measured by the coefficients in an input-output table. This is not to assert that producer services cause structural changes in firms that demand such services. Although the presence of producer-services firms provides potential cost-reducing opportunities for other firms, it would probably be more accurate to argue that it is typically the changing demands of firms that provide markets for specialized service functions, with the whole process increasing the division of labor. In any case, the essential point is not whether or not producer services are the prime mover. It is rather that in an information-dominated economy the expansion of producer services—whether within manufacturing firms or by the creation and growth of independent specialized firms—provides a key indicator of the degree to which the division of labor is expanding.

About one-fifth of the total capital invested by U.S. manufacturing firms is in facilities outside of the United States, and effective coordination of the international operations of large manufacturing firms and of many smaller companies

468   JOURNAL OF REGIONAL SCIENCE, VOL. 30, NO. 4, 1990

depends heavily on services. Moreover, economies of scale in international operations are less a matter of plant scale economies than of the firm's services capabilities with respect to such matters as logistics, technology transfer, marketing, and finance. The competitive positions of international firms are now largely determined by their capacity to manage information worldwide (Quinn and Doorley, 1988). The evolution toward a just-in-time global economy can be seen in General Electric's recent announcement of concrete plans to create its own international telecommunications network, which will enable its employees to communicate globally using voice, video, and computer data. Industry analysts expect a growing number of international corporations to build private international networks in the next decade as they increase the flow of information abroad and seek tighter control over their foreign operations (Sims, 1989).

Recognition of the increasing interdependence of manufacturing and services renders obsolete the emphasis that traditional economic-base theory gave to manufacturing exports as the key to regional growth. Without denying that manufacturing exports from a region can have significant local multiplier effects, there is nevertheless mounting evidence that service exports also provide a catalyst for regional growth. For example, a study of new service firms in Minnesota found that such firms—and producer services in particular—had higher sales outside the state than did manufacturing firms (Birch, 1987). Beyers, Alvine, and Johnsen (1985) estimated that producer-service firms in the Central Puget Sound Region did 36 percent of their business outside of the region and that the employment resulting from their exported services plus other service export activity (e.g., shipping/port functions, tourism) was collectively as large as the number of regional export-tied manufacturing jobs. Evidence also clearly indicated that the services structure of the Central Puget Sound Region was similar to that of other large U.S. metropolitan areas, suggesting that the findings for this particular area could likely be duplicated elsewhere. Other empirical studies that emphasize the importance of service exports to regional economies are summarized in Gillis (1987).

3.   EXPANDING THE DIVISION OF LABOR AND PRODUCTIVITY

The division of labor is the division of a process or of employment into parts, each of which is carried out separately. This includes both the division of labor that takes place within an establishment or within an industry and the separation of employment within society at large. Division of labor is associated with specialization and cooperation and their consequences for productivity. The degree of division of labor is closely related to the degree of increasing returns. A technology exhibits increasing returns to scale if a proportionate increase in all inputs results in a more than proportionate increase in outputs. In the single-output case, this implies a decreasing average cost curve. However, as Young (1928) pointed out in his path-breaking article on the relations between increasing returns and economic development, the mechanism of increasing returns is not to be discerned adequately by observing the effects of variations in sizes of particular firms or industries. Rather, the progressive division and specialization of industries are an essential part of the process by which increasing returns are realized. Industrial activities need to be seen as an interrelated whole. Moreover, the securing of increasing returns depends on the progressive division of labor, which creates external economies by using labor in ever more roundabout or indirect ways. While the division of labor depends upon the extent of the market, as Adam Smith observed, the extent of the market also depends upon the division of labor. Increasing division of labor, by breaking up complex industrial processes into simpler parts, not only invited a larger use of existing technologies, but also prompted the invention of new technologies.

In pre-industrial low-productivity societies, factors of production, firms, and localities are relatively unspecialized as well as undifferentiated in space. When industrial urbanization takes place, factors, firms, and localities become increasingly specialized and, within their respective market areas, more differentiated from each other. The progressive division of labor yields higher returns to individuals and firms, as well as to the economy as a whole. Specialized activities on a larger scale at one stage of production create opportunities for innovation and specialization at other stages, through backward and forward linkages. Firms in an expanding industry benefit from cost reductions as a result of external economies in the Marshallian sense; that is, the relevant economies (service facilities, special skills and education, etc.) are external to the firm but internal to the industry. As economic development proceeds, external economies become more general in nature. In the broader sense, then, the concept applies to all services, facilities, or activities that exist outside the firm but reduce the firm's costs. External economies so conceived are external to the firm but internal to the locality, region, or nation. The specializations and interdependencies of towns, cities, and metropolitan areas reflect the same specialization-differentiation-reintegration tendency that yields increasing returns to scale and (internalized) external economies to firms. Thus, the vertical re-integration of specialized activities is realized at three levels of functional organization: in work processes, in business organization, and in the urban system.

Unless integration has costs as well as benefits vertical integration would have no limits. The principal limiting factor has traditionally been ascribed to *bureaucratic failure*. Assessment of bureaucratic failure is an interdisciplinary and institutional issue. Economists, however, lack detailed knowledge of internal organization and its concrete problems, while sociologists, who often do have such knowledge, are seldom interested in comparative analyses of organizational differences in efficiency. Grossman and Hart (1986), using a property rights approach, have invoked differential efficacy of incentives in firm and market contexts in assessing the limits of vertical integration, while Williamson (1985) has taken a transactions costs approach, involving a combination of incentive and bureaucratic constraints. Nevertheless, the organization costs associated with vertical integration remain very imperfectly understood. For present purposes, the vertical integration issue may be posed in a somewhat different manner. Of the activities that a firm could potentially integrate, what are the distinguishing features of those activities that are integrated and of those that are not?

Large-scale corporate enterprise may be viewed as a means to concentrate (vertically integrate) specialized but technologically interrelated processes, as well as to create larger and more unified systems of finance and control. Recent industrial organization research indicates that vertical integration is likely to result when transactions involve firm-specific know-how and technological complementarities. In such instances, internal transactions costs are lower than external transactions costs. However, when internal transactions costs exceed external transactions costs vertical disintegration is the likely outcome. There are a variety of circumstances that can encourage vertical disintegration (Scott, 1986; Scott and Storper, 1987). It can arise where there are segmented labor markets in which some work tasks can be subcontracted out from firms in primary labor-market sectors to firms in secondary labor-market sectors. When markets are uncertain or unstable, as when peak output levels vary from stable and certain markets, firms will tend to disintegrate in order to avoid the backward transmission of production irregularities through their vertical structure. Vertical disintegration can be common when a firm needs a specialized input that an integrated firm cannot produce as efficiently as can a specialized firm. When significant specialization economies exist and when minimal optimal scales of output vary among different production stages, subcontracting may be replaced by complete disintegration, where independent producers sell to each other.

Vertical disintegration has clearly played a prominent role in the expansion of the producer-services sector (Kutscher, 1988). The complexity of managing large conglomerates means that management must increasingly rely on business management and other consulting services in order to ensure efficient operations. The volume and complexity of government regulations pose specialized problems with respect to banking, construction, the environment, labor relations, safety, transportation, and other areas, problems that often can be dealt with most efficiently by independent experts in the producer-services sector. Moreover, the concomitant growth of producer-services employment and of demand for more information allows producer-service firms in such fields as business consulting, law, engineering, and architecture to spread the high investment and development costs of their computer and data processing technologies over many users, thus realizing economies of scale. While many local and niche markets can be covered by independent small firms, economic organization is increasingly not so much a matter of large firms versus small firms, but one of a wide variety of interactions between large and small firms enabling them to benefit from their respective strengths, e.g., through joint ventures (Case, 1989). And the expansion of the entire production complex increases the division of labor, external economies, and productivity. Thus, for example, the data presented in Table 1 might suggest, from the perspective of neoclassical production theory, that productivity has been declining in the producer services sector because employment grew more rapidly than value of output between 1970 and 1986. But, as Leijonhufvud (1986) has pointed out, the neoclassical production function does not describe production as a complex process, but is rather more akin to a recipe for bouillabaisse, where the ingredients (K, L) are dumped into a pot; heated, $f(\bullet)$; and the output, X, is ready. This abstraction from production processes misses Young's (1928) insight, discussed earlier, that economic activities need to be seen as an interrelated whole. The total contribution of producer services is not reflected in this sector alone, but also in its role in expanding the more general division of labor and thereby generating the external economies that show up as increasing returns throughout the economy.

Technological progress and new forms of economic organization have created not only structural changes in the ways in which the economy produces goods and services but also changes in the educational requirements needed in the marketplace. The quality of the labor force must be improved so that new levels of skill can be combined in novel ratios with the complex, increasingly roundabout technologies that have been evolving. The flexible production paradigm—so successfully employed by the Japanese and numerous imitators around the world—indicates that the division of labor is not exhausted in the fragmentation and simplification of linear tasks performed in Adam Smith's pin factory. The use of a more sophisticated division of labor between skillful, flexible workers and intricate, flexible technologies has rendered obsolete Smith's fear that laborers would be reduced to stupidity and ignorance by endless repetition of simple tasks. This is particularly the case with respect to producer services. Many product innovations in manufacturing in turn become process innovations in producer services; and the needs of producer services feed back to induce product innovations in manufacturing. These complex, mutually interacting relationships require a producer-service employment mix with above-average education and skills.

Beyers et al. (1986) have shown that the occupational structure of firms in the producer services sector is dominated by professional and technical employees, and that the labor force of such firms appears to be becoming more sophisticated over time. Moreover, higher-education systems and producer services have a rich variety of interdependencies that promote economic development. Other empirical evidence indicates that higher education provides a critical catalyst in the transformation of economies from a traditional manufacturing basis to a more information-oriented basis, and that those areas with better educational systems are making the transformation more effectively in terms of more employment and a higher-paying job structure (Jones and Vedlitz, 1988).

4. EMPIRICAL ANALYSIS

The foregoing discussions have suggested that a growing economy (larger extent of the market) will be associated with an increasing division of labor, not only within firms but also among firms. It has been argued that in an increasingly information-oriented economy, quantitative and qualitative enlargements of the division of labor are reflected in expansion of *independent* producer services—often in small- and medium-sized enterprises—and of nonproduction employment within manufacturing firms. The expanding, complex coordination of ever larger numbers of specialists shows up as increasing productivity and higher per capita income. In addition, interdependencies between higher education and the expansion of producer services suggest a direct relationship between higher education, productivity, and per capita income. Nevertheless, not all of the positive externalities that arise from growing mutual interdependencies between manufacturing and services and among firms and industries will be captured by examining only producer services and higher education. Thus, population size will be regarded as at

472   JOURNAL OF REGIONAL SCIENCE, VOL. 30, NO. 4, 1990

least an approximate surrogate for more generalized economies resulting from an expanding extent of the market and division of labor, which, in relation to the vague term *agglomeration economies,* capture more accurately the dynamic nature of the process of economic development.

These hypotheses are evaluated using data for U.S. Metropolitan Statistical Areas (MSAs) and Primary Metropolitan Statistical Areas (PMSAs). The data sources were the *State and Metropolitan Area Data Book* 1986 (U.S. Bureau of the Census, 1986) and the *1982 Census of Services* (U.S. Bureau of the Census, 1984). The former used metropolitan definitions as of 1984, whereas the latter used the 1982 definitions. Almost one-third of the metropolitan areas had boundary changes between these years. Producer services data were not available for counties that were added to MSAs and PMSAs between 1982 and 1984 if there were fewer than 300 such establishments in the county. The present data set excludes areas for which relevant data were not available. This left 240 MSAs and PMSAs with identical boundaries and comparable data for 1982 and 1984. Regressions were, in fact, run for all MSAs and PMSAs ignoring boundary changes, but the results were not substantially different from those reported here.

The results are presented in Table 2 by region and for the United States as a whole, excluding Alaska and Hawaii. Nominal per capita income in these states greatly overstates real per capita income; and, since price indexes are available only for a relatively small number of metropolitan areas, they could not be used to adjust the nominal values for the data set. The regional groupings of states are those of Howe and Stabler (1989b), who used a regionalization method previously applied to Canada (1989a) to identify a globally optimal aggregation of states into regions within the U.S. economy. These regions are: (1) Pacific Coast: California, Oregon, Washington; (2) Northwest: Idaho, Montana, Wyoming; (3) Southwest: Nevada, Utah, Arizona, New Mexico, Colorado; (4) Dakotas: North Dakota, South Dakota; (5) Texas; (6) North Central: Iowa, Minnesota, Wisconsin, Missouri; (7) Central South: Arkansas, Mississippi, Louisiana, Kentucky, West Virginia, Alabama, Tennessee, Kansas, Nebraska, Oklahoma; (8) Northeast: New Jersey, Pennsylvania, New York, Indiana, Ohio, Illinois, Michigan; (9) South Atlantic: Maryland, Washington, D.C., Delaware, North Carolina, South Carolina, Virginia, Florida, Georgia; and (10) New England: New Hampshire, Vermont, Maine, Connecticut, Rhode Island, Massachusetts. Regions (2), (3), and (4) were not analyzed separately because they contained too few metropolitan areas, but their MSAs and PMSAs were included in the analysis of the nation as a whole.

Two functions were estimated, using the SAS ordinary least squares general linear models procedure with all variables in logarithmic form, for the relevant regions and for the United States.

(1) $$PCI = f(HIED, PSER)$$

(2) $$PCI = f(HIED, PSER, POP)$$

where *PCI* is metropolitan per capita income in 1983 (U.S. Bureau of the Census, 1986).

TABLE 2:   Regression Results for U.S. Metropolitan Areas, by Region and for the United States, with 1983 Per Capita Income as the Dependent Variable

Region		Intercept	HIED	PSER	POP	R^2	F-Value
Pacific Coast	(1)	7.211	0.295**	0.140**		.822	71.52**
(n = 35)		(41.10)	(5.45)	(5.01)			
	(2)	7.098	0.283**	0.111**	0.030*	.851	56.95**
		(41.78)	(5.59)	(3.83)	(2.40)		
Texas	(1)	5.324	0.352**	0.354**		.640	18.67**
(n = 23)		(8.33)	(3.25)	(4.39)			
	(2)	5.726	0.373**	0.376**	−0.52	.672	13.66**
		(8.31)	(3.49)	(4.67)	(−1.39)		
North Central	(1)	7.391	0.129**	0.171**		.737	28.04**
(n = 22)		(30.94)	(3.93)	(5.98)			
	(2)	7.102	0.130**	0.165**	0.028	.767	20.82**
		(23.99)	(4.10)	(5.89)	(1.55)		
Central South	(1)	7.474	0.196**	0.131**		.436	10.05**
(n = 28)		(18.48)	(3.67)	(2.81)			
	(2)	7.271	0.091**	0.112*	0.030	.469	7.37**
		(16.84)	(3.60)	(2.32)	(1.25)		
Northeast	(1)	7.685	0.188**	0.116**		.497	31.16**
(n = 65)		(32.65)	(5.95)	(4.09)			
	(2)	7.630	0.164**	0.074*	0.036**	.572	27.59**
		(34.74)	(5.46)	(2.53)	(3.28)		
South Atlantic	(1)	7.843	0.272**	0.069		.303	6.09**
(n = 30)		(17.24)	(2.86)	(1.18)			
	(2)	7.482	0.250*	0.048	0.047	.354	4.92**
		(14.65)	(2.64)	(0.82)	(1.45)		
New England	(1)	6.924	0.269	0.183		.698	13.84**
(n = 14)		(13.440)	(1.91)	(2.11)			
	(2)	6.505	0.217	0.165*	0.056*	.793	14.06**
		(13.49)	(1.76)	(2.19)	(2.25)		
United States	(1)	7.307	0.214**	0.153**		.491	114.91**
(n = 240)		(56.77)	(9.36)	(9.71)			
	(2)	7.187	0.204**	0.131**	0.026**	.513	83.14**
		(54.64)	(9.03)	(7.72)	(3.24)		

Notes: **Significant at the .01 level. *Significant at the .05 level.
The numbers in parentheses are t-values.

   HIED is the proportion of persons 25-years old and over who had completed 16 or more years of school in 1980 (U.S. Bureau of the Census, 1986).
   PSER is the sum of manufacturers' nonproduction payroll outlays in 1982 (U.S. Bureau of the Census 1986) and producer services (SIC 73) receipts in 1982 (U.S. Bureau of the Census, 1984) divided by MSA or PMSA private nonfarm

474 JOURNAL OF REGIONAL SCIENCE, VOL. 30, NO. 4, 1990

employment in 1982 (U.S. Bureau of the Census, 1986). *PSER* is, thus, a producer-services variable that combines the value of *independent* producer services and the nonproduction payroll outlays of manufacturing firms, because, as discussed previously, producer-service firms and corporate offices need to be examined in conjunction with one another in view of the strong complementary and substitutability between their outputs. The division by employment means that *PSER* provides an indication of the relative richness or density of producer services in the division of labor of the local economy. It should be pointed out that poor regression results were obtained when only producer services (SIC 73) density and only manufacturers' nonproduction payroll outlays density were used as independent variables. This points out the need to consider these activities jointly. Change in *PSER* between 1977 and 1982 was also tested and gave results similar to those shown in Table 2 for level of *PSER* in 1982. Because the rapid growth of producer services is a relatively recent phenomenon, it might be expected that there would be a strong correlation between growth of *PSER* and level of *PSER*.

POP is metropolitan population in 1980 (U.S. Bureau of the Census, 1986). Population size, which gives an indication of the extent of the market and consequent opportunities to expand the division of labor, may reflect productivity and income enhancing externalities not captured in *HIED* and *PSER*.

For the United States as a whole, the regression results summarized in Table 2 indicate that all of the coefficients in Equations (1) and (2) were positive and significant at the .01 level. However, the addition of POP in Equation (2) did not substantially increase the R^2-value of .491 obtained in Equation (1), and in Equation (2) the t-value for *POP* (3.24) was lower than those for *HIED* (9.03) and *PSER* (7.72). The simple Pearson correlation coefficients for *PCI* with *HIED*, *PSER*, and *POP* were, respectively, .54, .55, and .42. The correlation coefficient for *HIED* and *POP* was only .21, while that for *PSER* and *POP* was .43. Somewhat surprisingly, the correlation coefficient for *PSER* and *HIED* was only .21 at the national level; however the corresponding value was .71 for New England and .62 for the Pacific Coast, the two regions most noted for interactions between education and information-oriented activities. In contrast, the correlation coefficient for *PSER* and *HIED* was $-.06$ in the relatively economically lagging Central South.

With the exception of the two southern regions (Central South and South Atlantic), the regional R^2-values ranged from .497 to .822 for Equation (1) and from .572 to .851 for Equation (2). The R^2-values in both equations were higher than the corresponding U.S. values in all regions except the two southern regions. Thus, these simple models display considerable robustness when applied in different regional contexts.

The only region where the coefficient on *HIED* was not significant in both Equations (1) and (2) is New England, but this may be related to small sample size. The coefficient on *PSER* was not significant in either Equations (1) or (2) for the South Atlantic or in Equation (1) for New England; however, it was significant for Equation (2) for New England and for both equations in all other regions. Even though the coefficient on *POP* was significant at the national level, it was significant for only three of the regions, the Northeast, New England, and the Pacific Coast.

5. CONCLUSIONS

Do producer services induce regional economic development? It has been maintained here that goods production and services have become increasingly integrated within a flexible, information-oriented system of production organization. Producer services clearly have not been the sole cause of the newly emerging system. Nevertheless, the empirical results obtained strongly suggest that producer services—carried out both within manufacturing firms and by *independent enterprises*—do play an important role in expanding the division of labor, productivity, and per capita income. No attempt was made to measure productivity directly, but it is assumed that there is a direct association between productivity and metropolitan per capita income. Relatively high per capita incomes in some metropolitan areas may in part reflect such phenomena as disamenity premiums or the presence of oligopoly power in large corporations; but when the entire spectrum of metropolitan areas is considered, it seems reasonable to suppose that variation in productivity is the principal factor accounting for the variation in per capita income. Education, through its numerous interdependencies with producer services and flexible production systems, has also been an essential element in recent regional economic development processes. Population size of metropolitan area has had a significant positive effect on per capita income considering the United States as a whole, but its influence in this regard has not been as great as that of producer services density or education. As in many other instances, the overall results presented here indicate that efforts to achieve a better understanding of developmental processes need to take into account the differing regional contexts that nest within the undifferentiated national context.

REFERENCES

Bailly, Antoine S. and Denis Maillat. 1988. *Le Secteur Tertiare en Question.* 2nd ed. Paris: Economica.

Beyers, William B., Michael J. Alvine, and Erik G. Johnsen. 1985. *The Service Economy: Export of Services in the Central Puget Sound Region.* Seattle: Central Puget Sound Economic Development District.

Beyers, William B., John M. Tofflemire, Harriet A. Stranahan, and Erik G. Johnson. 1986. *The Service Economy: Understanding Growth of Producer Services in the Central Puget Sound Region.* Seattle: Central Puget Sound Economic Development District.

Birch, David L. *Job Creation in America.* 1987. New York: The Free Press.

Case, John. 1989. "Sources of Innovation," *Inc.,* June, p. 29.

Gillis, William R. 1987. "Can Service-Producing Industries Provide a Catalyst for Regional Economic Growth?," *Economic Development Quarterly,* 1, 249–256.

Grossman, S. J. and O. D. Hart. 1986. "The Costs and Benefits of Ownership: A Theory of Vertical Integration," *Journal of Political Economy,* 94, 691–719.

Hansen, Niles. 1990. "Innovative Regional Milieux, Small Firms, and Regional Development: Evidence from Mediterranean France," *Annals of Regional Science,* 24, 107–123.

Howe, Eric C. and Jack C. Stabler. 1989a. "Canada Divided: The Optimal Division of an Economy into Regions," *Journal of Regional Science,* 29, 191–211.

———. 1989b. "The Regional Structure of the United States Economy," unpublished paper.

Illeris, Sven. 1989a. "Producer Services: The Key Sector for Future Economic Development?," *Entrepreneurship and Regional Development,* 1, 267–274.

———. 1989b. *Services and Regions in Europe.* Brookfield, Vermont: Gower.

Jones, Bryan D. and Arnold Vedlitz. 1988. "Higher Education Policies and Economic Growth in the American States," *Economic Development Quarterly,* 2, 78–87.

476 JOURNAL OF REGIONAL SCIENCE, VOL. 30, NO. 4, 1990

Kutscher, Ronald E. 1988. "Growth of Services Employment in the United States," in Bruce R. Guile and James Brian Quinn (eds.), *Technology in Services*. Washington, D.C.: National Academy Press, pp. 47–75.

Leijonhufvud, Axel. 1986. "Capitalism and the Factory System," in Richard N. Langlois (ed.), *Economics as a Process*. Cambridge, U.K.: Cambridge University Press, pp. 203–223.

Martin, Fernand. 1986. "Le Rôle du Secteur Tertiare dans la Stratégie de Développement Economique," in Donald J. Savoie and André Raynauld (eds.), *Essais sur le Développement Régional*. Montréal: Les Presses de l'Université, pp. 123–134.

Monnoyer, Marie-Christine and Jean Philippe. 1985. *L'Interaction entre les Prestataires de Services et les PMI et le Développement Régional*, Vol. 1. Aix-en-Provence: Centre d'Economie Régionale d'Aix-Marseille.

Noyelle, Thierry J. and Thomas M. Stanback, Jr. 1984. *The Economic Transformation of American Cities*. Totowa, New Jersey: Rowman and Allanheld.

Pedersen, Poul Ove. 1986. "The Role of Business Services in Regional Development: A New Growth Centre Strategy," *Scandinavian Housing and Planning Research*, 3, 167–182.

Perez, Carlota. 1985. "Microelectronics, Long Waves and World Structural Change: New Perspectives for Developing Countries," *World Development*, 13, 441–463.

Perroux, François. 1964. *L'Économie du XXᵉ Siècle*. 2nd ed. Paris: Presses Universitaires de France.

Quinn, James Brian. 1988. "Technology in Services: Past Myths and Future Challenges," in Bruce R. Guile and James Brian Quinn (eds.), *Technology in Services*. Washington, D.C.: National Academy Press, pp. 16–46.

Quinn, James Brian and Thomas L. Doorley. 1988. "Key Policy Issues Posed by Services," in Bruce R. Guile and James Brian Quinn (eds.), *Technology in Services*. Washington, D.C.: National Academy Press, pp. 211–234.

Rones, Philip L. 1986. "An Analysis of Regional Employment Growth, 1973–85," *Monthly Labor Review*, 109, 3–14.

Scott, Alan J. 1986. "Industrial Organization and Location: Division of Labor, the Firm and Spatial Process," *Economic Geography*, 62, 215–231.

Scott, Alan J. and Michael Storper. 1987. "High Technology Industry and Regional Development: A Theoretical Critique and Reconstruction," *International Social Science Journal*, 39, 215–232.

Sims, Calvin. 1989. "Global Communications Net Planned by GE for Its Staff," *New York Times*, May 31, p. 25.

Stabler, Jack C. and Eric C. Howe. 1988. "Service Exports and Regional Growth in the Post-industrial Era," *Journal of Regional Science*, 28, 303–316.

U.S. Bureau of the Census. 1978. *Statistical Abstract of the United States: 1978*. Washington, D.C.: U.S. Government Printing Office.

———. 1984. *1982 Census of Service Industries, Geographic Area Series*, SC82-A-52, United States. Washington, D.C.: U.S. Government Printing Office.

———. 1986. *State and Metropolitan Area Book 1986*. Washington, D.C.: U.S. Government Printing Office.

———. 1987. *Statistical Abstract of the United States: 1988*. Washington, D.C.: U.S. Government Printing Office.

Williamson, Oliver E. 1985. *The Economic Institutions of Capitalism*. New York: The Free Press.

Young, Allyn A. 1928. "Increasing Returns and Economic Progress," *Economic Journal*, 38, 527–542.

[15]

Interregional Trade in Producer Services: Review and Synthesis

JAMES W. HARRINGTON
ALAN D. MACPHERSON
JOHN R. LOMBARD

ABSTRACT   This paper reviews some of the past decade's studies of producer or intermediate-services exports from local regions. After a discussion of conceptual and methodological problems and inconsistencies, we present these studies according to the three basic methodologies: surveys, location quotients, and input-output. Overall, our sense is that these studies support limited but important conclusions: (1) If intermediate services are defined broadly, certain of these activities have as their major function interregional or international transfer or trade. By nature, these distributive services have widespread clients, and benefit from locations with substantial physical and communications infrastructure. (2) Among most business- and financial-service activities, most offices are established to serve a local region, but may derive some revenues from beyond this expected zone. (3) The exceptions —the activities and establishments that derive much of their revenue beyond such "normal" zones—are particularly specialized, particularly large, or parts of multi-regional enterprises. (4) Such firms tend to locate in larger or more specialized urban places, probably because of the labor force, the corporate connections, and the rapid dissemination of ideas, contacts, and information within and among the largest metropolitan areas. These conclusions lead to some general policy recommendations.

Introduction

SINCE BEYERS AND ALVINE (1985) reported that most Seattle-area producer service establishments had clients far beyond Seattle's immediate hinterland, the role of the service sector in regional economic development has been reconceptualized by many researchers in many places. Findings have varied widely, as have the conceptualization and even purposes of the research undertaken. As a result, the very dimensions of study differ significantly across

James W. Harrington is an associate professor of geography and public policy at George Mason University, Fairfax VA 22030; Alan D. MacPherson is an associate professor of geography at the University at Buffalo, NY 14261; John Lombard is a consultant with Moran, Stahl & Boyer, New York NY 10017. The authors wish to express appreciation for the assistance of John Burkhardt and Andrea Stoldt and for the comments and suggestions of the editor and anonymous reviewers.

papers and reports that have similar foci. After nearly a decade of these studies, their categorization, synthesis, and assessment are in order.

This paper reviews empirical studies of provision of producer services across sub-national regions. Its major goals are to present issues of non-conformity, to note the different methodologies employed, and to compare findings across studies. The focus of the review is the extent to which producer services play a "basic" role in regional economies, generating revenue from nonlocal sources. Three empirical methodologies are reviewed: surveys of service providers, analyses of regional location quotients for service industries, and analyses of regional input-output models. One major finding is that the differing methodologies and categories used in these studies have reflected the researchers' very different purposes. Therefore, only limited empirical synthesis of their results is possible.

What are Producer Services, and [Why] Should We Care?

Despite the use of the phrase "producer services" in most of the works reviewed here, the sectors studied, and the mix of intermediate versus final clients are far from standardized.

Since Greenfield (1966), there has been an increasing tendency to dichotomize intangible goods production on the basis of intermediate versus final markets. While this market-based distinction is conceptually reasonable, the output of producer service establishments often combines final services to households with intermediate inputs to businesses. The proportion of this combination varies by sector and location, and this variation has created disagreements about which service sectors to call "producer services." Allen (1988) argued that the mixed-output problem is worst for service providers whose role may be defined as the interface between producers and consumers: distribution networks of wholesalers and retailers, and financial intermediaries (banks, insurers) who collect financial capital at the retail level and invest it in productive and consumption activities. This suggests that a fundamental problem with the producer/consumer service dichotomy is the presence of a third role for services: intermediation. Most often, this entails a buffer between production (of goods or services) and consumption. However, the burgeoning field of personnel services provides a packaging of labor services on a contract basis to goods or service producers, another form of intermediation.

In the studies of Stanback et al. (1981), producer services are distinguished from five other groups of service activities: distributive, retail, consumer, nonprofit, and government. In this scheme, producer services entail financial and business-service activities. Most studies surveyed below use this narrow, but still problematic, delineation of producer services.

INTERREGIONAL TRADE IN PRODUCER SERVICES   77

One source of confusion is that the primary basis for the category "producer services" does not coincide with the rationale for focusing on these activities in studies of regional exports.   The consumer/producer distinction hinges on differences in the nature and calculation of multipliers for intermediate versus final services.   Rather, the studies to be surveyed here generally assume *differences in the locational needs and tendencies* of consumer- versus producer service establishments and employment.   (The assumption is usually implicit. See Daniels [1985: 6-8, 105, 157, 278] for brief, explicit discussion.) Consumer services are assumed to be locationally tied to the center of a consumer market of adequate size.   Indeed, central-place hierarchies are generally measured by the location of consumer services for nested regions of larger and larger size. Consumer services define, and thereby reinforce, existing hierarchies. While the location of producer service activities reflect central-place hierarchies, these activities also locate to benefit from agglomeration of similar establishments or proximity to specialized clients (Ó hUallacháin 1989). The regional-development interest in producer services stems from the observations of their export from smaller places to larger centers (Bailly et al. 1987), and from centers outside their usual hinterlands (Polèse 1982; Beyers and Alvine 1985; Michalak and Fairbairn 1988). Thus, "in theory, the less populated, peripheral regions should be able to develop export-oriented producer services" (Coffey and Polèse 1989: 15).

Our review of the empirical literature on regional exports of services must take what has been given.   While this encompasses a fairly standardized range of activities, the levels of detail and breadth vary dramatically.   Most studies reviewed here focus on some subset of finance, insurance, real estate, business services (advertising, engineering, accounting), legal services, and miscellaneous professional services.   Government services (especially education) and medical services have been included on occasion (MacPherson 1988b).   The image is of highly schooled professionals and their support staffs, providing information- and capital-based services to other business people from CBD offices.   The reality, of course, is more mixed.   Even more mixed are the other industry categories often included (for example, repair activities and membership organizations). The greatest source of heterogeneity and incongruence, however, is the sectoral scale of investigation.   For example, "finance, insurance, and real estate" may be presented as one sector (Smith 1984; Goe and Shanahan 1988), as seven two-digit SIC sectors, or as a non-exhaustive set of "key" industries such as commercial banking, investment banking, commercial insurance, and commercial real-estate development (Keil and Mack 1986; Ley and Hutton 1987; Harrington and Lombard 1989).

Problems in Measuring Regional Exports of Producer Services

Alternative methodologies. Empirical study of producer service exports from regions can rely on primary or secondary data. The main primary-data methodology is to *survey establishments* to determine the geography of their service linkages. Published results report postal as well as interview surveys. Users of services may be surveyed, or service providers may be asked about their sales and clients. Survey methods allow characteristics of individual service-providing or service-client establishments to be related to their out-of-region linkages. Therefore, these methods have been used when a researcher desires to investigate organizational aspects of producer service exports: most often, the influence of establishment size or of corporate linkages on the propensity to sell or obtain services outside the local area.

The most commonly available secondary-source data are employment statistics by industry and region. From these data, *location quotients* can be calculated to determine the relative specialization of regions in particular service activities. Unfortunately, such estimates typically ignore cross-trade in the same industry: highly differentiated service products are in fact imported into regions with very large location quotients in that service industry.

While location-quotients can provide some insight into the extent to which local services are purchased by local export-oriented activities, estimates based upon this approach ought ideally to be collated with *regional input-output* data. To date, however, relatively few published accounts examine the interregional export contribution of the service sector from an input-output perspective. This is not terribly surprising, given the complexity and cost of creating and updating matrices. Because of their explicit focus upon inter-industry flows, however, structural models often provide the best answers to the extent of intermediate-services' linkages to export activity.

Regional scale. The geographic scale of the "region" severely affects the extent of sales outside that region. The differing purposes of service-export studies have yielded different delineations of local regions. A research question about the possibility that service activities can bring income into a local labor market would be answered by estimating sales outside of a metropolitan area or non-metropolitan county. Clearly, any attempt to demonstrate the inapplicability of central-place theory to producer services would require estimates of sales beyond a larger central-place hinterland (Blumenfeld 1955).

While differences in geographic scale affect the estimates developed for service sales out of regions, such differences also affect other relationships of interest to services researchers. For example, Ashton and Sternal (1978) found that very small service firms were locally oriented while large firms were more likely to export out of New England. These findings contrast with those of

Beyers and Alvine (1985) and Michalak and Fairbairn (1988), who found no relationship between firm size and extra-regional export propensity among firms in the extended metropolitan Seattle area and metropolitan Edmonton, respectively. The studies' basic methodologies were similar—all three relied on survey responses by producer service firms. However, the New England region is a large national region, not a metropolitan (even an extended metropolitan) area. In a study of such long-distance service exports, there may well be a relationship between size of establishment and extra-regional exports. However, such a relationship would still vary by service industry and organizational status of service establishments.

Services embodied in other exports. Services are clearly exported from a region if they are provided for a client outside the region or paid for by funds that originate out of the region. In such cases, a survey of service companies could discern these extra-regional sales. However, services can bring income and jobs into a region if their clients export. In those cases, a survey of service companies would not likely discern the embodied or indirect exports (Patton and Markusen 1991). These embodied exports of services are, of course, a traditional way of viewing services' role in regional economies: services have been seen as increasing the income multiplier associated with exports of manufactures. Income or employment multipliers estimated via location-quotient and input-output analyses do include embodied exports of services. Given that producer services are defined by their intermediate nature, these embodied or indirect exports should be a large part of their regional economic impact.

The implications of indirect service exports for regional economies depend on the purpose and methodology of each study. The results of survey-based studies are particularly useful for understanding the possible spatial extent of service linkages. However, estimating the importance of producer services to other exporting sectors in a regional economy requires other methods. In this regard, Gilmer et al. (1989) suggested that service industries that have widely varying location quotients across regions, but whose location quotients are highly correlated with the location quotients of other (especially manufacturing) industries, are indirect exporters that add to the economic base of regions where their location quotients are high. According to these authors, service industries of this ilk should not be proposed as free-standing bases for regional export development.

Intra-corporate exports of services. The corporate or divisional headquarters of a multi-facility company provides services to the entire company or division. If the geographic extent of the company or division exceeds the "region" of interest to the researcher, these flows of services may have a substantial impact on employment and income in the region of interest. However, different research methodologies will discern these flows differently.   A survey of service companies will not detect intra-corporate flows of services within manufacturing companies. At the same time, location-quotient or input-output estimates based on establishment-level data will not detect services that are sourced in establishments classified as manufacturing.

Some of the points noted above can be illustrated with reference to recent Canadian evidence. For example, Polèse (1982) surveyed a variety of establishment types in eastern Quebec, thirty-five percent of whom were part of multi-facility companies. A major finding was that "over half of the regional service demand is satisfied by imports [largely from Montreal]," and that "almost 45 percent of the service imports are in the form of intra-firm flows." However, "locally purchased services are, by contrast, composed of over 95 percent inter-firm market transactions" (p. 158).

Several implications can be drawn from these findings. First, surveys and input-output studies that focus on service exports without inspecting imports are missing a great deal of the interregional picture. They can only tell us what we know by now: that producer services have the potential for a wide market area. Such partial studies cannot tell us about the region's position in the provision of its (and other regions') service needs. Second, the large proportion of imported services is not surprising, given the study area's position outside Montreal but within its hinterland. While traditional theory has relatively little to say about intra-corporate flows, the origin of specialized or expensively produced services in large regional centers is to be expected. It would be useful to employ a similar research methodology over a large region, with sufficient survey detail to discern the market versus intra-corporate flows of services, by type, among establishments in centers at all levels in the regional central-place hierarchy. Third, intra-firm service flows are important for any region with a sizable representation of multi-establishment firms (35 percent of the sample, in this case). Fourth, long-distance service linkages are more likely to be intra-firm, especially in the case of small producer service clients. There is a severe distance decay in the information about available producer services, which intra-firm linkages more easily overcome.

Comparison of Empirical Findings

Survey-based estimates. Because survey instruments are custom-designed, the greatest heterogeneity of measures and definitions is present among these studies. Respondents have been asked to report whether or not they have extra-regional sales or sources of particular services, or may be asked for percentages of extra-regional sales or sources. The region may be defined at one or more of several functional scales ("this county," "this metropolitan area," "this state," "this multi-state region") or distance ranges (1-10 miles or 1-30 kilometers versus 11-50 miles or over 30 kilometers). The distribution of responses may be reported, or summary statistics may be reported.

For example, Ashton and Sternal (1978) reported the proportion of respondents in a given producer service industry who claimed that 10 to 50 percent of their revenues came from clients outside of New England and the proportion who claimed that over 50 percent of their revenues were externally sourced. Most other studies reported the proportion of extra-regional revenues averaged across all respondents in a producer service industry. In some cases the averages were weighted by the relative size of the respondents in each industry: some investigators weighted respondents by revenue size (van Dinteren 1987), others by employment size (Beyers and Alvine 1985). In other cases the responses were not weighted before averaging (Michalak and Fairbairn 1988; Harrington and Lombard 1989). Of course, many of the difficulties and inconsistencies discussed earlier in this paper can be found in the survey-based literature, including different regional scales and different service typologies.

Ashton and Sternal (1978) surveyed 1500 firms in six New England states in six service industries: advertising, management consulting, research and development, equipment rental, engineering/architecture/surveying, and accounting/auditing. The sectors are highly specific (defined at the 4-digit SIC level), and represent services whose professional employees make relatively high salaries. Of the 607 respondents, 317 (52 percent) indicated that they provided services in more than one of these industries.

The questions concerned sales outside New England. This regional scale meant that Boston-area firms, heavily represented in the sample, would be considered service exporters only if they had clients outside of the region (New England) for which Boston is the highest-order service center. Overall, 37 percent of the respondents derived at least 10 percent of their revenues from clients in the U.S. but outside New England. The results varied widely across the industries: out-of-region clients accounted for at least 10 percent of sales for three-quarters of the R&D and of the management-consulting respondents, and for one half of the multiple-service firms, but only four percent of the accounting firms. Equipment leasing, advertising, and engineering/architecture industries had moderate proportions of firms with at least 10 percent extra-regional sales: 34 percent, 28 percent, and 27 percent, respectively. When the threshold is raised to 50 percent of revenues from U.S. clients outside the region, 65 percent of the R&D firms responded positively, compared to only 47 percent for management-consulting firms. Of the other industries, only in the multiple-service group did over a quarter of respondents (33 percent) report over half of their revenues from U.S. clients outside New England.

While only 27 percent of the 321 small-firm respondents (annual sales under $500,000) gained over 10 percent of their revenues from extra-regional (but domestic U.S.) sales, 46 percent of the next size category (the 120 respondents with annual sales between $500,000 and $1 million) gained over 10 percent of their revenues from U.S. customers outside New England. This proportion increased steadily through three more size categories to 64 percent of the 14 respondents with annual sales of $20 million or more. A similar pattern was revealed for the threshold of 50 percent of revenues from extra-regional sources: larger size categories had higher proportions of firms surpassing the threshold (only 13 percent of the smallest firms, but 50 percent of the firms with sales of between $10 and $19.9 million), except for the largest size category. Only 3, or 21 percent, of the 14 largest firms exceeded the 50 percent extra-regional sales threshold. A similar pattern appeared again when size categories were determined by employment size: steady increases in the proportions of firms in each size category that gained more than 10 percent or more than 50 percent of their revenues from U.S. sales outside New England, through the first five size categories. However, while all three of the firms with 500-999 employees received over 50 percent of their revenues from outside New England, only two of the six 1,000-plus employee firms met that threshold.

Finally, Ashton and Sternal (1978) reported that the 48 respondents which are owned by U.S. companies outside New England are more likely to gain at least 10 percent of their sales from extra-regional sources than are the regionally-owned respondents. The 87 respondents that have U.S. subsidiaries outside New England are much more likely to gain at least 10 percent of their revenues from beyond the study region than are the respondents without extra-regional subsidiaries.

Marshall (1983) received 353 responses from business-service offices in Birmingham, Leeds, and Manchester. Computer-service establishments received only 22 percent of their revenues from within 10 miles. In contrast, solicitors, finance companies, and insurance brokers were dependent on local sources for 50 to 70 percent of revenues. Computer services, management consultants and advertising agents derived 25 to 33 percent of revenues from a national market, more than 50 miles distant. While large extra-regional revenues were related to employment size and to headquarters status, "more detailed analysis of the relationship suggests that number of employees was the main determining factor," especially for independent offices (p.1350).

Beyers and Alvine (1985) contacted 2,200 central Puget Sound-area establishments (four counties, centered on the cities of Seattle, Tacoma, and Everett) in services sectors deemed likely to have substantial extra-regional revenues (these sectors included transport services as well as a range of business and financial services). Half of these establishments reported at least 10 percent of their revenues from establishments outside the region. Fifty-five percent of the sales accounted for by these 1,100 exporting offices were outside the region; 39 percent were outside the state of Washington. (Among the *other* 1,100 offices contacted by telephone, an average of two percent of sales were external to the region.) The sectors with over 47 percent of sales out of state were transport carriers, transport services, real estate, computer services, and research and development. At the other extreme, over half the sales of advertising, legal, equipment rental, accounting, and "other business services" offices (all offices selected on the basis of at least some extra-regional sales) were within the four-county region. The authors reported that there was no relationship between establishment size and export orientation, when all 1,100 exporting establishments were considered as a group.

Van Dinteren (1987) surveyed business-service establishments in 13 Dutch cities with populations between 50,000 and 200,000. Of the 459 postal respondents, the most export-oriented sectors were computer services and advertising services, each of which had half their revenues (weighted by size of respondents' revenues) from outside the local region, i.e., more than 30 kilometers away. Advertising services had the greatest proportion of revenues from other parts of the Netherlands well beyond their large regions. Legal and accounting services were the most locally oriented. According to van Dinteren, larger offices had more external sales, but this was largely explained by the larger size of multi-site service firms' head offices, which were more export oriented than independent or branch offices.

Goe and Shanahan (1988) surveyed 1,025 firms in metropolitan Akron (Ohio) by telephone, covering a broad range of service sectors (including transport and utilities, retail trade, and the sectors more commonly termed producer services). Based on information provided by the 678 respondents, the authors assigned each firm into a category determined by the firm's primary customer base: consumers, manufacturers, or service providers (or some combination of the three). Goe and Shanahan presented detailed information about the 179 respondents exhibiting rapid growth during 1970-1986: eating and drinking retailers, business services, and health services. Establishments in the first two sectors were primarily oriented toward local consumer markets. Among the 61 respondents in the business-service sector (SIC 73), 13 (21 percent) relied primarily on a local consumer market, while 14 (23 percent) relied primarily on a local service-firm market. Seventeen firms (28 percent) sold more outside the region than within; the largest respondent firms were not part of this externally-oriented group. All 17 export-oriented business service firms were single-site enterprises.

84 GROWTH AND CHANGE, FALL 1991

While the studies outlined above varied considerably in terms of research design, regional scale, and purpose, several broad regularities appear through the haze of differing methods and findings. In all cases, management consulting establishments sold large proportions of output to clients outside the region. R&D establishments showed even greater export orientation, but fewer studies computed this industry separately. Business services (including the more detailed industries of advertising and R&D) exhibited fairly high export propensities. "Other" producer services tended to export substantial proportions of output, especially in the one study (Ashton and Sternal, 1978) in which that term had a coherent meaning (establishments that combined more than one business-service activity, usually some combination of management consulting, R&D, and engineering). Architecture and engineering services had high proportions of extra-regional revenues, except in Ashton and Sternal's (1978) New England study. On the other hand, legal, advertising, rental and leasing services, accounting, and banking/lending establishments had smaller export linkages (but still noteworthy: often 10 to 20 percent of revenues). Advertising services, insurance services, and real estate services exhibited mixed results.

For most service industries, Beyers and Alvine's (1985) study of metropolitan Seattle services and van Dinteren's (1987) study of interregional and international exports from service establishments in 13 medium-sized Dutch cities yielded higher estimates of export propensities than did the other studies. However, these two studies used the smallest definitions of the "local region" of all the studies: "exports" are defined as out of that extended metropolitan region in the Seattle case, or outside of a 30-kilometer radius in the Netherlands study. Given the distance decay that seems to be present in the marketing and sales of services, the higher numbers of these studies are reasonable.

Illeris' review (1989: Appendix III) of nine surveys (eight in Europe, one in Canada) of producer service users found great variation in the questions asked by the surveys and in the answers found. The three surveys that asked for respondents' sources of externalized market-research services found very low proportions of those services obtained in the respondents' local area. On the other hand, accounting services and personnel administration, when provided outside the responding corporation, were very likely to be provided locally. These purchasing patterns correspond loosely with generalized findings of service establishments' patterns of sales (previous paragraph). Advertising, data processing, design, insurance, and research and development exhibited broad variation across the studies Illeris reviewed.

Location-quotient estimates. The studies surveyed exhibited a wide variety of methodologies, reflecting major differences in the research goals of individual contributors. The most frustrating aspect of this subset of projects is the different sectoral categories used—again, because of the various authors' different purposes. To understand the distinct economic roles of different parts of Great Britain, Marshall et al. (1987) compared the 1981 location quotients of 19 local labor market areas for services overall, for the broad category of producer services, and for business services. The variation across regions or size classes was examined to determine which types of services were being traded across regions. Not surprisingly, the variation among regional location quotients increased dramatically as the sectoral scale narrowed. Peripheral regions with "services" location quotients of 0.40 to 0.69 had producer service location quotients of 0.54 to 0.78. Regions in southeast England had business-service location quotients of 1.05 to 1.85, producer service location quotients of 1.03 to 1.61, and all-service location quotients of 0.99 to 1.19. An important conclusion drawn by Marshall et al. (1987) was that metropolitan locations in the core regions of the southeast dominated the national system of producer service trade at both the interregional and international levels, suggesting a strong and continuing role for agglomeration economies and spatial concentration.

One would expect that large metropolitan areas should have service-industry location quotients greater than 1.0, reflecting their service provision for a hinterland larger than their metropolitan boundaries. In this regard, Austrian and Zlatoper (1988) compared the 3-digit SIC service-industry location quotients (based on establishment employment data) of each of 89 U.S. metropolitan areas (1984 population greater than 1 million) to the average for all 89 areas. If an area's industry-specific location quotient exceeded 120 percent of the 89-area average for the industry, exports from the area were assumed. The area's employment in the industry, beyond the employment that would account for a location quotient 20 percent greater than the all-area average, was assumed to be export-oriented employment. The five metropolitan areas with the highest absolute amount of export-oriented employment in services were the high-order coastal centers of New York, Washington, Los Angeles, San Francisco, and Boston, followed by Chicago in the Midwest. The other midwestern metropolitan areas measured had much lower numbers of estimated service-export employment. Their rankings appeared essentially the same as their population rankings: Pittsburgh, Detroit, Cleveland, Indianapolis, Columbus, Buffalo, and Rochester.

Austrian and Zlatoper (1988) identified the most widely exported service industries as those for which the metropolitan areas' location quotients had a coefficient of variation greater than 1.0. Of these, the highest coefficients were for the air transport, securities brokerage, lodging, motion picture production, and life insurance industries.

To study the dominance of Canada's largest metropolitan areas, Coffey and Polèse (1987b) compiled aggregate location quotients for five size classes of Canadian urban areas (the highest-order class combining areas with 1981 populations over 300,000; the lowest-order class combining areas with populations from 10,000 to 29,999). Their sectoral scheme was relatively disaggregated: from the large sectors of wholesale trade and retail trade to smaller industries such as advertising, legal services, and engineering/architecture. The ratio of location quotients for highest-order versus lowest-order places was greatest (1.32/0.12 = 11.0) for "commercial research, management, and data services." Such a high ratio suggests strong centralization of these activities in high-order places—implying "exports" to the local areas around those places. Two other service sectors had very large disparities between the location quotients of highest-order and lowest-order places (ratios of 5.0 or more): management consulting and personal services. In contrast with Marshall et al. (1987), Coffey and Polèse (1987a&b) have suggested that the specialized labor pools that are required for export-oriented producer service development need not necessarily reside in the largest cities; partly because of the transportability of certain types of services, but also because of the desirability of non-metropolitan locations for skilled professionals.

Keil and Mack (1986) and Gilmer et al. (1987; 1989) developed a methodology for analyzing interregional variation in location quotients as a way of determining which service industries are prone to be exported from some regions and imported into others. Unlike most other approaches toward location quotient analysis, these authors controlled for some of the service exports to areas within the hinterland of the given region by using the sector's employment share in urbanized areas as the denominator of the quotient. In this way, the employment share of a sector in one urbanized region can be compared to the sector's average share across all urbanized regions, rather than to an average that includes hinterland areas. "For a given place, an exporting industry is indicated by the combination of a large location quotient and a large standard deviation when measured across like-sized places" (Gilmer et al., 1989: 6). In addition, the authors noted that by computing location quotients across a set of regions and sectors, with, and then without the non-urbanized component of regions (in the numerator and the denominator), the difference indicates the nature of implied importing or exporting. Specifically, "agglomerative sectors which serve lesser places will have standard deviations which fall significantly when rural areas are shed." For the largest urban areas, these sectors have location quotients over 1.0 because they serve smaller areas. If, however, only large urban areas are used in the calculation of a base for location quotients, these sectors' quotients fall back toward 1.0. Such sectors concentrate in urban areas primarily to serve those areas and their hinterlands, rather than to export more widely (Gilmer et al. 1989: 7; Gilmer 1990: 4-5).

Using these criteria—large variation of sectoral location quotients across metropolitan areas (tradeability), large changes in the variation when only urbanized areas were considered (tradeability beyond hinterland), and relatively low location quotients in Tennessee Valley metropolitan areas (regional under-representation)—Gilmer et al. (1987) identified nine two-digit service sectors as having the greatest potential for import substitution: the component sectors in the finance, insurance, and real estate group, miscellaneous business services, membership organizations, miscellaneous professional services, and museums. Except for museums, these sectors form the constant core of the sectors often labelled ''producer services.''

The authors (Gilmer et al. 1989) used a similar methodology to study these producer services at greater sectoral disaggregation, using 1984 rather than 1979 employment data. The 23 detailed (three- and four-digit) sectors with greatest location quotient variability were ''almost all...specialized financial services. News syndicates, research and development labs, mail services, and personnel supply were the only business services on the list of traded services'' (Gilmer et al. 1989: 11). In almost all sectors, variability in location quotients declined when only urbanized areas were considered, implying exports that primarily served hinterlands.

Gilmer (1990) reported a location-quotient analysis (based on wage-and-salary earnings, rather than on employment) of two-digit sectors (services and non-services) across the 44 U.S. metropolitan areas with populations over 1 million, using 1987 data. When the location quotients were calculated, using a base of those 44 metropolitan areas, the sectors with the greatest standard deviation (implying the greatest differentiation across these large cities) entailed earnings from pipelines, military bases, and mining. The services with the greatest standard deviation were air transport, museums, rail transport, security/ commodity brokers, real estate, educational services, and hotels. The location quotients for durable manufacturing earnings had greater variation than real estate or education, but less variation than security/commodity brokers or air transport.

Aside from brokerages and air transport, location quotients for most of the other producer services exhibited moderate standard deviations across the country's 44 largest metropolitan areas. The location quotients of these finance, insurance, and real estate sectors, as well as the business service, legal service, and motion picture sectors, declined the most when they were calculated using the 44 large cities as a base rather than all U.S. metropolitan areas. These two findings strongly suggest that these sectors face moderate specialization, localization, and exports across large metropolitan areas, but that their major locational characteristic is concentration in these large areas to serve these areas' hinterlands. The smallest deviations in location quotients (calculated using only the 44 large areas as the base) were among the more consumer-oriented services: health services, retail, personal services, insurance agents, state and local government.

Gilmer (1990) also compared the location quotients (again, computed using 1987 earnings data for the country's 44 largest metropolitan areas) for the four Texas metropolitan areas with populations over one million (Dallas, Houston, San Antonio, and Fort Worth), across all sectors. The differences among the four cities' economies were striking. The most important comparison for our purposes is the near-total lack of producer service sector location quotients above 1.1 in either of the two smaller cities (San Antonio and Fort Worth). Only in rail and air transport, insurance carriers, and hotels did either of the two smaller cities exhibit disproportionately high earnings. Gilmer takes this to conclude that "technical and agglomerative economies in the service economy are depleted quickly as we move down the urban ladder by population size" (p. 14).

Across all these location-quotient studies, the broad category of finance, insurance, and real estate exhibited high variation, along with its specific, constituent sectors of insurance underwriters and trust companies. Outside of that sector, advertising, R&D, and miscellaneous professional services had large variations in location quotients across regions. Public administration (especially Federal civilian and Federal military) showed large variation in some studies.

Input-output-based estimates. Beyers and Alvine (1985) reported briefly on sectoral-input changes between the 1958 and 1977 input-output tables of the Puget Sound economy. Overall, the region demanded 11.4 cents of local services per dollar of output in 1977, up from 8.78 cents in 1958. However, this change was greater for service-output demand for services (14.3 cents in 1977, 12.4 cents in 1958) than for manufacturing's demand for the region's services (6.8 cents in 1977, up from 5.5 cents in 1958). Evidence from Canada (Gardner, 1983; MacPherson, 1988b) suggests that industries in the manufacturing sector increased their consumption of producer services *over the 1970s* at roughly the *same* pace as most other parts of the economy (80 percent between 1971-1979). Over the same period, however, the relative share of total producer service income that was directly generated by sales to the manufacturing sector increased from 18 percent to 22 percent. This suggests that manufacturing gained a lead role in the growth of producer service revenues. An implication of this is that regional exports of merchandise have become increasingly dependent on producer service support (Blumenfeld 1955; Daniels 1985; Ontario Ministry 1986). In this regard, it should be noted that Tschetter's (1987) recent analysis of U.S. occupation-by-industry and input-output data suggested that: (1) intermediate service inputs have become increasingly important to the international marketing efforts of firms in all sectors; and (2) use of externally provided producer services as an input to industrial export growth has been complemented by a commensurate increase in producer service occupations across all sectors of the economy.

One of the strengths of the input-output approach to estimating extra-regional linkages of producer services is the method's focus on indirect exports, and its ability to ascertain the flow of products through intermediaries (Patton and Markusen 1991). Further evidence from Canada (Stabler and Howe 1988) suggests that input-output tables can also be used to track direct and indirect exports of services at the interregional and international scales. Using the recent provincial disaggregation of Statistics Canada's structural model of the Canadian economy, Stabler and Howe estimated the sectoral distribution of export activity for Canada's four western provinces over the 1974-1979 period. To avoid the assumption that industries produce only one major commodity, the authors employed a rectangular industry-by-commodity input-output model. Their results were noteworthy in three respects. First, the importance of service exports increased dramatically in Canada's four western provinces over the period— faster than interregional exports of merchandise. Second, for direct service exports, sales to foreign markets increased faster than service exports to other parts of Canada. Third, service exports accounted for at least 25 percent (and possibly as much as one-half) of the export-induced portion of the region's overall economic growth. While earlier input-output work by Beyers (1983) revealed a comparable export-base role for services across several U.S. regions, Stabler and Howe's (1988) findings are especially notable in light of western Canada's reputation as a merchandise-oriented economy (exporting mining, petroleum, forestry, and agricultural products.

Unfortunately, few of the recently published studies provide specific information on the relative sizes of the export coefficients for different service sectors. Valuable information about this structural element of regional economies is available to the users of these regional models, and needs to be published.)

Conclusions

In addition to the general interest in the rapid growth of service activities, students of regional development are concerned with the prospect of increasing regional economic welfare via the provision and export of service products. Following the above review of interregional service provision, we want to ask three sets of questions. First, which service sectors, establishments, and regions are most likely to obtain revenues from clients outside the region? Second, what are the implications of extra-regional service sales for the regional *imports* of producer services? Third, how and why should regional development policy be affected by interregional trade in services?

Characteristics of interregional service exports.   In sectoral terms, interregional trade in services is most common and most pronounced when establishments optimize with great specialization or agglomeration. Specialization is most important in sectors that rely on *or create* expensively collected and analyzed, non-standardized information—such as technical R&D, market research, computer programming or management consulting. Agglomeration in producer services often results from external economies of shared labor training, and probably accounts for the extra-regional sales from securities brokerages, specialized financial services, and insurance carriers in a relatively few locations. In the case of goods-handling services—like the air and rail transport sectors which exhibit substantial interregional exporting—agglomeration economies stem from shared physical infrastructure and the logistical benefits of centralized transfer points.   Advertising services presented decidedly mixed results in the studies surveyed. Could this reflect the heterogeneity of local-media-buying versus creative activities in that sector?

In establishment terms, the evidence that larger establishments are more likely to export services is substantial, though not conclusive. Organization affects this relationship; the export orientation of independent, single-establishment firms seems to depend on their size. Elements of business strategy, especially specialization, probably influence this relationship between size and linkages, as well. Controlling for size and sector, head offices of multi-site firms have more extra-regional sales.

The findings with respect to regional characteristics are as mixed as the types of regions studied. However, the range of study areas (Appalachia, England, New England, nonmetropolitan Quebec) helps us see the importance that central-place hierarchy plays in the provision of most services. Except for the services based on specialized and non-standardized information, service linkages largely reflect urban and regional hierarchies. The sectoral and establishment exceptions —and there are many—remind us that industry-specific agglomeration *and* firm-specific capability, strategy, and linkages are powerful influences on location and linkages. Patton and Markusen (1991) have cautioned that the location of service establishments can be dependent upon the location of a major client, even if the service establishments have some extra-regional sales.

Service imports. If producer service establishments have clients outside their local regions, then regions import services as well as export them, and our models as well as our policies must recognize this explicitly. Decades ago, Blumenfeld (1955: 123) commented that ''Half a loaf is certainly better than no loaf; but half a (regional) balance-of-payments analysis may well be worse than none." Which regions import which intermediate service? What determines the rate of regional service imports? What are the results of too much or too little service importing?

Regional imports of intermediate or business services have been studied in the context of "truncated" or "branch-plant" economies, largely via surveys of procurement patterns. Illeris (1989: 195) generalized that the greater service-import propensity of branch plants is not only a function of their service imports from headquarters, but of their extra-organizational linkages as well. Mac-Pherson (1991) found these more general linkages of externally owned establishments to be an important correlate of their service importing.

Import substitution. Surprisingly, though, the issue of service imports has not often been addressed by advocates of service development as a form of regional policy, since such writers have been more concerned with the export potential of certain services. Gillis (1987) noted that "import substitution" in services is as important a regional-development goal as export promotion. The principle can be viewed as simply reducing leakages from the local economy or as increasing economic development by increasing the interconnectedness or articulation of the local economy.

After their determination that the Tennessee Valley region exhibited a shortfall of financial-services establishments, Gilmer et al. (1989) asked whether the overrepresentation of certain sectors in places like Atlanta may reflect more than happenstance. Perhaps such sectors require proximity to corporate headquarters, or require intense intra-sectoral agglomeration, or perhaps there just aren't enough large Tennessee Valley cities.

Import development. The postwar experience of nations employing an import substitution development strategy clearly suggests that small countries cannot attempt self-sufficiency. Within countries, even large countries like the U.S., regions may be better suited for specialization and trade in services rather than producer service autarky. Given that greater regional imports are the logical corollary to interregional export development, the reality of interregional service imports should figure in our economic-development planning.

Policy attention should turn to the ability of small companies to hear about and contract with top-notch services. The role of service provision in the economic competitiveness of goods and service production is increasingly well documented (Marshall 1982; Wood 1987; MacPherson 1988a, 1988b; Tucker and Sundberg 1988). The extent to which a region's productive activities can find and make use of appropriate, efficient, and effective services may well be more important to overall economic well-being than whether those services are exported or imported. How could such information and interaction be increased, to the benefit of the service exporter (and its region) and the remote service client (and its region)? Britton (1989) has presented a series of problems to be overcome, from the irrelevance of consultant services to stagnant small firms to the lack of problem identification or perceived need for services on the part of other small firms.   In the U.K., the Department of Trade and Industry has developed a program of Business and Technical Advisory Services to approach small businesses, identify their potential gains from technical or marketing consulting, identify potential consultants, and subsidize each business's first use of a consultant. While regionally dispersed consultant brokers are better able to establish contacts among businesses, Britton noted the benefits of central government's prestige, consultant contacts, and money. In the U.S., individual state initiatives for technology transfer might well be augmented by interstate or Federal networking.

At the regional as well as the national level, we need to bid farewell to mercantilist policies of export dominance and to recognize that domestic value added is the goal.   Information, interaction, market communication, market development, and quality are key variables in increasing local value added, whether the services used are local or external.

REFERENCES

Allen, J. 1988. Service industries: Uneven development and uneven knowledge. *Area* 20 (1): 15-22.

Ashton, D.J. and B.K. Sternal. 1978. *Business services and New England's export base.* Boston: Research Department, Federal Reserve Bank of Boston.

Austrian, Z. and T.J. Zlatoper. 1988. The role of export services. *REI Review* (Case Western Reserve University), Fall: 24-29.

Bailly, A.S., D. Maillat, and W.J. Coffey. 1987. Service activities and regional development: Some European examples. *Environment and Planning A* 19: 653-668.

Beyers, W.B. 1983. The interregional structure of the US economy. *International Regional Science Review* 8: 213-231.

Beyers, W.B. and M.J. Alvine. 1985. Export services in post-industrial society. *Papers of the Regional Association* 57: 33-45.

Blumenfeld, H. 1955. The economic base of the metropolis: Critical remarks on the basic-nonbasic concept. *J. of the American Institute of Planners* 21: 114-132.

Britton, J.N.H. 1989. Innovation policies for small firms. *Regional Studies* 23: 167-173.

Coffey, W. and M. Polèse. 1987a. Intrafirm trade in business services: Implications for the location of office-based activities. *Papers of the Regional Science Association* 62: 71-80.

———. 1987b. Intrafirm trade of product services: A Canadian perspective. *Environment and Planning A* 19: 597-611.

INTERREGIONAL TRADE IN PRODUCER SERVICES   93

————. 1989.   Producer services and regional development: A policy-oriented perspective. *Papers of the Regional Science Association* 67:   13-28.

Daniels, P.W. 1985. *Service industries: A geographical perspective.* London: Methuen.

Gardner, R.L. 1983. *Industrial development in metropolitan Toronto: Issues, prospects, and strategy.* Economic Development Office of the Chairman, Municipality of Metropolitan Toronto.

Gillis, W.R. 1987. Can service-producing industries provide a catalyst for regional economic growth? *Economic Development Quarterly* 1 (3): 249-256.

Gilmer, R.W. 1990. Identifying service-sector exports from major Texas cities. *Economic Review,* Federal Reserve Bank of Dallas (July): 1-16

Gilmer, R.W., S.R. Keil, and R.S. Mack. 1987.   Export potential of services in the Tennessee Valley. *Regional Science Perspectives* 17 (2).

————. 1989. Export potential of business and financial services: Methodology and application to the Tennessee Valley. Paper presented at the 36th North American meeting of the Regional Science Association, Santa Barbara, 10-12 November.

Goe, W.R. and J.L. Shanahan. 1988. Analyzing the implications of service sector growth for urban economies: Evidence from the Akron PMSA. Presented at the annual meeting of the Association of Collegiate of Planning, Buffalo NY, October.

Greenfield, H.I. 1966. *Manpower and the growth of producer services,* New York: Columbia University Press.

Harrington, J.W. and J.R. Lombard. 1989. Producer-service firms in a declining manufacturing region. *Environment and Planning A* 21: 65-79.

Illeris, S. 1989. *Services and regions in Europe.* Aldershot, England: Avebury.

Keil, S.R. and R.S. Mack. 1986. Identifying export potential in the service sector. *Growth and Change* 17(2): 1-10.

Ley, D. and T. Hutton. 1987. Vancouver's corporate complex and the producer services sector: Linkages and divergences within a provincial staple economy. *Regional Studies* 21: 413-424.

MacPherson, A. 1988a. New product development among small Toronto manufacturers: Empirical evidence on the role of technical service linkages. *Economic Geography* 64 (1): 62-75.

————, 1988b. *Service-to-manufacturing linkages and industrial innovation in Toronto.* Unpublished doctoral dissertation, Department of Geography, University of Toronto.

————. 1991. Interfirm information linkages in an economically disadvantaged region: An empirical perspective from metropolitan Buffalo. *Environment and Planning A* 23 (4): 591-606.

Marshall, J.N. 1982. Linkages between manufacturing industry and business services. *Environment and Planning A* 14: 1523-1540.

————. 1983. Business-service activity in British provincial conurbations. *Environment and Planning A* 15: 1343-1359.

Marshall, J.N., P. Damesick, and P. Wood. 1987. Understanding the location and role of producer services in the United Kingdom. *Environment and Planning A* 14: 1523-1540.

94   GROWTH AND CHANGE, FALL 1991

Michalak, W.Z. and K.J. Fairbairn. 1988. Producer services in a peripheral economy. *Canadian Journal of Regional Science* 11: 353-372.

Ó hUalláchain, B. 1989. Agglomeration of services in American metropolitan areas. *Growth and Change* 20 (3): 34-49.

Ontario Ministry of Treasury and Economics. 1986. *Background notes on the service sector in Ontario.*

Patton, W. K. and A. Markusen. 1991. The perils of overstating service sector growth potential. *Economic Development Quarterly* 5 (3): 197-212.

Polèse, M. 1982. Regional demand for business services and interregional service flows in a small Canadian region. *Papers of the Science Association* 53: 151-163.

Smith, S. 1984. Export orientation of non-manufacturing business in non-metropolitan communities. *American J. of Agricultural Economics* (May).

Stabler, J.C. and E.C. Howe. 1988. Service industries and regional growth in the postindustrial era. *J. of Regional Science* 28 (3): 303-315.

Stanback, T.M., P.J. Bearse, T.J. Noyelle, and R.A. Karesek. 1981. *Services: The new economy.* Totowa, NJ: Rowman and Allanheld.

Tschetter, J. 1987. Producer services industries: Why are they growing so rapidly? *Monthly Labor Review* (Dec): 31-40.

Tucker, K. and M. Sundberg. 1988. *International trade in services.* London: Routledge.

van Dinteren, J.H.J. 1987. The Role of business-service offices in the economy of medium-sized cities. *Environment and Planning A* 19: 669-686.

Wood, P.A. 1987. Producer services and economic change: Some Canadian evidence, in *Technical Change and Industrial Policy,* edited by K. Chapman and G. Humphrys. Oxford: Basil Blackwell.

[16]

The role of services in production

by Stephen Britton

A proposition arising out of a recent review by Daniels (1989: 432) is that 'services do not displace manufacturing, and manufacturing does not compete with services; rather they reinforce each other'. This perspective is a more sophisticated conceptualization than long-held interpretations of the relations between goods production and services. Commonly used classifications of services have been based on traditional notions of the economic role and industrial segmentation of services – such as intermediate and final demand services or producer and consumer services. Extensive discussions of these classifications made elsewhere make it unnecessary to review them here (e.g., Daniels, 1985; Fuchs, 1986; Gershuny and Miles, 1983; Riddle, 1986). From these reviews there are convincing reasons to seek more comprehensive and rigorously theorized approaches to services (Daniels and Thrift, 1987; Gershuny and Miles, 1983; Nusbaumer, 1987; Petit, 1986; Urry, 1987; Walker, 1985). Rather than enter the debates on typologies and definitions of services as such, this paper explores the interpretation of the relationships between services and production implied in our opening quotation. It is insufficient, and in many instances misleading, to treat services simply as inputs into material goods production when it is the interdependencies between the two sectors, and their common status as distinct arenas of capitalist accumulation in their own right, that are conceptually important.

Before addressing the relations between services and goods production, we can note three contexts where this issue is of relevance to contemporary economic geography research. First, there has been much recent work on the nature, dynamics and geography of 'producer' services. The very category of producer services implies they have a particular structural relation to both goods production and 'consumer' services that in many instances becomes debatable and ambiguous on detailed investigation (e.g., Allen, 1988a). Secondly, for those investigating the composition and role of services in national or regional economic structure (e.g., Daniels, 1989: 431; Britton, 1989; Perry, 1989), it is important to recognize that aggregate patterns reflect two levels of causal processes. On the one hand will be general societal dynamics such as the systemic properties of capitalist accumulation mediated by the concrete local peculiarities of markets, capital formation, commercial practices, state regulation, political struggles or demography. From such specific national or regional histories will derive the size and types of service industries, companies and occupations in the

530   *The role of services in production*

social formation under scrutiny. On the other hand, territorial patterns are also shaped at the microlevel from processes and practices at work within industries, enterprises and labour markets. Such trends as the externalization of service functions from companies, the integration within a diversified industrial group of finance and banking activities, the value-adding strategies of companies, or developments in corporate organization and administration, can all have consequences for the growth and role in a territory of what are enumerated as stand-alone services, or discrete service occupations. Thirdly, there is the problem of conceptualizing the role of services within the primary social institutions of production and accumulation – enterprises and corporate groups. In past, less complicated economies, there was a reasonably close correspondence between an industry, product group, a market and an enterprise. This correspondence has in many industries broken down with technology advances and the advent of the large diversified corporation. Large corporations straddle several industries and production functions at once, and in doing so link technical and social conditions of production (diverse occupations and labour forces, forms and extent of competition, networks of inputs and outputs, sources of buyers and sellers) that range far beyond traditional commercial practices and academic conceptions of industrial structure. This reality of the marketplace raises important questions regarding the role and function of services in these units of accumulation, especially in a period of rapid industrial restructuring and altered competitive conditions.

I am not concerned with certain traditional themes to do with services and accumulation such as: the relative productivity and labour intensity of service industries compared to manufacturing industries (Leverson, 1985); the relationships between *per capita* income growth and demand for services (Gershuny and Miles, 1983; Kuznets, 1971); or the structural shift to 'self-servicing' (Allen, 1988b; Gershuny and Miles, 1983). But the discussion does touch on some fundamental issues: how accurate is the notion that (producer) services outputs are essentially intermediate inputs to primary and secondary sector industries? Does the apparent increasing domination by services of employment in late twentieth-century capitalist societies represent what Japanese planners call the 'softization' of advanced economies, which implies that services are less capable of triggering productivity gains, technological advances, tradable exports and interindustry multipliers than are manufacturing industries (Kolko, 1988: 95)? Is it correct to characterize service labour and functions, as is done in the neoclassical economics literature and by Marxists (e.g., Mandel, 1975) as being 'unproductive' and 'parasitical'? Or, alternatively, is Riddle (1986: 21–28) right when she argues that services do not play a peripheral, or even a supportive, role *vis-á-vis* goods production, but rather 'lie at the heart' of any economy and provide the 'facilitative milieu' in which other, especially market-orientated, production activities become possible. One place to begin dealing with these issues is to consider the role and character of services in the various production arrangements of capitalist society.

I The primacy of goods production?

The status of many services as intermediate inputs into industrial production has long been recognized. A significant proportion of what is categorized as the service sector – distribution, transport, construction, utilities, business or producer and many government services – is in fact related to an evolving division of labour within primary and secondary industries. Early US studies indicated that 10% of service sector employment expansion in the 1950s was accounted for by producer services. Data for the UK, Australia, Canada and the USA in the 1970s showed that one-third (22-38%) of tertiary sector output (share of GDP) took the form of intermediate services to the 'productive' sectors (Gershuny and Miles, 1983: 30). More recently, the OECD analysed GDP data for eight member countries by classifying services (i.e., excluding 'goods' and 'government') into those 'directly linked to goods production' (those which 'are a necessary adjunct to the process of producing goods') and 'free-standing services' (which are 'bought by households in their capacity as final consumers') (Blade, 1987: 164–65). It was found that, on average, production-related services contributed 25% of GDP and 'free-standing services' 20%. Taken together, primary and secondary sector output and production-linked services contributed around 65% of GDP. Another indication of this economic role of services is from input-output data on seven OECD countries (calculated from Petit, 1986: 123). Over 50% of the output, on average, of transport, communications, banking and insurance, and 'services to firms' industries goes to intermediate consumption, that is to enterprises, as does over 25% of distribution and 'various' other services output.

Other studies have also demonstrated the vital function of services within manufacturing: approximately 75% of the total value added in the US goods sector is created by service activities within that sector (Quinn and Gagnon, 1986: 101); about 25% of US GNP was accounted for (in 1980) by services used as inputs by goods-producing industries – more than the total value added to GNP by the manufacturing sector (Riddle, 1986: 22); and that services were responsible for 10% of value added in US agriculture, and at least 20% in US mining industries (Riddle, 1986: 22). The historic relation between services as intermediate inputs is also commonly expressed in patterns of expenditure by the state in capitalist societies on public goods. Government funding of transportation, communications and utilities infrastructure, advisory and trade promotion agencies, finance market regulation, or labour recruitment (immigration) and training all suggest the critical role of the state in supplying critical inputs to production without which much capitalist investment would never be initiated. This is a point omitted from the analysis by Blade presumably on the grounds that such goods are not supplied by market mechanisms, an indication of the author confusing the function of a service in the economy with its mode of provision (Urry, 1987: 15).

Certainly from the Marxian perspective, the structure of contemporary capitalist economies has never been other than based on the centrality of

532   *The role of services in production*

industrial goods production, with many services being important intermediate inputs: but a different analytical framework is employed. Without denying that there has been an expansion of what appear as 'stand-alone' or 'free-standing' service industries, Walker (1985) and Mandel (1975) argue that what has occurred in the latter half of this century is an elaboration of the industrial goods economy rather than a qualitative redirection towards a services economy. The increasing complexity of capitalist goods production (i.e., a dramatic elaboration of the social division of labour) has meant not only an increasing number of specialist economic activities indirectly, yet fundamentally, related to goods production, but an equally important development of the technical division of labour *within* goods production. Thus, many of what are conventionally categorized as service occupations or industries are part of the ever-lengthening production sequences necessary to conceive, plan, enable, supervise, produce and maintain the production and distribution of goods.

Holding to the view that it is misleading to classify production occupations on the assumption that they must generate finished material output, Walker offers a typology for an extended (industrial) division of labour which may be used to distinguish labour services as such from occupations related to goods (Table 1). From this perspective we can appreciate the diverse strategic roles of service occupations and activities not only within production, but also to units of capital, that is the enterprises themselves (a theme expanded on below). There are layers of supporting (supplementary, secondary, tertiary and quaternary) labour that is functionally related, yet to varying degrees removed from direct labour working directly on tangible goods production. This schema serves to illustrate the fact that conventional classifications understate the extent to which goods production is, directly or indirectly, responsible for the generation of services employment and changes to the structure of the economy. In fact the argument can be taken right back to its logical starting point by insisting that all occupations and industries are but elaborations of technical and social divisions of labour the foundation of which is the transformation of nature into use and exchange values.

Whether a Marxian or non-Marxian framework is used to analyse economic structure, it is difficult to refute the idea that '[f]ar from being 'service economies', OECD economies remain firmly anchored in the production of goods' (Blade, 1987: 166). This interpretation also reinforces the traditional notion that an important part of the services sector is essentially determined by demand generated within manufacturing. Hence the justifiable conclusion, drawn by analysts with quite divergent theoretical perspectives, that there are stronger grounds for treating the services sector as an integral part of goods production than is often supposed. The arguments of these authors are convincing, but they underestimate other important components of the service sector, particularly producer services.

Analysis of input-output data on OECD countries by Petit (1986: 123) revealed other functions of the services sector. Services can be an important element of international trade: while 90% of services output was consumed domestically, foreign trade accounts on average for a significant 8% of output. There are also

Table 1   Extended division of labour within production*

1. Primary (direct) labour	a) Immediate workplace – processing, transfer, assembly
	b) Supplementary – transport, repairs etc.
2. Secondary (indirect) labour	a) Auxiliary labour to immediate primary labour – inventory and clerical staff, quality controllers, supervisors, engineers etc.
	b) Preproduction or preparatory labour – product development (design, testing, research), cleaners, clerical
	c) Postproduction labour – packaging, wholesaling, transport, installation, maintenance, repair
3. Complementary labour	a) Construction labour – buildings, land improvements, infrastructure (overlaps 2 and 4)
4. Tertiary labour	a) Circulation and management – trade, management, advertising, banking, leasing, renting, some transport, communications, insurance etc.
5. Quaternary labour	a) Knowledge production (pure research), labour reproduction scientists, educational and health workers etc.

Note:
*This table makes no assumptions as to the internal workplace or external enterprise location of the tasks listed.
Source: compiled from Walker (1985: 74–79)

variations in the quantum of output attributable to different groups of services. In absolute terms, about 32.5% of average total services output came from distribution industries, 20.5% from transport and communications, 29.6% from banking, insurance and 'service to firms', and 9% from 'various' services industries. Another pattern is that each 'sector' or group of services acquired most of its demand from one source: distribution and various services from final consumers; transport, communications, banking and insurance and 'services to firms' from intermediate demand. But these matters aside, there are two particular patterns which appear at odds with both the notion of services being intermediate inputs to goods production, and conventions for categorizing final demand services.

First, it is clear from the data that all services groups serve both intermediate *and* final markets. What are classified as final demand services in the OECD data-distribution and various personal, leisure and recreation services, in fact direct over 30% of their output into intermediate markets (e.g., software, building supplies, and print media retail outlets serving home and trade customers

534   *The role of services in production*

simultaneously). A second pattern is that a substantial volume of transactions are generated within and between service industries themselves: the output of many producer service industries goes to other services, which can be a significant component of national accumulation in its own right. One only has to think, for instance, of the linkages between finance institutions and legal and accountancy services, or between advertising agencies, market consultants and other service firms. Other UK input-output figures show that more of the output from producer service industries went to other services (22%) than went to manufacturing (18%) (Marshall, *et. al.*, 1987: 588; Producer Services Working Party, 1986: 53). And Riddle (1986: 25) argues that one of the fastest-growing segments of the service sector is those services that either distribute the product of, service the input needs of, or act as market intermediaries for, other service industries. These trends reinforce the point that some components of producer service industries, and many consumer services as well, have market niches and economic roles that are either independent of goods production except in a most indirect fashion (such as large scale data processing for information-intensive public and private institutions, reservations agencies, leisure parks), or straddle the producer and consumer services sectors (e.g., hotel, travel, banking, legal, consultancy and insurance service companies).

Such patterns reveal one of the key definitional and conceptual difficulties of dealing with a group of service industries which are central to the production of goods, and hence classifiable as producer services, but which also provide essential consumer services. On the one hand, data supports conventional ways of categorizing and conceptualizing the economic function of services, but on the other hand, the same data reveal ambiguities in these practices. Lumping together, or weakly differentiating among, activities and categories as diverse as producer, intermediate, final demand and consumer services industries can seriously hinder our appreciation of the particular dynamic of each group of services, the conditions which determine their expansion and contraction, and the function(s) they perform. It has been the growing appreciation of the diverse nature of services that has led to an awareness that the role and contribution of services to production and accumulation generally is both more extensive and complex than previously supposed. There are strong grounds for reconsidering the assumption that the extent and form of the supply of many services is dependent on, or spinoffs from, demand generated by manufacturing. Arguments that the ultimate determinant of accumulation rests with goods production, or has shifted to services as 'postindustrial' theorists would have it, underestimate the interdependencies between these components of economic structure.

II Interdependencies between services and goods production

It is evident that at the most elementary level in the organization of capitalist economies, services and material goods production are interdependent. Walker

(1985) notes that not only does the production of all goods require the input of labour services, but most labour services cannot be performed without the use of material goods – whether they be buildings, pieces of equipment, or the output of service labour in the form of tangible goods (books, software manuals, video cassettes). Similarly, the role of the state in supplying 'public goods' – those which are collectively consumed, which require long time horizons over which return on investment must be calculated, or where benefits would be captured 'free' by others so preventing the provider of the good from controlling commercial distribution rights and hence a market return on investment – illustrates additional fundamental independencies. Here it is not so much that many public goods are inputs into goods production, because that is clearly the case. Rather, without supply by the state of energy supplies, transportation and communication networks, or whatever, then capitalist production of many material goods *and* labour services may not even proceed because of the inability or unwillingness of private investors to enter these markets.

It has been the rise in interest in producer services, however, that has encouraged a reassessment of the relation between services and goods production. Daniels (1987) has noted the move towards integration between the major sectors of advanced capitalist economies, with increasing overlap between manufacturing and services, and between services themselves. In similar vein the Producer Services Working Party (1986: 2–5), while recognizing that the 'tertiarization' of the goods sector has undoubtedly occurred (by which they meant the observed rise in importance of service occupations and service tasks necessary for the production of goods), suggested that the traditional relationship of manufacturing 'demand' determining services 'supply' is no longer applicable for important parts of the two sectors because of various interdependencies between them. Riddle (1986: 183) has suggested that in corporations both the integration and specialization of production and services functions is occurring. And Taylor and Thrift (1983) recognized the progressive intermeshing of the circuits of industrial, commercial and banking capital within large enterprises which makes it harder to distinguish financial institutions from industrial corporations. We can explore these suggestive observations in the context of three units of analysis.

1 *Enterprises and corporations*

The ability to compete for many firms is increasingly dependent on the quality of knowledge (information services) at the disposal of management. The comparative advantage enjoyed by any unit of individual capital is found in the nature and quality of service inputs into production. It is the dramatic shift in the social and technical division lf labour – the trend towards extended prodcution systems – brought about by the forces noted in the previous points that Walker (1985; 1988) considers to be the primary cause of the growth of services.

Service inputs are vital to the maintenance of a unit of capital or enterprise,

536   *The role of services in production*

irrespective of the commodities it trades in. The survival strategies of enterprises in uncertain trading conditions can hinge on the quality of externally or internally supplied services. The last 15 years has been an era of heightened internationalization of (goods, finance, property, securities and services) markets, de(re)regulation and austerity policies of governments, depressed demand and increasingly intense competition, volatile exchange and interest rates, and the pursuit of coping strategies by capital. In this context there has been a rapid growth in demand for, or renewed strategic appreciation of, advice and information on merger and takeover options, portfolio investments, product design, diversification possibilities, commercial and international law, marketing strategies and advertising. In turn, one geographic expression of the importance of services to the survival of enterprises has been the surge in supply of producer services in key metropolitan areas of the OECD countries, (Allen, 1988c; Daniels, 1989; Marshall *et al.*, 1987).

The importance of services to competitive strategy is no more evident than in the way the development of services has transformed how goods-producing enterprises and industries are organized and operated. The managerial coordination of multiestablishment or chain enterprises and franchises, the adoption of multidivisional and matrix forms of corporate organization, the computerization of production technology, and the internationalization of production (and indeed the geographic extension of capitalist relations generally) would not be possible without certain service industries, products and occupations. The 'annihilation of space by time' is essentially a function of advances in 'services technology'. For instance, the phenomenon of the 'decentralization of administration' by goods producers, to use Daniels and Thrift's term, is related to the organizational and locational opportunities which the new information-handling technology and services offer corporations (Hepworth, 1986). In turn, this has enabled corporations to allocate their activities geographically in line with the social relations and labour requirements of each business function (e.g., Dicken, 1986; Massey, 1984; Nelson, 1986). Thus at the level of structural change within Fordist production regimes, there occurred a shift from large-scale industrial agglomerations based on sector specialization to dispersed geographic specializations based on corporate divisions of labour. More recent structural shifts are now being identified with the evolution of neo (post?) Fordist flexible accumulation regimes which have different geographic arrangements such as functionally disintegrated or externalized networks of lead and subcontracting firms (Amin, 1989; Moulaert and Swyngedouw, 1989; Sayer, 1986; Scott, 1988), or the reclustering of R & D and production units of firms (Schoenberger, 1988). All these rearrangements of the geography of enterprises and production are founded on enabling developments in the services components of goods production, and information handling and communications technology industries. The direction of causal links in these developments, however, will have been quite diverse, and it is not safe to assume that innovation or 'needs' in goods production has simply led innovation in services and the supply of services.

To add to the complexity of interpreting the role of services in accumulation, in any one enterprise (as in any one industry) there can occur the substitution of material goods for service products in order to maintain rates of profit. Within the range of production activities and tasks – or the 'value chain' to use Porter's (1985) phrase – of a single product firm, there will be alternative sources of value creation. A publisher, for instance, has the option to obtain revenue from advertising (a service), or publication rights (proprietary ownership of information – itself a labour service output), rather than from the sale of newspapers or magazines (goods) solely. Other enterprises will diversify into service products for a variety of reasons, partly depending on the nature of the unit of capital itself. A company may make a strategic move to control forward or backward linkages in a production chain (for example, aircraft manufacturers purchasing research and development companies; breweries moving forward into taverns, supermarkets or liquor outlets; 'cola' drink producers buying into fast food franchises). A similar action might be taken to ensure the more rapid circulation of goods inventories (automobile manufacturers owning car retail chains and finance houses from which to supply consumer credit), or to achieve diversification into adjacent markets (say from newspapers into television stations) where economies of scope and the degree of crosselasticity of consumer demand suggest such moves are likely to be profitable or necessary for strategic reasons. Investment vehicles like asset traders (corporate raiders), conglomerates, finance and insurance institutions (and diversified industrial corporations to a degree), will shift surplus capital to commercial property, tourism, leisure, transport or rental and leasing services as relative rates of profit and shareholders' imperatives dictate. Finally, service industries may be considered as alternative investment avenues for manufacturing corporations at times when rates of profit in any one industry are declining because of reduced demand, when markets are saturated, or when competition intensifies. Thus, at the level of the central economic units of accumulation – enterprises – there is interdependence of goods and services.

2   Industries

The conceptual distinction between goods production and intermediate services is far from clear-cut in reality. In some industries it is very difficult to draw a boundary between goods and services production, since outputs incorporate, indivisibly, both types of product. Such is the case with data-processing equipment where the utilization and marketing of hardware is inextricably linked with the nature and supply of software, and with video cassette recorders and compact disc players which are dedicated to the products of the film and music (service) industries.

Contrary to common assumptions about the intermediate status of services, there are also circumstances where demand from services has led manufacturing investment. Technological breakthroughs in some services have sparked the expansion of important manufacturing industries, as for example with research and development (scientific instruments), health care (medical equipment), information processing (typewriters, photocopiers, computers) and transport and communication (vehicles, transmitting and receiving equipment). Similarly, the transformation of the form of provision and consumption of some services has led to dramatic surges in demand for a variety of goods, such as household appliances, leisure equipment, medical diagnosis and home improvement supplies. There are perhaps two ways of interpreting these inter-related trends. One is the move towards 'self-servicing' (Gershuny, 1978), where rising costs of labour services has encouraged households to substitute goods for paid services (in other words there has been a change in the mode of services provision). The second has been an expansion of capitalist relations of production by commodifying hitherto nonexchange goods, especially of public services such as in the transport and health arenas (Blackburn *et al.*, 1986; Mandel, 1975).

To further undermine the notion of services as intermediate inputs is the fact that the products of several goods and services industries are to varying degrees substitutable where there is a degree of crosselasticity of demand. In other words, services and tangible goods can be in competition with each other, as for example, with newspapers, radios and television, or between video cassette recorders and movie theatres. While they may be complementary, it is not appropriate to see these products in terms of a linear sequence of input-output linkages. In fact, in the examples cited, the complex interdependence of some elements of the goods and services sectors highlighted in the two points just made are fully revealed; which are the intermediate or final demand products is quite unclear (is it the television or the programme which is the intermediate product?); equally unclear is what is being substituted (is it newspapers substituted for televisions, or the type and format of information presented through the two mediums?).

Finally, and turning to the origin of value-added in goods production, in a number of product markets it is the 'services' end of the production chain – design, styling, research, marketing, delivery, packaging, consumer credit – which determines the competitiveness of agricultural and manufacturing investment. As the length of production chains increases, so services are responsible for a greater share of value added to products. At some point in the production of many goods, services will account for the majority of added value, although there will be variations in the origin of this contribution; that is, it will either be from in-house occupations and task units within the firm, inputs purchased externally to complement the in-house production process (which may include putting-out and subcontracting arrangements), or from downstream external services once the commodity leaves the producer.

3   Circuits of capital

The notion of interdependence between goods and services, that is the production and circulation of commodities, is well developed in Marxian analysis, where the physical movement of goods, and the velocity and turnover time of capital locked up in commodities, are seen as central determinants to the realization process and rates of accumulation. When put in the context of this high order of abstraction, the role of services is essentially to reduce the indirect costs of production and to minimize the time-space barriers to the turnover time of capital. Hence banks and other credit institutions facilitate the availability of money in advance of sales, while advertising, distribution and retail industries facilitate the rate of consumption of commodities and hence the rate of profit realization. But theories of the role of services using structuralist perspectives contain conceptual ambiguities when they are applied at lower levels of abstraction. In this regard, three issues come to mind: 1) the debate over whether services labour is productive or not; 2) conceptualizing the conditions of accumulation pertaining to specific circulation industries; and 3) treating the structural role of circulation capital as simply complementary to production capital.

Following the orthodox Marxian position, Mandel (1975, 403–406) defines productive labour as that 'which creates surplus value', with the boundary between productive and nonproductive labour runnning between '. . . wage-labour which increases, changes, or preserves a use-value, or is indispensable for its realization – and wage-labour which makes no difference to a use-value, i.e., to the *bodily form* of a commodity, but merely arises from the specific needs involved, i.e., *altering* (as opposed to *creating*) the form of an exchange value'. These statements, in the absence of any discussion of how 'changes' to a use value differ from 'altering' a use value, are unclear and contradictory. Nonetheless, an elaboration of this formulation leads to the conclusion that the 'exchange of personal services for revenues' and costs of circulation which 'originate in a mere change of form of value' constitute services labour and service capital which also are not productive. Without getting into semantic debates, there is an important problem with this argument.

At the level of capital in general, that is for capitalists in the aggregate, it may well be appropriate to distinguish between labour and capital in this manner since, if the source of all surplus value is ultimately in the creation of commodities, then any labour or capitals which compete for a share of total value without adding to that stock of value can reasonably be defined as unproductive. But Mandel himself recognizes that this logic does not hold if we shift our attention to the level of individual capitals. As was argued in a previous section, services of all kinds are indispensable to enterprises. Tucked away in a footnote, Mandel (1975: 406) acknowledges this when he says that '[f]or the *individual capitalist* all wage labour – even in the sector of circulation and services – is obviously productive, since it enables him (sic) to appropriate a part of the over all social surplus-value'. Hence, for example, advice from financial consultants to a proprietor on whether to reinvest profits in the firm or to put assets into securities or property during a recession (that is a service which involves 'merely a change of form of value') may be critical to the long-term survival of that

540 *The role of services in production*

individual firm. In the same way, advertising, which does nothing to enhance the value or affect the technical specifications of a commodity is a vital element in competition between enterprises. And a third example, the phenomenon of companies hiving off part of their operations, in part consists of creating stand-alone business units designed to facilitate the 'exchange of personal services for revenues'. The accrual of specialist skills within an enterprise (e.g., marketing, personnel management, 'trouble shooting', junk bonds, currency management or loopholes in commercial law), where these skills are also of utility to other companies, can represent opportunities for the externalization of these skills, which are then offered on the open market and become a supplementary source of profit accumulation for the parent company. So, in the everyday reality of individual enterprises, there is no clear-cut, unambiguous definition of what constitutes productive and unproductive labour.

The second matter for consideration is the treatment of fractions of circulation capital. From a Marxian position, tangible goods production in general can be conceptualized straightforwardly as relating to the sphere of production. Similarly, at first glance circulation capitals, which are directly or indirectly involved with the movement of goods and the velocity of money (including banking, other finance, insurance, transport, retailing and communications), could profitably be analysed within a schema similar to that advocated by Walker. But when the focus is shifted down a notch to specific industries, it is clear from Allen's (1988a) arguments that this would be insufficient because the commercial logic and imperatives of industries such as banking, and the nature of the markets in which they operate, cannot be reduced simply to the circulation requirements of goods production. To do so would misrepresent the nature of much of the activity of such industries. Foreign exchange, stocks, securities and property markets, for instance, are arenas of accumulation and speculation in their own right with their own dynamics. Nor can they be reduced to just producer services, since the term 'producer' service does not deal adequately with either the structural relations involved in the notion of circulation as interpreted through Marxian theory, or with the diversity of market behaviour and competitive strategies exhibited by service industries firms within the various spheres of circulation.

As to the last issue, it is important for Marxian theory to recognize that at a lower level of analysis, it is not always correct to treat circulation capital as being complementary to the needs of production capital. Individual capitals and fractions of capital (irrespective of whether they are manufactures, banks or retailers) compete for the surplus value generated in the various stages and alternative pathways of the circulation process. The interests of industrial goods capital and its means of accumulation has historically differed from financial and commercial capital (Harvey, 1982: 68–74). As Allen (1988a) notes for instance, merchant capital (import and export intermediaries, wholesalers and retailers) cannot be seen as solely geared to the 'needs' of goods producers, but has a dynamic that is increasingly leading to it competing with, and controlling, goods production (e.g., major retailers dominating networks of subcontracted manufacturers). This calls into question the conventional assumption that, say retailers, 'serve' the interests of manufacturers by providing the means to realize the surplus value inherent in the latter's commodities. Linkage networks and production chains can be so mobilized as to enhance the capacity of retailers to extract a share of surplus value produced in the manufacturing sphere that would otherwise go to (manufacturing) labour or other (manufacturing) capitalists. It does not seem apt to label such retailers, as social science convention would have it, a 'consumer service', when they are increasingly efficient extractors of profit from both consumers and producers, as well as from labour and other fractions of capital. In such instances it is reductionist to treat commercial capital as functionally subordinate to production capital, at least at the empirical level of analysis.

Similarly there may be a divergence between industrial and finance capital. During periods of crisis the two tend to be in competition with, rather than complementary to, each other and to have different geographies (Gordon, 1988: 59). In times of economic expansion financial institutions and investment fund managers allocate capital largely according to the demand from, and hence geography of, investments made by industrial corporations. During recession, however, finance capital flows take quite a different distribution path, as funds are moved around the globe seeking speculative opportunities from currency differentials, stock and bond markets and commercial property.

When considering the relations between industrial and services capital, however, complementarities are equally important. Mandel (1975: 406) suggests that there has been a long-term trend since the 1950s for industrial corporations and investment institutions to divert excess profits into services to counter a secular fall in the average rate of profit. The same trend may be argued from the perspective of the regulationist school, in that profit ceilings imposed on industrial producers to prevent them from reaching the internal limitations of Fordist production techniques have triggered diversification into other markets such as tourism, publishing, telecommunications, rental cars, movie production, fast food franchises or the music and video entertainment industries.

These principles still hold if we move further down the ladder of levels of abstraction and aggregation to consider components of a production or value chain (encompassing the sourcing, transformation, distribution and exchange of commodities) within diversified and vertically integrated corporations. Control over one strategic position within an externalized chain, or internalized control over several vital links in a chain (especially knowledge, finance or buying and selling outlets) gives the corporate entity power to alter practices up- or downstream, and to extract (compete for) a share of the surplus generated at various stages in the chain. Such strategic manoeuvres can be interpreted as extensions of the geographic and structural reach of a lead corporation as it moves forwards or backwards into allied or additional markets. Where the segments of a production chain are distributed in different countries, or where horizontal

542 *The role of services in production*

integration involves investing in offshore markets, these tactics of a corporation contribute to the widely observed internationalization of production.

At the empirical level of analysis, then, a case can be made for a sharper conceptualization of the structural roles of sub-groups of services within the accumulation process, and of their competing or complementary interests. A distinction can be made, for example, between clusters of services geared in the first instance to the circulation of goods (e.g., transport, advertising, wholesaling, commodities markets, retailing, consumer credit, consumer information agencies), money (finance and investment institutions, foreign exchange markets), information and monitoring (investment analysts, accountants and auditors, management consultants, marketing agencies, business publications), property rights (share, commodities and bond markets, legal services) and labour (corporate or clerical employment agencies, training schools, mass transit systems, immigration agencies). Thrift (1987) has gone some way to unpacking the category of finance capital into its constituent components: banking (interest-bearing) capital, commercial capital, which is subdivided into merchant capital which mediates the circulation of commodities for a fee, and money-dealing capital which mediates in the circulation of money and credit for a fee. Such advances help clarify some definitional problems: they can also reveal the degrees of autonomy or interdependence of different capitals, the separation or interpenetration of product (services) markets, and the degree of interindustry boundary spanning of individual service enterprises that exist.

In passing, it must be remembered that resolution of any of these issues is dependent on investigation being specified with respect to scales of resolution, units of analysis and levels of abstraction. For example, the role played by financial or commercial capital with respect to production will take on a certain complexion if viewed from the perspective of capital in general, with the orthodox Marxian notion of circuits of capital providing an essential theoretical tool with which to reveal important structural interdependencies. But if one shifts focus to the accumulation strategies of integrated corporations or conglomerates, or to capital movements between industries and territories, then the relationships between goods, services and capital take on a different hue which will require appropriate theorization. The pitching of one's analysis at any particular level of abstraction will lead to the identification of a variety of relationships which may or may not be directly transferrable between levels.

III Conclusion

The economic roles of services in capitalist accumulation discussed above suggest that much more attention needs to be directed at conceptualizing services on at least two levels: 1) the relationships between goods manufacture, services and value added in commodity production in general (and arrangements and practices which have evolved within specific industries and territories); and 2) the function and contribution of various types of services to the accumulation strategies of enterprises and corporate groups.

On the first theme, an accurate identification of the relative contribution of certain service and production activities with respect to competitive advantages is most important. It would seem that the role services play in profit generation and accumulation generally has been underestimated. The origin and nature of the competitive advantages enjoyed by many goods-producing industries, enterprises and territories may have long centred on the services component of their production systems, but this has gone unrecognized in academic analysis.

This omission has not been made in the commercial sphere, as the recognized market value of patents, intellectual property, goodwill, high-performing staff and brand names testifies. A variety of political, economic and management repercussions have followed this market reality. Nations, regions and companies are going to great expense and effort to capture and foster the conditions and requirements necessary to develop advanced service industries and skilled service labour. Political attempts in specific territories to attract high-tech industries, international finance markets, advanced communications or research and development institutions, can be interpreted as one manifestation of the fact that services (especially information- and knowledge-based segments of production and circulation chains) are seen as the key determinants of competitive advantage and continued accumulation.

When the enterprise or business organization is the focus of analysis, three generic ways in which services assist accumulation can be identified. First, services may be incorporated (from internalized or externalized sources) into a company because of the technical requirements of a production process (that is, as part of an extended division of labour). Secondly, services may be integrated within the firm to ensure reproduction by securing required flows of inputs, turnover of capital, and realization of profit. Such services can be acquired by developing them in-house, or via forward integration involving open market transactions, tied arrangements or equity holdings with external suppliers. A third objective role of services is to maximize accumulation and return on investment capital in the face of incessant competition: this is an important reason for the trend for more extended production sequences within companies since it increases opportunities for profit realization, cost and quality control, product development and production stability. But raising these points is to confine ourselves to single product enterprises.

In large diversified corporations, particularly conglomerates, services become an investment option in their own right, irrespective of any role in a production process. Service activities, in the organizational form of pre-existing companies, are purchased or sold as part of an investment portfolio purely on the grounds of financial performance; there is no necessity for service activities so purchased to perform any intermediate input function for the group. (In practice, however, corporations and conglomerates will purchase finance, property development and other such units for multiple reasons, including the internalization of functions that are strategically important to the group's operations and goals.) The concern

544   *The role of services in production*

with financial performance by industrial corporations has been particularly evident during the current economic crisis. The rapid growth of certain services, notably stockbrokers, money market dealers, property investors and law firms in the major cities of OECD countries, has largely resulted from the dramatically heightened speculative activity of corporations (as well as private and institutional investors) as they liquify and switch assets out of goods production and convert them into financial investments at a time when recession has depressed profit levels in industry (Gordon, 1988).

One final comment: for geographers it is no easy task to identify the most appropriate unit of analysis for investigating the multiple roles that services play in the accumulation process and the various complementarities and interdependencies to be found between services and goods production. Unfortunately, many of the conventional analytical perspectives and most existing databases at our disposal do not always reveal critical dimensions of services that such analyses would require. It is necessary to develop research frameworks, for instance, which are predicated on the multifaceted interdependence of components of modern services and goods production, particularly within large corporations and conglomerates. It is also necessary to recognize the limiting nature of official statistics which treat the sectors in a one-dimensional fashion by divorcing the organizational and functional dimensions and contexts of services. As it stands, for example, there is the well-known problem that if service products are produced within manufacturing enterprises they are enumerated as part of the goods-producing sector: when the same products are supplied externally by specialist service firms they are enumerated as part of the services sector. In similar fashion, Coffey and Polese (1987) have identified three types of trade in services – direct exports (sales to other firms) by producer service enterprises, intraenterprise transactions between producer service establishments, and intraenterprise transactions between manufacturing establishments – which cannot be distinguished from official data sets. Until these sorts of measurement and conceptual problems are overcome, both the interdependence between different economic activities and the economic contribution of services to accumulation in territories and production systems which have been discussed here, will continue to be underestimated and misrepresented.

University of Auckland, New Zealand

IV   References

Allen, J. 1988a: Service industries: uneven development and uneven knowledge, *Area* 20(1), 15–22.
   1988b: Towards a post-industrial economy? In Allen, J. and Massey, D., editors, *The economy in question*, London: Sage and Open University.
   1988c: The geographies of services. In Massey, D. and Allen, J., editors, *Uneven re-development: cities and regions in transition*, London: Hodder and Stoughton

and Open University.

Amin, A. 1989: Flexible specialisation and small firms in Italy: myths and realities. *Antipode* 21(1), 13–34.

Blackburn, P., Coombs, R., and **Green, K.** 1986: *Technology, economic growth and the labour process.* London: Macmillan.

Blade, D. 1987: *Goods and services in OECD economies.* Paris: OECD.

Britton, S.G. 1989: Understanding the 'services economy' a preliminary review of theory. Working Paper on Auckland's Producer Service Industries No. 2, Department of Geography, University of Auckland.

Coffey, W.J. and **Polese, M.** 1987: Trade and location of producer services: a Canadian perspective. *Environment and Planning A* 19, 597–611.

Daniels, P.W. 1989: Some perspectives on the geography of services. *Progress in Human Geography* 13(3), 427–33.

1987: Producer services research: a lengthening agenda. *Environment and Planning A* 19, 569–74.

1985: Service industries: a geographical appraisal. London: Methuen.

Daniels, P.W. and **Thrift, N.** 1987: The geographies of the UK service sector. A survey. Working Paper on Producer Services No. 6, Departments of Geography, University of Bristol and University of Liverpool.

Dicken, P. 1986: *Global shift: industrial change in a turbulent world.* London: Harper and Row.

Fuchs, Y.R. 1968: *The service economy.* New York: National Bureau of Economic Research Inc. and Columbia University Press.

Gershuny, J. 1978: *After industrial society? the emerging self-service economy.* London: Macmillan.

Gershuny, J and **Miles, I.D.** 1983: The service economy. The transformation of employment in industrial societies. New York: Praeger.

Gordon, D.M. 1988: The global economy: New edifice or crumbling foundations? *New Left Review* 169, 24–65.

Harvey, D. 1982: *The limits to capital.* London: Basil Blackwell.

Hepworth, M. 1986: The geography of technological change in the information economy. *Regional Studies* 20(5), 407–24.

Kolko, J. 1988: *Restructuring the world economy.* New York: Pantheon.

Kuznets, S. 1971: *Economic growth of nations.* Cambridge, MA: Harvard University Press.

Leverson, I. 1985: Services in the US economy. In Inman, R.P., editor, *Managing the service economy: prospects and problems,* Cambridge: Cambridge University Press.

Mandel, E. 1975: *Late capitalism.* London: Verso.

Marshall, J., Damesick, N. and **Wood, P.** 1987: Understanding the Location and Role of Producer Services in the United Kingdom. *Environment and Planning A* 19, 575–93.

Massey, D. 1984: *Spatial divisions of labour: social structures and the geography of production.* London: Methuen.

Moulaert, F. and **Swyngedouw, E.A.** 1989. A regulation approach to the geography of flexible production systems. *Environment and Planning D: Society and Space* 7, 327–45.

Nelson, K. 1986: Labour demand, labour supply, and the suburbanisation of low-wage

546   *The role of services in production*

office work. In Scott, A. and Storper, M., editors, *Production, work, territory: the geographical anatomy of industrial capitalism*, Boston: Allen and Unwin.

Nusbaumer, J. 1987: *The service economy: lever to growth*. Boston: Kluwer.

Perry, M. 1989: *New Zealand's service economy 1956–1986: a preliminary examination of employment and output trends*. Working Paper on Auckland's Producer Service Industries No. 1, Department of Geography, University of Auckland.

Petit, P. 1986: *Slow growth and the service economy*. New York: St Martin's Press.

Porter, M.E. 1985. *Competitive advantage*. New York: Free Press.

Producer Services Working Party, 1986: *Uneven development in the services economy: understanding the location and role of producer services*. London: Institute of British Geographers.

Quinn, J.B. and **Gagnon, C.E.** 1986: Will services follow manufacturing into decline? *Harvard Business Review* 86(6), 95–106.

Riddle, D.I. 1986: *Service-led growth: the role of the service sector in world development*. New York: Praeger.

Sayer, A. 1986: New developments in manufacturing: the just-in-time system. *Capital and Class* 30, 43–72.

Schoenberger, E. 1988: From Fordism to flexible accumulation: technology, competitive strategies, and international location. *Environment and Planning D: Society and Space* 6, 245–62.

Scott, A. 1988: *New industrial spaces*. London: Pion.

Taylor, M. and **Thrift, N.** 1983: The role of finance in the evolution and functioning of industrial systems. In Hamilton, F.E. and Linge, G.J.R., editors, *Spatial analysis and the industrial environment*; Volume 3, *Regional economies and industrial systems*, Chichester, John Wiley & Sons.

Thrift, N. 1987: The fixers: the urban geography of international commercial capital. In Henderson, J. and Castells, M., editors, *Global restructuring and territorial development*, London: Sage.

Walker, R. 1985: Is there a service economy? The changing capitalist division of labour. *Science and Society* 69(1), 42–83.

1988: The geographical organisation of production. *Society and Space* 6(4), 377–408.

Urry, J. 1987: Some social and spatial aspects of services. *Society and Space* 5, 5–26.

[17]

Revue d'Economie Régionale et Urbaine n° 4 (1989)

THE DIFFUSION OF PRODUCER SERVICES IN THE URBAN SYSTEM

par
Riccardo CAPPELLIN
Professeur associé d'Economie Régionale
Università L. Bocconi, Milan

- I -
INTRODUCTION

Traditional theories of the growth of service activities have always stressed the relationships with the demand, while they have almost neglected to analyse the factors which on the supply side affect the competitivity and the growth of service productions. In fact, even empirical researches based on sample surveys have almost always aimed to study the factors which determine the increase in the demand of services by industrial firms. On the contrary, very few empirical researches, both in Italy and in other countries, have aimed to analyse the characteristics of the firms of the tertiary sectors (DANIELS and HOLLY, 1983).

The development of service activities in a metropolitan area does not only depend on the development of the local market but rather on the capacity of the local supply, in the framework of the competition at the national and at the international level with other urban centers. The growth of service activities is especially affected by the existence of specific advantages in terms of costs of production, of quality of the production factors and of the labor force employed, of agglomeration economies, of access to the communication networks, of availability of informations, of local know-how and entrepreneurship capabilities. Therefore, the development of services in a particular urban center depends on the capability of removing the different obstacles which on the supply side may hinder the development of the capacity of exporting services to other areas.

This study aims, first of all, to illustrate some recent theoretical contributions which allow to extend the analysis of the location factors of service activities in the urban centers beyond the limits of the traditional theories, such as the central place model, the export base model or the stage of development theory. While these theories were mainly considering the demand side, recent contributions consider both the factors which affect the demand and those which affect the supply of tertiary activities. Secondly, this study will present the results of two surveys on service firms of various tertiary sectors, aiming to examine the structure of employment in service firms and the process of innovation adoption.

642 The diffusion of producer services in the urban system

- II -

INNOVATIONS, TRANSACTION COSTS AND SERVICE ACTIVITIES

The relationships between service activities and innovations can be analysed according to three different perspectives (CAPPELLIN, 1983). First of all, the use of new services by industrial firms can be considered as an organisational or a process innovation within these latter firms. Secondly, the production of new services by the existing service firms or the birth of new service firms in a specific area may be considered as a product innovation. Finally, service firms may adopt process or organisational innovations, in order to increase their productivity and/or to improve the quality of the service provided (MOMIGLIANO and SINISCALCO, 1986).

These different relationships between the adoption of innovations and service activities are clearly interdependent among themselves. In fact, the production of new services by a particular service firm does not only represent a product innovation, but it usually requires also the adoption of important process and organisational innovations by these firms. Moreover, the development of new services or the improvement of the quality of the existing services are often a necessary condition in order to expand the use of these services by the industrial firms.

Tightly related to the concept of innovation is a precise definition of the so called "advanced" services. These may be defined as those services which satisfy at least one of the following two criteria. First of all, the production of the "advanced" services should require advanced technological know-how or high skilled labor force or large fixed investments per employees, such as in the case of computer and telecommunication services. Secondly, "advanced" services should be capable to promote the adoption of product, process, organisational and market innovations in the firms using them, as is the case of R&D and consulting services. Clearly some services may be defined "advanced" according to both these criteria. On the other hand, some "modern" services, such as some new personal services, seem not be capable to satisfy any of these criteria and can hardly be defined "advanced" services.

In a post industrial economy, as that of the Western European countries, the main export base activity of an urban center is represented by business service activities. In fact, while manufacturing activities are diffused even in small urban centers, the most qualified business services and also the service functions of industrial firms, such as the headquarters of large manufacturing firms, are usually concentrated in the largest urban centers (CAPPELLIN, 1980).

The input-output relationships of business service activities are rather different from those of manufacturing activities, as inputs of raw material, of intermediate products and of capital goods are much less important for service activities (CAPPELLIN et al., 1987). On the other hand, due to their increasing specialisation, service firms are tightly related one with the others through input and output flows of intermediate services. As service firms provide specialised services to manufacturing firms, they are also tightly related to the internal functions of manufacturing firms, performing a service activity. Finally, the most important input of service firms compete one with the others in the labour markets of the most qualified occupations. Therefore, the choice of business service firms between the location in larger more than in smaller urban centers or the dual problem of the specialisation of each urban center in the supply of particular services are affecting the characteristics of : a) the transactions of services between different firms, b) the transactions of labour inputs (CAPPELLIN, 1988).

Transaction costs (WILLIAMSON, 1979 and 1981) are usually higher for service firms than for industrial firms, due to the immaterial nature of the output of service firms and due to the need of a tight and active relationship and of bilateral exchanges of informations between the supplier and the user in the process of producing a service. As stocks are almost impossible in the case of services, service transactions are more frequent than those of goods. Service quantity, quality and productivity are harder to be defined and are often uncertain. Therefore, service transactions are usually more complex and require an higher reciprocal trust than transactions of industrial products. Finally, service activities often imply very special human skills and high immaterial, human capital investments which may bind together the buyer and the seller of the service considered.

As transaction costs decrease the lower is the distance between the buyer and the seller or the higher is their concentration in the specific urban centers, cities or central locations have a comparative advantage, with respect to rural or peripheral locations, in those economic activities which, as services, imply high transaction costs.

Apparently the urban concentration of service firms could decrease as the progress in transportation and communications has increased the possibility to export services from a particular center to other even very distant locations. In fact, transportation services, banking and financial services and also consulting services, such as engeneering and management consulting, may be supplied to firms located in other countries, regions and urban centers.

However, it seems necessary to distinguish the exchanges between a service firm and the firms using that service from the exchanges occuring between different service firms, which are tightly interdependent and perform different functions in the joint production of a particular service. Exchanges which are uphill of service production seem to imply greater transactions costs than exchanges which are downhill of service production. In fact, the sources of the inputs of service firms are usually more diversified than the buyers of their outputs. The purchase of inputs by service firms requires frequent contacts with many different firms. Service firms, such as transportation firms, banks or consulting firms require intermediate inputs which should be provided by many other service firms, such as communication, legal, fiscal, technical consulting services, financial intermediaries, research and higher education institutions, etc... Therefore, even when the output of a service firm can be supplied to non local and distant users, the objective to minimize transaction costs on the exchange of the inputs determines the concentration of this firm together with many other service activities in (large) urban centers.

644   The diffusion of producer services in the urban system

The importance of transaction costs increases the higher is the quality of a service, as advanced services require a tight bilateral exchange of informations also in the execution phase. Therefore, the progress in communications has a lower impact on those services which require frequent "face to face" contacts, while it may make the routine and more standardized services almost "footloose". However, as high quality services and low quality services are tightly interdependent, also these latter services may be led to concentrate in the largest urban centers, since they may have an easy access to high quality services and they can reach peripheral locations using modern communications and computer networks.

- 111 -
THE STRUCTURE OF TWO EMPIRICAL SURVEYS ON SERVICE FIRMS

Many empirical studies in various countries have interpreted the factors of the development of service activities by analysing the pattern of the demand of services by industrial firms. Other studies have analysed the distribution of service employment or production at the regional or urban level mainly using census data or national account data (CAPPELLIN and GRILLENZONI, 1983 ; CAPPELLIN, 1986a and 1986b). Very few are the empirical studies of service firms, although it seems clear that a thorough analysis of the development of service activities would require a direct investigation of the structure and performance of service firms, as all other sources of informations are certainly either rather indirect and very often inadequate. For these reasons, two empirical surveys on service firms have been elaborated and will be reported in this study. Moreover, two other surveys are currently being undertaken with similar methodology (Umbria et Veneto regions).

The first of these surveys concerns three mayor urban centers of the Lombardy region : Milan, which represents the largest urban center of the regional urban system, Como which is located in an old industrialised area and Brescia which is located in an area of more recent industrialisation (BOSCACCI and CAPPELLIN, 1987). This survey consists in the direct interview of 207 service firms belonging to the following sectors : 1) trade intermediaries of industrial machines and materials, 2) transport and custom services, 3) accounting and fiscal consulting services, 4) technical services, 5) advertising and public relation services, 6) marketing services, 7) management consulting services, 8) soft-ware and computer services, 9) private research services. The data refer to the situation existing at the beginning of 1986. The size of the firms interviewed correspond to the average size of the service firms in the Lombardy region and is rather limited since 56 % of them have less than 6 employees.

The second survey, elaborated within the Milan Project (CAPPELLIN and POLO, 1987) concerns only the Milan Metropolitan Area (MMA). Also in this survey data refer to the situation existing at the beginning of 1986. However, this survey differs from the previous one as the questionnaire is much more detailed and the firms interviewed may be considered as the "leader" firms in their respective sector according to the opinion of experts, due to their size and growth rate. Therefore, the average size of these firms is much larger than that of the survey on the Lombardy urban centers and all firms have more than 50 employees and in various service sectors the firms considered have more than 100 employees.

The sectors considered have been choosen in order to represent all the productive branches, according to which the tertiary activities are classified by the Italian Official Statistis (ISTAT). In particular, the following sectors have been considered : 1) large food shops, 2) large department stores, 3) cloth shops, 4) computer shops, 5) cathering services, 6) trading companies, 7) truck transports, 8) tour operators, 9) banks, 10) factoring services, 11) leasing services, 12) insurance brokers, 13) software services, 14) administration consulting, 15) certified accountants, 16) advertising services, 17) marketing services, 18) engeneering services.

The questionnaire of this survey has considered the following aspects of the structure of service firms : the characteristics of the founder, the mode of the firm birth, the mix of services produced, the characteristics of the customers, the problems faced in the adoption of innovations, the structure of employment, the characteristics of hired and dismissed workers, the procedures of labour training, the forms of collaboration and joint-ventures among service firms, the factors of the firm location.

– IV –
THE CHANGES IN THE DEMAND OF SERVICES

The development of service activities is certainly affected by various factors which determine the demand of services by industrial and also tertiary sectors.

According to the product life cycle theory, the different ages of the particular products determine a different importance of particular production factors. It is interesting to observe that the typology of these factors seems rather similar to the typology of service activities classified according to the function which they perform in the hierarchical organisation of the firms.

In fact, in the "initial phase" of the product life cycle, a strategic role is played by "orientation services", which are connected with the identification of the long term prospects of the firm, of technology, of markets and of the local environment, such as the R&D services or other "advanced" consulting services. In the "development phase" of the product life cycle, the crucial services required are technical, organisational, financial and marketing services, which may defined as "planning services". These services aim to implement the strategic objectives which have been decided in the orientation phase of the decision making process. Finally, in the "maturity phase" of the product life cycle, a crucial role is played by "programming services", which are routine services connected with the daily organisation and control of the production process, such as production, personnel, accounting, buying, selling and transport services.

Various studies on the location of service activities have indicated that each of these three types of services requires different types of contacts (face to face, telephone, mail, computer networks, etc...). Therefore, each of these three types of services has a different optimal location pattern within the various centers of the urban hierarchy of a region or a country (GODDARD, 1975).

646 The diffusion of producer services in the urban system

In fact, "orientation services" tend to localise in the metropolitan areas, where "face to face" contacts with many different economic agents are more easy. "Planning services" tend to locate in medium size urban centers, as they require frequent contacts among a more limited number of agents, which often are internal to the individual firms or belong to the different firms of the same sector. These urban centers often are the main urban centers industrial specialised districts and are characterised by the development of a set of very specialised producer services. Finally, "programming services" can be localised even in small urban centers of peripheral regions, near to the production plants and/or to the final markets, since they require a lower volume of informations, mainly concerning frequent transactions between these plants and the respective clients and suppliers.

The existence of specific location factors for each of these services and the strategic role of these latter in the development of specific productions indicates that the relationship between the demand and the supply of services has an interdependent character. In fact, on the one hand, the technological characteristics of local productions affect the type of services which are demanded. On the other hand, considering the supply side, the existence of particular services in particular areas is affected by the local availability of specific factors, affecting the location of the particular service considered. Therefore, the existence of an adequate supply of specific service may represent the necessary condition in order to develop particular new industrial productions and to reconvert the local economic system from traditional to other technologically more advanced productions (CAPPELLIN, 1986b).

A second type of factors which may affect the demand of services is related to the forms of the relationships among the various firms within a regional economy. In fact, the crucial role of service activities is to establish links between the different production units and their respective suppliers, their competitors and their markets. An higher division of labor among the industrial firms implies a tighter network of relationships among these firms and an increased role of service activities. In fact, the role of producer services is similar to that of transportation services, as even they aim to overcome the distance between the different firms, by establishing networks of financial, technological and commercial relationships among these firms. The forms of these relationships among the firms may be different, ranging from direct financial partecipation, to family relationships among the respective entre-preneurs, to informal and temporary agreements, to sub-contracting, etc...

In particular, a factor affecting the form of these relation-ships and the demand of services consists in the development stage of the local economy considered. In fact, in an initial phase of the development process, the firms are weakly integrated one with the others, as it is indicated by the case of the Italian Mezzogior-no. Therefore, strategic services are those which organize the relationships between the local firms, for example specialised in the sectors of construction or of agriculture, and their respective local sources of raw material and the local markets of their outputs, such as transport and retail trade services.

In an intermediate development phase, when specialised industrial districts become important, as in the case of the "Third Italy" (FUA' and ZACCHIA, 1983), the strategic function of services is to organize the complex flows of intermediate products among tightly integrated firms. Communications and wholesale services and especially internal services within the industrial firms become the most important services in these areas.

In fact, in these areas characterized by small and medium size firms, the relationships among the firms are often organi ed in an informal way and the supply of services is often not organized by market relationships but by a system of social relations and by various types of public or cooperative institutions. For example, labour training is mainly based on learning by doing and the know-how is diffused through the frequent mobility of skilled workers among the firms whithin these industrial specialized districts. Financial relationships are also affected by family and friendship relationships among the entrepreneurs. Technological innovations diffuse through a gradual process of imitation of the technology adopted by the firms which are more advanced.

Finally, when a local economy enters in a post-industrial phase, as in the case of large metropolitan areas, such as the Lombardy region, the crucial flows among the firms do not seem to be the physical flows of inputs and outputs but the immaterial flows of financial resources and the flows of informations on new technological opportunities and on the evolution of markets. The relationships of the firms expand both in an intersectoral and in an interregional perspective. The crucial objective of the firms becomes the fast access to process, product, market and organisational innovations, rather than the achievement of economies of scale through a better production integration with other firms, as it was the case in an intermediate phase of development.

In this third phase of development, the growth of new producer services determines "urbanisation economies" for the local firms, while it decreases the role of "localisation economies", within a particular sector of specialization as it promotes a greater sectoral diversification of the local economy. In fact, new advanced services may promote cooperation agreements with non local firms and facilitate the access to new markets and to new technologies, thus decreasing the role of the flows of intermediate products within the individual sectors of the local economy.

When the local economy becomes more developed and the problems created by the increasing international competition and by the fast change of tecl.nology become crucial, then, the internal organizations of the firms becomes more complex and the demand of services increases. Therefore, service functions which were originally performed by the entrepreneur himself are delegated to service workers within the firms and services, which were obtained through informal contacts with other firms or with public institutions, are bought through market transactions from external specialised firms. Therefore, the growth of services is mainly due to a process of increasing division of labor, rather than to the growth of completely new service functions.

The two empirical surveys indicated above confirm the importance of demand side factors of the development of service

648   The diffusion of producer services in the urban system

activities. However, contrary to a widely believed opinion, according to which services would be mainly demanded by large firms, the survey on Lombardy urban centers indicates that the most important customers of the service firms interviewed are first of all the medium size industrial firms and then the tertiary firms, the small industrial firms, the large industrial firms and the public administration. From the sectoral point of view, the industrial sectors are the most important customers of the service firms (56 %). However, the service sectors are also rather important and are indicated by 42 % of the firms.

The survey on the Milan Metropolitan Area (MMA), differently from that on Lombardy, indicates that for the "leader" service firms interviewed the demand by industrial firms is very important and it exceeds 75 % of the turnover for the sectors of truck transports (88 %), leasing (86 %), cathering (81 %), insurance brokers (76 %), and it exceeds 50 % for the following sectors : engeneering (73 %), advertising (73 %), trading companies (65 %), factoring (61 %), accounting (56 %), and marketing (52 %). Moreover, the customer firms with more than 200 employees represent on average 57 % of the turnover of the service firms interviewed. Low values are indicated only by the computer shops (13 %), administration consulting (10 %), leasing (9 %) and factoring (5 %). Also the receptivity of the customers to the supply of new services seems to be higher for industrial sectors (62 %) and for large firms.

These results seem to confirm that the technological level of the customers affects the demand of services. Moreover, the role of demand by industrial firms and large firms seems to increase the larger is the size of the services firms considered.

– V –
PRODUCT INNOVATIONS AND BIRTH OF NEW FIRMS

The growth of services does not authomatically follow the growth of the demand in the individual areas considered. In fact, the continuous technological progress in communications allows an urban center to produce services not only for the local firms but also for firms located in other rather distant areas. Therefore, the demand of qualified services, necessary in order to innovate the production processes in a particular area, may be satisfied by service firms located in other areas. One the other hand, a particular urban center may develop the supply of particular services to a larger extent than that required by the demand of the local firms as these services may be exported to other areas. In other cases, various obstacles on the supply side may hinder the growth of service firms, notwithstanding the level of local demand and this latter may be satisfied by the import of services from other areas. Therefore, it is important to analyse the factors which, on the supply side, affect the birth and the competitivity and growth of the production and export of services (BAILLY et al., 1985).

According, the survey on Lombardy, only 23 % of the firms have exclusively a local market. 24 % of the firms sell more than 2/3 of their turnover outside of their respective province. 45 % sell more than 1/3 outside of their province. 48 % of the firms sell also to other regions and 15 % also abroad. The share of exports is significant and on the average equal to 7 %. It achieves high values for the trade intermediaries of industrial machines and materials (25 %). However, the export propensity is not homogenous for all the three urban centers considered, but it is larger for Milan and Como than for Brescia.

According to the survey on the MMA, sales outside the MMA represent 56 % of the turnover, on average. Important exceptions are represented by some sectors for which the local market is very important : insurance brokers (51 %), software services (53 %), marketing (57 %), computer shops (72 %), large foods stores (85 %) , administration consulting (89 %). On the contraru, for trading companies (88 %) and engeneering services (49 %) exports are very important.

The demand and the supply of producer services may become rather autonomous one from the other, since the demand of services by the local firms, especially the large ones, becomes oriented toward service firms external to the area considered, while local service firms may be capable to export significant shares of their turnover toward other regions and also abroad. These results disprove the widely believed opinion according to which services are mainly oriented toward the local market.

Another widely believed opinion is that service sectors would be not very innovative. On the contrary, the survey on Lombardy indicates that the firms interviewed consider as very important for their competitivity the adoption of innovations, such as product, process and organisational innovations. Moreover a large share of them (42 %) has adopted some type of innovations in the last three years. The innovation level increases for larger firms, however it is not significantly different in the three urban areas considered.

The survey on the MMA indicates that the adoption of innovations represents a strategic factor in determining the competitivity of service firms. In particular, the most important forms of innovations are represented by : 1) the production of new services (30 %), 2) the sale into new markets (25 %), 3) the adoption of new processes (24 %), 4) the organisational changes (21 %). These results indicate the great importance in the service sectors of non price competitivity factors with respect to the price competitivity, as qualitative changes in the characteristics of services may be more important than quantitative changes in production costs.

The most important obstacles to the introduction of new services can be found in the low initial receptivity of the customers (31 %) and on the other hand in the problems faced in evaluating the potential demand (24 %). Only in the case of leasing and of computer shops, important obstacles derive from financial problems and, in the case of engeneering and truck transportation, from project elaboration costs.

Various factors affect the adoption of product innovations. These latter may be consist either in the introduction of new services by the individual tertiary firms or in the birth of new service firms in a specific urban area.

The introduction of new services is related to the fact that each service firm usually produces a set of different services,

650   The diffusion of producer services in the urban system

which are tightly interdependent as they are complementary in their production or in their use. Even industrial firms always jointly produce both goods and services, as each industrial firm employs workers which produce services as accounting, personnel organization, research and development, marketing, etc...

The integration of different services within the same firm depends on the existence of "economies of scope", which may be defined as the situation when the cost of production for all outputs is less than the cost of producing each output separately (TEECE, 1982).

Economies of scope, often occurr due to the optimization in the use of a common resource in two different productions. In fact, the access to common sources of informations, the exploitation of a particular common technological or organisational know-how or the access to particular common services and infrastructures may explain both a decrease of production costs and the urban concentration of various service activities. Moreover, as economies of scope may determine a decrease of the price of the individual services, they may promote the urban concentration of the users of these services.

The economies of scope may exist not only in the production costs but also in the costs of marketing of different services which are tightly complementary. In fact, the use by a firm of different complementary services, produced by a single other firm may imply an important saving of transaction costs, connected to the procedures of negotiating and executing of these services. Similarly, the use of complementary services produced by various firms all localised within the same urban center, may facilitate the exchanges of informations between the firms producing these services, thus promoting a better reciprocal integration and a greater effectiveness of the services considered in solving the problems of the firms using them.

According a widely believed opinion the creation of new firms would be especially related to the process of externalisation of services which were previously produced in other firms, such as less specialized service firms or industrial firms. This process is related to the role of economies of scope. In fact, economies of scope, in the joint production of services with other industrial or service outputs, may become lower than economies of scale, to be achieved when the production of services is concentrated in few specialized firms.

This process of externalisation of services, previously jointly produced or integrated with industrial production, may lead to the "filtering upward" (PRED, 1988 ; NOYELLE and STANBACK, 1984 ; CAPPELLIN, 1986b) of some services in the urban hierarchy. In fact, small cities may lose some high quality services, which were previously produced within less specialized and traditional service firms or within industrial firms localised in these cities, if these services are increasingly concentrated in large cities, for example due to acquisition of small local firms by large multiregional firms.

According to a different interpretation the birth of new service firms is not due to the aim of a greater exploitation of economies of scale and to changes in the organization of production. On the contrary, it may consist in the spin-off from the original firms of entrepreneurial initiatives, which become completely autonomous with respect to these firms, as the new services may be sold in new markets and to new users. In this case, the birth of new service firms responds to the aim of exploiting technological and organisational competences, which have been developed within the original firms.

Therefore, economies of scope may also be interpreted in a dynamic framework as a factor explaining the process of diversification of the production of a firm or the growth of new sectors in an urban economy. In fact, the existence of a particular know-how in the production of a specific service by a tertiary firm but also by an industrial firm or by a particular urban center, may imply lower costs in the production of specific new services, thus facilitating the entry by the original firm into new markets. These dynamic relationships between two different services seem rather similar to the complementary relationships explained by economies of scope.

In fact, the existence of tacit elements in the technology used, of learning by doing factors and of internal organisational routines usually hinders the transfer to new firms and to different urban centers of the know-how learned in the specific productions within particular firms or urban centers. In these cases, the identification of the new possible applications of a particular know-how is easier within the same firm or the same urban center, as it is not necessary to reveal to others particular production secrets and appropriate human resources may be more easily transfered from old to new productions (TEECE, 1982 ; AYDALOT, 1986).

Both surveys elaborated disprove the widely believed opinion that service firms are normally created as externalisation of service function previously produced within industrial firms. On the contrary, they indicates that entrepreneurship in service sectors mainly derives from other service firms and only in few cases from spin-offs and process deverticalisation by industrial firms.

According to the survey on Lombardy, the birth of tertiary firms due to the externalisation of functions of other firms represents a very rare case (5 %), which is relevant only in the sectors of technical services, of informatics and of administrative consulting.

According to the survey on the MMA the new services are almost always (86 %) complementary with respect to those which were already produced in the respective firms. Moreover, the birth of new firms seems to be the effect of the start of new activity by a single entrepreneur (48 %) or of the diversification toward new production of firms which were active in other sectors in the same area (18 %). Rather important (18 %) is also the creation of firms by other firms active in the same sector but in different areas, as it is indicated by the case of the location of branches of various international service firms. Only few firms (6 %) have been born as the externalisation of services previously produced in already existing industrial or tertiary firms.

652   The diffusion of producer services in the urban system

- VI -
PROCESS INNOVATIONS AND ORGANISATIONAL CHANGES

Another important type of innovations in the service firms is represented by the adoption of process or organisational innovations. The most important obstacle to these types of innovations does not consist in the financial cost of new investments (16 %) but in the need to requalify the personel (29 %), in the resistances to the modification of organisational routines (23 %) and in the need to hire new qualified personel (16 %). Therefore, a crucial factor, which explains the capability to innovate and the competitivity of the service firms is given by the availability of high qualified labour resources and their appropriate organization modes.

The survey on Lombardy indicates that, notwithstanding the widely believed opinion that tertiary firms should have a rather simple internal organisational structure this latter is rather complex, since an high share of firms (between 25 % and 50 %) internally produce the following services : research, personnel selection, economic studies and marketing research, organization, professional training, accounting, advertising and public relations.

Another widely believe opinion is that the qualification of the labor force should be lower in tertiary firms than in industrial firms. On the contrary, the survey on Lombardy indicates that 75 % of the entrepreneurs has at least an high school degree and 40 % has an university degree.

Also according to the survey on the MMA the university degree is the most common education level of the entrepreneurs in all the sectors considered (42 %). The high education level of the labor force in service firms is also indicated by the fact that the overall share of entrepreneurs, managers and employees with university degree in most sectors is greater than 30 %. Moreover, the turnover ration (hired + dismissed / employed workers) in the last four years is rather high and it is 120 % in accounting and advertising firms and 80 % in computer software firms.

The market of high skilled labor force active in the tertiary sectors is a typical case of segmented labor market. In particular, the urban centers, especially those which dominate the urban hierarchy, are characterised with respect to rural areas and smaller urban centers, by the concentration of high skilled workers, such as entrepreneurs, managers, consultants and various other professional profiles in service and in industrial firms.

This concentration of high skilled workers in urban centers may be explained by factors which are specific to the working of the labour market and which have a microanalytic rather than a sectoral character. In this respect the concentration of high skilled workers in urban centers may represent a factor, rather than the effect, of the urban location of particular economic activities.

In fact, the growth of service activities depends, first of all, on the existence of appropriate entrepreneurial capabilities in the various areas, as the total employment in service sectors is made especially by selfemployed workers. Moreover, the spatial mobility of entrepreneurs and of the firms in the service sectors is rather limited, since service activities are linked to the local environment more than industrial activities, due to technical and institutional reasons. In particular, the creation of new service activities depends on a gradual process of learning by doing occurring in traditional service activities, as entrepreneurs of new service firms often have been working as employees in other tertiary firms or in the headquarters of industrial firms. Therefore, the urban labor markets of high qualified workers have the typical characteristics of the "internal labor markets" (DOERINGER and PIORE, 1971).

The service sectors have an internal hierarchical structure, since the workers and the firms may be distinguished in different levels, of which some have an operational and routine function and concern the production of services of lower quality, while others have strategic roles and produce services which are more complex and technologically advanced. Secondly, these markets are rather closed with respect to the outside world, since it is possible to enter in these markets only at the lowest levels of their hierarchical structure. The mobility from and to firms of other sectors and of other urban centers is very limited, while the mobility from firm to firm within the same sector and within the same urban center may be rather high.

These characteristics of the urban labour markets of skilled workers may be explained by three factors which have been indicated by the theory of the internal or dual labor markets : 1) these occupational profiles are very specific with. respect to the individual environments considered, 2) the professional skills are learned through on the job training, 3) the internal organisation of these labor markets is regulated by specific rules for each professional profile.

The results of the two empirical surveys confirm the hypothesis that the characteristics of the labour markets of service activities are similar to that indicated by the theories of the internal or dual labour markets. In fact, the segmented nature of the labour market of service activities is confirmed by the fact that, notwithstanding the high mobility from one firm to the other, a very large share of the entrepreneurs originate from other service firms.

The survey on the MMA indicates that the originating sectors of the entrepreneurs are very often other service sectors (75 %). Only for software (50 %) and engeneering (50 %), the previous professional experience has occurred to a large extent in industrial firms. Also this result confirms the low importance of the externalisation process of service functions, which were previously performed within industrial firms.

Also in the Lombardy survey the most common origin (69 %) of the entrepreneurs is the need that of selfemployed or dependent worker in the tertiary sectors. Less important is the origin as employee in industrial firms (16 %). This latter origin is more common in the case of technical services and of private research services. Moreover, the spin-offs from industrial firms are more common in Milan, where internal services of industrial firms are more important, than in Brescia and Como.

These results on the sectoral origin of the entrepreneurs may be explained by the fact that according to the survey on the MMA the most important characteristics demanded to new hired workers

654   The diffusion of producer services in the urban system

is the knowledge of the problems of the sector (30 %). Another important requirement is the level and length of the previous work experience (23 %). Moreover, the most important mode for professional training in the case of entrepreneurs and other high qualified workers is represented by the one the job experience (39 %), and the organization of internal courses (23 %), especially in the largest firms (more than 250 employees). These results confirm the importance of on the job training with respect to formal education curricula.

The flexible internal organisational structure of the service firms indicates the need that the individual workers demonstrate an adequate autonomy in their work. In fact, among the most demanded requirements to new hired workers is the inventive and coordination capability (23 %), especially in software and certified accountant services, where the share of employees with university degree is important.

Also according to the survey on Lombardy, the most commonly used mode of professional training is the one the job experience, integrated with internal education courses in the case of large firms. On the contrary, in smaller firms the relationships with customers and other firms are considered as especially important.

The theories of internal and dual labor markets may explain why young workers are attracted to large urban areas. In fact, these workers are attracted by the high internal mobility and the better carrier prospects which characterize the labor markets of these areas. Therefore, positive characteristics of the physical, social and cultural environment may facilitate the immigration of qualified workers in the urban centers and the development of service activities which require this type of labor force. In particular, these characteristics of the urban labor markets seem coherent with the indications of the "incubator hypothesis", according to which new firms, especially in the high technology sectors, prefer a location in urban areas during the first phases of their life (LEONE and STRUYCK, 1976).

- VII -
THE SUPPLY OF SERVICES AND THE ECONOMIES OF AGGLOMERATION

The growth of services in an area depends on the demographic and employment size of the urban center considered, not only because a greater size indicates greater revenues and greater demand of the services considered, but also because this indicates the existence of greater external economies, which are determined by the existence of appropriate infrastructures, by the contiguous location of numerous service and industrial firms and by the possibility of access to a larger market of qualified labor.

As indicated above, one of the most important inputs of service firms and also one of the most important factors affecting their location consists in the inputs of other services and in the transaction costs required by these exchanges of services between different firms.

Since service firms require a tight and active relationship between the supplier and the user of a service, geographical distance and communications costs have a greater importance in affecting the exchanges of services, than in the case of industrial products. Therefore, the objective to minimize the transportation and communication costs implies the urban concentration of services.

However, the exchanges of services imply also important transaction costs, which are different from transportation and communication costs and which should also be minimized as these latter. Transaction costs are affected by the level of geographical concentration, as they are related to the reciprocal knowledge, to the similarity of language, culture, technological level and socio-political institutions existing between the two parties of a transaction of services.

In particular, the respective advantage of an urban concentration of service activities with respect to a greater spatial diffusion may change according to the evolution of technology and the changes in the characteristics of the relationships between the service firms and the other firms supplying inputs or buying their outputs (CAPPELLIN, 1988).

These factors may be particularly important in explaining the location of new service firms, since these latter may prefer a location in smaller urban centers, if the transaction costs incurred in their contacts with their respective suppliers and users were lower in smaller centers than in large urban centers. On the contrary, the concentration in a large urban area may be more usefull for those firms, which are older and which normally produce technologically more advanced services. In fact these services usually require more complex relations among the various suppliers and users. Thus, their concentration in large urban centers is important in order to minimize transaction costs.

Milan represent by far the most important concentration of service activities in Lombardy. However, the process of diffusion of service activities is confirmed by various indicators, beside the analysis of the employment changes in the two census 1971 and 1981. In fact, the survey on Lombardy indicates that firms where new hired workers in the last three years represent 100 % of the employed workers have been 39 % in Como, 35 % in Brescia and 30 % in Milan. This latter center presents an higher share (31 %) of firms with low rate of hired workers (less than 25 %) than Como (10 %) and Brescia (6 %).

The firms interviewed are often rather young, since 55 % has been founded after 1975 and 29 % after 1980. However, the firms founded after 1980 are more frequent in Brescia and Como than in Milan. The average age of the entrepreneur, when the firm is founded, is between 31 and 40 years old (42 %). Como is the area which indicates the highest share of entrepreneurs less than 30 years old and Milan the area with the highest share of entrepreneurs more than 31 years old.

The importance of economies of agglomeration is indicated by the level of integration among service firms, as the increasing integration between service and industrial firms is accompanied by an increasing integration among the service firms themselves.

The survey of Lombardy indicates that 40 % of the firms use inputs of "advanced" services and that 80 % of these firms consider this use as a strenght points of their competitive strategy. The external use concerns not only services, which the firms interviewed are not capable to develop autonomously, but also services, which are internally produced by these firms.

656   The diffusion of producer services in the urban system

This survey indicates that services which are most commonly used are rather traditional services, such as legal services (83 %), fiscal (73 %) and cleaning (69 %) services. However, there are numerous firms which use external services more rare, such as computer services (25 %), professional training (18 %), certified accounting (23 %), advertising (28 %) and technical services (20 %). Very low percentages of use are those of personel recruitment and selection, management organization, financial control and public relation services. The use of external services is more common in Milan, although the percentage of use are not very different from the other areas. This may be due to an higher technological level of service firms in the Milan area and to the clearly higher availability of services in this area : a factor which may facilitate the use of these services.

As indicated by various surveys on the demand of services by industrial firms, also this survey on service firms indicates a positive relationships between the number of the services used and the size of the firms. In fact, all firms with more than 20 employees use more than 8 external services, while only 36 % of the firms with 2-3 employees use more than 8 external services. Moreover, the empirical results confirm the hypothesis that a greater size of the firm does not imply a decrease of external services and a substitution with internal services, as the use of external and internal services appears as complementary.

The intensity of the relationships with the external environ-ment is also indicated by the use of external collaborations. The flexibility of the labour organization, which characterizes service firms, allows complex links between the functions performed by employees and those performed through the collaboration with workers external to the firms. In fact, external collaborations represent an important share of employees (30 %) in many firms (40 %) and for 19 % of the firms the number of external collabora-tions is greater than the number of employees. However, many firms do not use external collaborations (41 %). This result should not be interpreted as the effect of the decentralisation of the most routine functions, as the sectors where external collabora-tions are most important are rather qualified, such as marketing services, organization consulting, technical services and private research services. Therefore, it seems that rather qualified activities are forced to search outside of the firms professional capabilities which are rather rare and may not be easily organized in the framework of a contract of dependent labour.

- VIII -
STRENGHT AND WEAKNESS POINTS OF SERVICE FIRMS

It is possible to analyse the crucial factors in the growth of service firms by analysing the strenght and weakness points indicated by the firms interviewed in the two surveys. In the survey on Lombardy, the strenght factors are first of all the quality of the service produced (99 %), then the inputs of advanced services (79 %), the large scope of the services supplied (76 %) and the price levels (70 %). On the contrary, strenght factors, indicated by a lower number of firms, are the search of employees (41 %), the search of customers (46 %) and the financement of activities (52 %). The order of importance of these factors is rather similar for all service sectors considered.

Riccardo CAPPELLIN   657

Therefore, it seems that the qualitative characteristics of the service supplied are rather high, but the greatest problems are to be faced in the labour market and in the markets of the specific services, where the firms face important transaction costs in their relationships with the clients and various obstacles hinder an adequate circulation of informations on the characteristics of the demand and of the supply of services.

The strength factors indicated by the firms interviewed in the survey on the MMA confirm the importance of non price factors in the competition on the markets of services. In fact, the strength factors consist in the high quality of services (31 %), in the large scope of the service supplied (18 %) and in the customisation of services supplied (16 %). These results demonstrate the importance of processes of horizontal and vertical product diversification (POLO, 1986) and of the need to introduce services which are complementary to those already supplied in order to exploit the existence of economies of scope. In all these cases it seems that an important factor is the control of the transaction costs in the relationships between the supplier and the user of services, since the quality of a service seems to consist mainly in the correspondence between the characteristics of the service supplied with the need of the users.

On the contrary, the weakness points indicated in this survey are the low price competitivity of the services supplied (23 %) and the inadequate capabilities in advertising and public relations (24 %). Also these results indicate the importance of non price factors, which should compensate the greater costs characterizing the "leaders" firms interviewed in the survey on the MMA with respect to the smaller firms interviewed in the survey on Lombardy. The low transparency of the demand is indicated both as an obstacle to the introduction of new services and by the lack of advertising and public relations, and it is certainly related to the importance of transaction costs and to the imperfect circulation of informations in the market of services.

- IX -
CONCLUSIONS

The results of these two surveys on the service firms may be considered as rather representative of the problems and trends of the development of service activities in Italy, due to the relative high development level of the urban areas considered and the wide spectrum of the sizes of the firms interviewed. Certainly, these results seem to disprove various widely believed opinions on the characteristics and factors of the development of service activities.

In fact, the development of service activities is tightly related to the adoption of process and organisational innovations by the firms, which are using the services, and with the adoption of product, process, and organisational innovations in the service firms.

The demand of services is related to the technological level of the firms and to the stage in the product life cycle which characteristics these firms. However, it is also related to systemic factors, such as the forms of the relationships linking among

658　The diffusion of producer services in the urban system

themselves the various firms, using the services, and the modes of organization of the various industrial sectors and of the overall regional economy.

The local demand is not an adequate explanation of the development of service activities in the different areas and service firms export a large share of their output outside their respective area of location. Therefore, the growth of service activities, as in the case of industrial productions, should be related to the quality and costs of the services supplied by the various areas in the framework of an increasing interregional and international competition.

The competition in the market of services is mainly based on non price factors. The improvement of the quality of the existing services and the introduction of new services have a crucial role. These factors may be more important than the economies of scale and the costs of transportation, which have usually been considered by the traditional theories on the growth of services, such as the central place theory (MULLINGAM, 1984 ; PRED, 1977).

The adoption of process and organisational innovations is rather frequent in service firms, notwithstanding a supposed lower productivity of service activities. The adoption of these innovations is mainly related to the characteristics of the labour market of service activities, which presents the typical characteristics of the internal and dual labour markets.

These empirical results seem to indicate that the development of service activities corresponds to a pattern of "endogenous growth" (CAPPELLIN, 1983). In fact, service firms mainly arise as spin-offs from other service activities and from the development of local entrepreneurship capabilities. Their growth is promoted by the tight interdependance existing among the service firms within the same urban area. However, the growth of new service firms may be greater in smaller urban centers, due to the existence of agglomeration diseconomies. The growth of new services is related to the valorisation of the know-how which has been accumulated in specific sectoral productions, which characterize the particular area considered. Therefore, it is possible to promote a specialisation of the various urban centers in different type of services and a non hierarchical distribution of service activities among larger and smaller urban centers.

Regional and national policies should mainly aim to stimulate the local supply of services, to qualify the local labour force, to promote the valorisation of the local entrepreneurship capabilities, thus aiming to stimulate the birth of new local service firms, rather than aim to achieve an unfeasible relocation of the services already existing in some areas toward the less developed areas.

The empirical results of these two surveys seem to confirm the explanatory power of the recent theoretical contributions which have been indicated in this study. In particular, they seem to indicate three fields which seem worth further research : 1) the widening of the market area of the service activities and the need to study the interaction between local capabilities and external stimulus in the framework of an increasing internationalisation of service firms, 2) the segmented characteristics of the labour markets of service activities, which are rather different from the labour markets of industrial activities, 3) the very imperfect circulation of informations between producers and users of services and the importance of transaction costs in the exchanges occurring in the market of producer services.

BIBLIOGRAPHIE

AYDALOT P., 1986, "Trajectoires technologiques et milieux innovateurs", in P. Aydalot (ed.), "Milieux innovateurs en Europe", Paris, GREMI

BAILLY A.S., MAILLAT D. et REY M., 1985, "Tertiaire moteur et développement régional : le cas de petites et moyennes villes", Revue d'Economie Régionale et Urbaine, n° 1.

BOSCACCI F. and CAPPELLIN R., 1987, "La diffusione dei servizi per la produzione in un sistema regionale", Paper presented at the VIII Italian Conference of Regional Science, Cagliari, 11-13 november 1987.

CAPPELLIN R., 1980, "Teorie e modelli dello sviluppo spaziale delle attivita' di servizio", Giornale degli Economisti ed Annali di Economia, n° 3-4, pp. 205-321.

CAPPELLIN R., 1983b, "Productivity growth and technological change in a regional perspective", Giornale degli Economisti ed Annali di Economia, n° 7-8, pp. 459-482.

CAPPELLIN R., 1986a, "The development of service activities in the Italian urban system", in S. Illeris (ed.), "The present and future role of services in regional development", Bruxelles : D.G. for Science, Research and Development, Commission of the E.C., FAST Occasional Papers, n° 74, pp. 17-49.

CAPPELLIN R., 1986b, "Disparita' regionali nel processo di terziarizzazione", in L. Pasinetti (ed.), "Mutamenti strutturali del sistema produttivo : integrazione tra industria e settore terziario", Bologna, II Mulino, pp. 81-99.

CAPPELLIN R., 1988, "Transaction costs and urban agglomerations", Revue d'Economie Régionale et Urbaine, n° 2.

CAPPELLIN R., CHIZZOLINI B. and SANTANDREA V., 1987, "A multiregional econometric model of the Italian economy : the growth of service employment", Papers of the Regional Science Association, pp. 3-19.

CAPPELLIN R. and GRILLENZONI C., 1983, "Diffusion and specialization in the location of service activities in Italy", Sistemi Urbani, vol. 5, pp. 249-282.

CAPPELLIN R. and POLO M., 1987, "Innovazione ed occupazione nei settori terziari dell'area metropolitana milanese", in AAVV, "Progetto Milano : Sottoprogetto Struttura Econoomica", Milano : F. Angeli, I.Re.R., in print.

DANIELS P.W. and HOLLY B.P., 1983, "Office location in transition : observations on research in Britain and North America", Environment and Planning, Vol. 15, pp. 1293-1298.

DOERINGER P.B. e PIORE M.J., "Internal labor markets and manpower analysis", Boston : D.C. Heath.

660   The diffusion of producer services in the urban system

FUA' G. e ZACCHIA C. (eds.), 1983, "Industrializzazione senza fratture", Bologna : II Mulino.

GODDARD J.B., 1975, "Office location in urban and regional development", Oxford : Oxford U.P.

LEONE R. and STRUYK R., 1976, "The incubator hypothesis : evidence from five SMSA", Urban Studies, vol. 13.

MOMIGLIANO F. and SINISCALCO D., 1986, "Mutamenti della struttura del sistema produttivo ed integrazione tra industria e terziario", in L. Pasinetti (eds.), Mutamenti Strutturali del sistema produttivo: integrazione tra industria e settore terziario, Bologna : II Mulino, pp. 13-59.

MULLINGAM G.F., 1984, "Agglomeration and central place theory : a review of the literature", International Regional Science Review, vol. 9, pp. 1-42.

NOYELLE T. and STANBACK T.M., 1984, "The economic transformation of American cities", Totowa, N.J. : Rowman & Allaheld.

POLO M., 1986, "Recenti sviluppi nell'analisi della differenziazione del prodotto", Giornale degli Economisti, n° 3-4, pp. 171-200.

PRED A., 1977, "City systems in advanced economies", London : Hutchinson

TEECE D., 1982, "Toward an economic theory of the multiproduct firm", Journal of Economic Behaviour and Organisation, vol. 3, pp. 39-63.

WILLIAMSON O.E., 1979, "Transaction-cost economics : the governance of contractual relations", The Journal of Law and Economics, vol. 22, pp. 233-261.

WILLIAMSON O.E., 1981, "The modern corporation : origins, evolution, attributes", Journal of Economic Literature, vol. 19, pp. 1537-1568.

SUMMARY

   The study analyses recent theoretical approaches which explain not only the level of demand but also the competitivity of supply of services. The study demonstrates that various mythes on the service sectors are contradicted by empirical evidence. The demand of service by small industrial firms and by service firms is more important than that of large firms. Services are increasingly exported to other regions and countries and are not only addressed to the local economy. The adoption of product and process innovation is very diffused in service firms. Service firms mainly grow as spin-off from other service firms and not as externalisation of service functions from industrial firms.

[661]

[18]

Regional Studies, Vol. 24.4, pp. 327–342.

Producer Services, Trade and the Social Division of Labour

W. R. GOE

Centre for Economic Development, Carnegie Mellon University, Pittsburgh, PA 15213, USA

(Received August 1989; in revised form February 1990)

GOE W. R. (1990) Producer services, trade and the social division of labour, *Reg. Studies* **24**, 327–342. Several hypotheses have been advanced to explain the growth in employment and output of producer services industries in US metropolitan and regional economies. One hypothesis contends that this growth is attributable to the increasing externalization of service activities by corporate managerial offices to independent producer services firms. This has contributed to the growth of corporate complex agglomerations in urban regions. Manufacturing industries have traditionally been viewed as being the motivating force underlying this growth. A second hypothesis contends that the growth of producer services industries is attributable to their evolution into basic industries and the growth of export trade. This paper examines the validity of these hypotheses using data collected from a survey of business establishments in producer services industries located in the four metropolitan areas of the northeast region of Ohio (Cleveland, Akron, Canton and Youngstown/Warren). The findings indicate that the primary role of producer services industries in each metropolitan area is to provide their products of labour to other industries in the service sector rather than manufacturing. Additionally, producer services industries in each metropolitan area are characterized by a dual structure: (1) a larger tier of establishments that is primarily dependent upon local markets and linked into local corporate complex agglomerations; and (2) a smaller tier of establishments that is primarily dependent upon export markets and linked into the broader spatial division of labour.

Producer services   Indirect production activities   Corporate complexes   Export of services
Social division of labour

GOE W. R. (1990) Les services aux entreprises, les échanges commerciaux et la division sociale du travail, *Reg. Studies* **24**, 327–342. Plusieurs hypothèses ont été avancés pour expliquer la croissance de l'emploi et de la production dans les services aux entreprises dans les économies métropolitaines et régionales aux Etats-Unis. Un hypothèse soutient que cette croissance s'explique par le fait que de plus en plus la direction des entreprises fait faire les activités de services par des prestataires indépendants. Cela a contribué à la croissance des agglomérations d'entreprises complexes dans les zones urbaines. L'explication reçue c'est que les entreprises industrielles en sont le moteur. Un deuxième hypothèse prétend que l'essor des services aux entreprises est dû à leur évolution dans les industries de base et à la croissance des exportations. L'article examine le bien-fondé de ces hypothèses à partir des données provenant d'une enquête des établissements commerciaux offrant des services aux entreprises et localisés dans les quatre zones métroploitaines au nord-est de Ohio (à savoir, Cleveland, Akron, Canton et Youngstown/Warren). Les résultats laissent voir que le rôle primordial des services aux entreprises dans chaque zone métropolitaine c'est de fournir leurs produits aux autres branches du secteur tertiaire plutôt qu'aux entreprises industrielles. En plus les services aux entreprises dans chaque zone métropolitaine se caractérisent par une structure dualiste: (1) un niveau d'établissements plus nombreux qui en premier dépend des marchés locaux et est relié aux agglomérations d'entreprises complexes; et (2) un niveau d'établissements moins nombreux qui dépend en premier

W. R. GOE (1990) Produzentendienstleistungen, Handel und die soziale Arbeitsteilung, *Reg. Studies* **24**, 327–342. Es gibt mehrere Hypothesen zur Erklärung der Zunahme der Arbeitsstellen und des Umfangs der Produzentendienstleistungindustrien in den grosstädtischen und regionalen Industrien der USA. Eine behauptet, das Wachstum sei der zunehmenden Aussenverlagerung von Dienstleistungstätigkeiten von Unternehmensgeschäftsstellen auf unabhängige Firmen für Produzentendienstleistungen zuzuschreiben. Dies hat zum Anwachsen von Unternehmenskomplexballungen in städtischen Gebieten beigetragen. Eine zweite Hypothese behauptet, das Anwachsen der Produzentendienstleistungsindustrien sei auf deren Entwicklung zu Rohstoffindustrien und die Zunahme des Exporthandels zurückzuführen. Dieser Aufsatz untersucht die Gültigkeit beider Hypothesen, wobei Daten einer Erhebung von Geschäftsniederlassungen in Produzentendienstleistungsindustrien in den vier Grosstadtgebieten des Nordostens von Ohio (Cleveland, Akron, Canton und Youngtown/Warren) benutzt werden. Die Befunde deuten darauf hin, dass es die Hauptrolle der Produzentendienstleistungsindustrien in jedem Grosstadtgebiet ist, ihre Arbeitsprodukte vermehrt anderen Industrien im Dienstleistungssektor zur Verfügung zu stellen, als der herstellenden Industrie. Darüberhinaus sind Produzentendienstleistungsindustrien in jedem Grosstadtgebiet durch ihre Doppelstruktur gekennzeichnet: (1) eine grössere Firmenschicht, die in erster Linie vom örtlichen Markt abhängt und mit örtlichen Unternehmenskomplexballungen verknüpft ist,

328   *W. R. Goe*

des marchés d'exportation et est relié à la division spatiale du travail plus large.

Services aux entreprises
Activités de production indirectes
Complexes d'entreprises   Services à l'exportation
Division sociale du travail

und (2) eine kleinere, die in erster Linie von Exportmärkten abhängt, und mit der breiteren räumlichen Arbeitsteilung verknüpft ist.

Produzentendienstleistungen
Indirekte Produktionstätigkeiten
Unternehmenskomplexe   Export von Dienstleistungen
Soziale Arbeitsteilung

INTRODUCTION

Over the past several decades, many urban regions in the United States have experienced significant shifts in the structure of their economies. The decline of America's industrial competitiveness and the loss of jobs in the manufacturing sector has received much attention as has the growing concentration of employment in the set of industries defined as the 'service sector' (see, for example, BLUESTONE and HARRISON, 1982; COHEN and ZYSMANN, 1987; HARRISON and BLUESTONE, 1988; NOYELLE and STANBACK, 1984; STANBACK *et al.*, 1981). The structural shifts underlying these employment trends have had differential consequences for US urban regions as a new spatial division of labour is emerging (STORPER and WALKER, 1984; MASSEY, 1984).

Some urban regions that were highly dependent upon manufacturing industries have been subject to a wrenching downward spiral of deindustrialization as they have suffered substantial losses of manufacturing jobs while realizing little or no service sector growth (for example, see PERRY, 1987). Other regions have been more successful in undergoing structural transition and have substituted, with varying degrees of success, new employment opportunities in the service sector (for example, see GOE and SHANAHAN, 1989).[1] This has been the predominant trend for the nation as a whole as aggregate data indicate an absolute decline in US manufacturing employment since 1979 along with substantial growth of employment in the service sector.[2]

An important component of the growth in the service sector has been intermediate producer services (GERSHUNY and MILES, 1983). The rate of employment growth in producer services industries has outpaced that in total nonagricultural employment since the 1950–60 period (GREENFIELD, 1966; TSCHETTER, 1987).[3] Further, the share of producer services industries in US GNP expanded at a greater rate than that for any other sector of the economy (including the service sector as a whole) over the 1947–77 period (STANBACK and NOYELLE, 1982). The growth of employment and output in producer services industries signals a marked increase in demand for the products of labour of these industries. It has been argued that this reflects a fundamental shift in *how we produce*, i.e. the way production systems are organized and executed (WALKER, 1985).

Over the past decade, increased attention has been focused in both the US and UK on examining the growth of producer services industries and its implications for urban and regional development (BEYERS *et al.*, 1985a; DANIELS, 1983, 1985; GILLIS, 1987; GILLESPIE and GREEN, 1987; GERSHUNY and MILES, 1983; HUTTON and LEY, 1987; ILLERIS, 1989; MARSHALL, 1982, 1983, 1985, 1989; NOYELLE and STANBACK, 1984; OCHEL and WAGNER, 1987; STANBACK and NOYELLE, 1982; STANBACK *et al.*, 1981; TSCHETTER, 1987; WOOD, 1986). Out of this growing body of literature, several hypotheses have been advanced to explain the growth in producer services. One hypothesis contends that the growth in producer services is attributable to shifts in the social division of labour characterized by the increasing externalization of service activities from corporate offices to independent producer services firms.[4] (WALKER, 1985; DANIELS, 1985; GERSHUNY and MILES, 1983; GILLESPIE and GREEN, 1987; ILLERIS, 1989; KUTSCHER, 1988; MARSHALL, 1985, 1989; NOYELLE and STANBACK, 1984; STANBACK and NOYELLE, 1982; STANBACK *et al.*, 1981; WOOD, 1986). This has contributed to the growth of corporate complex agglomerations in urban regions (HUTTON and LEY, 1987; NOYELLE and STANBACK, 1984). Manufacturing industries have generally been viewed as being the motivating force underlying this growth (COHEN and ZYSMAN, 1987). A second hypothesis contends that the growth in producer services is attributable to their evolutionary development into basic industries and the growth of export trade (AUSTRIAN and ZLATOPER, 1988; BEYERS *et al.*, 1985a, 1985b; GILLIS, 1987; GROSHEN, 1987; KEIL and MACK, 1986; SHELP, 1981).

The purpose of this paper is to examine the validity of these hypotheses using data collected from a survey of business establishments in producer services industries located in the four metropolitan areas of the northeast region of Ohio (Akron, Canton, Cleveland and Youngstown/Warren). This urban region provides an appropriate context for examining these hypotheses given its historical dependence upon heavy manufacturing and recent growth in producer services. The survey findings indicate that the primary role of producer services industries in each metropolitan area is to provide their products of labour to other industries in the service sector *rather* than manufacturing. Additionally, producer services industries in each metropolitan area are characterized by a dual structure: (1) a larger tier of establishments that is primarily dependent upon local markets and linked into local corporate complex agglomerations; and (2) a smaller tier of establishments that is primarily dependent upon export markets and linked into the broader spatial division of labour.

The paper is organized as follows. The first section discusses theoretical and methodological indeterminacies that characterize much of the research on producer services industries. The purpose is to establish a foundation for: (1) further advancing the use of more precise theoretical concepts for describing the role of producer services industries in the economy (see WALKER, 1985; GILLESPIE and GREEN, 1987); and (2) providing a more rigorous data analysis by circumventing methodological problems that have confounded previous research efforts. The second section examines the aforementioned hypotheses in greater detail and discusses key issues associated with the growth of producer services industries. The third section examines economic restructuring in the northeast Ohio region to provide a broader context in which to place the findings from the survey. The fourth section describes the research methodology used in the study. The subsequent sections present and discuss the findings from the survey. Finally, the implications of the study for economic development policy are discussed.

THEORETICAL AND METHODOLOGICAL INDETERMINACIES IN PRODUCER SERVICES RESEARCH

The concept of producer services is an extension of Kuznets' taxonomic scheme of producer goods and consumer goods to service sector industries. As succinctly stated by GREENFIELD, 1966: 'The basic distinction between consumer and producer services needs little elaboration. Those services which at destination are used by households or individuals fall clearly under the former, and those services used ultimately by business firms and other productive enterprises are included in the latter'. The concept of producer services has entered popular economic thought with little critical examination. In recent years, however, it has come under increased scrutiny due to dissatisfaction with its inherent limitations in theory and application (see, for example, WALKER, 1985; GILLESPIE and GREEN, 1987).

One criticism concerns the lack of fit between definitions of *services* and the product of labour from industries that are normally grouped in the service sector. WALKER, 1985, distinguishes between goods and *labour services* with the latter not taking the intervening form of a material product.[5] The limitation is that the products of labour of many industries grouped under the category of producer services are

not labour services and take the intervening material form of a good. Others may produce joint products involving both goods and labour services. Therefore, the term *service* is conceptually inappropriate for describing the common property of these industries. This alludes to a second problem of determining what industries should be categorized as producer services.

There has been no consensus over what set of industries comprises the producer services. Generally, the producer services are defined as including a combination of banking and finance, insurance, real estate, engineering, architecture, accounting, book-keeping, business services and legal services (see BEYERS, 1989; BROWNING and SINGELMANN, 1978; GILLESPIE and GREEN, 1987; GREENFIELD, 1966; HUTTON and LEY, 1987; STANBACK, 1979; TSCHETTER, 1987). However, there has been no consistency across studies in defining a precise set of industries. Another problem is that many of these industries (e.g. banking, insurance, real estate) market their products of labour (labour services, goods, joint products) to consumers as well as businesses and other productive enterprises. National input/output analyses for both the US and a number of EC countries indicate that consumer markets can provide a substantial component of demand for producer services industries (BEYERS, 1989; OCHEL and WAGNER, 1987). In these cases, it generally cannot be determined which producer service industries or firms within a particular industry that are serving both markets should actually be classified as consumer services due to a greater dependency on consumer markets.

An important factor contributing to this problem is the interrelated use of the Standard Industrial Classification (SIC) code as a means of defining industry categories in research application. The SIC code classifies firms into industry groups that are based upon the product of labour that provides the greatest source of revenue. Given this underlying basis, the categories of the SIC code do not consistently distinguish between producer and consumer markets for a particular product of labour.[6] The end result is that the theoretical construct of producer services cannot be precisely translated into a specific subset of SIC categories by which most economic data is grouped.

The problems that have been outlined require both methodological and theoretical solutions. From the methodological standpoint, more rigorous criteria are needed to determine whether industries and/or firms within service sector industries are indeed producer services, regardless of their SIC categorization. From the conceptual standpoint, theoretical development needs to move beyond the unresolvable problem of the lack of fit between definitions of services and the products of labour resulting from industries categorized in the service sector. This problem ostensibly exists due to the evolutionary development of the SIC code, the particular divisions in which it partitions the economy and its use to define the service sector. In using the SIC code to define the service sector, industry categories exhibit little consistency regarding the nature of their products of labour. In turn, this has obscured the development of a more rigorous theoretical framework for analysis.

In response to these problems, WALKER, 1985, argues that 'the concept and theory of *services* are so badly misconceived as to merit rejection in further analytic work' (p. 83). Instead, he contends that industries within the service sector should be conceptualized as indirect labour within an increasingly complex and extended social division of labour. This suggests that further conceptual development of producer services industries must be based upon an understanding of the role of these indirect production activities in the social division of labour of production systems. Following GILLESPIE and GREEN, 1987, the term indirect production activities will therefore be used throughout the remainder of the paper to describe the economic role of the products of labour from producer services industries. The concept of producer services industries will be retained only out of familiarity to describe a specific subset of industries within a broader division of the economy that has been inappropriately labelled the service sector, i.e. producer services industries provide indirect production activities which may take the form of a labour service, good or joint product.

THEORETICAL HYPOTHESES REGARDING THE GROWTH OF PRODUCER SERVICES

In examining the role of producer services industries in urban development, NOYELLE and STANBACK, 1984, describe the growth of corporate complexes which consist of agglomerations of corporate managerial offices (headquarters, divisional head offices and regional sales headquarters) and firms from local producer services industries that serve the infrastructure of corporate offices. In essence, the growth of producer services industries in urban regions containing corporate complexes is primarily due to the formation of local market linkages with the infrastructure of corporate managerial offices.

The concept of corporate complex agglomerations aligns with the contention that the growth of producer services over the past several decades is attributable to shifts in the social division of labour. That is US firms have increasingly subcontracted indirect production activities from independent firms rather than providing them in-house. For example, instead of relying solely on internal departments, firms may purchase such functions as advertising and software consulting from independent firms. The *externalization* of indirect production activities potentially involves

several dimensions. One dimension has become known as *unbundling*.

Unbundling refers to a reduction or elimination of the internal provision of indirect production activities by businesses coupled with the tranfer of provision to independent firms who specialize in those activities (TSCHETTER, 1987; KUTSCHER, 1988). Given that many US firms have initiated restructuring strategies aimed at reducing overhead costs, it has been argued that the growth of producer services is primarily attributable to unbundling (see, for example, PIORE, 1986; NOYELLE and STANBACK, 1984). However, due to a lack of economic data needed for precise testing, little statistical evidence has been uncovered to support the unbundling thesis. For example, using occupational employment data, TSCHETTER, 1987, and KUTSCHER, 1988, found that unbundling within the US manufacturing sector accounted for only a very small portion of the growth in US producer services industries.[7] Whether or not unbundling is the primary force behind the growth of producer services industries, such growth implicitly assumes that from the demand side, firms have elected *not* to internalize the provision of a growing volume of indirect production activities within their organizational structures. Thus, the externalization of indirect production activities has increased over and above particular corporate strategies for internal provision. In turn, this indicates that externalization could represent a means of meeting new requirements for indirect production activities, a means of meeting previously established requirements in new ways that does not involve cutbacks in internal provision, or unbundling.[8]

The externalization of indirect production activities is motivated by several needs. The most obvious is the desire to reduce costs. The externalization of indirect production activities from corporate offices can reduce overhead such as wages, benefits and capital requirements. Perhaps even more important than the reduction of overhead costs in some cases is the need for specialized knowledge regarding particular indirect production activities. Firms in producer services industries tend to specialize in specific indirect production activities, e.g. international trade law, investment banking, management consulting. COHEN, 1981, argues that the specialized knowledge of indirect production activities provided by producer services industries is often needed to help business firms adapt more easily to changing economic conditions. For example, specialized marketing consultants facilitate the adaption of firms to shifts in markets by devising new marketing strategies (e.g. regional marketing). Producer services industries therefore play a buffering role in the economy by facilitating adaptation to the changing conditions and complexities of the global economy. In effect, the growth of producer services is also a response to the expanding need for specialized knowledge regarding indirect production actitivies which in many cases cannot be easily and efficiently produced within firms lacking this expertise.

Finally, as noted by COHEN, 1981; MARSHALL, 1985; and PIORE, 1986, among others, the externalization of indirect production activities from corporate offices provides greater flexibility for firms contracting out for these activities. This occurs along two primary dimensions. First, during economic downturns, firms can more easily reduce their level of expenditures for contracted indirect production activities compared to carrying the economic burden of supporting these activities internally. Second, changing needs for specialized knowledge regarding indirect production activities can be more quickly and easily met as they arise by contracting with appropriate producer services firms. Thus, greater flexibility can be created in meeting firms' changing needs for specialized knowledge. Examples that fall across both of these dimensions include contracting with specialized architects to meet periodic needs in building design or with employment agencies to meet temporary needs for accounting or secretarial assistance. In these respects, corporate complexes represent a form of industrial organization that facilitates *flexible control*.[9]

In describing corporate complexes, NOYELLE and STANBACK, 1984, place major emphasis on the external demand created for indirect production activities by the managerial offices of large, multilocational corporations whose administrative offices and auxiliary operations are located separately from production activities. It should be noted that the managerial offices of smaller, single site firms could provide an equally important structural component of corporate complexes. This could be especially true in smaller metropolitan areas with few managerial offices of large, multilocational corporations. Thus, the externalization of indirect production activities represents a strategy that could potentially be used by all businesses, regardless of size or organizational complexity.

An important underlying issue in the debate about the service sector concerns what types of industries are directly responsible for motivating the growth of corporate complexes in US urban regions through the externalization of indirect production activities. The traditional viewpoint dating back to Adam Smith is that service sector industries represent nonproductive labour and are parasitic to goods-producing industries. It is manufacturing that provides the *engine of economic growth*. This viewpoint has heavily influenced perceptions of the service sector in the UK (e.g. see KALDOR, 1966; BACON and ELTIS, 1976) as well as in the USA. This perspective is convincingly argued by COHEN and ZYSMAN, 1987:

> At the heart of our argument is a contention that

> ... tight linkages tie a broad core of service jobs to manufacturing—but on a much larger scale. Shift out of manufacturing and it is more likely that you will find that you have shifted *out of* such services as product and process engineering, than *into* those services. This is true of a large number of high-level service activities ... These services are complements to manufacturing, not potential substitutes or successors (p. 7).

This argument suggests that growth of corporate complexes in US urban regions is primarily attributable to the formation of direct linkages between producer services firms and the managerial offices of manufacturing firms.

The externalization of indirect production activities represents a potential strategy for industries in the service sector as well as in manufacturing. This potential is described by WOOD, 1986, who states, 'as the size of the service sector and its internal complexity have grown, more jobs have become based upon the service expertise offered to *other* service functions' (p. 40). This presents an alternative hypothesis that the growth of urban corporate complexes is primarily attributable to the formation of direct linkages between producer services firms and the managerial offices of firms in service sector industries. Thus, the growth of producer services industries is only loosely tied to the manufacturing sector.[10]

The description of corporate complexes by NOYELLE and STANBACK, 1984, contends that these agglomerations are self-contained within an urban region. That is, they depend primarily upon local market linkages between producer services firms and corporate managerial offices which require close physical proximity. This perspective aligns with the traditional viewpoint that service sector industries are nonbasic industries that depend upon local markets and the production of goods within the region for the wealth needed to support them.

There is a growing body of evidence that indicates that trade by producer services industries extends beyond the confines of the local region in which the industries are located (e.g. see BEYERS *et al.* 1985a, 1985b; GOE and SHANAHAN, 1988).[11] While the view of producer services as nonbasic industries may hold true at earlier historical points, this research suggests that producer services industries are evolving into basic industries as the development of their markets is extending beyond the urban regions in which they are located. The development of an export base can contribute to employment growth in producer services industries. Additionally, this suggests that the spatial division of labour underlying corporate complexes may be more intricate than described by NOYELLE and STANBACK, 1984. That is, corporate complexes may spatially extend across urban regions and be characterized by nonlocal market linkages. The following analysis examines the validity of these

332   W. R. Goe

hypotheses in an urban region that has undergone
extensive economic restructuring involving growth
in producer services industries.

THE STUDY REGION

Due to its declining manufacturing base and recent
growth in producer services industries, the economy
of the northeast Ohio region provides an appropriate
context in which to examine the research hypotheses.
The study region consists of an eleven-county area
that subsumes four adjacent metropolitan statistical
areas (MSAs): Cleveland—Cuyahoga, Lake, Geauga
and Medina counties; Akron—Summit and Portage
counties; Canton—Stark and Carroll counties; and
Youngstown/Warren—Mahoning and Trumbull
counties (see Fig. 1). The population of the region in

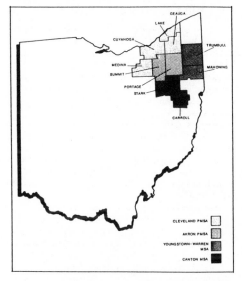

Fig. 1. *The Northeast Ohio Region*

1985 was 3·43 million, down from 3·67 million in
1970. Slightly over one half of the region's population
is concentrated in the Cleveland PMSA (1·87 million
in 1985). The Akron PMSA is the next largest
metropolitan area (648,496 persons), followed by the
Youngstown/Warren MSA (515,498 persons) and the
Canton MSA (403,884 persons).

The northeast Ohio region is located in the heart of
the so-called 'rustbelt'. The region's economy has
historically been highly dependent upon heavy manufacturing in industries such as steel (Cleveland,
Canton, and Youngstown), industrial machinery and
bearings (Cleveland and Canton) and tyres and rubber
products (Akron). Over the past several decades these
key industries have undergone extensive restructuring
involving plant closings and the shifting of production
out of the northeast Ohio region.

During 1974–86, all four of the MSAs in the
northeast Ohio region experienced a decline in manufacturing employment. Combined, these losses
amounted to 168,000 manfacturing jobs (see Table 1).
This total represented 15% of the net loss of manufacturing jobs endured by the nation as a whole (1·1
million jobs) over the identical time period. The
Youngstown/Warren MSA suffered the most severe
decline as it lost over 40% of its manufacturing job
base. The other three metropolitan areas lost slightly
less than 30% of their manufacturing jobs.

Over the same time period, all four of the MSAs
experienced net employment growth in service sector
industries. In combination, a net 148,900 service
sector jobs were created in the four MSAs.[12]
However, only in the Cleveland and Akron metropolitan areas did service sector job growth offset the loss
of manufacturing jobs in absolute number. Further,
the rate of service job growth in all four of the MSAs
was far below the national rate of 40·2%. Overall, the
US experienced a net gain of 21·5 million new jobs in
service sector industries during 1974–86. The service
sector jobs created in the four metropolitan areas of
the northwest Ohio region accounted for less than 1%
of this total.

Producer services industries were an important

Table 1. *Employment shifts in manufacturing and the service sector in the Northeast Ohio Region, 1974–86*

	Manufacturing employment (000s)				Service sector employment (000s)			
	1974	1986	Net change 1974–86	% change 1974–86	1974	1986	Net change 1974–86	% change 1974–86
Cleveland PMSA	287·1	204·9	(82·2)	(28·6)	558·6	646·9	88·3	15·8
Akron PMSA	94·2	67·2	(27·0)	(28·7)	156·2	184·4	28·2	18·1
Canton MSA	62·2	43·7	(18·5)	(29·7)	83·5	101·8	18·3	21·9
Youngstown/Warren MSA	92·0	51·7	(40·3)	(43·8)	113·9	128·0	14·1	12·4
Total for four MSAs	535·5	367·5	(168·0)	(31·4)	912·2	1,061·1	148·9	16·3
USA	20,077	18,965	(1,112·0)	(5·5)	53,471	74,967	21,496	40·2

Sources: Ohio Bureau of Employment Services, *Labor Market Review*, 1984, 1987; US Department of Labor, *Employment and Earnings*, (August 1988).

component of the service sector growth in the northeast Ohio region. Employing the classification of producer services industries developed by GILLESPIE and GREEN, 1987, the rate of job growth in producer services industries outpaced that for the service sector as a whole in the northeast Ohio region over the 1974–86 period (see Table 2). Combined, the rate of job growth for the four MSAs in producer services industries was 36·9% compared to the 16·3% rate for the service sector as a whole (see Table 3). Producer services industries accounted for roughly 30% of all new service sector jobs in the four MSAs over the 1974–86 period.[13]

Business services (SIC 73) accounted for the largest job gains in producer services over the 1974–86 period. This classification category subsumes a diverse array of industries including: advertising; credit reporting and collection; mailing, reproduction and stenographic services; services to buildings (cleaning and extermination); personnel supply services; computer and data processing services; and miscellaneous business services such as research and development laboratories, management consulting and public relations. In aggregate, a net 20,323 new jobs were created in business services across the four MSAs (see

Table 3). The next largest sources of job gains were in real estate and legal services.

The data that have been presented indicate that economic restructuring within northeast Ohio over the 1974–86 period involved a downward, cyclical ratcheting of the regional economy (BERGMAN and GOLDSTEIN, 1983). The extensive decline in manufacturing employment over this time period had yet to be offset in 1986 by employment growth in service sector industries. Nonetheless, service sector industries provided the predominant source of new jobs that were created. Further, producer services industries provided a substantial component of this growth. With the loss of manufacturing jobs and the shift of production out of northeast Ohio, producer services industries have become increasingly more important to the regional economy.

RESEARCH METHODOLOGY

A survey of business establishments from producer services industries located in the four metropolitan statistical areas of northeast Ohio was undertaken in order to gain insight into factors influencing the growth of producer services industries within each metropolitan area. A proportional stratified sample of service sector business establishments was selected from each MSA. With this sampling design, the number of establishments selected from each producer services industry in each MSA was proportional to the percentage of establishments in each producer services industry relative to *all* service sector establishments in each metropolitan area.[14] In total, a sample of 1,397 establishments was selected across all four MSAs.[15]

Data were collected via a telephone survey administered through a Computer-Assisted Telephone Interviewing system.[16] Overall, a 56·4% response rate was achieved for the producer services industries.[17] Establishments agreeing to participate in the study were given a structured questionnaire designed to measure a wide range of characteristics including sources of

Table 2. Classification of producer services industries

SIC Code	Description
60	Banking
61	Credit agencies other than banks
62	Security, commodity brokers and services
63	Insurance carriers
64	Insurance agents, brokers and service
65	Real estate
73	Business services[1]
81	Legal services
89	Miscellaneous services[2]

Notes: 1. Includes advertising, market research, consulting, research and development and other business services.
2. Includes engineering and architectural services and accounting, auditing and bookkeeping.

Source: Adapted from GILLESPIE and GREEN, 1987.

Table 3. Employment change in producer services industries, Northeast Ohio Region, 1974–86

		Cleveland PMSA		Akron PMSA		Canton PMSA		Youngstown/ Warren MSA		Total for four MSAs	
SIC	Industry	Net change	% change	Net change	% change	Net change	% change	Net change	% change	Net change	% change
60	Banking	1,035	9·1	235	8·2	(637)	(30·3)	393	17·1	1,026	5·5
61	Credit agencies other than banks	1,346	23·8	238	21·4	566	72·6	631	63·7	2,781	32·6
62	Security, commodity brokers	562	32·1	203	126·1	38	69·1	90	91·8	893	43·2
63	Insurance carriers	2,776	33·4	(616)	(21·0)	1,294	289·5	188	18·6	3,642	28·7
64	Insurance agents, brokers	2,579	99·9	236	33·5	179	39·1	233	39·4	3,227	74·4
65	Real estate	3,961	45·4	278	20·7	(9)	(1·2)	1,350	106·6	5,580	46·2
73	Business services	12,497	40·2	2,764	50·5	2,863	143·2	2,199	93·0	20,323	49·6
81	Legal services	3,512	94·3	572	80·2	307	91·6	283	66·8	4,674	90·0
89	Miscellaneous services	(125)	(0·9)	1,051	91·9	490	118·6	679	124·1	2,095	13·6
	Total producer services	28,143	32·5	4,961	30·2	5,091	69·3	6,046	63·0	44,241	36·9

Source: County Business Patterns, 1974, 1986.

revenue, location of markets and the types of market groups purchasing their product(s) of labour.[18]

Establishments responding to the survey that identified themselves as private, for-profit businesses were asked whether or not they marketed their product(s) of labour to: (1) consumers; (2) government agencies and public institutions; and (3) businesses. They were then asked to estimate the percentage of their total business revenues that came from each of these three market groups. This data was used as criteria to determine whether each establishment was truly engaged in the provision of indirect production activities (sales to businesses plus government agencies and public institutions). Establishments obtaining the majority of their revenues from consumers were classified as providing consumer activities and were eliminated from further analysis. Establishments obtaining the majority of their revenues from businesses and government agencies were classified as providing indirect production activities and were retained for further analysis. This classification procedure permits a more rigorous data analysis by allowing establishments that derive the majority of their revenues from producer markets to separated out from those primarily dependent upon consumer markets.

Establishments engaged in the provision of indirect production activities were asked to list the types(s) of businesses, government agencies and public institutions to which they marketed their product(s) of labour. These responses were coded into SIC categories at the one-digit level. This data was used to broadly delimit the positioning of the producer services firms in the social division of labour on the basis of direct forward market linkages.

Establishments were also asked to estimate the percentage of their customer base from each of the three market groups that were located within the local metropolitan area versus areas outside the MSA in which the establishment was located.[19] This data was used to determine the percentages of producer services establishments with export markets in areas outside the MSA in which the firm was located. Additionally, this data was combined with the percentages of business revenues from indirect production activities to calculate percentage estimates of revenue from export markets for each establishment. These estimates were derived as follows:

$$E_{ij} = (P_{cj}^g * P_r^g) + (P_{cj}^b * P_r^b)$$

where: E_{ij} = percentage estimate of export revenue for establishment i from location j

P_{cj}^g = percentage of government agency and public institution customer base from location j

P_r^g = percentage of total revenues derived from government agencies and public institutions

P_{cj}^b = percentage of business customer base from location j

P_r^b = percentage of total revenues derived from business

FINDINGS

The classification of establishments in the sample revealed that the majority of establishments in six of the eight producer services industries derived the major proportion of their revenues from consumers rather than businesses, government agencies and public institutions. Only in business services (SIC 73) and miscellaneous services (SIC 89) did the majority of establishments receive their primary source of revenue from indirect production activities (see Table 4). This pattern was consistent across all of the MSAs with two exceptions. First the majority of legal services establishments located in the Cleveland PMSA were classified as providing indirect production activities. Second, the majority of business services establishments located in the Youngstown/ Warren MSA were classified as providing consumer activities.

The breakdown of the classifications by metropolitan area indicates that the majority of establishments in the Cleveland and Akron PMSAs received their primary source of revenue from indirect production activities. This is primarily attributable to the large number of establishments sampled from business services and miscellaneous services. In contrast, the samples from the Canton and Youngstown/Warren MSAs predominantly consisted of establishments that derived the major source of their revenues from consumer markets. These findings suggest that the Cleveland and Akron PMSAs are the dominant centres of trade in indirect production activities within the northeast Ohio region.

The establishments from each metropolitan area that were found to derive their dominant source of revenue from indirect production activities were retained for further analysis since their primary role is to provide their products of labour to businesses and other productive enterprises rather than consumers. The survey data for direct forward market linkages indicates that a much larger percentage of these establishments provide their product(s) of labour to businesses and productive enterprises in other service sector industries rather than manufacturing, primary (agriculture, forestry, fishing, mining) and construction industries. Additionally, a much larger percentage of establishments had direct forward market linkages with manufacturing industries compared to primary and construction industries. This pattern was consistent across all four of the metropolitan areas (see Table 5).[20]

Over twice as many establishments in the Akron and Canton metropolitan areas had direct forward

Table 4. *Distribution of establishments in producer services industries that receive their dominant source of revenue from indirect production activities versus consumer activities*

Industry (SIC)	Primary source of revenue	Cleveland PMSA No.	Cleveland PMSA (%)	Akron PMSA No.	Akron PMSA (%)	Canton MSA No.	Canton MSA (%)	Youngstown/ Warren MSA No.	Youngstown/ Warren MSA (%)
Banking (60)	Consumer activities	9	75·0	5	71·4	1	100·0	0	0·0
	Indirect production activities	3	25·0	2	28·6	0	0·0	1	100·0
Credit agencies other than banks (61)	Consumer activities	4	57·1	7	100·0	4	80·0	5	100·0
	Indirect production activities	3	42·9	0	0·0	1	20·0	0	0·0
Security, commodity brokers and services (62)	Consumer activities	12	70·6	3	100·0	1	100·0	0	—
	Indirect production activities	5	29·4	0	0·0	0	0·0	0	—
Insurance carriers (63)	Consumer activities	2	66·7	6	85·7	1	100·0	3	100·0
	Indirect production activities	1	33·3	1	14·3	0	0·0	0	0·0
Insurance agents brokers and services (64)	Consumer activities	16	69·6	18	78·3	15	65·2	14	82·4
	Indirect production activities	7	30·4	5	21·7	8	34·8	3	17·6
Real estate (65)	Consumer activities	25	83·3	13	68·4	14	87·5	8	88·9
	Indirect production activities	5	16·7	6	31·6	2	12·5	1	11·1
Business services (73)	Consumer activities	10	8·5	20	22·5	16	41·0	13	59·1
	Indirect production activities	107	91·5	69	77·5	23	59·0	9	40·9
Legal services (81)	Consumer activities	12	48·0	16	69·6	18	78·3	2	50·0
	Indirect production activities	13	52·0	7	30·4	5	21·7	2	50·0
Miscellaneous services (89)	Consumer activities	2	4·0	6	17·1	4	26·7	2	40·0
	Indirect production activities	48	96·0	29	82·9	11	73·3	3	60·0
Total producer services	Consumer activities	92	32·4	94	44·1	73	59·3	47	71·2
	Indirect production activities	192	67·6	119	55·9	50	40·7	19	28·8

Table 5. *Percentage of producer services establishments with direct forward market linkages to other sectors of the economy*

	Manufacturing industries	Only manufacturing industries	Ratio of market specialization[1]	Service sector industries	Only service sector industries	Ratio of market specialization	Primary and construction industries[2]	Only primary and construction industries	Ratio of market specialization
Cleveland PMSA	45·6	18·4	0·404	79·1	48·7	0·616	8·2	1·3	0·159
Akron PMSA	28·6	12·1	0·423	85·7	61·5	0·718	6·6	2·2	0·333
Canton MSA	34·2	13·2	0·386	81·6	55·3	0·678	13·2	5·3	0·402
Youngstown/ Warren MSA	46·2	15·4	0·333	76·9	38·5	0·501	15·4	7·7	0·500

Notes: 1. Calculated by dividing percentage of establishments with direct forward market linkages to manufacturing industries by the percentage of establishments with direct forward market linkages only to manufacturing.

2. Includes Agriculture, Forestry, Fishing, Mining and Construction.

market linkages with other service sector industries compared to manufacturing. This ratio was slightly less for the Cleveland and Youngstown/Warren samples, although large differences were found. The ratios of market specialization indicate a greater tendency among establishments with direct forward market linkages to other service sector industries to provide their product(s) of labour *only* to industries in the service sector. Thus, there was a greater tendency among establishments with direct forward market linkages to manufacturing to also provide their product(s) of labour to industries outside of manufacturing. This tendency was slightly more pronounced

for establishments with direct forward market linkages to primary and construction industries.

The data for market locations revealed that over 75% of the establishments in the Cleveland, Akron and Youngstown/Warren samples had developed export markets for indirect production activities. This compared to 66·7% of the establishments in the Canton sample. Broken down by location, a proportion of establishments in each metropolitan area had developed export markets in the other MSAs of the northeast Ohio region, other locations in Ohio and the USA, and in international locations (see Table 6). The largest proportions of establishments from the

Table 6. Producer services firms with export markets for indirect production activities by location (%)

From	To							
	Cleveland PMSA	Akron PMSA	Canton MSA	Youngstown/ Warren MSA	Other areas in Ohio	Remainder of USA	Internatonal locations	% total firms with export markets
Cleveland PMSA	—	38·4	27·7	19·5	41·5	59·1	20·8	78·0
Akron PMSA	61·3	—	39·6	20·8	13·2	41·5	11·3	79·2
Canton MSA	26·2	50·0	—	23·8	21·4	35·7	14·3	66·7
Youngstown/ Warren MSA	60·0	40·0	40·0	—	40·0	40·0	20·0	80·0

Cleveland metropolitan area had developed export markets in other locations in the USA and Ohio, i.e. developed markets outside the northeast Ohio region. This finding was in contrast to the other three metropolitan areas.

The largest percentage of establishments from the Akron and Youngstown/Warren metropolitan areas had developed export markets in the Cleveland PMSA while the largest proportion of establishments from the Canton metropolitan area served export markets in the Akron PMSA. In each of these MSAs, the second largest proportion of establishments had developed export markets in other locations in the USA. These findings suggest that a proportionally greater number of producer services establishments located in the Cleveland PMSA had developed export markets outside the northeast Ohio region compared to those located in the other three metropolitan areas.

The estimates of mean percentage revenues from the export of indirect production activities revealed that, on average, producer services establishments in the Cleveland, Akron and Youngstown/Warren samples derived over 35% of their revenues from exports. This is in contrast to establishments in the Canton sample which derived an average of 27·7% of total business revenues from exports (see Table 7).[21]

From the standpoint of regional markets, establishments located in the Cleveland and Youngstown/Warren metropolitan areas tended to derive the dominant portion of their export revenues from markets outside the northeast Ohio region. However, export revenues from markets in other areas of Ohio and international locations tended to be much smaller compared to those from markets in other US locations. Establishments located in Youngstown/Warren

tended to obtain their second largest source of export revenues from markets in the Cleveland PMSA. In contrast, all export markets within the northeast Ohio region tended to be smaller than those outside the region for establishments located in the Cleveland metropolitan area.

Producer services establishments located in the Akron and Canton metropolitan areas tended to derive the largest source of export revenues from markets within the northeast Ohio region. Establishments located in Akron tended to receive the largest source of export revenues from markets located in the Cleveland PMSA. Export revenues for establishments located in Canton tended to be more evenly distributed across markets in the other three metropolitan areas with Akron providing the largest source. Markets in other locations of the USA also tended to provide an important source of export revenue for establishments in both of these metropolitan areas.

While the *average* proportion of total revenue from exports was less than 50% for establishments in all metropolitan areas, there were a number in each of the metropolitan areas that received their primary source of revenue from exports. Approximately one-third or more of the establishments in the Cleveland, Akron and Youngstow/Warren samples received their primary source of revenue from export markets (see Table 8). In addition, 25% of the establishments in the Canton sample exhibited a primary dependency on export markets.

DISCUSSION

The findings from the survey demonstrate in further detail that analyses of producer services industries that

Table 7. Estimates of mean percentage revenues from exports of indirect production activities by location

From	To									
	Cleveland PMSA	Akron PMSA	Canton MSA	Youngstown/ Warren MSA	Total within NE Ohio	Other areas in Ohio	Remainder of USA	International locations	Total outside NE Ohio	% total revenue from exports
Cleveland PMSA	—	3·5	2·0	0·7	6·2	7·0	19·5	3·6	30·1	36·3
Akron PMSA	16·8	—	3·8	1·3	21·9	4·2	13·1	1·0	18·3	40·2
Canton MSA	4·6	6·3	—	3·0	13·9	2·8	10·7	0·3	13·8	27·7
Youngstown/ Warren MSA	7·9	2·0	2·7	—	12·6	4·6	21·3	3·4	29·3	41·9

Table 8. Distribution of establishments in producer services industries that receive their dominant source of revenue from exports versus local markets (%)

Primary source of revenue	Cleveland PMSA	Akron PMSA	Canton MSA	Youngstown/ Warren MSA
Export markets	32·5	37·5	25·0	40·0
Local markets	67·5	62·5	75·0	60·0

rely solely on secondary data grouped by SIC categories are confounded by an inability to distinguish between establishments whose primary function is to serve consumers rather than businesses and other productive enterprises. In the four metropolitan areas of the northeast Ohio region, a number of establishments from all the producer services industries were found to derive their primary source of revenue from consumers rather than indirect production activities. All of the finance, insurance and real estate industries in each metropolitan area were found to be predominantly composed of establishments with a primary dependency on consumer markets. This was also found to be true for the legal services industry with the exception of that in the Cleveland metropolitan area. The survey findings demonstrate that it cannot be accurately assumed that a particular set of SIC categories represents the producer services industries since the potential exists for a dominant proportion of business establishments within each industry to primarily serve consumer markets rather than provide indirect production activities to businesses.

With regard to those establishments that derive their primary source of revenue from indirect production activities, the data suggests that the primary role of these establishments within the social division of labour of the four metropolitan economies is to provide their products of labour to other service sector industries. Therefore, direct forward linkages with manufacturing industries are of less importance to the welfare of producer services industries within the northeast Ohio region. A caveat must be attached to this interpretation since the data cannot fully distinguish the importance of individual linkages in terms of revenue provided to the producer services establishments. They do show, however, that a larger number of businesses and productive enterprises in service sector industries provide revenue (of whatever magnitude) for the establishments in the sample compared to businesses in manufacturing industries.

These findings imply that the dominant force affecting recent growth in producer services industries within the four metropolitan areas of the northeast Ohio region is the externalization of indirect production activities by firms in service sector industries. Thus, the extension of the social division of labour underlying the growth of producer services industries has been motivated primarily by service sector industries. Further, the major force underlying recent

growth of corporate complexes in the four metropolitan areas of the northeast Ohio region is the formation of direct linkages between establishments in producer services industries and firms in other service sector industries.[22] This growth is only loosely tied to the manufacturing sector. The formation of direct linkages with manufacturing industries is of lesser importance in the growth of corporate complexes.

This interpretation of the data supports the position that growth in service sector industries may be attainable without extensive *direct* forward market linkages to manufacturing industries (see COHEN and ZYSMAN, 1987).[23] However, such a pattern of service sector growth must be evaluated in the context of aggregate economic performance. That is: can the growth of producer services industries driven primarily by demand from other service sector industries provide the engine of economic growth within a regional or metropolitan economy? Based on the performance of the regional economy in northeast Ohio, the magnitude of the export of indirect production activities from the four metropolitan areas has not been sufficient to counteract the effects of deindustrialization and manufacturing decline. The growth of producer services industries as well as other service sector industries has yet to stimulate a major economic expansion and elevate each metropolitan economy to a higher plateau of economic growth. Rather, this growth has only contributed toward stabilizing the decline in each metropolitan area.

The data analysis revealed that the majority of producer services establishments in each metropolitan area engaged in the export of indirect production activities. However, the mean estimates of export revenues indicate that establishments in each of the four MSAs tended to derive the dominant proportion of their business revenues from local markets rather than from exports. This indicates that the majority of establishments in each metropolitan area are primarily linked into local corporate complex agglomerations. For these establishments, export markets represent a secondary source of revenue that augments their dominant role in the local metropolitan economy.

Within each of the metropolitan areas, however, there was a smaller tier of producer services establishments that received the dominant proportion of their revenues from export markets. This indicates that infrastructures of producer service industries in metropolitan economies cannot be entirely characterized as being linked into local corporate complex agglomerations. Producer services industries in each of the four metropolitan areas of the northeast Ohio region were found to be interlinked with businesses located in all the other metropolitan areas with Cleveland providing the major intraregional export market. The producer services infrastructures in the Akron and Canton metropolitan areas were found to be the most oriented toward intraregional export markets.

338   *W. R. Goe*

Additionally, producer services industries in all of the metropolitan areas were found to be interlinked with businesses in other Ohio, US and international locations. The infrastructures in the Cleveland and Youngstown/Warren metropolitan areas were found to be the most oriented towards export markets outside the northeast Ohio region. These findings suggest that producer services industries in both large metropolitan areas (Cleveland) and smaller metropolitan areas (Akron, Canton, Youngstown/Warren) are characterized by a dual structure: (1) a larger tier of producer services establishments that is primarily linked into local corporate complex agglomerations; and (2) a smaller tier of establishments that is primarily linked into the broader spatial division of labour. These findings suggest that producer services industries in all the metropolitan areas are contributing toward economic growth, both within and outside the northeast Ohio region. The patterns of export trade suggest that producer services industries are contributing toward further integration of the four metropolitan economies within the northeast Ohio region. Moreover, export trade by producer services industries is also furthering economic integration with regions outside northeast Ohio. However, this predominantly involves further integration with regional economies within the USA rather than at the international level.

IMPLICATIONS FOR ECONOMIC DEVELOPMENT POLICY

The particular form of industrial organization evolving in the USA that involves the externalization of indirect production activities from corporate administrative and decision-making functions (thereby stimulating the growth of producer services industries) is primarily the product of market forces rather than an explicit industrial policy. A debate continues over whether or not an explicit industrial policy is needed in the USA (see, for example, BLUESTONE and HARRISON, 1982; JOHNSON, 1984; SCHULTZE, 1983; THUROW, 1985; REICH, 1983; VERNON, 1988). Thus far, the involvement of the federal government in economic development has consisted of an array of fragmented programmes implemented by different agencies. Further, these programmes have focused primarily on facilitating the revitalization of the manufacturing sector rather than promoting the development of service sector industries. The greatest influence of the federal government in recent years regarding the service sector has been the deregulation of a number of industries including transportation, communication and banking.

The onus of economic development has been the primary responsibility of state and local governments where it has pitted state against state and locality against locality in an effort to attract transplant businesses, develop new industries and retain existing economic infrastructures (FLORIDA *et al.*, 1988). Regional approaches to economic development have yet to become commonplace in the USA. While the study presented in this paper is limited in geographic scope, the findings do have several implications for economic development policy in US regions or metropolitan areas regarding producer services industries.

First, a regional or local economic development policy toward producer services industries should emphasize the importance of developing markets provided by service sector industries in addition to manufacturing industries. The externalization of indirect production activities by businesses in service sector industries can provide a greater source of demand for producer services industries. This could be especially critical in regions with a declining local manufacturing base (such as northeast Ohio) as the study findings suggest that such a pattern of growth is attainable under these conditions. Thus, the growth of producer services industries driven by demand from other service sector industries can provide a stabilizing influence in a regional economy by providing new jobs, adding to a region's export base and by facilitating the success of local businesses in adapting to changing economic conditions.

Second, a regional or local economic development policy toward producer services industries must facilitate the development of the export potential of indirect production activities. The findings of the study strongly suggest that the costs of communication and/or transportation involved in obtaining indirect production activities over distances are absorbed by outsourcing businesses when they require particular expertise or specialized knowledge regarding indirect production activities. Therefore, economic development policy should focus on developing trade programmes that call attention to the particular strengths and expertise offered by local or regional firms in producer services. Such programmes should not only be targeted toward businesses located outside the local region or metropolitan area in order to expand exports, but also should be targeted toward other local businesses in order to maximize important substitution of indirect production activities. A regional or local economic development policy toward producer services industries that incorporates these strategies can strenthen the increasingly important role being played by these industries in regional and metropolitan production systems.

Acknowledgements—This research is part of a three-year study of the service economy in northeast Ohio being conducted by the Center for Urban Studies at The University of Akron. The research is funded by the Northeast Ohio Inter-Institutional Research Program supported by the Ohio Urban University Program and the

Ohio Board of Regents. The author would like to thank the reviewers for their helpful comments and James Shanahan, Shara Davis, Melanie Carpenter and Steve Hambley of the Center for Urban Studies.

NOTES

1. This, of course, does not address the issue of the extent to which new jobs within the service sector provide adequate *replacements* for lost manufacturing jobs in terms of wages, benefits and quality of work.

2. US manufacturing employment declined by 1·98 million jobs between 1979 and 1987, although cyclical gains have been realized since the end of the last recession in 1983. Simultaneously, 14·2 million new jobs were created in the service sector (US DEPARTMENT OF LABOR, 1988, p. 43).

3. GREENFIELD, 1966, found that the rate of employment growth in producer services industries was greater than that for total employment over the 1950–60 decade. TSCHETTER, 1987, found that the average annual rate of growth in producer services industries was greater than that for total nonagricultural employment over the 1959–72, 1972–82, 1982–86 periods. It should be noted that Greenfield's analysis specified a broader set of industries as comprising producer services compared to Tschetter's. The lack of consensus over an operationalized definition of producer services industries is discussed further below.

4. The social division of labour refers to the complex network of linkages across industries and work groups that form a production system (see WALKER, 1985, p. 52).

5. WALKER, 1985, states, 'A good is a material object produced by human labor for human use . . . In its simplest form, it is tangible, discrete and mobile. A labor service, on the other hand, is labor that does not take the intervening form of a material product, such as a play or a lecture' (p. 48).

6. For example, using the US version of the SIC code, commercial photography (SIC 7333), classified under business services (SIC 73) and photographic studios (SIC 7221), classified under personal services (SIC 72), clearly distinguishes between business and consumer markets for photographic services. This is also the case with personal credit institutions (SIC 614) and business credit institutions (SIC 615) in relation to financial credit services. However, this differentiation is infrequently and haphazardly employed throughout the SIC schematic. For example, interior decorating services, which obviously could have a substantial consumer market, are classified only under business services, nec (SIC 7399). A separate category was not created under personal services or private households (SIC 88). Another example is disinfecting and pest control services (SIC 7342) which is also classified only under business services.

7. There are a number weaknesses in the analyses of TSCHETTER, 1987, and KUTSCHER, 1988, which make them fall short of a complete and precise test of the unbundling thesis. First, both focus only on unbundling in the manufacturing sector. This does not discount the possibility of unbundling in service sector industries.

Second they use aggregated occupational data which can obscure unbundling by individual firms. Therefore, it is impossible to examine the characteristics of firms that did engage in unbundling versus those that did not. Finally, given the use of occupational data, it is impossible to tell the precise nature of the types of indirect production activities that are being unbundled versus those being provided internally by manufacturing firms.

8. A number of authors have noted the importance of information technology (IT) in stimulating demand for producer services industries (for example, see BEYERS, 1989; DANIELS, 1985; GERSHUNY and MILES, 1983; OCHEL and WAGNER, 1987). The integration of IT into production systems has created demand for data processing, software development, systems integration and other forms of computer consulting (all defined as producer services according to the SIC code). Thus, technological innovation can play an important role in the development of new requirements for indirect production activities. Firms employing technological innovations may opt to contract out for the expertise of related indirect production activities rather than attempt to produce such expertise internally within the firm. This represents one way in which externalization could increase without unbundling. Additionally, the specialized knowledge provided by producer services industries can complement the indirect production activities provided internally by firms. For example, a firm may maintain a fully staffed personnel department while simultaneously contracting with personnel consultants and employment agencies to obtain needed labour. Assuming that a firm is growing, this suggests the potential for externalization and internal provision of indirect production activities to increase simultaneously.

9. The term *flexibility* is not being used in the sense of supporting the notion of *flexible specialization* (PIORE and SABEL, 1984) as the emergent dominant model of industrial organization. Rather, the term is used only to indicate that externalization allows firms to have greater control over fixed costs while meeting their requirements (either in a periodic or more continuous fashion) for indirect production activities involving specialized knowledge (e.g. legal services, management consulting) and/or those involving more routine functions (e.g. building maintenance, stenographic help). In turn, this allows firms to more easily maintain profitability, weather economic downturns and/or to survive, even while perhaps being uncompetitive in the larger international economy. A broader important issue is whether the growth of corporate complexes represents a dimension of a *regime of accumulation* that will allow the US economy to regain its competitive edge? Or, is it a feature of its decline?

10. By 'loosely tied' I mean that the growth of producer services industries is not predominantly due to direct forward market linkages with manufacturing firms. Even in this case, however, producer services are tied to the manufacturing sector in several ways. First, the firms in other service industries that represent their predominant customers may depend directly on manufacturers for their markets. Second, all producer servi-

ces industries are dependent upon manufacturing for technologies to be used as means of production, e.g. computers and office equipment. Thus, the growth in such producer services industries would be indirectly linked to manufacturing in relation to both upstream and downstream activities.

11. The cited studies are ones that rely on primary data collection from producer services industries to establish the presence of export trade. Other studies such as AUSTRIAN and ZLATOPER, 1988; GROSHEN, 1987; and KIEL and MACK, 1986, rely on secondary data analysis and the use of location quotients to establish such evidence. Unfortunately, the presence of export trade can only be implied by this approach.

12. This figure was derived by using the *residual* definition of the service sector which includes all one-digit SIC divisions outside of agriculture, mining, manufacturing and construction.

13. This estimate was derived by dividing net job growth in producer services industries for the four MSAs combined (listed in Table 3) by the net job growth in the service sector for the combined MSAs (listed in Table 1, i.e. 44,241/148,900). A caveat must be attached to the accuracy of this estimate since the data for the numerator and denominator are derived from different sources, i.e. *County Business Patterns* and *BLS Employment, Hours and Wages*. One of the fundamental differences between these datasets is that *County Business Patterns* does not enumerate government employment. Interestingly enough, net job growth in the service sector for the four MSAs combined over the 1974–86 period using *County Business Patterns* was 185,294 new jobs—approximately 36,394 more jobs than estimated by BLS data. The BLS data estimates a net growth of 8,000 jobs in government. This does not account for the large difference in estimates. Using *County Business Patterns* data for net job growth, producer services accounted for 24% of service sector growth (44,241/185,294).

14. With this sampling design, statistical estimates are derived for each individual MSA and not the region as a whole. A proportional stratified sample for the region as a whole would be dominated by establishments located in the Cleveland PMSA since it has a much larger economic base. This design was not selected since it would provide less information on producer services industries in the three smaller metropolitan areas.

15. Overall, 4,443 establishments were sampled from *all* service sector industries across the four MSAs. Therefore, the sample of establishments from producer services industries represented a subset of the entire sample. The sampling frames for the Cleveland PMSA, Akron PMSA and Canton MSA were obtained from the data files of Leadsource, Incorporated, an information service firm that specializes in compiling business listings. The sampling frame for the Youngstown/Warren MSA was obtained from Dun & Bradstreet's 'Dun's Market Identifiers' data file. Establishments from each two-digit SIC category in the service sector were randomly drawn from all establishments in that category that were listed in each data file. A provision was included in the selection process for firms with both headquarters and branch establishments located within

an MSA. If these conditions were met, only the headquarters location was included in the sample. Both Leadsource and Dun & Bradstreet purport that their files cover the major proportion of all businesses in each MSA since they are periodically updated. However, given that their coverage is less than 100%, all producer services firms in each MSA did not have a chance of being selected for inclusion in the sample. This was especially true of recent start-up firms that had gone into business following the last update.

16. Computer-Assisted Telephone Interviewing systems employ microcomputer technology to reduce the amount of time required in collecting, coding and analysing survey data. This methodology offers numerous advantages over conventional paper-and-pencil methods (see DOORN and DECKER, 1985; GROVES and MATHIOWETZ, 1984; and SHANGRAW, 1986).

17. In total, 788 of the 1,397 producer services establishments in the sample responded to the survey. For the four MSAs combined, the highest response occurred in Banking (SIC 60) with an 82·8% response rate (24/29 establishments). The lowest response occurred in Insurance Carriers (SIC 63) with a 46·9% response rate (15/32 establishments). The response rates for the remaining producer services industries ranged between 52·1% and 62·7%.

18. Before administering the questionnaire, interviewers were instructed to identify and engage a company officer who possessed the information needed to effectively respond to the questionnaire. If such a person was unavailable at that time, appointments were made to call back when the appropriate person was available to be interviewed.

19. Establishments were asked to estimate the percentage of their customer base from each market group that was located in: (1) international locations; (2) US locations outside the state of Ohio; (3) within the state but outside northeast Ohio; (4) the Youngstown metropolitan area; (5) the Cleveland metropolitan area (6) the Canton metropolitan area, and (7) the Akron metropolitan area.

20. Respondents could provide multiple responses in specifying the types of businesses, government agencies and public institutions to which they provided their product(s) of labour. The frequency distribution of these responses was aggregated into broader categories of direct forward market linkages: (1) manufacturing industries; (2) other service sector industries; and (3) primary (agriculture, foresty, fishing and mining) and construction industries. Distributions of establishments with direct forward market linkages to only one of these broad sectors were also calculated.

21. Although pertaining to a slightly different set of industries and smaller geographic areas, these figures are roughly consistent with the estimate calculated by BEYERS *et al.*, 1985. In examining a wider range of industries including transportation, communications and other services, they found that 36·2% of total sales came from exports in a sample of 2,666 service sector firms located in the central Puget Sound region of Washington.

22. Caveats must also be attached to generalizations concerning the causes of growth in producer services

industries since they involve longitudinal assumptions based on cross-sectional data.

23. An important related issue that cannot be addressed by the survey data is the spatial attributes of the *indirect* forward linkages from producer service establishments to manufacturing industries. Therefore, no insight can be provided into what extent the demand for indirect production activities from other service sector industries is indirectly dependent upon the local versus nonlocal manufacturing base. Thus, it is possible that the growth of producer services industries driven primarily by demand from other service sector industries is still indirectly dependent on the local manufacturing base. However, if the frequency of export activity by the producer services establishments in the survey is an indication, indirect forward linkages to manufacturing may be nonlocal as well.

REFERENCES

AUSTRIAN Z. and ZLATOPER T. J. (1988) The role of export services, *REI Review* (Autumn), pp. 24–9.

BACON R. and ELTIS W. (1976) *Britiain's Economic Problem: Too Few Producers*. Macmillan, London.

BERGMAN E. M. and GOLDSTEIN H. A. (1983) Dynamics and structural change in metropolitan economies, *Am. Plann. Ass. J.* (Summer), 263–79.

BEYERS W. B. (1989) *The Producer Services and Economic Development in the United States: The Last Decade*. Economic Development Administration, Technical Assistance and Research Division, US Department of Commerce, Washington, DC.

BEYERS W. B., ALVINE M. J. and JOHNSON E. G. (1985a) The service sector: a growing force in the regional export base, *Econ. Dev. Commentary* **9**, 3–7.

BEYERS W. B., ALVINE M. J. and JOHNSON E. G. (1985b) The service economy: export of services in the Central Puget Sound region, Central Puget Sound Economic Development District, Seattle, WA.

BLUESTONE B. and HARRISON B. (1982) *The Deindustrialization of America*. Basic Books, New York.

BROWNING H. and SINGELMANN J. (1978) The transformation of the US labor force: the interaction of industry and occupation, *Politics and Society* **8**, 481–509.

COHEN R. B. (1981) The new international division of labour, multinational corporations and urban hierarchy, in DEAR M. and SCOTT A. J. (Eds) *Urbanization and Urban Planning in Capitalist Society*, pp. 287–315. Methuen, London.

COHEN S. S. and ZYSMAN J. (1987) *Manufacturing Matters! The Myth of the Post-Industrial Economy*. Basic Books, New York.

DANIELS P. W. (1983) Business service offices in British provincial cities: location and control, *Environ. Plann. A* **15**, 1,101–120.

DANIELS P. W. (1985) *Service Industries: A Geographic Appraisal*. Methuen, London.

DOORN P. K. and DEKKER F. (1985) Computer-assisted telephone interviewing: an application in planning research, *Environ. Plann. A* **7**, 795–813.

FLORIDA R., KENNEY M. and MAIR A. (1988) The transplant phenomenon: Japanese auto manufacturers in the United States *Econ. Dev. Commentary* **12**, 3–9.

GERSHUNY J. and MILES I. (1983) *The New Service Economy: The Transformation of Employment in Industrial Societies*. Frances Pinter, London.

GILLESPIE A. E. and GREEN A. E. (1987) The changing geography of producer services employment in Britain, *Reg. Studies* **21**, 397–411.

GILLIS W. R. (1987) Can service-producing industries provide a catalyst for regional economic growth?, *Econ. Dev. Quart.* **1**, 249–56.

GOE W. R. and SHANAHAN J. L. (1988) Analyzing the implications of service sector growth for urban economies: evidence from the Akron PMSA, paper presented at the ACSP 30th Annual Conference, State University of New York, Buffalo.

GOE W. R. and SHANAHAN J. L. (1989) Patterns of economic restructuring in industrial-based metropolitan areas, Center for Urban Studies, The University of Akron.

GREENFIELD H. I. (1966) *Manpower and the Growth of Producer Services*. Columbia University Press, New York.

GROSHEN E. G. (1987) Can services be a source of export-led growth? Evidence from the fourth district, *Econ. Rev. Fed. Res. Bank of Cleveland* **3**, 2–15.

GROVES R. M. and MATHIOWETZ N. A. (1984) Computer-assisted telephone interviewing: effects on interviewers and respondents, *Public Opinion Quart.* **48**, 356–69.

HARRISON B. and BLUESTONE B. (1988) *The Great U-Turn*. Basic Books, New York.

HUTTON T. and LEY D. (1987) Location, linkages, and labour: the downtown complex of corporate activities in a medium size city, Vancouver, British Columbia, *Econ. Geogr.* **63**, 126–41.

ILLERIS S. (1989) *Services and Regions in Europe*. Gower, Brookfield, VT.

JOHNSON C. (1984) *The Industrial Policy Debate*. ICS Press, San Francisco.

KALDOR N. (1966) *Causes of the Slow Rate of Growth of the United Kingdom*. Cambridge University Press, Cambridge.

KEIL S. R. and MACK R. S. (1986) Identifying export potential in the service sector, *Growth and Change* (April), pp. 2–10.

KUTSCHER R. E. (1988) Growth of services employment in the United States, in GUILE B. R. and QUINN J. B. (eds.) *Technology In Services: Policies for Growth, Trade and Employment*, pp. 47–75. National Academy Press, Washington, D.C.

MARSHALL J. N. (1982) Linkages between manufacturing industry and business services, *Environ. Plann. A* **14**, 523–40.

MARSHALL J. N. (1983) Business-service activities in British provincial conurbations, *Environ. Plann. A* **15**, 1,343–59.

MARSHALL J. N. (1985) Business services, the regions and regional policy, *Reg. Studies* **19**, 353–64.

MARSHALL J. N. (1989) Corporate reorganization and the geography of services: evidence from the motor vehicle aftermarket in the west midlands region of the U.K., *Reg. Studies* **28**, 139–150.

MASSEY D. (1984) *Spatial Divisions of Labour*. Macmillan, London.

NOYELLE T. J. and STANBACK T. M. (1984) *The Economic Transformation of American Cities*. Rowman and Allanheld, Totowa, NJ.

OCHEL W. and WAGNER M. (1987) *Service Economies in Europe: Opportunities for Growth*. Westview, Boulder, CO.

PERRY D. C. (1987) The politics of dependency in deindustrializing America: the case of Buffalo, New York, in SMITH M. P. and FEAGIN J. R. (Eds) *The Capitalist City*, pp. 113–37. Basil Blackwell, New York.

PIORE M. (1986) Perspectives on labor market flexibility, *Ind. Rel.* **25**, 146–66.

PIORE M. and SABEL C. (1984) *The Second Industrial Divide*. Basic Books, New York.

REICH R. B. (1983) *The Next American Frontier*. Times Books, New York.

SCHULTZE C. (1983) Industrial policy: a dissent, *Brookings Review* **2**, 1–13.

SHANGRAW R. F. (1986) Telephone surveying with computers: administrative, methodological and research issues, *Evaluation and Program Planning* **9**, 107–11.

SHELP R. K. (1981) *Beyond Industralization*. Praeger, New York.

STANBACK T. M. (1979) *Understanding the Service Economy*. The Johns Hopkins University Press, Baltimore.

STANBACK T. M. and NOYELLE T. J. (1982) *Cities in Transition*. Allanheld Osmun, Totowa, NJ.

STANBACK T. M., BLAUE P. J. NOYELLE T. J. and KONASEK R. A. (1981) *Services: The New Economy*. Allanheld, Osmun, Totowa, NJ.

STORPER M. and WALKER R. A. (1984) The spatial division of labor: labor and the location of industries, in TABB W. and SAWYERS L. (eds.) *Sunbelt/Snowbelt: Urban Development and Regional Restructuring*, pp. 19–47. Oxford University Press, New York.

THUROW L. C. (1985) A world-class economy: getting back into the ring, *Technol. Rev.* (August/September) pp. 27–37.

TSCHETTER J. (1987) Producer services industries: why are they growing so rapidly, *Monthly Lab. Rev.* (December), pp. 31–9.

US DEPARTMENT OF LABOR (1988) Employees on nonagricultural payrolls by major industry, 1936 to date, *Employment and Earnings* **35**, 43.

VERNON R. (1988) A strategy for international trade, *Issues in Science and Technology* **5**, 86–91.

WALKER R. A. (1985) Is there a service economy? The changing capitalist division of labor, *Science Soc.* **49**, 42–83.

WOOD P. A. (1986) The anatomy of job loss and job creation: some speculations on the role of the 'producer service' sector, *Reg. Studies* **20**, 37–46.

[19]

Flexible Production, Externalisation and the Interpretation of Business Service Growth

MARTIN PERRY

*Increasing interest in the creation of flexible systems of pro-
duction has led to an interpretation of business service employment as an outcome largely of changes in the reorganisation
of production. This interpretation is challenged because
of its conceptual weakness and its over-simplification of
the advantages of subcontracting services. Data from New
Zealand and the UK reveal that both internalisation and
externalisation trends are taking place within industry, but
with no marked increase in subcontracting.*

INTRODUCTION

The continuing growth of literature on service employment expansion
has tended to widen rather than resolve the meaning and significance of
this trend. While researchers whose interests lie in global employment
changes [for example Rowthorn and Wells, 1987] remain convinced
that differential productivity rates are the main explanation of the
rising service sector employment share, service sector specialists are
unable to agree on the salient causes of growth. More careful attempts
to measure the productivity performance of services have revealed
a rate of increase as impressive as many manufacturing activities
[Mark, 1982]. The extension of markets as a result of technological
and organisational innovation and the consequent demand for services
to integrate sprawling business empires has undoubtedly been part of
absolute increase in demand [Marshall, 1988]. The importance of
growing demand between service activities has been emphasised in the
case of UK property consultants [Daniels *et al.*, 1988]. The increasing
role of product differentiation strategies based on the conjunction of
material and non-material goods has also been identified as a further
source of growth [Enderwick, 1989].

Into this maelstrom of competing explanations has recently been

Martin Perry is at the Department of Geography, National University of Singapore, Kent
Ridge Crescent, Singapore 0511.

The Service Industries Journal, Vol.12, No.1, (January 1992), pp.1–16
PUBLISHED BY FRANK CASS, LONDON

2   THE SERVICE INDUSTRIES JOURNAL

added the possibility that 'productive decentralisation' is driving the rapid expansion of business services [Lewis, 1988; Scott, 1988]. The thrust of the decentralisation argument is to shift the focus of explanation from the structure of post industrial society to the analysis of labour processes within a new 'regime of accumulation'. The main link being the subcontracting of producer service employment from within industrial enterprises to independent, specialist suppliers. Clearly it is iimportant to disentangle the relative contribution of these and related processes to business service growth because of their quite different implications.

The importance of industry occupation shifts has been recognised for some time. Analysis of employment change in various European countries during the 1960s and 1970s indicated that the greatest proportion of the growth in 'service' occupations resulted from the occupational shift within manufacturing industries, rather than the disproportionate growth of service industries [Gershuny and Miles, 1983]. In turn some of this 'occupational disaggregation' was expected to be reconcentrated into new, specialised 'intermediate producer services' [Gershuny and Miles, 1985]. The difference between this line of argument and the proponents of more recent productive decentralisation interpretations of service growth is partly the elevation of externalisation to a prime cause of producer service growth. More fundamentally, however, is the attempt to link the expansion of business services into a wider account of economic change. The main thrust of the argument being that capitalist industry has undergone a major qualitative shift toward a flexible system of production based around a network of subcontracting relationships in place of large scale, mass production systems [Scott, 1988].

This paper considers how far a shift to a new regime of flexible production provides a substantial explanation of the rapid rise of business service employment. The paper is in three parts: part one provides a brief outline of the productive decentralisation model; part two discusses the empirical evidence on the extent of business service subcontracting, including recent survey data from New Zealand on the demand and supply of business services in the Auckland Region; part three outlines the influences shaping the mode of service procurement and the reasons why no single direction of change is occurring. The main message of the paper is that both internalisation and externalisation processes are occurring with a modest net impact on the overall growth in business service employment. More detailed explanations, attuned to individual circumstances and locations are demanded than are supplied by the decentralisation account.

BUSINESS SERVICE GROWTH   3

FLEXIBLE PRODUCTION

Over the past decade increasing attention has been paid to the idea that more flexible systems of production are taking root. The character of this reorganisation has been summarised by various labels including 'postfordism', 'flexible specialisation' and 'productive decentralisation'. In the present article 'decentralisation' will be used to denote the changed form of capitalist economies. The arguments surrounding the shift in western capitalism toward a more decentralised system of production can be summarised at three levels. First, the basis of the crisis in capitalist economies that demanded a qualitative reorganisation; second, the concept of flexible production systems as a 'solution' to this crisis; three, the significance of vertical disintegration and subcontracting as one aspect of flexibility is explained.

According to supporters of the decentralisation thesis, the 1960s and 1970s represent a significant rupture in the capitalist regime of accumulation [Piore and Sabel, 1984; Scott, 1988]. Prior to this watershed, mass production industries were dominant and sustained by productivity-related pay increases and Keynesian economic management which ensured a continuing demand for the output of industry. This regime was thrown into crisis by the failure of Keynesian economic management to manage the combined impact of industrial recession, the build up of labour resistance in mass production sectors and rising oil prices which created an hitherto unknown phenomenon, stagflation. Coincidentally, competition from Japan and newly industrialising countries intensified and further weakened western industrial capital. Politically, a new conservative consensus emerged, dedicated to dismantling the welfare institutions and demand management mechanisms associated with Keynesian modes of social regulation. In the vacuum created by these events, an alternative regime emerged based on flexible forms of production.

The resolution of this crisis lay in the introduction of new labour processes aligned with technologies based on micro electronics and computers. The central feature of the reorganisation of capitalism is held to be the growth of flexible forms of production. Flexibility is achieved in several ways, but a basic distinction is between functional and numerical flexibility. Functional flexibility is achieved through the development of workforces characterised by few occupational boundaries, multiskilling and flexible work hours. Numerical flexibility seeks to maximise the potential labour force available to the employer, while minimising the 'core' workforce for whom the employer is permanently responsible. The flexible firm is, therefore, associated with the development of a

4 THE SERVICE INDUSTRIES JOURNAL

dual labour market comprising an inner core of stable, skilled employees with secure employment based on their importance to the organisation's key, firm-specific activities. The 'peripheral' workers, by contrast, have less firm-specific skills and can be recruited from the open market or released into it as the firm's demand changes. Both types of flexibility are facilitated by several additional forms of flexibility affecting working practices (for example, a reduction in demarcation restrictions) and machinery (allowing short production runs across a wider range of products).

One way flexibility is achieved is through the vertical disintegration of production. The breaking of formerly self-contained organisations into a myriad of new industrial subsectors enables producers 'to combine and recombine together in loose, rapidly shifting coalitions held together by external transactional linkages' [Scott, 1988]. The increased use of subcontracting over internal production assists labour market flexibility by providing a further mechanism for reducing the permanent workforce. The main drawback is the transaction costs associated with selecting and managing subcontracting relationships. Such costs are minimised by close physical proximity which leads to a further characteristic of the flexible production regime, namely the emergence of new growth centres. This alleged growth of externalisation has been interpreted as providing an explanation for the rapid growth of business services: in short, producer service employment within industrial enterprises is being replaced by contracting-in the required services from outside [Lewis, 1988; Scott, 1988].

The decentralisation model provides an explanation of the 'growth' of services in terms of labour process changes; there are also researchers who support the importance of externalisation from other perspectives. As a pragmatic response to the exigencies of recession, it has been argued that companies have become more conscious of the cost of their administrative overheads and have cut back their internal service provision and bought in this expertise as required [Howells and Green, 1986; Marshall, 1988]. Similarly it has been suggested that increased technical complexity has made it too costly for firms to retain internal sources [Daniels, 1985]. Complementary to this last point is the possibility that the accrual of specialised skills within an enterprise can create profitable opportunities for the externalisation of these skills [Britton, 1989].

The present article does not seek to deny the existence of externalisation processes. The issue addressed is whether a watershed has been crossed in the attitudes toward service provision away from internal provision. Before proceeding further with this argument, however,

BUSINESS SERVICE GROWTH   5

a firmer definition and description of the externalisation process is required.

Externalisation refers to the shift of a particular set of goods and services from being generated within a firm to outside it [Howells and Green, 1986]. Recent research has concentrated on the employment implications and advantages of externalisation, but as Howells [1989] notes, the process raises more issues. There are multiple motivations influencing the internalisation/externalisation balance and several routes through which a change in this balance might be achieved. It is also possible that externalisation may arise by 'default' where services originate through the innovation of service suppliers in respect of new functions that are bought in from the outset. In the latter case an increase in externalisation occurs without any transfer of activities.

A summary of the motivations for externalisation and the mechanisms by which it might be achieved is given in Table 1. Howells and Green [1986] distinguish three possible strategies: (1) decentralisation to a subsidiary or associate company; (2) devolution of the activity to separate enterprises via licence or franchise agreements; and (3) disintegration where no ownership links are retained. A fourth alternative is also possible whereby the internal service is rationalised with no surviving identity, which is most probable when small units are involved. The decentralisation model is not precise in indicating which of these processes is consistent with the new mode of accumulation, although they can be associated with quite different motivations. Decentralisation may mainly be to facilitate the more extensive marketing of a internal service function that has spare capacity or has developed sufficient expertise to warrant diversification of the group's income base. Disintegration may occur because the service is no longer utilised or to obtain cost savings and/or an enhanced quality of service. Externalisation may reflect a strategic company decision, equally it may result from a management/ worker buy-out. For the purposes of the present paper the focus is on externalisation that causes a transfer of employment across sectors. This will occur when the service is devolved or disintegrated and possibly where it is decentralised depending on the nature of the organisational link retained.

As noted, the focus of the present article is on externalisation as an explanation for the growth of business service employment. It is, however, interesting to note how restructuring trends within the service sector are partly in contradiction to the decentralisation model. This is evident, for example, in the concentration of ownership associated with the development of synergistic combines across complementary activities

6   THE SERVICE INDUSTRIES JOURNAL

TABLE 1

A TYPOLOGY OF SERVICE EXTERNALISATION

Mechanism[1]

Principal motives	Decentralisation	Devolution	Disintegration	Rationalisation
Cost saving		X	X	X
Increased accountability	X	X		
Reduce overheads		X	X	X
Obtain more specialised service			X	X
Improve quality			X	X
Exploit external market potential	X	X		

[1]See text for definition

such as marketing, advertising, public relations and management consultancy [Perry, 1990a]. Another interesting feature of business services is their low use of part time labour [Marshall, 1988].

EMPIRICAL EVIDENCE

Evidence identifying the significance of service subcontracting is limited. Rajan and Pearson [1986] estimated that 43 per cent of business service employment growth in the UK during 1979–85 was the result of externalisation. This finding was derived from ambiguous survey evidence [Perry, 1990b] and a small number of case studies. The employment estimate should, therefore, be treated with some caution. Other surveys of subcontracting activity have found little or no evidence of an increase in this form of production flexibility. Mason *et al.* [1988] reveal in their study of flexible employment strategies in the Southampton region of the English 'sunbelt' that there has been no major increase in subcontracting by manufacturing firms during the 1980s. Marginson *et al.* [cited in Pollert, 1987] in a survey of multi-establishment companies with over 1000 employees in the UK found that 61

BUSINESS SERVICE GROWTH   7

per cent of respondents had made no change in the overall level of subcontracting over the previous four years. A high level of subcontracting was found; 83 per cent of establishment managers reported that they subcontracted at least one service, but this was part of a well-established pattern.

The surveys by Mason *et al.* and Marginson *et al.* agree that cleaning is an activity which has been increasingly externalised. The unique character of the contract cleaning industry needs to be highlighted in explaining this trend. Contract cleaning is dominated by a handful of large multinational companies. With few opportunities to increase labour productivity by capital investment, competition is on the basis of minimum labour costs by reducing the hours and number of cleaners allocated to tasks [Brosnan and Wilkinson, 1989]. The fierce competition results from the ease of entry to the industry which a few large companies are seeking to counter by forcing low profit margins. Once dominance has been established, the surviving firms hope to increase their returns [Brosnan and Wilkinson, 1989]. Organisations which have subcontracted cleaning are, therefore, reaping the economic benefits of a particular stage in the development of the industry. The incipient changes in the structure of contract cleaning, alongside a decline in the quality of the end product, suggests that the recent popularity of contracting-out may not endure.

Similarly, the recent examples of externalisation cited by Howells [1989] mostly comprise the decentralisation of in-house computing departments where particular forces are at work. The motivation has been to participate in a rapidly growing industry rather than to exploit the advantages of 'malleable external linkages'. In some instances the parent group may not even continue to use its subsidiary service operation. Of course, it might be suggested that the growth of computer services results from externalisation by other companies, but the overwhelming trend has been for an increased internalisation of data processing activities [Weil, 1982; Keeble and Kelly, 1986].

If part of the explanation for the recent 'growth' in business services is the decentralisation of these functions to independent service firms, a diminution in business service occupations within manufacturing might be expected. In fact the evidence is far from clear on this point. In the UK, the long-term trend has been for the share of administrative, technical and clerical jobs (ATCs) in manufacturing to increase. Since 1980, there has been an absolute and percentage decline in the number of ATCs in manufacturing, but this coincides with a fall in total manufacturing capacity [Marshall,

8   THE SERVICE INDUSTRIES JOURNAL

1988]. In New Zealand, a similar decline in manufacturing ATCs was recorded during a recession in the early 1980s, subsequently the proportion has increased again [Perry, 1989]. Further investigation of externalisation in New Zealand suggests that recession rather than a re-evaluation of internal services was the main influence on trends in ATCs [Perry, 1990b]. In the latter survey, changes in the mode of procurement of 17 business services were examined amongst Auckland-based manufacturing industries. The survey identified the presence of both internalisation and externalisation processes, but neither was a significant influence on service employment trends. In brief, the main findings were [see Perry, 1990b for further discussion]:

1. Almost half the sample of 145 businesses had externalised expenditure on at least one service, but the shift was rarely more than 10 per cent of the total expenditure on that item;
2. Almost one third of the respondents had internalised more expenditure on at least one service, although once again the extent of the shift was generally modest;
3. Firms undertaking no changes or a combination of greater internalisation and externalisation across different services were the most numerous, accounting for 72 per cent of respondents;
4. Changes in procurement policy were concentrated in five services: data-processing, advertising, road haulage, payroll and accounting. In the case of other services, over 90 per cent of respondents had made no change in the mode of procurement;
5. In two of the five most 'fluid' services, data-processing and accounting, the most significant trend was to internalise more expenditure;
6. Larger firms (over 100 employees) did not have a significantly more active strategy of externalising expenditure, neither were those services accounting for the largest share of a firm's expenditure more likely to be externalised; and
7. As regards an overall strategy towards the procurement of services, the majority indicated that they had no strategy (36.5 per cent) or that each service was reviewed separately (55 per cent). Consequently, those with a consistent policy to externalise or internalise service demands were a small minority (6 per cent and 2.5 per cent respectively).

An estimate of the significance of externalisation within the current employment of Auckland's business service sector was derived from the survey evidence and interviews with service suppliers in three industries. The results indicated that externalisation accounted for around 15 per cent of the employment increase in data processing, 4.5 per cent in engineering and technical consultancies and 13.5 per cent in advertising and other marketing services. Two important comments need to be added to these estimates. First, most of the 'growth' derived from the contracting-out of public services. As in the UK, the externalisation of services from the public sector has been a more significant trend than from private companies. In both countries, however, an increase in subcontracting has been driven by political motives and the goal of privatisation, so that it is misleading to interpret the public and private sectors as responding to the same stimuli [Pollert, 1987]. There is a greater uniformity of pressure upon public services compared with the enormous diversity of considerations affecting private companies [Pinch, 1989]. Second, the estimates related to current employment, rather than the level of employment at the time of externalisation. The latter was often substantially less where a parent company had continued to invest in a decentralised service.

Empirical evidence therefore provides little support to the decentralisation explanation of the rapid growth in business service employment. It is clear that a range of sometimes conflicting influences are shaping internalisation/externalisation decisions. Figure 1 summarises the main factors potentially generating changes in the mode of service procurement, distinguishing between influences that arise internally in the service user organisation and externally, for example through changes in service technology. For some firms, dramatic market changes and the need to increase sensitivity to the changing demands of their customers encourages the internalisation of critical market-related services. Technology has also influenced procurement: on the one hand by expanding the range of services in-house service workers can perform and, on the other hand, creating new demands for external services. The myriad influences at work emphasise the difficulties of conflating a complex problem into a single, uni-directional model of change. The next section outlines four main areas where the decentralisation model may be questioned.

EXTERNALISATION: CONCEPTUAL AND PRACTICAL LIMITATIONS

The reasons for this lack of fit between the decentralisation model and actual patterns of change are addressed at the following levels:

10   THE SERVICE INDUSTRIES JOURNAL

FIGURE 1

INFLUENCES ON SERVICE PROCUREMENT CHANGE

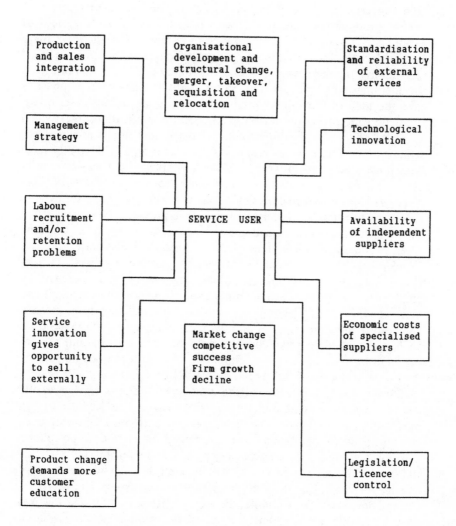

1. the concept of flexibility;
2. the questionable efficiency of subcontracting relationships;
3. the benefits of internalisation; and
4. the nature of technological change.

Flexibility

The suggestion that western capitalism has entered a new phase of organisation based around a more decentralised, flexible system of production has attracted a wide range of criticism. On one level there is considerable doubt that mass production industries have experienced any relative demise, especially when Japanese as well as western mass production is taken into account [Sayer, 1989]. Pollert [1987] emphasises how the idea of flexibility contains an uneasy alliance of description, prediction and prescription with strong political motivations intertwined by those advocates seeking to convert the model into a management strategy. The internal contradictions in the concept of flexibility have been illustrated by MacInnes [1987], for example in the way job security for core workers may conflict with the drive to contract out work. One response of firms to recession has been to use their own 'core' staff whom they wish to retain to undertake tasks done previously by contractors. This implies that subcontracting might fall in a recession, at the time when the financial advantages of using outside suppliers are greatest. Conversely, in a boom subcontractors can exploit a sellers' market, encouraging internalisation. Flexibility may be a goal pursued by employers, but they have many other goals which often cut across it and limit its practical application. Finally, the alleged flexibility of modern technology and associated suitability for small scale production has been challenged. Flexible production systems tend to be costly and require continuous operation to be profitable and for both reasons lie beyond the investment capacity of small enterprise [Schonberger, 1987].

A more specific difficulty in the context of business services is the distinction between core and peripheral activities. The decentralisation model proposes that firms seek to differentiate between a core workforce employed on a permanent and privileged basis and a peripheral workforce comprising part time, temporary and subcontracted labour. In other words, a strategic choice is made regarding the businesses' core activity and employment conditions are made accordingly. But the 'core' can and does shift. For example, the core of British Rail's workforce was once its drivers and signalmen; today platform attendants and station personnel are the key groups because of the importance attached to customer relations [Pollert, 1987]. On the other hand, there are key skills such as legal advice, without which a company could not function, that are subcontracted. In short, concepts such as core and periphery hold little concrete substance.

Efficiency and subcontracting

The capacity to internalise and to centralise service provision has been viewed as one reason for the success of multi-divisional corporations [Williamson, 1981]. Internalisation overcomes the risk of 'adverse selection' associated with the uncertainties of small-firm contract relationships. The problem of quality control is particularly severe in relation to service purchases [Holmstrom, 1985]. Three 'moral hazards' jeopardise service purchases: ascertaining the quality of the service, the inability to observe the actions of the provider and difficulty in establishing an incentive to obtain the desired level of effort [Holmstrom, 1985]. In the case of physical goods, delivery standards can be more readily established, overcoming these three hazards. Moreover, where quality can be judged, services are still less easily returned for improvement than physical commodities.

As a consequence, the contracting-out of services is favoured only under certain specific conditions. Marshall [1989] identified a number of principles governing the mode of service procurement that are similar to those identified earlier by Williamson [1979]

1. Vital or commercially confidential services tend to be carried out in-house.
2. Services demanding specialist knowledge or expertise tend to be internalised where the knowledge or skills held by the user are important in the service, or if the user has evolved expertise in the particular service.
3. Infrequently used services tend to be contracted out because they do not justify an in-house capacity.
4. Unpredictable service needs tend to be more internalised than routine or programmed services.
5. Where it is important to ascertain precise costs, external contracts tend to be favoured as they provide a clear measure of expenditure.

The Advantages of Internalisation

Recent trends have increased the advantages of integrating production, marketing and after-sales services [Burstein, 1986]. Product differentiation strategies are now based partly on the conjunction of material and non material goods [Enderwick, 1989]. This development is illustrated by the advances in computing which have rendered technical aspects of the hardware less critical influences on user purchases than the associated software. As a consequence, hardware manufacturers are internalising software activities [Keeble and Kelly, 1986]. In the case of other innovatory products which require significant market-making expenditures and buyer education, producers hold unique knowledge of their product. For reasons of economy and to protect their expertise, the producer is the best equipped to undertake buyer instruction [Enderwick 1987]. The application of technology to service activities and the creation of significant economies of scale implies that large enterprises could reap major gains by internalising these functions: this has already occurred in the case of financial services and oil companies [Enderwick, 1987] and a number of large enterprises with major advertising expenditures are internalising the purchase of media space [Perry, 1990a].

If subcontracting was increasing for the alleged advantages of exploiting a more peripheral workforce this would imply not only an increase of external service purchases but also a qualitative change in the nature of subcontracting relationships. In relation to advertising, for example, a firm may subcontract separately each element in the production of advertising (market research, copywriting, production, campaign organisation and monitoring of the impact) or it may employ a single agency. The former approach more closely relates to the flexibility model in that inputs are purchased as required from fragmented suppliers with minimum bargaining power. Where a single agency is used it can become a powerful influence over company strategy. Consequently the search for flexibility in service inputs may be obtained through changes in the nature of subcontracting, rather than absolute levels of subcontracting.

Technological Change

Technology plays a critical role in shaping the balance of internalisation and externalisation and here again the main impact is to enhance the fluidity of choices rather than to create a uni-directional flow of change. Of course, judging the impacts of technical change is hazardous because the initial use of new technology is rarely its ultimate configuration. The economics of computer technology, for example, initially encouraged bureau services but with the cheapening and simplification of computer technology, demand has shifted towards in-house facilities [Weil, 1982]. Similarly, while office technology was directed originally at back office functions, it is increasingly being used to integrate all office functions and to serve/sell to customers [Daniels, 1987]. It seems, therefore, that technology has expanded the range of in-house services whilst

14   THE SERVICE INDUSTRIES JOURNAL

also expanding the demands for external services to assist in the implementation and maintenance of office technology.

CONCLUSION

The main message of this article is that the exploration of externalisation and its contribution to employment change needs to be addressed in less sweeping terms than the decentralisation model. The model provides inadequate guidance on the relative efficiency of internal/external service provision. Traditionally these problems may have been answered within a transaction cost framework that assessed the relative economic costs and benefits of internal/external purchases. This approach has limitations as cost structures are difficult to determine in absolute terms outside the organisational context in which firms operate [Sayer, 1989]. For example, the vastly different organisation of Japanese and western economies, with the former's much greater preponderance of subcontracting to small firms, reflects organisational forms rather than contrasting transaction costs. This alerts us to the need to study service employment in the context of the structure of their national economies. The proportion of internalised services varies between countries, presumably reflecting traditions, social institutions and the varying demand and capacity for in-house staff within manufacturing. No one common factor or development sequence is able to explain the extent or growth of producer services, instead a combination of influences connected to the economic, demographic, historical and institutional context require identification. These influences can best be revealed through micro level studies across a wide range of services and user organisations.

There is one change in the social institutional context which is currently affecting the provision of services in many countries; namely the withdrawal of the state from direct participation in many service activities. One aspect of this has been to enforce the subcontracting of services, particularly in such activities as cleaning, transport, catering and computing. The investigation of this experience provides the opportunity for an assessment of the impact of externalisation. Work in this area has so far concentrated on the relative quality of employment conditions pre and post externalisation [Spencer, 1984; Mohan, 1988]. Research into the efficiency consequences of externalising services should provide more realistic insights into the benefits, and costs of increased subcontracting. This evaluation should encompass quality and equity considerations as they are felt by the communities affected by the changes in provision.

The changes occurring in the public sector are one aspect of the policy

BUSINESS SERVICE GROWTH   15

importance of studying externalisation/internalisation processes. There are other economic policy consequences across a range of issues. Will, for example, the liberalisation of international trade in services affect the internal/external procurement of services amongst multinational enterprises? Internal service transfers are currently a substantial, but unmeasured component of international exchange. What are the trends toward more local service purchases in overseas markets and can host country governments manipulate these trends to their own advantage? Is the distribution of service activities within firms changing with a shift of occupations towards market areas and away from head offices? Is externalisation encouraging a more dispersed distribution of business service employment? What are the economic benefits of large service contractors based on low-wage labour? How can workers within contracting organisations be protected from marginal employment conditions? Such questions underline the importance of a much closer examination of externalisation/internalisation processes.

REFERENCES

Britton, S., 1989, 'Understanding the Service Economy: A Preliminary Review of Theory', University of Auckland: Occasional Paper No. 24, Department of Geography.
Brosnan, P. and F. Wilkinson, 1989, 'Low Pay and Industrial Relations: the Case of Contract Cleaning', *New Zealand Journal of Industrial Relations*, Vol. 14, No. 1.
Burstein, M., 1986, 'The Business Service Industry Sets Pace in Employment Growth', *Monthly Labour Review*, April.
Daniels, P., 1985, *Service Industries a Geographical Appraisal*, London: Methuen.
Daniels, P., 1987, 'Technology and Metropolitan Office Location', *Service Industries Journal*, Vol. 7, No. 3.
Daniels, P., A. Leyshon and N. Thrift, 1988, 'Trends in the Growth and Location of Professional Producer Services: UK Property Consultants', *Tijdschrift voor Econ en Soc Geografie*, Vol. 79, No. 3.
Enderwick, P., 1987, 'The Strategy and Structure of Service Sector Multinationals: Implications for Host Regions', *Regional Studies*, Vol.21, No. 3.
Enderwick, P., 1989, 'Some Economics of Service-Sector Multinational Enterprises', in Enderwick, P. (ed.), *Multinational Service Firms*, London: Routledge.
Gershuny, J. and I. Miles, 1983, *The Service Economy: The Transformation of Employment in Industrial Societies*, New York: Praeger.
Gershuny, J. and I. Miles, 1985, 'Towards a New Social Economics', in Roberts, B., R. Finnegan and D. Gaille (eds.), *New Approaches to Economic Life*, Manchester: Manchester University Press.
Holmstrom, B., 1985, 'The provision of services in the market economy', in Inman, R. (ed.), *Managing the Service Economy: Prospects and Problems*, Cambridge: Cambridge University Press.
Howells, J. and A. Green, 1986, 'Location, Technology, and Industrial Organisation in UK Services', *Progress in Planning*, Vol. 26, No. 2.
Howells, J., 1989, 'Externalisation and the Formation of New Industrial Operations: A Neglected Dimension in the Dynamics of Industrial Location', *Area*, Vol. 20, No. 3.
Keeble, D. and T. Kelly, 1986, 'New Firms and High Technology Industry in the United Kingdom: The Case of Computer Electronics', in Keeble, D. and E. Wever (eds.) *New Firms and Regional Development in Europe*, London: Croom Helm.

16   THE SERVICE INDUSTRIES JOURNAL

Lewis, J., 1988, 'Services Post Industrial Transformation or Flexible Production', in Marshall, J. *Services Uneven Development* Oxford: Oxford University Press.

MacInnes, J., 1987, *Thatcherism at Work*, Milton Keynes: Open University Press.

Mark, J., 1982, 'Measuring Productivity in Service Industries', *Monthly Labour Review*, June.

Marshall, J., 1988, *Services Uneven Development*, Oxford: Oxford University Press

Marshall, J., 1989, 'Corporate Reorganisation and the Geography of Services: Evidence from the Motor Vehicle Aftermarket in the West Midlands Region of the UK', *Regional Studies*, Vol. 23, No. 2.

Mason, C., C. Pinch and S. Witt, 1989, 'Inside the Sunbelt": Industrial Change in Southampton', in M. Breheny and P. Congdon (eds.), *Growth and Change in the South East of England*, London Papers in Regional Science 20, London: Pion.

Mohan, J., 1988, 'Spatial Aspects of Health Care Employment in Britain: 1. Aggregate Trends', *Environment and Planning A*, Vol. 20, No. 1.

Perry, M., 1989, 'New Zealand's Service Economy 1956–1986; A Preliminary Examination of Employment and Output Trends', University of Auckland: Occasional Paper No. 22, Department of Geography.

Perry, M., 1990a, 'The Internationalisation of Advertising', *Geoforum*, Vol. 22, No. 1.

Perry, M., 1990b, 'Business Service Specialisation and Regional Economic Change', *Regional Studies*, Vol. 24, No. 3.

Pinch, S., 1989, 'The Restructuring Thesis and the Study of Public Services', *Environment and Planning A*, Vol. 21, No. 7.

Piore, M. and C. Sabel, 1984, *The Second Industrial Divide*, New York: Basic Books.

Pollert, A., 1987, 'The "Flexible Firm": A Model in Search of Reality (or a Policy in Search of a Practice)?', University of Warwick, Warwick Papers in Industrial Relations 19, School of Industrial and Business Studies.

Rajan, A. and R. Pearson, 1986, *UK Occupational and Employment Trends to 1990*, London: Butterworths.

Rowthorn, B. and J. Wells, 1987, *De-industrialisation and Foreign Trade*, Cambridge: Cambridge University Press.

Sayer, A., 1989, 'Postfordism in Question', *International Journal of Urban and Regional Research*, Vol. 13, No. 4.

Schonberger, R., 1987, 'Frugal Manufacturing', *Harvard Business Review*, Vol. 87.

Scott, A., 1988, 'Flexible Production Systems and Regional Development: The Rise of New Industrial Spaces in North America and Western Europe', *International Journal of Urban and Regional Studies*, Vol. 22, No. 2.

Spencer, K., 1984, 'Assessing Alternative Forms of Service Provision', *Local Government Studies*, Vol. 10. March/April.

Weil, U., 1982, *Information Systems in the 80s*, Englewood Cliffs: Prentice Hall.

Williamson, O., 1979, 'Transaction Cost Economics: The Governance of Contractural Relations', *Journal of Law and Economics*, Vol. 22, No. 2.

Williamson, O., 1981, 'The Modern Corporation: Origins, Evolution, Attributes', *Journal of Economic Literature*, Vol. 19, No. 4.

[20]

Consultancy Services and the Urban Hierarchy in Western Europe[1]

P.W. Daniels, J.H.J. Van Dinteren and M.C. Monnoyer

Abstract

A cross-national survey of the relationship between the evolving organization and structure of consultancy service enterprises and the urban hierarchy in Europe has been undertaken. Primate cities in Europe are still the preeminent foci for business services performing strong national and international control. The relationship between markets for consultancy services and the urban hierarchy is complex, but it is possible to suggest a typology of firms on the basis of client characteristics and location. Caution is necessary about assuming that the provision of consultancy services through networks is organized along hierarchical lines that mirror administrative hierarchies.

Introduction

In a growing number of publications the importance of the service sector for national and regional economic development is stressed (for example, see Beyers, 1989; Daniels and Moulaert, 1991; Illeris, 1989; Marshall *et al.*, 1988). In recent years the research efforts in this field have grown significantly. In almost all cases the studies are concentrated on the national level because it is difficult to collect comparable official statistics for different countries, and the collection of primary data is almost impossible. Nevertheless, the international perspective is of growing importance because of the internationalization of the service sector, the transition to an integrated European market post-1992, and the inevitable need to explore economic processes and their associated spatial outcomes at the wider European level. In an effort to cooperate internationally a number of researchers have established a network: the 'Réseau Européen Services et Espace' (RESER) which was founded in 1989. In order to test the scope for collaborative research the members of the network embarked on a cross-national survey in 1990 of the relationship between the evolving organization and structure of consultancy service enterprises and the urban hierarchy in Europe. It is expected that not only will cities near the top of the urban hierarchy attract a disproportionate share of intermediate services, they will also tend to attract those service organizations that are larger than competitors lower down the hierarchy as well as attracting firms that command much larger market areas, including those serviced by intermediate services in lower order urban centres. With respect to the differences between [1731] countries, the study was limited to establishing a few significant differences in characteristics. The number of respondent consultancy firms in each country was too small (see below) to carry out a cross-national analysis into the functioning of these companies.

The survey was focused on a selected number of consultancy services in cities at different hierarchical levels. Consultancy services that are strongly orientated towards other firms (business to business) were chosen: management, engineering, and computer software consultants. We focused on establishments in three main types of cities (Figure 1). First, the primate city in each country. Next, two cities selected from the next-largest five cities in each country (ranked by population); the so-called second-tier cities. Finally two cities in the range 50 000 –100 000 inhabitants were chosen: one city located in an old industrial region and the other located in a rural region. These two cities are referred to as third-tier cities.

An enterprise register from which a representative random sample could be drawn was only available for the Netherlands. It was therefore not possible to draw a representative sample. Hence, it was decided to include an equal number of establishments in each type of city in the survey. The intention was to hold six interviews within each selected service group in a particular type of city. The six establishments in each group were further subdivided into two establishments serving mainly the regional market, two providing services to national clients, and two operating in the international market. As we have selected three groups of consultancy services and three types of cities the intended number of interviews was 54 for each country. Consultancy firms, traced from diverse sources, were initially approached by telephone. This was to identify those establishments that satisfied the above criteria, a process that continued until the full quota was obtained.

Because of the selection of establishments as described above, the survey is not by any means representative of the universe of consultancy service establishments in the selected cities. Because of this, at least three relationships between variables cannot be discussed later in this paper:

1. the geographical market in relation to type of city;
2. type of city in relation to the composition of the consultancy service sector;
3. composition of the consultancy service sector in relation to the geographical market of these establishments.

This was unfortunate, particularly when this concerned the geographical market (in which a triple division was made into local or regional, national, and international), and certainly in relation to the centrally placed question about the meaning of urban hierarchy in the functioning of business service firms. This allows the question to remain unanswered about whether the percentage share of the market areas in turnover shows differences between, among other things, the three separate urban levels.

The aim of taking 54 interviews per country, and the intended division of each group by the market served, has not been achieved for every country (Table 1). There are 292 valid cases available for analysis. Denmark, Spain, and the United Kingdom are overrepresented. In Denmark, only the group of computer consultants were approached. In

- ●   Primate city   (population 692 000–8 707 000)
- ●   Second-tier city   (population 191 000–3 061 000)
- ·   Third-tier city   (population 24 000–108 000)

Figure 1   Cities included in the survey.

the Netherlands, the population was nearly twice as large as intended.

More important than the differences between countries is the question about whether the controlling variables in the setup of the data file have achieved the ratios aimed for.

Table 1.   Distribution of respondents by type of city and by country

City type	Denmark	Italy	France	UK	Netherlands	Spain	All countries
Primate	36	34	30	27	25	40	30
Second-tier[a]	36	33	43	63	31	42	39
Third-tier[a]	28	33	26	10	44	18	31
Total	100	100	100	100	100	100	100
Number of respondents	14	52	53	30	103	14	292

Note: [a] Two such cities chosen in each country.

If the study had been organized on the basis of a random sample, we might have expected primate cities to have the majority of respondent establishments. However, because the survey method required a specific number [1732] of establishments in each city, and also because of the varying inclinations of establishments in different kinds of city to respond, second-tier cities have a relatively larger share than intended, at the expense of primate and third-tier cities (Table 1). Furthermore, the consultancy firms serving an international market are somewhat underrepresented, with a share of 26 per cent, and there is a larger share of nationally active companies (43 per cent) than intended. There are also rather fewer management consultancy firms (30 per cent) than intended (33 per cent), and engineering consultancy firms, with a share of 39 per cent, are somewhat overrepresented. [1733]

Consultancy Firms in European Cities: A Profile

As expected on the basis of secondary data on the size distribution of service sector establishments in general, small firms (1–10 employees) predominate (39 per cent), with large firms (more than 50 employees) composing almost 25 per cent of the respondents. However, it is possible that there is some bias towards larger establishments because of the effort put into segmenting respondents into those with local, national, and international markets located in each of the cities targeted for the survey in each country.

There is a significant difference between the type of firm (management, engineering, or computer software consultants) in relation to the number of employees (size). Engineering consultancies and computer software consultancies are considerably larger than the average (30 per cent have more than 50 people employed) whereas 52 per cent of the management consultancies employ fewer than ten persons. The relationship between size of establishment and market served is statistically significant; in other words, large establishments are more likely to service international markets (Table 2). It should be noted, however, that one in three international market establishments is small (ten employees or fewer). Some 43 per cent of the large establishments are in primate cities, and overall there is a statistically significant relationship between type of city (primate, second-tier, third-tier) and size of establishment (Table 3). [1734]

Table 2.   Market served, by size of the establishment (number of employees)

Market type	Size			Total
	1–10	11–50	>50	
International	21	18	43	26
National	40	52	36	43
Local or regional	39	30	21	31
Total	100	100	100	100
Number of respondents	113	98	72	283

Table 3.   Type of city (hierarchical level) and size of the establishment (number of employees)

City type	Size			Total
	1–10	11–50	>50	
Primate	24	28	43	30
Second-tier	34	46	36	39
Third-tier	42	26	21	31
Total	100	100	100	100
Number of respondents	113	98	72	283

Organizational Status

Some 43 per cent of the firms in the study are autonomous (that is, single-site, independent organizations). The remainder are multi-site firms; the majority are national headquarters (28 per cent), followed by international headquarters (17 per cent), and branches (12 per cent). Organizational status and the city location of respondent establishments also broadly conform with expectations. Autonomous offices are more likely to be located in second-tier and third-tier cities (Table 4). But it is not clear why in some countries there are

Table 4.   Status of consultancy service establishments by type of city

Status	City type			Total
	primate	second-tier	third-tier	
International headquarters	18	20	12	17
National headquarters	40	23	22	28
Branches	7	14	13	12
Autonomous offices	35	43	52	43
Total	100	100	100	100
Number of respondents	89	112	90	291

relatively so many international and national headquarters establishments in third-tier cities. Denmark, Italy and France have no international headquarters in such cities, but the United Kingdom has one, the Netherlands four, and Spain six. Perhaps this is caused by the distance between the cities selected and the national economic centres of gravity, or it might be explained by historical inertia (that is, some of the firms started business in the cities concerned and have continued to exert control from the same locations, even if they have grown and diversified at national or international level).

There is also a highly significant difference in the size of establishments with respect to organizational status: 61 per cent of the establishments that employ 50 or more people are (inter)national headquarters, and 67 per cent of those employing ten persons or fewer represent autonomous firms; 61 per cent of the establishments control offices at other locations. Organizational status influences the likelihood that an establishment will control other offices. Four out of every five international headquarters control other offices, whereas only one in three branches performs this role. National headquarters occupy an intermediate position. In the present sample there is only a marginal difference in the propensity of establishments to control other offices according to where they are positioned in the urban hierarchy. In another study, however, differences in these organizational networks between French regions were much more pronounced (Léo and Philippe, 1991). In our study the number of establishments and employees controlled is highest in primate cities; the differences between second-tier and third-tier cities in this respect is of almost no importance (Table 5). Because the primate cities also have a larger number of office establishments than the other types of cities, they remain the most important centres of control. By comparison with second-tier and third-tier cities the proportion of establishments and jobs abroad that are controlled by offices in the primate cities is also relatively higher (Table 5). [1735]

Table 5. The control of other offices, by type of city

City type	Establishments controlling other offices (%)	Mean number of establishments controlled	Mean number of employees controlled	Offices abroad[a]	
				establishments	employees
Primate	62	5.2	229	25	16
Second-tier	63	2.4	44	8	2
Third-tier	58	2.4	34	17	9
Total	61	3.4	109	21	13

Note: [a] As a percentage of all offices or employees controlled.

On the basis of the complete data provided by 107 respondents, we can say that an establishment that is controlling offices elsewhere typically controls one establishment in the region in which it is located, two establishments elsewhere in the country, and the equivalent of less than one establishment abroad. Overall, therefore, each controlling establishment is responsible (statistically) for 3.4 establishments elsewhere. The total number of offices controlled within regions is 100, within countries 211, and abroad 67, giving a total of 352 offices controlled by the respondent establishments. These offices employ 11 095 workers, of which 50 per cent are located in establishments elsewhere in the country, 37 per cent in establishments controlled within the region, and 13 per cent are controlled in offices located abroad. There is an inverse relationship between the number of persons per establishment controlled by the firms in the survey and location. The establishments controlled within regions average 42 persons per establishment, 28 per establishment in the country, and 21 per establishment controlled from abroad.

Employment

The establishments in the survey employed a total of 19 137 staff with an average size of 68 employees and a median of 16; the largest employs 2035. The median proportion of female employees is 25 per cent, with a mean of 29 per cent, and a maximum of 100 per cent. The median proportion of nonpermanent employees within an establishment is only 1 per cent, with a mean of 13 per cent. Some 30 per cent of the engineering consultancies employ 50 or more staff, compared with 35 per cent of computer software consultancies and 15 per cent of management consultancies. As noted earlier, management consultancies are dominated by small establishments, with 52 per cent employing ten persons or fewer.

As a general rule the larger the market served, the larger the number of employees in an establishment. The average number of employees in establishments operating internationally is 84 (mean 29), for offices operating on the national market it is 67 (mean 18), and 55 (mean 11) for offices serving clients mainly in their own region. Thus, the average international headquarters has 147 employees, followed by national headquarters (98), branch offices (45), and autonomous offices (25). These differences are mainly caused by the presence of some large establishments within the categories distinguished here, for the medians are almost the same for the first three categories (some 40 employees) whereas for autonomous offices the median size is seven employees. Because there is to some extent a relationship between status and type of city the largest offices are found in the primate cities (mean 126, median 31), followed by the second-tier cities (47 and 16, respectively), and the third-tier cities (37 and nine, respectively).

In the average establishment, 13 per cent of all employees work part time. There is no significant difference between the proportion of nonpermanent employees in individual establishments and in the firm as a whole. The higher up the urban hierarchy an establishment is located the more likely it is to have a higher proportion of nonpermanent employees. This is possibly a product of labour-market conditions, especially of competition between employers and the greater opportunities for workplace mobility in the more diverse business environments of the larger cities, where there is a greater choice of jobs, especially for the more skilled workers. [1736] It is also the case that in some countries nonpermanent employees may cost less to employ than permanent employees; social security obligations may be reduced, for example. It is also likely to be more difficult to get temporary specialist staff in second-tier and third-tier cities and there is therefore a tendency to employ permanent staff if at all possible. Management consultancies employ a higher proportion of nonpermanent staff than the other two activities, perhaps because these offices are smaller and tend to bring in specialists to fulfil contracts on a temporary basis as they cannot afford to retain such staff on a permanent basis.

Linked with the higher proportion of nonpermanent employees in primate cities is the much higher proportion of female employees in the same establishments. This may reflect the greater maturity of primate-city labour markets. The share of female employees shows no relationship with occupational structure, but there is a significant difference in the share of female employees according to the type of firm, reaching the high level of 43 per cent in management consultancy firms. The share of female employees also varies significantly between countries. Only 22 per cent of employees in the Dutch firms are female, compared with 42 per cent in Italy and 39 per cent in the United Kingdom.

Turnover

It was anticipated that the collection of financial information about individual firms would be difficult. In the event, the level of response was better than expected, with only 44 respondents (15 per cent) failing to provide data on turnover and expenditure. Turnover is positively correlated with size of establishment, but the differences in average turnover by type of company and type of city are not statistically significant. Again, however, these averages are affected by a small number of establishments which have a very high turnover. Use of the median for turnover by country shows that Spanish establishments have the highest turnover, followed by Danish and French firms, and a third group comprising Italian, UK, and Dutch firms. Even more interesting is turnover per employee, which shows a range from 76 000 ecu in Italy, to 145 000 ecu in Spain. These national differences in turnover do not change significantly if the values are weighed to take account of nonpermanent employees, even though the turnover per employee does increase slightly (it is assumed that nonpermanent employees work half a week).

Contrary to expectations, branches perform better than either international or national headquarters and significantly better than autonomous offices (Table 6). The majority of branch offices employ staff engaged primarily in the delivery and support of services to clients whereas office staff at headquarters are largely concerned with the internal administration of the firm and its more general orientation to the external business environment. Turnover per employee in branches is 340 000 ecu compared with 125 000 ecu and 106 000 ecu, respectively, for international and national headquarters. It is interesting to note that in a study of business service firms in intermediate cities in the Netherlands, branches also had the highest turnover per employee, followed by headquarters and autonomous offices (Van Dinteren, 1989). Similar conclusions have been arrived at in French studies: branches had a 20–50 per cent higher turnover than autonomous firms (for example, see Léo and Philippe, 1991).

The difference between multi-site firms and autonomous offices is also very striking (Table 6). Autonomous offices have higher overheads than branches and related multi-site firms (as these will, at least in part, be supported by headquarters), but they must work with smaller margins than branches just to survive. Branches can bill clients at levels reflecting the national or international image or reputation of the parent firm. It may be,

Table 6. Mean and median turnover (in thousands of ecu), by establishment and per employee

	Turnover		Turnover per employee
	mean	median	
Type of company			
Management consultants	6 649	696	69
Engineering consultants	7 666	1522	114
Computer software consultants	13 616	1395	165
Significance	ns		ns
Type of city			
Primate	21 780	2609	118
Second-tier	3 989	1084	79
Third-tier	3 096	580	158
Significance	ns		ns
Country			
Denmark	55 885	2500	119
Italy	3 087	600	76
France	3 922	1333	105
United Kingdom	25 521	772	75
Netherlands	3 592	783	142
Spain	13 571	3436	145
Significance	*		ns
Status			
International headquarters	16 074	3049	125
National headquarters	17 639	1791	106
Branches	8 643	4345	340
Autonomous offices	1 416	394	68
Significance	*		**
Size (employees)			
1–10	762	249	135
11–50	2 361	1455	95
>50	27 709	9348	115
Significance	**		ns
Total	9 238	116	126

Note: ** significant at 0.01 level; * significant at 0.05 level; ns, not significant.

of course, that branch offices are simply more [1737] efficient than autonomous firms. If a small autonomous firm is having to respond to new tasks every time it is difficult to contemplate that firm charging fees with a large margin based on its reputation for earlier (similar) work.

Changes in the Supply of Consultancy Services

The typical consultancy service firm became established at its present location during the late 1970s (mean 1978). The mode year, however, is 1985. Either the establishments in the survey are relatively youthful or a number have changed location recently. This would accord with other evidence that business services in general have mainly been a growth phenomenon of the 1980s (for example, see Elfring, 1988). This being the case, it is interesting to establish how dynamic they actually are by using changes in the services which they provide as an index. Although some caution is necessary, because there was no time limit specified, 28 per cent of the respondents indicated that the services they provided had changed since the establishment first began operating from its present location. Most involved [1738] diversification, either within the same area of business (33 per cent) or into other, possibly new or different, services (27 per cent). Twenty two per cent of the firms indicated that they had become more specialized, and 25 per cent had even attempted to change their core service. It seems that the favoured response to changes in markets and to competition has been diversification of output rather than changes of direction or attempts to identify niches. This also corroborates the findings of other researchers who have explored the organizational development strategies of intermediate service firms (Dunning, 1989; Leyshon *et al.*, 1988). In many cases, acquisition and merger have largely led to increased diversification rather than to greater specialization.

The propensity to diversify the services supplied from individual establishments is not related to type of company, type of city, or organizational status. There are, however, significant differences according to the market served, with national market offices showing the smallest number of changes (20 per cent) compared with an above-average 37 per cent of international market offices and 29 per cent of local or regional offices. Perhaps local or regional market offices need to be more flexible than is indicated by the data; they do not occupy the established market niches of national or international market firms, which can afford some of the risks associated with flexibility. It is clear, however, that autonomous offices tend to be much more conservative than their larger, multi-site counterparts. But this is, of course, the opposite of the hypothesis discussed earlier concerning the relationship between propensity to make changes and the market that is served. It seems, then, that in the context of the development of consultancy services and the European urban hierarchy there is no statistically significant relationship between change in the supply of consultancy services and type of city in which an establishment is located.

Geographical Markets for Consultancy Services

In selecting companies, the aim has been for an equal share of consultancy firms that claim to be regionally, nationally, or internationally active. If one looks at the actual division of the turnover among markets served, this does not mean that it definitely leads to equal shares. It seems that the regional market contributes 54 per cent on average to the total turnover, 29 per cent is contributed from the parent city, and, in addition, 25 per cent from the rest of the region. The national market (excluding the region) has a share of 38 per cent and the international market has 8 per cent. It appears from Table 7 that the companies who see themselves as 'operating internationally', achieve an average of 27 per cent of their turnover abroad.

Table 7. Typology of companies on the basis of market sales (specified by respondent) according to market served

Market	Local or regional	National	International	Total
Parent city	51	19	19	29
Regional	36	21	19	25
National	12	59	35	38
International	1	1	27	8
Total	100	100	100	100
Number of respondents	85	113	71	269

Some establishments claim to have no income from clients in the home city (8 per cent of all firms), 18 per cent claim no income from the region, 15 per cent have no income from the national market, and 64 per cent have no income from the international market. Notably, some 10 per cent of establishments obtained 20 per cent or more of their total turnover in the [1739] last financial year from international clients. These figures suggest that, in general, more than 50 per cent of turnover comes from outside the region in which an establishment is located. As in other studies, this shows that business services are exported nationally (for example, see Beyers *et al.*, 1986; Marshall, 1983; Van Dinteren, 1987, 1989) and to a growing extent at the international level (for example, see Leyshon *et al.*, 1988; Marshall *et al.*, 1988). By doing so, these firms undoubtedly contribute to the economic development of the city and region in which they are located.

This contribution is not dependent on the size of the consultancy firm in the local economy. As indicated earlier with regard to the market served, small firms do have international clients: 7 per cent of the turnover of firms employing ten employees or fewer is attributable to international clients compared with 13 per cent of firms employing 50 or more. This difference is not as large as might be expected from the size range of firms in the survey. Moreover, 41 per cent of the turnover of small establishments is attributable to clients outside the region. This must be encouraging for second-tier and third-tier cities. Nevertheless, if measured in absolute terms, the contribution of large firms towards the local and regional economy is still the most important.

The key variables accounting for some significant differences in the geographical spread of markets are the country, the status of establishments, and the market served (see Table 8).

Table 8. Market served, by country, establishment status, size, and type of city

	Parent city	Region	National	International	Total	Number of respondents
Country						
Denmark	13	22	62	3	100	13
Italy	39	27	28	6	100	52
France	30	30	34	6	100	51
United Kingdom	32	23	29	16	100	23
Netherlands	20	24	47	9	100	93
Spain	42	22	32	5	100	37
Significance	**	ns	**	ns		
Status						
International headquarters	31	20	36	13	100	44
National headquarters	26	21	42	11	100	76
Branch offices	30	36	30	4	100	31
Autonomous offices	31	27	38	5	100	117
Significance	ns	**	ns	*		
Size (employees)						
1–10	32	26	34	7	100	106
11–50	31	25	40	4	100	90
>50	22	24	41	13	100	66
Significance	*	ns	ns	*		
Type of city						
Primate	32	19	38	11	100	82
Second-tier	29	27	39	5	100	102
Third-tier	27	29	37	7	100	85
Significance	ns	**	ns	*		

Note: see Table 6.

However, the influence of these variables varies, depending on the kind of market served. Thus, intercountry variations are most marked in relation [1740] to the home-city market and the national distribution of clients. The share of international clients contributing to turnover does not vary significantly between countries. An overrepresentation of the regional market is characteristic of branches because they are an integral part of the regional network strategy of firms. Headquarters, both national and international, are orientated rather less towards the regional market and more towards national and international markets.

There are also differences in the division according to type of city, particularly in the regional and international share of the turnover. The international share is, as expected, highest in the primate city. The second-tier and third-tier cities have a higher than average regional orientation, but these lower-ranking cities also have firms exporting abroad. If we had not intended to select an equal division of regional, national, and international companies, then the differences between the three divisions of cities would probably have been larger, so much so that the role of the primate cities in national and international markets would have been emphasized, in contrast to the third-tier cities. Research on business services in the Netherlands, on the basis of a representative random sample, shows the occurrence of internationalization outside the metropolitan areas. Among the business service firms in the four largest cities, 47 per cent export their services. In the rest of the metropolitan area (the Randstad) this is 43 per cent, in the intermediate zone bordering the Randstad it is 31 per cent, and in the remainder of the Netherlands 27 per cent. An average business-service firm in one of the four largest cities in the Randstad will obtain 13 per cent of its turnover from sales to foreign purchasers. Outside the metropolitan area, this is 9 per cent, without any great differences between the regions concerned. Furthermore, it appears that during the past few years an increasing number of business firms outside the metropolitan region have begun to operate in foreign markets (Van Dinteren, 1988).

In relation to the actual countries where international clients are located, there does appear to be a distance-decay effect and/or an EC–non-EC division of international clients. Thus, the countries most frequently mentioned as the locations for international clients are Belgium, West Germany, the United Kingdom, Scandinavia and France. Outside Europe, the United States, South East Asia, Africa, and South America are the most frequently cited client locations (Figure 2). At present, Eastern Europe is conspicuous by its absence, with only three respondents citing clients in that area, but this will very likely change during the 1990s. As might be expected, the principal locations of international clients for firms grouped by home country do show differences, and a distance-decay effect is apparent. Hence, Danish computer service firms have most of their international clients in Scandinavia or in West Germany, whereas most of the international clients of the French consultancies are in West Germany, Belgium, Iberia, or in regions of the world where there are colonial connections, such as Africa in the case of France or South East Asia in the case of the Netherlands. For the United Kingdom and the Netherlands, the United States is an important source of international business, but it is a relatively insignificant market for the respondent establishments in the other countries in this study.

An examination of turnover by status of clients in the national markets of each establishment shows that 45 per cent are local (autonomous) firms, 21 per cent are headquarters, 20 per cent are in public administration, and 14 per cent are branches. Engineering consultancies have a relatively higher proportion of turnover resulting from public administration (27 per cent). To some extent there is a relationship between status of client and type of city in which the consultancy service establishment is situated. Thus, offices in third-tier cities have a higher proportion of clients that are local firms (56 per cent); the equivalent proportion is much lower in primate cities (33 per cent). Such an inverse relationship exists for headquarters; 31 per cent of the turnover of consultancy service [1741] offices in primate cities comes from headquarters. In second-tier cities this is 22 per cent and 11 per cent in third-tier cities. As a general rule, small consultancy firms have the largest proportion of local clients whereas the large establishments have a greater proportion of public firms and headquarters as clients. The status of clients also shows some significant variations in

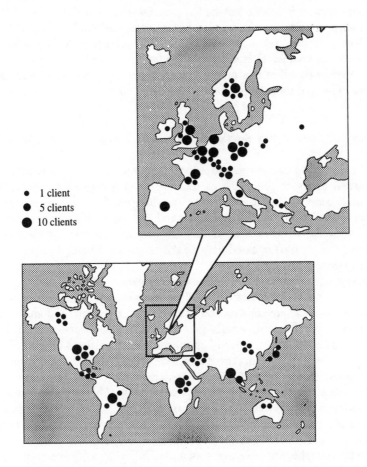

*Figure 2.   The distribution of the most important foreign clients for some Western European
        consultancy services.*

relation to the status of the office; autonomous offices have a higher proportion of local
clients (57 per cent), whereas international and national headquarters have a higher share
of headquarters (34 per cent and 26 per cent, respectively).

The activity sectors of the five main clients of the participating establishments are not
by any means dominated by manufacturing (for example, see Marshall, 1983; Van Dinteren,
1987). Indeed, only 39 per cent of the respondents name their five main clients as manufacturing firms; the equivalent figures for private-sector and public-sector services are
25 per cent and 22 per cent, respectively. Private-sector and public-sector services are
particularly important, as they form the main clients for management consultants. Engineering

consultants, as might be expected, have a [1742] higher proportion of main clients in the construction sector. It is notable that the five principal clients of 49 per cent of the consultancy offices in third-tier cities are in manufacturing, compared with 36 per cent in second-tier cities and only 30 per cent in primate cities. That primate cities are indeed much more diverse as service complexes is shown by the proportion of private-service-sector clients. For firms in primate cities this proportion is 32 per cent, compared with 26 per cent in second-tier cities and only 20 per cent in third-tier cities.

A Typology of Consultancy Service Clients, and Location in the Urban Hierarchy

In an effort to derive useful generalizations from such a diverse international data set it may be useful to try to group the establishments in a way which identifies those with characteristics most similar to each other and different from groups of other firms. One method for achieving this is cluster analysis and this has been applied to the 184 establishments that provided complete data on their geographical market and the characteristics of their clients. The analysis is based only on the responses relating to the national clients of each firm (Tables 9 and 10).

Four groups of establishments have been distinguished. The 72 establishments in group 1 (39 per cent) rely mainly on local firms for their turnover. The majority of their clients employ fewer than 50 persons, are construction or manufacturing firms, and are located primarily in the same city as the establishments in group 1 (Table 9). Of course there are other variables that can be examined for each group of establishments. Significant differences occur when a distinction is [1743] made with regard to market served, country, establishment status, and size of the establishment (Table 10). The establishments in the first group have relatively more local and regional clients than those in the other groups. They are also characterized by an overrepresentation of small and autonomous offices which are located mainly in third-tier cities.

A second group of 74 establishments (40 per cent) is very strongly orientated towards clients that are national public-sector firms. In many respects, the establishments belonging to this group resemble the 'average establishment' with reference to the characteristics shown in Table 10, although national headquarters and establishments with more than 50 employees are somewhat overrepresented.

The third group (13 per cent) comprises 23 establishments whose main turnover comes from headquarters of other firms, from firms which employ more than 200 staff, and firms in private services or in manufacturing. The large majority of these clients are located outside the region in which the supplying establishments are situated. Group-3 establishments are overrepresented in primate cities, and a significant number are national headquarters and/or medium-sized offices. Most are primarily orientated towards national markets, but 30 per cent also serve international markets.

The fourth group is the smallest, with 15 establishments (8 per cent). For a large proportion of their turnover they rely on branches, large firms (more than 200 employees), and/or firms located abroad. One in two clients is a manufacturing firm and one in three clients a construction firm. Almost half are nevertheless located in third-tier cities even though several provide services to international markets. There is a relative overrepresentation of international headquarters. [1744]

Table 9.   Some characteristics of consultancy firm clients, by market groups

	Market groups				Total
	1	2	3	4	
Status[a]					
Local	80	31	8	21	46
Branches	7	12	4	65	13
Headquarters	8	21	70	9	21
Public administration	6	37	18	4	20
Size[a]					
≥200	31	44	87	61	46
50–150	23	32	7	19	24
<50	46	24	6	20	30
Type of firm[b]					
Manufacturing	58	18	46	52	40
Construction	21	8	5	1	12
Private services	18	27	33	37	25
Public sector	3	47	16	10	23
Market served[c]					
Home city	37	28	24	11	30
Region (excluding city)	27	28	10	28	25
Nation (excluding region)	33	39	60	27	38
Abroad	3	5	7	33	7
Number of firms	72	74	23	15	184
Percentage in each group	39	40	13	8	100

Notes:
Columns sum up to 100 per cent for each variable; market groups are defined in the text.
[a] National market only.
[b] Main clients only.
[c] Proportions in total turnover.

The need for proximity between a consultancy service and its clients is one of the reasons for the concentration of these activities in capital cities as well as in the large metropolitan areas in regions where there is strong economic development. Statistics confirm that this is generally true of all European countries (Illeris, 1989). Our study underlines the importance of the concentration of client markets in the region where consultancy services are set up.

In countries which cover a wide geographical area, 60 per cent of the markets are found in the region, and this ratio still lies between 35 per cent and 40 per cent in smaller countries, where the concept of region does not have the same connotation in terms of geographical distance. In the larger countries, the national market (beyond the area of localization) typically only represents less than one third of market opportunities. The transformation in the management practices of companies has brought about a widening

Table 10. Some characteristics of the consultancy service establishments, by market groups

	Market groups				Total
	1	2	3	4	
Geographical market[a]					
International	19	15	30	67	23
National	33	49	57	33	42
Local, regional	47	37	13	0	35
Type of city					
Primate	15	28	52	27	26
Second-tier	40	43	39	27	40
Third-tier	44	28	9	47	34
Status					
International headquarters	3	10	13	20	8
National headquarters	17	35	48	27	29
Branch offices	10	14	13	13	12
Autonomous offices	71	42	26	40	51
Size (employees)					
1–10	56	40	17	55	45
11–50	32	37	48	18	35
>50	11	27	35	27	20
Number of firms	72	74	23	15	184
Percentage in each group	39	40	13	8	100

Notes:
See Table 9.
[a] As mentioned by respondents.

in the demand for consultancy both in industrial and in tertiary activities, without really having any effect on original practices. The internationalization of the markets for consultancy services is, in fact, only at its very beginning, as it is only UK firms, and to some extent Dutch firms, which realize a significant part of their turnover in this field (16 per cent for the United Kingdom, 9 per cent for the Netherlands). However, these observations must be qualified. There are two criteria which modify the way that clients are sought: the status of the establishment within the company hierarchy and the size (number of salaried workers) of the establishment or company. The status of the establishment will have an effect on the efforts made to participate in the regional and international market. In fact, in all European countries it is found that national head offices, regional seats of management, and independent companies all operate in a similar fashion when targeting the clients of their area or the large companies of the country. However, only establishments with the status of international head office or national seat of management obtain significant results abroad. Conversely, it is the regional seats of management which obtain the best results in regional markets.

These observations are not surprising, for they reflect strategic choices by large consultancy firms and a consideration of their consequences for material and immaterial investments. Lasting success in foreign markets presupposes large investments as well as efforts regarding communication and presence which are too much for most companies which have weak structures. The decision to create regional branches corresponds to the desire to reproduce, in those geographically distinct markets, services which are highly perfected and standardized. This then allows reductions in cost which might open other markets which would otherwise be less receptive to consultancy services. The competitive capacity of these establishments is often better than that of independent establishments (Léo and Philippe, 1990). The influence of the size of an enterprise can be seen chiefly in the importance that consultancies with more than 50 salaried workers attribute to international markets. In one way, foreign clients 'replace' the home-town markets where companies with fewer than 50 salaried workers concentrate their human and material resources.

The considerable development that consultancy services underwent during the 1980s, both in turnover and in the number of salaried workers, led to the idea that these activities would undergo a rapid and relatively harmonious expansion in other European countries. The reality has proved to be more complex. The demand for consultancy services has spread throughout different economic activities. Fewer than 40 per cent of the consultancy services questioned include clients from the industrial sector among their top five customers. Industrial clients do not dominate the market, at least in large cities, whereas the public sector has become a regular client. However, the geographical concentration of the supply of consultancy remains steady [1745] (Illeris, 1989), as does the concentration in the demand from large-scale enterprises which have dynamic management methods. Consultancy services experience a geographical stratification in their markets, just as they have a segmentation in their markets, just as they have a segmentation in their clientele according to sector and status.

As a consequence of the newness of the market for demand in consultancy, these services have therefore made a diversified penetration according to the sector of activity, their organizational characteristics, and their geographical coverage.

Conclusions

The RESER group embarked on this study knowing that business services in general have been tending to locate their establishments or to initiate expansion, especially headquarters and regional office functions, in or near to primate and second-tier cities. To some extent this behaviour can be explained by historical inertia and managerial preferences, and most observers are agreed that if it continues it will reinforce even further the dichotomy between the economic development of core and peripheral cities and regions in Europe (or elsewhere, for that matter). The main reason for the anxiety about the disbenefits that this location behaviour implies is that business services have become increasingly important for successful product development and innovation, marketing, and distribution; in other words they contribute to the competitiveness of other firms in the local or regional economic environment. They are also important to the economies of towns and cities because, being one of the main sources of national job growth in recent years, they will bring more highly skilled (higher income) new jobs as other more traditional economic activities are contracting. Moreover, many of the business service firms contribute to the economic development of a city by exporting their services outside the region in ways which increase the scope for multiplier effects.

From this paper it appears that the primate cities are still preeminent centres of business services in the urban hierarchy. One finds an overrepresentation of large offices, and, in particular, the larger offices are also more likely to be internationally active. Furthermore, there is also a strong external supervision from those cities, both nationally and internationally. The consultancy firms in the primate cities also have their own typical customers that mainly comprise head offices and public-sector offices. Lower in the hierarchy, especially in the third-tier cities, the clientele is more strongly determined by industrial and/or locally active companies, the external supervision is less, and the consultancy firms are generally smaller and, relatively speaking, more likely to be autonomous. This confirms existing ideas about the relationship between the urban hierarchy and the performance and behaviour of the business service sector.

These generalizations can also be derived from a typology of consultancy firms on the basis of the sales market (characteristics of the clientele). The typology consists of four groups. The first three groups show a clear and coherent pattern, so much so that moving from group 1 to group 3:

(a) the market served becomes larger;
(b) the size of the consultancy firm becomes larger;
(c) the share of the primate city as the location where firms are established increases and that of the third-tier city decreases;
(d) the share of the head offices increases and that of the autonomous offices decreases;
(e) among the clientele, the share of the head offices increases and that of local firms decreases;
(f) among the clientele, the size of the establishment increases. [1746]

The fourth group of consultancy firms does not fall in line with this linear pattern. This small group (8 per cent of the total) is nationally and internationally orientated and is rather strongly represented in third-tier cities. It is important to remember a general point here, that consultancy firms in second-tier and third-tier cities work in international markets. As regards volume, however, this does not compare with the international sales of consultancy firms in the metropolitan areas.

The survey results suggest that the relationship between market and urban hierarchy is complex. Thus, third-tier cities have an important regional market role because of the significance of branch and autonomous establishments in their complement of firms; these establishments are in direct competition at this market level. But autonomous firms are not by any means excluded from international markets (about 33 per cent had some international clients) so that second-tier and third-tier cities can participate in those markets as, it may be recalled, autonomous firms are prominent in those cities.

What this suggests is that we should beware of assuming that the provision of consultancy services through networks of establishment is organized along hierarchical lines which mirror administrative hierarchies. On the contrary, networks can be controlled or developed from second-tier or third-tier cities, and even branch establishments (as our data show) can control other establishments (also see Pred, 1977). Networks are not exclusively controlled from the primate cities; some 42 per cent of establishments with predominantly regional markets are in control of other parts of the same organization. It also seems that all three types of consultancy service examined in this paper have an equal propensity to create networks. If, as our evidence suggests, networks develop in response to demand in regional markets, then the prospects for autonomous firms would seem limited, unless they set up their own system of branches and become a multi-site firm.

This paper gives nothing more than a cross-sectional view of firms and their behaviour at a given moment in time. Nevertheless, there is the question of the future relationships within the urban system. Will there be increasing differences between cities and regions or will it be a question of convergence? In various studies (among others, see Bade, 1986; Gillespie and Green, 1987; Illeris, 1991; Monnoyer and Philippe, 1985; Moulaert *et al.*, 1991; Van Dinteren, 1987) it has been shown that there is already a strong growth of business services outside the traditional economic centres. However, there needs to be more information about the qualitative aspects of that growth. Does it mainly concern businesses regionally active, for instance, or autonomous or subsidiary establishments, or will consultancy firms lower in the urban hierarchy play an increasing role in the national and international urban system? Are the internationally operating consultancy firms already located in second-tier and third-tier cities there by chance or are they the forerunners of a structural shift?

The congestion in metropolitan areas and the stricter demands made on their environment by people with a higher education, also helped by the quality of national infrastructural networks (rail, motorways, telecommunications), lead to a physical enlargement of the national economic centres in the direction of neighbouring regions that become dominated by second-tier and third-tier cities with an attractive style of living and residential facilities.

There still remains further research to be carried out, as can be seen from the above questions. It will be a particular task of RESER to conduct cross-national analyses, for instance, into the differences in the functioning of service groups in the participating countries and the resulting urban networks. But of more importance is the research into the effect of European integration on national urban systems and the role of the service sector in this process. [1747]

Note

1. For the purpose of the project being undertaken by Réseau Européen Services et Espace, both primary and secondary data were collected. This paper is limited to an analysis of some of the primary data. The researchers involved in this survey were Antoni Soy (Centro de Estudios de Planificación, Barcelona), Lanfranco Senn (Groupo CLAS, Milano), Sven Illeris (University of Roskilde), Peter Daniels (Service Industries Research Centre, University of Portsmouth), Jacques Van Dinteren (Kolpron Consultants, Rotterdam), and Marie-Christine Monnoyer (University of Bordeaux).

References

Bade, F.J. (1986), 'The economic importance of small and medium-sized firms in the Federal Republic of Germany', in D. Keeble and E. Wever (eds), *New Firms and Regional Development in Europe* (Croom Helm, Andover, Hants), 256–74.

Beyers, W.B. (1989), *The Producer Services and Economic Development in the United States: The Last Decade*, Central Puget Sound Economic Development District, Seattle, WA.

Beyers, W.B., Tofflemire, J.M., Stranahan, H.A. and Johnson, E.G. (1986), *The Service Economy: Understanding Growth of Producer Services in the Central Puget Sound Region*, Central Puget Sound Economic Development District, Seattle, WA.

Bonnet, J. (1990), *Les Ancrages Territoriaux des Services*, Colloque Plan Urbain, Métropoles en Déséquilibre; copy available from Geographic Secretariat, LA260-Université Lyon III, Lyon.

Daniels, P.W. and Moulaert, F. (eds) (1991), *The Changing Geography of Advanced Producer Services. Theoretical and Empirical Perspectives* (Belhaven Press, London).

Dunning, J.H. (1989), 'Multinational enterprises and the growth of services', *Service Industries Journal*, 9, 337–46.

Elfring, T. (1988), *Service Employment in Advanced Economies* (Gower, Aldershot, Hants).

Gillespie, A. and Green, A. (1987), 'The changing geography of producer services in Britain', *Regional Studies*, 21, 397–412.

Illeris, S. (1989), *Services and Regions in Europe* (Avebury, Aldershot, Hants).

Illeris, S. (1991), 'Location of services in a service society', in P.W. Daniels and F. Moulaert (eds), *The Changing Geography of Advanced Producer Services* (Belhaven Press, London), 91–107.

Léo, P.-Y. and Philippe, J. (1990), *Réseaux et Services aux Entreprises*, notes de recherche, Centre d'Économie Regionale, Université d'Aix-en-Provence, Aix-en-Provence.

Léo, P.-Y. and Philippe, J. (1991), 'Networked producer services: local markets and global development', in P.W. Daniels (ed.), *Services and Metropolitan Development: International Perspectives* (Routledge, Chapman and Hall, Andover, Hants), 305–24.

Leyshon, A., Daniels, P.W. and Thrift, N.J. (1988), 'Large accounting firms in the UK and spatial development', *Service Industries Journal*, 8, 317–46.

Marshall, J.N. (1983), 'Business-service activities in British provincial conurbations', *Environment and Planning A*, 15, 1343–59.

Marshall, J.N., Wood, P., Daniels, P.W., McKinnon, A., Bachtler, J., Damesick, P., Thrift, N., Gillespie, A., Green, A. and Leyshon, A. (1988), *Services and Uneven Development* (Oxford University Press, Oxford).

Monnoyer, M.C. and Phillipe, J. (1985), *L'Interaction Entre les Prestataires de Services et les PME et le Développement Régional*, Centre d'Économie Régionale, Université d'Aix-en-Provence, Aix-en-Provence.

Moulaert, F., Chikhaoui, Y. and Djellal, F. (1991), 'Locational behaviour of French high tech consultancy firms', *International Journal of Urban and Regional Research*, 15 (1), 5–23.

Pred, A.R. (1977), *City-systems in Advanced Economics* (Hutchinson Education, London).

Van Dinteren, J.H.J. (1987), 'The role of business-service offices in the economy of medium-sized cities', *Environment and Planning A*, 19, 669–86.

Van Dinteren, J.H.J. (1988), 'De regionale dimensie van internationale dienstverlening' (The regional dimension of international operating service firms), *Economische Statistische Berichten*, 73, 528–30.

Van Dinteren, J.H.J. (1989), *Zakelijke Diensten en Middelgrote Steden* (Business service firms and medium-sized cities), Krips Repro, Meppel (in Dutch, with extensive English summary). [1748]

ENTREPRENEURSHIP & REGIONAL DEVELOPMENT, 5 (1993), 265–277

Business networks, small firm flexibility and regional development in UK business services

JOHN BRYSON[1], PETER WOOD[2] and DAVID KEEBLE[3]

[1]Institute of Earth Studies, University of Wales, Llandinam Building, Penglais, Aberystwyth, Dyfed, SY23 3DB;

[2]Department of Geography, University College London, 26 Bedford Way, London WC1H 0AP;

[3]Department of Geography and Small Business Research Centre, University of Cambridge, Downing Place, Cambridge CB2 3EN, UK

Since 1980, the UK has experienced a dramatic growth in firms and employment in information-intensive business services, such as management consultancy and market research. Recent expansion of new and small firms operating in these sectors is the focus of a major ESRC-sponsored research project currently under way at Cambridge University Small Business Research Centre.

Small business service firms are able to compete successfully with large firms due to the imperfect nature of the market which characterizes business services demand and supply, together with specialization of expertise. The success of small business service firms depends on informal person-to-person networks, word-of-mouth recommendation and repeat business based on successful earlier assignments or personal contacts acquired, for example, while working in a large consultancy or market research company. This paper examines the types of networks utilized by small business service firms and argues that two distinct types exist: demand- and supply-related networks; the former involves links with clients, the latter links and co-operation between complementary small business service firms.

Keywords: networks; small firms; business services; management consultancy; market research.

1. Introduction

During the 1980s, turnover, employment and the stock of firms in a range of business service activities in the UK have all grown spectacularly (Keeble *et al.* 1991). Overall employment in 'other business services' (SIC 8395, which includes management consultants, market research, public relations consultants, employment agencies, translators, document copying services, etc.) more than doubled between 1981 and 1990, growing by 354,000 or +122%. This compares with a growth rate of +3.5% for all industries and services, and a decline in manufacturing employment of –17.5%. Both large and small firms are involved. During the late 1980s, the annual turnover of large consultancy firms grew on average by 25–30%. Indeed, a survey of the UK's 37 top management consultancy firms, those with turnovers of more than £1.5 million, shows that this group recorded an average expansion in turnover in the single year 1988–89 to 1989–90 of 35%, with an average growth in number of professional staff of 20% (Management Consultancy 1990). Total turnover of this group of large and medium-sized firms increased by £225 million, to nearly £1 billion (£943 million).

Much of this growth in the stock of business service firms has been dominated by small enterprises and has been most dramatic in information-intensive business services such as computer services and management consultancy. The growth of business services must be seen as part of a general phenomenon of small firm expansion in UK services

0898-5626/93 $10·00 © 1993 Taylor & Francis Ltd.

and the economy generally during the 1980s (Bannock and Daly 1990, p. 256, Dunne and Hughes 1990, Keeble 1990). Between 1985 and 1990, the number of small firms expanded rapidly, with increases in the total stock of businesses of 114 % for management consultancy, 106 % for personnel recruitment and employment agencies, and 37 % for advertising and market research. During this period the growth of business numbers in 12 'fast-growth small-firm' business service sectors (those with above-average business growth rates and above-average shares of small businesses) was on average over twice as fast as in 15 comparable consumer service sectors (Keeble *et al.* 1992a). Information-intensive business services generally showed even higher rates of new firm formation than either financial services or manually based support services.

A more detailed analysis of management consultancy firms shows that the numbers of firms with turnovers of up to £1 million increased by no less than 7204, or 113 %, in the five years 1985 to 1990 alone (Business Statistics Office 1990). This growth in numbers of very small businesses represents 99 % of the total net growth in the stock of all businesses in this sector over the period. The small size of most professional business service firms is indicated by the fact that, in 1990, 77 % of management consultancy firms employed 12 or fewer professionals. In market research, 83 % of all firms registered with the Market Research Society (MRS) employed 12 or less professional staff, while 77 % employed 24 or less workers overall (Bryson *et al.* 1993).

The growth of small firms in professional business services thus stands out as the single most important component of the rapid growth of small service sector businesses in the 1980s (Keeble *et al.* 1991). Equally rapid employment growth reflects in part at least the intrinsically high labour-intensity of information-based business services, 'professional expertise' being a commodity whose production and delivery cannot easily be automated. This paper examines the characteristics of small business service firms which help explain their competitive success, focusing in particular on the nature of the 'networks' entrepreneurs utilize to acquire clients and to create and maintain organizational flexibility.

2. Methodology

The findings presented in this paper are based on detailed interviews with 120 small independently owned and managed business service companies, equally divided between management consultancy and market research organizations. Choice of these two sectors as case studies reflects their strategic importance in providing specialized and essential information to a wide range of private and public sector organizations, their rapid recent growth rates, and the large number of small firms operating within them. Small firms are defined, following an industry-wide consensus, as those employing approximately 10 or fewer professional staff, or 25 or fewer total staff (Keeble *et al.* 1991). Equal numbers of firms in each sector were interviewed in inner London, south-east England outside London (mainly Berkshire, Hertfordshire and Surrey), and northern England (the North West and Yorkshire and Humberside), randomly selected from industry registers. The survey was carried out between January and July 1991, and achieved a response rate of 75 %.

The sample populations were drawn from a database of 869 management consultancy firms derived from professional directories (including the Institute of Management Consultants) and 366 companies registered with the MRS. By definition, the survey sample thus consists of independently owned companies, virtually all of which employ less than 25 staff in total, with a mean of 6.5 employees (including owners/directors). The fundamental importance of professional expertise to the commercial success of these firms is indicated by a professional/support staff ratio of nearly 2:1 (65% professional, 35% support). Most firms are relatively new, young enterprises, no less than two-thirds (65%) having been established since 1980, with a further 31% since 1970. Over half (53%) increased their employment between 1985 and 1990, with an average growth for the whole sample of +2% employees. Ten per cent grew rapidly, by between six and 27 extra staff. A significant minority (37%), however, remained static in employment numbers, often by deliberate choice.

3. Flexibility, networks and networking

The small firm sector is inherently flexible in being able to respond rapidly and flexibly to changing client requirements. An inherent part of this flexibility is a consequence of the relatively intangible and personal nature of the services these firms provide. Small business service firms are also able to satisfy client requirements by employing the complementary services of other small or large consultancy firms or even sole practitioners. Small business service firms which specialize in particular industries, techniques or regions may also be employed as subcontractors by large organizations. The central argument of this paper is that small business service firms, or even individuals, are able to compete successfully – by price and by expertise – with large firms through the use of a variety of personal contacts, associates and business contacts. This type of organizational flexibility, frequently termed 'networking', or a 'network' of contacts/associates, enables small firms to offer a wide range of services without employing a substantial full-time professional or support staff.

The term 'network' or 'networking' was originally developed in relation to formal exchanges of information within large organizations, especially under the influence of modern information technologies. Given this background two different and conflicting definitions of 'networking' have been developed in the academic literature. First, 'networking' and 'networks' have become increasingly fashionable conceptual devices for theorizing the internal organization of large businesses (see Bressand *et al.* 1989). For example, a recent paper by Leo and Philippe (1991) examines the geographical networks, or branch plants, of service companies and attempts to understand the localization of business services within France. Second, entrepreneurship has been conceptualized as a dynamic process which requires for its successful development linkages or networks between key components of the process (Aldrich and Zimmer 1986, p. 3). In this approach entrepreneurship is viewed as 'embedded in a social context, channelled and facilitated or constrained and inhibited by people's positions in social networks' (Aldrich and Zimmer 1986, p. 3). It is the second approach which is examined in this paper.

In recent papers Curran *et al.* (1991, 1992) argue that networks and networking 'have emerged as fashionable conceptual devices for theorizing and researching a number of important aspects' of small businesses, but that much recent work is 'conceptually and methodologically poorly realized' (Curran *et al.* 1991, p. 1). To overcome this theoretical confusion they argue that 'networks' and 'networking' can be usefully divided into two types: compulsory and voluntary networks. Compulsory networks are those which an organization must belong to in order to survive and operate successfully, for example banks or accountants, while participation in the local chamber of commerce or golf club would be classified as voluntary networking. Many of these 'networks' are support networks (for example banks, enterprise agencies and business advisers), which function to provide advice, information and capital (Curran *et al.* 1992, pp. 3–4). This study's emphasis on support networks is hardly surprising as it was funded by one of the high street banks to ascertain the significance of local economic networks as a vehicle for improving the bank's services to the small business sector.

One difficulty with this model of networks rests on the identification of voluntary and compulsory networking. A particular firm's membership of the local chamber of commerce or professional association may be considered by its managing director as a compulsory activity vital for the company's success or its public image. For another company, membership of these organizations might be considered as voluntary and even unnecessary networking. A related criticism is that a voluntary, infrequently used network might be more important for the survival of a company during times of crisis than a compulsory, frequently used network; for example the firm's market research or management consultancy advisers as against its bank. The two types of network identified by Curran *et al.* overlap with those identified by Birley (1985) who divides 'networks' into two types: formal and informal. Formal networks include banks, accountants, lawyers and the local chamber of commerce, while informal networks include family, friends, previous colleagues and previous employers (Birley 1985, p. 109).

Curran *et al.* used their definition of networking in a study of 350 small service firms to ascertain the use they make of compulsory and voluntary networks. The key finding of this work is that such firms have relatively small networks, with limited use either of 'compulsory' external advisers, for example accountants and bank managers, or voluntary networks, based on the family and social groups. This study concludes by stating that 'small business owners do have contacts with their environment – it would be impossible to run the business otherwise – but these are much more limited and much less proactive than notions such as "networks" and "networking" as used in the literature imply' (Curran *et al.* 1991; Curran *et al.* 1992, p. 57). This conclusion is a direct consequence of the definitional problems identified above. It is not surprising that Curran *et al.* found that very few small firms identified membership of the golf club, the chamber of commerce or even the bank manager as important network contacts. We would argue that for most small service firms, these types of support networks are relatively insignificant compared with network relationships with clients and with other supply-side companies.

For small firms the definition of 'networking' and 'networks' must be founded on the relationship they have with the external environment. As far as this paper is concerned the informal networks, including those embodied within formal relationships (for example, with clients or banks), identified by Birley appear to be the most important and can be usefully further divided into three types depending on the nature of the relationship the firm has with the external environment. The first comprises 'networks' associated with clients, obtaining new business and the maintenance or establishment of contacts with clients, in order words *demand-related networks*. The second type covers 'networks' associated with the co-operative supply of a service or product – *supply-related networks*. Finally, there are networks which can loosely be defined as *support functions*: for example banks, business advisers, the founder's family and friends. This paper examines the demand- and supply-related networks of small business service firms. Support networks are not investigated as these have already been examined by Curran *et al.* (1992) and found to be of limited importance.

Within this refined definition of networks possible measures of their importance in relation to specific firms can be considered. First, as far as *demand-related* networks are concerned the frequency of contact between the client and the supplier of a service is an excellent indication of the strength of this relationship. This can be measured as the proportion of repeat business a firm receives over a given period of time. Second, the number of referrals obtained from existing clients provides a good indication of the perceptions a firm's clients have of its services. For firms which provide intangible services high levels of referrals reduce the necessity of advertising for new clients and increase the success of obtaining new business. Finally, the level and type of service performed by a business service firm is a good indicator of the symmetry of the relationship with the client. If the service is routine and low order the relationship between the supplier and the client is asymmetrical, with the client having most of the power in the relationship. If the service is specialized and strategic, however, the relationship between the supplier and the client will be more symmetrical and is likely to lead to the development of a more interdependent relationship. A client of a cleaning company must simply know that the company can clean efficiently, whereas employing a strategic management consultancy firm often requires great personal trust and confidentiality. It is obvious which of these two examples is likely to result in the development of a strong service–client networking relationship.

The strength and symmetry of a firm's *supply-related* networks can also be measured. First, strength is reflected in the frequency and types of co-operative ventures with other service firms. As far as frequency is concerned a useful measure is the proportion of a firm's projects, in any one year, which involves the use of another company or self-employed individual. Perhaps more significant, however, is the symmetry of the transaction, reflected in the level of skills acquired in this way. A market research firm which subcontracts its data processing is less dependent on the supply network than a firm which subcontracts a complete project to a specialist. A second measure of the symmetry of supply networks is the number of referrals obtained from rival firms. This is a good indication of the firm's reputation amongst its competitors. Some of these measures of demand- and supply-related networks will be used in the next two sections to determine the importance of demand-related and supply-related networks for small management consultancy and market research firms.

4. Demand-related networks

The growth of small business service firms must be related to the part they play in wider changes in business organization, and especially in satisfying the needs of clients. The significant role played by small information-intensive business service enterprises in the wider economy is indicated in Table 1, which shows that clients of the surveyed firms are drawn from a wide range of sectors, but with manufacturing and business services accounting for three-fifths of sales. These sectors, along with financial services (13%), are especially important for national and regional economic growth. Moreover, the clients

Table 1. Markets and clients of small business service firms.

| | Means % of business firms | | | | | | |
	Financial services	Business services	Other services	Manu-facturing	Local govt.	Central govt.	Other
Total firms	12.7	20.6	15.2	39.6	3.4	5.5	3.4

| | Client size (%) | | |
	Small firms	Medium firms	Large firms
Total firms	12.7	15.7	71.6

of small business service firms are predominantly large firms (with over £5 million turnover). In fact, the lists of clients served by management consultancy and market research firms are dominated by major 'blue-chip' clients. Thirty-eight (63%) of the small management consultancy firms surveyed depended on large firms for over half of their turnover, and only five (8%) had no large clients. Conversely, over half have no small clients (with less than £1 million turnover) (Wood *et al.* 1991, p. 10). Market research firms are even more dependent on large clients, with no less than 50 (83%) of the sample firms deriving over half their turnover from them. Again, over half have no small clients (with less than £1 million turnover).

The intangible nature of the products supplied by business service firms makes it difficult to acquire clients simply by advertisements. A client's selection of a management consultancy or market research firm is more of 'an art rather than a skill' (Aucamp 1978). Factors which a potential client must take into consideration when selecting a business service firm are its reliability, its experience in a particular area, its potential ability to work productively with the client's personnel, the competition, the quality of its work and its cost. These factors are impossible to measure in advance, since business service firms sell skills, expertise and experience which result only in future, and maybe unclearly defined gains. The large number of management consultancy and market research firms, and the specialized intangible nature of their expertise create an imperfect market-place for their services. This is a direct result of clients' lack of information about the services, and quality of any business service firm (Holmstrom 1985, p. 187). Consultancy and research firms also usually have very little knowledge of their competitors, and client choice of external advisers is dependent on personal recommendation and on an informal selection procedure.

The growth of small information-intensive business service firms reflects the often strategic nature of their advice and its relatively intangible nature, embodied in experienced individuals. These individuals provide a personal or 'customized' service to clients, based on their own reputations, experience, track records and contact client networks. Business service firms thus employ highly educated and qualified individuals whose professional expertise is not tied strongly to the firm in which it is developed. Such expertise is highly mobile and coupled with low barriers to entry, requiring little capital or equipment, enables individuals to leave established firms to set up new firms or to act as sole practitioners. These characteristics encourage the continuing fragmentation of the market research and management consultancy industries, enhancing organizational flexibility. The most important attributes possessed by the entrepreneur who establishes a small research/consultancy firm are professional expertise, an existing reputation and a network of client contacts. These essential requirements for competitive success explain the concentration of founders' previous employment in same-sector or client firms, and into large rather than small companies (Table 2). Thus 90% of the 184 founders involved were previously employed in either market research (28%), management consultancy (21%) or client companies (41%), while 63% were employed in large firms (over £5 million turnover), with only 20% coming from other small firms (less than £1 million turnover).

Regional differences are important here with a large proportion of inner London and southern firms spinning off from established consultancy firms and market research firms (Wood *et al.* 1991). In northern Britain new management consultancy and market research firms more often spin off from client companies which are the obvious training grounds in areas which do not possess a large base of established business service firms. Small business services firm founders thus acquire their reputation and initial client contacts whilst working for either a large supply or client company.

Table 2. The process of new business service firm formation.

Type	A	B	C	D	E	F
	No. of firms					
Market research	28	7	6	3	6	3
Management consultancy	21	17	8	4	0	1
Total firms	49	24	14	7	6	4

Notes:
A = worked for existing MR/MC firm and decided they could do it for themselves;
B = worked for an existing client firm and decided they could do it for themselves;
C = redundancy;
D = spin-off, of 2–3 founders jointly from MR/MC firm;
E = housewife with children re-entering profession/work;
F = externalization, of 2–3 founders jointly from client company's in-house service department.

An important measure of the relationship between a business service firm and its clients is the level of repeat business. Repeat business reflects a client's satisfaction with an earlier assignment. In this case the only measure of the success of an earlier assignment is the client's perception of its success or failure. A 'successful' project will probably lead to further assignments. As far as all 120 firms are concerned, repeat business provided on average just under two-thirds (61%) of small firm assignments by value (proportion of annual turnover), although this rate was lower for management consultancy firms (Table 3). For management consultancy firms based in the rest of the South East outside London repeat business provides a significant majority (73%) of their business by value (Table 3). In contrast repeat business for consultancy firms based in northern Britain represents only 40% of their turnover. Market research firms are even more dependent on repeat business with 70% of the turnover of firms based in the rest of the South East and northern Britain coming from former clients.

Table 3. Repeat business as a proportion of annual turnover.

Type	UK	Inner London	Rest of the South East	North
Management consultancy	57	56	73	40
Market research	64	68	70	70

The importance of repeat business for small business service firms is further emphasized in an analysis of how firms obtained their last three clients (Table 4). Some 67% of the last three assignments of market research firms and 40% of those of management consultancy firms were obtained from former clients. The nature of their work means that market research firms generally serve more clients than management consultancy firms and in consequence are likely to be more dependent on repeat business than management consultancy firms. This is especially important for market research firms based in the outer South East and for management consultancy firms based in inner London. For both sectors the lowest level of repeat business was for firms based in the north. Table 4 also provides evidence for another measure of the importance of demand-related networking for small business service firms, that of referrals between client companies. A significant minority of management consultancy firms (22%) obtained their last three projects from referrals between clients. This was particularly important for firms based in the rest of the South East, excluding London. In contast only 12% of market research firms' recent projects had been obtained via client referral, with only

Table 4. Could you perhaps describe how your firm obtained its last three assignments?

| | *No. of mentions* | | | | | | | |
| | *Management consultancy* | | | | *Market research* | | | |
Source	*UK*	*IL*	*OSE*	*N*	*UK*	*IL*	*OSE*	*N*
Referrals from clients	38	11	16	11	21	7	6	8
Referrals from other supply firms	11	5	4	2	12	7	1	4
Repeat business	70	29	23	18	116	37	45	34
Directories/advertisements	16	4	6	6	5	0	1	4
Cold calls	11	5	0	6	13	3	5	5
DTI	21	4	2	15	2	0	1	1
New business	9	2	5	2	5	3	1	1
Total	176	60	56	60	174	57	60	57

Notes:
UK   = United Kingdom;
IL   = inner London;
OSE   = outer South East, excluding London;
N   = North West and Yorkshire and Humberside.

10% of projects being obtained in this way by firms based in the rest of the South East. Client referral as a method for obtaining new clients is thus most important for consultancy firms, which obtain a significantly lower proportion of their business from repeat business than market research firms. Thus personal contacts which have developed either between a business service firm and its clients or between clients account for 61% of consultancy firms' and 76% of market research firms' last three assignments. Given these figures, the importance of personal contacts and an established reputation for business service firms cannot be overestimated.

The final measure of the importance of demand-related networks is the symmetry of the relationship. In serving client needs, the expertise offered by small business service firms must complement the client's own, in-house capabilities (Wood 1991). These will have been developed through staff training and career development programmes and will generally respond slowly to changes in organizational structure and in the commercial market-place. Specialized outside assistance is increasingly sought from business service firms to help companies respond to economic and political turbulence effectively. For our sample of small firms, taking on work which could have been carried out by a client's own in-house staff occurred in only a minority of cases (Wood *et al.* 1991, p. 14). Firms were asked to describe in detail their last three projects. Most clients required advice which either did not exist inside the firm or an independent view of a particular issue or problem. In the majority of cases the types of projects undertaken by consultancy and market research firms were specialist, and in many cases strategic, in their focus, whose success depended to a great extent on the relationship that existed between the client and the business service firm. The strategic nature of these projects is perhaps best demonstrated by the most frequently used type of management consultancy expertise, human resource management (Wood *et al.* 1991). The management of human resources is one of the most important aspects of corporate planning, but it is also one of the most difficult tasks for internal appraisal. A particular need arises for authoritative and experienced outside experts, able to take an independent view separate from the personal and political involvement of most 'insiders'. If successful, such projects would lead clients to seek further advice, when required, from the business service firm and to recommend the company to other potential clients.

5. Supply-related networks

Small business service firms are able to satisfy specialized client demand by co-operating with other business service firms or even with individuals. By using a network of contacts and associates, small business service firms are able to compete, by expertise and price, with large firms by being able to offer a wide range of services without employing a substantial full-time professional staff. These supply-related networks enable small business service firms to be extremely flexible in their responses to the demands of clients and to offer many of the services and facilities provided by large firms.

Supply-related networks can be divided into two types. First, small business service firms network with other small firms, or even individuals, to increase the range of services and advice they can provide. Many of these are national networks, but increasingly small business service firms are developing formal links with complementary firms based in other European countries. Second, sole practitioners combine together into a network to provide a formal vehicle for their activities. This type of network may be either an informal relationship between a small number of individuals, or a formal relationship involving many individuals governed by a series of rules and regulations. The most well-known network, the Richmond Group, has over 80 participating members. Both these types will be examined below.

Table 5 reveals that a significant proportion of surveyed firms (74%) regularly use outside researchers or consultants to enhance the skills of their in-house staff. Management consultancy firms use associates (85%) more than research companies (64%). In both sectors more firms based in inner London or in the outer South East use external associates than northern-based companies. This is probably due to the low level of specialization and the limited number of research and consultancy companies based in the north (Wood *et al.* 1991). The number of associates used regularly by consultancy or market research companies is fairly small (Table 6), the majority of companies (77%) having networks of 10 or less associates. Those supporting northern-based management consultancy companies are much smaller than for inner London or outer south-eastern firms. Just under one-third of northern-based management consultancy companies do not use associates, while 30% regularly use only between one and five associates. Exactly half of the firms based in inner London regularly use between six and 10 associates. Over the last five years both management consultancy and market research firms have increased their use of associates. Just over one-third of firms increased their use of associates, but a small minority (16%) decreased their use. A small minority (21 firms) do not use associates, either because they do not need outside expertise, or they consider the quality of associates' work is poor compared with their in-house expertise.

Table 5. Does your firm use associates?

Response	*UK*	*%*	*IL*	*%*	*OSE*	*%*	*North*	*%*
Management consultants:								
Yes	51	85	19	95	18	90	14	70
No	9	15	1	5	2	10	6	30
Total	60	100	20	100	20	100	20	100
Market research:								
Yes	37	64	14	70	13	68	10	53
No	21	36	6	30	6	32	9	47
Total	58	100	20	100	19	100	19	100

Table 6. Roughly what size is your network of associates?

Size of network	UK	%	IL	%	OSE	%	North	%
Management consultancy:								
0	9	15	1	5	2	10	6	30
1–5	13	22	4	20	3	15	6	30
6–10	23	38	10	50	10	50	3	15
11 +	15	25	5	25	5	25	5	25
Total	60	100	20	100	20	100	20	100
Market research:								
0	22	37	6	30	7	35	9	45
1–5	21	35	6	30	8	40	7	35
6–10	12	20	5	25	3	15	4	20
11 +	5	8	3	15	2	10	0	0
Total	60	100	20	100	20	100	20	100

Table 7 records the six most important reasons for firms using associates. Responses were unprompted and classified after interview. The most common reason identified by 48% of management consultancy firms and 61% of market research firms was to extend their existing in-house expertise (Table 7). The second reason for using associates was during a period of work overload. Market research and management consultancy companies typically exhibit a cyclical work pattern related to economic cycles. This cyclical pattern may be accentuated by the limited time available for marketing the company and extending networks of potential client contacts during busy periods. The third reason, related to the first two factors, was to reduce costs and enhance flexibility. Perhaps the most important aspect of Table 7 is that it suggests that business service firms use associates and other firms primarily to obtain high-order professional expertise, specialist advice and assistance rather than to buy in low-order services, for example data processing. This suggests that networks are a powerful component in the assembly of expertise to manage business change.

Table 7. What role do associates play in your business?

| | Management consultancy: | | | | Market research: | | | |
Role	UK	IL	OSE	N	UK	IL	OSE	N
Extend expertise	50	22	20	8	38	18	12	8
Work overload	26	9	9	8	13	7	3	3
Reduce costs/increase flexibility	15	5	4	6	4	0	2	2
Marketing	6	4	2	0	1	0	1	0
Data collection	2	0	1	1	3	0	0	3
Extend geographic range	6	3	3	0	3	1	1	1
Total	105	43	39	23	62	26	19	17

We have argued that reputation and knowledge which reside in individuals rather than in companies is the basis of the market research and management consultancy industries. These characteristics encourage individuals to leave companies and establish themselves as sole practitioners. Both the management consultancy and market research industries have high proportions of sole practitioners. Sole practitioners can undertake work directly for clients, but sometimes operate in a network with other sole practitioners or as subcontractors. This latter type of individual-centred supply-related network is well illustrated by the example of a sole practitioner management consultant based in Berkshire. This consultant left a large management consultancy firm to establish his own client base to obtain greater control over his working life. Thirty per cent of the projects this consultant is offered by clients, however, are too large to be undertaken successfully by an individual. This difficulty has been overcome by establishing a limited management consultancy company, with a network of sole practitioners. While still predominantly operating as independent sole practitioners this company provides the 'resources' and formal company image to enable the individual professionals involved to undertake large projects. The sole practitioners use the company vehicle only when they are in danger of losing a project because the client considers it to be too big for an individual. This method of organization enables sole practitioners to compete, by open tender, with small and even large consultancy companies. It gives sole practitioners flexibility working together either as a formal group or as individuals.

In spite of their small size, many market research firms interviewed as part of this study claimed to be 'full service' companies, prepared to undertake the whole range of design, survey and analysis skills. In practice this widens their appeal to clients, but depends on a network of supporting contacts. Such companies are particularly active in both inner London and the north (Table 8). Many of the projects are, in fact, quite specialized, and in fulfilling broadly specified contracts they often subcontract part, or even all, of the project to other market research companies or sole practitioners. At a very basic level many market research companies subcontract their field work to larger companies, or even specialized field-work companies, which possess an efficiently organized, large and geographically dispersed network of field interviewers. A small company is unable to support such a network without undertaking interview work for other market research firms or even client companies. A small proportion (8%) of market research companies are solely field-work companies. Four of these are located in the outer South East and undertake field work for market research companies based in inner London and in the north. All market research companies must have access to a network of freelance survey staff either run indirectly by a field-work company or employed directly. Similarly all quantitative market research companies must have access to either external or internally based data processing facilities.

Table 8. Type of expertise offered by market research companies.

Type	UK	IL	OSE	N
Quantitative	10	1	7	2
Qualitative	9	5	2	2
Full service	35	13	7	15
Field work	5	1	4	0

The final measure of supply-related networking is that of referrals between business service firms. This, in fact, is not very important, accounting for only 6% of the last three projects obtained by management consultancy firms, and 7% of market research projects (Table 4). This low level suggests a reluctance to co-operate with potential competitors, perhaps affected by the current recession. This type of network also depends on the availability of associates to undertake specialist parts of projects which cannot be performed by the firm's professional staff. On the other hand six management consultancy firms argued that associates are extremely useful contacts, occasionally hearing about projects which they cannot undertake themselves. In these circumstances they may advise the potential client to seek the advice of the consultancy firm which has given them the most employment opportunities.

6. Conclusion

This paper has shown that supply- and demand-related 'networks' of informal personally based contacts are an inherent and vital component of the relationship which a small business service firm has with its clients and other business service firms. They are also extremely important for specialist companies attempting to fill particular market niches. Without their ability to 'network' with other firms many small business service firms would be unable to offer a wide range of services at a competitive price. To survive and compete successfully with large companies small business service firms must occupy a web of fairly well-developed demand- and supply-related 'networks'. Networking thus appears to have been an important element in the recent growth of small companies in information-intensive business services.

The imperfect market which characterizes the demand and supply of business services implies that 'networking' and 'networks' are especially useful operational tools for small management consultancy and market research companies. Consultancy and research firms have very little knowledge of their competitors while client choice of external advisers is dependent on personal recommendation and on an informal selection procedure (Table 4). 'Networking' is a useful approach as it allows the role and function of small firms to be judged in the context of their overall activities and in relation to their external environment. It emphasizes the interactive nature of the activities of business service firms, interactive with clients and with other business service firms, and highlights the importance of an individual's reputation and expertise.

Note

We wish to acknowlege the financial contributions to the work of the Cambridge University Small Business Research Centre from the Economic and Social Research Council, Arthur Andersen & Co Foundation, Barclays Bank, Commission of the European Communities (DGXXIII), Department of Employment, and the Rural Development Commission. Any views expressed do not necessarily reflect those of the sponsoring organizations.

References

Aldrich, H. E. and Zimmer, C. R. 1986, Entrepreneurship through social networks. In Sexton, D. and Smilor, R. (eds) *The Art and Science of Entrepreneurship* (Cambridge: Ballinger).

Aucamp, J. 1978, How to locate and select a marketing research consultancy. In Rawnsley, A. (ed.) *Manual of Industrial Marketing Research* (Chichester: Wiley).

Bannon, M. J. 1973, *Office Location in Ireland: the Role of Central Dublin* (Dublin: An Foras Forbartha).

Bannock, G. and Daly, M. 1990, Size distribution of UK firms, *Employment Gazette*, **98**, 255–258.

Birley, S. 1985, The role of networks in the entrepreneurial process, *Journal of Business Venturing*, **1**, 107–117.

Bressand, A., Distler, C. and Nicolaidis, K. 1989, Networks at the heart of the service economy. In Bressand, A. and Nicolaidis, A. (eds) *Strategic Trends in Services: An Inquiry into the Global Service Economy* (New York: Harper & Row), 17–33.

Bryson, J., Keeble, D. and Wood, P. 1990a, The performance of small services: are small management consultancies an undervalued sector? *Management Consultancy*, November, 29–31.

Bryson, J., Keeble, D. and Wood, P. 1990b, Survey of small market research companies: some preliminary findings, *MRS Newsletter*, December, 36–37.

Bryson, J., Keeble, D. and Wood, P. 1993, The creation, location and growth of small business service firms in the United Kingdom, *Service Industries Journal* (forthcoming, April).

Business Statistics Office 1985, 1990, Size analysis of United Kingdom businesses, 1985, 1990, *Business Monitor*, PA 1003.

Curran, J. and Blackburn, R. A. 1992, *Small Firms and Local Economic Networks: Relations Between Small and Large Firms in Two Localities*, Kingston Business School, Business Paper 19, Kingston University.

Curran, J., Jarvis, R., Blackburn, R. and Black, S. 1991, Small firms and networks: constructs, methodological strategies and some preliminary findings, paper presented at the UKEMRA conference, Blackpool.

Dunne, P. and Hughes, A. 1990, Small businesses: an analysis of recent trends in their relative importance and growth performance in the UK with some European comparisons, Cambridge University Small Business Research Centre, Working Paper I.

Holmstrom, B. 1985, The provision of services in a market economy. In Inman, R. (ed.) *Managing the Service Economy: Prospects and Problems* (Cambridge: Cambridge University Press), 183-213.

Johannisson, B. 1986, Network strategies: management technology for entrepreneurship and change, *International Small Business Journal*, 5, 19-30.

Johannisson, B. 1991, Designing supportive contexts for emerging enterprises, paper presented at the international workshop, The Formation, Management and Organization of Small and Medium Sized Enterprises, Jönköpking, Sweden.

Keeble, D. 1990, Small firms, new firms and uneven regional development in the United Kingdom, *Area*, 22, 234-245.

Keeble, D., Bryson, J. and Wood, P. 1991, Small firms, business services growth and regional development in the United Kingdom: some empirical findings, *Regional Studies*, 25, 439-457.

Keeble, D., Bryson, J. and Wood, P. 1992a, The rise and role of small business service firms in the United Kingdom, *International Small Business Journal*, 11, 11-22.

Keeble, D., Bryson, J. and Wood, P. 1992b, Entrepreneurship and flexibility in business services: the rise of small management consultancy and market research firms in the United Kingdom. In Caley, K., Chittenden, F., Chell, E. and Mason, C. (eds) *Small Enterprise Development: Policy and Practice in Action* (London: Paul Chapman).

Leo, P. and Philippe, J. 1991, Networked producer services: local markets and global development. In Daniels, P. W. (ed.) *Services and Metropolitan Development: International Perspectives* (London: Routledge).

Management Consultancy 1990, UK management consultancy industry shows good growth, *Management Consultancy*, May, 22-26.

Thorngren, B. 1970, How do contact systems affect regional development? *Environment and Planning*, 2, 409-427.

Wood, P. 1991, Flexible accumulation and the rise of business services, *Transactions, Institute of British Geographers*, NS 16, 160-172.

Wood, P., Bryson, J. and Keeble, D. 1991, Regional patterns of small firm development in the business services: preliminary evidence from the UK, Small Business Research Centre, Cambridge University, Working Paper No. 14.

[22]

PAPERS IN REGIONAL SCIENCE: *The Journal of the RSAI* 75, 3: 351–374
© 1996 by Regional Science Association International

EXPLAINING THE DEMAND FOR PRODUCER SERVICES: IS COST-DRIVEN EXTERNALIZATION THE MAJOR FACTOR?

William B. Beyers

Department of Geography
University of Washington
Seattle, WA 98195
USA

David P. Lindahl

Department of Geography
University of Washington
Seattle, WA 98195
USA

ABSTRACT Producer services employment has grown rapidly within advanced economies in recent years. The bases of demand related to this growth are not well understood by regional scientists. A common view is that this growth is largely attributable to cost-driven factors and vertical disintegration processes on the part of producer service users. This paper demonstrates that cost-driven externalization is not the most important force underlying growth in demand for producer services. The need for specialized knowledge is by far the most important factor behind producer services demand, combined with a variety of other cost, quasi-cost, and non-cost-driven forces.

1. EXPLAINING THE DEMAND FOR PRODUCER SERVICES

The contemporary regional science literature suggests that processes of internalization and externalization of producer service functions are driven by the search for ever more cost-effective industrial organizational structures (Scott 1988; Goe 1990, 1991; Perry 1990, 1992). It has been argued by some that the rapid growth of the producer services sector has been driven by this changing social division of labor (Goe 1990, 1991; Coffey and Bailly 1991, 1992; Coffey, Drolet and Polèse 1994; Martinelli 1991), which is manifested in a growing demand in the marketplace for the producer services. However, it has also been argued that there are "changing business practices," associated in part with innovations in the types of producer services offered in the marketplace (Tschetter 1987; Kutscher 1988; Beyers, 1992). These innovations have been facilitated, *inter alia*, by technological changes in information processing and telecommunications capabilities. At the same time, the rise of networks of offices of regional, national, and international producer services firms has been argued to lead to reconfigurations in the locus of provision (i.e., production inhouse or purchase from an outside supplier) of service functions (Daniels 1985; Martinelli 1991).

This paper explores the bases of demand for producer services from theoretical and empirical perspectives and provides insights into the relative importance of externalization and/or internalization processes in the development of producer service businesses. We first present a review of work describing possible explanations for producer services demand. This review emphasizes cost-driven motivations for marketplace purchases by the clients of producer service firms, as well as reasons that go beyond narrowly-defined cost bases for demand. This section is followed with survey-based empirical evidence on the motivations behind the founding of new firms and whether processes of vertical disintegration are responsible for these births; evidence on the relative importance of specific factors driving clients to seek outside service provision; and evidence of inhouse capabilities and internalization and/or externalization of activities on the part of service users. These results demonstrate that pure cost-driven motivations for external purchase *is not* perceived by the suppliers of a wide variety of producer services as the *dominating* force motivating clients to seek their services. Instead, we find that the demand for specialized technical expertise, that is often unavailable to the client at practically any reasonable cost, is a far more important factor. Cost-driven factors *are* evident, but they are rarely cited as the sole reasons driving producer service demand. Most often these factors are interwoven with a complex set of other quasi-cost and non-cost reasons. Moreover, there is only limited evidence that service users are shifting services once performed inhouse to outside producer service suppliers, and where this tendency does exist, it is mainly a recent phenomenon and cannot explain the sustained growth in producer services demand seen over the course of the past two decades. This paper will present this evidence in the aggregate and for individual producer services, but we will be unable to explore these issues from a geographical, organizational, age, and size of firm perspective. In other recent work we have reported on the geographical and organizational dimensions (Lindahl 1994; Beyers 1994; Beyers and Lindahl, 1997).

It is important to note at the outset that our emphasis on demand-related factors in this paper provides only partial understanding of the development bases for the current rapid expansion of the producer services. Supply-side considerations are noticeably absent in this paper, as well as locational, technological, and other firm-environment relations that bear on development of producer service businesses. Each of these other factors is also considered as highly important, and we do not wish to ignore the important literature that addresses these factors (O'Farrell, Hitchens and Moffat 1992; Coffey and Bailly 1991; Bryson, Keeble, and Wood 1992). However, we considered it a priority to explore the demand side in this paper, as much recent theoretical debate has centered on this issue. In sum, we wish to answer two basic questions: 1) what are the major forces contributing to the demand for producer services? and 2) is cost-driven externalization a major force contributing to this demand?

2. COST, QUASI-COST, AND NON-COST DRIVEN FACTORS OF DEMAND

A number of factors are associated with the decision to purchase a service from a producer service firm. Existing conceptualizations of the organization of the production process emphasize cost considerations in solving the question of whether to producer a service internally or purchase it in the open

market. However, there are other more "quasi-cost" and "non-cost" factors
which also influence the decisionmaking process, including questions of quality and institutional context. Each of these factors should be regarded as a
proximate factor conditionally explaining the choice to externally purchase a
producer service, or, to the contrary, be an explanation for decisions to have
inhouse departments or capabilities for producing these services. In addition,
it is possible to imagine firms having inhouse departments and also acquiring
the same or similar producer services externally.

Pure Cost-Driven Considerations

There are a number of explanations that are largely cost-related in nature
for decisions on the locus of supply of producer services by users of these
services (the "make or buy" decision; Coffey, Drolet and Polèse (1994)). We
now turn to a brief review of a number of these cost-driven considerations.

Transactions Costs. The model of industrial production offered by Scott
(1988) presents a set of principles regarding the organization of production
and the decision as to whether to produce a function internally or to procure
it externally. Utilizing a transactions cost approach, Scott argues that in cases
where external provision is less expensive, firms will turn to the marketplace
for the acquisition of input factors, including producer services. Scott argues
that there is a continuous process of analysis in capitalist societies of the organization of the production process, with producers constantly seeking opportunities to reduce costs. These costs include the internal costs for wages,
administration, and overhead, or external costs for search, procurement, and
bargaining, for instance. Often this means shifting supply to an external supplier, who is able to exploit scale economies to a greater extent than a firm
using these inputs, thus leading to a process of vertical disintegration. Scott
argues when these restructuring processes occur, the redeployment of capacity
is often in an agglomeration in which new and more specialized producers
can serve a number of territorially agglomerated clients and can obtain needed
inputs from suppliers (Scott, 1988: pp. 26-60). He interprets the growth of the
modern office core in major cities to be an example of the outcome of such
processes but does not discuss the broader use of producer services by all
sectors of production (Scott, 1988: pp. 85-89). A number of scholars writing
about the producer services have also discussed internal versus external costs
of acquiring producer services as a critical factor in explaining the locus of
their production (O'Farrell, Moffat, and Hitchens 1993; Perry 1992; Goe 1991,
1990; Coffey and Bailly 1991, 1992). If producer services are acquired in the
open market, O'Farrell, Moffat, and Hitchens (1993) argue, then the purchaser
of these services will have a more accurate estimate of the cost of provision
in many cases than if the firm attempted to produce the service inhouse. This
ability to obtain firm cost estimates, they argue, is another factor driving businesses to purchase from specialized producer service firms. Harrison (1994)
argues that strategic downsizing, cost-cutting, and the desire to be "lean and
mean," especially on the part of large firms, has led to the proliferation of
new firms. While his arguments are largely concentrated on manufacturing-
oriented activities, he holds that these processes are also relevant for service
industries.

Thus, *if there has been a pure cost-driven process of vertical disintegration on the part of clients, leading to a shift from inhouse to outside service provision, we would expect clients to have shed themselves of these functions (i.e., downsized).* This represents the most "pure" form of cost-driven externalization, although there are also possible "non-cost" factors that may lead to downsizing. Another indicator of cost-driven externalization that is a bit less "pure" would be an indication that clients sought outside services because of a perception that outside provision is cheaper. The reason that such a factor is a bit more muddied is that a firm could hold such a view regardless of whether they had existing capabilities (or could even conceivably acquire such capabilities) to produce the service internally. Moreover, this view (that an outside provider is less expensive) may or may not be based on an actual comparison of the costs of internal provision or external purchase. In spite of these caveats, *where clients are driven to an outside provider because of a perception that such provision is less expensive suggests, but does not confirm, that transactions-cost-driven motivations are an important factor driving producer service demand.* Thus, these two factors—downsizing and perception that outside provision is less expensive—are what we deem to be the best indicators of cost-driven externalization.

Quasi-Cost Considerations

There are other demand factors that we label "quasi-cost" in nature. These are factors that in some cases may be interpreted in a transactions-cost framework, but in others are more related to issues of strategy, scope, and motivations that are indirectly related to the service user's desire to reduce costs.

Factors of Flexibility. Several authors have argued that producers are attempting to lower their costs through a flexible approach to production, which may mean turning to outside suppliers of producer services to a greater extent (Christopherson and Noyelle 1992; Hatch 1987; Coffey 1992). Coffey and Bailly (1992) argue that flexible production systems built around the utilization of producer services are likely to emerge, especially:

> ...where the required service inputs involve highly diverse and constantly shifting mixes of information and expertise, and where the demand for these inputs is both sporadic and unpredictable, it may not be economically feasible for a firm to engage sufficient personnel to deal effectively with the entire range of demand. (Coffey and Bailly, 1992: p. 860).

Goe (1990) also emphasizes the tendencies towards flexibility, which may lead firms to purchase from producer service specialists. He argues this will give firms greater flexibility for their clients by allowing them to quickly change specialist purchases in downturns and as internal needs change (Goe, 1990: p. 331). By acquiring producer services in the open marketplace, producer services clients thus are able to adapt quickly to changing business circumstances without having to endure internal commitments to staff and capital investments. Hansen (1991) has documented the importance of a flexible production system involving producer services for Danish manufacturers, including both localized and distant procurement of specialist services. Three aspects of flexibility are discussed here: strategies for risk reduction, strategies to deal with infrequent demand, and strategies related to a desire to concentrate on core skills.

1) *Risk Reduction.* For reasons similar to a flexible production strategy, it has been suggested that by externalizing service purchases, client firms can reduce internal risks (O'Farrell, Moffat, and Hitchens 1993; Coffey and Bailly 1991, 1992). Here the notion is that by purchasing from outside specialists, firms do not need inhouse departments for these services, thereby not having responsibility for payment into social insurance programs for these employees, and avoiding the commitment to capital investment and training associated with having these inhouse departments. If demand for services fluctuates for these potential clients of producer service firms, then the need for these inhouse departments could fluctuate, causing capacity problems (e.g. not enough or too much).

2) *Infrequent demand.* If demands for producer services are only sporadic, then it may not be feasible to have an inhouse department, quite apart from questions of the risk of carrying staff related to such infrequently demanded functions. In these cases, if firms decide they actually need to use services of this type, then they will likely turn to outside specialists unless it is very easy to develop inhouse capacity for the duration of the need (Porter, 1990: p. 247; O'Farrell, Moffat, and Hitchens, 1993: p. 389; Coffey and Bailly, 1992: p.860; Perry 1992: p. 9). The quotation above by Coffey and Bailly in the section on flexibility by Coffey and Bailly speaks to this issue.

3) *Concentration on core skills.* While many firms could have inhouse departments producing given producer services these functions are often peripheral to the primary business activity of the firm. Beyond the concerns about flexibility, risk, and predictability of cost discussed already, it is argued that firms may chose to purchase these services in the marketplace because the activities are too distant from firms' core expertise (Coffey and Bailly, 1992: p. 860; Wood, 1993: p. 166; Goe, 1991; Porter, 1990: p. 244; O'Farrell, Moffat and Hitchens, 1993: p. 389; Quinn, 1992). Porter argues it this way: "In firms, busy managers no longer want to worry about noncritical activities, even if the services could be performed equally well inhouse." (Porter, 1990: p. 244). In addition to these arguments, it is possible that firms could also downsize to concentrate on core skills, to become "lean and mean," and in the process purchase more services in the marketplace.

This discussion of issues surrounding flexibility leads to expectations that sellers of producer services will have clients seeking their services to reduce risks, cope with infrequent needs, and make it possible for the purchaser of producer services to concentrate on skills core to the industry and markets served by these firms.

Non-Cost Considerations

Lack of Expertise. If firms do not have inhouse expertise to produce a service they need, then they can either develop an inhouse department to produce this service, or decide to purchase it in the marketplace. A number of scholars have identified these inhouse limitations as reasons for external purchase. Coffey and Bailly (1992: p. 860; 1991: p. 101) identify knowledge, personnel, and cost limitations as impediments leading to external purchase, as well as the difficulties in keeping up with the pace of technical change in the provision of certain services. Perry (1992) argues that firms may have not developed expertise internally in certain services, thereby leading them to external purchase. Goe argues that this factor is a major force associated with the growth of the producer services:

> In effect, the growth of producer services is also a response to the expanding need for specialized knowledge regarding indirect production activities which in many cases cannot be easily and efficiently produced within firms lacking this expertise. (Goe, 1990: p. 330-331).

> The real issue at hand is whether firms possess any internal capability to produce a particular function that is needed. If firms do possess some internal capability, the issue becomes one of whether this capability is adequate to meet the particular demand requirements at hand. (Goe, 1991: p. 122).

The factors associated with this dimension are numerous and interdependent with many of the other factors already identified in this section of the paper. For example, if the barriers to entry (in terms of *cost* and *time*) were low to become proficient in a particular expertise, it would seem likely that firms would develop this inhouse capability quickly—such as knowledge of software for word processing and accounting. However, it may be that the variety of types of knowledge have proliferated so rapidly that this force has become a relatively important basis for producer services firm growth. *This leads us to expect this factor—the lack of technical expertise on the part of clients—to be an important basis for demand for producer services.*

Buyer/Supplier Dynamics. Related to the factor just described, Porter (1990) has argued there is a dynamic relationship between changes in services supplied and the demands of buyers for these services which has, over time, expanded the volume and range of external service purchases. He writes that there is:

> ...rising buyer sophistication leading to more and broader service requirements; ...(and) technological changes that have upgraded service quality or made entirely new services feasible. (Porter 1990: p. 243).

O'Farrell, Moffat, and Hitchens (1993: p. 387) make a similar argument, as do Coffey and Bailly (1991), Perry (1990), and Beyers (1989). One force, then, that may be an important contributor to greater demand for producer services has been changes in the technological and organizational environments of the *purchasers* of producer services, at the same time as there has been change in production environments of producer services firms. The evolution of the marketplaces in these circumstances has fueled growth of producer services, but at the same time the inhouse departments of their clients have also probably been changing. *We should expect to see evolving relationships between producer service firms and their clients in terms of services offered, and the relative importance of external purchase versus internal provision.*

Third-party information needs. In some circumstances it is necessary for a firm to acquire independent evaluations of work it may have done inhouse, or of work performed by another producer services firm. Perry (1992) has argued that this is yet another basis for growth in demands for marketed producer services. Examples of demands of this type include the need for independent audits and appraisals, expert testimony in legal cases, or specialist qualifications needed to undertake a project or task.

Growing complexity of management. Coffey and Bailly (1992) have noted the growing complexity of national and international business environments, leading to the need for more specialists. The increased turbulence in the production environment caused by shorter product life-cycles may also increase the complexity of the management environment. Porter (1990) also argues this is a major force associated with the growth and evolution of the producer services:

> In firms and institutions, the growth in the underlying need for services is driven by the increasing sophistication, internationalization, and complexity of management. Specialized forms of services have proliferated as has the complexity of needs in such established service industries as advertising, accounting. ... More complex products and more sophisticated technologies throughout the value chains of firms require more design, operational, and maintenance services. The internationalization of competition is powering the growth of services needed to support trade and the management of dispersed corporate facilities. Technological and regulatory changes are opening up entirely new service fields, such as hazardous waste disposal and nondestructive testing. (Porter 1990: p. 243).

Other factors. There are a variety of other factors that are largely non-cost in nature. O'Farrell, Moffat, and Hitchens (1993: p. 389) suggest that in some cases certain services are simply not of importance to the firm (as distinct from not frequently demanded or not related to core activities), so they do not pursue their internal provision. They also observe that there are organizational variations in the use of producer services, with small and very large organizations argued to be less demanding users than medium sized firms. Increased government regulations and the development of regulations governing international trade in goods and services is another factor leading to the growth in demands for service specialists (Coffey and Bailly, 1992). Other factors include new needs stemming from participating within an international context and the influence of changing technologies. *Thus, we may expect that these non-cost factors related to the growing complexity of the business environment, government regulations, the need for third-party information, and other factors stimulating the demand for producer services not centrally linked to cost considerations, are of importance in explaining the demand for producer services.*

Summary. In this section of the paper we have identified a wide variety of cost, quasi-cost, and non-cost-driven factors which may be related to the relatively rapid growth in demand for the producer services. These factors range from neoclassical cost-driven explanations to a much broader inventory of reasons why businesses, governments, and households might demand the services of producer service enterprises. It is important to recognize that cost and non-cost motivations may be embedded in any of these factors, regardless of our categorizations. Yet, testing the importance of factors within these three categories can contribute to answering the key questions, to be addressed in the next section of this paper: (1) whether existing demand or growth in demand for producer services has been fueled by externalization processes driven by cost considerations, and, if not, (2) what the contribution of other factors are to this demand.

3. EMPIRICAL EVIDENCE

We now present results from extensive survey research that focuses on the conceptual explanations for growth in the demand for producer services discussed in the preceding section of this paper. We first discuss our sources of data, then turn to three categories of evidence that bear on the issues discussed in section II of this paper. Our first category of evidence involves information on firm founders, especially as it relates to possible processes of vertical disintegration. In this section, we are trying to determine whether new firm births have been driven by cost-motivated outsourcing and flexible behavior on the part of servicing-using businesses. We then report on the importance of the specific cost, quasi-cost, and non-cost factors for producer service establishments' clients. This evidence is then extended by an analysis of the role of inhouse departments of producer service clients and the extent to which clients are externalizing or internalizing service functions in recent years.

We should also note that our analysis of service users (i.e., demand) is based upon the perspective of the suppliers who serve these users. We realize that *purchasers* of the output of producer services firms could have divergent perspectives on the reasons why they seek the services of producer service firms, but we are encouraged by the convergence of results to be presented in this paper with the findings of other scholars who have probed some of these issues from surveys of service users (Coffey, Drolet, and Polèse 1994; Coffey 1995; O'Farrell, 1993; Tordoir 1994; O'Farrell, Hitchens, and Moffat 1992, 1993; Bryson, Keeble, and Wood 1992).

Data Sources

The data presented in this paper are based on a survey of firms interviewed in 1993 in Chicago, the Central Puget Sound region, Spokane, and in some rural counties in the Pacific Northwest. We purposefully sought out businesses located in very high order metropolitan centers, a medium sized city, and in rural areas. These firms were large and small, single and multiple establishment, and situated in a wide variety of producer service businesses, as shown in Table 1. The typical firm was small, with median employment being eight people. Some 61% of the establishments were single-establishment firms, 18% were headquarters, and the balance were either branches, franchises, or other organizational forms. This sample included interviews with 446 establishments; responses from most of these firms are used in this paper. The data were gathered through in-depth telephone interviews, which focused upon a variety of basic characteristics of these firms, factors related to sources of competitive advantage, the demand-related factors reported upon in this paper, growth indicators, patterns of marketing from an industrial and geographical perspective over time, employment histories, founder histories, uses of subcontractors and collaborative tendencies, modes of producing and communicating their work, changes in services offered over time and reasons for these changes, and locational behavior. This paper is confined only to those aspects directly related to issues of demand and client externalization. This information was gathered in both quantitative and qualitative ways, and considerable open-ended text was recorded which helped enormously in developing the results reported upon in this paper.

TABLE 1. Industries Included in this Study

Standard Industrial Classification (SIC) CODE	Industry Title	Number of interviews
61	Nondepository Credit Institutions	18
62	Security and Commodity Brokers, Dealers, Exchanges, and Services	27
63/64	Insurance Carriers, Agents, Brokers, and Services	19
736	Personal Supply Services	16
737	Computer Programming, Data Processing, and Other Computer Related Services	46
7389	Business Services, Not Elsewhere Classified	50
81	Legal Services	58
871	Engineering, Architectural, and Surveying Services	69
872	Accounting, Auditing, and Bookkeeping Services	57
873	Research, Development, and Testing Services	21
874	Management and Public Relations Services	52

The growth of employment in the producer services has been largely associated with a proliferation of business establishments, as opposed to growth in the average size of establishments. In the 1982 to 1992 time period, U.S. County Business Patterns reports that employment in producer services grew from 10.4 to 15.8 million persons. The number of producer service establishments grew from .85 million to 1.29 million between 1982 and 1992, and average employment per establishment remained stable at 12.2 persons per establishment. At any point in time, the population of establishments includes a mix of businesses of differing ages, who are the surviving businesses from the various age-cohorts of which they are a part. We should expect the sample of businesses we interviewed to be composed of establishments of varying age, with a large proportion being relatively new businesses. This was in fact the case. The sample of establishments had a median age of twelve years, with 48% of the establishments being started since 1982. Thus, our sample has a proportion of newer firms not unlike what we would expect, given national trends in producer service establishment populations.

Founder Information Who is starting this expanding population of businesses, and why are they doing so? Let us turn to some critically important information on founders to answer these questions. When founders were asked to identify why they started their firms, the most frequently cited reason was to be their own boss, with financial considerations taking a secondary position such as identification of a market opportunity or to increase personal income, as shown in Table 2. Thus, many of the relatively new single establishment or headquarters firms in this sample of producer service businesses appear to have been started by people wishing to have some degree of control over what they are doing in their lives, although market and income opportunities are also perceived to be important. The reasons cited here do not lend much support to founders as leading agents of externalization processes. Founders of the single-establishment and headquarters businesses relied overwhelmingly on personal capital sources to start their businesses. Although male

TABLE 2. Top Reasons for Starting Single Establishment
or Headquarters Business

Reasons for Starting Firm:	Most Important Reason (%)	Secondary Reason (%)
	n=280	n=106
Desire to be own boss	42%	24%
Market opportunity identified	20%	32%
As an alternative to unemployment	9%	2%
To increase personal income	7%	17%
Less travel	<1%	1%
Other	21%	25%

founders started 80% of these businesses in the entire sample, there is a clear inverse relationship between the proportion of women founders and age of firm.

The most common previous business activity of founders was to be employed in the same occupation in the same industry (42%) or in a different industry (13%), but not by a firm that is a current client. Only 3% were previously employed by a current client, while 14% reported an occupational shift when founding, and 7% came from school or in the military. "Other" reasons accounted for another 20% of the cases; these tended to be personal factors, related to the desires to be more independent, to seize a market opportunity, or because of negative aspects associated with their prior business.

This founder information shows little movement of firm founders from inhouse departments of their clients, suggesting that from the firm founder perspective there is little downsizing by clients that is related to start-ups of producer service businesses. Instead we find personal motivations, coupled with visions of business opportunities, to be the most important motivations for starting new producer service businesses. In many cases these businesses are created to fill a "niche," related to quasi-cost or non-cost motivations on the part of clients to purchase producer services. The next section examines the importance of these demand factors.

Demand Factors

As we discussed in Section 2, this paper seeks to answer what seems at first glance a simple question: what are the primary factors driving the demand for producer services? Table 3 sheds light on this question, summarizing answers to reasons why clients sought the services of producer services firms. This table highlights (*with a box*) the five most important reasons in each sector, with the percentages being the proportion of respondents identifying the factor to be highly important as a reason why clients seek their services. Respondents were also asked whether these factors had become more or less important in the past five years, and this information is also found in Table 3.

It is immediately evident that there are major differences in the overall patterns of response across these sectors. On the one hand, this demonstrates the tremendous complexity of forces contributing to the demand for these types of services; there are no simple explanations, even within particular

TABLE 3. Reasons Why Clients Seek Outside Producer Services[a]

		Non-Dep. Credit	Security Brokerage	Insurance	Personnel Supply	Computer Services	Misc. Bus. Svcs.
		n=18*	n=27*	n=17*	n=12*	n=42*	n=49*
		61	62	63/64	736	737	7389
Non-Cost	Lack of technical expertise	39%	89%+	77%	58%	86%+	53%
Non-Cost	Size of client is too small to produce services	39%	52%	47%	67%	60%	43%
Cost	Perception that outside firm can perform task more cheaply	39%	41%	35%+	67%	50%	51%
Non-Cost	Increased government regulation	28%++	37%++	59%+++	17%+	12%+	18%+
Quasi-Cost	Avoidance of risks associated with inhouse provision	44%	67%+	59%+	25%	24%	31%
Cost	Lack of financial resources to perform such services	61%	22%	53%	33%	41%	31%
Quasi-Cost	Infrequent need for services	11%	11%	18%	33%	31%	39%
Non-Cost	Need for unbiased, 3rd party opinion or expert testimony	6%	15%	6%	17%	12%	33%
Non-Cost	Need to stay abreast of changing technologies	6%++	4%	18%	0%	55%+	33%+
Quasi-Cost	Service provided not related to strategically central function	33%	11%	18%	8%	14%	16%
Non-Cost	Need to stay abreast of rapidly changing economic conditions	22%	41%	29%++	17%+	24%+	12%
Cost	"Downsizing" by clients or desire to be "lean and mean"	17%+	0%	24%+	17%++	36%+++	20%++
Non-Cost	Increasing complexity of managing a firm	0%	15%	0%	8%	10%	10%
Non-Cost	Changes in nature of client's business	11%	7%	6%	8%	19%	4%
Non-Cost	Increasing complexity of doing business in intntl. context	0%	11%+	0%	0%	2%	10%
Variable	Other reasons	22%+++	30%NA	12%	75%++	12%	16%

% of respondents noting factor as highly important - SIC Code and Industry

Responses are based on a question asking respondents, "On a scale of 1-5 (1=no importance and 5=highly important), please rate the most important reasons why clients seek your services".

Percentages equal the number of 4 and 5 responses divided by the total number of valid responses.

Percentages in bold denote 5 most important reasons in each sector.

"+", "++", "+++", and "..." denote the degree of change in the relative importance of the factor over the past 5 years.

[a] n is based on approximate number of valid responses for each sector. These may vary by individual factor.

** Total n of sample will be greater than sum of sectors due to inclusion of a few respondents in other misscellaneous producer services SIC codes.

Table 3. Reasons Why Clients Seek Outside Producer Services^a (continued)

Variable		n=59* 811 Legal Services	n=68* 871 Arch. & Eng.	n=57* 872 Account- ing	n=21* 873 Researc h &Test- ing	n=50* 874 Mgmt. Consult- ing	n=403* TOTAL**
Non-Cost	Lack of technical expertise	88%++	88%	91%	81%	74%	77%
Non-Cost	Size of client is too small to produce services	34%	24%	58%	43%	36%	42%
Cost	Perception that outside firm can perform task more cheaply	10%	21%	35%	67%	58%+	37%
Non-Cost	Increased government regulation	14%+++	27%+++	63%++	48%++	36%++	31%++
Quasi-Cost	Avoidance of risks associated with inhouse provision	7%	19%++	30%	38%	40%	30%
Cost	Lack of financial resources to perform such services	3% -	24%	32%	33%	18%	26%
Quasi-Cost	Infrequent need for services	9%+	28%	30%	38%	40%	26%
Non-Cost	Need for unbiased, 3rd party opinion or expert testimony	12%	6%	51%	67%	52%+	26%
Non-Cost	Need to stay abreast of changing technologies	0%	6%	19%	52%	40%++	22%+
Quasi-Cost	Service provided not related to strategically central function	5%	13%	19%	5%	34%+	17%
Non-Cost	Need to stay abreast of rapidly changing economic conditions	0%	3%	11%	10%	34%++	16%
Cost	"Downsizing" by clients or desire to be "lean and mean"	3%	12%++	11%+	5%	18%++	15%++
Non-Cost	Increasing complexity of managing a firm	2%	0%	11%	10%	24%++	11%
Non-Cost	Changes in nature of client's business	0%	2%	5%	5%	34%++	10%
Non-Cost	Increasing complexity of doing business in intntl. context	2%	0%	11%+	10%	24%++	8%
Variable	Other reasons	7%	19%++	21%++	14%	30%+++	19%++

a. % of respondents noting factor as highly important - SIC Code and Industry
Responses are based on a question asking respondents, "On a scale of 1-5 (1=no importance and 5=highly important), please rate the most important reasons why clients seek your services".
Percentages equal the number of 4 and 5 responses divided by the total number of valid responses.
Percentages in bold denote 5 most important reasons in each sector.
"+", "++", "+++", and "-" denote the degree of change in the relative importance of the factor over the past 5 years.
* n is based on approximate number of valid responses for each sector. These may vary by individual factor.
** Total n of sample will be greater than sum of sectors due to inclusion of a few respondents in other misscellaneous producer services SIC codes.

industrial sectors. On the other hand, certain factors do emerge as highly important across most of the sectors

Lack of technical expertise, deemed a non-cost factor, is the most frequently cited reason as to why clients seek respondents' services. This pattern is consistent across each of the 11 sectors, with the exception of Non-Depository Financial Institutions (SIC 61) and Temporary Help Agencies (SIC 736). Over 85% of the establishments in Accounting (SIC 872), Security Brokerage (SIC 62), Architecture and Engineering (SIC 871), Legal Services (SIC 81), and Computer Services (SIC 737) noted this factor as highly important. Some of the qualitative comments associated with these responses provide a bit more insight: "most of our clients don't even understand standard bookkeeping" noted one accountant; "clients come to us because they lack local knowledge" according to a surveying firm; and "I'm very specialized. There's really no one else in the country that does what I do," said a consultant who provides specialized studies for the mining industry. This high degree of specialization is evidenced in Table 3, which provides some examples of the niches identified by survey respondents. For many of these services, the question of a "make or buy" decision (Coffey, Drolet, and Polèse 1994) is never even a consideration by clients; the service needed is so specialized or completely out of the scope of a client's internal capabilities that cost-driven factors are absent from the equation. This is particularly the case for Legal Services (SIC 81) where few factors emerge other than *lack of technical expertise* as a primary reason driving client demand.

The second most frequently cited reason for the entire sample is *size of client is too small to produce services,* a quasi-cost factor, with over 50% of the Temporary Help Agencies (SIC 736), Computer Services (SIC 737), Accounting (SIC 872), and Security Brokerage (SIC 62) establishments identifying this fac-

TABLE 4. Examples of Descriptions of "Niches"

Industry	
Security Brokerages	"Investment services for Native American organizations - Lutheran communities"
Computer Services	"Software development and support for the fruit accounting industry" "Computer software for the waste industry"
Architecture & Engineering	"High-pressure water-jet technology" "K-12 school design"
Management Consulting	"Shutdown of plants, especially paper mills and gold mines" "Education media consulting -- our niche is that we know how to manipulate our main client: IBM"
Miscellaneous Business Services	"Polygraph analysis, especially for sex offenders" "Export consulting and intermediary for firms doing business in the Arab world"

364 PAPERS IN REGIONAL SCIENCE, VOL. 75, NO. 3, 1996

tor as a highly important source of client demand. The high relative importance of this factor speaks to two issues: (1) the majority of clients of producer services establishments are small firms, and, as noted above, (2) the decision to seek external services by these smaller firms is associated far less with a purposeful internal/external provision decision (although there are a number of instances where this is important), but has more to do with the general lack of or inability to acquire such capabilities internally. Counteracting this tendency, however, is the increased internalization of certain routine functions by clients due to the adoption of various information technologies. A large number of accountants, for instance, noted that smaller clients are performing more of the bookkeeping and payroll-oriented tasks that had once been provided by an outside establishment with the advent of user-friendly and readily available software packages. This has allowed, and forced, many accounting firms (and other types of businesses experiencing similar trends) to "ratchet up" the types of services they perform, providing more specialized financial or management counseling, for example.

Increased government regulation is another non-cost-driven factor holding moderate importance for a number of sectors, especially Accounting (SIC 872), Insurance Carriers/Brokers (SIC 63/64) and Research, Development, and Testing Services (SIC 873). New tax laws, environmental regulations, financial institution regulation stemming from the late 1980s banking and thrift crisis, and other local, state and Federal government activities have fueled much demand for certain types of services. Some of this demand is derived directly from government expenditures (approximately 11% of all respondents' revenues were from government clients); however, most is due to the impact of regulations on non-government clients. This factor also was identified by a substantial percentage of respondents in each sector as becoming more important as a basis of demand over the past five years.

Other non-cost-driven factors (such as *need for unbiased 3rd party opinion or expert testimony, need to stay abreast of changing technologies, need to stay abreast of rapidly changing economic conditions, changes in nature of client's business,* and *increasing complexity of doing business in an international context*) demonstrate moderate to weak importance in the aggregate; however, there is a great degree of variability between (and within) sectors. *Need for 3rd party opinion,* for instance, is noted by over 50% of the establishments in Accounting (SIC 872), Research, Development, and Testing Services (SIC 873) and Management Consulting and Public Relations (SIC 874) as highly important, while other sectors identify this factor as either of weak or moderate importance.

Cost and quasi-cost-driven factors associated with a cognizant internal provision or external purchase decision emerge in Table 3 as moderately important reasons for service demand. *The perception that outside providers can perform tasks more cheaply* is cited by over 35% of the establishments as highly important for each of the sectors, with the exception of Legal Services (SIC 81) and Architecture and Engineering (SIC 871). Some qualitative comments from respondents who cited this factor as important include: "it's cheaper for them to go to us than to hire a receptionist," said a telephone answering service; and "clients know we're expensive but realize that in the end we save them money," noted a management consultant. One accountant echoed a

theme indicated by a number of other respondents: "clients don't often recognize the reality that we're more cost-effective, but we are trying to educate
them more about this and use it as a selling point." In this regard, then, the
cost-driven decision to procure a service externally is initiated by the provider
and not the user. Overall, though, this factor was not identified as becoming
more important in recent years (with the exception of Insurance (SIC 63/64)
and Management Consulting and Public Relations (SIC 874), where there was
a small proportion of respondents who believed this factor had become more
important).

Another cost-driven factor, *lack of financial resources to perform such services,*
indicates moderate importance in the aggregate. This factor may not represent
the most appropriate indicator of cost-driven motivations, as it captures the
population of small firm clients (who, again, may never even consider performing a service internally) and the particular characteristics of certain
respondent industries where financial resources are an integral part of the service (such as Non-Depository Financial Institutions (SIC 61) and Insurance
(SIC 63/64)). Other sectors where financial resources are not a central part
of the service delivered rate this factor as either of low or moderate importance
(with the exception of Computer Services (SIC 737) which is the only sector
that demonstrates consistent evidence of cost-driven motivations and vertical
disintegration tendencies).

A quasi-cost-driven factor that demonstrates moderate importance is *avoidance of risks associated with inhouse provision.* Respondents citing this factor as
highly important noted a number of types of risk that clients may seek to
transfer to an outside contractor, including financial and administrative risks
of hiring new personnel, risks associated with performing the service properly,
and liability risks such as those associated with specialized technical studies
or analyses (i.e., hazardous waste testing). Thus, some of these risks are
directly cost-oriented and others are not. A sizable proportion of Architecture
and Engineering businesses (SIC 871) noted that this factor had become more
important over the past five years.

A key finding in Table 3 is the low frequency of responses associated with
"downsizing" or the desire to be "lean and mean." This factor represents the strictest interpretation of the vertical disintegration/externalization thesis. In the
aggregate and across most sectors, this turns out *not* to be an important factor
of service demand, with only one sector (Computer Services, SIC 737) having
greater than 30% of the establishments noting this factor as highly important.
We will confirm this result in the next section of this paper, where we find
weak evidence for externalization of demand. It is important to note, though,
that this factor was noted by a high proportion of respondents across most
sectors as becoming more important as a source of client demand. Thus, while
this factor is not currently a primary driver of service demand for most producer service establishments (and, we assert, has not been a major contributor
to the rapid employment growth in producer services during the past two
decades), its influence will likely be greater in the future (unless these trends
are due to short-term recessionary restructuring).

Finally, the *other* category includes a variety of reasons, most related to
non-cost and quasi-cost factors, such as industry-specific needs (i.e., residential

realtors that require the services of a mortgage broker for all transactions) and the demand for a quick turnaround in service delivery faster than a client's internal capabilities. Many respondents noted that these individualized factors had become more important.

The results in Table 3, then, suggest that there are a complex variety of factors contributing to the demand for outside provision of producer services. While cost-driven factors do emerge as important in some sectors (and the influence of these factors may be increasing), the preponderance of sectors show quasi-cost or non-cost factors, especially that related to lack of expertise on the part of a client, as the overwhelming demand motivations across all sectors. The next section provides further detail on the inhouse capabilities of clients and externalization/internalization tendencies.

Competition with Inhouse Departments

In addition to developing information on reasons why clients sought the services of the producer service firms we interviewed, we also sought information on the existence of and competition with inhouse departments of client firms. This question was intended to help clarify relationships between producer service clients and suppliers, and to help us better understand factors surrounding internal versus external procurement of producer service functions. Table 5 presents results by sector and for the sample as a whole. We asked the producer service firms if their client had an inhouse department which provided the same types of services as they supplied. In the majority of cases (63%), clients have inhouse departments providing services similar to those supplied by the producer service firms, but as Table 5 shows there was direct competition in only 25% of the overall sample, while in 38% of the cases there was not competition with the client's inhouse departments. This suggests that the client's inhouse departments are frequently providing a service similar to but not identical to the producer service suppliers, or that the producer service supplier may be providing additional capacity for the client firm.

Sectoral variations are evident in Table 5, with sectors such as Computer Services (SIC 737), Management Consulting and Public Relations (SIC 874), Research, Development, and Testing Services (SIC 873), and Miscellaneous Business Services (SIC 7389) indicating that almost all clients have inhouse departments. At the other extreme, relatively few of the clients of Architecture and Engineering (SIC 871), Security Brokerage SIC 62), and Nondepository Financial Institutions (SIC 61) have inhouse departments providing services similar to those supplied by the producer service firms. In these sectors when an inhouse department is present it tends to be noncompetitive. For sectors in which clients tend to have inhouse departments, Table 5 shows a stronger tendency for competition with these inhouse departments, and in some cases, there is more competition between inhouse departments than noncompetitive relationships (such as in Miscellaneous Business Services (SIC 7389), and Research, Development and Testing Services (SIC 873).

TABLE 5. Inhouse Departments of Clients and Competition With Service Providers[a]

| | n=18 | n=26 | n=18 | n=15 | n=44 | n=45 | n=57 | n=67 | n=55 | n=19 | n=45 | n=422 |
| | 61 | 62 | 63/64 | 736 | 737 | 7389 | 811 | 871 | 872 | 873 | 874 | TOTAL* |
	Non-Dep. Credit	Security Brokerage	Insurance	Personnel Supply	Computer Services	Misc. Bus. Svcs.	Legal Services	Arch. & Eng.	Accounting	Research & Testing	Mgmt. Consulting	
Clients Do Not Have Inhouse Departments	72%	62%	50%	27%	5%	16%	53%	69%	31%	16%	13%	37%
Clients Have Inhouse Department and They Compete with it	6%	12%	6%	33%	43%	44%	18%	9%	40%	53%	40%	25%
Clients Have Inhouse Departments and No Competition	22%	27%	44%	40%	52%	40%	30%	22%	47%	32%	47%	38%

a. SIC Code and Industry
* Total n of sample will be greater than sum of sectors due to inclusion of a few respondents in other miscellaneous services SIC codes.
Table based on question asking respondents, "Do your clients typically have an inhouse department that provides the same types of services you do, and, if so, do you compete for business directly with that department?"

TABLE 6. Changes in the Locus of Provision of Service[a]

	n=18 61 Non-Dep. Credit	n=23 62 Security Brokerage	n=17 63/64 Insurance	n=14 736 Personnel Supply	n=27 737 Computer Services	n=42 7389 Misc. Bus. Svcs	n=56 811 Legal Services	n=66 871 Arch. & Eng.	n=55 872 Accounting	n=18 873 Research & Testing	n=43 874 Mgmt. Consulting	n=390 TOTAL*
The Client Never Performed the Services	67%	57%	59%	21%	0%	21%	67%	64%	13%	50%	14%	39%
Client Once Performed, Now Some Purchases are External	6%	4%	29%	50%	67%	33%	15%	14%	20%	22%	40%	25%
Client Once Performed, Now All Purchases are External	0%	4%	0%	0%	4%	7%	2%	5%	2%	0%	5%	3%
Client Now Performs the Service, Previously Did Not	0%	0%	0%	7%	0%	12%	2%	0%	21%	0%	5%	6%
Client Now Performs the Service to a Greater Extent	11%	17%	12%	0%	0%	5%	11%	6%	29%	6%	16%	11%
No Change in Balance of Internal/External Provision	17%	17%	0%	21%	30%	21%	4%	12%	14%	22%	21%	16%

a. SIC Code and Industry
Columns sum to 100%
Table based on question asking respondents, "In general, have your clients been seeking companies for services once performed or are they performing more of these services inhouse over the past few years?"
*Total n of sample will be greater than sum of sectors due to inclusion of a few respondents in other miscellaneous producer services SIC codes.

Changes in the locus of provision of services.

The relationships between inhouse departments and producer service firms reported in Table 5 were documented for *current* business relationships. We also sought information on *changes* in the clients' tendencies to buy these services in the marketplace over time, to further develop trend information on internalization and externalization of demand. Table 6 reports findings on these relationships. In the aggregate, some 39% of the respondents indicate that their clients have never performed the producer service supplier's service, a percentage similar to the share without inhouse departments (37%). In some 16% of the cases there has been no change in the share of inhouse versus market purchase of producer services, while in 28% of the cases some degree of externalization is reported, and in 17% of the cases tendencies towards internalization are reported. Table 6 shows considerable variation among sectors, and consistency with tendencies reported in Table 5. The responses in this table show that externalization tends to be partial, and in no sector does complete externalization exceed that of partial externalization in the acquisition. In the cases reporting internalization, it appears to be much more common to find expansion of *existing* internal provision, rather than the *initialization* of internal provision. Sectors with few clients having inhouse departments also tend to report that their clients had never performed their service. For example, 69% of the Architecture and Engineering (SIC 871) firms reported their clients did not have inhouse departments, and 64% said they never had performed their service. At the other extreme, sectors such as Management Consulting and Public Relations (SIC 874) typically face clients with inhouse departments--typically top managers--and most of these have previously performed services similar to the management consulting and public relations firms.

Sectors in which most clients have inhouse departments show varying tendencies towards externalization or internalization of these services. Temporary Help Services (SIC 736) Computer Services (SIC 737), Miscellaneous Business Services (SIC 7389), and Management Consulting and Public Relations (SIC 874) show relatively strong tendencies towards clients expanding their external acquisition of these services. In contrast, Accounting (SIC 872) shows a stronger tendency for clients to be performing accounting services inhouse over time. Research, Development, and Testing Services (SIC 873) clients often have inhouse departments that undertake the same functions as the service provider. They seek outside services often for liability reasons (when there is a need for a 3rd party opinion), in times of recession (when they will downsize a department), and when there is a need for research in a geographic area out of the clients' reach.

Inhouse departments and changes in locus of service provision

When we look simultaneously at the presence of and competitive relationships with inhouse departments *and* at changes in where clients have been obtaining services, we gain additional insights into the dynamics of producer service markets. Table 7 shows results for the 372 establishments that provided information on both dimensions. Thirty one percent of the establishments clients do not presently have inhouse departments, nor have they ever performed

TABLE 7. Cross Tabulation of Inhouse Departments
and Changes in the Locus of Provision[a]

	Clients do Not Have Inhouse Departments	Clients have Inhouse Depts. and Compete	Clients have Inhouse Depts. but not Compete	Percent of Total Row Categories
They Never Performed the Service	30.9%	1.1%	7.8%	39.8%
They Have Partially Externalized	3.8%	11.3%	10.2%	25.3%
They Have Fully Externality	0.5%	0.8%	1.9%	3.2%
The Client Now Performs, Used to Not Perform	0.8%	1.6%	3.2%	5.6%
The Client Now Performs to a Greater Extent	1.9%	3.5%	5.4%	10.8%
No Change in Internal/External Balance	3.0%	4.8%	7.3%	15.1%
Percent of Total Column Categories	40.9%	23.1%	36.0%	100%

a. Center Box Shows Percent of Total Cases, N = 372

the services supplied by the producer service firms. On the other hand, some seventy percent of the sample has had some type of relationship in which there was an inhouse department, and in which there may or may not have been a change in marketplace relationships with clients of the producer service firms. It should be noted that the lack of technical expertise was an important factor related to each of the alternative situations described in Table 7.

Table 7 shows a variety of combinations of tendencies for externalization or internalization, along with differing relationships with clients inhouse departments. Analyses of comments gathered as a part of the survey help interpret these various situations. Businesses indicating that *their clients never performed their services* and *do not have inhouse departments* supplying these services tend to be specialized services which are in infrequent demand by clients, or simply not central to the functions of the client firm. A number in this group indicated the need to buy outside expertise to satisfy regulatory requirements. For those who say their *clients never performed their service*, but who *have inhouse departments that do not compete* (8% of the cases), it is clear that specialization within the services marketplace has occurred. Clients may perform certain routine functions, such as bookkeeping within inhouse departments, but simultaneously they demand accounting services they cannot produce (Wood 1993).

Externalization cases. For those who have enjoyed growth in demand due to clients' externalizing, we see three situations. Where *clients do not have an inhouse department now* (4% of the cases), externalization has been driven by small size, lack of financial resources, infrequent need, or a feeling that external suppliers can provide the service more cheaply than they can. Lack of time, and changes in computer technology which allow specialization in service delivery were also mentioned as forces leading to changes in demand by this group of establishments. In cases where *clients* do *have an inhouse department* and *compete with it* (12% of the cases)—the situation where producer service firms are seemingly winning business from their clients—the key factor appears to be lower cost of provision externally, but also a desire to gain access to new technologies, strategies to downsize and externalize risks by clients, and the fact that the client is too small to provide the service. Clients in these cases seek to avoid the long term obligations associated with inhouse departments, sometimes have conflicts-of-interest that make them go external, or find inhouse departments simply overworked. Other comments suggest that this is a cyclical matter, with externalization and internalization occurring as overall business levels of clients fluctuate. In cases where externalization has occurred and there is *not now competition with clients' inhouse departments* (12% of the cases) we see differentiation of capabilities and needs between producer service firms and their suppliers. Specialization of tasks, lack of centrality to client firms' work, risk externalization, and downsizing of client firms were also mentioned as reasons for noncompetitive externalization.

Internalization cases. Establishments internalizing service functions supplied by producer services firms *with competing inhouse departments* (5% of the cases) tended to be growing client firms, who felt that as their size expanded they could more efficiently provide these services through an inhouse department. Prevalent among comments for this group were remarks about ways in which advances in computer technologies have facilitated these shifts in service provision. In contrast, establishments internalizing service functions where there was *not competition with inhouse departments* (9% of the cases) show a mix of reasons for these tendencies, in some cases noting again the role of computers to drive inhouse these activities, and alternatively institutional situations such as banks now accepting financial statements produced inhouse.

Balanced cases. The groups which have had no change in the balance of internal and external provision, but variation in the role of inhouse departments account for 15% of the total cases. Here we again find that information technologies play a key role. Those where the *clients do not have an inhouse department* against which they compete, yet claim there is no change in the balance of internal/external acquisition tend to say that the client is too small to produce the service, or it is not central to the client's function, or indicate increasing government regulation or externalization of risks are important bases of demand, yet they also indicate that computerization has spared them from internalization. Those *with competing inhouse departments* show no clear basis for their responses, while those *with noncompeting inhouse departments* indicate a mixture of reasons driving and offsetting demand for their services. On the one hand, they suggest the need for more specialized information, often for confidentiality reasons or due to lack of knowledge on the part of the clients, but then too they note that information technologies have helped develop inhouse capabilities.

The groups showing internalization or balance often describe relationships suggestive of changing buyer-supplier relationships, as argued by Porter (1990) and Wood (1993). Wood (1993) emphasizes the need for this interaction in the "management of change," with fluidity in relationships and responsibilities performed by clients and producer service suppliers.

This analysis of inhouse capabilities of clients and their tendencies towards internalization or externalization of service functions presents limited evidence of "pure" externalization--where a specific service previously performed inhouse has been shifted to an external supplier. In far more cases we find complementary relationships between inhouse departments and suppliers, where producer service establishments are providing increasing or decreasing amounts of services similar but not identical to the services provided by the inhouse departments of their clients. When clients do not have formal inhouse departments, most have never performed the service provided by an outside supplier.

"*Summary* The empirical evidence just presented can be summarized as follows. Demand for producer services has not been fueled by employees of downsizing companies founding new business and serving their former employees as clients. Rather, the overwhelming explanation is associated with non-cost and quasi-cost factors, particularly the lack of expertise on the part of clients firms and the creative packaging of these capabilities in new and expanding producer service business. There are differences in the importance of these factors across individual lines of producer services, and in some instances cost-related factors are influential in the demand for these services. Firms often perform their services in the presence of an inhouse department, but competition is less frequent than complementarity between services produced inhouse and those acquired in the marketplace".

4. CONCLUDING REMARKS

This paper provides critically needed empirical evidence on forces underlying the demand for producer services. We have evaluated three categories of evidence: motivations for firm creation, cost and non-cost factors related to the demand for outside service provision, and dynamics between clients' inhouse capabilities and outside service suppliers. Although we find some recent evidence of vertical disintegration and cost-driven externalization on the part of service users, this is not the major force driving producer services demand or new firm births. Instead, the demand for specialized technical expertise, in combination with a myriad of other non-cost, quasi-cost, and cost-driven factors, is far more important.

These results extend the findings reported by O'Farrell, Moffat, and Hitchens (1993) for a sample of manufacturers in the U.K.; the work of Tordoir (1994) for a diversified sample of U.S. and Dutch producer service clients; the research conducted by Wood, Bryson and Rotheram (1994) on the use of consultants by large British corporations; Perry's (1990) analyses of New Zealand users and suppliers of producer services; and Coffey, Drolet, and Polèse (1994) analyses of Montreal users of services. Based on the findings of these other scholars, and the evidence in this paper, it should now be unequivocally clear that cost-driven externalization is not responsible for most of producer services employment growth in recent decades. We do, however, find evidence that such processes represent more than a minor force within certain sectors (such as computer services), and that for many other sectors instances of downsizing and outsourcing (for cost and other reasons) have increased noticeably in recent years. It is unclear as to whether this trend will be sustained over the next decade or if it represents merely a temporary phenomenon. Continued empirical research in this regard will help us understand the magnitude and longevity of these and other trends.

Finally, the complexity of forces that contribute to demand for services requires a better understanding as to which types of forces yield different outcomes—from a supply perspective and from a regional view. Do different types of demand motivations, for instance, favor one type of organizational form, size, age or other characteristic (from a supplier's perspective) over another? Do certain demand forces manifest themselves within different geographies? Where forces of externalization and downsizing do exist, are they mainly a metropolitan phenomenon that are possibly diffusing down the urban hierarchy or are such forces widespread? We hope this research has laid the foundation for answering these and a host of other related questions.

ACKNOWLEDGMENTS

We would like to acknowledge the support of the National Science Foundation through grant number SES-9224515 and a related REU supplement for the research which is reported in this paper. We also acknowledge our undergraduate student assistant, Ezra Hamill, for his help with statistical and textual analysis.

REFERENCES

Beyers, W. 1989. *The producer services and economic development in the United States: The Last Decade.* U.S. Dept. of Commerce, Economic Development Administration, Technical Assistance and Research Division.

Beyers, W. 1992. Producer services and metropolitan growth and development. In *Sources of Metropolitan Growth*, eds. E.S. Mills and J.F. McDonald, pp. 125-146. New Brunswick: Rutgers University Press.

Beyers, W. 1994. Producer services in urban and rural Areas: contrasts in competitiveness, trade, and development. A paper given at the North American Regional Science Meetings, Niagara Falls, Ontario, November 1994.

Beyers, W. and Lindahl, D. 1997. Strategic behaviour and development sequences in producer service business. *Environment and Planning A*, 29, forthcoming.

Bryson, J., Keeble, D., and Wood, P. 1992. *Business networks, flexibility and regional development in UK business services.* Small Business Research Centre, University of Cambridge. Working Paper 19.

Bryson, J., Wood, P., and Keeble, D. 1993. The creation and growth of small business service firms in post-industrial Britain. Small Business Research Centre, University of Cambridge. Working Paper No. 26.

Christopherson, S. and Noyelle, T. 1992. The U.S. path toward flexibility and productivity: the remaking of the U.S. labour market in the 1980's. In *Regional Development and Contemporary Industrial Response*, eds. H. Ernste and V. Meier, pp.163-178. London: Belhaven Press.

Coffey, W. 1992. The role of producer services in systems of flexible production. In *Regional Development and Contemporary Industrial Response*, eds. H. Ernste and V. Meier, pp. 133-146. London: Belhaven Press.

Coffey, W. 1995. Forward and backward linkages of producer service establishments: evidence from the Montreal metropolitan area. A paper presented at the Association of American Geographers Meetings, Chicago, Illinois, March 1995.

Coffey, W. and Bailly, A. 1991. Producer services and flexible production: an exploratory analysis. *Growth and Change* 22: 95-117.

Coffey, W. and Bailly, A. 1992. Producer services and systems of flexible production *Urban Studies* 29: 857-868.

Coffey, W., Drolet, R., and Polèse, M. 1994. Make or Buy?: Internalization and externalization of producer service inputs in the Montreal metropolitan area. A paper prepared for the North American Meetings of the Regional Science Association International, Niagara Falls, Ontario, November 1994.

Daniels, P. 1985. *Service industries, a geographical appraisal*. London: Methuen.

Goe, W. 1990. Producer services, trade and the social division of labor. *Regional Studies* 24: 327-42.

Goe, W. 1991. The growth of producer services industries: sorting through the externalization debate. *Growth and Change* 22: 118-141.

Hansen, N. 1991. Factories in Danish fields: how high-wage, flexible production has succeeded in peripheral Jutland. *International Regional Science Review*. 14: 109-132

Harrison, B. 1994. *Lean and mean, the changing landscape of corporate power in the age of flexibility*. New York: Basic Books.

Hatch, C. 1987. Leaning from Italy's industrial renaissance. *The Entrepreneurial Economy* 1: 4-11.

Lindahl, D. 1994. Market differentiation and competitiveness in the producer services: can local firms compete with large multi-establishment firms. A paper given at the North American Regional Science Meetings, Niagara Falls, Ontario, November 1994.

Kutscher, R. 1988. Growth of services employment in the United States In *Technology In Services: Policies For Growth, Trade, And Employment*, eds. G. R. Guile and J.B Quinn, pp. 47-75. Washington: National Academy Press.

Martinelli, F. 1991. A demand orientated approach to understanding producer services. In *The Changing Geography Of Advanced Producer Services*, (eds.) P. Daniels and F. Moulaert, pp.15-29. London: Bellhaven Press.

O'Farrell, P. 1993. The performance of business-service firms in peripheral regions: an international comparison between Scotland and Nova Scotia. *Environment and Planning A*, 25: 1627-1648.

O'Farrell, P., Hitchens, D. and Moffat, L. 1992. The competitiveness of business service firms: A matched comparison between Scotland and the South East of England. *Regional Studies*, 26: 519-533.

O'Farrell, P., Hitchens, D. and Moffat, L. 1993. The competitive advantage of business service firms: a matched pairs analysis of the relationship between generic strategy and performance. *Service Industries Journal*. 13: 40-64.

O'Farrell P., Moffat, L. and Hitchens, D. 1993. Manufacturing demand for business services in a core and peripheral region: Does flexible production imply vertical disintegration of business services. *Regional Studies* 27: 385-400.

Perry, M. 1990. Business service specialization and regional economic change. *Regional Studies*, 24: 195-210.

Perry, M. 1992. Flexible production, externalization and the interpretation of business service growth. *The service industries journal* 12: 1-16.

Porter, M. 1990. *The competitive advantage of nations*. New York: Free Press.

Quinn, J. 1992. *Intelligent enterprise*. New York: Free Press.

Scott, A. 1988. *Metropolis. from the division of labor to urban form*. Berkeley: University of California Press.

Tordoir, P. 1994. Transactions of professional business services and spatial systems. *Tijdscrift Voor Economische En Sociale Geografie* 85:322-32.

Tschetter, J. 1987 Producer services industries: why are they growing so rapidly. *Monthly Labor Review*. 110: 31-40.

Wood, P. 1993 Regional patterns of business service externalisation in the uk: an expert labour approach. Paper presented at the International RESER Conference, Siracusa Sicily, Sept. 1993.

Wood, P., Bryson, J., Rotheram, D. 1994 Consultant Use and the Management of Change: Insights into Expertise. Paper presented at the International RESER Conference, Barcelona, Sept. 1994.

[23]

ENTREPRENEURSHIP & REGIONAL DEVELOPMENT, 9 (1997), 93–111

Business service firms, service space and the management of change

JOHN R. BRYSON

School of Geography, University of Birmingham, Edgbaston, Birmingham
B15 2TT, UK

The growth of business service firms represents the latest stage in a continuing twentieth century process of technological and organizational restructuring of production and labour skills. It is associated with the rising information intensiveness of production and the development of an economy of signs. Business service activities located in service spaces drive innovations both in production technology and in management systems. The co-presence of business service firms with their clients as well as other business service firms shapes the possibilities of trust between them. A detailed case study of the way in which large client firms utilize the services of independent business service companies is provided. This is followed by an examination of the relationship between small firms and business service expertise. A dual information economy may be developing in which large firms are able to search for specialist business service expertise irrespective of its location, while SMEs are tied into local providers of more generalist expertise.

Keywords: business services; service space; co-presence; embedded knowledge; management consultancy; consultant-client relationship; untraded interdependencies.

1. Introduction

The role of service functions in the advanced economies has grown dramatically in recent decades. In Britain employment in services rose from 61.5% of the total workforce in 1981 to 72.1% in 1994. In some interpretations, this has been seen as a challenge to the prime position of manufacturing as a source of innovation and economic growth, with the resultant 'post-industrial society' characterized by the dominance of service employment and output (Bell 1974). Against this, however, the fastest growth in services during the 1980s and 1990s took place in 'business services' such as management consultancy, computer services, and technical and financial services (Bryson et al. 1996d). To the extent that these activities are inextricably linked to, if not dependent on, manufacturing and other production sectors, the growth of business services thus reflects not only the decline of industry, but also the growing complexity of production functions and organizations. It represents an extension of the division of labour within the wider production system. Investigating the role and growth of business service enterprises is thus arguably of central importance for understanding contemporary economic change in the advanced capitalist economies.

This paper relates the growth of business service firms to the part they play in wider changes in business organization, and especially in satisfying the needs of their clients. Its purpose is to place detailed empirical research into the context of theoretical debates over business service activity, and the development of service spaces (Allen and Pryke 1994). The analysis draws on material from three related research projects. First, an investigation into the growth of small management consultancy and market research firms in the United Kingdom, hereafter referred to as the Business Service

0898-5626/97 $12·00 © 1997 Taylor & Francis Ltd.

Survey (BSS) (Bryson *et al.* 1996d). This research is based on in-depth interviews with 120 small, independently-owned business service companies (see Bryson *et al.* 1993 for the methodology). This research project provided an insight into the role and functioning of small business service firms. It revealed nothing, however, about the ways in which such companies were used by client companies. Second, an exploration into the reasons why large client companies choose to employ the services of independent business service professionals, hereafter referred to as the Client Survey (CS) (Wood *et al.* 1994). A postal survey of 123 large UK-based firms (Table 1) was undertaken in 1993 and 1994, followed by 40 in-depth interviews. The sample was broadly representative of the target population, seeking a balance between manufacturing and service-based firms, and between those in the 'south' and 'north' of England. Third, on-going research investigating the ways in which small and medium-sized enterprises (SMEs) utilize expertise and information available from either private sector business service firms or from state agencies. The SME project has just started, and one purpose of this paper is to develop thinking about the ways in which both complex (large) and simple (SMEs) organizations acquire and utilize external expertise (Bryson, *et al.* 1996a,b).

This paper is divided into three sections. The first section develops a understanding of the relationship between service space and co-present interaction. It also develops an enterprise approach to understanding the growth of business service firms and the utilization of their expertise by clients. The second section presents some of the findings of the client survey. This explores the ways in which external expertise is incorporated into the production process of both large manufacturing and service companies. Finally, section three examines SMEs in relationship to the business

Table 1. Characteristics of respondents to the client company survey.

	No.	%
Employment size		
< 1500	20	16
1,501–3,000	23	19
3,000–6,000	18	15
6,000–18,000	31	25
> 18,000	23	19
Missing data	9	7
Sector		
Utilities	15	12
Financial and business services	26	21
Manufacturing	40	33
Consumer services	15	12
Primary, construction and transport	21	17
Other	6	5
Total	123	
Location of headquarters		
London	37	32
South East	25	22
Rest of England	43	37
Wales/Scotland/Ireland	10	9

service debate suggesting that a dual information economy may be developing in the United Kingdom.

2.   Embedded knowledge, service space and organizational change

2.1   *An enterprise approach to the growth of business service firms*

The evolution of capitalism during the nineteenth century in Europe and America is associated with the gradual transformation of artisan production and small family firms into large-scale business enterprises (Church 1993). This transition is associated with a growth in management complexity and the development of specialist management expertise. In the evolving family firms of the nineteenth century ownership and management control was predominantly restricted to family members. Thus, management tasks in the firm of Cadbury Brothers Ltd were divided between George and Richard Cadbury; George was responsible for manufacturing, buying and advertising, and Richard for accounts, sales and correspondence (Williams 1931: 68). Management activity at this time consisted of a combination of production and support activities. These support activities are, in fact, internalized business service activities wrapped around the production process. The current debate into the role of information in the economy (Hepworth 1989), with claims that an information economy now exists, is misplaced, as information and its interpretation has always being an important prerequisite for competitive success (Arrighi 1994: 39).

The growing size, complexity and geographical spread of business enterprises necessitated the introduction of new and increasingly sophisticated forms of management practice (Clegg *et al.* 1986). A new class of salaried executives emerged organized into hierarchies of upper, middle and lower management. Such hierarchies were frequently subdivided into management functions, for example, marketing, personnel and strategy. The development of multinational companies is associated with the transfer of ownership away from individuals to financial institutions. To support corporate expansion capital was increasingly raised on the stock markets. Institutional investors, such as insurance companies and pension funds, held an increasing proportion of corporate stock resulting in the development of new structures of corporate control. The divorce of ownership and control is thus an important feature of the emergence of the large corporation (Bearle and Means 1932). This development is associated with greater corporate accountability, and the development of modern accountancy as a device to monitor the financial performance and hence profitability of the capitalist enterprise (Roslender 1992).

From the late 1970s the structure of management regulation and employment altered as a reaction to macro-forces external to business organizations. As companies were forced to compete in the global economy production was rationalized and employees were transformed into human resources to be used for the benefits of the organization. These changes are associated with the transformation of the hierarchical organization into the heterarchical organization (Hedlund and Rolander 1990). This involves the geographical diffusion of core strategic activities and co-ordinating roles, and the replacement of hierarchical control with a wide range of governance modes. Such organizations internalize some of their activities, engage in joint ventures to develop and manufacture specific products, as well as subcontracting elements of the production process and support activities. The ideal heterarchical organization is one that performs each function in the most effective and competitive manner. Heterarchy involves a reliance on out-sourcing and the use of external business service suppliers. In-house support functions are down-sized, and replaced by formal or informal relationships with independent external suppliers. A just-in-time approach to specialist knowledge and expertise is introduced that may lead to a growing dependency on external business service suppliers.

Heterarchy, however, does not imply rigidity as enterprises will internalize previously externalized functions on the basis of cost or production efficiency. The company becomes more flexible and cost efficient, resulting in pressures on employees to increase productivity. Management layers are removed resulting in individual managers having greater responsibilities and higher workloads. Ideas and innovations flow not from the top of the hierarchy, but horizontally within the organization, as well as from either formal or informal relationships with external agents.

A career in a heterarchical organization is no longer a career for life (Kanter 1993). Increasingly employees have to rely on their own abilities, reputations and professional accreditation to structure their experience of work in a number of different corporate environments. Professional careers replace careers structured around a single company's promotional hierarchy. Individual employees have to develop reputational capital rather than company-specific organizational capital. All of these alterations result in the establishment of a different set of relationships between the organization and its external environment, and between the organization and its employees. Thus, a study by Wiersema (1995) found that unexpected executive turnover can significantly alter the perspective of a management team and is an important mechanism by which firms adapt to the changing competitive environment. A new chief executive or manager may identify a problem, and hire a consultant they had previously employed while working for another organization. Hofer suggests that a necessary 'precondition for almost all successful [company] turnarounds is the replacement of current top management' (Hofer 1980: 25–26, also see Kesner and Dalton 1994).

Since the late 1970s a reorganization of the production process has occurred as a consequence of international competition, technological change, recessionary forces and changes in the requirements of organizations. These pressures created a demand for specialist business service firms who could satisfy the short- or long-term needs of both small and large enterprises. Large companies must decide whether to develop and retain such expertise in-house, or identify suitable external information providers. In this case transaction cost theory is frequently applied, in spite of criticisms (Hepworth 1989; Jacquemin 1987), as a framework in which to explain the development of flexible production systems. The organization of the firm resolves itself into a conflict between the costs of providing a service within the firm (hierarchies) and the cost of purchasing the service from an independent supplier (markets) (Dahlman 1979; O'Farrell et al. 1992). The relationship is, however, not as simple as this as the decision to internalize or externalize a function will be determined by the culture of the organization, the internal politics and the nature of the expertise required.

The growth of business service firms represents the latest stage in a continuing twentieth century process of technological and organizational restructuring of production and labour skills. This has required increasing managerial inputs, the expansion of the management division of labour, and the development of specialized management expertise in areas such as marketing, market research and personnel. These new management areas acquired their own terminologies and methodologies and have gradually transformed themselves into recognized professions (Perkins 1989). The history of capitalist production is thus associated with a constant division and specialization of activity and the growth of a professional middle class. It is this class that is at the centre of the modern service economy (Urry 1986, Savage *et al.* 1988).

2.2   Embedded knowledge and the question of brokerage

The out-sourcing of management support activities and the increasing precarious nature of management employment has important implications for organizational behaviour besides a reduction in overheads. Internalized management functions, for example marketing, construct knowledge that is embedded within the organization's cultural and social system. Location within a particular cultural and social structure constrains individuals as it prevents the possibility of certain types of action. It is also enabling as it orders the individual's understanding of the world and of themselves, by constructing their identities, goals and aspirations, and 'by rendering certain issues significant or salient and others not' (Emirbayer and Goodwin 1994: 1441). Such knowledge engenders a considerable degree of trust as it creates individual reputations and identities that are known throughout the organization. The transfer of such expertise to independent business service companies enhances organizational flexibility, but it also allows knowledge and expertise created within a different environment to be transferred between organizations. Such knowledge may alter the organization, or be rejected by it. However, the embeddedness of knowledge in social and cultural formations implies that all successful relationships between individual actors are determined by 'concrete personal relations and structures (or 'networks') of such relations [which are involved] in generating trust and discouraging malfeasance' (Granovetter 1985: 490). This results in the formation of what Eccles (1981) has termed the 'quasifirm' arrangement of extensive and long-term relationships between organizations and their subcontractors. These long-term relationships of trust between actors occupying positions in different organizations, for example the relationship between a consultancy company and its clients, is a organizational form that exists somewhere between a pure market relationship and the vertically integrated company. The argument is that to understand the business service relationship involves the recognition that all business transactions are determined by and influenced by networks of personal relationships. These relationships range from close ties of friendship (the 'old boy' network) through direct experience of the way in which a particular organization conducts its business activities (Bryson *et al.* 1993).

The externalization of support services, and the increased requirement by organizations for external expertise involves the evolution of organizational 'brokers' (or gatekeepers) (Gould and Fernandez 1989, Knoke and Pappi 1991). Brokers occupy 'a structural position that links pairs of otherwise unconnected actors' (Fernandez and Gould 1994: 1455). The notion of brokerage has implications for the position of actors within a network for the development of transactions between unrelated organizations. Access and control of resources are central to the nature of power in any relationship. Burt (1977) assumes 'that actors are purposive in that they use their control of resources in order to improve their individual well-being'. Influence is thus defined as the possession or control of scarce resources. Control and access to resources, especially information, are thus important dimensions of a broker's power.

In Granovetter's terms brokers operate as a crucial bridge between different parts of the social system (Granovetter 1973, 1982). Granovetter's work on the strength of weak-ties shows that individuals possess a number of close friends or acquaintances, and are thus embedded in a closely-knit social structure. Any two friends will, however, possess different friends and acquaintances and, therefore, friendship represents a crucial bridge between two different groups of individuals. Such weak-ties between different parts of the social system provide individuals with access to information and expertise that is unavailable from their own friends or from within the organization in which they work. Thus, 'it follows that individuals with few weak-ties will be deprived of information from distant parts of the social system and will be confined to the provincial news and views of their close friends' (Granovetter 1982: 106). The implications for this perspective on organizational behaviour is that it transfers some power from the organization to individuals or groups of individuals responsible for the identification of external business service companies. Individual brokers will occupy a particular position in the information network, and thus will tend to implicitly or explicitly favour particular types of business service organization, and/or individual professionals. It also has important implications for the success of independent business service professionals as this will largely be determined by the number of weak-ties they possess. Research needs to focus on how such brokers mediate between client companies and external providers of business service firms.

2.3   Service space and co-present interaction

The nature of commodity production altered with the crisis experienced by Fordist factory production systems (Bryson *et al.* 1996c). To encourage and maintain consumption of mass-produced commodities the service element of commodities has increased. Associated with this trend is a 'rising information intensiveness of production in all industries, including manufacturing' (Hepworth 1989: 23). Thus, to Lash and Urry (1994: 4) 'what is increasingly produced are not material objects, but signs'. Such signs are either informational or aesthetic. The design process and business service activities such as advertising and market research now comprise a much higher proportion of the value of a finished commodity. Market research, advertising and design now drive the innovation process in both manufacturing and business and financial services. A good example of this is the development of Jaguar car's XK8 sports car. Research undertaken by Jaguar identified that up to 25% of all XK8s would be purchased by women, and that in the important USA market this would rise to over 33% of consumers. Jaguar ensured that the design team for this new car consisted of both male and female designers and that the car's ergonomics would produce a comfortable drive for both males and females. Thus, door clearances have been designed so that a woman wearing a skirt or a dress can get in and out without difficulties, and door pulls, release catches and switches were designed so that they can be used without breaking nails (Freeman 1996). These alterations to the design of the car, and the targeting of women purchasers by female Jaguar marketing and promotion executives may appear to be minor changes, but they represent a significant transformation in the way in which car companies are constructing the symbolic and design content of their products. Rather than engineers designing cars, designers, market researchers and marketing experts are instructing engineers in what they should design.

These business service driven innovations are the result of in-house business service support functions, or the deployment of external independent business service companies. A high proportion of external business service firms are located in London and the South East, with their initial establishment and continued operational success dependent on interaction with the London information nexus. For example, in 1993 33% of management consultancy firms were located in London, and 61% in the whole of the South East (Keeble *et al.* 1994). There are two dimensions of this interaction. First, both small and large business service firms regularly use external associates to undertake specialist components of a larger project. Such networking enables business service companies to offer a wide range of services without employing a substantial full-time professional staff. London-based business services firms use associates much more frequently than companies based elsewhere in the United Kingdom (Bryson *et al.* 1993). This may be explained by the operation of co-present interaction, as well as by the availability of expertise. Second, the intangible nature of the products supplied by business service firms makes it difficult to acquire clients simply by advertisements. This is a direct result of clients' lack of information about the services and quality of any business service firm. This explains the significance of repeat business for business services firms as it reflects a client's satisfaction with an earlier assignment, with a 'successful' project leading to a further assignment. It also demonstrates the embeddedness of the client business service relationship. The BSS study found that on average repeat business provided just under two-thirds of firm assignments by turnover. Repeat business was also much more important for London-based business service companies (Wood, *et al.* 1993).

Such findings suggest that the spatial fragmentation of business organizations, with externalized business service support functions increasingly located in global or information-rich cities, is producing a distinctive service space (Allen and Pryke 1994). Service space generates new knowledge and expertise that can be consumed by any client, no matter where they are located, as long as the client possesses the capability to identify, access and utilize such service expertise effectively. Such information-rich environments also offer opportunities for individuals to create a reputation for a particular type of service expertise that may become of global significance.

Service spaces consist of information-intensive companies functioning as innovation, information and expertise transfer agents. Effectively they operate as pivotal information nodes in the global economic system. Information technology has loosened the relationship between certain types of activity and location leading to the dispersal of back-office functions to locations remote from centres of corporate control (Stanback 1991). New technologies only loosen some of these locational relationships, agglomerations of information analysts are still required to interpret and control information (Sassen 1994). According to Boden and Molotch (1994), the most effective way to interpret and implement new knowledge acquired from the use of new information technologies is by co-present interaction. Such interaction, however, is much more complex than just face-to-face interaction as it includes the advantages that may accrue to a company from a location surrounded by similar companies or business service firms. Untraded interdependencies may develop that produce innovations as a consequence of tacit knowledge and expertise transfer (Storper 1995). Co-present interaction thus includes 'inadvertent' meetings that 'occur when people of the same ilk frequent the same spaces' (Boden and Molotch 1994: 274). It also is assisted by the location of the headquarters of professional organizations in global cities. The presence of these institutions offers possibilities for co-present interaction leading to the acquisition of new clients, the formation of new companies, and the development of new innovations, and of course for untraded interdependent interaction. Such interaction creates trust, and results in the transfer of embedded knowledge (Granovetter 1985). Even where geographical dispersion separates people who need to be constantly in touch, conferences and business meetings enable them to maintain an element of this interaction. The frequency of such conferences appears to have increased 'because specialists need to tell each other what they are doing' (Boden and Molotch 1994, Rubalcaba-Bermejo and Cuadrado-Roura 1995).

The co-presence of business service firms with some of their clients 'shapes the possibilities of trust between them' (Friedland and Boden 1994, Friedland and Palmer 1994). It also determines the extent to which client firms develop strategies and structures to cope with market uncertainty (Beck 1992). The employment by clients of business service experts is an attempt to remove uncertainty and reduce exposure to risk (Scott 1988). It does this in two ways. First, by reducing employment overheads by only employing experts when they are required. Large companies are thus able to maintain their competitiveness because some information development costs are externalized to business service firms. They are also able to recruit 'temporary' employees who have been trained in different corporate environments and cultures. The possibility always exists for a client to 'head-hunt' a business service employee internalizing their expertise. This has the advantage for the business service company as their 'inside' professional will generate new business, and continue to promote the reputation of the company.

Second, by acquiring access to a range and depth of expertise that cannot be created inside a company. Firms thus become dependent on knowledge and expertise that exists outside their borders. Firms have been transformed into 'extended' or flexible firms in which the boundaries between externalized and internalized management expertise has become increasingly blurred. Such external business service expertise acts to reinforce expertise available from interlinkages between corporations at Board level. Useem (1984) suggests that such board room interlinkages operate to gather information about corporate practices, regulatory and political changes, and macroeconomics expectations (Mizruchi 1991, Scott 1979). Explicit board room linkages, and implicit linkages as a result of using the same business service expertise, allow companies to exchange information, innovate and retain their competitive position. Such linkages allow the continual benchmarking of organizational performance and behaviour, as well as the transfer of information and expertise. They are also another form of untraded interdependency (Storper 1995). Related to this argument is that active participation in the social networks that drives this form of interaction is essential for its existence. Long distance interaction will not work as the nature of the relationship will deteriorate over time, as well as over space (Nohria and Eccles 1992).

Three dimensions of service space can be identified as innovation transfer nodes. First, the relationship between a client and business service firm depends on personal contact between two individuals. The movement of managers between client companies transfers both expertise as well as tacit knowledge (business service contacts). This is supported by the client survey, which found that the main reason (31% of firms) for employing a particular consultancy company was previous experience (Table 2). The transfer of a manager from a company that regularly employs external business service firms will also transfer this style of management, as well as the information available from a particular subset of business service firms. It will also result in a different relationship between the organization and service space.

BUSINESS SERVICE FIRMS, SERVICE SPACE AND THE MANAGEMENT OF CHANGE   101

Table 2.   Reasons given by clients for employing a particular consultancy company.

	No.	%
Previous experience	45	31
Recommendation	14	10
Reputation/prestige	32	22
Location/local availability	3	2
Offered specialist expertise	24	16
Ability to work closely with own staff	26	18
Offered more competitive rates	2	1

Second, the transfer of information between client companies occurs when ideas generated internally are transferred to another company as a consequence of the employment of business service companies. This may result in continuous change and improvement in an industrial sector as all organizations will gradually obtain access to the same organizational and production innovations. For any one company to enhance its profitability will require alterations to business practices that are currently not accepted behaviour within that sector. Business service firms, by operating as innovation transfer agents, may be responsible for the dynamic nature of organizational structures and operational procedures. Change has become the norm, with this change being driven increasingly by independent business service enterprises.

Third, the growing importance of multinational business service enterprises (Daniels 1993), and the export behaviour of nationally-based companies, has led to the transfer of innovations between countries. This has led to the development of weak-ties between individuals at a global level. The United Kingdom's business service companies have closely followed innovations developed in the USA, and transferred these to their UK clients. Recent examples of such transfers are the introduction of Business Process Reengineering into the UK from the USA, the introduction of the system of annual hours from Sweden (Lynch 1985), and the transfer of management practices and procedures from the advanced economies into the restructuring economies of the former Soviet Union. The transfer of management practices between countries by business service professionals has its advantages as it can result in beneficial alterations to current business practices. It also, however, has its dangers as practices developed within one country may be inexpertly altered to fit another business culture (Gertler 1995). Thus, some business service companies have sold business process reengineering as the latest management practice or fashion, to companies that did not require it.

3.   Business service expertise and client interaction

To understand the growth and significance of business service activities in the advanced economies necessitates an analysis of the role that business service activities play in changes in business organizations, and especially in satisfying the needs of clients. This section explores the results of the client survey by providing an analysis of the client business service relationship.

The client survey showed that 62% of companies routinely used consultants in the management of change, and 71% (87 companies) provided details of particular recent change programmes. Consultants frequently contributed to projects that clients regarded as of strategic importance. Such projects often concerned changes in management structure and process, organizational culture, and personnel capabilities. In 60% of cases changes in performance were also involved (Table 3). Changes in particular tasks and activities, including products and markets, image, and especially technology were less commonly described, reflecting the strategic focus of this enquiry (Wood *et al.* 1994). Such changes are often implicated in the process of organizational change, and frequently require the use of outside expertise. Overall, consultants are also used more frequently by growing companies (Table 4). This is because growth produces a demand for temporary assistance to fill gaps in the availability of internal staff, or it may reflect differences in management practices between growing and declining companies. This relationship between turnover and use of consultancy needs to be investigated further.

The use of business service consultancies reflects various forms of relationship between internal and external managerial expertise. Four types of client-consultant relationship have been identified from this research. First, a relationship of 'substitution' of external expertise for a recognized internal inexperience or incapacity. This usually involved technical skills, for example market research, information technology applications, and occasionally financial and administrative systems. Substitution is also very common in the routine out-sourcing of logistics, training, catering and security services. Second, the 'addition' of consultant expertise and experience to well-established client's capabilities. Companies with good in-house

Table 3. **Main components of organizational change.**

	Components ranked as 'significant' or 'highly significant'	
Changes in	*No. of firms*	*%*
Set up organization	47	41.6
Tasks and activities	49	43.4
Technology used	22	19.5
Management structures and processes	95	82.6
Organizational culture	93	80.2
People	82	71.9
Organizational performance	68	59.7
Image of the organization	48	42.5

Table 4. **Proportion of clients using external consultancy companies by change in turnover, 1990–1994.**

	No. using consultancy companies	*No. not using consultancy companies*	*% using consultancy*
> 40% growth	9	3	75
21–40% growth	16	5	76
Up to 20% growth	19	11	63
0–20% decline	11	13	46
> 20% decline	3	3	50

expertise will engage consultants with similar expertise. This was the most common relationship identified from this study and was most frequent in the management of broad strategic and organizational change programmes. Consultants engaged for this type of relationship must be sensitive to the cultural and political nature of the client's internal operating environment. Third, 'augmentation' of client skills, within particular sectors. In this case consultants complement clients' in-house resource in particular areas, for example information technology and environmental policy. Fourth, consultant employed as facilitator. This type of relationship is very different from the first three as it does not specifically involve knowledge transfer. Instead an ability to organize the client's own in-house resources is required. Such a role may be necessary as a consequence of an over-heated internal political debate, or a lack of management time. In one case consultants were employed to ensure that a client-formulated change programme kept to its implementation timetable.

The first three types of exchange accord respectively with Tordoir's 'selling', 'sparring', and 'jobbing' relationships (Tordoir 1993). They are not, however, discrete alternatives, nor do they determine the nature of the interaction process. First, they reflect both consultant and client contribution to managing different types of expertise. Any consultant or client will combine different modes of engagement, even in the same project. A client may even employ three or four consultancy firms to provide different types of expertise for the same change programme. This, however, requires that the client has an ability to divide the change process into clearly defined segments. The various kinds of client–consultant interaction will have common operational elements. Both 'substitution' and 'addition' require in-house management time to manage the consultancy relationship. Facilitation may be the most difficult form of interaction as it involves consultant identification of the client's political and cultural structures. During this process new methodologies and management techniques may have to be learned by the organization that were previously not recognized as an in-house deficiency. The process of exchange is dynamic, so that the different forms of relationship interact with each other. Thus, consultant expertise that is 'substituted' for an in-house deficiency may be most successful when such skills and expertise are also transferred into the internal labour market. .

These four types of interaction depend on cultural and power relations. Success or failure will not be related to the quality of the expertise, but the way it is articulated by the consultants, and by the client. A project will fail because insufficient in-house management time has been deployed to identify the dimensions of the problems, and the way in which expertise will be transferred during the relationship. Also, the success of the relationship will be strongly determined and influenced by the form and nature of the social interaction. This influences the way in which trust, mutual confidence, understanding, and expectations are constructed during the course of a consultancy project. Successful social interaction depends on the clear identification by the client of its requirement as well as a comprehensive understanding by the consultant of the client's needs. A successful consultancy project is thus one in which the consultant persuades the client that the finished project has met these requirements, and that the client's organization appears to be more efficient or effective.

The postal questionnaire identified a number of reasons why clients employed consultants (Table 5). Four primary reasons can be identified, but these are not mutually exclusive. First, the client required special knowledge and skills (58%) reflecting either an interaction of 'substitution' or 'addition'. Second, to obtain an impartial, independent view point (41%). This reflects one of the most important

Table 5. Reasons why client companies use external consultants.

	No. of firms	%
Required special knowledge and skill	68	58.1
Required intensive help on a temporary basis	44	37.6
For an impartial, outside viewpoint	48	41.0
To confirm an internal management decision	11	9.4
Timescale did not allow for skills development internally	18	15.4
Good past experience of using consultants	14	12.0
Unable to recruit appropriate staff	2	1.7

reasons for using external expertise in that it enables in-house staff to distance themselves from a decision that may be perceived to be politically unacceptable by the organization. It is a requirement by the regulators of the controlled industries (water, etc.) that independent consultants are employed to substantiate in-house claims. This reason is also used by a client to acquire some of the credibility or prestige attached to some of the global consultancy companies, for example, McKinsey or Bain. Third, consultants are employed because of their ability to provide temporary intensive help (38%), and also their ability to provide assistance for projects with short time-scales, for example a take-over bid (15%). Fourth, consultants are employed because the company has had a satisfactory experience of using consultants (12%). This explanation is related both to culture and experience. Clients can acquire a consultancy culture in which past experience indicates that external advice may be beneficial for the development of a rapid solution to a problem, or that working with individuals one-step removed from the organization enables in-house staff to examine the company's internal dynamics from a fresh perspective.

Consultants were not employed because the management expertise already existed in-house (Table 6). Another reason for the exclusive use of an in-house resource was the understanding that successful change management could only be undertaken by individuals familiar with the company's practices, style and culture (16%). This may be related to experience of a unsuccessful consultancy project in which a consultant failed to read the in-house culture in the right way. Related to these reasons is the perceived requirement by a small number of companies for confidentiality (7%).

Overall the postal questionnaire identified a selective acceptance of the need to employ consultants. Such acceptance is conditional on the internal cultural and political environment of the organization. The in-depth interviews revealed a learning

Table 6. Reasons for not employing consultants.

	No. of firms	%
Rapid response required	6	5.2
Appropriate management expertise available in-house	30	26.1
Need for familiarity with company practices, style, culture	18	15.7
Confidentiality/security reasons	8	7.0
Higher cost of external consultants	6	5.2
Poor past experience of using consultants	5	4.3

process through which individual managers and companies must progress if they are to make effective use of consultancy interaction. During the early 1980s consultants were employed to provide a 'blueprint' for change, but were not involved with implementation. Such projects were ineffective as the reports were not implemented as their findings were never integrated with the cultural and power structure of the client organization. During the 1980s, large companies have learnt by this mistake and the majority will now utilize their in-house resources before employing consultants, and ensure that consultant interaction is controlled by the client, rather than by the consultant.

Issues of corporate control, ownership of change and empowerment are all important aspects of a successful interaction with external expertise. This argument is based on the understanding that the only individuals with the power to transform an organization are its staff, and that consultants are employed as an extension (addition) of the internal labour market. Effectively, this implies that a new management skill has been developed, which is the ability to manage a relationship with an external information/expertise provider. Use of consultants may be periodic or a permanent feature of any one company's management style. However, use, non-use and the nature of the interaction is dynamic, changing as the management structure alters. In most cases consultants were expected to work closely with the in-house staff (43%), or carry out specific elements of a larger project (32%) (Table 7). Sometimes they offered specialist technical advice (31%), including staff development and training (21%). In 26% of cases the consultant provided a 'blueprint for change', with clients expecting their in-house staff to implement the proposal. Such a strategy will work if the internal staff have been actively involved in the construction of the 'blueprint'.

Dynamic processes are at work in the way in which clients choose consultancy firms. This is related to the imperfect nature of the business service market, as well as to the personal basis of consultancy interaction. A strong relationship also exists between the use of consultants and the length of the change programme. Thus, 32 of the projects planned over more than one year used consultants, while only 6 did not. Longer projects most commonly involved changes in management structures and process, or operational changes, including the introduction of new technology, new tasks and activities, or improvements in performance (Wood *et al.* 1994). For such projects, the use of consultants was often based on previous experience of them, even though more time was available for the assessment of alternatives. This reflects the importance of trust and mutual understanding in the client consultancy relationship. It also is a

Table 7. Use made by clients of consultants.

	No. of firms	%
Provided the 'blueprint for change'	30	25.9
Carried out specific sections or elements of the change project	37	31.9
Involve directly with the implementation of change	17	14.7
Worked in partnership with internal staff (including secondment)	50	43.1
Provided specialist, technical advice	36	31.0
Provided specialist human resource management advice	11	9.5
Provided specialist market research advice	9	7.8
Trainer/educator role	24	20.7

measure of the client's perceived importance of the change. Important change programmes cannot be given to companies or individuals of which the client does not
have previous experience.

Overall, the choice of consultants depended heavily on three related characteristics
(Table 2). First, previous client experience of working with the consultancy. In most
cases this will reflect experience of working with a particular consultant rather than a
company. The establishment by a client of a working relationship with a particular
consultant frequently leads to repeat business. In this case, enforced client consultancy
co-presence as a consequence of working on a project may engender trust and the
formation of weak-ties between individuals. These weak-ties bind managers and consultants together, and result in the manager transferring tacit knowledge of specific
consultants with them when they move within or between companies. The movement
of managers between and within large companies thus alters that organization's relationships with service spaces, the main locations for business service expertise. Second,
the reputation and prestige of the company or the consultants. In many respects, the
reputation of a business service professional is tied closely to the concept of trust. Trust
is a form of capital investment that the individual makes in establishing a particular
reputation. The client has to trust the professional's expertise, ability and interpretations of the benefits that may eventually accrue from a particular project. Trust is also
private knowledge that is only available to a restricted group of individuals and is
impossible to transfer completely between individuals, but is transferred with them.

Third, the ability to work closely with the in-house staff. In the majority of case
studies this was one of the most important factors in the choice of consultants, and
usually depended on whether it was considered that the consultants would fit in with
the culture of the client organization. This is perceived by clients to be an important
factor as a consultant that does not understand the company culture may produce
recommendations that will be rejected by those in positions of power in the internal
labour market. The location, or local availability, of consultants was only a minor
influence on the choice of consultants. This suggests that large companies will search
nationally and globally for the right type of expertise. However, search strategies
appear to be restricted by the notions of co-presence and embeddedness explored
above. Search strategies are thus partially determined by the existence of previous
personal contact between the client's management team and the consultant.

The important point that must be made is that good consultancy depends on the
establishment of effective personal and social relations. It is thus dependent on the
establishment of a relationship of trust between two individuals, operating within two
different institutions, who have different motivations for engaging in the relationship.
A successful project should improve the effectiveness of the client organization, and the
consultant should augment an existing reputation leading to new projects.

4. Business services and small and medium-sized enterprises

The management of large companies consists of a complex interplay between complementary in-house and external expertise. This exchange of expertise appears to be
increasingly important for successful survival and competitiveness. The growth of
specialist business service firms has thus been based on a growing demand for specialist
expertise by large client companies, and is a symptom of wider changes that have
occurred in the organization of production. Business service firms play an important

role in the management of change by providing expertise that either existed previously inside organizations, or expertise that by its very nature can only be provided by an outside agency. In this case, an independent impartial viewpoint may be sought to resolve a management difficulty.

Most successful business service firms work in the main for large corporate clients, preferring to ignore the less profitable SME sector (Bryson *et al.* 1994). Of the 2.5m firms operating in Britain, however, only 9,000 employ more than 200 people, with 96% having fewer than 20 staff. Between 1989 and 1991 firms with fewer than 20 employees created nearly half a million new jobs while the workforce of large firms declined. Together these small and medium-sized enterprises (SMEs) account for 50% of UK non-government employment (Department of Trade and Industry 1995a).

In contrast to large companies SMEs have limited management resources and are thus more likely to require the services of outside experts, but are less likely to be able to afford them. Small businesses frequently excel in their core business areas, but have little management expertise, and are thus prone to failure as a result of poor financial planning, marketing, planning or personnel management (Bryson *et al.* 1996a).

Owing to the cost of external expertise many SMEs rely on government funded or subsidized expertise, advice from banks and accountants and on informal advice obtained via friends and families (Department of Trade and Industry 1995b, Marshall *et al.* 1993). In July 1992 the Department of Trade and Industry (DTI) announced that it was radically changing its system of support for SMEs. The new policy is designed to help SMEs compete in world markets by establishing a network of 'one stop shops for business', marketed under the name 'Business Link' (DTI 1993). Business Link is an attempt to improve the acquisition of outside expertise by SMEs by simplifying the provision of advice at a local level. It provides SMEs with access to a range of services formerly available from a confusing welter of different agencies, for example Chambers of Commerce, Enterprise Agencies, Local Authorities, Training and Enterprise Councils, the DTI and the Department of Employment. A Business Link 'one stop shop' should provide SMEs with a single point of contact in an area to the services available from all independent local agencies. By the end of 1995, a network of 80 Business Link companies with 200 outlets was operating in England providing advice and services to SMEs. To be successful, however, SMEs must be persuaded that the Business Link chain has something to offer them in the form of improved productivity and competitiveness. In September 1995, telephone interviews with 825 SMEs identified that the main source of advice was their accountant (34%) followed by independent consultants (19%) (Department of Trade and Industry 1995b). Only 2% of companies stated that they would approach a Business Link company for advice. This suggests that the DTI's Business Links initiative is failing to persuade it target audience of the value of its services.

SMEs lack the time and skilled specialist staff to develop in-house managerial skills, and for sorting the mass of publicly or privately available managerial, technical, or market information. Many managers or owners of SMEs lack management skills and are often unsure whether the problems they face can be solved, and where they can obtain information and critical expertise. This is one of the reasons why new SMEs are so vulnerable and prone to high failure rates (OECD 1993). The externalization or transaction cost debate does not hold true for SMEs as in most cases they cannot afford to develop in-house expertise in all management areas. They thus have no choice, but employ business service firms, obtain information from state agencies, or continue to survive without the information. Loss of potential opportunities or competitiveness due to inefficient organizational decision-making procedures or lack of information represents an information opportunity cost. SMEs must reach an equilibrium between the amount of management time, or cost, of acquiring necessary information, and day-to-day management and business tasks. In comparison to large firms, it is likely that SMEs will be dependent on local suppliers of business services, and thus may not be able to obtain the best advice. A *dual information economy* may be developing within the UK with large firms searching for specialist business service expertise irrespective of its location, while SMEs are tied into local or regional providers of more generalist expertise. A postal survey of 147 small and medium-sized manufacturing and service firms revealed that 51% used local consultancy companies for business planning, and a further 21% used firms located in the surrounding region (e.g. North West) (Bryson *et al.* 1996b). The Business Link network will reinforce the dominance of local suppliers for SMEs, but might encourage the establishment of regional and national networks of SMEs and business service advisers that would provide SMEs with access to specialist expertise. In addition, the regional diffusion of business service activities away from London and the South East is being encouraged by the devolution of management control by large organizations. Regional branches of service firms established to service the branch networks of global companies may diversify their activities and develop regional specialisms targeted at the wider regional market.

Comparatively little is known about the ways in which SMEs utilize information. Implicit in the development of the Business Link network is the assumption that successful SMEs know which external expertise they require to remain competitive and possess the management capabilities to control and manage the relationship with an external professional. Equally there is an assumption that business service suppliers must recognize their contribution to innovation adoption or management practice and they must themselves be innovative and constantly re-assessing their expertise and services. It also suggests that there is a need to consider less successful client firms and the policies needed to enhance their competitiveness by encouraging them to make more effective use of external expertise.

5. Conclusions

This paper has argued that the growth of business service firms represents the latest stage in a continuing process of technological and organizational restructuring of production and labour skills. It is associated with the rising information intensiveness of production and the development of an economy based around the symbolic content of commodities. Business service companies are increasingly driving innovations in the wider production system. They provide expertise that represents the accumulation of knowledge from experience of working for a variety of different companies and in different countries. The development of a sophisticated business service sector, with global companies located in service spaces and global cities, provides opportunities for the transfer of management ideas and innovations between individual companies as well as countries. Thus, management ideas developed in the USA and Japan are transferred into British companies by global consultancy companies.

The employment by clients of external business service expertise reduces employment overheads by allowing the client access to just-in-time knowledge without the cost rigidity of a full-time employee. Clients also obtain access to a range and depth of expertise that cannot be created and maintained inside their organizations. External business service firms operate in the same way as board room linkages in that they provide companies with access to information developed within different cultural and political environments. The internal political and cultural environment of the client organization is both 'enabling' and 'constraining'. It provides employees with a particular language (Boden 1994) and accepted work practices, but it can also prevent the internal development and introduction of certain ideas and innovations. External business service firms provide a mechanism for embedding new ideas into a client's internal political and cultural environment.

An important dimension of the business service client relationship rests on the establishment of 'weak-ties' between individuals employed by client companies and by business service professionals. The business service client relationship is dependent on the establishment of trust between individuals operating within different institutions. The work of Granovetter on 'weak-ties' provides one way of understanding the ways in which a client company identifies an external business service provider. The 'weak-tie' approach is useful as it highlights the social, cultural and political nature of the client business service relationship. It also draws attention to the role 'brokers' play in mediating between client companies and external providers of business service expertise. When change is driven within an organization by external expertise, such expertise will be chosen in a particular way, relate to the organization in a particular way, and have generated the knowledge it uses in a particular way. All of this implies that while business service employment may be a small proportion of total employment in the United Kingdom, their activities have important implications for the operation, structure and performance of both manufacturing and service firms, as well as the public sector.

Acknowledgements

This paper arises from research findings from three funded research programmes. First, the business service survey was supported under the Economic and Social Science Research Council (ESRC) Small Firms Initiative by contributions from the ESRC, Barclays Bank, Commission of the European Communities (DGXXIII), the Employment Department and the Rural Development Commission. This research was undertaken with Dr David Keeble, University of Cambridge, and Dr Peter Wood, University College London. The client survey was funded by the ESRC and was undertaken in collaboration with Dr Peter Wood. The small firm survey is funded by the ESRC and the NatWest Group Charitable Trust. It is jointly directed by Professor P.W. Daniels (University of Birmingham). All of this support is gratefully acknowledged.

References

Allen, J. and Pryke, M. 1994 The production of service space, *Environment and Planning, D: Society and Space*, **12:** 453–475.
Arrighi, G. 1994 *The Long Twentieth Century: Money, Power, and the Origins of our Times* (London: Verso).
Bearle, A.A and Means, G.G. 1932 *The Modern Corporation and Private Property* (New York: Macmillan).
Beck, U. 1992 *Risk Society* (London: Sage).
Bell, D. 1974 *The Coming of the Post-Industrial Society* (London: Heinemann).

Boden, D. 1994 *The Business of Talk: Organisations in Action* (Cambridge: Polity Press).
Boden, D. and Molotch, H.L. 1994 The compulsion of proximity, in Friedland, R. and Boden, D. (eds) *Space, Time and Modernity* (Berkeley: University of California Press), 257–286
Bryson, J.R., Churchward, S. and Daniels, P.W. 1996a Small and medium-sized firms, strong ties and the acquisition of managerial knowledge and expertise, Small Firms Business Services Project, Working Paper No. 1, University of Birmingham, Birmingham.
Bryson, J.R., Churchward, S. and Daniels, P.W. 1996b Preliminary findings of an investigation into the use by small and medium-sized firms of external expertise provided by the private sector, or via the Business Link network, *Service Sector Commentary*, 3 (2), Service Sector Research Unit, University of Birmingham, Birmingham, forthcoming.
Bryson, J.R., Daniels, P. and Henry, N. 1996c From widgets to where? A region in economic transition, in Gerrard, A.J. and Slater, T.R. (eds) *Managing a Conurbation: Birmingham and its Region* (Birmingham: Brewin Books).
Bryson, J.R., Keeble, D and Wood, P. 1994 *Enterprising Researchers: The Growth of Small Market Research Firms in Britain*, Business Services Monograph, Series 1, No. 2, Small Business Research Trust, city.
Bryson, J.R., Keeble, D. and Wood, P. 1996d The creation and growth of small business service firms in post-industrial Britain, *Small Business Economics*, forthcoming.
Bryson, J.R., Wood, P. and Keeble, D. 1993 Business networks, small firms' flexibility and regional development UK business services, *Entrepreneurship & Regional Development*, 5: 265–277.
Burt, R.S. 1977 Power in a social topology, *Social Science Research*, 6: 1–83.
Church, R. 1993 The family firm in industrial capitalism: international perspectives on hypotheses and history, in Jones, G. and Rose, M.B. (eds) *Family Capitalism* (London: Frank Cass).
Clegg, S., Boreham, P. and Dow, G. 1986 *Class, Politics and the Economy* (London: Routledge & Kegan Paul).
Dahlman, C. 1979 The problem of externality, *The Journal of Law and Economics*, 22, 141–162.
Daniels, P.W. 1993 *Service Industries in the World Economy* (Oxford: Blackwell).
Department of Trade and Industry 1993 Business Link: A prospectus for one stop shops for Business, Department of Trade and Industry, London.
Department of Trade and Industry 1995a Small firms in Britain, HMSO, London.
Department of Trade and Industry 1995b Business advice among small and medium sized enterprises and the 'Business Links' Campaign, DTI, London.
Eccles, R. 1981 The quasifirm in the construction industry, *Journal of Economic Behaviour and Organisation*, 2: 335–357
Emirbayer, M. and Goodwin, J. 1994 Network analysis, culture, and the problem of agency, *American Journal of Sociology*, 99, 1411–1454.
Fernandez, R.M. and Gould, R.V. 1994 A dilemma of state power: brokerage and influence in the national health policy domain, *American Journal of Sociology*, 99: 1455–1490
Freeman, V. 1996 Jaguar's XK8: the female of the species, *The Times*, Saturday, 2 March, 1996.
Friedland, R. and Boden, D. 1994 NowHere: an introduction to space, time and modernity, in Friedland, R. and Boden, D. (eds) *Space, Time and Modernity* (Berkeley: University of California), 1–60.
Friedland, R. and Palmer, D. 1994 Space, corporation, and class: towards a grounded theory, in Friedland, R. and Boden, D. (eds) *Space, Time and Modernity*, (Berkeley: University of California Press), 287–334.
Gertler, M.S. 1995 "Being there": proximity, organisation, and culture in the development and adoption of advanced manufacturing technologies, *Economic Geography*, 71 (1): 1–25.
Gould, R.V. and Fernandez, R.M. 1989 Structures of mediation: a formal approach to brokerage in transaction networks, *Sociological Methodology*, 19: 89–126.
Granovetter, M. 1973 The strength of weak ties, *American Journal of Sociology*, 78: 1360–1380.
Granovetter, M. 1982 The strength of weak ties: a network theory revisited, in Marsden, P.V. and Lin, N. (eds) *Social Structure and Network Analysis* (London: Sage).
Granovetter, M. 1985 Economic action and social structures: the problems of embeddedness, *American Journal of Sociology*, 91(3): 481–510.
Hedlund, G. and Rolander, D. 1990 Action in heterarchies – new approaches to managing the MNC, in Bartlett, C.A., Doz, Y. and Hedlund, G. (eds) *Managing the Global Firms* (London: Routledge), 15–46.
Hepworth, M. 1989 *Geography of the Information Economy* (London: Pinter Publishers).
Hofer, C.W. 1980 Turnaround strategies, *Journal of Business Strategy*, 1: 19–31.
Jacquemin, A. 1987 *The New Industrial Organisation*, (Cambridge, MA: MIT Press).
Kanter, R.M. 1993 *Men and Women of the Corporation* (New York: Basic Books).
Keeble, D., Bryson, J. and Wood, P. 1994 *Pathfinders of Enterprise : The Creation, Growth & Dynamics of Small Management Consultancies in Britain*, Business Services Research Monograph, Series 1, No. 2, Small Business Research Trust, Milton Keynes.
Kesner, I.F. and Dalton, D.R. 1994 Top management turnover and CEO succession: an investigation of the effects of turnover on performance, *Journal of Management Studies*, 31(5): 701–713.
Knoke, D. and Pappi, F. 1991 Organisational action sets in the US and German labor policy domains, *American Sociological Review*, 56: 509–523.
Lash, S. and Urry, J. 1994 *Economies of Signs and Space* (London: Sage).
Lynch, P. 1985 Annual hours – an idea whose time has come, *Personnel Management*, November.

Marshall, J.N., Alderman, N., Wong, C. and Thwaites, A. 1993 The impact of government-assisted management training and development on small and medium-sized enterprises in Britain, *Environment and Planning C: Government and Policy*, 11: 331–348.

Mizruchi, M.S. 1991 Market relations, interlocks, and corporate political behaviour, *Research in Political Sociology*, 5: 167–208.

Nohria, N. and Eccles, R. 1992 Face-to-face: making network organisations work, in Nohria, N. and Eccles, R.G. (eds) *Networks and Organisations: Structure, Form, and Action* (Boston, MA: Harvard Business School Press).

O'Farrell, P.N., Hitchens, D.M. and Moffat, L.A.R. 1992 The competitiveness of business service firms: a matched comparison between Scotland and the South East of England, *Regional Studies*, 26(6): 519–533.

OECD 1993 *Small and Medium-sized Enterprises: Technology and Competitiveness* (Paris: OECD).

Perkins, H. 1989 *The Rise of Professional Society: England since 1880* (London: Routledge).

Roslender, R. 1992 *Sociological Perspectives on Modern Accountancy* (London: Routledge).

Rubalcaba-Bermejo, L. and Cuadrado-Roura, J.R. 1995 Urban hierarchies and territorial competition in Europe: exploring the role of fairs and exhibitions, *Urban Studies*, 32(2): 379–400.

Sassen, S. 1994 *Cities in a World Economy* (London: Pine Forge Press).

Savage, M., Dickens, P. and Fielding, T. 1988 Some social and political implications of the contemporary fragmentation of the 'service class' in Britain, *International Journal of Urban and Regional Research*, 12: 455–475.

Scott, A.J. 1988 *Metropolis: from the Division of Labor to Urban Form* (Berkeley: University of California Press).

Scott, J. 1979 *Corporations, Classes and Capitalism* (London: Hutchinson).

Stanback, T.M. 1991 *The New Suburbanization: Challenge to the Central City* (Boulder: Westview Press).

Storper, M. 1995 The resurgence of regional economies, ten years later: the region as a nexus of untraded interdependencies, *European Urban and Regional Studies*, 2 (3): 191–221.

Tordoir, P.P. 1993 *The Professional Knowledge Economy: the Management and Integration of Professional Services in Business Organisations* (Academisch Proefschrift: University of Amsterdam).

Urry, J. 1986 Capitalist production, scientific management and the service class, in Scott, A.J. and Storper, M. (eds) *Production, Work and Territory: The Geographical Anatomy of Industrial Capitalism* (London: Allen and Unwin), 43–66.

Useem, M. 1984 *The Inner Circle: Large Corporations and the Rise of Business Political Activity in the US, and UK* (Oxford: Oxford University Press).

Wiersema, M.F. 1995 Executive succession as an antecedent to corporate restructuring, *Human Resource Management*, 34 (1): 185–202.

Williams, I.A 1931 T*he Firm of Cadbury, 1831–1931* (London: Constable).

Wood, P.A., Bryson, J. and Keeble, D. 1993 Regional patterns of small firms' development in the business services: evidence from the United Kingdom, *Environment and Planning A*, 25: 677–700.

Wood, P., Bryson, J. and Rotherham, D. 1994 Consultant use and the management of change: insights into expertise, Business Services Research Project, Working Paper No. 3, University College London.

Part III
Multinational Service Firms

[24]

TRANSNATIONAL CORPORATIONS AND SERVICES: THE FINAL FRONTIER

Frederick F. Clairmonte and John H. Cavanagh *

Part one. The setting

In the literature on the world economy, comparatively little attention has been paid to what is, in fact, its largest and most dynamic sector—services, and even less analytical work has been devoted to the role of transnational corporations (TNCs) in this sector.

* Frederick F. Clairmonte is a staff member of UNCTAD and John H. Cavanagh is a Fellow of the Institute for Policy Studies in Washington, D.C. The views expressed in this article are their own and not necessarily those of their institutions. The authors express their gratitude to Miss Judy Mann for her assistance in the preparation of this article.

This enquiry marks the beginning of an overall synthesis of the role of corporate power in the proliferation of the various branches of the service sector.

The *internationalization* of the output of goods and services[1] has its origin in the efflorescence of the world market since the Renaissance. The extent to which any particular commodity is internationalized has fluctuated considerably from time to time in the course of the evolution of the capitalist system. The trade in tea, cane sugar, tobacco, cotton and animal furs expanded from domestic markets in the sixteenth century into international ones by the end of the eighteenth century, the high-water mark in the fortunes of mercantilism. This internationalization was further intensified in the nineteenth century, in the heyday of economic liberalism.

However, the progress from internationalization to transnationalization occurred only at the turn of the present century, when transnational corporations began exporting capital, goods and services in large volume. Transnationalization marks a specific stage in the higher evolution of mature capitalism, in which a given sector's output falls within the controlling ambit of the transnational corporation. By the 1960s, with the ascendancy of conglomeration[2] on a massive scale, the TNC became the principal vehicle of internationalization.

A. CENTRAL CURRENTS

Four central elements in the transformational process constitute the foundation of the present enquiry:

(*a*) The heterogeneous service sector has eclipsed agriculture and manufacturing as the leader in the global economy, and can be expected to gather momentum over the remaining years of the century.

(*b*) Until the last decade, services were the least internationalized of the major sectors and the least penetrated by transnational corporate capital.

(c) The internationalization of services is being strongly encouraged by two sets of corporate phenomena. The first is what may be designated as the formation of *Transnational Service Conglomerates* (TSCs), which operate in two or more service sectors. The second is the formation of *Transnational Integral Conglomerates* (TICs), which span a large spectrum of both service and industrial sectors, whose highest expression to date are the huge and powerful Japanese conglomerate groupings (e.g., Mitsubishi, Mitsui, Sumitomo, etc.).

---

[1] Internationalization refers to the extent to which production of a given sector is exported. This is in contrast to "transnationalization", which refers to the degree to which the output and marketing of a given sector are controlled by transnational corporations. While the terms "output" and "production" are conventionally used to describe the generation of material products, in this work they are also used to refer to the generation of services.

[2] Conglomerate mergers are those between companies which are neither direct competitors nor in a buyer-seller relationship with one another.

An analytical differentiation must be made between giant industrial corporations (e.g. Bayer and Toyota) and the large service conglomerates (e.g. Dentsu and Sears). Economies of scale in industry proper can be realized by the production of a large number of standardized units in one location. In contrast, services often do not lend themselves to operations in standardized units. Rather, in the case of services, economies of scale are achieved by organizing individual units (e.g. Hertz car rental centres) into chains, and managing them from a central office through computerized operations. Effectively, TSCs combine a high degree of centralization in overall administration and finance with a propensity for decentralization by means of their far-flung distribution network operating through franchises.

The spectrum ranging from absolute centralization to absolute decentralization is broad, and a given firm's position on that spectrum is largely determined by the nature of the commodity or service bought and sold and the technology employed. Hence the degree of centralization or decentralization, as the case may be, is not the decisive determinant of the relative power of corporate capital.

The distinction drawn between service and manufacturing corporations ought not to be construed as implying that these two economic categories are separated by rigid boundaries. Actually, in consequence of the growth of TICs, these once separate categories are tending more and more to be amalgamated under a single corporate roof. The global power which this form of integration confers on the TICs is unprecedented, inasmuch as it facilitates the meshing of initial output with various techniques of sophisticated marketing and promotion of products for sale to the consumer. Under the impetus of these combined forces, internationalization of services is being prodigiously speeded up.

(*d*) The fourth key element to be noted is that the internationalization of services is fast permeating all economic sectors and corporate groupings in both capitalist (developed and developing) and centrally planned economies, particularly in reshaping both their labour force and the overall trajectory of these economies.

These momentous changes that are taking place in corporate ownership and control are blurring the once neat boundaries that used to demarcate the familiar categories of the service sector.

B. TOWARDS A REDEFINITION OF SERVICES

The distinction between services and the vast range of material products harks back to the physiocrats' *tableau économique,* Adam Smith and Karl Marx. The first serious attempt to define services as a distinct activity, however, was made by Professor Colin Clark in his pioneering study.[3] Essentially, he subdivided the economic universe into three categories: primary (mainly agriculture and fishing), secondary (mining and manufacturing), and a residual

---

[3] Colin Clark, *The Conditions of Economic Progress* (London, Macmillan, 1940).

tertiary or services sector including commerce, transport, communications, finance, insurance, real estate, government[4] and professional[5] services. This third category can be further broken down into "producer services" for intermediate demand and "consumer services" for final consumption.

Not merely is the substance of services heterogeneous, but views on its definitional boundaries are even more diverse. In Professor Stigler's words: "there exists no authoritative consensus on either the boundaries or the classification of the service industries."[6] Professor Simon Kuznets, for example, modified his definition between 1958 and 1966 by including transportation, communications and public utilities in services in his early work and eliminating them in his later work.[7]

More recently, with the onset of the microprocessor revolution and the opening up of entirely new and previously unexplored frontiers beyond manufacturing, classification has become more intractable. Japan's Ministry of Finance, for example, has now revised its industrial classification formula to take into account new tertiary industries, particularly those associated with software, information, business services, culture and sports.

There is little point in entering into these methodological disputes. The various definitions or classifications proposed are analytically limited in that they embrace only formal economic aggregates, while ignoring corporate structures that, in the last analysis, are the providers and determinants of services. What matters for the purpose of the present study is that the largest corporations now transcend the sectoral categories of primary, secondary and tertiary. In their production, finance and marketing operations the frontiers of another time, and soon of another age, will have become meaningless. Despite these definitional problems, it is nevertheless possible to demarcate the boundaries of services in common-sense terms. Schematically, services can be said to comprise the range of activities beyond the confines of agriculture, mining and manufacturing. This would comprise the broad categories of government services (civilian and military), personal consumption services, and business support services.

---

[4] Government services span the entire gamut of a country's civil and military administration.

[5] Professional services comprise the technical, legal, commercial, and medical services produced by engineers, lawyers, accountants, physicians, and other professionals.

[6] George Stigler, *Trends in Employment in the Service Industries* (New Jersey, Princeton University Press, 1956), p. 47.

[7] Compare his "Quantitative Aspects of the Economic Growth of Nations: Industrial Distribution of Income and Labour Force by States. United States 1919-21 to 1955", *Economic Development and Cultural Change*, July 1958, with his *Modern Economic Growth* (Heinemann, London, 1966).

Victor Fuchs illustrated the difficulty of framing a definition when he noted that "a dentist who makes a false tooth and places it in the patient's mouth is certainly delivering a tangible product, but dentistry is invariably classified as a service. It is difficult to make a sharp distinction between the activities of an auto assembly plant and those of an automobile repair shop, but the former is invariably classified in industry and the latter is usually regarded as a service." Victor Fuchs, *The Service Economy* (New York, Columbia University Press, 1968, p. 15).

C. GROWTH OF SERVICES GLOBALLY

Already by the turn of the century, a large proportion (20 per cent on the average) of the labour force in developed countries was absorbed by services. By the end of the Second World War, the United States became the world's first so-called service economy, with less than half of the labour force engaged in the output of food and manufactured goods.

The 1960s witnessed a vast expansion of services. In the case of five major economic groupings (table 1), the share of services in GDP and the labour force grew in all of them during the last two decades, albeit at unequal rates. No social class or country remains untouched by the growth of services at the expense of manufacturing and agriculture.

The evidence suggests that it would be fallacious to assume that services as a whole are more labour-intensive than manufacturing or agriculture, for the relative labour intensity of services varies greatly from one country or grouping to another. It is no less relevant to note that just as the boundaries between

TABLE 1

Services: share of GDP and labour force

Economic grouping	Services as percentage of GDP		Services as percentage of labour force	
	1960	1981	1960	1980
Industrial market economies	54	61	44	56
of which:				
United States	58	63	57	66
Japan	42	53	37	49
High income oil exporters[a]	...	23	25	35
of which:				
Saudi Arabia	...	20	19	25
Libyan Arab Jamahiriya	...	29	30	53
Middle income economies[b]	46	48	23	34
of which:				
Indonesia	25	34	17	30
Brazil	49	53	33	46
Low income economies[c]	27	29	14	15
of which:				
China	20	20	...	12
India	30	37	15	18
Eastern Europe[d]	17	22[e]	28	39
of which:				
USSR	17	22[e]	29	41
Poland	17	21[e]	23	30

Sources: Compiled from data in World Bank, *World Development Report, 1982* and *ibid.,* 1983 (New York, Oxford University Press, 1982 and 1983).

[a] Per capita GNP over $5,760.

[b] Per capita GNP of $401-$5,760.

[c] Per capita GNP of $400 and less.

[d] Poland, Bulgaria, Hungary, USSR, Czechoslovakia and German Democratic Republic.

[e] 1980.

sectors are vanishing, so the conventional distinction between labour-intensive and capital-intensive industries is losing much of its former meaning, owing to the changing form and content of technology.

D. LABOUR FORCE: CHANGING CONFIGURATIONS

An examination of the shifting structure of the labour force in two advanced industrialized countries of different sizes brings out clearly the sectoral specificities. In both the United States and Switzerland (see tables 2 and 3), the service sector as a whole experienced rapid but unequal growth over the past decades, with banking and insurance the pace-setters. Services made gains at the expense of employment in both agriculture and manufacturing in both countries.[8]

E. THE CAUSAL EXPLANATIONS

There can be no such thing as a single causal explanation for the growth of services. The multiplicity of the factors contributing to the upsurge is as diverse as the various service sectors themselves, although the predominant ones can be singled out.

A major factor has been the role of the state. Among the most dynamic elements in the post-war economies of most developed market economies (DMEs) have been welfare programmes (notably in health) and the military complex, whose outlays have given rise to a myriad of service jobs. Another has been the changing structure of global manufacturing in consequence of the internationalization of output of TNCs. Since 1970, veritable global factories have been established in the automobile, consumer electronics and textile/apparel industries. This has only been made possible by gigantic leaps in applied sciences, conspicuously in the information services, transport and communications.[9]

The growth and proliferation of services is organically related to such globalization, for global manufacturing requires the dovetailing of such diverse services as information and telecommunications; shipping and other forms of transport to link the diverse production units; as well as a promotional technology coupled to wholesale and retail networks serving the consumer. The process necessitates the employment of large numbers of white-collar workers, ranging from relatively low paid office workers to teams of highly paid corporate lawyers. The onset of the computerized microelectronic era has not only tightened the co-ordination of a numerically vast number of services, but has also reinforced the historical relationship between services and manufacturing.

---

[8] In the United States, the increase in the mining labour force was attributable to the shift to coal after the oil price hikes in 1973 and 1979.

[9] The automobile industry is a vivid illustration: a "global car" is now assembled from parts manufactured in as many as 16 different countries.

TABLE 2

United States: structure of the labour force

	1972		1982		
	Thousands	*Per cent*	*Thousands*	*Per cent*	*1972 = 100*
Primary					
Agriculture	3 484	4.5	3 401	3.7	97.6
Secondary					
Manufacturing	19 151	24.8	18 849	20.3	98.4
Mining	628	0.8	1 122	1.2	178.7
Construction	3 889	5.0	3 912	4.2	100.6
Tertiary					
Transportation and public utilities . . .	4 541	5.9	5 057	5.4	111.4
Wholesale and retail trade	15 949	20.7	20 547	22.0	128.9
Finance, insurance and real estate . . .	3 908	5.1	5 350	5.8	136.9
Other services	12 276	15.9	19 000	20.4	154.8
Government	13 333	17.3	15 784	17.0	118.4
Total	77 159	100.0	93 022	100.0	120.6
Total labour force[a]	82 153		99 528		

Source: Computed from data in *Economic Report of the President* (U.S. Government Printing Office, Washington, D.C., February 1983).

[a] Including the self-employed.

TABLE 3

Switzerland: structure of the labour force

	1972		1982		
	Thousands	*Per cent*	*Thousands*	*Per cent*	*1972 = 100*
Primary	255	8.0	214	7.0	83.9
Agriculture	222	7.0	180	5.9	81.1
Secondary	1 438	45.1	1 174	38.7	81.6
Food, beverages and tobacco	123	3.9	111	3.6	89.7
Textiles and apparel	138	4.3	86	2.8	62.6
Chemicals, mineral oils	74	2.3	70	2.3	94.5
Metals	196	6.2	169	5.6	85.9
Watchmaking	88	2.7	55	1.8	62.8
Machinery and equipment	279	8.7	252	8.3	90.5
Construction	270	8.5	195	6.4	72.2
Tertiary	1 496	46.9	1 646	54.3	110.0
Retail trade	274	8.6	289	9.5	105.7
Banking, insurance	100	3.2	141	4.6	141.7
Hotel and restaurant business	170	5.3	177	5.8	104.1
Public entities, teaching	206	6.5	230	2.6	111.7
Public health	115	3.6	169	5.6	146.7
Total labour force	3 189	100.0	3 033	100.0	95.1

Source: Swiss Federal Office for Statistics, quoted in Union Bank of Switzerland, *Business Facts and Figures*, June 1983, p. 11.

F. Influence of urbanization

Historically, services have been concentrated in urban areas, a state of affairs which is likely to continue in the future. The causal relationship between the growth of cities and services is a complex one shaped by several elements, including agriculture's inability to absorb rural population increases, the mounting capital intensity of manufacturing and the sheer imperative of survival. Moreover, cities, as the centres of transnational corporate networks and state bureaucracies, have generated a constant flow of new service jobs.

The cities' share of the world's population has grown rapidly in the last three decades, and the share is projected to continue to increase and to account for over half of the world's population by the turn of the century (table 4). The implication is that global services will likewise continue to grow, both in relative and in absolute terms.

To the foregoing contributory factors can be added the entry of giant corporations into the services sector with their techno-financial capabilities. What this implies is that the prospective growth of the sector and of its attendant branches will be greater upon the entry of such services giants as Sears, Dentsu and Mitsubishi than could ever have been visualized in earlier periods when firms were atomized.

The foregoing description and analysis have concentrated on the growth of what is merely one segment of the service economy—namely officially recorded flows. The picture would be incomplete, however, without some reference to the subterranean economy.

G. The subterranean economy [10]

The Clarkian/Kuznetsian framework is flawed in that it covers exclusively officially recorded flows. Ever since the industrial revolution, a segment of all national economies has comprised an unrecorded element which, in recent times, has been variously designated as the black market, the underground economy, the submerged economy, the subterranean economy, the informal sector, the unrecorded economy, and like terms. These marginal activities include:

Prostitution, drug trafficking, larceny, theft and white collar crime;

Illicit currency transactions;

Illicit unrecorded work; [11]

Tax evasion.

---

[10] Although analysis of the services sector in this study is focused on market economies—developed and developing—a substantial underground economy is said to exist also in the centrally planned economies.

[11] Raffaele de Grazio, *Le travail clandestin: Situation dans les pays industrialisés à économie de marché* (Geneva, International Labour Office, 1983). The author defines subterranean work as *"une activité professionnelle, unique ou secondaire, exercée en marge ou en dehors des obligations*

TABLE 4

The upsurge of urbanization by major regions of the world

	1950		1980		2000 (projected)	
	Total population (millions)	Urban pop. as percentage of total	Total population (millions)	Urban pop. as percentage of total	Total population (millions)	Urban pop. as percentage of total
World	2 526	28.9	4 432	41.1	6 119	51.2
United States	152	64.2	223	77.0	264	83.4
Western Europe . . . . of which:	392	55.4	484	70.5	512	78.4
Germany, Fed. Rep. of . .	50	72.3	61	84.7	59	89.3
United Kingdom	51	84.2	56	90.8	55	93.7
France	42	56.2	54	77.9	56	85.4
Latin America . . . . of which:	164	40.8	364	65.4	566	75.7
Brazil	53	34.5	122	67.0	187	79.2
Mexico	27	42.7	70	66.7	116	77.4
Argentina	17	65.3	27	82.4	33	87.9
USSR	180	39.3	265	63.2	310	74.1
Asia	1 389	. . .	2 579	. . .	3 550	. . .
East Asia	673	16.8	1 175	32.7	1 475	45.3
South Asia . . . . of which:	716	16.2	1 404	24.8	2 075	37.1
China	557	11.1	995	25.7	1 257	39.1
India	368	17.3	684	22.2	961	33.9
Indonesia	80	12.4	148	20.2	199	32.3
Philippines	21	27.1	49	36.2	77	49.0
Africa . . . . of which:	220	14.8	470	28.8	853	42.4
Nigeria	33	10.5	77	20.4	150	33.4
South Africa	14	42.2	29	49.6	51	60.3
Egypt	20	31.9	42	45.4	64	57.4
Zaire	14	19.1	28	39.5	50	56.3

Sources: Compiled from data in United Nations Demographic Indicators of Countries (New York, 1982). United Nations Department of International Economic and Social Affairs, Selected Demographic Indicators by country 1950-2000; *Demographic Estimates and Projections as Assessed in 1978* (CST/ESA/SER.R/98) and *ibid., Estimates and Projections of Urban, Rural and City Populations 1950-2025: The 1980 Assessment* (ST/ESA/SER.R/45).

NOTE. Calculated on the basis of medium variant of population growth.

Since the onset of the global economic depression in the mid-1970s and the slowdown of the legal economy, these activities have proliferated the world over.

légales, réglementaires ou conventionnelles, à titre lucratif et de manière non occasionnelle" (p. 9). According to diverse estimates quoted by the author, the subterranean labour force accounted for the following percentages of the total labour force in the years or periods mentioned: France (1979-1982), 3-6 per cent; Federal Rep. of Germany (1981), 8-12; Italy (1979), 10-35; Denmark (1974-75), 11; Sweden (1979), 13-14; Belgium (1979), 15-20; Norway (1981), 40. The percentage contribution of clandestine work to GNP was also estimated for the following countries: Denmark (1974-1975), 6; Sweden (1978), 6-16; Norway (1980), 7-17; Italy (1977), 8; Australia (1978-1979), 10; Federal Republic of Germany (1981), 13; UK (1980), 15; Belgium (1981), 15; and USA (1979), 28.

Just as a multiplicity of interrelated factors accounted for the growth of officially recorded services, so there are several elements which go far to explain the growth of the subterranean economy. The first is the large number of government fiscal and other regulations, restrictions and prohibitions. The avoidance of these enactments can be very lucrative. The temptation to flout the law has become almost irresistible, and the prospect of illicit gain, tax-free, has attracted many shady operators, the Mafia being a prime example.

Another cause of the spread of the underground economy has been the impact of the world-wide depression since the mid-1970s. The consequent layoffs and redundancies have raised the officially acknowledged unemployment level in the OECD countries to around 35 million. Driven out of the legitimate economy, many workers have no other recourse than to find some job in the underground economy, invariably with sub-minimum wages and no pension or welfare payments. Likewise, the protectionist barriers that have been raised because of the depression have made smuggling a profitable (if unlawful) occupation.

H. THE INTERNATIONALIZATION OF SERVICES

Of the three major sectors of the world economy, the services sector may be said to be the least internationalized, a contention that must be evaluated in a global setting. In the decade of the 1970s, the overall share of world GDP exported jumped from 16 to 27 per cent (see figure I and table 5). This rise reflected the entry of large quantities of output of manufacturing, mining, and agriculture into the world market through the marketing and promotional networks of TNCs.[12] The decade also witnessed lesser but significant strides in

---

[12] For an elaboration, see F. F. Clairmonte and J. H. Cavanagh, "Transnational Corporations and Global Markets: Changing Power Relations", *Trade and Development, An UNCTAD Review* (No. 4, Winter 1982), United Nations publication, Sales No. E.83.II.D.1.

TABLE 5

The internationalization of the world economy[a]

	1970			1980		
	World GDP (billion dollars)	World exports (billion dollars)	Exports as percentage of GDP	World GDP (billion dollars)	World exports (billion dollars)	Exports as percentage of GDP
Agriculture	181.9	57.8	31.8	602.8	273.2	45.3
Mining and manufactures . . .	726.7	217.5	29.9	2 769.5	1 522.1	55.0
Services	1 457.6	99.9	6.9	5 644.0	610.4	10.8
TOTAL	2 366.2	375.2	15.9	9 016.3	2 405.7	26.7

Sources: Calculated from data in UNCTAD, *Handbook of International Trade and Development Statistics, 1983* (United Nations publication, Sales No. E/F.83.II.D.2) and from tapes of the United Nations Department of International Economic and Social Affairs.

[a] Excluding socialist countries.

FIGURE I

Structure of the world economy GDP and exports[a]
1970-1980

(*Percentages*)

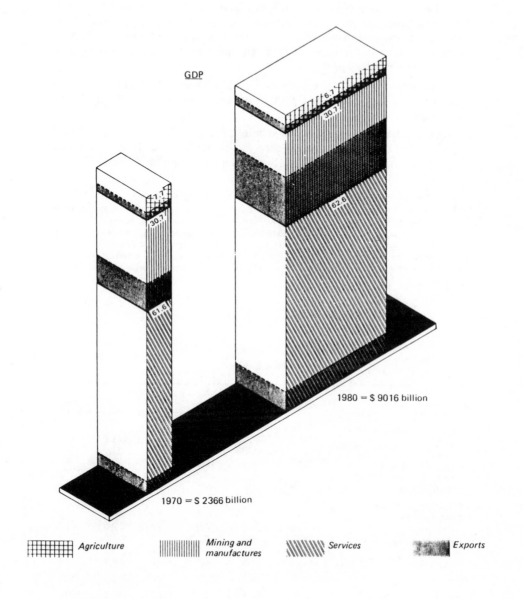

| Agriculture | Mining and manufactures | Services | Exports |

Source: Table 5.

[a] Excluding socialist countries.

225

the internationalization of services, with service exports jumping from 7 per cent to 11 per cent of the service sector's GDP; exports of agricultural products rose from 32 per cent to 45 per cent, and those of the mining and manufacturing industries from 30 per cent to 55 per cent of the GDP of the sectors in question.

The internationalization of different sectors and sub-sectors followed differentiated patterns, as United States data suggests. Of 14 leading United States service sectors, foreign revenues as a share of total revenues ranged from less than 1 per cent in the case of health services to over a third in the case of maritime transportation.[13]

As one turns from the generalized world picture to look at the particular importance of services in the exports of selected countries, one perceives some very suggestive trends (tables 6-8).

(i) Out of an estimated recorded total of $585 billion of service exports (1981), over half was accounted for by the top five developed market economies, with the United States alone accounting for one fifth.

---

[13] Foreign revenues as a percentage of total 1981 revenues varied as follows: financial services, 23; equipment lending and rental, 22; air transportation, 17; motion pictures, 16; computer and data processing, 15; insurance, 9; hotels and motels, 8; consulting and management, 7; construction and engineering, 4; communications, 3; education, 1; and franchising, 1. The overall average for these 14 sectors was 8 per cent, with total foreign revenues exceeding $109 billion. See US International Trade Commission, *The Relationship of Exports in Selected US Service Industries, to US Merchandise Exports* (Washington, D. C., USITC Publication 1290, September 1982).

TABLE 6

Services: leading exporters, 1981

(*Billion dollars*)

Country	Transport	Travel	Investment income	Other services	Total	Per cent
Developed market economies						
United States	15.2	12.2	82.3	11.4	121.1	20.8
France	10.7	7.2	23.2	14.5	55.6	9.5
United Kingdom	12.3	6.0	18.4	13.0	49.7	8.5
Germany, Fed. Rep. of	9.4	6.3	9.2	15.0	39.9	6.8
Belgium/Lux.	4.8	1.6	23.1	5.1	34.6	5.9
Developing economies						
Mexico	0.5	6.2	1.3	2.2	10.2	1.8
Singapore	3.0	1.7	0.9	3.4	9.0	1.5
Rep. of Korea	2.1	0.4	0.5	3.0	6.0	1.0
Kuwait	0.8	0.5	3.0	0.0	4.3	0.7
Saudi Arabia	1.9	1.6	0.0	0.8	4.3	0.7
Other	73.5	55.4	61.3	59.8	250.0	42.7
World	134.2	99.1	223.2	128.2	584.8	100.0

Source: Computed from data in: UK, Committee on Invisible Exports, *World Invisible Trade* (London, June 1983).

TABLE 7

Balance of service trade: major surplus and deficit countries, 1981

(*Billion dollars*)

	Transport	Travel	Investment income	Other services	Total	Per capita surplus or deficit (dollars)
Surplus countries						
United States	−0.9	0.7	46.1	7.4	53.2	232
United Kingdom	0.7	−0.6	3.4	8.0	11.6	207
Switzerland	−0.3	1.3	5.1	0.8	6.9	1 078
France	−1.3	1.5	0.8	3.7	4.6	85
Singapore	1.6	1.4	−0.4	2.0	4.6	1 917
Deficit countries						
Japan	−3.2	−3.9	−5.7	−7.4	−20.2	−172
Germany, Fed. Rep. of	−1.8	−11.4	−2.7	−2.5	−18.5	−300
Saudi Arabia	−5.5	−1.2	−6.8	−3.2	−16.7	−1 796
Brazil	−1.7	−0.2	−10.3	−0.6	−12.8	−106
Canada	−0.1	−0.9	−9.6	−1.5	−12.0	−496

Source: As for table 6.

(ii) As regards the balance of services trade, some countries record enormous surpluses (United States and United Kingdom)[14] and others very large deficits (Japan, Federal Republic of Germany and Saudi Arabia).

(iii) In general, DMEs are running surpluses on service accounts, while the developing economies are accumulating mounting deficits. Earlier forecasts by Prof. Leontief[15] suggested that developing economies would have service deficits of the order of $30 billion by the year 2000. As a study by the UNCTAD secretariat reveals, however, this figure has already been easily exceeded: the net deficit of the developing countries' trade in services climbed from $14 billion to $80 billion between 1967 and 1980, at an average annual rate of 25 per cent.[16] There appears no reason why this unbroken upward climb should not continue.

(iv) It is not fortuitous that the countries with the biggest surpluses in their service trade are precisely the most vociferous proponents of a liberali-

---

[14] Since 1794, when foreign trade records were first established, the United Kingdom's service trade has been in surplus every year in peace time. A sizeable segment of this surplus was formerly earned by trade with the colonies, and even now continues to the present, thanks largely to United Kingdom trade with Hong Kong, which contributes materially to the surplus.

[15] Wassily Leontief *et al.*, *The Future of the World Economy: A United Nations Study* (New York, 1977), p. 60.

[16] *Trends in World Production and Trade* (TD/B/887/Rev.1), pp. 20-21 (United Nations publication, Sales No. E.82.II.D.13).

zation of this trade.[17] In the United States, it is the huge earnings from service exports (and to a lesser extent from farm exports) which offset the huge deficit on merchandise account.[18]

(v) It should be apparent from the colossal deficits of developing countries on their service accounts that a liberalization of the international trade in services would swell their deficits and benefit primarily DMEs. Under a régime of liberalization, developing countries would be committed to boost their services imports whereas they would realize only marginal gains from their almost negligible service exports.

(vi) The significance of the service trade is reflected also in the per capita surplus of certain countries, notably Singapore ($1,917 in 1981) and Switzerland ($1,078) in their international trade in services.

(vii) The share of services in total exports also varies widely, ranging from 3 per cent in Saudi Arabia to 78 per cent in Greece.[19]

(viii) Although recorded service exports as a percentage of goods exports shrank slightly between 1970 and 1980, for the top 15 exporters of services the share edged up from 34 to 37 per cent.

Previous sections sketched the numerical framework in which the growth and prospects of the trade in services can be understood. But such a numerical framework, in itself, can give no indication of the determinants of the future evolution of this trade. This can only be done by taking stock of the rapidly changing institutional power relations in the global service economy.

The mainsprings of corporate power are examined, first, from the point of view of the structure, performance and strategies of leading corporations in six major activities of the services sector: finance capital, insurance, tourism, shipping, advertising and accountancy. Inasmuch as it is not uncommon for individual corporations to carry on several of these activities, this analysis should be supplemented by specific case studies of transnational conglomer-

---

[17] The philosophical justification of such liberalization was lucidly formulated by the Liberalization of Trade in Services Committee (LOTIS) of the United Kingdom Committee on Invisible Exports, in the paper "Liberalization of Trade and Services" (London, November 1982), p. 6. "LOTIS considers that it is logical as well as wise that the UK should support and be seen to support any initiative for the gradual removal of barriers to trade in services. It believes that greater freedom in this area will lead to benefits for the users of services through greater competition and choice. Moreover, such freedom will help to foster a continuing growth of world trade in services which will encourage economic development in all participating countries, instead of leading simply to a transfer of wealth or redistribution of existing benefits." An International Committee on Trade and Services, chaired by ex-President Carter's trade representative, was set up after the November 1982 GATT Ministerial meeting to promote the idea of liberalization. See *Financial Times,* 18 April 1983.

[18] Between 1946 and 1981, the United States merchandise account changed from a net surplus of $6.7 billion to a net deficit of $27.9 billion. However, when services transactions were taken into account, the balance changed to $7.8 billion (1946) and to $11.1 billion (1981) (*Economic Report of the President,* transmitted to the Congress (Washington, D. C., February 1983), p. 276).

[19] In Greece, this is mainly accounted for by shipping and tourism. It should be noted that these service export totals include only recorded transactions. In the case of Greece and a few other countries, this figure would be much higher if it included shipping revenues of local shipowners who register their ships in tax-haven countries.

ates. It is only by combining these two methods of investigation that the social scientist can understand the operations of modern capitalist enterprises which affect services and the hundreds of millions of persons who earn their livelihood in this sector.

Part two. Emergence of service conglomerates

The modern transnational corporation began to take shape after 1875. In the ensuing decades, a transition from relatively competitive conditions to monopolistic and oligopolistic output and market structures was realized by pooling arrangements, the financial holding company, and a legal framework congenial to the concentration of corporate power. Essentially, the principal activities of these transnational corporations were manufacturing, mining and plantation agriculture, e.g. American Tobacco Co., Lever Bros., Union Minière, De Beers, United Fruit Co., Tate and Lyle.

The earliest service transnationals were companies engaged in banking, transport (shipping and railroads), and insurance whose overseas expansion was related to the colonial world and the semi-colonial worlds of China and Latin America. Outstanding examples include giants such as Barclay's Bank, Lloyds Bank, Jardine Matheson, the P and O Shipping Lines, the Deutsche Bank, the East Asiatic Company, La Banque d'Indochine, the Hamburg Amerika Line and the United Africa Company.

Between the end of the First World War and the 1960s, transnational corporations began to enter other service sectors, notably advertising, telecommunications, tourism, retailing and accountancy. None the less, their role was still on a relatively modest scale compared with the concentration and transnationalization of capital in the manufacturing sector.

Since the 1960s, the transnationalization of both services and manufactures has gathered momentum—albeit at different tempos. The profoundest changes in the services sector were those experienced or undertaken by corporations directly linked to tourism, multi-commodity trading companies and the rapidly diversifying financial corporations (e.g. American Express) which benefited from deregulatory measures, notably in the United States.

A. SERVICE AND MANUFACTURING TNCs: THE JUXTAPOSITION

The combined sales of the world's top 200 corporations,[20] which in 1982 exceeded $3 trillion, or the equivalent of one third of the world's GDP, indicate the magnitude of corporate power (see table 9).

---

[20] Excluded from the top 200 are family-owned enterprises, of which Cargill (with annual sales running at $30-35 billion) is perhaps the leading example. Other family-owned or private firms include Continental Grain, Bunge and Born, André, Dreyfus and Marc Rich.

TABLE 8

Leading exporters of services

	1970				1980			
	Service exports (billion dollars)	Percentage of world total	Goods exports (billion dollars)	Service exports as percentage of goods exports	Service* exports (billion dollars)	Percentage of world total	Goods exports (billion dollars)	Service exports as percentage of goods exports
United States	21.5	23.2	42.6	50.5	105.1	19.3	216.7	48.5
France	6.0	6.5	17.9	33.7	51.3	9.4	111.3	46.1
United Kingdom	10.9	11.7	19.4	56.2	51.3	9.4	115.4	44.5
Germany, Fed. Rep. of . . .	6.3	6.8	34.2	18.4	41.2	7.6	192.9	21.3
Belgium/Luxembourg . . .	2.8	3.1	11.6	24.6	32.5	6.0	64.1	50.7
Italy	5.6	6.0	13.2	42.4	27.7	5.1	77.7	35.7
Netherlands	3.7	4.0	11.8	31.7	27.6	5.1	73.9	37.4
Japan	3.3	3.6	19.3	17.2	26.2	4.8	129.3	20.2
Switzerland	2.6	2.8	5.2	50.5	13.7	2.5	29.6	46.1
Austria					13.3	2.4	17.5	75.9
Spain					11.9	2.2	20.7	57.3
Canada	3.2	3.5	16.1	19.9	9.9	1.8	64.3	15.3
Sweden					8.5	1.6	30.9	27.6
Mexico					8.4	1.5	15.4	54.7
Singapore					6.6	1.2	19.4	34.0
Top 15	65.9	71.1	191.3	34.4	435.2	80.0	1 178.9	36.9

Rep. of Korea	. . . .				4.8	0.9	17.6	27.5
Australia	. . . .				4.2	0.8	22.1	19.0
Greece	. . . .				4.0	0.7	5.1	78.4
South Africa	. . . . . .				3.9	0.7	12.7	30.7
Kuwait	. . . . . .				3.8	0.7	20.0	19.0
Saudi Arabia	. . . . . .				3.7	0.7	109.1	3.4
Brazil	. . . .				3.1	0.6	20.1	15.3
Taiwan Province of China	. . . .				3.0	0.5		
Argentina	. . . . . .				2.7	0.5	7.5	36.0
Venezuela	. . . . .				2.5	0.5	20.6	12.3
Nigeria	. . . . . .				1.5	0.3	26.0	5.9
Chile	. . . . .				1.5	0.3	4.8	31.3
New Zealand	. . . . .				0.9	0.2	5.4	16.3
Malaysia	. . . .				0.8	0.2	13.8	6.0
Turkey	. . . . . .				0.7	0.1	2.6	26.9
Second 15	. . . . . .	26.8	28.9	124.0	21.6			
					41.2	7.6	287.3	14.4
Others		92.7	100.0	315.3	29.4			
					67.8	12.4	543.3	12.5
TOTAL . . .					544.2	100.0	2 009.5	27.1

Sources: Computed from data of the UNCTAD secretariat and the United Kingdom Committee on Invisible Exports.

^a Except for Switzerland, excludes miscellaneous government transactions and transfers. Blank spaces: figures not available.

TABLE 9

Top 200 transnational corporations: services v. manufactures, 1982[a]

Country[b]	Service TNCs			Manufacturing TNCs			Total TNCs		
	Number	Revenues (million dollars)	Per cent of top service TNCs	Number	Revenues (million dollars)	Per cent of top manufacturers	Number	Revenues (million dollars)	Per cent of top 200
United States	30	392 187	32.9	50	910 268	49.1	80	1 302 455	42.8
Japan	21	487 567	40.9	14	169 742	9.2	35	657 309	21.5
United Kingdom	9	99 548	8.4	9	165 174	8.9	18	264 722	8.7
Germany, Fed. Rep. of	4	45 034	3.8	13	162 507	8.8	17	207 541	6.8
France	9	92 904	7.8	7	89 733	4.8	16	182 637	6.0
Netherlands	–	–	–	4	86 377	4.6	4	86 377	2.8
Italy	1	10 150	0.8	4	74 331	4.0	5	84 481	2.8
Canada	5	38 772	3.2	2	16 309	0.9	7	55 081	1.8
Brazil	1	8 442	0.7	1	18 937	1.0	2	27 379	0.9
Spain	–	–	–	2	21 574	1.2	2	21 574	0.7
Switzerland	–	–	–	2	20 427	1.1	2	20 427	0.7
Israel	2	17 463	1.5	–	–	–	2	17 463	0.6
Others[c]	–	–	–	10	118 233	6.4	10	118 233	3.9
TOTAL	82	1 192 067	100.0	118	1 853 612	100.0	200	3 045 679	100.0
World GDP[d]								9 421 452	
Top 200 as percentage of GDP									32.3

Source: Computed from data in *Forbes*, 9 May 1983 and 4 July 1983.

[a] A service TNC is any TNC deriving over half of its revenues from services; a manufacturing TNC is any TNC deriving half of its revenues from manufacturing.

[b] Ranked by combined sales of top service and manufacturing TNCs.

[c] Including ten countries with one TNC in the top 200: Mexico, Venezuela, Iran (Islamic Republic of), Kuwait, Sweden, Austria, Belgium, Republic of Korea, India and South Africa.

[d] Excluding socialist countries.

Of these 200 corporations, 116 have their headquarters in just five countries: the United States (80), Japan (35), the United Kingdom (18), the Federal Republic of Germany (17), and France (16). These 116 corporations have acquired over 85 per cent of the aggregate sales of the 200.[21] Corporations from the developing world are not entirely absent, as eight firms from seven developing countries figure in the 200.

Out of the 200 corporations, 118 are predominantly (i.e. over half of sales) engaged in manufacturing, and 82 could be classified as service corporations. These service TNCs accounted for two fifths of the combined revenues of the 200 in 1982. It is noteworthy that there is an even higher level of geographical concentration among the service TNCs: around three quarters of their revenues were accounted for by corporations in two countries: Japan (41 per cent) and the United States (33 per cent).[22]

Recent data compiled from *Fortune*'s tabulation of the top 500 corporations indicate the financial leverage of the big service corporations. The combined assets of merely the top 50 TNCs in each of the four leading service sectors in the United States were equivalent to more than 14 per cent of GNP and 4 per cent of total capital stock,[23] with commercial banking by far the leading service sector (table 10).

---

[21] The United States corporations, however, account for over two fifths of the top 200's revenues; next in the order of shares of revenues are companies having their headquarters in Japan (22 per cent) and in the United Kingdon (9 per cent).

[22] The average size (in terms of assets) of leading service TNCs differs greatly from country to country; the 21 Japanese companies average $23 billion as opposed to $13 billion for the United States corporations and around $8 billion for the five Canadian TNCs.

[23] Assets consist of specific property and claims against others which possess commercial or exchange value. Caution should be exercised in any comparison of assets with GDP, inasmuch as the contribution of an individual firm to GDP is only the value added by that firm, a sum which is only a fraction of the firm's assets. Since value-added data for *Fortune*'s top 500 companies are almost impossible to obtain, assets and revenues have been used in the comparison to give an order of magnitude of the size of these firms.

TABLE 10

USA: major service TNCs, 1982

Service sector	Assets of top 50 TNCs in each sector (billion dollars)	Per cent of total USA capital stock
Commercial banking	1 144.4	11.9
Diversified financial	495.6	5.2
Utilities	448.2	4.7
Life insurance	436.8	4.5
Retailing	128.4	1.3
Diversified service	116.9	1.2
Transportation	87.6	0.9
Total USA capital stock	9 602.4[a]	100.0

Source: Computed from data in *Fortune*, 13 June 1983.

[a] Estimated by the authors.

233

Whereas 100 years ago, most services were transacted by highly specialized firms that provided single service lines, at present the boundaries between services are crumbling in consequence of corporate diversification and of the evolution of corporations that could be designated as financial supermarkets. It is for this reason that the label "service TNC" should be used with great caution, for this omnibus designation covers the three very different groupings which are discussed below.

1. *Single-line service TNCs*

While the food retailer McDonald's is a paramount example of this species of single-line service firms, this grouping is actually on the road to extinction owing to the enhanced power (financial and marketing) and capacity for survival that conglomeration offers, particularly in times of economic crisis.

2. *Transnational service conglomerates (TSCs)*

Single-line firms have to diversify mainly because corporate capital seeks new outlets to sustain profitability. At first, they usually expand into a complementary line that can build successfully on the firm's existing technical and marketing expertise. In the case of services, such complementarities exist between banking, insurance and other financial services; between advertising, public relations, the media and telecommunications, etc. As distinct from the single-line firms, the TSCs can be expected to make much headway in the future.

3. *Transnational integral conglomerates (TICs)*

The third category represents what may be described as the supreme embodiment of modern capitalism. The logic of uninhibited corporate growth is perhaps nowhere more frankly stated than in a report by R. J. Reynolds Industries Inc. (1981 sales: $13.8 billion) which straddles manufacturing, plantation agriculture and service sectors:

> First, having captured one-third of the United States cigarette market, the company could see a point of diminishing returns for growth potential. Second, significant cash was being generated which could be invested advantageously elsewhere. [Adopting] an unrestricted approach towards diversification, Reynolds moved into entirely new areas — shipping and petroleum, on the theory that it made sense, when appropriate, to supply cash to any strong, well-established business.[24]

There is yet another force—external to the corporation proper—promoting the mergers and acquisitions that are the essence of conglomerate expansionism, namely the activities of commercial and investment banks. "One of

---

[24] R. J. Reynolds Industries Inc., *Our 100th Anniversary, 1875-1975*, Winston-Salem, North Carolina, 1975. See also *Marketing and Distribution of Tobacco*, study prepared by the UNCTAD secretariat (TD/B/C.1/205), United Nations publication, Sales No. E.78.II.D.14.

the favourite pastimes of concentrated financial power," noted Congressman Wright Patman, ex-Chairman of the United States House Subcommittee on Banking and Currency, "is promoting concentration in non-financial industries. There is substantial evidence that the major commercial banks have been actively fuelling the corporate merger movement."[25]

Since this statement was made more than a decade ago, events have moved apace. First, merger activity has embraced not only non-financial industries but increasingly financial ones as well. Secondly, investment banks like Goldman Sachs and Salomon Brothers have become rivals to commercial banks by arranging mergers on an unprecedented scale. In 1982, United States investment banks earned $221 million in fees for services performed in connection with merely 33 mergers and 17 debt and equity offerings. Such merger promotion by these large banks, as one banker warned, "is helping to change the face of corporate America," often at the expense of "the long-term health of their clients."[26] It is precisely in this area that the impact of banking on other services and on manufacturing is most noticeable.

The interaction of service corporations in six major service sectors— financial services, insurance, tourism, shipping, advertising and accounting—is discussed below.[27]

B. THE MAJOR SECTORS

Six sectors have been selected for analysis on the grounds that a substantial volume of their output has been internationalized. It is on the basis of the value of international transactions that these sectors have been ranked. It needs to be restressed that such a sequential sectoral analysis should not be construed as in any way suggesting that there are rigid boundaries dividing them.

---

[25] Wright Patman, "Other People's Money", *The New Republic,* 17 February 1973. He went on: "A 1971 congressional report, for example, found that the major banks financed acquisitions, furnished key financial personnel to conglomerates and were even willing to clean out stock from their trust departments to aid in takeover bids. Thus Gulf & Western, one of the most aggressive conglomerates of the 1950s and 1960s (92 acquisitions involving almost a billion dollars in 11 years), expanded hand in glove with Chase Manhattan. Friendly representatives of Chase made funds available and provided advice and services that assisted Gulf & Western in its acquisitions. In return, in addition to the customary business charges for Gulf & Western's accounts and loans, Chase secured banking business generated by the newly developing conglomerates that formerly had gone to other banks, and was recipient of advance inside information on proposed future acquisitions."

[26] *Financial Times,* 16 May 1983.

[27] The ensuing analysis excludes foreign investment earnings, a major item on service account, because it is qualitatively different from other service sectors. This exclusion is justified inasmuch as such earnings originate from the heterogeneous foreign operations of transnational corporations in all sectors. For an elaboration, see F. F. Clairmonte and J. Cavanagh, "Transnational ...", *op. cit.,* pp. 168-169.

1. *Towards the financial conglomerate*

It would be difficult to find a better portrayal of the changes now revolutionizing financial services than that of the American insurance periodical *Best's Review:* "The financial services world is an intricate one of competing conglomerates, interlocking directorates, foreign and domestic subsidiaries and spin-off companies, all interwoven with provincial and federal legislative policies that can present a daunting prospect for newcomers to the field."[28] What all this adds up to is the eradication of distinct categories or definitions and the emergence of new conceptions of a bank and even of money. The driving force behind these changes is what has been labelled the financial conglomerate or the financial supermarket. Such institutional hybrids span, amongst other services, commercial banking, securities broking, insurance services, the issue of traveller's cheques and credit cards, money market funds, point-of-sale debit systems and financial futures operations.

The conglomeration of financial services is being facilitated and promoted by the interaction of electronic technology, government deregulation and the corporate striving for the dismantlement of existing barriers. Thanks to the technological revolution, world-wide financial transactions can now take place at the speed of light and corporations can operate effectively in dozens of financial markets simultaneously. What remains to be done to consummate the truly global financial conglomerate is the dismantling of State regulation. Such a process is already well under way in Japan, the Federal Republic of Germany, Switzerland, Singapore, Hong Kong and the Philippines, and also in the United States. Given the sheer size of United States finance capital and the deregulation battles now raging in that country, attention will be focused on changes within the United States.

(a) *Definitions*

Financial services embrace a vast spectrum of activities of which the major ones are commercial banking,[29] brokerage and securities dealings,[30] the operation of thrift institutions (composed of savings banks and savings and loan associations),[31] the issue of traveller's cheques and credit cards, the management of cash accounts,[32] financial futures operations and insurance.[33]

---

[28] *Best's Review*, July 1983.

[29] A commercial bank is an institution which specializes in demand deposits and commercial loans.

[30] Brokerage houses, investment banking houses and securities companies are firms whose functions overlap. Their common denominator, however, is that they all buy and sell securities, i.e. stocks and bonds.

[31] Thrift institutions specialize in accepting consumer deposits and reinvesting them in mortgages. In 1981, the combined assets of United States thrift institutions were estimated at $800 billion, second only in financial institution rankings to commercial banks. See J. M. Rosenberg, *Dictionary of Banking and Finance* (New York, John Wiley & Sons, 1982), p. 495.

[32] Merrill Lynch pioneered managed cash accounts at the end of the 1970s and at present is the market leader. By 1983, it was managing assets of around $75 billion in 950,000 separate accounts. It has now extended the offering of these accounts internationally from Western Europe to Asia.

[33] An insurance company is an institution which, in exchange for premiums, issues policies which guarantee reimbursement for losses caused by legally designated contingencies.

236

Laws governing banking, financing and insurance differ, at times considerably, between countries. In the United States, a rigid separation between banking and other financial dealings has been a basic principle of banking law since the early 1930s. The walls, however, are crumbling, or, in the summation of *The Financial Times:* "Hardly a month goes by without another major development—another brick knocked out of the wall. Banks, particularly the major ones, are buying brokers and most recently banks. Big non-bank commercial and industrial companies are buying everything."[34]

(b) *Profile of the top 100*

Notwithstanding these diversities, the principal institution providing financial services has been and remains the big commercial bank. The assets of the world's top 100 banks indicate the extent of their financial power (table 11). In 1982, their combined assets of $4.5 trillion were almost half of global GDP and more than one and a half times the combined sales of the top 200 corpo-

---

[34] *Financial Times,* 24 May 1983.

TABLE 11

Profile of top 100 banks, 1982

Headquarters[a]	Number of banks	Assets (billion dollars)	Percentage of total assets
Japan	24	1 161.0	25.8
USA	15	743.9	16.5
France	8	514.3	11.4
Germany, Fed. Rep. of	11	466.1	10.4
UK	5	355.6	7.9
Italy	8	263.3	5.9
Canada	5	247.5	5.5
Netherlands	4	154.5	3.4
Switzerland	3	138.6	3.1
Belgium	4	91.7	2.0
Brazil	1	61.7	1.4
Hong Kong	1	57.1	1.3
Australia	2	49.1	1.1
Israel	2	42.6	1.0
Spain	2	41.6	0.9
Iran (Islamic Rep. of)	1	27.1	0.6
India	1	23.6	0.5
Austria	1	19.6	0.4
Sweden	1	19.1	0.4
Iraq	1	18.6	0.4
	100	4 496.6	100.0

Source: Computed from *The Banker,* June 1983.

[a] Ranked by banks' assets.

rations. Big Japanese and United States banks alone control over two fifths of the total assets of these 100 firms with 24 Japanese banks having over a quarter of this.[35]

Although transnational operations began to be undertaken by banks as early as the 1870s, the bulk of their operations and profits in the ensuing century were related to domestic operations. Their international expansion really "took off" during the 1970s when the top 100 banks became the major intermediaries for recycling petrodollars. This dramatic change is reflected in the figures for the seven biggest United States banks, whose profits from foreign operations soared from 22 per cent of total profits in 1970 to 55 in 1981, and to a record 60 per cent in the following year alone (table 12).

TABLE 12

Growth in foreign profits of leading United States banks

Bank[a]	Foreign profits (million dollars)			Percentage of total profits		
	1970	1981	1982	1970	1981	1982
Citicorp	58	287	448	40	54	62
BankAmerica	25	245	253	15	55	65
Chase Manhattan	31	247	215	22	60	70
Manufacturers Hanover	11	120	147	13	48	50
J. P. Morgan	26	234	283	25	67	72
Chemical New York	8	74	104	10	34	39
Bankers Trust New York	8	116	113	15	62	51
TOTAL	167	1 323	1 563	22	55	60

Source: Calculated from data from Salomon Bros. in *The Economist,* 14 January 1978, and *Forbes,* 5 July 1982 and 4 July 1983.

[a] Ranked on basis of 1982 assets.

The financial bonanza of the 1970s, springing largely from transactions in petrodollars, gave a powerful impetus to the Eurocurrency market, whose combined volume now hovers around $2 trillion. This Eurocurrency market, which trades any country's currency on deposit outside that country, expanded enormously both the volume and variety of banking services globally. The expansion of the banks' international operations was accompanied by a remarkable increase in the mobility of financial resources (sometimes including embezzled funds), which in its turn was aided by the anonymity and secrecy that protect bank accounts in a number of countries.

The most recent participant in offshore banking is the United States, whose Federal Reserve Board authorized the creation of international banking facil-

---

[35] Colossal economies of scale exist in commercial banking, with estimates of optimal bank size beginning at $15 billion worth of assets. This is one of the reasons for mergers of large-scale banks. Merely in the first half of 1983, 10 banks in the United States with assets of over $1 billion each were taken over by other banks. This represents a giant stride, with the value of major bank acquisitions rising from $475 million in 1980 to $1.4 billion in 1981 and $3.6 billion in 1982, (*Fortune,* 19 September 1983).

ities (IBFs) in United States territory to siphon off some of these funds from offshore banking centres.[36] Proliferation of offshore banking facilities exercises a nefarious impact on developing countries. These tax havens—old and new— have become the silent receptacles of billions of dollars from the third world which, by definition, have been subtracted from the development process.

By 1983, developing countries were indebted to the tune of $850-900 billion; the payment of interest on the debt (not to speak of the reimbursement of principal) was diverting most developing countries' resources away from national development to the transnational banking system. Approximately $300 billion of this total is owed to commercial banks.[37] The immense profitability of developing country operations is exemplified by the case of Brazil, which produced over one fifth of Citicorp's profits in 1982, although the bank's loans to Brazil accounted for only 5 per cent of the bank's total assets.[38]

Offshore banking is one important component of the transnationalization of banking. There are yet others,[39] including large-scale international takeovers of big banks by other banks. Five recent annexations illustrate this mode of transnationalization:

Chase Manhattan Bank acquired 31.5 per cent of the fifth largest Dutch commercial bank (Nederlandes Crediet Bank) and is striving to raise its stake by another 27.5 per cent.[40]

Citibank has moved to finalize its control over the holding company of Grindlay's, having acquired nearly 49 per cent of its equity. Lloyds Bank is the other major owner.

In 1980, the Midland Bank acquired a large interest (acquisition price: $820 million) in the 11th largest United States bank, Crocker National of California. In 1983, it boosted its shareholding to 57 per cent. Thus annexationism can either take the form of a 100 per cent takeover or be phased over time.

The Fuji Bank, part of the Japanese Fuyo Group (which also includes the Marubeni Sogo Shosha and dozens of other companies), bought out two of

---

[36] The IBFs are freed from several restrictions that hamper United States banks: they can accept time deposits from foreigners free of reserve requirements and interest rate ceilings; they are exempt from paying deposit insurance and are not liable to the various regulatory assessments imposed by the Federal Deposit Insurance Corporation. By April 1983, there were 269 IBFs in the USA, with 142 of these located in New York, followed by California, Florida, Illinois and Texas. It is estimated that the assets of the IBFs are rapidly approaching $200 billion (*Financial Times*, 16 May 1983).

[37] According to Mr. Paul Volcker, Chairman of the Federal Reserve Board, the developing countries' debt to commercial banks of non-OPEC countries has soared to $285 billion (Bank for International Settlements, *Press Review*, 28 October 1983). Their debt to banks of the OPEC countries probably exceeds $50 billion.

[38] *The Economist*, 19 March 1983.

[39] One other component of transnationalization is what is known as the interbank system. This system, through which banks place deposits with other banks, is the vital lubricant which prevents the entire world banking system from seizing up. It is more than ten times larger than the 1982 international syndicated loan market of $82 billion and is thought to involve around one trillion dollars of bank-to-bank deposits (*Financial Times*, 1 March 1983).

[40] *Financial Times*, 31 March 1983.

239

the commercial financing subsidiaries of Walter E. Heller International (USA) for $425 million.[41]

In the largest Japanese acquisition ever of a United States bank, the Mitsubishi Bank (Japan's fourth biggest) bought the BanCal Tri-State Corporation,[42] which in turn owns the oldest bank in California, the Bank of California. The deal substantially enhanced Mitsubishi's service and manufacturing leverage in that country. Inevitably, such a Japanese transnationalization drive is triggering demands by United States finance capital to break into the Japanese market—a move resisted by the Japanese Government.[43]

(c) *The crumbling of the walls*

These forms of corporate annexationism so well advanced in banking are increasingly finding a congenial legal climate, particularly in the United States, where the legal walls that separate financial services are crumbling. Over the past half a century the foundations of this wall were laid essentially in three major pieces of legislation.

In 1927, the McFadden Act was enacted prohibiting banks from having branches outside their home states. Six years later, in the aftermath of the Great Depression, the Glass-Steagall Act was enacted at the time of the Roosevelt New Deal Administration, which debarred banks from carrying on investment business, the object being to protect depositors from excessively risky uses of their money. In 1956, the provisions of the Glass-Steagall Act were supplemented by the Bank Holding Company Act, which defines a bank as an institution that takes deposits and makes commercial loans, but is prohibited from other commercial activities.

The first signs of the crumbling of the separating walls occurred during the Carter administration; the dismantling of barriers proceeded apace under President Reagan. Merely in the two years since 1981, three major reforms have been instituted:

Interest rate ceilings for banks have been effectively abolished[44] with the result that banks may now pay higher interest and so can win back deposits and compete more effectively with the unregulated money market funds;

The division between banking and other financial services is disappearing as banks have already begun to move into stockbroking;

---

[41] In a similar move, Sumitomo Bank and the Bank of Tokyo bought 37 branches of the Bank of California.

[42] In terms of assets, the Bank of California ranks 63rd in the United States. It possesses the strategic advantage of operating branch banks in the states of Washington and Oregon, which were set up before the 1927 enactment of the McFadden Act prohibiting banks from operating branches outside the home state (*Japan Economic Journal,* 30 August 1983).

[43] The Japanese Ministry of Finance, for example, is hostile to a proposed joint venture between Nomura Securities and Morgan Guaranty Trust to set up a joint trust company in Japan.

[44] The Garn-St. Germain Depository Institutions Act, rushed through Congress in 1982, freed both commercial banks and thrift institutions to offer competitive interest rates. It was designed

Regulators have suspended the fifty-year ban on interstate branching by authorizing strong banks to take over weaker ones in other states in crisis conditions. Already two precedents have been set: Citicorp has rescued and taken over a $3 billion California savings bank and the Bank of America has taken over Seafirst, the largest bank in the state of Washington.[45]

Such a loosening of regulations in the United States and elsewhere has given rise to a variety of combinations of financial service corporations that would have been unimaginable a decade ago. It is revealing to look at the data covering selected mergers of the early 1980s; the trend towards amalgamation can be expected to gather momentum in the rest of the decade (see table 13).

---

primarily to save the thrifts from bankruptcy or "shotgun mergers". Another provision of the Act authorized banks with assets of under $50 million to write insurance. This flung open the doors to insurance for 2,300 of the 3,500 banks that came under the Federal Reserve Board's jurisdiction.

[45] Facilitating this process of national unification in the banking system are certain coordinated actions by state legislatures. For example, New England lawmakers are creating the first regional interstate banking system by introducing reciprocal banking legislation among the six states concerned. For a legal overview of the financial services industry in the United States, see *Hearings before the Committee on Banking, Housing and Urban Affairs. Problems, options and issues currently facing the financial services industry and the agencies that regulate and supervise these entities*, parts I and II. 98th Congress, 1st Session, April, May and June 1983, Washington, D.C.

TABLE 13

Selected financial mergers, recent years

Acquirer	Million dollars	Acquired
Bank		*Bank*
Citibank (USA) and Lloyds (UK) ...	n.a.	Grindlays Bank (UK)
Midland Bank (UK)	820	Crocker National (USA)
Mitsubishi Bank (Japan)	282	BanCal Tri-State (USA)
First Chicago (USA)	275	American National (USA)
Bank of Montreal (Canada)	547	Harris Bankcorp (USA)
		Investment bank/brokerage house
Bank of America (USA)	53	Charles Schwab (USA)
Citicorp (USA)	30	Vickers da Costa (UK)
		Futures company
Lloyds, National Westminster, Barclays, Midland, William & Glyn's (UK) ...	n.a.	International Commodity Clearing House (UK)
		Financial conglomerate
Fuji Bank (Japan)	425	Walter E. Heller, two subsidiaries (USA)
Financial conglomerate		*Bank*
American Express (USA)	550	Trade Development Bank (Luxembourg)

TABLE 13 *(continued)*

Acquirer	Million dollars	Acquired
		Investment bank/brokerage house
American Express (USA)	930	Shearson Loeb Rhodes (USA)
		Insurance
Alexander and Alexander (USA) . . .	300	Alexander Howden (UK)
		Media firm
American Express (USA)	175	Warner Communications Cable subsidiary (USA)
Investment bank/brokerage house		*Investment bank/brokerage house*
Lehman Brothers (1977, USA)	n.a.	Kuhn Loeb (USA)
		Trading company
Goldman Sachs (USA)	n.a.	J. Aron (USA)
Insurance		*Insurance*
Marsh and McLennan (USA)	n.a.	C. T. Bowring (UK)
Winterthur (Switzerland)	n.a.	Republic Financial Services (USA)
Winthertur (Switzerland)	n.a.	Provident Insurance (UK)
Connecticut General (USA)	n.a.	INA (USA)
		Investment bank/brokerage house
Prudential Insurance (UK)	385	Bache Group (UK)
Prudential Insurance Co. (USA)	n.a.	Hambro Bank (UK)
Aetna Life & Casualty (USA)	n.a.	Samuel Montagu (UK)
Mutual fund		*Bank*
Dreyfus Corporation (USA)	n.a.	Lincoln State Bank (USA)
Retail company		*Investment bank/brokerage house*
Sears Roebuck (USA)	600	Dean Witter Reynolds (USA)
		Real estate brokerage house
Sears Roebuck (USA)	n.a.	Coldwell, Banker & Co. (USA)
Trading company		*Investment bank/brokerage house*
Phibro (USA)	550	Salomon Brothers (USA)
		Insurance
Jardine Matheson (HK)	30	Bache Insurance Services (USA)
Industrial corporation		*Investment bank/brokerage house*
Dow Chemical Co. (USA)	n.a.	Arbuthnot Latham (UK)
Texaco (USA)	n.a.	Charles Fulton Holdings (UK)
Bechtel Engineering (USA)	n.a.	Dillon Read & Co. (USA)
Société Générale de Belgique (B) . . .	n.a.	Tanks Consolidated (UK)

242

TABLE 13 *(concluded)*

Acquirer	Million dollars	Acquired
	Insurance	
Engelhard Minerals (USA)	278	Northwestern National Insurance (USA)
ITT (early 1970s, USA)	n.a.	Hartford Insurance (USA)
BAT (UK)	1 200	Eagle Star (USA)
American Brands (USA)	352	Southland Life Insurance (USA)

Sources: Compiled from trade sources.

The drive towards a concentration of financial power in the United States has its parallels elsewhere. In the United Kingdom, for example, larger merchant banks are watching this American movement, and are now themselves actively seeking to break into the brokers' business and related financial services. The move of the Rothschild Investment Trust Group (RIT) to merge with the United Kingdom's third largest merchant bank (the Charterhouse Group) is indicative.[46] The mounting presence of giant United States and Japanese financial service corporations in world markets also contributes to the momentum of concentration of financial services in other developed market economies.

What is therefore emerging is not only a conflict between TNCs and the developing countries, but also heightened conflicts between the capitalist centres manœuvring to acquire ascendancy on global financial markets. In this struggle for the conquest of financial markets, the United States and Japanese financial conglomerates are far better poised than their smaller rivals in the United Kingdom and elsewhere.[47]

2. *The insurance realm*

In recent decades, the world's insurance and reinsurance[48] business has changed more radically than any other service sector, and is likely to be further

---

[46] The merged firm becomes the largest merchant bank in the United Kingdom, with combined shareholders' funds of around £360 million, dwarfing the previous leaders Kleinwort Benson and Hill Samuel. Another institutional change influencing the entire shape and direction of British banking is the large-scale intrusion of building societies into the market for consumer deposits.

[47] An indication of this disparity in financial power is seen in a comparison of market capitalization (in million pounds) of the three leading investment houses in these countries. The United Kingdom: Kleinwort Benson (235), Hill Samuel (184) and Charterhouse Group (171), which merged with RIT. The United States: American Express (4,800), Merrill Lynch (2,648), Phibro-Salomon (1,392). Japan: Nomura Securities (3,278), Nikko Securities (1,356) and Daiwa Securities (1,219). (*Sources:* RIT and *Financial Times,* 4 November 1983.)

[48] A lucid definition is that given in a United Nations document: "Insurance companies cede part of their risks to reinsurers. Thus, a reinsurance company is an insurance company's insurance company. This situation enables insurers to underwrite a larger amount of business than would otherwise be possible by protecting them both from a series of small losses and from a single big loss arising out of a major catastrophe." *Transnational Reinsurance Operations: A Technical Paper* (ST/CTC/15), United Nations publication, Sales No. E.80.II.A.10, para. 4.

243

changed by the year 2000. The first major breach in the phalanx of specialized insurance companies opened up in the 1950s, when numerous mergers occurred between life and non-life insurance companies, a pattern of vertical integration characterized by takeovers of insurance brokers and reinsurance companies.

By the mid-1960s, yet another far-reaching change in the structure of the insurance industry occurred. This was the rise of new transnational service conglomerates operating through holding companies with subsidiaries in insurance, banking, data processing, engineering, mutual fund management, real estate appraisal and other activities. While there were internal dynamics propelling insurance companies in this direction, external stimuli were also at work, such as the opportunity to minimize taxes through the setting up of holding companies.

The 1970s witnessed another attack on "pure" insurance companies from an entirely different flank: industrial transnational corporations. One major variant of this encroachment is the acquisition of well-established insurance firms by TNCs. The size of some of these buyouts has now reached almost astronomic proportions, seen in the unprecedented $1.2 billion takeover by the British American Tobacco Company (BAT) for the United Kingdom's sixth largest composite insurer, Eagle Star.[49]

Another trend is the practice of certain TNCs to try to economize on premiums and minimize taxes by creating their own "captive" insurance subsidiaries in such tax havens as Bermuda and the Cayman Islands. This trend has become so pronounced that by 1983, more than 300 of the 500 largest United States firms had set up captive insurance subsidiaries in Bermuda. In addition, some United States banks that are now being freed from the regulatory shackles of an earlier era are entering the insurance industry. The remaining single-line insurers are apprehensive that the banks' huge customer bases and extensive branch networks will allow them to offer a variety of underpriced insurance products thanks to high volume turnover and low start-up costs. Retailers such as Sears (1982 sales: $31 billion), which operates one of the world's biggest insurers, Allstate, are armed with similar firepower and have also mounted the attack.

---

[49] Certain industrial TNCs have taken over one or more insurance companies. For example, American Brands, one of the world's leading tobacco and alcohol producers, which acquired Franklin Life Insurance in 1979 and Southland Life Insurance in 1983 (see table 13); Gulf & Western has acquired 18 insurance companies; Teledyne owns 15 and Control Data owns 14. Insurance companies are desirable acquisitions not merely because of their profitability but because of the volume of their daily cash flows and the assets under their control. A conglomerate can use funds generated by the premiums of insurance subsidiaries to buy long-term bonds issued by other corporate bodies. Moreover, since insurance premiums are tax deductible, corporations have yet another incentive to buy up insurance companies or to form their own captive ones. Several corporations are so large and diversified that they can bear substantial risk without insurance. If they have their own insurance companies, however, they can, without costs, insure themselves for as much as they wish, and charge the premiums against tax. See "Thriving on Insecurity: A Look at the Insurance Industry", *Dollars and Sense,* May/June 1983, and Andrew Tobias, *The Invisible Banker* (Alexandria, Virginia; National Insurance Consumer Organization, 1983).

The insurance industry is differentiated from other service industries not merely by the growing intrusion of corporations not previously active in this industry, but also by its vulnerability to indigenization by both the private and the public sectors in developing countries. In contrast to tourism, the takeover, nationalization or expulsion of TNC insurers is feasible as it will not result in a revenue loss due to competition from abroad. While repelling a transnational hotel chain may lead to a loss of business as the tourist flow is directed else-where, a nationalized insurance company can adequately provide all or almost all the insurance requirements of domestic firms and individuals. Reinsurance, however, requires far greater financial resources than most developing country companies can mobilize, and thus the only countervailing alternative to con-tinued domination by transnational reinsurance companies is the formation of regional reinsurance organizations that service several countries.

The expansion of insurance services world-wide since 1950 was stimulated by, and paralleled the implantation of TNC subsidiaries overseas, and the growth of world trade from $52 billion in 1950 to over $2 trillion by 1982. The disintegration of the colonial empires in the postwar era created openings for newcomers, notably insurers and reinsurers from the Federal Republic of Ger-many and Switzerland, as well as indigenous firms from the newly independent countries.

A brief look at world insurance markets over the past 20 years shows that estimated global property/casualty (i.e. non-life) insurance premiums have climbed almost eightfold, from $40 billion to over $300 billion, while reinsu-rance premiums have risen from $5.6 billion to more than $40 billion. By 1983, policies world-wide insured a sum of around $5 trillion, the equivalent of a little over half of world GDP.[50] These figures reflect a prodigious growth of the insurance industry in all regions since the mid-1960s. A regional breakdown of premiums (direct insurance[51] and reinsurance), indicates a decline of the share accounted for by United States insurers from almost three fifths of the world total (1965) to under half at present.

The share of Western European insurers, in contrast, has risen slightly from 32 to 35 per cent over this period. The rest of the non-socialist world doubled its share, from 9 per cent to 18 per cent.[52] Direct insurance and reinsurance, the two major segments of the insurance business, vary in relative importance from one region to another (see table 14). In Eastern Europe, reinsurance accounts for almost a third of direct insurance, as against well under one tenth in the United States.

---

[50] These global totals are computed on the basis of data in *Best's Review,* June 1983, and *The Economist,* 25 September 1982 and 8 October 1983.

[51] Direct insurance consists of life insurance and an omnibus category of non-life insurance, whose four major segments are motor, accident/liability, fire and marine insurance.

[52] Premiums on direct insurance for Asia, Africa and Latin America rose from $3 billion to $21 billion between 1970 and 1981. Swiss Reinsurance Company (Swiss Re.), "The insurance industry in Africa, Asia and Latin America", *Sigma,* No. 8, August 1983, p. 3.

TABLE 14

Regional distribution of world insurance and reinsurance premiums[a]

	Western Europe			United States			Other regions		
	Total (billion dollars)			Total (billion dollars)			Total (billion dollars)		
Year	Direct	Re	Percentage Re/Direct	Direct	Re	Percentage Re/Direct	Direct	Re	Percentage Re/Direct
1965	10.8	3.7	34.4	25.3	1.4	5.5	3.5	0.5	13.6
1970	17.5	5.7	32.6	42.5	2.2	5.2	8.4	1.3	16.0
1975	39.5	11.4	28.9	66.2	4.1	6.2	18.4	3.1	16.9
1981	80.7	25.5	31.6	131.1	9.6	7.3	49.3	6.0	12.2

Sources: Swiss Reinsurance Co., *Sigma*, No. 2, February 1977, p. 10, and correspondence with *Sigma* (1983).

[a] Excluding socialist countries.

Among the world's four major regions, there are marked divergences in the sectoral composition of insurance (see figure II). Structurally, there is a clear discrepancy between developed countries, where life insurance is predominant, and the developing world where motor, marine and fire insurance policies are more common.[53]

Corporations based in five countries dominate the international insurance market: the United States, the United Kingdom, the Federal Republic of Germany, Switzerland and France. Firms headquartered in these countries have about 75 per cent of all overseas insurance offices. Big insurance corporations from five other countries are also leading actors on the world market: Japan, Italy, the Netherlands, Belgium and South Africa.

Unlike most sectors where it is possible to construct a fairly coherent picture of the world's leading corporations,[54] in the case of insurance the compilation of a comparative global table is, at present, beyond the authors' capabilities. In the absence of comparable data, the authors have constructed five tables listing 71 of the world's largest insurance companies from the United States, Western Europe, Japan and South Africa (table 15).

With the world's biggest insurance sector, the United States exhibits a relatively concentrated structure, as the top 42 life insurance companies accounted for over half of the insurance policies issued in that country in 1982. Both life insurance and property/casualty insurance are dominated by three

---

[53] The pie chart for Asia is misleading as it combines Japan (whose insurance pattern is similar to that of the OECD countries) with developing countries more akin to Africa and Latin America.

[54] As has happened in almost all economic sectors world-wide, there has been a reduction in the number of insurance firms over a relatively short time span: from 14,457 in 1968 to 12,941 in 1982. This conclusion is based on a research survey in 81 countries conducted by the Swiss Reinsurance Company ("Changes in the international insurance structure", *Sigma*, No. 7, July 1983).

FIGURE II

Breakdown of insurance in major regions, 1981

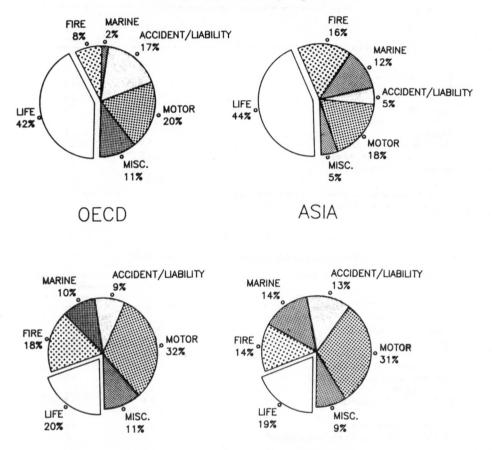

OECD

ASIA

LATIN AMERICA

AFRICA

Source: Swiss Re., "The Insurance Industry in Africa, Asia and Latin America", *Sigma,* No. 8, August 1983, p. 5.

large corporations which, in both cases, account for over 55 per cent of the top ten's business. Certain United States industrial corporations have been pioneers in the creation of captive insurance companies. Under the leadership of such corporations as Exxon and Mobil, the captive insurance market has grown from 150 companies with premium incomes of $50 million (1970) to over 1,500 at present with annual premiums of $7 billion, at an annual compound growth rate of 62 per cent.[55] The extent of foreign penetration of the United States

[55] In Bermuda alone there are over 1,200 such companies, having more than $5 billion of premium income, followed by the Cayman Islands with 200-250 captive companies. See "Insurance in developing countries: developments in 1980-1981, study by the UNCTAD secretariat" (TD/B/C.3/178), and *Financial Times,* 9 September 1983.

TABLE 15A

The ten largest US life insurance companies, 1982

| | Assets | |
Company	Billion dollars	Per cent
Prudential	66.7	22.6
Metropolitan	55.7	18.9
Equitable Life Assurance	40.3	13.6
Aetna Life	28.6	9.7
New York Life	22.5	7.6
John Hancock Mutual	21.7	7.3
Travelers	17.4	5.9
Connecticut General Life	15.7	5.3
Teachers Insurance & Annuity	13.5	4.6
Northwestern Mutual	13.3	4.5
TOTAL	295.4	100.0

Source: Compiled from data in *Fortune,* 13 June 1983.

TABLE 15B

The ten largest US property/casualty insurers, 1982

| | Consolidated revenues | |
Company	Billion dollars	Per cent
Aetna Life & Casualty Co.	14.2	23.1
CIGNA Corp.	11.8	19.2
The Travelers Corp.	11.4	18.6
The Hartford Insurance Group	5.1	8.3
American International Group	3.6	5.8
The Continental Corp.	3.5	5.7
Fireman's Fund Insurance Co.	3.3	5.5
CNA Financial	3.1	5.2
American General Corp.	2.9	4.8
United States Fidelity Guaranty Company	2.3	3.8
TOTAL	61.2	100.0

Source: Compiled from data in *Business Insurance,* 14 March 1983.

TABLE 15C

South Africa: major insurance companies, 1982

| | Net premium income | |
Company	Million dollars	Per cent
Sanlam	752.0	42.0
Old Mutual	741.5	41.4
Liberty Life	296.5	16.6
TOTAL	1 790.0	100.0

Source: Compiled from data in *International Herald Tribune,* 2 September 1983.

TABLE 15D

Japan: major life insurance companies, 1982

Company	Major Japanese group	Assets	
		Million dollars	Per cent
Nippon	Sanwa Bank	34 677	24
Dai-Ichi	Dai-Ichi Kangyo Bank	21 963	15
Sumitomo	Sumitomo	18 381	12
Meiji	Mitsubishi	12 376	8
Asahi	Dai-Ichi Kangyo Bank	11 556	8
Mitsui	Mitsui	8 501	6
Taiyo	—	7 484	5
Yasuda	Fuyo	7 299	5
Others	....	25 056	17
	TOTAL	147 293	100

Source: Computed from data supplied to UNCTAD by the Life Insurance Association of Japan, October 1983.

TABLE 15E

Western Europe's top 40 insurance firms, 1981

Country	Number of firms	Market capitalization	
		Million dollars	Per cent
UK	17	9 995.5	44.6
Germany, Fed. Rep.	10	4 323.0	19.3
Italy	5	3 758.9	16.8
Switzerland	4	3 033.0	13.5
Netherlands	3	1 173.8	5.2
Belgium	1	125.0	0.6
TOTAL	40	22 409.2	100.0

Source: Computed from data in *Financial Times*, 21 October 1982.

market is still relatively small: only 1.7 per cent of the premium volume in life, accident and health insurance, and 4.7 per cent of the property/casualty market.[56]

The paramountcy of a few leading corporations is also seen in the United Kingdom, the Federal Republic of Germany,[57] Italy and Switzerland, which are

---

[56] *Best's Review,* June 1983.

[57] The FRG and Switzerland are also the headquarters of the world's largest reinsurance corporations. Of the world's 15 largest reinsurance companies, six are from FRG, five are American and one each is from Switzerland, the United Kingdom, France and Japan. The top two alone, however, Munich Re. and Swiss Re., account for over half of the top 15's total net premiums. (Calculated from 1981 data supplied by Swiss Re.)

the headquarters of 36 of Europe's top 40 private insurance firms.[58] Almost all these powerful insurance groups are deriving increasing amounts of their income from overseas.[59] In Japan, eight firms dominate insurance, all but one of them belonging to one of the big six Japanese conglomerate groups. In the history of capitalism, it could well be that the Republic of South Africa has attained the highest degree of industrial, mining and service concentration. Four fifths of the value of the shares listed on the Johannesburg Stock Exchange are held by merely seven companies, three of them insurance groups.[60]

By contrast with the progressive internationalization and transnationalization of insurance in most developed countries,[61] an opposite movement is discernible in the developing world. In Africa and Asia, the number of countries which nationalized the insurance industry or restricted the operations of foreign insurance companies rose tenfold from 1968 to 1982. No less remarkable is that the number of countries whose insurance markets were dominated by foreign firms (50-100 per cent) dropped from 43 to 18.[62]

3. *Tourism*

As in the financial services and insurance industries, so also in the tourism industry an entirely new galaxy of corporate actors is making its appearance. What is striking is that in all of them the corporate entities are undergoing a metamorphosis from single-line firms to transnational service conglomerates.

---

[58] These include 12 corporations which rank among Europe's top 100 corporations by market capitalization; see *Financial Times,* 21 October 1982. Figures in parentheses give their ranking among the top 100. UK: Prudential Corporation (44), Royal Insurance (56), Commercial Union (64), General Accident (72), Eagle Star (80), and Guardian Royal Exchange (89). FRG: Allianz Versicherung (35) and Allianz Lebens (50). Italy: Assicurazioni Generali (18). Switzerland: Zurich Versicherung (38), Swiss Reinsurance (86), and Winterthur Versicherung (100). Netherlands: Nationale Nederlanden (95).

[59] In the Netherlands, to take but one example, about two fifths of the income of the second largest insurance company (the result of a 1983 merger of Ennia and Ago) comes from overseas.

[60] These include Anglo American, Sanlam Insurance, Barlow Rand, Old Mutual Insurance, Liberty Life Insurance, Anglo-Vaal and the Rupert/Rembrandt/Rothman's holding company. Old Mutual, the largest insurance group in South Africa, owns equity in more than 200 companies. It is already the principal shareholder in Barlow Rand, the industrial and mining house, and has now acquired a majority stake in Rennier, the hotels and transport conglomerate. Sanlam is the controlling stockholder of Gencor, the second biggest mining house. Gencor in turn has annexed (1983) Tedelex (consumer electronics) and Samancor (ferro alloys). Its Kohler subsidiary has bought the local operations of DRG and Xactos in the packaging sector. Liberty Life has close corporate links with the republic's second largest bank, the Standard Bank. It became a leading actor in consolidating the beer industry in South Africa.

[61] France is one of the few developed market-economy countries that have nationalized the insurance industry.

[62] Foreign companies still account for over half of the total number of insurance companies in: Ireland, Luxembourg, Portugal, Canada, Japan, Australia, New Zealand, Cyprus, Uruguay, Cameroon, Gabon, Ivory Coast, Malawi, Senegal, Zimbabwe, Hong Kong, Lebanon and Singapore. (Swiss Re., "Changes in the international insurance structure", *Sigma,* No. 7, July 1983.)

Deregulation will also be making its impact on airline consolidations. By 1990, in the United States alone, it is predicted that "there will be four or five giant airlines and a host of specialized, although not necessarily tiny, ones."[63]

The tourism sector's basic ingredient, the tourist, includes, in the colourful idiom of *The Economist*, "everything from the Pope and his entourage to backpackers."[64] The principal and increasingly overlapping subsectors of tourism comprise hotels, airlines and tour operators/travel agents.

In the course of the past decades, despite economic crises, receipts from international tourism have burgeoned from $10 billion (1964) to $100 billion in 1982 (see table 16). When, however, domestic tourism is added to this, global tourism receipts rise to between $500 billion and one trillion dollars.[65] The size of the gap between these two estimates is an indication of the ignorance which still shrouds most of the world's service sectors. Given the industry's dimension it is not surprising that it has become a major source of foreign exchange and employment in many developing countries.

A notable feature of the overall picture of tourism is the movement towards service conglomeration. Although specialized transnationalized hotel

---

[63] *Business Week*, "Special Report: Deregulating America", 23 November 1983. See also United States Senate, *Financial Services Industry, Hearings before the Committee on Banking, Housing and Urban Affairs*, Parts 1 and 2, 98th Congress, Washington, D.C., April and May 1983.

[64] *The Economist*, 16 October 1982.

[65] World Tourism Organization (statement by Mr. Robert C. Lonati, Secretary-General of the World Tourism Organization, on the state of tourism on the threshold of 1983, Madrid, January 1983).

TABLE 16

International tourism receipts[a]

(*Million dollars*)

Region[b]	1964	1975	1979	1982
Europe	6 000	26 363	53 974	58 860
North America	1 700	6 410	10 345	15 500
Latin America	1 500	3 809	7 141	10 150
East Asia and Pacific	600	2 524	5 683	9 000
Middle East	180	438	1 283	3 500
Africa	250	1 127	1 692	1 915
South Asia	— [c]	329	710	1 000
TOTAL	10 230	41 000	80 828	99 925

Sources: International Union of Official Travel Organizations, *World Travel*, June 1965, p. 8; and World Tourism Organization, *Regional Breakdown of World Tourism Statistics, 1975-1979*, Madrid, 1981; and information supplied by the World Tourism Organization in 1983.

[a] Excluding international fare receipts.

[b] Ranked by 1982 receipts.

[c] Included in figure for East Asia and Pacific.

chains continue to exist,[66] they are increasingly superseded by more complex forms of TSCs and TICs. Pre-eminent among the former are hotel chains related to airlines either through equity investment, loan capital or referral systems (e.g. the case of Swissair and United Airlines). Indeed, airlines have become the driving force in tourist activities, with the majority of them exercising varying degrees of control over tour operators and hotel interests. Several, including Aer Lingus, SAS and UTA, derive over a quarter of their revenues from non-airline activities (see table 17). A second set of TSCs in this field are travel agents/tour operators also related to hotels.

The TICs have penetrated the hotel industry through such conglomerates as Grand Metropolitan (United Kingdom), whose corporate empire straddles retailing, alcoholic beverages, tobacco manufacturing and the Intercontinental Hotel chain. Airlines,[67] tour operators, and car rental agencies[68] also span the gamut from single-line firms to TSCs and TICs.

The TNCs can be expected to continue to expand in the tourist industry thanks to computerized reservations systems, brand names and massive promotion. In the battle to attract tourists, developing countries increasingly face a crucial choice: either join the TNC tourist circuit, or lose sizeable tourist income to those competing countries that do.

4. *The shipping industry*

Unlike all other economic sectors—service and non-service—shipping, by its very nature, is wholly internationalized. Its size can perhaps best be measured by total freight costs in world trade which topped $120 billion in 1981, of which about nine tenths are shipping costs.[69]

The shipping universe consists mainly of three categories: shipbuilding, shipowners, and trading companies which, in turn, draw on a host of ancillary services ranging from handlers to brokers to charterers. This section is concerned principally with the service sectors of shipowning and trading companies, although shipbuilding is relevant in those cases where it impinges directly upon, or is corporately associated with, these two service sectors.

---

[66] More than half (53 per cent) of the hotels controlled by TNCs were located in DMEs in 1978, the remainder in developing countries. See United Nations Centre on Transnational Corporations, *Transnational Corporations in International Tourism* (ST/CTC/18), United Nations publication Sales No. E.82.II.A.9, table 6.

[67] Eight airlines dominated tourist travel (outside the socialist countries), each with over $10 billion revenue passenger miles (rpm) in 1977 (i.e. including domestic passengers): United Airlines, American Airlines, TWA, British Airways, Japan Airlines, Air France, Air Canada and Lufthansa.

[68] Hertz Corporation, the biggest car rental company, is a subsidiary of the media conglomerate RCA.

[69] "Review of maritime transport, 1982", report by the UNCTAD secretariat (TD/B/C.4/258), table 23 (to be issued as a United Nations publication). While the entire gamut of global service sectors is characterized by varying degrees of concealment and non-accountability, none approaches shipowners in the extent and refinement of applied secrecy.

TABLE 17

Selected airlines: patterns of related activities fiscal year 1982

Airlines	Operating revenues (million dollars)	Tour operations	Hotel interests	Car rentals	Association with other airlines[a]	Other related interests[b]	Ancillary activities as percentage of total 1980 revenue
DME							
Aer Lingus[c]	224.2	X	X		X	X	36.0
Air Canada[c]	1 756.1	X			X	X	7.7[d]
Air France	2 812.0	X	X		X	X	n.a.
Alitalia[c]	1 529.7				X	X	3.6
American Airlines	3 977.8		X		n.a.	X	4.5[e]
British Airways[c]	3 621.9	X	X		X	X	5.0
British Caledonian Airways	614.5	X	X	X	X	X	13.9
CP Air	688.1	X	X		n.a.	X	4.7
Eastern Airlines	3 769.2				X	X	n.a.
Finnair[c]	353.8	X	X		n.a.	X	n.a.
Iberia	1 516.5		X		n.a.	X	11.6
Japan Air Lines	2 887.5	X	X		X	X	7.3[d]
KLM	1 708.0	X	X		X	X	17.0
Lufthansa	2 903.5	X	X	X	X	X	13.4[d]
Pan Am	3 471.4		X		X	X	8.3[d]
Qantas[c]	1 255.7		X		n.a.	X	10.0
Sabena[c]	767.0	X	X		X	X	13.1[e]
SAS	1 459.3	X	X		X	X	32.0
Swissair	1 424.7	X	X		X	X	14.3
Trans World Airlines	3 236.2	X	X		n.a.	X	9.2[d]

TABLE 17 *(continued)*

Airlines	Operating revenues (million dollars)	Tour operations	Hotel interests	Car rentals	Association with other airlines [a]	Other related interests [b]	Ancillary activities as percentage of total 1980 revenue
DME (continued)							
United Airlines	4 613.9	X	X		n.a.	X	11.7[e]
Union de Transports Aeriens-UTA	795.9	X	X		X	X	26.8[d]
DE							
Air India[c]	748.7	X	X		X	X	2.2[e]
Avianca	413.4	X			n.a.	X	1.6
Korean Airlines	153.0				n.a.	X	3.0
Pakistan International[c]	663.9	X	X		X	X	n.a.
Philippine Airlines	565.8	X		X	n.a.	X	3.3
Singapore Airlines[c]	1 231.8	X	X		X	X	1.1[e]
VARIG	964.3	X	X		n.a.	X	n.a.

Sources: Compiled from Annual Reports; ICAO, *Financial Digest*, 1982; *World Air Transport Statistics, No. 27,* 1982; UN Centre on Transnational Corporations, *Transnational Corporations in International Tourism (op. cit.).* DME = developed market economy. DE = developing economies.

NOTE: n.a. denotes information not available. X signifies activity in this sector.

[a] Refers to ownership and other links among airlines.

[b] Including such miscellaneous activities as catering, airport ground services, world-wide aviation insurance and re-insurance, international merchant banking, etc.

[c] Wholly state-owned.

[d] 1982.

[e] 1981.

Shipowners are a heterogeneous category spanning the so-called "independents", industrial TNCs, state shipowners in the centrally planned economies, and banks. Trading companies are equally heterogeneous in that they are part of mining and industrial TNCs, assorted multi-commodity traders, banks, the Japanese *sogo shosha* and other variants of TICs, state trading companies and mammoth retailers. Many of the shipowning and trading firms are family-owned, and hence are not subject to the strict requirements of accountability that apply to public or state companies.

UNCTAD, recognizing that most shipowners are headquartered in developed economies, has attempted to solicit support for an extension of developing countries' participation in shipowning.[70] While generous in their intentions, declarations in this sense tend to ignore that shipowners based in developing countries are subject to the same drives to capital concentration, and pursue the same commercial practices, as their counterparts in the developed ones. The discussions on the shipping industry all too often leave out the essence of corporate power relations in world shipping and related services.

(a) *Shipowners*

The corporate power of the firms that dominate world shipping, and the conflictual relations they have generated, should be projected against the backdrop of the current economic crisis: world shipping is ailing from the largest tonnage surpluses since the Second World War.[71] One of the spin-offs of this crisis will be the liquidation of small and medium-sized shipowners and traders, which in turn will greatly enhance the power of the big survivors.[72]

By contrast with other service sectors, it is at present impossible to give a detailed panorama of the world's shipowners, since about half of world shipping is controlled, in the words of Mr. Robert Ramsay, by "faceless men".[73] Notwithstanding this anonymity, it is none the less possible to patch together an impressionistic picture of the ownership structure. First, around 8 per cent of the world's shipping capacity (693 million deadweight tons in 1982)[74] is owned by state shipping companies in the centrally planned economies; the remainder is privately owned. Within the latter there are essentially two groups: the so-called "independents", which are principally shipowners; and trading companies and other TNCs, which carry on shipowning as a relatively minor operation.

---

[70] Indicative of the imbalance between developing countries' export capacity and carriage capacity is that they have acquired only 13 per cent of the world's fleet, whereas they generate around two fifths of the world's seaborne trade and three fifths of the world's seaborne exports. See "UNCTAD activities in the field of shipping", report by the UNCTAD secretariat (TD/278).

[71] See UNCTAD's yearly *Review of Maritime Transport* for detailed data.

[72] In the words of one shipping company executive: "Ten to 15 per cent of the shipping world, the owners, brokers, handlers, charterers, is at the breaking point" (*International Herald Tribune*, 18 January 1983).

[73] Quoted in the shipping magazine *Fairplay*, 16 June 1983. Mr. Ramsay is a former member of the Shipping Division of the UNCTAD secretariat.

[74] This total is broken down as follows: tankers (47 per cent), oil and bulk carriers (30), general cargo ships (16), container ships (2), and other ships (5). (See UNCTAD, *Review of Maritime Transport, 1982, op. cit.* table 8.)

Perhaps as much as 40 per cent of the world shipping fleet is owned by the "independents", led by shipping magnates in Hong Kong and Greece. Foremost among these are Sir Yue-kong Pao, C. Y. Tung, T. Y. Chao, the Onassis family and the Niarchos family. The Hong Kong "independents" are the leading owners, accounting for 10 per cent of the world's fleet, of which Sir Yue-kong Pao owns almost half. Pao's meteoric rise shows how misleading it is to use the term "independent" to designate such shipowners, most of whom have diversified into real estate and other ventures.

Pao's modest beginnings more than a quarter of a century ago date back to the most recent expansionary phase of capitalism, during which the barriers to entry were considerably lower than they are at present. Over the years, his World-Wide Shipping Group has built up a fleet of over 200 vessels operated by a network of holding companies, associated shipowning groups, management companies, agencies and financial concerns. From shipping, Pao has shifted a sizeable amount of his assets into property, including two thirds of the shareholders' funds from his largest subsidiary, World International. The Group's estimated annual (and largely tax-free) turnover is around $US1-1.5 billion. In recognition of this massive financial/shipping power base, Pao has been elected to the international advisory council of Chase Manhattan Bank and to the presidency of Intertanko, the powerful group of independent tanker owners. Pao's links to finance capital have, more than anything else, been a key to his shipping success; in his own words, "the whole game [of shipping] is about finance".[75]

The effective shipping power of the "independents" should not, however, be exaggerated. Some of them are mainly banking and finance companies which act as "fronts" for the real shipowners. In a typical transaction, a Hong Kong shipowner may own a mere 5 per cent of the equity of a given ship, with 70 per cent of the ship's cost being advanced by the Export/Import Bank of Japan and the remaining 25 per cent by Hong Kong finance houses.[76]

Independents have spearheaded the practice of benefiting from a special kind of tax haven through "open-registry" or flag-of-convenience (FOC) fleets. Liberia, Panama, Cyprus, Bermuda and the Bahamas offer the maritime equivalent of offshore banking and insurance units through the incentives of low taxes and anonymity.[77] Additional advantages enjoyed by FOC fleets are the possibility of recruiting cheap non-union labour and of avoiding liability in the event of accidents. Understandably, already almost a third of the world's shipping fleet operates under flags of convenience.

---

[75] *Far Eastern Economic Review,* 29 January 1982.

[76] Thorsten Rinman and Rigmor Brodefors, *Sjöfartens Historia* (Rinman & Lindén, Gothenberg, 1982), p. 186.

[77] Not only is a geographical concentration perceived among countries offering tax havens for FOC fleets, but also among countries where the beneficial owners of these fleets reside. According to the UNCTAD secretariat, the ownership of FOC fleets is dominated by three countries and one territory: the USA (29.7 per cent of total dwt), Hong Kong (20.7), Greece (11.6), and Japan (10.6). "Beneficial ownership of open-registry fleets—1982", report by the UNCTAD secretariat (TD/B/C.4/255).

FOC fleets are but one stratagem mastered by Sir Yue-kong. *The Far Eastern Economic Review* neatly sums up others:

What makes the World Wide Shipping Group seem so mysterious is the vast maze of private and joint venture companies behind which the billion dollar empire is run. It is so secret and tangled that even World Wide's close bankers often do not fully understand what is going on. Registered in Bermuda, Panama, London and Hong Kong, the World Wide group's major holding companies, agencies and hundreds of ship-owning companies give Pao considerable flexibility in running his operation. That it confused bankers, brokers, shareholders and competitors is beside the point.

The interplay within the private empire allows ships to be swapped between companies without anyone having to answer to inquiring shareholders or provide independent ship valuations to justify sale prices. This moving of assets can generate significant amounts of cash flow by, for example, the selling of vessels into a cash rich World Wide company to boost less mature entities in the group.[78]

Among shipowners, however, Sir Yue-kong Pao belongs to a small powerful élite. The result of this concentration of power is that any attempt on the part of most ship operators in developing countries to carve out a bigger slice of world shipping markets faces almost insuperable barriers. Prominent among the barriers against new entrants are:

The intimate working relationship of shipowners with TNC buyers and traders;

Self-reinforcing agreements such as pools, cartels, and consortia; and

The liner conference system, which "institutionalizes barriers to entry and removes price competition".[79]

The other major group of shipowners are trading companies and other TNCs which also own shipping lines. Goods carried on such lines are referred to as "captive cargoes", which may be either directly owned by the TNC concerned or indirectly owned through intermediaries that the company controls.[80] This indirect ownership, whereby TNCs can dissimulate their shipping interests, makes possible a great variety of transfer pricing, of which one form is incisively described by Mr. Robert Ramsay:

[These TNCs] can easily inflate freight rates and pretend that they have negotiated rates at arm's length with "independent shipowners". By doing this, the TNCs can use high shipping costs as an argument for depressing the f.o.b. prices which they pay to exporting countries and reduce the levels of tax which they pay at both ends of a trade ... The ultimate in tax avoidance sophistication is reached when a TNC operates so close to bankruptcy that it has to borrow working capital overseas at a high rate of interest—omitting, of course to disclose to the taxation authorities that the money it is borrowing happens to be its own, and that the recipient of the high rate of interest is itself.[81]

---

[78] *Far Eastern Economic Review,* 29 January 1982.

[79] "UNCTAD activities in the field of shipping", *op. cit.,* para. 17.

[80] A common practice is for TNC executives to buy up shares in their own names and operate them as though they were part of the TNC. By this very simple stratagem an important segment of the world's fleet ownership is concealed.

[81] Robert A. Ramsay, "Shipping: Regulations or the Market? The Effect on Trade" (unpublished lecture given in Canberra, July 1983).

While specific illustrations of indirect ownership are unavailable, prominent examples of direct ship ownership by TNCs include: the seven petroleum sisters; Cargill's subsidiary Tradax and Dreyfus (each with an estimated 1 per cent of the world's shipping fleet); Alcoa; Reynolds Metals; Alcan; several steel companies; and the six major Japanese conglomerate groups, each with its own extensive maritime network.

It is logical to supplement the foregoing discussion of the shipowning community with a discussion of the other major branch of maritime commerce—trading companies—inasmuch as, in some countries, e.g. Japan and the Republic of Korea, some corporations are both shipowners and trading companies. The authors have identified five categories of major trading institutions: multi-commodity traders mining and industrial TNCs, transnational integral conglomerates (TICs), state trading companies[82] and retailers.

(b) *Multi-commodity traders*

Of the thousands of trading companies world-wide, fewer than 50 dominate world trading, in that they account for over four fifths of primary commodity trade. These are the progeny of the quasi-monopolistic trading companies that reigned from the seventeenth to the nineteenth centuries. With the exception of the years from the middle of the 1850s (which marked the demise of the British East India Company) to the end of the 1880s, there was never a period when big trading companies did not exercise some form of control over commodity prices and markets.

In the intervening interval of a century, trading companies graduated from specialized commodity traders (e.g. the former United Fruit Company) to firms paramount in several commodity markets. To be sure, far-reaching changes, including those in finance and banking, computer and telecommunications technology and transportation, have left the current majors very different from their forbears. Multi-commodity traders can be further subdivided into the vertically integrated[83] (including Cargill, Continental Grain, Bunge, Dreyfus and André), and those that are essentially traders (including Marc Rich, Toepfer, and Phibro).

Most multi-commodity traders are family-owned and non-accountable, no less in developing than in developed countries. In this framework, intimate relationships have been forged between the trading companies and transnational banks. Several of the biggest have at their disposal credit lines of up to $120 million each with one bank and, in some cases, a trader may have as many as 12-15 such credit lines. A growing number of banks are also acquiring trading companies. Banks bring not only assets to these takeovers, but almost all of the supporting facilities and services which the purer species of trading houses

---

[82] State trading companies dominate the external sector of centrally planned economies, although, in certain cases, multi-commodity traders are involved in consummating deals with market economies, and even at times handle trade between centrally planned economies. Also in certain capitalist economies state traders handle a segment of primary commodity trade, e.g. India's tea exports and Canadian grain.

[83] Such extensions include transportation equipment, grain elevators, processing facilities and ocean transportation.

normally do not possess. Such financial institutions as the Hong Kong and Shanghai Banking Corporation (with a 33 per cent interest in Hutchison Whampoa), Midland Bank (with controlling interests in three trading companies), Barclay's Bank, Crédit Lyonnais and Banco do Brasil are heavily involved in trading companies.

(c) *Mining and industrial TNCs*

Transnational trading affiliates of industrial and mining TNCs constitute another sizeable group of trading institutions that have materialized over the past century. Indeed, two fifths of world trade consists of intra-firm transfers. In turn, these transfers have given rise to the now widespread technique of transfer pricing.

The role of industrial TNCs as traders has been enhanced by increasing recourse to two specific forms of trade: international subcontracting and barter. The former is exemplified by the practice of firms such as Levi Strauss farming out the processing of unprocessed cloth to a firm in another country and bringing back the finished product, i.e. jeans. Subcontracting now embraces a vast range of textile, electronic, automobile and other products, accounting for over $18 billion worth of United States imports alone in 1982.

Barter has blossomed in response to global indebtedness, which leaves both developing economies and centrally planned economies hard pressed to allocate foreign exchange for imports. An innovation of the late 1970s has been the creation of special barter or counter-trade departments within such TNCs as General Electric and General Motors to cultivate markets and deals that dispense with cash transactions. As the crisis deepened in the early 1980s, counter-trade rose to as much as 25-30 per cent of world trade.

(d) *Transnational integral conglomerates (TICs)*

If the criterion of trading companies' effectiveness is their capacity to penetrate and retain foreign markets, then it would appear that no group matches the TICs. Japan's *sogo shoshas,* which are joined to finance and industrial corporations and the central state machinery, best exemplify this capacity. In the last 100 years, they have become the most dynamic machine of Japan's impressive growth—at home and abroad. Their corporate power has transcended the geo-political frontiers of the island empire, with banks providing financing; the *shoshas* ensuring the purchasing, marketing, carrying out of inventory and market research; and industrial subsidiaries being the production arm. Currently, there are nine giant *sogo shoshas,* whose 1982 aggregate revenues exceeded $342 billion, a figure which excludes revenues from their financial and industrial affiliates (see table 18).[84]

---

[84] In the latter half of the 1970s, their share of Japan's foreign trade (exports plus imports) at times outstripped 60 per cent. Each *sogo shosha* handles 20,000-25,000 products—evidence of the organizational breadth of these conglomerates which have long ceased to be purely trading corporations. The *sogo shoshas* are a dominant force not only in Japanese trading, but also in the trade of certain of its major trading rivals. By the early 1980s, they already handled a tenth of total United States exports (*Forbes,* 4 July 1983).

TABLE 18

The *sogo shoshas*: global sales

(*Billion dollars*)

Corporations	1974	1982	1982 (1974 = 100)
Mitsubishi	32.5	63.3	195
Mitsui	27.1	62.8	232
C. Itoh	17.8	52.9	297
Marubeni	19.4	48.2	248
Sumitomo	17.8	44.6	251
Nissho-Iwai	13.7	30.1	220
Toyo Menka	8.3	15.1	182
Kanematsu-Gosho	7.9	13.4	170
Nichimen	7.1	11.9	168
TOTAL	151.6	342.3	226

Source: Computed from annual company reports.

In view of Japan's market power and prowess, several countries, both developed and developing, are striving to emulate this model of conquest of the world market. Whether they will succeed, in view of Japan's cultural and historical specificities, remains problematical. In the vanguard of the emulators are the *changhap sangsa* (general trading companies), the trading arms of the Republic of Korea's conglomerates. It is an indication of the trading dimensions of the *changhap sangsa* that in 1981 the top ten accounted for just under half of the country's exports of over $20 billion, with three leaders—Daewoo, Hyundai, and Samsung—accounting for one fifth of the total.[85] As in Japan, these trading conglomerates enjoy privileged relationships with the state[86] and with sources of finance.[87] Other Asian traders have followed the example of the *sogo shosha* and the *changhap sangsa*. In Malaysia, with the Government's support, four major Malaysian corporations have formed a joint trading agency, Nastra.[88]

---

[85] *South,* October 1982.

[86] Samsung's chairman of the board, Mr. Lee Byung Chull, organized his business associates into the Federation of Korean Industry, which became a central pillar of support for the late President Park Chung Hee.

[87] Several years ago, Samsung owned shares in half of the nation's commercial banks, including 85 per cent of what is now Hamil Bank, almost 50 per cent of Choheung Bank, and 30 per cent of the Commercial Bank of Korea (*Far Eastern Economic Review,* 4 June 1982).

[88] The four include: Petrona, the national oil company; Felda, the state land development authority and owner of over one million acres of rubber and palm oil plantations; Malaysian Mining Corporation, the world's biggest tin mining group; and Kuok Brothers, whose interests range from shipbuilding, hotels and property to large-scale sugar trading in Asia (*Financial Times,* 31 December 1981).

With a view to counter the loss of export markets for United States firms to these integrated Asian trading companies, legislation has been enacted in the United States authorizing banks and other corporations to participate in the formation of United States trading companies.[89] While they may never attain the same degree of cohesiveness that the *sogo shosha* and the *changhap sangsa* enjoy with their governments and banking systems, there is little doubt that the United States trading companies will make their presence felt in world markets in the furure.[90]

(e) *Retailers*

Retail firms likewise have established close links with financial, trading, advertising and other services sectors. Large corporate retailers have entered the world market in two ways: through the establishment of trading subsidiaries which purchase merchandise directly, and through the transnationalization of their outlets. This transnationalization takes the form of setting up supermarkets, department stores and mail order companies which can realize gains by purchasing goods in bulk directly instead of through intermediaries and by penetrating new markets and profit centres.

Like some industrial TNCs that have entered trading, many retailers use subcontracting trading arrangements covering such products as clothing, footwear and toys. Invariably, in their bulk purchases from developing countries they enjoy considerable power over "captive suppliers", as they are in a position to dictate both output and prices. Prominent among those that are both traders and transnational retailers are C & A Brenninkmeyer,[91] Marks & Spencer, K-Mart, Daiei, Mitsubishi and the five leading department stores in the Federal Republic of Germany.

None of these retailers, however, can rival the sales volume of Sears Roebuck. Many of the goods offered for sale in its 850 stores in the United States and 130 overseas outlets are supplied through the company's five main foreign buying offices, whose bulk purchases are effected at sizeable discounts. In 1983, Sears formed a trading company which "intends to be a trading house along the lines of Minneapolis' Cargill, Inc., or New York's Phibro-Salomon Inc."[92] In

---

[89] The Export Trading Company Act of 1979 (S. 1663) defines an export trading company as a firm "organized and operated principally for the purpose of (a) exporting goods or services produced in the US and (b) facilitating the exportation of goods and services produced in the US by unaffiliated persons by providing one or more export trade services" (US Senate, Committee on Banking, Housing and Urban Affairs, *Export Trading Companies, Trade Associations and Trade Services*, 96th Congress, 2nd Session, 15 May 1980, p. 5).

[90] There are, of course, some existing TICs in the United States with major trading arms. For example, Sea-Land Services, the largest United States maritime cargo carrier, is part of R. J. Reynolds Industries Inc., whose other subsidiaries also straddle a whole range of primary commodities (Del Monte, Aminoil), manufactures (Tobacco International and Heublein) and services (Kentucky Fried Chicken).

[91] This estimated $6 billion family-owned retailer exemplifies the backward linkages developed by transnational retailers. Much of what C & A sells is manufactured in about 20 plants operated by its Canada International subsidiary.

[92] *Business Week*, 22 August 1983.

261

line with this blueprint, Sears World Trade Inc., the new trading and counter-trading arm of the parent, acquired (1983) Price and Pierce, one of the world's largest forest product companies. (Price and Pierce was itself a component of a larger British holding company, Tozer Kemsley & Millibourn.) As the chairman of the Sears trading subsidiary has said, this expansion was "a significant step in becoming a major world trading company".[93]

That this latest strategic takeover is part of a still larger corporate design is shown by the fact that it had been preceded by the setting-up of a joint venture trading company with First Chicago Corp. (the parent of First National Bank of Chicago), and by a no less strategic joint venture with Schenkers International Forwarders, one of the world's top cargo management companies.

Thanks to these strategic annexations, Sears is now in a commanding position not only in its traditional lines of business (merchandising, insurance and financial services) but also in certain novel activities—shipping, cargo management, world-wide trading in commodities and manufacturing.

The ramifications of Sears' appropriations transcend an individual corporation, in the sense that its case history is like the proverbial drop of water that gives a clue to the chemical composition of the sea. Its theoretical and empirical significance is that it illumines the complexity of the interacting elements of capital accumulation in general and the direction of corporate service sectors in particular.

5. *Advertising*

World-wide mass advertising, now primarily controlled by transnational service conglomerates (TSCs), is at once a major component of the services sector and a stimulator of the trade in goods and services. An idea of the impact of advertising is conveyed by the figure for advertising billings world-wide, which exceeded $118 billion in 1982.[94] The United States, with roughly $61 billion in advertising outlays in 1982, accounts for fully one half of the advertising universe. Five other centres of corporate power—Japan, the Federal Republic of Germany, the United Kingdom, France and Canada—plus the United States account for four fifths of the total.

A comparison of the world's 50 biggest advertising agencies with the world's 50 biggest TNCs in 1982 illustrates the proportionately greater United States dominance in advertising than in other sectors: whereas only 20 of the 50 biggest TNCs are based in that country, 35 of the top 50 advertising corporations are American.

Expenditure on advertising varies greatly from market to market; for example, in 1982 yearly advertising outlays amounted to $265 per capita in the United States but to only a few cents in some developing countries of Asia. To

---

[93] *International Herald Tribune*, 15 November 1983.

[94] Figures from the International Advertising Association, as quoted in *The San Francisco Chronicle*, 26 August 1983.

put it another way, over 2.3 per cent of United States GNP is allocated to advertising, but less than one tenth of 1 per cent in most of the developing world (see table 19). One inference that may be drawn is that developing countries now offer more scope than developed market economies for the future expansion of advertising agencies. The extent to which world markets have so far been penetrated by these agencies is reflected in the overseas earnings of the ten leading United States advertising agencies: their foreign income averaged more than two fifths of their 1982 aggregate income (see table 20).

TABLE 19

Global advertising, 1982

	Population[a] (millions)	GDP[a] (billion dollars)	Advertising outlays (billion dollars)	Per capita advertising outlays (dollars)	Advertising as percentage of GDP
USA	230.1	2 603.3	61.0	265.1	2.3
Japan	119.1	1 054.2	11.0	92.4	1.0
EEC	266.8	2 810.5	27.3	102.3	1.0
ASEAN[b]	277.9	172.3	0.2	0.7	0.1
Others	3 681.5	2 466.1	18.5	5.0	0.8
World	4 575.4	9 106.4	118.0	25.8	1.3

Source: Calculated from data of UNCTAD, United Nations Department of International Economic and Social Affairs, and the International Advertising Association.

[a] Estimated from 1980 data of UNCTAD and the United Nations Department of International Economic and Social Affairs.

[b] The Philippines, Singapore, Thailand, Malaysia and Indonesia.

TABLE 20

USA and UK: top ten advertising agencies, 1982

Agency[a]	World billings	Income (million dollars) In USA	Income (million dollars) In non-USA	Non-USA income as percentage of world income
Young & Rubicam	2 512	247	130	34.5
Ted Bates Worldwide	2 374	233	123	34.6
J. Walter Thompson Co.	2 315	167	180	51.9
Ogilvy & Mather	2 151	177	138	43.8
McCann-Erickson	1 841	82	194	70.3
BBDO International	1 606	155	83	34.9
Leo Burnett Co.	1 487	136	85	38.5
Saatchi & Saatchi Compton[b]	1 303	69	118	63.1
Doyle Dane Bernbach	1 235	129	49	27.5
Foote, Cone & Belding	1 196	127	49	27.8
TOTAL	18 020	1 522	1 149	43.0

Source: Computed from data in *Financial Times*, 13 October 1983.

[a] Ranked by world billings.

[b] United Kingdom.

263

One important caveat, however, must be added in interpreting these numbers. Considerably more advertising can be bought per monetary unit in some countries than in others. A firm can reach the same number of newspaper readers, say, in Sweden at one thirtieth of the price it would pay in the United States. In the Netherlands, a firm could reach the same number of radio listeners at one twentieth of the United Kingdom price.[95] In other words, the depth of penetration in various countries cannot be gauged solely by the size of the advertising outlay.

The data concerning expenditures on publicity need to be further qualified, in that they do not take into account the cost of technical operations (composing, fabricating) or sums spent on certain sports events. It is known, furthermore, that some industries (tobacco, soap, cosmetics) spend large sums advertising their wares.[96]

The giant advertising agencies have become an indispensable adjunct of business activities in all sectors. Led by Japan's Dentsu and the United States firms Young & Rubicam and J. Walter Thompson, 14 advertising agencies operating world-wide (each with yearly billings exceeding one billion dollars) jointly account for over one fifth of total world expenditures on publicity. It is precisely these agencies that secure the bulk of contracts awarded by the biggest TNCs. This dovetailing of marketing and advertising technique with corporate strategies is clearly elucidated by remarks by the chairman of one of the world's biggest brewers, Mr. August A. Busch III: "In 1977, we installed a programme which we call 'Total Marketing' which combines all of the key marketing elements into a single orchestrated thrust. Advertising was joined by sales promotion, merchandising, field sales, sales training and sports programming, enabling us to market not only on a national plan, but also at the grass-roots level. This 'in the trenches' approach, coupled with our national programs, will prove vital to our growth in the 1980s."[97]

Within a relatively short time, after their emergence in the prosperous 1920s, a handful of United States advertising agencies entered the international market. In certain cases, these agencies were offshoots of industrial corporations which had done much of their own promotional work. Lintas, for example, now part of the huge Interpublic Group of companies, grew out of in-house Unilever operations (1929) to become an independent advertising agency. Lintas' legal separation from Unilever never signalized a commercial separation. Up to the present, Unilever remains the agency's largest client, accounting for slightly under half of its total billings.

The period of greatest international growth for advertising agencies was that of the 1960s and 1970s, when their corporate clients experienced their most

---

[95] For 1982 media cost comparisons for Western Europe and the United States, see *Financial Times,* 9 December 1982.

[96] According to N. M. Tilley, *History of the R. J. Reynolds Tobacco Co.* (Commerce, Texas, 1976, mimeo.), with the exception of two years (1929 and 1932), advertising's share of R. J. Reynolds' net earnings never fell below 40 per cent, and in one year (1934) it exceeded 80 per cent.

[97] *Brewers Digest,* January 1981.

rapid international growth. By 1982, international billings had risen to the point where they accounted for as much as 70 per cent of McCann-Erickson's operations and those of other leading agencies. The 14 leading advertising agencies are active in both developed and developing countries. In Latin America, for example, J. Walter Thompson is the foremost advertising agency in Argentina, Chile and Venezuela, number two in Brazil, number four in Mexico.[98]

In several cases, advertising TNCs possess a far greater knowledge of consumer behaviour in local and national markets than governments. Even certain centrally planned economies are not immune to the lure of advertising. In 1980, Dentsu set up a Beijing office and brought Chinese trainees to Japan "to deepen their understanding and knowledge of advertising in the industrial democracies."[99]

As has happened in other service sectors, the internationalization of the operations of advertising agencies has been accompanied by a spate of mergers and annexations that are reshaping the industry. In 1982, the top ten were realigned. Ted Bates Worldwide, formerly number six, became number three after its buy-out of William Esty. The United Kingdom's foremost agency, Saatchi & Saatchi, broke into the top ten by the acquisition of Compton Advertising (formerly the 14th largest United States agency). Advertising power was further concentrated through the formation of holding companies, of which the Interpublic Group of Companies is the largest.[100] It amalgamated McCann-Erickson, Marschalk, Campbell-Ewald, SSC & B and Lintas into a single management agency. The financial and marketing leverage that such unification confers is a formidable deterrent to entry for smaller and medium-sized firms attempting to carve out a niche in the market.

Another no less effective form of concentration is the creation of joint ventures between the biggest advertising agencies in different countries. This is evidenced in the world's two largest advertising markets, the United States and Japan. The pioneers were Dentsu and Young & Rubicam, the world's two biggest agencies, that established a joint venture in Japan and are planning similar ventures elsewhere. Such joint ventures, because of the power they represent, triggered a spate of acquisitions[101] and joint ventures[102] by their chief competitors.

The discussion so far has been confined to the growth of advertising agencies through transnationalization, annexations of and link-ups with other agencies. A new movement, familiar enough in other services, is surfacing, leading to diversification into TSCs and TICs. Some majors have entered the

---

[98] *Advertising Age,* 25 May 1981.

[99] *Advertising Age,* 14 December 1981.

[100] In 1982, its combined global billings were $3.7 billion.

[101] Examples of the first are Leo Burnett buying out its Japanese partner Leo Burnett/Kyodo; Doyle Dane Bernbach raising its stake in Dai-Ichi Kikaku; and Foote Cone & Belding exploring the possibility of setting up a wholly owned subsidiary in Japan.

[102] Among the big agencies studying possible link-ups in Japan are BBDO International, Saatchi & Saatchi Compton Worldwide, and Ogilvy & Mather (*Advertising Age,* 21 March 1983).

related service activities of public relations and the media. Others have become active in entirely unrelated fields, Havas of France being a prime example.[103]

Perhaps no world-wide advertising firm better exemplifies the totality of the sectors than Dentsu, which accounts for a quarter of all advertising in Japan. Dentsu was born (1902) a service conglomerate coupling news services with advertising. Today, as *Fortune* notes: "Dentsu's power over the media is out in the open and unabashed."[104] Its properties include several newspapers and TV stations. It has bailed out faltering newspapers, such as the *Mainichi Shimbun*, by extensive subsidies in the form of advertising. Dentsu's strategy further involves buying huge blocks of newspaper and magazine pages in advance, along with about half of commercial TV's prime time. In advertising proper, it serves 3,000-odd corporate clients, including many of *Fortune's* top 500. Beyond the confines of the media and advertising, Dentsu's activities range from managing sports tournaments to beauty contests, and from planning traffic on Okinawa to the Pope's trip to Japan. In words which might apply to the vision of the other advertising majors, Dentsu's president Hideharu Tamaru proclaimed the agency's role in the twenty-first century to be "organizer, producer, and consultant in the field of culture by maintaining closer ties with the government, public enterprises, academic bodies, international organizations, and private corporations."[105] In short, advertising has moved well beyond consumer manipulation into the political arena. Dentsu, for example, has close links with Japan's ruling Liberal Democratic Party.[106] Likewise, Saatchi & Saatchi is employed by the United Kingdom's Conservative Party and has, in the words of *The Economist,* "made abuse an art".[107] A prominent client for McCann-Erickson in 1982 was the Salvadorian politician Roberto d'Aubuisson; the agency's image-building campaign contributed to his election as head of his country's national assembly.[108]

Some agencies have not confined their political promotions to a national level, but have even commented on the activities of United Nation bodies. By no means atypical is the language of the Interpublic Group's 1982 annual report: "UNESCO and other bodies are encouraging government control and ownership of the media—a concept that is anathema to freedom-loving people

---

[103] Havas is a holding company of 27 other companies, many of them in unrelated fields (Centre on Transnational Corporations, *Transnational Corporations in Advertising: A Technical Paper* (ST/CTC/8), United Nations publication, Sales No. E.79.II.A.2, para. 20).

[104] *Fortune,* 1 November 1982. Japan's two leading news services, Kyodo and Jiji, still own 48 per cent of Dentsu's stock.

[105] *Ibid.*

[106] Liberals see "Dentsu as a master manipulator", writes *Fortune,* "working in open and hidden ways with all the tricks of its trade to maintain the dominance of the ruling elite's conservative ideology. In this view the taxpayers are paying for their own brainwashing" (*Fortune,* 1 November 1982).

[107] *The Economist,* 18 June 1983.

[108] John Cavanagh and Kathy Selvaggio, "Who's behind the media blitz?", *Multinational Monitor,* August 1983, p. 20.

and to the communications business, of which advertising is an integral part."[109]

6. *The accounting establishment*

Accounting[110] today is a multi-billion dollar world service that has grown in concert with the swift expansion of the transnational corporation over the last three decades. Like their clients, the accounting firms themselves—most often based in the United States—carry on their activities throughout the world.

The notion of public accountability for corporations first became a subject of serious concern at the time of the Roosevelt New Deal administration, during the great depression, in the same political setting which led to the legislative separation of commercial from investment banking. In the words of a United States study that has not lost its pungency:

> In the Securities Act of 1933 and the Securities Exchange Act of 1934, Congress directed the SEC [Securities and Exchange Commission] to protect the public from false and misleading information by requiring publicly-owned corporations to disclose financial and other information in a manner which accurately depicts the results of corporate activities ... The "Big Eight" and other large accountant firms have prospered from this Federal requirement because they are retained as the auditors for the Nation's major corporations ... This study finds little evidence that they serve the public or that they are independent in fact from the interests of their corporate clients.[111]

In the ensuing five decades, most of the advanced capitalist countries, and certain developing ones, also enacted legislation for the accountancy profession which, while varying from country to country, was nowhere more rigorous than in the United States. In response to widespread disclosure of questionable payments and bribes on a mass scale by TNCs in the 1960s and 1970s, the United States Congress passed the Foreign Corrupt Practices Act of 1977, which declared certain illicit acts to be criminal offences and which reinforced the New Deal legislation. By the early 1980s, in the fierce struggle for shrinking markets, even this relatively innocuous legislation was being dismantled.[112]

Overview of the accounting market

The profession of accountancy could be defined as embracing everything from small-scale bookkeeping to the sophisticated systems of accounts of multi-commodity trading companies. For the purpose of this study, however, the

---

[109] The Interpublic Group of Companies, Inc., *Annual Report, 1983.*

[110] Accounting may be defined as the application of the principles and practice of systematically recording, interpreting and presenting financial information. Further, it is the business of the accountant to audit financial statements and business records to verify their accuracy in order to ensure public accountability.

[111] United States Senate, Subcommittee on Reports, Accounting and Management of the Committee on Government Operations, *The Accounting Establishment: A Staff Study,* 95th Congress, 1st Session, 31 March 1977, pp. 1, 4, and 17.

[112] By 1982, the SEC had already withdrawn at least 14 rules governing the profession, and instead was relying to a greater extent on the American Institute of Certified Public Accountants to police the activity of its 174,000 members. In effect, this was tantamount to asking the fox to guard the chicken coop.

analysis of the accounting realm is restricted to those large accounting firms which were supposed to comply with the legal guidelines for the accountancy profession.

In the post-war world, eight large United States-based accounting firms— the "Big Eight"—came to dominate the world's corporate accounting business.

	Million dollars		*Million dollars*
Coopers & Lybrand (1981 fees)	998	Arthur Young (1980)	750
Peat, Marwick, Mitchell	979	Ernst & Whinney (1980)	706
Arthur Andersen	973	Deloitte, Haskins, Sells	800
Price, Waterhouse	850	Touche Ross	700

In time the big names have been joined by a few others, notably the European firms KMG and Binder Dijker Otte. Like funeral parlours and the law business, the majors have discovered that accountancy is immune to economic downswings. World-wide fee income for Peat, Marwick, Mitchell, for example, jumped 17.5 per cent in 1982. Jointly, the fees of the Big Eight surpassed $7 billion.

Within the largest accounting firms, a process of slow diversification into TSCs is at work, as they are now providing "add-on" services to their corporate clients, notably financial consulting, the development of computer systems and tax accounting. Yet another indication of the Big Eight's rapid growth is the increase in numbers of their United States partners: from 1,070 (1960) to over 7,000 by 1981.[113] An index of their internationalization is that almost half of Peat, Marwick, Mitchell's fees originate outside North America.[114]

Although the modern accountancy establishment was originally conceived as an instrument for defending the public interest, the growth of these giants and their symbiotic relations with transnational corporations have produced a result very unlike that originally intended. To be sure, they have become superb craftsmen in the arts of manipulating corporate accounts through a wide variety of techniques ranging from transfer pricing to bribes, and a plethora of tax evasion devices.

It is inadequate merely to report, as *Fortune* has done,[115] that 117 of the top 1,043 United States companies were charged with at least one federal offence over the last decade. What the survey ignored is that, in many cases, these offences were committed with the knowledge of the accountancy establishment working in conjunction with financial officers of the companies concerned.

---

[113] *The American Almanac of Jobs and Salaries* reported that, as of 1980, partners in New York accountancy firms earned an average of $104,500 and senior partners $242,700 a year. Because these firms are legal partnerships, they are not obliged to disclose profits, a major factor in their non-accountability.

[114] Peat, Marwick, Mitchell, with about 2,000 partners and 23,100 employees in 66 countries, earns about four fifths of its revenues from accounting, 14 per cent from tax advice and the rest from management consultancy (*The Economist*, 28 November 1981).

[115] *Fortune* survey reported in *International Herald Tribune*, 14 November 1980. "The big cases are often shockers ... big business crime hasn't been swept away in a tide of post-Watergate morality ... the list would have been longer had it included foreign bribes and kickbacks."

The very nature of the relationship between the two, the supposed custodian of the public interest being paid by the parties it is supposed to monitor, vitiates its original purpose, for the accountant who exposes financial malpractice loses his client and risks self-liquidation. The ostensible independence of the profession and hence public accountability are further eroded when the federal United States agency responsible for monitoring accounting practices itself recommends that the prevailing system should be made even less accountable. The SEC suggested that the 1977 Foreign Corrupt Practices Act should be changed so that "corporations not be liable for accounting provision violations which were without senior management's knowledge or involvement".[116]

For so long as this climate of tolerance prevails and the rules of accountancy are not strictly observed in the spirit in which they were originally conceived, the public interest will not be safeguarded.

Part three. The future

The world economy is undergoing a momentous structural change. Services, moving to the centre of the stage, already account for almost two thirds of world GDP.

A. SUMMING UP

Internationalization is the crux of this transformation, with the overall share of the world's GDP exported advancing from 16 per cent to 27 per cent during the 1970s. During this period, services also became prominent in global markets, with exports rising from 7 per cent to 11 per cent. The main beneficiaries of the international services trade, and the most vocal proponents of its liberalization, have been a small number of developed market economies, with the United States its foremost protagonist.

A tiny number of large TNCs that entered the services sector are the driving force behind this internationalization, contributing to an accelerated liquidation of medium and small-scale firms that traditionally dominated the field. No less rapid have been the disintegration of barriers between individual service sectors and the rise of transnational service conglomerates (TSCs) and transnational integral conglomerates (TICs).

For several reasons the services sector was the last of the main sectors to fall under the hegemony of transnational conglomerates. Economies of scale and related technologies in most services did not lend themselves to the concentration and centralization of capital until recent decades. In addition, the marketing of many services was carried out through small, widely dispersed, individually owned units. When the TNCs attained dominance (which happened at different times and in varying degrees of intensity in different sectors), it was

---

[116] *New York Times,* 17 June 1981.

269

United States and Japanese corporations that were in the *avant garde*. TNCs from these two countries exercise a far more pervasive control over services in the world market than they do over agriculture, mining and manufacturing.

At present, TNCs are impelling the service sector forward at a faster pace than any other sector. The expansion of services has also been accompanied by a serious decline in corporate accountability, due to service companies' access to tax havens, flags of convenience, bank secrecy laws and a large array of legal and illegal arrangements.

B. TNC POWER: OMINOUS IMPLICATIONS

What, it may be asked, will the internationalization and transnationalization of services, and indeed of capital, imply for the world capitalist economy as a whole, and for the developing economies in particular? A response to this question can only be formulated within the framework of the unequal development of capitalism. In the services sector, the penetration of TNCs is already well advanced in advertising, accounting, tourism, and banking, while in other sectors, such as health and retailing, it is still at an incipient stage.

With the exception of a few developing countries, the gains derived from services on the international market have bypassed the developing world. In short, these countries simply cannot compete. The reaction of governments of developing countries to such an unequal distribution of power varies widely. In most cases, under the spur of economic liberalism espoused by GATT and certain other international organizations, these governments have opened their economies to TNCs. Perhaps the most extreme cases are those offering tax and investment havens and the incentives of offshore banking units, captive insurance companies, flags of convenience and subcontracting *maquiladoras*. A less extreme form of such "openness" is the welcome extended to transnational advertising, hotel chains, tourist enclaves, etc. It is debatable whether this receptivity has contributed to the development process in the developing world as a whole. More to the point, it has been a source of immense enrichment for the members of only a small oligarchy who channel their (lawful or illicit) gains abroad.

In the world economy as a whole, the future of service TNCs and services in general is inseparable from technological revolutions in computers, word processors, electronic office equipment and telecommunications systems.

The swift introduction of these new technologies is slashing jobs in service and industrial sectors. In United Kingdom banking, for example, employment is forecast to drop 12 per cent between 1983 and 1990, owing to the widespread introduction of automated teller machines, cashier-operated note dispensers and other labour-saving devices.[117] Since knowledge and information constitute a major facet of power, those able to harness these technologies and to

---

[117] Automated teller machines installed in United Kingdom banks grew from 3,466 in June 1982 to 5,480 by the end of 1983, a rise of almost 60 per cent (*Labour Research*, vol. 72, No. 11, November 1983, p. 284).

disseminate them on a large scale become even more powerful. In this realm, it is precisely the largest service TNCs which have the easiest access to advanced technologies, both nationally and internationally.

These new technologies are swiftly reshaping not only international economic relations but cultural ones as well. Telecommunications satellites are being used by advertising and media TNCs to project corporate images and ideology world-wide. This form of publicity is based largely on a Western élitist ideology and on a complex of values antithetical to cultural pluralism. The propagation of these images acquires a political force as they implicitly drive home the desirability of a specific economic and social order. Indubitably, technology in this perspective, along with the values it transmits, can never be a neutral force. Wedded to mass advertising and the media, it is deployed to reshape the size, composition and evolution of world trade and consumption patterns.

The foregoing description of the impact of new technologies and of the values spread by them should be seen in the context of the current economic crisis. Certainly, the unequal nature of capitalist development is replicated in the unequal impact of the crisis on different economies, sectors and corporations. Within the services universe, for example, shipping is stagnating, while accountancy, insurance and tourism are momentarily weathering the storm.

Big banking, while surviving thus far with relatively high earnings, is now approaching a critical phase. Its major profit centres of the 1970s, namely the developing economies, are foundering under a staggering burden of indebtedness and agonizing from a political instability born of austerity measures imposed in a desperate bid to break out of the debt grip. As the big banks diminish their exposure to the developing economies, they are confronted with shrinking geographical opportunities for profitable investment. With the debt squeeze marginalizing much of the potential market of the developing world for service TNCs, increasingly the economic war for world service markets will be fought within the OECD countries. Financial service conglomerates are already being mobilized as spearheads in struggles between major developed countries for power and wealth. In this sense, transnational conglomerates are in the forefront of a virtual economic war characterized by a proliferation of corporate takeovers, price wars, cartel arrangements, state subsidization, protectionist measures and other means.

Another by-product of the rise of the service TNC has been a revolution in the workplace as large centralized industrial units are replaced by smaller, fragmented and decentralized service units. These service units, while decentralized at certain levels, are in no way incompatible with a highly centralized corporate structure that retains firmer control over its labour force than its industrial counterparts.

The world trade union movement, and indeed the labour movement as a whole, built up over the last century and a half with the blue-collar industrial worker as its core, has thus far proved unable to organize white-collar workers on any significant scale. The main reason is the heterogenity of service workers, who include large numbers of a low-wage and a deliberately de-skilled labour force at one end of the spectrum and a coterie of high-income lawyers and

271

finance experts, scientists, technologists, researchers, managers and engineers at the other end. Those at the lower end appear unlikely to organize due to their replaceability, while those in the upper echelons have identified themselves with the goals of corporate capital. As a consequence, services, with all their complex technical and corporate interrelationships, have contributed to raise corporate power to unprecedented heights despite the global economic depression and to no less unprecedented control over the labour force and the world economy.

C. Countervailing strategies

One of the central principles of the entire United Nations system is the right of every nation to use its economic resources in conformity with the interests of the people. The power of transnational capital, epitomized in the service conglomerates, tends to erode this national sovereignty. Yet, despite the widening gap between TNC power and that of the governments and people of developing countries, this process of erosion is not irreversible. Countervailing strategies at the national, regional and international levels can be worked out which could contribute to narrow the gap. Certain policy measures which have the potential to be realized are outlined schematically below for the six service sectors that have been studied.

Several of these sectors lend themselves to rigorous action at the national level that would tend to reinforce economic sovereignty. Both banking and insurance are sectors whose needs at the national level can effectively be met by nationalized enterprises. Indeed, an increasing number of developing countries have augmented public sector control over these two sectors during the past decade. In the external trade sector, the formation of specialized state trading corporations for primary commodity exports is but another logical step which, when coupled to public sector control of financial services, would strengthen a country's bargaining leverage *vis-à-vis* transnational power.

In the case of advertising, strict controls on penetration by foreign companies can counteract the harm done to the cultural heritage. In those countries in which tourism is important, cultural autonomy can be better safeguarded by increased national control over airlines, hotels and other tourist enterprises. With respect to the information revolution, developing countries should take steps to enter the industry by training the technical cadres and developing software and hardware capabilities.

In those cases where national capabilities are inadequate to meet the challenge, inter-country co-operative ventures may prove desirable (in much the same manner as certain common production, marketing and research arrangements between TNCs have proved effective). In a sector like reinsurance, where major financial resources are required, regional reinsurance pools can be effective. Likewise, in the marketing of primary commodities, regional multinational marketing enterprises in the public sector can become more potent forces in securing and retaining foreign markets.

272

Certain actions by developing countries can only become effective if taken at an international level. In view of the mobility of transnational capital, any individual move that may be construed as jeopardizing the profitability of TNCs is likely to provoke an adverse response on their part. Attempts should be made, for example, to staunch revenue losses due to transfer pricing by imposing more stringent accounting practices; if such efforts are to be successful, the developing countries concerned should strive to enact appropriate legislation simultaneously.[118]

A model that merits serious study on this score is the unitary taxation legislation recently pioneered in the state of California which assesses firms for taxation based on the proportion of their world-wide profits, which corresponds to the firm's in-state assets, payroll and sales figures. A similar formula adapted to the requirements of developing countries could go a long way towards halting the most flagrant abuses of transfer pricing, and would also open corporate operations to ethical public scrutiny.

International action by developing countries is also the only feasible countermeasure to the transnationalization of culture and the media which threatens to eclipse national values and information in some of them. UNESCO's initiative for a "New International Information Order" has addressed itself to this power. Not surprisingly, it has thereby become the target of a barrage of abuse by the service TNCs and their governments.

All of these measures singly and in their totality, at the national, regional and international levels, must be imbued with an understanding of the pervasive political and economic power of transnational service conglomerates, which are strenuously resisting such policy orientations. International commodity agreements based on buffer stocks, for example, can be frustrated in certain cases by individual or collective dumping of the corporations' own commodity stocks on international markets.

Knowledge of the existence of such power need not lead to defeatist conclusions, but should rather stimulate a response; for while the implementation of effective countervailing strategies is bound to encounter formidable obstacles, in the long run such strategies can be successful.

---

[118] The perils of individual action are illustrated by the recent case where Japanese corporations threatened to halt investments in those states of the USA which apply the unitary method of collecting taxes from TNCs (*Financial Times*, 11 October 1983).

[25]

Regional Studies, Vol. 21.3, pp. 215–223.

The Strategy and Structure of Service–Sector Multinationals: Implications for Potential Host Regions

PETER ENDERWICK

Department of Economics, The Queen's University of Belfast, Belfast BT7 1NN, UK

(Received March 1986; in revised form June 1986)

ENDERWICK P. (1987) The strategy and structure of service-sector multinationals: implications for potential host regions, *Reg. Studies* **21**, 215–223. At the regional level increased consideration is being given to the attraction of tradeable service investments. Successful attraction requires understanding of the defining characteristics of service-sector multinational enterprises. In the light of these characteristics potential hosts may need to alter their policies with respect to targeting, assessing likely economic impact and the provision of infra-structure support. The dynamic nature of the world market in services necessitates careful monitoring. While producer services in particular offer attractive investment prospects, such job creation is likely to be both limited and spatially uneven.

Service-sector   Multinational enterprises   Regional development   Inward investment

ENDERWICK P. (1987) La stratégie et la structure des multinationales du secteur tertiaire: effets sur les régions potentielles d'accueil, *Reg. Studies* **21**, 215–223. Au niveau régional on accorde de plus en plus d'importance aux perspectives d'attirer les investissements des services ayant une valeur marchande. A cet effet, ill faut comprendre les caractéristiques qui distinguent les entreprises multinationales du secteur tertiaire. A la lumière de ces caractéristiques les zones d'accueil pourront avoir besoin de modifier leurs politiques en ce qui concerne le ciblage, l'évaluation des effets économiques probables et l'établissement d'une infrastructure de soutien. La nature dynamique du marché mondial dans les services nécessite une surveillance attentive. Tandis que les services de production en particulier offrent des perspectives d'investissements attrayantes, une telle création d'emplois risque d'être à la fois limitée et spatialement répartie de façon disparate.

Secteur tertiaire   Entreprises multinationales
Développement régional   Investissement interne

ENDERWICK P. (1987) Die Strategie und Struktur der multinationalen Unternehmen des Dienstleistungssektors: Implikationen für potentielle Gastgeberregionen, *Reg. Studies* **21**, 215–223. Auf regionaler Ebene wird der Anziehungskraft verkäuflicher Dienstleistungsinvestierungen zunehmend Aufmerksamkeit geschenkt. Erfolgreiche Anziehungskraft verlangt Verständnis der bestimmenden Merkmale der multinationalen Unternehmen des Dienstleistungssektors. Im Lichte dieser Merkmale müssen potentielle Gastgeber unter Umständen ihre Bestrebungen bezüglich Zielsetzung, Abschätzung wahrscheinlicher wirtschaftlicher Wirkung und der Bereitstellung von Unterstützung in Form einer Infrastruktur abändern. Die dynamische Natur des Weltdienstleistungsmarktes macht sorgfältige Überwachung notwendig. Obschon besonders Produzentendienstleistungen attraktive Aussichten für Investierungen bieten, wird die Schaffung von Arbeitsplätzen wahrscheinlich begrenzt und auch räumlich ungleichmässig bleiben.

Dienstleistungssektor   Multinationale Unternehmen
Regionalentwicklung
Nach innen gerichtete Investierung

INTRODUCTION

For those regions of the UK which achieved rapid employment and output growth in the 1960s and early 1970s through the attraction of overseas investment, the last few years have seen a deterioration in prospects and performance. The slowing down in growth rates of mobile manufacturing investment (OECD, 1981), increased locational competition at both the national and intra-national levels and rapid job loss within the manufacturing sector (HOOD and YOUNG, 1982; NORTHERN IRELAND ECONOMIC COUNCIL, 1983; O'MALLEY, 1986) have reduced the attractions of this development strategy. Furthermore, rising labour costs have forced procurement agencies to seek industries offering higher value-added per head. In this context, investments in internationally tradeable services offer considerable potential. They are generally labour-intensive and many (e.g. computer software, consultancy etc.) offer

216   *Peter Enderwick*

high value added. In addition, services typically exhibit low import content, increasing their domestic income and employment multipliers.

Two other developments reinforce the case for service investments. The first is the growing importance of service output and employment in the advanced industrial economies. The majority could be described as 'post-industrial' with the tertiary sector dominating employment. This suggests possible compatibility between incoming factors (management, capital, service technologies) and locational factors such as skilled labour. The ability to assimilate service technologies should be at least as high as that which existed for manufacturing investments in the 1960s. Second, on the supply side, international service transactions are of increasing significance. In 1982 invisibles to the value of $602 bn accounted for one-quarter of non-governmental international payments (Table 1). Insurance, banking, construction, consultancy, advertising and other professional services amounted to over $150 bn or 7% of world trade. The share of invisibles in total trade rose from 23·4% in 1960 to 26·2% in 1982 (ENDERWICK, 1987a). Despite this, international market penetration in services is low. US affiliates in the non-petroleum goods producing industries had 1974 sales equivalent to 16% of the value of commodity production in the OECD nations (excluding the USA). The comparable figure for US service industry affiliates was 3%. However, the recent performance of many large service firms has provided them with sufficient resources and resilience to consider overseas markets. Between 1973 and 1983, the Fortune Service 500 increased their profits at a rate 124% in excess of the rise of the consumer price index, clearly outperforming the 500 leading industrials.

Table 1. World trade by main categories 1982, in $USm

Total trade (excluding government and transfers)	2,301,400
Visible trade	1,699,100
Invisible trade, of which:	602,300
Transport	126,400
Foreign travel	97,300
Investment	227,800
Other services[1]	150,800

Note: 1. Other services comprises primarily insurance, banking, construction and consultancy, advertising and other professional services.
Source: Committee on Invisible Exports, World Invisible Trade, London.

If the potential economic contribution of service investment is to be realized, prospective host governments need to understand the dynamics of service-sector investment. This paper attempts to shed some light on this poorly researched area. The second section discusses the nature and tradeability of international services. This is followed by an analysis

of the distinguishing characteristics of service multi-nationals. Drawing on this, section four considers the major implications for government agencies. The concluding section sets out a number of caveats to the discussion.

THE NATURE AND TRADEABILITY OF SERVICES

Definitions of service activity follow two principal methods. The first focuses on the characteristics of service output, particularly its intangibility and often impermanence. The second approach emphasizes the sectoral nature of economic activity defining service output as the residual unaccounted for by primary (agriculture, mining) or secondary (manufacturing) activities. Both approaches leave much to be desired. The first is overly restrictive excluding those activities which result in material goods, such as construction, while the residual approach fails to specify the particular characteristics of service production. These problems of definition are compounded by the heterogeneity of the service sector. Even within the subgroup of industries concentrating on marketed services, diversity is evident in the source of demand for such services. Thus, there are those industries such as wholesale distribution and advertising providing predominantly producer services, and others (retail distribution, hotel provision) supplying final or consumer services. A number of industries (telecommunications, banking) offer 'mixed' output, since they sell both final and intermediate services. (For a fuller discussion of this question see MARSHALL, DAMESICK and WOOD, 1985).

The difficulties of categorizing service sector output are compounded in the international context. Particularly pertinent is the degree to which services are internationally tradeable. A useful classification is provided by BODDEWYN, 1987, who distinguishes between: (1) foreign-tradeable services which create a commodity distinct from the productive process itself and which lend themselves to exporting; (2) location-bound services that necessitate a foreign presence, generally because consumption cannot be separated from production, for example hotel accommodation; and (3) combination or 'mixed' services where locational substitution is possible.

With regard to tradeability two additional considerations are important. The first is the role of price competitiveness. Almost any service is tradeable at the right price. Indeed, in the presence of marked price differences, individuals may incur considerable time and travel costs to consume location-bound services where this is feasible. This suggests that cost competitiveness will be an important determinant of the propensity to trade services. Second, innovations in microelectronics and communications technology have greatly enhanced opportunities for trade in services, making possible international exchange of electronically encodeable data. Furthermore, the conjunction of communications, information processing and storage technologies enable both locational and temporal separation of service production and consumption (FEKETEKUTY and HAUSER, 1985).

Multinational enterprises are most widespread in the producer service sector. While it is difficult to quantify the size or growth pattern of this sector, WOOD, 1986, estimates that the 'external' producer service industries accounted for around 18% of total British employment in 1981. When allowance is made for 'internal' producer service employment (service occupations within manufacturing), this sector rivals production in accounting for around one-third of total employment. Furthermore, there is widespread agreement that the producer service sector has enjoyed significant growth in the last few years, albeit from a relatively small base (HARRIS, 1985). In the United States business services was the fastest growing industry in the past decade (HOWE, 1986).

THE DISTINGUISHING CHARACTERISTICS OF SERVICE-SECTOR MULTINATIONALS

While service-sector multinationals display a number of traits which distinguish them from their manufacturing counterparts (see ENDERWICK, 1987a), here we focus on those characteristics of primary interest to procurement agencies.

First, it is important to note the extent to which overseas markets for services are met by direct investment rather than exporting. In 1974, of the estimated $50 bn of services sold overseas by US companies, $43 bn (86%) was attributable to affiliate sales. The importance of overseas production in comparison to exporting is much greater for service industries when contrasted with goods producing industries.

Second, service-sector multinationals display considerable product specialization. Their competitive assets are likely to be of low technological complexity as this concept is normally understood. Rather, the major sources of competitive advantages are found in differential access to and ability to process and apply information and the existence of government-induced market imperfections (e.g. differential regulation, minimum standards etc.). Technical conditions associated with information markets (tendency towards monopoly provision, economies of learning and doing, high 'experience' content of information etc.) suggest that many services will exhibit barriers to entry built upon first-mover advantages and benefits of incumbency.

Third, for many service firms production economies of scale are relatively unimportant, although

greater reliance may be placed on economies of agglomeration. For services heavily dependent on specialized information sources and specific skills, location may be dictated by such considerations. With financial services like insurance and banking, a central business district location within the major city is often a prerequisite (DUNNING and NORMAN, 1983). There are some grounds for believing that, compared with national firms, multinational affiliates may be less dependent on agglomeration effects. This follows from both their larger than average size, which allows the internal exploitation of economies previously consumed as externalities, and their privileged access to parent services.

Fourth, like manufacturing investment, service multinationals display marked international spatial concentration. The advanced economies account for almost 70% of the total stock of service investment. For service industries like retail trade or communications, very little investment occurs outside the most advanced economies. Developing countries, particularly tax-haven and offshore banking centres, host little service investment outside banking and insurance (Table 2). Within host economies geographical concentration is often coupled with multi-location affiliates suggesting benefits of a concentrated presence deriving perhaps from economies of regional promotion and the reinforcement effects of multiple representation.

Fifth, the uneven development of service industries internationally may be replicated at the national level. The marked geographical concentration of service industry both between and within regions has long been recognized (DANIELS, 1982). Similarly, inequalities have been raised by the centralization of key business functions (R & D, financial control, senior management etc.) within core regions and cities (GODDARD and SMITH, 1978; HOWELLS, 1984; MALECKI, 1981). Even within the USA there is clear evidence of uneven development in high-technology services with New York City displaying comparative advantage in applications software while the computer time-sharing industry is centred on Atlanta, Georgia.

Table 2. *Service sector direct investment abroad as a percentage of total stock of direct investment*

Country	Year	Services as a % of all direct investment		
		All	Developed economies	Developing economies
Canada	1974	28·7	–	–
Italy	1976	38·2	89·3	10·7
Japan	1974	38·8	65·3	34·7
United Kingdom	1974	26·8	80·2	19·8
USA	1976	28·7	68·3	31·7
West Germany	1976	22·4	59·4	40·6

Source: UNITED NATIONS, 1978, Table III–38.

Finally, the relationships between service multinationals and client industries are of interest. A number of studies suggest that around 50% of marketed service demand is intermediate rather than final (GERSHUNY and MILES, 1983). Four principal factors account for the growth of producer services. First, the extension of the inter-industry division of labour has resulted in the expansion of industries such as distribution, banking, insurance and finance serving the needs of material producers. Second, managerial occupations have grown as organizations pursuing geographical and industrial diversification have faced increasingly complex problems of administration and control. Third, product differentiation strategies are increasingly based on the conjunction of material and non-material goods, for example computer hardware and software. Fourth, the demand for services such as advertising has grown with the rapid development of new user industries, for example investment management and computers and data processing.

Linkages appear to be particularly close in the case of high-technology services which exhibit a tendency to locate physically close to user industries (often high technology goods industries), where joint access to a pool of skilled labour, major government departments and universities is crucial (BROWNE, 1983).

IMPLICATIONS FOR HOST GOVERNMENT AGENCIES

Drawing on the foregoing discussion we derive policy implications in five major areas: the targeting of investments; the bargaining position; the likely impact of service investments; required local infra-structure; and the changing environment for international services.

The targeting of service multinationals

In identifying potential service investors, some changes in orientation will be required. There is evidence, certainly in the case of business services, that direct investment is generally preceded by exports from the source nation (DUNNING and NORMAN, 1983). Some familiarity with the local market through initial servicing by export reduces investment risk, which is often significant in the case of services with the need to impose immediate and strict quality control or the attainment of minimum critical mass. Furthermore, investors appear to enjoy privileged access to some of their host nation market where customers are affiliates of existing clients in the home market. This suggests that targeting should focus on those firms currently serving the local market through some non-equity mode (exporting, licensing etc.). If 'gradualism' in international operations applies to service industries such firms are the key target group. In addition, where there exists a foreign-owned

sector, investigation of parent company service purchases in the home market should be undertaken. There is likely to be a high degree of accordance between parent and affiliate loyalties in areas such as banking, accounting and advertising services.

Second, the attraction of foreign-based services should focus on the direct investment mode. Although generalizations from the US experience with service affiliate sales dominating exports may be misleading (SAPIR, 1985), there are grounds for believing that service technologies supplied on a non-equity basis will be on restrictive terms. Technology transfer in services involves the transfer of skills rather than disembodied information. Its time-intensive nature means that the transferring organization and transferee will seek to develop some form of long term relationship. This is particularly likely in the case of differentiated services where buyer perceptions are based on the interaction of the firm's output, reputation and image, as in the construction industry (ENDERWICK, 1987b). In such a case buyers cannot separate the inputs and contribution of licensor and licensee. Underperformance by the licensee could impose significant external costs on the licensor.

Third, the geographical focus of investment attraction should shift. While the principal manufacturing investment source nations encompass the major service multinationals, there are some differences. France, West Germany, the UK and USA together account for more than 40% of 'other services'. Service multinationals appear to be of lesser significance in the case of Japan and the Netherlands. The Japanese case is the most interesting. While 85% of all registered Japanese establishments in Europe (LOEVE *et al.*, 1985) are in commercial and service activities, these tend to be trade supporting and are unlikely to be self-standing service investment. Competitively, the Japanese are weak in services such as construction and software (FRANKO, 1983). However, some services (insurance, securities) are being pulled overseas in the wake of Japanese manufacturing firms (MARSH, 1984). Finally, a number of developing nations are rapidly achieving internationally competitive service industries particularly in banking, construction, shipping and trading (LECRAW, 1986)—see Table 3.

The bargaining position

To a degree, the economic impact of inward investment is dependent on the terms negotiated. Where host governments enjoy a strong bargaining advantage, they are able to impose their preferences over such matters as local content, technology transfer and earnings remittance. In the case of multinational service firms, there exist opposing influences on relative bargaining strength. The limited capital inflow, minimal technology transfer and marginal impact on labour market skills associated with

Table 3. Main countries in 'other services' invisible trade, 1982 ($USm)

Country	Receipts	Payments	Balance
United Kingdom	12,434	5,000	7,434
United States	11,728	4,032	7,696
Belgium/Luxembourg	7,282	5,680	1,602
France	22,997	16,463	6,534
Italy	7,164	6,910	254
Netherlands	5,647	5,301	346
West Germany	14,768	17,104	−2,336
Japan	6,369	13,193	−6,824
Korea	3,422	1,378	2,044
Singapore	4,405	1,455	2,950
Total 'top 10'	96,216	76,516	19,700
World	150,848	150,077	−6,229

Source: Committee on Invisible Exports, World Invisible Trade,
London.

traditional services places host governments, particularly those in the advanced nations, in a strong position (COWELL, 1983). In addition, the riskiness of multinational service investments (demands of quality maintenance and high rates of expropriation) means that investors are likely to prefer location in the advanced economies.

Offsetting these considerations, the difficulties of licensing some service technologies restrict the sources of supply to potential hosts. Furthermore, in many developing countries, the resource costs of cultivating indigenous service industries are so high in terms of committing scarce skilled labour resources to areas of relatively low value added and employment creation, that such nations are likely to make considerable efforts to buy in services expertise. Clearly, relative bargaining strength is a pragmatic question requiring careful investigation.

The economic impact of service investments

In calculating investment incentives, host governments need some assessment of the likely economic impact of inward investment. Service investments raise a number of interesting issues.

First, doubts have been cast on the propulsive effects of service industries. The small size of the producer services sector in most regions, its low export propensity, limited linkages and poor innovative record do not suggest the existence of characteristics conducive to the emergence of growth poles (HARRIS, 1985). Offsetting these arguments the possession of a vibrant producer services sector may be valuable in the diffusion of innovations (ANTONELLI, 1985) and in the adjustment to structural change.

Second is their likely employment effects. For a number of reasons employment creation is unlikely to be very considerable. In the USA tradeable services accounted for only 1·8 million jobs or 37% of all export related employment in 1982 (BENZ, 1985).

Although tradeable services display higher labour content than manufacturers (SAPIR and SCHUMACHER, 1984) the small average size of investing firms, their need for skilled labour and preference for entry by acquisition to ensure both more rapid entry and the achievement of critical mass, all militate against sizeable direct employment creation. Indirect employment creation depends on the ease with which service technologies are diffused and absorbed (SHELP, 1985) and the extent to which multiplier effects are retained within the host economy. While precise estimates of these values are not available it is unlikely that multinational service sector employment would approach the magnitudes associated with foreign-owned manufacturing firms.

Third, the export contribution of service multinationals may be low. In 1979, around 11% of the UK's gross output of services was exported, compared to 33% of the gross output of manufacturing. Existing evidence suggests that investments in business services (management consultancy, selection agencies, banking, insurance) are prompted by the desire to service mainly local markets (DUNNING and NORMAN, 1983). In the case of more readily exportable services (shipping, reinsurance) existing favoured locations (Liberia, Cyprus, Cayman Islands, Bermuda) appear to enjoy almost insurmountable advantages built around the virtual absence of regulation. There may be an indirect export impact from those services which enhance the competitiveness of the goods export sector (MILLER, 1985).

Fourth, there are grounds for concern over the likely durability of service investments. Narrow domestic markets mean that many service multinationals are dependent on overseas earnings. For example, overseas affiliate revenues within advertising are equivalent to almost 13% of US domestic earnings. The comparable figure for banking is nearly 20%. The rapid relative price rise (and poor productivity performance) of services encourages substitution of capital goods for increasingly uncompetitive services. Rapid innovation in high technology services has had a two-fold effect in displacing labour: capital-intensity has risen as 'new technology' has been applied; in addition, changes in the capital-component of output has reduced employment. For example, computer software products increased their market share from 12%–25% between 1980 and 1985 at the expense of labour-intensive software services (MARKUSEN, 1985). Economies of scale in the provision of financial services is encouraging some large enterprises such as oil companies, to internalize these functions. Finally, the UK's share of world service exports has declined suggesting its decreasing attractiveness as a location for the production of world services. Consideration of these factors suggests areas of potential vulnerability within service multinationals.

Fifth, the geographical impact of service multinationals is probably to accentuate national spatial inequalities. Their clustering within metropolitan centres of the most developed regions (DANIELS, 1982) suggests the possibility of dualistic development. In the case of high technology business services offering wage levels often 50% above the service sector average, both spatial and wage inequality may be increased (BROWNE, 1983).

Sixth, the contribution of service investments will be related to the existence and structure of non-service production. Clearly, in the case of producer services suppliers will seek out potential clients in large and fast growing manufacturing sectors. But the relationship is more complex than this. The efficient provision of services to non-service firms may generate positive externalities for these firms enhancing their competitive edge (MILLER, 1985). But it is important to consider both the size and ownership structure of the goods sector. Where foreign ownership and entry by acquisition are significant, there is a higher probability of centralization or external regional sourcing of service functions (MARQUAND, 1983). This results from the propensity of acquiring firms to centralize and internalize their service functions both nationally and internationally (COHEN, 1981; MARSHALL, 1979).

Finally, there may be indirect benefits from the presence of service multinationals. The accumulation of host government experience with such firms creates expertise which may be increasingly required in dealing with manufacturing firms pursuing appropriation through contractual and technical services. It is also possible that the existence of comprehensive and competitive business services may act as an inducement to mobile manufacturing firms, reinforcing the linkages between service and goods producing industries (MARSHALL, 1985). The regional distribution of R & D services appears to be an important influence on spatial variations in innovative performance (OAKEY, THWAITES and NASH, 1980). The underprovision of business services in peripheral regions may result in a communications cost disadvantage for such regions. In addition, the initial application of new communications technologies in core regions characterized by a high volume and density of business information provision serves to exacerbate spatial variations in communications costs (CURDS, 1983).

Infra-structure support

The provision of appropriate infra-structure is a major element in the successful attraction of overseas investment. In the case of service multinationals support may assume novel forms.

First, as highlighted at a number of points, there is a correlation between the existence of a vigorous goods sector and the likelihood of attracting service—particularly producer service-multinationals. Complementarity appears to be absolutely crucial in the case of high technology services (BROWNE, 1983). This does not necessarily imply close physical location. For a nation as small as the UK, inter-regional trade in business services is perfectly feasible.

Second, tangible infra-structure required by service multinationals is likely to differ from that normally offered. Service firms require a ready pool of highly educated labour. In the United States computer and management services industries, 40% of employees are in professional and technical occupations. This compares with an all industry average of 15% (BROWNE, 1983). Location appears to be a critical factor for service firms. Many seek close proximity to major education, communications and research centres (viz. Boston and Stanford in the USA, Cambridge and the 'M4 corridor' in England). More difficult to identify is the importance of intangible support in the form of an accommodative industrial policy encouraging collaboration between service users and suppliers (GONENC, 1984) and an atmosphere conducive to academic/industrial collaboration (BULLOCK, 1983; LOWE, 1985; SEGAL QUINCE and PARTNERS, 1985). Such centres may be a necessary, but not sufficient condition, for high technology services growth.

Third, there may be a case for public subsidy of key capital goods, particularly information transmission systems. Their high initial capital and scale requirements suggest a possible barrier to entry. To date, only the very largest organizations (banks, oil companies, construction and consultancy firms and trading companies) have been able to establish private networks. The existence of industry (SWIFT in banking, airline information) and public data networks suggests that shared networks are both technically and economically feasible. The limited evidence on the adoption of international data telecommunications systems suggests that diffusion rates are fastest for the largest multinationals possessing in-house telecommunications skills. For smaller companies the existence of independent technical and service advisory companies are an important stimulus to adoption (ANTONELLI, 1985).

The changing environment for international services

The dynamism of the service sector inevitably means that aspiring host agencies will need to monitor closely a changing environment. The following are some of the principal areas of likely change.

First, the current interest in lowering barriers to trade in services suggests that the direct investment/export mix could shift dramatically for some service industries. The present pervasive restrictions discourage arms length trade and encourage overseas production (SHELP, 1981). This prediction may be less valid for knowledge-based innovatory services where there are further incentives to internalization (ENDERWICK, 1986a).

Second, problems of targeting prospective investors are compounded by the impact of continuing deregulation and new technologies. Deregulation has a disturbing effect on established industrial structures accelerating both entry, exit and amalgamation. One effect of new micro-electronics based technologies has been to raise the returns from both close collaboration between users and suppliers and joint utilization of infrastructure. The result has been a growth in 'corporate clusters' centred around core high technology firms. The distinction between service and non-service multinationals is increasingly blurred.

Third, competition among service suppliers is becoming more fierce. This is occurring as service firms diversify into related areas (e.g. Saatchi and Saatchi's purchase of the New York-based management consultants, the Hay Group) and as a number of very large traditionally goods producers acquire major service arms (e.g. General Motors in software, General Electric, Dow Chemical and Texaco in banking and credit). This implies the future existence of large, heavily backed competitors with non-service sector origins.

Fourth, the area of government protectionism with regard to international data and technology flows is very fluid. Intensified control of outward information flows could complement import protectionism in an increasingly autarkic world (BERTSCH, 1985).

CONCLUSIONS

In conclusion we note some limitations of the foregoing discussion and outline a limited way forward for potential host regions.

First, while there has been increased interest in the possible attraction of service investments to peripheral regions (INDUSTRIAL DEVELOPMENT BOARD, 1985) there must be doubts about the ability of services to compensate for the enormous manufacturing job losses which a number of regions have experienced (WABE, 1986). There is a danger in generalizing from well documented success stories such as New England (HOWELL, 1985). The fallacy of composition cautions against the likely existence of an almost infinite number of service-based growth poles.

Second, there is a danger of generalizing from experiences with non-service multinationals. As suggested in a previous section, service multinationals display a number of very distinctive characteristics. As an example, consider the case of peripheral host regions which have succeeded in attracting manufacturing branch plants in the later stages of their product cycle. The cycle concept may not apply to high technology goods (OAKEY, 1985) or services

(GONENC, 1984), or may be so brief as to be non-operationable. Those commentators who suggest that areas not blessed with the relevant infrastructure to attract stage one establishments should focus on the mature stages (HOWELL, 1985), may be over-optimistic.

Third, the marked national geographical inequality in service provision suggests that attraction policies based at the regional level may not be the most effective arrangement. Apart from wasteful competition there may be a case for a nationally based policy incorporating some selective direction of service investments. Tentative evidence suggests that service firms may have a locational preference for those areas which have not had a history of manufacturing industrialization or high unionization (SEGAL, 1985). If this is the case, service firms would appear to offer little to those regions seeking to restructure in the face of rapid deindustrialization.

Finally, the above analysis offers a limited proposal for aspiring host economies. A useful first step would be an attempt to attract more of the service functions (R & D, financial control, design etc.) of existing investors. This would not be without its difficulties. For example, the limited empirical evidence on the decentralization of R & D activity suggests that this is negatively related to the existence of export-oriented branch plants and underdevelopment of local scientific and technical infrastructure (BEHRMAN and FISCHER, 1980; HIRSCHEY and CAVES, 1981). Nevertheless, the spillover effects of acquiring such functions are considerable.

Where feasible it may be advantageous to confine service investments to distinct geographical enclaves. Many of the areas most successful in attracting multinational services have ensured the continuing minimization (or absence) of regulation. For developed host economies this could be accommodated within existing initiatives such as free ports or export processing zones. While high technology services will exhibit clear spatial preferences they may be attracted to science parks located in core areas. Concepts of this type are being increasingly embraced by a number of governments. Despite the dangers of enclave development they would provide a useful testing ground for the acquisition of critical core expertise.

Finally, theoretical analysis of the MNE offers some insights into the form of advantages possessed by service MNEs as well as the probable mode of their exploitation. Where advantages relate to commercial know-how (e.g. banking) and close contact with turbulent market environments (e.g. international financing) their defining characteristics include opportunities for economies of learning and doing, their tacit or uncodified form and the importance of quality maintenance. The internal exploitation of ownership advantages is encouraged by a number of considerations. The high frequency of exchange for services of an intangible or transient form serve to offset the formation costs of overseas affiliates. A significant overseas presence may strengthen protection over intangible assets such as trademarks and copyright. Internalization of service outputs may also bring advantages to potential buyers. Multinational branding of services conveys valuable information about the quality and performance of services.

In the case of knowledge based innovatory services there are further incentives to internalization. When innovators must undertake market-making expenditures demand creation and diffusion require buyer education. Innovators, often with unique knowledge of their services, may be the best equipped to undertake buyer instruction. This suggests at least vertical integration of production and sales (BURSTEIN, 1984).

Alternative modalities of international operations such as licensing are discouraged by a number of facets of service sector activity. There are problems of debundling the 'technology' package of many services. Studies of insurance and retailing suggest that effective transfer necessitates the sharing of experience and provision of on-the-job training (SHELP, 1985). The importance of the tacit elements of the technology bundle restrict the effectiveness of arms length transfer. Similarly, the product specialization of many service firms creates problems of small numbers exchange as potential licensees are limited.

These considerations suggest that it may be difficult for host governments to obtain selected elements of the service package. Rather, there exist incentives for the possessors of service industry advantages to internalize these and exploit them overseas in the form of direct investment.

Acknowledgement—I have benefitted from the helpful comments of two anonymous referees of this journal.

REFERENCES

ANTONELLI C. (1985) The diffusion of an organisational innovation: international data telecommunications and multinational industrial firms, *Int. J. Ind. Organis.* **3**, 109–18.

BEHRMAN J. N. and FISCHER W. A. (1980) *Overseas R & D Activities of Transnational Companies.* Oelgeschlager, Gunn and Hain, Cambridge, MA.

BENZ S. F. (1985) Trade liberalisation and the global service economy, *J. World Trade Law* **19**, 95–120.

BERTSCH G. (1985) US export controls, trade and technology transfer, paper presented to the Academy of International Business, UK Regional Meeting, Manchester.

BODDEWYN J. J. (1987) Service multinationals: conceptualisation, measurement and theory, *J. Int. Bus. Studies* (forthcoming).

BROWNE L. E. (1983) High technology and business services *New England Econ. Rev.* July–August, 5–17.

BULLOCK M. (1983) *Academic Enterprise Industrial Development and the Development of High Technology Financing in the US.* Brand Brothers, New York.

BURSTEIN M. L. (1986) The business services industry sets pace in employment growth, *Monthly Lab. Rev.*, April, 29–36.

CENTRE FOR URBAN AND REGIONAL DEVELOPMENT STUDIES (1983) *Study of the Effects of New Information Technology on Less-Favoured Regions of the Community.* Report to the Regional Policy Directorate of the Commission of the European Communities, CURDS, Newcastle upon Tyne.

COHEN R. B. (1981) The new international division of labour, multinational corporations and urban hierarchy in DEAR M. J. and SCOTT A. J. (Eds.) *Urbanization and Urban Planning in Capitalist Society*, pp. 287–315. Methuen, London.

COWELL D. W. (1983) International marketing of services, *Serv. Ind. J.* **3**, 308–28.

DANIELS P. (1982) *Service Industries: Growth and Location.* Cambridge University Press, Cambridge.

DUNNING J. H. and NORMAN G. (1983) The theory of the multinational enterprise: an application to multinational office location, *Environ. Plan. A.* **15**, 675–92.

ENDERWICK P. (1987) Some economics of service-sector multinational enterprises in ENDERWICK P. (Ed.) *Multinational Service Industries* (forthcoming). Croom Helm, London.

ENDERWICK P. (1987b) Multinational contracting in ENDERWICK P. (ed.) *Multinational Service Industries* (forthcoming). Croom Helm, London.

FEKETEKUTY G. and HAUSER K. (1985) Information technology and trade in services, *Econ. Impact* **52**, 22–8.

FRANKO L. (1983) *The Threat of Japanese Multinationals—How the West Can Respond.* Wiley, Chichester.

GERSHUNY J. and MILES I. (1983) *The New Service Economy: The Transformation of Employment in Industrial Societies.* Frances Pinter, London.

GODDARD J. B. and SMITH I. J. (1978) Changes in corporate control in the British urban system, 1972–77, *Environ. Plann. A* **10**, 1,073–84.

GONENC R. (1984) Software—a new industry, *OECD Observer* **131**, 20–3.

HARRIS R. I. D. (1985) The role of manufacturing in regional growth, Occasional Paper No. 23, The Queen's University of Belfast Working Papers in Economics.

HIRSCHEY R. C. and CAVES R. E. (1981) Internationalisation of research and transfer of technology by multinational enterprises, *Ox. Bull. Econ. Statist.* **42**, 115–30.

HOOD N. and YOUNG S. (1982) *Multinationals in Retreat: The Scottish Experience.* Edinburgh University Press, Edinburgh.

HOWE W. J. (1986) The business services industry sets pace in employment growth, *Monthly Lab. Rev.* April, 29–36.

HOWELL J. M. (1985) The economic renaissance of New England, *Econ. Impact* **51**, 16–23.

HOWELLS J. R. L. (1984) The location of research and development: some observations and evidence from Britain, *Reg. Studies* **18,** 113–29.

INDUSTRIAL DEVELOPMENT BOARD (1985) *Encouraging Enterprise: A Medium Term Strategy for 1958–1990.* HMSO, Belfast.

LECRAW D. J. (1986) Third world multinationals in the service industries, in ENDERWICK P. (Ed.) *Multinational Service Industries* (forthcoming). Croom Helm, London.

LOEVE A., DEVRIES J. and DESMIDT M. (1985) Japanese firms and the gateway to Europe, *Tijdschr. Econ. Soc. Geogr.* **76,** 2–10.

LOWE J. (1985) Science Parks in the UK, *Lloyds Bank Rev.* **156,** 31–42.

MALECKI E. J. (1981) Recent trends in the location of industrial research and development: regional development implications for the United States, in REES J., HEWINGS G. J. D. and STAFFORD H. A. (Eds.) *Industrial Location and Regional Systems,* pp. 217–37. Croom Helm, London.

MARKUSEN A. R. (1985) High-technology jobs, markets and economic development prospects: evidence from California in HALL P. and MARKUSEN A. (Eds.) *Silicon Landscapes,* pp. 35–48. George Allen and Unwin, Hemel Hempstead, Herts.

MARQUAND J. (1983) The changing distribution of service employment in GODDARD J. B. and CHAMPION A. G. (Eds.) *The Urban and Regional Transformation of Britain,* pp. 99–134. Methuen, London.

MARSH F. (1984) Future trends in Japanese overseas investment, *Multinat. Bus.* **2,** 1–11.

MARSHALL J. N. (1979) Ownership, organisation and industrial linkage, *Reg. Studies* **13,** 531–58.

MARSHALL J. N. (1985) Business services: the regions and regional policy, *Reg. Studies* **19,** 352–63.

MARSHALL J. N., DAMESICK P. and WOOD R. (1985) Understanding the location and role of producer services, paper presented to Regional Science Conference, University of Manchester.

MILLER R. R. (1985) International competition in services: an American perspective, Working Paper 85/5, Strathclyde International Business Unit.

NORTHERN IRELAND ECONOMIC COUNCIL (1983) The duration of industrial development assisted employment, Report No 40, NIEC, Belfast.

OAKEY R. (1985) High-technology industries and agglomeration economies, in HALL P. and MARKUSEN A. (Eds.) *Silicon Landscapes,* George Allen and Unwin, Hemel Hempstead, Herts.

OAKEY R., THWAITES A. T. and NASH R. (1980) The regional distribution of innovative manufacturing establishments in Britain, *Reg. Studies* **14,** 235–54.

OECD (1981) *Recent International Direct Investment Trends.* OECD, Paris.

O'MALLEY E. (1986) Foreign-owned industry in Ireland: performance and prospects, in BACON P. (Ed.) *Medium Term Outlook, 1986–1990.* The Economic and Social Research Institute, Dublin.

SAPIR A. (1985) North–south issues in trade in services, *World Econ.* **8,** 27–42.

SAPIR A. and SCHUMACHER D. (1984) *The Employment Impact of Shifts in the Composition of Commodity and Services Trade.* OECD, Paris.

SEGAL N. (1985) The Cambridge Phenomenon, *Reg. Studies,* **19,** 563–78.

SEGAL, QUINCE AND PARTNERS (1985) *The Cambridge Phenomenon. The Growth of High Technology Industry in a University Town.* Segal, Qince and Partners, Cambridge.

SHELP R. K. (1981) *Beyond Industrialisation: Ascendancy of the Global Service Economy.* Praeger, New York.

SHELP R. K. (1985) Service technology and economic development, *Econ. Impact.* **52,** 8–13.

WABE J. S. (1986) The regional impact of de-industrialisation in the European community, *Reg. Studies* **20,** 23–36.

WOOD P. A. (1986) The anatomy of job loss and job creation: some speculations on the role of the 'producer service' sector, *Reg. Studies* **20,** 37–46.

UNITED NATIONS (1978) *Transnational Corporations in World Development: A Re-Examination.* UN, New York.

[26]

Multinational Enterprises and the Growth of Services: Some Conceptual and Theoretical Issues

by

John H. Dunning*

This article sets out to identify first, the main competitive advantages of multinational enterprises (MNEs) in providing services; second, the way in which these advantages are used to best advance the strategic goals of MNEs and the reasons why the value added activities which these advantages generate are undertaken outside the home country of the MNE. The article also identifies some of the reasons for the growth of MNE involvement in the service sector over the last two decades and, in particular, why foreign direct investment (FDI) has been the preferred route for organising cross-border activities involving services.

A multinational enterprise (MNE) is an enterprise which owns or controls value-adding activities in two or more countries. These activities might lead to production of tangible goods (e.g., washing machines) or intangible services (e.g., an audit) or some combination of the two (e.g., the transmission of data).[1] This output might be sold to other firms or used by the same firm for further value-adding activities, i.e., take the form of intermediate goods (e.g., pharmaceutical chemicals) or services (e.g., a warehousing facility or a patent right). Or it might be sold to final consumers, i.e., take the form of consumption goods (e.g., a bar of chocolate) or services (e.g., a haircut), or indeed items that might belong in both categories (e.g., a car or airline journey).

In some senses, the distinction between goods and services is a false one; indeed one observer [Levitan, 1985] claims that it is a statistical artifact. First, most goods purchased are intended to provide a service or a function; food is bought to assuage hunger, for its nutritional qualities and for its appeal to the palate, a bicycle is a form of transport, a TV set is a means of entertainment, shoes are for walking, and so on. Second, there are few 'pure' goods or services. Not only do virtually all goods embody non-factor services in the course of their production, and most services require physical assets and intermediate goods; but *at the point of sale,* most are jointly and simultaneously supplied with each other. Sampson and Snape

*University of Reading, Department of Economics, Whiteknights, Reading, RG6 2AA, UK

[1985] refer to such services as 'separated' services; Bhagwati [1984] prefers the expression 'splintered' services. Hirsch [1986] grades services according to the proportion of their total costs incurred by the producer and user during their interaction – what he calls the simultaneity factor.[2] The lower these costs in cross-border transactions, the greater the tradability of services is likely to be.

The essential differences, then, between the nature of goods and services appear to be twofold. First, in the case of services, there is a direct, and frequently a simultaneous, association between the acts of production, exchange and consumption; whereas, in the case of goods, these acts are normally separate and discrete activities. Second, there is the question of ownership. The transaction of goods implies an exchange of ownership, except where it is internalised within a hierarchy. For most services, which involve a joint supply of goods and services, only part of the price paid is for a transfer of ownership. Take, for example, the purchase of a theatre ticket. In conjunction with the entertainment being provided (the production and consumption of which are simultaneous), the customer, along with other theatregoers, buys the temporary right of use of physical assets, e.g., the seat and theatre facilites necessary for that entertainment. The same analogy could be made to a range of other services, and particularly those which are part of a collective or, as Shelp [1984] would put it, mass purchase; and/or which require substantial fixed, but shared assets; and/or service segmented markets, in which firms may wish to practise price discrimination.

The distinction between a service and a good becomes further obscured when one considers the options available to consumers to buy or acquire the right to use (enjoy the service) of goods. A telephone conversation is a service; but the rental paid by the subscriber to the telephone company includes a contribution towards both the cost and maintenance of the physical assets necessary to provide the service, and that of the service *per se*. Yet, what is the difference between *buying* a telephone and a share of the communications network as a packaged product and that of acquiring a right to use these assets? The question seems to revolve around the ownership of the assets. The same applies to a car rental compared with a car purchase. Car rental companies are classified as service producers, while automobile companies are treated as goods producers. Yet, in both cases, the customer is acquiring a right to a particular mode of travel. However, while in the former instance, the right is time limited and may be circumscribed by the owner of the asset; in the second, there are no restrictions on the buyer, as the asset itself has changed hands.

In summary, the output of economic activity may range from that of pure goods to pure services. However, most (indeed an increasing proportion of) goods embody some non-factor intermediate services, and most services embody some intermediate goods. And even pure services require people to supply them [Grubel, 1987]. For the purposes of this article, we shall take a service to mean a product, the *main* purpose of which is to provide a service; where these services also require goods we shall refer

MULTINATIONAL ENTERPRISES AND SERVICES GROWTH   7

to them as *goods-embodied services*. Likewise, we shall think of a good as a product the main purpose of which (at the time of sale) is to supply a tangible commodity; where these goods require services (other than factor services) we shall refer to them as *service-embodied goods*. We shall also treat a service as an *output* rather than an input; although many services take the form of intermediate outputs, i.e., those which are subsequently embodied in downstream value-adding activities.

Foreign direct investment (FDI) in services may be undertaken both by service and non-service MNEs. In 1982, no less than 82.2 per cent of the assets of US wholesale trading foreign affiliates were owned by parent companies whose main activities were in manufacturing and petroleum production; the corresponding percentages for finance (excluding banking) insurance and real estate were 55 per cent and business and other services 53.3 per cent. By contrast, 88.8 per cent of the assets of manufacturing affiliates were owned by parent companies whose main activity was also in manufacturing. In analysing FDI in services, therefore, it may be helpful to distinguish between *service activities* and *MNE service industries*.

THE GROWTH OF SERVICES IN THE WORLD ECONOMY

The share of services in a country's gross national product (GNP) primarily depends on:

  (i)   the level and pattern of demand for final (i.e., consumer) services,
  (ii) the extent to which services enter into the exchange economy,
  (iii) the extent of the 'roundaboutness' of the production process and the role of services in that production,
  (iv) the organisation of the production of services, e.g., between specialist service companies and non-service companies,
  (v)   the economic structure of the country, i.e., the types of goods and services produced, and the way in which they are produced; this, in turn, depends on the indigenous resources available and the system for organising their improvement and deployment, and
  (vi) the state of technology in supplying services or goods-embodied services.

In the past 20 years, the share of services in the gross national product of 58 out of 83 countries which provide data to the World Bank has increased. In 1985 it averaged 61 per cent for developed market economies, compared with 55 per cent in 1985; for developing countries the respective figures were 47 per cent and 42 per cent. However, this increased share has been mainly at the expense of primary, rather than secondary production; indeed, in both developing and developed countries, the rate of growth of manufacturing output has exceeded that of services.[4] The growing importance of services in most national economies has been examined by various scholars in recent years. [Daniels, 1982; Shelp, 1981, 1984, 1985; Gershuny and Miles, 1983; and Riddle, 1986 and 1987]. It reflects a combination of both *demand-* and *supply*-led factors. These include:

(i)   the growth of per capita output and the high income elasticity of demand for at least some 'discretionary' consumer services (particularly in industrialised countries);[5]

(ii) the increasing role of intermediate or producer services in the value-added process. In particular, advances in telematics have helped firms incorporate new information-based services within their own structures and to diversify the services they are able to offer their customers. One example is the way in which supermarket chains have used data networks established for inventory control to support a variety of other service activities (e.g., travel) [UNCTAD, 1985];

(iii) the increasing tendency of firms in non-service sectors to hive off (externalise) less productive service activities (accounting, auditing, transport, business consultancy); one recent example is the relinquishment by Exxon of its international transport services;

(iv) the growing importance of marketing, distribution and after-sales maintenance and servicing activities to the value of a physical product (e.g., a copying machine, an aircraft), or encouraging the production of both intermediate services (education and telecommunications), and final services (health); and of services directly related to the functions of government (civil service, tax collection, social security, etc.);

(v)   the growth of finance, banking, legal, insurance, transport and other support services necessary for the efficient functioning of modern society;

(vi) the emergence of new intermediate markets for services (the Euromarket, reinsurance, securitisation, new forms of data transmission, etc.).

In general, there is some evidence to suggest that, although the quality and variety of services vary more than that of goods, the demand for services, for example as between consumers from different countries at a given level of income, is likely to be less heterogeneous.[6] *Inter alia,* this helps explain the current trend toward the globalisation of some services, such as investment banking, insurance, hotels, advertising and airlines.

The question now arises, what is the role of MNEs in the supply of these services? Data currently being processed by the UNCTC indicate that the share of MNEs of the total service activities undertaken both in developed and developing countries is increasing quite rapidly. And certainly, as Table 1 shows, the growth of the FDI stock in most service sectors has risen much faster than in the primary or secondary sectors. The following sections seek to offer an explanation for these phenomenon by drawing upon one of the most widely accepted paradigms of international production. In particular, it argues that the involvement of MNEs in the service sectors has risen over the past two decades, partly because of the *general* demand and supply-led characteristics identified above, and partly because these characteristics have *particularly* favoured FDI as a modality

MULTINATIONAL ENTERPRISES AND SERVICES GROWTH 9

TABLE 1
ANNUAL AVERAGE GROWTH RATES OF THE STOCK OF INWARD DIRECT
INVESTMENT BY REGION, 1975-82 (%)

	Europe (9 countries)[1]	North America (2 countries)[2]	Other Industrialied (2 countries)[3]	Total Industrialised (13 countries)
Primary	10.8	8.6	18.9	9.7
Secondary	6.7	13.9	13.9	10.0
Tertiary	10.8	22.3	18.4	16.5
Construction	7.4	19.5	7.6	12.8
Transport & communications	4.2	17.8	6.2	11.5
Distributive trade	10.7	22.1	19.0	16.6
Property	9.8	40.2	19.2	17.8
Banking & finance	14.1	18.6	18.9	16.6
Other services	5.1	19.4	23.7	16.1
TOTAL	8.3	15.8	16.6	12.3

Source: Original host country sources as cited in J.H. Dunning and J.A. Cantwell, *The IRM Directory of Statistics of International Investment and Production* (London: Macmillan, and New York: New York University Press, 1987), and where necessary author's estimates based on these sources.

1. Austria, France, W. Germany, Italy, Netherlands, Norway, Portugal, Spain, and the UK.
2. Canada and the UK.
3. Australia and Japan.

for organising the cross-border production and transaction of these services.

THE THEORY OF INTERNATIONAL PRODUCTION: ITS RELEVANCE TO THE GROWTH OF SERVICES

There is now a general agreement in the literature that the extent and pattern of international production – production undertaken by MNEs outside their national boundaries – is dependent on:

(i) the extent and nature[7] of their technological, managerial and marketing advantages *vis à vis* those of indigenous firms in the country in which they are producing or contemplating value-added activities;[8] and also those which arise from the geographical diversification of such activities;

(ii) the benefits of combining these advantages with immobile factor endowments, in a foreign or the home country, to produce further value-adding activities[9] (which reflect the location specific or comparative advantages of these countries);

(iii) the advantages of internally controlling and co-ordinating (i) and (ii) with other assets owned by the MNE, rather than selling this right to indigenous firms located in the country of production.

It is further accepted that the configuration of these ownership, location and internalisation (OLI) advantages, and the response of them by firms will vary according to *industry, country* or *region* (or origin and destination) and *firm* specific characteristics; this latter incorporating the perceived competitive positions of firms and their strategies for growth.

It is also worth observing that while a majority ownership (i.e., a 51 per cent or more equity stake in a foreign affiliate) confers a *de jure* right of the MNE to control the use of the ownership advantages it transfers, and of locally sourced resources, *de facto*, such control might be assigned to the seller by the contract concluded between it and a foreign buyer. In consequence, international production, i.e., the foreign value-adding activities of MNEs, should embrace non-equity activities, including strategic alliances, wherever the agreement between the parties allows the non-resident partner some control or influence over the terms of the agreement, and the way in which it is executed.

We now consider the relevance of the three elements of the eclectic paradigm of international production just outlined to the service sector. In particular we shall be interested in identifying whether or not there are distinctive OLI characteristics of service-producing MNEs, compared with goods-producing MNEs. Is there any reason to suppose that service-based MNEs possess unique competitive advantages, or that FDI in services is likely to play a more important role as a means of exploiting foreign markets; or that the markets for intermediate services are likely to be more (or less) imperfect than those of goods?

THE FACTORS MAKING FOR MULTINATIONALITY OF SERVICES: THE COMPETITIVE (OR OWNERSHIP SPECIFIC) ADVANTAGES OF MNEs

Some general issues

The concept of corporate competitive advantage (elsewhere referred to as ownership advantages) refers to the ability of enterprises to satisfy the needs of their or potential customers.[10] Usually, the literature identifies three main criteria:

1. the characteristics and range of goods or services supplied, loosely referred to as 'quality': these embrace the components of a service which makes it desirable for the customer to possess and include such attributes as design, comfort, usefulness, performance, reliability, durability, efficiency of personal service, degree of professionalism, attitude, itineraries (as in the case of a shipping cruise);
2. price (less discounts, but including expected after-sales costs, e.g., repairs and maintenance);
3. services associated with the purchase and use of product, e.g., delivery times, frequency and reliability of services (as in transport services), up-to-dateness (as in news agencies), information and advice on product or service qualities, the number and location of

selling outlets, after sales repair and maintenance facilities, the ability of replacements and spares, and so on.

To produce and market goods and services more successfully than their competitors, MNEs must either have an exclusive or privileged access to specific assets which enables them to produce a particular good or service at lower cost; and/or to organise more efficiently a set of complementary assets to produce a range of value-adding activities, (so-called common governance advantages); and/or be more discerning choosers of *where* to engage in production (so-called locational choice advantages). The literature has identified these ownership specific advantages – primarily from the viewpoint of primary product or manufacturing firms – in some detail; these are set out in Appendix 1. For our purposes, each of the three needs of purchasers identified in the previous paragraphs rests on the supplying firms' having access to some core technological, managerial, financial or marketing assets so that they can produce and sell specified services at the lowest production costs; and/or their capacity to co-ordinate these with other assets so that they can produce the right volume, type and range of products (including intermediate products) in the right locations.

The questions of interest which we seek to answer in the following paragraphs are threefold:

1. What are the particular ownership specific advantages likely to apply in the production and marketing of services?
2. In what respects and to what extent do these vary *between* service sectors?
3. Under what conditions are MNEs (either generally or from particular countries) better able to supply these services than non-MNEs?

The nature of competitive advantages of MNEs in service sectors

We have already suggested that there are very few 'pure' services, in that the consumption of services does not also entail, in part at least, the coincident consumption of goods. Where goods and services are jointly supplied, it could be that a firm's competitive advantages rests in its ability either to produce goods and/or services, e.g., private medical treatment. Perhaps even more important is the fact that there are many firms (and particularly MNEs) supplying services (whether they be pure or not) which also supply goods (i.e., they are diversified goods and services producers). This would suggest that some of the co-ordinating advantages of supplying services may arise because of the firm's goods-producing activities; and as we have already observed a substantial proportion of services are supplied by manufacturing or primary product enterprises. For example, the involvement in the freight shipping business by companies like Unilever and Royal Dutch Shell, arises partly because of the nature of the products transported and partly because of the perceived advantages of logistical management [Van Rens, 1982]; while the ability of foreign exchange dealers and news agencies to meet the needs of their clients satisfactorily rests crucially on the availability of sophisticated telecommunications equipment which can transmit information instantaneously from any part of the world.

What of the advantages specific to supplying 'pure' services? We have seen that the nature of a pure *consumer* service is that it is perishable or near perishable, has little or no storage value and its consumption is coincident with its production. Most *producer* or intermediate services are different in the sense that they are not directly consumed but are embodied in products or other services; moreover, exactly the same service may be used over and over again. A chemical formula may be used to generate $1 million or $100 millions of products; a TV advertising commercial can be used repeatedly; the same architecture and interior design can be used to build a hotel in Bangkok or Buenos Aires. Let us now examine some of the competitive advantages identified in the literature and see how they apply to the service sector.

i. Quality: product differentiation

Many services are complex and involve a strong human content. Indeed, in the strictest sense of the word, all services are embodied either in goods or people. Because of this, their quality is more likely to be variable than that of goods [Grubel, 1986]. Obvious examples include personal, business and professional services, entertainment and retail services, where the service provided is either customer-specific (e.g., a legal consultation or a repair of a car) or collectively idiosyncratic (e.g., a theatre performance or a train journey). The ability to ensure a high and consistent quality of service is particularly likely to appeal to business customers whose own reputation may be affected by the service.

Several writers, notably Caves [1982], have suggested that in consumer goods industries, the ability to create and sustain a successful brand image – and the goodwill attached to it – is one of the key competitive advantages of MNEs. Casson and others [1982] prefer to emphasise the capability of firms to monitor quality and reduce buyer transaction costs by offering services from multiple locations. Likewise, in consumer service sectors, MNEs such as Hilton and Holiday Inn (hotels), American Express and Visa (credit cards), McDonalds and Kentucky Fried Chicken (fast food chains), Avis and Hertz (car rentals), Saatchi and Saatchi and J. Walter Thompson (advertising agencies), are each recognised for their trademarks and/or by the kind of markets they seek to serve. Since many of these services are 'experience' rather than 'inspection' goods, the availability of pre-purchase advice about foreign tours or the experience of related services may guide consumer choice. Similarly, the location and (perceived) quality of after sales and repair and maintenance outlets may affect the selection of durable goods bought by both business and private customers.

MULTINATIONAL ENTERPRISES AND SERVICES GROWTH 13

ii. Economies of scope

The availability and price of several services rests on the economies of scope of the seller. An obvious example is the services provided by a retail establishment. The larger the range and volume of products stocked, not only may the retailer be able to bargain for lower prices from the supplier, but he can help lower the transaction costs of his customers. The greater bargaining power of chain stores and multiples also enables them to exert more control over the quality and process of the goods they purchase, and to offer this service to their customers. The worldwide referral systems of many airlines and hotel chains can also be a major advantage to international customers. Economies of scope are also common in shipping and among business consultants; they are inherent in insurance and many banking activities and, perhaps, are widest of all in brokerage-type services, such as those provided by travel agents, and investment analysts and commodity dealers.They are particularly important in that they help link marketing knowledge with production flexibility and promote a geocentric attitude towards international production.

iii. Economies of scale and specialisation

In principle, there is no difference between the economies of *plant* scale and specialisation enjoyed by firms in manufacturing and those in some service sectors. The lower unit costs of providing air transport by a 747 Jumbo compared with a 727, or accommodation by a 500-bed hotel compared with a 30-bed hotel, or medical services by a large compared with a small hospital, are directly comparable with the eocnomies of large scale production of motor vehicles, pharmaceuticals or micro-chips. Similarly, large international business consultants, the merchant and investment banks, and the hotel chains can profit from the economies of specialisation of personnel and the economies of common governance arising from their ability to move people, money and information between different parts of the same organisation, and to take advantage of differential factor costs and environmental flexibility. Often too, large service companies can gain from raising finance on favourable terms and buying goods and services at quantity discounts in exactly the same way as a manufacturing firm. Shipping is another industry characterised by high fixed costs, with relatively low marginal costs of operation. Nowhere are the advantages of spreading risks, which size and scope confer, better seen than in the insurance and investment banking sectors. Size, indeed, is the main ticket of entry to transnational activities in both of these sectors, and, without such transnationality, each would be smaller than it is.

iv. Technology and information

The 'knowledge' component of production techniques and tangible goods (which is itself an intermediate service) varies between industrial sectors and is usually measured by such indices as the proportion of sales accounted for by innovatory (e.g., research and development) activities or the proportion of professional, scientific and engineering personnel in the total labour force. The ability to invent new products and to produce existing products more cheaply, or of a better and more reliable quality, is a key competitive advantage in many goods industries.

In some service sectors, it is the capability to acquire, produce, assemble, store, monitor, interpret and analyse information (and to do so at the least possible cost), which is the key intangible asset or core competitive advantage. As one would expect, this is especially so in those sectors whose main service *is* the acquisition, assembling and transmitting of information (stockbroking, foreign exchange and securities dealing, business consultancy), commodity broking and the various data-providing processing and service bureaux (Extel, Reuters, etc.), and transmitting networks (Euronet). Here again, the ability to provide services goes hand in hand with the equipment and physical goods and the knowledge of *how* to produce and disseminate that information.

v. Some special features of knowledge as an asset in the service sector

Knowledge as a service has another characteristic: it need not be perishable, and it may be repeatedly used to the benefit of the purchaser at low or no cost. It is an intangible asset which helps create and sustain the production and sale of a stream of goods which embody that knowledge. Similarly, the production of some services, notably information and human capital-intensive services (finance and banking, telematics, business and professional services) embody a common pool of codifiable and tacit knowledge, which is specific to the firm (or more particularly to the collective wisdom, intellect and experience and judgemental capabilities of the personnel of the firm), plus inherited knowledge (as contained in documents, tapes, discs, films, etc.).

The large service firms in information-intensive sectors trade on their name (and sometimes on the specific services they offer) in the same way as do the large manufacturing companies. Chase Manhattan Bank, Coopers and Lybrand, A.G. Nielsen, Prudential Insurance Co., McKinsey, Salomon Brothers, Foster Wheeler, Nomura, Extel, Heidrick and Struggles, are all as well known by their clients, and equally valued for the knowledge intensity of their services, as ITT, Monsanto, Philips, Texas Instruments, Boeing, or Ciba Geigy in the provision of technologically intensive goods.

In manufacturing industry, the provision of modern process and product technology is becoming increasingly expensive while its rate of dissemination and/or obsolescence is fast accelerating [Ohmae, 1985]. No less important is the fact that technology requires the possession of, or access to, complementary assets (e.g., modern production facilities, sales and distributing networks); the good embodying the technology is to be successfully commercialised [Teece, 1987].

Two results of these trends are, first, that technology intensive firms are increasingly having to widen their markets in order to absorb the huge fixed costs and reap the economies of scale associated with the production and marketing of technology for technology-intensive goods; and, second, that there is increasing pressure on even the largest MNEs to enter into collaborative arrangements with other firms (including their competitors) to reduce the risks of expensive research and development commitments, to capture the economies of technological synergy, and to broaden the application of technology to different processes, products and markets [Contractor and Lorange, 1987].

vi. *Favoured access to inputs or markets*

A secure and privileged access to inputs and/or distribution outlets and market access afford many manufacturing firms a competitive advantage over their less favoured rivals. Sometimes (especially where markets are seasonal, uncertain or hazardous) these advantages can only fully be exploited by firms where these same markets are internalised; in other cases, an adequate futures market, a comprehensive knowledge about sourcing and marketing outlets, a satisfactory contractual relationship with suppliers or customers may achieve the same result. In both cases, however, these advantages can only be sustained by MNEs when some kind of market failure exists. Such failure has itself helped create international brokerage or arbitrage-linked service firms whose main purpose is to act on behalf of buyers and/or sellers to find an appropriate seller or buyer for their products and services. Security, insurance and commodity broking, estate agencies, and travel agents fall into this category. Such competitive advantages as they possess rest on their capabilities to minimise the transaction costs of their clients and advise them of how best to meet their requirements.

In some cases, the competitive advantages of service firms rest in their knowledge of the sourcing of essential inputs, and an ability to reduce the associated search negotiating and monitoring costs, in the same location. Moreover, some intermediate services need to draw upon each other, and frequently they are jointly demanded by customers (e.g., shipping and insurance, banking and finance) which is an added reason for agglomerating economies and, in recent years, for mergers and/or diversifications. The concentration of globally oriented business and financial activities in a few major cities of the world (e.g., London, New York, Paris, Tokyo, Hong Kong, etc.) and within these cities in a very particular location (e.g., City of London, Wall Street, etc.) is explained by the need to gain and sustain this particular form of competitive advantage. In the airline business, the acquisition of rights to particular routes (an essential prerequisite to offering travel to the places in question) is also an important property right. And the very rationale of executive search agencies rests on their capability to recruit the kind of personnel needed from a world market.

As regards access to markets, there are numerous examples of firms having advantages over their competitors. The early venturing abroad of multinational insurance, banking, advertising, accounting and executive search companies was primarily to supply migrating individuals or branch firms of MNEs with services they had previously supplied to their parent companies. With the globalisation of markets and production, these firms have found it increasingly desirable to be multinational to win or retain the business of their international clients; and in this respect advances in telematics have advanced the competitive position of firms best able to offer an integrated package of services, once the necessary data network has been established [Sauvant, 1986]. American and European hotel chains and construction companies, experienced in meeting the needs of domestic customers, knew exactly what these customers wanted when they first went abroad (particularly to unfamiliar places). In the mass tourist business, hotels, airlines, and tour operators frequently combine to ensure each other a ready-made market of each other's services. More generally, the growth of international bulk shipping services has followed that of MNE activity, particularly in those sectors (e.g., oil, chemicals and agribusiness) where propensity for intra-firm trade is high.

A totally different category of service companies are the sales subsidiaries, import and export merchants, the general trading companies and the buying agents of large retail chains or goods-producing enterprises. These, in fact, account for the largest amount of service investments by MNEs. Their function is primarily to promote or sustain markets or to seek out and acquire inputs for their domestic activities. In some cases, notably the Japanese general trading companies (the Sogo Shosha), they have developed into huge conglomerates which have integrated backwards or horizontally into a wide range of non-trading activities or have established long-term and close contractual relationships with manufacturing and/or primary producers. Their main ownership advantages arise from their control over a global network of activities, their immense bargaining power (particularly in respect of the terms and conditions of trade), their unsurpassed knowledge of market conditions for the products they buy and sell, their ownership of wholesale and retail trading outlets, and their ability to reduce foreign exchange risks and environmental turbulence by diversifying their trading portfolios. In addition, the last two decades or so have seen a growth in specialist multinational buying groups or consortia, representing leading wholesale or retail outlets in Europe and the US (e.g., Sears Roebuck, C & A, Marks and Spencer).

THE FACTORS MAKING FOR MULTINATIONALITY OF SERVICES: THE COMPARATIVE OR LOCATIONAL SPECIFIC ADVANTAGES OF COUNTRIES

Some general issues

Service firms possessing competitive advantages identified in the previous sections usually have a choice of *where* they (or the firms to which they sell the right to use these advantages) engage in value-adding activities.

MULTINATIONAL ENTERPRISES AND SERVICES GROWTH   17

Sometimes, the nature of the services provided, the technology of production, or government regulations restrict the locational options; and it should be recalled that because of their nature, it is only possible to transport services if they are embodied in goods or people. This would suggest that trade in services is, at least, partly dependent on the transportability of the goods in which they are embodied (or which they embody) and on their production costs. The behaviour or anticipated behaviour of competitors may also affect locational decisions in oligopolistic service sectors.

To what extent can the transnationalisation of the service sector be explained by the desire to exploit competitive advantages from a foreign rather than a domestic location? Are there specific characteristics about services, which make for more or less transnationality of value-adding activities than in the case of goods?

International involvement in services or goods embodied services usually takes three forms. The first is the exports of final services sold to independent buyers; these may be

> (a) earned by exporting directly to a foreign country (e.g., Lloyds of London insuring a Norwegian ship, a New York stockbroker buying or selling shares for a German client, or a Canadian telecommunications company paying a Spanish telecommunications company a share of the price of a personal telephone call made by a Canadian to a Spanish citizen);
> (b) earned by a foreign customer travelling to the exporting country and buying the service from there (e.g., the main form of export of personal services);
> (c) services embodied in material substances which are exported from the home country.

The second comprises intermediate services sold to independent buyers. These represent the services of technology, marketing, management skills, etc., transacted through non-equity licensing or 'other' contractual agreements. The goods content of these services vary from virtually zero (e.g., a chemical formula) to substantial (a turnkey project). Third, there is foreign direct investment; this embraces the sale of services produced by the foreign affiliates of MNEs (which is essentially the subject matter of this report). In turn, these affiliates may buy intermediate services from their parent company or other affiliates (i.e., intra-firm services), or final goods for resale. They may also earn invisible exports in the form of interest, dividends and fees,[11] while overseas workers (e.g., Korean construction employees employed by Korean constructional MNEs in the Middle East, artists, military personnel, etc.) may repatriate part of their wages and salaries.

The export v FDI alternative

There are two main types of goods which do not normally enter international trade. They are those which involve prohibitively high transport costs and those which must require a simultaneity of production and consumption. Governments, however, by a whole range of import restrictions or regulatory regimes can also make it unprofitable for foreign firms to export to their territories. In the service sector, there are six types of services which are not usually tradable (i.e., location bound). These are:

1. those the sales of which are dependent upon the presence of people, goods, or other services which are located in the country of use. These include hotel and most local tourist facilities, restaurants, car hire, construction development, motion picture production, real estate and news agencies;
2. transport facilities;
3. telecommunication and public utility services, though some services (e.g., water, electricity) in one country may be part of a grid location in another country, and TV programmes can be 'exported' by satellite;
4. warehousing, wholesaling, and retailing services, including repair and maintenance services;
5. most forms of public administration and social and related community related services (e.g., libraries);
6. services which require a face-to-face contact between buyer and seller.

In addition, in practice, education, health services, and most personal and household services are traded only to a limited extent – in as much as the foreign purchaser may avail himself of such services at the location of production.

Second, there are other services where the international transaction costs (either to the buyer or seller, or to both) are, in practice, too high to allow much trade; these include most business consultancy services, professional services, and commercial banking.

Third, there are services which are widely traded. These include most intermediate services but, most notably, all kinds of codifiable information and technology, investment banking, insurance, commodity broking, advertising, services, and a variety of property rights (e.g., firms, broadcasting, patents, architectural drawings, tape recordings, etc.). A large proportion of these services are transferred *within* MNEs; that is to say, direct investment is a necessary prerequisite for trade in services to occur. It is in this group of services that tradability over the last decade or more has been revolutionised by advances in data-transmitting devices and techniques [UNCTC, 1982].

Since the opportunities for trade in services are more limited than those for goods, it might be reasonably supposed that the relative involvement of MNEs activity in the former sector would be that much greater. In practice, however, this does not occur, simply because in many sectors (social services, public utilities, many personal services, much of wholesaling, warehousing and retailing, building and construction, and ground transport services), the competitive advantages of foreign MNEs seeking to establish a local presence are unlikely to be as great as those of domestic companies or are insufficient to compensate for the additional costs of servicing a foreign market [Hirsch, 1976]. Another reason is that government strictly controls foreign investment in strategically and politically sensitive service sectors, such as transport, telecommunications, banking, community services (education, health, and public utilities), and, by a variety of discriminatory measures or non-tariff barriers (e.g. procurement and standards policies) favours indigenous companies.

At the same time as the information and knowledge component of other services (banking, finance, insurance, advertising, tour operators, etc.) has been increasing, so has the presence of MNEs. Moreover, as firms seek to globalise their supply of services in an attempt to meet the needs of their multinational customers and/or to promote a distinctive brand image, the tendency for competitive advantages to become more firm-specific increases. This explains the growth of US, European and Japanese MNE involvement in the 'up-market' sectors of many professional services, some education and health services, real estate, and in those consumer services where 'brand names' or 'trademarks' are important (hotels, fast food chains, some retail stores, etc.).

As we have described, the main reasons for the increase in MNE service activity in the last two decades has been the growth in demand for consumer services following a rise in real incomes, technological advances which have increased the demand for and supply of services and their tradability, the expansion of telecommunication and other service support facilities as goods have become technically more complicated, the expansion of trade in goods associated with increased geographical process or product specialisation, the increasing complexity and uncertainty of modern society leading to the need for insurance and professional advisory services, the increasing specialisation and round-aboutness in production, and the increasing role of government. We also suggested that MNEs, relative to other firms, have been well placed to benefit from these developments.

Which particular locational variables influence FDI in services?

While transport costs are obviously not such an important factor in the export v foreign production choice in services as in goods, being near to the customer and adapting the service to his local customs and needs probably play a more important role. The size and character of the market and real wage rates are also significant in influencing the siting of business and professional services and also of tourist-related activities.

The availability of key human and natural resources, however, is of crucial relevance in some sectors. The siting of tourist hotels depends on the location of the scenery, climate and physical amenities which the visitors are seeking; the siting of financial and insurance institutions, particularly when intended to serve a region or when they are part of a global network of activities, rests on an adequate supply of premises, communication facilities, and suitably trained labour. There are also agglomerative economies in being close to competitors, suppliers and customers. More generally, the provision of most industrial and high-income consumer service activities tend to concentrate in the larger and wealthier countries, and in the leading cities in these countries. Where these activities supply a regional or global market, they tend to be fairly footloose between alternative locations. Indeed, it is worth noting that the fastest growing service sectors are currently those which

(a) are subject to increasing economies of scale and scope;
(b) tend to be geographically concentrated;
(c) are regionally or globally oriented;
(d) generate a substantial amount of intra-firm trade.

The role of government in influencing the location of service activities is of particular significance. The same kind of incentives, controls and regulations that affect trade and foreign direct investment in goods also abound in services; indeed, it is generally agreed that the regulation over service activity is considerably greater than over goods. Though there has been a strong movement towards deregulation and liberalisation of some services (e.g., telecommunications, finance and insurance) in recent years, many others remain strongly under government control or surveillance. In addition, foreign MNEs may face a range of non-tariff barriers and are sometimes treated less favourably than indigenous companies. These issues are currently the subject of much debate in the EEC, OECD, GATT and other international fora.

On the other hand, some governments are making deliberate attempts to attract inward investment in services, particularly in infrastructure projects. Examples include Chile's efforts to attract US MNEs in the health care and sanitation sectors; Brazil's invitation to foreign MNEs to participate in some of the multi-billion highway, port and railroad construction schemes; Greece's decision to invite bids from foreign investors to build a new international airport and subway system in Athens and an expressway linking Athens with Thessalonika. Other governments are seeking to attract financial and business services. For example, Curacao and Luxembourg are making a bid to develop offshore financial facilities; Barbados, Jamaica and Ireland are trying to create a comparative advantage for themselves in the supply of well trained and motivated labour for business services; while China, India, Jamaica, Mexico and the Philippines are attempting to attract offshore data entry services for MNEs [Riddle, 1986; 1987].

Summary of forces influencing the location of MNE activity

Some 84 per cent of the stock of FDI by service MNEs is located in developed countries, compared with 75 per cent of all kinds of investment. But the *structure* of service activity in developed market economies is very different from that in developing countries. In the former, intermediate services purchased by capital or technologically advanced industrial sectors, financial, business and professional services, and services competing for the discretionary income of consumers play a much more important role. In the latter, there is a higher proportion of investment in trade and distribution, building and construction, public utilities, tourism, and some basic financial services.[12] The variation *within* developing countries is no less marked. The pattern of service activity in Singapore and Hong Kong is totally different from that in most other developing countries. In these latter countries, the structure of markets and resources, and the role played by government are crucial factors influencing the level and pattern of service output. To give one or two obvious examples: MNEs in tourist related activities dominate the service sectors in island economies like Seychelles, Barbados and Fiji; Singapore and Hong Kong are becoming the leading international financial and business centres in Asia; while the larger populated developing countries (e.g. India, Brazil and Indonesia) have attracted a wider a more balanced composition of service activities. Regulations and controls on service activities also differ widely between developing countries. In general they are more relaxed in East Asia and more stringent in Latin America.[13]

The most significant features affecting the changing of location of service activity by MNEs in recent years have undoubtedly been (i) changes in regulatory patterns, including the deregulation and liberalisation of the financial sector in some countries, and (ii) advances in the technology of transborder data flows. As far as developing countries are concerned, one of the reasons for a more liberal attitude towards inward investment in services is the growing realisation that without such investment (e.g. in infrastructure projects) e.g., hydro-electric power, telecommunications and roads, national development goals could be stunted. Examples include Greece, Turkey and Brazil [Riddle, 1987]. At the same time, by assisting trade in goods-embodied services, technical advances in data collection, assembly, processing and transmission may lead to a relocation and reorganisation of service activities by MNEs [UNCTAD, 1985; Sauvant, 1986]. While, on the one hand, they may lead to more decentralisation of routine service activities, on the other, by reducing the transaction costs of cross-border activities, they may pave the way for more economic integration among service (as well as manufacturing) MNEs, and more intra-firm trade between different parts of the MNE network.[14]

FACTORS MAKING FOR THE MULTINATIONALITY OF SERVICES: THE ORGANISATION OF TRANSACTIONS THROUGH MNE HIERARCHIES (INTERNALISATION ADVANTAGES)

Some general issues

Why should firms located in one country wish to exploit their competitive advantages in another country by engaging in vertical or horizontal integration, rather than lease the rights to those advantages to indigenous firms in a foreign country? For service firms to become MNEs in the traditional sense of the word, they must engage in foreign direct investment. Such investment is assumed to be necessary for firms to exercise authority over the way in which their competitive advantages are used across national boundaries, or, in some cases, to acquire an advantage in the first place. The fact that they choose to do so rather than contract this right to foreign firms suggests that they perceive there are certain costs associated with the latter mode of exchange which impede them from securing the full economic rent on their assets. By internalising the market (i.e., co-ordinating the use of its assets with other value adding activities),the firm believes it can protect its position, and, in so doing, it becomes an MNE[15] or increases the extent of its multinationality.

The literature suggests that the mode of organising cross-border exchanges of services will depend first on the relative contractual and hierarchial costs involved, and second on the extent and pattern of government intervention. The transaction costs include:

1. those relating to the transaction *per se*, e.g., search (for the right buyer or seller), identification and negotiating costs;
2. those relating to the *terms* of the contract; these include (a) price: as information is often asymmetrical, the buyer may be prepared to pay the seller less than the good or service is worth; (b) specification of the good or service to be supplied; (c) control over use made of the good or service supplied; (d) frequency and timing of deliveries (including inventory and warehousing costs);
3. those relating to the monitoring of the performance of the contractee;
4. those relating to the uncertainty of whether the terms of the contract will be adhered to and the costs of (a) their being broken (e.g., disruptions to the production process through untimely or irregular delivery schedules, loss of competitiveness through dissipation or abuse of property rights) and (b) litigation to recoup the costs associated with (a);
5. those relating to the external costs (and benefits) of the transaction (i.e., accruing to other than the parties directly involved in the exchange).

As for the role of governments, this may vary between outright control over the form of foreign involvement (e.g., no foreign direct investment is usually allowed in broadcasting or airlines, while only franchise agreements might be permitted between domestic hoteliers and foreign hotel chains), to various fiscal and other devices designed to tilt the balance of advantage away from one modality to that of another. For example, deregulation of financial markets might be expected to lead to more equity investment by financial institutions and fewer contractual agreements, while, by aiding intra-firm transactions, improvements in information mining and monitoring and communications technology, might lead to the reverse situation (e.g., in advertising and commodity broking). Tariff and non-tariff barriers, including union and other restrictions on the employment of foreign workers, might lessen the ability of firms to exploit the economies of common governance.

The literature further identifies the types of situations in firms are likely to wish to internalise market transactions (see Appendix 1). They vary between the nature of the activity (i.e., good or service being exchanged), the firms organising the transaction, and the market conditions specific to the countries engaged in the transaction. Competitive advantages which are idiosyncratic, non-codifiable and comprise the core assets of firms, and/or which are used to produce goods and services, the quality and reputation of which are of especial appeal to consumers, are not likely to be traded externally, while the more volatile and hazardous the international environment in which they are produced and traded, the more likely firms will prefer to internalise transactions.

The question now arises: how important are transaction costs a factor in explaining the growth of multinational service activities? Moreover, to what extent do different services incur different kinds of transaction costs?

Such fragmentary evidence as is available on the significance of the various vehicles of cross-border transactions among services suggests that not only that all forms of transactions have increased in the last 20 years, but that the modalities vary as much as – and perhaps even more than – those within the primary and secondary sectors.[16] Later we shall summarise some of the main variables affecting transactional modes and how they affect different service sectors.

There are three groups of services, the cross-border supply of which tends to be organised via foreign direct investment rather than by contractual relationships. The first comprise banking and financial services and most kinds of information-intensive business and professional services (e.g., management and engineering consultancies, computer-related services, data-based services, travel agents and airlines). Here the main reasons for integrating either vertically along the value-added chain or horizontally across value-added chains are because (a) much of the proprietary knowledge and information is tacit, expensive to produce, complex and idiosyncratic, but easy to replicate, and (b) there are substantial synergetic advantages to be gained from the geographical diversification of productive activities (e.g., those that arise from risk-spreading and the arbitraging of people, goods, money and information) which can best be accomplished within MNE hierarchies.

The second group comprise firms which engage in forward integration to ensure productive efficiency, and/or to protect the quality of the end product (and hence the customer's goodwill). Very often such companies are known by their brand name or image. The advertising, market research, executive search, international construction companies, some business consultants and some consumer-oriented services (e.g., fast food chains) and car rentals (where foreign direct investment does take place) and some goods-related personal services (e.g., motor vehicle maintenance and repair facilities) fall into this category.

The third group are trade-related services affiliates which are often owned by non-service MNEs, the purpose of which is to obtain inputs for the parent companies (or, like Japanese trading companies, for other home-based companies) on the best possible terms or to attain or develop markets for goods produced and exported by parent (and/or home-based) companies. In the first case, the protection of the supply position of the importing company and the assurance of the right quality at the right price is the dominant motive; in the second, the belief that fully or majority-owned subsidiaries are likely to be more efficient and better motivated to serve the exporting company's interests than independent sales agents is the main reason for internalisation [Nicholas, 1983]. Included in this group might be realtor companies whose purpose is to advise and act as brokers to foreign clients in the purchase of real estate.

By contrast to the above sectors, there are others, where minority joint ventures or non-equity agreements tend to be the preferred route of foreign participation. We might identify four groups of service companies which typify this entry or expansionary mode of MNE activity.

The first are hotels, restaurants and car rental companies. In these cases, the performance requirements of the contractor can often be satisfactorily codified in a management contract or franchising agreement. A UNCTC study on tourism [UNCTC, 1981] also emphasised that synergistic advantages of global reservation and referral systems could also be obtained without an equity capital stake, which in the hotel business could be both substantial and, in some parts of the world, highly risky. Moreover, although the customers for hotel, restaurant, and car rental companies were often from the investing countries, local knowledge of such things as food preferences, accommodation needs, decor and ancillary services made a substantial local managerial input desirable.

The second group typifies the need for local specialised knowledge even more, and the fact that products required specific customisation. These include range of business services (e.g., engineering, architectural and technical services), and some types of advertising (where local tastes and product images may be very different from those of the investing country), recreational activities, and accounting and legal services (where again knowledge of local standards and procedures may be acquired). But, perhaps, most significant in this group would be civil lengineering, oil and chemical constructional companies who engage in turnkey projects. Although sometimes the larger of these companies may have permanent offices in the countries they serve, the main part of their business is likely to be of a transitory nature.

Thirdly, because of the marketing and distribution costs, newly established or smaller manufacturing MNEs may wish to join forces with, or use as licensees, local selling agents or service firms. The presence of a local partner both reduces capital risk of the foreign investor and helps to buy complementary competitive assets or advantages necessary to exploit those of the foreign company. In other sectors (e.g., engineering and construction), a joint venture with a local firm can help an MNE win contracts from the host government and/or lessen the risks of expropriation.[17]

Lastly, in some sectors (e.g., investment banking and property/casualty insurance), the risks borne in providing particular services are such that they have to be shared by, or syndicated among, a consortium of firms. Sometimes these may involve firms from only one country, and, in other cases, from several countries.

Recent changes in organisational form

There have been several forces making for more cross-border hierarchial activity in services, and several which have operated in the opposite direction over the last decade or so. Of the former, two deserve especial mention. The first is the liberalisation of the attitudes and policies of several developed and developing country governments towards inward direct investment; and the movement towards deregulated markets in the financial and insurance sector. The second has been advances in the technology and management of information collecting, handling and storage (e.g., sophisticated computing monitoring systems), data-processing (e.g., system integration services, facilities management, remote computing services), and of data-transmission (e.g., satellite and optic cables). Both these developments, by reducing the cost of co-ordinating decision-making across national boundaries, have tended to increase the need for centralised control. It is seen in service sectors, such as engineering and project control through computer-aided design and graphic systems, and in the operations of such services as those conducted in series, such as banking services, insurance sales, airline reservations, and hotel room bookings [UNCTAD, 1985]. Some excellent examples of the ways in which this is being achieved are given by Feteketuky and Hauser [1985].[18]

On the other hand, there have been forces making for an increase in minority ventures or contractual arrangements. We might identify four of these. The first is the increasing specialisation among suppliers of finance capital, information and people related services (e.g., employment agencies). When considered alongside the maturation of some kinds of intermediate services and the increasing ability of sellers to exercise control over their proprietary rights through an appropriately worded contract, firms in such diverse sectors as hotels, telecommunications and construction are increasingly opting for the technical service agreement, management contract or franchise as a modality of operation. Second, as economic development proceeds, so will the necessary indigenous capabilities required by foreign MNEs in the service sector to conclude joint ventures or non-equity agreements to become available. Third, the assets required to provide some services, particularly those which are information-intensive, are either too costly or require different skills and technology for any one firm to possess. In consequence some service firms are either merging or collaborating on particular projects. Cross-border acquisitions and mergers have been particularly marked in the communications, banking, insurance and advertising sectors [UNCTAD, 1985]. Such co-operative arrangements help their participants to reduce the risks but capture the advantages of joint information and technical synergies. The fourth reason (and this is the same as the second reason for making for more direct investment) is the reduction in market failure brought about by improved information and data flows. The hypothesis here is that this could ease the possibility of non-equity arrangements for specific projects, even though it made for more equity involvement by large and diversified MNEs pursuing a global strategy.

Summary of points about organisational form

MNE activity, as well as depending on competitive advantages of the investing companies and locational advantages of producing in two or more countries is dependent on the extent it is beneficial to exploit these two advantages by using internalised markets. Indeed, the way in which firms organise their international activities may itself be a crucial competitive advantage.

As a broad generalisation, there is reason to suppose that the exchange of tangible services through the market is likely to involve higher transaction costs (relative to total costs of production and transaction) than that of goods. There are six reasons for this:

1. most services contain a larger element of customer tailoring than do goods, and they are more idiosyncratic;
2. since there is generally a greater human element in their production, their quality is likely to vary more than those of many goods (e.g., one can control the quality of refined oil or the tolerance of an electronic component by machine), but the pure service element attached to a legal consultation, restaurant meal, or shipping cruise may vary on each occasion;
3. until very recently, at least, a major proportion of the information provided and the certain knowledge and experience connected with interpreting and evaluating the information was tacit and non-codifiable;
4. partly because of (3) and the fact that information or knowledge related to service activities may be inexpensive to replicate, the possibility of abuse or dissipation of that knowledge is a real threat to the firm possessing it;
5. since markets for many services are highly segmented, the opportunities for price discrimination, which can be best exploited via hierarchies, other than markets are considerable;
6. the control of some service activities may be perceived to be a crucial element in the success of non-service producing companies; for example, some shipping lines may be owned by manufacturers to ensure delivery of goods on time, while the prosperity of large

MULTINATIONAL ENTERPRISES AND SERVICES GROWTH 27

retail outlets may be dependent on their expertise and goodwill of their buyers of foreign goods.

Together with the fact that many services are impossible or difficult to trade over space, the above reasons explain both the presence and the rapid growth of MNE activity in this sector. The facts that as incomes rise both people and firms spend more on services; that technology, information and software services are becoming increasingly significant to the production process of all types of goods and services; that non-service firms are becoming increasingly involved in service activities (examples include the large MNE petroleum companies diversifying into banking, computer hardware companies into the provision of software, etc.); and that, as the provision of some services becomes more complex, specialist service companies are being set up;[19] all help to explain an intensification of international activity in its varied forms.

Table 2 sets out the competitive advantages of MNEs in various service sectors; the more important characteristics which favour a home or foreign location for the value adding activities using such advantages; and the leading considerations affecting the modality by which MNEs exploit their competitive advantages. The final columns of the table give some indication of the way in which foreign markets are penetrated; and also of the extent to which organisation of cross-border transactions differs between service sectors.

CONCLUSIONS

Our aim has been to identify the main competitive advantages of MNEs in providing services, the way in which these advantages are used to best advance the strategic goals of MNEs, and the reasons why, at least for some, the value-added activities which these advantages generated are undertaken outside the home country of the MNE. We have also identified some of the reasons for the growth of MNE involvement in the service sector over the last two decades and, in particular, why foreign direct investment has been the preferred route for organising cross-border activities involving services than others. Special attention has been paid to the increasing needs of firms, both in service and non-service sectors, to integrate, vertically or horizontally, their domestic activities with services obtained from, or sold to, foreign countries; and the fact that, over recent years, both demand- and supply-led forces have intensified the advantages from the common governance of inter-related activities involving services. Moreover, new opportunities for industrial and geographical diversification have created their own locational and ownership advantages which have strengthened the position of MNEs in an increasing number of service sectors. We expect this trend to continue in the 1990s, providing that governments take a reasonably liberal attitude to both trade and investment in services and service-related activities.

TABLE 2

ILLUSTRATIONS OF OWNERSHIP, LOCATION AND INTERNALISATION ADVANTAGES RELEVANT TO TNC ACTIVITY IN SELECTED SERVICE SECTORS

	O (Competitive Advantages) Ownership	L (Configuration Advantages) Location	I (Coordinating Advantages) Internalisation	Foreign Presence Index[1] (U.S. Data)[2]	Organisational Form
Accounting/ Auditing	• Access to multinational clients • Experience of standards required • Professional expertise • Branded image of leading accounting firms	• On the spot contact with clients — F • Accounting tends to be culture sensitive — F • Adaptation to local reporting standards and procedures — F • Oligopolistic interaction — F	• Limited inter-firm linkages — E • Quality control over (international) standards — I • Government insistence on local participation — E	• High (92%) • Little intra-firm trade	• Mostly partnerships or individual proprietorships • Overseas subsidiaries loosely organized, little centralised control • Few jvs
Advertising	• Favoured access to markets (subsidiaries of clients in home markets) • Creative ability; image and philosophy • Goodwill • Full range of services • Some economies of coordination • Financial strength	• On the spot contact with clients — F • Adaptation to local tastes, languages — F • Need to be close to mass media — F	• Quality control over advertising copy — I • Need for local inputs — E • National regulations — E • Globalisation of advertising intensive products — I • To reduce transaction costs with foreign agencies — I	• High (85%) • Some intra-firm trade	• Mainly 100%; some jvs; limited non-equity arrangements
Commercial Banking	• Access to multinational clients, foreigners abroad • Professional expertise • Access to capital • Effective distribution networks • Intrinsic value of reserve currencies	• Person-to-person contact required — F • Government regulations — F • High value activities often centralised — H • Lower costs of foreign operations — F • Psychic distance (Islamic banks) — F	• Quality control — I • Economics of scope — I • Economics of coordinating capital flows — I • Importance of international arbitraging — I	• High (virtually 100%) • Some intra-firm trade in information and finance capital	• Mostly branches or subsidiaries, some agencies • Some jvs – notably, where governments insist • Some consortia
Computer Software/ Data Processing	• Linked to computer hardware • Highly technology/information intensive • Economics of scope • Government support	• Location of high skills & agglomerative economics often favours home country — H	• Idiosyncratic knowhow: need for protection against dissipation — I • Quality control — I • Coordinating gains — I		
Construction Management	• Size, experience and reputation • Government assistance • Low labour costs (developing country TNCs)	• Economics of concentrating technology intensive activities — H • On-the-spot interaction with clients and/or building firms — F	• Need for complementary local assets, risk spreading on large projects — E • Quality control — I • Good deal of subcontracting — E	• Favours exports (39%) (but n.b. often foreign receipts include local subcontracting element)	• Mixture; joint ventures favoured to gain access to markets, or where partner(s) bring complementary assets to the venture

TABLE 2 (CONTINUED)

Educational Services	• Country-specific, related to stage of economic development and role of government • Experience of client needs (Japanese schools in London)	• largely invisible exports through student visiting supplying countries H • Some foreign affiliates of private schools to cater for citizens of home country abroad • Need to expose students to foreign cultures F	• Quality control I • Integration with curricula in home country I • Exposure of foreign curricula/teaching methods E	• Low (2%) • Little intra-firm trade	• Originally 100% subsidiaries, but increasingly more jvs with foreign educational establishments
Engineering, Architecture Surveying Services	• Experience in home and other foreign markets • Economics of size and specialisation • Economics of scope/coordination	• Customisation to local tastes and needs L • Need for on-the-spot contact with customers and related producers L	• Joint ventures, to gain local experience expertise E • Quality control I • Knowledge often very idiosyncratic and tacit I	• Fairly high (75%) • Substantial intra-firm trade (in technology) and management skills)	• Mixture, but often professional partnerships • Some licensing
Information Services: Data Transmission	• Highly capital and human skill intensive • Sometimes 'tied' to provision of hardware • Considerable economics of scope and scale • Quality of end product/services provided	• Varies according to type of information being sold and transmission facilities between countries H/F • Where 'people' based, clients or firms may visit home country or firms supply services in client's countries H/F • News agencies are location bound, i.e., where the news is! H/F	• In case of 'core' assets, need for protection from dissipation I • Quality control I • Substantial gains from internalising markets, to capture externalities of information transactions I • Cognitive market failure, asymmetry of knowledge I	• Balanced (50%) • Some intra-firm trade	• Mixture, but 100% where market failure pronounced
Insurance	• Reputation of insurer; image (Lloyds of London) • Economics of scale and scope; and, sometimes, specialised expertise (e.g., marine insurance) • Access to multinational clients	• Need to be in close touch with insured (e.g., life insurance and related services (shipping finance)) F • Oligopolistic strategies among larger insurers F • Governments prohibit direct imports; extent to which there is freedom to trade F • Economics of concentration (in reinsurance) H	• Economies of portfolio risk spreading I • Tacit knowledge I • Need for sharing of large scale risks (reinsurance syndication) I • Government requirements for local equity participation E	• High (78%) • Some intra-firm trade	• Mixture: strongly influenced by governments, types of insurance and strategy of insurance companies
Investment Banking (brokerage)	• Reputation and professional skills (I.B. is an 'experience' service) • Substantial capital base • Knowledge of and interaction with international capital markets • Financial innovations	• Need to be close to clients H/F • Need to be close to international capital/finance markets, and also main competitors F • Availability of skilled labor H/F	• Complex and organic character of services provided I • Protection against exchange/political risks I • Need to pursue global investment strategy I • Quality control I	• High (84%) • A lot of intra-firm trade in form of control/coordination from H.O.	• Mainly via 100% subsidiaries

TABLE 2 (CONTINUED)

Hotels	• Experience in home countries in supply up-market services • Experience with training key personnel • Quality control • Referral systems • Economics of geographical specialisation, access to inputs	• Location bound when selling a 'foreign' service F • Exports through tourists, businessmen visiting home country H	• Investment in hotels is capital intensive E • Quality control can generally be ensured through contractual relationships (e.g., a purchase or management contract E • Governments usually prefer non-equity arrangements E • Referral systems can be centrally coordinated without equity control E	• Favours non-equity involvement, but exports of knowledge/management	• Vary, but mainly through minority ventures or contractual relationships
Legal Services	• Access to multinational clients and knowledge of their particular needs • Experience and reputation	• Need for face-to-face contact with clients F • Foreign customers may purchase services in home country H • Need to interact with other local services F • Restrictions on use of foreign barristers in courts F • Extent of local infrastructure H/F	• Many transactions highly idiosyncratic and customer specific I • Quality control I • Need for understanding of local customers and legal procedures E	• Low (2%) (mainly because trade in legal services is 'people embodied')	• Some overseas partnerships, but often services are provided via movement of people (clients to home country lawyers or vice versa)
Licensing	• (By definition) ability to supply technology; but most technology supplied by non-service firms	All exported H	• To protect licensor and to exploit economics of scope I • Quality control I	• All exports (100%) • Largely intra-firm. 70% in U.S. cases	
Management Consultants, & Public Relations	• Access to market • Reputation, image, experience • Economics of specialisation, in particular, levels of expertise. etc. skills, countries	• Close contact with client; the provision is usually highly customer specific F • MNE clients might deal with H.O. H • Mobility of personnel H/F	• Quality control, fear of underperformance by licensee I • Knowledge sometimes very confidential and usually idiosyncratic I • Personnel coordinating advantages I	• Balanced (55%) • Some intra-firm trade. H.O often coordinates assignments	• Mostly partnerships or 100% subsidiaries • A lot of movement of people
Medical Services	• Experience with advanced/specialised medicine; high quality hospitalisation • Modern management practices • Supportive role of government	• Usually consumers travel to place of production; but some foreign owned hospitals or medical facilities H/F	• Quality control I	• Favours exports (39%) • Little intra-firm	• A people oriented sector; overseas operations, mainly 100% owned subsidiaries
Motion Pictures (Production and rental receipts); Live Entertainment (theatre)	• Experience in home markets, good domestic communication (e.g. broadcasting) facilities • Government subsidies of arts	• Location bound (motion picture production) F • Sometimes customers visit place of production and sometimes vice versa H/F	• Quality of film production and TV programmes I • Theatre production usually involves non-equity contracts E	• Balanced (50%) • Little intra-firm trade	• Mixed • Again services embodied in people or bought by people who are internationally mobile

MULTINATIONAL ENTERPRISES AND SERVICES GROWTH 31

TABLE 2 (CONTINUED)

Regional Offices	• Part of MNE network; need and functions of office vary according to nature of MNEs business and extent of foreign operations	• Depends on labour, office, communication costs where R.O.s are located H/F • Work permits, taxes, etc. • Location of goods-producing units of MNEs	• All advantages relate to economies of coordination, and acting as agent on part of parent company I	• Entirely via fdi • Virtually all intra-firm trade	• All 100% owned
Restaurants, Car Rentals	• Brand name, image of product (service) • Reputation and experience • Referral systems • Economics of scale and scope • Tie up deals with airlines and hotels	• Location bound F • Foreign earnings through tourists and businessmen visiting exporting countries H	• Franchising can protect quality control E	• As with hotels	• As with hotels
Telecommunications	• Knowledge intensive • Technology, capital, scale economies (e.g., ability to operate an international communications network) • Government support	• Government regulation of trade and production H • Sometimes location bound (telephone communications) H/F	• Large costs often require consortia of firms • Quality of 'goods' part of service often needs hierarchical control (e.g., by companies like AT&T); otherwise service usually provided on leasing basis, or exported	• Balanced (50%) • Some intra-firm trade	• Mixture, but a good deal of leasing
Tourism	• Reputation in providing satisfactory experience goods • Economics of scope (kind of travel portfolio offered) • Bargaining power • Quality of deals made with airlines, hotels, shipping companies, etc.	• Need for local tour agents and support facilities F • Customers initially originate from home country H • Costs of supplying local facilities usually lower F	• Coordination of itineraries, need for quality control of ancillary services for tourists I • Preferences of host governments for local support facilities E • Economics of transaction costs from vertical integration	• 90% plus exports either of final or intermediate services	• Large tour operators have local offices, others may use agents
Transportation Shipping & Airlines	• Highly capital intensive • Government support measures, and/or control over routes of foreign carriers • Economics of scope and coordination • Linkages with producing goods firms (in shipping)	• Essentially location linking H/F • Need for local sales office, terminal maintenance and support facilities (at airports and docks) F	• Logistical management • Advantages of vertical integration I • Quality control I	• Favours exports (39%) • A lot of intra-firm trade involving non-service companies	• Mostly 100% owned subsidiaries • Some consortia of TNC's

[1] The % in brackets represents proportion of sales of U.S. foreign affiliates to U.S. exports plus sales of foreign affiliates.

[2] From U.S. Office of Technology Assessment (1986)

PARTICULAR FEATURES OF SERVICE ACTIVITIES AS THEY AFFECT THE OLI VARIABLES INFLUENCING INTERNATIONAL PRODUCTION

1. Because of the greater human element in the provision of services; and because each service is a 'one-off' operation, *quality variability* is the most important feature which distinguishes the competitive or ownership-specific advantages of the providers of services, compared with those of goods. This characteristic further suggests that where firms perceive they can best control the quality of their intermediate products by owning these products, they will prefer the hierarchial to the market route of marketing this asset.

2. The *economies of scope* are an 'inherent' competitive advantage of some service sectors, e.g. wholesale and retail trading, insurance and securities dealing. These advantages result from the common governance of separate activities, and hence cannot be marketed to independent firms.

3. The *intangibility and perishability* of pure services mean they require face to face contact for an exchange. Trade can then only take place where a foreign buyer or seller is in the same place as a domestic seller or buyer. This suggests that the locational choice of companies supplying services may be more constrained than that facing goods-producing firms.

4. Because some services are regarded as strategically and/or culturally sensitive, their markets tend to be more *highly regulated* than their goods counterparts. In the past, this has restricted the activities of MNEs and/or encouraged non-equity alliances between foreign and domestic firms, in such sectors as banking, insurance, railways, education, health and broadcasting and television. Recent moves towards the deregulation of some service markets, e.g. finance and insurance, have been followed by a marked increase of MNE activity in these sectors.

5. Rather more than in most goods sectors, services are much more *differentiated* and geared to supplying particular niche markets. Thus it is possible for MNEs to exist side by side with companies in supplying different segments of the same market. This is particularly true of services such as banking, construction, hotels, accounting, legal and personal services; with MNEs catering for the international and/or top end of these markets.

6. Services, more than goods, have the property of being jointly demanded and/or supplied; examples include tourist-related services, banking and financial services, and trade-related services. Often this property leads to agglomerative economies of location; while economies of scope, transaction costs associated with buyer or seller uncertainty (services are 'experience' rather than 'inspection' products) lead to internalisation of intermediate product markets.

APPENDIX I

THE ECLECTIC PARADIGM OF INTERNATIONAL PRODUCTION

1. *Ownership Specific Advantages* (of enterprises of one nationality (or affiliates of same) over those of another)

MULTINATIONAL ENTERPRISES AND SERVICES GROWTH   33

    a. Property right and/or intangible asset advantages
    Product innovations, production management, organisational and marketing systems, innovatory capacity; non-codifiable knowledge; 'bank' of human capital experience; marketing, finance, know-how, etc.
    b. Advantages of common governance
      i. which those branch plants of established enterprises may enjoy over *de novo* firms. Those due mainly to size and established position of enterprise, e.g. economies of scope and specialisation; monopoly power, better resource capacity and usage. Exclusive or favoured access to inputs, e.g., labour, natural resources, finance, information. Ability to obtain inputs on favoured terms (e.g., due to size or monopsonistic influence). Exclusive or favoured access to product markets. Access to resources of parent company at marginal cost. Economies of joint supply (not only in production, but in purchasing, marketing, finance, etc., arrangements).
     ii. which specifically arise because of multinationality. Multinationality enhances above advantages by offering wider opportunities. More favoured access to and/or better knowledge about international markets, e.g. for information, finance, labour, etc. Ability to take advantage of geographic differences in factor endowments, markets. Ability to diversify or reduce risks, e.g., in different currency areas and/or political scenarios.
2. *Internalisation Incentive Advantages* (i.e. to protect against or exploit market failure)
  Avoidance of search and negotiating costs.
  To avoid costs of enforcing property rights.
  Buyer uncertainty (about nature and value of inputs (e.g., technology) being sold).
  Where market does not permit price discrimination.
  Need of seller to protect quality of intermediate or final products.
  To capture economies of interdependent activities (see b. above).
  To compensate for absence of future markets.
  To avoid or exploit government intervention (e.g., quotas, tariffs, price controls, tax differences, etc.).
  To control supplies and conditions of sale of inputs (including technology).
  To control market outlets (including those which might be used by competitors).
  To be able to engage in practices, e.g., cross-subsidisation, predatory pricing, leads and lags, transfer pricing, etc., as a competitive (or anti-competitive) strategy.
3. *Location Specific Variables* (these may favour home or host countries)
  Spacial distribution of natural and created resource endowments and markets.
  Input prices, quality and productivity, e.g. labour, energy, materials, components, semi-finished goods.
  International transport and communications costs.
  Investment incentives and disincentives (including performance requirements, etc.)
  Artificial barriers (e.g. import controls) to trade in goods.
  Infrastructure provisions (commercial, legal, educational, transport and communication).
  Psychic distance (language, cultural, business, customs, etc., differences).
  Economies of centralisation of R & D production and marketing.
  Economic system and policies of government; the institutional framework for resource allocation.

APPENDIX II

THE OECD ECONOMIC CLASSIFICATION OF SERVICES

I. *Services comprising mainly the transport of passengers,*
  goods or information
   A. *Transport of passengers*
        of freight, by various means (sea,
        air, road, rail, inland waterway,
        pipeline transport etc.)
   B. *Broadcasting and telecommunications*

II. *Services comprising mainly in making goods available*
     to users
     A. *Provision of tangible goods*
         1. *Real estate*
         −rental
         −storage, warehousing
         2. *Equipment* (rental, leasing, etc)
     B. *Provision of intangibles*
         −licensing
         −franchising
         −supply of information, documentation
III. *Services comprising mainly in making capital available*
      to clients
      A. *Temporarily:* banking, credit and loans
      B. *Permanently, but only on an event-linked basis:*
          insurance
IV. *Services for insuring the preservation, maintenance or*
      renovation of existing goods
 V. *Services linked mainly to the capabilities or specific*
      expertise of the service provider
      A. *Services usually rendered by individuals*
          (e.g.: performing artists, members of para-legal
             professions, consultants, architects, phys-
             icians, accountants)
      B. *Services usually rendered by undertakings*
          −engineering
          −advertising
          −computer services (software)
          −organisation
          −security
VI. *Intermediation services* (consisting mainly in bringing
       together producer and consumer economic agents)
       −broking
       −estate agencies
       −travel agencies
       −certain banking services

NOTES

This paper is based on work carried out for the UN Centre for Transnational Corporations
and presented at the World Economics Conference, Keele. I am grateful for being allowed to
use some of the material. A revised version of the paper was also presented to a conference on
Trade and Investment in Services organised by the Instititut für Weltwirtschaft in June 1988.

   1. For the purpose of this paper, we define a product as the output of productive activity, a
      good as a *tangible* product, and a service as an *intangible* product.
   2. Where U = total cost of a service to the user, P_i and R_i are costs incurred by the producer
      and the user independently of each other, as P_s and R_s are the costs incurred by the
      producer and consumer during their interaction, then the simultaneity factor (S) is equal
      to $P_s + R_s/U$.
   3. Unique in the sense that it may not be exactly repeated, although it may be 'consumed' by
      a large number of consumers at the same time (e.g. a lecture or packaged tour).
   4. But only some. An unpublished paper by Grubel and Hammes (1987) suggests that in
      industrial countries the demand for services has remained a constant fraction of real
      consumption. The authors argue that this demand has been sustained as a result of the
      increased female participation ratio in the labour force and the monetisation of
      household activities most of which involve the production of services. In some sectors,

goods have replaced services (e.g. vacuum cleaners and washing machines for domestic and laundry services, and television and video recorders for cinema entertainment).

5. Compare, for example, the widely different patterns of demand for food, clothing, furniture and cars compared with a computer print-out, an advertising campaign, an airline journey or an insurance policy.

6. Writers such as Porter [1980, 1985, 1986] refer to the advantages which one competitor has over another competitor (or another competitor) as competitive advantages, but, to the industrial economist, these are more accurately described as monopolistic (in the sense that for some time period at least) the firm possessing the advantages has an exclusive or privileged right to them [Lall, 1977]. But even this latter nomenclature can be misleading when such advantages arise from the superior co-ordinating advantages which one firm may possess over another [Casson, 1987].

7. The word 'ownership' is preferred to 'firm' as it emphasises the generic characteristic of competitive advantages. We accept, of course, that these may vary according to particular attributes of firms (e.g. size, age, management strategy, etc.). We reserve the term firm-specific characteristics (rather than advantages) to embrace these.

8. Including 'potential' as well as actual competitors. Here the theory of contestable markets is directly relevant.

9. This may be based on 'natural' resources, or 'engineered' by economic or political institutions indigenous to the country in question [see Scott and Lodge, 1985].

10. For a detailed elaboration of the concept of competitive advantage, see Porter [1980, 1985 and 1986] and Dunning [1981: 80].

11. While payments for technology, management and administrative services are usually included as 'trade in services', profits from foreign direct investment are not. This is not really satisfactory as part of the profits (i.e. over and above the opportunity cost of risk capital) should be thought of as a payment for the services of real assets provided by MNEs. For a reasoned case of why the earnings on foreign direct investment should be included as services, see Rugman [1986].

12. As Dorothy Riddle points out in her book (1986a) and her paper for UNCTC (1987), the role of services in economic development has been inaccurately described as an adjunct to industrialisation rather than as an engine of growth in themselves. The classification of economies into pre-industrial, industrial and post-industrial is then unhelpful; services, particularly producer services, act as a crucial part of a country's infrastructure whatever its level of development. What varies is *which* services are provided and *the way* in which these services are provided.

13. But, as Dorothy Riddle notes [1987: 57], the Andean Pact nations have recently 'reversed their conservative stance on FDI in services'.

14. The question of the extent to which the recent expansion of output of services has led to a centralisation or decentralisation of the location of these services has received scant attention in the literature. Neither is there any literature on the comparative locational economics of high value compared with low value service activities or of innovatory compared with mature services, as there is in the case of the manufacturing sector.

15. One definition of a MNE is that it is a firm which internalises intermediate product markets across national boundaries [Casson, 1986]. These products might take the form of goods or services. Strictly speaking, *cross-border* internalisation can take place only when a firm adds value-creating activities in a foreign country to those it undertakes in its home economy; in this case, foreign direct investment automatically leads to intra-firm trade in goods or services. In fact, an MNE may sometimes achieve the same effects of internalisation without ownership, in the sense that some contractual agreements assign control over the use of intermediate products to one or other of the contracting parties.

16. Dorothy Riddle [1987] makes the interesting point that 'service companies have more legal options regarding their forms of foreign investment than do manufacturing companies, as the latter by the very nature of their services are forced to establish manufacturing plants and distribution centres abroad'. By contrast Riddle adds 'service companies may establish more outposts of the corporation managed by a small number of skilled employees, operate joint ventures or set up subsidiaries'.

17. For example, a US Department of State Study [1971] reported that the financial sector, and notably banking and insurance, was second only to the extractive industry in the

incidence of expropriation. More recently evidence by Kobrin [1984] suggests that this incidence has not declined [Enderwick, 1986].

18. In banking, for example, modern information technology has made it possible for managers to centralise information resources in areas such as foreign currency and economic forecasting on a global scale. In computing, IBMs worldwide communications network allows it to introduce design changes in all its manufacturing facilities around the world in a single day. Similarly, the Bechtel Group has set up a computer and communications network, which enables it to co-ordinate the activities of engineers in India, project managers in San Francisco and construction supervisors on site in Saudi Arabia.

19. An example, quoted by Fetetekuty and Hauser [1985], is that of the Mcdonnell Douglas Corporation, a manufacturing firm that developed a data-base for its internal research and development activities, and now has a separate subsidiary that provides on-line data services to the general public both in the US and abroad.

REFERENCES

Anderson, E. and H. Gatignon, 1986. 'A Transaction Costs Approach to Modes of Market Entry', *Journal of International Business Studies*, Vol.17, Fall.

Basche, J.R., 1986. *Eliminating Barriers to International Trade and Investment in Services*, New York Conference Board Research Bulletin, No.200.

Bhagwati, J., 1984, 'Splintering and Disembodiment of Services and Developing Nations', *The World Economy*, June.

Boddewyn, J.J., M.B. Halbrich, and A.C. Perry, 1986, 'Service Multinationals: Conceptualisation, Measurement and Theory', *Journal of International Business Studies*, Vol.16, Fall.

Browne, L.E., 1987, 'Services and Economic Progress: An Analysis', *Economic Impact*, Vol.57, No.1.

Buckley, P. and M.C. Casson, 1985, *The Economic Theory of the Multinational Enterprise*, London: Macmillan.

Casson, M.C., 1982, 'Transaction Costs and the Theory of the Multinational Enterprise', in A.M. Rugman (ed.), *New Theories of the Multinational Enterprise*, New York: St. Martins Press.

Casson, M.C. and associates, 1986, *Multinationals and World Trade*, London: Allen & Unwin.

Casson, M.C. 1987, *The Firm and the Market*, Oxford: Basil Blackwell.

Caves, R.E., 1974, 'Causes of Direct Foreign Investment: Foreign Firms' Share in Canadian and United Kingdom Manufacturing Industries', *Review of Economics and Statistics*, Vol.56, August.

Caves, R.E., 1982, *Multinational Enterprise and Economic Analysis*, Cambridge: Cambridge University Press.

Cho, K.R., 1986, 'Determinants of Multinational Banks', *Management International Review*, No.1.

Contractor, F.J., 1980, 'The Composition of Licensing Fees and Arrangements as a Function of Economic Development of Technology Recipient Nations', *Journal of International Business Studies*, Vol.XI, Winter.

Contractor, F.J. and P. Lorange, 1988, *Cooperative Strategies in International Business*, New York: Praeger.

Daniels, P.W., 1982, *Service Industries: Growth and Location*, Cambridge; Cambridge University Press.

Davidson, W.H., 1980, 'The Location of Foreign Direct Investment Activity: Country Characteristics and Experience effects', *Journal of International Business Studies*, 11, Fall.

Dunning, J.H., 1981, *International Production and the Multinational Enterprise*, London: Allen & Unwin.

Dunning, J.H., 1983, 'Market Power of the Firm and the International Transfer of

MULTINATIONAL ENTERPRISES AND SERVICES GROWTH 37

Technology', *International Journal of Industrial Organisation*, Vol.1.

Dunning, J.H., 1988, 'The Eclectic Paradigm of International Production: A Restatement and Some Possible Extensions', *Journal of International Business Studies*, Vol.19, Spring.

Dunning, J.H. and M. McQueen, 1981, 'The Eclectic Theory of Production: A case study of the international Hotel Industry', *Managerial and Decision Economics*, Vol.21, December.

Dunning, J.H. and G. Norman, 1983, 'The Theory of the Multinational Enterprise: An Application to Multinational Office Location', *Environment and Planning*, A, Vol.15.

Dunning, J.H. and G. Norman, 1987, 'The Location Choice of Offices of International Companies', *Environment and Planning*, A, Vol.19.

Enderwick, P., 1986, *Some Economies of Service-Sector Multinational Enterprises* (mimeo).

Feketekuty, G. and G. Hauser, 1985, 'Information Technology and Trade in Services', *Economic Impact*, Vol.52.

Gershuny, J. and I. Miles, 1983, *The New Service Economy: The Transformation of Employment in Industrial Societies*, London: Frances Pinter.

Gray, H.P., 1987, *International Trade in Services: Four Distinguishing Features* (mimeo).

Grubel, H., 1968, 'Internationally Diversified Portfolios: Welfare Gains and Capital Flows', *American Economic Review*, Vol.58, December.

Grubel, H., 1986, *Direct and Embodied Trade in Services*, Service Project Discussion Paper, 86–1, Vancouver: The Fraser Institute.

Grubel, H., 1987, 'Traded Services are Embodied in Materials or People', *The World Economy*, Vol.10, September.

Grubel, H. and D.L. Hammes, 1987, 'Household Service Consumption and Monetization' (mimeo).

Hill, P.T., 1977, 'On Goods and Services', *Review of Income Wealth*, Vol.23, December.

Hirsch, S., 1976, 'An International Trade and Investment Theory of the Firm', *Oxford Economic Papers*, Vol.28, July.

Hirsch, S., 1986, *International Transactions in Services and in Service Intensive Goods* (mimeo).

Hymer, S., 1960 and 1976, *The International Operations of National Firms: A Study of Direct Foreign Investment*, Ph.D. dissertation (1960), published by M.I.T. Press 1976.

Johnson, H., 1970, 'The Efficiency and Welfare Implications of the Multinational Corporation', in C.P. Kindleberger (ed.), *The International Corporation: A Symposium*, Cambridge, MA: M.I.T. Press.

Knickerbocker, F., 1973, *Oligopolistic Reaction and the Multinational Enterprise*, Boston: Harvard University Press.

Kobrin, S.J., 1984, 'Expropriation as an Attempt to Control Foreign Firms in LDCs: Trends from 1960 to 1979', *International Studies Quarterly*, Vol.28.

Kojima, K., 1978, *Direct Foreign Investment*, New York: Praeger.

Kojima, K., 1982, 'Macroeconomic versus International Business Models of Foreign Direct Investment', *Hitosubashi Journal of Economics*, Vol.25.

Lall, S., 1980, 'Monopolistic Advantages and Foreign involvement by U.S. Manufacturing Industry', *Oxford Economic Papers*, Vol.32.

Levitan, S.A., 1985, 'Services and Long-term Structural Change,' *Economic Impact*.

Livingston, S., 1982, 'The Role of Services in Trade', *The Fletcher Forum*, reprinted in *Economic Impact*, 1985.

Lancaster, K., 1971, *Consumer Demand: A New Approach*, New York: Columbia University Press.

Magee, S., 1977, 'Information and Multinational Corporations: An Appropriability Theory of Direct Foreign Investment', in J. Bhagwati (ed.), *The International Economic Order*, Cambridge, MA: M.I.T. Press.

Mannisto, M., 1981, 'Hospital Management Companies Expand Foreign Operations', *Journal of the American Hospital Association*, Vol.55, No.3.

Nicholas, S.J., 1983, 'Agency Contract, Institutional Modes, and the Transaction of Foreign Direct Investment by British Manufacturing Multinationals before 1939', *Journal of Economic History*, Vol.43.

Oman, C., 1984, *New Forms of International Investment in Developing Countries*, Paris: O.E.C.D.

Porter, M.E., 1980, *Competitive Strategy: Techniques for Analyzing Industries and Competitors,* New York: Free Press.

Porter, M.E., 1985, *Competitive Advantage: Creating and Sustaining Superior Performance,* New York: Free Press.

Porter, M.E. (ed.), 1986, *Competition in Global Industries,* Boston: Harvard Business School Press.

Riddle, D.I., 1986a, *Service Led Growth: The Role of the Service Sector in World Development,* New York: Praeger.

Riddle, D.I., 1986b, *The Service Audit: A Key to National Competitive Positioning* (mimeo).

Riddle, D.I., 1987, *The Role of Service Transnational Corporations in the Development Process* (mimeo).

Root, F.R. and Ahmed, A.A., 1978, 'The Influence of Policy Instruments on Manufacturing Direct Foreign Investment in Developing Countries', *Journal of International Business Studies,* Vol.9, Winter.

Rugman, A.M., 1979, *International Diversification and the Multinational Enterprise,* Lexington, MA: Lexington Books.

Rugman, A.M., 1981, *Inside the Multinationals: The Economics of Internal Markets,* New York: Columbia University Press.

Rugman, A.M., 1986, *A Transaction Cost Approach to Trade in Services* (mimeo).

Sampson, A., 1982, *The Money Leaders,* New York: Viking Press.

Sampson, G.P. and R.H. Snape, 1975, 'Identifying the Issues in Trade in Services', *The World Economy,* June.

Sauvant, K.P., 1986, *International Transactions in Services,* Boulder and London: Westview Press.

Seymour, H., R. Flanagan, and G. Norman, 1985, *International Investment in the Construction Industry: An Application of the Eclectic Approach,* University of Reading, Discussion Papers in International Investment and Business Studies, No.87, July,

Schwamm, H. and P. Merciai, 1985, *The Multinationals and the Services,* Geneva: I.R.M. Multinational Report, No.6, October–December.

Scott, B.R. and G.C. Lodge (eds.), – *U.S. Competitiveness in the World Economy,* Boston: Harvard Business School Press.

Shelp, R.K., 1981, *Beyond Industrialization: Ascendancy of the Global Service Economy,* New York: Praeger.

Shelp, R.K., 1984, *Service Industries and Economic Development,* New York: Praeger.

Shelp, R.K., 1985, 'Service Technology and Economic Development', *Economic Impact 52.*

Teece, D., 1983, 'Technological and Organisational Factors in the theory of the Multinational Enterprise', in M.C. Casson (ed.), *One Growth of International Business,* London: Allen and Unwin.

Teece, D., 1986, *Capturing Value from Innovation, Integration, Strategic Partnering and Investment Decisions* (mimeo).

UNCTAD, 1985, *Services and the Development Process,* New York: UN E.85.II,D.13.

UNCTC, 1979, *Transnational Corporations in Advertising,* New York: UN, Sales No. E.79.II,A.2.

UNCTC., 1982, *Transnational Corporations and Trans Border Data Flows,* New York: UN, Sales No. 82.II,A.4.

UNCTC, 1983, *Transnational Corporations in World Development,* New York.

UNCTC, 1987a, *Role of Transnational Banks,* New York: UNCTC E/C.10/1987/13, 29.1.87.

UNCTC, 1987b, *Ongoing and Future Research: The Role of Transnational Corporations in Services, Including Transborder Data Flows,* New York: UNCTC, E/C,10/1987/ 11,26.1.87.

UNCTC, 1988, *Transnational Corporations in World Development,* UNCTC E.88.II, A. 7 June.

US Department of Commerce, 1985, *U.S. Direct Investment Abroad: 1982 Benchmark Survey Data,* Washington: Government Printing Office.

US Department of State, 1971, *Nationalization, Expropriation and Other Takings of U.S. and Certain Foreign Property Since 1960,* Washington Bureau of Intelligence and Research.

MULTINATIONAL ENTERPRISES AND SERVICES GROWTH   39

US Office of the U.S. Trade Representative, 1984, *U.S. National Study on Trade in Services,* Washington: Government Printing Office.

US Office of Technology Assessment, 1986, *Trade in Services. Exports and Foreign Revenues,* Washington: Government Printing Office.

Vaitsos, C.V., 1986, *Transnational Rendering of Services, National Development and the Role of TNCs,* paper prepared for UNDP/UNCTAD/ECLA Project RLA/82/012, 1986.

Van Rens, J.H.P., 1982, *Multinational in the Transport Industry,* paper produced for Conference on Multinationals in Transition, Paris: I.R.M., 15–16 November 1982.

Vernon, R., 1966, 'International investment and international trade in the product cycle', *Quarterly Journal of Economics,* Vol.80, May.

Vernon, R., 1979, 'The Product Cycle Hypothesis in a New International Environment', *Oxford Bulletin of Economics and Statistics,* Vol.41, November.

Yannopoulos, G.N., 1983, 'The Growth of Transnational Banking', in *The Growth of International Business,* edited by M.C. Casson, London: Allen & Unwin.

International Journal of Advertising, 1994, **13**, 77–92

International Advertising Strategies by NIC Multinationals: The Case of a Korean Firm

Dong-Sung Cho, Jinah Choi & Youjae Yi

Seoul National University, Korea

INTRODUCTION

As the firms in the developing nations globalize their business, they tend to put more emphasis on advertising in the international market. For instance, most international advertisements by Korean firms had been either one-time product advertisements or co-operative advertisements involving distributors in the 1960s and 1970s. At the time these firms had typically conducted OEM (original equipment manufacturer) brand-orientated businesses. Since the 1980s, however, the firms have begun to depend more heavily on the corporate advertising which builds up brand image and company awareness. This trend manifests itself of their business practices from the OEM brand-orientated business to the business with their own brands.

A number of studies have dealt with the advertising practices of multinational corporations (MNCs) based in advanced nations (Aaker and Myers, 1989; Killough, 1978; Onkvist and Shaw, 1987; Peebles *et al.*, 1976). Although less frequent, there is still a substantial volume of research conducted in the general area of international marketing practices of MNCs based in either developing countries or newly industrialized countries (NICs) (Levy, 1988; Wortzel and Wortzel, 1981). Nevertheless, to date not much attention has been given to the international advertising strategies of the firms in developing countries. This article attempts to fill this gap by studying the international advertising strategies of NIC-based firms.

This article develops a conceptual model to describe how the international advertising strategy changes as a firm progresses through the sequential stages of internationalization. This conceptualization is based on the literature survey regarding the components of advertising strategy at each stage of internationalization of marketing (export marketing, multinational marketing and global marketing). A case of one Korean international firm is used to validate the proposed model.

We chose a case method as a research methodology, due to both the exploratory nature of the subject and a very limited number of truly internationalized firms in NICs. There are a handful of NICs around the world, but among them, Korea has the most large-sized multinationals. In the 1990 Fortune Listing of the 500 largest industrial companies outside the US, Korea had eleven firms listed, outnumbering other NICs. As a representative case, we chose Samsung Electronics Co. This is one of the largest Korean firms that are already internationalized and that have production and sales outlets in various foreign locations with substantial experiences on mass marketing. The case study is based on extensive interviews with members of international departments in Samsung Electronics and its advertising agency, Cheil Communications. In addition, considerable literature such as periodicals of Cheil Communications, monthly and yearly reports of Cheil Communications to Samsung Electronics, and the *Korea Advertisement Almanac* were used as references (Cheil Communications, 1986, 1988, 1990; Samsung Electronics, 1989).

CONCEPTUAL FRAMEWORK

Dimensions of international advertising strategy
This study defines international advertising strategy as an integrated approach of the following three sequential processes: (1) establishment of the advertising objectives which are to be co-ordinated with the business objectives and overall goals of the firm; (2) generation of alternative plans on various dimensions of international advertising by taking into account internal business environment (such as past results of advertising, budget and organizational structure) and external environment (such as demand conditions, target segments, competition, and economic, social, cultural, and technological factors); (3) selection of the best strategy among alternative plans (Colvin *et al.*, 1980; Jain, 1990; Keegan, 1989; Miracle, 1968).

The most fundamental issue of international advertising strategy is a firm's choice among three alternative strategies: extension, adaptation, and creation (Keegan, 1989; Quelch and Hoff, 1986; Sorenson and Wiechmann, 1975). The three basic strategies mentioned above can be applied to various dimensions of advertising such as appeals, visuals (illustration and layout), and copy. The manager of an international advertising department has to decide on the choice of advertising message and agency, media, organizational structure, and budget. The manager also has to measure and analyse advertising effectiveness and decide whether or not to use co-operative advertising with distributors.

This study focuses on decision variables of international advertising strategy, namely, selection of message, organization, advertising agency, and media. It excludes factors that are external to the development of strategy such as setting advertising budget or measuring advertising effectiveness. However, this study addresses the issue of using corporate advertising versus product advertising. The summary of descriptions on the various dimensions of international advertising is presented in Table 1.

One important dimension of the international advertising strategy is whether to standardize the contents of advertising message internationally or to adapt to individual markets (Britt, 1974; Donnelly and Ryans, 1969; Levitt, 1983). The decision on this issue guides the direction of the international advertising strategy as well as other dimensions such as organizational structure and advertising agency selection.

Under the assumption that consumer preferences are homogeneous across different countries, and that these preferences can be satisfied under similar purchase patterns, the standardization strategy has many advantages such as clarity of decision-making, ease of implementation, low cost, efficient operation, co-ordinated image, and world-wide usage of good advertising ideas (Fatt, 1967). On the other hand, the adaptation strategy is preferred on the grounds that economic, social, and cultural environments vary widely in different countries, that the stages on the product life cycle patterns differ for each product, and that media practices and consumer tastes change across national borders. More recently, however, the mixed strategy between the two approaches is becoming more acceptable in the international advertising field (Buzzel, 1968; Onkvist and Shaw, 1987).

The organizational form of advertising may vary; it is sometimes centralized, sometimes decentralized or sometimes in the form of combination. In the case of centralization, advertising functions such as preparation of advertising, selection of media and advertising agency and budgeting are controlled by the head office. This structure is appropriate when the business area is not geographically large. In the case of decentralization, decisions regarding advertising functions are delegated to local offices or subsidiaries in foreign countries. This helps them to find the advertising strategy that fits foreign market situations, while solving communication problems between the head office and the branch offices. Under the combination of the above two structures, the budget and the main direction of advertising are determined at the head office while advertising production and agency selection are performed by the branch offices.

An international firm can select the advertising agency among domestic agencies, foreign agencies and branch agencies of multinational agencies. A firm may use more than one type of agency by hiring local agencies for managing the respective foreign markets and by employing a domestic agency for co-ordinating the foreign operations.

The media for international advertising consist of global media and local media. The global media (such as *Time* or *Newsweek*) have a world-wide distribution to highly educated and high income readers, and have high credibility. The local media, on the other hand, have the advantage of attracting a more specific target audience. Types of media can be divided into print media such as newspapers and magazines, audio-visual media, and outdoor displays (see Table 1).

Table 1 *Dimension of global advertising strategy*

Dimension		Alternative		
Type of advertisement	corporate advertisement			product advertisement
Message	standardization	→[1]	mixed	→ adaptation
Organization	centralization			decentralization
Agency	domestic agency		local agency	global agency
Media	local media			global media
	print		audio-visual	others (outdoor/bus etc.)

1 Arrows represent the evolutionary process

Factors influencing the international advertising strategy

A firm's choice on the international advertising strategy is influenced by both internal and external factors (Jain, 1990; Keegan, 1989). The internal factors are defined as the internal conditions faced by a firm. They include the firm's perspective on internationalization, the top executive's perspective on international advertising, the firm's marketing objectives, type and extent of the foreign market penetration, the firm's resources allocated to advertising (mainly budget and manpower), four Ps of marketing, and international marketing organization. The external factors are defined as the international environment faced by the advertising industry. They can be divided into three parts: socio-cultural factors such as culture, language, education, religion, attitude, beliefs, and class structure; economic factors such as size and characteristics of domestic and international market; and political and legal factors.

Since the firm's internal factors are different for individual firms and for different stages that the firms are in, it is generally regarded that the internal factors cannot be used as independent variables. However, a study by Cho (1987) concluded that the internal factors could be used as independent variables to explain the international marketing strategy by the Korean firms. This is because Korea's typical firms went through the internationalization process at about the same time, with very similar motives and behaviours, thus experiencing similar development phases. Among the internal factors, the firm's perspective on internationalization and the type and extent of the foreign market penetration can be categorized according to the stage of the globalization process. This research will take these two factors as independent variables and examine their influence on the Korean companies in developing the international advertising strategy.

Before going on to the next section, it should be noted that Korea is a developing country whose export market at the beginning of internationalization was larger than the domestic market. Therefore, the international advertising by Korean companies was not an extension or adaptation of domestic advertising as would be the case with advanced nations. Rather, it progressed independently without much influence by domestic advertising from the beginning. The discussion on stages of international advertising presented below should be viewed from this perspective.

STAGES OF INTERNATIONALIZATION BY KOREAN FIRMS

Korean firms have gone through internationalization from the domestic-orientated stage to the export-orientated stage, then to the multinationally-orientated stage, and will eventually move toward the globally-orientated stage (Cho, 1989). The summary in Table 2 of the stages of internationalization by the firms of developing countries has been supported by numerous studies (e.g. Keegan, 1989; Wortzel and Wortzel, 1981).

At the first stage, a firm performs only domestic marketing and limits its activities within the nation without doing any international marketing activities. The firm interacts with foreign markets through importation of parts and materials, semi-finished and finished products. Slowly moving to the second stage, the firm starts to engage in indirect exportation through middlemen or indirect distributors who take care of all the marketing efforts abroad. At the third stage, a firm enters foreign markets

Table 2 *Types of marketing and advertising performed by Korean firms at each stage of internationalization*

Stage of internationalization	Type of marketing	Type of advertising
1. Import	Domestic marketing	Domestic advertising
2. Indirect export		
3. Direct export	Export marketing	Export advertising
4. Overseas branches		
5. Foreign direct investment (in simple assembly line operation)	Multinational marketing	Multinational advertising
6. Full scale operation in foreign country (production and marketing adaptation)		
7. Co-operative contracts, foreign licensing, franchising, joint investment		
8. Joint production in third country		
9. Multinational mergers and alliances		
10. Formation of the global firm	Global marketing	Global advertising

directly and starts to conduct export marketing. It first organizes an export department at the headquarters, then establishes sales branches or subsidiaries overseas, thus moving to the fourth stage. At the fourth stage, the firm still focuses more on managing production processes and deals with large distributors rather than analysing and penetrating into foreign markets itself.

At the fifth stage, a firm starts to relocate production facilities either in advanced nations to overcome trade protectionism and get market access, or in third-world countries to minimize production costs. At this stage, the firm also restructures production configuration to fit to the specific market environments in foreign countries and adapt to the needs of foreign customers. The firm usually establishes a local marketing subsidiary to take care of distribution functions in each local market. In the course of the firm's continued direct investments overseas, the number of in-dependently operating local marketing subsidiaries grows, forming a multinational marketing system. A firm advances the foreign operation through the sixth stage to the ninth stage, as shown in Table 2.

The firm enters the tenth stage of global marketing during this period. At this stage, nationalistic interests take less priority, and more firms make international mergers and alliances and ultimately form global corporations which produce products at low-cost locations and distribute them throughout the world (Porter, 1986; Cho, 1984, 1989). The firm at this stage makes the marketing plans that reflect the differences in the economic environments and the competitive situations in various foreign countries.

It could be said that Korea's representative firms in the electronics industry (namely, Samsung, Gold Star and Daewoo) have entered the threshold of globalization. At the globalization stage, the firms adopt an aggressive 'push strategy' toward distributors, focus on direct advertising to consumers, and actively market their own brands by developing new products or improving the existing products for foreign markets.

International advertising strategy of Korean firms by stage

Along with the stages of internationalization of the Korean firms, international advertising can also be divided into three stages: export advertising, multinational advertising, and global advertising (see Table 2).

Export advertising (1960s–late 1970s)
Under the export promotion policy adopted by the government in the 1960s, Korean firms took an active role in exporting products such as textile and garments. The Korean firms at the time were unable to enter foreign markets by themselves, but relied on professional traders and foreign buyers through OEM brand exportation. As a result, most of the marketing activities were directed toward the distributors and middlemen in trade.

Entering the late 1970s, the Korean firms experienced difficulties in the export market due to waves of oil shocks, escalating materials costs, global recessions and growing protectionism in the advanced nations. To overcome these barriers, many Korean firms opened branch offices in foreign countries to perform international marketing activities more aggressively. According to Wortzel and Wortzel (1981), this stage is part of the multinational marketing stage and includes progressive marketing based on production concept and part of product concept. At this stage, a firm tries to maintain control on distribution channels by adopting a 'push strategy' aimed at distributors, and by introducing product advertising aimed at general consumers to increase sales of own-brand products (Wortzel and Wortzel, 1988). In a number of major export markets, the Korean firms established local subsidiaries to penetrate the market more effectively through stock sales and other approaches. Examples of such cases include Gold Star Electronics Inc, a marketing subsidiary of Gold Star founded in 1978 in the US, and Samsung Electronics in New York.

Although international advertising was commenced in the 1960s, the advertising functions performed at this stage were very limited in nature to export, with most advertising targeted at foreign buyers using trade journals. Among the multinational firms, companies in export trading or international construction did not engage in much international advertising for two reasons. They either did not realize the importance of international advertising for the reasons cited above or they thought the boom in the Middle East would continue. On the other hand, the service

Service Industries in the Global Economy II

industries such as airlines and hotels showed more interest in international advertising. For example, Korean Air Lines, hotels, travel agencies and travel bureaux actively engaged in international advertising.

At the later part of this stage, many of the large Korean business groups known as 'Chaebols' established general trading companies as an international frontier of the groups' affiliated companies. Some of these groups also established in-house advertising agencies. In fact, most of the advertising agencies in Korea were in-house agencies. At this stage, most of the firms used domestic in-house agencies. Development of international advertising was the main objective of these in-house agencies of Korea's big business groups. The firms without in-house agencies such as Sunkyong, Ssangyong and Daewoo generally performed production and implementation by themselves and advertised in well-known international media by contacting media representatives (Koh, 1981). One of the tasks of these general trading companies and in-house advertising agencies was to organize advertising at the group level. The majority of their advertisements were corporate advertisements rather than product advertisements, because the main purpose of advertising at that time was to increase the awareness and credibility of the corporation and to improve its image.

In the late 1970s, Gold Star began to export home appliances such as televisions, radios and cassette players under its own brand name and started product advertising with emphasis on dependable quality at low cost. Soon the other competitors followed.

In each of these companies, the organizations responsible for international advertising consisted of two categories: (1) non-specialized departments such as advertising, planning, international advertising, or international trade, which carried out planning functions; and (2) international divisions at the headquarters of the company and the domestic advertising agency which carried out media selection and implementations. As a result, most of the responsibilities involving budget, production and implementation were centralized under the authority of the head office in the homeland, and rarely did local branch offices or foreign subsidiaries carry out local advertising independently of the head office. The advertising messages were standardized, rather than adapted to local situations, and the media with international coverage were selected over those with local coverage. Across the industries, over 90 per cent of advertisements were placed in printed media with magazines being used the most, followed by newspapers (Koh, 1981). The rate of using audio-visual media such as television and radio was less than 10 per cent.

Multinational advertising (early 1980s–late 1980s)

Many Korean firms started to build production facilities in the foreign countries during the first half of 1980s, and they began to perform marketing functions actively in foreign markets. For example, Gold Star established a production subsidiary, Gold Star of America Inc, in 1983 in order to overcome the growing trade protection regulations undertaken by the US government and to access the end market more easily. Hyundai founded Hyundai Auto Canada Inc in Canada, and Samsung Electronics set up a production facility for television in Portugal in 1982 for the penetration into the EC market and founded Samsung International Inc in New Jersey in 1984.

During this period, a number of Korean firms such as Hyundai Motor Co, Samsung and Gold Star went into multinational operations. According to the current statistics

84   INTERNATIONAL JOURNAL OF ADVERTISING, 1994, 13

on foreign direct investment made by the Korean firms (e.g. KIET, 1990; KTPC, 1990), Samsung Electronics has thirteen production facilities in eleven countries, Gold Star nine factories in countries including Thailand, Mexico, and Indonesia, and Daewoo four production facilities in Hong Kong, France, the UK and mainland China. These Korean firms had to compete head-to-head with other multinational companies in foreign markets. The Korean firms chose to build up brand images through advertising in an effort to increase brand awareness and to differentiate their products from those produced by other companies. The proportion of product advertising, relative to corporate advertising, increased sharply and the contents of advertising messages became more confined to product images.

At this stage, the firms tended to delegate some of their advertising responsibilities to foreign subsidiaries as they developed networks of their foreign subsidiaries in their major markets. These delegations were the result of the inability of Korean advertising agencies due to their lack of international experiences. The head offices usually controlled the international advertising activities by sending staff members to international marketing or sales divisions in foreign subsidiaries.

Due to subsidiaries' lack of manpower, local or multinational advertising agencies typically carried out planning and implementation of the advertisements at the foreign subsidiaries. Consequently, most of the advertisements tended to take the form of adaptation which reflected the local conditions. The contents of the message also tended to take the form of adaptation for the same reason. For corporate advertising and new product advertising, both of which were generally controlled by the main office, standardized advertising was used. The firms at this stage still depended on newspapers and trade journals in terms of medium. However, they started to utilize more of the outdoor media (Koh, 1987).

Global advertising since the late 1980s

Korean firms gained a good deal of international advertising skills during the stage of multinational advertising. Nevertheless, the firms began to encounter problems as the advertising activities were dominated by the foreign subsidiaries. Specifically, the head offices of Korean multinational firms had difficulty in controlling the international advertising which tended to focus only on short-term gains. They also had difficulty in co-ordinating message formats and logos among the advertisements used by the subsidiaries in different countries. The main method of control used was reporting to the main office for approval at the beginning of the year for advertising plans and outdoor displays and each time for event advertising. Another method often used was to give the main office the responsibility of approving advertising budgets. At this stage, controlling and co-ordinating the activities of local subsidiaries became an important issue.

Technological advances as well as increased competition from the firms of other developing countries caused the Korean firms to realize that their international marketing capabilities had to be strengthened. Thus, they started to establish globally integrated multinational marketing and advertising networks which would build their brand images and advance their corporate identities in the global scale. At this stage, the Korean firms started to put considerable effort into co-ordinated global advertising by employing the international advertising agencies who were able to integrate their advertising activities throughout the world.

Table 3 *Characteristics of international advertising strategies at each stage*

	Stage	Export advertising	Multinational advertising	Global advertising
Dimension of advertising strategy	Main message	Corporate	Corporate + Brand	Corporate + Brand
	Message format	Standardization	Adaptation	Combination
	Advertising organization	Centralization	Decentralization	Mixed
	Agency	House agency/Main office	Local agencies	Local agencies + global agencies
	Media	Newspapers/magazines (trade journals)	Newspapers/ magazines other media	Newspapers/ magazines other media
Factors influencing strategy	Internationalization	Export-orientated	Foreign-market orientated	Global-market orientated
	Importance of international advertising	Less important	Begin to emphasize the importance	Important
	Sales organization	Export department	International department	Foreign subsidiaries
	Power given to branches	—	Not much	Production function
	Relationship to 4Ps of marketing	• Low level of product competitiveness • Price competition • Heavy dependence on existing distribution channels	• Increasing product competitiveness • Price competition • Development of new channels	• Competitiveness on quality • Non-price competitiveness • Co-ordination of distribution channels

The changes made by the Korean firms toward globalization were also influenced by the trends that were taking place in the global environment such as the economic integration in many regions of the world (such as the European Community and the American Free Trade Agreement) and the increasing globalization of the market. The global or globalized market is defined as one which can be attained by a particular product with a unique advertising appeal and message. In the global market, global firms compete with each other. The competitive environments of the electronics or automobile industries, where major Korean multinational companies compete, have already become globalized to a greater extent. Naturally, the need for integrated corporate image for the firms serving the global market has increased. The major task for the Korean firms which have reached the third stage of international advertising would be to co-ordinate the advertising format and the headline copy. This becomes an important responsibility, especially when the firms advertise in the global media. Probably one of the most successful cases in the recent history of advertising would be NEC's Davis Cup or Toyota's 'Fun to Drive'.

Many Korean firms are using global agencies to reduce the co-ordination costs while increasing the level of control. These firms can implement the globalized

Figure 1   Degree of involvement by the head office in advertising

advertising strategy by efficiently using the global agencies that have a network of agencies throughout the world. The Korean firms increasingly utilize global media by diversifying into outdoor media or telecommunication channels from their traditional dependence on print media. Table 3 summarizes the firm's internal factors that influence the dimensions of global advertising strategy, and these are listed by stage of advertising.

Figure 1 depicts the degree of involvement and control required by the head office at each of the three stages. The head office involvement is high at the first stage, decreases at the multinational advertising stage, then increases back up at the global advertising stage, but less than the first stage. The curve is shaped like a mirror image of the letter J (see Figure 1).

A CASE OF SAMSUNG ELECTRONICS COMPANY

Samsung Electronics Company was selected as a representative case for field observation and to validate the proposed framework. Samsung was chosen because it is typical of multinational firms in Korea, with an extensive network of international subsidiaries. It has a relatively long history of multinational advertising with a fairly sizeable budget allocated to overseas advertising. This case study divides the international advertising strategies of Samsung Electronics Company into three development stages. The characteristics of the international marketing strategies as well as the dimensions of advertising strategies are identified at each stage, based on the internal company statistics as well as the secondary data (e.g. Samsung Electronics, 1989).

Export advertising (early 1970s–early 1980s)

Samsung Electronics is one of the major companies of the Samsung Group, a representative of Korea's big business groups, and was established in 1969 with a main focus on exportation. Before 1977, the firm's international business organization consisted of the export section, which was established as a part of general affairs department in 1971 to perform simple export activities such as attracting foreign buyers or operating export administrations. In 1977, the export planning department was established under the electronics business division to perform product development, demand forecasting, market surveys and sales functions. Most international business activities depended heavily on the hands of foreign buyers at that time. Several foreign branches were set up to promote communication with the foreign buyers as the export quantity increased.

Samsung Electronics had a high proportion of OEM branded exportation at this stage. Samsung Electronics exported 80 per cent of its total exports in OEM brands to the large buyers in the US and Europe. OEM was a quick and easy way of increasing the quantity of exports for the firm that was relatively new, without heavy investment in consumer marketing or in building brand awareness. On international advertising, Samsung Electronics began full-scale export advertising in 1977.

The firm saw a need for export marketing as the export activities intensified. An international department was thus established in 1977 to perform its international advertising within the in-house agency, Cheil Communications Inc. Samsung Electronics founded the international promotion section in 1979 to shoulder the responsibility for international advertisements, promotions, and exhibitions, and the firm started to engage actively in its international advertising activites.

During the early period of export advertising from 1977 to 1979, the advertising done by Samsung Electronics consisted of corporate advertising which emphasized the firm's business areas, production capabilities and technological abilities, and product advertising which emphasized the particular brands of the foreign exporters or the manufacturers. The corporate advertising focused on importers and manufacturers of the electronics industry as a primary target, and foreign buyers and the international economic community as a secondary target. The company used international trade journals such as *Business Week*, *Time* and *Asian Business* and professional journals such as *Asian Electronics Union*. The campaigns used the headline, 'Advancing technology to accelerate growth', with the goal of enhancing the corporate credibility and awareness. Due to the high proportion of OEM brand exporting, the product advertisement focused on distributors in the US, Asia, Europe, the Middle East and Central and South America, mainly through trade journals, the message emphasizing high value for low cost.

The advertisements were primarily made up of products such as black and white and colour televisions, radios and cassette players. However, from 1981, advertisements featured microwave ovens and VCRs, and these products rapidly took the leading roles. With the changes in product composition, Samsung Electronics needed to strengthen its image as a technologically advanced firm and it therefore changed the direction of the advertising strategy toward Corporate Identity Programme (CIP).

This intensive CIP was used as an indication that the firm had reached the second stage. At that stage, most of the international advertisements had been developed and implemented jointly by the main office and its agency, Cheil Communications. International media (mostly magazines) were used with the global market as the major target. Consequently, the strategy used for the message format was standardization without much variation in different countries (see Table 4).

Table 4 *Characteristics of international advertising during the early years at Samsung Electronics*

	Late 1970s	Early 1980s	Mid-1980s
Product	Colour television, radio/cassette players	Colour television, microwave oven, VCR	VCR, microwave oven
Target	Importers, wholesalers and distributors	Importers, wholesalers and distributors	Consumers
Main media	Trade magazines, international media (*Time, Vision,* etc.)	trade magazines, international media (*Time, Vision,* etc.)	International media, some local media
Appealing point	Introduction of corporation	Corporate identity (CI)	Low cost/high quality
	(size, revenue, etc)	Introduction of local subsidiary	Familiarity with local market

Multinational advertising (early 1980s–late 1980s)

With its increasing share of international operations, Samsung Electronics started to experience difficulties in its export markets, due mainly to trade protectionism in many advanced nations. As a result, the firm actively set up subsidiaries in the foreign countries. The first subsidiary was set up in the US in 1978, followed by others in Germany in 1981, Portugal in 1982 and the United Kingdom in 1984. Lacking appropriate knowledge on local markets, the head office delegated much of the local marketing activities to these foreign subsidiaries. Personnel sent by the main office were usually in charge of making contacts with the distributors. For distribution in the advanced countries, the firm depended heavily on the large-scale dealers and distributors.

From the mid-1980s, however, Samsung Electronics switched its export strategy from OEM brand exporting to its own-brand exporting, in order to strengthen its image and improve profitability in the long run. With these motives, the firm started to increase the proportion of exports under its own name in areas like Central and South America, Southeast Asia and the Middle East, where economic conditions were at a relatively lower level and where they were able to build their own strong distribution channels. As a result of the new strategy, the firm recorded about 35 per cent of the total export value under its own brand in 1988.

The firm supported small-scale advertising and promotional activities through local agencies in order to introduce its local subsidiary and product lines. As the export quantity increased and the product lines and export markets diversified, the firm increased the advertising and promotional budgets.

The advertisements can be divided into main office-sponsored ones and local office-sponsored ones, depending on who performed the marketing functions at this stage. The main office-sponsored advertisements were developed by Cheil Communications. They were mainly either corporate advertisements to enhance overall company image or launching advertisements to introduce new and high-end products. These advertisements appeared in the airline's in-flight magazines or in the international magazines using the headline, 'Welcome to Samsung's 3As Family', which emphasized modern technology. The local office-sponsored advertisements were mainly product advertisements developed by small-scale local agencies. The firm did not hire large-scale global agencies due to budgetary limitations. For example, SISA, a sales subsidiary of Samsung Electronics in the US, selected a PR agency named Regis McKena Inc, which ranks in the top fifty among the US agencies for producing their advertisements.

Only the budget-related decisions were made by the main office and the rest of the functions, such as planning and production of the advertisements, were delegated to local offices. The head office considered that it did not have enough market- or advertising-related information to carry out effective advertising plans. Moreover, although the staff at the local office had mostly sales-related experiences, they lacked marketing abilities. Thus most of the planning and production activities were performed by the local agency.

The CI campaigns were not synchronized, because the acting bodies were different and the creative guidelines were not uniform at various locations. Therefore, the advertisements suffered from the problem of a globally unco-ordinated corporate image. In terms of media, main office-sponsored advertisements were placed in internationally well-known economics or news magazines such as *Time*, or listed in famous airlines' in-flight magazines. The firm used local media in the areas where the international media space was difficult to obtain, such as in Central and South America and the Middle East. Among the major media types, magazines were used most, followed by economics newspapers. Due to the budget limitations, tele-communication channels were used infrequently by a small number of subsidiaries and foreign traders. Outdoor media have begun to receive attention since the Asian Games in 1986 and were used more often in major cities.

At this stage, the main objective was again increased company awareness and the improved branch image rather than boosted short-term sales. The company targets have been changed from traders and distributors to general consumers. But due to budgetary limitations and contact problems for obtaining the space in foreign media, the selected media did not cover general consumers well. As a result, the advertising targets were narrowed down to opinion leaders who read economics newspapers or news magazines.

The appealing point of the message was 'low-cost, high-quality' under the theme of introducing technological capabilities and overall product qualities, because the firm's products did not have obvious competitive advantages against others. Examples of such advertisements can be quoted from the *Asian Wall Street Journal*, 'The better you know us, the better for us', 'The world's sophisticated electronics markets prefer Samsung', or 'No matter where in the world you are, you have a good partner in Samsung'.

In terms of advertising organization, the strategic planning department and the production department continued to have difficulties in maintaining co-ordinated advertising strategies for the firm.

Global advertising (since the late 1980s)

Although the total export revenue was increasing, Samsung Electronics experienced decreased profitability from the late 1980s because of the increased cost of labour and materials, as well as the strengthened value of domestic currency. Rapidly spreading block economies and import regulations adopted by the US and EC nations were also causing problems in export markets. The firms from developed nations, including the Japanese firms which located production facilities in the low-wage Southeast countries, were entering the low-cost market. The domestic labour costs were also increasing. As a consequence, Samsung could not maintain the low-cost strategy or the OEM brand export strategy. The firm had to reduce the proportion of OEM brand exporting and change its low-cost strategy toward high-quality strategy with an increased share of brands under its own name. For a reading on the past effects and future direction of OEM exportation, see KIET, 1989.

In late 1988, Samsung announced a new global strategy in an effort to eliminate overlapping investments and to co-ordinate electronics businesses within the group. The company's intention was to promote synergy effects, with the long-term goal of being one of the top five electronics companies in the world. More specifically, this strategy called for market diversification through actively participating in trade opportunities in the previously Eastern bloc countries as a response to the changing global political environment.

Samsung expects to ultimately capture a significant share of the world market with this global strategy. As of the end of 1990, it planned to double the number of its thirty overseas sales subsidiaries within three years and to increase its regional headquarters from three to five, thus strengthening the global network of management. It also planned to expand the sales force at the local subsidiaries and to broaden the scope of approaches from sales-orientated marketing toward customer-orientated marketing.

Through the changes in the global strategy, Samsung Electronics was able to improve its corporate image internationally and to differentiate its image from the others. The headline copy presently used is 'Our name is a little longer'. At the same time, a global advertising strategy was established. The company was making commitments to internationalize its market by establishing the global advertising strategy which would produce co-ordinated corporate and brand images enabling the firm's products to be differentiated from those of its competitors through appeals made continuously to the global consumer.

The globalization of advertising could be made possible by the internationalization of Korean advertising agencies and by the recent joint ventures of Korean agencies and global agencies with a network of multinational branches. Cheil Communications began to internationalize by establishing overseas branch offices starting with an office in Tokyo in 1988, followed by others in New York and San José. In February 1989, it formed a joint venture company with Bozell Inc of the US and started to co-ordinate its international advertising functions by using Bozell's global network of branches.

In addition, the firm put marketing manpower in its regional headquarters located in Southeast Asia, North America, Central and South America and Europe, and is planning to adopt the grouped localization strategy which co-ordinates the activities by region for more efficient control. The summary of the characteristics at each stage is listed in Table 5.

Table 5   *Characteristics of strategies at each stage*

Stage/ strategy	Export advertising	Multinational advertising	Global advertising
Type	Corporate + product	Corporate + product + brand	Corporate + product + brand
Message	Standardization	Standardization + adaptation	Regional adaptation
Organization	Centralization	Decentralization	Grouped centralization
Agency	Domestic	Domestic + foreign local	Global
Media	Newspapers, magazines	Newspapers, magazines, outdoor media, others	Increased use of telecommunication network, outdoor media, others

CONCLUSION

A Korean international firm was selected in this research to analyse the changes that were taking place in the advertising strategies adopted by firms in developing countries that behave differently to the firms of the advanced nations. This study explored the dimensions of international advertising strategy and identified external and internal factors that influence the dimensions of advertising strategy. The literature survey and analysis were used to formulate a model on the internationalization process of Korean firms. As Korean international firms were making progress toward the globally-orientated stage from the export-orientated and multinationally-orientated stages, it was found that the international advertising strategies were also evolving and showed unique characteristics at each stage. It was also discovered that factors such as establishment of foreign subsidiaries and adoption of global marketing strategy were the driving forces underlying the evolutionary process.

Some caution is needed in interpreting the results of this study. The international firms of Korea were just beginning to adopt a global advertising strategy, and at the present time only a few Korean firms have entered the global advertising stage. Most firms were still at the export advertising stage or at the multinational advertising stage. Even the firms in the global advertising stage were not following the pattern used by the global firms of advanced nations, but exhibited the combination of characteristics which were shown in the prior stage.

As more Korean firms make progress toward globalization, they are expected to follow the stage model developed in this study. It is expected that this model will be applied to more cases in the future, particularly as Korean firms have a strong tendency to imitate the pioneers in the relatively new area of international advertising. Due to the accumulated effort in international advertising and learning from the pioneering companies, the followers are expected to shorten the first two stages to the minimum, and proceed rapidly to the final stage as soon as their finances permit.

92 INTERNATIONAL JOURNAL OF ADVERTISING, 1994, **13**

REFERENCES

Aaker, D. A. & Myers, J. G. (1989) *Advertising Management,* 3rd edn. Englewood-Cliffs, NJ: Prentice-Hall.

Britt, S. H. (1974) Standardizing marketing for the international market. *Columbia Journal of World Business,* **9,** 39–45.

Buzzel, R. D. (1968) Can you standardize multinational marketing? *Harvard Business Review,* **46,** 102–113.

Cheil Communications (1986) International advertisement of Korea. *Company Magazine of Cheil Communications* June, 43-49.

Cheil Communications (1988) *History of 15 Years at Cheil Communications.* Seoul: Cheil Communications.

Cheil Communications (1990) Internationalization of Korean firms and their global marketing strategy. *Company Magazine of Cheil Communications,* 12–15.

Cho, D. S. (1984) *Cases of Korean Companies on International Management.* Seoul: Kyung Moon Publishing Co.

Cho, D. S. (1987) *The General Trading Company: Concept and Strategy.* Lexington, MA: Lexington Books.

Cho, D. S. (1989) *International Business,* 2nd edn. Seoul: Kyung Moon Publishing Co.

Colvin, M., Heeler, R. & Thorpe, J. (1980) Developing international advertising strategy. *Journal of Marketing,* **44,** 73–79.

Donnelly, J. H. & Ryans, J. K. (1969) Standardized global advertising: a call as yet answered. *Journal of Marketing,* **33,** 57–60.

Fatt, A. C. (1967) The danger of 'local' international advertising. *Journal of Marketing,* **31,** 60–62.

Jain, S. (1990) *International Marketing,* Boston, MA: PWS-Kent.

Keegan, W. J. (1989) *Global Marketing Management,* 4th edn. Englewood-Cliffs, NJ: Prentice-Hall.

KIET (1989) *Current Situation and Future Direction of OEM Exportation in the Korean Electronics Industry.* Seoul: KIET.

KIET (1990) *Causes and Counterplans for Stagnation in Exportation to the USA, Japan and EC.* Seoul: KIET.

Killough, J. (1978) Improved payoffs from transnational advertising. *Harvard Business Review,* **56,** 102–110.

Koh, K. (1981) A study on international advertising strategy adopted by the Korean companies. Unpublished MA dissertation. Seoul: Yonsei University.

Koh, K. (1987) A study on standardization of international advertising. Unpublished Ph.D. dissertation. Seoul: Soongsil University.

Korean Trade Promotion Corporation (KTPC) (1990) *Comparison of Competitiveness Among Strategic Export Products to the USA.* Seoul: Korean Trade Promotion Corporation.

Levitt, T. (1983) The globalization of markets. *Harvard Business Review,* **61,** 92–102.

Levy, B. (1988) Korean and Taiwanese firms as international competitors: the challenges ahead. *Columbia Journal of World Business,* **23,** 43–51.

Miracle, G. E. (1968) International advertising principles and strategies. *MSU Business Topics,* Autumn, 29–36.

Onkvist, S. & Shaw, J. J. (1987) Standardized international advertising: a review and critical evaluation of the theoretical and empirical evidence. *Columbia Journal of World Business,* **22,** 43–55.

Peebles, D. M., Ryans, J. K. & Vernon, I. R. (1976) Coordinating international advertising. *Journal of Marketing,* **42,** 28–34.

Porter, M. E. (1986) *Competition in Global Industries.* Boston, MA: Harvard Business School Press.

Quelch, J. A. & Hoff, E. J. (1986) Customizing global marketing. *Harvard Business Review,* **64,** 59–68.

Ricks, D. A., Arpan, J. S. & Fu, M. (1974) Pitfalls in advertising. *Journal of Advertising Research,* **14,** 47–51.

Samsung Electronics (1989) *History of 20 Years at Samsung Electronics.* Seoul: Samsung Electronics.

Sorenson, R. Z. & Wiechmann, U. E. (1975) How multinationals view marketing standardization. *Harvard Business Review,* **53,** 38–44.

The Korean Economic Daily Newspaper (1990) Special edition on electronics industry. 16 October.

Wortzel, H. V. & Wortzel, L. H. (1988) Globalizing strategies for multinationals from developing countries. *Columbia Journal of World Business,* **23,** 27–35.

Wortzel, L. H. & Wortzel, H. V. (1981) Export marketing strategies for NIC and LDC-based firms. *Columbia Journal of World Business,* **16,** 51–60.

[28]

The Perceived Advantages, Disadvantages and Strategic Responses of International Stockbroking Firms in ASEAN Countries

KIM WAI HO, YAN CHIN LIM and
THIAN SER TOH

This paper presents the findings of a questionnaire survey of stockbroking firms in five countries in the Association of South East Asian Nations (ASEAN): Singapore, Malaysia, Thailand, Philippines and Indonesia. The main focus of the study is twofold: first, to investigate the advantages and disadvantages of the presence of international stockbroking firms in ASEAN, as perceived by local stockbroking firms; and second, to survey the strategies of these firms in response to the competition posed by international broking firms. We find that local firms believe that there are benefits arising from the entry of foreign firms in the region. Among the more important benefits cited are higher quality research, increase in trading volume and market liquidity. The most important strategies of local firms are to improve their research capability and to provide better staff training. This augurs well for the stockbroking industry in the ASEAN region.

There has been an increasing trend in the globalisation of financial markets in the last two decades, globalisation being defined as 'the integration of financial markets throughout the world into a universal financial market' [Fabozzi and Modigliani, 1992]. As part of this globalisation trend, the international stockbroking industry has also become more inter-connected. Some of the factors contributing to this globalisation trend in stockbroking include technology, convergence in international monetary policy and the growing presence of international fund management [Toh, Ho, and Lim, 1993].

The authors are in the Nanyang Business School, Nanyang Technological University, Nanyang Avenue, Singapore 639798.

The Service Industries Journal, Vol.17, No.2 (April 1997), pp.264–277
PUBLISHED BY FRANK CASS, LONDON

Stock markets in ASEAN (Association of South-East Asian Nations) have responded to this process of globalisation. Trading mechanisms and regulations have been updated to ensure efficient execution and settlement of trades [Ghon Rhee and Chang, 1992]. For example, the stock exchanges in Singapore, Malaysia and Thailand have been expanding their capacity through automated trading systems.

Other developments in some of the ASEAN equity markets include the introduction of scripless settlement, extension of trading hours, introduction of new traded securities such as options and warrants, and measures to liberalise the stockbroking industry, such as the admission of international broking houses as members on the exchanges and the permission of equity participation of foreign broking firms in local firms [Toh, Ho, and Lim, 1993]. For example, the Stock Exchange of Singapore has granted membership to seven foreign stockbroking firms in 1992. Several international broking firms have also established offices in most of the ASEAN markets (as well as other Asia–Pacific markets). The motivation of this study is to examine the effects of the growing presence of international broking firms in the ASEAN markets on the stockbroking industry in these markets. The strategies of local broking firms in ASEAN in response to the growing challenge posed by international broking firms will be of interest to the international stockbroking community.

Thus, the main focus of this paper is twofold: first, to study the perceptions of ASEAN stockbroking firms with respect to the advantages and disadvantages of the presence of international firms; and second, to survey the strategies of ASEAN broking firms in response to foreign competition. This research is based on a questionnaire survey of stockbroking firms in five countries in ASEAN (i.e. Singapore, Malaysia, Thailand, Philippines and Indonesia) conducted at the end of 1993 and in early 1994. Presentation of the survey results is preceded by a discussion of possible advantages and disadvantages of the presence of foreign broking firms, strategic responses by local firms, methodology used in this study and hypotheses to be tested and is followed by some concluding remarks.

ADVANTAGES AND DISADVANTAGES OF THE PRESENCE OF FOREIGN BROKING FIRMS AND STRATEGIES OF LOCAL STOCKBROKING FIRMS

Disadvantages

Globalisation and deregulation of financial markets have increased the degree of competition in the ASEAN stockbroking industry, especially in the more open markets such as Singapore. As shown in a survey by *Global*

Investor [May 1993], the majority of the top-ranked broking firms in Asian stock markets in terms of research and equity execution have international connections. Since international investors are more likely to place their deals with these firms, the threat to local firms is obvious. The presence of foreign broking firms may increase the likelihood of local firms losing local corporate clients as well as existing foreign institutional clients. Protectionists will regard the stifling of the growth of local firms as a disadvantage of opening up one's market to foreign competition.

Another problem that may be associated with the increased presence of foreign firms is the problem of rising operating costs. Poaching of experienced research and dealing staff from local firms by foreign firms in order to achieve quick start-ups may not be viewed favourably. Losing experienced staff may also mean a possible loss of client base, since clients usually follow the move of dealing staff to their new employers. In order to retain their staff, firms will have to pay competitive salaries and other benefits.

The presence of foreign firms may also contribute towards higher market volatility due to the shifting of institutional funds from one market to another in this region when one market is perceived to be overvalued relative to others.

Benefits

While competition may have increased operating costs, it may also be desirable in raising the level of market sophistication. Foreign firms, with their expertise and skills, may lead to greater use of advanced technology and higher quality research. A few of the local firms in markets which are more open to foreign competition have managed to make it to the top rankings in terms of equity research and execution. Some examples are Kim Eng and GK Goh in Singapore, Peregrine in Hong Kong, and Rashid Hussain in Malaysia [*Global Investor*, May 1993].

The presence of foreign firms, with their international connections and institutional client bases, may have a positive impact on trading volume, liquidity and depth of the ASEAN markets. Trading volumes have surged in the ASEAN markets from 1988 to 1993 [Pacific Rim Stock Markets Review by Barings Securities, July 1993]. However, the rise in volume may also be due to bull market conditions.

The presence of foreign broking firms in ASEAN stock markets may also increase market confidence in these markets. International institutional investors may feel more confident in the market if the market is more transparent with good research information. Foreign firms may provide a good link between the markets and overseas investors.

Globalisation of financial markets may also have a favourable impact on the development of financial reporting in the region. The more sophisticated listed companies may have incentives to provide more information about their companies in order to cultivate better relations with analysts.

Strategies

Toh and Chua [1992] identified four types of strategic responses to the entry of foreign firms by local firms: 'head-on competition', formation of alliances, going deeper into the local market, and switching focus to position taking (i.e. seeking trading profits). 'Head-on-competition' refers to the establishment of dealing or research offices in the region, and in leading financial centres such as London and New York. This is often done to satisfy the needs of institutional clients.

The process of establishing a foothold in overseas markets requires heavy investment in human resources and technology. It is therefore important for local firms to be adequately capitalised. Local firms can either enlarge their capital base by injecting more equity, merging with other local firms, admitting foreign partners or seeking listing status to tap capital from the stockmarket. Joint ventures with regional or international firms may bring about benefits from synergies in capital, customer base and market knowledge.

'Going deeper into the local markets' means expanding the retail business, setting up more local branches and extending financing and margin loans to larger clients. Switching focus to one of position-taking is a strategy that requires a larger capital base.

Other than the strategies identified by Toh and Chua [1992], local firms could also strive to be more competitive by upgrading their research capability, using more up-to-date technology and providing better staff training. Because of differences in market characteristics, local firms in different countries in the ASEAN region may adopt different strategies.

METHODOLOGY AND HYPOTHESES

To gauge the views of the stockbroking community on the issues discussed above, we conducted a questionnaire survey of the stockbroking firms in the ASEAN region. Questionnaires were sent to all member firms of the Stock Exchange of Singapore, the Kuala Lumpur Stock Exchange in Malaysia, the Stock Exchange of Thailand and the Manila Stock Exchange in Philippines. As for Indonesia, we sent the questionnaire to 45 firms out of the top 60 companies in Indonesia, because of the large number of businesses in that country.

Respondents were asked to indicate the importance of the benefits and disadvantages of the presence of international firms discussed above. Local firms were asked to indicate the importance of various strategies on a a five-point scale, 1 being the least important and 5 the most important.

Since this paper concentrates on the local stockbroking firms, analysis will be based on the responses of firms which are either 100 per cent locally owned or majority locally owned ('local firms'). The responses of local firms using the mean score for each of the disadvantages, benefits and strategies in each country are summarised and ranked according to the computed mean.

To find out whether some disadvantages, benefits or strategies are more important than others within each country, we use the Friedman two-way analysis of variance of ranks test to measure the null hypothesis that the responses of local firms in each country come from the same population:

H_0 : *Responses in respect of disadvantages (and benefits and strategies, respectively) within each country come from the same population.*

Empirical studies show that in regulated environments, such as the airline [Cheng and Kesner, 1988; Snow and Hrebiniak, 1980] and banking industries [Lenz, 1990], alternative strategies do exist. Since the stockbroking industry in the ASEAN countries can be considered a regulated industry, we would expect to observe some preferred strategies.

Since the five countries do not share identical characteristics in terms of the degree of protection of local stockbroking industry and liberalisation, we would expect some inter-country differences in the responses. We use the Kruskal–Wallis one-way analysis of variance test to test the null hypothesis that responses of local firms between each country come from the same population:

H_0 : *Responses between countries come from the same population.*

Since a significant Kruskal–Wallis test does not reveal which countries are significantly different, we use Mann–Whitney test to make multiple comparisons between each pair of countries in cases where the null is rejected. The Mann–Whitney test is the most frequently used follow-up to the Kruskal–Wallis test [Huck, Cormier, and Bounds, 1974]. Since the response rate from the Indonesian firms is rather poor (see Table 1), we will exclude Indonesian firms in the multiple comparisons. This will also reduce the number of multiple comparisons to a more manageable level.

DATA ANALYSIS AND RESULTS

Preliminary Analysis

The number of firms surveyed and the response rate in each country are shown in Table 1. A total of 237 firms were surveyed and the overall

INTERNATIONAL STOCKBROKING FIRMS IN ASEAN COUNTRIES 269

response rate is 41 per cent. The response rate from Indonesia firms (16 per cent) is low while that from the other countries are more reasonable, ranging from 39 per cent to 67 per cent. Thus, less weight will be attached to the responses from Indonesian firms in discussing the results of the study.

TABLE 1
NUMBER OF STOCKBROKING FIRMS IN SAMPLE

Country	Number of Firms Surveyed	Number of Firms Responded	Response Rate (%)
Singapore	33[a]	22	67
Malaysia	56[a]	22	39
Thailand	40[a]	16	40
Philippines	63[b]	29	46
Indonesia	45[c]	7	16
TOTAL	237	96	41

a   represents all firms in the respective country.
b   represents member firms of the Manila Stock Exchange.
c   selected from the top 60 firms in terms of volume.

As shown in Table 2, there are very few foreign broking firms in the sample. For instance, there are no foreign firms in the sample of companies in Malaysia and Thailand. As mentioned previously, we only analyse the responses of local firms in this study.

TABLE 2
OWNERSHIP OF RESPONDENT FIRMS

Country	100% locally owned or majority locally owned*	100% foreign owned or majority foreign owned	Ownership not indicated	Total
Total				
Singapore	15	7	-	22
Malaysia	22	-	-	22
Thailand	14	-	2	16
Philippines	26	3	-	29
Indonesia	4	3	-	7
TOTAL	81	13	2	96

* Further breakdown of these figures are shown in Table 3.

An analysis of the characteristics of local firms is shown in Table 3. In Singapore and Malaysia, 47 per cent and 32 per cent respectively, of the respondent local firms have foreign shareholders whereas the proportion of local firms with foreign shareholders in Thailand and Philippines is much smaller, 21 per cent and 19 per cent respectively. A large proportion (71 per cent) of the respondent firms in Thailand have some affiliations to banks. Slightly more than half (53 per cent) of the respondent firms in Singapore are connected to some banking groups. The presence of banks in the broking industry in Malaysia and Philippines is less significant. As for the number of firms that have set up offices overseas, Singaporean firms have the highest proportion (60 per cent), followed by Malaysian and Thai firms, 45 per cent and 43 per cent respectively. Only 12 per cent of the respondent firms in Philippines have offices overseas.

TABLE 3
CHARACTERISTICS OF RESPONDENT FIRMS WHICH ARE 100% LOCALLY OWNED OR
MAJORITY LOCALLY OWNED

| | Ownership | | | | Bank Affiliation | | | | Overseas Offices | | | |
| | 100% Local | | Majority Local | | Without Bank Affiliation | | With Bank Affiliation | | Without Overseas Offices | | With Overseas Offices | |
	No.	%	No.	%	No.	%	No.	%	No.	%	No	%
Singapore	8	53	7	47	7	47	8	53	6	40	9	60
Malaysia	15	68	7	32	17	77	4	18	12	55	10	45
Thailand	11	79	3	21	4	29	10	71	8	57	6	43
Philippines	21	81	5	19	22	85	3	12	23	88	3	12
Indonesia	3	75	1	25	3	75	1	25	4	100	-	-
TOTAL	58	72	23	28	53	65	26	32	53	65	28	35

Note: One firm each in Malaysia and Philippines did not indicate whether they are affiliated to any banking group.

Disadvantages of the Presence of Foreign Firms

The results of the statistical analysis are shown in Table 4. The Friedman test is not significant at 5 per cent level, in the case of Malaysia, Thailand, Philippines and Indonesia. Thus, respondents in these countries are indifferent to the disadvantages listed. In Singapore, the null hypothesis that the responses come from the same population is rejected at 1 per cent significance level. Loss of existing foreign institutional clients and rising costs arising from competition seem to be the main concerns of the Singaporean firms. This is consistent with the fact that the Singapore stockbroking industry is the most liberalised among the five countries.

INTERNATIONAL STOCKBROKING FIRMS IN ASEAN COUNTRIES 271

TABLE 4
DISADVANTAGES OF THE PRESENCE OF FOREIGN FIRMS
MEAN SCORES OF RESPONDENT FIRMS WHICH ARE 100% OR MAJORITY LOCALLY OWNED

Disadvantages	Singapore (N = 15) Mean Score		Malaysia (N = 22) Mean Score		Thailand (N = 14) Mean Score		Philippines (N = 26) Mean Score		Indonesia (N = 4) Mean Score		Kruskal–Wallis Test Chi- Square	P- Value
Increased market competition	3.67	4	2.90	5	3.25	2	2.83	5	3.00	6	3.066	0.547
Increased market volatility	2.53	7	2.86	7	2.44	7	3.17	3	3.33	3	3.703	0.448
Growth of local firms stifled	2.73	6	2.89	6	3.00	4	2.57	6	3.00	6	3.362	0.499
Loss of staff due to poaching	3.73	3	3.86	1	3.38	1	3.23	2	3.14	5	4.509	0.342
Loss of corporate clients to foreign firms	3.60	5	3.38	4	2.69	6	2.52	7	3.71	2	11.121	0.025*
Loss of existing foreign institutional clients	4.00	1	3.43	2	2.75	5	2.87	4	4.00	1	10.403	0.034*
Rising costs arising from competition	3.93	2	3.43	2	3.25	2	3.36	1	3.17	4	1.955	0.744
Friedman Test												
Chi-Square	19.73		7.02		11.76		6.16		6.99			
p-value	0.003**		0.319		0.068		0.405		0.322			

N is the number of sample firms in each country. The score is based on a scale of 1 to 5, 1 being least important and 5 most important. Numbers in italics are the ranks of disadvantages in each country. The rank is based on the mean score within each country. The Kruskal–Wallis one-way analysis of variance tests the null hypothesis that the responses for each disadvantage between countries come from the same population. The Friedman two-way analysis of variance of ranks tests the null hypothesis that the responses within each country come from the same population.

* significant at 5% level ** significant at 1% level

The results of the Kruskal–Wallis test show that the null hypothesis that the responses between countries come from the same population cannot be rejected at 5 per cent significance level for all except two disadvantages: loss of corporate clients to foreign firms, and loss of existing foreign institutional clients. The results of the follow-up tests (see Panel A in Table 7) again suggest that Singapore firms are more concerned with loss of clients to foreign firms. Apart from the exceptions noted, firms in the ASEAN countries are generally neutral in their assessment of the disadvantages of the presence of foreign broking firms. This is probably because there is certain degree of protection given to local stockbroking firms in most of the ASEAN countries. Thus, with the exception of Singapore, the threats posed by foreign firms are not so imminent.

Benefits of the Presence of Foreign Firms

Table 5 summarizes the results of the statistical tests. The Friedman tests are significant at 5 per cent level for Malaysia and at 1 per cent level for Singapore, Thailand and Philippines. In general, promoting higher quality research, increased trading volume and increased market liquidity seem to the main benefits of the presence of foreign broking firms, as perceived by the ASEAN local firms.

TABLE 5

BENEFITS OF THE PRESENCE OF FOREIGN FIRMS -MEAN SCORES OF RESPONDENT FIRMS
WHICH ARE 100% OR MAJORITY LOCALLY OWNED

	Singapore (N = 15)		Malaysia (N = 22)		Thailand (N = 14)		Philippines (N = 26)		Indonesia (N = 4)		Kruskal–Wallis Test	
Benefits	Mean Score		Mean Score		Mean Score		Mean Score		Mean Score		Chi-Square	P-Value
Increased market depth	3.38	6	4.10	2	3.81	4	4.29	4	3.50	6	11.238	0.024*
Increased market liquidity	3.80	4	4.05	3	3.75	5	4.32	3	3.86	4	7.838	0.098
Promote higher quality research	3.93	2	4.38	1	4.38	1	4.40	2	4.14	3	4.565	0.335
Promote better corporate reporting	2.67	8	3.76	7	3.31	8	3.57	8	3.57	5	9.821	0.044*
Promote use of technology	2.57	9	3.65	8	3.19	9	3.59	7	2.86	8	11.841	0.019*
Increased market confidence	3.07	8	3.90	4	3.81	3	4.19	5	3.57	5	9.365	0.053
Increased market sophistication	3.67	5	3.76	6	3.50	6	3.86	6	3.14	7	5.826	0.213
Increased trading volume	4.00	1	3.86	5	4.00	2	4.58	1	4.29	2	13.401	0.010**
Increased competition	3.87	3	3.52	9	3.38	7	3.00	9	4.43	1	12.832	0.012*
Friedman Test												
Chi-Square	25.63		17.32		21.78		31.98		9.28			
p-value	0.001**		0.027*		0.005**		0.000**		0.319			

N is the number of sample firms in each country. The score is based on a scale of 1 to 5, 1 being least important and 5 most important. Numbers in italics are the ranks of benefits in each country. The rank is based on the mean score within each country. The Kruskal–Wallis one-way analysis of variance tests the null hypothesis that the responses for each disadvantage between countries come from the same population. The Friedman two-way analysis of variance of ranks tests the null hypothesis that the responses within each country come from the same population.

* significant at 5% level
** significant at 1% level

The results of the Kruskal–Wallis test show that there are inter-country differences in the perceived importance of some benefits. Results of the follow-up test to the Kruskal–Wallis test (see Panel B in Table 7) suggest that Singapore firms do not think that promoting better corporate reporting and promoting use of technology are benefits from the presence of foreign firms, probably because Singapore is already relatively advanced in these areas. Local firms in Malaysia and Philippines (and to a lesser extent in Thailand) consider increased market depth as an important benefit of the presence of foreign firms.

Another observation is that firms in Philippines put greater importance to the benefit of increased trading volume relative to firms in the other countries in ASEAN. This is probably due to the greater reliance of foreign interests in their stock markets.

Strategies of Local Firms

The results of the statistical tests are summarized in Table 6. The Friedman test is significant in all five countries, implying that certain strategies are preferred over others. The results of the Kruskal–Wallis test show that there is agreement among firms in the five countries that *improving research capability* is the top priority strategy that they would adopt. This reflects their recognition of the importance of having good research capability in order to compete with international broking firms. The local firms in the ASEAN countries also feel that *better staff training* is an important strategy, probably because of the need to retain their staff in the face of competition from foreign broking firms.

Establishing a strategic alliance with foreign firms is considered an important strategy by firms in Thailand, Philippines and Indonesia although their scores are not statistically different from those of firms in Singapore and Malaysia. In contrast, merging with other local firms is generally considered not an important strategy by firms in all the five countries. This is consistent with the view that local firms prefer to grow by joining forces with foreign firms (instead of other local firms) so as to benefit from the higher quality research capability and international connections of foreign firms.

The ASEAN local firms, especially Singaporean firms, believe that expanding the retail sales force is an important strategy. However, establishing more local branches does not seem to be rated highly, probably due to institutional restrictions (for example, broking firms not allowed to set up branches in Singapore).

Firms in Singapore and Malaysia seem to put more emphasis on establishing overseas offices or ventures as compared to firms in the other three countries (although the Kruskal–Wallis test is not significant at 5 per cent level). This is consistent with the observation that more firms in Singapore and Malaysia have already set up offices overseas (see Table 3).

TABLE 6

STRATEGIES IN RESPONSE TO FOREIGN COMPETITION: MEAN SCORES OF RESPONDENT FIRMS WHICH ARE 100% OR MAJORITY LOCALLY OWNED

	Singapore (N = 15) Mean Score		Malaysia (N = 22) Mean Score		Thailand (N = 14) Mean Score		Philippines (N = 26) Mean Score		Indonesia (N = 4) Mean Score		Kruskal–Wallis Test	
Test											Chi-Square	P-Value
Establish overseas offices/ventures	3.79	*4*	3.85	*7*	3.15	*8*	3.05	*9*	2.20	*11*	9.247	0.055
Strategic alliance with foreign firms	3.21	*7*	3.59	*9*	4.00	*2*	4.12	*3*	4.20	*2*	5.255	0.262
Expand retail sales force	4.27	*2*	3.86	*6*	3.33	*6*	3.65	*6*	4.00	*3*	7.754	0.101
Establish more local branches	2.42	*12*	3.20	*10*	3.40	*5*	2.96	*10*	2.60	*8*	4.168	0.384
Improve research capability	4.47	*1*	4.57	*1*	4.40	*1*	4.44	*1*	4.80	*1*	2.534	0.639
Provide financing for large clients	2.80	*9*	3.95	*5*	3.13	*9*	3.38	*7*	3.80	*6*	9.810	0.044*
Use up-to-date technology	3.71	*6*	4.14	*4*	3.93	*4*	3.71	*5*	3.20	*7*	5.080	0.279
Take positions to improve profit	3.00	*8*	2.86	*12*	3.29	*7*	3.18	*8*	2.40	*10*	2.188	0.701
Increase capital base	3.73	*5*	4.41	*2*	2.93	*11*	3.92	*4*	4.00	*3*	16.367	0.003**
Seek public listing	2.79	*10*	3.73	*8*	3.07	*10*	2.29	*12*	2.60	*8*	13.885	0.008**
Provide better training for staff	3.86	*3*	4.27	*3*	3.93	*3*	4.22	*2*	4.00	*3*	3.661	0.454
Merge with other local firms	2.57	*11*	2.91	*11*	2.40	*12*	2.36	*11*	2.20	*11*	2.811	0.590
Friedman Test												
Chi-Square	29.72		39.18		41.50		47.34		19.81			
p-value	0.002**		0.000**		0.000**		0.000**		0.048*			

N is the number of sample firms in each country. The score is based on a scale of 1 to 5, 1 being least important and 5 most important. Numbers in italics are the ranks of strategies in each country. The rank is based on the mean score within each country. The Kruskal–Wallis one-way analysis of variance tests the null hypothesis that the responses for each disadvantage between countries come from the same population. The Friedman two-way analysis of variance of ranks tests the null hypothesis that the responses within each country come from the same population.

* significant at 5% level
** significant at 1% level

In general, firms are fairly neutral when answering the question on position-taking to improve profit. One interpretation is that they regard

INTERNATIONAL STOCKBROKING FIRMS IN ASEAN COUNTRIES   275

position-taking as too risky a strategy. However, their responses may not be an accurate indication of the extent of risk-taking through trading on own accounts because of the sensitivity of the question concerned.

Another strategy that receives consensus among firms in the five countries is that of using up-to-date technology. The importance of information technology in modern management is well-known.

TABLE 7

MULTIPLE COMPARISONS BETWEEN COUNTRIES USING MANN–WHITNEY TEST
(FOLLOW-UP TESTS FOR SIGNIFICANT KRUSKAL–WALLIS TEST RESULTS)

	Singapore vs Malaysia p-value	Singapore vs Thailand p-value	Singapore vs Philippines p-value	Malaysia vs Thailand p-value	Malaysia vs Philippines p-value	Thailand vs Philippines p-value
PANEL A (Disadvantages)						
Loss of corporate clients to foreign firms	0.667	0.031 *	0.021 *	0.074	0.042 *	0.519
Loss of existing foreign institutional clients	0.088	0.006 **	0.033 *	0.104	0.234	0.838
PANEL B (Benefits)						
Increased market depth	0.011 *	0.118	0.003 **	0.187	0.413	0.048 *
Promote better corporate reporting	0.008 **	0.099	0.031 *	0.109	0.601	0.356
Promote use of technology	0.006 **	0.048 *	0.006 **	0.137	0.764	0.238
Increased trading volume	0.607	0.917	0.025 *	0.515	0.001 **	0.040 *
Increased competition	0.283	0.255	0.062	0.846	0.213	0.411
PANEL C (Strategies)						
Provide financing for large clients	0.008 **	0.396	0.173	0.019 *	0.101	0.521
Increased capital base	0.044 *	0.028 *	0.608	0.000 **	0.115	0.009 **
Seek public listing	0.027 *	0.571	0.176	0.076	0.001 **	0.040 *

p-value: These are *p-values* of the Mann–Whitney tests corrected for ties.
* significant at 5% level
** significant at 1% level

Comparisons between Indonesian firms and firms from other countries are omitted because of the very small sample of Indonesian firms.

There are three strategies on which we observe some disagreement statistically. The Kruskal–Wallis test is significant at the 1 per cent level with regard to the two strategies related to capital-raising – that is, increasing capital base and seeking public listing. The null hypothesis that responses of firms between countries come from the same population is also rejected at the 5 per cent level with regard to 'providing financing for large clients'. The results of multiple comparisons in Table 7 (Panel C) show that the significance of the Kruskal–Wallis test is mainly due to the high scores from Malaysian firms in these three strategies. This may reflect the aggressiveness of Malaysian local firms in striving to achieve a higher level of business in view of the opportunities arising from the strength of the Malaysian economy and the growing market capitalisation of the Malaysian stock exchange.

Another observation from Table 7 is that Thai firms do not see a need to increase their capital base. This is not surprising in view of the dominance of banks in the broking industry in Thailand (see Table 3). Local firms in Philippines regard public listing as relatively unimportant, probably due to the fact that there is less requirement for capital in view of the small trading volume on the stock exchanges in Philippines.

CONCLUSION

Globalisation and deregulation of financial markets in recent years have brought about a growing presence of international stockbroking firms in the ASEAN countries. In this paper we present evidence from a questionnaire survey on broking firms in ASEAN on two main issues: the perceptions of local firms on the disadvantages and benefits of the presence of international firms; and the strategies of local firms in response to foreign competition.

The main results of the survey can be summarised as follows. Local firms in the region are generally neutral with regards to the disadvantages of the presence of broking firms although we observe that Singaporean firms are more concerned with the loss of clients to foreign firms than other local firms in the region, reflecting the relatively more competitive environment in Singapore. The main benefits of the presence of international firms are perceived to include higher quality research, increase in trading volume and market liquidity. This is a result that would interest regulators in countries which are still relatively closed to foreign broking firms.

Local firms seem to agree that improving research capability and providing better staff training are the most important strategies in response to foreign competition, suggesting that local firms are prepared to upgrade in areas where they are currently at a disadvantage. Another important strategy is to establish strategic alliance with foreign firms, especially for firms in Thailand, Philippines and Indonesia. Other strategies which are relatively important include expanding retail sales force and use of up-to-date technology. Malaysian firms seem to have an appetite for new capital for expansion.

INTERNATIONAL STOCKBROKING FIRMS IN ASEAN COUNTRIES   277

The results of this study are important considerations for the international stockbroking firms when they make further inroads in the broking industry in the ASEAN region. Local broking firms could also obtain useful information from this survey with regard to the common strategies adopted or to be adopted by other local firms. Further research can be conducted to assess how performance of local firms are affected by the strategies they adopt. However, the difficulties of obtaining reliable performance measures cannot be underestimated.

ACKNOWLEDGEMENTS

The authors would like to thank Nanyang Technological University for funding this research and Dr Hun Tong Tan for his comments. Any errors are the authors' responsibility.

REFERENCES

Barings Securities, July 1993, *Pacific Rim Stock Markets Review.*

Cheng, J.L.C. and I.F. Kesner, 1988, 'Responsiveness to environmental change: The interactive effects of organizational slack and strategic orientation', *Academy of Management Proceedings.*

Ghon Rhee S. and R.P. Chang, 1992, 'The Microstructure of Asian Equity Markets', *Journal of Financial Services Research*, pp.437–54.

Global Investor, May 1993, Euromoney Publications.

Fabozzi F.J. and F. Modigliani, 1992, *Capital Markets – Institutions and Instruments*, Prentice-Hall.

Huck, S.W., W.H. Cormier, and W.G. Bounds, 1974, *Reading Statistics and Research*, Glasgow: Harper Collins Publishers.

Lenz, R.T., 1980, 'Environment, strategy, organization structure and performance: Patterns in one industry', *Strategic Management Journal*, Vol.1, pp.209–26.

Snow, C.C. and L.G. Hrebiniak, 1980, 'Strategy, Distinctive Competence, and Organizational Performance', *Administrative Science Quarterly*, Vol.25, pp.317–36.

Toh T.S. and P.S. Chua, 1992, 'Stockbroking "Heavyweights": Implications for Regional Markets', unpublished manuscript, Nanyang Business School, Nanyang Technological University.

Toh T.S., K.W. Ho and Y.C. Lim, 1993, 'The Impact of Globalisation on ASEAN Stockmarkets', paper presented at the Joint SES–CREFS Conference on Current Issues in Equity Markets, Singapore, November.

Part IV
Services, Technological Change and Globalization

[29]

Comparative Advantage and Trade in Services

Brian Hindley and Alasdair Smith

OES the theory of comparative advantage, developed over two centuries to clarify thought about trade in goods, apply to trade in services? An economist who has not thought about the issue might stare blankly if confronted with the question. His problem would be to understand why comparative-advantage theory might *not* apply to services. There is a well-defined (which is not to say, perfect) conceptual framework for the study of international trade. No obvious characteristic of that framework limits its applicability to tangible goods rather than intangible services. [1]

Certainly it is from others than professional economists that the question seems to come, but it comes sufficiently persistently to deserve a more considered response than the one given above. Ronald Shelp, of the American International Group in New York, in a chapter entitled 'Economic Theory: a History of Neglect', remarks:

'Whether the theory of comparative advantage is applicable to international service trade is a striking illustration of the failure of economic theorists to come to grips with services. Where in the economic literature on comparative advantage can a discussion of the service sector be found? Can even one example using a service product to illustrate comparative advantage be recalled?' [2]

The underlying premise in that kind of comment is that services are different from goods — which may, indeed, be so. But a bunch of flowers, a ton of coal and a jet airliner are very different things as well. It may be true that no economist has discussed international trade in brussels sprouts or used that vegetable to illustrate comparative advantage, but that surely does not raise any substantial question as to whether the conceptual apparatus of the theory of comparative advantage is applicable to brussels sprouts.

BRIAN HINDLEY is Counsellor for Studies at the Trade Policy Research Centre, London, and a Senior Lecturer in Economics at the London School of Economics and Political Science, University of London, and ALASDAIR SMITH is Professor of Economics at the University of Sussex, United Kingdom.

BRIAN HINDLEY AND ALASDAIR SMITH

That services are different from goods — whatever that means in a particular context — does not in itself provide any basis for a supposition that the theory of comparative advantage (which is also referred to as the theory of comparative cost) does not apply to services. For that, it is necessary to point to differences which make the *logic* of the theory inapplicable to services, a much more stringent requirement than mere 'differences'.

WHAT IS THE THEORY OF COMPARATIVE ADVANTAGE?

The first step towards a full answer to the question of whether the theory of comparative advantage applies to trade in services is to clarify what economists mean by the term 'comparative-cost theory'. There is rather widespread misunderstanding of what comparative-cost theory implies. In particular, it is often taken to imply support for — indeed, to be almost synonymous with — free trade (or *laissez-faire* policies in general). This is not the case.

The theory of comparative cost comes in two parts. The first is a positive or descriptive theory; the second, a normative or prescriptive one. It is of central importance to keep the distinction between the two clear.

Positive theory attempts to explain why production of particular goods is cheaper (relative to other goods) in one location than in another and, therefore, why some classes of goods are exported from, and others imported to, a particular location.

Normative theory asks whether the pattern of production and specialisation which results from international cost differences is economically efficient and socially desirable and investigates what are the optimal government policies towards international trade.

In some cases, the answer to the central question of the positive theory of comparative cost is straightforward. There is no particular difficulty in explaining why Sweden, for example, imports oranges and bananas. In other cases, including most manufactured goods and probably most services, fully satisfactory explanations of the comparative advantage attaching to particular locations are more difficult to obtain.

The model most widely used by trade theorists to 'explain' trade flows is the Heckscher-Ohlin-Samuelson model. In the textbook version of this model the direction of trade is determined by capital and labour endowments at different locations. Economists concerned with testing theories of trade flows, however, have found it necessary not only to extend the Heckscher-Ohlin-Samuelson model to take account of additional factors of production, such as skilled labour, but also to develop new theories which turn on such variables as technological differences, economies of scale and market imperfection. [3]

This broad and expanding menu of hypotheses might reasonably be taken to suggest that no one current theory is capable of explaining satisfactorily flows of trade in goods; it might even be taken to suggest the possibility that there will never be one satisfactory theory into which all others may be subsumed. Theories of international trade in goods face major problems in explaining the available data on goods flows. Even so, data on service flows, theories which explain them and the testing of such theories are all in a very much more problematic state than their counterparts in goods trade.

These problems will be discussed in detail below. It is worth noting at this point, however, a common error. The fact that it may be difficult to disentangle the determinants of trade — that is to say, the fact that it may be difficult to develop a convincing *description* of the sources of comparative advantage — does not in any sense invalidate the *prescriptions* of the theory of comparative cost.

On one level, the position that ignorance of the determinants of comparative advantage gives an intellectual justification for ignoring the normative component of the theory of comparative cost is vacuous. We do not have to know *why* the butcher, the baker and the candlestick-maker are better at their craft than us to know that it *is* so and to draw appropriate policy conclusions.

It is more generous to the argument, however, and more instructive, to view it as focussing on the intersection of two questions:

(a) What determines comparative advantage?

(b) Are there policies available to governments which will enable them to change the comparative advantage of their countries in an advantageous way?

Evidently the answer to question 'b' might be conditional on the exact answer to 'a'. In fact, however, almost all the affirmative answers to question 'b' appear to be one variant or another of the infant-industry argument (or, as it appears in its current North American and West European guise, the argument that senile industries can be rejuvenated by kind treatment); and that argument, discussed below, does *not* depend on the precise specification of the source of comparative advantage. Unless some different answer to question 'b' appears which is conditional on 'a', it follows that difficulties in empirical testing of theories do not provide intellectual justification for ignoring the normative component of the theory of comparative cost.

To state the point alternatively, suppose that it was possible to identify those service industries in which a country was likely, for whatever reason, to develop a comparative advantage. What would be the policy implications of such an observation? Consider, *as an example*, the textbook Heckscher-Ohlin-Samuelson theory.

It is often supposed that the textbook explanation of trade patterns in which countries well endowed with capital relative to labour are predicted to specialise in capital-intensive goods, while labour-abundant ones specialise in labour-

372   BRIAN HINDLEY AND ALASDAIR SMITH

intensive goods, implies that developing countries *should*, in some sense, concentrate their development efforts on labour-intensive activities. Such an interpretation is mistaken (i) because it confuses 'is' with 'ought', (ii) because it reverses the true order of causation and (iii) because it misunderstands what type of information is required for economic decision taking. Specifically:

(a) If it is observed that the market tends to favour the development of labour-intensive activities, the relevant policy question is whether such favouring will be of a greater or lesser degree than is socially desirable. There is no general presumption that market choices will be biassed in one way or the other.

(b) To interpret the Heckscher-Ohlin-Samuelson theory as a policy prescription is to misunderstand the direction of causation in the sense that the theory is demonstrating a *consequence* of the optimal choice of technique rather than providing a defining characteristic of that technique.

(c) To say that a low-wage country will, and should, adopt techniques and activities which are more labour intensive than those in use in high-wage countries is not to give a well-defined prescription to the economic decision taker who is faced with much more specific questions.

To put this last point in another way, usable economic prescriptions are either general policy prescriptions, such as 'the government should give special encouragement to sectors which generate positive externalities, for example by subsidising the training of new workers'; or they are very detailed and specific prescriptions, such as 'a steel plant of the most modern specification and of minimum efficient scale should be constructed on a coastal site'. Any conclusions derived from the positive theory of comparative advantage are too specific to be the first type of prescription and too general to be the second.

The foregoing observations apply to the services sector as well as to manufacturing and they apply to all explanations of comparative advantage. Thus, even if it were possible to establish that a particular type of country had characteristics which would make it an efficient producer of, say, shipping services, that is not in itself an argument for special encouragement or discouragement of this type of activity.

The only policy implication of the positive theory, then, is a modest one. Public-sector planners concerned with the appropriate size and shape of publicly-provided infrastructure will want to forecast future developments in the private sector. Understanding the sources of comparative advantage will be of some help in this respect.

In addition to being clear about the distinction between the normative and the positive theory of comparative cost, it is important to understand the logical structure of the normative theory itself. The starting point of that theory is David Ricardo's classic discussion of the gains from trade.

COMPARATIVE ADVANTAGE AND SERVICES 373

If two parties enter a voluntary transaction, there is a strong presumption that each regards himself as gaining thereby. A question relevant to the issue of whether individuals should be allowed to proceed freely with voluntary transactions, however, is whether others will be harmed by that activity. For the important class of transactions involving the purchase of goods from abroad, Ricardo demonstrated that other members of the country cannot in aggregate be worse off (and will in general be better off) if such transactions are freely allowed than if they are totally prohibited. The underlying force of the observation is very great; too great to be lost from sight. It stands to this day and nothing in the logical structure of its proof excludes international transactions involving services from its scope.

Nevertheless, the Ricardian proposition that free trade is better than no trade has only limited applicability to the trade policies of most countries, which typically seek to control and regulate trade flows rather than to eliminate them. Control and regulation are more defensible, in terms of economic efficiency, than prohibition. Thus the normative theory of comparative advantage goes on to investigate whether such interventions can be justified.

It is essential to be clear about whether one is discussing the policy objective of improving the welfare of a single country or the objective of improving the welfare of all countries considered together. *Global* welfare cannot be maximised when countries maintain border controls such as tariffs. From a cosmopolitan point of view, therefore, tariffs and other trade-restrictive measures cannot be good instruments of policy. From a *national* point of view, however, trade restrictions may be desirable instruments of policy. When a country can raise the price of a good which it exports, or reduce the price of a good which it imports, by restricting the quantities which it trades, maximisation of national welfare requires that it should exploit its monopoly or monopsony power in that way. This, however, will entail the cost from a cosmopolitan point of view of reducing *global* welfare. Essentially such a country can shift the distribution of global income in its favour by means of tariffs and emerge a winner from a negative-sum game: it may have a positive optimal tariff.

Even from a national point of view, this kind of argument does not justify wholesale protectionism. As a practical matter, the level of trade restrictions which is justifiable on the basis of this optimal-tariff argument, for most countries and most goods, is likely to be zero or almost zero. Only the very largest countries such as the United States are likely to have much impact on the import prices they face and, while it is easier to find examples of countries which can influence their export prices (Saudi Arabia for oil and Brazil for coffee), even that list quickly becomes difficult to fill.

A further set of issues is whether trade restrictions are useful tools from the standpoint of domestic policy objectives. One notable conclusion of the theory of optimal international economic policy is that, even from a national point of view, the efficient attainment of policy goals very rarely requires the imposition of trade restrictions (the major exception being the optimal-tariff argument cited above), although it may well require the use of non-border measures such as taxes on, or subsidies to, output. Hence the difficulties in levying border taxes on services, frequently cited in official documents, do not imply any difficulty in applying efficient economic policies to the services sector.

DO THE PRESCRIPTIONS OF COMPARATIVE-COST THEORY APPLY TO SERVICES?

A first answer to this question, therefore, must be 'yes'. Economists embarking on proofs of the proposition that the world as a whole gains from free trade do not normally specify the characteristics of the 'goods' (x_1, x_2, x_3 . . .) which enter their analysis; and even the typical use of the word 'goods' is a matter of tradition, not deliberately designed to exclude services. Had Ricardo in his classic example specified wine and insurance policies instead of wine and cloth, his demonstration of the gains from trade would have still succeeded, it being dependent only on one country being able to produce insurance policies at a lower cost relative to wine than the other country. Nothing in the logical structure of his proof *ipso facto* excludes international transactions involving services from its scope.

All of this notwithstanding, certain classes of both goods and services have characteristics which raise doubts about the applicability to them of the Ricardian proposition or of other propositions from the body of comparative-cost theory.

First, many service industries are subject to fiduciary regulation and, in many others, sellers are required to possess appropriate licences and/or qualifications. These ubiquitous facts could be interpreted as a challenge to the major premise of the Ricardian argument; as deriving from a belief that, without such restrictions, one party to a voluntary transaction may be wrong to regard himself as having gained from it. This issue is considered in the next sub-section.

Secondly, the Ricardian argument is about trade. But in some industries, and notably in some service industries, foreign markets are most efficiently served by a permanent presence in the market — by the establishment of a local branch or subsidiary. In a review of eighteen service industries, the Department of Commerce in the United States identified eight industries in which investment is the dominant mode for international transactions (accounting, advertising, automobile and truck leasing, banking, employment agencies, equipment leasing, hotels and motels and legal services), eight industries in which both trade and investment flows are important (communications, computer services, construction and engineering, educational services, franchising, health services, insurance and motion pictures) and only two industries in which trade flows dominate (air and maritime transport).[4] This raises the question of how foreign direct investment as a substitute for trade, or as a necessary condition for trade, should enter the analysis.

From the observation that trade and foreign direct investment may be close substitutes in the case of some services (such as insurance) and that trade and mobility of labour may be close substitutes in other cases (such as management services), some people have drawn the conclusion that there are problems in the application of standard trade theory, as developed for trade in goods, to the services sector. It is not at all clear why this should be so. Certainly, there is a particular problem for the positive theory, in that it may be hard to predict whether a comparative advantage will manifest itself as a trade flow, an investment flow or a labour flow. But from the viewpoint of the normative theory there is less of a problem. A country gains from importing services *or* allowing immigration of labour *or* receiving foreign direct investment if the terms on which these transactions take place are more favourable than the terms available on domestic transactions. The basic reasoning is the same in each case. To the extent that the three modes of commerce are close substitutes, the welfare effects of the three should also be almost the same. Nevertheless, the view that there is a problem here is sufficiently widespread to deserve more detailed attention and we consider this point later in the section.

Turning now to the other strands of the normative theory identified in the previous section, it can similarly be considered whether services deserve exceptional treatment.

Is the optimal-tariff argument especially applicable to the services sector? On the contrary, it seems unlikely that there are many countries (or even many groupings of countries acting in concert) which have available to them in the services sector trade-restrictive policies that would have an appreciable effect in reducing the cost to the country of services purchased from abroad (unless that cost had previous been raised by poor policy, which is certainly possible).

Indeed, it was argued above that, where countries have world market power to exploit, it is likely to be in their export markets rather than their import markets. Such power is better exploited by taxes on exports than by taxes on imports. And, in so far as trade policies are designed to exploit monopoly power in international markets, the difficulty of taxing imports at the border does not make a sound economic case for imposing alternative forms of restrictions on imports of services.

This is a suitable point at which to deal with the possibility that the *foreign* country has monopoly power which it is exploiting. This is quite different from the optimum-tariff argument, for that argument is concerned with how the *home* country should exercise its monopoly power, if it has any. Let us suppose, therefore, that we are concerned with policy choice in a country which does not have market power itself, but is faced by a monopolistic supplier which is offering goods or services at a price significantly above the marginal cost of production. In such a situation, there is an incentive for the country to promote (by protection or

376   BRIAN HINDLEY AND ALASDAIR SMITH

direct subsidy) the development of domestic suppliers, even if they are less efficient than the foreign monopolist, for their very existence will (i) reduce the foreign supplier's monopoly power, (ii) lower the price faced by the country and (iii) transfer some of the monopoly profits from the foreign supplier to the home country.

Of course, the application of this argument is strictly limited. It cannot be in a country's interest to produce at a cost greater than the *marginal import cost* at which supplies are obtainable from the foreign monopolist (although that marginal import cost will exceed the price charged by the monopolist which, in turn, will exceed the monopolist's cost of production). It has to be said, however, that the scenario in which a foreign supplier has significant monopoly power seems, at least in the area of services, fairly implausible. The mark-up over marginal cost must surely give an incentive to potential competitors to enter the market and to drive down the price. It may be that there are barriers to entry in particular cases, so that one foreign supplier is in a privileged and protected position, perhaps as a consequence of past colonial links. Then, there is a simple and powerful policy response, namely to remove the barriers to entry by other foreign suppliers and by domestic firms. In general, the adoption of policies which facilitate entry, whether by domestic or foreign competitors, into allegedly monopolistic markets seems likely to be a socially less costly means of curbing monopoly power than the promotion of inefficient domestic firms.

The discussion now turns to the theory of optimal policy intervention in the presence of distortions. There are two major cases, or groups of cases, in which policy interventions affecting trade flows, but by means other than tariffs, can be defended on economic grounds.

The first group of arguments was alluded to earlier, namely the presence of distortions in domestic factor markets. Factor markets may, indeed, be badly distorted in many countries, especially developing countries, with the result that the services sector is larger or smaller than it would be if resources were efficiently allocated. But there is no *a priori* means of determining whether, in practice, the effect is likely to be that the services sector is too small or too large. Moreover, application of this set of ideas to the services sector seems to raise no special conceptual difficulties. The analysis appears to apply whether the industry is producing a 'service' or a 'good'. But one member of this group of arguments is the infant-industry argument; and that argument is sufficiently important for special attention to be devoted to considering its specific relevance to the services sector (see below). Balance-of-payments arguments for protecting domestic service industries might also be included in this group. One of the authors has discussed that issue elsewhere in the context of insurance.[5] There is little to add to that discussion for services in general.

The second group of arguments for intervention also raises issues that are not, in principle, specific to service industries, although they may, in practice, have a

COMPARATIVE ADVANTAGE AND SERVICES   377

more direct relevance to certain ones than to goods industries. These are arguments for intervention based on the existence of externalities in production or consumption. Appropriate policy in either case will typically entail subsidies to activities generating positive externalities and taxes on those activities generating negative externalities. Again, as with factor-market distortions, the analytical framework is as relevant to services as to goods. If a side-effect of a service activity is to 'pollute' the environment with, say, pornographic displays then it is desirable to discourage the activity, just as it is desirable to reduce the output of goods whose production pollutes the air with smoke.

There is a case for a tax on imports only when it is imports as such which generate the negative external effects. Particular service industries (cinema and video film, popular music and advertising) provide examples of such putative negative external effects attached to imports. Such imports are often said to have deleterious effects on local cultures (in both developed and developing countries). If that is so, then there may be an economic efficiency case for border measures or restrictions on use.

This kind of externality argument raises profound issues which are not appropriately discussed in this article. For example, observers may disagree on the sign of the external effect. The necessarily large subjective element entailed in conjectures about consumption externalities in general means that it is very difficult to separate alleged externalities from bigotry (others ought to have what I think they ought to like), simple conservatism or the interests of those engaged in the domestic industry.

There are therefore three problems in the application of the normative theory of comparative cost to service industries that merit further discussion: (i) the issues involved in regulation and licensing, (ii) issues arising from foreign investment and (iii) the infant-industry issue. They will be discussed in turn.

Regulation and Licensing

It is very striking that at the domestic level, in almost all economies, the services sector is the target of government intervention and regulation of a nature and degree which is different from the intervention to which non-service activities are subject. The motivation and nature of this regulation deserves close scrutiny, first in case it reveals a genuine need for interventions specifically targeted at services or at particular services, then in order to investigate whether such interventions should affect international transactions to a greater or lesser extent than domestic transactions and, finally, to investigate the implications for international trade of the regulation which, whether for good or bad reasons, exists and is likely to continue to do so.

The fact that the services sector is subject to more detailed government intervention than other sectors is most easily seen by consulting any account of the

BRIAN HINDLEY AND ALASDAIR SMITH

economics of regulation.[6] Overwhelmingly, it is services which are subject to regulation. It may take the following forms: (i) control of the rates charged by utilities, (ii) control of entry into and of rates charged in various modes of transport, (iii) control by licensing and/or numerical restriction of entry into many services such as the law, accountancy, medicine, hairdressing and taxi driving, (iv) government ownership or control of telecommunications, broadcasting, cable television and other media and (v) detailed supervision of the structure and practices of banks, insurance companies, security traders and other financial companies.

It would be an exaggeration to suggest that there is an entirely uniform pattern to these examples of regulation. Nevertheless, two common and connected themes do emerge. The first is the danger of 'destructive competition' and the second is the need to protect the interests of ill-informed buyers.

The argument that competition will be destructive is very commonly offered in transport, being based on the alleged tendency for industries in which there are large fixed costs and fluctuating demand to be subject to competition of an intensity that leads to frequent bankruptcy and to constant changes in the services offered to consumers. Thus such cartels as the International Air Transport Association (IATA) and shipping conferences flourish under the sponsorship, and with the protection, of government. A related argument is that there will be 'cream-skimming' — a situation in which some firms are willing to supply only the most lucrative markets, so that competition leads to a deterioration or loss of service in the less lucrative markets.

It is probably true to say that economists, by and large, find these arguments less persuasive than members of the industry said to be subject to these problems. For example, arguments that competition will be destructive typically require a continuing stream of entrants into an industry, even though their presence will lead to negative profits in equilibrium. Few economists would find this absolutely inconceivable. Rather more might find it difficult to accept that the conjunction of circumstances is probable or likely to be of practical importance. Similarly, the 'cream-skimming' argument requires that protected firms should be willing to provide service to a market in which they will incur losses. An alternative and more economically plausible hypothesis is that the 'non-cream' markets are in fact profitable.

There is no particular virtue in the intuitions of economists on empirical matters. Fortunately, however, evidence from the United States of the effects of de-regulation is now available.[7] De-regulation of domestic passenger air transport has brought about a significant reduction in fares and a fair degree of both exit from and entry into the industry, but there has been very little evidence of competition of a degree that would harm consumer interests in the long run or of loss of service to marginal markets. Similarly, the relaxation of regulation of the New York Stock Exchange has brought about significant gains to the consumers of

COMPARATIVE ADVANTAGE AND SERVICES 379

its services and no evidence of the destructive competition which the stock exchange itself had predicted on the basis of the (scarcely credible) argument that its members had a high ratio of fixed to variable costs. (As any economist would have predicted, the most striking single effect of de-regulation was on the price of a 'seat' on the stock exchange, that price reflecting the value of the anticipated monopoly rents available from the limitation on entry and competition.) These, admittedly limited, examples give some grounds for adopting a sceptical approach to arguments of destructive competition, especially when they are offered by those with a clear self-interest in the restriction of competition.

The second major argument for regulation rests on the imperfect information of buyers, a problem which seems to be greater when it is an intangible service rather than a tangible good that is being purchased. But imperfect information on the part of buyers does not *ipso facto* make a case for *regulation* of suppliers. In principle, it would be possible to ensure that the relevant information was available so that buyers could make their own choice between alternative suppliers on the basis of it. This raises the problem, however, that it might be expensive for buyers to interpret such information (the balance sheets of insurance companies, for example). Moreover, when the basic information required is the same for all buyers, the duplication involved in each buyer seeking and interpreting the same information for himself is wasteful. There is a case for just one agency or person to acquire and process the information and to disseminate it to all other potential buyers. This does not have to be a government agency, although 'free-rider' problems emerge when it is not. Nor, if it is a government agency, is it necessary on this ground that it should be equipped with powers to compel suppliers rather than powers to inform buyers.

But a case for regulation starts to take shape when the information requirements of buyers are uniform, when all are likely to act in the same way on the basis of that information and when it is expensive to convey the information to them. Suppose that no fully-informed buyer would buy insurance, deposit money or fly in the aircraft of a company with characteristics below a certain level. If it is expensive to inform all potential buyers of the fact that a company's characteristics have fallen below the required level then there is a possible case for ruling that any company taking deposits, selling insurance or providing air passenger transport should display the appropriate characteristics. Companies which are unwilling or unable to attain the required level should be refused the opportunity of offering the service.

It is worth emphasising that this case rests (i) on the costs to buyers of acquiring information, (ii) on homogeneity of the information requirements of buyers and homogeneity of reactions to particular pieces of information and (iii) on the high costs to an information-gathering and information-interpreting agency of disseminating information. These conditions are quite restrictive.

The argument is not exclusive to services. Many traded goods are subject to health, safety and technical standards, presumably on identical grounds. Indeed, this fact constitutes an increasingly important problem in trade policy (especially, perhaps, within the European Community where, as with trade in services, the possibility of affecting imports by tariffs is limited). In trade in goods, as in trade in services, the basic objectives of regulation are widely seen as legitimate. But there is an important difference between goods and services. A regulatory agency can forbid a supplier of goods to sell 'sub-standard' items while permitting it to continue to sell its other lines, but in many services the distinction between the standard of the product and the acceptability of the supplier does not exist. An unsatisfactory bank is one which seems likely to default on all its obligations, a doctor of dubious competence cannot be required to supply only competent medical care and so on. Thus when the case for regulation is accepted it becomes a case for *regulating entry into the industry*. The next step is to recognise that often the natural people to police standards of entry are the existing suppliers of the product, for who can judge the competence of a prospective lawyer, accountant or hairdresser better than a professional qualified in the field? Once the industry is given a key role in setting standards of entry, or even advising on the appropriate standards of entry, the regulatory agency is in imminent danger of 'capture' by the industry, of being more concerned with protecting the interests of suppliers than those of consumers.

Then the problem of equity arises if there is ever a proposal to de-regulate or to relax standards of entry. Those who entered the industry under regulated conditions will normally have paid some form of entry fee which reflects the value of the super-normal profits associated with the restriction. A proposal which has the effect of cutting the resale value of a stock-exchange seat or a taxi licence will be seen as inequitable by those who thought that they had purchased a permanent right to operate in a protected market. The implication is that market regulation will have a 'ratchet' effect, with de-regulation being rarer than increases in regulation.

At the very least, all of this must lead one to suspect that in a regulated industry, even if there exists a good case for *some* regulation, there will be a systematic tendency for regulation to be taken too far.

What is the relevance of all this to the application of the theory of comparative cost to the services sector? Given the existence of a case for government intervention, the central question is whether *international* transactions should be treated differently from domestic transactions. On the face of it, there is no such case. If consumers need protection from over-optimistic, stupid or fraudulent suppliers, they need that protection independently of the nationality of the suppliers. The existence of a case for regulation in no sense invalidates prescriptions deriving from the theory of comparative advantage. To the extent that consumers benefit from competition, more competition seems better than less competition and foreign countries may be an important source of potential and actual competition. The established reputations of foreign suppliers may be an important source of assurance to customers. This is as true of services as of goods and such considerations argue for regulation of service industries in ways that are neutral as between domestic and foreign suppliers and that are specifically designed to avoid exclusion of foreign competition.

This, it must be recognised, is a counsel of perfection. In practice, even a well-intentioned government will find it difficult to regulate service industries in ways that do not accidentally discriminate against foreign competitors. For example, a common requirement in the banking and insurance industries is that a firm should have an adequate capital base relative to its level of operation. To require that a foreign subsidiary show evidence of such assets *in the country of operation* may be to under-estimate the possibilities of risk spreading and risk sharing among the different parts of a multinational enterprise and to impose costly restrictions on the investment policy of the firm. On the other hand, to allow the assets of the parent firm or other foreign-held assets to be used to meet solvency requirements exposes one to the danger that if the same assets are used to guarantee the solvency of several independent operations, they may be inadequate cover against the independent risks to which the multinational enterprise as a whole is subject. No doubt there is much to be gained by the adoption of methods of protecting consumers which do not discriminate against foreign competitors, but it seems impossible to avoid all conflict between the objectives of free competition and the objectives of consumer protection.

In addition, there is the problem that governments normally do not *want* to be even-handed between domestic and foreign firms and, in their attempts to protect domestic firms against foreign competition, will welcome the opportunity to design domestic policies whose ostensible purpose is to protect consumers, but which really serve to exclude, or hamper, foreign competition.

The problem of *recognising* misuse of regulatory powers may be exaggerated. It should not be difficult to test whether a measure whose supposed intention is to protect consumer interests does in fact fulfil such an objective.

Foreign Investment in Service Industries

The point has already been briefly made that, in principle, foreign investment is susceptible to the same type of analysis as international trade. An international investment will be made when both investor and recipient see in it better opportunities than they see elsewhere and this transaction, which is apparently to the private mutual benefit of the parties involved, will fail to be socially beneficial under precisely the conditions discussed earlier in the context of trade. This will be as true of investment in the services sector as of investment in the goods sector.

382   BRIAN HINDLEY AND ALASDAIR SMITH

The fact that in the services sector investment flows may be of greater relative importance than trade flows is then of no particular significance.

There is, however, the following issue which has not yet been considered in this article. If some non-optimal policies are being followed by a government, might it not be the case that other policies should be adjusted to take account of the distortions created by the first set of policies? This issue is of some practical importance in relation to the effects of trade policies on investment flows. For example, if a multinational enterprise is induced to invest in a host country only by the need to get round the host's restrictions on imports of goods, will such a 'tariff-hopping' investment necessarily be beneficial to the host? In fact, it might not be so, precisely because of the existence of the trade restriction. An import restriction benefits the producers within a country of import-competing goods at the expense of consumers. The earnings of producers are raised above the social productivity of the inputs of producers because they include a component which is simply a transfer from consumers. If foreign firms invest in an economy because the returns to such investment are raised by the presence of the import restriction, then the cost to the host country of the investment may well exceed the benefit, for the returns to the investor will exceed the true social productivity of the investment. [8] Another way to view the potential loss in this case is as a reduction in tariff revenue as imports (subject to tariffs) are replaced by the output associated with the foreign investment.

A further possibility is that inward investment, although not harmful in itself, may cause a deterioration in the terms of trade — by expanding production of exports and reducing the prices received by existing exporters. [9]

It seems implausible that either of these effects would be adverse in the case of inward investment in the services sector. In a country importing services an adverse terms-of-trade effect would require the investment to have the effect of increasing the volume of exports through the industrial relocation of any domestic factors displaced from the services sector. Such an effect, if it occurs, is likely to be small and in any event is unlikely to have an effect on the terms of trade which is sufficient to offset the positive effects of the investment. In a country which is an exporter of services, it seems equally implausible that the effects would be significant. As has already been argued, it is unlikely that many countries can influence their terms of trade in services.

Nor does it seem likely that losses from tariff-hopping investment will occur in the services sector. This is because imports of services are typically not subject to tariffs. There may be a variety of other barriers to trade which give rise to behaviour analogous to tariff-hopping investment and such barriers may generate 'rents' which correspond to the tariff revenue. For example, where there are quotas rather than tariffs, the owners of import licences earn rents from their ability to buy cheaply abroad and sell expensively at home. In so far as the direct result of foreign investment in the services sector is a reduction in imports of the service that were previously *not* taxed at the border, there is less likely to be an adverse social effect, for the rents of importers are not likely to be as socially valuable as tax revenue received by the government. To this extent, inward investment in service industries is more likely to give rise to gains to the host country than inward investment in tariff-protected goods industries (which, in practice, seems itself unlikely to give rise to losses, given taxation of profits). This conclusion applies *a fortiori* to investment in those industries (which may only occur in the services sector) in which foreign suppliers can serve the market *only* through foreign direct investment.

Finally, it is worth noting a range of general issues which arise concerning foreign direct investment and which are extensively discussed in the vast literature on the multinational enterprise. There is the possibility that foreign investment in the services sector generates positive externalities in the host country. In so far as many service industries rely on human skills and 'know-how' for their comparative advantage and in so far as many service industries can be entered on a relatively small scale (compared with manufacturing industry), contact with multinational enterprises may provide the quickest route for local residents to acquire the relevant knowledge and skills and to create a locally-based industry which does not have to rely on protection of one form or another for its existence.

On the other hand, there are the concerns which many have about foreign direct investments: transfer of technology, interference in host-country politics, transfer pricing and so on. Perhaps only in the case of communications and computer services are there issues of particular relevance to the services sector, but these general issues are beyond the scope of the article.

By contrast to the widespread feeling that foreign investment raises particular problems in the services sector, our general conclusion is that, from an economic point of view, inward investment in service industries seems more likely to give rise to economic gains to the host country than inward investment in goods industries (which, in practice, seems unlikely to give rise to losses, given sensible policy in the host country).

It has also been noted that labour migration may be a substitute for trade in services. This, however, is a form of international transaction which raises major issues which again go far beyond the scope of the article.

Infant-industry Case in Services

The essentials of the infant-industry case — and its difficulties — are the same for goods and services.[10] It is not necessary, therefore, to differentiate between goods and services in setting out the issues.

The infant-industry argument starts from the postulate that a country has an inherent comparative advantage in some activity. Nevertheless, the output of that

384   BRIAN HINDLEY AND ALASDAIR SMITH

activity is imported. The inherent comparative advantage does not display itself in current production because the local industry cannot come into existence, or expand consistently with its inherent comparative advantage, because of competition from established firms abroad.

Hence, it is said, there is a case for protection. Were the 'infant' allowed a competition-free space in which to grow, there would be a process of learning by doing and the comparative advantage would be revealed. At the end of the process the local industry would be viable without protection and this, it is said, would give rise to a net gain to the country as a whole.

Appropriate protection will expand the scale of the domestic activity and, therefore, will lead to more local residents possessing the requisite skills of the activity than would otherwise be the case. Were the argument for possession of the activity on national soil based on some externality — the needs of national defence, say — this would be sufficient. Local residents would then be bearing a cost for some specified purpose. But the attraction of the infant-industry case is exactly that it maintains that, in the aggregate, local residents will not bear a cost for supporting the activity. There will be social returns to the initial costs of protection which justify those costs in pure economic terms.

Two statements are necessary for the infant-industry argument to arrive at its conclusion that protection is justified in economic terms:

(a) Encouragement of the industry by protection is socially worthwhile. The expected social gains from protection outweigh the expected social losses when both are appropriately discounted.

(b) Without protection it is not privately worthwhile for producers to enter the industry. The expected private gains from entering the industry are outweighed by the expected private losses when both are appropriately discounted.

The problem for proponents of this argument is to explain how these two states of affairs can co-exist. The social gains from establishing the activity all accrue, in the first instance, to local producers. In the absence of protection the social losses entailed in the establishment of the industry would also accrue to them as private losses (and, depending on the form of protection, they might be smaller than the social losses from protection). If it is socially worthwhile to establish the industry by protection, therefore, it seems that it must also be privately worthwhile. The question which advocates of the infant-industry case must answer is why private producers do not act on this incentive: why protection is necessary to establish the industry.

Several answers might be given to this question. They include, for example, a social rate of discount that is lower than the private rate, different social and private attitudes towards risk and the blanket case of uninformed potential producers and well-informed members of governments. Perhaps the most important answer focusses on 'first-mover disbenefits' within the industry where the returns to the investments of those first entering the industry — for example, their investments in research and development — do not accrue to those who made the investment, but are spread over later entrants also, who, for example, acquire at low cost the knowledge which the early entrants acquired at a high cost. The optimal policy response to such problems will vary with the imperfection alleged; but the key point here is that none of the justifications for giving special assistance to infant industries is a justification for protection from foreign competition. There is always a policy response that is economically more efficient than a trade restriction.

The first point to be borne in mind when applying the infant-industry argument to services is this: the difficulties of applying a tariff to some service imports does not preclude efficient policy responses to infant-industry cases. Nor will it be an efficient response to any of the above conditions to prohibit or restrict foreign investment in the industry (which, it might be noted, will provide a possible solution to problems of first-mover disbenefits, since such disbenefits might then accrue to foreign investors to the benefit of local or potential local producers).

Applying the infant-industry argument to service industries essentially calls for answers to two questions. The first is whether the conditions required for the argument to be valid are likely to apply to service industries. The second, if they do, is what policies are appropriate?

The answer to the question of whether the circumstances of the infant-industry case apply to service industries is obviously empirical, not appropriately answered in *a priori* terms. Nevertheless, one might conjecture, first, that since entry into many service industries can be made on a relatively small scale, attitudes towards risk are likely to be a less important determinant of entry and establishment than in manufacturing industry. Second, it is difficult to think of reasons why government officials might have better sources of information on the potential of enterprises in service industries than potential entrants into those industries. Third, it is difficult to think of first-mover disbenefits that might affect service industries. Each of these points provides some ground for scepticism that the conditions of the infant-industry case will be met in service industries.

If this is incorrect, and those conditions do exist, however, neither differences between social and private rates of discount nor attitudes towards risk provide a good ground for policies specific to service industries. Both call for policies that correct the underlying problem in general — for goods and services. This might entail, for example, general policies towards capital markets or in the provision of capital for new firms. In the case of first-mover disbenefits, there will typically be some defect in the economic structure and an efficient policy will be to correct that defect so that those who invest in research or in training labour are appropriately rewarded. Only adherence to the position that government officials know best might suggest actions specific to the services sector (in the event that what they know is that entry into their domestic services sector will yield profits for entrants). Even then, the appropriate policy is a subsidy to output of the domestic services sector. It does not entail discrimination against foreign firms supplying services, whether by trade or investment.

Conclusion on the Normative Theory

This section has addressed the question of the applicability of the *normative* theory of comparative cost to the services sector. It is concluded that none of the potential difficulties in applying the normative theory of comparative cost to trade and investment in service industries appears to yield any *a priori* reason to suppose that the theory does not apply. Or, to put it more positively, the theory of comparative cost does provide a useful framework in which to analyse the particular issues which arise in the services sector. Attention now turns, therefore, to the positive issue of what actually determines comparative advantage in service industries.

WHAT DETERMINES COMPARATIVE ADVANTAGE IN SERVICE INDUSTRIES?

Evidently this is a question which ultimately requires answers based on empirical analysis. Conjecture may generate hypotheses, but hypotheses need empirical support in order to be translated into potentially useful statements about reality. In the area of trade and investment in services, however, the data necessary to test more than the most sweeping hypotheses are usually absent. Nevertheless, it seems possible to make some observations about the likely pattern of comparative advantage between developed and developing countries.

In the present context, the basic stylised fact of trade and investment in services is that services, and service-related investment, tend to flow from developed to developing countries. There are exceptions to this statement. Were the global civil aviation industry to be liberalised, for example, it is very likely that some airlines based in developing countries would expand at the expense of airlines based in developed countries. Nevertheless, it is in general true that developing countries import, and developed countries export, services.

Service industries engaging in international transactions tend to be organised around information and its exploitation. This strongly suggests that countries with a relatively large skilled labour force will have a comparative advantage in the production of services. In addition, the production of some services (especially transport) requires substantial capital. Few internationally-traded services require large amounts of labour *per se*. Where they do (shipping, construction and engineering), the companies involved are often able to find means of combining their physical assets and skills with developing-country labour. With this partial

COMPARATIVE ADVANTAGE AND SERVICES 387

exception, all of these considerations suggest that developed countries have a comparative advantage, and developing countries have a disadvantage, in the production of services.

In principle, these hypotheses are easy to test. In practice, though, there is a major problem with the availability of data and only one brave attempt has been made to break through that barrier, by André Sapir and Ernst Lutz in a study for the World Bank.[11] The study uses only a small range of industries (freight transport, passenger transport and insurance) and is typically for only a small sample of countries. It sometimes uses constructed variables that are at best an uncertain approximation of what they are attempting to proxy. Finally, it deals with trade flows only, so that any interrelationship between trade and investment flows is ignored. All these deficiencies (which are recognised and highlighted by the authors) are due to lack of data.

In spite of that problem, however, the results of the econometric analysis are in broad and sometimes strong conformity with the conjectures set out above. Professor Sapir and Dr Lutz conclude that 'the main factors shaping comparative advantage in services trade are the availability of physical and human capital'. Moreover, 'developing economies that are successful in accumulating capital have good prospects for exporting services. Nevertheless, for most developing countries, emphasizing the export of services does not appear to be a realistic prospect.'[12]

As against this, however, there are particular areas within the services sector where the development of micro-electronic technology may hold significant prospects for developing countries. Micro-electronics is advanced technology, but the 'technological gap' between developed and developing countries may be of less importance here than in other areas. The rate of diffusion of technological knowledge between firms in micro-electronics is quite unprecedented which means that one should expect a rapid rate of international diffusion also. The number of people in an electronically-based enterprise who are required to have advanced expertise will in some cases be a very small proportion of the labour force; and the levels of skill required from most of the labour force may be quite modest.[13]

A further aspect of the micro-electronic revolution is that it greatly facilitates communication between different locations, to the extent that it is now possible for a worker in one country with access to a computer terminal to receive information, instructions and 'raw materials' electronically from another country, to perform the tasks assigned to him and then to deliver the 'product' back to the distant employer or customer.[14]

A concrete example is as follows. In recent years the typesetting stage of book production has been increasingly performed in developing countries in the Middle East and Asia. The source of this apparent comparative advantage is a simple one. Typesetting is labour intensive and wages of print workers in the developed countries are particularly high relative to skilled wages in developing countries. The comparative advantage of developing countries in this area can be expected to grow as electronic transmission of data reduces transport costs and delays and as more stages of the printing process are incorporated electronically into the typesetting stage. (This example assumes that typesetting itself will remain a significant part of the printing process and is not supplanted by direct input from the writer of the material. The general point, however, will apply to any process requiring keyboard input of a routinised kind.)

CONCLUSIONS

One of the most important features of services is their role as an intermediate good. Services purchased by other producers will typically be complementary to their production and trade. To raise the price of such services, or to reduce their quality, by inappropriate policy is therefore to tax production and trade in service-using industries as well as to tax final consumers of services. Such taxation will often occur, however, without any corresponding revenue to the national treasury. The 'tax revenue' will pass directly to local producers of protected services, absorbed either in inefficient operation or in augmented profits of local producers.

Such taxation of consumers and users of services requires strong justification. In this article we have offered some reasons for being sceptical of the existence of such justification. In so far as local producers of services need protection or subsidisation to survive (which, of course, is unlikely to be the case for all of them), in so far as there is no basis in infant-industry-type externalities to expect that protection will permit a sufficient rate of increase in their acquisition of comparative advantage to justify the costs of production and in so far as there is not a positive external effect deriving from the industry (as, surely, there is not for most service industries) then the protection of local producers is simply a burden on the economy — developed or developing — that employs it. Similarly, domestic regulation of service industries needs justification and the relevant question is whether the correct balance is struck between the costs and benefits of regulation to users of services. It has been argued that, although a good case potentially exists for some regulation, there may be a systematic tendency for regulation to take forms which are sub-optimal and to go too far.

The size of the services sector suggests the possibility that the burdens implied by incorrect policy are large. The nature of service industries and of the data on their operations that are currently available — and that are likely to be available in the near future — makes any attempt at quantification a far from easy task.

This article has argued, however, that from a *conceptual* point of view there is no difficulty about applying the standard toolkit of the international economist to the

COMPARATIVE ADVANTAGE AND SERVICES 389

problems of trade and investment in services. Services are different from goods in ways that are significant and that deserve careful attention, but the powerful logic of the theory of comparative advantage transcends these differences.

---

1. This article is based on an extract from a longer paper prepared for the Secretariat of the United Nations Conference on Trade and Development (UNCTAD) on the role of services in the development process. The UNCTAD Secretariat has given permission to publish the extract as a contribution to the current debate on the services issue. An earlier version of the article was discussed at an international conference on Restrictions on Transactions in the International Market for Services convened by Wilton Park and the Trade Policy Research Centre at Wiston House, near Steyning, West Sussex, in the United Kingdom, on 30 May to 2 June 1984. We are grateful to participants in the conference, and particularly to Professor Jagdish Bhagwati, who was the discussant of the paper, for their valuable comments.

2. Ronald K. Shelp, *Beyond Industrialization: Ascendency of the Global Service Economy* (New York: Praeger, 1981) ch. 4, on 'Economic Theory: a History of Neglect', p. 85.

3. For a convenient recent survey of the empirical testing of trade theories, see Alan V. Deardorff, 'Testing Trade Theories and Predicting Trade Flows', in R.W. Jones and Peter B. Kenen (eds), *Handbook of International Economics* (Amsterdam: North-Holland, 1983) Vol. I.

4. *US Service Industries in World Markets: Current Problems and Future Policy Development* (Washington: US Government Printing Office, for the United States Department of Commerce, 1976), cited in Shelp, *op. cit.*, p. 100.

5. Brian Hindley, *Economic Analysis and Insurance Policy in the Third World*, Thames Essay No. 32 (London: Trade Policy Research Centre, 1982) pp. 23-28.

6. See, for example, Alfred E. Kahn, *The Economics of Regulation: Principles and Institutions* (New York: John Wiley, 1971) Vol. 2.

7. See, for example, Leonard W. Weiss and Michael W. Klass, *Case Studies in Regulation: Revolution and Reform* (Boston: Little Brown, 1981).

8. This argument was made rigorously in a two-sector model in Richard Brecher and Carlos Diaz-Alejandro, 'Tariffs, Foreign Capital and Immiserizing Growth', *Journal of International Economics*, November 1977.

9. A full decomposition of the welfare effects of inward investment is given in J.R. Markusen and J.R. Melvin, 'Tariffs, Capital Mobility and Foreign Ownership', *Journal of International Economics*, August 1979.

10. The classic reference on these issues is Harry G. Johnson, 'Optimal Trade Intervention in the Presence of Domestic Distortions', in Robert E. Baldwin *et al.* (eds), *Trade, Growth and the Balance of Payments* (Chicago: Rand McNally, 1965).

11. See André Sapir and Ernst Lutz, *Trade in Services: Economic Determinants and Development-related Issues*, World Bank Staff Working Paper No. 480 (Washington: World Bank, 1981).

12. *Ibid.*, p. 31.

13. See Luc Soete, 'Long Waves in Economic Growth and the International Diffusion of Technology', mimeograph, Science Policy Research Unit, University of Sussex, 1983.

14. For further discussion and related points, see Jagdish N. Bhagwati, 'Splintering and Disembodiment of Services and Developing Nations', *The World Economy*, June 1984.

'The orthodox economists have been much preoccupied with elegant elaborations of minor problems'

— Joan Robinson, *An Essay on Marxian Economics* (1947)

Regional Studies, Vol. 20.5, pp. 407-424.

The Geography of Technological Change in the Information Economy

MARK HEPWORTH

Centre for Urban and Regional Development Studies, University of Newcastle upon Tyne,
Newcastle upon Tyne NE1 7RU, UK

(Received April 1985; in revised form November 1985)

HEPWORTH M. (1986) The geography of technological change in the information economy, *Reg. Studies* **20**, 407-424. Innovations in information technology are transforming urban and regional systems through their impacts on production and distribution processes. Case studies of Canadian multi-locational firms are used to examine this spatio-economic transformation in the context of the new information-based service economy. By focusing on computer networks as spatial systems of information technology, it is shown that these innovations can lead to centralized and decentralized patterns of direct production and office activity. New insights are also developed into the telecommunications–transportation trade-off and the key role of telecommunications in regional development.

Information technology   Information economy   Services   Regional development

HEPWORTH M. (1986) La distribution spatiale de l'évolution technologique dans l'économie de l'information, *Reg. Studies* **20**, 407-424. Les innovations nées de la technologie de l'information sont à même de transformer les systèmes urbano-régionaux par suite de l'effet sur les procédés de production et de distribution. A partir des cas d'étude sur des entreprises canadiennes à localisations multiples il s'ensuit une analyse de cette mutation spatiale et économique dans le cadre d'une nouvelle économie orientée vers les services et fondée sur l'information. En concentrant sur les réseaux informatiques en tant que systèmes spatiaux de la technologie de l'information, on montre que ces innovations peuvent entraîner une répartition centralisée et décentralisée de l'activité dans les fabriques et aux bureaux. Il se développe aussi une meilleure compréhension de l'échange télécommunication–transportation et du rôle-clé des télécommunications dans le développement régional.

Technologie de l'information
Économie de l'information   Services
Développement régional

HEPWORTH M. (1986) Die Geographie technologischen Wandels in der Informationswirtschaft, *Reg. Studies* **20**, 407-424. Durch Auswirkungen auf Produktions- und Verteilerprozesse bewirken Innovationen in der Informationstechnologie die Umgestaltung städtischer und regionaler Systeme. Fälle kanadischer Firmen mit einer Vielzahl von Standorten werden untersucht, und dazu benutzt, diesen räumlich-wirtschaftlichen Wandel im Zusammenhang der neuen, auf Information basierenden Dienstleistungswirtschaft zu prüfen. Indem die Aufmerksamkeit auf Komputernetze als räumliche Systeme der Informationstechnologie konzentriert wird, wird gezeigt, dass diese Innovationen zu einem zentralisierten wie dezentralisierten Vorbild direkter Produktions- und Bürowirklichkeit führen können. Es werden auch neue Einsichten in die Wechselwirkung von Fernverbindungen und Transportwesen und die Schlüsselstellung von Fernverbindungen bei der regionalen Enfaltung herausgearbeitet.

Informationstechnologie   Informationswirtschaft
Dienstleistungen   Regionale Entwicklung

INTRODUCTION

This paper is a vivid illustration of how innovations in information technology will transform urban and regional systems. Case study evidence on Canadian firms indicates that the use of computer networks,[1] as spatial systems of information technology, may lead to a spatial reorganization of both manufacturing production and office activity. This arises from the technology's potential for overcoming time and distance constraints on production and distribution processes, controlling dispersed operations, and converting material intermediate inputs into electronic form such that they are transmittable over telecommunications lines.

It is shown that computer network innovations have enabled Canadian firms to penetrate new regional markets which, at the international level, are 'unprotected' by tariff barriers. Here, the telecommunications–transportation trade-off is of greater significance than previously assumed, owing to its applicability to both the movement of material production inputs and people.

Finally, analysis of the spatial organization of work in computer-related, printing and publishing, and research and development occupations, suggests that job opportunities in different regions are potentially affected by the 'distance-shrinking' effects of computer networking. Specifically, networking can lead to centralized and decentralized patterns of job-creation, such that today's distributional issues centre on who gets what information and where. This follows from a contextual analysis of occupational change at the national and regional level, which indicates that Canada is an information-based service economy. As a result, network innovations have far-reaching implications for scholarly research and government policy alike.

GEOGRAPHICAL RESEARCH

Most geographical literature on the so-called 'information revolution' is still anticipatory (BERRY, 1970; GODDARD, 1980) or lacks substantive evidence (RICHARDSON and CLAPP, 1985). Although 'historical contexts' for situating information technology abound (ROTHWELL, 1984; HALL, 1985), there is a paucity of empirical work on the current spatial impacts of technical change.

Thus far, innovations in information technology have not led to re-evaluations of traditional theories of regional development, which rest on key propositions about the role of information space and contact systems, the hierarchical structure of diffusion processes, and the locus of corporate control in urban and regional systems (THORGREN, 1970; TORNQVIST, 1977; PRED, 1977; BORCHERT, 1978). Yet, case study and survey research on Canadian multi-locational firms indicates that computer networks enhance head office control over dispersed operations (HEPWORTH, 1985) and distributed processing technology may induce firms to decentralize management decision-making (LANGDALE, 1983). Also, network innovations are enlarging information space owing to their 'global reach' and usage by new industries which sell variegated information to firms and governments in the international 'network marketplace'[2] (HELLEINER and CRUISE O'BRIEN, 1982). Therefore, it is incumbent on researchers to re-evaluate the roles of communications technology and information as a resource and commodity in regional development (ABLER and FALK, 1980).

Like telex and the ordinary telephone (POOL, 1977) computer network innovations will transform the space economy. Although some geographers have recognized that telecommunications' role in this transformation is linked to its technological convergence with computers (GODDARD et al., 1985), few researchers have proceeded to make computer networks the explicit focus of their empirical work (BAKIS, 1985). As a result, the telecommunications-transportation trade-off has remained an elusive and speculative concept (NILLES et al., 1976). By focusing on network innovations, fresh insights can be obtained into the key role of telecommunications in regional development. It becomes evident that telecommunications has two vital functions. First, it enables organizations to share centralized computer resources (data, programmes and processing capacity) between dispersed users through a process of information transfer—voice, data, video, and facsimile communications (TANENBAUM, 1981). And second, it enables increases in labour productivity generated by the application of computer technology at one place to be transmitted to and exploited at any other. Thus far, researchers have only considered the potential spatial impacts of voice communications (GODDARD, 1975; GODDARD and PYE, 1977) and, by considering telecommunications in isolation, have overlooked the importance of the second process. However, it is new non-voice applications of telecommunications technology and the second process (productivity transmission) that basically affect the spatial organization of labour and capital at the regional level.

Research on Canadian firms indicates that computer networks tend to be highly centralized structures, although it is now technically feasible to distribute data processing hardware (HEPWORTH, 1985). In a sample of 117 multi-locational firms from different sectors of the Canadian economy, about 90% of computing capacity was concentrated in metropolitan cities where head offices were located. Users in other cities and regions gained access to central computing resources through telecommunications lines. Assuming that usage of computer power raises labour productivity and given that head offices tend to be concentrated in a few cities, it follows that regional variations in productivity will bear little relation to the spatial distribution of capital investment. As such, networking raises serious questions as to how regional economies are modelled, productivity changes are spatially assigned and, by corollary, how and why interregional income and unemployment differentials and factor movements arise.

The above questions assume great significance in the light of new evidence on occupational change in the labour force of advanced industrialized countries. In contrast with the secular decline of direct production employment, there has been significant job growth in occupations which primarily involve producing, processing, and distributing information. By 1981, between 40% and 50% of the labour force in OECD nations worked in information occupations, or occupations considered to be immediately affected by innovations in information technology (OECD, 1981, 1985).

The horizontal (industry-wide) and vertical (function-deep) dimensions of computer networking account for its original description by BELL, 1973, as the 'transforming resource' of the post-industrial economy. Researchers have only partially used Bell's conceptual schema by sharing his emphasis on the role of knowledge (basic research) as the 'strategic resource' (BRITTON and GILMOUR, 1978). This bias reflects 'text-book' thought about the specialized role of information in regional development—that is, information as innovation diffusion (HÄGERSTRAND, 1967) and control over organizations and regions (GODDARD and SMITH, 1978).

While these traditional approaches are valid, it remains to consider not only the 'transforming resource' of the post-industrial economy but also the vast majority of its constituent labour force. By focusing on 'knowledge', researchers have emphasized the role of scientific and technical occupations in regional development (MALECKI, 1980), but generally tended to treat what BELL, 1978, later called 'information workers' as a residual category—that is, 'non-production' employment. However, the centrality of computer networks as key process technologies derives from their transformation of production and distribution processes in which information workers are intensively involved—such as clerical and scientific tasks. Therefore, in analysing the regional employment impacts of the innovation process, it is necessary to classify occupations by their information content.

While geographical research on information technology exhibits a traditional emphasis on manufacturing industry (REES *et al.*, 1983) and particularly the locational characteristics of its 'high tech' component (HALL and MARKUSEN, 1985), recent work has drawn attention to the economic prominence of services in regional development (GERSHUNY and MILES, 1983; STANBACK *et al.*, 1981). These studies have highlighted the heterogeneity of service sector activities and, by applying new taxonomies (SINGELMANN, 1978), have made conceptual and empirical distinctions between component industries—produce services, consumer services, and so on.

In this paper, an economic context for analysing computer network innovations is developed by complementing these new approaches for classifying service industries with new taxonomies for classifying occupations by their information content (PORAT, 1977). This two-dimensional perspective on labour force trends indicates that Canada is an information-based service economy.

TECHNICAL CHANGE IN THE INFORMATION ECONOMY

Innovations in information technology and the secular decline of 'blue-collar' manufacturing employment have drawn attention to the growing importance of information and services in advanced industrialized economies. These processes of economic and technical change, which are consistent with Bell's post-industrial model, are examined in the Canadian context. The changing industrial and occupational structure of Canada's labour force between 1971 and

1981 is used as a basic indicator of the services–information dimension of economic development. And, spatial analysis of the innovation process focuses on the changing regional distribution of computer capacity in the 1970s and early 1980s.

Labour force trends

Bell based his original analysis of 'post-industrial' occupational change on a simple white-collar/blue-collar dichotomy. More precise ways of defining and measuring the information component of the labour force were developed later by PORAT, 1977. The latter's work force analysis begins with settling on an 'operational' definition of information occupations:

> Does this worker's income originate *primarily* in the manipulation of symbols and information? Clearly all human endeavour contains some component of information processing. Without information processing, all cognitive functions would cease and there would be no human activity. But that definition is operationally useless. We are not saying that information workers deal exclusively in information and that other kinds of workers never deal in information. Rather we assert that certain occupations are primarily engaged in the manipulation of symbols, either directly, at a high intellectual content (such as the production of new knowledge) or at a more routine level (such as feeding computer cards into a card reader). And for other occupations, such as in personal services or direct manufacturing, information handling appears only in an ancillary fashion. It is a distinction of degree not kind (*ibid.*, p. 3).

Based on job descriptions used for the United States Population Census, Porat created an inventory of information occupations which is disaggregated into information producers, processors, distributors and infrastructure workers (Fig. 1). The information sector of the labour force is constructed by extracting information workers from all industries to form a single heterogeneous category. Residual labour forces in each industry make up the non-information sector, for example: miners in the primary sector; welders in the secondary sector; and truck drivers, hairdressers and sales counter persons in services.

Porat's taxonomy was applied to cross-tabulated 1971 and 1981 Census data on the industrial and occupational distribution of Canada's national and regional labour force. From this analysis, it was found that the proportion of information workers in the national labour force increased from 44·1% to 48·9% during the 1970s and that 60% of net growth was concentrated in information occupations (Table 1). Similar trends occurred at the regional level, although the economic base of Canada's constituent provinces differ considerably. Over the same period, service industries accounted for about 78% of net job growth and the sector's share of the national labour force

410   *Mark Hepworth*

Information producers

Scientific and technical
Examples: chemists and engineers

Market search and co-ordination
Examples: salesmen and buyers

Information gatherers
Examples: surveyors and quality inspectors

Consultative services
Examples: accountants and lawyers

Health-related consultative services
Examples: doctors

Information processors

Administrative and managerial
Examples: production managers and senior civil servants

Process control and supervisory
Examples: factory foremen and office supervisors

Clerical and related
Examples: clerks and bank tellers

Information distributors

Educators
Examples: school teachers and university lecturers

Public information disseminators
Examples: librarians and archivists

Communication workers
Examples: newspaper editors and TV directors

Information infrastructure

Information machine workers
Examples: computer operators and printing pressmen

Postal telecommunications
Examples: mail carriers and telegraph operators

Fig. 1. *Taxonomy of information occupations*

Table 1. *The occupational distribution of the labour force in Canada and the Canadian Provinces, 1971 and 1981 (%)*

		Information Sector	Non-information sector				
			Primary	Secondary	Tertiary	Quaternary	Quinary
Canada	1971	44·1	7·8	18·3	4·2	8·6	16·6
	1981	48·9	5·5	16·1	3·7	8·7	17·0
British Columbia	1971	44·6	6·2	17·3	5·1	9·2	17·2
	1981	48·4	5·1	15·1	4·3	9·3	17·7
Alberta	1971	42·3	14·6	12·0	4·1	9·0	17·7
	1981	50·1	8·9	12·3	4·0	8·9	15·9
Saskatchewan	1971	33·8	29·7	7·5	3·9	8·2	16·6
	1981	40·9	20·2	8·7	3·8	9·1	17·3
Manitoba	1971	41·7	13·3	13·6	5·0	8·6	17·5
	1981	46·0	9·1	12·4	5·1	9·0	18·4
Ontario	1971	46·6	5·0	20·5	3·5	8·6	15·5
	1981	51·0	3·7	17·7	3·2	8·5	15·8
Quebec	1971	45·0	5·5	20·4	4·4	8·3	16·0
	1981	49·4	3·6	17·4	3·7	8·5	17·4
New Brunswick	1971	38·3	8·1	18·7	6·0	9·0	19·6
	1981	42·3	6·7	17·5	4·6	9·1	19·7
Prince Edward Island	1971	32·2	19·6	13·9	4·5	8·6	21·0
	1981	37·8	14·3	13·8	4·1	8·8	21·3
Nova Scotia	1971	38·5	7·3	17·3	4·9	8·7	22·8
	1981	43·3	6·2	15·3	4·1	9·4	21·6
Newfoundland	1971	36·5	10·2	19·7	6·7	9·3	17·4
	1981	39·6	9·0	19·6	4·4	9·3	18·1

Source: Special tabulations of labour force data from the 1971 and 1981 Census of Population, Canada and the Provinces, Statistic Canada.

increased from 62·2% to 67·2% (HEPWORTH, 1985). Again, regional economies underwent similar changes in their industrial structure, such that about two-thirds of the labour force in every Canadian province worked in services by 1981.

A more integrated view of these labour force trends can be developed by characterizing industries according to Singelmann's taxonomy and their information component (Table 2). It becomes clear that the basic difference between producer and consumer services is that the former's outputs are information (documents, advice, etc.) whereas the latter's are largely a non-information service (hairstyles, sports, laundry facilities, car repairs, food and drink, etc.).

Importantly, job growth in these qualitatively different components of the service sector has highlighted the degree to which regional labour markets are becoming increasingly 'segmented' (GORDON et al., 1982). On the one hand, job growth in producer services has been concentrated in relatively well-paid and intellectually-satisfying information occupations but, on the other, job-creation in consumer services has been concentrated in low-paid, mostly part-time occupations carried out by a female-dominated labour force, for example, fast food, shop

Table 2. Changes in the information component of Canada's labour force between 1971 and 1981, by Singelmann's Industrial Classification

	% change in total labour force	% information workers in total labour force		
	(1971–81)	1971	1981	Difference
Agriculture extractive and transformative industries	−0·7	6·0	13·4	7·4
Mining	52·8	34·7	42·4	7·7
Construction	39·7	23·7	30·2	6·5
Manufacturing	29·9	38·2	39·3	1·1
Services				
Distributive services				
Transportation, communications, other utilities	39·9	50·2	53·8	3·6
Wholesale trade	61·0	61·7	62·3	0·6
Retail services	52·0	42·8	45·5	2·7
Non-profit services				
Health and welfare	66·9	32·3	35·4	3·1
Education	35·8	84·5	86·0	1·5
Religion	30·4	21·8	23·2	1·4
Producer services				
Finance, insurance, and real estate	74·6	91·7	94·0	2·3
Business services	130·2	85·8	86·0	0·2
Mainly consumer services				
Amusement and recreation	76·2	39·8	44·8	5·0
Personal services	2·0	9·6	12·0	2·4
Accommodation and food	96·6	21·1	23·7	2·6
Miscellaneous services	109·5	47·8	50·3	2·5
Public administration	38·8	54·2	62·1	7·9

sales, and laundry work (HEPWORTH, 1985). The latter process is indicated by stable growth in the non-information component of quaternary and quinary services (see Table 1).

Similar patterns of occupational change are evident in primary and secondary industry. While 'blue-collar' occupations have declined in both sectors, there has been consolidated growth in the substantial information component of Canada's manufacturing labour force. By 1981, about two-fifths of the manufacturing labour force was involved in information occupations, with this share rising to nearly 50% and above in specific industries, that is: petroleum and coal products (58·2%); chemical and chemical products (57·9%); electrical products (51·2%); and non-electrical machinery (49·3%). Essentially, information workers in primary and secondary industries (and other sectors) constitute the 'in-house' component of producer service activity, and their information outputs are embodied in final products and services as intermediate inputs of production. For example, numerous accountants, lawyers, scientists, personnel and advertising specialists are 'hidden' in the total labour force of the textile, motor car, and entertainment industry.

In sum, Canada is emerging as an information-based service economy, at least in terms of the character of work carried out by the bulk of its labour force. These workforce developments indicate not only the changing character of production in all industries, but also growing similarity in the occupational profile of service and non-service industries. The latter trend suggests that, with respect to job-generation in high-unemployment economies, the debate over which sector is the 'engine of growth' is both unnecessary and anachronous. Clearly, job options for 'blue-collar' work are declining, lower-order service occupations are poor alternatives, and what remains is a large supra-industry information sector 'located' squarely in the path of the innovation process. This is the current economic context in which innovations in information technology are occurring in Canada.

The innovation process

Canada's first computer was installed at the University of Toronto, Ontario in 1952. Between June 1966 and December 1983, the national computer population increased from 710 to 16,643, and by now 75% of all computers are used in services, 15% in manufacturing, and the remainder are in primary industries (mainly, oil and gas). The diffusion process has followed the familiar 'S' curve pattern in Canada as a whole and most provinces—that is, a low rate of adoption in the early 1970s, acceleration in the rest of the decade, and slow-down in the early 1980s as the technology matured (Table 3). This pattern is consistent with the findings of survey research on the

412   *Mark Hepworth*

Table 3. The diffusion of computer technology in Canada, 1971 to 1983, by province

	Computers per 1,000 labour force			
	5-Year Average Growth Rate 1971–6	4-Year Average Growth Rate 1977–80	3-Year Average Growth Rate 1981–3	12-Year Average Growth Rate 1971–83
Canada	2·7	12·1	5·6	8·0
British Columbia	6·7	13·2	8·8	13·2
Alberta	2·7	13·6	11·2	11·2
Saskatchewan	3·6	27·3	10·9	19·0
Manitoba	7·6	7·9	6·7	9·9
Ontario	1·7	12·4	5·5	7·4
Quebec	2·9	4·3	4·4	4·4
New Brunswick	7·2	9·1	9·8	11·7
Prince Edward Island	26·2	4·1	7·4	11·4
Nova Scotia	1·1	18·4	4·8	9·1
Newfoundland	8·0	12·7	4·9	11·9

Source: Canadian Computer Census, 1971 to 1983 (annual); Canadian Information Processing Society.

technology's use in large Canadian companies, which indicated that major capital investments in computer networks were concentrated in the second half of the 1970s.

Aggregate data on computer networks used by individual organizations do not exist. Consequently, the regional distribution of computer capacity was inferred through a sample of Canadian multi-locational firms and all federal government agencies. Data on the city location, capacity (as indicated by main memory size) and broad applications of computers used by these organizations is recorded annually by the Canadian Computer Census.[3] It was found that about 64·5% of total computer capacity used in the sample—or the dominant users of network technology—was concentrated in Ontario in 1983 (Table 4). This is consistent with the findings of a similar analysis carried out by the Federal Department of Communications.[4]

There are significant inter-sectoral differences in provincial shares of total computer capacity. Ontario which dominates national corporate and government activity, has consolidated its large share of the technology's usage. However, there has been a significant 'catching-up' effect in Western Canada, where rapid rates of economic and population growth occurred during the 1970s. In contrast, there is little evidence of spatial convergence with respect to the under-developed resource economies of the Atlantic Provinces. The most significant trend is the decline in Quebec's share of national computer capacity which occurred in all sectors.

The key factors that explain this pattern of regional

Table 4. Regional distribution of computer capacity, by sector and province, 1978 and 1983 (%)

		Manufac-turing	Oil	Agriculture, forestry, mining	Trans-portation	Finance, insurance, real estate	Trade	Computer services	Federal government	All sectors
British Columbia	1978	5·1	0·1	15·3	2·5	3·4	11·0	1·3	4·0	4·5
	1983	3·8	0·9	20·4	3·8	5·7	13·6	7·9	3·0	6·2
Alberta	1978	3·1	50·8	2·4	0·8	1·9	3·5	0·8	0·8	3·9
	1983	3·5	63·5	9·7	0·5	2·5	1·4	2·0	2·5	7·5
Saskatchewan	1978	0	0	12·1	0	0·2	0·9	8·3	0·4	2·0
	1983	0	0	15·5	0	0·4	0·1	14·4	0·2	3·9
Manitoba	1978	0·4	0	8·3	0·8	9·9	2·3	13·7	2·0	4·8
	1983	0	0·1	4·0	8·4	11·2	2·8	4·6	1·1	3·8
Ontario	1978	78·4	46·8	37·0	3·6	52·9	67·9	57·7	84·7	60·1
	1983	82·4	34·5	31·8	32·7	66·6	69·4	60·4	80·1	64·5
Quebec	1978	12·8	2·3	24·8	92·0	30·4	14·2	15·7	5·5	19·7
	1983	10·1	0·8	9·9	54·5	11·8	11·5	6·3	8·5	12·1
New Brunswick	1978	0	0	0	0·1	0·1	0	0	0·9	0·1
	1983	0·1	0·1	0	0	0	0	0	0·3	0·1
Prince Edward Island	1978	0	0	0	0	0	0	0	0	0
	1983	0	0	0	0	0	0	0	0·1	0
Nova Scotia	1978	0	0·2	0	0	1·2	0·1	0·2	1·1	0·4
	1983	0·1	0·1	0·1	0	1·6	1·2	0·3	3·3	0·8
Newfoundland	1978	0	0	0	0·1	0	0·1	1·2	0·3	0·2
	1983	0	0	0	0	0	0	4·0	0·1	0·7
Total capacity	1978	179·6	18·5	21·3	25·2	83·8	25·2	80·5	57·3	491·5
	1983	1,001·2	296·8	177·3	281·4	621·0	329·3	705·3	432·5	3844·9

Note: Computer capacity is measured by main memory size, in kilobytes.
Source: Sample from Canadian Computer Census, 1978 and 1983; Canadian Information Processing Society, Toronto.

concentration are the head office locations and centralized networking strategies of Canadian multi-locational enterprise. About 90% of private corporations concentrated the vast bulk of computing capacity—80% to 100% on average—at their head offices. Further, this level of concentration did not change significantly between 1978 and 1983, although most firms had decentralized some computer hardware. Thus, Ontario's dominant share of total computing capacity is explained by the structural characteristics of the Canadian urban system, in which Toronto and Ottawa function as national centres of corporate and federal government head office activity respectively (SEMPLE and SMITH, 1981). Similarly, Quebec's falling share is attributable to the 'exodus' of corporate head offices from Montreal to Toronto over the last two decades, and Alberta's increasing share reflects Calgary's emergence as a head office centre in the Canadian oil and gas industry (SEMPLE and GREEN, 1983).

The head office concentration of computer power clearly indicates that networks are essentially instruments of organizational control. A mail survey of Canadian firms confirmed this central role of the technology, which is reflected in the growing importance of strategic network applications (for example, decision-support analysis) relative to routine transactions and administrative applications such as payroll processing and electronic mail.

The same mail survey confirmed that most companies are pursuing centralized networking strategies, although distributed processing architectures are technically feasible. Economies of scale in data processing, which arise from intensive use of mainframe computers, proved to be the salient reason for maintaining centralized networks. Importantly, scale economies are realized by making central computing resources accessible to dispersed users through data communications channels. At present, the overall costs associated with information transfer are of secondary importance and line costs are minimized through the widespread use of concentrators, multiplexers, and other specialized devices. Finally, decentralizing tendencies arising from the adoption of more powerful and cheaper minicomputers at remote locations are not clearly evident. Although some companies have taken this option, networks constructed with mini-computer technology either have specialized applications (for example, Imperial Oil's secondary network for monitoring gas station supplies), or shared public networks and service bureau facilities are used as primary or 'backbone' transmission systems.

With the growth of information occupations and the emergence of powerful computer and telecommunications technologies, some researchers have attempted to take explicit account of the innovation process by suggesting revisions to orthodox economic models (JONSCHER, 1983). In particular,

PORAT, 1980, has suggested changing the conventional two-factor production model, $Y = f(K, L)$, as follows:

$$Y = F(KI, KN, LI, LN)$$

where: Y = output

KI = information capital inputs (e.g. computers)

KN = non-information capital inputs (e.g. lathes)

LI = information labour inputs (e.g. managers)

LN = non-information labour inputs (e.g. welders)

In other words, the corollary of distinguishing between information and non-information workers is that they use different forms of capital in carrying out their respective tasks. For example, a secretary uses a word-processor to produce a typescript and a carpenter uses a saw to create a table. In conceptual terms, Porat's model is preferable to two-factor production models, which have been traditionally used by geographers to analyse the dynamics of regional development, because the technical parameters of the production process are defined more precisely (WARSKETT, 1981).

However, evidence on diffusion patterns indicates that the spatial organization of the primary form of information capital—computers—creates a fundamental dilemma for inter-regional analysis based on traditional or Porat-type production function models. Although computing resources tend to be spatially concentrated, access to these resources is not location-dependent because they can be used over telecommunications lines. As such the primary form of information capital is unlike all other forms of non-information capital (for example, factory machinery) because workers and the bulk of their working materials can be separated by vast distances. The ultimate outcome of this spatial discontinuity, or the dis-articulation of labour and capital in given regional production functions, is that spatial variations in labour productivity will bear little relation to the spatial distribution of capital investment. Further, as information and network technology become more central to production in all sectors, this relation will become progressively weaker. Therefore, it is suggested that revisions to macro models for inter-regional analysis should be based on prior and in-depth knowledge of the innovation process itself. For this reason, our empirical analysis is situated at the micro level and investigates the process of computer network in individual companies.

CASE STUDIES OF COMPUTER NETWORKING

The case studies presented are part of a ten-firm sample which included: IBM Canada, Labatt

Breweries, and Massey-Ferguson (manufacturing); Canadian Imperial Bank of Commerce; Imperial Oil Canada (resources); Sears Canada (trade); Air Canada (transportation); and I. P. Sharp, QL Systems, and Infoglobe (computer services). All research material was collected through 1984 from two-stage personal interviews, correspondence, and follow-up telephone conversations. For each company, information was obtained on:

1. The *organizational context* in which the technology is embedded, including the locus of management decision-making and the company's competitive environment
2. The *topology* of the computer network implemented by the company, focusing on the spatial and technical characteristics of the 'backbone' system
3. The *applications* of the network, including routine and strategic applications, such as payroll-processing and decision-support functions
4. The geographical distribution of the company's informatics *manpower*, including all higher- and lower-order personnel associated with operating the network to produce in-house computer and communications services, for example, systems analysis and data entry operators.

The topology of a computer network describes the geographical configuration of its components, including computers and terminals, telecommunications lines (for data transmission), and communication processing equipment (e.g. concentrators). As 'maps' showing the spatial organization of electronic information capital used by an organization or group of organizations (e.g. banks), they are usually technical and abstract documents and resemble graph-theoretical representations of other real network systems (e.g. railroads). Topologies are likened to geometrical forms—stars, trees, loops, etc.—which indicate the spatial and functional organization of information technology. For illustration, the topologies of computer networks currently operated by companies in the Canadian oil and food-processing industries are presented (Fig. 2). Both networks have 'star' topologies, implying that information processing is highly centralized and carried out exclusively on 'host' computers at corporate head offices. In the case of the food-processing firm, multiplexers are used to economize on data communications costs, by merging traffic to and from distant ('remote') terminals into single high-capacity channels. Generally, topologies indicate the spatial organization of a network's backbone system (the main computers, communications-processing devices, and trunk lines) and imply how diverse operations are integrated and controlled within the user organization. The strategic role of the technology, however, can only be identified by further analysis of organizational structure, behaviour, and strategy.

The case study research focused on a specify cat-

egory of information occupations—computer-related or informatics jobs—although other types of occupations entered into the analysis. Informatics occupations include higher- and lower-order jobs related to the operation and development of computer-communications technology such as computer operators and data control clerks (lower-order), and systems analysts, programmers, and user training specialists (higher order). Employment in these occupations has grown rapidly in all countries, as firms and governments have developed 'in-house' informatics capabilities and new industries have evolved to sell equivalent computer-communications services in the 'network marketplace' (BARR and KOCHEN, 1984). As such, informatics jobs have been created directly by the innovation process and, along with manufacturing jobs, can be regarded as the 'first wave' of employment impacts associated with information technology.

While some economists have pointed to job-creation in informatics occupations as a positive sign (PEITCHINIS, 1981), survey research indicates that large Canadian companies have concentrated the bulk of these new jobs in head office cities (HEPWORTH, 1985). Given the distributional issues arising from this pattern of job-concentration, spatial analysis is used here to develop insights into key technical and economic factors affecting the geography of job-creation in informatics and other information occupations.

Case study one: newspaper publishing

The Globe and Mail, a Toronto-based newspaper, began operating a satellite publishing network in October 1980 following two years of research and development in California, where the *Los Angeles Times* was also experimenting with the technology. The economic motive for networking, whereby laser scanners and earth stations function as specialized computers and terminals, was to increase circulation outside the company's traditional Southern Ontario market, when it faced growing competition from two other regional newspapers, *The Toronto Star* and *The Toronto Sun*. Before the network was established, *The Globe* was printed in Toronto only and about 20,000 copies were distributed outside Ontario by air and road. The basic constraints on regional market expansion were high transportation costs (relative to printing costs and price) and distributing the newspaper in time to meet morning commuter traffic in distant Canadian cities.

The satellite network is integrated into a highly computerized process of newspaper production at *The Globe*'s central printing plant and editorial offices in Toronto (Fig. 3). A new by-product of this process is electronic material for the newspaper's on-line data base subsidiary, Infoglobe.[5] However, the final pre-printing stages are more relevant here, because they

PETROLEUM COMPANY

Network applications: market research, customer services, inventory control accounts, message services, and refinery simulation models

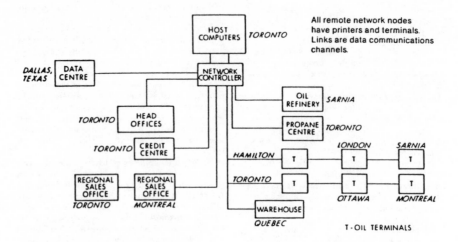

FOOD PROCESSING COMPANY

Network applications: financial control, business planning, customer services, inventory control, accounts, payroll, order entry.

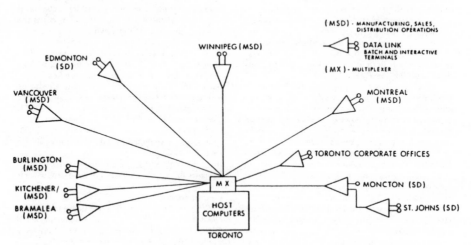

Fig. 2. *Examples of computer network topologies*

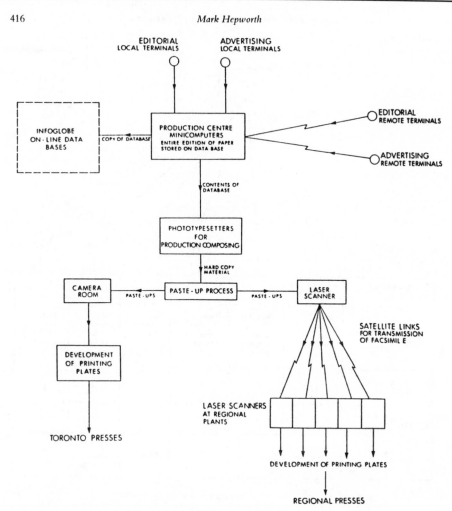

Fig. 3. *The organization of newspaper production at* The Globe and Mail

involve the creation of an electronic facsimile of each edition of the newspaper and is broadcast to distant printing plants (Fig. 4). Satellite signals are received simultaneously by all plants and converted to photographic negatives from which offset plates for the local presses are developed. This system enables the newspaper to be printed simultaneously across several time zones and distributed from six production sites to different regional markets.

Computer networking has increased *The Globe*'s daily circulation outside Ontario to about 130,000 copies. The average cost of selling the newspaper in other regions has fallen by up to 25% owing to scale economies in satellite transmission. At a cost of $700 per hour for transponder capacity, it takes only one and a half hours to broadcast the entire facsimile. Further, with wider circulation, the newspaper has attracted higher-priced national advertising, so that the immediate benefits include lower distribution costs and greater advertising revenue. In the longer term, market entry barriers have been created at the regional level and further expansion will involve outlays only on extensions to the ground segment of the network. The initial investment (excluding research and development expenditures) amounted to about $1·5 million mainly on laser scanners, but three-

Service Industries in the Global Economy II

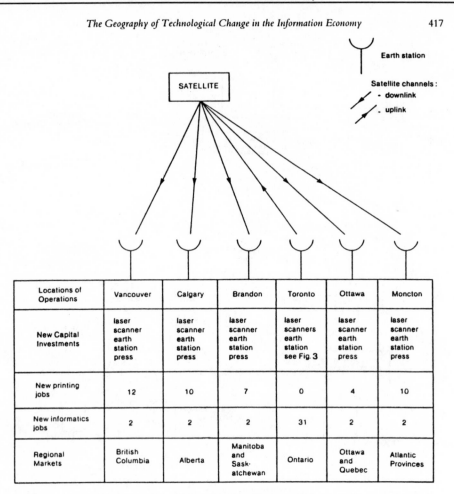

Fig. 4. *The topology of* The Globe and Mail *satellite communications network*

quarters of these capital costs had been recouped by June 1984.

Additional capital and labour is all informational, however there are important qualitative differences between these resources which are expressed spatially. New investments in traditional capital used by the industry—specifically, printing presses—have been concentrated outside Ontario. The bulk of new electronic capital is centralized in Toronto, where computer technology is used in the pre-printing stages of production, to create facsimiles, and to control all operations. Similarly, all forty-five plus new jobs in traditional printing occupations (e.g. pressmen) have

been created outside Ontario, but two-thirds of informatics jobs, including all higher-order jobs, are concentrated in Toronto. As such, the relative numbers and types of information employment generated at each location reflect the spatial organization of old and new forms of information capital.

Thus, computer networking has transformed production and distribution processes in Canada's largest newspaper. It has led to radical expansion in market areas, new loci of production, and a geographically dichotomized pattern of job-creation, whose qualitative variations reflect parallel variations in the new information capital deployed.

Case study two: research and development in electronics products

Bell Northern Research (BNR), whose head offices and main laboratories are located in Ottawa (Ontario), carries out research and development (R & D) on telecommunications and office automation products for its Montreal-based parent companies, Bell Canada and Northern Telecom. The latter manufactures three product lines which currently take up three-quarters of BNR's manpower resources—telephone switches, circuit-board design, and office automation equipment. R & D is a computer-based, labour-intensive process and 70% of all laboratory work involves creating the software embodied in Northern Telecom's electronic products.

R & D activity is distributed across several research sites in North America and Europe, because marketing of Northern Telecom's products requires that BNR's research teams work directly with the manufacturing company's dispersed customers. Face-to-face contacts are essential for identifying user requirements, ensuring products are correctly installed, and providing post-sales support. These locational imperatives have led BNR to establish new laboratories outside Canada, in the parent company's high-growth American and European markets (Table 5).

Between 1977 and 1978, a computer network was set up to co-ordinate an R & D process with a unique spatial organization (Fig. 5). A layered approach to product development enables each laboratory to specialize in only part of the work carried out for a specific product line (Fig. 6). For example, base software and hardware for telephone switches are designed and engineered in Ottawa, but user-oriented application software for the same product is developed in Texas and North Carolina. Owing to this inter-regional division of highly-skilled labour, research teams must be kept perfectly informed of changes in product specifications that arise elsewhere. As a result, network traffic consists mainly of very large volumes of R & D information being exchanged between laboratories.

Before the network was established, BNR depended on road and air transport for transferring computer tapes on which product-related information was stored. However, the increased spatial scale and complexity of R & D, arising from BNR's support of Northern Telecom's foreign market expansion, made traditional modes of information transfer inefficient. More trained personnel were required for carrying computer tapes between Ottawa and other cities and supervising customs clearance; more 'paperwork' had to be prepared for customs authorities, placing further demands on technical staff; as new products evolved and international high technology markets grew more competitive, the security risks of transferring R & D information increased accordingly; and, information had to be exchanged in faster time to direct, monitor, and control more dispersed and complex operations. As a 'transport' medium, the current BNR network is a timely and labour-saving system for directly transmitting R & D information between laboratory sites. Transborder data flows are neither detected nor subject to customs scrutiny so that intermediate inputs of Northern Telecom's products are not subject to national tariffs.

In addition to its transport function, the BNR network is used in the direct production of software. Until recently, when some laboratories were allocated computers, all software was developed over telecommunications lines on host systems located at a multi-site complex in Ottawa. Some research teams still depend on terminals, which interact with the Ottawa computer systems, and all systems software for R & D computers is developed centrally and distributed over the network. Further, computer systems at distributed sites are maintained through remote diagnostics carried out over telecommunications lines from Ottawa.

Although the spatial scale and complexity of BNR's operations have increased considerably, the bulk of informatics manpower and computer resources used to support R & D activity is still concentrated in Ottawa. There are three main reasons for this centralized pattern of informatics resource management. First, scale economies are realized in

Table 5. *Recent trends in Northern Telecom's sales and employment by geographic region*

	Sales ($ million)			Total employment		
	Canada	USA	Total	Canada	USA	Total
1982	1,248	n.a.	3,036	18,964	13,377	34,449
1981	1,335	1,047	2,571	20,776	12,737	35,444
1980	1,084	807	2,055	18,634	11,479	31,915
1979	1,001	740	1,901	18,511	14,147	33,301
1978	1,008	447	1,505	17,487	12,607	31,756
1977	1,014	193	1,222	18,303	4,048	23,577

Source: Evans Research Corporation; EDP in-depth reports (Toronto)

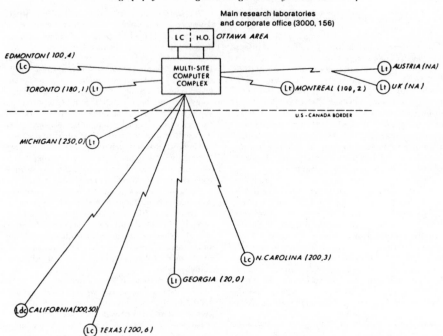

KEY: L   = Research laboratory with computer (c) or terminals (t)
        Ldc   = BNR Inc has own data centre (legally separate company)
        Z   = data communication link
        (X,Y) = (Total employment, Informatics employment)

Fig. 5.   The topology of the B N R computer network

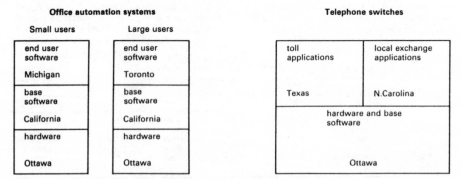

Fig. 6.   The spatial organization of research and development at Bell Northern Research

data processing, software development, and purchasing telecommunications services and computer equipment. Second, all product-related information has to be consolidated on central data bases to co-ordinate research work. And third, physical contacts are needed not only between informatics workers, owing to the problem-solving nature of software development, but also between higher order informatics personnel and line management, to assess user requirements, develop company-wide standards in computing and communications services and contribute to audit and long-range planning functions.

Computer networking has enabled BNR to maintain a centralized approach to informatics resource management because dispersed computer-based R & D can be supported directly from Ottawa. More specifically, scale economies in data processing and software development are realized by distributing the costs of providing these services over all locations. By corollary, the productivity gains of informatics workers themselves are transmitted over the network. Indeed, the number of informatics personnel employed by BNR has hardly changed since 1978, so that the same manpower has been used to provide computer and communications services to new research teams based in the United States and Europe. The employment outcomes of these spatio-economic processes are that 90% of BNR's 200+ informatics jobs is concentrated in Ottawa; however, led by Northern Telecom's foreign market expansion, 500+ research and development jobs and a 'handful' of 'machine-minding' informatics jobs (for the new distributed systems) have been created outside Canada since the network was installed.

In sum, this case study shows how computer networking can lead to decentralization of production. It has enabled BNR to decentralize the production of intermediate inputs into Northern Telecom's electronic products, because the informational characteristics of these inputs allows for their transmission over telecommunications lines. In this respect, the technical basis of these spatio-economic processes is identical to that identified in *The Globe and Mail* study, where intermediate inputs in newspaper production —editorial, advertising and computing services —were transmitted by satellite as an electronic facsimile. Unlike the *Globe* study, networking did not lead directly to regional expansion in BNR's 'markets' (because R & D services are effectively intra-corporate transactions), but indirectly the company has supported Northern Telecom's own foreign market expansion based on decentralized manufacturing and R & D activity. Finally, the geography of job-creation in informatics and production occupations (printing and software-creation) exhibited similar spatially-dichotomized patterns.

IMPLICATIONS OF THE CASE STUDY ANALYSIS

The case study findings are extremely relevant to geographical research and government policy, because the analysis has provided solid evidence of information technology's potential impacts on urban and regional systems. These implications are listed below, empirical questions are posed for future research, and other case studies are mentioned to support specific points.

1. The technical focus of geographical research on information technology should be computer networks, because the spatial reorganization of capital and labour associated with these innovations derives from the use of telecommunications and computers as 'companion' technologies.

2. The spatial organization of information capital undermines traditional theories of regional development based on closed production function models of economic growth. Specifically, the spatial distribution of capital investment, at the urban or regional level, may bear little relation to the geography of productivity change arising from the application of computer technology.

3. The increased significance of the telecommunications–transportation trade-off derives from its equal applicability to the movement of people and material inputs into production. By focusing on computer networks, it is evident that the expanded role of telecommunications arises from its integration into direct production processes, as will its traditional function as a distribution medium.

4. Network innovations have created a new form of inter-regional 'trade' in information services, which occurs in an intra-corporate and market context (I.P. Sharp, QL Systems, Infoglobe). As with merchandise trade, the balance of trade in information services will determine how different urban and regional economies are affected in terms of employment, balance of payments (at the international level), local taxation revenues, and industrial development based on local linkage-creation processes. With the growing importance of information services in all sectors, the 'stakes' of developing a comparative advantage in network-based trade increase accordingly.

5. Information-based economies are 'open' economies, in the sense that inter-regional transactions are not yet subject to national tariff policies. Although the General Agreement on Trade and Tariffs (GATT) will shortly consider services trade, the development of multilateral regulatory policies is likely to be outpaced by technological developments which are eroding national boundaries (SPERO, 1982; YUROW, 1983; TOBIN FOUNDATION, 1982).

New types of transborder services are emerging

as computer network applications are commercially exploited. For example, the WINC network operated by Mohawk Data Systems is used to collect and deliver 'electronic mail' sent between Canadian cities via the company's central 'post office' or computer centre in the United States. The 'network marketplace' is also organized on an international basis (I.P. Sharp, QL Systems, Infoglobe) and existing non-tariff barriers are poor substitutes for systematic regulation of commercial transborder data flow (ANDERLA, 1982). Similarly, although the *Globe and Mail* example is intra-national in scope, identical satellite technology is used by the world's largest newspapers, such as the *Herald Tribune*, for same-day publishing in different countries. In this instance, regional market expansion may be viewed, according to one's ideological orientation, as a new form of 'cultural imperialism' (GALTUNG, 1982) or as further evidence of the emerging 'global village' (McLUHAN, 1964). The fundamental questions raised by the case studies are: what types of information services will become increasingly network-based and traded in tariff-free sectors of the international economy?; and, what are the implications of these technologically-led processes for international trade theory, which has conventionally focused on manufacturing production? (JUSSAWALLA, 1982).

6. While computer networking creates opportunities for decentralizing factory- and office-based activities, policy-oriented analysis should consider these new opportunities in the basic context of corporate structure, behaviour, and strategy. In other case studies, organizational factors explain why programmers at Air Canada's financial offices in Winnipeg (Manitoba) work on computer systems located in Montreal (Quebec), and why all Massey-Ferguson's North American employees depend on computer systems located in the United Kingdom. In the former case, Air Canada's historical links with Winnipeg and the politics of 'high tech' job-location in Canada's crown corporations were key factors in networking strategies and overall informatics resource management. Adverse conditions in North American markets for agricultural machinery has led to corporate restructuring and substantial streamlining of Massey's operations. As a result, computer systems located in Toronto, which formerly supported all Canadian and United States operations, were closed down and satellite communications channels are now used to link North American users to computer systems in England, where Massey has centred its global network.

7. Similarly, while technological developments in distributed processing have led some researchers to suggest that large companies will decentralize

management decision-making (LANGDALE, 1979), Canadian evidence indicates that private companies are currently using hierarchical systems to maintain and support centralized organizational structures. For example, Sears Canada currently operates a Toronto-centred point-of-sale terminal network which supports the retail chain's centralized and mature merchandising strategy. At the local level, terminals provide individual stores with remote access to computer power and information that is essential to routine operations, such as credit authorization and inventory control; nationally, the terminals provide head office management with 'eyes' at all operations sites through an on-going process by which transactions data is recorded, relayed to Toronto, and stored in central data bases. The obvious question is whether Sears' Canadian competitors, who are adopting identical technology, will copy this model and centralize branch office managerial, administrative, and clerical functions? More broadly, how will computer networking affect the regional distribution of information service employment in multi-locational organizations, given the characteristic branch structure of economic activity in Canada, and what will be the cumulative effects of organizational restructuring? Clearly, empirical research on these questions is urgently needed owing to the growing importance of information services in all regional economies, but it should account for both the technological capabilities of computer networking and the organizational context in which the innovation process is embedded.

8. As the BNR study showed, computer networking can be used to establish a complex spatial division of labour, by serving as a passive medium for transferring information as work material and an active mechanism for controlling and integrating work processes at different locations. It is extremely plausible that network innovations, when used directly to reduce overall labour costs, will lead multi-locational corporations to exploit low-wage markets for information labour, 'de-skill' certain occupations through fragmentation and standardization of work tasks, and re-evaluate the need for face-to-face contacts in selective occupations. For example, access software for Infoglobe's on-line data bases is developed by programmers who work in Toronto computer systems from their homes in Kingston (Ontario), and IBM Canada has conducted a 'work-at-home' experiment with its Toronto-resident word-processing staff. Most importantly, the case studies indicate that 'home' can be in another city or country, as long as telecommunications channels can be used to access working materials—computer power and information. In

other words, computer network innovations have drawn attention to the extreme mobility of information at a time when nearly half of Canada's labour force depends on this intangible resource as working material.

9. Finally, the 'information space' in which multi-locational organizations operate has been greatly enlarged by computer network innovation. This is brought about directly by physical expansion of private networks, the commercial activities of the 'network marketplace' and government economic-technology policies. For example, BNR's research teams in the United States and Europe have the added responsibilities of monitoring R & D and marketing activities carried out by Northern Telecom's competitors. In Canada, government agencies are using networks to bring together domestic suppliers and buyers, in the belief that 'improvements' to the basic signalling functions of local product markets will lead to new patterns of linkage-creation in the national economy. And, case study research on the 'network marketplace' (I.P. Sharp, QL Systems, Infoglobe) indicates that public data base services are primarily used by multinational enterprise to monitor their global, political, economic and financial environments.

CONCLUSIONS

In-depth understanding of the technical capabilities and economic uses of computer networks is essential for various fields of geographical research—such as industry and office location, inter-regional trade, labour and capital markets, innovation diffusion, and transportation and communications. In this respect, it should be emphasized that this paper has focused on wide area networks, which are used for inter-city communications, because these innovations are relatively mature and their spatio-economic impacts are already materializing.

However, for future research, it should be recognized that the innovation process has two further inter-related stages. The first stage involves the implementation of local area networks (LANs) in offices, factories, and other operations sites; and the second is projected to be the interconnection of LANs through wide area networking to create fully-integrated, two-level systems for controlling the entire process by which goods and services are produced and distributed. Currently, most large organizations are using wide area networks for a growing range of applications (the technical focus of this paper), and widespread use of LAN technology is expected to come about through the late 1980s. In Canada and other countries, uncertainty surrounding technical standards has led to a 'wait and see' situation—particularly with respect to IBM's new LAN

technology—that has slowed down the innovation process (MOKHOFF, 1982). However, as LAN innovations accelerate, computer networking will figure as the key process technologies through which the reindustrialization of manufacturing economies and 'automation' of office economies will come about.

It has also been emphasized that the profound significance of computer networking arises from the economic context in which it is occurring. With the substantial and growing information service component of the modern economy, it is clear that network innovations will radically affect production and distribution processes in all sectors. Spatial analysis of these transformations, which will produce a new geography of economic opportunity, would benefit from thorough knowledge of the innovation process. In this regard, revisions to traditional urban and regional economic theory should not be based on an uncritical acceptance of Porat-type 'adjustments' to neo-classical equations, which cannot account for crucial spatio-economic and spatio-technical processes. It is clear that the significant 'distance-shrinking' and 'space-adjusting' characteristics of new information technology has increased rather than diminished geography's potential contribution to public debate on the distribution issues raised by the so-called 'information revolution'.

NOTES

1. A computer network is a group of independent computers and terminals which communicate with one another over telecommunications lines. Networks are classified by their main applications (e.g. point-of-sale network), topology (spatial and functional organization) and architecture (the distribution of functions between network components and the hierarchical rules that govern communications).

2. The concept is described by DORDICK, NANUS and BRADLEY, 1981, as follows:

   A network marketplace will result from the establishment of low-cost computer communications metworks . . . These networks will provide the transportation system for information processing products and services so that a mass production, mass distribution, mass marketing and mass consumption information processing industry can develop, much like the developments that followed other historic advances in transport.

3. The Canadian Computer Census (Annual: 1963–83) is carried out and published by the Canadian Information Processing Society. It lists computers by individual organization, city location, broad applications, memory size (supplementary and main memory), manufacturer and other technical features (e.g. number of data communications lines). The detailed listing covers computers which have a monthly rental value of £2000+ and overall coverage is considered to be about 80% of total capacity and 60% of the machine population.

4. See *Datacom '76*, Department of Communications, Communications Research Centre (CRC), CRC Report No. 1306, Supply and Services Canada, Ottawa, April 1977.
5. In 1981, *The Globe and Mail* began operating an on-line information retrieval service called Infoglobe. An electronic copy of each edition of the newspaper is taken off the minicomputer data base, stored on the host computer systems of a Toronto service bureau and distributed in packaged form through the latter's nation-wide network. Thus, computer networking is used by *The Globe* to produce and distribute newspaper information in traditional and new forms.

REFERENCES

ABLER R. and FALK T. (1980) Intercommunications, distance, and geographical theory, *Geografiska Annaler Series B* **62**, 59–67.
ANDERLA G. (1983) The international data market revisited, OECD Directorate for Science, Trade and Industry, OECD Paris.
BAKIS H. (1985) *Telecommunication and Organisation of Company Work Space*. Centre National d'Etudes des Télécommunications, Paris.
BARR C. and KOCHEN M. (1984) Computer-related labour in the 1980s: supply and demand, *Inf. Soc. J.* **2**, 155–80.
BELL D. (1973) *The Coming of Post-Industrial Society*. Basic Books, New York.
BELL D. (1978) The social framework of information society, in DERTOUZOS M. and MOSES J. (Eds.) *The Computer Age: A Twenty Year View*, pp. 163–211. MIT Press, Cambridge, MA.
BERRY B. (1970) The geography of the United States in the year 2000, *Trans. Brit. Inst. Geogr.* **51**, 21–54.
BORCHERT J. (1978) Major control points in American economic geography, *Ann. Am. Ass. Geogr.* **62**, 214–32.
BRITTON J. and GILMOUR J. (1978) *The Weakest Link*. Science Council of Canada, Supply and Services Canada, Ottawa.
DORDICK H., NANUS B. and BRADLEY H. (1981) *The Emerging Network Marketplace*. Ablex, Norwood, NJ.
GALTUNG J. (1982) The new international order: economics and communication, in JUSSAWALLA M. and LAMBERTON D. (Eds.), *Communication Economics and Development*, pp. 133–43. Pergamon, New York.
GERSHUNY J. and MILES I. (1983) *The New Service Economy*. Francis Pinter, London.
GERTLER M. (1984) Regional capital theory, *Progr. Hum. Geogr.* **8**, 50–81.
GODDARD J. (1975) *Office Location in Urban and Regional Development*. Oxford University Press, Oxford.
GODDARD J. (1980) Technological forecasting in a spatial context, *Futures* **12**, 90–105.
GODDARD J., GILLESPIE A., ROBINSON F. and THWAITES A. (1985) The impact of new information technology on urban and regional structure in Europe, in THWAITES A. and OAKEY R. (Eds.) *The Regional Impact of Technological Change*, pp. 215–41. Francis Pinter, London.
GODDARD J. and PYE R. (1977) Telecommunications and office location, *Reg. Studies* **11**, 19–30.
GODDARD J. and SMITH I. (1978) Changes in corporate control in the British urban system, 1972–77, *Environ. Plann. A* **10**, 1,073–84.
GORDON D., EDWARDS R. and REICH M. (1982) *Segmented Work, Divided Workers*. Cambridge University Press, Cambridge.
HÄGERSTRAND T. (1967) *Innovation Diffusion as a Spatial Process*, translated by A. PRED. University of Chicago Press, Chicago.
HALL P. (1985) The Geography of the fifth Kondratieff, in HALL P. and MARKUSEN A. (Eds.) *Silicon Landscapes*, pp. 1–19. George Allen and Unwin, New York.
HALL P. and MARKUSEN A. (Eds.) (1985) *Silicon Landscapes*. George Allen and Unwin, New York.
HELLEINER G. and CRUISE O'BRIEN R. (1982) The political economy of information in a changing international economic order, in JUSSAWALLA M. and LAMBERTON D. (Eds.) *Communication Economics and Development*, pp. 100–32. Pergamon, New York.
HEPWORTH M. (1985) Geography of the information economy, doctoral dissertation in progress, Department of Geography, University of Toronto.
JONSCHER C. (1983) Information resources and economic productivity, *Inform. Econ. Policy* **1**, 13–35.
JUSSAWALLA M. (1982) International trade theory and communication, in JUSSAWALLA M. and LAMBERTON D. (Eds.) *Communications Economics and Development*, pp. 82–99. Pergamon, New York.
LANGDALE J. (1979) The role of telecommunications in information economy, Seminar on Social Research and Telecommunications Policy, Background Papers, Telecom Australia.
McLUHAN M. (1964) *Understanding Media*. Routledge and Kegan Paul, London.
MALECKI E. (1980) Corporate organisation of R & D and the location of technological activities, *Reg. Studies* **14**, 219–34.
MARTIN J. (1981) *Computer Networks and Distributed Processing*. Prentice-Hall, Englewood Cliffs, NJ.
MOKHOFF N. (1982) Untying the office knot, *Telephony* **1**, 22–41.
OECD (1981) Information activities, electronics, and telecommunications technologies, OECD ICCP Series No. 6 (2 vols.) OECD, Paris.
OECD (1985) Update of information sector statistics, ICCP Committee Report, OECD, Paris.
PEITCHINIS S. (1981) *The Employment Implications of Computer and Telecommunications Technology*. University of Calgary Press, Calgary.
POOL I. DE S. (Ed.) (1977) *The Social Impact of the Telephone*. MIT Press, Cambridge, MA.

424   *Mark Hepworth*

PORAT M. (1977) *The Information Economy: Definition and Measurement.* Special Publication 77–12 (1), Office of Telecommunications, United States Department of Commerce, Washington.

PORAT M. (1980) Policy uses of a macroeconomic model of the information sector and microeconomic production functions, Discussion Paper, OECD Directorate for Science Technology and Industry (ICCP), OECD, Paris.

NILLES J., CARLSON F., GRAY P. and HANNEMAN G. (1976) *The Telecommunications–Transportation Trade-Off.* Wiley Interscience, New York.

PRED A. (1977) *City Systems in Advanced Economies.* Wiley, New York.

REES J., STAFFORD H., BRIGGS R. and OAKEY R. (1983) Technology and regional development in the American context, Collaboration Paper, International Institute for Applied Systems Analysis, Laxenburg, Austria.

RICHARDSON H. and CLAPP J. (1984) Technological change in information processing industries and regional income differentials in developing countries, *Int. Reg. Sci. Rev.* **9**, 241–56.

ROTHWELL R. (1984) Technological innovation and long waves in economic development, Seminar on Cambio Technologico j Desarollo Economico, University Internacional Menendez Pelayo, Santander, Spain.

SEMPLE R. and GREEN M. (1983) Interurban corporate headquarters relocation in Canada, *Cahiers de Geographie du Quebec* **27**, 389–406.

SEMPLE R. and SMITH W. (1971) Metropolitan dominance and foreign ownership in the Canadian urban system, *Can. Geogr.* **25**, 4–26.

SINGELMANN J. (1979) *From Agriculture to Services.* Sage, Beverly Hills CA.

SPERO J. (1982) Information: the policy void, *Foreign Policy* **48**, 139–56.

STANBACK T., BEARSE P., NOYELLE T. and KARASEK R. (1981) *Services: The New Economy.* Rowan and Allanheld, Totowa NJ.

TANENBAUM A. (1981) *Computer Networks.* Prentice Hall, Englewood Cliffs NJ.

THORGREN B. (1970) How do contact systems affect regional development? *Environ. Plann.* **2**, 409–27.

THE TOBIN FOUNDATION (1982) *Structural Issues in Global Communications.* The Tobin Foundation, Washington.

TORNQVIST G. (1977) Comment, in OHLIN B., HESSELBORN P. and WYJKMAN P. *The International Allocation of Economic Activity,* pp. 445–51. Macmillan, New York.

WARSKETT G. (1981) The role of information activities in total Canadian manufacturing: separability and substitution, *ICCP Series No. 6 2*, OECD, Paris.

YUROW J. (1983) Differing national perspectives on data protection, 11th annual Telecommunications Conference, presentation paper, Washington, April 27.

[31]

FOREIGN BANKS AND METROPOLITAN DEVELOPMENT: A COMPARISON OF LONDON AND NEW YORK

by

P. W. DANIELS*

Liverpool, U.K.

Foreign banks and world cities
Foreign banks have been highly selective in their choice of location for international operations; metropolitan areas which are well integrated into the global network of financial centres are favoured (Reed 1981). They are major contributors to urban change which is increasingly driven by the global economy rather than local or national economies. Friedmann (1986) has suggested that this contributes to the world city hypothesis (see also Friedmann & Wolff 1982). Although intended mainly as the starting point for political enquiry into the urbanization process the concept of the world city also suggests an economic entity in which the concentration of corporate control or financial services implies a growing, and possibly disproportionate, influence over investment and other decisions across large geographical areas and an enhancement of the dichotomy between cores and peripheries with respect to occupational structures, employment opportunities, or access to information liable to stimulate economic growth and development.

International finance has been prominent in promoting world city formation (Kindleberger 1979, Reed 1983, Langdale 1985) along with other intermediate services such as legal, advertising or computer services (Noyelle & Stanback 1984), corporate headquarters (Cohen 1981) or the global network

of telecommunications and transport services (see for example Rimmer 1986). New York and London occupy the top of the world city hierarchy (Reed 1983, Friedmann 1986) both in terms of population size and the diversity of services represented there. The macro-scale processes which have been responsible for the development of such cities are likely to be complemented by more local impacts but these have not received much attention (although see for example Cohen 1984, Mollenkopf 1984, Noyelle 1984). Does the selective location decision-making by foreign banks, for example, generate location-specific demand for output of intermediate services such as marketing, advertising, management consulting, real estate or computer services? In the medium and long term, if successful, there is also the prospect of foreign banks expanding their operations in the host country but little is known about the actual or potential impacts of these changes on labour demand or increase in the range and quality of intermediate services required. This is but one symptom of a more general hiatus in our knowledge of the role of intermediate services in contemporary urban and regional development.

Foreign banks in London and New York: some questions
The number of foreign banks directly represented (i.e. branch, representative office, or subsidiary) in New York (mainly Lower Manhattan) has increased from 114 to 307 between 1974 and 1984 and in London (mainly the City) from 264 to 403 during the same

* Department of Geography, University of Liverpool, Roxy Building, P.O. Box 147, Liverpool L69 3BX, UK.

Received, August 1986; revised, September 1986.

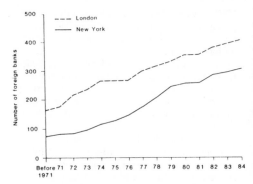

Fig. 1. *Growth of foreign banks in London and New York, 1971-1984.*
Source: Data published annually in *The Banker.*

period (Fig. 1). The New York foreign banks had 20,689 employees (mean size = 64) in early 1985 while the foreign banks in London employed 31,689 (mean = 74). In view of the rise of specialist financial or world cities, the major contribution of intermediate services such as banking to this development, and the indirect and direct effects of foreign banks on national economic well-being, especially through the very limited number of metropolitan areas in which they agglomerate, this article explores the hypothesis that the growth of foreign banks has a location-specific impact on the distribution of clients, on the demand for intermediate services, and on the demand for labour in a way which enhances the comparative advantage of those cities. Furthermore, the characteristics of any local impacts will be very similar in metropolitan areas that are major international financial centres.

There are a number of questions which can usefully be addressed in the context of this hypothesis. Firstly, do the principal reasons for the location of foreign banks in London and New York conform with the expectations generated by the world city hypothesis (Friedmann 1986) or the corporate complex hypothesis (Cohen 1979)? A related question is whether other cities are considered within the same national urban system and, if so, why are they rejected. Secondly, which segments of the market (corporate, government, private) do foreign banks in London and New York service and what is the geographical distribution of clients in these market segments? Are bank clients mainly other firms located in

Manhattan or the City (thus reinforcing the comparative advantage of these locations within the national and global urban system)? Thirdly, to what extent do foreign banks in New York and London 'buy in' other services rather than provide them from internal sources such as via headquarters in the parent country? Which intermediate services, such as advertising or insurance services, are used and what is the geographical location of the principal suppliers (by value of purchases)? What are the reasons for purchasing services externally and, as the banks become established in Manhattan or in the City, are they generating additional demand for external intermediate services? Fourthly, to what extent do foreign banks recruit staff from the local labour market and are there particular types of occupational skills required? Finally, how do foreign banks envisage developing their activities in New York and London and will any changes be largely confined to these cities or will there be 'ripple' effects as they begin to extend representation into other US and UK cities?

Foreign bank expansion in context
The last decade has witnessed an inexorable growth of international trade in services. Exports of service sector GDP increased from 7 to 11% between 1970 and 1980 and the services share of world GDP exported increased from 16 to 27% (Clairmonte & Cavanagh 1984, Herman & Van Holst 1984). Transport services and travel (business and tourism) between them account for almost 11% of world trade in goods and services while other services (including financial services, consultancy, etc.) represent some 7.5% of the total (Bank of England 1985a). Many of these are intermediate (or producer) services; in terms of average annual growth rates between 1968 and 1983 they have been performing much better than physical services such as shipping. Rapid advances in information technology, for example, have helped to lower the barriers to trade in 'invisibles' such as insurance, commodities, banking or trading in securities (Malmgren 1986, Morris 1986). As these services have become more specialized and deregulation of national and other financial markets has accelerated in recent years, both the attraction of international operations and the need to protect the specialized knowledge/expertise previously made available (in some instances) on licence

270

to overseas customers had led to a notable increase in direct representation of many intermediate service organizations at overseas locations (Daniels & Thrift 1986).

The development of a world banking system is but one symptom of these trends. Until the end of the 1960s commercial banks were only really involved in providing short-term trade finance. The provision of medium-term loans, for example, had been confined to domestic markets and the possibilities for extending these to international activities were not appreciated until the early 1970s, well after Eurocurrency lending or Eurobond operations had become established (Bank of England 1985b, Committee of London Clearing Bankers 1978). International activities offer banks the prospect of achieving corporate objectives based on balance sheet expansion funded mainly by purchasing funds in the wholesale money markets (Bank of England 1985a). Bankers must respond to a number of trends including deregulation of financial markets, the integration of global dealing as a result of new technology (Hewlett 1985, Read 1983) and the preference amongst banking clients for finance through securities markets rather than loans (Fforde 1983, Rhoades 1983). US banks led the way in responding to these trends and were followed by other foreign banks. Banks looked overseas because domestic market practices and/or domestic laws and regulations would not permit certain activities to be undertaken in local markets (see for example, Berger 1981). Reliance on domestic markets also makes banks vulnerable to the effects of fluctuations in the business cycle; diversification into overseas based operations, while not eliminating this problem, spreads the risks. Another important factor which encouraged US and other banks to expand internationally was the behaviour of their corporate customers, many of whom were multinational manufacturing and service enterprises requiring financial services to assist with the establishment and growth of overseas production, research and development or sales and marketing activities. Only the largest US banks recognised these opportunities in the late 1960s but they have since been followed on a large scale by UK, Japanese, other West European, Australasian and, most recently, banks representing Third World countries.

Technology has also encouraged greater global integration of markets (Langdale 1985). The relative costs of information processing and the related innovations in telecommunications and computer technology have steadily fallen. This not only speeds up the volume and complexity of transactions but encourages adaptation of traditional instruments and markets in government securities or foreign exchange, for example, or the 'explosion' of new financial instruments.

Direct representation in overseas markets has therefore become a prominent feature of the banking industry since the early 1970s. American banks have tended to lead the way; in London, for example, by 1950 they had 11 branches and one representative office (out of a total of 53), rising to 13 branches and 2 representative offices by 1960 (total 77) and 37 branches and 2 representative offices by 1970 (total 159) (Wilson Committee 1980). Apart from the major clearing banks such as Barclays, National Westminster or Lloyds (but not Midland), most of the UK banks in New York did not become established there until after the mid-1970s. The drive towards representation overseas is not just important for the corporate objectives of the banks, it also generates benefits for the economies in which the growth is taking place (Committee of London Clearing Bankers 1978, Brinckmann 1986). Domestic industry benefits from the high level services offered by foreign banks with the quality of these services to some extent linked to the scale and diversity of the leading national financial centre. There are indirect effects on the national economy: foreign banks are large-scale employers (71 US banks in London employed 10,972 in 1984; 25 UK banks in New York employed 3091 in 1985), they pay substantial property taxes and rents as well as business taxes such as corporation tax in the UK (it has been estimated, for example, that about half of all tax paid by banks in the UK is related directly to their international business in London), about one-third of the property tax income of the City of London comes from banks largely engaged in international transactions (Committee of London Clearing Bankers 1978). Overseas banks made an important contribution to the balance of payments, and support the overseas trading activities of the host country's industry by providing trade finance, foreign exchange services, international payments services and guarantees and performance bonds. Foreign banks are also undertaking more domestic business and play a central role in providing essential services to other markets such as insurance, commodities or the Stock Exchanges in the City or in Lower/Midtown Manhattan.

There are four main types of foreign banks. The first group represents geopolitical/strategic interests of the parent country such as looking after the interests of national companies or in some cases multinationals. A second group comprises banks which follow and provide services to multinationals in general. Subsidiaries are independent from the parent bank, usually provide retail banking, and compete on a more equal footing with the host country banks. Finally, investment banks which bring together the users and the sources of capital are becoming more important as financial markets have become more sophisticated.

Basic data

The principal source of information used for this study is the listing of foreign banks in London and New York published annually in *The Banker*. It must be stressed that the statistics derived from this source (name of bank, address, status, number of staff, name of chief representative or manager, date of entry) are only broadly indicative of the scale of foreign bank operations in New York and London (see also Haney 1985, Blanden 1984). The New York listings exclude the investment banking or securities/consumer finance and leasing subsidiaries of foreign banks. US banks involved mainly in domestic banking, such as Barclays Bank of New York, but owned by foreign banks are not included, along with members of consortia such as Nordic American which includes four Scandinavian banks (Haney 1985). More than one form of representation is common amongst foreign banks in London: banks with London-based subsidiaries in addition to branches, European representative offices using the same premises as a UK branch, banks which are London-based and UK-registered but owned by groups of shareholders rather than an institution with an ultimate country of origin other than the UK, banks which are part of consortia or joint ventures, and foreign securities houses (Blanden 1984). Joint ventures, for example, are recognised banks or deposit-taking institutions which are registered in the UK with more than one bank,

mostly foreign, among the principal shareholders. In 1984 the 27 joint ventures in London employed 2,342 staff (Blanden 1984).

Foreign bank offices are concentrated in relatively small areas of Manhattan and the City. Over half (226) of the London banks have offices in the EC2 postal district and almost 25% of these are located in Gresham Street, London Wall and Bishopgate. In the case of the latter, one building (99 Bishopgate) housed 1,398 foreign bank staff in 1985. In Manhattan almost one-third of the foreign banks have their offices in the 10022 postal district and just over 22% of the jobs are located along Park Avenue (107 banks), closely followed by Fifth Avenue with 15% (32 banks). Madison Avenue and the World Trade Center also have significant numbers of foreign banks which together account for 55% of total employment. Another notable feature in New York, but not London, is the geographical concentration of national banks; just under 50% (15) of the Japanese banks are in the World Trade Centre and 9 of the 25 UK banks are in one of two buildings: 520 and 535 Madison Avenue in Midtown.

The survey

All the banks employing more than 5 staff were included in a postal survey conducted in 1985. This was followed with a small number of face-to-face interviews with bank principals in New York and London undertaken in April-June 1986.

One-third of the banks included in the survey provided useable responses with a slightly higher level of response from London (Table 1). A follow-up procedure was not used because of the prohibitive cost, especially in relation to the New York banks. The size distribution of the respondent banks broadly represents that for the total population in which a small number of banks employ a large proportion of total employees; just 26 large banks (> 250 employees) account for 49% of London's total employment (48% of survey respondents) and 21 banks for 47% of the New York total (58% of survey respondents). Canada, Switzerland and the UK comprise the majority of the large foreign banks in New York, as do Australia, Canada and the US in London. Approximately one in four of all foreign banks in both cities employ five or fewer staff.

Branch offices are over-represented amongst the respondent banks (Table 2). The

Table 1. *Employment in foreign banks: survey population and respondents, London and New York.*

City		Bank employment[1]					
		<5	6 – 60	61 – 250	251 – 500	>500	Total
London:	All	338	5665	9980	5936	9918	31805
		(128)	(194)	(81)	(17)	(9)	(429)
	Survey[2]	–	1762	3671	2049	3027	10509
		–	(51)	(30)	(5)	(4)	(90)
New York:	All	229	4248	6480	5169	4563	20689
		(87)	(157)	(57)	(15)	(6)	(322)
	Survey	10	948	1733	1428	2348	6467
		(2)	(36)	(15)	(4)	(3)	(60)

Note: [1] Values in brackets denote number of banks.
   [2] The survey excluded foreign banks with <5 employees; two of the New York respondents had reduced staff
   numbers below this threshold after the original data base had been compiled.
Source: Survey population: *The Banker*, November 1984 and March 1985.
   Survey respondents: Questionnaire survey, Summer/Fall 1985.

Table 2. *Status of foreign banks: survey population and respondents, London and New York.*

City		Status of bank									
		Branch		Represen- tative office		Agency		Subsidiary or other		Total	
		No.	%	No.	%	No.	%	No.	%	No.	%
London:	All	238	55	146	34	–	–	44	10	428	100
	Survey	70	78	3	3	–	–	17	19	90	100
New York:	All	157	48	96	29	50	15	19	5	322	100
	Survey	41	68	4	7	12	20	3	5	60	100

Source: see Table 1.

principal reason is the low response from representative offices, although many were excluded because they fell below the employee threshold for inclusion in the survey. Representative offices simply provide information to potential customers and the chief representative may well not have had ready access to some of the information requested. Agencies, which unlike branches cannot accept domestic deposits but may be more flexible in other respects, are not necessary in London but under us banking and tax laws they are a legitimate mode of operation for banks which are not competing for domestic deposits. Subsidiaries are over-represented in the London sample but in the appropriate proportion in New York. The sample of respondent banks in both cities is therefore broadly comparable with the survey population in respect of distribution by size and status if it is assumed that the agencies in New York are essentially the same as branches (in the sense that they have very similar powers).

Reasons for opening an office in the us/uk
The two reasons cited most frequently by banks for opening an office in the uk and us are to diversify the activities of the parent bank and to improve corporate and private client access (Table 3). Almost half of the banks citing diversification as the motivating factor ranked it as '1', producing weighted ranks (Table 3) which are almost identical for each country. However, although only 38% of the respondents cited 'other factors' as reasons for opening an office, a much higher proportion indicated that these were more important than those listed in the questionnaire. Indeed, the weighted rank is highest for 'other reasons' amongst banks in the us and has the second highest ranking amongst the reasons given by the banks located in the uk.

   Respondents were asked to specify these 'other reasons' and many gave more than one. A number of banks in both the uk and us stressed the importance of access to the international financial market (especially the

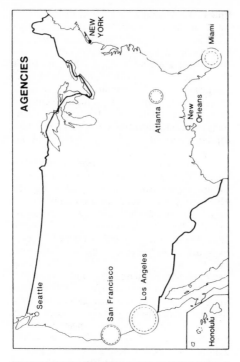

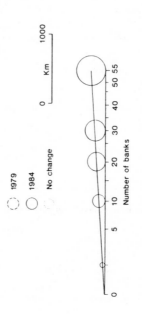

Fig. 2. *Other US representative offices, agencies and branches of foreign banks in New York, 1979 and 1984. Source:* As for Fig. 1.

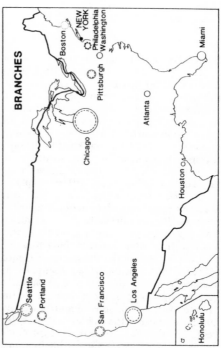

Table 3. Reasons for opening an office, foreign banks in UK and US.

Reason[1]	Proportion of all banks citing reason		Proportion ranking reason as '1'[2]		Overall rank (weighted)	
	UK	US	UK	US	UK	US
a	47	42	5	16	4.33	3.20
b	33	33	7	15	3.83	3.25
c	47	37	17	27	3.33	2.86
d	48	44	14	20	3.48	3.50
e	84	70	49	48	1.91	1.90
f	36	32	9	21	4.12	3.68
g	78	77	33	48	2.19	1.91
h	38	38	68	78	1.94	1.39

Notes: [1] a. Prestige
　　　b. Relaxation of controls on foreign bank operations
　　　c. To retain control over the specialist services you provide
　　　d. A response to the location behaviour of other foreign banks
　　　e. To diversify the activities of the parent bank
　　　f. To take advantage of the opportunities offered by enhanced international telecommunications and computer technology
　　　g. To improve corporate and private client access
　　　h. Other reasons
[2] Proportion of those banks actually citing the reason

Source: Questionnaire survey, Summer/Fall 1985.

Eurodollar market) and the pivotal role of the two cities in that market. Several banks had opened an office to expedite trade between the parent country and the US/UK or to provide financial services to corporations based in the parent country or to their US/UK parents/subsidiaries. The profitable business opportunities available were cited as the only reason for opening an office by six of the US-based respondents and two of those in the UK. Foreign banks open offices in places where their clients expect them to be; their absence from a major international financial centre might somehow make them less attractive. Yet prestige does not rank highly amongst the factors listed in Table 3, along with the suggestion that banks have opened offices in the UK or the US in response to the location behaviour of other foreign banks. A notably larger proportion of the banks in the UK cite these two reasons although a larger number of those in the US ranked them as '1'. Perhaps London's status within the UK and at the global scale as *the* largest international

financial market makes more of the banks located in the UK generally aware of prestige and the behaviour of other foreign banks. A number of the UK-based respondents also cited its time zone advantages which makes it surprising that so few banks saw the opportunities offered by enhanced international telecommunications and computer technology as an important reason for opening an office; this factor has the lowest weighted rank for both sets of respondent banks (see Table 3).

In most instances the London and New York offices are the headquarters for US or UK operations. But in order to fully gauge the extent of foreign bank participation in national banking markets it is necessary to assess the distribution of any other offices. In 1985 the major concentrations of foreign bank offices in the US outside New York were Los Angeles (97 offices), Chicago (71), Houston (53), San Francisco (51) and Miami (35) (Fig. 2). The number of offices outside New York has increased in almost every city where foreign banks were already represented in 1979 and some locations, especially in the Sun Belt states, such as Dallas, Atlanta and Miami have experienced substantial growth in the number of banks between 1979 and 1984. The 90 banks with offices outside New York in 1979 employed 8,857 staff, rising to 152 banks in 1985 with 19,762 employees (Cohen 1986). Although New York undoubtedly dominates the distribution of foreign bank offices and employment in the US it does so at a much lower level than London (Fig. 3). There are more foreign bank offices outside London but most are small offices with principal concentrations in Birmingham, Manchester, Glasgow and Edinburgh. In 1979 there were 251 offices employing 1,547 staff outside London compared with 175 offices and 2,459 employees in 1984.

However, the location patterns shown in Figs. 2 and 3 almost certainly understate the extent of foreign bank activities outside New York and London. The information used is obtained from foreign banks represented in each city; any banks with offices elsewhere in the US/UK but not represented in New York or London are not included. Amongst the banks in the survey, only 37% of those in New York have no other offices in the US; the equivalent proportion for London is 82%. Some 22% of the New York banks have one office in some other US city and 12% have offices in

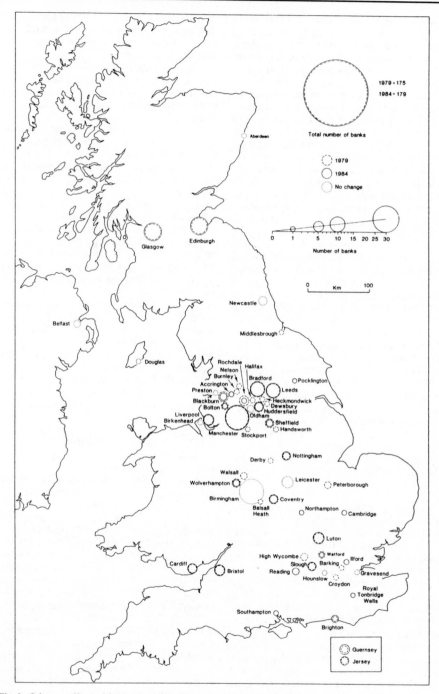

Fig. 3. *Other US offices of foreign banks based in London, 1979 and 1984.*
Source: As for Fig. 1.

four other cities. The bank with the largest number of offices in other US cities is represented in no less than 21 separate locations. The highest level of representation outside London is 8 cities (one bank) and only 6% have an office in one other UK city.

Some care is needed when interpreting the apparent expansion of foreign banks to locations outside New York and London. In most cases the decision to establish these offices may reflect a desire to improve client services or the colonization of new markets after becoming firmly established in the initial location. But the regional economies which the banks are seeking to serve are vulnerable, as are any other markets, to changing economic fortunes; the depressed state of the Texas economy following the sharp fall in crude oil prices or the deceleration in the resource-driven economic development of the Denver region all represent a reduction in foreign bank business opportunities. Yet there has been no noticeable decrease in the number of bank offices or employees in areas of this kind. Once established outside New York, foreign banks are reluctant to move their offices because of the loss of credibility with other banks and with existing or potential clients. Even though it may cost a million dollars or more to keep offices open in Houston and Chicago (both of which are currently 'quiet' locations) this is a small price to pay for continued visibility relative to total bank assets. Hence, the patterns in Fig. 2 and Fig. 3 probably incorporate a 'residual' component of offices which foreign banks are reluctant to close even if markets have contracted.

The choice of London and New York
There will inevitably be some overlap between the rationale for opening an office in the UK and the US and the factors considered when choosing London or New York as the centre for operations. It can be assumed that location decision-making involves an initial step in which a suitable country/market is identified, followed by a search for the most suitable location within that market which is best able to meet the objectives defined for a new overseas branch, agency, representative office or subsidiary. Since it has already been suggested that foreign banking involves a relatively small number of metropolitan areas the location choice decisions will very likely be highly circumscribed irrespective of the

countries offering new market opportunities. The location behaviour of other banks already established in overseas markets will also act as a constraint.

With these caveats in mind, it is not surprising that agglomeration economies are a powerful influence on the choice of London or New York as locations for foreign banks (Table 4). Proximity to US/UK banks and other financial institutions has a weighted rank of 1.59 for London and 1.46 for New York with 90% of all the banks citing the factor and 60% assigning the rank of '1' to this factor. The agreement between the statistics for the two independent samples is striking and lends a great deal of credibility to the importance of proximity and linkage potentials stressed in the office location literature (see for example Armstrong 1972, Alexander 1979, Goddard 1975, Daniels 1975, 1979). The weighted ranks for proximity to other foreign banks (1.83 for London and 2.37 for New York) reveal a similar level of importance for this factor but it is cited by almost twice as many London banks. The lower weighting may, to some extent, reflect a tendency to take this factor as 'given' when the evidence relating to the concentration of foreign banks and related employment in a small number of districts within the City or Manhattan is taken into account. Almost half the New York banks cited proximity to the headquarters of manufacturing corporations as a location factor but only 25% of the London banks did so. As a result, the weighted rank is almost 3 for New York but 4 for London, though if the scores for the 'proximity' factors are summed and averaged they are very similar: 2.47 for London and 2.30 for New York.

The commonality between London and New York in the weight attached to intra-metropolitan proximity is replicated for external linkages. The proportion of banks citing transport and telecommunications links with financial centres outside the US or UK is almost identical (Table 4) and a similar proportion of these rank this location factor as '1', producing a weighted rank which is also identical (3.83). There is less agreement about the importance of good transport links with locations elsewhere in the country. Overall, it is cited by fewer respondents and none of the US banks rank this as a first order factor. No doubt the differences between London and New York arise both from the con-

Table 4. *Ranking of factors affecting choice of London and New York for banking operations.*

Factor[1]	Proportion of all banks citing factor		Proportion ranking factor as '1'[2]		Overall rank (weighted)	
	London	New York	London	New York	London	New York
a	26	15	9	–	4.82	5.55
b	16	15	–	–	7.42	4.89
c	79	53	37	23	1.83	2.37
d	89	91	60	60	1.59	1.46
e	25	45	14	27	4.00	3.08
f	62	34	13	–	3.22	4.45
g	28	34	8	4	4.80	2.40
h	45	31	13	6	4.28	3.83
i	28	26	20	–	5.16	4.33
j	54	52	10	10	3.83	3.83
k	24	32	81	68	2.05	1.56

Notes: [1] a. Availability of suitable office space
b. Satisfactory rental arrangements
c. Proximity to other foreign banks
d. Proximity to US/UK banks and other financial institutions
e. Proximity to headquarters of manufacturing corporations
f. Availability of suitable qualified labour
g. Access to intermediate services, e.g. advertising, business services, computer services
h. Prestige
i. Good transport links with other US/UK metropolitan areas
j. Transport and telecommunications links with financial centres outside the US/UK
k. Other factors

[2] Proportion of those banks actually citing the reason

Source: Questionnaire survey, Summer/Fall 1985.

trasting scales of the urban systems of which they are a part and the relatively small number of New York foreign banks with other offices elsewhere in the United States. Of the remaining location factors (apart from 'other factors') it is worth noting that only approximately one-third of the respondents included access to a pool of intermediate services such as advertising or computer services as a location factor and less than 10% in both cities considered this to be of first order importance. There is, however, a substantial discrepancy in weighted ranks (4.80 for London, 2.40 for New York). Thus, for those banks, in New York at least, that do purchase services from external sources ready availability is an important consideration. It remains to be seen why this should not also be the case for the London foreign banks.

For approximately one in four of the banks, 'other' location factors were more significant than those listed on the survey schedule. In the case of London, five banks cited the regulatory requirements of the Bank of England whereby recognized banks must have an office within the City of London

capable of receiving notices. The attraction of London as the premier international financial centre, especially for Euromarket operations, is also of overriding importance to three banks. The dominance of New York as the unrivalled financial centre within the United States is the principal location factor in the list of 'other factors'.

None of the London foreign banks considered any other UK city as a base for the UK operations. This underlines London's primate status at national level as already revealed by the limited representation of other foreign bank offices in cities such as Manchester, Birmingham and Edinburgh. As might be expected from the earlier evidence pertaining to foreign banks outside New York, some 18% (9) of the respondents (51) who were able to say whether any other cities had been considered indicated that cities other than New York had been examined. The majority of the banks involved only considered one alternative (most frequently Chicago or Los Angeles) but one bank did examine three possibilities. The principal reasons given for rejecting possible alternatives to New

York were their inadequate facilities and lower status as international financial centres.

Type and location of bank clients

Corporate clients are the major source of business for foreign banks (i.e. the number of banks with such clients) (Table 5). Only 42% of the New York respondents indicated that they had private clients compared with 61% of those in London. The significance of this difference is difficult to assess unless the overall distribution of private business, which is to some extent governed by the type of bank, amongst all foreign banks in each city is known. A similar proportion of the New York banks have government (local, state, national or overseas) clients compared with 71% of their London counterparts. The difference between London and New York in this respect may arise from the historical associations between the London banks and Commonwealth countries.

If the corporate complex thesis is correct we would expect the geographical distribution of bank clients to be oriented towards the location of the office providing the banking services. This is broadly confirmed (Table 5) although there are some deviations which probably arise from the pivotal role of banks in the global economy. Each bank was asked to estimate the proportion of total turnover for each type of client (corporate, private, government) disaggregated according to the location of those clients. Between 25 and 30% of the banks with corporate clients did not have transactions with Manhattan or City-based firms. Approximately 10% had more than 70% of their corporate clients located in these two areas but for the majority of banks they accounted for less than 25% of their corporate clients. More than half of the New York banks have clients elsewhere in the New York region but all represent less than 25% of total corporate clients and there are no banks with more than 70% of their clients in the New York region outside Manhattan. More than 30% of the London banks have no clients in the metropolitan region (compared with 21% for New York) but three banks have more than 70% of their corporate clients located there.

The London-based banks are more likely to have corporate clients in the rest of the UK or overseas than New York-based banks but

Table 5. *Location of clients of foreign banks in London and New York.*

Type of client and location	Number of banks and proportion of all clients[1]							
	New York				London			
	Nil	<25%	>70%	Total	Nil	<25%	>70%	Total
Corporate								
Manhattan/City	12	19	5 (2)	48	25	20	7 (1)	81
NY Reg/London Reg	10	29	–		24	31	3	
Rest US/Rest UK	11	14	3 (1)		14	43	4 (1)	
Elsewhere	25	10	7 (4)		18	24	15 (4)	
Private								
Manhattan/City	12	5	4 (1)	25	30	13	7 (2)	55
NY Reg/London Reg	12	8	1		21	15	8 (2)	
Rest US/Rest UK	15	7	1 (1)		21	24	3 (1)	
Elsewhere	10	3	11 (6)		16	12	17 (5)	
Government								
Manhattan/City	20	4	2 (1)	26	38	12	6 (3)	64
NY Reg/London Reg	20	3	1		35	17	–	
Rest US/Rest UK	19	3	2 (1)		34	18	1	
Elsewhere	8	1	16 (16)		9	6	36 (15)	

Notes: [1] Number of banks specifying proportion of total turnover (100) for each type of client, i.e. 19 of the New York banks with corporate clients located in Manhattan indicated that this represented <25% of total turnover from corporate clients.
[2] Values in ( ) are number of banks specifying 100% of client type in location specified, i.e. 2 New York banks have 100% of their corporate clients located in Manhattan.

Source: Questionnaire survey, Summer/Fall 1985.

a striking feature for both cities is the large number of banks with more than 70% of their corporate clients outside the host country. Indeed, a larger number of the London banks have corporate clients elsewhere than have corporate clients in the City. As noted earlier, this no doubt reflects the longstanding involvement of the UK in financing overseas trade and encouraging foreign banks to set up there much earlier than the US with its more protectionist and highly fragmented banking system. This is one reason why US banks, anxious to escape the restrictions holding bank national expansionist policies, have often been in the forefront of the establishment of foreign bank nuclei at offshore locations. It is also the case that because of the increasingly competitive financial environment in which they now operate, the banks must engage in market-making by sending out staff to initialize contracts and to promote business.

Although taken together private clients are fewer in number, there is a consistent increase from the City/Manhattan outwards in the number of banks with such clients (Table 5). More than 53% of the London banks have overseas clients and two-thirds of these have > 70% of their private business from these sources. The proportions are almost identical for New York overseas private clients. More than 54% of the London banks in the sample do not have any local (i.e. City) private clients.

The discrepancy between metropolitan region clients and those from further afield in the rest of the US/UK or elsewhere is most clearly demonstrated in relation to government transactions. A larger number of banks indicated an involvement in such transactions but 77% of the New York respondents and 60% of those in London have no metropolitan region clients and for those that do they represent less than 25% of all government clients. Although 30% of the New York respondents had no overseas government clients, almost all those with such business (65%) indicated that it represented 100% of all the government transactions which they handled. 66% of the London banks with government clients overseas also tend to rely heavily on these clients since most represent > 70% of all their transactions in this category.

This overseas orientation of government clients is less surprising, given functions such

as assisting national companies operating in the host economy performed by many foreign banks, than the high frequency of banks with overseas private clients. Only linkages with corporate clients are numerically significant within the two metropolitan regions but large-scale dependence (> 70%) on business from firms located in these areas is smaller than for those banks with clients (whether corporate, private or government) located overseas. It would, of course, be unwise to conclude from this that the foreign bank/local market (metropolitan) client relationship is weak since there is no information available on the value of the transactions represented by the clients in each of the geographical areas. The smaller number of metropolitan clients may well result from subdivision of a very large market (by total value of transactions) amongst a large number of competing banks. Individual transactions may still, therefore, be worth much more than those undertaken further afield. The overseas connections may reflect historical or national associations with clients who may not necessarily represent a large share of all foreign bank business by value. It would clearly be interesting, but very difficult to obtain suitable disaggregated data, to transform the absolute proportions summarized in Table 5 to the value of bank transactions which they represent. This would provide a more reliable indication of the impact of foreign banks on the supply of banking services to the local (metropolitan) as opposed to national or international markets.

Use of intermediate services
Information technology and modern air communications ensure that foreign banks can compete in spatially extensive markets; the corporate complex of which they are an integral part need not necessarily dominate client location. This situation is less likely to prevail in relation to the inputs required by the banks in order to market or advertise their services, to monitor their performance, to recruit personnel, or to identify suitable office accommodation and company housing for executives. The much more direct impact of foreign banks on the demand for intermediate services will depend on the degree to which they externalize the purchase of these services rather than providing them in-house. Each bank was therefore asked to indicate the proportion (by value) of each of seven inter-

mediate services provided from internal sources and the proportion of the remainder purchased from suppliers in specified geographical areas (Tables 6 and 7). Given the size of some of the banks in the survey it is inevitable that the figures provided can only be broadly indicative but they reveal a clear dichotomy between a group of intermediate services provided largely with in-house resources and those mainly purchased from external suppliers.

Three types of intermediate service, marketing, accounting and computing are primarily provided in-house (Table 6). The proportion of banks obtaining > 70% of these services internally is very similar in both cities; marketing (90%), accounting (78%), computing (75%); indeed the proportion obtaining all these services in-house is also very similar. The decision to commit in-house resources to these three services is clearly an 'all or nothing' choice for the majority of banks. Only 10-15% of the service not obtained in-house is sought from other sources. Internal accounting or computing allows the banks to keep close control over functions which are commerically sensitive, are important to their competitors, or liable to security problems, in particular tasks in-

volving the use of computers. The much smaller number of banks purchasing marketing, accounting and computing services externally are most likely to obtain them from service firms located in the City or in Manhattan but in many cases the expenditure involved represents < 25% of total expenditure on that particular service. Again however, where banks have chosen to externalize > 70% of accounting or marketing services they make a total commitment rather than sustaining a more balanced mix between internal/external supply. The London banks reveal this tendency most strongly for the use of accounting services while for computing services it is a notable characteristic in both metropolitan areas.

The balance between in-house provision and external purchasing of intermediate services is almost completely reversed with respect to insurance, legal and real estate services; advertising seems equally likely to be provided in-house or purchased externally (Table 7). More than 90% of the New York banks and 85% of the London banks do not use insurance services from internal sources; the equivalent figures for legal services are 67% and 64% respectively and 65% and 70% respectively for real estate service. Al-

Table 6. *Number of banks in New York and London obtaining selected services primarily from internal sources.*

Type of service and source location	Services obtained (% by value)							
	New York				London			
	Nil	<25%	>70%	Total	Nil	<25%	>70%	Total
Marketing services								
Internal	2	1	46 (41)	51	4	2	70 (59)	80
Manhattan/City	44	4	1 (1)		68	6	3 (3)	
NY Reg/London Reg	49	1	–		74	4	1	
Rest US/Res UK	50	–	1		78	2	–	
Elsewhere	47	4	–		74	3	–	
Accounting services								
Internal	3	–	43 (31)	54	15	–	66 (44)	87
Manhattan/City	35	12	2 (2)		52	19	11 (11)	
NY Reg/London Reg	53	1	–		80	4	2 (2)	
Rest US/Rest UK	54	–	–		87	–	–	
Elsewhere	51	2	–		84	2	1	
Computing services								
Internal	7	1	37 (24)	50	14	4	62 (41)	85
Manhattan/City	29	10	5 (4)		52	16	12 (7)	
NY Reg/London Reg	46	2	–		77	4	3 (2)	
Rest US/Rest UK	47	–	1		81	3	1 (1)	
Elsewhere	45	3	–		79	4	1 (1)	

Source: Questionnaire Survey, Summer/Fall 1985.

Table 7. *Number of banks in New York and London obtaining selected services primarily from external sources.*

Type of service and source location	Services obtained (% by value)							
	New York				London			
	Nil	<25%	>70%	Total	Nil	<25%	>70%	Total
Insurance services								
Internal	46	–	4 (3)	51	74	2	7 (5)	87
Manhattan/City	9	3	34 (33)		10	4	66 (60)	
NY Reg/London Reg	43	–	4 (4)		80	1	4 (3)	
Rest US/Rest UK	49	–	1 (7)		84	2	1 (1)	
Elsewhere	43	1	4 (2)		83	1	2 (1)	
Legal services								
Internal	37	8	5 (2)	55	56	8	8 (1)	87
Manhattan/City	3	5	40 (32)		5	7	58 (46)	
NY Reg/London Reg	49	3	–		73	9	3 (3)	
Rest US/Rest UK	48	3	–		83	4	–	
Elsewhere	48	3	–		83	3	–	
Real estate services								
Internal	30	3	11 (9)	46	53	3	10 (6)	76
Manhattan/City	11	3	27 (24)		13	5	48 (43)	
NY Reg/London Reg	39	2	1 (1)		63	5	5 (5)	
Rest US/Rest UK	44	2	–		73	2	–	
Elsewhere	43	1	–		74	1	1 (1)	
Advertising services								
Internal	24	3	13 (11)	42	41	6	27 (21)	78
Manhattan/City	17	4	15 (10)		38	7	27 (24)	
NY Reg/London Reg	37	2	–		62	3	9 (5)	
Rest US/Rest UK	39	1	–		76	1	1 (1)	
Elsewhere	31	4	7 (5)		70	–	5 (3)	

Source: Questionnaire, Summer/Fall 1985.

most all the external demand for these services is focussed on the most readily accessible sources: Manhattan or the City of London. For the majority of banks this represents at least 70% of their total purchases by value and in 75-80% of cases all such expenditure is made in these areas. Concentration of external purchases is most strongly developed in New York, especially for real estate and legal services. There are a limited number of suppliers to London banks located in the metropolitan region but they comprise less than 5% of the contacts with external suppliers. Intermediate service located in other parts of the US or the UK hardly benefit at all (directly at least) from foreign bank service purchasing behaviour. If existing foreign banks continue to expand and new ones become established in London and New York, then provided that they continue to externalize certain service requirements it is likely that this will enhance further the complex of supporting activities already well developed

in the two prime downtown locations and, to a lesser degree, in the surrounding metropolitan regions.

Advertising services are less readily identified as external rather than in-house requirements (Table 7). Just over half of the banks in both samples do not obtain these services internally but if they do there is a preference for at least 70% of expenditure remaining in-house. More than half of the banks purchase external advertising and, again, the majority rely almost completely on these sources. Advertising agencies with local (Manhattan/City) offices are the principal beneficiaries although more than 10% of the London banks have strong links (> 70% of expenditure on advertising) with firms located elsewhere in the metropolitan region. Advertising is also the service most likely to be obtained from overseas agencies, reflecting the influence of head office contacts with advertisers, the likelihood that advertising strategies are international rather than national or local in the sense that many of the target clients are participants in the activities located in the other supranational and international financial centres around the world, and the recent prominence of international mergers and takeovers by leading advertising agencies.

Increased use of external intermediate services?

The majority of the banks have increased the proportion of their expenditure on intermediate services obtained from external suppliers since they were first established in New York and London. Almost 52% of the New York banks are in this category and 62% of those in London. Only 13% of the New York respondents indicated that the proportion of expenditure had decreased. The equivalent figure for London is 8%. This leaves a group of banks where expenditure on external intermediate service has remained constant since they were established: 28% in New York and 29% in London.

Table 8. *Factors influencing increases in expenditure on external purchase of services.*

Factor[1]	Ranking			
	No. of banks assigning rank as '1'		Weighted rank	
	New York	London	New York	London
a.	1 (6)[2]	8 (20)	2.33	2.05
b.	4 (9)	5 (24)	1.89	2.67
c.	16 (22)	29 (43)	1.45	1.63
d.	– (2)	2 (10)	3.00	3.40
e.	5 (12)	4 (19)	1.75	2.68
f.	2 (11)	5 (25)	2.45	2.44
g.	4 (5)	11 (13)	1.40	1.23

Notes:[1] a. Bank policy changes have encouraged use of external services
b. Autonomy of New York/London office in choice of services
c. More specialized services required by New York/London office
d. Marketing by suppliers of specialized services
e. Services purchased external to the organization are obtainable at lower cost
f. Improved knowledge of the range and quality of services available
g. Other factor/s

[2] Values in brackets are total number of banks citing each factor

Source: Questionnaire survey, Summer/Fall 1985.

There are a number of factors which might influence decisions to purchase services from external sources and these have been ranked by those banks reporting an increase in the proportion of such expenditure (Table 8). Factors not included in the list given on the survey schedule have the highest weighted average for New York and London although only 16% and 23% respectively of the eligible respondents mentioned 'other reasons'. The high weighting may arise from the tendency for respondents not to include the 'other reasons' in a ranking from 1 to n in the way typical of those respondents referring only to the list provided. An increase in the size of the office or growth in business is most frequently specified as an 'other reason' by London banks. In one case it is suggested that as the number of intermediate services required has increased it has proved more difficult to provide them from within a branch of the present size; another bank describes externalization of service consumption as a natural tendency as business has grown. Internal expertise has been assembled where appropriate but, when this is not cost-effective, external relationships are developed. Similar reasons, increased business and a related tendency to look more carefully at external suppliers, are also cited by the small number of New York banks specifying 'other reasons' (Table 8).

By far the most frequently mentioned reason, and the factor with the second highest weighted rank, for increased expenditure on external services is the requirement for more specialized services. As Greenfield (1966) has observed, specialized intermediate service suppliers can usually offer their expertise at lower unit cost and in a more prompt and effective manner than multi-functional or multi-service enterprises such as, in this case, banks. They will also, in the interests of sustaining competitiveness, be at the leading edge of any developments or innovations associated with the service they provide. As intermediate services have become increasingly specialized it clearly becomes difficult, even for large international organizations, to retain the necessary personnel with the requisite skills and knowledge to provide highly specialized inputs required infrequently, often at short notice and certainly not on a day-to-day basis. In such circumstances, it makes more sense to bring in specialist suppliers who are engaged at different times (and therefore made viable) by a large number of client organizations. Thus, 77% of the London banks cited the need for more specialized services (with 67% ranking it as '1') and 71% (73% ranking it as '1') in New York. A related factor is the lower cost of services purchased externally and this is ranked third (1.75) by London banks but only fifth by the New York banks. Improved knowledge of the range and quality of intermediate services available is cited by more than a third of the respondents in both cities and has an almost identical weighted rank (Table 8). But this is somewhat lower than the rank ascribed to conscious policies by foreign banks to encourage use of external services and the related factor of greater autonomy of the New York/London offices in the choice of service sources.

Local labour demand

The number of jobs in foreign banks has grown steadily as the number of offices in each city has increased (see Fig. 1). While it might be expected that some of the most senior and specialized personnel would be assigned to overseas locations using the resources of the parent organization, the majority of middle and lower management together with workers engaged primarily in routine work will be recruited from local labour markets. Staff recruitment is undoubtedly dictated by cost but there are additional considerations. Clients may prefer to deal with UK or US employees rather than expatriates. On the other hand clients may be reassured if they deal with senior expatriates who confirm the 'foreign' character of the banks and can provide authoritative assessments of their own national economy,

strength of the currency or investment opportunities. In some countries, especially those with a shortage of suitably qualified personnel, foreign banks are required to recruit almost all their staff from local sources and limits are set on the number of expatriates allowed.

The actual proportion of current (Summer/Fall 1985) staff recruited from the local labour market varies considerably between banks. The majority of the New York banks in the survey obtained 75-100% of their employees from local sources, mainly the metropolitan region. The average of 77% somewhat understates the position because one bank only obtained 7% of its staff locally. The picture is much the same for London although the average is higher at 87% and eight banks recruited all their staff from the London area (compared with just three in New York). The proportion given by each bank for staff recruited locally can be used to estimate the absolute number of employees obtained by the banks in the sample. The figure for New York is 7,857 (89% of total staff) and 9,343 for London (70% of total staff). About a third of all the staff recruited in London are sought by US banks (17/90) and in New York the UK banks (6/60) account for a large share of total demand (3,785). Japanese banks are prominent amongst the respondents in both cities but require much smaller numbers of staff: 840 and 622 in London and New York respectively.

The absolute level of local demand for labour is an important measure of the impact of foreign bank growth but even more significant is the occupational structure of demand. This will influence the level of local incomes, the scope for raising skill levels, and the at-

Table 9. *Proportion of total local recruits in selected occupation categories.*

Occupation	Proportion of local recruits							
	New York[1]				London[1]			
	Nil	<10%	11−25%	>70%	Nil	<10%	11−25%	>70%
Managerial	12	24	12	1	11	40	25	−
Professional	19	15	12	1	20	25	27	1
Technical	20	18	9	1	22	38	15	−
Clerical	−	1	1	15	−	1	5	27
Other	43	7	4	1	50	30	3	−

Note: [1] N = 55 (New York) and 85 (London)

Source: Questionnaire survey, Summer/Fall 1985.

Tijdschrift voor Econ. en Soc. Geografie 77 (1986) Nr. 4

tractiveness of the metropolitan economy for other economic activities wanting to draw upon the pool of occupational skills in the local labour market. The proportion of staff in five broad occupation groups recruited by each bank in the local labour market reveals a substantial emphasis on demand for clerical and related staff rather than employees in managerial, professional and technical occupations (Table 9). Approximately 30% of the banks in London and New York recruited more than 70% of their staff for clerical positions. Most of the remainder sought to fill 50-60% of their vacancies with clerical workers. While direct comparision is difficult, these proportions are higher than the share of office and clerical workers in financial services and the securities industry in New York City in 1981: 52.7% and 55.0% respectively (Cohen 1984). Of particular concern in New York is that both the investment bank and legal services industries employ much smaller numbers of workers from minority and ethnic groups than represented in the metropolitan population as a whole (Cohen 1984, Mollenkopf 1984). This means that the impact of any growth in these industries, and the associated demand for clerical workers, is transmitted mainly to the middle and outer suburbs rather than to the inner-city neighbourhoods. It is not known to what extent the foreign banks in New York fit this model but it is likely that their recruitment patterns are similar to those explored by Cohen (1984) for investment banks.

All the foreign banks recruit clerical workers but one in three in New York have not recruited any staff in professional or technical occupations and one in four of those in London. For the majority of the banks recruiting staff in these occupations they represent less than 25% of the total staff required. Much will depend on the size of the office and the services which it provides; small establishments will have more polarized occupational structures in which managerial and clerical staff will predominate. It is also possible that professional and technical staff are brought in from overseas locations because of their familiarity with their employer's operational, computing or legal procedures, for example. It may be more costly and time consuming to hire and train local specialists although as the scale of foreign bank operations increases the pool of suitably trained labour should also grow and make local recruitment more attractive.

The majority of banks do recruit staff in managerial positions from the metropolitan labour markets but they usually comprise less than 10% of all staff required. This suggests that, if the share of managerial staff in the labour force at large is between 15-20% (see, for example, Cohen 1984), many managers are imported from the parent country of the foreign bank. Since a smaller proportion of London-based banks (less than 13%) do not recruit any managers locally it may well be that the pool of potential employees at this level is superior to that found in New York where 22% of the foreign banks do not obtain any managerial personnel from local sources.

Conclusion

The results of this study suggest a degree of parallelism in the behaviour of foreign banks in London and New York with respect both to location decision-making and the demands placed upon the local metropolitan economy. Foreign banks are highly selective when choosing locations from which to operate in overseas markets and there are indications that a cumulative effect ensures that only a very few 'world cities' are favoured. A few of the London and New York banks have other offices elsewhere in the UK or the US but concentration, especially in London relative to other UK cities, is well established.

A more decentralized pattern of foreign banks could emerge if their representation increases in host countries. Almost all the banks participating in the survey expected their activities in the US and the UK to increase over the next five years. There is, however, a significant difference between New York and London ($\chi^2 = 19.97$, pb = .0005) with respect to the expected location of these increases. Almost 35% of the foreign banks in New York indicated that any changes will largely involve the establishment of agencies, branches or representative offices in other US cities; only 7% of the London foreign banks anticipated expansion at UK locations other than London and the City in particular. Some 5% of the banks in both cities thought that the changes would involve both the metropolitan areas in which they are currently concentrated and locations elsewhere in the US and the UK. In view of the relative flexibility permitted by telecommunications and the increasing tendency for the banks to seek out their clients, rather than *vice versa*, a number of the New York banks are considering decentralizing some of their functions within the Tri-State region or beyond. The high cost of New York is a disincentive but the relaxation of bank controls and related incentives in states such as Delaware are also influential.

For most foreign banks, however, agglomeration economies ranked highly with reference to the choice of New York and London as bases for US/UK operations. This is confirmed by the pattern of foreign bank demand for intermediate services which are primarily obtained from external sources: insurance, legal and real estate services. Some 50% of the banks using these services channel more than 70% of their expenditure to suppliers in Manhattan or the City. Some demand extends to suppliers in the surrounding metropolitan regions but not much further. Advertising services are equally likely to be provided from internal as external sources while marketing, accounting and computing services are primarily obtained in-house. The limited number of banks purchasing these services externally do, however, favour City and Manhattan suppliers.

The majority of banks in both cities are increasing their use of external intermediate services. The principal reason is cost, the increasing specialization of service inputs required and the difficulty of obtaining and/or retaining suitably qualified personnel. A number of banks indicated that as the scale of their operations increased it was inevitable that external demand for services would also expand although some expressed the opposite; that as they become larger they expect to externalize less. An example often quoted is the hiring of a UK or US legal specialist to replace counsel from head office.

A large proportion of the foreign banks' demand for labour in the local labour market is directed towards clerical workers. They also recruit staff in managerial occupations, partly because of the pool of suitably qualified labour created by the presence of other banks. There is only limited demand for professional and technical staff and this may reflect the functional characteristics of foreign bank offices and, if they use external intermediate services, many of the inputs from staff in these occupations will clearly be supplied from elsewhere.

Acknowledgements:

A grant towards the cost of interviewing foreign bank principals in New York from the United States Information Agency is gratefully acknowledged. The author is also greatly indebted to the bank vice-presidents in London and New York who generously gave their time for interviews and provided comments on an earlier draft of this paper.

References:

ALEXANDER, I. (1979), *Office Location and Public Policy.* London: Longman.
ARMSTRONG, R. B. (1972), *The Office Industry: Patterns of Growth and Location.* Cambridge, Mass.: MIT Press.
BANK OF ENGLAND (1985a), Services in the UK Economy. *Bank of England Quarterly Bulletin* 25, pp. 404-414.
BANK OF ENGLAND (1985b), Managing Change in International Banking: A Central Banker's View. *Bank of England Quarterly Bulletin* 25, pp. 553-558.
BERGER, F. E. (1981), The Emerging Transformation of the US Banking System. *The Banker* 131, pp. 25-39.
BLANDEN, M. (1984), Foreign Banks in London: Newcomers to the City. *The Banker* 134, pp. 93-105.
BRINCKMANN, J. H. (1986), The Force of the Foreign Threat. *International Correspondent Banker,* pp. 16-18.
CLAIRMONTE, F. & J. CAVANAGH (1984), Transnational Corporations and Services: The Final Frontier. *Trade and Development* 5, pp. 215-273.
COHEN, R. B. (1979), The Changing Transactions Economy and its Spatial Consequences. *Ekistics* 274, pp. 7-15.

COHEN, R. B. (1981), The New International Divison of Labour, Multinational Corporations and the Urban Hierarchy. *In:* M. J. DEAR & A. J. SCOTT, eds., *Urbanization and Urban Planning in Capitalist Society.* London: Methuen.
COHEN, R. B. (1984), The Investment Banking Industry. New York: Conservation of Human Resources (mimeo).
COHEN, E. (1986), Japanese and Nordic Influence. *The Banker* 136, pp. 102-134.
COMMITTEE OF LONDON CLEARING BANKERS (1978), *The London Clearing Banks.* London: Longman.
DANIELS, P. W. (1975), *Office Location: An Urban and Regional Study.* London: Bell.
DANIELS, P. W., ed. (1979), *Spatial Patterns of Office Growth and Location.* Chichester: Wiley.
DANIELS, P. W. & N. J. THRIFT (1986), UK Producer Services: The International Dimension. Paper prepared for IBG Limited Life Working Party on Producer Services in Britain (mimeo).
FFORDE, J. S. (1983), Competition and Regulation in British Banking. *Bank of England Quarterly Bulletin* 23, pp. 363-376.

FRIEDMANN, J. (1986), The World City Hypothesis. *Development and Change* 17, pp. 69-83.

FRIEDMANN, J. & G. WOLFF (1982), World City Formation: An Agenda for Research and Action. *International Journal for Urban and Regional Research* 6, pp. 309-344.

GODDARD, J. B. (1975), *Office Location in Urban and Regional Development.* London: Oxford University Press.

GREENFIELD, H. I. (1966), *Manpower and the Growth of Producer Services.* New York: Columbia University Press.

HANEY, S. (1985), Foreign Banks: More New Names in New York. *The Banker* 135, pp. 109-113.

HERMANN, B. & B. VAN HOLST (1984), *International Trade in Services: Some Theoretical and Practical Problems.* Rotterdam: Netherlands Economic Institute.

HEWLETT, N. (1985), New Technology and Banking Employment in the EEC. *Futures* 17, pp. 34-44.

KINDLEBERGER, C. P. (1979), *The Formation of Financial Centers.* Princeton: Princeton University Press.

LANGDALE, J. (1985), Electronic Funds Transfer and the Internationalisation of the Banking and Finance Industry. *Geoforum* 16, pp. 1-13.

MALMGREN, H. B. (1986), Negotiating International Rules for Trade in Services. *Economic Impact* 53, pp. 27-32.

MOLLENKOPF, J. (1984), The Corporate Legal Services Industry. New York: Conservation of Human Resources (mimeo).

MORRIS, F. E. (1986), The Changing World of Central Banking. *New England Economic Review* March/April, pp. 3-19.

NOYELLE, T. J. (1984), The Management Consultancy Industry. New York: Conservation of Human Resources (mimeo).

NOYELLE, T. J. & T. M. STANBACK (1984), *The Economic Transformation of American Cities.* Totowa, NJ: Rowman and Allanheld.

READ, C. N. (1983), Information Technology in Banking. *Long Range Planning* 16, pp. 21-30.

REED, H. C. (1981), *The Pre-Eminence of International Finance Centres.* New York: Praeger.

REED, H. C. (1983), Appraising Corporate Investment Policy: A Financial Centre Theory of Foreign Direct Investment. *In:* C. P. KINDLEBERGER & D. B. AUDRETSCH, eds. *The Multinational Corporation in the 1980s,* pp. 219-244. Cambridge, Mass.: MIT Press.

RHOADES, S. A. (1983), Concentration of World Banking and the Role of US Banks Among the 100 Largest, 1956-80. *Journal of Banking and Finance* 7, pp. 427-437.

RIMMER, P. J. (1986), Japan's World Cities: Tokyo, Osaka, Nagoya and Tokaido Megalopolis. *Development and Change* 17, pp. 121-157.

WILSON COMMITTEE (1980), *Evidence on the Financing of Industry and Trade* (Submission by American Banks Association of London). London: Her Majesty's Stationery Office.

[32]

Urban Studies (1987), **24**, 534–546
© 1987 Urban Studies

Telecommunications, World Cities, and Urban Policy

Mitchell L. Moss

[*First received March 1987; in final form, July 1987*]

Introduction

Cities are the communication centers of our civilization yet, we know remarkably little about how information and telecommunications technologies affect central cities and their surrounding metropolitan areas. Many observers believe that new information systems will ultimately lead to the demise of cities by allowing electronic means of communication to substitute for face-to-face exchanges. (Webber, 1973; Downs, 1985; Kellerman, 1984). Technologies, such as telecommuting, teleconferencing, and electronic mail will, it is argued, eliminate the differences between home and office and city and country by providing the benefits of urban life without confronting the problems of the city — such as commuting, crime, congestion, and pollution. This article explores the way that telecommunications technologies are leading to the centralization of business services in a small number of principal world cities, while simultaneously leading to the dispersion of routine information-based activities to the periphery of the metropolitan regions surrounding the largest central cities. The article consists of three parts: 1) a discussion of the communications deregulation and its effects on telecommunications infrastructure; 2) an analysis of the office location for advanced 'producer services' in major world cities; 3) a reconsideration of urban policy and economic development strategies for information-intensive cities.

Cities and Communications

The rise of the modern city is integrally linked to advances in communications technology: the telephone was essential to the development of the office building, the key architectural innovation of the twentieth century city. Prior to the telephone, human messengers were the primary means of bringing information into and out of office buildings. As one observer wrote in 1908, 'Suppose there was no telephone and every message had to be carried by a personal messenger. How much room do you think the necessary elevators would leave for offices? Such structures [skyscrapers] would be an economic impossibility.' (Pool, 1980).

Despite the contribution of communications to urban growth, far more attention has been given to transportation systems than to communications systems in the study of cities. 'There exists a considerable geographical literature on the analysis and design of transportation networks, but there is no comparable literature on communication networks' (Abler, 1974). Although investing in urban infrastructure is widely regarded as a means to stimulate urban development, urban infrastructure policies have primarily focused on physical systems for the movement of people, water, cargo, and vehicles. 'As compared to all other major urban infrastructure investments, the telephone impact is the least documented, even though it is just about the oldest and the most familiar' (Meier, 1985).

Mitchell L. Moss is Director of the Urban Research Centre, New York University, New York.

The telecommunications infrastructure — which includes the wires, ducts, and channels that carry voice, data, and video signals — remains a mystery in most cities. In part, this is due to the fact that key components of the telecommunications infrastructure, such as underground cables and rooftop microwave transmitters, are not visible to the public (Blazar, Spector, and Grathwol, 1985). Unlike airports and garbage disposal plants, telecommunications facilities are not known for their negative side effects, and, until recently, have not been the source of public disputes and controversy. Moreover, the predominant role of either regulated monopolies or central government agencies in the design and development of communication facilities has meant that there have been few opportunities for local governments to intervene, whether through land use regulation or capital assistance. Airports, highways, and subways, by contrast, regardless of their funding source, are highly visible elements of the urban infrastructure that typically fall under the jurisdiction of one or more local and regional agencies. This situation is gradually changing, as public agencies have come to recognize the importance of communications in economic development and, as citizens groups have expressed concerns about potential health hazards from telecommunications facilities.

More than a quarter of a century ago, Meier observed that 'an intensification of communications, knowledge and controls seemed to be highly correlated with the growth of cities' (Meier, 1962). Although Meier emphasized the need for systematic measures of the transactions that occur in cities, with the notable exception of Abler, Pred, Goddard and Gottmann remarkably little empirical work on communications within and among cities has been done. One area which has received considerable attention has been the relationship of communications to the location of offices (Goddard, 1975; Goddard and Pye, 1977; Hepworth, 1986; Pye, 1979; Thorngren, 1977).

Alternative Approaches to Communications and Urban Growth

There are two major schools of thought regarding the effects of communications technology on office location (Bakis, 1981). The conventional wisdom is that new information and communications technologies will eliminate the need for central cities since technology makes it possible to transact business without requiring face-to-face contact. Abler observed that with the shift from industrial to information activities, the locational advantages of a city would diminish. 'Advances in information transmission may soon permit us to disperse information-gathering and decision-making activities away from metropolitan centers, and electronic communication media will make all kinds of information equally abundant everywhere in the nation, if not the world. When that occurs, the downtown areas of our metropolitan centers are sure to lose some of their locational advantages for management and governmental activities' (Abler, 1970).

More recently, a study of office location concluded that 'the central city is continuing to lose its locational advantage and uniqueness within the metropolitan spatial structure. Technological changes continue to lower the necessity for concentration. Emerging telecommunications technologies promise an even greater freedom of locational choice' (Kutay, 1986). The proposition that cities and communities need not be defined by a sense of physical place and that accessibility through communications systems would replace propinquity in the creation of communities was raised by Webber who observed that 'the glue that once held the spatial settlement together is now dissolving, and the settlement is dispersing over ever widening terrains' (Webber, 1968). Although Webber was a pioneer in recognizing the significance of communications in extending the boundaries of social communities, he overestimated the degree to which technology would erode the need for cities and the potential for remote areas to replace metropolitan centers.

"For the first time in history, it might be possible to locate on a mountain top and to maintain intimate, real-time, and realistic contact with business or other associates. All persons tapped into the global communications net would have ties approximating those used today in a given metropolitan region" (Webber, 1968).

The second approach has been taken by Gottmann who argues that the telephone has had a 'dual impact' on office location: '... first it has freed the office from the previous necessity of locating next to the operations it directed; second, it has helped to gather offices in large concentrations in special

536   MITCHELL L. MOSS

areas' (Gottmann, 1977). The effects of telecommunications systems on cities depends on the
functions that urban centers perform. The shift from
the factory to the office and the concomitant growth
of white-collar work beginning in the nineteenth
century had enormous consequence for cities. 'The
growth of white-collar occupations of all kinds,
then, is without doubt the most important single
explanation for the growth of the world cities in the
period since 1850' (Hall, 1984). In the future, it will
be the computer and telecommunications system,
rather than the white collar which drives urban
growth, and, in certain cases, decline.

While advances in transportation and communications technologies have long made it possible to
disperse both the headquarters and production of
manufacturing activities to suburban locations,
cities that are centers for 'information-intensive
services', (e.g. accounting, advertising, banking, law,
management consulting, publishing) are likely to
benefit from the greater use of sophisticated information and telecommunications technologies. The
opportunities that communications technologies
present for multinational firms to engage in the
provision of global services has also heightened the
value of information to co-ordinate international
activities. 'If the possession of product, process, or
material technology is one of the foundations of
ownership advantages in manufacturing industry,
then that of information and management, organizational and marketing technology, is the key to
success in the provision of business services' (Dunning and Norman, 1983). In fact, the greater the
extent of geographic decentralization, the greater
the need for centralization of key control activities.
'Telecommunications has eliminated the dichotomy
between centralization and decentralization and
allowed decentralization with centralization' (Keen,
1986). Not all cities will benefit from 'telecommunications technologies; rather, those cities whose
economic life is based on the exchange of information, both face-to-face and electronically, will be
strengthened by the capacity to participate in the
increased global marketplace for business services
through communications technologies. Indeed,
Chinitz suggests that communications technologies
will improve the efficiency with which information is
transmitted in central cities; '... technological developments and capital investments which facilitate
interaction within the CBD and reduce congestion

favor the CBD by expanding its holding capacity. ...
the new CDP [computer and data processing]
technologies, by facilitating communication within
the CBD will expand its capacity' (Chinitz, 1984).

International Information Capitals

New telecommunications technologies, in conjunction with the internationalization of services and
finance, are strengthening a handful of world cities
such as New York, London, Tokyo, Los Angeles,
and Hong Kong. These cities, at one time centers for
the manufacture of goods, are now the centers for
the production of information that is distributed
electronically around the globe. In reviewing the
changing economic fortunes of industrial cities,
Newton has identified a similar trend in urban
transformation, without explicitly considering the
role of telecommunications technology:

> ...western cities may have lost their supreme
> importance as centers of industry and production,
> but they have gained as the centers of the
> coordination and control of production, and as
> centers of consumption. ...As the production and
> the distribution of goods becomes more complex,
> more differentiated and more spatially specialized,
> so the need for centralized integration and
> planning becomes more essential, and the office
> block tends to replace the factory in the city
> (Newton, 1986).

Communications technology, by extending the
global reach of cities that are centers for information-based services, also affects the relationship of a
city to its home nation. The world information
capitals increasingly resemble the 'city-states' of
ancient Greece, for their destiny is remarkably
independent of their own domestic national economies. Such cities are intricately linked to each
other through sophisticated telecommunications networks that operate on an around-the-clock basis.
The face-to-face activities that occur in these cities
have not been made obsolete by new technology;
rather, technology has extended the geographic
reach of the individuals and firms that transact
business in these world capitals. The operational
boundaries of a city are no longer defined by
geography or law, but by the reach of phone lines
and computer networks. As McLuhan stated, 'a
speed-up in communications always enables a

central authority to extend its operations to more distant margins' (McLuhan, 1964).

The emergence of such international information capitals is not measured by traditional criteria such as population size, land area, or employment. The world's top ten cities in terms of population are not the principal world cities with regard to amount of economic activity, location of information industries, or the flow of communication messages. The number of people living in a city may be an adequate measure of a city's importance in a nation-state, but it does not fully measure the significance of a city in today's global economy. Population size was critical to city growth when the purpose of cities was to provide large numbers of laborers to work in factories devoted to the manufacture and assembly of goods; today, the location of foreign banks, number of long distance telephone calls, and penetration of telex machines may be a more appropriate barometer of a city's economic health and vitality.

Telecommunications Policy and Infrastructure

The deregulation of the telecommunications industry in the United States and the privatization of telecommunications in other advanced industrial nations is leading to the creation of a new telecommunications infrastructure designed to serve the information — intensive activities of large metropolitan regions. Decisions concerning investment in new telecommunications systems are no longer made solely by governmental agencies concerned with uniformity of service; rather, in today's competitive telecommunications environment, decisions concerning telecommunications infrastructure are increasingly based upon market demand.

There are three main components to the telecommunications infrastructure: long-distance or inter-city systems; regional or local distribution systems; and intra-building or intra-complex communications systems, such as local area networks or 'smart building' systems. While competition in the United States first appeared in the provision of long distance service, deregulation and technological innovation are also leading to competition at the local and regional level (Moss, 1986). For cities such as London, Tokyo, and New York, that are centers for information and financial services, understanding how the new infrastructure will help or hinder their

capacity to attract and retain growing information — intensive industries has enormous importance.

Optical Fiber Systems and Cities

In the United States, a telecommunications infrastructure is being built that relies on optical fiber rather than traditional pairs of copper wire. Among the advantages of optical fiber systems are their large carrying capacity, the speed at which they transmit information, their signal strength, and their high security. The current state of the technology and the economics of fiber favor high-volume point-to-point communications — from one hub to another hub. As a result, the new optical fiber systems are initially being built to serve the heavily used communication routes, typically those linking major cities, further enhancing the comparative advantages possessed by these centers. This pattern of development is in sharp contrast with communication satellites, where the technology favors traffic from one point to multiple points or vice versa. 'Geostationary satellites lean towards the creation of a more equitable and decentralized communications network. …optical fibers lean more to the heavy routing of messages and to more centralized patterns of communication, preferring only fixed sources and receivers' (Podmore and Faguy, 1986).

Just as telegraph systems were installed alongside railroad tracks in the nineteenth century, optical fiber systems are being installed along the transportation rights-of-way of railroads, waterways, highways, and even bicycle paths (Moss, 1986a). In the United States, MCI has built its Northeast fiber system along the AMTRAK right-of-way; Cable and Wireless is using the right-of-way of the Missouri-Kansas-Texas Railroad to connect the Texas cities of Austin, San Antonio, Dallas, and Forth Worth; and optical fiber has also been installed along the Ohio Turnpike. The US Department of Transportation has proposed that the rights-of-way of the federal interstate highway system be made available for communication systems.

Fiber optic systems are also being built for intraurban and intra-building communications. New York Telephone has built three fiber optic networks around Manhattan and an interborough fiber network that links the counties adjacent to Manhattan. At the same time, Teleport Communications

Inc. has installed 150 miles of fiber in the New York-New Jersey Metropolitan Area that not only provides access to their communications satellite park, but also serves as an alternative to the intra-regional public switched network. In Washington, D.C., an optical fiber communications network linking federal government offices is to be built using the rights-of-way of underground steam tunnels, and in Chicago, a fiber optic is being installed in the coal tunnels below Chicago's business district. 'Once primarily a physical crossroads, the new metropolis is likely to become more important to us as an electronic crossroads for information processing and exchange' (Hicks, 1985).

A parallel pattern of infrastructure development is underway in the United Kingdom where the new competitor to British Telecom, Mercury Communications, anticipates that its 'initial customers will be businesses located within the city of London' (Jonscher, 1984). Mercury Communications is building a fiber system with hubs in London, Manchester, and Birmingham, that uses the rights-of-way of British Rail to link cities, and the unused ducts of the London Hydraulic System for its fiber system within London. In Western Europe as a whole, the emergence of new communications technologies is heightening the regional differences in the availability of advanced telecommunications. As is the case in the United States, the new optical fiber systems will not serve all cities initially, and may even exacerbate the disparities that exist between information-based cities and the declining manufacturing cities. "There is little to indicate that development in telecommunications networks are likely to disadvantage the largest cities relative to small towns and rural areas in any national urban and regional system. The incremental modernization of networks and the logic of density will ensure that the inner parts of large cities will have an initial advantage. ...In an increasingly commercial environment, PTTs will not continue to provide services in advance of demand if that demand fails to come forward; lagging regions will therefore find themselves at greater disadvantage" (Goddard, Gillespie, Thwaites, and Robinson, 1986).

Front and Back-Offices

The growth of information services has not only led to a new infrastructure for transmitting information

over long distances, but to a significant reconceptu-alization of the modern office building (Black, Roark, and Schwartz, 1986). Office buildings are not just places of employment, but structures within which information is generated, processed, and disseminated. As a result, there is a growing recognition of the need to design buildings that incorporate advanced telecommunications and computer systems, e.g., 'local area networks'. The modern office building must be able to accommodate elaborate technical systems to support computer and information processing functions that operate on a 24-hour basis. Moreover, financial institutions that participate in global markets require elaborate trading rooms that are linked to the major exchanges around the world; such trading rooms occupy large floor areas, often in multi-level settings, that are not available in the narrow skyscraper or traditional office structure. For data processing functions, the intense use of information technology is leading to the movement of routine clerical functions out of the central city to lower cost locations that are within close proximity to the large metropolitan region (Nelson, 1986).

The specialized information functions that rely extensively on face-to-face transactions with access to international telecommunications systems are being centralized in highly innovative buildings, such as the Lloyd's Bank in London, and the Hong Kong Shanghai Bank in Hong Kong. At the same time, banks and securities firms are moving their back-office activities to buildings specifically designed for high energy loads, large floor areas, and round-the-clock operations located in suburban areas or on the periphery of the central business district (Moss and Dunau, 1986). This has not led to the obsolescence of the central city, but to the increased specialization of function within large metropolitan areas. The trend toward 'centralized decision making and dispersing routine data processing' has, of course, been evolving since the 1960s (Cowan, 1969). What is particularly notable is the internationalization of control functions and the integration of functions among a handful of world cities (Friedmann, 1986). This has intensified the demand for space in the core of major cities. 'Even with the considerable suburbanization of office activities that has taken place in the recent past, it is evident that central cities have continued to hold their own as foci of office functions, that is, as foci of management and control operations within the national economy as a whole' (Scott, 1982).

The new communications technologies, whether they be teleports, optical fiber systems, mobile telephones, 'smart buildings', or radio paging systems are initially being built to serve the major information users located in large cities and metropolitan areas. Moreover, the very cities that are the centers for face-to-face communication are also the ones which will benefit most from the spread of advanced telecommunications systems. For, as electronic means of communications are used to control and co-ordinate geographically dispersed activities, there will be less face-to-face decision making in outlying areas and the city's role as a hub for the interpersonal exchange of information will be even more important. As Netzer presciently noted, 'there is a texture and subtlety in three-dimensional face-to-face communications that cannot be reproduced in any other way, so much so that past advances in telecommunications technology appear to have increased, not substituted for, some aspects of the demand for face-to-face communication'. This suggests that the demand for traditional clusters of office and service activities will not simply disappear.

...As long as there is some real remaining demand for the essential economic characteristic that central cities offer, the decline in the total demand for cities will not take the form of a proportionate decline in the size of all cities: there will be winners and losers, as some cities fare very badly indeed while some hold their own, or better (Netzer, 1977).

The new urban-based telecommunications infrastructure is, in concert with the internationalization of services and the deregulation of financial markets, reinforcing the economic position of the major cities that are already the leading information hubs. Although the availability of telecommunications technologies is not a determinant of economic development, the presence of advanced telecommunications systems is a permissive factor, which can facilitate the growth of information-intensive firms (Goddard et al, 1986). Furthermore, the absence of a sophisticated telecommunications infrastructure may act as a deterrent in attracting information-based service firms. Certainly, there is the possibility of a synergistic relationship between

telecommunications infrastructure and information-intensive industries. The infrastructure may be built to serve existing firms, but access to sophisticated telecommunications services may stimulate new uses and users, generating even further expansion of the telecommunications infrastructure.

Business Services and Global Cities

In order to understand the effect of new urban-based telecommunications systems on future patterns of growth, it is necessary to recognize the types of activities and firms that are concentrated in a handful of world cities. Hall has described the trend toward agglomerating services in cities and moving manufacturing to non-urban areas. ...'Especially when the non-routine, quaternary services are included, the service sector can be seen to have an urban location pattern, in stark contrast to the increasingly rural pattern found in manufacturing' (Hall, 1985). A new urban hierarchy based on the presence of 'advanced producer services' (e.g. finance, law, accounting, management consulting, and advertising) that provide services to businesses has been explicitly identified for American cities (Noyelle and Stanbach, 1984). Drawing upon their framework, it is possible to understand the role of telecommunications in leading to the concentration of key business services in large world cities. Before the advent of modern communications technology, most services had to be produced where they were consumed.

The production of business services, for example, was highly dependent on timely information inputs and outputs, and this made geographic proximity necessary. Most business services had to be performed where the manufacturing took place. With modern communications and data storage and processing, however, it is possible to receive and deliver information instantly over great distances, and this means that the two activities can be separated geographically (Feketekuty and Hauser, 1986).

Telecommunications systems facilitate both the global decentralization of manufacturing and the agglomeration of financial, legal and advertising services within a relatively limited number of urban hubs. This has been noted by Daniels who states, 'In contrast to consumer services the location of producer services is dominated by centralization in a small number of major employment centers which offer the range of agglomeration and urbanization economies which seem prerequisites for the effective provision of the specialized outputs from such services' (Daniels, 1985).

While technological innovations allow firms to overcome the constraints of time and space, the concentration of information-based activities in global cities continues to intensify (Cohen, 1981). By locating in these major urban centers, commercial banks and related enterprises benefit from the economies of scale inherent in centrally processing the actions of globally based lenders and borrowers. Nicol recognized this trend in noting, 'The introduction of information technology into the banking sector has not led to the dispersal of its activities. On the contrary, the current trend seems to be centralization, along with new functional and spatial divisions of labor'.

This implies, in particular, the gradual reduction in market-oriented, multiservice branches in favor of more specialized centers that can make efficient use of new communications technologies (Nicol, 1985).

New York's role as a global city has resulted in its attracting 405 foreign bank offices, which is 43 per cent of the 940 such offices in the United States, (see Figure 1). This dominance is even more significant considering the fact that foreign bank assets in New York amount to over $248 billion for a total of 59 per cent of all such assets in the U.S. Although New York City plays a dominant role in the global economy, other US cities act as important gateways for location-specific international trade and finance activities. Indeed, of the 55 cities in which offices are located, 83 per cent of the offices and 89 per cent of the assets are located in just six cities; New York, Los Angeles, San Francisco, Chicago, Houston, and Miami.

London's role as the largest center for Euromarket activity has resulted in the United Kingdom having the largest concentration of US bank branch locations and assets; in fact, as a percentage of European countries, the United Kingdom contains

Fig. 1. U.S. Locations of Foreign Banks: all Types of Offices.
Source: American Banker. February 14, 1986.

74 per cent of American branch assets and 38 per cent of American branch offices. The capacity of telecommunications systems to integrate the operation of financial markets in different geographic locations has contributed to London's continued prominence as an international financial capital. 'London's position in between the US and Far Eastern Time Zones make it a useful center for arbitrage between financial markets in those zones (chiefly the markets of the U.S.A., Japan and Hong Kong); dealings on all those markets can be orchestrated from London in the course of one deal day' (Hewlett and Toporowski, 1985). Thus, the use of new communications sytems represents an example of how telecommunications technology can give new meaning to existing locational assets, in this case the decision to put London at the locus of Greenwich Mean Time.

Apart from financial institutions, additional producer services are also migrating to those cities that serve as international financial centers. In the case of advertising, the growth of multinational firms has created a demand for agencies which can 'shadow'

their areas of distribution. The globalization of advertising incorporates both a centralized structure and centralized strategy. '...Because successful advertising must reflect national and cultural differences, extensive decentralization seems essential to the development of effective local campaigns. This tendency toward decentralization may occur simultaneously, however, with centralized development of advertising concepts and strategies in a few locations, as part of the trend toward "world advertising" for worldwide consumer agents' (Noyelle and Dutka, 1986). The merger and consolidation trend within the international advertising industry resembles that of the banking industry in the United States in which local communities are increasingly served by extensions and outposts of service providers based in global cities.

According to the American Association of Advertising Agencies, 1985 Roster, 166 of the 679 member agencies had more than one office. 750 of these branch offices were located outside of the US in 163 foreign cities. The global map in Figure 2 depicts the world cities with the largest concentrations of

Fig. 2.   *Worldwide Locations of U.S. Advertising Agencies.*

Source: 1985/86 Roster and Organization of the American Association of Advertising Agencies.

542   MITCHELL L. MOSS

branch offices. In both Europe and the Pacific Rim
there is a remarkably even distribution of offices
between the largest information hubs of nation-
states. This locational pattern is consistent with the
notion that information hubs, as the locus for the
greatest amount of communications technology, are
the most efficient and effective centers for voice,
video, and data transmission.

The Location of Law Firms

The emergence of global information hubs is also
demonstrated in an analysis of the global location of
law firms. The location of US law firms was
traditionally determined by the need for access to
the local courthouse; today, law firms are behaving
like other service industries and are increasingly
following their clients to locations far removed from
their home city or nation. This branching effect
mirrors the movements of multinational enterprises
to information hubs where clients form agreements
and draft contracts.

    A survey by the *Legal Times* of the 500 largest
American law firms reveals that 48 law firms have 72
offices in 11 European cities, and 19 law firms have
33 offices located in 10 Pacific Rim cities. Figure 3
demonstrates that these firms are largely concentrated in approximately the same cities as those for
American branch banks. These cities are the largest
information hubs which bring together the greatest
amount of global business activities. In the case of
the Pacific Rim, Tokyo's role as a global city
suggests that more law firms would be expected to
have a presence there; however, foreign lawyers
have, until recently, been restricted from practicing
in Japan.

International Accounting Firms

In contrast to law firms and advertising agencies, the
accounting profession in the United States has long
had an international character; for example, Peat,
Marwick, Mitchell and Co., and Price, Waterhouse
and Co. were originally founded in England, while
Coopers and Lybrand represents a merger of
British, Canadian, and American firms. Figure 4
portrays the location of the offices of the top 13
international accounting firms, and demonstrates an

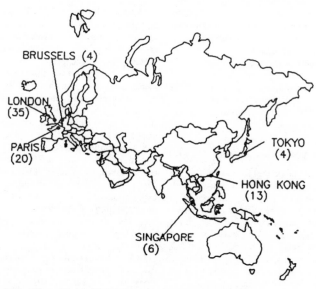

Fig. 3. European and Asian Offices of the top 500 U.S. Lawfirms (Cities with 4 or more Offices).
Legal Times. '500 Largest Lawfirms,' Washington, D.C. 9/15/85.

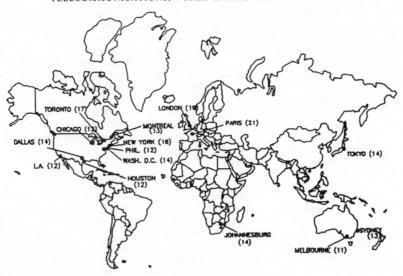

Fig. 4.   Number of Offices of the Top 13 International Accounting Firms by Location, (1981).
Data drawn from Leyshon, Daniels and Thrift, 1986.

even greater tendency towards urban consolidation in a limited number of world cities. The dual process of internationalization and urban concentration is demonstrated clearly, and reflects the fact that '...it is vital for an accountancy firm dealing with a large multinational corporation to be able to offer a worldwide network of offices and, especially offices in the big international financial centers where most of the corporate action still is' (Leyshon, Daniels, and Thrift, 1986).

Urban Policy in an International Context

It has previously been noted that the problems of the central city are no longer local, but national, (Scott, 1982a). The evidence presented here suggests that urban development policy requires an understanding of economic and technological forces which are international in character. 'The major arena of activity determining regional resource allocation is after all neither the locality, nor the region, nor even the national economy, but rather the international environment beyond. The structural parameters which determine local effects in the last analysis are well beyond the purview of local activity' (Ross,

Shakow and Susman, 1980). Further, urban development policy needs to go beyond the 'brick and mortar' approach to rebuilding downtowns and attracting new business. Public officials have traditionally encouraged private firms to expand their operations and to attract new firms with a variety of mechanisms that lower the cost of land or make sites more accessible and attractive. These policies emphasize the location of land within a city rather than the location of a city within a world economy. This article has highlighted the synergistic role of technological and international forces in fostering growth and development in cities linked by advanced communications systems (Donaghy and Warren, 1986). Urban development policies can improve local conditions only if they are based on a full understanding of the factors that influence local economic development, and telecommunications technology is clearly a powerful, if often invisible force.

In fact, one can argue that almost all of the land use conflicts and social policy problems of large cities in the 1980s are related to the growth of information-intensive service industries. Whether it be the gentrification of urban neighbourhoods, the growth of office buildings in the suburbs, or the lack of jobs for unskilled inner city residents, the technological and economic forces that have shaped the global city have contributed to these urban development problems (Dowall, 1984). The so-called 'Manhattanization' of San Francisco and the traffic congestion in downtown Los Angeles are the by-products of the intense demand for central city office space by international banks and the corporate services that they support. For decades, planners have sought to create a 'central business district' in the City of Los Angeles with very limited success; it was not until Los Angeles emerged as a world financial center that the downtown central business district emerged as a vibrant office hub. 'Central business district was stimulated by considerable expansion of financial and headquarters functions, many keyed directly to the operation of international capital, especially within the Pacific Rim' (Soja and Scott, 1986).

In the United Kingdom, the decline of traditional manufacturing cities such as Manchester, Birmingham and Newcastle has occurred concurrently despite the growth of banking and business services in London and the communities within close proximity to London. The recent deregulation of financial markets in London has led to the massive immigration of foreign banks into the City of London and provided the impetus for the renewal of the London Docklands, where a teleport and financial service operations are to be located. It is especially ironic that the deployment of new computer systems has led to the obsolescence of the London Stock Exchange while simultaneously stimulating demand for technologically-intensive 'trading rooms', labelled the 'cockpit of the financial services revolution', that cannot be accommodated in London's modest-sized office buildings (*The Banker*, 1986). The revision of the London City Plan reflects the pressure for office space in the Square Mile and the way in which deregulation and technology have generated new demands for office development in London that were not initially planned for or anticipated by local authorities (Cochrane, 1986).

A Telecommunications-Based Urban Policy

In light of the diminished role of regulated monopolies and central government authorities in control-

ling the shape of new telecommunications systems, the challenge for urban policy is to determine how cities can maintain and attract communications-intensive economic activities. For some communities, 'teleports' are regarded as a 'technological fix' that can stimulate business and jobs. In the 1960s, many cities thought that cable television could solve the urban problems of poverty and participation; in the 1980s, teleports are being treated as the high technology solution to the economic development problems of the metropolis. In a technologically-driven industry, characterized by enormous regulatory change and technological advance, there is no basis for urban policies that favor a specific technology over another.

A telecommunications-oriented urban policy should recognize the way in which telecommunications technology imposes new demands on labor skills, office location and design, and even on transportation infrastructure. Planners and policy makers should monitor advances in telecommunications technology, and where appropriate, become active participants in telecommunications policy making concerning pricing, availability of services, and infrastructure development. Local governments, as large users of telecommunications systems, (i.e., signalization of traffic lights, emergency response systems, and operation of educational systems) could also leverage their telecommunications activities to create a telecommunications infrastructure for use by individuals and firms.

The fundamental challenge, though, is to recognize the pervasive impact of telecommunications in all aspects of urban growth and development, despite the fact that the design and development of communications systems fall outside the purview of local government authorities. '...The new electronic highways of the information society are ... not public thoroughfares, but a myriad of private roads' (Gillespie and Hepworth, 1986). This article has emphasized the extent to which telecommunications is creating a new urban hierarchy, in which those cities that are already information-intensive are becoming even stronger as telecommunications hubs. New communications technologies can also be used to foster economic growth in outlying communities; however, taking advantage of those opportunities requires a recognition of the specific, and often subtle, needs of information-based industries.

Understanding the importance of telecommunications systems and role of market values in guiding the telecommunications infrastructure is a necessary first step for an informed urban policy. For scholars, one of the key issues deserving of research is the relationship of telecommunications to other factors that affect urban economic development, such as the quality of the labor force and the transportation infrastructure. Finally, a framework that allows the movement of information to be considered as important as the movement of people and goods will be required to improve our understanding of cities in the twenty-first century.

REFERENCES

ABLER, R. F. (1974). "The Geography of Communications", in *Transportation Geography: Comments and Readings*. New York, NY: McGraw-Hill. pp. 327–347.

ABLER, R. F. (1970). "What Makes Cities Important", in *Bell Telephone Magazine*, Vol. 49, No. 2, pp. 10–15.

ABLER, R. F. (1980). "Effects of Space-Adjusting Technologies on the Human Geography of the Future", in Abler, R. F., Janelle, D., Philbrick, A. and Sommer, J. (eds.), *Human Geography in a Shrinking World*. Duxbury, Mass.: Duxbury Press. pp. 25–36.

BAKIS, H. (1981). "Elements for a Geography of Telecommunication", *Geographical Research Forum*, No. 4, pp. 31–45.

THE BANKER. (1986). *"Banking Tomorrow"*, Vol. 136, No. 727, pp. 93–97.

BLACK, J. T., ROARK, K. S. and SCHWARTZ, L. S. (eds.). (1986). *The Changing Office Workplace*. Washington D.C.: Urban Land Institute and Builders Owners and Managers Association International.

BLAZAR, W., SPECTOR, M. E. and GRATHWOL, J. (1985). "The Sky Above", *Planning Practice*, Vol. 51, No. 12, pp. 22–26.

CHINITZ, B. (1984). "The Influence of Communications and Data Processing Technology on Urban Forum", in Ebel, R. D. and Ross, J. P. (eds.), *Research in Urban Economics*, Greenwich, Conn.: JIA Press Inc.

COCHRANE, W. (1986). "City of London: Vistas on Expansion", *Financial Times*, October 27.

COHEN, R. (1981). "The New International Division of Labor, Multinational Corporations and Urban Hierarchy", in Dear, M. and Scott, A. J. (eds.), *Urbanization and Urban Planning Capitalist Society*, New York: Methuen Inc.

COWAN, P. (1969). "Communications", *Urban Studies*, Vol. 6, No. 3, pp. 436–446.

DANIELS, P. W. (1985). *Service Industries: A Geographical Appraisal*. London and New York: Methuen.

DONAGHY, K. and WARREN, R. (1986). "Telecommunications and the Use of Urban Space", Paper presented to the Canadian Institute of Planners National Conference.

DOWALL, D. E. (1984). *The Suburban Squeeze*. Berkeley, Ca.: University of California Press.

DOWNS, A. (1985). "Living with Advanced Telecommunications", *Society*, Vol. 23, No. 1, pp. 26–34.

DUNNING, J. H. and NORMAN, G. (1983). "The Theory of the Multinational Enterprise: an Application to Multinational Office Location", *Environment and Planning*, Vol. 15, pp. 675–692.

DUKTA, A. B. and NOYELLE, T. J. (1986). "The Economics of World Market for Business Services: Implications for Negotiations", *The University of Chicago Legal Forum*, Vol. 1986, pp. 57–96.

FEKETEKUTY, G. and HAUSER, K. (1986). "The Impact of Information Technology on Trade", in Faulhaber, G., Noam, E., and Tasley, R. (eds.), *Services in Transition*, Cambridge, Mass.: Ballinger Publishing Company.

FRIEDMANN, J. (1986) "The World City Hypothesis", *Development and Change*, Vol. 17, No. 1; pp. 69–84.

GILLESPIE, A., GODDARD, J., ROBINSON, F., SMITH, I. and THWAITES, A. (1984). *Effects of New Information Technology on the Less-Favoured Regions of the Community*. Commission of the European Economic Communities, Regional Policy Series, No. 23, Brussels.

GILLESPIE, A. E. and HEPWORTH, M. E. (1986). *Telecommunications and Regional Development in the Information Society*. Working Paper No. 1, Newcastle Studies of the Information Economy, The University of Newcastle-upon-Tyne.

GODDARD, J. B., GILLESPIE, A., THWAITES, A. E. and ROBINSON, F. (1986). "The Impact of New Information Technology in Urban and Regional Structure in Europe", *Land Development Studies*, Vol. 3, No. 1, pp. 11–32.

GODDARD, J. B. and PYE, R. (1977). "Telecommunications and Office Location", *Regional Studies*, Vol. 11, pp. 19–30.

GOTTMANN, J. (1977). "Megalopolis and Antipolis: The Telephone and the Structure of the City", in Pool, I. de S. (ed.), *The Social Impact of the Telephone*. Boston: MIT Press.

GOTTMAN, J. (1983). *The Coming of the Transactional City*. University of Maryland, Institute of Urban Studies, College Park.

HALL, P. (1984). *The World Cities*. New York: Weidenfeld and Nicolson.

HALL, P. (1985). "The World and Europe", in Brotchie, J., Newton, P., Hall, P. and Nijkamp, P. (eds.), *The Future of Urban Form*. Sydney: Croom Helm.

HEPWORTH, M. (1986). "The Geography of Technological Change in the Information Economy", *Regional Studies*, Vol. 20, No. 5, pp. 407–423.

HEWLETT, N. and TOPOROWSKI, J. (1985). *All Change in the City*, Economist Publications, Special Report, No. 222, London.

HICKS, D. A. (1985). *Advanced Industrial Development Restructuring Relocation and Renewal*. Boston: Oelgeschlager, Gunn & Hain Inc.

HOLLY, B. P. and STEPHENS, J. D . (1981). "City Systems Behaviour and Corporate Influence: The Headquarters Location of US Industries Firms, 1955–75", *Urban Studies*, Vol. 18, pp. 285–289.

JONSCHER, C. (1984). "Telecommunications Liberalization in the United Kingdom", in Snow, M. (ed.), *Marketplace for Telecommunications: Regulation and Deregulation in Democracies*. New York: Longman. pp. 153–166.

KEEN, Peter, *Competing in Time*. Ballinger Publishing Co. Cambridge, Mass. 1986.

KEEN, P. G. W. (1986). *Competing in Time: using Telecommunications for Competitive Advantage*. Cambridge, Mass.: Ballinger.

KELLERMAN, A. (1984). "Telecommunications and the Geography of Metropolitan Areas", *Progress in Human Geography*, 8(2).

KUTAY, A. (1986). "Effects of Telecommunications Technology on Office Location", *Urban Geography*, Vol. 7, No. 3, pp. 243–257.

LEYSHON, DANIELS and THRIFT, (1986). "Geographical Impacts of Producer Service Conglomerates", A Working Paper. University of Liverpool.

MCLUHAN, M. (1964). *Understanding Media: The Extension of Man*. New York: McGraw-Hill.

MEIER, R. L. (1962). *A Communication Theory of Urban Growth.* Boston, Mass.: MIT Press.

MEIER, R. L. (1985). "Telecommunications and Urban Development", in Brotchie, J., Newton, P., Hall, P., and Nijkamp, P. (eds.), *The Future of Urban Forum, The Impact of New Technology.* Sydney: Croom Helm. pp. 111–120.

MOSS, M. L. (1986). "A New Agenda for Telecommunications Policy", *New York Affairs,* Vol. 9, No. 3, pp. 81–93.

MOSS, M. L. (1986a). "Feasibility of Allowing Fiber Optic Cable Along the Interstate System", Congressional Testimony Before US House of Representatives, Joint hearing before the Subcommittee on Economic Development and the Subcommittee on Surface Transportation of the Committee on Public Works and Transportation; Ninety-Ninth Congress, Second Session.

MOSS, M. L. and DUNAU, A. (1986). *The Location of Back Offices: Emerging Trends and Development Patterns.* Sylvan Lawrence Research and Data Center, Real Estate Institute, New York University.

NELSON, K. (1986). "Labor Demand, Labor Supply and the Suburbanization of Low-wage Office Work", in Scott, A. J. and Storper, M. (eds.), *Production, Work, and Territory.* Boston: Allen and Unwin.

NETZER, D. (1977). "The Economic Future of Cities: Winners and Losers", *New York Affairs,* Winter, Vol. 4, No. 4, pp. 81–93.

NEWTON, K. (1986). "The Death of the Industrial City and the Urban Fiscal Crisis", *Cities,* pp. 213–218.

NICOL, L. (1985). "Communications Technology: Economic and Spatial Impacts", *High Technology, Space, and Society.* Vol. 28, pp. 191–209. Urban Affairs Annual Reviews, Beverly Hills, Ca.: Sage Publications.

NOYELLE, T. J. and DUTKA, A. B. (1986). "The Economics of the World Market for Business Services: Implications for negotiations on Trade in Services", *The University of Chicago Legal Forum 1986,* pp. 57–96.

NOYELLE, T. J. and STANBACH, JR., T. M. (1984). *The Economic Transformation of American Cities.* Towanda, N.J.: Rowman and Allenheld Inc.

POOL, I. DE S. (1980). *Forecasting the Telephone: A Retrospective Technology Assessment.* Ablex Publishing Corporation, Norwood, New Jersey.

PODMORE, C. and FAGUY, D. (1986). "The Challenge of Optical Fibers", *Telecommunications Policy,* Vol. 10, No. 4, pp. 341–351.

PRED, A. (1973). *Urban Growth and the Circulation of Information: The United States System of Cities 1790–1840.* Cambridge, Mass.: Harvard University Press.

PRED, A. (1979). "Industry, Information and City-System Interdependencies", in Hamilton, F. E. I, (ed.), *Spatial Perspectives on Industrial Organization and Decision Making.* New York: John Wiley & Sons. pp. 105–139.

PYE, R. (1979). "Office Location: The Role of Communications and Technology", in Daniels, P. W. (ed.), *Spatial Patterns of Office Growth and Location.* London: Wiley.

ROSS, R., SHAKOW, D. M. and SUSMAN, P. (1980). "Local Planners — Global Constraints", *Policy Sciences,* Vol. 12, pp. 1–25.

SCOTT, A. J. (1982). "Production System Dynamics and Metropolitan Development", *Annals of the Association of American Geographers,* Vol. 72, No. 2, pp. 185–201.

SCOTT, A. J. (1982a). "Locational Patterns and Dynamics of Industrial Activity in the Modern Metropolis", *Urban Studies,* Vol. 19, pp. 111–134.

SOJA, E. W. and SCOTT, A. J. (1986). "Los Angeles: Capital of the Late Twentieth Century", *Environment and Planning,* Vol. 4, pp. 249–254.

THORNGREN, B. (1977). "Silent Actors — Communication Networks for Development", in Pool, I. de S. (ed.), *Social Impact of the Telephone.* Boston, Mass.: MIT Press.

WEBBER, M. M. (1973). "Urbanization and Communications", in Gerbner, G., Gross, L. P. and Melody, W. H. (eds.), *Communications Technology and Social Policy.* New York, NY: John Wiley & Sons.

WEBBER, M. M. (1968). "The Post-City Age", *Daedalus,* Vol. 97, No. 4, pp. 1091–1110.

[33]

Professional Geographer, 41(3), 1989, pp. 257-271
© Copyright 1989 by Association of American Geographers

TELECOMMUNICATIONS AND THE GLOBALIZATION
OF FINANCIAL SERVICES*

Barney Warf

Port Authority of New York-New Jersey

Financial services are undergoing a major period of internationalization. National markets are interlinked by telecommunications, a process induced through deregulation and new communications technologies. This paper reviews the recent, intertwined trends in the finance and telecommunications industries in light of urban and regional restructuring theory, cites several company-specific examples, explores the impacts on the international urban hierarchy and the labor process (e.g., back offices), and assesses the role of teleports. Finally, it offers an agenda for further research. **Key Words: telecommunications, financial services, international linkages.**

Geographers have paid scant attention to financial services, particularly since they have been revolutionized by telecommunications systems, despite the fact that capital flows exert an enormous influence over the creation and destruction of economic landscapes (see Thrift 1987; Green 1988). Wheeler (1986) and Holly (1987) examined the spatial linkages within the banking industry in the United States, but not their reliance upon telecommunications. Chinitz (1984), Goddard and Pye (1977), Kellerman (1984), and Kutay (1986) studied the role of telecommunications in office location patterns and urban form, but did not specifically consider the financial sector. Hepworth (1986), conversely, assessed the effects of technological change in communications on Canadian banks, but not their impacts on capital and labor markets. These studies provide insights into an enormously complicated set of issues, but they do not address the international

scale, an important void in light of the rapid linking of national markets (globalization) of finance currently in progress.

This paper summarizes recent structural and spatial trends in the financial industry and their linkages to telecommunications. It considers in particular the internationalization of financial firms as part of an emerging global division of labor. The shift toward globalization has been well documented (Dicken 1986), especially with regard to industry and trade. The role of finance capital, however, has been largely overlooked, despite the fact that banking, insurance, and securities are significant industries in their own right.

This paper approaches the topic on the analytical basis of restructuring theory, articulated in various forms by Scott (1986), Scott and Storper (1986), Markusen (1985), and Massey (1984). Restructuring theory is concerned with the geographic and social evolution of the labor process and capitalist production, and thus stands in contrast to neoclassical theory, which emphasizes demand. Urban areas in this conception are organized around the locational demands of firms, them-

* The author sincerely thanks Ulrike Zilz, two anonymous reviewers, and the editors for their helpful comments and suggestions.

selves mediated by a changing pattern of forward and backward linkages. Under the compelling force of market competition, firms adopt new technologies that affect their levels of output, profits, wages, and their reliance upon agglomeration and economies of scale. Recent restructuring theory has focused on vertical integration and disintegration as adaptive strategies in this context.

By changing their locational strategies (i.e., patterns of inputs and outputs), new investments alter the geographic distribution of advantages and disadvantages among individual places and thus affect the spatial division of labor as a whole. Telecommunications play a powerful role in this regard, although the consequences of their introduction have not been fully anticipated by researchers or even by those who have come to rely upon them so heavily. In certain sectors, particularly banking and securities, however, telecommunications clearly have facilitated the formation of worldwide markets. While restructuring theory has been concerned with the transition from monopoly to global capitalism (e.g., Graham et al. 1988), of which the internationalization of finance is a significant part, neither it nor competing modes of explanation in economic geography (e.g., the product cycle) has explicitly addressed the role of telecommunications in the recent evolution of the global economy.

This paper includes several themes. The current wave of internationalization may be attributed to the numerous deregulatory changes in the finance and telecommunications industries in the 1970s. These changes profoundly affected both industries, contributed to the emergence of new technologies, and accelerated the expansion into the global market. A variety of empirical examples will substantiate this theme. Financial globalization has greatly affected the international urban system (particularly New York, Tokyo, and London, which lie at the apex of the global financial hierarchy), the emergence of secondary centers, and the dispersal of back offices. Teleports serve as vital parts

in regional and international telecommunications infrastructures. I will conclude with some research questions for further investigation.

Deregulation and Globalization in the Finance and Telecommunications Industries

A conceptual foundation necessary for understanding the communications and capital markets in the 1980s is the series of technological and deregulatory changes that began in the 1970s. These changes profoundly altered the competitive structure of both industries, encouraged new entrants, unleashed new sources of investment funds, and accelerated their expansion in the international marketplace (Walter 1988).

The deregulation, and subsequent wave of globalization, of financial services arose in part from the 1973 collapse of the Bretton-Woods agreement and the subsequent shift to floating exchange rates (Pecchioli 1983). The new regulatory regime that ensued permitted unprecedented transnational capital flows that progressively undermined the regulatory controls designed to protect national currencies. Deregulation accelerated in the OECD nations in a series of steps, including relaxation of controls on foreign investment and interstate banking, rules governing pension fund portfolios, abolition of fixed commission rates on stock markets, and approval of foreign members. The process continues in the United States with the debate over the potential repeal of the 1933 Glass-Steagall Act that effectively separated banking and securities markets. London followed the American lead and underwent the "Big Bang" round of deregulation in 1986, spurring multiple "Little Bangs" elsewhere in Europe, Canada, and Australia. Japan in 1987 began to permit foreign investors on the Tokyo stock exchange, the world's largest. The deregulation of financial sectors, in short, increased competition, liberated new sources of investment funds, encouraged the entrance of institutional investors, raised the levels of volatility, and accelerated the quest by banks and securities firms to cross national borders to escape restrictive home regulations.

Simultaneously, the wave of deregulation engulfed other industries, particularly communications (Moss 1988). The most important deregulatory event in telecommunications in the United States was the 1984 divestiture of the American Telephone and Telegraph monopoly (Brock 1981; Langdale 1982). The 1984 decision created a "new" ATT that was precluded from offering local phone service, and seven Regional Bell Operating Companies that were precluded from offering long distance service. The erosion of ATT's monopoly position opened new opportunities for competitors, such as MCI and US Sprint, and encouraged other firms to install private telecommunications systems. In Great Britain, the privatization of British Telecommunications and the entrance of the Mercury Corporation, which serves the financial complex in London, was a similar process. Japan in 1987 likewise licensed three new companies to compete with Nippon Telegraph and Telephone (NTT).

The deregulation of the telephone industry is important because telephones are the most important form of telecommunications, even at the international scale (Downs 1985; Moss 1986, 1987a). The telephone is the workhorse of financial firms: for example, the number of calls emanating daily from Wall Street increased from 900,000 in 1967 to 3 million in 1987 (Magnier 1987). As US long distance telephone rates declined (Fig. 1), financial firms, by far the heaviest users of long distance data transmission services, benefitted disproportionately from deregulation through lower costs and new opportunities (Shrivastava 1983; *Telephony* 1984).

New Telecommunications Technologies and Financial Services

The acceleration of technological change in telecommunications was one consequence of deregulation. As the microelectronics revolution dramatically lowered the costs of computing, the relatively slow transmissions systems employed by telephone companies (especially copper cables) became increasingly expensive bottlenecks. Telecommunications users spent much more on communications technologies than for computing (Fig. 2). Financial firms turned to three alternative technologies—satellites, microwaves, and fiber optics—to circumvent copper cable systems.

The emergence of satellite transmission technology on a commercially viable basis profoundly affected the telecommunications industry and its users. Satellite transmission costs are insensitive to distance, and they achieve a time-space convergence: from the point of view of a satellite, every place is the same distance from all others (Nichol 1985). The telephone network is deeply intertwined with satellite transmission, particularly at the global scale: one-half of all international financial deals, for example, are negotiated through telephone calls transmitted via satellite (Forbes 1985; Buyer 1983). Satellites suffer a disadvantage, however, in that signals relayed between an earth station and a satellite 23,000 miles high in geosynchronous orbit incur a propagation delay of one-quarter second each way, or one-half second per round trip transmission. Such delays render satellites more appealing for international transmissions of computer data than for voice traffic.

The deregulation of the US satellite market began with the Federal Communications Commission's "open skies" decision in 1971. International satellite traffic, however, is still strictly regulated due to the domination by the International Telecommunications Satellite Organization (Intelsat). Intelsat, a consortium established in 1964 and owned by 166 nations, controls 100% of international television traffic and 75% of international telephone traffic. Several competitors, such as IBS and Pan American Satellite, entered the market as alternative providers of international satellite transmission

260   THE PROFESSIONAL GEOGRAPHER

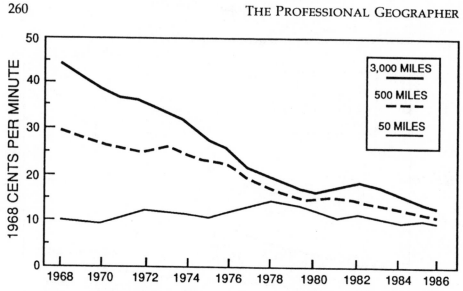

Figure 1.   US long distance telephone communications costs, 1968–86 (*Economist* 1987).

service as the banking community became increasingly reliant upon satellites in the 1980s (*Communications News* 1986).

Microwave transmission is a relatively inexpensive alternative to the telephone and is used intensively by financial firms and others at the local level. Private microwave networks remain illegal in Europe. Microwave technology, however, suffers the disadvantage of requiring line-of-sight transmission, rendering it useless in the international market, and has not emerged as the mode of choice among high volume users over long distances.

Fiber optics provide the most promising alternative to the copper cables of the telephone system. Fiber optics technology has existed since 1975, but only in the deregulated climate of the 1980s did it receive attention as a tamper-proof and error-free transmission mode that can communicate high volumes of information without interference. Fiber optics systems also possess considerable amounts of redundancy (multiple transmission paths), an important feature for users greatly concerned about minimizing downtimes in the event of system failure

(US Dept. of Commerce 1985). The majority of fiber optics lines have been installed in metropolitan areas, where they enhance the attractiveness of large cities to financial firms (Moss 1986, 1987b). Fiber optic lines are also increasingly important in the international markets. The world's first international fiber optic line, the "TAT-8" trans-Atlantic cable connecting New York and London, was completed in 1988 through a joint effort of ATT, US Sprint, MCI, and British Telecommunications. Rapid growth in fiber optics systems will occur throughout the 1990s in the Pacific Rim, connecting growing financial centers such as Tokyo, Singapore, and Taiwan (Fig. 3).

Financial Services and Telecommunications— Empirical Examples

The heaviest users of telecommunications systems are financial services firms (Korek and Olszewski 1979; Schiller 1982). The growth in demand for telecommunications must be seen in the context of the broader shift toward a service-based economy. Banks, securities brokers, and in-

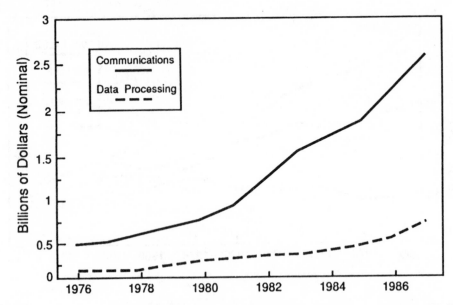

Figure 2. Communications and data processing expenditures, 400 largest US brokerage firms, 1976–87 (Securities Industry Association 1988).

surance companies have invested the most heavily in new telecommunications technologies and have reaped the greatest returns. These investments raised productivity and slowed employment growth in financial services (Gurwitz and Rappaport 1985). More dramatically, telecommunications have altered the patterns of linkages among and within financial firms and their clients. The financial sector is highly information-intensive, and it would be impossible for banks, securities firms, and insurance companies to provide the services they do without extensive telecommunication systems, including, in the United States, the annual processing of 37 billion checks, 3.5 billion credit card drafts, and the trade of 30 billion shares of securities (*Economist* 1987).

The rewards to these investments have been tremendous, increasing the volatility of investment capital and easing the problems associated with massive paper flows. The electronic funds transfer system, for example, eliminated the 16-hour float that cost banks billions of dollars annually in lost interest (Mandeville 1983) and rapidly accelerated the business of check processing (Forbes 1985; *Insight* 1988). Electronic fund transfers facilitated interstate banking during the period of deregulation (Berger and Humphrey 1986). At the international level, telecommunications have allowed banks to increase their loan activities (*Bank Administration* 1987) and to adjust instantaneously to exchange rate fluctuations (Marion 1986; Walton 1983).

The rising importance of telecommunications to financial firms can be seen in the increasing commitment they have made to acquire information transmission services. The 1000 largest US banks between 1972 and 1985 increased the proportion of their operating expenses dedicated to telecommunications from 5 to 13%; for smaller banks, such expenses increased from 4 to 7% (Fig. 4). A marked rise in telecommunications investments is evident among the largest banks in the

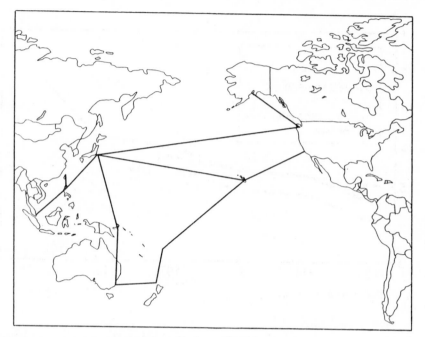

Figure 3. Pacific Rim fiber optics links proposed or under construction, 1988 (*Financial Times of London* 1988).

1980s, many of which installed private networks as they expanded into the global marketplace. Citicorp's Global Telecommunications Network (GTN), for example, is the largest private telecommunications network in the world. It links offices in 94 nations, transmits over 800,000 calls per month, allows Citicorp to trade $200 billion daily in foreign exchange markets around the world, and spawned other applications such as Citimail, an electronic mail service (Forbes 1985). GTN expanded further in 1986 when Citicorp purchased Quotron, the world's leading provider of securities data (Shale 1987). Security Pacific National Bank, similarly, established a subsidiary, Data Transmission Corporation, to serve the same purposes.

Securities firms have also invested heavily in new telecommunications technologies. Integrated work stations on the trading floors, which cost up to $70,000 each, give brokers rapid access to multiple clients and to the computerized trading programs with which they can buy and sell large blocks of stocks, in turn raising the volatility of the market considerably. Merrill Lynch, the largest American securities firm, spends $400 million annually on its telecommunications system (*Business Week* 1988). These investments made the equities markets increasingly vulnerable to disruptions. When Hurricane Gloria forced Wall Street's closure in 1985, for example, the Midwest and Pacific Exchanges also closed, unable to function without the Securities Information Automation Corporation, the financial markets' nervous system (US Department of Commerce 1985).

The globalization of finance has been advantageous to vendors of financial data (Walton 1983). The world's largest such vendor, Reuters' Monitor Dealing Trader System in London, allows securities brokers in 79 nations to communicate directly with one another (Schiller 1982).

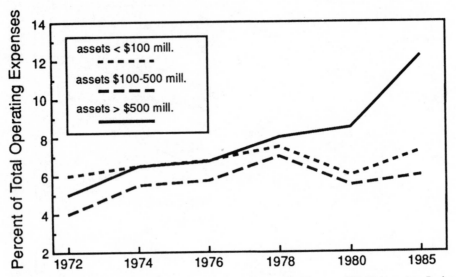

Figure 4.   Telecommunications expenditures of US banks by size of assets, 1972–85 (American Bankers Association 1988).

Reuters and the Chicago Board Options Exchange jointly created Globex, a global electronic system to allow dealers to trade futures and futures options 24 hours per day in markets in 100 different nations (Norris 1989; Siler 1989). The largest American vendor of financial market data, Dow Jones' Telerate (Telecommunications Systems Financial Information Network), provides data on securities, futures, and exchange rates to 50,000 subscribers in 41 nations (Schiller 1982).

Another strategy financial firms have adopted in their quest to maximize access to instantaneous information on the global market is to join consortia that process transactions and distribute data to their members. In the United States, the Clearing House Associations' Interbank Payments System (CHIPS) processes 90% of all US dollars exchanged in international commerce (Lingl 1981; *Transition* 1983). IBM and Merrill Lynch formed a joint venture, Inmet (International Marketing Network), that allows personal computer users to receive financial data via satellite. In 1973, 239 banks in 15 nations established the Society for Worldwide Inter-

bank Financial Telecommunications (SWIFT), a nonprofit cooperative organization designed to meet the growing demand for rapid, standardized interbank communications (Winder 1985; Parry 1987). SWIFT membership grew to include 1000 banks in 51 nations in 1983 (Forbes 1985).

In the same vein, international securities brokers established a means to connect buyers and sellers in different nations through the National Association Dealers Automated Quotation System (NASDAQ). NASDAQ's trading volume grew from 1.5 billion shares in 1975 to 20.5 billion in 1985, making it currently the world's third largest stock market after Tokyo and New York (*Financial Times of London* 1987). NASDAQ's growth is closely linked to the Euromarket, where it was originally confined to the trade in Eurocurrencies. It has since expanded to include all trade in financial instruments located outside of their domestic national boundaries. (For example, the Euroyen market includes trade in all yen-denominated equities, currency, bonds, and commercial paper located outside of Ja-

TABLE 1

PERCENT DECLINE IN INDICES FOR MAJOR
WORLD STOCK MARKETS, OCTOBER 19, 1987

New York	22.6
Tokyo	2.3
London	10.8
Mexico City	16.5
Paris	6.1
Milan	6.3
Amsterdam	7.8
Frankfurt	7.5
Toronto	9.1
Hong Kong	9.3

Source: *New York Times*, October 20, 1987, 1.

pan.) Unlike other stock exchanges, where most of the buying and selling of shares occurs on the trading floor, NASDAQ lacks a specific physical location. While it is nominally centered in London, NASDAQ buyers and sellers are spread throughout the world and linked through telecommunications systems.

The extensive internationalization of the securities industry was painfully evident on October 19, 1987, when stock markets throughout the world experienced a precipitous, nearly simultaneous decline in prices (Bennett and Kelleher 1988). The Dow Jones index plunged 508 points (22%) and was immediately followed by large drops in other financial centers (Table 1). The long term effects of "Black Monday" have been negligible: the Dow Jones index has regained much of the post-crash losses, and layoffs of roughly 11,000 employees by securities firms, mostly in New York, were far less than originally projected. The crash, nonetheless, illustrated the unprecedented volatility and degree of internationalization in the equities markets.

Financial firms are not the only institutions to invest in new telecommunications networks. The Federal Reserve Bank relies heavily upon its Securities Transfer Wire to process government notes and bonds, handling more than $300 billion per day in government paper (Stevens 1984; *Insight* 1988). Many manufacturers have also installed telecommunications systems to provide better inventory con-

trol and closer monitoring of prices (Porter 1988). General Motors' Electronic Data Systems, for example, links the company's 550,000 terminals in 18,000 locations worldwide. Texas Instruments, with 41,500 workstations worldwide, sends 160,000 electronic messages every day on its private network. IBM links its 400,000 employees in 145 nations with satellites leased from private companies. Virtually all large airlines use private networks to make reservations and monitor flights around the globe. Maritime and air cargo carriers employ the Electronic Data Interchange (EDI) and FastFlow, respectively, to track cargo movements. The surge in demand for telecommunications has also prompted growth in the sales of Telex and facsimile ("fax") machines (Moss 1988), giving rise to new circuits of electronic mail. Telecommunication systems have reduced the uncertainty inherent in all location and investment decisions, even as they have raised the volatility of capital flows by allowing instantaneous access to large quantities of information on markets, costs, and competition.

Geographic Aspects of Finance-Telecommunications Integration

The increasing internationalization of financial markets in the 1980s has had important spatial repercussions. Capital flows acquired an unprecedented level of mobility that allows financial firms to scan the globe in search of maximum profit rates, to switch vast funds instantaneously to take advantage of differential interest rates and currency fluctuations, or to react to political events. More than one trillion dollars per day now circulates around the planet, mostly driven by speculation (*Insight* 1988). The overlapping time horizons of the major financial trading centers allow for continuous circulation throughout the day (Fig. 5). Far from eliminating the importance of location in the world system, telecommunications have altered the meaning of place, particularly with respect to location in time, a critical variable given the enormous vol-

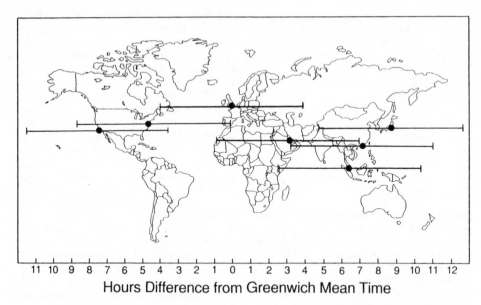

11 10 9 8 7 6 5 4 3 2 1 0 1 2 3 4 5 6 7 8 9 10 11 12

Hours Difference from Greenwich Mean Time

Figure 5.   Trading hours of major world financial centers (calculated by author).

atility of finance capital and the emergence of the 24 hour trading day.

The internationalization of capital markets via telecommunications may entail a progressive loss of control by nation-states over their money supply, impairing their ability to influence inflation and interest rates and currency fluctuations. A stream of revenue data arriving in New York from a tax haven in Bermuda, for example, is virtually impossible to detect. Global telecommunications have increasingly made central bank interventions problematic by giving greater locational freedom to private financial institutions (*Economist* 1988). The easing of technological restrictions increased the importance of locations unfettered by regulatory restrictions. Consequently, foci of offshore banking, such as the Virgin Islands, Cayman Islands, and Netherlands Antilles, are significant secondary areas of activity (Pecchioli 1983). Tax havens, particularly Panama, Bahrain, and Luxembourg, reap enormous advantages from relaxed fiscal policies (*Economist* 1988).

The processes of deregulation, tech-

nological change, and internationalization have clearly imparted a series of differential advantages throughout the international urban hierarchy. In particular, three major centers—Tokyo, London, and New York—have emerged as "world cities," the primary centers of global capital in the 1980s (Marion 1986; Moss 1987a, 1987b). Each metropolitan area offers a formidable array of agglomeration economies, a vast complex of corporate headquarters, financial and business services, a major stock market, a national bank, and state-of-the-art telecommunications facilities.

A brief glance at the distribution of international banking confirms the primacy of these centers. London and New York, for example, contained the largest concentrations of foreign banking in the world in 1987, with 400 and 351 foreign banking branches, respectively (compared to 96 in Los Angeles and 75 in Chicago). Half of all foreign banking deposits in the United States are situated in New York (Damanpour 1986). Foreign banks are spread over several national markets and rely extensively on telecommunications to communicate with their home offices, clients, and investors.

London, New York, and Tokyo are the leading edge of the internationalization of the national and continental economies in which each is situated as they become progressively tied to global financial circles. London's growth, for example, is due in large part to the Euromarket and its linkages to New York and Tokyo. Its growth accentuated the bifurcation between southeastern Britain and the depressed, industrialized northeast (Daniels and Thrift forthcoming). London has witnessed the rapid growth of domestic and foreign financial firms, the creation of large numbers of well paying jobs, escalating housing prices, and the gentrification of the inner city (e.g., the Docklands).

Similarly, the rising linkages between New York and the international financial community closely connected it to the global economy, with important implications as far as its exposure to national and global business cycles (Drennan 1987; Warf 1988b). New York's housing prices have become the highest in the United States as the number of finance related jobs (particularly in foreign-owned firms) skyrocketed and numerous inner city communities were gentrified. The growth of New York's banking and securities sectors has been accompanied by an enormous telecommunications infrastructure: for example, Manhattan alone has twice the telecommunications switching capacity of the average nation, more computers than Brazil, and more word processors than all of Europe combined (Moss 1986).

The globalization of finance also profoundly affected Tokyo, the least understood member of the tripartite axis. The Tokyo metropolitan area grew quickly in the 1980s to include one-quarter of Japan's total population. Tokyo's status reflects Japan's preeminence in international capital markets. Japan is the world's largest creditor with external assets greater than OPEC's at its apogee (Vogel 1986). Concomitantly, Tokyo has emerged as the center of a vast conglomeration of financial firms, including the world's ten largest banks by assets, the largest stock market, and enormous securities firms (e.g., Nomura, Daiwa, Yamaichi, and Nikko). Tokyo also has a highly sophisticated telecommunications infrastructure, including the CAPTAIN (Character and Pattern Telephone Access Information Network) system (Nakamura and White 1988), a teleport, and fiber optics linkages to other cities in Japan and East Asia, and to Los Angeles (Far Eastern Economic Review 1987). ATT and the Kokusai Denshin Denwa, for example, will soon finish a Los Angeles-Tokyo connection (Fig. 3).

As telecommunications services become increasingly ubiquitous, however, a growing tier of "second order" urban centers challenges the primacy of these three centers. Los Angeles has emerged as the center of Pacific Rim capital circuits in the United States, including foreign banking, generating many of the social predicaments that plague New York (e.g., high housing prices and serious congestion) and fears of a "bicoastal" national economy. Toronto recently emerged as the international banking center of Canada, and has witnessed mounting housing problems. Hong Kong and Singapore are now the bankers of Southeast Asia; Bahrain serves much of the Middle East; Paris, Zurich, and Frankfurt are increasingly important to banking operations in Europe as it enters a period of marked economic integration. Although they do not exhibit the massive agglomeration economies found in London, New York, and Tokyo, and thus do not loom quite as prominently as centers of headquarters activity, these metropolitan areas will surely become increasingly important in the global financial landscape of the future.

Telecommunications enhance the attractiveness of large metropolitan areas for headquarters' functions. They also reshape the locational strategies used by firms to place their back offices, the relatively capital-intensive branches that perform clerical functions such as bookkeeping, payroll, billing and claims processing (Nelson 1986). Satellites, and to a lesser extent, microwave systems, allow many firms to detach their back offices from their headquarters, encouraging back offices with few external linkages to be relocated to suburban locations with lower rents and frequently better skilled labor (Moss and Dunau 1986). For example, American Express moved its back offices from New York City to Salt Lake City, UT, Fort Lauderdale, FL, and Phoenix, AZ; Citibank shifted its Mastercard and Visa divisions to Tampa, FL, and Sioux Falls, SD; Hertz relocated its data entry jobs to Oklahoma City, while Avis went to Tulsa, OK; and Eastern Airlines moved its back offices to Miami, FL. Yet other firms have moved their back offices to the Caribbean (Office of Technology Assessment 1985) and Ireland (Lohr 1988), leading to the emergence of the "global office."

In the context of restructuring theory, telecommunications accelerate a spatial bifurcation within many large finance firms by enhancing the attractiveness of downtown areas for skilled managerial activities while simultaneously facilitating the exodus of low wage, back office sectors. This process mimics the separation between headquarters and branch plant functions widely noted in manufacturing. In both cases, a vertical disintegration of production takes place, accompanied by the dispersal of standardized, capital-intensive functions and the concomitant reorganization of skilled, labor-intensive functions around large, densely populated urban areas.

Teleports, Regional Development, and International Finance

Telecommunications have received considerable attention in the regional development literature (e.g., Goddard and Gillespie 1986; Estabrooks and Lamarche 1987; Lesser 1987). Within this context, an increasingly important telecommunications facility for cities seeking to reap benefits from the internationalization of global capital is the teleport, a suburban office park equipped with satellite earth stations and often linked to a fiber optics network (Lipman et al. 1986). The World Teleport Association defines a teleport as follows:

> An access facility to a satellite or other longhaul telecommunications medium, incorporating a distribution network serving the greater regional community and associated with, including, or within a comprehensive related real estate or other economic development (Hanneman 1987, 15).

Just as ports facilitate the transshipment of cargo and airports are necessary for the movement of people, so too are teleports vital information transmission facilities in the age of global capital. Because telecommunications exhibit high fixed costs and low marginal costs, teleports offer significant economies of scale to small users unable to afford private systems (Blazar 1985).

In 1986, there were 36 teleports in the United States and 54 in the world (Fig. 6) (Hanneman 1987). The uneven distribution of teleports is likely to have several geographic repercussions. The current concentration in industrialized nations, particularly the United States, will perpetuate the advantages they enjoy in information-intensive financial services, particularly in highly skilled headquarters' functions. As secondary centers of financial capital acquire them, however, teleports may contribute to a more dispersed pattern of banking, insurance, and securities employment, particularly among smaller firms that rely heavily on the economies of scale they offer. Finally, as third world countries that currently have very few teleports acquire such facilities, they may become increasingly attractive as centers of back office operations.

The world's largest and most sophisticated teleport is The Teleport on Staten Island, NY. It has become increasingly important to that metropolitan region's access to global capital and information markets (Tyson 1986). For example, Recruit USA, a Japanese financial services firm, uses the site to transmit securities information between New York and To-

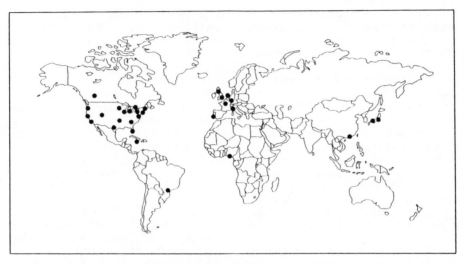

Figure 6.   Distribution of teleports, 1986 (Hanneman 1987).

kyo by satellite: during the daylight hours in New York, it sends data to be processed by computers at the cheaper night rates in Tokyo and retrieves the results instantaneously; the process is then reversed at night in New York or daytime in Tokyo (Warf 1988a), another reflection of the rising importance of time as a locational determinant in international capital markets.

Concluding Comments and a Research Agenda

The process of internationalization in the financial markets accelerated in the 1980s with dramatic effects on local communities. Banking and securities firms, which arguably constitute the most globalized of all industries, have adapted to the world market through large scale telecommunications networks, including private systems and those erected through consortia. The integration of financial and telecommunications services contributed markedly to the emergence of dispersed markets without an overt physical location (e.g., NASDAQ), new information services, and a heightened volatility in

the stock market. One implication of this process for nation-states is a progressive loss of control over their money supply. As the technological barriers to capital flows decline, the importance of political and regulatory ones rises accordingly (Marion 1986).

Geographically, the increasing dependence of banks and securities firms on telecommunications has entailed the centralization of some activities and the decentralization of others. The comparative advantage of cities such as London, New York, and Tokyo in financial services was accentuated by the presence of fiber optics networks and teleports. Simultaneously, satellites and fiber optics systems permitted the decentralization of unskilled back office activities. Both trends have reinforced the transformation of these cities into repositories of skilled, white-collar labor and accentuated the bifurcation of the regional labor market. Telecommunications systems, therefore, neither obliterate the importance of space nor iron out uneven development, but serve to replicate both phenomena, and all the social predicaments they entail, to new forms at different spatial scales. The restructuring theory articulated earlier, which has found a growing currency among urban and economic geographers, has yet to address these issues seriously.

What issues will be significant to future inquiries into this subject? Several major topic areas are suggested below, each of which contains many possibilities for further research.

1. The social consequences of telecommunications have received relatively little scrutiny. To avoid the mechanistic interpretations that confined this issue to largely technical terms, researchers must keep in mind the differential patterns of advantages and disadvantages that new technologies create among users, workers, and places.

2. The labor market effects of the widespread adoption of telecommunications systems deserve more attention. Of particular interest is the globalization of office functions. Does the flight of back offices measurably reduce the job opportunities for inner city populations, especially minorities? Does this same process generate meaningful development in places such as the Caribbean and Ireland, or does the internationalization of clerical labor markets reduce wages in both sets of nations?

3. What are the locational dynamics and regional effects of the securities industry? Although stock and bond brokers and investment banks are some of the heaviest and most important users of telecommunications, the literature on the geography of this sector is remarkably sparse.

4. More needs to be known about the political economy of teleports. Who funds them? Why are they so heavily concentrated in the United States? What are their regional impacts and role in the international service economy? Do viable alternative systems exist? What are their geographic repercussions?

5. What is the likely role of telecommunications in the global economy of the future? Will satellites and fiber optics systems link regions more to international business cycles than to the rhythms of their domestic economies? How will the rapid transfer of enormous quantities of funds affect patterns of trade, exchange and interest rates, and production? Will regulatory restrictions continue to be the most important factor in the growth of offshore banking?

The answers to these questions will not come easily. Necessary data are often lacking, and telecommunications do not mesh comfortably with the dominant research traditions in geography. Yet in attempting to confront such issues, exciting realms are opened for investigation.

Literature Cited

American Bankers Association. 1988. *1986 National Operations Automation Survey.* New York: American Bankers Association.

Bank Administration. 1987. Bank increases loan activity through telecommunications network. May, 80–81.

Bennett, P., and J. Kelleher. 1988. The international transmission of stock price disruption in October 1987. *Federal Reserve Bank of New York Quarterly Review* 13(2):17–26.

Berger, A., and D. Humphrey. 1986. The role of interstate banking in the diffusion of electronic payments technology. In *Technological Innovation, Regulation, and the Monetary Economy,* ed. C. Lawrence and B. Shay, 114–32. Cambridge, MA: Ballinger.

Blazar, W. 1985. Telecommunications: Harnessing it for development. *Economic Development Commentary* 9(3):8–11.

Brock, T. 1981. *The Telecommunications Industry.* Cambridge, MA: Harvard University Press.

Business Week. 1988. A scramble for global networks. March 21, 140–48.

Buyer, M. 1983. Telecommunications and international banking: The political and economic issues. *Telecommunications* 17(May):5–11.

Chinitz, B. 1984. The influence of communications and data processing technology on urban form. In *Research in Urban Economics* (Vol. 4), ed. R. Ebel, 78–91. Greenwich, CT: JAI Press.

Communications News. 1986. Bank speeds its international transactions and cuts telecom costs with IBS satellite service. Vol. 23:54.

Damanpour, F. 1986. A survey of market structure and activities of foreign banking in the United States. *Columbia Journal of World Business* Winter:35–46.

Daniels, P., and N. Thrift. Forthcoming. The

city of London and restructuring of large professional producer services. In *Services and Metropolitan Development: International Perspectives*, 12–31. London: Methuen.

Dicken, P. 1986. *Global Shift*. London: Harper and Row.

Downs, A. 1985. Living with advanced telecommunications. *Society* 23(1):26–34.

Drennan, M. 1987. New York in the world economy. *Survey of Regional Literature* 4:7–12.

Economist. 1987. Telecommunications: Rewiring the world. October 17, 1–31.

Economist. 1988. 1992: A survey of Europe's internal market. July 19:1–22.

Estabrooks, M., and R. Lamarche, eds. 1987. *Telecommunications: A Strategic Perspective on Regional, Economic and Business Development*. Moncton, Ontario: Canadian Institute for Research on Regional Development.

Far Eastern Economic Review. 1987. Japan banking and finance. Vol. 136:47–110.

Financial Times of London. 1987. World telecommunications. October 19, section 3.

Financial Times of London. 1988. Telecom groups weave web across Pacific. March 17, 6.

Forbes, C. 1985. Electronic banking today and tomorrow. *Bankers' Monthly Magazine*, Jan. 15, 19.

Goddard, J., and A. Gillespie. 1986. *Advanced Telecommunications and Regional Development*. Newcastle-upon-Tyne: Centre for Urban and Regional Development Studies.

Goddard, J., and R. Pye. 1977. Telecommunications and office location. *Regional Studies* 11:19–30.

Graham, J., K. Gibson, R. Horvath, and D. Shakow. 1988. Restructuring in US manufacturing: The decline of monopoly capitalism. *Annals of the Association of American Geographers* 78:473–90.

Green, G. 1988. *Finance Capital and Uneven Development*. Boulder, CO: Westview Press.

Gurwitz, A., and J. Rappaport. 1985. Structural change and slower employment growth in the financial services sector. *Federal Reserve Bank of New York Quarterly Reviews* 9(4):39–45.

Hanneman, G. 1987. Teleports: The global outlook. *Satellite Communications*, May, 29–33.

Hepworth, M. 1986. The geography of technological change in the information economy. *Regional Studies* 20:407–24.

Holly, B. 1987. Regulation, competition, and technology: The restructuring of the US commercial banking system. *Environment and Planning A* 19:633–52.

Insight. 1988. Juggling trillions on a wire: Is electronic money safe? February 15, 38–40.

Kellerman, A. 1984. Telecommunications and the geography of metropolitan areas. *Progress in Human Geography* 8:222–46.

Korek, M., and R. Olszewski. 1979. *The Changing Structure of the U.S. Telecommunications Industry*. Menlo Park, CA: SRI International.

Kutay, A. 1986. Effects of telecommunications on office location. *Urban Geography* 7:243–57.

Langdale, J. 1982. Competition in the United States' Long Distance Telecommunications Industry. *Regional Studies* 16:393–409.

Lesser, B. 1987. *Telecommunications Services and Regional Development*. Halifax, NS: Institute for Research on Public Policy.

Lingl, H. 1981. Risk allocation in international inter-bank electronic fund transfers: CHIPS and SWIFT. *Harvard International Law Journal* 22:630–31.

Lipman, A., A. Sugarman, and R. Cushman, eds. 1986. *Teleports and the Intelligent City*. Homewood, IL: Dow Jones-Irwin.

Lohr, S. 1988. The growth of the global office. *New York Times*, Oct. 18, D1.

Magnier, M. 1987. Communications held key to NY's future. *Journal of Commerce*, November 9, 1.

Mandeville, T. 1983. The spatial effects of information technology. *Futures* 15(1):67.

Marion, L. 1986. The rocky road to globalization. *Institutional Investor* 1:31.

Markusen, A. 1985. *Profit Cycles, Oligopoly, and Regional Development*. Cambridge: MIT Press.

Massey, D. 1984. *Spatial Divisions of Labor*. London: Methuen.

Moss, M. 1986. A new agenda for telecommunications policy. *New York Affairs* 9(3):81–93.

Moss, M. 1987a. Telecommunications and international financial centers. In *The Spatial Impact of Technological Change*, ed. J. Brotchie, P. Hall, and P. Newton, 116–29. London: Croom Helm.

Moss, M. 1987b. Telecommunications, world cities, and urban policy. *Urban Studies* 24:534–46.

Moss, M. 1988. Telecommunications: Shaping the future. In *America's New Market Geography: Nation, Region and Metropolis*, ed. G. Sternlieb and J. Hughes, 255–75. New Brunswick, NJ: Center for Urban Policy Research.

Moss, M., and A. Dunau. 1986. Offices, information technology, and locational trends. In *The Changing Office Workplace*, ed. J. Black, K. Roark, and L. Schwartz, 171–82. Washington, DC: Urban Land Institute.

Nakamura, H., and J. White. 1988. Tokyo. In *The Metropolitan Era, Volume 2: Mega-Cities,* ed. M. Dogan and J. Kasarda, 123–56. Newbury Park, CA: Sage Publications.

Nelson, K. 1986. Labor demand, labor supply and the suburbanization of low-wage office work. In *Production, Work, Territory*, ed. A. Scott and M. Storper, 149–71. Boston, MA: Allen and Unwin.

Nichol, L. 1985. Communications technology: Economic and spatial impacts. In *High Technology, Space, and Society*, ed. M. Castells, 191–209. Beverly Hills, CA: Sage Publications.

Norris, F. 1989. Computers for the futures pits. *New York Times*, Feb. 13, D1.

Office of Technology Assessment. 1985. *Effects of Information Technologies on Financial Services Systems*, OTA-CIT-322. Washington, DC: US Government Printing Office.

Parry, J. 1987. Swift restructures its operating framework. *American Banker* 152(April 23):2.

Pecchioli, R. 1983. *The Internationalization of Banking: The Policy Issues*. Paris: OECD.

Porter, J. 1988. New technology in communications may save billions. *Journal of Commerce*, Feb. 29, 1–2.

Schiller, D. 1982. Business users and the telecommunications network. *Journal of Communications* 32:84–96.

Scott, A. 1986. Industrialization and urbanization: A geographical agenda. *Annals of the Association of American Geographers* 76:25–37.

Scott, A., and M. Storper, ed. 1986. *Production, Work, Territory*. Boston, MA: Allen and Unwin.

Securities Industry Association. 1988. *National Membership Operations Survey*. New York: Securities Industry Association.

Shale, T. 1987. Keeping risk at bay in the global banking era. *Euromoney* 4:70–79.

Shrivastava, P. 1983. Strategies for coping with telecommunications technology in the financial services industry. *The Columbia Journal of World Business* 18:19–25.

Siler, J. 1989. 24-hour trading is planned. *New York Times*, March 24, D1.

Stevens, E. 1984. Risk in large dollar transfer systems. *Federal Reserve Bank of Cleveland Economic Review*, Fall, 2–16.

Telephony. 1984. Telecommunications and the financial services industry. Vol. 207: 153.

Thrift, N. 1987. The fixers: The urban geography of international financial capital. In *Global Restructuring and Territorial Development*, ed. J. Henderson and M. Castells, 203–33. Beverly Hills, CA: Sage Publications.

Transition. 1983. CHIPS: More than just a clearing system. Feb., 20.

Tyson, D. 1986. Fiber-optic network links firms to New York teleport. *American Banker*, Jan. 29, 1.

US Department of Commerce, Office of Telecommunications. 1985. *Issues in Domestic Telecommunications: Directions for National Policy*. Washington, DC: US Government Printing Office.

Vogel, E. 1986. Pax Nipponica? *Foreign Affairs* 64:752–67.

Walter, I. 1988. *Global Competition in Financial Services: Market Structure, Protection, and Trade Liberalization*. Cambridge, MA: Ballinger Books.

Walton, P. 1983. A boom for the money markets. *Financial Times*, Dec. 14, 28.

Warf, B. 1988a. Japanese investments in the New York metropolitan region. *Geographical Review* 78:257–71.

Warf, B. 1988b. The New York region's renaissance. *Economic Development Commentary* 12(2):13–17.

Wheeler, J. 1986. Corporate spatial links with financial institutions: The role of the metropolitan hierarchy. *Annals of the Association of American Geographers* 76:262–74.

Winder, R. 1985. Too swift for comfort. *Euromoney*, Jan., 55–56.

BARNEY WARF is an Analyst for the Port Authority of New York-New Jersey and adjunct Assistant Professor of Geography at Hunter College. His interests include regional development, social theory, and the international economy.

[34]

Regional Studies, vol. 24.6, pp. 495–512

The Internationalization of R & D and the Development of Global Research Networks

J. HOWELLS

Centre for Urban and Regional Development Studies, University of Newcastle upon Tyne, Newcastle upon Tyne NE1 7RU, UK

(Received October 1989; in revised form February 1990)

HOWELLS J. (1990) The internationalization of R & D and the development of global research networks, *Reg. Studies* **24**, 495–512. The paper considers processes associated with, and conceptualization of, the internationalization of R & D, using the pharmaceuticals and chemical/energy sectors as ways of illustration. Wider issues relating to research internationalization are considered, including changes in the macro research and technological environment and the growth of inter-organizational research collaboration. Other wider organizational changes are considered, including the impact of information and communication technologies, in relation to research location and structure, before the paper concludes with a re-assessment of current conceptualization of R & D in light of these changes.

Research and development   Internationalization   Technological innovation   Location

HOWELLS J. (1990) L'internationalisation de la R et D, et le développement de réseaux mondiaux pour la recherche, *Reg. Studies* **24**, 495–512. Cet article met en considération les démarches nécessaires à l'internationalisation de la R et D et la conceptualisation de celle-là, en se servant des industries pharmaceutiques et de l'énergie comme études de cas. Des questions d'une plus grande envergure concernant l'internationalisation de la recherche sont considérées, y compris les changements dans l'environnement de la macro-recherche et de la technologie, et la croissance de la collaboration inter-entreprise. D'autres changements de grande portée sont considérés, y compris l'impact des technologies de l'information et de la communication par rapport à la localisation et à la structure de la recherche. Pour conclure l'article réévalue la conceptualisation actuelle de la R et D à la lumière de ces changements.

R et D   Internationalisation
Innovation technologique   Localisation

HOWELLS J. (1990) Die Internationalisierung von Forschung und Entwicklung, und die Entwicklung der globalen Vernetzung der Forschung, *Reg. Studies* **24**, 495–512. Dieser Aufsatz behandelt das Konzept der Internationalisierung von Forschung und Entwicklung, und Vorgänge, die damit in Verbindung stehen, wobei der pharmazeutische und der chemische/bzw. Energiesektor zur Illustration benutzt werden. Weitreichendere Fragen, die sich auf die Internationalisierung der Forschung beziehen, werden erwogen, wie der Wandel, der in der Forschung, der technologischen Umwelt und der Zunahme interorganisatorischer Zusammenarbeit in der Forschung stattgefunden hat. Andere weitreichende organisatorische Veränderungen werden in Betracht gezogen, einschliesslich der Auswirkung der Informations-und Kommunikationstechnologie im Verhältnis zu Standorten und Struktur von Forschungs vorhaben, bevor der Aufsatz mit einer Neubewertung der gegenwärtigen Konzeptualisierung von Forschung und Entwicklung im Lichte dieser Veränderungen abschliesst.

Forschung und Entwicklung   Internationalisierung
Technologische Innovation   Standort

INTRODUCTION

Although research investigating the nature and distribution of inward investment in the UK and other advanced industrial economies dates back to the late 1960s (see, for example, DE SMIDT, 1966; RAY, 1971; BLACKBOURN, 1972, 1974; DICKEN and LLOYD, 1976; WATTS, 1980), few studies have sought to analyse the locational operations of firms and industries in an overall global context. There have however been a number of notable exceptions, including work on transnational corporations and spatial production systems (YANNOPOULOS and DUNNING, 1976; STEED, 1978; CLARKE, 1982; DICKEN, 1986; see also TAYLOR and THRIFT, 1982, 1986) and in terms of the international dimension to service location (DUNNING and NORMAN, 1983; DANIELS *et al.*, 1986; MORRIS, 1987; HOWELLS, 1988). In a wider context, work by Dunning (see, for example, DUNNING, 1958) and others (KINDLEBERGER, 1970; CAVES, 1971, 1982; KNICKERBOCKER, 1973; HOOD and YOUNG, 1979; BUCKLEY and CASSON, 1976; RUGMAN, 1981; CASSON, 1983) have sought to analyse and develop theories for the internationalization of production and trade and analyse the role of multinationals in this development process. The conceptualization of the internationalization of production has centred around separate sets of theories and models relating to trade, foreign investment and multinationals (industrial organization). Despite attempts to provide a more integrated analysis and model of international development in production (DUNNING, 1977), research and analysis of these two strands of global production system has still tended to be undertaken separately.

Work analysing the growth and development of R & D on an international scale has been focused on the internal organization of research laboratories within major, mainly US, multinational corporations (CREAMER, 1976; RONSTADT, 1977; BEHRMAN and FOSTER, 1980; HOOD and YOUNG, 1982). More particularly such studies have generally neglected other aspects of the globalization of research activities which are increasingly becoming important. These relate to: the growth and development of international inter-organizational collaboration covering the range of public/private sector institutions; the *flows* of research and technology inputs across national boundaries (as well as just considering the static organization of research laboratories); the supply and migration of *scientific and technical personnel* within and between organizations and countries; the links between R & D laboratories and *other corporate functions*; and, associated with this, the role of communication and information flows in the research process. This paper seeks to shed further light on the process of R & D internationalization by taking up the issues outlined above and viewing them against a background of a number of major trends in scientific research that are seen to be taking place in the late 1980s and 1990s. The study focuses on R & D in the pharmaceutical industry and wider chemical and energy sectors (as part of an ongoing research project by the author using primary survey data) to illustrate some of these wider internationalization processes. The paper will therefore review and develop existing notions and models relating to the internationalization of research activity, then move on to highlight some of the major trends that are occurring within research activity on a global basis and finally, on the basis of preceding discussion, reassess our current conceptualization of R & D internationalization.

Global R & D activity: conceptual frameworks and theoretical approaches

Trade and foreign direct investment theories have largely seen research and technology as an important but exogeneous factor in the process of the internationalization of industrial production. R & D and technology have therefore been seen here as an important 'input' or 'tool' for multinational companies (as a means of exploiting or defending oligopolistic or 'ownership' advantages in foreign markets) but remaining largely as a 'black box' in such analyses. By contrast the more specific conceptualization and modelling of the actual process of R & D globalization has focused almost entirely on organizational issues to do with research requirements within multinational companies and has been treated largely in isolation to more general theories relating to foreign trade and investment.

There have therefore been basically two alternative theoretical strands that have been used to relate the internationalization of R & D to the wider process of the globalization of industrial production. The first relates to the former point, noted above, that research and technology is treated as a tool which firms use to defend and develop their market power across national boundaries. On this basis R & D is seen as a corporate weapon in terms of a *demand or market* control mechanism. The organization and location of R & D abroad has therefore largely been seen as a response process (associated with 'market pull') where R & D is deployed in the most optimal way to defend and secure market power. Multinationals seek to extend their oligopolistic control of a market by foreign direct investment, and one element in the maintenance and extension of oligopoly control is technology. In order to extend oligopolistic control in new and existing foreign markets, foreign multinationals set up research laboratories to support product differentiation through product innovation and development. This view of R & D globalization has grown up with monopolistic competitive theories of foreign direct investment (HYMER, 1972; KNICKERBOCKER, 1973). Thus, in short, enterprises need some form of 'monopolistic advantage' to compete in highly imperfect markets for products and factors and that one of the most important of these monopolistic advantages is technological superiority and sophistication which depends in turn on R & D activity (LALL, 1979, p. 313). The types of research laboratories located abroad in response to these pressures were envisaged to be technology transfer units undertaking minor product modifications and development work to adapt the product to local market conditions. In addition these support laboratories could feed back into the corporate research process the particular market needs of these national markets.

The second perspective, relating to the latter point, has been to focus on the needs and requirements of R & D in order to fulfil its role as an element in the competitive advantage of corporations which happen to be multinational rather than national in character. The focus here is therefore on *supply side* requirements of R & D and the problems associated with organizing these inputs to optimize research output and efficiency. The main issue of R & D internationalization here is on the increasing scale and complexity of organizing R & D at this (multinational) level compared with national or sub-national firms, rather than wider issues to do with the globalization of production itself. The ability to tap into pools of scientific and technical labour and the attraction of low cost research bases have also been seen as key elements in this process. The importance of being able to recruit scarce scientific talent is not new (LIEBENAU, 1984, p. 339), however in the post-war period major companies began to become less reliant on international recruitment and migration and instead started to locate R & D laboratories abroad in order to gain access to research talents in short supply (see DUNNING, 1988, p. 128). On a more radical level these moves to tap pools of skilled labour on a global basis by multinational corporations could be seen to reflect the wider process of the new international division of labour (FROBEL *et al.*, 1980). With the development of corporate functional hierarchies evident in both national (THORNGREN, 1970; PARSONS, 1972; WESTAWAY, 1974) and international scales (HYMER, 1972; LIPIETZ, 1986), multinational companies are seen, under the model, as seeking to exploit valuable supplies of scarce skilled labour as well as the much larger supplies of low-skilled, low cost, less militant workers in the more general production process (SCHOENBERGER, 1988, pp. 108–9). A further element in these supply side factors is the attraction by multinationals of low cost but competent research capacity overseas. The UK, for example, has always been an attractive research environment for US multinationals because of its low cost, as well as for other factors such as widely acclaimed scientific reputation, common language and cultural background (NEDO, 1973, p. 8, CREAMER, 1976, p. 72).

It could be argued that the product life cycle model offers a conceptual framework that integrates both the demand (market) and the supply side requirements of production and technology into an integrated framework. Moreover it succeeds in both fusing trade and foreign investment elements together in a single integrated form. The product life cycle model stemming from the 'law of industrial growth' is associated with three stages of production, where manufacturing capacity will shift from innovating markets to foreign markets as products move from an 'early' or 'development' phase through to a 'growth' stage and into a 'mature' phase of their life cycles (see, for example, VERNON, 1966). A number of studies have suggested that R & D (or at least the development side of R & D) may lag behind the internationalization phases of the production process. However, leaving aside the considerable (if not insurmountable) inconsistencies and problems associated with the product life cycle model (TAYLOR,

1986), the model itself provides an explanation of why multinationals do *not* shift their research abroad. As VERNON, 1977, pp. 41–5, notes, the need in the early stages of the major technological work is to co-ordinate scientific, engineering planning, financial and marketing activities and to keep a close watch on expensive and high risk investments will induce both R & D and the initial stages of production to be kept at home. According to the model, by the time this phase is over and overseas production is planned, the research and technology inputs associated with the product will have fallen to such a level that additional R & D capacity abroad will not be required. However, as LALL, 1979, pp. 319–20, notes, the product life cycle model is concerned with *national* firms (*a priori*) starting out with a new product rather than (existing) multinationals (*a posteriori*) which have a stream of products being marketed abroad. In summary, the conceptualization of the product life cycle model remains weak and often inconsistent with little conceptualization of the role of the firm. Above all, in this context, little or no consideration is given to the role or pattern of R & D, on a national or international level.

Another set of conceptual frameworks related to the internationalization of R & D revolves around more recent studies trying to classify the organization of R & D. In particular, these schema centre on the products and the organizational structure of the firms concerned, relating this in turn to the geographical orientation of the company and the types of R & D units involved (Table 1). The main focus of these classifications is on the geographical market orientation of the products that the firm produces (column 1) and how this is translated into the types of R & D units established abroad (columns 2A and 2B). A final element in transnational R & D that has been focused is the organizational structure of R & D employed by the firm in its transnational activities (column 3).

According to BEHRMAN and FISCHER, 1980, pp. 15–22, the geographical market scope of the products that the firms produce is reflected in the type and status of the R & D units located abroad. 'Home market' companies if they have R & D laboratories abroad will tend to establish only low level technical support or test facilities. By contrast 'world market' companies involved in global product markets will establish global or corporate product units, which are internationally independent to oversee long-term basic product research. Such 'world market' firms may also, however, establish low level research support centres as well as their higher global corporate research units. 'World market' companies can therefore often operate the whole spectrum of research facilities globally according to their market presence and research requirements. BURSTALL *et al.*, 1981, pp. 132–3 and pp. 99–100, in a study of the

Table 1. *Schema for transnational R & D*

Geographical market orientation	Types of R & D unit: mission, content and geographic scope				Organizational structure of foreign R & D activities
Home market companies	Technology transfer units	Support laboratory	Regional scientific and chemicals staffs	Specialized/ limited research capacity	Decentralized R & D—lead divisions
	Indigenous technology units	Legally integrated R & D laboratory	Animals and farm facilities		Decentralized R & D—corporate supervision
					Three-level responsibility
Host market companies	Global product units	International	Applied R & D laboratory new product		Domestic product line and foreign geographic management
					Independent R & D units
					Centralized control and co-ordination
					Committee R & D
					Centralized R & D with domestic R & D matrix
World market companies	Corporate technology units	Independent R & D laboratory	Research mission laboratory	Comprehensive research capacity	Centralized R & D with product co-ordination
					Centralized R & D
BEHRMAN and FISCHER, 1980	RONSTADT, 1977	HOOD and YOUNG, 1982	BEHRMAN and FISCHER, 1980	BURSTALL et al., 1981	BEHRMAN and FISCHER, 1980

international pharmaceutical industry, link the evolution of a research laboratory's capability from a specialized or limited unit to that with comprehensive research capacity to the scientific and industrial capacity of the host economy. They in turn relate this with the technological capacity of a foreign affiliate moving from a 'first order capacity' unit which only receives and adapts research and technology to a 'second order capacity' which can develop and transmit on new technologies to other affiliates (*ibid.*, pp. 129–31).

A final element that researchers have identified is that of the management style relating to R & D (column 3). BEHRMAN and FISCHER, 1980, pp. 125–38, found the managerial styles at each of the ends of the management control spectrum, absolute centralization and total freedom, to be unusual, although they did find a firm's management style to be partially determined by market orientation and this was reflected in the organization of transnational R & D. Thus world market firms tended to have tightly co-ordinated and centralized international R & D activities, whilst host market firms tended to have a more decentralized 'supervised freedom' management styles (*ibid.*, pp. 63–4 and pp. 75–6).

These schema provide valuable insights into the forces shaping the structure of transnational R & D activity and how firms respond to their different market circumstance. In turn it has been suggested that as more firms move towards a global market orientation this will be reflected in the types of R & D unit established abroad, i.e. more global/international/corporate R & D laboratories. Although the *dynamics* of the process of R & D internationalization

are not explicitly revealed in these studies, BEHRMAN and FISCHER, 1980, pp. 26–7, suggest an evolutionary process as laboratories move along the spectrum of R & D work. This evolutionary approach is interestingly taken up by YOUNG *et al.*, 1988, developing the more dynamic approaches set out by WHITE and POYNTER, 1984, and PORTER, 1986a, in multinational and affiliate development. YOUNG *et al.*, 1988, p. 493, taking a 'bottom-up' perspective of multinational subsidiaries operating in Scotland, outline the prospects of role-evolution for foreign affiliates particularly in relation to their R & D capability (although they point out that divestment or 'exiting' in research can also occur).

Finally, work by LALL, 1979, pp. 324–9, and HIRSCHEY and CAVES, 1981, pp. 117–28, using aggregate inter-industry statistics, and by HAKANSON, 1981, and HAUG *et al.*, 1983, using firm-based data, have tried to evaluate some of the more general trends associated with overseas R & D. Their separate analyses revealed that overseas R & D activity was more likely if: overall research expenditures were higher; there were high levels of sales by foreign affiliates or need to respond to market signals (i.e. higher overseas market involvement and experience); the types of products the industry produced needed local adaptation; and if domestic research costs were high (i.e. by implication research costs abroad would be lower making overseas R & D more attractive). Overseas R & D activity was found to be less likely if there appeared to be scale economies in research activity (i.e. on the assumption that this would restrict the ability of firms to decentralize their research activity into (smaller) units overseas). It was also found that technology transfer flows complimented, rather than were a substitute for, overseas R & D (i.e. higher technology flows were associated with higher levels of R & D). In addition, HAKANSON, 1981, p. 55, found that the propensity to undertake R & D abroad also increased with corporate size (i.e. degree of internationalization) and the amount of R & D devoted to new product development, whilst HAUG *et al.*, 1983, p. 391, found that the propensity of a foreign affiliate to have a R & D unit attached to it increased with its age. These results provide some interesting insights into the overall parameters of the propensity to undertake research abroad and suggest that the overall scale and nature of R & D, the types of products produced, the level of overseas investment and cost considerations all play a part in the level of overseas research activity.

THE CHANGING DYNAMICS OF GLOBAL R & D

Although the above studies have yielded valuable insights into the organization of overseas research activity, they were based on observations and trends of multinational R & D in the 1970s and before. Moreover, a number of major changes are now occurring in the nature and scale of research activities internationally which are altering the operation of transnational R & D. These changes, outlined below in turn, can be seen at three levels of analysis: the macro research environment level; intra-organizational developments (particularly relating to the evolution of R & D structures within multinationals); and inter-organizational changes (associated with research collaboration and technology transfer).

The changing macro research environment

There have been a number of wider, some would argue fundamental, changes that have occurred in the macro research and scientific environment that are in turn influencing the growth of global R & D systems. One such development is the recent rise of new pervasive enabling technologies, in particular information and communication technologies (ICT), biotechnology and advanced materials, which are seeping deeply and broadly into the economic and social fabric of advanced industrial economies through the creation of new products, processes and services, via productivity improvements and new work practices. Some observers go so far as to link this with a new economic and social paradigm, in turn relating this to long wave theory and the rise of the fifth Kondratieff (see KONDRATIEFF, 1935; SCHUMPETER, 1939; KUZNETS, 1930; MENSCH, 1979). What is not in doubt is that these technologies have very wide and far-reaching applications and impacts on the economy as a whole and that they in turn

require a broad and diverse range of scientific disciplines and technological inputs to develop them (this in turn has had an impact on the internal and external research requirements of the firm—see below).

Associated with this the traditional barriers between scientific and technological disciplines are being broken down, as the interchange between basic research and applied and development work grows. This in turn is a reflection of commercial and time pressures on R & D activity. Thus, in the field of high-temperature superconductors basic research is being undertaken with a view to future applications right from the beginning. Equally, in some areas of biotechnology substantial progress in applications will not be possible without breakthroughs in the understanding of basic biology and biochemistry (COMMISSION OF THE EUROPEAN COMMUNITIES, 1989, p. 6). The pressure to improve the interface between basic research on the one hand, and applied and development work on the other, stems from the increasing complexity, cost and time taken to develop new innovations. In the pharmaceutical industry, as in other research intensive industries, the task of R & D is becoming much harder. Increasingly, medical research is having to be directed to much more complex and little understood systems in the physio-chemical processes which control the operation of the human body. The search for new pharmaceutical compounds through appropriate biological tests therefore becomes increasingly lengthy. Thus BERDE, 1980, quotes the experience of Sandoz in Switzerland, which synthesized and screened over 10,000 entities in a two to three year period, 99·9% of which never reached the stage of human evaluation. Of the seven that did, only one was eventually adopted and introduced into the market. As a result the rate of phramaceutical innovation discovery, as represented by New Chemical Entities (NCEs) worldwide has steadily dropped from a yearly average of 86·2 during 1961–5 to a yearly average of only 55·6 for the period 1981–5 (REIS ARNDT, 1987).

The increasing complexity of research is also reflected in the time taken to develop new discoveries. The length of time to develop an innovation and the costs of undertaking R & D have risen dramatically during the 1970s and 1980s, as the complexity of the research operation has increased. At the same time the rate of technological change is speeding up as the life span of new innovations is being steadily eroded. In 1970 the average time taken to make a new medicine generally available was six years; by 1985, however, this had been increased to twelve (NEDO, 1987, p. 21). This lengthening in development times has been a reflection of increased safety, testing and validation requirements, in many fields such as aerospace or biotechnology. However, although the rate of development now takes much longer, the rate of change in terms of the life span of new products is speeding up. In the pharmaceutical industry, because development times have increased, the effective 20-year patent life of a new drug has been effectively reduced to eight years. In other industries the rate of technological change is also continuing to speed up, particularly in the field of ICT. Thus, the time-scale between two generations of semiconductor devices (from 4 megabyte memories to 16 megabyte memories) has fallen from four to three years, while the associated investment in R & D has doubled the cost. The establishment of support costs of R & D laboratories has grown considerably in recent years as research teams demand more sophisticated equipment and facilities, whilst the sheer cost of producing a major new technological breakthrough has risen during the 1970s and 1980s. In particular, the development costs have risen fastest. Thus in the pharmaceutical industry, approximately 50% of total R & D resources were spent on development in 1970, however by 1983 this figure had risen to 70%, with development expenditure per unit of research having more than doubled over this period (*ibid.*, p. 12). Equally in the case of public switches in the telecommunications industry the level of R & D investment in absolute terms that is required to develop a product has been growing rapidly and this is rising for each new generation of switch systems (CHARLES *et al.*, 1989, p. 25).

The increasing development costs and lengthening development times, combined with shortening product life spans, has put pressure on all firms undertaking research. In order to recoup such costs as rapidly as possible (whilst still retaining their monopolistic position), firms have sought to launch their new products in as large a geographical market area as possible, increasingly on a global market basis. For large firms this is via the development or extension of their multinational networks. In the pharmaceutical industry such pressures have been reflected in recent merger and acquisition activity aimed at building up a stronger research base as well as gaining a truly international sales and marketing team (for example the mergers between SmithKline and Beecham and Bristol Myers and Squibb). For smaller firms, however, such forces have meant moves towards increased external development and marketing collaboration. Even though small and new firms have been successful at the invention stage they have increasingly been forced into seeking collaboration with large multinational firms who can fund high development and launch costs of their inventions and/or offer a worldwide sales and marketing network. The field of biotechnology is a good example of this. In the early 1980s, new biotechnology firms were seen as a major threat to established pharmaceutical and chemical multinationals, subsequently however these companies have had to enter into collaborative or joint venture agreements, or have been acquired, through lack of sufficient funds and adequate sales networks of their own.

Associated with these major changes in the R & D environment has been the overall growth, and shifts in, global research activity. The bulk of research activity is highly concentrated, with OECD countries holding the dominant share of research effort (by contrast, developing countries only had 12·6% of total world scientists and engineers in 1973 and in expenditure terms this was even smaller; OECD, 1981, p. 45). In turn, within the OECD area research activity is highly concentrated, with the United States (US) accounting for nearly *half* of the OECD total in 1985 with an expenditure of $112 billion (Fig. 1). R & D expenditure has also grown rapidly with the knowledge and information intensification of the economy. Thus, the Gross Expenditure on R & D (GERD) within the total OECD area grew by 4·5% between 1981–3 and by 8% in 1983–5 amounting to some $229 billion and with an employment level of 1,670,000 (OECD, 1987, p. 3). Within the overall concentration and growth of R & D activity there have been a number of significant shifts. In particular, Japan recorded an R & D growth twice the average for the European Community as a whole, whilst by contrast the UK and the Netherlands recorded almost negligible growth rates over this period.

A final element here is the role of government policy in shaping the international pattern of R & D. Studies by RONDSTADT, 1977; BEHRMAN and FISCHER, 1980; and BURSTALL *et al.*, 1981, have all revealed the importance of government policies and their regulatory and purchasing patterns in helping to influence the location of research activity. The pharmaceutical industry is again no exception. In France, for example, the prices which foreign drug firms are allowed to charge are based on the extent to which they undertake research activity within the country, whilst more indirectly some development and clinical trial work by US companies has been shifted abroad, particularly to the UK, because the registration and drug final practices of the Food and Drug Administration (FDA) were seen as being slow and cumbersome (WARDELL and LASAGNA, 1975). Finally governments throughout the world have established more direct incentives for attracting R & D activity either through tax or funding programmes aimed at supporting R & D in general or more targeted national research programmes which seek to develop the research base of a country in a particular field. These latter targeted research programmes can have an important effect in switching the research programmes of multinational companies between counties. Thus, both Unilever and Shell in the early 1980s are believed to have moved out active involvement in many areas of biotechnology in Britain and switched their effects to the Netherlands

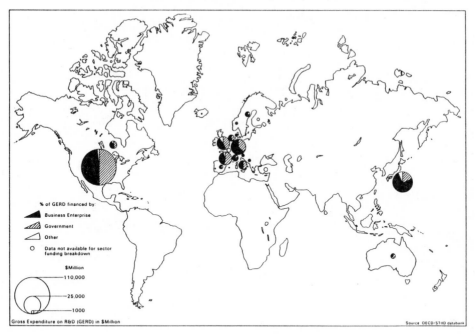

Fig. 1. National R & D expenditure for OECD countries, 1985

as the Dutch national biotechnology programme took shape (SHARP, 1986, p. 41). However HAUG *et al.*, 1983, p. 390, confirming BEHRMAN and FISCHER's, 1980, pp. 109–10, work, found that positive inducements at least in terms of government subsidies were unimportant in attracting foreign research activity.

Global R & D and intra-organizational dynamics: the role of multinationals

The number of multinationals undertaking R & D abroad in the pre-Second World War era was restricted to an elite few. Even by 1965 it was estimated that, for US multinationals (which have had the highest propensity to locate abroad), only 6·5% of their total R & D expenditure was undertaken abroad (US TARIFF COMMISSION, 1973). Indeed this expenditure was highly concentrated sectorally in three industries—transport equipment, electrical and non-electrical machinery which accounted for 62% of the total. More recent estimates by CREAMER, 1976, p. 35, put the figure much lower for 1966 at 4·6% of US parent companies' expenditure and only 3·4% of total US industrial R & D. By 1972, these shares had risen to 7·9% and 6·2% respectively, however it has only been since the mid 1970s that sizeable research operations have begun to be located

abroad and significant global R & D networks established.

These global R & D networks, given favourable financial circumstances, can grow rapidly. Glaxo, a major UK pharmaceutical company provides a good example of such developments (Figs. 2–5). In 1968, it employed just over 750 in R & D, overwhelmingly centred on two sites in the UK. By 1978, employment had increased to over 1,500 but with the main focus of R & D operations still centred on the UK. However, by 1988, employment had grown to nearly 5,000 focused on four main sites: Greenford and Ware (UK); Research Triangle Park, North Carolina (US); and Verona (Italy), with a set of secondary centres located in France, Switzerland, Canada and Japan. Only 63% of total employment in R & D by this date was located in the UK. By 1992 with the relocation of its main research laboratory from Greenford to Stevenage, Glaxo will have a fully integrated international research operation (Fig. 5).

Undoubtedly the often dramatic shift in the internationalization of research within companies has been part of their more general move towards a global operating environment. This is most evident in the fact that a sizeable proportion of companies with R & D establishments abroad gained them indirectly through the acquisition of a company in the overseas markets (BEHRMAN and FISCHER, 1980,

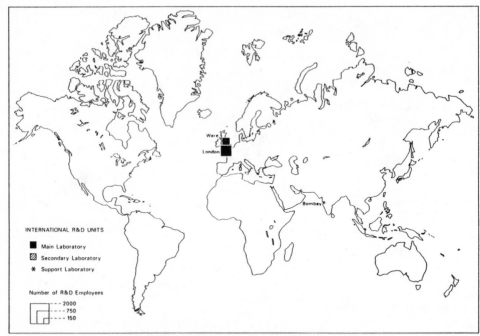

Fig. 2. *Development of Glaxo's global R & D network I, 1968*

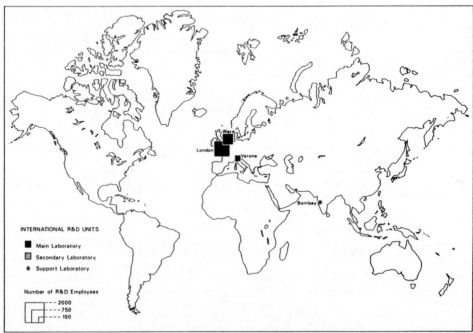

Fig. 3. *Development of Glaxo's global R & D network II, 1978*

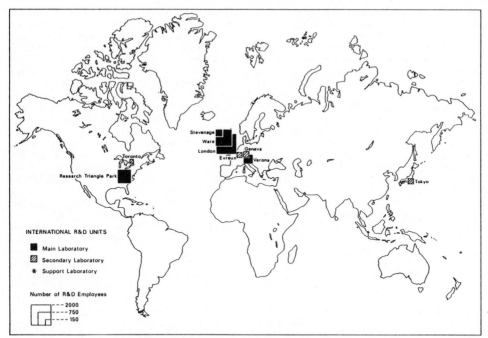

Fig. 4. *Development of Glaxo's global R & D network III, 1988*

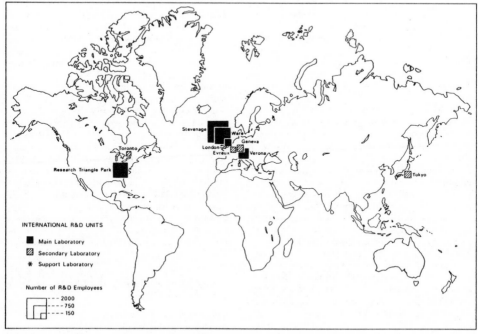

Fig. 5. *Development of Glaxo's global R & D network IV, 1992*

pp. 24–5, estimate that about 25% of all R & D laboratories located abroad arose through acquisition). However it has been more specifically associated in the context of R & D, with the desire to gain and maintain market power and monopoly rights in an increasingly international marketplace and the need to tap pools of scientific and technical manpower and expertise. As more companies move from being 'host market' to 'world market' firms, the role of R & D has moved from a direct but secondary role of helping to serve the market via product modification towards a much more integrated mechanism in gaining new markets. Increasingly the sources of new ideas for new products and innovations are coming from the user firms and industries and if firms are to remain competitive and be able to move into new markets they must be able to maintain close relationships with their existing and potential customers (VON HIPPEL, 1980, pp. 55–6; see also VON HIPPEL, 1976, 1977). According to ABERNATHY and TOWNSEND, 1975, pp. 392–31, such user-denomination of the innovative process can be particularly expected in the early stages of a technology's evolution where '. . . innovative insight comes from those individuals or organizations that are intimately familiar with the . . . process, rather than those intimately familiar with new technologies'. The other key factor in encouraging the build up of transnational research activities is the increasing demand and competition for skilled scientists. In the US alone it has been estimated that there will be a potential shortfall of 500,000 scientists and engineers in 2010 as a result of demographic trends and the pattern of university enrolment (COMMISSION OF THE EUROPEAN COMMUNITIES, 1989, p. 6). As a result, companies are having to widen their research networks in order to tap more geographically dispersed scientific talent (Doz, 1987).

As the size and complexity of overseas R & D operations has grown, multinational companies have become increasingly concerned with the co-ordination and integration of research tasks (see also on a wider level PORTER's, 1986b, configuration and co-ordination debate). Up until the Second World War problems of maintaining transport and communication links with overseas research laboratories, severely hampered the proper functioning of integrated research between 'home' and overseas research establishments. In the post-war period these problems have substantially eased, with new opportunities arising from the development of computer-communication networks allowing multinationals to improve the efficiency and effectiveness of their R & D activities. A number of UK and US pharmaceutical and chemical companies are using computer-communication networks to facilitate the co-ordination of their research operations (HOWELLS, 1990). One such company is Wellcome, which is pioneering

work on AIDS with its drug Retrovir. The research is centred on two main centres, the Beckenham and Dartford sites in the UK and the Research Triangle Park laboratory in North Carolina. Smaller research facilities are in Sophia Antipolis and Greenville (US) and on a new site in Kobe High Tech Park, Japan. Other related research activities are based in a joint research facility in Rochester and a biomedical facility in Vancouver. A computer-communication network has been established, centred on Dartford which links with all the main research and manufacturing facilities in the company (Fig. 6). The introduction of a computer-communication network has brought particular benefits to the research process in Wellcome where the two main research centres in the UK and the US both work on the same therapeutic areas, but are operated and managed on a local basis. The network has therefore helped to avoid costly research duplication, allowed improved co-ordination of projects with an international potential and speeded up the information and data flows between the two main research centres. In addition it has increased the opportunity for contact between research and other corporate functions within the firm. Sanofi, a French pharmaceutical company controlled by Elf Aquitaine, operates a similar computer-communication network linking its main research laboratories in France centred at Montpellier with facilities also in Montrouge (Paris), Toulouse and Labiege to the other main research establishments in Milan and Brussels (Fig. 7). Pfizer in the US and Glaxo have also developed networks and on-line information systems which are providing increasing support for their global research operations. Outside the chemicals industry, BAKIS, 1980, pp. 44–53, has provided a detailed analysis of IBM's global communications network and how it has allowed IBM to develop a high degree of research and production between different sites in Europe. Similarly, HEPWORTH, 1986, p. 418, has outlined the impact of the introduction of a computer network by Bell Northern Research, which allowed its research laboratories spread across Canada and the US to specialize in their research work. Computer-communication networks can also facilitate the growth of external R & D contracts by organizations (ESTRIN, 1986). In particular, such networks have been fostered by third parties, primarily government departments and agencies to encourage national and international research synergies and often date back quite a long way (see, for example, PAGE, 1967).

The growth of global inter-organizational research contracts

Inter-organizational research contact and flows are becoming an increasingly important element in the overall globalization of research. Transnational inter-

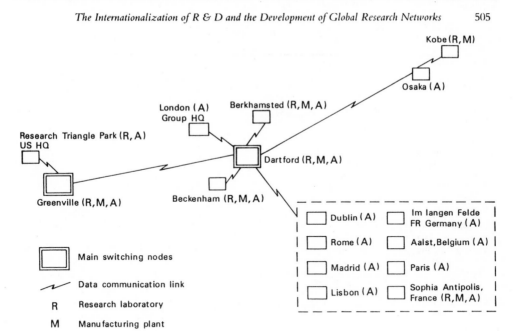

Fig. 6. Topology of Wellcome's computer communication network

organizational research contacts and technical agreements have generally received little attention until recently, although in the chemical industry such agreements were common in pre-First World War and inter-war periods (during the inter-war period, ICI and Du Pont had very close research links— HOUNSHELL and SMITH, 1988, pp. 198–209). However, since the late 1970s the growth of international research and technical co-operation has increased dramatically (FUSFIELD, 1986, p. 794; THOMAS, 1988, p. 176). Thus (CHESNAIS, 1988, pp. 63–4) reviewing a series of studies investigating the inter-firm research and technology agreements (Table 2) concludes, 'The numbers provided by different case studies, surveys or general databanks ... illustrate the trend and all appear to coincide in showing a sharp increase in the early 1980s'. Work by RICOTTA, 1987, quoted in CHESNAIS, 1988, indicates that the US dominates these patterns of geographical agreements. This reflects a number of factors: the move by US firms towards 'strategic partnering' among both domestic and foreign firms (TEECE, 1986); the fact that the US represents the overwhelming dominant force in research and advanced technology in the OECD; and its relatively easy and open agreements for the acquisition of equity participation in, and co-operation with, US firms.

Such agreements can take a variety of forms varying from non-equity agreements associated with one-way or two (or more) way licensing, through to more structured joint venture agreements, equity participation or consortium. Equally they range from pre-competitive, basic research agreements to competitive R & D and technological co-operation and more general manufacturing and marketing ventures (i.e. covering the whole range of R & D to commercialization process—CHESNAIS, 1988, p. 58). These *flows* and initiatives between firms in relation to R & D and technology have largely been ignored in the past when considering the internalization of R & D even though for some major corporations they remain the only form of their transnational research and technical activities. This is particularly true of Japanese companies which have traditionally been reluctant to establish research establishments abroad. For example for Takeda (the largest pharmaceutical company in Japan and ranked sixth in the world in 1989) its only research activities outside Japan until 1988 were via its agreements with Abbott in its joint venture in Tap Pharmaceuticals and through its central research facilities located in Chicago. By contrast, it had more extensive research and licensing links with a range of European and US companies, including two joint ventures with Grunnenthal and licensing deals with Cyanamid, Roche, Ciba-Geigy, Glaxo, Bayer and Yoshitomi (Fig. 8). However with

Table 2. *Trends in the growth of interfirm agreements*

Author and type of agreement	1974	1975	1976	1977	1978	1979	1980	1981	1982	1983	1984	1985
HLADICK, 1985 Joint ventures by US firms in high income countries	37	14	16	15	14	27	34	40	35	—	—	—
RESEAU MILAN, 1985 Electronics industry using only				(131)[1]					69	104	118	—
HACKLISCH, 1986 Forty-one largest world merchant semi-conductor firms	—	—	—	—	2	1	4	22	19	16	42	—
LAREA-CEREM, 1986 Agreements involving European firms in a R & D intensive industry	—	—	—	—	—	—	15	31	58	97	131	149
VENTURE ECONOMICS, 1986 Corporate venture capital investment agreements	—	—	—	—	30	30	30	60	100	150	195	245
SCHILLER, 1986 International agreements with US small biotechnical firms	—	—	—	—	—	—	—	22	58	49	69	90

Source: CHESNAIS, 1988, p. 63.
Note: 1. 1977–8 figure.

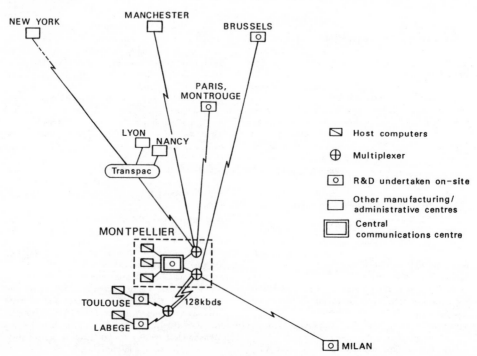

Fig. 7. *Topology of Sanofi's computer communication network*

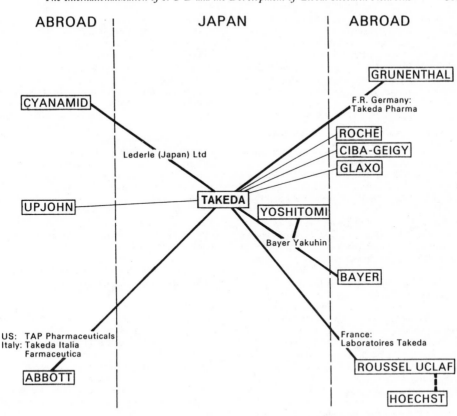

Fig. 8. *Takeda's international collaborative ventures*

the growing links of its European operations centred in Germany, in 1988 it decided to establish a European Research and Development Centre at its new European headquarters (Takeda Europe Gmbh) in Frankfurt and other research facilities may follow over the next ten years. Wider marketing and production deals in terms of patent cross-licensing and joint ventures can therefore be important in influencing what countries (and where within those countries) a company may select to set up their international research facilities. As with the indirect effect of acquisition on overseas research patterns, commercial rather than purely research considerations are often important in delimiting where an eventual R & D unit may be set up overseas.

However, international research flows and collaboration have not only operated on an inter-firm basis. The 1980s has also witnessed increasing

industry–academic–public research establishment contacts on a transnational basis. Again the US has been the base where firms have sought Higher Education Institute (HEI) and public research institute contact because of the relative ease and openness of its HEIs and other research institutes and because of its pre-eminent scientific base. Canada, the UK and some other European countries, such as the Netherlands, have also been significant targets for research link-ups. Again, for Japanese companies without a strong overseas R & D presence, such collaborations have represented an attractive means for gaining access to major scientific and technical expertise abroad. It also stems from the fact that collaboration with public universities in Japan still remains extremely difficult. A further factor in encouraging such trends has been government and inter-governmental research programmes designed to improve the science and technology base of a nation or grouping of countries (SCIBERRAS, 1987). Indeed, by 1987, the European Commission alone estimated that it had created over 364 international joint projects within the Community involving over 2,500 research scientists belonging to 950 different teams (COMMISSION OF THE EUROPEAN COMMUNITIES, 1988).

DISCUSSION AND CONCLUSIONS

This paper has sought to provide an overview of some of the current processes that are involved in the internationalization of R & D activity, linking this with an earlier theoretical review of the literature in this field. Arising from this, there are a number of conceptual or theoretical themes which are highlighted here. The first relates to the 'evolutionary' models of transnational R & D, where the establishment of research overseas is seen to go through a series of stages. Such concepts go back to the product life cycle model and have sought to outline the development of R & D overseas as a progression from domestic-based R & D units, transferring technical know-how to overseas subsidiaries, towards the introduction of small support laboratories abroad and finally the creation of full-blown international R & D laboratories. As R & D units are established overseas, technical transfer is seen to decline accordingly. However, it is here considered that such a smooth progression is too unidimensional and deterministic. Shifts towards overseas research by a company can be extremely 'lumpy' whilst it has also been shown that international technical flows tend to increase rather than decrease as research laboratories are located abroad. Secondly the progression or build-up of research facilities overseas is seen as one way. No notion of a 'reverse' de-internationalization of R & D is conceived, even though from the late 1970s onwards there have been a series of major divestments by major corporations, such as Chrysler, involving closure of their research facilities abroad (WELCH and LUOSTARINEN, 1988, p. 37). Even if these clear phases of R & D expansion do exist, they are becoming increasingly blurred with 'telescoping' of multinational development. VERNON, 1979, himself suggests that there is telescoping of the product life cycle as all products move to a world market status. If so, the product market schema outlined by BEHRMAN and FISCHER, 1980, as being so important to R & D overseas development patterns, will become less relevant over time as the requirements for local development and adaptation are reduced. How this would in reality affect the development paths of R & D though is difficult to predict.

The telescoping of the expected pattern of transnational R & D expansion in turn has implications for the flow of technology transfer overall described above. If the nature of product markets is increasingly towards global status and progression of R & D towards overseas operations is speeded up, the technological lag between the home market and foreign markets will increasingly disappear (VERNON, 1979, p. 259). In a survey of 954 new products introduced in the US and transferred abroad, Vernon found that the number of products transferred abroad within one year rose from 8·1% in 1946–50 to 35·4% in 1971–5 (VERNON and DAVIDSON, 1979). Such speeding up of technology transfer is rapidly eroding the hierarchical notion of 'superior home' versus 'inferior overseas' research capability. Indeed MANSFIELD and ROMEO, 1984, have raised the issue of reverse technology transfers from overseas subsidiaries to American firms. They discovered that far from overseas research units transferring little of their work back to the US, 47% of their 1979 R & D effort was transferred back to the US (*ibid.*, p. 123).

The growth of external R & D contacts on an international basis has received little interest in terms of multinational R & D or the wider internationalization of R & D. Part of the explanation for this rapid growth in external R & D contact may be explained by a re-evaluation by multinationals of their internalization efficiencies and transactions costs associated with undertaking R & D (WILLIAMSON, 1981, p. 1,565). It may also be related to two more fundamental factors that are occurring in the technological environment at the present time. Based on earlier notions of long wave theory and business cycles, the emergence of a new set of technologies and industries (which in the case of biotechnology is having important ramifications for the pharmaceuticals and chemical/energy sectors) do not emerge smoothly from existing firms and sectors. Instead they rely upon what Schumpeter terms the 'process of creative destruction', whereby much of the knowledge needed to implement such change must be sought from *outside* the firm. Secondly, more directly, it has been suggested that the increasingly blurred boundary between basic and strategic research, and shorter lead times to commercialization, have made industry more willing to fund external research. These more fundamental pressures have also been reflected in a more practical (and defensive) response by major multinationals to the challenge of new and small research-based companies who were able to exploit changing scientific opportunities present in the late 1970s via niche research strategies (see PISONO et al., 1988, p. 218). As a result, major multinationals have been increasing their licensing activity in order to strengthen their technological capabilities and to reduce their competitors' ability to overtake them in key technological fields.

Although the rise of multinational corporations

through the exploitation of local labour markets has been evaluated in the context of the 'new international division of labour', little consideration has been given to their impact on international migration. Multinationals not only seek to locate R & D establishments to tap pools of scientific talent, but they also have a profound impact on the international movement of scientific labour both external and internal to the firm. The role of Internal Labour Markets (ILMs) within the multinational firm is therefore having an increasingly important impact on the global movement of scientific and technical personnel (SALT, 1988). Indeed, since personnel movements are seen as the most effective way of transferring and communicating technical know-how, such movements must be more effectively monitored if we are to gain an understanding of the functioning of the international research system.

Surprisingly little attention has been focused on organizational strategies and structures in the context of international R & D. The internal requirements for the effective running of R & D operations, associated with scale and scope requirements, minimum efficient size and communication/integration trade-offs which are important on a national scale (see, for example, MALECKI, 1980; HOWELLS, 1984), are also of vital importance on an international level. This is at a time when multinationals are both seeking to effectively expand their global R & D operations, as well as coping with the problems of successfully rationalizing and integrating separate R & D communities on a global basis, as with the case of the SmithKline Beecham merger. PRAHALAD and DOZ, 1987, see these organizational capabilities as of primary concern in maintaining competitive advantage. They believe multinationals must abandon their traditionally rigid organization structures — either centralized or decentralized — and instead find new ways of exploiting 'interdependencies' which link their disparate businesses. ICT will obviously have a role here to play. Up until now, developments in ICT in relation to research have tended to respond to and facilitate organizational and generalized pressures associated with globalization, rather than being used more actively to change the organization and location of R & D on a multinational basis (HOWELLS, 1990).

A final issue in the internationalization of R & D is that of the role of research in leading to economic growth and development. In the past, R & D was treated as operating within a closed 'spatial economic system', where research inputs and outputs were seen as remaining within a given regional or national setting (*ibid.*). However with the growing internationalization and inter-dependency of research establishments, research itself has become more 'spatially fluid' with the benefits of research being undertaken in one locality no longer necessarily remaining in that area. With the rise of international R & D centres, research undertaken in a laboratory may have little or no integration with the local economy within which it is based, even if it is located near to a manufacturing plant owned by its parent company associated with the 'technological isolation effect' (PARKER, 1974, p. 206; HOWELLS, 1983, p. 153). Although in the 1960s and 1970s there was concern that foreign investment attracted little additional research or technical support with it (truncation), there has been a growing awareness that attracting research facilities by themselves will not necessarily further the economic and technological base of a region or country. Indeed there is growing concern that foreign located R & D establishments in the UK and Europe are part of a wider 'technological leakage' effect, where the economic benefits of research undertaken in these laboratories do not reside within the local or national economy but are transferred and exploited abroad (HOWELLS and CHARLES, 1989, pp. 41–7). Increasingly, R & D facilities have to be viewed within the context of *internal* information and technical transfers (between sites of major multinational companies), the ownership and acquisition patterns associated with R & D, and the way that research activity is integrated with manufacturing and other corporate activities within a local area.[1] It is only with a better understanding of how R & D operates and interacts on a global basis, that public policies can be designed to improve the technological and industrial competitiveness of both national and regional economies.

Acknowledgements — The research is funded under the UK Economic and Social Research Council; thanks go to all the company executives in Europe, Japan and North America who have been involved in the study and the helpful comments of two anonymous referees. This paper is a shortened version of a paper presented at a 'Six Countries Programme' Workshop on the Internationalization of R & D in Ottawa on 16–17 October 1989.

NOTE

1. See the wealth of Canadian studies on this topic relating to technology and economic development on a range of spatial scales (CORDELL, 1971; BRITTON and GILMOUR, 1978; SCIENCE COUNCIL OF CANADA, 1979; BRITTON, 1980, 1985; STEED, 1982, 1989).

REFERENCES

ABERNATHY W. J. and TOWNSEND P. L. (1975) Technology, productivity and process change, *Technol. Forecast. Social Change* **7**, 379–96.

ADVISORY BOARD FOR THE RESEARCH COUNCILS (ABRC) (1989) *Science and Public Expenditure, 1989*. ABRC, London.

BAKIS H. (1980) The communications of larger firms and their implications on the emergence of a new industrial order, Contributing Report, Commission on Industrial Systems, International Geographical Society, Chuo University, Tokyo, 26–30 August.

BEHRMAN J. N. and FISCHER W. A. (1980) *Overseas R & D Activities of Transnational Companies.* Oelgeschlager, Gunn & Hai, Cambridge, MA.

BERDE B. (1980) The experimental and the medical scientist in the pharmaceutical industry, *Prog. Drug Res.* **9**, 83–100.

BLACKBOURN A. (1972) The location of foreign-owned manufacturing plants in the Republic of Ireland, *Tijdschr. Econ. Soc. Geogr.* **63**, 438–43.

BLACKBOURN A. (1974) The spatial behaviour of American firms in Western Europe, in HAMILTON F. E. I. (Ed.) *Spatial Perspectives on Industrial Organisation and Decision-Making,* pp. 245–64. Wiley, London.

BRITTON J. N. H. (1980) Industrial dependence and technological underdevelopment: Canadian consequences of foreign direct investment, *Reg. Studies* **14**, 181–99.

BRITTON J. N. H. and GILMOUR J. M. (1978) The weakest link — a technological perspective on Canadian industrial development, Background Study 43, Science Council of Canada.

BUCKLEY P. J. and CASSON M. C. (1976) *The Future of the Multinational Enterprise.* Macmillan, London.

BURSTALL M. L., DUNNING J. H. and LAKE A. (1981) *Multinational Enterprises, Government and Technology: Pharmaceutical Industry.* OECD, Paris.

CASSON M. S. (Ed.) (1983) *The Growth of International Business.* Macmillan, London.

CAVES R. E. (1971) International corporations: the industrial economics of foreign investment, *Economica* **38**, 1–27.

CAVES R. E. (1982) *Multinational Enterprises and Economic Analysis.* Cambridge University Press, Cambridge.

CHARLES D., MONK P. and SCIBERRAS E. (1989) *Technology and Competition in the International Telecommunications Industry.* Frances Pinter, London.

CHESNAIS F. (1988) Technical co-operation agreements between firms, *STI Review* **4**, 51–119.

COMMISSION OF THE EUROPEAN COMMUNITIES (1988) *Researchers Europe: Stimulation of the International Co-operation and Interchange needed by European Research Scientists,* COM (ST) 44 Final, Commission of the European Communities, Luxembourg.

COMMISSION OF THE EUROPEAN COMMUNITIES (1989) *A Framework for Community RTD Actions in the 90s.* Discussion Document, CEC, Brussels.

CREAMER D. (1976) *Overseas Research and Development by United States Multinationals, 1966–1975: Estimates of Expenditures and A Statistical Profile.* The Conference Board, New York.

CLARKE I. M. (1982) The changing international division of labour within ICI, in TAYLOR M. J. and THRIFT N. J. (Eds.) *The Geography of Multinationals,* pp. 90–116. Croom Helm, London.

CORDELL A. J. (1971) The multinational firm, foreign direct investment and Canadian science policy, Special Study No. 22, Science Council of Canada, Ottawa.

DANIELS D. W., LEYSHON A. and THRIFT N. J. (1986) Producer services in an international context, Working Papers on Producer Services 1, University of Liverpool and St. Davids University College Lampeter.

DE SMIDT M. (1966) Foreign industrial establishments located in the Netherlands, *Tijschr. Econ. Soc. Geogr.* **57**, 1–19.

DICKEN P. (1986) *Global Shift: Industrial Change in a Turbulent World.* Wiley, London.

DICKEN P. and LLOYD P. E. (1976) Geographical perspectives on United States investment in the United Kingdom, *Environ. Plann. A* **8**, 685–706.

DOZ Y. (1987) International industries: fragmentation versus globalisation, in GUILE B. R. and BROOKS M. (Eds.) *Technology and Global Industry,* pp. 00–00. National Academy Press, Washington.

DUNNING J. H. (1958) *American Investment in British Manufacturing Industry.* Allen & Unwin, London.

DUNNING J. H. (1977) Trade, location of economic activity and the multinational enterprise: a search for an eclectic approach, in OHLIN B., HESSELBORN P. O. and WIJKMAN P. J. (Eds.) *The International Allocation of Economic Activity,* pp. 395–418, Macmillan, London.

DUNNING J. H. (1981) *International Production and the Multinational Enterprise.* Allen & Unwin, London.

DUNNING J. H. (1988) *Multinationals, Technology and Competitiveness.* Unwin Hyman, London.

DUNNING J. H. and NORMAN P. (1983) The theory of the multinational enterprise: an application to office location, *Environ. Plann. A* **15**, 675–92.

ESTRIN D. L. (1986) Access to inter-organization computer networks, Department of Electrical Engineering and Computer Science, Massachusetts Institute of Technology, Cambridge, MA (mimeo).

FROBEL F., HEINRICHS J. and KREYE O. (1980). *The New International Division of Labour: Structural Unemployment in Industrialised Countries and Industrialization in Developing Countries.* Cambridge University Press, Cambridge.

FUSFIELD H. I. (1986) *The Technical Enterprise: Present and Future Patterns.* Ballinger, Cambridge, MA.

HAKANSON L. (1981) Organisation and evolution of foreign R & D multinationals. *Geogr. Annaler* **63B**, 47–56.

HAUG P., HOOD H. and YOUNG S. (1983) R & D intensity in the affiliates of US owned electronics manufacturing in Scotland, *Reg. Studies* **17**, 383–92.

HEPWORTH M. (1986) The geography of technological change in the information economy, *Reg. Studies* **30**, 407–24.

HIRSCHEY R. C. and CAVES R. E. (1981) Research and transfer of technology by multinational enterprises, *Oxf. Bull. Econ. Statist.* **43**, 115–30.

HOOD N. and YOUNG S. (1979) *The Economics of Multinationals Enterprise.* Longman, London.

HOOD N. and YOUNG S. (1982) US multinational R & D: corporate strategies and policy implications for the UK, *Multinat. Bus.* **2**, 10–23.

HOUNSHELL D. A. and SMITH J. K. (1988) *Science and Corporate Strategy: Du Pont R & D, 1902–1980.* Cambridge University Press, Cambridge.

HOWELLS J. (1983) Filter-down theory: location and technology in the UK pharmaceutical industry, *Environ. Plann. A* **15**, 147–64.

HOWELLS J. (1984) The location of research and development: some observations and evidence from Britain, *Reg. Studies* **18**, 13–29.

HOWELLS J. (1988) *Economic, Technological and Locational Trends in European Services.* Avebury, Aldershot.

HOWELLS J. (1990) The location and organization of research and development: new horizons, *Res. Policy* **19**, 133–46.

HOWELLS J. and CHARLES D. (1989) Research and technological development and regional policy: a European perspective, in GIBBS D. C. (Ed.) *Government Policy and Industrial Change*, pp. 23–54, Routledge, London.

HYMER S. (1972) The multinational corporation and the law of uneven development, in BHAGWATI J. N. (Ed.) *Economics and World Order*, pp. 80–106. Macmillan, London.

KINDLEBERGER C. P. (Ed.) (1970) *The International Corporation.* MIT Press, Cambridge, MA.

KNICKERBOCKER F. T. (1973) *Oligopolistic Reaction and the Multinational Enterprise.* MIT Press, Cambridge, MA.

KONDRATIEFF N. (1935) The long waves in economic life, *Rev. Econ. & Statist.* **17**, 101–15.

KUZNETS S. S. (1930) *Secular Movements in Production and Prices.* Houghton Mifflin, London.

LALL S. (1979) The international allocation of research activity by US multinationals, *Oxf. Bull. Econ. Statist.* **41**, 313–31.

LIBENAU J. (1984) International R & D in pharmaceutical firms in the early twentieth century, *Bus. Hist.* **26**, 329–46.

LIPIETZ A. (1986) New tendencies in the international division of labor: regimes of accumulation and models of regulation, in SCOTT A. and STORPER M. (Eds.) *Production, Work, Territory: The Geographical Anatomy of Industrial Capitalism*, pp. 16–40, Allen & Unwin, New York.

MALECKI E. J. (1980) Corporate organization of R and D and the location of technological activities, *Reg. Studies* **14**, 219–34.

MANSFIELD E. and ROMEO A. (1984) 'Reverse' transfers of technology from overseas subsidiaries to American firms, *IEEE Trans. Eng. Mgt.* **EM-31**, 122–7.

MENSCH G. (1979) *Statement in Technology: Innovations Overcome the Depression.* Ballinger, New York.

MORRIS J. (1987) The internationalization of banking, technological change and spatial patterns: a case study in South Wales, *Geoforum* **18**, 257–67.

NATIONAL ECONOMIC DEVELOPMENT OFFICE (NEDO) (1973) *Innovative Activity in the Pharmaceutical Industry.* Pharmaceuticals Working Party, Chemicals Economic Development Committee. NEDO, London.

NATIONAL ECONOMIC DEVELOPMENT OFFICE (1987) *Pharmaceuticals: Focus on R & D.* Pharmaceuticals Economic Development Committee, NEDO, London.

ORGANIZATION FOR ECONOMIC CO-OPERATION AND DEVELOPMENT (1981) *North/South Technology Transfer: The Adjustments Ahead.* OECD, Paris.

ORGANIZATION FOR ECONOMIC CO-OPERATION AND DEVELOPMENT (1987) STI Indicators Newsletter 10, OECD, Paris.

PAGE J. R. U. (1967) Planning and development of the European Space Documentation Service, in DE REJCK A. and KNIGHT J. (Eds.) *Communication in Science*, pp. 146–55, Churchill, London.

PARKER J. E. S. (1974) *The Economics of Innovation: The National and Multinational Enterprises in Technological Change.* Longman, London.

PARSONS G. F. (1972) The giant manufacturing corporations and balanced regional growth in Britain, *Area* **4**, 99–103.

PISANO G. P., SHAW W. and TEECE D. J. (1988) Joint ventures and collaboration in the biotechnology industry, in MOWERY D. C. (Ed.) *International Collaborative Ventures in US Manufacturing*, pp. 183–222. Ballinger, Cambridge, MA.

PORTER M. E. (1986a) Changing patterns of international competition, *Calif. Mgt. Rev.* **28**, 9–40.

PORTER M. E. (1986b) Competition in global industries: a conceptual framework, in PORTER M. E. (Ed.) *Competition in Global Industries*, pp. 15–60. Harvard Business School Press, Boston, MA.

PRAHALAD C. K. and DOZ Y. L. (1987) *The Multinational Mission: Balancing Local Demands and Global Vision.* Free Press, New York.

RAY D. M. (1971) The location of United States manufacturing industries in Canada, *Econ. Geogr.* **47**, 389–400.

REIS ARNDT E. (1987) A quarter of a century of pharmaceutical research: new drug entities, 1961–1985. *Drugs Made in Germany* **30**, 105–12.

RICOTTA E. (1987) Accordi di Collaborazione: strumenti flessibidi per strategie global, unpublished report, FOR-START, Rome.

RONSTADT R. (1977) *Research and Development Abroad by US Multinationals.* Praeger, New York.

RUGMAN A. M. (1981) *Inside the Multinationals: The Economics of Internal Markets.*

SALT J. (1988) Highly-skilled international migrants, careers and internal labour markets, *Geoforum* **19**, 387–99.

SCIBBERAS E. (1987) Government sponsored programmes for international technological exchanges and applied collective research, *R & D Management* **17**, 15–23.

SHARP M. (1986) The evolution of policy towards biotechnology in Britain and France, Science Policy Research Unit, University of Sussex (mimeo).

SCHOENBERGER E. (1988) Multinational corporations and the new international division of labor: a critical appraisal, *Inst. Reg. Sci. Rev.* **11**, 105–19.

SCHUMPETER J. A. (1939) *Business Cycles: A Theoretical, Historical and Statistical Analysis of the Capitalist Process.* McGraw-Hill, London.

SCIENCE COUNCIL OF CANADA (1979) Forging the links—a technological policy for Canada, Report No. 29, Science Council of Canada, Ottawa.

STEED G. P. F. (1978) Global industrial systems—a case study of the clothing industry, *Geoforum* **9**, 35–47.

STEED G. P. F. (1982) Threshold firms: backing Canada's winners, Report No. 48, Science Council of Canada, Ottawa.

STEED G. P. F. (1989) Not a long shot: Canadian industrial science and technology policy, Background Study 55, Science Council of Canada, Ottawa.

TAYLOR M. (1986) The product-cycle model: a critique, *Environ. Plann. A* **18**, 751–61.

TAYLOR M. and THRIFT N. (Eds.) (1982) *The Geography of Multinationals*. Croom Helm, London.

TAYLOR M. and THRIFT N. (Eds.) (1986) *Multinationals and the Restructuring of the World Economy*. Croom Helm, London.

TEECE D. (1986) Profiting from technological innovation: implications for integration, collaboration, licensing and public policy, *Res. Policy* **15**, 285–305.

THORNGREN B. (1974) How do contact systems affect regional development?, *Environ. Plann. A* **2**, 409–27.

THOMAS L. G. (1988) Multinational strategies in the US pharmaceutical industry, in MOWERY D. C. (Ed.) *International Collaborative Ventures in US Manufacturing*, pp. 147–81. Ballinger, Cambridge, MA.

US TARIFF COMMISSION (1973) *Implications of Multinational Firms for World Trade and Investment and for US Trade and Labor.* Government Printing Office, Washington, DC.

VERNON R. (1966) International investment and international trade in the product cycle, *Q.J. Econ.* **80**, 190–207.

VERNON R. (1977) *Storm over the Multinationals: The Real Issues.* Macmillan, London.

VERNON R. (1979) The product cycle hypothesis in a new international environment, *Bull. Econ. Stats.* **41**, 255–67.

VERNON R. and DAVIDSON W. H. (1979) Foreign production of technology-intensive products by US-based multinational enterprises Working Paper No. 79–5, Division of Research, Graduate School of Business Administration, Harvard University.

VON HIPPEL E. (1976) The user's role in industrial innovation, in the scientific instrument innovation process, *Res. Policy* **5**, 212–39.

VON HIPPEL E. (1977) The dominant role of the user in the semiconductor and electronic subassembly process innovation, *Trans. Eng. Mgt.* **EM-24**, 60–71.

VON HIPPEL E. (1980) The user's role in industrial innovation, in DEAN B. V. and GOLDHAR J. L. (Eds.) *Management of Research and Innovation*, pp. 53–65, North Holland, Amsterdam.

WARDELL W. M. and LASAGNA L. (1975) *Regulation and Drug Development*. American Enterprise Institute for Public Policy Research, Washington, DC.

WATTS H. D. (1980) The location of European investment in the United Kingdom, *Tijdschr. Econ. Soc. Geogr.* **71**, 3–14.

WELCH L. S. and LUOSTARINEN R. (1988) Internationalization: evolution of a concept, *J. Gen. Mgt.* **14**, 34–55.

WESTAWAY J. (1974) The spatial hierarchy of business organisations and its implications for the British urban system, *Reg. Studies* B, 145–55.

WHITE R. E. and POYNTER T. A. (1984) Strategies for foreign-owned subsidiaries in Canada, *Bus. Quart.* (Summer), 59–69.

WILLIAMSON O. E. (1981) The modern corporation: origins, evolution, attributes, *J. Econ. Lit.* **19**, 1,537–68.

YANNOPOULOS G. N. and DUNNING J. H. (1976) Multinational enterprises and regional development: an exploratory paper, *Reg. Studies* **10**, 389–99.

YOUNG S., HOOD N. and DUNLOP S. (1988) Global strategies, multinational subsidiary roles and economic impact in Scotland, *Reg. Studies* **22**, 487–97.

Geoforum, Vol. 21, No. 1, pp. 35–50, 1990
Printed in Great Britain

The Internationalisation of Advertising

MARTIN PERRY,* Auckland, New Zealand

Abstract: Increasing attention is being paid to the internationalisation of service industries. This article adds to this interest through an examination of the advertising industry. A profile of the world's largest agencies is given and three phases in the international expansion of these agencies are described. A case study in New Zealand examines the response of domestic agencies to the competition from multinational firms. Previous studies have emphasised how the internationalisation of producer services results from the growth of multinational corporations in other sectors. Account alignment is a feature of the advertising industry, but due to the uncertain tenure in which agencies hold their clients other organisational responses have evolved to support the global advertising empires that now characterise the industry. The most recent innovation is the formation of holding group structures; these overcome previous limitations on the expansion of agencies and have laid the basis for further concentration in the industry.

Introduction

Service activities as a whole remain the least internationalised segment of the world economy when considered in terms of export trade. In 1980, 55% of the world GDP in mining and manufactured goods was exported compared with 11% for services (CLAIRMONTE and CAVANAGH, 1984). Multinational business organisations have also been more prominent in manufacturing than services. On the other hand, the internationalisation of service activity is increasing and recent research has indicated that its importance has been undervalued. GRUBEL (1987) argues, for example, that when account is taken of the service component embodied in traded commodities, international trade in services is much greater than recorded data show. Banking and finance have experienced rapid internationalisation over the past two decades and the importance of this trend for other services is increasingly evident. Out of the world's top 200 corporations in 1982, 82 were predominantly service organisations and these accounted for 40% of the combined revenue of the top 200 corporations (CLAIRMONTE and CAVANAGH, 1984). THRIFT (1987) has charted the

growth of multinational accountancy and real-estate firms, and demonstrated their affinity to the world's financial capitals. In the present article the attention is on advertising.

Advertising is part of a cluster of service activities that support other sectors of the economy. Their role is to create and sustain markets. Advertising agencies date from the 1820s, but it was not until the 1880s that agencies came into their own, spurred on by the growth of mass consumption goods and the establishment of popular newspapers which gained much of their revenue from advertising (FRASER, 1981). Advertising agencies encouraged the use of their services and sought a permanent position in the new capitalist order by transforming their image into professional specialists, offering 'salesmanship in print' through the application of scientific knowledge (SINCLAIR, 1987). Leading American agencies expanded overseas in the 1920s, but it is since the 1960s that the internationalisation of advertising accelerated. The worldwide growth of television provided a vehicle for multinational companies to promote their overseas expansion at a time when their domestic markets were becoming increasingly saturated. Advertising agencies established a direct presence in overseas markets, rather than centralise advertising production, because locally-created

*Department of Geography, University of Auckland, Private Bag, Auckland, New Zealand.

advertising generated more income from multinational advertisers. While the overseas expansion of agencies and producers was linked, in that the agencies represented a home client in foreign markets, the rapid expansion of both was not always coordinated. One multinational company, for example, was reported to be working with 1200 separate agencies (LANIGAN, 1984). The desire to rationalise advertiser-agency relations led to the stricter alignment of international accounts to a smaller number of larger agencies. Like other producer services, therefore, the internationalisation of advertising results from more than the growth strategies of individual agencies. It is integrated with the growth of multinational corporations in other sectors.

Changes in the organisation of the market for services provide one explanation for the internationalisation of service organisations. CLAIRMONTE and CAVANAGH (1984) also suggest that economies of scale and related technologies in most services were not conducive to the concentration and centralisation of service capital until recent decades. With new technologies, the corporate diversification of service organisations facilitated expansion due to the enhanced power (marketing and financial) over single-line transnationals. Transnational service conglomerates emerged through the expansion into complementary activities so as to gain economies of scope. One set of complementary links exists between banking, insurance and other financial services; another group links advertising, public relations, market research and a range of business consultancy activities.

The present article reviews the internationalisation of advertising in terms of the industry's links with transnational advertisers and its own internal expansion. The focus is on understanding the reasons for the dominance of transnational advertising agencies and their changing organisational structure. The worldwide domination of the present industry by transnational, usually American-based, agencies will be demonstrated by reference to recent industry data. While the growth of multinational advertisers and the alignment of their global advertising accounts to individual agencies facilitated expansion, it will be shown how the client base of individual agencies remains precarious and unstable. In the 1980s, the industry has been transformed through the emergence of a small number of holding groups. These holding groups are fundamentally reshaping the relationship between agencies, advertisers and the media, and linking advertising to a range of other marketing and business consultancy services. The final part of this paper is a brief case study of the reaction of local agencies in New Zealand to the internationalisation of the industry.

The Development of Advertising

Advertising agencies are hired by firms who wish to advertise in order to devise and direct the campaign. A few enterprises, notably retail organisations, create and administer their own advertising, but the vast majority rely on agencies. The tasks performed by agencies include market research to identify the appropriate promotional strategy; creative input to design the form of the campaign and the brand image; production of the advertisement, in print, film or other media; implementation of the strategy; and finally the monitoring of the campaign. Not all these tasks are usually performed within an agency. Production and the collection of market research and monitoring information are typically subcontracted to specialists. Before outlining the reasons for the internationalisation of advertising, some further understanding of the industry's evolution is required.

KALDOR (1950) defined advertising as a cost element supported by the manufacturer to raise demand to the level of supply. Since advertising is supplied jointly with goods and services, and since consumers cannot indicate directly their willingness to pay for it, Kaldor argued that too much advertising is produced. "The information supplied in advertisements . . . attempts to influence the behaviour of the consumer, not so much by enabling him to plan more intelligently through giving more information, but by forcing a small amount of information, through its sheer prominence to the foreground of consciousness" (KALDOR, 1950). Advertisers choose to advertise in order to increase their share of a market or to raise barriers to the entry of new firms. COMANOR and WILSON (1974), in a more recent empirical study, found similarly that relative advertising expenditures appear to be more important than prices in allocating sales amongst industries. Advertising, therefore, has a major impact on consumer spending decisions, and hence on the allocation of resources.

In Marxist theory, the role of advertising is interpreted similarly, but with a different emphasis. Once the basic needs of food, shelter and clothing are satisfied for most people, capitalism faces the problem of 'realisation', of making sure that the volume of production beyond this minimum level is consumed.

Geoforum/Volume 21 Number 1/1990 37

If capitalism cannot overcome this, a crisis will eventuate caused by the loss of profit, and in turn investment. In other words, capitalism must stimulate demand and advertising plays a vital role in this function. MANDEL (1978) therefore explained the expansion of the service sector by "an unmistakable expression of the growing difficulties of realisation in late capitalism". This interpretation of service sector expansion does not sufficiently account for the complexity of recent changes in service activity. In the specific context of advertising, expenditure growth was not spectacular during the 1970s and early 1980s in most Western economies and tends to grow faster in expanding economies (Table 1). While the general function of advertising is undoubtedly to stimulate demand, its ability to do this is limited. The crisis of 'late capitalism' has required reform of the productive sector and labour relations as the primary responses to the crisis of consumption (LIPIETZ, 1987).

The growth and internationalisation of services has been interpreted in the context of the function and survival of commercial capital (THRIFT, 1987). Commercial capital, of which advertising is one part, mediates in the circulation of commodities for a fee,

without retaining any long-term interest in the commodities. The reduction in the barriers to capitalist production through internationalisation may have been expected to lessen the need for 'parasitic' services, which absorb rather than create surplus value, but commercial capital has thrived. THRIFT (1987) gives several reasons for the prosperity of commercial capital. It has actively created new markets for its services, particularly connected with the international credit system. The institutional and market barriers which characterise international trade generate demand for service expertise. Finally, commercial capital is integral to the process of speculation and new market acquisition.

A second dilemma is why commercial capital has retained its independence from banking and industrial capital. As THRIFT (1987) points out, there is no reason why service functions, such as advertising and marketing, should not be performed internally by the corporations they serve. Two general reasons explain why commercial capital has not been absorbed by other sectors: first, that external provision is more efficient, and second that service providers protect their position by institutional controls. Each of these reasons apply to advertising and are worth

Table 1. Advertising expenditure in selected nations*

Country	Advertising expenditure		Number of 10 top agencies overseas-owned 1987
	% change in real prices, 1970–1983	% of GDP 1983	
Australia†	78.9	1.48	7
Austria†	73.3	0.47	5
Brazil	212.0	1.05	5
France	138.0	0.55	6
Greece‡	113.2	0.35	8
Hong Kong§	144.1	0.72	9
India	136.6	0.21	3
Italy	69.5	0.50	8
Japan	42.4	0.99	1
Malaysia‖	161.7	0.55	10
Netherlands	36.7	0.88	7
New Zealand‖	30.3	1.30	8
Spain¶	67.0	0.71	10
Sweden‡	21.0	0.64	4
Switzerland	34.9	1.00	8
U.K.	40.9	1.39	6
U.S.A.	47.7	1.48	2

*Source: JWT UNILEVER (1985) and *ADVERTISING AGE* (1988a).
†1971–1983.
‡1975–1983.
§1976–1983.
‖1977–1983.
¶1973–1983.

38   Geoforum/Volume 21 Number 1/1990

illustrating to understand the role and organisation of agencies.

Originally advertising was retained within the advertiser's organisation. The first advertising agents arose in the late nineteenth century as subcontractors to newspapers and magazine publishers. Agents bought space from publishers at a discount and sold it on to advertisers at the open market book rate. Advertisers could deal with publishers directly and buy their own space, but the new range of household products sold in national markets needed the service of agencies because they required promotion beyond the locality familiar to the advertiser (LEISS *et al.*, 1986). Large advertisers also sought assistance to produce the copy for advertising, particularly as the print outlets expanded to magazines which allowed more creative use to be made of advertising space than the rigid, column-based format of newspapers.

From the turn of the century, agencies consolidated their specialist niche by the application of research into consumer behaviour and the circulation of the media. Knowledge of regional and sectoral fluctuations in markets and their relationship to readerships for particular publications became the expertise of agencies. The continued success of agencies was based on providing a range of design, copy and marketing advice to advertisers, and in advocating the need for new media that could then support the promotion of branded goods nationally. LEISS *et al.* (1986) outline four phases to the evolving role of advertising agencies that has ensured the industry's separation from advertisers and expanded the market for its services.

Stage 1 (1890–1925) was characterised by the development of new styles of appeal, away from the 'announcements' of earlier periods, to persuasion. In stage 2 (1925–1945) the professionalisation of advertising enabled agencies to influence public policy on the development of commercial radio. Diversification into audience research broadened the marketing services offered by agencies and facilitated improved campaign planning and monitoring. Products were presented less and less on the basis of their performance, and more by appeals based on the social reasons for consumption. Stage 3 (1945–1965) was dominated by the harnessing of television to advertising needs. The potential of this new media enabled more complex advertising, developed through the application of psychological concepts and techniques. At the same time, agencies influenced the realignment of older media to assist their continu-

ing advertising relevance. In stage 4 (1965–1985) advertising adapted to the multi-media conditions of the present market place. More sophisticated television advertising techniques were devised so as to retain the relevance of the most profitable medium in competition from cheaper media offering better access to specialised markets. The emphasis is now on identifying market segments, through statistical and marketing research.

The relationship between agencies and the media exemplifies Thrift's second reason for the continuing independence of service functions; namely, institutional barriers. Accredited agencies alone have the status to buy media space at a discount from broadcasters and publishers. This position has been protected by the media because of the incentive it gives agencies to attract advertising and because the media save transaction costs by dealing with fewer, larger buyers. To the advertiser, the agencies have been effective lobbyists in the commercialisation of the media so as to serve the interests of the advertiser. As LEISS *et al.* (1986) demonstrate, it is impossible to write a history of the media without giving significant attention to the role of advertising, and at the heart of this story is the relationship between media and advertisers, as established by agencies.

The early growth of advertising was based on branded household products. Expenditure on advertising continues to vary between sectors. Industries that have well-defined product differentiation, high profitability, oligopolistic control and are based on nondurable products with low price elasticity of demand tend to have the highest expenditure (COMANOR and WILSON, 1974). In 1987, the 100 leading American advertisers comprised 39 food, drink and tobacco companies, 17 communication and entertainment companies, 10 automobile manufacturers, 10 toiletry, cosmetic and cleanser companies, five electrical and office equipment companies, five pharmaceutical manufacturers, five oil and chemical companies, four financial institutions, three retail organisations and three miscellaneous organisations, including the U.S. government (*ADVERTISING AGE*, 1988b). In the U.K. in 1983, the top five product groups by advertising expenditure were retailing, household and leisure, finance, food drink and tobacco (FULOP, 1988).

The proportion of world advertising expenditure paid for by transnational companies has not been calculated, but it is certainly important, particularly in respect of television advertising. One estimate

Geoforum/Volume 21 Number 1/1990 39

suggests that between 65 and 77% of the worldwide television advertising at popular viewing times derives from transnational companies (SINCLAIR, 1987). In New Zealand, transnational companies accounted for 22% of all advertising expenditure amongst the 40 highest advertising spenders in 1987 (ADMEDIA, 1988a). When television advertising only is measured, the proportion rises to almost 50%.

The Organisation of Agencies

The advertising industry has several unusual characteristics which set it apart from other service activities. Advertising agencies are restricted from specialising because clients insist that simultaneously they do not work for one of their competitors. Some clients go further and will never work for an agency that has worked with a competitor. Thus although J. Walter Thompson lost the account for Ford's European advertising they were prevented from obtaining another automobile client under threat of losing other regional accounts with Ford. This sensitivity reflects the advertiser's concern that their marketing plans may become known to a competitor. The consequence is that agencies are unable to specialise according to product group. The exception tends to be retail advertising which demands a high volume of print advertising with little strategic marketing content.

As all agencies tend to be generalists, advertisers are relatively free to shift their business. To counter this, agencies seek to be distinctive by devising research techniques, market consultancy services and special management assistance to key clients. Other forms of specialisation are possible by targeting specific consumer groups or advertising media.

The broad similarity between agencies nonetheless remains and coupled with the no-competing-accounts rule leads to a high turnover of clients. According to the American Association of Advertising Agencies, 7.2 years is the average period advertisers have been with their present agencies. Some advertising agencies have worked for individual clients over several decades. J. Walter Thompson has worked with Unilever for 85 years, Kodak 56 years and Ford for 44 years, NW Ayer and American Telegraph and Telephone have been linked for 80 years, and McCann-Erickson has been advertising Coca-Cola since 1942. These relationships are the exception. Typically the relationship between advertiser and agency is highly volatile, being one of the first marketing elements to be reviewed at a time of economic stress.

There is no contractual restriction on clients shifting their account at short notice and the motivations for shifting agencies are numerous. Clients may be lost through merger and acquisition activity which transfers a product to a company using a different agency. The loss of a single large client can represent a substantial revenue decline, while the limitation of holding directly competing accounts restricts expansion or buying other agencies. For example, the acquisition of Ted Bates by Saatchi & Saatchi in 1986 led Colgate Palmolive, one of the world's largest advertising spenders, to leave Ted Bates after a long-standing association because of the clients held by Saatchi & Saatchi. When Saatchi & Saatchi purchased New Zealand's second largest agency (McKay King) in 1988, 10 clients, representing almost a quarter of the acquired income, were lost from the combined agency because of account conflicts. Agencies may themselves resign accounts, so that they are able to pursue a conflicting client or because a new client has made this a condition of their business. When Leo Burnett purchased full ownership of their New Zealand agency in 1987, the local manager was instructed to resign the Pizza Hut account so that it was clear to seek another fast-food client who are internationally aligned to the agency (McDonald's). At the time Pizza Hut accounted for 7% of the local agency's income while it may be several years before McDonald's business can be captured from their existing New Zealand agency. Agencies are also vulnerable to a loss of key staff, as client allegiances can lie with individual account directors rather than the agency. It is possible for employees to establish their own agency and take clients with them, so the penalty for alienating key agency staff can be a loss of business.

Where long-term relationships exist, they are not usually exclusive. The advertiser typically maintains an account for a specific region or brand range so that several agencies are used to service their whole activities. Philips NV, for example, work with seven of the world's largest agencies (BBDO International, DMB&B Ogilvy & Mather, Publicis, Saatchi & Saatchi, Lintas and J. Walter Thompson) while Nestle Foods operate with nine (Bozell, Jacobs, Kenyon & Eckhardt, Eurocom, Foote Cone & Belding and McCann-Erickson in addition to four of the agencies used by Philips NV). The reason for these multiple relationships are partly the divisional structure of large corporations which may provide autonomy to regional or product managers. The wide product range of transnationals means that several agencies are usually required to undertake all the advertising for multinational conglomerates because it is unlikely that one agency will not have account conflicts for some of the products. Advertisers also prefer to retain a number of 'club' agencies so that the threat of account loss can be made effective.

The Globalisation of Advertising

The total worldwide expenditure on advertising was estimated as U.S.$150 billion in 1987: 50% of this expenditure was in North America, 28% in Europe, and 19% in Asia/Pacific (SAATCHI & SAATCHI, 1988). The total worldwide advertising billings (roughly equivalent to expenditure) controlled by the world's top 50 advertising agencies was close to U.S.$60 billion in 1986. These global billings generated an income of U.S.$8800 million. Of the income to these global agencies, less than half came from the U.S.A., which is the headquarters for the overwhelming majority of the world's largest advertising agencies. The internationalisation has been both rapid and comprehensive. In 1970, the U.S.A. had accounted for 62% of the world advertising expenditure (MATTELART, 1979). In 1954, the top 30 U.S. advertising agencies earned only a little over 5% of their total income from overseas (BARNETT and MULLER, 1974).

Table 2 provides a profile of the world's 20 largest agencies. A global network is a feature of all these top advertising agencies with the exception of Japan. Overseas agencies have made little impact on the Japanese advertising market because of cultural and economic obstacles, so that indigenous agencies have been able to grow large on the basis of domestic domination. At the same time Japanese agencies have not expanded successfully overseas. The two Japanese agencies included in Table 2 control over a third of all advertising expenditure in that country. More usually, a multinational organisation is the basis for gross income over U.S.$100 million, which was the threshold distinguishing the world's top 20 agencies. In some cases, these multinational structures have been assembled entirely since the 1960s. Ted Bates had no overseas presence in 1963, Ogilvy & Mather had one foreign subsidiary, Leo Burnett had two, while Young & Rubicam had seven (MATTELART, 1979).

The ownership of the 10 largest agencies in the sample of countries for which advertising expenditure data are available is given in Table 1. These data show a high level of overseas ownership across widely dispersed regions. Moreover, the data tend to under-record the extent of overseas agency interests due to the importance of non-financial affiliations, as well as

Table 2. Profile of the world's top 20 advertising agencies in 1986*

Agency	HQ	Gross income		No. of countries operating in†	Worldwide employment
		Worldwide (U.S.$ million)	% U.S.A.		
Dentsu Inc.	Tokyo	681.0	0	1	na
Young & Rubicam	New York	628.4	57.0	43	10,844
Saatchi & Saatchi Compton Worldwide	New York	490.5	39.6	43	na
Ted Bates Worldwide	New York	486.0	58.1	29	5517
J. Walter Thompson	New York	471.0	55.1	41	7662
Ogilvy & Mather Worldwide	New York	459.6	54.3	49	7449
BBDO Worldwide	New York	445.1	69.0	38	5005
McCann-Erickson Worldwide	New York	427.7	34.3	46	7412
DDB Needham Worldwide	New York	375.0	66.7	20	5335
DMB&B	New York	336.3	57.1	21	6077
Foote, Cone & Belding	Chicago	323.0	75.0	29	5105
Hakuhodo International	Tokyo	309.6	0	1	na
Grey Advertising	New York	309.1	65.8	31	4725
Leo Burnett	Chicago	292.3	64.3	25	4064
SSC&B: Lintas Worldwide	New York	237.0	29.1	39	4083
Bozell, Jacobs, Kenyon & Eckhardt	New York	175.6	89.4	21	2068
DFS Dorland Worldwide	New York	165.1	97.0	25	3900
N. W. Ayer	New York	125.5	73.4	8	2558
Publicis International	Paris	119.6	0	8	na
HCM	Paris	106.0	22.8	10	1396

Geoforum/Volume 21 Number 1/1990

direct ownership. In India, for example, six of the largest 10 agencies are linked to overseas firms in addition to those with foreign ownership. The geographic spread of agencies extends beyond the countries with first- and second-order international financial centres (REED, 1983) to which international real-estate and accountancy firms tend to limit their expansion (THRIFT, 1987). For example, the largest U.K. real-estate consultancies do not expand beyond 20 countries, while an advertising agency may span 40 countries including the Middle East, Africa, Latin America and South East Asian countries in addition to those with international financial centres.

The reasons for the internationalisation of advertising lie partly in the process of account alignment. While geographical interest in this subject is recent, the actual process is well established. J. Walter Thompson were the progenitors of the alignment trend. In 1927, General Motors requested them to represent them internationally and open an office wherever the company operated. In this way J. Walter Thompson opened offices in Europe, Australia, Canada, India, South Africa and Latin America in the 1920s and 1930s. Other U.S. companies requested J. Walter Thompson to act similarly on their behalf, including Kraft and Kodak, who remain clients today. McCann-Erickson and Lintas were originally the in-house advertising departments for Standard Oil and Unilever, which followed their parents around the globe, becoming autonomous units in the 1930s.

This early period of agency growth has been termed the 'imperialist' phase by MATTELART (1979). The geographical expansion of agencies is still influenced by the investment strategy of multinationals. Proctor & Gamble recently acquired a major Brazilian company and, in response, Saatchi & Saatchi are expanding their presence in Latin America to maintain their association with Proctor & Gamble. By the 1960s, however, the major multinationals had selected agencies and, while these relationships were subject to review, it became harder to expand by obtaining an unaligned transnational advertiser. As overseas markets became saturated with agencies seeking multinational clients, the 'nationalisation' model became the more usual basis for expansion (MATTELART, 1979). The pattern was characterised by overseas growth through the partial acquisition of foreign agencies. The motivations were to lower the profile of the multinational agency at a time of economic patriotism while simultaneously providing access to the local market. Now that expansion was often in the Far East or Latin America, away from the culturally more similar regions of America and Europe, working with a local agency also became a practical advantage. The partnership approach was a means of maintaining income growth by fuller exploitation of the countries of earlier expansion and newer, less familiar markets.

While the expansion of multinationals provided the impetus for the 'nationalisation' of agencies, agency expansion had a logic of its own. Overseas expansion offered freedom from the exclusive dependence on the saturated U.S. market and its recessionary cycles, as well as the pull of higher profits and in more open and less demanding environments (MATTELART, 1979). Agencies had been displaced from television production in the U.S.A. by broadcasting networks, while the international spread of commercial television offered lucrative new markets. From the second half of the 1960s into the early 1970s, the international billings of the top 10 U.S. agencies grew at 12.6%, compared with less than 1% in the U.S.A. {Worthington [cited in SINCLAIR (1987)]}.

In a host country, agencies do not concentrate solely on overseas clients but they are their most important income source. In New Zealand, for example, overseas-owned agencies have the highest proportion of foreign, multinational accounts although they still form only 28% of their clients (Table 3). This profile is not necessarily in conflict with the objectives of the agency. According to PEEBLES and RYANS (1984) an important consideration for multinational advertisers selecting an overseas agency is evidence of their ability to communicate to local consumers, as indicated by an indigenous client base. When income, rather than client numbers, is examined the connection between overseas agencies and multinational enterprise is more evident. An interview survey of New Zealand agencies by the author[1] found that multinational accounts generated around two-thirds of the income to most overseas agencies. In contrast, local agencies rarely had more than a fifth of their income from overseas-owned multinationals. These income differences are reflected in the higher proportion of income overseas agencies derive from television advertising (Table 3).

Account alignment has been an important process enabling the internationalisation of advertising, but in itself does not explain the overseas expansion of agencies. Other marketing services used by transnational companies are much less internationalised

Service Industries in the Global Economy II

42

Geoforum/Volume 21 Number 1/1990

Table 3. Market base of the largest 40 advertising agencies in New Zealand by ownership status 1987*

No. of agencies by ownership	Billings 1987 (N.Z.$000)	Total No. of accounts	Accounts from non-New Zealand firms	% total billings from TV
25–100% overseas 15	361,160	413	118	58
1–24% overseas 8	192,370	241	48	58
100% New Zealand 23	257,940	426	80	43

*Source: ADMEDIA (1988a, b).

than advertising. In the U.S.A., the top 100 advertisers in 1987 had a total marketing expenditure of U.S.$28.4 billion, of which U.S.$13 billion was spent on non-media forms of promotion (*ADVERTISING AGE*, 1988a). These 'below-the-line' promotion activities are still performed largely by national companies, although this is changing. As a whole the top 50 market research agencies in the U.S.A. earn 32% of their revenue overseas, but three firms are responsible for 93% of this overseas income (*ADVERTISING AGE*, 1988c). Moreover, two of these firms are now part of the same parent group (Dun and Bradstreet). The majority of the largest marketing organisations have little overseas income, including the second largest U.S. market research firm which earned 97% of its 1987 revenue in the U.S.A. (*ADVERTISING AGE*, 1988c). The international market companies which do exist tend to result from technical expertise, such as the scanner-based data collection services provided by A. C. Nielsen and Audits of Great Britain. Alternatively, they are based on the domination of a particular industry such as IM International's specialisation in the pharmaceutical market. Rather than direct overseas investment, there is a significant export trade in market research methods through the licensing of particular techniques.

The explanation for the greater internationalisation of advertising over other marketing activities needs to consider two issues; why transnationals seek to minimise their agency associations and why advertising is devolved to subsidiary countries, rather than being produced by one centrally-located agency.

From the transnational advertiser's perspective, agency alignment is preferred because of economic administrative efficiencies. Alignment helps to establish an uniform worldwide image for a company's products. In turn, this facilitates production economies by creating a standard product design that will sell worldwide (QUELCH and HOFF, 1986). Agency alignment facilitates the transfer of successful marketing strategies between locations (SORENSON and WIECHMANN, 1975) and standard promotional campaigns are more economic than numerious national ones. Agency alignment provides the transnational leverage over an agency in a region where their advertising expenditure is relatively modest, because a poor performance in one market can lead to a review of their overall account.

An aligned account does not mean that the same campaign is replicated in every location or even more than one geographical region. The extent to which it is desirable and practical to integrate the advertising activities of their national subsidiaries is disputed in the management literature. In the 1960s, business strategists tended to argue in favour of marketing standardisation, pointing to a number of successful examples. Moreover, it was believed that consumer interests were becoming uniform and that a consistent brand image worldwide would hasten market similarities (BUZELL, 1968). Experience indicated that these claims were premature. Partly as a consequence of the political and cultural resistance to multinational capital which emerged in the 1970s, transnational companies found it more effective to disguise their operations behind locally-produced advertising. Advertising standardisation also proved to be less effective than locally-produced campaigns because the dissimilarities between national markets, especially for consumer goods, were greater than supposed. As a consequence, SORENSON and WIECHMANN (1975) found that, while a majority of surveyed multinationals exercised a high degree of centralisation in such areas as the product, the name and packaging, less control was exercised in the area of pricing, distribution and advertising. More recent

Geoforum/Volume 21 Number 1/1990   43

evidence indicates that the decentralisation of advertising continues.

In a survey of 418 of the 'Fortune 500' business firms conducting international trade, HITE and FRASER (1988) found that of those firms advertising internationally (two-thirds of the population), 9% relied solely on standardised advertising. In contrast, 54% used a combination of centrally- and locally-created advertising, while 37% utilised solely localised advertising. Where advertising is adapted to the local market, this invariably involves the use of an agency located in that market.

The influences which determine how far a multinational company standardises its advertising are related to the type of product, the managerial autonomy of local establishments and the character of the local market. Durable products, where production advantages derive from research and development and where price differentials have a long-term marketing relevance, are more susceptible to a standardised approach than packaged goods (HARRIS, 1984). Products or services connected with international travel are also amenable to standardisation. The benefits are less easily achieved for packaged goods, which can be more readily matched by a local producer in terms of price and quality. In this sector, which it was noted earlier is the major advertising spender, there is a greater need for flexibility in advertising campaigns, including greater local freedom to devise and plan promotional strategies.

Successful standardisation requires particular management structures that cannot always be achieved within corporations. Subsidiary managers who joined a company because of its apparent commitment to local autonomy may be alienated by a rapid removal of their strategic decision making. The expansion of centralised control risks reducing the speed with which local management can respond to national opportunities and competitive situations. Slow response time is a serious problem in markets with low barriers to the entry of local competition. Experience also indicates that marketing standardisation requires an international career structure for executives so that country managers and centralised product directors can communicate effectively. Such integration takes time and investment to achieve. Local advertising regulations, such as controls on the origin of the products displayed, can also affect the marketing approach. Some countries insist, for example, that products displayed in local advertising must be of local manufacture when they are produced in that

country. Other characteristics of the local market which influence the use of locally-produced advertising are reported to be consumer eating patterns, attitudes to work and authority, and education levels. The closer these patterns are to American norms, the greater the likelihood of advertising standardisation (HITE and FRASER, 1988). [A more sinister motivation to the actions of agencies, not pursued here, has been given by MATTELART (1979) who emphasises the political role of advertising and the close links between some agencies and U.S. foreign relations.]

The position of advertising agencies in respect to the development of uniformly-marketed brands has been ambivalent. Universal brands tend to strengthen the role of large multinational agencies, but generate less income from overseas markets than where each agency office creates its own advertising. SINCLAIR (1987) relates how advertising agencies resisted the strategy of the U.S. television networks to cooperate in the creation of a centralised medium supported by multinational advertisers, so that all advertising would be created in the U.S. and networked across the world. The agencies opposed this approach and successfully fought in favour of locally-generated advertising which provided a greater role for their own services. New communication technologies are changing the attitudes of larger agencies, as they offer the possibility of both centralised and segmented advertising. Satellite and cable television communicates to specific audiences across several countries and agencies see this as an opportunity to reduce locally-produced advertising while still differentiating the campaign to target specific interest groups. A further motivation behind the enthusiasm of multinational agencies for the new media is its lack of regulation compared with television, including, for example, the allowance of tobacco advertising. This interest in new communication media partly explains the recent further expansion of overseas agencies in Europe where new broadcasting operations are becoming available to serve a continental market.

The contrast in the extent of internationalisation between advertising and other marketing services relates partly to the closer links between advertising and corporate management than other marketing services. While advertising requires knowledge of the advertiser's business strategy and directly assists in its formulation, a large amount of market research activity is geared to the assembly of 'raw' information. There is, therefore, less concern to align research accounts. Other promotional activities such as sponsorship, in-store promotion and direct marketing tend to be organised around specific events and are developed in line with the campaign devised by an advertising agency. Moreover, a significant proportion of other marketing activities are organised through an advertising agency, rather than being engaged directly by the client. Through this link, the contrast in the extent of internationalisation is declining. The next section indicates that international agencies are establishing marketing firms to mirror their own operations.

Global Holding Groups

The previous profile of agency sizes (Table 2) was based on individual firms. A further degree of concentration is revealed when the common ownership of individual agencies is considered and they are linked together in their holding group structures. A profile of the five mega groups which now dominate the industry is given in Table 4. Saatchi & Saatchi are the largest with an income margin of almost U.S.$700 million over the Interpublic Group. The European-based WCRS/Beller Group is the sixth largest group but with a total income of less than a third of the Ogilvy Group. In the U.S.A., these five holding groups controlled almost 55% of media advertising expenditure in 1987. These groups began to emerge in the 1960s with the formation of the Interpublic Group, but it is in the 1980s that ownership concentration has accelerated. In 1986, Saatchi & Saatchi purchased Ted Bates, Dancer Fitzgerald Simple and Backer & Spielvogel, respectively, then ranked number 4, 17 and 32 in the world in terms of gross income. The reported goal of Saatchi & Saatchi is to operate the world's largest advertising network which will encompass one of the top five agencies in the 10 most important markets in the world. This is currently

being achieved with the exception of Canada. Omnicom was formed in 1986 through the merger of three agencies (Needham Harper, Doyle Dane Bernbach and BBDO). The latest mega group to emerge is the U.K.-based WPP which controls two international marketing organisations and expanded into advertising with the acquisition of J. Walter Thompson in 1987. Out of the world's top 10 agencies, only two (Young & Rubicam and Leo Burnett) are not owned by a holding group, although both control their own subsidiaries and operate joint venture agreements. While the five groups now dominate, smaller-scale holding group structures, uniting separate agencies and agencies to other marketing activities, are increasingly typical of all multinational agencies.

The motivation behind the formation of holding group structures is the greatly increased profits made possible through more control of their client base and by expansion that would otherwise be frustrated by the limitations of account conflicts. The earlier phases of internationalisation did not resolve the instability of individual agencies caused by the fragile tenure in which clients are held and the inability to enhance control through specialisation. As the scale of individual advertisers has grown, the vulnerability of agencies to the loss of a single client has risen accordingly. By retaining the separate identity of agencies, and maintaining competition between them, the holding group can control a larger client base than is possible within the individual firm. Holding group structures are a feature of other services. HOLLY (1987) shows that in the U.S.A. banking organisations are adopting this structure to permit growth that would otherwise be frustrated by government regulation. Before outlining the nature of advertising holding groups, some further explanation of the motives behind their formation is given.

Table 4. Top five advertising holding groups 1987*

Holding group	Income (U.S.$ million)		% of total U.S. advertising expenditure†	No. of offices in:		No. of subsidiary advertising agencies
	U.S.A.	Rest of world		U.S.A.	Rest of world	
Saatchi & Saatchi	822.5	862.1	17.2	na	na	15
Interpublic	390.2	602.7	8.0	25	196	7
Omnicom	549.9	346.1	11.9	97	160	11
WPP Group	491.5	401.0	10.0	100	198	2
Ogilvy Group	365.9	358.0	7.6	76	268	7

*Source: *ADVERTISING AGE* (1988a, d).
†Holding group billings as a proportion of total U.S. advertising expenditure on media advertising. These data are a guide only as the group billings include some non-media advertising.

Geoforum/Volume 21 Number 1/1990   45

The concentration of expenditure in the 10 leading spenders in the U.S.A. was 27% in 1987. In the U.K., the 20 enterprises with the highest expenditure were responsible for 17% of the total expenditure in 1983. Concentration is not a recent phenomenon. In 1938, six or less firms accounted for 80% of the total expenditure in the case of the large majority of commodities in the U.K. (KALDOR and SILVERMANN, 1948). In the 1950s and 1960s advertising expenditure devolved more widely, but, with the increasing concentration of industrial ownership, a small number of major advertising spenders have once again emerged. The current world's highest spender on advertising is Philip Morris, a U.S. food, drink and tobacco conglomerate, which exceeded Proctor & Gamble in 1987 following its takeover of General Foods. Proctor & Gamble had previously been the leading spender for 24 years (*ADVERTISING AGE*, 1988a). The merger between R. J. Reynolds (RJR) and Nabisco in 1985 created a further degree of concentration with the combined conglomerate now the fifth highest spender on advertising in the U.S.A. Between 1984 and 1987 the proportion of total advertising expenditure in the U.S.A. paid for by the top five advertisers rose from 12.5 to 17.5%. The merger proposed between Philip Morris and RJR Nabisco will further accentuate the concentration of global advertising. Large agencies derive the majority of their income from large advertisers and as these reduce in number, agency growth depends on getting a larger share of the total business of these major conglomerates. Unless the agency is able to work with several of these large advertisers, it

risks becoming dependent on a smaller number of clients.

The vulnerability of individual agencies to account losses can be illustrated by reference to a number of recent examples. In 1987, Ted Bates Denmark, the largest agency in that country, lost three client accounts which represented 8% of their national income. The loss of business caused 25 redundancies out of a total staff of 205. In 1988, Saatchi & Saatchi lost the business of RJR Nabisco after producing a campaign for a North American airline announcing an in-flight smoking ban. RJR Nabisco, whose interests include tobacco, objected to their agency acting against their interests and in response they sacked Saatchi despite their 18-year association with Nabisco. At the time, RJR Nabisco generated 7% of Saatchi's U.S. income on an account that employed 200 agency staff. As a further illustration of agency vulnerability, the extent of client turnover amongst New Zealand's leading agencies in the last 2 years is shown in Table 5. In many cases close to half the existing client base is new, but net expansion is minimal or even negative due to the client losses. (The figures in Table 5 tend to exaggerate client gains as they include short-term assignments, while these are excluded from the client losses.) The high turnover is a characteristic of overseas and local agencies, but creates more difficulties for overseas agencies as they tend to have fewer, larger clients.

The formation of holding groups provides a mechanism for reducing the impact of client losses by the

Table 5. Client turnover amongst the top 15 advertising agencies in New Zealand 1986–1988*

Agency	No. of clients 1988	Clients gained post 1986:		Clients lost 1986–1988
		No.	% of total clients in 1988	
Colenso	31	12	38	4
McKay King	37	18	49	9
Haines	49	na	na	7
Ted Bates	27	9	33	10
DDB Needham	31	11	35	10
Saatchi & Saatchi	70	27	38	11
DMB&B	25	12	48	15
Rialto	32	13	41	3
Ogilvy & Mather	29	8	27	11
McCann-Erickson	37	8	22	12
Carlton Carruthers du Chateau	79	21	26	17
Leo Burnett	24	6	25	6
Campbell	11	6	54	2
Lintas	25	12	48	6
J. Walter Thompson	22	8	36	9

*Source: ADMEDIA (1987, 1988b).

46   Geoforum/Volume 21 Number 1/1990

greater financial resources available to the parent organisation. It is also possible to overcome the restriction imposed by advertisers, that they do not work with a competitor, by passing 'conflicting' clients to separate agencies within the group. For example, when WPP purchased J. Walter Thompson it established a separate agency, Conquest Europe, to handle an existing automotive client (Alfa Romeo) so that Ford's relationship with J. Walter Thompson could be maintained.

Holding groups are also a basis to provide clients with a fuller range of promotional activities that usually take place alongside an advertising campaign, including public relations and direct marketing. These activities have tended to grow at a faster rate than advertising because they are more economic, are more accountable (the results of a direct marketing exercise can be evaluated by the number of coupon returns or orders received), and they are suited particularly to retailing promotion, which is the fastest growing area of advertising expenditure (FULOP, 1988). Although most retailers have always advertised, their expenditure tended to be limited because their shop windows, local press advertising and leaflets adequately promoted their business. Over the past three decades the fundamental changes which have occurred in the organisation, ownership and technological capacity of distribution have stimulated a demand for more advertising. The increased buying power and concentration in retailing has reduced the power of manufacturers compared with retailers. To obtain a place in the retail store, manufacturers now commonly offer incentives to the retailer which include advertising allowances to promote a particular brand through a specific store. Industry sources indicate that the manufacturer may pay between 50 and 100% of the advertising costs, and that retailers may sometimes charge over 100%, thereby making a profit out of their advertising (*MARKETING, 1984*).

Advertising agencies have responded to the growth of 'below-the-line' advertising by establishing their subsidiary firms to service this market or by purchasing existing firms. The Ogilvy Group, for example, acquired the world's second largest market research company in 1987, while WPP own one of the largest international public relations firms (Hill & Knowlton) and acquired the seventh largest market research organisation (MRB International) in 1987. Increasingly international agencies establish local branches of their marketing subsidiaries in all their international locations. For example, Young & Rubicam assist the establishment of their four subsidiaries Cato

Johnson (sales promotion), Burson-Marsteller (public relations), Sudler & Hennessey (specialist health care agency) and Wundermann International (direct marketing) in all their agency locations. The separation between advertising and these other activities is maintained partly in the hope that the image of independence reduces client suspicions toward referral between the various activities. The inclusion of a specialist health care promotions firm in the Young & Rubicam group is not unique; other agencies have diversified into this sector because of the growing importance of medical and pharmaceutical advertising.

Holding groups are diversifying beyond marketing activities to include a wider range of business consultancy services. By involvement in strategic planning, agencies intend to influence the direction of the firm's investment and marketing strategy, and secure a place for itself in this work. Saatchi & Saatchi's consulting divisions now include strategic business planning, market research, human resources, technology development, transition and crisis management. Over 50 of their clients work for the company across three or more service activities, and over a fifth of all new projects are gained via referral from subsidiary organisations within the group (SAATCHI & SAATCHI, 1988). These subsidiary activities are being added to the group through the takeover of established consultancy firms. The acquisition of strategic planning expertise is also to assist the growth of the group itself; this factor was, for example, a consideration in WPP's purchase of the Henley Forecasting Centre in 1988.

A further motivation behind the formation of holding group structures is to centralise the buying of media space into one separate company. Under this arrangement agencies in the same holding group no longer buy the media time or space for clients, instead this is subcontracted to another subsidiary serving all the agencies in the group. Advertisers insist that their agency does not work with competitors, but they are generally less sensitive to being part of a combined media buying operation. Some advertisers, notably Nestle, are opposed because they fear a loss of priority in having their media demands met. In most cases advertisers are cooperating with the incentive of lower costs. This willingness has made it possible for Omnicom and the Ogilvy Group to plan a joint media buying operation to counter the dominance of Saatchi & Saatchi. The joint Omnicom–Ogilvy operation is to commence in Europe in 1989 with buying power equal to the Saatchi group. To the agencies, separate,

Geoforum/Volume 21 Number 1/1990   47

high-volume media brokerage increases profits because of the ability to obtain discounts from media vendors and because of increased productivity derived from the computerisation of this activity. In the U.K., the Saatchi group's combined media space purchasers represents 20% of the total market and this is to come under the control of one firm.[2]

Can Local Agencies Survive?

With the forces of internationalisation and concentration so powerful, it is interesting to consider how local agencies responded to the expansion of multinational agencies and to consider their future. This discussion is addressed by examining the New Zealand advertising industry which, like most countries outside of the U.S.A., is dominated by overseas agencies. In 1987, there were 43 accredited advertising agencies in New Zealand of which 23 were partially or fully overseas-owned. In terms of industry billings, overseas holding groups controlled 72% of all advertising expenditure (ADMEDIA, 1988a).

The internationalisation of New Zealand's advertising industry occurred in the late 1970s. Overseas agencies had been present in New Zealand since the 1930s when Lintas was established, primarily as Unilever's in-house agency, but it was not until 1968 that the next overseas agency moved in. By 1974, another three overseas agencies had established offices, while a similar number of New Zealand agencies had initiated ownership links with international firms. In the early 1970s, 80% of industry billings were still controlled by New Zealand agencies, but this was to fall by more than a half over the next decade. By the mid 1970s, for example. Ogilvy & Mather had 27 clients, 16 of whom were international business handled by the agency elsewhere and previously represented in New Zealand by a local agency (*NBR MARKETPLACE, 1974*).

Indigenous agencies responded to the overseas competition in three ways. One method was to buy into a multinational agency group, while retaining local managerial control. Other agencies sought to market their national sovereignty as a means of retaining large domestic clients. The final method was to attempt to become multinational by opening overseas offices. Of these three strategies, the first has proved the most successful and is exemplified by Colenso which has been New Zealand's largest agency for almost a decade. In 1973, Colenso sold 20% of its equity to an Australian agency, which in turn was owned 35% by the American-based BBDO who are one of the two main division of the Omnicom group. Although BBDO have only a small direct link to Colenso, it nonetheless gave the latter access to all the international network's services and expertise, as well as the New Zealand business of BBDO's international clients. Amongst current clients are three of BBDO's international accounts, namely Pepsi Cola, Philips NV and Bayer. A further important basis for the agency's success was the expansion of Colenso's New Zealand operations by the purchase of two other local agencies. Accounts that would otherwise be conflicting (for example, Pepsi Cola and Fresh Up, or the Bank of New Zealand and Post Bank) can be retained within the Colenso/BBDO group, allowing expansion beyond that possible in a single firm, and providing a more stable income base.

The second strategy to counter overseas agencies, of using New Zealand ownership as a positive marketing attribute, has been followed by several larger agencies but only one of the top 10 remains 100% locally owned. In 1986 McKay King, then the second largest agency in New Zealand, bought back the share of their company sold to an Australian partner. This independence was short lived as 2 years later they merged with the local Saatchi & Saatchi agency, partly because of the need to service international clients. The weakness of staying independent was also shown when the former Australian partner responded by establishing two subsidiary agencies in New Zealand. Local ownership tends to survive amongst smaller agencies only.

The third strategy of New Zealand companies establishing their own multinational network proved to be an unsuccessful experiment. In 1972, three local agencies established a separate firm with offices in America, Asia and the U.K. The venture did not survive because of inadequate business from both New Zealand enterprises selling in these overseas markets and overseas-based enterprises attracted by the New Zealand link. A few agencies have opened offices in Australia to service particular New Zealand clients operating in both markets, but these have also tended to be short-lived investments because of their dependency on a single key client. Rather than establish branches, independent agencies have tended to affiliate non-financially with international networks of independent agencies to provide a means of servicing transnational accounts.

These three strategies allowed local agencies to retain some multinational business and the higher billings they generate, but their position is increasingly threatened. In 1988, only one of the overseas agencies had succeeded in attracting all its main international accounts, but the number of unaligned accounts is declining. The degree of managerial autonomy that has existed amongst local establishments, enabling them to select their own preferred agency, is declining now that 100% ownership of multinational subsidiaries has been made easier by changes in foreign exchange regulations (BOLLARD and BUCKLE, 1987). The loss of local autonomy contributed to at least 10 major account shifts in 1988 in favour of the internationally aligned agency away from locally-owned agencies. At the same time several foreign agencies have exploited the relaxed foreign exchange regulations to obtain full ownership of their New Zealand subsidiary. The strategy pursued by Colenso, of obtaining a minority overseas partner is, therefore, increasingly vulnerable.

Overseas holding groups are planning the introduction of combined media buying organisations. In anticipation of this competition, the two largest locally-owned agencies and a small third have established their own joint media buying operation to commence in 1989. The local group have current billings equivalent to 13% of the total industry, but this share is still small in comparison to the potential control of the overseas holding groups. Already Saatchi & Saatchi control 20% and Omnicom and the Ogilvy Group combined control 33% of current billings. In 1988 a further international trend also affected New Zealand with the establishment of an international agency specialising in retail advertising. Retail advertising has been important to local agencies because its emphasis on non-television media made the sector unattractive to most multinational agencies. Within 4 months of operation the new agency obtained four major retail accounts previously held by local agencies and had established a sister agency to facilitate further expansion. The inescapable conclusion is that increasing overseas control of the local advertising industry is inevitable. As the trends affecting New Zealand are not unique, this conclusion equally applies to most other nations.

Conclusion

Service industries have generally been perceived as important employers, but with relatively minor economic significance compared to more 'basic' sectors. Advertising is of relatively minor direct employment importance but exerts a major influence on economic

development. Advertising agencies have facilitated the growth of transnational capital by the provision of marketing expertise. Without a mechanism for the distribution of information about products, the significant economies of scale achieved by multinational capital might have not been realised so readily. Initially, the internationalisation of advertising was a response to the demands of advertisers. This allowed agencies to expand but still left them exposed to the inherent instability of their market. Increasingly the expansion of agencies has had an impetus of its own, giving advertising a more proactive role in economic development. In New Zealand, for example, Young & Rubicam estimate that about one in five new accounts now results from new product launches suggested by the agency to their clients. The new products are identified in the reports of other Young & Rubicam branches, backed up by market impact assessment from their overseas experience. The diversification of the holding groups into related marketing and business consultancy services, is designed to provide greater influence over the development of advertiser's corporate strategy. The goal of leading agencies, such as Saatchi & Saatchi, is to redirect the marketing strategy of transnational agencies towards more emphasis on universal world brands rather than decentralised, culturally specific campaigns. To this end they are investing considerable research to identify international market segments to which centrally-created advertising will be directed and seeking to exploit new forms of broadcasting, via satellites and cable networks and the growth of international publications (WINRAM, 1984). If successful, the spatial centralisation of advertising would occur alongside the ownership concentration of international advertising within the holding groups as the proportion of locally-produced advertising declined.

The formation of the mega corporations represents a significant adjustment to the relations between advertisers, media and agencies. The ultimate effectiveness and long-term consequences are a matter of speculation, but some reaction from advertisers and the media is probable. Transnational advertisers are likely to react against the increased profits of their agencies and the reduced freedom to select agencies as the trend to concentration in agency ownership accelerates. Some multinational advertisers are reported to be investigating their own media buying operations now that the financial advantages have become appreciated. A number of large corporations have not been persuaded that holding groups provide member agencies with sufficient independence. In

Geoforum/Volume 21 Number 1/1990   49

consequence, they have moved their accounts to independent agencies. Media organisations have suggested that the commission paid to holding groups may be reduced so that they can share the increased profits. A further reaction may be the takeover of agencies by transnational conglomerates. To finance their expansion, holding companies have become public companies, making themselves vulnerable to acquisition. The control of advertising by other activities has not yet emerged, neither has advertising diversified into unrelated areas or even media ownership (although there are exceptions here in the case of Japanese agencies).

The growing influence of agency holding groups is one example reinforcing the importance now attached to producer services in generating economic change. The continuing evolution of the advertising industry should be monitored. As we have seen in the case of New Zealand, the survival of remaining local agencies is increasingly threatened. The implication of this for domestic manufacturers may be a weakening of their market share as transnational agencies and their clients strengthen their dominance. There are also implications for the location of service activity if holding groups are successful in shifting the marketing effort of transnational advertisers away from locally-produced advertising. Such a shift would affect both those directly employed in agencies and the more numerous jobs involved in the production of advertising. The dynamic relationships between agencies, advertisers and media offers considerable scope for further study of the restructuring of the service sector and its impact on other sectors of the economy.

Acknowledgements—The author has received financial support from the N.Z. Social Science Research Fund Committee. Permission from Crain Communications Inc. to reproduce the data from *Advertising Age* is gratefully acknowledged.

Note

1. The survey covered 19 of the 43 accredited agencies existing in 1987 and was conducted by personal interview between June and September 1988.
2. Subsequent to the drafting of this article, the WPP Group acquired the Ogilvy Group in May 1989.

References

ADMEDIA (1987) Advertising agency billings 1986, March, 25–48.

ADMEDIA (1988a) Advertising agency billings 1987, March, 35–49.

ADMEDIA (1988b) *Agencies and Clients* 1988. AdMedia, Auckland.

ADVERTISING AGE (1987) 43rd annual agency income report, 26 March.

ADVERTISING AGE (1988a) 26th foreign agency income survey, 9 May.

ADVERTISING AGE (1988b) 33rd 100 leading national advertisers report, 28 September.

ADVERTISING AGE (1988c) 14th annual industry review, 23 May.

ADVERTISING AGE (1988d) 44th annual agency income report, 30 March.

BARNETT, R. and MULLER, R. (1974) *Global Reach.* Simon & Schuster, New York.

BOLLARD, A. and BUCKLE, R. (1987) *Economic Liberalisation in New Zealand.* Allen & Unwin, Wellington.

BUZELL, R. (1968) Can you standardize multinational marketing?, *Harv. Business Rev.* **68**, 102–113.

CLAIRMONTE, F. and CAVANAGH, J. (1984) Transnational corporations and services: the final frontier, *Trade Dev.* **5**, 215–273.

COMANOR, W. S. and WILSON, T. A. (1974) *Advertising and Market Power.* Harvard University Press, Cambridge, MA.

FRASER, W. H. (1981) *The Coming of the Mass Market 1850–1914.* Macmillan, London.

FULOP, C. (1988) The role of advertising in the retail marketing mix, *Int. J. Advertising*, **7**, 99–117.

GRUBEL, H. G. (1987) All traded services are embodied in materials or people, *Wld Econ.*, **10**, 319–330.

HARRIS, G. (1984) The globalisation of advertising, *Int. J. Advertising*, **3**, 223–234.

HITE, R. and FRASER, C. (1988) International advertising strategies of multinational companies, *J. Advertising Res.*, **28**, 9–17.

HOLLY, B. P. (1987) Regulation, competition, and technology: the restructuring of the US commercial banking system, *Envir. Plann. A*, **19**, 633–652.

JWT UNILEVER (1985) Trends in total advertising expenditure in 10 countries 1970–1983, *Int. J. Advertising*, **4**, 173–184.

KALDOR, N. (1950) The economic aspects of advertising, *Rev. econ. Stud.*, **18**, 1–27.

KALDOR, N. and SILVERMANN, R. (1948) *A Statistical Analysis of Advertising Expenditure and the Revenue of the Press.* Cambridge University Press, Cambridge.

LANIGAN, D. (1984) Agency alignment, *Marketing*, November, 97–98.

LEISS, W., KLINE, S. and JHALLY, S. (1986) *Social Communication in Advertising.* Methuen, London.

LIPIETZ, A. (1987) *Mirages and Miracles.* Verso, London.

MANDEL, E. (1978) *Late Capitalism.* New Left Books, London.

MARKETING (1984) Biggest ad spenders in '83, February, 29–33.

MATTELART, A. (1979 *Multinational Corporations and the Control of Culture.* Harvester Press, Brighton.

NBR MARKETPLACE (1984) Filling another square on their global chessboards, March, 11–15.

PEEBLES, D. and RYANS, J. (1984) *Management of International Advertising.* Allyn & Bacon, Boston, MA.

QUELCH, J. A. and HOFF, E. J. (1986) Customizing

global marketing *Harv. Business Rev.*, May–June, 59–68.

REED, H. C. (1983) Appraising corporate investment policy; a financial centre theory of foreign direct investment, In: *The Multinational Corporation in the 1980s*, C. P. Kindleberger and D. B. Audretsch (Eds). M.I.T. Press, Cambridge, MA.

SAATCHI & SAATCHI (1988) *Annual Report 1987*. Saatchi & Saatchi, London.

SINCLAIR, J. (1987) *Images Incorporated: Advertising as Industry and Ideology*. Croom Helm, London.

SORENSON, R. S. and ULRICH, E. W. (1975) How multinationals view marketing standardization, *Har. Business Rev.*, May–June, 38–48.

THRIFT, N. (1987) The fixers: the urban geography of international capital, In: *Global Restructuring and Territorial Development*, J. Henderson and M. Castells (Eds). Sage, London.

WINRAM, S. (1984) The opportunity for world brands, *Int. J. Advertising*, **3**, 17–26.

[36]

Telecommunications and the Changing Geographies of Knowledge Transmission in the Late 20th Century

Barney Warf

[Paper first received, March 1994; in final form, July 1994]

Summary. Recent innovations in telecommunications and computing, enhanced by a global wave of deregulation and the emergence of post-Fordist production regimes, have unleashed profound transformations of various service sectors in the global economy. This paper first reviews the geographical repercussions of the explosion of information services, including the birth of electronic funds transfer systems, the growth of global cities and the dispersal of back offices to low-wage sites across the globe. Secondly, it explores the political economy and spatiality of the largest of these systems, the Internet. Thirdly, it summarises how the global division of labour has recently engendered the birth of 'new information spaces', places whose recent growth is contingent upon the introduction of telecommunications, citing as examples Singapore, Hungary and the Dominican Republic.

The late 20th century has witnessed an explosion of producer services on an historic scale, which forms a fundamental part of the much-heralded transition from Fordism to post-Fordism (Coffey and Bailly, 1991; Wood, 1991). Central to this transformation has been a wave of growth in financial and business services linked at the global level by telecommunications. The emergence of a global service economy has profoundly altered markets for, and flows of, information and capital, simultaneously initiating new experiences of space and time, generating a new round of what Harvey (1989, 1990) calls time–space convergence. More epistemologically, Poster (1990) notes that electronic systems change not only what we know, but how we know it.

The rapid escalation in the supply and demand of information services has been propelled by a convergence of several factors, including dramatic cost declines in information-processing technologies induced by the microelectronics revolution, national and worldwide deregulation of many service industries, including the Uruguay Round of GATT negotiations (which put services on the agenda for the first time), and the persistent vertical disintegration that constitutes a fundamental part of the emergence of post-Fordist production regimes around the world (Goddard and Gillespie, 1986; Garnham, 1990; Hepworth, 1990). The growth of traditional financial and business services, and the emergence of new ones, has ushered in a profound—indeed, an historic—transformation of the ways in which information is collected, processed and circulates, forming

Barney Warf is in the Department of Geography, Florida State University, Tallahassee, FL 32306-2050, USA.

0042-0980/95/020361-18 © 1995 Urban Studies

what Castells (1989) labels the 'informational mode of production'.

This paper constitutes an ambitious overview of the development, spatial dynamics and economic consequences of international telecommunications in the late 20th century as they arise from and contribute to the expansion of a global service economy. It opens with a broad perspective of recent changes in trade in producer services, particularly international finance, as the propelling force behind a large and rapidly expanding telecommunications infrastructure. Secondly, it explores the political economy of one of the largest and most renowned electronic systems, the Internet. Thirdly, it dwells upon the spatial dimensions of the mode of information, including the flowering of a select group of global cities, offshore banking centres, and the globalisation of clerical functions. Fourthly, it traces the emergence of what is called here 'new informational spaces', nations and regions reliant upon information services at the core of their economic development strategies. The conclusion summarises several themes that arise persistently in this discussion.

The Global Service Economy and Telecommunications Infrastructure

There can be little doubt that trade in services has expanded rapidly on an international basis (Kakabadse, 1987), comprising roughly one-quarter of total international trade. Internationally, the US is a net exporter of services (but runs major trade deficits in manufactured goods), which is one reason why services employment has expanded domestically. Indeed, it could be said that as the US has lost its comparative advantage in manufacturing, it has gained a new one in financial and business services (Noyelle and Dutka, 1988; Walter, 1988). The data on global services trade are poor, but some estimates are that services comprise roughly one-third of total US exports, including tourism, fees and royalties, sales of business services and profits from bank loans.

From the perspective of contemporary so-cial theory, services may be viewed within the context of the enormous series of changes undergone by late 20th-century capitalism. In retrospect, the signs of this transformation are not difficult to see: the collapse of the Bretton-Woods agreement in 1971 and the subsequent shift to floating exchange rates; the oil crises of 1974 and 1979, which unleashed $375b of petrodollars between 1974 and 1981 (Wachtel, 1987), and the resulting recession and stagflation in the West; the explosive growth of Third World debt, including a secondary debt market and debt–equity swaps (Corbridge, 1984), the growth of Japan as the world's premier centre of financial capital (Vogel, 1986); the explosion of the Euromarket (Pecchioli, 1983; Walter, 1988); the steady deterioration in the competitive position of industrial nations, particularly the US and the UK, and the concomitant rise of Japan, Germany and the newly industrialising nations, particularly in east Asia; the transformation of the US under the Reagan administration into the world's largest debtor, the emergence of flexible production technologies (e.g. just-in-time inventory systems) and computerisation of the workplace; the steady growth of multinational corporations and their ability to shift vast resources across national boundaries; the global wave of deregulation and privatisation that lay at the heart of Thatcherite and Reaganite post-Keynesian policy; and finally, the integration of national financial markets through telecommunications systems. In the 1990s, one might add the collapse of the Soviet bloc and the steady integration of those nations into the world economy. This series of changes has been variably labelled an 'accumulation crisis' in the transition from state monopoly to global capitalism (Graham *et al.*, 1988), or the end of one Kondratieff long wave and the beginning of another (Marshall, 1987). What is abundantly clear from these observations is the emergence of a new global division of labour, in which services play a fundamental role.

The increasing reliance of financial and business services as well as numerous multinational manufacturing firms upon telecommunications to relay massive volumes of information through international networks has made electronic data collection and transmission capabilities a fundamental part of regional and national attempts to generate a comparative advantage (Gillespie and Williams, 1988). The rapid deployment of such technologies reflects a conjunction of factors, including: the increasingly information-intensive nature of commodity production in general (necessitating ever larger volumes of technical data and related inputs on financing, design and engineering, marketing and so forth); the spatial separation of production activities in different nations through globalised sub-contracting networks; decreases in price and the elastic demand for communications; the birth of new electronic information services (e.g. on-line databases, teletext and electronic mail); and the high levels of uncertainty that accompany the international markets of the late 20th century, to which the analysis of large volumes of data is a strategic response (Moss, 1987b; Akwule, 1992). The computer networks that have made such systems technologically and commercially feasible offer users scale and scope economies, allowing spatially isolated establishments to share centralised information resources such as research, marketing and advertising, and management (Hepworth, 1986, 1990). Inevitably, such systems have profound spatial repercussions, reducing uncertainty for firms and lowering the marginal cost of existing plants, especially when they are separated from one another and their headquarters over long distances, as is increasingly the case.

Central to the explosion of information services has been the deployment of new telecommunications systems and their merger with computerised database management (Nicol, 1985). This phenomenon can be seen in no small part as an aftershock of the microelectronics revolution and the concomitant switch from analogue to digital information formats: the digital format suffers less degradation over time and space, is much more compatible with the binary constraints of computers, and allows greater privacy (Akwule, 1992). As data have been converted from analogue to digital forms, computer services have merged with telecommunications. When the cost of computing capacity dropped rapidly, communications became the largest bottleneck for information-intensive firms such as banks, securities brokers and insurance companies. Numerous corporations, especially in financial services, invested in new communications technologies such as microwave and fibre optics. To meet the growing demand for high-volume telecommunications, telephone companies upgraded their copper-cable systems to include fibre-optics lines, which allow large quantities of data to be transmitted rapidly, securely and virtually error-free. By the early 1990s, the US fibre-optic network was already well in place (Fig. 1). In response to the growing demand for international digital data flows beginning in the 1970s, the United Nation's International Telecommunications Union introduced Integrated Service Digital Network (ISDN) to harmonise technological constraints to data flow among its members (Akwule, 1992). ISDN has since become the standard model of telecommunications in Europe, North America and elsewhere.

The international expansion of telecommunications networks has raised several predicaments for state policy at the global and local levels. This topic is particularly important because, as we shall see, state policy both affects and is affected by the telecommunications industry. At the international level, issues of transborder data flow, intellectual property rights, copyright laws, etc., which have remained beyond the purview of traditional trade agreements, have become central to GATT and its successor, the International Trade Organization. At the national level, the lifting of state controls in telecommunications had significant impacts on the profitability, industrial organisation and spatial structure of information services. In the US, for example, telecommunications underwent a profound reorganisation following the dissolution of ATT's monopoly in 1984, leading to secular declines in the price

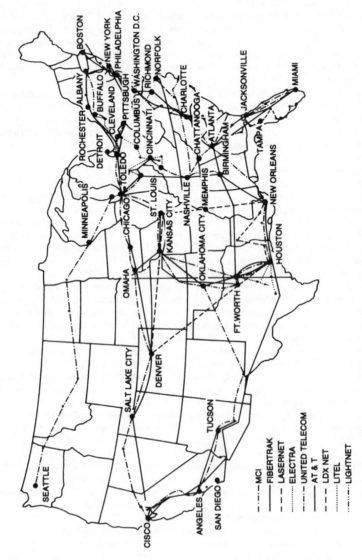

Figure 1. The US fibre-optics network, 1992. *Source:* Office of Technology Assessment (1993).

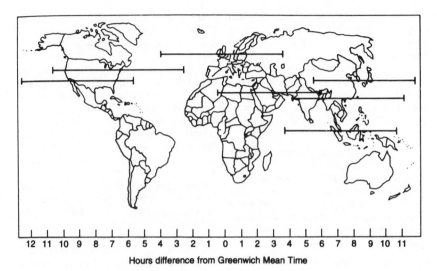

Figure 2. Trading hours of major world financial centres.

of long-distance telephone calls. Likewise, the Thatcher government privatised British Telecom, and even the Japanese began the deregulation of Nippon Telegraph and Telephone.

Telecommunications allowed not only new volumes of inter-regional trade in data services, but also in capital services. Banks and securities firms have been at the forefront of the construction of extensive leased telephone networks, giving rise to electronic funds transfer systems that have come to form the nerve centre of the international financial economy, allowing banks to move capital around a moment's notice, arbitraging interest rate differentials, taking advantage of favourable exchange rates, and avoiding political unrest (Langdale, 1985, 1989; Warf, 1989). Citicorp, for example, erected its Global Telecommunications Network to allow it to trade $200bn daily in foreign exchange markets around the world. Such networks give banks an ability to move money—by some estimates, more than $1.5 trillion daily (*Insight*, 1988)—around the globe at stupendous rates. Subject to the process of

digitisation, information and capital become two sides of the same coin. In the securities markets, global telecommunications systems have also facilitated the emergence of the 24-hour trading day, linking stock markets through the computerised trading of stocks. Reuters and the Chicago Mercantile Exchange announced the formation of Globex, an automated commodities trading system, while in 1993 the New York stock exchange began the move to a 24-hour day automated trading system. As Figure 2 indicates, the world's major financial centres are easily connected even with an 8-hour trading day. The volatility of stock markets has increased markedly as hair-trigger computer trading programmes allow fortunes to be made (and lost) by staying microseconds ahead of (or behind) other markets, as exemplified by the famous crashes of 19 October 1987. It is vital to note that heightened volatility, or the ability to switch vast quantities of funds over enormous distances, is fundamental to these capital markets: speculation is no fun when there are no wild swings in prices (Strange, 1986).

Within the context of an expanding and ever more integrated global communications network, a central role in the formation of local competitive advantage has been attained by teleports, which are essentially office parks equipped with satellite earth stations and usually linked to local fibre-optics lines (Lipman *et al.*, 1986; Hanneman, 1987a, 1987b and 1987c). The World Teleport Association defines a teleport as:

> An access facility to a satellite or other long-haul telecommunications medium, incorporating a distribution network serving the greater regional community and associated with, including, or within a comprehensive real estate or other economic development. (Hanneman, 1987a, p. 15)

Just as ports facilitate the transshipment of cargo and airports are necessary for the movement of people, so too do teleports serve as vital information transmission facilities in the age of global capital. Because telecommunications exhibit high fixed costs and low marginal costs, teleports offer significant economies of scale to small users unable to afford private systems (Stephens, 1987; Burstyn, 1986). Teleports apparently offer a continually declining average cost curve for the provision of telecommunications services. Such a cost curve raises important issues of pricing and regulation, including the tendency of industries with such cost structures to form natural monopolies. Government regulation is thus necessary to minimise inefficiencies, and the pricing of telecommunications services becomes complex (i.e. marginal revenues do not equal marginal costs, as in non-monopolistic, non-regulated sectors) (Rohlfs, 1974; Saunders *et al.*, 1983; Guldmann, 1990).

In the late 1980s there were 54 teleports in the world, including 36 in the US (Hanneman, 1987a). Most of these are concentrated in the industrialised world, particularly in cities in which data-intensive financial and business services play a major economic role. In Europe, London's new teleport in the Docklands will ensure that city's status as the centre of the Euromarket for the near future; Hamburg, Cologne, Amsterdam and Rotterdam are extending telematic control across Europe.

Tokyo is currently building the world's largest teleport. In the 1980s, the Japanese government initiated a series of high-technology 'technopolises' that form part of a long-term 'teletopia' plan to encourage decentralisation of firms out of the Tokyo region to other parts of the nation (Rimmer, 1991). In 1993 the city initiated the Tokyo Teleport on 98 ha of reclaimed land in Tokyo harbour (Tokyo Metropolitan Government Planning Department, 1993). The teleport's 'intelligent buildings' (those designed to accommodate fibre optics and advanced computational capacity), particularly its Telecom Centre, are designed to accommodate ISDN requirements. Wide Area Networks (WANs) provide local telecommunications services via microwave channels, as do Value Added Networks on fibre-optic routes. The site was originally projected to expand to 340 ha, including office, waterfront and recreational functions, and employ 100 000 people, but may be scaled back in the light of the recent recessionary climate there.

The world's first teleport is named, simply, The Teleport, located on Staten Island, New York, a project jointly operated by Merrill Lynch and the Port Authority of New York and New Jersey. Built in 1981, The Teleport consists of an 11-acre office site and 16 satellite earth stations, and is connected to 170 miles of fibre-optic cables throughout the New York region, which are, in turn, connected to the expanding national fibre-optic network. Japanese firms have taken a particularly strong interest in The Teleport, comprising 18 of its 21 tenants. For example, Recruit USA, a financial services firm, uses it to sell excess computer capacity between New York and Tokyo, taking advantage of differential day and night rates for supercomputers in each city by transmitting data via satellite and retrieving the results almost instantaneously (Warf, 1989).

In addition to the US, European and

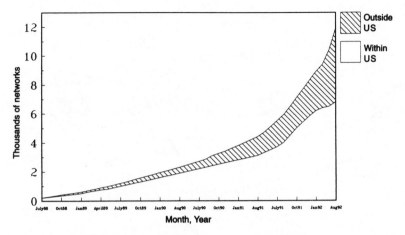

Figure 3. Growth of Internet. *Source:* Broad (1993).

Japanese teleports, some Third World nations have invested in them in order to secure a niche in the global information services economy. Jamaica, for example, built one at Montego Bay to attract American 'back office' functions there (Wilson, 1991). Other examples include Hong Kong, Singapore, Bahrain and Lagos, Nigeria (Warf, 1989).

The Internet: Political Economy and Spatiality of the Information Highway

Of all the telecommunications systems that have emerged since the 1970s, none has received more public adulation than the Internet. The unfortunate tendency in the popular media to engage in technocratic utopianism, including hyperbole about the birth of cyberspace and virtual reality, has obscured the very real effects of the Internet. The Internet is the largest electronic network on planet, connecting an estimated 20m people in 40 countries (Broad, 1993). Further, the Internet has grown at rapid rates, doubling in networks and users every year (Figure 3); by mid 1992, it connected more than 12 000 individual networks worldwide. Originating as a series of public networks, it now includes a variety of private systems of access,

in the US including services such as Prodigy, CompuServe or America On-Line (Lewis, 1994), which allow any individual with a microcomputer and modem to 'plug in', generating a variety of 'virtual communities'. By 1994, such services connected almost 5m people in the US alone (Lewis, 1994).

The origins of the Internet can be traced back to 1969, when the US Department of Defense founded ARPANET, a series of electronically connected computers whose transmission lines were designed to withstand a nuclear onslaught (Schiller, 1993). Indeed, the very durability and high quality of much of today's network owes its existence to its military origins. In 1984, ARPANET was expanded and opened to the scientific community when it was taken over by the National Science Foundation, becoming NSFNET, which linked five supercomputers around the US (Figure 4). The Internet, which emerged upon a global scale via its integration with existing telephone, fibre-optic and satellite systems, was made possible by the technological innovation of packet switching, in which individual messages may be decomposed, the constituent parts transmitted by various channels (i.e. fibre optics, telephone lines, satellite), and

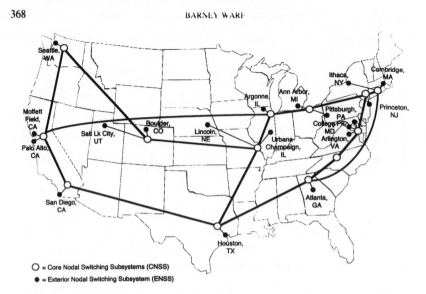

Figure 4. Distribution of NSFNET Backbone Service. *Source:* Office of Technology Assessment (1993).

then reassembled, seamlessly and instantaneously, at the destination. In the 1990s such systems have received new scrutiny as central elements in the Clinton administration's emphasis on 'information superhighways'.

The Internet has become the world's single most important mechanism for the transmission of scientific and academic knowledge. Roughly one-half of all of its traffic is electronic mail, while the remainder consists of scientific documents, data, bibliographies, electronic journals and bulletin boards (Broad, 1993). Newer additions include electronic versions of newspapers, such as the *Chicago Tribune* and *San Jose Mercury News*, as well as an electronic library, the World Wide Web. In contrast to the relatively slow and bureaucratically monitored systems of knowledge production and transmission found in most of the world, the Internet and related systems permit a thoroughly unfiltered, non-hierarchical flow of information best noted for its lack of overlords. Indeed, the Internet has spawned its own unregulated counterculture of 'hackers' (Mungo and Clough, 1993). However, the

system finds itself facing the continuous threat of commercialisation as cyberspace is progressively encroached upon by corporations, giving rise, for example, to new forms of electronic shopping and 'junk mail' (Weis, 1992). The combination of popular, scientific and commercial uses has led to an enormous surge in demand for Internet capacities, so much so that they frequently generate 'traffic jams on the information highway' as the transmission circuits become overloaded (Markoff, 1993).

Despite the mythology of equal access for everyone, there are also vast discrepancies in access to the Internet at the global level (Schiller, 1993; Cooke and Lehrer, 1993). As measured by the number of access nodes in each country, it is evident that the greatest Internet access remains in the most economically developed parts of the world, notably North America, Europe and Japan (Figure 5). The hegemony of the US is particularly notable given that 90 per cent of Internet traffic is destined for or originates in that nation. Most of Africa, the Middle East and Asia (with the exceptions of India, Thailand and Malaysia), in contrast, have little or no access. There is, clearly, a reflection here of the long-standing bifurcation between the First and Third Worlds. To this extent, it is apparent than the geography of the Internet reflects previous rounds of capital accumulation—i.e. it exhibits a spatiality largely preconditioned by the legacy of colonialism.

There remains a further dimension to be explored here, however, the bifurcation between the superpowers following World War II. As Buchner (1988) noted, Marxist regimes favoured investments in television rather than telephone systems: televisions, allowing only a one-way flow of information (i.e. government propaganda), are far more conducive to centralised control that are telephones, which allow multiple parties to circumvent government lines of communication. Because access to the Internet relies heavily upon existing telephone networks, this policy has hampered the emerging post-Soviet 'Glasnet'. Superimposed on top of the landscapes of colonialism, therefore, is the landscape of the Cold War.

A rather curious yet revealing byproduct of the Internet's expansion concerns the international transmission of computer viruses, programmes written deliberately to interfere with the operations of other software systems. Although viruses are not new to users of computers, the rapid growth of electronic systems in the 1980s has markedly accelerated their capacity to travel internationally, indicating both the extent and speed with which knowledge circulates through such networks as well as the vulnerability of these systems to unwanted intrusions. In 1992, for example, the Michelangelo virus disrupted software systems of users ranging from South African pharmacists to the San Francisco police department. More ominous is the 'Bulgarian virus machine' (Mungo and Clough, 1993). In the 1980s, Bulgaria was the designated computer producer for the Soviet bloc, and Sofia University produced large numbers of skilled engineers and programmers to serve it. As communism collapsed in the late 1980s, many of such

individuals, including bored young men who comprise the vast bulk of hackers, took to writing viruses and releasing them on international networks, including those of the UN. Simultaneously, Sofia University began to export its anti-virus software on the world market. Although some of the worst excesses of Bulgarian hackers have been curtailed, some indications are that they are being joined by Russian, Thai and other counterparts.

Geographical Consequences of the Mode of Information

As might be expected, the emergence of a global economy hinging upon producer services and telecommunications systems has led to new rounds of uneven development and spatial inequality. Three aspects of this phenomenon are worth noting here, including the growth of world cities, the expansion of offshore banking centres and the globalisation of back offices.

World Cities

The most readily evident geographical repercussions of this process have been the growth of 'world cities', notably London, New York and Tokyo (Moss, 1987a; Sassen, 1991), each of which seems to be more closely attuned to the rhythms of the international economy than the nation-state in which it is located. In each metropolitan area, a large agglomeration of banks and ancillary firms generates pools of well-paying administrative and white-collar professional jobs; in each, the incomes of a wealthy stratum of traders and professionals have sent real estate prices soaring, unleashing rounds of gentrification and a corresponding impoverishment for disadvantaged populations. While such predicaments are not new historically— Amsterdam was the Wall Street of the 17th century (Rodriguez and Feagin, 1986)—the magnitude and rapidity of change that global telecommunications have unleashed in such cities is without precedent.

London, for example, boomed under the

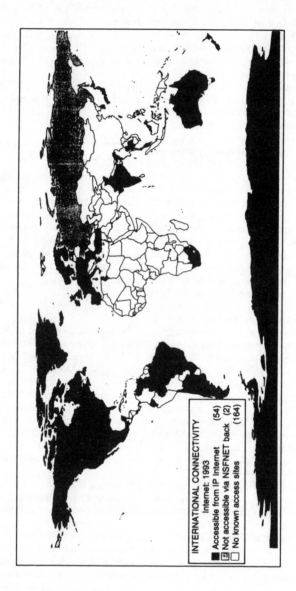

Figure 5. The geography of access to the Internet, 1993. *Source:* unpublished data from the Internet Supervisory Oversight Committee.

impetus of the Euromarket in the 1980s, and has become detached from the rest of Britain (Thrift, 1987; Budd and Whimster, 1992). Long the centre of banking for the British Empire, and more recently the capital of the unregulated Euromarket, London seems to have severed its moorings to the rest of the UK and drifted off into the hyperspaces of global finance. State regulation in the City— always loose when compared to New York or Tokyo—was further diminished by the 'Big Bang' of 1986. Accordingly, the City's landscape has been reshaped by the growth of offices, most notably Canary Wharf and the Docklands. Still the premier financial centre of Europe, and one of the world's major centres of foreign banking, publishing and advertising, London finds its status challenged by the growth of Continental financial centres such as Amsterdam, Paris and Frankfurt.

Similarly, New York rebounded from the crisis of the mid 1970s with a massive influx of petrodollars and new investment funds (i.e. pension and mutual funds) that sustained a prolonged bull market on Wall Street in the 1980s (Scanlon, 1989; Mollenkopf and Castells, 1992; Shefter, 1993). Today, 20 per cent of New York's banking employment is in foreign-owned firms, notably Japanese giants such as Dai Ichi Kangyo. Driven by the entrance of foreign firms and increasing international linkages, trade on the New York stock exchange exploded from 12m shares per day in the 1970s to 150m in the early 1990s (Warf, 1991). New York also boasts of being the communications centre of the world, including one-half million jobs that involve the collection, production, processing, transmission or consumption of information in one capacity or another (Warf, 1991). This complex, including 60 of the largest advertising and legal services firms in the US, is fuelled by more word-processing systems than in all of Europe combined. The demand for space in such a context has driven an enormous surge of office construction, housing 60 headquarters of US Fortune 500 firms. Currently, 20 per cent of New York's office space is foreign-owned, testi-

mony to the need of large foreign financial firms to establish a presence there.

Tokyo, the epicentre of the gargantuan Japanese financial market, is likely the world's largest centre of capital accumulation, with one-third of the world's stocks by volume and 12 of its largest banks by assets (Masai, 1989). The Tokyo region accounts for 25 per cent of Japan's population, but a disproportionate share of its economic activity, including 60 per cent of the nation's headquarters, 65 per cent of its stock transactions, 89 per cent of its foreign corporations, and 65 per cent of its foreign banks (Cybriwsky, 1991). Tokyo's growth is clearly tied to its international linkages to the world economy, particularly in finance, a reflection of Japan's growth as a major world economic power (Masai, 1989; Cybriwsky, 1991). In the 1980s, Japan's status in the global financial markets was unparalleled as the world's largest creditor nation (Vogel, 1986; *Far Eastern Economic Review*, 1987). Tokyo's role as a centre of information-intensive activities includes a state-of-the-art telecommunications infrastructure, including the CAPTAIN (Character and Pattern Telephone Access Information Network) system (Nakamura and White, 1988).

Offshore Banking

A second geographical manifestation of the new, hypermobile capital markets has been the growth of offshore banking, financial services outside the regulation of their national authorities. Traditionally, 'offshore' was synonymous with the Euromarket, which arose in the 1960s as trade in US dollars outside the US. Given the collapse of Bretton Woods and the instability of world financial markets, the Euromarket has since expanded to include other currencies as well as other parts of the world. The recent growth of offshore banking centres reflects the broader shift from traditional banking services (loans and deposits) to lucrative, fee-based non-traditional functions, including debt repackaging foreign exchange transactions and cash management (Walter, 1989).

Today, the growth of offshore banking has occurred in response to favourable tax laws in hitherto marginal places that have attempted to take advantage of the world's uneven topography of regulation. As the technological barriers to capital have declined, the importance of political ones has thus risen concomitantly. Several distinct clusters of offshore banking may be noted, including, in the Caribbean, the Bahamas and Cayman Islands; in Europe, Switzerland, Luxembourg and Liechtenstein; in the Middle East, Cyprus and Bahrain; in southeast Asia, Singapore and Hong Kong; and in the Pacific Ocean, Vanuatu, Nauru and Western Samoa. Roberts (1994, p. 92) notes that such places "are all part of a worldwide network of essentially marginal places which have come to assume a crucial position in the global circuits of fungible, fast-moving, furtive money and fictitious capital." Given the extreme mobility of finance capital and its increasing separation from the geography of employment, offshore banking can be expected to yield relatively little for the nations in which it occurs; Roberts (1994), for example, illustrates the case of the Cayman Islands, now the world's fifth-largest banking centre in terms of gross assets, where 538 foreign banks employ only 1000 people (less than two apiece). She also notes that such centres are often places in which 'hot money' from illegal drug sales or undeclared businesses may be laundered.

Offshore markets have also penetrated the global stock market, where telecommunications may threaten the agglomerative advantages of world cities even as they reinforce them. For example, the National Associated Automated Dealers Quotation System (NASDAQ) has emerged as the world's fourth-largest stock market; unlike the New York, London, or Tokyo exchanges, NASDAQ lacks a trading floor, connecting half a million traders worldwide through telephone and fibre-optic lines. Similarly, Paris, Belgium, Spain, Vancouver and Toronto all recently abolished their trading floors in favour of screen-based trading.

Global Back Offices

A third manifestation of telecommunications in the world service economy concerns the globalisation of clerical services, in particular back offices. Back offices perform many routinised clerical functions such as data entry of office records, telephone books or library catalogues, stock transfers, processing of payroll or billing information, bank cheques, insurance claims, magazine subscriptions and airline frequent-flyer coupons. These tasks involve unskilled or semi-skilled labour, primarily women, and frequently operate on a 24-hour-per-day basis (Moss and Dunau, 1986). By the mid 1980s, with the conversion of office systems from analogue to digital form largely complete, many firms began to integrate their computer systems with telecommunications.

Historically, back offices have located adjacent to headquarters activities in downtown areas to ensure close management supervision and rapid turnaround of information. However, under the impetus of rising central-city rents and shortages of sufficiently qualified (i.e. computer-literate) labour, many service firms began to uncouple their headquarters and back office functions, moving the latter out of the downtown to cheaper locations on the urban periphery. Most back office relocations, therefore, have been to suburbs (Moss and Dunau, 1986; Nelson, 1986). Recently, given the increasing locational flexibility afforded by satellites and a growing web of inter-urban fibre-optics systems, back offices have begun to relocate on a much broader, continental scale. Under the impetus of new telecommunications systems, many clerical tasks have become increasingly footloose and susceptible to spatial variations in production costs. For example, several firms fled New York City in the 1980s: American Express moved its back offices to Salt Lake City, UT, and Phoenix, AZ; Citicorp shifted its Mastercard and Visa divisions to Tampa, FL, and Sioux Falls, SD, and moved its data processing functions to Las Vegas, NV, Buffalo, NY, Hagerstown, MD, and Santa Monica, CA; Citibank moved its cash management services to New Castle, DE; Chase Manhattan housed its credit card operations in Wilmington; Hertz relocated its data entry division to Oklahoma City; Avis went to Tulsa. Dean Witter moved its data processing facilities to Dallas, TX; Metropolitan Life repositioned its back offices to Greenville, SC, Scranton, PA, and Wichita, KS; Deloitte Haskins Sells relocated its back offices to Nashville, TN; and Eastern Airlines chose Miami, FL.

Internationally, this trend has taken the form of the offshore office (Wilson, 1991). The primary motivation for offshore relocation is low labour costs, although other considerations include worker productivity, skills, turnover and benefits. Offshore offices are established not to serve foreign markets, but to generate cost savings for US firms by tapping cheap Third World labour pools. Notably, many firms with offshore back offices are in industries facing strong competitive pressures to enhance productivity, including insurance, publishing and airlines. Offshore back office operations remained insignificant until the 1980s, when advances in telecommunications such as trans-oceanic fibre-optics lines made possible greater locational flexibility just when the demand for clerical and information processing services grew rapidly (Warf, 1993). Several New York-based life insurance companies, for example, have erected back office facilities in Ireland, with the active encouragement of the Irish government (Lohr, 1988). Often situated near Shannon Airport, they move documents in by Federal Express and the final product back via satellite or the TAT-8 fibre-optics line that connected New York and London in 1989 (Figure 6). Despite the fact that back offices have been there only a few years, Irish development officials already fret, with good reason, about potential competition from Greece and Portugal. Likewise, the Caribbean has become a particularly important locus for American back offices, partly due to the Caribbean Basin Initiative instituted by the Reagan administration and the guaranteed access to the US market that it provides. Most back offices in the Caribbean

have chosen Anglophonic nations, particularly Jamaica and Barbados. American Airlines has paved the way in the Caribbean through its subsidiary Caribbean Data Services (CDS), which began when a data processing centre moved from Tulsa to Barbados in 1981. In 1987, CDS opened a second office near Santo Domingo, Dominican Republic, where wages are one-half as high as Barbados (Warf, forthcoming). Thus, the same flexibility that allowed back offices to move out of the US can be used against the nations to which they relocate.

New Information Spaces

The emergence of global digital networks has generated growth in a number of unanticipated places. These are definitely not the new industrial spaces celebrated in the literature on post-Fordist production complexes (Scott, 1988), but constitute new 'information spaces' reflective of the related, yet distinct, mode of information. Three examples—Singapore, Hungary and the Dominican Republic—illustrate the ways in which contemporary telecommunications generate repercussions in the least expected of places.

Singapore

Known best perhaps as a member of the East Asian newly industrialised countries (NICs), Singapore today illustrates what may be the most advanced telecommunications infrastructure in the world, creating an 'intelligent island' with high-speed leased circuits, a dense telephone and fibre-optic network, household teleboxes for electronic mail and ubiquitous remote computer access (Dicken, 1987; Corey, 1991). Singapore's government has led the way in this programme through its National Computer Board and Telecommunications Authority. This transformation has occurred as part of a sustained shift in the island's role from unskilled, low-wage assembly functions to exporter of high value-added business services and as the financial hub of south-east Asia, a process hastened by the flight of capital from Hong Kong

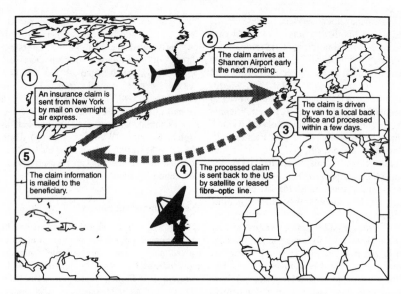

Figure 6. Mechanics of back office relocation to Ireland.

(Jussawalla and Cheach, 1983). Exports of services have now become Singapore's largest industry in terms of employment and foreign revenues. Reuters, for example, uses Singapore as its news hub in south-east Asia. In part, this transformation reflects the island's relatively high wages and fears of competition from its larger neighbours. Today, more than one-third of Singapore's labour force is engaged in skilled, white-collar employment. In addition, Singapore uses its telecommunications network for advanced Electronic Data Interchange (EDI) services to facilitate maritime shipping, in congruence with its status as the world's largest port.

Hungary

Before the collapse of the Soviet Union, Hungary suffered many of the same telecommunications problems as other underdeveloped nations: outdated technology, unsatisfied demand and few advanced services. Today, largely due to deregulation and

foreign investment, the Hungarian telecommunications system is the most advanced in the former Soviet bloc, subsuming 10 per cent of the nation's total investment capital. The leader in this process has been the postal service, Magyar Posta, and its successor, the Hungarian Telecommunications Company (Matav), which introduced innovative pricing based on market, not political criteria, fees for telephone connections, time-differentiated and distance-sensitive pricing and bond financing. Concomitantly, an administrative reorganisation decentralised control of the firm, breaking the inefficient stranglehold of the bureaucratic, Communist *apparatchik* (Whitlock and Nyevrikel, 1992). The birth of the new Hungarian telecommunications network was invaluable to the nation's emerging financial system, centred in Budapest, which has expanded beyond simple loans and stocks to include database management and stock transfers (Tardos, 1991). Thus, in this respect, Hungary serves as a model for other nations making the transition from state socialism to market economies.

The Dominican Republic

In the 1980s, the Dominican government introduced a policy designed to develop non-traditional exports, particularly tourism and information services, as part of a strategy to reduce the country's reliance upon agricultural exports. For a small, relatively impoverished nation, the nation possesses a well-endowed information services infrastructure (Warf, forthcoming). The national telephone company Codetel (Compania Dominicana de Telecommunicaciones), for example, has provided the Dominican Republic with near-universal telephone access, high-speed data transmission services on fibre-optics lines, digital switching equipment, cellular telephones and microwave service to all neighbouring nations except Cuba. Codetel also sells a variety of high value-added services such as electronic mail and databases, telex, remote terminals, facsimile services, Spanish–English translations and leased lines. This infrastructure has made the Dominican Republic the most advanced nation in telecommunications in Latin America and has attracted numerous foreign firms. IBM-Santo Domingo, for example, engages in a complex, worldwide system of sub-contracting with its subsidiaries, purchasing, for example, printers from Argentina, disk drives from Brazil, CPUs from the US or Brazil and software, written in Canada, the US and Denmark, through its distributor in Mexico. A similar firm is Infotel, which performs a variety of computer-related functions for both domestic and international clients, including compilation of telephone directories, photo-composition, data conversion, computerised, on-line sale of advertising images, desktop publishing and map digitising. Infotel serves a variety of domestic and foreign clients, including Dominican utilities and municipal governments, the GTE telephone-operating companies, the US Geological Survey and the Spanish telephone network. Another service attracted to the Dominican Republic is back offices. American Airlines, and its subsidiary Caribbean Data Services, processes medical and dental insurance claims, credit card applications, retail sales inventories, market surveys and name and address listings at a Free Trade Zone near the capital.

Concluding Comments

What lessons can be drawn from these observations about the emergence of a globalised service economy and the telecommunications networks that underpin it? As part of the broad sea-change from Fordist production regimes to the globalised world of flexible accumulation, about which so much has already been said, it is clear that capital—as data or cash, electrons or investments—in the context of global services has acquired a qualitatively increased level of fluidity, a mobility enhanced by the worldwide wave of deregulation unleashed in the 1980s and the introduction of telecommunication networks. Such systems give banks, securities, insurance firms and back offices markedly greater freedom over their locational choices. In dramatically reducing the circulation time of capital, telecommunications have linked far-flung places together through networks in which billions of dollars move instantaneously across the globe, creating a geography without transport costs. There can be no doubt that this process has real consequences for places, as attested by the current status of cities such as London, New York, Tokyo and Singapore and the Cayman Islands. Generally, such processes tend to concentrate skilled, high value-added services, e.g. in global cities, while dispersing unskilled, low value-added services such as back offices to Third World locations.

In short, it is vital to note that, contrary to early, simplistic expectations that telecommunications would 'eliminate space', rendering geography meaningless through the effortless conquest of distance, such systems in fact produce new rounds of unevenness, forming new geographies that are imposed upon the relics of the past. Telecommunications simultaneously reflect and transform the topologies of capitalism, creating and rapidly recreating nested hierarchies of spaces technically articulated in the architecture of computer networks. Indeed, far from eliminating variations among places, such systems permit the exploitation of differences between areas with renewed ferocity. As Swyngedouw (1989) noted, the emergence of hyperspaces does not entail the obliteration of local uniqueness, only its reconfiguration. That the geography engendered by this process was unforeseen a decade ago hardly needs restating; that the future will hold an equally unexpected, even bizarre, set of outcomes is equally likely.

References

AKWULE, R. (1992) *Global Telecommunications: The Technology, Administration, and Policies.* Boston: Focal Press.

BLAZAR, W. (1985) Telecommunications: harnessing it for development, *Economic Development Commentary,* 9, pp. 8–11.

BROAD, W. (1993) Doing science on the network: a long way from Gutenberg, *New York Times,* 18 May, B5.

BUCHNER, B. (1988) Social control and the diffusion of modern telecommunications technologies: a cross-national study, *American Sociological Review,* 53, pp. 446–453.

BUDD, L. and WHIMSTER, S. (Eds) (1992) *Global Finance and Urban Living: A Study of Metropolitan Change.* London: Pergamon.

BURSTYN, H. (1986) Teleports: at the crossroads. *High Technology,* 6(5), pp. 28–31.

CASTELLS, M. (1989) *The Informational City.* Oxford: Basil Blackwell.

COFFEY, W. and BAILLY, A. (1991) Producer services and flexible production: an exploratory analysis, *Growth and Change,* 22, pp. 95–117.

COOKE, K. and LEHRER, D. (1993) The Internet: the whole world is talking, *The Nation,* 257, pp. 60–63.

CORBRIDGE S. (1984) Crisis, what crisis? Monetarism, Brandt II and the geopolitics of debt, *Political Geography Quarterly,* 3, pp. 331–345.

COREY, K. (1991) The role of information technology in the planning and development of Singapore, in: B. BRUNN and T. LEINBACH (Eds) *Collapsing Space and Time,* pp. 217–231. London: HarperCollins.

CYBRIWSKY, R. (1991) *Tokyo: The Changing Profile of an Urban Giant.* Boston: G.K. Hall and Co.

DICKEN, P. (1987) A tale of two NICs: Hong Kong and Singapore at the crossroads, *Geoforum,* 18, pp. 151–164.

DICKEN, P. (1992) *Global Shift: The Internationalization of Economic Activity,* 2nd edn. New York: Guilford Press.

FAR EASTERN ECONOMIC REVIEW (1987) Japan banking and finance, 9 April, pp. 47–110.

GARNHAM, N. (1990) *Capitalism and Communication: Global Culture and the Economics of Information.* Beverly Hills: Sage.

GILLESPIE, A. and WILLIAMS, H. (1988) Telecommunications and the reconstruction of comparative advantage, *Environment and Planning A,* 20, pp. 1311–1321.

GODDARD, J. and GILLESPIE, A. (1986) *Advanced Telecommunications and Regional Development.* Newcastle-upon-Tyne: Centre for Urban and Regional Development Studies.

GRAHAM, J. *ET AL.*(1988) Restructuring in U.S. manufacturing: the decline of monopoly capitalism, *Annals of the Association of American Geographers,* 78, pp. 473–490.

GULDMANN, J. (1990) Economies of scale and density in local telephone networks, *Regional Science and Urban Economics,* 20, pp. 521–533.

HALL, P. and PRESTON, P. (1988) *The Carrier Wave: New Information Technology and the Geography of Innovation, 1846–2003.* London: Unwin Hyman.

HANNEMAN, G. (1987a) The development of teleports, *Satellite Communications,* March, pp. 14–22.

HANNEMAN, G. (1987b) Teleport business, *Satellite Communications,* April, pp. 23–26.

HANNEMAN, G. (1987c) Teleports: the global outlook, *Satellite Communications,* May, pp. 29–33.

HARVEY, D. (1989) *The Condition of Postmodernity.* Oxford: Basil Blackwell.

HARVEY, D. (1990) Between space and time: reflections on the geographical imagination, *Annals of the Association of American Geographers,* 80, pp. 418–434.

HEPWORTH, M. (1986) The geography of technological change in the information economy, *Regional Studies,* 20, pp. 407–424.

HEPWORTH, M. (1990) *Geography of the Information Economy.* London: Guildford Press.

Insight. (1988) Juggling trillions on a wire: is electronic money safe? 15 February, pp. 38–40.

JUSSAWALLA, M. and CHEAH, C. (1983) Towards an information economy: the case of Singapore, *Information Economics and Policy,* 1. pp. 161–176.

KAKABADSE, M. (1987) *International Trade in Services: Prospects for Liberalisation in the 1990s.* London: Croom Helm.

LANGDALE, J. (1985) Electronic funds transfer and the internationalisation of the banking and finance industry, *Geoforum,* 16, pp. 1–13.

LANGDALE, J. (1989) The geography of international business telecommunications: the role of leased networks, *Annals of the Association of American Geographers*, 79, pp. 501–522.

LEWIS, P. (1994) A boom for on-line services, *New York Times*, 12 July, C1.

LIPMAN, A., SUGARMAN, A. and CUSHMAN, R. (1986) *Teleports and the Intelligent City*. Homewood, IL: Dow Jones.

LOHR, S. (1988) The growth of the global office, *New York Times*, 18 October, D1.

MARKOFF, J. (1993) Traffic jams already on the information highway, *New York Times*, 3 November, p. 1, C7.

MARSHALL, M. (1987) *Long Waves of Regional Development*. London: Macmillan.

MASAI, Y. (1989) Greater Tokyo as a global city, in: R. KNIGHT and G. GAPPERT (Eds) *Cities in a Global Society*. Newbury Park, CA: Sage.

MOLLENKOPF, J. and CASTELLS, M. (Eds) (1992) *Dual City: Restructuring New York*. New York: Russell Sage Foundation.

MOSS, M. (1987a) Telecommunications, world cities and urban policy. *Urban Studies*, 24, pp. 534–546.

MOSS, M. (1987b) Telecommunications and international financial centres, in: J. BROTCHIE, P. HALL and P. NEWTON (Eds) *The Spatial Impact of Technological Change*. London: Croom Helm.

MOSS, M. and DUNAU, A. (1986) Offices, information technology, and locational trends, in: J. BLACK, K. ROARK and L. SCHWARTZ (Eds) *The Changing Office Workplace*, pp. 171–182. Washington, DC: Urban Land Institute.

MUNGO, P. and CLOUGH, B. (1993) *Approaching Zero: The Extraordinary Underworld of Hackers, Phreakers, Virus Writers, and Keyboard Criminals*. New York: Random House.

NAKAMURA, H. and WHITE, J. (1988) Tokyo, in: M. DOGAN and J. KASARDA (Eds) *The Metropolitan Era, Volume 2: Mega-Cities*. Newbury Park, CA: Sage.

NELSON, K. (1986) Labor demand, labor supply and the suburbanization of low-wage office work. in: A. SCOTT and M. STORPER (Eds) *Production, Work, Territory*. Boston: Allen Unwin.

NICOL, L. (1985) Communications technology: economic and spatial impacts, in: M. CASTELLS (Ed.) *High Technology, Space, and Society*, pp. 191–209. Beverly Hills, CA: Sage.

NOYELLE, T. and DUTKA, A. (1988) *International Trade in Business Services*. Cambridge, MA: Ballinger.

OFFICE OF TECHNOLOGY ASSESSMENT (1993) *Automation of America's Offices*. Washington, DC: US Government Printing Office.

PECCHIOLI, R. (1983) *The Internationalization of Banking: The Policy Issues*, Paris: OECD.

POSTER, M. (1990) *The Mode of Information: Poststructuralism and Social Context*. Chicago: University of Chicago Press.

QUINN, J., BARUCH, J. and PAQUETTE, P. (1987) Technology in services. *Scientific American*, 257(6), pp. 50–58.

RIMMER, P. (1991) Exporting cities to the western Pacific Rim: the art of the Japanese package, in: J. BROTCHIE, M. BATTY, P. HALL and P. NEWTON (Eds) *Cities of the 21st Century*. Melbourne: Longman Cheshire.

ROBERTS, S. (1994) Fictitious capital, fictitious spaces: the geography of offshore financial flows, in: S. CORBRIDGE, R. MARTIN and N. THRIFT (Eds) *Money Power Space*. Oxford: Basil Blackwell.

RODRIGUEZ, N. and FEAGIN, J. (1986) Urban specialization in the world-system, *Urban Affairs Quarterly*, 22, pp. 187–219.

ROHLFS, J. (1974) A theory of interdependent demand for a communications service, *Bell Journal of Economics and Management Science*, 5, pp. 13–37.

SASSEN, S. (1991) *The Global City: New York, London, Tokyo*. Princeton, NJ: Princeton University Press.

SAUNDERS, R., WARFORD, J. and WELLENIUS, B. (1983) *Telecommunications and Economic Development*. Baltimore: Johns Hopkins University Press.

SCANLON, R. (1989) New York City as global capital in the 1980s, in: R. KNIGHT and G. GAPPERT (Eds) *Cities in a Global Society*. Newbury Park, CA: Sage.

SCHILLER, H. (1993) 'The information highway': public way or private road? *The Nation*, 257, pp. 64–65.

SCOTT, A.J. (1988) *New Industrial Spaces*. London: Pion.

SHEFTER, M. (1993) *Capital of the American Century: The National and International Influence of New York City*. New York: Russell Sage Foundation.

STEPHENS, G. (1987) What can business get from teleports? *Satellite Communications*, March, pp. 18–19.

STRANGE, S. (1986) *Casino Capitalism*. Oxford: Basil Blackwell.

SWYNGEDOUW, E. (1989) The heart of the place: the resurrection of locality in an age of hyperspace, *Geografiska Annaler*, 71, pp. 31–42.

TARDOS, A. (1991) Problems of the financial information system in Hungary, *Acta Oeconomica*, 43, pp. 149–166.

THRIFT, N. (1987) The fixers: the urban geography of international commercial capital, in: J. HENDERSON and M. CASTELLS (Eds) *Global Restructuring and Territorial Development*. Beverly Hills: Sage Publications.

TOKYO METROPOLITAN GOVERNMENT PLANNING DEPARTMENT (1993) *Tokyo Teleport*. Tokyo: Tokyo Metropolitan Government Information Centre.

VOGEL, E. (1986) Pax Nipponica? *Foreign Affairs*, 64, pp. 752–767.

WACHTEL, H. (1987) Currency without a country: the global funny money game, *The Nation*, 26 December, 245, pp. 784–790.

WALKER, R. (1985) Is there a service economy? The changing capitalist division of labor, *Science and Society*, Spring, pp. 42–83.

WALTER, I. (1988) *Global Competition in Financial Services: Market Structure, Protection, and Trade Liberalization*. Cambridge, MA: Ballinger.

WALTER, I. (1989) *Secret Money*. London: Unwin Hyman.

WARF, B. (1989) Telecommunications and the globalization of financial services, *Professional Geographer*, 41, pp. 257–271.

WARF, B. (1991) The internationalization of New York services, in: P. DANIELS (Ed.) *Services and Metropolitan Development: International Perspectives*, pp. 245–264. London: Routledge.

WARF, B. (1993) Back office dispersal: implications for urban development, *Economic Development Commentary*, 16, pp. 11–16.

WARF, B. (forthcoming) Information services in the Dominican Republic, *Yearbook of the Association of Latin American Geographers*.

WEIS, A. (1992) Commercialization of the Internet, *Electronic Networking*, 2(3), pp. 7–16.

WHITLOCK, E. and NYEVRIKEL, E. (1992) The evolution of Hungarian telecommunications. *Telecommunications Policy*, pp. 249–258.

WILSON, M. (1991) *Offshore relocation of producer services: the Irish back office*. Paper presented at the *Annual Meeting of the Association of American Geographers*, Miami.

WOOD, P. (1991) Flexible accumulation and the rise of business services, *Transactions of the Institute of British Geographers*, 16, pp. 160–172.

Name Index

The International Library of Critical Writings in Economics